Prophet of Truth

Martin Gilbert was born in London in 1936 and educated at Highgate School and Magdalen College, Oxford. In 1962 he joined Randolph Churchill's research team, collecting material for the official Life of Sir Winston and in 1968 he succeeded Randolph as official biographer.

THE CHURCHILL BIOGRAPHY IS COMPLETE IN
EIGHT VOLUMES:

Volume I. Youth, 1874–1900 *by Randolph S. Churchill*
  Volume I. Companion (in two parts)
Volume II. Young Statesman, 1900–1914 *by Randolph S. Churchill*
  Volume II. Companion (in three parts)
*Volume III. The Challenge of War, 1914–1916 *by Martin Gilbert*
  Volume III. Companion (in two parts)
*Volume IV. World in Torment, 1917–1922 *by Martin Gilbert*
  Volume V. Prophet of Truth, 1922–1939 *by Martin Gilbert*
  Volume V. Companion, The Exchequer Years 1923–1929
  Volume V. Companion, The Wilderness Years 1929–1935
  Volume V. Companion, The Coming of War 1936–1939
*Volume VI. Finest Hour, 1939–1941 *by Martin Gilbert*
*Volume VII. Road to Victory, 1941–1945 *by Martin Gilbert*
*Volume VIII. 'Never Despair', 1945–1965 *by Martin Gilbert*

OTHER BOOKS BY MARTIN GILBERT

The Appeasers (*with Richard Gott*)
The European Powers, 1900–1945
The Roots of Appeasement, 1900–1945
Recent History Atlas, 1860–1960
British History Atlas
American History Atlas
Jewish History Atlas
First World War Atlas
Russian Imperial History Atlas
Soviet History Atlas
The Arab–Israeli Conflict: Its History in Maps
Sir Horace Rumbold: Portrait of a Diplomat
Churchill: A Photographic Portrait
The Jews of Russia: Their History in Maps and Photographs
Jerusalem Illustrated History Atlas
Exile and Return: The Struggle for Jewish Statehood
Children's Illustrated Bible Atlas
Auschwitz and the Allies
Atlas of the Holocaust
Churchill's Political Philosophy
The Jews of Hope: The Plight of Soviet Jewry Today
Shcharansky, Hero of our Time
The Holocaust, the Jewish Tragedy
Second World War

Editions of documents

Britain and Germany Between the Wars
Plough My Own Furrow, the Life of Lord Allen of Hurtwood
Servant of India: Diaries of the Viceroy's Private Secretary, 1905–1910

*Available in Minerva

PROPHET OF TRUTH

WINSTON S. CHURCHILL
1922–1939

Martin Gilbert

Minerva

PROPHET OF TRUTH

A Minerva Paperback

PROPHET OF TRUTH
First published in Great Britain 1976
by William Heinemann Ltd
This Minerva edition published 1990
by Mandarin Paperbacks
Michelin House, 81 Fulham Road, London sw3 6rb

Minerva is an imprint of the Octopus Publishing Group

A CIP catalogue record for this title
is available from the British Library
ISBN 0 7493 9103 0

Printed and bound in Great Britain by
BPCC Hazell Books
Aylesbury, Bucks, England
Member of BPCC Ltd.

Dedicated to the Memory of
Peter Gilbert

Contents

Illustrations

Preface

THIS volume covers sixteen years of Churchill's life, for two of which he was out of Parliament, for nearly five of which he was Chancellor of the Exchequer and for ten of which, leading up to the outbreak of war in 1939, he was out of office.

Throughout these years the originality and boldness of Churchill's intellect and character impressed itself forcefully upon his contemporaries. As Chancellor of the Exchequer from October 1924 to June 1929 he introduced five budgets, launched important measures of social reform, brought Britain back on to the Gold Standard, organized the Government's newspaper at the time of the General Strike, led the Government's negotiations for a settlement in the coal industry, and embarked upon a vast scheme of the de-rating of industry in order to stimulate and revive the economy. He also took a leading part in the Cabinet's discussions on defence and foreign affairs. These five years at the Exchequer marked a high point of Churchill's political influence, of his parliamentary skills, and of his personal contentment.

With the fall of the Conservative Government in 1929, Churchill's career entered a stormy and often lonely decade, the so-called 'wilderness years'. Yet despite the obloquy to which he was frequently subjected, and his exclusion from the Cabinet, his actions during this period were founded throughout upon his belief in the Parliamentary system and his concern for national safety and survival, and his arguments gained wide public support, increasing from year to year. From 1929 to 1939 calculations of political advantage were irrelevant to Churchill; indeed, he saw clearly that both his opposition to the Government's India policy after 1930 and his campaign for vigorous rearmament after 1933 could only undermine his chances of a return to the Cabinet. During these long-drawn-out and at times bitter struggles he was prepared to challenge repeatedly the National Government not in order to overturn it, but in a determined effort to persuade its leaders to change their policies. 'It is nothing to me whether I am in Parliament or not,' he wrote to his wife on 8 March 1935, 'unless I can defend the cause in which I believe.'

Churchill's five-year opposition to the Government's India policy was sincere and passionate, although individual Ministers sought to portray him as an enemy of Indian aspirations, and as a political wrecker. Churchill was in fact concerned throughout with the future welfare and unity of India, and was worried about the social and political difficulties which would be created by the dominance of the Congress Party. The Government argued that the Federal Scheme of self-Government proposed in the India Bill was the sole means of keeping India within the Empire, but Churchill pointed out that it would only stimulate demands for full independence, an outcome which the Government Ministers themselves rejected, and which they believed would be averted by their proposals. Churchill himself favoured full provincial autonomy for the Indians, with adequate safeguards for the minority rights of the Muslims and the Untouchables, and he urged a vigorous social reform and a more liberal administration. Above all, he saw the unity of the Empire as an indispensable element of Britain's security in the forthcoming struggle with Germany.

As the India controversy developed, Churchill was deeply disturbed by the way in which the Government used its policy as a political lever in Britain itself, and resorted to what he believed were dubious and at times anti-constitutional methods to advance it. But as soon as the India Bill became law he accepted defeat, and personally encouraged Gandhi both in his campaign on behalf of the Untouchables and in his plans for a prosperous and self-reliant society.

From 1933 the problems of defence, and of the Nazi danger, were uppermost in Churchill's mind, dominating his Parliamentary speeches, his literary work, his newspaper articles and much of his private correspondence. In foreign policy, he urged the close cooperation of the League of Nations' states for the collective security of all countries threatened by Germany. He rejected the policy of seeking a direct accommodation with the Nazis at the expense of the smaller states of Europe. The full extent of Nazi persecution was evidence, as he saw it, that there would never be any meaningful accommodation between Nazism and Parliamentary democracy. From the earliest successes of the Nazi movement, even before 1933, he expressed his repugnance of Nazi excesses, and he continued to do so after 1933, despite repeated German protests at his articles and speeches. Nothing could persuade him to accept the possibility of compromise with evil at the expense of others, or to abandon his faith in the rule of law, the supremacy of elected Parliaments and the rights of the individual. His moral precepts were clear but unalterable, underlined first by his researches into the politics of the early eighteenth century, and then by his study of the history of the English-speaking people. 'Thus I condemn tryanny in whatsoever guise' he wrote to one of his research assistants on 12 April 1939, 'and from whatever quarter it presents itself.'

In order that Britain would be sufficiently strong both to resist direct threats and to lead an alliance of threatened states, Churchill urged upon the Government a series of measures which they either rejected or delayed in taking up: in February 1934 he pressed for the immediate reorganization of civil aircraft factories so that they could, when needed, be converted rapidly to war production; in March 1934 he urged the formation of a Ministry of Defence; in March 1935 the drawing-in of Russia to the problems of European security; in August 1935 the creation of a National Assembling Plant for aircraft in order to manufacture as many as five hundred machines a month; in April 1936 the establishment of a Ministry of Supply, and, throughout this period, a higher rate of defence spending, a faster rate of aircraft production, closer cooperation with France, and a greater public and Government awareness of the scope and scale of the German danger.

In his continued forecasts of the potential German air strength, Churchill has often been accused of exaggeration. Yet it will be seen from the evidence in this volume that his forecasts and warnings, accurate in themselves, were concerned not merely with the numbers of German first-line aircraft but with the overall nature of Germany's industrial capacity, and with Germany's ability to produce, after 1937, as many aeroplanes as she chose above the existing British schemes, and to organize those aeroplanes into first-line squadrons far in excess of British plans.

Although the Government and the Air Ministry sought to weaken the impact of Churchill's warnings by accusing him of exaggeration, within four years they were forced to recognize that the true situation was as he had forecast. On 25 October 1938 the Secretary of State for Air, Sir Kingsley Wood, admitted to the Cabinet: 'It is clear that in our previous programmes of expansion we have not taken a sufficiently long range view and have underestimated both the capacity and intentions of Germany.'

'How often I find myself called wrong,' Churchill had written to his wife on 17 April 1924, 'for warning of follies in time.' Yet over a wide range of defence matters in the 1930s—military, naval, industrial, as well as aerial—Churchill's fears, some expressed publicly, the more secret and detailed of them confided privately to those in authority, were justified by events. The Government's repeated response, however, even after October 1938, was to continue to attack his motives and judgement, and to seek to minimize the importance of his information. 'No doubt it is not popular to say these things,' Churchill had written to his wife on 26 September 1935, 'but I am accustomed to abuse and I expect to have a great deal more of it before I have finished. Somebody has to state the truth.'

During the nine years that he was out of office, Churchill could find few Members of Parliament willing to support him openly in the many defence debates. On one occasion, on 26 October 1938, when he appealed for fifty Conservatives to support his call for the immediate establishment of a Ministry of Supply, only Harold Macmillan and Brendan Bracken joined him in the opposition Lobby. The activities of the Party Whips were continually turned against him, in repeated and successful attempts to lessen the impact of his warnings and to erode his support. Churchill remained staunchly attached to those who had shared his isolation; thus on 2 June 1940 after King George VI had opposed the appointment of Brendan Bracken to the Privy Council, Churchill wrote to the King's private secretary, Sir Alexander Hardinge:

Mr Bracken is a Member of Parliament of distinguished standing and exceptional ability. He has sometimes been almost my sole supporter in the years when I have been striving to get this country properly defended, especially from the air. He has suffered as I have done every form of official hostility. Had he joined the ranks of the time-servers and careerists who were assuring the public that our Air Force was larger than that of Germany, I have no doubt he would long ago have attained high Office.

In July 1935, after Churchill had repeatedly expressed his anxiety about the state of Britain's anti-aircraft defences, Baldwin invited him to join the Air Defence Research sub-committee of the Committee of Imperial Defence. Henceforth Churchill was aware of all the scientific developments of air defence, and, from the moment of joining, contributed his own ideas and energy to the many projects moving forward, including radar. Churchill's continual pressure on the sub-committee for a greater pace, scale and range of research led to resentment and friction, but so highly was Churchill regarded by those who were aware of the true gravity of the situation that the inventor of radar himself, Robert Watson-Watt, appealed to him privately in June 1936 to obtain a more rapid moving forward of experiments.

Within the main Government departments Churchill's views and anxieties were well known. During 1936 the Permanent Under-Secretary of State at the Foreign Office, Sir Robert Vansittart, and the head of the News Department, Reginald Leeper, disturbed at the weakness of the democracies in face of Nazi propaganda, themselves turned to Churchill, and were able secretly to use him to try both to revive public morale and to bring together in private conclave and on public platforms many leading figures from the Labour Party, the Trade Union movement, the League of Nations Union and other concerned bodies. This semi-official role, never publicly disclosed or even hinted at, led Churchill to work with many disparate groups to try to influence public opinion towards the need for greater vigilance in defence of democracy, faith in the moral tenets of the anti-totalitarian cause, the closest possible Anglo-French cooperation and a willingness to take up arms, if necessary, in order to ensure the survival of democratic civilization.

Other civil servants, politicians and serving officers also approached Churchill, with equal secrecy, but on an entirely unofficial basis. In this volume I have tried to tell the story of those individuals who provided Churchill with information and encouragement while he was out of office. Churchill did not seek out these individuals; it was they who, alarmed by what they considered to be the dangerous neglect of Britain's national interest, took the initiative in going to see him, or in sending him secret material. More then twenty civil servants and Government officials took this course, principal among them being Major Desmond Morton from 1934, Ralph Wigram in 1935 and 1936, and Wing-Commander Torr Anderson from 1936. To Desmond Morton, Churchill wrote thirteen years later, on 15 October 1947, while preparing his war memoirs:

I am anxious to make some mention in my memoirs of all the help you gave me—and I think I may say the country—in the critical pre-war years. . . . When I read all these letters and papers you wrote for me and think of our prolonged conversations I feel how very great is my debt to you, and I know that no thought ever crossed your mind but that of the public interest.

On 21 October 1947 Desmond Morton replied: 'you are good enough to say that you think I helped our country. It certainly was my hope and desire, but unfortunately those in power then would not listen to me. Nevertheless I am more than happy to feel that the little I could do for you, either in those pre-war days or during the war, was of any service to you.'

In his memoirs, written so soon after the war, Churchill could not tell the story of the help which Morton and others had given him. Yet without the information provided by Morton, Wigram and Anderson, and by many other officials whose contact with Churchill is described in this volume, each of whom risked his career by telling Churchill what they knew of Britain's defence weaknesses, it would have been very difficult, if not impossible, for him to have kept up his sustained pressure on the Government, to have kept himself so fully informed on a day-to-day basis of the true defence situation in all its aspects, to have aroused public opinion through his detailed and accurate warnings, or to have been so well prepared to take up once more the responsibilities of a member of the War Cabinet on the outbreak of war in September 1939.

Acknowledgements

I T would have been impossible to try to give a fair or accurate picture of Churchill's life during the seventeen years covered by this volume without the evidence and documents preserved in a wide range of public archives and private collections. As well as the documents in Churchill's own archive, I have found important material in the Royal Archives at Windsor; the archives of the Air Ministry, the Cabinet Office, the Committee of Imperial Defence, the Foreign Office, the Prime Minister's Office and the Treasury, at the Public Record Office (London and Ashridge); the archive of *The Times*; the German Diplomatic Archives captured by the Allies in 1945; the Blenheim Palace archives, and the archives of the BBC. In addition, I have drawn upon further contemporary material in sixty-seven private archives, those of Lord Addison, L. J. Alber, L. S. Amery, Stanley Baldwin, Lord Balfour, Bernard Baruch, Lord Beaverbrook, W. H. Bernau, Lord Birkenhead, G. D. Birla, Lord Boothby, Lord Camrose, Lord Cecil of Chelwood, Austen Chamberlain, Neville Chamberlain, Lord Cherwell, M. G. Christie, Randolph Churchill, Sir Stafford Cripps, Sir Henry Page Croft, Anthony Crossley, Lord Derby, Sir Patrick Donner, Lord Dundee, P. J. Grigg, Sir Henry Goschen, Shiela Grant Duff, Lord Halifax, Lord Hankey, Sir James Hawkey, Lady Blanche Hozier, Michael Hutchison, Lord Islington, Lord Keyes, Harold Laski, Walter Lippmann, Lord Lloyd, David Lloyd George, Countess Lloyd-George, Lord Lothian, Louis Loucheur, Ramsay MacDonald, Lord Margesson, Sir Edward Marsh, Paul Maze, Sir Harold Nicolson, Lord Norwich, Sir Eric Phipps, Lord Quickswood, Lord Reading, Lord Rosebery, Sir Horace Rumbold, Lord Salisbury, C. P. Scott, Lord Selborne, Sir E. L. Spears, Baroness Spencer-Churchill, Lord Swinton, Lord Templewood, Sir Colin Thornton-Kemsley, Lord Thurso, Lord Vansittart, Viscountess Waverley, Lord Wedgwood, Lord Weir and Lord Willingdon. I am grateful to all those who helped me to locate these archives, who gave me permission to consult them, and who allowed me to quote from copyright material contained in them. Should any copyright holders have been inadvertently overlooked, I should like to apologize.

I am particularly grateful to the many people who knew Churchill during the inter-war years, who worked with him, or who were themselves involved in the issues and controversies described in this volume. For their kind help, for their patience in answering my questions, and for their valuable reminiscences I should like in particular to thank Baroness Clementine Spencer-Churchill, Sir Richard Acland, the late Judge Waris Ameer Ali, the Earl of Ancaster, Group Captain C. T. Anderson, Maurice Ashley, the late Frank Ashton-Gwatkin, Fred Astaire, Sarah Lady Audley, the Earl of Avon, Lord Balogh, Ronald Bell, G. D. Birla, Sir Robert Birley, Lord Boothby, Viscount Boyd of Merton, Lord Brockway, Sir Richard Brooke, Lord Bullock, His Excellency Fritz Caspari, Lord Coleraine, Sir Colin Coote, Sir Christopher Courtney, Sir F. W. Deakin, Sir Patrick Donner, Lord Duncan-Sandys, the Earl of Dundee, Douglas Fairbanks, R. E. Fearnley-Whittingstall, Sir Keith Feiling, Desmond Flower, Richard Fry, Lord Geoffrey-Lloyd, Air Marshal Sir Victor Goddard, Lord Gordon-Walker, Shiela Grant-Duff, Sir Derrick Gunston, the late Lord Hailes, Miss Grace Hamblin, Norman Hamilton, Lord Harvey of Prestbury, Sir John Hathorn Hall, Professor Agnes Headlam-Morley, Edward Heath, the Hon Sylvia Henley, Mrs Kathleen Hill, David Hindley-Smith, Major-General F. E. Hotblack, Sir Edward Hulton, Dr Thomas Hunt, Michael Hutchison, Michael Huxley, Sir Archibald James, Lajos Lederer, James Lees-Milne, the late Sir Tresham Lever, Kenneth Lindsay, Stefan Lorant, Malcolm MacDonald, Air Commodore L. L. MacLean, Harold Macmillan, Commander Sir John Maitland, Sir John Masterman, Paul Maze, Sir Oswald Mosley, Earl Mountbatten of Burma, Sir Godfrey Nicholson, the late Sir Otto Niemeyer, Admiral Sir Reginald Portal, the Hon Terence Prittie, Count Edward Raczynski, Sir Victor Raikes, Raja Hathisingh, Dr Emery Reves, Cecil Roberts, Sir Folliott Sandford, the Hon Lady Soames, A. F. K. Schlepegrell, Sir Victor Seeley, Sir Geoffrey Shakespeare, Shiva Rao, Professor C. A. Siepmann, John Spencer-Churchill, Sir Raymond Streat, Sir Cecil Syers, Sir Charles Taylor, Lord Thorneycroft, Sir Colin Thornton-Kemsley, Sarita Lady Vansittart, the late Ava Viscountess Waverley, the late Sir John Wheeler-Bennett, John Wheldon, A. E. Woodward-Nutt, Lieutenant-General Sir George Wrisberg and John Zinkin.

I am also grateful to all those who gave me access to information or archives, who answered queries on factual points, and who provided material for use both in the volume itself and in the biographical notes. For help in providing this material I should like to thank the staffs of the Bodleian Library, the Cambridge University Library, the Imperial War Museum, the India Office Library and the Library and Archives of Churchill College, Cambridge, as well as many individuals, including Sir Max Aitken; J. R. L. Anderson; Robert Armstrong; F. Bailey, Naval Historical Library, Ministry of Defence; I. A. Baxter, India Office Records; René Bell; Benedict S. Benedikz, Head of Special Collections, University of Birmingham; J. G. Bevington; Denis Bird; the late Lord Birkenhead; Mrs D. M. Birks, Radleian Society; A. & C. Black Limited, Publishers; Geoffrey D. M. Block, Conservative Research Department; R. Marshall Bond; Jean-Loup Bourget, Cultural Attaché, French Embassy, London; Mrs M. C. Bowyer; J. K. Bradbury, Assistant Editor the *Birmingham Post*; Mrs Pat Bradford, Archivist, Churchill College, Cambridge; Lord Bradwell; Philip A. H. Brown, Assistant Keeper, the British Library; David Butler; H. A. Cahn; Viscount Caldecote; Miss J. M. R. Campbell, Archivist, National Westminster Bank Ltd; Mrs K. F. Campbell, Library and Records Department, Foreign and Commonwealth Office; David Carrington, Librarian, *Jewish Chronicle*; Graham Cawthorne; Eric Ceadel, Librarian, Cambridge University Library; M. H. Chambers; Paul Channon; Sir John Clark; Miss A. M. Colquhoun, Librarian, Australian Reference Library, London; W. E. Cook, Ministry of Defence; Dr J. G. Cormie; H. E. Cox, Chief Librarian, Mirror Group Newspapers; Lord Croft; Mrs Clare Crossley; Professor David Dilks; Lord Dowding, Organizing Secretary, The Navy League; T. H. East, Home Office; G. Van der Espt, Cultural Counsellor, Belgian Embassy; Lady Falkender; Alderman Donald L. Forbes; J. W. Ford, Departmental Record Officer, Treasury Chambers; Carl Foreman; R. C. Fox, Ministry of Defence; A. J. Francis, Office Services, Ministry of Defence; Frederica F. Freer; Eileen Fuller; Gilbert de Goldschmidt-Rothschild; J. Gordon, Secretary, Army & Navy Club; Sir Arnold Hall; B. Hallowell, Ministry of Defence, Adastral House; G. P. M. Harrap; Lord Hartwell; Robert P. Hastings; the late Sir Roger Hawkey; Christopher Hibbert; David Higham; Ann Hoffman; Kenneth G. Holden; His Honour Judge Holdsworth; Dr Michael Hoskin, Keeper of the Archives, Churchill College, Cambridge; Katie Hunter; H. Montgomery Hyde; Ronald Hyde, Editorial Director, *Evening Standard*; T. L. Ingram; Lord Ironside; D. H. Johnson, Secretary, Barclays Bank; Jacqueline Kavanagh, Written Archives Officer, BBC Written Archives Centre; David Kessler; Lord Keyes; Professor C. A. Macartney; Alan F. Mack, Director, Manchester Chamber of Commerce and Industry; Lord Mancroft; David Marquand; Lieutenant-Commander G. R.

Marr, RN, Ministry of Defence; Mrs J. Forbes Meiklejohn; E. Menhofer, Press Attaché, Austrian Embassy, London; L. H. Miller, Librarian, Ministry of Defence; Miss E. Mitchell, Secretary to the Librarian, Royal College of Surgeons of England; Mario Montuori, Director, Istituto Italiano di Cultura, London; Lord Moyne; Maurice Nadin; His Excellency B. K. Nehru, High Commissioner for India, London; His Excellency Albano Nogueira, Portuguese Ambassador; Miss M. Offermans, Goethe Institut, London; Alan W. Palmer; the Hon Helen Pease; Gordon Phillips, Archivist, *The Times*; Robert H. Pilpel; Major R. D. Raikes; Cyril Ray; the Marquess of Reading; Ashley Redburn; William Rees-Mogg; Christopher Reith; Gordon Richardson; Lieutenant-Commander J. A. Roberts, Ministry of Defence; Miss Judith H. Robertson; Captain Stephen Roskill; R. Rothschild, Ambassador of Belgium, London; Mrs A. P. Rowe; David Satinoff; Lord Selborne; Philippe Selz, Private Secretary, French Embassy, London; Mrs J. E. Senior; Peter Shea, Sales Director, A. A. Sites Ltd; Lord Sherfield; Hilde Sloane; N. H. Smith; M. Spalinski, Press Counsellor, Embassy of the Polish People's Republic; A. Spollone, Librarian, Istituto Italiano di Cultura, London; Patrick Strong, Keeper of College Library and Collections, Eton College; Charles Stuart; C. M. Stuart, Naval Historical Library, Ministry of Defence; D. Taylor, Local History Librarian, City of Manchester Cultural Services; N. V. Tilley, Principal Librarian, Information Services, Bradford Metropolitan District; Margaret Townsend, Editor's secretary, *News of the World*; Basil H. Tripp; F. L. Tyler; Mike Unger, Liverpool Daily Post & Echo Ltd; Hugo Vickers; Ralph C. Vickers; Nigel Viney; V. H. Wallis, Establishment Division, Home Office; Colin Watson, Obituary Department, *The Times*; Graham Watson; Anne Westover, Secretary to the Chairman, *Daily Express*; Charles Wintour, Editor, *Evening Standard*; John Womersley, Assistant Editor, *Daily Mail*; Judith A. Woods, Archivist, The Labour Party Library; and J. Wynn.

I have listed the printed sources which I have consulted, most of them published diaries and autobiographies, as part of the list of sources beginning on page 1117. I have also made frequent use of Hansard for the texts of Parliamentary speeches, and also of speeches reported in and editorial opinion, from the following newspapers and magazines: *Answers*, *The Birmingham Post*, the *British Gazette*, the *British Worker*, *Colliers*, the *Daily Despatch*, the *Daily Express*, the *Daily Herald*, the *Daily Mail*, the *Daily Mirror*, the *Daily News*, the *Daily Telegraph*, the *Daily Worker*, the *Democrat*, the *Evening News*, the *Evening Standard*, the

Glasgow Herald, the *Hertfordshire Mercury*, the *Leicester Mail*, the *Leicester Daily Mercury*, *The Listener*, the *Manchester Guardian*, the *Morning Post*, *Nash's Pall Mall*, the *Nation and Athenaeum*, the *New Leader*, the *New Republic*, the *New Statesman*, the *News Chronicle*, the *News of the World*, the *Observer*, the *Review of Reviews*, the *Spectator*, the *Star*, the *Strand Magazine*, the *Sunday Chronicle*, the *Sunday Express*, the *Sunday Gazette*, the *Sunday Graphic*, the *Sunday Pictorial*, the *Sunday Times*, *Time and Tide*, *The Times*, the *Weekly Dispatch*, the *Westminster Gazette* and the *Yorkshire Post*.

I should very much like to thank all those who scrutinized the volume when it reached the proof stage: Professor A. J. L. Barnes, Dr T. A. B. Corley, Dr Christopher Dowling, Joe Haines, Wing-Commander Norman MacMillan, Ivor Samuels, R. W. Thompson and Miss Mary Tyerman. For the chapter on the Committee of Privileges I am indebted to Jeremy Carver for the benefit of his legal expertise; Sir John Colville kindly scrutinized the footnotes in the proof stage; and Sue Townshend undertook the substantial task of typing the volume's final phases.

In preparing the revised 1990 edition, I am grateful to those who sent in notes of errors, or who suggested amendments: Sir Richard Acland, Judge James A. Brown, the Rev. Michael Gedge, Major Andrew A. Gibbs, Frank Hardie, Professor R.F.V. Heuston, David Littman, Colonel J.H. McGuinness, Stephen Parker, and Tom Weissenberg.

During years of increasing economic restriction the financial burden of producing this volume was lessened by the support and generosity both of Sir Emmanuel and Lady Kaye, and of Mrs Jerene Appleby Harnish, through the kindness of the Winston S. Churchill Association of the United States and its President, Dr Harry V. Jaffa. I am also grateful to the Winston Churchill Memorial Trust, who made it possible for me to visit India in search of documentary materials and personal recollections of Churchill's five-year opposition to the Government's India Bill in the 1930s.

During the three years in which this book has been written I received continual hospitality and understanding from Audrey and Michael Sacher, who provided the most warm and sympathetic of backgrounds for the work, and whose encouragement has meant much to me.

To my wife Susie, for her invaluable contribution to the research in all its stages, no words of praise are enough; for five years she has been the sole research assistant on the Churchill biography, its principal critic, and a devoted guide.

Merton College,
Oxford
18 April 1990

Part One

Return to Conservatism
1922–1924

1

Out of Parliament:
'Getting Much Better in Myself'

FOLLOWING his defeat at Dundee in the General Election of October 1922 Churchill was without a seat in Parliament for the first time in twenty-two years. After five years of unbroken Cabinet office, first as Minister of Munitions, then as Secretary of State for War and Air, and finally as Colonial Secretary, he welcomed the chance of a prolonged holiday. He was determined also to finish the first two volumes of his war memoirs, which he had begun while still a Cabinet Minister. In the second week of November his friend General Spears,[1] who had only just been elected to Parliament for the first time, offered to give up his seat in order that Churchill could return to the Liberal benches. But Churchill replied on 18 November, from his home at 2 Sussex Square:

My dear Louis,

I am greatly touched by the extreme kindness of yr offer & the willing sacrifice that it involves. It is a splendid proof of yr friendship. I cd not accept it from you. I want you to enjoy yr seat in Parliament & I shall like to feel I have one or two friends there. I am off to Rome for the winter; & meanwhile if I or my work are assailed in the House I shall rely upon you & Archie[2] to defend me.

[1] Edward Louis Spears, 1886–1974. Joined the Kildare Militia, 1903. Captain, 11th Hussars, 1914. Four times wounded, 1914–15 (Military Cross). Liaison officer with French 10th Army, 1915–16. Head of the British Military Mission to Paris, 1917–20. Brigadier-General, 1918. National Liberal MP for Loughborough, 1922–24; Conservative MP for Carlisle, 1931–45. Churchill's Personal Representative with the French Prime Minister, May–June 1940. Head of British Mission to de Gaulle, 1940. Head of Mission to Syria and the Lebanon, 1941. First Minister to Syria and the Lebanon, 1942–44. Knighted, 1942; created Baronet, 1953.

[2] Archibald Henry Macdonald Sinclair, 1890–1970. Educated at Eton and Sandhurst. Entered Army, 1910. 4th Baronet, 1912. Captain, 1915. 2nd in Command of the 6th Royal Scots Fusiliers, while Churchill was in command, January–May 1916. Squadron-Commander, 2nd Life Guards, 1916–18. Elected to the Other Club, 1917. Major, Guards Machine Gun Regiment, 1918. Private Secretary to Churchill, Ministry of Munitions, 1918–19. Churchill's

The Whips will find me a seat if I wanted one; but what I want now is a rest. . . .

On 2 December 1922 Churchill left England, not for Rome as he had originally planned, but for the South of France, staying for six months at the Villa Rêve d'Or near Cannes. Twice during those six months he returned briefly to England, in order to supervise the rebuilding of Chartwell, which he had purchased at the end of 1922, and to discuss the technical aspects of his memoirs with various naval experts.[1]

Writing to his wife on January 30, during his second visit to London, Churchill described his work in finishing his first volume. 'I am so busy,' he wrote, 'that I hardly ever leave the Ritz except for meals.' His main news was about the book's title, and the help which *The Times* was giving him on it:

Geoffrey Dawson,[2] the new Editor of the 'Times', came to see me yesterday and suggested himself the title of 'The Great Amphibian', but I cannot get either Butterworth[3] or Scribner[4] the American publishers to fancy it. They want 'The World Crisis' or possibly 'Sea Power and the World Crisis' or 'Sea Power in the World Crisis'. We have to settle tomorrow for certain.

The 'Times' is very friendly and helpful. They have turned some of their best men on to try to find mottoes for the chapter headings I have been unable to fill. Garvin[5] has read it all through and is absolutely satisfied with

---

personal Military Secretary, War Office, 1919–21. Churchill's Private Secretary, Colonial Office, 1921–22. Liberal MP for Caithness and Sutherland, 1922–45. Secretary of State for Scotland, 1931–33. Leader of the Parliamentary Liberal Party, 1935–45. Secretary of State for Air in Churchill's wartime Coalition, 1940–45. Created Viscount Thurso, 1952.

[1] Among those who gave Churchill advice were Lord Beatty and Sir Roger Keyes, he was helped principally by a retired Rear-Admiral, Sir Thomas Jackson, who had begun working for him while he was still at the Colonial Office. From 1912 to 1913, when Churchill was First Lord of the Admiralty, Jackson had been Director of Naval Intelligence.

[2] George Geoffrey Robinson, 1874–1944. Educated at Eton and Magdalen College Oxford. Fellow of All Souls, 1898. Private Secretary to Milner in South Africa, 1901–05. Editor of the *Johannesburg Star*, 1905–10. Editor of *The Times*, 1912–19 and 1923–41. Took the surname of Dawson, 1917.

[3] Thornton Butterworth, Churchill's publisher from 1919 to 1939. He published all five volumes of Churchill's *The World Crisis* (the first in 1923, the fifth in 1931), as well as the single volume abridged and revised edition (1931) and the Sandhurst edition (1933). He also published Churchill's *My Early Life* (1930); *India* (1931); *Thoughts and Adventures* (1932); *Great Contemporaries* (1937) and its enlarged edition (1938); and *Step by Step* (1939).

[4] Charles Scribner, 1890–1952. Joined his father's publishing house, Charles Scribner's Sons Ltd, 1913; Secretary, 1918–26; Vice-President, 1926–32; President, 1932–52. On active service as a 1st Lieutenant, France, 1917–18 (US Remount Service). Published Churchill's *Marlborough* in six volumes, but declined to publish *A History of the English-Speaking Peoples*.

[5] James Louis Garvin, 1868–1947. Editor, *The Observer*, 1908–42. An original member of the Other Club, 1911. Editor, *Pall Mall Gazette*, 1912–15. Editor-in-Chief, *Encyclopaedia Britannica*, 1926–9. His only son was killed in action in 1916 on the western front.

it. He is going to write a tremendous review in the 'Observer' when the time comes.

At the beginning of February, Churchill returned to the Rêve d'Or where, as he had hoped, he spent most of his time painting. He also corresponded with his brother Jack[1] about financial affairs, as he was expecting an advance payment of £5,000 for his memoirs, due to be paid at the end of February. 'Let us have a good scheme of investment,' he wrote. To his insurance broker, W. H. Bernau,[2] Churchill commented, on February 17, on a personal note: 'The weather here has been indifferent, but I am getting much better in myself.'

While he was in France, Churchill received two letters about political developments in England. On March 8 his brother Jack sent him news of the Labour Party's success in two by-elections, one at Mitcham, the other at Willesden. At Mitcham Labour had won the seat from the Conservatives; at Willesden East a Liberal fighting with Labour support had likewise won a previously Conservative held seat. Unless Liberals and Conservatives came together again in a Coalition, Jack warned, 'the Labour Party will be in in 4 years time'. On March 14 Sir James Stevenson[3], who had worked under Churchill at the Ministry of Munitions, the War Office and the Colonial Office, wrote to him praising his 'wonderful energy, high ideal and work for the State', and adding:

Don't lie low too long. Things are in the 'melting pot'. L.G.[4] is playing what *looks* like a good game but it isn't. Nobody trusts him. They are sick of

[1] John Strange Spencer Churchill, 1880–1947. Churchill's younger brother, known as Jack. Educated at Harrow. A stockbroker. Major, Queen's Own Oxfordshire Hussars, 1914–18. Served at Dunkirk, 1914; on Sir John French's staff, 1914–15; on Sir Ian Hamilton's staff, 1915; on General Birdwood's staff, 1916–18. In 1908 he married Lady Gwendeline Teresa Mary Bertie (1885–1941), known as 'Goonie', daughter of the 7th Earl of Abingdon.

[2] William Henry Bernau, 1870–1937. Started work at Cox & Co, bankers, 1889; in charge of the Insurance Department, 1910–35; retired 1935. Churchill's insurance broker.

[3] James Stevenson, 1873–1926. Managing Director of John Walker & Sons, Distillers. Director of Area Organization, Ministry of Munitions, 1915–17. Vice-Chairman, Ministry of Munitions Committee, 1917. Created Baronet, 1917. Ordnance Member of the Munitions Council, 1918. Surveyor-General of Supply, War Office, 1919–21. Member of the Army Council, 1919. Member of the Air Council, 1919–21. Personal Commercial Adviser to Churchill at the Colonial Office, 1921–22. Created Baron, 1924.

[4] David Lloyd George, 1863–1945. Educated at a Welsh Church school. Solicitor, 1884. Liberal MP for Caernarvon, 1890–1931. President of the Board of Trade, 1905–08. Privy Councillor, 1905. Chancellor of the Exchequer, 1908–15. Minister of Munitions, May 1915–July 1916. Secretary of State for War, July–December 1916. Prime Minister, December 1916–October 1922. Independent Liberal MP, 1931–45. Created Earl, 1945.

Simon[1] and Asquith.[2] They want a leader all right and if you would only formulate a programme and cast it on the breeze I am sure it would draw. There can only be *two* parties. That is the line of country to ride.

There are hundreds of thousands who wont vote at all at present. They have *no* party. But they are anti labour. Dont overlook the fact that they are *learning* to govern. The passivity of the present Govt is beyond belief. They *settle* nothing. Baldwin[3] is scared of the Treasury officials. . . .

Churchill did not respond to these promptings. 'It has been vy pleasant out here,' he wrote to his cousin the Duke of Marlborough[4] on April 7, '& such a relief after all these years not to have a score of big anxieties & puzzles on one's shoulders. The Government moulders placidly away. But I must confess myself more interested in the past than the present.'

The first volume of Churchill's war memoirs had been serialized in *The Times* from February 8, and was published on April 10, entitled *The World Crisis*. J. L. Garvin wrote the review he had promised, describing the book in the *Observer* as 'a whale among minnows', and expressing his confidence that Churchill had sent his critics 'to the bottom by the whacks of his tale'. In his Preface Churchill wrote: 'I hope that this account may be agreeable to those at least who wish to think well of our country, of its naval service, of its governing institutions, of its political life and public men; and that they will feel that perhaps after all Britain and her Empire have not been so ill-guided through the great convulsions as it is customary to declare'. A total of

[1] John Allsebrook Simon, 1873–1954. Educated at Fettes and Wadham College Oxford. Fellow of All Souls. Liberal MP for Walthamstow, 1906–18; for Spen Valley, 1922–31. Solicitor-General, 1910–13. Knighted, 1910. Attorney-General, with a seat in the Cabinet, 1913–15. Home Secretary, 1915–16, when he resigned in opposition to conscription. Major, Royal Air Force, serving in France, 1917–18. Liberal National MP for Spen Valley, 1931–40. Secretary of State for Foreign Affairs, 1931–35. Home Secretary, 1935–37. Chancellor of the Exchequer, 1937–40. Created Viscount, 1940. Lord Chancellor, 1940–45.

[2] Herbert Henry Asquith, 1852–1928. Educated at the City of London School and Balliol College Oxford. Liberal MP, 1886–1918 and 1920–24. Home Secretary, 1892–1905. Chancellor of the Exchequer, 1905–08. Prime Minister, 1908–16. Created Earl of Oxford and Asquith, 1925. His eldest son, Raymond, was killed in action in 1916.

[3] Stanley Baldwin, 1867–1947. Educated at Harrow and Trinity College Cambridge. Conservative MP for Bewdley, 1908–37. Financial Secretary to the Treasury, 1917–21. President of the Board of Trade, 1921–22. Chancellor of the Exchequer 1922–23. Prime Minister, 1923–24, and 1924–29. Lord President of the Council, 1931–35. Prime Minister (for the third time), 1935–37. Created Earl, and Knight of the Garter, 1937.

[4] Charles Richard John Spencer-Churchill, 1871–1934. Churchill's cousin. Known as 'Sunny'. Succeeded his father as 9th Duke of Marlborough, 1892. Paymaster-General of the Forces, 1899–1902. Staff Captain and ADC to General Hamilton during the South African War, 1900. Under-Secretary of State for the Colonies, 1903–05. Lieutenant-Colonel, Queen's Own Oxfordshire Hussars, 1910. An original member of the Other Club, 1911. Employed at the War Office as a Special Messenger, 1914–15. Joint Parliamentary Secretary, Board of Agriculture and Fisheries, 1917–18.

7,380 copies were printed, but the sales were so rapid that the publishers ordered a reprint of 2,500 three days later, and a third of 1,500 on May 3. The book received many reviews: the *Daily Telegraph* praised its 'exceptional frankness' and felt that it deserved a place 'on the best shelf' in the vast library of war books already published. The *New Statesman* was certain that history would vindicate Churchill's actions at the Admiralty. 'He has written a book which is remarkably egotistical,' it concluded, 'but which is honest and which certainly will long survive him.'

Churchill had sent copies of his book to many of his friends. One of the first to thank him was the Prince of Wales,[1] who wrote from St James's Palace on April 12 that he had already begun to read it, and added: 'I'm so glad you've had a lot of polo & are fit enough again to enjoy it. Its great news to hear you are playing in London this coming season & I hope we'll get lots of games together.' Another correspondent was Margot Asquith,[2] who wrote to him on May 4: 'I think your book a great masterpiece, written with a warmth of words, an economy of personal laudation, swiftness of current, selection, lucidity & drama unexcelled by Macaulay. I started and finished it in a night & having closed it determined to write this one line . . .' Margot Asquith ended with political advice:

Lie low; do nothing in politics, go on writing all the time & painting; do not join yr former colleagues who are making prodigious asses of themselves in every possible manner: Keep friends in every port—lose *no* one. Pirate Ships are no use in times of Peace.

Your man of war is for the moment out of action but if you have the patience of Disraeli with your fine temper glowing mind & real kind unvindictive nature you cd still command a great future.

Churchill returned to England from France in the second week of May, but he made no immediate effort to return to Parliament. In a speech to the Aldwych Club in London on May 24 he said, of his own political future: 'After seventeen rough years of official work I can assure you that there are many worse things than private life. To see so many things being done, or left undone, for which one cannot possibly be

---

[1] Edward Albert Christian George Andrew Patrick David, 1894–1972. Entered Royal Navy as a Cadet, 1907. Prince of Wales, 1910–36. 2nd Lieutenant, Grenadier Guards, August 1914. Attached to Sir John French's Staff, November 1914. Served in France and Italy, 1914–18. Major, 1918. Succeeded his father as King, January 1936. Abdicated, December 1936. Duke of Windsor, 1936.

[2] Emma Alice Margaret Tennant, 1864–1945. Known as Margot. She married H. H. Asquith (as his second wife) in 1894, and published four separate volumes of memoirs, including *The Autobiography of Margot Asquith* in 1921.

blamed oneself, for which other people are being most heartily blamed, has afforded me great refreshment. . . .'

On May 30 Churchill's political future was discussed by Lord Riddell[1] and Sir Robert Horne.[2] Riddell recorded in his diary:

Horne suggested to Baldwin that he would be wise to invite Winston to join the Government, as he would thus secure a powerful colleague and an excellent debater. Baldwin was evidently impressed by the idea, but doubtful of giving effect to it. Horne had lunch with Winston the other day and asked him where he stood politically. He replied, 'I am what I have always been—a Tory Democrat. Force of circumstance has compelled me to serve with another party, but my views have never changed, and I should be glad to give effect to them by rejoining the conservatives.'

At the beginning of August Churchill was offered a private commission which could greatly augment his finances. In return for a fee of £5,000 two oil companies, Royal Dutch Shell and the Burmah Anglo-Persian Oil Company, asked him to represent them in their application to the Government for a merger with the Anglo-Persian Oil Company, in which the Government held the majority share.[3] A year earlier, at the time of the Coalition Government, the Cabinet had turned down the companies' application following the recommendation of a Cabinet Committee presided over by Stanley Baldwin, then President of the Board of Trade. In May 1923 Baldwin had become Prime Minister. The two oil companies were eager to re-apply, and approached Churchill to be their representative. At first he hesitated, but following

[1] George Allardice Riddell, 1865–1934. Began work in London as a boy clerk in a solicitor's office. Solicitor, 1888. Chairman of the *News of the World*, 1903. Knighted, 1909. An original member of the Other Club, 1911. Liaison officer between the Government and the Press, 1914–18. Created Baronet, 1918. Created Baron, 1920. President of the Royal Free Hospital, 1925. Among his charitable bequests were £100,000 each to the Royal Free Hospital and the Eastman Dental Clinic. In his Will he also left £1,000 to Churchill.

[2] Robert Stevenson Horne, 1871–1940. Lecturer in Philosophy, University College of North Wales, 1895. Examiner in Philosophy, Aberdeen University, 1896. Active at the Scottish Bar, 1900–14. Assistant Inspector-General of Transportation, with the rank of Lieutenant-Colonel, 1917. Director of Department of Materials and Priority, Admiralty, 1917. Director, Admiralty Labour Department, 1918. Third Civil Lord of Admiralty, 1918–19. Knighted, 1918. Conservative MP, 1918–37. Minister of Labour, 1919. President of the Board of Trade, 1920–21. Chancellor of the Exchequer, 1921–22. Declined office under Bonar Law and turned to the City for employment, where he became Chairman of the Great Western Railway Company, the Burma Corporation and several other companies. Created Viscount Horne of Slamannan, 1937.

[3] In 1913, while First Lord of the Admiralty, Churchill himself had carried through the House of Commons the Anglo-Persian Oil Convention, whereby, in order to secure for the Royal Navy adequate oil supplies free from the risk of foreign control or private speculation, Britain became the majority shareholder in the Anglo-Persian Oil Company, holding 51% of the shares. The Government subsequently derived a substantial revenue from this source.

a further approach from Sir Robert Waley Cohen,[1] Churchill agreed to consider the oil companies' request.

That summer Churchill's wife and children stayed at Cromer, by the North Sea, while he himself remained at Sussex Square, working on the proofs of his second volume, and studying the oil merger documents. On August 13, writing to his wife, he expressed his 'general agreement' with the British Government's Note to France, in which Britain had rebuked France for its occupation of the Ruhr. Churchill had been told of the contents of the Note on the telephone by his friend Lord Beaverbrook.[2] 'It is a very strong Note,' Churchill added, 'and will produce serious internal reactions in the Conservative Party.' He felt that the Note should not be criticized publicly, telling his wife: 'I think when the Government deliberately take a step of this kind towards a foreign country, no one should try to weaken its effect.'

On August 14 Churchill went to see Baldwin at 10 Downing Street. It was their first meeting since Baldwin had become Prime Minister. On the following day Churchill sent his wife an account of the meeting, and of his other activities:

My interview with the PM was most agreeable. He professed unbounded leisure & recd me with the utmost cordiality. We talked Ruhr, Oil, Admiralty & Air, Reparations, the American Debt & general politics. I found him thoroughly in favour of the Oil Settlement on the lines proposed. Indeed he might have been Waley Cohen from the way he talked. I am sure it will come off. The only thing I am puzzled about is my own affair. However I am to see Cohen on Friday. It is a question of how to arrange it so as to leave no just ground of criticism. My talk with the PM was quite general & I did not raise the personal aspect at all at this preliminary & non-committal stage. Masterton[3] in whom I confided was vy shy of it on large

[1] Robert Waley Cohen, 1877–1952. Educated at Clifton and Emmanuel College Cambridge. Joined the Shell Company, 1901; subsequently Managing Director of the Shell Transport and Trading Co Ltd, and of United British Oilfields of Trinidad Ltd. Petroleum Adviser to the Army Council. Knighted, 1920. President of the United Synagogue. Vice-Chairman, University College London.

[2] William Maxwell Aitken, 1879–1964. A Canadian financier. Conservative MP, 1910–16. Knighted, 1911. Elected to the Other Club, 1912; resigned, 1930. Canadian Eye-Witness in France, May–August 1915; Canadian Representative at the Front, September 1915–16. Newspaper proprietor: bought the *Daily Express*, his largest circulation newspaper, in December 1916. Created Baron Beaverbrook, 1917. Chancellor of the Duchy of Lancaster and Minister of Information, 1918. Minister for Aircraft Production, 1940–41. Minister of State, 1941. Minister of Supply, 1941–42. Lord Privy Seal, 1943–45. Known as 'Max'.

[3] James Edward Masterton-Smith, 1878–1938. Educated at Harrow and Hertford College Oxford. Entered Admiralty, 1901. Private Secretary to five First Lords: McKenna, 1910–11; Churchill, 1911–15; Balfour, 1915–16; Carson, 1916–17; Sir E. Geddes, 1917. Assistant Secretary to Churchill, Ministry of Munitions, 1917–19; War Office, 1919–20. Knighted, 1919. Permanent Under-Secretary of State, Colonial Office, 1921–4.

political grounds. However I shall proceed further before making up my mind.

I entered Downing Street by the Treasury entrance to avoid comment. This much amused Baldwin. However Max rang up this morning to say he hoped I had had a pleasant interview, & that I had greatly heartened the PM about the Ruhr! He is a little ferret. He has to go to Scotland tonight so I am going to dine at the Vineyard instead of his coming here.

Keyes[1] came down last night & we had long jolly talks about the war & what they killed each other for. I purchased in London two delicious young lady grouses wh were the feature of dinner. This morning we rode. The rides on the common are lovely—but vy little grass. However there is beautiful park in wh we trespassed, but wh we can easily get permission to use. The work progresses quite well. I have just returned from a 3 hours inspection, wood sawing etc. The water flows. There will be lots for you to see when you return.

I did a further deal in the franc, realizing to date about £150 profit. I have 8 articles to write as soon as the book is finished £500, 400, & 200 = 1100. We shall not starve.

I do hope you are enjoying yrself my beloved & not tiring yrself out. The happy mean. . . .

While Chartwell was being rebuilt, Churchill rented a house near by —Hosey Rigge—on the road from Westerham to his new property. Churchill had nicknamed the house 'Cosy Pig', and in a letter to his wife on August 17 he told her of his plans to entertain their children there. 'I am going to amuse them on Saturday and Sunday,' he wrote, 'by making them an aerial house in the lime tree. You may be sure I will take the greatest precautions to guard against them tumbling down. The undergrowth of the tree is so thick it will be perfectly safe, and I will not let them go up except under my personal charge.'

At the end of August Clementine Churchill was taken ill with a throat infection. She therefore stayed at Hosey Rigge, where she supervised the work at Chartwell which her husband had put in train, while he left England for France, where he was the guest of his friend the

---

[1] Roger John Brownlow Keyes, 1872–1945. Entered Navy, 1885, Naval Attaché, Athens and Constantinople, 1905–07. Commodore in charge of submarines, North Sea and adjacent waters, August 1914–February 1915. Chief of Staff, Eastern Mediterranean Squadron (Dardanelles), 1915. Director of Plans, Admiralty, 1917. Vice-Admiral in command of the Dover Patrol (and Zeebrugge raid), 1918. Knighted, 1918. Created Baronet, 1919. Deputy Chief of the Naval Staff, 1921–25. Commander-in-Chief, Mediterranean, 1925–28; Portsmouth, 1929–31. Admiral of the Fleet, 1930. National Conservative MP, 1934–43. Director of Combined Operations, 1940–41. Created Baron, 1943. Churchill wrote the foreword to his memoirs, *Adventures Ashore & Afloat* (1939). His elder son was killed in action in Libya, leading a raid on General Rommel's headquarters, 18 November 1941.

Duke of Westminster,[1] aboard the Duke's yacht *Flying Cloud*. On September 2 he wrote to his wife from Bayonne, describing his surroundings. 'It is absolute quiet & peace,' he wrote. 'One need not do anything or see anybody.' Churchill also told his wife that he had at last decided to accept the oil companies' request to represent them, having talked the matter over with his former Civil Lord of Admiralty, Lord Southborough,[2] who, he wrote, 'considers it my duty & in every way appropriate'. If Baldwin were to agree, he added, 'I think I shall have no doubts about going forward'.

The rest of Churchill's letter concerned financial affairs, and the move to Chartwell. For several months his wife had worried about the move: she was uneasy about leaving London, and felt no special attraction towards the new house. 'At first,' she later recalled in a conversation with the author, 'I did not want to go to Chartwell at all. But Winston had set his heart on it.' Much of her worry was financial: the cost of the rebuilding had already risen from £13,000 to £15,000 and she doubted their ability to find such large sums, or to maintain the property as it ought to be maintained. But Churchill made a determined effort to set her mind at rest:

My beloved, I do beg you not to worry about money, or to feel insecure. On the contrary the policy we are pursuing aims above all at *stability*. (like Bonar Law!)[3] Chartwell is to be our *home*. It will have cost us £20,000 and will be worth at least £15,000 apart from a fancy price. We must endeavour to live there for many years & hand it on to Randolph[4] afterwards. We must

---

[1] Hugh Richard Arthur Grosvenor, 1879–1953. Known as 'Bendor'. Educated at Eton. Succeeded his grandfather as 2nd Duke of Westminster, 1899. ADC to Lord Roberts, South Africa, 1900–02. Commanded an armoured car detachment, Royal Naval Division, 1914–15. Personal Assistant to the Controller, Mechanical Department, Ministry of Munitions, 1917. His uncle, Lord Hugh Grosvenor, a Captain in the Household Cavalry, was killed in action in November 1914.

[2] Francis John Stephens Hopwood, 1860–1947. Assistant Solicitor, Board of Trade, 1885. Knighted, 1901. Permanent Secretary, Board of Trade, 1901–07. Member of the Transvaal and Orange River Constitutional Enquiry, 1906. Permanent Under-Secretary of State for the Colonies, 1907–11. Privy Councillor, 1912. Additional Civil Lord of Admiralty, 1912–17. Created Baron Southborough, 1917. Secretary to the Irish Convention, 1917–18. President of the Commission to India on Reform, 1918–19. President of the China Association.

[3] Andrew Bonar Law, 1858–1923. Conservative MP, 1900–23; Leader of the Conservative Opposition in the House of Commons, 1911–15. Chancellor of the Exchequer, 1916–18. Lord Privy Seal, 1919–21. Prime Minister, October 1922–May 1923. Two of his three sons were killed in action in the First World War.

[4] Randolph Frederick Edward Spencer Churchill, 1911–1968. Churchill's only son. His godfathers were F. E. Smith and Sir Edward Grey. Educated at Eton and Christ Church Oxford. On leaving Oxford in 1932, without taking his degree, he worked briefly for the Imperial Chemical Industries as assistant editor of their house magazine. Joined the staff of the *Sunday Graphic*, 1932; wrote subsequently for many newspapers, including the *Evening Standard* (1937–39). Reported during Hitler's election campaign of 1932, the Chaco War of

make it in every way charming & as far as possible economically self contained. It will be cheaper than London.

Eventually—though there is no hurry—we must sell Sussex & find a small flat for you & me. . . .

Then with the motor we shall be well equipped for business or pleasure. If we go into office we will live in Downing Street!

Churchill calculated that during 1924 he would receive £5,000 for the second volume of *The World Crisis* which 'will furnish Chartwell finally & keep us going for six or seven months with the surplus'; a further £8,000 for the third volume; and £1,200 for three articles he was writing. 'The cheaper we can live, of course, the better,' he wrote. 'But I am budgeting to spend about £10,000 p.a. apart from the capital expenditure on Chartwell, or the payment of bills . . .' His letter ended: 'Add to this my darling yr courage & good will and I am certain that we can make ourselves a permanent resting place, so far as the money side of this uncertain & transitory world is concerned. But if you set yourself against Chartwell, or lose heart, or bite your bread & butter & yr pig then it only means further instability, recasting of plans & further expense & worry.'

Churchill went on to report his good progress with the second volume of *The World Crisis*, on which he was working for three or four hours each day. He hoped to finish the proofs by the following day and had already sent a set to Garvin, who replied that he had been 'at the proofs all day, sombrely enthralled'. History, Garvin believed, would vindicate both the Dardanelles campaign and Churchill himself. Garvin added: 'Mind you true tragedy, supreme tragedy are not the worst in life, far from it: the squalid morass of unattempting impotence is the stifling of the soul and hope of man. It's wonderful how you've done it: again the technical part so sober, the imaginative part so throbbing.'

In a further letter to his wife on September 5, Churchill reported that both he and the Duke of Westminster had been 'vy successful at the tables', winning £500 by 'pursuing' as he put it, 'a most small & conservative game'. During the day he worked at a number of magazine articles: 'I write and work in bed all morning as usual,' he wrote. 'If the sun shines, I paint.' His only political comment was on the Italian decision to occupy the port of Fiume, despite the protests of the League

1935, and the Spanish Civil War. Unsuccessful Parliamentary candidate 1935 (twice) 1936, 1945, 1950 and 1951. Conservative MP for Preston, 1940–45. On active service, North Africa and Italy, 1941–43. Major, British mission to the Yugoslav Army of National Liberation, 1943–44 (MBE, 1944). Historian; author of the first two volumes of this biography.

of Nations. 'What a swine this Mussolini[1] is,' Churchill wrote, and he added: 'I am all for the League of Nations. Poor devil it is life or death for it now.' In mid-September Churchill returned to London, writing to his friend General Spears on September 20:

I have been at Bayonne & am just about to return thither to play a month's polo with Westminster. Here I have been gripped by my second volume wh is now finished & will be published in October. I shall be back in England in November & will look forward to seeing you then.

Politics continue to mark time & will do so for a while. I am vy content to have for the first time in my life a little rest, & leisure to look after my own affairs, build my house & cultivate my garden. It is nice for you & Archie being in Parliament & you shd take every opportunity of making good speeches. Then some day when I rejoin that assembly—if ever—I shall be able to back you up.

During the autumn Churchill continued his work on the oil merger. This involved him in long discussions with directors of the oil companies concerned, and with several Government Departments. In a private note written later in the year, Churchill recalled that it was Baldwin himself who had, at an early point in the course of the discussions, authorized him 'to see the President of the Board of Trade[2] & the First Lord of the Admiralty,[3] to whom he said he wd speak personally', and to fix a price for the sale of the Government's oil interest. According

---

[1] Benito Mussolini, 1883–1945. Socialist journalist and agitator before 1914; editor of *Avanti*. Founded the patriotic *Il Popolo d'Italia*, 1914. Served on the Austrian front, 1917. Founded the Fascist Party at the end of the war. President of the Council of Ministers, 1922–26. Minister for Foreign Affairs, 1924–29 and 1932–36. Prime Minister, 1926–43. Minister of War, 1926–29 and 1933–43. Fled from Rome, 1943. Head of the German-controlled Government of Northern Italy, 1944–45. Murdered by Italian anti-Fascists.

[2] Philip Lloyd-Greame, 1884–1972. Educated at Winchester and University College Oxford. On active service, 1914–17 (Military Cross). Joint Secretary, Ministry of National Service, 1917–18. Conservative MP for Hendon, 1918–35. Parliamentary Secretary, Board of Trade, 1920–21. Knighted, 1920. Secretary of the Overseas Trade Department, 1921–22. President of the Board of Trade, 1922–23, 1924–29 and 1931. Assumed the name Cunliffe-Lister, 1924. Created Viscount Swinton, 1935. Secretary of State for the Colonies, 1931–35; for Air, 1935–38. Cabinet Minister Resident in West Africa, 1942–44. Minister of Civil Aviation, 1944–45. Minister of Materials, 1951–52. Secretary of State for Commonwealth Relations, 1952–55. His elder son died of wounds received in action in 1943.

[3] Leopold Charles Maurice Stennett Amery, 1873–1955. A contemporary of Churchill's at Harrow. Fellow of All Souls College, Oxford, 1897. *Manchester Guardian* correspondent in the Balkans and Turkey, 1897–99. Served on the editorial staff of *The Times*, 1899–1909. Conservative MP, 1911–45. Intelligence Officer in the Balkan and eastern Mediterranean, 1915–16. Assistant Secretary, War Cabinet Secretariat, 1917–18. Parliamentary Under-Secretary, Colonial Office, 1919–21. First Lord of the Admiralty, 1922–24. Colonial Secretary, 1924–29. Secretary of State for India and Burma, 1940–45. Known as 'Leo'.

to Churchill's note, Baldwin had told him that he was 'on general grounds averse from the continued participation of the British Government in the Oil business' and that he believed that twenty million pounds 'wd be a vy good price for the Government to obtain for their shares'.

On September 29 Churchill took up Baldwin's offer to speak to the First Lord of the Admiralty, Leopold Amery, who recorded in his diary: 'He certainly made suggestions which might make the scheme more capable and promised to let me have them as draft heads in a fortnight or so.' Amery added: 'He sounded me very anxiously about what our intentions were on the tariff issue strongly urging us not to throw away a good position but to continue peacefully in office for the next two or three years. He told me that the Liberals were very anxious to have him back but that he was not having any and was enjoying his present holiday immensely.'

On October 8 *The Times* began its serialization of the second volume of *The World Crisis*, and the volume was published on October 30. In its own review, *The Times* criticized Churchill for distorting documents and deploying 'undue censure' in his account of the Dardanelles, declaring: 'His apologia is too much an impatient indictment of colleagues who were antagonized by hastiness of action; and it does not contribute to the "silence following great words of Peace". It rather sends the reader back to Pitt's profoundly wise remark that of all the qualities a statesman needs, patience is the first.'

Churchill sent copies of his new volume to more than fifty friends and former colleagues. On November 1 Baldwin wrote from 10 Downing Street:

My dear Churchill,

I have for many years, made a practice of buying every book written by a friend, and thinking I might include you in this category I was an early purchaser of your first volume.

And now, before I had time to secure the second, comes your delightful present!

Believe me I am grateful and shall value it as the gift of the author.

If I could write as you do, I should never bother about making speeches!

Yours sincerely
Stanley Baldwin

On December 23 T. E. Lawrence[1] wrote to Churchill: 'It's far & away

---

[1] Thomas Edward Lawrence, 1888–1935. Born in North Wales, Educated at Oxford. Travelled in Syria and Palestine while still an undergraduate. Obtained a first-class degree in

the best war-book I've yet read in any language,' and five days later Leopold Amery wrote: 'I have read it with the greatest admiration for the skill of the narrative itself, but with even greater sympathy for you in your struggle against the impregnable wall of pedantry or in the appalling morasses of irresolution.'

In the first week of November Churchill continued to prepare his notes on the oil merger, and consulted Leopold Amery, the First Lord of the Admiralty, about the navy's oil requirements. But before he could complete his work, political events in England took a totally unexpected turn. Speaking at Plymouth on October 25, Stanley Baldwin had argued that the reintroduction of protection was the only means of fighting unemployment, and on November 13 he announced that he would hold a General Election.

While the Conservative Party, which had been in office for only a year, was thrown into a turmoil by Baldwin's decision, Liberals saw Free Trade as the policy on which they could be united for the first time since the fall of Asquith in December 1916. Twenty years earlier Churchill himself had left the Conservative Party largely on this very issue, becoming one of the leading Liberal advocates of Free Trade.

On November 11, in a letter issued to the Press and widely published, Churchill, while declining to stand as the Liberal candidate at Central Glasgow, strongly upheld Free Trade as 'vital to the British people and indispensable to the recovery of their prosperity'. It was more, he added; it was an appeal to all those 'who sincerely wish to heal the wounds of war and make its immediate hatreds die'. His letter continued:

Accepting the verdict of the electors a year ago, I have taken no part in opposing the Conservative Government, nor in disparaging the new Ministers. I should have been perfectly content to remain for a much longer period in

---

history, 1910. On archaeological work at Carchemish, 1911–14. Explored, with Leonard Woolley, the Negev desert south of Beersheba, 1914. Served in the Geographical Section, General Staff, War Office, 1914–15; military intelligence, Egypt, 1915–16. Accompanied Ronald Storrs to Jedda, 1916, at the inauguration of the Arab revolt against the Turks. Liaison officer and adviser to the Emir Feisal, 1917–18. Took part in the capture of Akaba from the Turks, July 1917, and the capture of Damascus, October 1918. Accompanied Feisal to the Paris Peace Conference, 1919. Elected a Fellow of All Souls, Oxford, 1919. Joined the Middle East Department of the Colonial Office, January 1921; resigned, 1922. Enlisted in the Royal Air Force (as J. H. Ross), 1922 and again (as T. E. Shaw), 1923. Served in India, 1926–28. Retired from the RAF, 1935, Killed in a motor cycle accident.

private life. But an aggressive attack has been levelled needlessly and wantonly at the foundations of the people's livelihood. A monstrous fallacy is erected against us. Nearly all the trades of the country are threatened with injury. All business is subjected to unnecessary and prolonged disturbance and uncertainty. The nation, which was promised only a year ago tranquillity and recuperation, is plunged in violent international strife. The return of prosperity must be delayed. The cruel conditions of the Winter will certainly be aggravated, and the influence of the British Empire as an agent of reconciliation on the Continent of Europe will be woefully, and for a time fatally, impaired.

In these circumstances I agree with you that those who are opposed to this wild adventure and reckless experiment must stand together in real comradeship. . . .

Following Churchill's statement in favour of Free Trade, several more Liberal Associations at once asked him to stand as a Free Trade candidate; on November 13 those of both West Leicester and Manchester Exchange asked him if he were prepared to be a candidate. Following a press rumour on November 14 to the effect that he had agreed to stand for Manchester, Lord Rothermere [1] telegraphed from the South of France: 'Although leaning towards tariff reform shall instruct all my newspapers daily and Sunday in that area to urge your return as in the best interests of Manchester itself.' During November 14 three more Liberal Associations asked Churchill to be their candidate: West Salford, Rusholme and the Mossley Division of Manchester.

Churchill was now determined to try to return to the House of Commons, and to take a leading part in the Liberal campaign against Protection. On November 15 he saw Sir Robert Waley Cohen, and formally withdrew from all work on the oil merger. On the following day a further invitation reached him from the Aberavon Liberal Association, which wanted him to stand against the Labour Party Leader, Ramsay MacDonald. [2]

On Friday November 16 Churchill went by train to Manchester, where, in the Free Trade Hall, he made a fierce and sustained attack

[1] Harold Sidney Harmsworth, 1868–1940. Younger brother of Lord Northcliffe, with whom he had helped to establish the *Daily Mail* and *Evening News*. Created Baronet, 1910. Proprietor of the *Daily Mirror*, 1914. Created Baron Rothermere, 1914. Launched the *Sunday Pictorial*, 1915. Director-General of the Royal Army Clothing Factory, 1916. President of the Air Council, 1917–18. Created Viscount, 1919. Two of his three sons were killed in action in the first world war, one in November 1916, the other in February 1918.

[2] James Ramsay MacDonald, 1866–1937. Labour MP for Leicester, 1906–18, for Aberavon, 1922–29 and for Seaham, 1929–31. Leader of the Labour Party, 1911–14. Prime Minister and Secretary of State for Foreign Affairs, January to November 1924. Prime Minister, 1929–35. National Labour MP, 1931–35. Lord President of the Council, 1935–37.

against Protection. Baldwin's decision to 'assassinate' Free Trade, he declared, was a 'Party verdict, obtained by Party politicians, and exploited for Party purposes', not a measure of statecraft, but 'an act of faction'. It was quite untrue that foreign imports caused domestic unemployment, as Baldwin had stated at Plymouth. 'I have studied the trade of Britain,' Churchill said, 'for more than 20 years, and I have never heard such a doctrine seriously propounded by any high and responsible authority before.' Churchill went on to point out that one of Baldwin's Ministers, Neville Chamberlain,[1] had said that price rises resulting from the tariff on foreign goods could be offset by higher wages. This was a very 'reckless' argument, he warned: 'Surely they had had enough of this mad race between a rise in wages and a rise in cost of living?'

'There is no reason,' Churchill told a crowded luncheon meeting at the Manchester Reform Club on the following evening, 'why Mr Asquith should not head a Government comprising the experience and European prestige of Lord Grey,[2] and the immense and unequalled following, the social driving force and historic war record of Mr Lloyd George.' With a reunited Party, he declared, there were 'no limits' to Liberal prospects; and to stormy applause he described Liberalism as the only 'sure, sober, safe middle course of lucid intelligence and high principle'.

On November 19 Churchill informed the West Leicester Liberal Association that he was willing to be their candidate, and on the following evening he was adopted unanimously. His main opponent was F. W. Pethick-Lawrence,[3] the Labour Party's principal advocate of

[1] Arthur Neville Chamberlain, 1869–1940. Son of Joseph Chamberlain, his mother died in childbirth in 1875. Educated at Rugby and Mason College, Birmingham. In business in the Bahamas, 1890–97. Lord Mayor of Birmingham, 1915–16. Director-General of National Service, 1916–17 (when his cousin Norman, to whom he was devoted, was killed in action on the western front). Conservative MP for Ladywood, 1918–29; for Edgbaston, 1929–40. Postmaster-General, 1922–23. Paymaster-General, 1923. Minister of Health, 1923, 1924–29 and 1931. Chancellor of the Exchequer, 1923–24 and 1931–37. Prime Minister, 1937–40. Lord President of the Council, May–November 1940.

[2] Edward Grey, 1862–1933. 3rd Baronet, 1882. Educated at Winchester and Balliol College, Oxford. Liberal MP for Berwick-on-Tweed, 1885–1916. Foreign Secretary, 1905–16. Created Viscount Grey of Fallodon, 1916. Ambassador on a special Mission to the USA, 1919.

[3] Frederick William Pethick-Lawrence, 1871–1961. Educated at Eton and Trinity College Cambridge. Barrister and economist. Editor of The Echo, 1902–05; the Labour Record and Review, 1905–07. Joint-editor, Votes for Women, 1907–14; imprisoned for nine months in 1912 for conspiring in connection with militant suffragette demonstrations. Urged a negotiated peace with Germany, 1917. Labour MP for West Leicester, 1923–31; for Edinburgh East, 1935–45. Financial Secretary to the Treasury, 1929–31. Member of the India Round-Table Conference, 1931. Privy Council, 1937. Created Baron, 1945. Secretary of State for India and Burma, 1945–47. He published his memoirs, Fate Has Been Kind, in 1943.

the Capital Levy, whereby all individual capital of over £5,000 would be subject to a special tax.

Speculation about Churchill's future followed swiftly on his adoption. 'I am told it is settled among the leaders of the Liberal Party,' wrote a political commentator in the *Daily Sketch* on November 21, 'that *if* they return to power Winston is to go back to the Colonial Office . . . this great idea is that many of the Crown Colonies and Protectorates, if fully developed, can be made to carry immense populations and to supply the Mother Country with all the raw materials she may require.' Churchill's standing with the rank and file of the Liberal Party was likewise improved. On November 22 his portrait, and that of Lloyd George, which had been banished to the cellars of the National Liberal Club early in 1921, was brought upstairs again, and hung again among the other Liberal stalwarts.

Clementine Churchill was disappointed that her husband had chosen to fight West Leicester, instead of one of the Manchester seats. She was equally worried when he accepted an invitation to dine at Lord Beaverbrook's house with Lloyd George, writing to him on the morning of the dinner:

My Darling Winston,

I want to appeal to you to think again before you go to Max's this evening. Ll.G. is not in the same position as you—He is in not out & he shares or practically shares the throne with Asquith.

Now I am sure the old *real* Liberals will want you back but of course there *is* the shyness of a long estrangement. Do not give them cause (quite wrongly I know) for thinking that you would like a new Tory Liberal Coalition. That might cool them off.

Instinctively, one of the reasons I wanted Rusholme was that if you were to lose a seat I felt it would be better for you to be beaten by a Tory (which would rouse Liberal sympathy) than by a Socialist.

My Darling it is important—I shall say *nothing* if you go, but consider the imprudence of losing the offer of a good Wee Free Seat (as opposed to extinct Nat Liberal) for the sake of a pleasant evening.

From the outset of the campaign Churchill was hampered by Press hostility. Neither of the local newspapers, the *Leicester Mail* or the *Leicester Daily Mercury*, would support him. But the proprietor of the neighbouring *Nottingham Journal*, Sir Charles Starmer,[1] decided to

---

[1] Charles Walter Starmer, 1870–1933. Joined the *Northern Echo*, 1899; Manager, 1908. Mayor of Darlington, 1907–08. By 1914 he had obtained control of the *Sheffield Independent*, the *Birmingham Gazette*, the *Nottingham Journal*, and thirty other local newspapers. Knighted, 1917. Liberal MP for Cleveland, 1923–24.

throw his influence behind Churchill and instructed his editor, Cecil Roberts,[1] to do all he could to help Churchill win. Churchill himself enlisted the help of a young man whom he had recently met, Brendan Bracken,[2] whom he despatched to Nottingham to see what the newspaper could do. Following Bracken's visit, Cecil Roberts appointed three of his best reporters to cover Churchill's meetings, and organized a convoy of trucks to take the *Nottingham Journal* to Leicester early each morning. The campaign itself was a rowdy one: each of Churchill's meetings was disrupted by continual heckling, and some ended in complete disorder. Of one such meeting, on November 22, the *Leicester Mail* reported that Churchill and his wife 'were greeted by groans and hoots, not a single cheer being heard in the building'.

Cecil Roberts, who spent much of the campaign in Leicester, admired how, even when the heckling was at its height, Churchill was able to speak with a vehemence of conviction 'that silenced the enemy and evoked applause'. Roberts later recalled how 'Hatred of him was aflame', and he added: 'No insults were too gross to hurl at him. One, of course, the Dardanelles fiasco, regarded as his particular crime, was always brought up. . . . The opposition were determined to shout him down. He was always admirably self-controlled and good-tempered, and he never failed to quell the opposition and get a hearing.' Whenever Churchill spoke, he was confronted by a vociferous group of hecklers, whom he dubbed 'the Socialist travelling circus'. To one question about the Dardanelles, on November 27, he replied: 'What do you know about that? The Dardanelles might have saved millions of lives.' And he continued: 'Don't imagine I am running away from the Dardanelles. I glory in it.'[3]

[1] Cecil Edric Mornington Roberts, 1892–1976. Educated at Mundella Grammar School. Poet and novelist, he published his first book in 1912. Literary Editor, *Liverpool Post*, 1915–18, and naval correspondent with the Grand Fleet and Dover Patrol. Assistant Director of Munitions Overseas Transport, 1918. Editor *Nottingham Journal*, 1920–25. Unsuccessful Liberal candidate, 1922. Author of more than thirty books, novels and plays between 1922 and 1974.

[2] Brendan Bracken, 1901–1958. Educated in Australia and at Sedbergh School. Journalist and financier. Conservative MP for North Paddington, 1929–45; for Bournemouth, 1950–51. Elected to the Other Club, 1932. Chairman of the *Financial News*. Managing Director of the *Economist*. Chairman of the *Financial Times*. Parliamentary Private Secretary to the Prime Minister (Churchill), 1940–41. Privy Councillor, 1940. Minister of Information, 1941–45. First Lord of the Admiralty, 1945. Created Viscount, 1952.

[3] Douglas Jerrold, the official historian of the Royal Naval Division, went specially to Leicester to answer the accusations against Churchill about the Dardanelles. He told a crowded and hostile meeting on December 3: 'We tried Mr Churchill's policy, and we did not fail. . . . I venture to say that had the campaign been prosecuted as it should have been with enthusiasm, courage and energy, in the same spirit in which it was begun by Mr Churchill the war would have ended in 1917.'

On December 3 Churchill was in London, where he spoke to large, noisy meetings at Finsbury Park, Shepherd's Bush and Walthamstow. After his final speech, at Walthamstow, he had to be escorted from the hall to his car by mounted police. Then, as the *Leicester Daily Mercury* reported: 'A vast crowd closed round the car hooting and jeering. Despite the vigilance of the police, one man broke through and smashed one of the windows of Mr Churchill's car. The police took him into custody. When this fact became known more booing ensued, and many people spat upon the car as it drove away.'

While Churchill was in London, his wife continued to speak each day on his behalf in Leicester. She had been particularly angered by one heckler, who had described her husband as unfit to represent the working classes in Parliament. With the single exception of Mr Lloyd George, she replied, her husband had been responsible for more legislation 'for the benefit of the working classes than any other living statesman',[1] and she continued: 'A great many people think he is essentially military, but I know him very well, and I know he is not that at all. In fact one of his greatest talents is the talent of peace-making.'

Churchill returned to Leicester on December 5, the last day of the campaign. To a crowded meeting of women electors that morning he declared that Baldwin's sudden conversion to Protection, 'carries us back to the days when tyrannical Ministers sought to rule the country against its will', and he went on to ask: 'Who is Mr Baldwin to acclaim himself such a singularly honest man? He is a man whom we only know in the last few months through the eulogies of the newspapers. He has no achievements to his record. He is an unknown man.'

During the afternoon Churchill spoke to a meeting of Leicester business men. His final speech of the campaign, it was a strong denunciation of both of Protection and of the Capital Levy. The poll was held on December 6. Churchill had failed in his challenge.[2]

Pethick-Lawrence later recalled how, when the figures were announced, Churchill came up to him and said: 'Well, anyhow it is a victory for Free Trade.' A month later, on 3 January 1924, when Churchill wrote to thank Cecil Roberts for such 'energetic and cordial

---

[1] Among the legislation which her husband had framed between 1908 and 1910, Clementine Churchill pointed out, were the Sweated Industries Act, the Unemployment Insurance Act, the Coal Mines Regulation Act and the Shop Hours Act, 'which provides for early closing and a universal half-holiday'.

[2] The final result was: Pethick-Lawrence (Labour), 13,634. Churchill (Liberal), 9,236. Instone (Conservative), 7,696.

support', he added: 'We had every disadvantage to contend with: no local press; no organisation; universally interrupted meetings. . . .'

As soon as Churchill's defeat was known, his friends hastened to commiserate with him. On December 7 Sir William Tyrrell[1] wrote to him from the Foreign Office: 'Your defeat stamps this election & covers Leicester with shame, but I rejoice to see you stick to your platform of opposition to extremes on either side of politics. . . . From all sides I hear you made one of the best fights ever put up. You will have but a short breather before you are at it again. . . .' Churchill's aunt, Lady Sarah Wilson,[2] wrote to him on December 8:

Gordon & I lived near Leicester (at Brooksby) for 10 years & we always thought they were beastly people.

I was at the Carlton Club that foggy Election night & when your poll was announced, there was grim silence, & stodgy Lord Midleton,[3] who was sitting next me—said—'Well, I am genuinely sorry. We wanted Winston in the House of Commons.'

On December 10 Churchill was present at the Old Bailey for the opening of criminal libel proceedings against Lord Alfred Douglas,[4] who had accused him of issuing a false communiqué at the time of the battle of Jutland in order to manipulate the stock market. According to Douglas, Churchill had acted on behalf of a group of Jewish financiers who had, as a result of his help, made enormous profits, and who had then rewarded Churchill himself with £40,000. Douglas put forward

[1] William George Tyrrell, 1866–1947. Educated at Balliol College Oxford. Entered the Foreign Service, 1889. Private Secretary to Sir Edward Grey, 1907–15. Knighted, 1913. Assistant Under-Secretary of State at the Foreign Office, 1919–25; Permanent Under-Secretary, 1925–28. Privy Councillor, 1928. Ambassador in Paris, 1928–34. Created Baron, 1929. President of the British Board of Film Censors, 1935–47. His younger son, Hugo died of wounds received in action, February 1915; his elder son, Francis, was killed in action in February 1918.

[2] Lady Sarah Isabella Augusta Spencer-Churchill, 1864–1929. Eleventh and youngest child of the 7th Duke of Marlborough. Churchill's aunt. In 1891 she married Lieutenant-Colonel Gordon Chesney Wilson, Royal Horse Guards. Besieged with her husband in Mafeking, 1899. Her husband was killed in action in France on 6 November 1914.

[3] St John Brodrick, 1856–1942. Educated at Eton and Balliol College Oxford. Conservative MP, 1880–85 and 1885–1906. Privy Councillor, 1897. Secretary of State for War, 1900–03; for India, 1903–05. Succeeded his father as 9th Viscount Midleton, 1907; created Earl, 1920. He published his memoirs, *Record and Reactions 1856–1939* in 1939. In 1901 Churchill had attacked his military policy in a series of speeches published with the title *Mr Brodrick's Army*.

[4] Alfred Bruce Douglas, 1870–1945. Son of the 8th Marquess of Queensbury. Poet, and friend of Oscar Wilde. Received into the Catholic Church, 1911.

these accusations in a public lecture, which was also printed as a pamphlet of which over 30,000 copies were distributed in London. In August, Douglas had sent a copy of the pamphlet to Churchill himself, with a covering note in which he declared: 'I challenge you to show your face in the witness box, & answer the questions I shall put to you.'

During the trial, in which the State was prosecutor, Churchill had to produce detailed evidence of his wartime finances. The case for the prosecution was conducted by the Attorney-General, Sir Douglas Hogg,[1] and both Churchill and Balfour were called as witnesses. When Hogg asked Churchill directly: 'Is there a shadow of truth in any of the accusations made against you,' Churchill replied: 'Not the slightest. From beginning to end it is a monstrous and malicious invention.'

Douglas was found guilty and sentenced to six months in prison. The Jury had taken only eight minutes to reach their verdict. Several politicians wrote at once to congratulate Churchill on the outcome of the case. 'It seems almost insulting to congratulate you,' Austen Chamberlain[2] wrote, on December 14, '& yet the ways of the law are so strange to a layman & the license allowed in attacks on public men so extreme, that it is a matter for congratulation to us all when one of our number vindicates public honour, even from such groundless charges.' At the end of his letter Chamberlain added: 'I am very sorry that you are still out of Parl'. I could not on this occasion offer you public support nor would you have wished it, but I should like you to know that I declined on grounds of private friendship & our very recent association in Govt to send your opponent a letter wishing him success.'

'I cannot recall the case of any public man who has suffered such abuse & misrepresentation,' Churchill's former Admiralty Secretary,

---

[1] Douglas McGarel Hogg, 1872–1950. Educated at Eton. A West India merchant. On active service in South Africa, 1900. Called to the Bar, 1902. King's Counsel, 1917. Attorney-General to the Prince of Wales, 1920–22. Knighted, 1922. Conservative MP, St Marylebone, 1922–28. Attorney-General, 1922–24 and 1924–28. Privy Councillor, 1922. Lord Chancellor, 1928–29. Acting Prime Minister, August–September 1928. Created Baron Hailsham, 1928; Viscount, 1929. Secretary of State for War, 1931–35. Lord Chancellor, 1935–38. His brother Ian (a friend of Churchill at Sandhurst) died of wounds received in action in France on 2 September 1914. Both his brothers-in-law also died on the western front, one in action in 1915, the other of illness in 1918.

[2] Joseph Austen Chamberlain, 1863–1937. Educated at Rugby and Trinity College Cambridge. Conservative MP, 1892–1937. Chancellor of the Exchequer, 1903–05. Unsuccessful candidate for the leadership of the Conservative Party, 1911. Secretary of State for India, 1915–17. Minister without Portfolio, 1918–19. Chancellor of the Exchequer, 1919–21. Lord Privy Seal, 1921–22. Foreign Secretary, 1924–29. Knight of the Garter, 1925. First Lord of the Admiralty, 1931.

Sir William Graham Greene,[1] wrote to him on December 14. 'It is not possible to hope that your enemies will cease to deprecate your actions & motives, but at any rate this particular outrageous falsehood cannot be publicly repeated.' Greene commented: 'It is largely due to such unjustifiable attacks that you lost your seat at Dundee and failed at Leicester.' That same day Churchill's former Parliamentary Secretary at the Ministry of Munitions, Frederick Kellaway,[2] wrote to congratulate him on the result of the trial, and he added: 'I was sorry you did not succeed at Leicester. You must get back to the House. The outlook is dark and troubled; the country will need your energy and vision.'

The results of the election of 1923 were a serious blow to the Conservatives, whose number of seats fell from 346 to 258. Although the Conservatives still had a larger number of seats than either Liberal or Labour, the Liberal and Labour seats combined amounted to 349. Baldwin remained as Prime Minister, but at the head of a Government which had received only 5½ million of the 14½ million votes cast. Labour, with 191 seats, was the second largest party in the House of Commons and could, if joined by the 158 Liberal MPs, defeat the Conservatives with ease.

From the first days of 1924, it was evident that the Labour Party would soon bring a vote of no-confidence in Baldwin's minority Government. It was widely rumoured that the Liberals would support Labour's motion, in order to force Baldwin to resign. Once the Conservative Government had been defeated in this way, it was certain that the King would then send for the Labour leader, Ramsay MacDonald, and ask him to form a Government.

Asquith had already made it clear in a public statement on December 12 that he would not support the Conservatives to keep out MacDonald. On January 8 Churchill expressed his anger at the Liberal Party's imminent support for Labour in a long letter to Violet Bonham

[1] William Graham Greene, 1857–1950. Educated at Cheltenham College. Entered the Admiralty, 1881. Private Secretary to successive First Lords of the Admiralty, 1887–1902. Principal Clerk, Admiralty, 1902–07. Assistant Secretary, Admiralty, 1907–11. Knighted, 1911. Permanent Secretary, Admiralty, 1911–17. Secretary, Ministry of Munitions, 1917–20.

[2] Frederick George Kellaway, 1870–1933. Began work as a journalist in Lewisham, 1898. Liberal MP for Bedford, 1910–22. Joint Parliamentary Secretary, Ministry of Munitions, 1916–18. Deputy Minister of Munitions, 1918–19. Secretary, Department of Overseas Trade, 1920–21. Postmaster-General, 1921–22. Chairman and Managing Director, Marconi International Marine Communication Co, 1924–33. Vice-Chairman and Managing Director, Marconi's Wireless Telegraph Company. Deputy Governor, Cables and Wireless Ltd.

Carter.[1] Given Asquith's attitude, he wrote, there was 'no possibility of averting the great misfortune of a Socialist Government being formed'. But, he went on to ask, would the majority of Liberals continue to support their Party if it became the sole and essential instrument of a Labour Government's survival? 'I had a talk with Grey the other night,' Churchill wrote, 'and certainly did not think that he was very keen on keeping the Socialists in. Runciman[2] clearly has views in the same direction.' Churchill added: 'I am making no concealment of mine, though after all I do not delude myself by supposing that I count in any way in the situation.'

Churchill went on to warn that if Labour remained in power, with its threat to 'undermine the commercial and business activities of the country', some Liberal MPs 'will certainly co-operate with the Conservatives'. He also believed that, as the months passed, the Conservative Party would 'gradually gain in strength by the reaction caused in the country at the apparition of this Socialist monstrosity'. The Conservatives would then, he believed, win 'sixty or seventy seats', while at the same time, as a result of the Liberal support for Labour, all chance of the Conservatives agreeing to help a minority Liberal Government 'will have passed away'.

Churchill asked Violet Bonham Carter to show his letter to her father. 'I should like him to know how my mind is moving,' he wrote. But before receiving a reply, Churchill made a dramatic public declaration, in the form of a 'letter to a correspondent', a copy of which he sent to *The Times*, and which the newspaper published in full on January 18.

In his letter, Churchill began by stating that the 'currents of party warfare' between Liberals and Conservatives were 'carrying us all into dangerous waters'. He went on: 'The enthronement in office of a Socialist Government will be a serious national misfortune such as has usually befallen great States only on the morrow of defeat in war.' If a

[1] Helen Violet Asquith, 1887–1969. Elder daughter of H. H. Asquith. Educated in Dresden and Paris. Married, 1915, Sir Maurice Bonham Carter (who died in 1960). President of the Women's Liberal Federation, 1923–25 and 1939–45; President of the Liberal Party Organization, 1945–7. A Governor of the BBC, 1941–46. Member of the Royal Commission on the Press, 1947–49. Unsuccessful Liberal candidate, 1945 and 1951. DBE, 1953; created Baroness Asquith of Yarnbury, 1964. Published *Winston Churchill as I Knew Him*, 1965.

[2] Walter Runciman, 1870–1949. Educated at Trinity College Cambridge. Liberal MP, 1899–1900; 1902–18. Shipowner. President of the Board of Education, 1908–11. President of the Board of Agriculture and Fisheries, 1911–14. President of the Board of Trade, 1914–16. Liberal MP, 1924–29; 1929–31. Liberal National MP, 1931–37. President of the Board of Trade, 1931–37. 2nd Baron, 1937. Created Viscount Runciman of Doxford, 1937. Head of Mission to Czechoslovakia, 1938. Lord President of the Council, October 1938–September 1939.

Labour Government were to be in charge of elections, law and order would not be guaranteed, and the mere threat of such a situation would cast 'a dark and blighting shadow on every form of national life and confidence, and on every prospect of trade revival'.

The Parliamentary Liberal Party realized that Churchill's letter to *The Times* constituted his final break with them. Only two months earlier he had been one of their most energetic champions in the electoral fight against the Conservatives; now he was denouncing their decision to try to defeat the Conservatives in Parliament by tacit support for a Labour minority. Violet Bonham Carter wrote to him sorrowfully on the day his letter was published:

My dear Winston,

I was on the point of answering your letter when I read your Manifesto in the paper—& now I feel there is no more to be said.—I am very sorry you should have published it because it is a public definition of your difference of opinion with the rest of the Party—& I rather hoped that that difference might have been bridged & reconciled by events before it was known to the world at large.

But of course I recognize & respect the strength & the sincerity of your conviction—though I cannot share it.

To turn the Labour Party out a week after putting them in appears to me as a purely frivolous 'wrecking' action—We can—& clearly have—quite clearly defined our view of Capital Levy & Socialism—& they know that if they attempt either they will be turned out—It may be unwise for them to carry on on these lines, with their teeth drawn, but that is not our business. . . .

On the evening of January 21 the Conservative Government was defeated in the House of Commons by 72 Labour and Liberal votes, and on the following morning Ramsay MacDonald was summoned to Buckingham Palace. That same day he formed Britain's first Labour Government. Despite their fierce political differences, Churchill wrote at once to MacDonald to congratulate him on becoming Prime Minister. MacDonald replied on January 27 from 10 Downing Street:

My dear Churchill,

No letter received by me at this time has given me more pleasure than yours. I wish we did not disagree so much!—but there it is. In any event I hope your feelings are like mine. I have always held you personally in much esteem, & I hope, whatever fortune may have in store for us, that personal relationship will never be broken. Perhaps I may come across you occasionally.

On February 4 Churchill was again asked to stand for Parliament as a

Liberal. The request came from the Liberal Association of Bristol West, but he replied on the following day that he would not be prepared 'to embark upon a by-electoral contest against the Conservatives'. Such a contest, he asserted, could only strengthen the divisions among anti-socialists, who ought, at a time of a 'Socialist Minority Government', to be united.

On February 6 Churchill left England for a short holiday in France. After a week in Paris with his wife, he went on to Mimizan, south of Bordeaux, as the guest of the Duke of Westminster. On February 17 he wrote to his wife, who was at Eze, on the Riviera, four hundred miles to the east, that he had still not made up his mind about his political future. 'I want *time* to work,' he wrote. 'A few months, anyhow. . . .'

Churchill returned to England on February 19, and hurried to Chartwell to see the progress of the reconstruction. On February 20 he sent his wife a long account of the work that was being done. He was also working again, he explained, on the next volume of his war memoirs. 'I continue to read a great deal about the war,' he explained, 'consuming on the average a book a day.'

Now that he was in his second year without a seat in Parliament, Churchill was dependent more than ever upon his writings to provide him with an income. Anxious to make arrangements to sell his articles in the United States, he enlisted the help of Brendan Bracken, who placed them, not only in America, but also in France, India and even Malaya. The majority of the articles were attacks on Socialism; in the first, published in the *Sunday Chronicle* on February 17 while he was still in France, Churchill warned that the apparent calm which had followed MacDonald's premiership was a sham. Of course, he declared, there were some good things in Labour's victory, and no one 'would grudge the old Trade Union leaders, who have borne the battle and the breeze in Parliamentary and political life for a quarter of a century, at least a share in the amenities of power and allow them to taste the sweets, such as they are, of office'. But, he went on:

I do not think so poorly of the Socialist party or its leaders as to suppose that they have abandoned their principles or deserted their cause for the petty satisfactions of office. I credit them with the intention of using this interlude of power as a necessary manoeuvre to advance towards their goal.

If they have to bow the knee in what they would call the Temple of Rimmon, it is not in the desire to succeed to the position of the high priest-hood, but solely with the design of smashing up the Temple. . . .

As for the Liberals, Churchill concluded, their difference with Socialism was fundamental, despite present lip-service, and the feud between the two ways of life and thought could not be ended 'until Socialism has been discredited or Liberalism has been devoured'.

As soon as he returned to England, Churchill took the opportunity of a by-election at Burnley to attack all Labour attempts to win Liberal support. In a letter which he sent to the Conservative candidate at Burnley, H. Camps,[1] on February 24, and which was published in *The Times* on the following day, he urged Liberal voters not to vote for the only other candidate, the Labour leader, Arthur Henderson.[2] Commenting on Churchill's letter, the *Glasgow Herald* declared on February 26 that Churchill was without a doubt 'preparing the way of return to the party which he left many years ago'. This, the paper said, was natural; no other Liberal had offered 'such strenuously consistent opposition' to the Labour Party, and Churchill was right to respond to 'the promptings of a legitimate ambition'. The Liberals had, as he believed, betrayed him. Now, 'compelled by his temperament to be in the thick of the fighting, Mr Churchill seems a predestined champion of the individualism which he has served all his political life—under both of its liveries'.

---

[1] H. E. J. Camps. Stood as a Conservative candidate for Burnley in 1922, 1923 and 1924, but was never elected to Parliament.

[2] Arthur Henderson, 1863–1935. Apprenticed as a moulder; later active in the Trade Union movement. Labour MP, 1903–18; 1919–22; 1923; 1924–31. Chairman, Parliamentary Labour Party, 1908–10. Chief Whip, Labour Party, 1914; 1921–24; 1925–27. President of the Board of Education, May 1915–August 1916. Paymaster General, August–December 1916. Member of Lloyd George's War Cabinet, December 1916–August 1917. Government Mission to Russia, 1917. Home Secretary in the first Labour Government, 1924. Secretary of State for Foreign Affairs, 1929–31. President of the World Disarmament Conference, 1932–33.

2

1924: Towards the Conservatives

ON 22 February 1924, Churchill learned that a by-election was to be held in the Abbey Division of Westminster. He was tempted to stand as an Independent, and on the following night, when he dined with Lord Beaverbrook and Lord Rothermere, both newspaper owners encouraged him to do so. They even offered him—as Churchill wrote to his wife on the following day—'the full support of their press', and urged him 'to let it be known straight away that my cap was in the ring'. Churchill took this advice, announcing to the Press Association that he intended to stand as an Independent Candidate, and that he would seek the support of both Liberal and Conservative voters.

Churchill hoped that the local Conservative Association would adopt him as their candidate, despite the fact that he was not even a member of their Party. He was therefore delighted to find that at the Conservative Party's central headquarters there was enthusiastic support for his candidature, as well as acceptance of his independent position. Churchill gave an account both of the constituency and of his prospects in his letter of February 23. It was, he said, 'one of the choicest preserves of the Tory Party', and he added: 'I have had an interview with Colonel Jackson[1] their head whip wh was entirely satisfactory. He & Younger[2] are working tooth and nail to secure me the support of the official Unionist Assn, tho I made it clear I intended to stand as an Independent candidate with Liberal as well as Conservative supporters.'

[1] Francis Stanley Jackson, 1870–1947. Educated at Harrow and Trinity College Cambridge. On active service in South Africa, 1900–02. Conservative MP for Howdenshire, 1915–26. Financial Secretary, War Office, 1922–23. Chairman of the Conservative Party, 1923–26. Privy Councillor, 1926. Knighted, 1927. Governor of Bengal, 1927–32.

[2] George Younger, 1851–1929. Educated at the Edinburgh Academy, the son of a successful brewer. President of the National Union of Conservative Associations in Scotland, 1904. Conservative MP for Ayr Burghs, 1906–22. Created Baronet, 1911. Chairman of the Conservative Party Organization, 1916–23. Treasurer of the Conservative Party, 1923–29. Created Viscount, 1923. Chairman, George Younger & Sons, Brewers, Ltd.

Churchill pointed out to his wife that there were at least a hundred MPs living and voting in the constituency, which included Victoria, Westminster, Pall Mall, 'Drury Lane theatre & Covent Garden!' Among those whom he believed would support him publicly were two of his friends who lived in the constituency, Edward Grigg[1] and General Spears. Altogether, he noted, 'it is an exceedingly promising opportunity, & if it comes off I will hold the seat for a long time'.

One reason why the Conservative Party's central headquarters were anxious to see him elected for the Abbey Division, Churchill told his wife, was their hope that he would then give a lead, inside Parliament, to some thirty Liberal MPs who disliked Asquith's support for Labour. These Liberals, Churchill wrote, were those 'who wish to act with the Conservatives, & whom the Cons are anxious to win as allies'. The Conservative idea, he added, was that 'by making the gesture of giving me this seat, the whole of this movement will be focused around me'. His letter continued:

At Baldwin's suggestion I had a long talk with him yesterday of the friendliest character. He evidently wants vy much to secure my return & co-operation. Their eyes are fully open to the dangers that lie ahead. Mac-Donald is making a gt impression on the country, & there is no doubt that he is gaining numerous adherents—mostly at the expense of the Liberals.

I informed L.G. of my resolves. He said I was only acting in accordance with my convictions & made no reproaches of any kind. . . .

Of course if I stood as a Cons it wd almost certainly be a walk over. But I cannot do this, & it is far better for all the interests we are safeguarding that I shd carry with me moderate Liberals.

Clementine Churchill advised caution. During February 24, she wrote from the South of France: 'Do not however let the Tories get you too cheap. They have treated you so badly in the past & they ought to be made to pay.' The Tory Party, she wrote, was up to its neck in a 'quagmire of inefficiency & stupidity', but she urged:

My Darling do not stand unless you are reasonably sure of getting in— The movement inside the Tory Party to try & get you back is only just born

---

[1] Edward William Macleay Grigg, 1879–1955. Educated at Winchester and New College Oxford. Editorial staff of *The Times*, 1903–05; 1908–13. Served in the Grenadier Guards, 1914–18 (Churchill shared his frontline dugout in November 1915). Military Secretary to the Prince of Wales, 1919. Knighted, 1920. Private Secretary to Lloyd George, 1921–22. National Liberal MP for Oldham, 1922–25. Governor of Kenya, 1925–31. Elected to the Other Club, 1932. National Conservative MP, 1933–45. Parliamentary Secretary, Ministry of Information, 1939–40. Financial Secretary, War Office, 1940. Joint Parliamentary Under-Secretary of State for War, 1940–44. Minister Resident in the Middle East, 1944–45. Created Baron Altrincham, 1945. Editor of the *National Review*, 1948–55.

& requires nursing & nourishing & educating to bring it to full strength. And there are of course counter influences as none of the Tory Leaders want you back as they see you would leap over their heads—The Times I feel sure is against you at present or at any rate not helping—Couldn't we cultivate John Astor[1] gradually?

I feel that though no genius he would be quite as much help as Beaverbrook. The Times can really do more than the Daily Express. . . .

I feel very anxious about it all—I am sure with patience all will come right. . . . Perhaps your hour will come only after Labour has a big independent Majority & shews itself in its true colours.

In spite of Clementine Churchill's anxieties, the move inside the Conservative Party to bring Churchill back continued. On Sunday February 24 Baldwin drove to see Austen Chamberlain at his weekend home in the country, to consult him about Churchill's candidature. Two days later, Chamberlain explained to Churchill's friend Lord Birkenhead[2] the course and outcome of their discussion:

Briefly the position is this—that it is too early for Winston to come out as a Conservative with credit to himself. On the other hand, the Abbey Conservatives would be unwilling to adopt him as an Independent anti-Socialist candidate. I do not know whether the Central Office could force him upon them—probably not—but in any case this would involve a split and would not be in Winston's interest. Both the Liberal and Labour parties, for what they are worth, in the Division, would back an out-and-out Conservative against Winston. This being so, no friend of Winston would wish him to stand.

Baldwin proposes to see Winston again and to explain the position to him. We want to get him and his friends over, and though we cannot give him the Abbey seat, Baldwin will undertake to find him a good seat later on when he will have been able to develop naturally his new line and make his entry into our ranks much easier than it would be to-day.

Austen Chamberlain added: 'Our only fear is lest Winston should try and rush the fence. I am sure that you will agree with me that this would

[1] John Jacob Astor, 1886–1971. Educated at Eton and New College Oxford. 2nd Lieutenant, 1st Life Guards, 1908. ADC to the Viceroy of India, 1911–14. On active service, 1914–18 (severely wounded); Major, 1920. Conservative MP for Dover, 1922–45. Chief Proprietor of *The Times*. President of the Press Club, the Newspaper Press Fund, and the Commonwealth Press Union. Chairman of the Middlesex Hospital, 1938–62. Lieutenant-Colonel, 5th Battalion City of London Home Guard, 1940–44. Created Baron Astor of Hever, 1956.

[2] Frederick Edwin Smith, 1872–1930. Known as 'F.E.'. Conservative MP, 1906–19. With Churchill, he founded the Other Club in 1911. Head of the Press Bureau, August 1914; resigned, October 1914. Lieutenant-Colonel, attached to the Indian Corps in France, 1914–15. Solicitor-General, May 1915. Knighted, 1915. Attorney-General, November 1915–19. Created Baron Birkenhead, 1919. Lord Chancellor, 1920–22. Created Viscount, 1921. Created Earl, 1922. Secretary of State for India, 1924–28.

be a mistake and I want you to send this letter on to Winston, adding your appeal to mine that he should not destroy these happy chances by any rash attempt on Abbey.'

On the evening of February 28 the Westminster Conservative Association chose Otho Nicholson,[1] a nephew of the previous member, to be their candidate. But on March 1 the *Evening Standard* reported a strong feeling throughout the Constituency that Churchill should stand, nevertheless, as an independent anti-Socialist candidate. The movement in his favour, it added, 'was increasing'. In a statement to the Press on March 2 Churchill wrote that so many people had appealed to him to be a candidate that he felt it necessary 'to state briefly and plainly' where he stood. On the main questions of public policy, he asserted, he remained in the same position that he had occupied for nearly twenty years, but at the same time he wished 'to work effectually with the Conservative Party in resistance to the rapid advance of Socialism'. Such a position, he continued, was neither 'solitary nor singular'; indeed, he believed that there were 'hundreds of thousands of Liberals', throughout the country, who felt as he did, and who wished to 'co-operate with the Conservative Party' to bring down the Labour Government. 'There were 3,500 in Burnley alone,' he pointed out. And he went on: 'The present so-called three-party system is unhealthy, unnatural and absurd.'

When Churchill learnt from Lord Birkenhead that Austen Chamberlain was opposed to his standing at Westminster, he was much angered. On learning of Churchill's anger, Chamberlain tried to put Churchill's mind at rest, writing to him on March 3:

Don't let the sun go down upon your wrath, for this is not true. I found Baldwin much more friendly to you than I had expected & inclined to get you the seat *if he could*, & all I said was in agreement with his view ie that S.B. couldn't *force* you on the Association, but that if he could persuade the Asstn to take you, that would be the best thing possible for our party— quite apart from my personal feelings which would lead me to wish you back in any case.

My advice to you through F.E. not to fight against the Conservative Asstn may be right or wrong. For the chances of the constituency I am dependent on the reports of other men, & they were that you would be beaten. But believe me, I beg you, I have acted throughout as a friend, &, tho' you

---

[1] Otho William Nicholson, 1891–1978. Educated at Harrow and Magdalene College Cambridge. Lieutenant, Royal Engineers, 1914–18. Mayor of Finsbury, 1923–24. Conservative MP for Westminster, Abbey, 1924–32. Brigadier commanding the 40th Anti-Aircraft Group, 1938–41; the 54th AA Brigade, 1941–42. Assistant-Commandant, School of AA Artillery, 1942. Director of J. & W. Nicholson & Company, Distillers.

might think my judgment wrong, you would not question the friendship if you had heard every word that I have said on the subject.

On March 4, Austen Chamberlain described the situation in a letter to his wife:

All our little world is in a commotion because our Asstn in Westminster, having declined to take Winston on his terms & selected a young Nicholson, they are now rent by internal factions & all the other would-be Conservative candidates unite to declare that they wont have Nicholson anyway & will support Winston who has decided to stand 'on his own'. And all the wise men who yesterday said that Winston could scarcely win with our help & hadn't a ghost of a chance without it are now in a blue funk & declare that he will beat Nicholson out of the field. Oh dear, how wise we are! I had hoped that we might get Winston adopted & I shan't be sorry if he wins, but it will be a nasty shock for us. . . .

On the morning of March 4 Churchill formally announced that he would fight the seat, and in a second press statement that morning he declared: 'My candidature is in no way hostile to the Conservative Party and its leaders.' Sir Philip Sassoon[1] wrote to him at once: 'I am so glad you are standing. You are BOUND to get in.'

Churchill's campaign began in earnest on March 5, when his wife returned from the South of France to help him and both Lord Beaverbrook and Lord Rothermere swung their newspapers to his cause. But in its leading article on March 6 *The Times* denounced Churchill for having 'mistimed an important decision', and for having shown himself 'an essentially disruptive force'.

The Westminster election received enormous publicity. Almost daily, Press cartoons and photographs charted its course. Commenting on Churchill's popularity, the *Evening News* reported on March 6: 'Offers of help are coming in so numerously that the Paddington telephone exchange operators wish he had a dozen lines. He is being rung up at his house as few people ever have been in the history of the telephone.' On the following morning Churchill appealed privately to Baldwin for direct help in 'seeking a gt advantage for the cause we have at heart'. His letter continued:

Mr Nicholson's withdrawal or even the non-interference of the Central Office in the fight, wd result in a resounding victory for Conservative &

---

[1] Philip Albert Gustave Sassoon, 1888–1939. Educated at Eton and Christ Church Oxford. Succeeded his father as 3rd Baronet, 1912. Conservative MP for Hythe, 1912–39. Private Secretary to Sir Douglas Haig, 1914–18. Parliamentary Private Secretary to Lloyd George, 1920–22. Trustee of the National Gallery, 1921–39. Under-Secretary of State for Air, 1924–29 and 1931–37. Privy Councillor, 1929. First Commissioner of Works, 1937–39.

Imperial interests & for anti socialism. It will also lead directly to the creation of a Liberal wing working with the Cons party in the coming struggle.

I am sure you do not wish to be compelled by technicalities to fire upon the reinforcements I am bringing to our aid. Act now with decision, & we shall be able to work together in the national interest. I have no other thoughts but to muster & rally the strongest combination of forces against the oncoming attack.

'Do not let this opportunity slip away,' Churchill added, '& all of us be weakened thereby.' But Baldwin did not intervene, and on the same day that Churchill appealed to him for cooperation, the editor of the *Morning Post*, H. A. Gwynne,[1] writing from the Carlton Club, warned him that the by-election was the test of his leadership—'your "Jena or Austerlitz" make no mistake'. Gwynne's letter continued: 'If I were in your place, I should call for Horne & Austen and forbid them to speak for Winston. If they refuse, then it is open war but it will be a short war & you will win. If they obey, you are undoubted leader, to be feared & respected.'

Throughout the first week of the campaign, Churchill was helped in setting up his organization by his cousin, Captain Guest,[2] the former Chief Whip of Lloyd George's coalition, and by Brendan Bracken, who had helped him at West Leicester. During March 8 his campaign was further strengthened by the decision of a leading Conservative MP, Sir Burton Chadwick,[3] to take control of the canvassing department. 'As the campaign progressed,' Churchill later recalled, 'I began to receive all kinds of support. Dukes, jockeys, prize-fighters, courtiers, actors and business men, all developed a keen partisanship. The chorus girls of Daly's Theatre sat up all night addressing the envelopes and despatching the election address.' The address itself was issued on the evening of

[1] Howell Arthur Gwynne, 1865–1950. Reuter's chief war correspondent in South Africa, 1899–1902. Editor of the *Standard*, 1904–11. Editor of the *Morning Post*, 1911–37. One of Churchill's most outspoken public critics at the time of the siege of Antwerp in October 1914.

[2] Frederick Edward Guest, 1875–1937. The third son of 1st Baron Wimborne; Churchill's cousin. Served in the South African War as a Captain, Life Guards, 1899–1902. Private Secretary to Churchill, 1906. An original member of the Other Club, 1911. Treasurer, HM Household, 1912–15. ADC to Sir John French, 1914–16. On active service in East Africa, 1916–17. Patronage Secretary, Treasury (Chief Whip), May 1917–April 1921. Privy Councillor, 1920. Secretary of State for Air, April 1921–October 1922. Liberal MP, 1923–29. Joined the Conservative Party, 1930. Conservative MP, 1931–37.

[3] Robert Burton-Chadwick, 1869–1951. Spent ten years of his early life at sea. On active service in South Africa, 1900. Director of Munitions Overseas Transport, and Director-General of Stores and Transport, 1915–19. Conservative MP for Barrow-in-Furness, 1918–22; for Wallasey, 1922–31. Knighted, 1920. Parliamentary Secretary, Board of Trade, 1924–28. Created Baronet, 1925. Counsellor, British Embassy, Buenos Aires, 1939–46. His elder son was killed in air operations, 1941.

March 9. The existence of a Socialist minority Government, Churchill warned, was a challenge 'to our existing economic and social civilisation'. Baldwin himself, Churchill pointed out, had publicly appealed 'for the cooperation of Liberals. I support him in this policy of setting country before Party.'

On the same day that Churchill issued his election address, Baldwin, replying to a letter from a Conservative constituent, stated that as Otho Nicholson had been selected by the local Conservative association, 'there is no doubt in my opinion that he should receive the whole-hearted support of the Party'. But by March 10 each of Churchill's nine wards in the Abbey Division was being organized by a Conservative MP, and that evening, in a statement to the *Evening Standard*, Churchill pointed out that for five days at the end of February the Conservative Central Organization had tried to persuade the local Conservatives to accept his candidature. 'Colonel Jackson,' he said, 'was entirely favourable to my standing for the Abbey Division.'

On March 12 the campaign entered its final week. 'Everyone here is agog about the Westminster Election,' Austen Chamberlain wrote to his wife that day. And he added: 'If I can vote, I shall vote quietly for Winston and say nothing about it.' Chamberlain doubted whether Churchill could in fact win. 'It will be terrible for him if he is beaten again,' he wrote. 'I shall be very sorry.'

On the evening of March 13 the Labour Party candidate, Fenner Brockway,[1] attacked Churchill's record as Secretary of State for War. It was a charge repeated throughout the campaign. According to Brockway: 'Mr Churchill did all he could to maintain militarism in Europe and to march armies against Russia. He wasted £100,000,000 of the taxpayers' money of this country—money sorely needed to deal with unemployment, housing etc—in mad, stupid, wicked and suicidal adventures which not only failed to throw over Bolshevik Russia, but strengthened it because of the attacks made from outside.' Another persistent Labour charge, which Churchill sought strenuously to rebut, was of his personal recklessness during the Dardanelles campaign. On March 20—the day after polling day—the Deputy Secretary to the

[1] Archibald Fenner Brockway, 1888–1988. Labour publicist and pamphleteer. Editor, *Labour Leader*, 1912–17. Imprisoned three times, 1916–17, with hard labour, for refusing military service. Secretary of the No-Conscription Fellowship, 1917. Joint Secretary, British Committee, Indian National Congress, 1919. Organizing Secretary, Independent Labour Party, 1922; General Secretary, 1928 and 1933–39. Editor, *New Leader*, 1926–29 and 1931–46. Labour candidate, 1922 and 1924; ILP candidate, 1934, 1935, 1941 and 1942. Labour MP for East Leyton, 1929–31; for Eton and Slough, 1950–64, Chairman, British Centre for Colonial Freedom, 1954–67. Created Baron, 1964.

Cabinet, Thomas Jones,[1] noted in his diary: 'The Dardanelles pursues Churchill most unfairly, for it was one of the big conceptions of the war, and if put through with vigour might have shortened the war by a couple of years.'

On March 15 a former Conservative Minister, Leopold Amery, decided not only to give public support to Nicholson, but declared, in a public letter: 'The menace of Socialism is not to be fought by negatives, however brilliantly phrased.' Churchill had already asked for a letter of support from the former Conservative Prime Minister, A. J. Balfour,[2] who lived in the constituency. On reading Amery's letter, Churchill wrote to Balfour: 'A letter from you will in my judgment turn the scale', and he added: 'Thousands of Conservatives are supporting me, & other thousands hanging in the balance.' Churchill went on to explain why he now turned to Balfour for support:

There was a sort of understanding that Shadow Cabinet Ministers did not intervene on one side or the other; & as you know Austen told Neville that if he (N) spoke on Nicholson's platform Austen will speak on mine.

This sort of self-denying policy, has now been departed from by Amery who in the enclosed letter has definitely taken public action against me.

In these circumstances surely your letter would be permissible. . . .

The whole Sunday press—without exception—will support me tomorrow and if your letter could be issued today I am confident the result will be decisive.

On the evening of March 15, with Baldwin's permission, Churchill issued Balfour's letter to the Press. In it Balfour admitted that were he still Leader of the Conservative Party, he would have had to have acted as Baldwin had done, and supported the official candidate. But he went on to describe his 'strong desire' as a private individual that Churchill should again be able to use his 'brilliant gifts' in the House of Commons. 'Your absence from the House of Commons at such a time,' he added, 'is greatly to be deplored. . . .'

On March 18 Churchill addressed his final meeting, in the Victoria

[1] Thomas Jones, 1870–1955. Lecturer in Economics, Glasgow University, 1899–1909. Joined the Independent Labour Party, 1895. Special Investigator, Poor Law Commission, 1906–09. Professor in Economics, Belfast, 1909–10. Secretary, National Health Insurance Commissioners (Wales), 1912–16. Deputy-Secretary to the Cabinet, 1916–30. Companion of Honour, 1929. Member of the Unemployment Assistance Board, 1934–40.

[2] Arthur James Balfour, 1848–1930. Educated at Eton and Trinity College Cambridge. Conservative MP, 1874–85; 1885–1906; 1906–22 (City of London). Prime Minister, 1902–05. First Lord of the Admiralty, 1915–16. Foreign Secretary, 1916–19. Lord President to the Council, 1919–22 and 1925–29. Created Earl, 1922.

Palace. 'The candidate was subjected to much interruption,' *The Times* reported the next day, 'the main burden of which consisted of remarks on Gallipoli and taunts by women about "murders in Ireland".'

In his speech Churchill ruled out all idea of a Conservative–Liberal coalition to combat Socialism. The only 'practical step', he said, was to have a united Conservative Party 'with a Liberal wing'. Conservatism itself, he repeated, must show that it had 'constructive ideas', and that it was able to grapple effectively with 'the acute problems of social distress'. Speaking of what the Liberals had done before 1914, Churchill declared: 'We had already achieved a good deal in providing ladders for those who had the capacity and ability to rise.' Now, he added, 'besides the ladders, there must be nets to catch those that fall'. At this a woman called out: 'It wants a good net to catch you, old chap!' It was essential, Churchill went on, for any future Conservative Government to undertake 'an immense recasting' of the insurance system, especially as regards unemployment insurance. Another area in which progress must be made, he said, was in the provision of houses 'with proper State assistance', and he argued that these houses could be built 'with novel methods and materials, in much the same way as the shell problem was solved during the war'.

Referring to the British Empire, Churchill spoke ruefully about 'this great country, so powerful and splendid but a few years ago', now, under Labour rule, 'almost ready to apologise for our existence, ready to lay down our burden in any one of the great Oriental countries if a stick be shaken at us by any irresponsible chatterbox'.

Polling took place on March 19. To the last, many Conservatives were extremely nervous of the effect of Churchill's candidature on their chances. During the day Lord Derby[1] wrote to Lord Rawlinson:[2] 'the fear is that he may so split our vote that the Socialist will get in, in which case he is done for as far as any reconciliation with our Party is concerned'. Derby himself hoped that Churchill would be elected, as he

[1] Edward George Villiers Stanley, 1865–1948. Educated at Wellington College. Lieutenant, Grenadier Guards, 1885–95. Conservative MP for West Houghton, 1892–1906. Postmaster General, 1903–05. 17th Earl of Derby, 1908. Director-General of Recruiting, October 1915. Under-Secretary of State at the War Office, July–December 1916. Secretary of State for War, December 1916–18. Ambassador to France, 1918–20. Secretary of State for War, 1922–24. Member of the Joint Select Committee on the Indian Constitution, 1933–34. Clementine Churchill wrote to her husband about Lord Derby, on 3 February 1922: 'People think he is bluff & independent & John Bullish but he is really a fat sneak.'

[2] Henry Seymour Rawlinson, 1864–1925. Educated at Eton and Sandhurst. On active service in the Sudan (1898), South Africa (1899–1902) and in the First World War, 1914–18. Knighted, 1915. Commanded the British Forces in North Russia, 1919. Created Baron, 1919. Commander-in-Chief of the Army in India from 1920 to his death.

was 'a fine fighting force in the House and would be of great assistance'. This view, he wrote, was shared 'by the majority of our Party . . . but there are a certain number of die-hards, headed by Amery, who are prepared to go to any steps to prevent this happening'.

As the last packet of votes was being carried up to the table someone turned to Churchill and said: 'You're in by a hundred.' As the report of his victory spread around the room, his supporters burst into cheering. 'The sound was caught by the crowds waiting outside,' he later recalled, 'and the news was telegraphed all over the world.' But the news was wrong. When the official figures were announced, it was clear that Churchill had in fact been defeated. Nicholson's majority was announced as 33. After a recount, it rose to 43.[1]

'I was over-joyed to read the message that you were elected,' Sir Martin Conway[2] wrote from the House of Commons on March 20, '& plunged into the depths when the news of a recount, & finally of your failure by so narrow a margin came to my ears.' Conway continued: 'You deserved to win. You were never more wanted in the House than now. Every MP I have so far met has expressed to me regret at the result. . . .'

Following his defeat, Churchill received many letters of commiseration. 'If *only* just one more packet of votes could have been found at the recount!' Lady Birkenhead[3] wrote a few days later. 'But anyhow it has been the most wonderful fight you have ever made. To do what you did by your own personality with no organisation was a truly magnificent feat.' On the day of the defeat Alfred Duff Cooper[4] wrote to Churchill from the Foreign Office:

---

[1] The final result was: Nicholson (Conservative), 8,187; Churchill (Independent and Anti-Socialist), 8.144; Brockway (Labour), 6,156; Scott Duckers (Liberal), 291.

[2] William Martin Conway, 1856–1937. Educated at Repton and Trinity College Cambridge. Art Historian. Alpine, Latin American, Himalayan and Arctic explorer. Unsuccessful Liberal candidate, 1895. Chairman of the Society of Authors, 1895, 1898 and 1899. Knighted 1895. Professor of Fine Arts, Cambridge, 1901–04. Trustee of the Wallace Collection, 1916–24. Director-General of the Imperial War Museum, 1917. Conservative MP, Combined English Universities, 1918–31. Created Baron, 1931.

[3] Margaret Eleanor Furneaux, 1878–1968. Daughter of the classical scholar Henry Furneaux. In 1901 she married F. E. Smith (later 1st Earl of Birkenhead).

[4] Alfred Duff Cooper, 1890–1954. Educated at Eton and New College Oxford. On active service, Grenadier Guards, 1914–18 (DSO, despatches). Conservative MP for Oldham (Churchill's first constituency), 1924–29. Financial Secretary, War Office, 1928–29 and 1931–34. MP for St Georges Westminster, 1931–45. Financial Secretary, Treasury, 1934–35. Privy Councillor, 1935. Secretary of State for War, 1935–37. First Lord of the Admiralty, 1937–38. Minister of Information, 1940–41. British Representative, Singapore, 1941. Chancellor of the Duchy of Lancaster, 1941–43. British Representative, French Committee of National Liberation, 1943–44. Ambassador to France, 1944–47. Knighted, 1948. Created Viscount Norwich, 1952. In 1919 he married Lady Diana Manners.

My dear Winston,

I saw the first news on the tape this morning and sent you a telegram before the heart breaking correction appeared. I know you have the lion's courage which will enable you to make light of this cruel blow but it may possibly help you a little to know that there are a great number of young and eager Conservatives whose enthusiastic support you command and who while deploring this wretched misadventure have confidence that it is only an incident in what must be the most brilliant career of our time. They look forward to the time which cannot be far distant when you will be their inspired and inspiring leader.

'It was the finest fight there ever was,' General Spears wrote, '& shows what you can do. To have so deeply moved in so short a time this stodgy Division is almost unbelievable. But it is bitterly disappointing too. I wd have given my right hand to get you in.' Spears was hopeful for the future: 'the bad spell is broken', he wrote, 'the unpopularity is a thing of the past & the next time is a certainty'.

Conservative support for Churchill had been stimulated by the Westminster by-election. On March 24 Monteith Erskine,[1] the MP for Westminster St George's, who had supported him during the campaign itself, wrote direct to Baldwin:

I don't want you to think that there is any change in my expressed loyalty to you personally as Leader of the Party.

My conviction was & is that Winston Churchill would have done more to strengthen the Conservative Party than would his opponent. It seems a pity that the best interests of the country should often be at the mercy of a local Association divided in its own Councils & in no way representative of local opinion.

The 25 or 30 MP's who came out in the open for Winston in no way measure the actual feeling in the House. Any number told me they wanted him to win & were quietly working for his return.

Churchill's cousin Lord Londonderry[2]—who had canvassed on his behalf during the Westminster campaign—wrote to him on March 25, advising him to commit himself fully to Conservatism: 'I admire your spirit immensely and I hope the luck may be yours the next time—but

---

[1] James Malcolm Monteith Erskine, 1863–1944. Educated at Wellington College. Conservative MP for Westminster St Georges, 1921–29. Knighted, 1929.

[2] Charles Stewart Henry Vane-Tempest-Stewart, Viscount Castlereagh, 1878–1949. Educated at Eton and Sandhurst. Conservative MP for Maidstone, 1906–15. Succeeded his father as 7th Marquess of Londonderry, 1915. Served briefly on the western front as 2nd in Command, Royal Horse Guards, 1915. Under-Secretary of State for Air, 1920–21. Minister of Education and Leader of the Senate, Government of Northern Ireland, 1921–26. Returned to Westminster as First Commissioner of Works, 1928–29 and 1931; and as Secretary of State for Air and Lord Privy Seal, 1931–35. Churchill's second cousin.

I still say—that it would have been yours this time had you read the future as I did.' Londonderry's letter continued: 'Please Winston reflect—a half way house is no use to anyone, least of all to you.'

On March 28 Lord Birkenhead wrote to Lord Derby that the Conservative Shadow Cabinet were going to meet on April 2 to decide whether, without actually forming a Coalition with the Liberals, they would agree to accept 'the half of a Liberal wing under Winston'. Birkenhead believed that if Churchill would lead those Liberals who wanted close association with the Conservatives, probably 'about 30 Liberals could be got'. Before the Shadow Cabinet met, Churchill saw Baldwin, and had what he described to Balfour on April 3 as 'a very friendly talk'. During their discussion, Churchill pointed out to Baldwin that there were more than thirty Liberal MPs who would be willing to act with the Conservatives in Parliament, provided that they could receive assurance that their seats would not be contested by Conservative candidates at the next election. Churchill also told Baldwin that there were at least twenty Labour seats which could be won by Liberals, and only Liberals, at the next election, provided these Liberals enjoyed the tacit support of their local Conservative Association. He could therefore offer Baldwin, so he believed, some fifty Liberal supporters in the next Parliament; supporters who might easily tilt the balance of seats from Labour to Conservative.

Churchill's search for Conservative support was helped by Sir Martin Conway, who, immediately following Churchill's defeat at Westminster on March 19, had formed a group of some twenty Conservative MPs, to advocate close cooperation between the Conservative Party and the anti-Socialist Liberals. Conway saw Baldwin on March 31—shortly before the meeting of the Shadow Cabinet—and pressed him to agree to some special electoral arrangement such as Churchill had proposed. Baldwin was sympathetic, but deprecated any immediate decision. Conway reported his conversation to Churchill, who wrote at once to Baldwin, on April 1: 'While I quite agree that there is no need to make any sweeping declaration of policy at the present time, it is necessary to face the fact that an arrangement about seats is urgent and lies at the root of the matter.' Churchill added: 'It would be sufficient at the present time, in my opinion, if the Conservative Whips were told as a definite decision of policy to encourage sitting Liberals to act consistently with the Opposition against the Government by giving them assurances of immunity from Conservative attack to the greatest extent which may be honestly found possible in the next few weeks or months.'

The Shadow Cabinet met on April 2, when Churchill's proposals were given a favourable reception. Although no general plan was adopted to protect all anti-Socialist Liberals from Conservative challenge, it was agreed to deal with each seat individually, on its merits. 'I think this must just be allowed to work for a few weeks,' Churchill wrote in his letter to Balfour on April 3. 'Appetite may come in eating. On the whole, therefore, I am content with the movement of affairs.'

On April 3 Churchill's cousin the Duke of Marlborough sounded a note of caution. 'It is not easy,' he wrote, 'to probe into the immediate future, but I personally think you are wise to preserve a detached position from the Tory Party—till you can command your terms, and get hold of the title deeds.' But eight days later, on April 11, an opportunity arose which Churchill felt he could not neglect: the Chairman of the Liverpool Constitutional Association, Sir Archibald Salvidge,[1] sent him a 'unanimous invitation' from the Liverpool Conservatives to address them at a mass meeting at the beginning of May. Churchill had in fact asked Salvidge to try to procure this invitation, and was delighted when it came.

In the third week of April Churchill spoke again to Colonel Jackson, hoping that the support of Conservative headquarters, although withheld during the Abbey by-election, might still be forthcoming in the other Westminster constituency. The discussion with Jackson boded well for Churchill's plans. 'He is going to try to fix up St Georges for me,' Churchill wrote to his wife—who was at Dieppe—on April 17. 'The Liberal Party is in a stew,' he explained. 'They are disgusted with the position into wh they have been led & then left without leading. There is an intensely bitter feeling agst Labour, which everywhere is cutting Liberal throats in the constituencies.' And he added: 'How often I find myself called wrong, for warning of follies in time.'

Churchill's letter of April 17 was the first letter he had ever written from Chartwell. In it he described all that he was doing to make the house ready for her return from Dieppe:

The children have worked like blacks & Sergeant Thompson,[2] Aley, Waterhouse, one gardener & 6 men have formed a powerful labour corps.

---

[1] Archibald Tutton James Salvidge, 1863–1928. Chairman, Liverpool Conservative Workingmen's Association, 1892. Alderman, Liverpool City Council, 1898. Chairman of Council, National Union of Conservative and Unionist Associations, 1913–14. Chairman, Liverpool Advisory Committee on Recruiting, 1914–16. Knighted, 1916. Chairman of the Liverpool Constitutional Association.

[2] Walter H. Thompson. Detective Constable, Special Branch, Scotland Yard, 1913. Bodyguard to Lloyd George, 1917–20. Bodyguard to Churchill, 1920–32 and accompanied Chur-

The weather has been delicious, & we are out all day toiling in dirty clothes & only batheing before dinner. I have just had my bath in your de Luxe bathroom. I hope you have no *amour propre* about it! . . .

I drink champagne at all meals & buckets of claret & soda in between, & the *cuisine* tho' simple is excellent. In the evenings we play the gramophone (of wh we have deprived Mary[1]) & Mah Jongg with yr gimcrack set.

All yesterday & today we have been turfing & levelling the plateau, the motor mower acts as a roller and we have done everything now except from the yew tree to the Kn garden end. Here as you know there is more levelling & also the pathway made by the carts to make good. I hope to finish to-morrow.

In her reply on April 19, Clementine Churchill commented on her husband's news that he might be given Conservative backing at Westminster St George's. She was sceptical of Baldwin's motives, telling her husband:

I suppose that if there were a real Liberal move to the right Baldwin would not be in a hurry to provide you with a safe Tory seat such as St George's? He would probably suggest that you stand as a Liberal for a Liberal Seat with no Tory opposition. This would suit his book better as the minute you become a Conservative his Leadership is endangered—both by you & F.E. whom you would bring back with you as a possible Leader.

On the morning of May 7, accompanied by his wife, Churchill left London by train to give his speech in Liverpool, reaching the city early in the afternoon. Four hours later he made a major speech to an audience of over five thousand people. It was the first Conservative meeting at which he had spoken for twenty years, and yet, as he pointed out in his opening remarks, for nearly ten of those twenty years—first in Asquith's Coalition and then under Lloyd George—he had been working 'in close accord' with many of the principal leaders of the Conservative Party. Now, he said, Liberals and Conservatives found themselves with many things in common, not as a result of having

---

chill to the United States, 1931–32. Retired from the police force with the rank of Detective Inspector, 1936. Worked as a grocer, 1936–39. Recalled to the police force, 1939, and served as Churchill's personal bodyguard from September 1939 until May 1945.

[1] Mary Churchill, 1922–   . Churchill's fifth and youngest child. Served with the Auxiliary Territorial Service, 1940–45; accompanied her father on several of his wartime journeys. In 1947 she married Captain (later the Rt Hon Sir) Christopher Soames. They have five children.

changed their respective positions, but as a result of 'the deep and slow tide of events'. During his speech, Churchill attacked the Labour Government for saying that it would repeal the McKenna duties, a set of tariffs on luxury articles which had been introduced by the previous Conservative Government. These duties, which included foreign cars, clocks and watches, brought in £2½ million a year to the Exchequer. 'It is a very rough and harsh measure,' Churchill said, 'suddenly to strike away the duties and plunge the whole of the arrangements of the industries into confusion,' especially, he added, when it was the State which had created 'these artificial conditions'. Churchill went on to uphold the wisdom of imperial tariffs, pointing out that he himself, as Colonial Secretary, had supported the Preference on sugar imposed in 1922, to protect the West Indies sugar trade, and had promised to maintain that Preference for at least ten years, until 1932.

There was no longer any place, Churchill declared, for an independent Liberal Party. Only the Conservatives offered a strong enough base 'for the successful defeat of Socialism'. Liberals like himself must be prepared to join forces with the Conservatives, to support them at the Polls, and to be supported by them, sustained by a 'broad progressive platform'. Churchill repeated his arguments at a luncheon on the following day at the Liverpool Conservative Club.

The Conservatives responded with enthusiasm to Churchill's appeal. The Conservative Chief Whip, Colonel Jackson, wrote on May 8 to offer Churchill his congratulations 'upon your brilliant speech', and Sir Samuel Hoare[1] wrote on May 9:

I must write this line to congratulate you upon the success of your two Liverpool speeches. If I may say so, they have both greatly strengthened your position with the Conservative Party. Your Conservative friends are now looking with keen anticipation to the debate upon the McKenna duties, when they much hope that your friends in the House will follow your excellent lead.

On May 9 the Conservative Association of Ashton-under-Lyne asked Churchill if we would be willing to stand, under their aegis, as an anti-Socialist candidate. Further invitations came from both the

---

[1] Samuel John Gurney Hoare, 1880–1959. Educated at Harrow and New College Oxford. Conservative MP for Chelsea, 1910–44. Succeeded his father as 2nd Baronet, 1915. Lieutenant-Colonel, British Military Mission to Russia, 1916–17 and to Italy, 1917–18. Deputy High Commissioner, League of Nations, for care of Russian refugees, 1921. Secretary of State for Air, October 1922–January 1924 and 1924–29. Secretary of State for India, 1931–35; for Foreign Affairs, 1935. First Lord of the Admiralty, 1936–37; Home Secretary, 1937–39; Lord Privy Seal, 1939–40; Secretary of State for Air, April–May 1940. Ambassador to Spain, 1940–44. Created Viscount Templewood, 1944.

Kettering and Royston Conservatives. Although Churchill declined these invitations, his relationship with the Conservatives was now a close one, and on May 10 he informed Baldwin that he was helping to organize a group of Liberal MPs in the House of Commons—including Frederick Guest, Edward Grigg and General Seely[1] who would be ready to vote with the Conservatives on the next anti-Labour motion. He also reported on Guest's behalf 'that as many as twenty (and perhaps more)' Liberals might go into the Lobby against their own leadership, and in support of the Conservatives. 'I am glad you liked my line at Liverpool,' Churchill added, 'and am much obliged to you for your friendly reference to it.'

An incident in May confirmed Baldwin's growing friendship with Churchill. On Sunday May 17 the *People* published an interview with Baldwin, in which the Conservative leader was said to have spoken most disparagingly of 'this Churchill plotting'. That same evening Colonel Jackson pressed Baldwin to issue a firm denial about the accuracy of the report, and on May 20, in a handwritten note, Baldwin himself hastened to put Churchill's mind at rest:

My dear Churchill,
I hope you will treat the article in the 'People' with the contempt it deserves and accept my assurances that the offensive remarks were never uttered by me. I am looking forward to dining with you on Thursday and hope that our meeting may be productive of useful results. . . .

On May 30 Churchill wrote to Baldwin asking for help regarding his possible nomination for Westminster St Georges. He was, he wrote, under 'great pressure' to stand again, in spite of the continuing opposition of the local Constituency Association, and a Memorial signed by 1,500 Conservative electors was shortly to be presented to the Conservative Central Office. He was assured 'on all sides', he added, that he had only to form his own Organization and set to work in the Constituency 'to secure my return to Parliament at the General Election whatever line the Central Office may be directed to take'. But he did not wish to think only of his 'own inclinations', or merely of the local situation. He would much rather avoid any conflict 'with

---

[1] John Edward Bernard Seely, 1868–1947. Educated at Harrow and Trinity College Cambridge. Liberal MP, 1900–02; 1923–24. Under-Secretary of State for the Colonies, 1908–11. Secretary of State for War, 1912–14. Resigned in March 1914, following the Curragh incident. Commanded the Canadian Cavalry Brigade, 1915–18. Gassed, 1918, and retired from Army with rank of Major-General. Under-Secretary of State to Churchill, Ministry of Munitions and Deputy Minister of Munitions, 1918. Under-Secretary of State for Air, 1919. Created Baron Mottistone, 1933. Chairman of the National Savings Committee, 1926–43. His son Frank was killed leading his company at the battle of Arras, 1917.

the official Conservative Party whose victory at the polls I desire to help by every means'. He also wanted to be free, he wrote, from a 'hard-fought local contest' in order to render to the Conservatives 'more useful service' throughout the country, 'and particularly London'.

Churchill appealed to Baldwin to help him out of his predicament, and to suggest some means whereby he could either stand at Westminster with full Conservative backing, or be otherwise helped to a Conservative-supported Constituency: 'I write to ask you to consider whether you can suggest any course which will prevent the discord and dissipation of effort which otherwise seems to be inevitable.'

Baldwin had no desire to see another contest on the Westminster model, or to drive away Churchill's Liberal supporters. On June 2 he sent Churchill a handwritten note, promising to consider Churchill's request 'very carefully in consultation with a few of my friends'. Among those whom Baldwin consulted was Sir Samuel Hoare. On June 4 a deputation of Westminster Conservatives led by Oliver Locker-Lampson[1] went to see Baldwin to press Churchill's claims, and to present a Memorial signed by 1,700 electors 'of all classes and interests'. Two weeks later, on June 17, Hoare wrote to Churchill to explain the situation:

Dear Winston,

I made a point of seeing both Stanley Baldwin and Stanley Jackson yesterday. . . . From my talk with them it appears to be certain that there will be great trouble in Westminster if you stand there. I put it to them that if you stood down, we ought to find you some other constituency without any further delay. They both told me privately that they have a constituency in view, and I understand that Jackson has already asked you to see him on the subject. If I may make a suggestion, I would say that it will be better if you can carry on the negotiations yourself direct with Jackson and Baldwin. I am inclined to guess that Oliver Locker-Lampson's deputation did not assist the progress of a settlement.

Churchill's hopes of being chosen for Westminster were ended when Nicholson decided not to stand down. But he still saw himself as leading an independent pro-Conservative group at the Polls. In a letter to Hoare on June 18 he asked about what title he and those Liberals who felt like him should chose. 'What do you think of the name

---

[1] Oliver Stillingfleet Locker-Lampson, 1881–1954. Educated at Eton and Trinity College Cambridge. Editor of *Granta*, 1900. Called to the Bar, 1907. Conservative MP, 1910–45. Lieutenant-Commander, Royal Naval Air Service, December 1914; Commander, July 1915. Commanded the British Armoured Car detachment in Russia, 1916–17. Parliamentary Private Secretary to Austen Chamberlain, 1919–21. Churchill's Private Secretary, 1926.

Liberal–Conservative?' he asked, and he continued: 'It is novel in England but Sir John MacDonald[1] held power in Canada at the head of a Liberal–Conservative party, and such a party name is now, I understand, in wide use in Spain (a doubtful precedent!).' Something, he was convinced, had soon to be decided. 'Time is passing,' he told Hoare, 'and though the sea is calm and the ship's company lethargic we know that very dirty weather is approaching. . . .'

During July Churchill's political plans finally obtained the approval of the Conservative Central Office. Helped by Sir Samuel Hoare, and with encouragement from Colonel Jackson, Churchill persuaded Baldwin to allow him to stand at the next General Election as an independent 'Constitutionalist' candidate, with full Conservative support. Baldwin agreed that Churchill would be found a safe Conservative seat in or near London, thus leaving him free to play a leading part in the Conservative election campaign outside his constituency. If possible, a seat would be found for which there was no Liberal candidate, but a straight fight between Churchill and the Labour nominee. Although Churchill would not join the Conservative Party, he would speak along the lines of its declared policies. Opposition to Ramsay MacDonald's proposed Anglo-Soviet Treaty would form an important part of his platform, as would his continued denunciation of the perils of Socialism. At a dinner given by Hoare in the second week of July, Churchill and Baldwin discussed their alliance in detail. 'Winston, in private, accepts our policy,' Baldwin wrote to Austen Chamberlain on July 21. 'It is now up to him to address a meeting and say so.'

During August, before Churchill could make any public speech, Colonel Jackson selected two potential constituencies, Richmond and Epping, both of which seemed suitable to Churchill's needs. On August 5, the Epping Constituency Chairman, Sir Harry Goschen,[2] with Jackson's approval, wrote direct to Churchill to ask if he would allow his name to go forward to his Executive Committee. 'Should this idea appeal to you,' Goschen added, 'I presume I might tell them that you would stand as a supporter of the Conservative Party, their leaders & policy, & especially as regards Ireland the policy they have outlined . . .'

[1] Sir John MacDonald, Prime Minister of Canada from 1869 to 1872 and from 1878 until his death in 1891 (his Party remained in power until 1896).

[2] Harry William Henry Neville Goschen, 1865–1945. Educated at Eton. A Director of the Agriculture Mortgage Co-operative Ltd and of the Atlas Assurance Company. OBE, 1918. Prime Warden of the Goldsmiths Company, 1919–20. Chairman of the National Provincial Bank. Created Baronet, 1927.

Churchill replied to Goschen on August 11, thanking him for 'such a fine offer'. He intended, he said, to do his utmost 'to secure a victory for the Conservative and anti-Socialist forces at the General Election, and the programme of the Conservative leaders had his 'full concurrence'. He was, he went on, prepared to give a pledge on Ulster, to the effect that no boundary changes would be made without the approval of the Ulster Parliament, but he deprecated bringing the Irish issue into the election campaign. The principal need, he added, was that 'a decisive victory should be won over the Socialists at the next appeal'; it was to this end that they must choose their issues and marshal their forces.

On August 14 Churchill sent Goschen's letter to Colonel Jackson, asking for guidance and an early decision. 'Time is slipping away,' Churchill warned, 'and nothing is settled. . . . The fight may well be upon us in October and November.' This was also the feeling in the constituencies, and on August 15, the Deputy Chairman of the Epping Conservatives, A. J. Hawkey,[1] telephoned to Central Office to ask when a decision would be forthcoming; the likelihood of a General Election before the end of the year made the selection of a candidate an urgent one.

Churchill waited at Chartwell for a decision to be reached. Among his visitors was Sir Roger Keyes, one of the most outspoken supporters of the Dardanelles campaign. Writing to his wife on August 19, Churchill pointed out that Keyes was a resident in the Epping constituency, 'and tells me that there is a very favourable disposition among the Conservative notables. It looks one of the safest seats in the country. But you never can tell.'[2] Most of Churchill's letter concerned news of Chartwell itself:

Work on the dam is progressing. Owing to the fact that the months have got mixed and apparently we are having April instead of August, the water has been rising steadily. We have this evening seven feet. It will be completely

[1] Alfred James Hawkey, 1877–1952. Educated at Woodford Collegiate School. A baker; Chairman of Clark's Bread Company; Vice-Chairman, Aerated Bread Company. Elected to the Woodford Urban District Council, 1909; Chairman, 1916–34. Chairman of the Wanstead and Woodford UDC, 1934–37. Organized Food Control in Woodford, 1914–18. Deputy Chairman of the Epping Conservative Association, 1922–26; Chairman, 1927–52. Knighted, 1926. Mayor of Wanstead and Woodford, 1937–38 and 1943–45; responsible for emergency feeding and information services in the Borough during the blitz, 1940–41. Member of the Essex County Council. Created Baronet, 1945. In his war memoirs Churchill described Hawkey as 'my ever faithful and tireless champion'.

[2] At the 1922 General Election the Conservative candidate, General Nicholson, had secured 13,620 votes, as against only 2,444 Labour and 1,950 Independent votes; an overall majority of nearly 10,000. The seat was thus among the safest Conservative seats in Britain.

finished by next Tuesday, or eight weeks from its initiation. I am at it all day long and every day. . . .

Meanwhile the old lake is practically dry. There is an average of a foot of mud, and I am going to go at it hard with my railway to clear it out. Thompson and I have been wallowing in the most filthy black mud you ever saw, with the vilest odour, getting the beastly stuff to drain away. The moor hens and dab chicks have migrated in a body to the new lake and taken up their quarters in the bushes at the upper end. There are about eleven of them there now.

Churchill ended his letter on a financial note. 'The 9 elder swine,' he reported, 'are sold for £31. They have eaten less than £1 a week for 18 weeks of life—so there is a profit of £13. Not bad on so small a capital.'

Churchill remained at Chartwell throughout August. On August 22 he took his son Randolph—aged thirteen—to lunch with a former Liberal Prime Minister, Lord Rosebery.[1] During their talk, they spoke at length about Churchill's ancestor, the first Duke of Marlborough, and of Macaulay's attacks on Marlborough's reputation. The discussion, Churchill wrote to his wife later that day, 'has turned my mind very seriously to the great literary project which so many people are inclined to saddle me with—a full scale biography of "Duke John".'

At the end of August two leading Conservatives, Sir Robert Horne and Lord Carson,[2] urged Churchill to speak publicly, as Baldwin also wished, in the Conservative interest. Opposition to MacDonald's Russian Treaty was the theme they advised, and Carson agreed to take the chair for Churchill's forthcoming speech at Edinburgh. Sir Robert Horne likewise agreed to appear on the platform. 'The Russian issue is the one,' Churchill wrote to Horne on August 30, 'and with good handling might be decisive.'

On September 10 Churchill learnt from Colonel Jackson that, although the chance of the seat at Richmond had fallen through, Epping was 'at this moment, a long way the best one which is available'. At Epping Churchill would have a determined Liberal opponent,

[1] Archibald Philip Primrose, 1847–1929. Succeeded his grandfather as 5th Earl of Rosebery, 1868. Lord Privy Seal, 1885. Secretary of State for Foreign Affairs, 1886 and 1892–94. Prime Minister, 1894–95. In 1906 he published a short memorial volume, *Lord Randolph Churchill*. His younger son Neil Primrose was killed in action in Palestine, 18 November 1917.

[2] Edward Henry Carson, 1854–1935. Educated at Trinity College, Dublin. Barrister. Conservative MP, 1892–1921. Knighted, 1900. Solicitor-General, 1900–06. Leader of the Ulster Unionists in the House of Commons, 1910–21. Attorney-General, May–October 1915. First Lord of the Admiralty, December 1916–July 1917. Minister without Portfolio in the War Cabinet, July 1917–January 1918. Created Baron, 1921. A Lord of Appeal in Ordinary, 1921–29.

which made the Constituency, Jackson wrote, 'not exactly the kind of seat that I would have wished to have seen you offered'. Nevertheless, he added, 'I should be very pleased if you accepted this invitation, and can assure you every possible assistance from this Office.' Encouraged by this pledge of support from Conservative Central Office, and eager to reach a decision before an election became imminent, Churchill accepted Jackson's advice, and on September 11 he wrote to Sir Harry Goschen accepting the Epping invitation.

On the evening of September 25 Churchill made his much-heralded Edinburgh speech, to a crowded and enthusiastic meeting of Scottish Conservatives at the Usher Hall. He was introduced to the meeting by Balfour, who praised his 'great insight' into the real problems facing Britain. In his speech, Churchill again declared that there was now 'no gulf of principle' between Conservatives and Liberals. The Labour Party had become the enemy of both. Both must combine to defeat it. In the past twenty years, he said, 'we have seen it grow from a handful of Socialist freaks and a band of sturdy old trade unionist leaders into the foundation of a Government which is at this moment ruling the land'. The Soviet Treaty was proof of what they really stood for. 'I object to subsidising tyranny,' Churchill declared, and he continued:

Judged by every standard which history has applied to Governments, the Soviet Government of Russia is one of the worst tyrannies that has ever existed in the world. It accords no political rights. It rules by terror. It punishes political opinions. It suppresses free speech. It tolerates no newspapers but its own. It persecutes Christianity with a zeal and a cunning never equalled since the times of the Roman Emperors. It is engaged at this moment in trampling down the peoples of Georgia and executing their leaders by hundreds.

It is for this process that Mr MacDonald, himself acquainted with Georgia,[1] asks us to make ourselves responsible. We are to render these tyrannies possible by lending to their authors money to pay for the ammunition to murder the Georgians, to enable the Soviet sect to keep its stranglehold on the dumb Russian nation, and to poison the world, and so far as they can the British Empire, with their filthy propaganda. That is what we are asked to take upon ourselves. It is an outrage on the British name.

Churchill went on to contrast the Labour Government's enthusiasm for the Soviet Treaty with its coldness towards the Dominions. By giving

---

[1] In 1920 Ramsay MacDonald had visited Georgia (then an independent State) as a member of a delegation from the Second International. After Soviet Russia conquered Georgia in April 1921 he championed the Georgian cause, and at the Berlin Conference of the Three Internationals in 1922 he devoted a large part of his speech to attacking the Soviet delegate, Radek, about the destruction of the Georgian Republic.

up the naval base at Singapore, he said, MacDonald had made it impossible for Britain to come to the aid of Australia or New Zealand in any future emergency. Enlarging on the contrast between Labour's attitude to the Soviets and to the Empire, he told his audience, in a calculated peroration reminiscent of his father's oratory of thirty years before:

To the enemies of Britain, of civilisation, of freedom, to those who deserted us in the crises of the war—smiles, compliments, caresses, cash. But for Canada, Australia, New Zealand, South Africa who sent their brave men to fight and die by scores of thousands, who never flinched and never wearied, who ˙re bone of our bone and flesh of our flesh—to them nothing but frigid repulsion.

Our bread for the Bolshevist serpent; our aid for the foreigner of every country; our favours for the Socialists all over the world who have no country; but for our own daughter States across the oceans, on whom the future of the British island and nation depends, only the cold stones of indifference, aversion, and neglect.

That is the policy with which the Socialist Government confronts us, and against that policy we will strive to marshal the unconquerable might of Britain.

Churchill's Edinburgh speech marked his public emergence as a supporter of the Conservative Party, and heralded his return to full-time politics. On September 30 his mother-in-law, Lady Blanche Hozier,[1] wrote from Dieppe to a friend in England: 'So Winston is on the war path again—after a prolonged holiday that he has enjoyed. . . .'

In the two years since he had lost his Parliamentary seat, Churchill had become increasingly friendly with a German-born Oxford professor, Frederick Lindemann.[2] The two men had first met in August

---

[1] Lady Henrietta Blanche Ogilvy, 1852–1925. Daughter of the 7th Earl of Airlie. In 1873 she married Sir Henry Hozier (who died in 1907). Mother of Clementine, Nellie and William.

[2] Frederick Alexander Lindemann, 1886–1957. Born at Baden Baden (where his mother was taking the cure); son of Alsatian father who had emigrated to Britain in the early 1870s, and an American mother. Educated at Blair Lodge Scotland, Darmstadt 1902–05, and Berlin University 1906–10. Doctor of Philosophy, Berlin, 1910. Studied physical chemistry in Paris, 1912–14. Worked at the Physical Laboratory, RAF, 1915–18, when he helped to organize the kite balloon barrage. Learned to fly, 1916. Personally investigated the aerodynamic effects of aircraft spin. Professor of Experimental Philosophy (physics) Oxford, 1919–56. Student of Christ Church (where he subsequently resided), 1921. Elected to the Other Club, 1927. Published his *Physical Significance of the Quantum Theory*, 1932. Member of the Expert Committee on Air Defence Research, Committee of Imperial Defence, 1935–39. Unsuccessful by-election candidate at Oxford, 1937. Personal Assistant to the Prime Minister (Churchill)

1921, and quickly found encouragement in each other's company. Early in 1924 Churchill had enlisted Lindemann's help with a new and important literary venture, writing to him on April 3:

My dear Lindemann,

I have undertaken to write on the future possibilities of war and how frightful it will be for the human race. On this subject I have a good many ideas, but I should very much like to have another talk with you following on the most interesting one we had when you last lunched here. Do let me know when you are likely to be in London in the next few weeks, so that we can fix a lunch together.

Thank you so much for the letter which you wrote my wife about the Election. It was exciting but provoking.

Yours sincerely,
Winston Churchill

Lindemann helped Churchill with his article, and answered further queries as Churchill developed his themes and arguments. On April 21 Churchill wrote again:

I wish you would make enquiries about the man who is said to have discovered a ray which will kill at a certain distance. I meet people who say that it can actually be seen to kill mice etc. It may be all a hoax, but my experience has been not to take 'No' for an answer.

'There is an article in "John Bull" of May 3,' Churchill wrote again on May 10, 'which deals with the subject of the deadly ray, which it might be worth your while to look at, if only to despise it.'

On September 24 Churchill's article was published in *Nash's Pall Mall* magazine, entitled 'Shall We All Commit Suicide'. Of all his literary work at this time, it made the greatest impact. In it he warned of weapons yet to be invented, and appealed for a greater wisdom in human affairs to avert future catastrophe. 'Mankind has never been in this position before,' he wrote. 'Without having improved appreciably in virtue or enjoying wiser guidance, it has got into its hands for the first time the tools by which it can unfailingly accomplish its own extermination.' He continued:

That is the point in human destinies to which all the glories and toils of men have at last led them. They would do well to pause and ponder upon their new responsibilities. Death stands at attention, obedient, expectant,

1940–41; in 1953 Churchill's Private Secretary, John Martin, wrote to him: 'Those without experience in the inner circle will never know the size of Winston's debt to you and how much stimulus and inspiration of ideas flowed from your office.' Created Baron Cherwell, 1941. Paymaster General, 1942–45 and 1951–53. Privy Councillor, 1943. Viscount, 1956.

ready to serve, ready to shear away the peoples *en masse*; ready, if called on, to pulverise, without hope of repair, what is left of civilisation. He awaits only the word of command. He awaits it from a frail, bewildered being, long his victim, now—for one occasion only—his Master.

Churchill went on to warn of the dangers still remaining in Europe of another war. For the time being, he wrote, 'the horror of war, its carnage and its tyrannies, have sunk into the soul'. But the causes of war had in no way been removed. They had in some ways been aggravated 'by the so-called Peace Treaty', and the situation was still a dangerous one, as Churchill explained:

Two mighty branches of the European family will never rest content with their existing situation. Russia, stripped of her Baltic Provinces, will, as the years pass by, brood incessantly upon the wars of Peter the Great. From one end of Germany to the other an intense hatred of France unites the whole population. This passion is fanned continuously by the action of the French Government. The enormous contingents of German youth growing to military manhood year by year are inspired by the fiercest sentiments, and the soul of Germany smoulders with dreams of a War of Liberation or Revenge. These ideas are restrained at the present moment only by physical impotence. France is armed to the teeth. Germany has been to a great extent disarmed and her military system broken up. The French hope to preserve this situation by their technical military-apparatus, by their black troops, and by a system of alliances with the smaller States of Europe; and for the present at any rate overwhelming force is on their side. But physical force alone, unsustained by world opinion, affords no durable foundation for security. Germany is a far stronger entity than France, and cannot be kept in permanent subjugation.

Churchill next examined the materials of war. A 'German'[1] had recently told him that the next war would be fought with electricity. 'And on this,' Churchill wrote, 'a vista opens out of electrical rays which could paralyze the engines of a motor car, could claw down aeroplanes from the sky, and conceivably be made destructive of human life or human vision.' In addition, he wrote, there was the enormous power of explosives. 'Has science turned its last page on them?' he asked, and proceeded to try to answer his own question:

May there not be methods of using explosive energy incomparably more intense than anything heretofore discovered? Might not a bomb no bigger than an orange be found to possess a secret power to destroy a whole block of buildings—nay to concentrate the force of a thousand tons of cordite and blast a township at a stroke? Could not explosives even of the existing type be guided automatically in flying machines by wireless or other rays, without a

[1] This was in fact Professor Lindemann.

human pilot, in ceaseless procession upon a hostile city, arsenal, camp, or dockyard?

Other sinister developments, Churchill warned, would take place in the sphere of poison gas and chemical warfare. Even a study of disease, of 'Pestilences methodically prepared and deliberately launched on man and beast', was surely being carried out 'in the laboratories of more than one great country'. And he warned: 'Blight to destroy crops, Anthrax to slay horses and cattle, Plague to poison not armies only but whole districts—such are the lines along which military science is remorselessly advancing.'

In his article Churchill urged that the prevention of future war ought to be the 'paramount object' of all human efforts, and he appealed for world support of the League of Nations, as the sole organization capable of averting catastrophe. His appeal was tinged with foreboding. 'Against the gathering but still distant tempest,' he wrote, 'the League of Nations, deserted by the United States, scorned by Soviet Russia, flouted by Italy, distrusted equally by France and Germany, raises feebly but faithfully its standards of sanity and hope,' and was as yet 'incapable of guarding the world from its dangers'. But, Churchill went on: 'To sustain and aid the League of Nations is the duty of all. To reinforce it and bring it into vital and practical relation with actual world-politics by sincere agreements and understanding between the great Powers, between the leading races, should be the first aim of all who wish to spare their children torments and disasters compared to which those we have suffered will be but a pale preliminary.'

Churchill had not previously been regarded as a supporter of the League. But officials of the League at once published his article as a pamphlet in the United States, where, within two weeks, over 250,000 copies were distributed, and a second massive reprint put in hand. 'Just look at this,' Churchill wrote to Lord Robert Cecil[1] on November 25, when he learnt the news of the pamphlet's success. 'You see I am not so unregenerate as you suppose.' 'Who says you are unregenerate,' Cecil replied. 'I regard you on the contrary as a brand plucked from the burning!!'

[1] Lord Edgar Algernon Robert Cecil, 1864–1958. Third son of the 3rd Marquess of Salisbury. Educated at Eton and University College Oxford. Conservative MP for East Marylebone, 1906–10. Independent Conservative MP for Hitchin, 1911–23. Under-Secretary of State for Foreign Affairs, 1915–18. Minister of Blockade, 1916–18. Assistant Secretary of State for Foreign Affairs, 1918. Created Viscount Cecil of Chelwood, 1923. Lord Privy Seal, 1923–24. President of the League of Nations Union, 1923–45. Chancellor of the Duchy of Lancaster, 1924–27. Nobel Peace Prize, 1937.

3

Return to Parliament:
'The Jolliest Bit of News
for Months'

ON October 3 Churchill addressed his first public meeting in the Epping division, at Waltham Abbey. Once more he attacked the Labour Government's decision to lend money to the Soviets, and reiterated his belief that the regime in Russia was 'unquestionably one of the worst and meanest tyrannies which have ever existed in the world'. This attack on the Labour Party for its support of the Soviets was popular with the local Conservatives. Outside his constituency, Conservatives also welcomed Churchill's support, and on October 4 Colonel Jackson wrote to him, of the recent Party Conference at Newcastle: 'I was glad when your name was mentioned to hear it given a very good reception.' Three days later his cousin Lord Londonderry wrote of 'how delighted I am that we shall have the full value of your powerful support'. Londonderry added: 'As you know it is what I have always hoped, and yet the bridge seemed impossible to build.'

On October 7 Churchill issued a statement to the Press Association, supporting the Liberal demand for a full Parliamentary enquiry into the Campbell case—'this scandalous affair' as he called it. Some weeks before, Ramsay MacDonald had agreed to drop the Government's prosecution against a Communist editor, J. R. Campbell,[1] who had published an article urging soldiers not to obey orders. Churchill

[1] John Ross Campbell, 1894–1969. Educated at elementary school, Paisley. Joined the British Socialist Party, 1912. On active service, 1914–18 (Military Medal, 1917). Editor of the *Glasgow Worker*, 1921–24; acting editor of the *Workers' Weekly*, 1924–26. Member of the Executive Committee of the British Communist Party, 1923–64, and of the Communist International, 1925–35. Served six months in prison for 'seditious conspiracy', 1925–26. Editor of the *Daily Worker*, 1949–59.

53

believed that the Conservatives should support the proposed Liberal demand for a Select Committee, and thus force the Labour Government's resignation. Churchill's statement ended with a warning about the position of the moderates in the Labour Party: 'There are in the ranks of the Socialist Government many men of high reputation, men who stood by their country in the war, men who have lived their lives in the public eye and in the House of Commons for a whole generation. The position of these men is pathetic. They have been unable to keep their feet upon the slippery slopes on which they have tried to stand.'

The Government's handling of the Campbell case was debated in the House of Commons on October 8. Asquith, who demanded a Select Committee, was supported by Baldwin, and in the ensuing division the Labour Government was defeated by 364 votes to 198. MacDonald at once called for a General Election, which was fixed for October 29.

On October 12 Churchill issued his election manifesto. 'I give my wholehearted support,' he declared, 'to the Conservative Party', which alone could give Britain another period of 'calm, clean, sober government'. Socialism, he went on, was alien to the British way of life: 'Such desperate courses originate easily among the down-trodden peoples of Central and Eastern Europe. Whether under a Communist Republic or an Imperial War Lord, whether under a Lenin or a Ludendorff, they have always been accustomed to submitting to tyranny. But this famous island is the home of freedom and of representative government. We have led the world along these paths, and we have no need now to seek our inspiration from Moscow or from Munich.'

In his manifesto, Churchill warned that the money lent to Russia by MacDonald would never be repaid, any more than Russia's war debt to Britain had been repaid.[1] But, he continued: 'far more important than the loss of money is the loss of honour involved in making ourselves responsible for the wickedness that is going on in Russia. A tyranny of the vilest kind has been erected.' The prisons were filled with 'innumerable political captives'. Scores of thousands of people 'of both sexes and of every class have been executed or murdered in cold blood', and he went on: 'Live peaceably with the Bolsheviks if you can; trade with Russia if they will allow you and if you think you will get paid for what you sell, but do not degrade the manhood of Britain by taking on your shoulders and on the shoulders of your children a direct share of responsibility for crimes which have darkened the light of the sun.'

---

[1] The Labour Government's loan to the Soviet Government amounted to £50 million. The unpaid war loans to the Tsarist Government totalled £757 million.

Churchill's friends hastened to wish him success in the coming contest. 'May all good luck attend you & may you soon take your place—right at the top,' Hugo Baring[1] wrote from Paris on October 13. 'Looking forward to seeing you once again thump the familiar box in the House of Commons,' Esmond Harmsworth[2] wrote on October 14. That same day both Lord Carson and Lord Balfour sent Churchill letters of support for which he had asked three days before. One of Churchill's friends, Sir Ian Hamilton,[3] had at first doubted whether the campaign would succeed, but in a letter to Churchill on October 25 he wrote:

My dear Winston,
Moved by some anxiety I pulled out my little Wolseley & ran down to Epping this afternoon. Round about I know a farmer or two, a cowman or two and a couple of big wigs. As I went as a proclaimed non politician it may interest you to hear that the result of my touting was that I came back fairly comfortable in my mind. You may take it from me that your two last speeches, the one in the open air & the last one, turned the scale. As you must know your danger (like that of Dizzy) lies in the hard upper crust of the Diehards. . . .

Polling took place on October 29. When the result was announced on October 30, Churchill was once more a Member of Parliament, with a substantial majority of just under 10,000.[4]

---

[1] Hugo Baring, 1876–1949. Sixth son of the 1st Baron Revelstoke, and brother of Maurice Baring. Educated at Eton. Lieutenant, 4th Hussars; on active serve (with Churchill) in the Tirah Campaign, 1897. Severely wounded in South Africa, 1900. Captain, 10th Hussars, 1914; wounded at Ypres, November 1914. Served with the British Mission to Siberia, 1918–19. A Director of Parr's Bank, 1911–18; the Westminster Bank, 1918–45; Resident Director, Paris, 1920–39. His only son, born in 1909, was killed in action in France in June 1940.

[2] Esmond Cecil Harmsworth, 1898–1978. Only surviving son of the 1st Baron (later Viscount) Rothermere (whose other two sons were both killed in action on the western front). Served in the Royal Marine Artillery, 1917–18. ADC to Lloyd George at the Paris Peace Conference, 1919. Conservative MP for the Isle of Thanet, 1920–29. Supported Churchill at the Abbey by-election, 1924. Elected to the Other Club, 1928. Chairman of Associated Newspapers Ltd, 1932–71. Chairman of the Newspaper Proprietors' Association, 1934–61. Member of the Advisory Council, Ministry of Information, 1939. Succeeded his father as 2nd Viscount Rothermere, 1940. Chairman of the Daily Mail and General Trust Ltd.

[3] Ian Standish Monteith Hamilton, 1853–1947. Entered Army, 1872. Major-General, 1900. Knighted, 1900. Chief of Staff to Lord Kitchener, 1901–02. General, 1914. Commander of the Central Force, responsible for the defence of England in the event of invasion, August 1914–March 1915. Commanded the Mediterranean Expeditionary Force at Gallipoli, March–October 1915, after which he received no further military command.

[4] The voting figures were: Churchill (Constitutionalist), 19,843; G. Granville Sharp (Liberal), 10,080; J. R. McPhie (Labour), 3,768.

Nationally, the result of the election was a complete victory for the Conservatives, who won 419 seats, as against 151 for Labour. For the Liberals, with only 40 seats, the election was a disaster. Asquith himself was defeated, and the Liberals lost more than a million votes. Churchill's own return to Parliament was widely acclaimed. At Trafalgar Square, the *Sunday Times* reported on October 31, 'the great cheer of the day was reserved for Mr Winston Churchill's victory at Epping', and T. E. Lawrence wrote to him that same day:

This isn't congratulation, it's just the hiss of my excess delight rushing out. You've done it gloriously—all the conditions to your credit; two bye-elections, two books, to whet the public appetite, and then this smashing success. Tactically, it seems to me, the ground is all in your favour now: only let's hope there will be enemy enough to provide you with exercise. Probably there will be, since some of the very shell-back Tories will want cracking occasionally: and their own chiefs are mild. However this isn't my affair. Thank you for providing the jolliest bit of news for months.

There was much speculation about whether Churchill would be brought into the Government. Even before polling day some had assumed that, with a Conservative victory, he would be given Cabinet office. On November 1 Sir William Tyrrell sent Baldwin a 'Private & Secret' account of a dinner, given by Philip Sassoon on October 28, at which Churchill, Birkenhead, Beaverbrook, Sir Samuel Hoare and Sir Philip Lloyd-Greame had all been present. According to Tyrrell the conversation had gone as follows:

F. E. to Winston—'I suppose you expect to get Office?'
Winston replies—'that will depend very much on what I am offered'.
'No,' said F. E.—'You have been hungering and thirsting for Office for two years and you will take anything they offer you.'
On Winston showing resentment, F.E. proceeded to give the company a sketch of all the tricks and subterfuges he and Winston on occasions had resorted to in order to obtain Office. . . .
Beaverbrook . . . expressed the conviction that you would be bound to give Office to Winston sooner than see him become the nucleus of dissatisfaction in your own party.
My impression is that you have so many fools in your party wedded to the slogan that anybody as brilliant as Winston must be given Office, that it would be worth while to silence them.

Churchill himself, nearly 25 years later, dictated a private note of his own recollections of the occasion, in which he wrote:

Sam Hoare, who thought himself, and was supposed to be, deeply in Mr

Baldwin's confidence, was asked point-blank across the table, 'What do you think he is going to do about Winston?' Hoare replied that he was quite sure Stanley, as he was already affectionately called, was not the sort of man to try any experiments of that kind. This was my own opinion too. However, a considerable band of extreme Right-wing Conservatives, headed by Lord Carson, convened a dinner in my honour at the Constitutional Club and acclaimed me as the leading anti-Socialist figure. 'The Times' newspaper wrote a reproving leading article on such attempts to prejudice this decision of the 'Leader'. I buried myself at Chartwell and saw nobody.

'I hope to goodness the Tories have the good sense to offer you high office,' Churchill's cousin Lord Wimborne[1] wrote. 'It will be reassuring to think of a progressive mind among their counsels, as a majority such as theirs is hardly conducive to a programme of social reforms.' Wimborne hoped that Churchill would be made either Chancellor of the Exchequer, or Secretary of State for India, but Churchill was not hopeful, writing to Sir Alan Burgoyne[2] on November 4: 'I think it very likely that I shall not be invited to join the Government, as owing to the size of its majority it will probably be composed only of impeccable Conservatives.'

Baldwin did not share Churchill's view that he could confine his Cabinet to 'impeccable Conservatives'. Indeed he was much concerned with the question of what post should be given to Churchill. During the afternoon of November 4 he asked Thomas Jones to see him about Cabinet appointments. According to Jones' diary, Baldwin asked him at one point: 'What would you do with Winston?' Jones suggested sending Churchill to the Board of Trade or the Colonial Office, but Baldwin replied: 'I thought of putting him in India.' The conversation continued:

T.J.: For heaven's sake do not do that. I have seen him lose his head at critical moments in the Irish business, and but for L.G.'s intervention we

---

[1] Ivor Churchill Guest, 1873–1939. Churchill's cousin; a grandson of the 7th Duke of Marlborough. Educated at Eton and Trinity College Cambridge. Liberal MP for Plymouth, 1900–06; Cardiff, 1906–10. Created Baron Ashby St Legers, 1910. Privy Councillor, 1910. Paymaster-General, 1910–12. Succeeded his father as 2nd Baron Wimborne, 1914. Lord Lieutenant of Ireland, 1915–18. Created Viscount, 1918.

[2] Alan Hughes Burgoyne, 1880–1929. Traveller, company director and author. In 1902 he published his first book, A Short History of Submarine Navigation. Founder of the Navy League Annual, 1907 and its editor until 1914. Honorary Treasurer of the Navy League, 1909–13. Conservative MP for North Kensington, 1910–22. Honorary Secretary of the Parliamentary Air Committee, 1916–18; Treasurer, 1919–20. On active service, France, Italy, Palestine and India, 1915–19; Lieutenant Colonel, 1918. Controller of the Priority Department, Ministry of Munitions, 1918–19. Knighted, 1922. Conservative MP for Aylesbury, 1924–29.

would have had bloodshed on the Border more than once.[1] If you have to take drastic action in India through Winston, everyone would blame Winston, whereas he might be quite guiltless and his action entirely justified by the situation in India. I would put Birkenhead in India. He has a better judgement than Winston, and it will keep him pretty well occupied.

All of which Sidney Herbert[2] strongly confirmed.

S.B.: But where shall I put Winston?

T.J.: Shove him in the Army or Navy; it does not matter which. Give him the one with most work. . . .

At seven o'clock that evening the King sent for Baldwin, and asked him to form a Government. Later that evening Austen Chamberlain urged Baldwin to give Churchill some senior ministerial post. 'If you leave him out,' he argued, 'he will be leading a Tory rump in six months' time.' Chamberlain suggested that Churchill should be made Secretary of State for the Colonies—the post he had held under Lloyd George in 1921 and 1922—but Baldwin demurred. Chamberlain then suggested that Churchill might be made Minister of Health. Baldwin liked this idea; given Churchill's work at the Board of Trade from 1908 to 1910, he would be an ideal Minister to develop Baldwin's own plans for a major extension of social insurance. Baldwin at once sent à telephone message, asking Churchill to call on him on the following afternoon. Churchill himself, in his private note, later recalled:

This evidently meant I should be invited to join the Government. But in what capacity? I thought I might be asked to go back to the Dominions and Colonies which I had vacated two years before. My wife urged me strongly that if such an offer were made to me I should suggest instead the Ministry of Health where there was much to be done in housing and other social services with which in my Radical days I had been connected having passed important legislation—Trade boards, Labour Exchanges, Unemployment Insurance, Shop Hours' Regulation and the like. Accordingly I set out.

While Churchill was on his way to the Conservative Central Office on the afternoon of November 5, Baldwin was already discussing the Cabinet problem with Austen Chamberlain's half-brother, Neville. According to Baldwin's own account of the conversation, as told to

---

[1] For a full account of Churchill's part in the Irish policies of 1921 and 1922, see volume four of this biography, pages 663–749. The Belleek incident of June 1922, to which Jones was referring, is described on pages 723, 726–31 and 736 of volume four.

[2] Sidney Herbert, 1890–1939. Educated at Eton and Balliol College Oxford. On active service in the Royal Horse Guards, 1915–18 (wounded, despatches). Captain, 1918. Private Secretary to Churchill (then Secretary of State for War), 1919–20. Conservative MP for Scarborough and Whitby, 1922–31; for Westminster, Abbey, 1932–39. Parliamentary Private Secretary to the Prime Minister (Baldwin), 1923–24 and 1924–27. Created Baronet, 1936.

Thomas Jones four days later, Baldwin began the conversation by offering to make Neville Chamberlain Chancellor of the Exchequer—the post he had held in Baldwin's first Government. Baldwin also told Chamberlain that he had decided to give Churchill a place 'at once', and mentioned the Ministry of Health as a possibility. But Chamberlain told Baldwin that he himself would like to 'go back to Health'—another of the Cabinet posts he had held before. 'But who then could be Chancellor?' Baldwin asked. Neville Chamberlain's account of the conversation continued:

I enquired whether he had thought of S. Hoare. He said No, and I concluded the idea did not appeal to him. He mentioned Winston but said he supposed there would be a howl from the party. I said I thought there would, but that would be so if he came in at all, and I did not know if it would be much louder if he went to the Treasury than to the Admiralty. On the whole I was inclined to say that W. for the Treasury was worth further consideration.

Baldwin had already asked Churchill to see him, and Churchill was actually sitting in the waiting room while Neville Chamberlain was suggesting that he become Chancellor of the Exchequer. In his private note, Churchill recalled:

I was shown into the Prime Minister's office. After a few commonplaces I asked him whether he minded the smoke of a cigar. He said 'No,' and pulled out his famous pipe. Then he said 'Are you willing to help us?' I replied guardedly, 'Yes, if you really want me.'

I had no intention of joining the Government except in some great position, and I had no idea—nor had anyone else—what was in his mind. So when he said, 'Will you be Chancellor of the Exchequer?' I was astonished. I had never dreamed my credit with him stood so high. I replied at once, 'What about Horne?' (who was a great friend of mine). 'No,' said the Prime Minister, 'I offered him that post a year ago when I needed him, and he refused. He will not have it now. But, would you believe it, I have had him here this morning. I offered him the Ministry of Labour, and he refused! What do you think of that?' 'Well,' I said, 'he has been Chancellor of the Exchequer. The Ministry of Labour is a difficult and thankless task and ranks only as a minor office with £2,000 a year.' There was a pause. 'Well, anyhow,' said the Prime Minister, 'he has refused. And that's the end of that.' But from the tone it might well have been 'that's the end of him'.

There was another pause. Then he said 'Perhaps you will now tell me what is your answer to my question. Will you go to the Treasury?' I should have liked to have answered, 'Will the bloody duck swim?' but as it was a formal and important conversation I replied, 'This fulfils my ambition. I still have my father's robe as Chancellor. I shall be proud to serve you in this splendid Office.'

The immediate reaction to Churchill's appointment was one of disbelief. On his way out of Baldwin's room, he later recalled in an unpublished note:

I looked into Jackson's room. He was most curious to know what had happened. 'I hope you have got something you like?' he asked. I said 'Yes. I am Chancellor.' For a moment it seemed to me that he thought I meant Chancellor of the Duchy of Lancaster, which is a subordinate sinecure; but when the realisation came to him in a few more seconds, he nearly fell out of his chair. He pulled himself together and offered very sincere personal congratulations. His father had been my father's Financial Secretary when he resigned the Chancellorship of the Exchequer in 1886, and had stood by him against all comers.

The news of Churchill's appointment had to be kept secret for two days. He returned at once to Chartwell where, he recalled, 'I had great difficulty in convincing my wife that I was not merely teasing her.'

On learning of Baldwin's offer, Austen Chamberlain wrote to his wife: 'Meanwhile S.B. has made Winston Chancellor—last night he thought the CO too good for him!' Chamberlain had wanted Sir Robert Horne appointed Chancellor, and on the following morning, after having spoken to Lord Birkenhead, he wrote again to his wife: 'Beloved: S.B. is mad! F.E. is as much disturbed as I am & feels that W.'s appointment in place of H. will rouse great antagonism & is not good for W.'

On November 6 J. C. C. Davidson[1] wrote to Baldwin: 'Winston's appointment is genius—you have hamstrung him—so that his hairy heels are paralysed. He will do all right.' That same day Austen Chamberlain wrote to Baldwin: 'I am alarmed at the news that you have made Winston Chancellor, not because I do not wish Winston well but because I fear that this particular appointment will be a great shock to the Party. . . . You will remember that the first reason you gave me for not offering Horne the Treasury was that you wanted Neville there.' Neville Chamberlain himself wrote to Baldwin on November 7:

[1] John Colin Campbell Davidson, 1889–1970. Educated at Westminster and Pembroke College Cambridge. Private Secretary to successive Colonial Secretaries (Crewe, Harcourt, Bonar Law), 1910–15. Private Secretary to Bonar Law, 1916–20. Conservative MP for Hemel Hempstead, 1920–23 and 1924–27. Parliamentary Private Secretary to Stanley Baldwin, 1921–22; to Bonar Law, 1922–23. Parliamentary Secretary, Admiralty, 1924–27. Chairman of the Conservative Party, 1927–30. Chancellor of the Duchy of Lancaster, 1931–37. Chairman of the Indian States Enquiry Committee, 1932. Created Viscount, 1937.

I rather felt my breath go when I heard that Winston and Steel-Maitland[1] had been actually appointed. I didn't know you were going to be as quick as that! But I don't go back on my views as to the wisdom of your choice in either case, though they don't seem too popular.

Churchill's friends were much excited by his return to the Cabinet. Horne, who had hoped for the post himself, wrote to Churchill on November 6: 'I send you my warmest congratulations on your appointment to the Exchequer. It realises in 1924 what I urged L.G. to do in 1922. Thus belatedly do the Fates perform their ca' canny job!' 'I know that it has always been your ambition to succeed your father in this office . . .,' Consuelo Balsan[2] wrote on November 7. 'It is not a long step from the Treasury to the PM and I can see no serious rivals, so mind you move with circumspection and care.' 'I congratulate you,' wrote George Lambert,[3] 'but I congratulate the Country still more. You are in my judgment the fittest man in all England to be Ch of the Excheq'.' Lambert, like Consuelo Balsan, speculated on the future. 'Winston, my boy,' he wrote. 'I have got a fair instinct for politics. I think I shall live to see you Prime Minister.'

The Times believed Baldwin had made a mistake to give Churchill, who was not even a member of the Conservative Party, the second highest post in a Conservative Cabinet. But the political journalist Herbert Sidebotham,[4] writing in the *Daily Despatch*, described Churchill as 'not only by common consent the ablest commoner in the Conservative Party, but there is good reason to think that the Chancellorship of the Exchequer is the post that will best suit his abilities. Finance

[1] Arthur Herbert Drummond Ramsay Steel-Maitland, 1876–1935. Educated at Rugby and Balliol College Oxford. President of the Oxford Union Society, 1899. Fellow of All Souls College, Oxford, 1900. Conservative MP, 1910–18 and 1918–29. An original member of the Other Club, 1911. Parliamentary Under-Secretary, Colonial Office, 1915–17. Created Baronet, 1917. Head of the Department of Overseas Trade (Development and Intelligence), 1917–19. Minister of Labour, 1924–29.

[2] Consuelo Vanderbilt, 1877–1964. Born in New York. She married Churchill's cousin the 9th Duke of Marlborough in 1895, at the age of 18, and obtained a divorce in 1921 (after which she married Lieutenant-Colonel Jacques Balsan, CMG). Mother of the 10th Duke of Marlborough and Lord Ivor Charles Spencer-Churchill. In the 1920s and 1930s Churchill was a frequent visitor at her château, St George's Motel, near Dreux (some 50 miles to the north of Paris). In 1935 she published her memoirs, *The Glitter and the Gold*.

[3] George Lambert, 1866–1958. Liberal MP for South Molton, 1891–1924; 1929–31. Civil Lord of Admiralty, 1905–15. Privy Councillor, 1912. Chairman of the Liberal Parliamentary Party, 1919–21; Liberal National MP, 1931–45. Created Viscount, 1945.

[4] Herbert Sidebotham, 1872–1940. Educated at Manchester Grammar and Balliol College Oxford. Editorial Staff of the *Manchester Guardian*, 1895–1918. Military correspondent of *The Times*, as 'Student of War', 1918–21 (also Gallery Correspondent, as 'Student of Politics'). Political Adviser to the *Daily Chronicle*, 1922–23. Contributor to the *Daily Despatch*, the *Sunday Times* ('Scrutator') and the *Daily Sketch* ('Candidus').

in the hands of a real orator will become, as Gladstone made it in the old days, a glowing enthusiasm.'

Churchill had long wanted to vindicate his father's brief tenure of the Exchequer in 1886. On November 7 Austen Chamberlain's step-mother, Mrs Carnegie, commenting in a private letter on Churchill's triumph, wrote: 'No one expected he would have been given one of the first posts, least of all himself—but the ambition of his life had suddenly & unexpectedly been realized. I think that it is more than likely that he will do it well . . .' Writing to Randolph's housemaster, Colonel Sheepshanks,[1] on November 19, Churchill commented: 'Many thanks for your congratulations. No one was more surprised than I.'

Churchill believed that he could act as a moderating and reforming influence on the Conservative Party. On November 8 he had written to Lord Rosebery: 'Five years of steady sensible liberal (with a small "l" of course) Government will improve our affairs appreciably.' And he added: 'I am vy glad to go to the Exchequer, & on Wednesday next I propose to wear at the pricking of the Sheriffs, those robes wh have slumbered in their tin box since January 1887.'

On November 13 Churchill took part in his first official function as Chancellor of the Exchequer: the swearing in of Sheriffs. That same day he lunched with Reginald McKenna,[2] who wrote to Lord Beaverbrook on November 14: 'He tells me he means to master the intricacies of finance and I think he will succeed, though he will find it more difficult than he imagines.'

---

[1] Arthur Charles Sheepshanks, 1884–1961. Educated at Eton and Trinity College Cambridge. Assistant Master (Classics) at Eton, 1906–14. On active service in France, 1914–18 (despatches twice, wounded twice, DSO); Lieutenant-Colonel, 1917–18. Returned to Eton as Assistant Master (Classics), 1918–38. Housemaster, 1922–38.

[2] Reginald McKenna, 1863–1943. Educated at King's College London and Trinity Hall Cambridge. Liberal MP for North Monmouthshire, 1895–1918. President of the Board of Education, 1907–08. Privy Councillor, 1907. First Lord of the Admiralty, 1908–11. Home Secretary, 1911–15. Chancellor of the Exchequer, May 1915–December 1916. Chairman of the Midland Bank, 1919–43.

Part Two
Chancellor of the Exchequer
1924–1929

4

A Reforming Chancellor:
'Great Issues in the Social Sphere'

CHURCHILL'S principal concern on becoming Chancellor of the Exchequer was social reform, particularly in the sphere of insurance and pensions. Indeed, by making Churchill Chancellor, Baldwin both envisaged, and ensured, a substantial expansion of the existing social insurance schemes. In the summer of 1923 Baldwin, while himself Chancellor, had set up a Committee under Sir John Anderson[1] to examine the state of national insurance. The Anderson Committee, reporting early in 1924, had urged a substantial extension of contributory, and compulsory insurance, to which the Government would be the principal contributor.

Within two weeks of Churchill becoming Chancellor, he, Neville Chamberlain and Baldwin discussed the problem together. 'We received from you,' Churchill recalled later in a letter to Baldwin on 17 April 1925, 'the strongest possible encouragement to proceed.' As Chancellor, Churchill had not only to find the money for the scheme, but to coordinate the plans and suggestions of the Ministry of Labour and the Ministry of Health. Armed with Baldwin's support, he sought to frame his first budget in such a way that he would be able to finance an even more comprehensive insurance scheme than that proposed by

[1] John Anderson, 1882–1958. Educated at Edinburgh and Leipzig Universities. Entered the Colonial Office, 1905; Secretary, Northern Nigeria Lands Committee, 1909. Secretary to the Insurance Commissioners, London, 1913. Secretary, Ministry of Shipping, 1917–19. Knighted, 1919. Chairman of the Board of Inland Revenue, 1919–22. Joint Under-Secretary of State to the Viceroy of Ireland, 1920. Permanent Under-Secretary of State, Home Office, 1922–32. Governor of Bengal, 1932–37. MP for the Scottish Universities, 1938–50. Lord Privy Seal, 1938–39. Home Secretary and Minister of Home Security, 1939–40. Lord President of the Council, 1940–43. Chancellor of the Exchequer, 1943–45. Chairman of the Port of London Authority, 1946–58. Created Viscount Waverley, 1952. Order of Merit, 1957. Member of the BBC General Advisory Council.

Anderson, and one which would also cover the previously untouched area of pensions for both widows and orphans.

During his first month as Chancellor, Churchill examined every aspect of Government finance and Treasury administration. As had always been his custom on entering a new Ministry, he submitted his officials to a barrage of written questions, in which he sought both to find out about the routine of departmental business, and to set the tone for his own policies. On Sunday November 16, having studied a series of Treasury papers and tables, he dictated at Chartwell a number of memoranda to his senior Treasury advisers. Writing to the Controller of the Supply Services, Sir George Barstow,[1] about the future payment of war pensions, he urged the need to consider 'the continuous pressure of Parliament for a more compassionate administration'.

On November 26 Churchill wrote to the Permanent Head of the Treasury, Sir Warren Fisher,[2] urging a careful examination of the Anderson Committee report on Insurance, and in particular of the proposed sixpenny increase in the contributions by both employers and employed. Should there be a general decline in national prosperity, Churchill felt that the Government should have the power to reduce benefits. 'I see great difficulties in this,' he wrote, 'but yet great need for it if we are not to bind the future almost beyond what our title warrants.' 'I am deeply interested in all these projects,' Churchill added, 'and I should like to meet the Committee one day next week or as many of them as are available. "Security for 6d" is an impressive motto.'

Churchill was anxious to make substantial reforms in the tax system. During his work at Chartwell on November 16 he had written to the Chairman of the Board of Inland Revenue, Sir Richard Hopkins:[3]

---

[1] George Lewis Barstow, 1874–1966. Entered Local Government Board, 1896; Treasury, 1898. A Principal Clerk, Treasury, 1909. Controller of Supply Services, Treasury, 1919–27. Knighted, 1920. Government Director, Anglo-Iranian Oil Company, 1927–46. Chairman, Prudential Assurance Co., 1941–53. One of his two sons was killed on active service in 1941.

[2] Norman Fenwick Warren Fisher, 1879–1948. Educated at Winchester and Hertford College Oxford. Entered the Inland Revenue Department, 1903. Seconded to the National Health Insurance Commission, 1912–13. Deputy Chairman, Board of Inland Revenue, 1914–18; Chairman, 1918–19. Knighted, 1919. Permanent Secretary of the Treasury, and Official Head of the Civil Service, 1919–39. Member of the Committee on Ministers' Powers, 1929–32. Subsequently a Director of several companies, including the Anglo-Iranian Oil Co.

[3] Richard Valentine Nind Hopkins, 1880–1955. Educated at King's Edward School Birmingham and Emmanuel College Cambridge. Member of the Board of Inland Revenue, 1916; Chairman, 1922–27. Knighted, 1920. Controller of Finance and Supply Services, Treasury, 1927–32; Second Secretary, Treasury, 1932–42; Permanent Secretary, 1942–45. Member of the Imperial War Graves Commission. Chairman of the Central Board of Finance of the Church Assembly.

'Calculate the cost of 1925–26 & 1926–27 of putting the super-tax on the nett basis, & simultaneously reducing the standard rate of Income tax (a) by 6^d & (b) by 1/-.' Replying on November 21, Hopkins had estimated the cost to the Exchequer of a sixpenny reduction as £31 million in a full year. A shilling reduction would cost £62 millions. A week later, in the course of a nine-page letter to Hopkins written on November 28, Churchill set out his view of the principles on which taxation should operate:

I do not desire sensibly to diminish the Super Tax burdens resting upon the greatest fortunes, nor on the other hand to increase the burden of Death Duties upon them. On many grounds this class may well be left to stand where they do. I wish to relieve chiefly the lower and medium classes of Super Tax payers, giving the greatest measure of relief to the lowest class comprising professional men, small merchants and business men—superior brain workers of every kind. Where these classes possess accumulated capital in addition to their incomes, the increase of Death Duties operating over the same area will reclaim a substantial portion of the relief afforded by the reform of the Super Tax.

The doctor, engineer and lawyer earning 3 or 4 thousand a year and with no capital will get the greatest relief; the possessor of unearned income derived from a capital estate of 2 or 3 hundred thousand pounds, the smallest relief; while the millionaire will remain substantially liable to the existing scales of high taxation.

'As the tide of taxation recedes,' Churchill explained, 'it leaves the millionaires stranded on the peaks of taxation to which they have been carried by the flood. The smaller class of Super Tax payers get a progressive relief . . .' As for the 'great mass' of income tax payers, it was Churchill's desire that they should have progressive relief, until they would 'subside into the refreshing waters of the sea'. Lower income tax, he stressed, was entirely in the interests 'of a revival of enterprise'. For those in the poorest groups he wanted to organize further financial help. 'I contemplate,' he told Hopkins, 'an additional burden placed upon employers for the purposes of widows and earlier old age insurance.' These notes, he concluded, 'should enable you to carry our discussion a stage further'.

After three weeks as Chancellor of the Exchequer Churchill had come to certain definite conclusions about the details of a reform programme. He wanted to see a progressive reduction of income tax; the provision of widows' pensions and a major extension of old age insurance, as well as the development of cheap housing. He even hoped to be able to reintroduce the penny post. To finance these measures, he felt that it was not only essential to recover a good proportion of the war debt owed to Britain by France and Italy,[1] but also to prevent any unnecessary increase in defence expenditure.

On November 26 Churchill explained his plans to the Cabinet, asking his colleagues to assist him 'to the utmost by careful financial administration'. It was essential, he added, for 'excessive taxation' to be avoided; and to that end, as the minutes recorded:

... he urged that the Government should concentrate on a few great issues in the social sphere, such as the solution of the housing problem and an 'all-in' insurance scheme, rather than fritter away our resources on a variety of services which, though possibly good in themselves, were not of vital national importance.

In urging a careful scrutiny of defence expenditure, Churchill was insistent that Britain's security must in no way be impaired. During the Cabinet of November 26 he explained to his colleagues that the opportunities for holding defence expenditure steady were limited. Indeed, he stressed, 'some increase in the Royal Air Force must be faced in order to secure the safety of the country'. The Army, likewise, offered little scope for economy, except in the cost of administration. 'There was little, if any, room for reduction in the size of the Army,' he said bluntly. Only the Royal Navy seemed to Churchill to be demanding greater funds than it needed, having already put forward a programme of expansion both for the development of a naval base at Singapore and for a substantial number of new cruisers. Some 'investigation' was needed, Churchill believed, 'as to the rate at which these projects could be undertaken consistently with our financial situation and the desirability from a political point of view of avoiding any increase in armaments in the forthcoming financial year'. The Cabinet agreed with Churchill that the rate of growth of naval expenditure would have to be examined carefully.

At the end of the meeting Churchill proposed that the Committee of Imperial Defence should undertake a 'fresh survey' of the whole problem of Empire defence. He also wanted a study made of 'the desirability and practicability of renewing the decision taken by the Cabinet Committee on Finance on August 11th, 1919, that the Fighting

---

[1] On 31 March 1924 Britain was owed £2,000 million by her wartime Allies. The Allied debts to Britain were: Russia, £757 million; France, £698 million; Italy, £592 million; Yugoslavia, £28 million; Rumania, £24 million; Greece, £23 million; Portugal, £21 million; the Belgian Congo, £3 million and Poland, £95,000. The Bolsheviks having declared that they would not honour Tsarist or Kerensky war debts, the sum owed by Russia was considered unrecoverable. Britain owed the United States more than £900 million in war debts.

Services should proceed on the assumption that no great war is to be anticipated within the next ten years', although, Churchill insisted, 'provision should be made for the possible expansion of trained units in case of an emergency arising'. He also wanted an examination of the 'rate of growth' of the construction of the Singapore base, and of the naval programme.

That same day, Churchill discussed his schemes with Neville Chamberlain, the new Minister of Health. With the proposed reductions in income tax, Churchill explained, the employing classes would be better able to defray their share of higher insurance contributions. Two days later Churchill sent Baldwin a five-page account of his conversation with Chamberlain. 'I told him,' Churchill wrote, 'that I did not know whether the Budget this year would be "Hope" or "Humdrum". If the expenditure of the Departments increased . . . it would be no use trying to make petty remissions of taxation, and it would be better to wait until 1926 when a respectable surplus might be available.' As to housing, Churchill wrote, he and Neville Chamberlain had found themselves 'in the most complete accord'. The building trade, they were agreed, should be left to expand 'the existing profitable building' without help or hindrance, while the Government should devote its energies and resources to experiment with new methods of construction for the lower classes, 'who cannot afford to pay at the existing prices'.

In his letter of November 28 Churchill told Baldwin that he did not yet know whether it would be possible to embark upon their reform schemes in 1925 or 1926. 'I hope myself greatly that 1925 will be possible,' he wrote, 'because the relief to the direct taxpayer will stimulate trade revival, and the beginning of the pensions scheme will make a profound impression on the social life of the country and particularly on the position of women.'

Neville Chamberlain recorded his reaction to Churchill's ideas in his diary on November 26, 'It seemed plain to me,' he wrote, that Churchill 'regretted that he was not Minister of Health'. Indeed, he had told Chamberlain during their discussion of how he envied him. 'You are in the van,' Churchill declared. 'You can raise a monument. You can leave a name in history.'

On November 28 Churchill sent for the Deputy Secretary to the Cabinet, Thomas Jones. 'I saw him alone,' Jones recorded in his diary on November 28. 'He was drinking some whisky-and-soda, and he got some tea for me. He was very confidential.' According to Jones' account, Churchill said to him:

I understand you talk a lot with the PM and that you give him advice—good advice, I have no doubt. Well, I want this Government not to fritter away its energies on all sorts of small schemes; I want them to concentrate on one or two things which will be big land-marks in the history of this Parliament, and if you are doing anything for a speech at the Albert Hall I would like you to fix on two things and make them stand out—Housing and Pensions. I think I see my way to help both of these if I can stop the Departments spending in other directions.

I was all for the Liberal measures of social reform in the old days, and I want to push the same sort of measures now. Of course I shall have to give some relief to the taxpayers to balance these measures of reform. If trade improves I can do that, but we cannot have a lot of silly little cruisers, which would be of no use anyway. . . .

For the whole of December Churchill continued his search for means to check Government expenditure in such a way as to ensure that extra funds would be available for pensions, insurance and housing. On December 1 he asked Sir George Barstow to prepare a memorandum for the Cabinet, opposing the 'most unwarrantable demand' by the Admiralty for marriage allowances. His reasons, he explained that same day in a personal letter to the First Lord of the Admiralty, William Bridgeman,[1] was that even without a marriage allowance, the naval officer already received more money in pay and allowances than his army or air force equivalent. 'I am sorry,' Churchill wrote at the end of his letter, 'that it should be my duty to be so contentious in these matters.' That same day he wrote to Austen Chamberlain, to explain that he would soon have to ask for 'substantial repayments' of French and Italian war debts, already more than six years overdue. Churchill told Chamberlain: 'I expect to be rather a heavy burden to you in your diplomacy.' The process of demanding payment, he wrote, 'will mean worry for you—sulky instead of smiling Ambassadors'; and he continued:

We can avoid all this trouble by throwing up the sponge, by sitting still and putting up with being fleeced. Then there will be lots of compliments about the good feelings which we have established in Europe and about what a very agreeable and friendly nation we are. But I think this is a pretty thin diet to give to the taxpayers of this country in their present circumstances.

[1] William Clive Bridgeman, 1864–1935. Educated at Eton and Trinity College Cambridge. Conservative MP for Oswestry, 1906–29. A junior Opposition Whip, 1911. A Lord Commissioner of the Treasury, 1915–16. Assistant Director, War Trade Department, 1916. Parliamentary Secretary Ministry of Labour, 1916–19; Board of Trade, 1920–22. Home Secretary, 1922–24. First Lord of the Admiralty, 1924–29. Created Viscount, 1929. A Governor of the BBC, 1933–35 and its Chairman, 1935.

The situation about debts has vastly altered since we were last in office together. Europe is recovering. France and Italy as they become richer will become increasingly desirous for financial respectability. The same sort of influence that made us settle the American debt will be operative upon them about our debt. I do not see why we should not get a substantial annual payment from both France and Italy if we use to the full the great advantage of our position.

Chamberlain agreed that Churchill should go to France in January to seek to negotiate the repayment of at least a part of France's war debt. Meanwhile, on December 2, Churchill circulated all his Cabinet colleagues with a memorandum which he had written more than two years before, on 3 August 1922, in which he had set out his attitude towards inter-Allied debts:

We have suffered hitherto by foreign countries thinking that we have no will of our own in these matters. The United States has a will of its own, very clearly and obstinately expressed, namely, to exact payment from Great Britain. France has a will of her own, equally clearly expressed, namely, to pay nobody. If Great Britain remains a sort of spongy, squeezable mass, on which these two conflicting wills may imprint their stamp, our fundamental interests will suffer . . .

During the first week of December Churchill examined many possibilities to curb expenditure for at least two years. On December 2 he asked his Financial Secretary, Walter Guinness,[1] to look into the question of withholding any increase in teachers' salaries at least until 1927. That same day he asked the Secretary to the Cabinet, Sir Maurice Hankey,[2] whether it was really necessary for the number of submarines based at Hong Kong to be increased from six to twenty-one. 'I should have thought,' he wrote, 'it was very provocative to build up a large submarine base in close proximity to the Japanese coast. Suppose the Japanese owned the Isle of Man, and started putting 21 submarines

---

[1] Walter Edward Guinness, 1880–1944. 3rd son of the 1st Earl of Iveagh. Educated at Eton. Wounded while on active service in South Africa, 1900–01. Conservative MP for Bury St Edmunds, 1907–31. On active service 1914–18 (despatches thrice). Under Secretary of State for War, 1922–23. Financial Secretary, Treasury, 1923–24 and 1924–25. Minister of Agriculture and Fisheries, 1925–29. Created Baron Moyne, 1932. A director of Arthur Guinness, Son, and Company, brewers. Elected to the Other Club, 1934. Secretary of State for the Colonies, 1941–42. Minister Resident, Cairo, 1944 (where he was murdered by Jewish terrorists).

[2] Maurice Pascal Alers Hankey, 1877–1963. Entered Royal Marine Artillery, 1895. Captain, 1899. Retired, 1912. Secretary to the Committee of Imperial Defence, 1912–38. Lieutenant-Colonel, Royal Marines, 1914. Knighted, February 1916. Secretary to the War Cabinet, 1916–18; to the Cabinet, 1919–38. Created Baron, 1939. Minister without Portfolio, September 1939–May 1940. Chancellor of the Duchy of Lancaster, 1940–41. Paymaster-General, 1941–42. His brother Hugh was killed in action in South Africa in March 1900. His brother Donald was killed in action on the western front in October 1916.

there!' Another enquiry which Churchill instituted on December 2 was into the cost of Foreign Office telegrams from Persia and the Persian Gulf. 'Every day,' he wrote to Barstow, 'pages and pages are sent out about obscure matters which only very rarely eventuate in action of any kind.'

Despite the pressure for economy, Churchill accepted the need for the steady development of the Air Force. 'I expect Trenchard[1] is pretty good in getting value for money,' he wrote to Barstow on December 4. At first he hoped that the Air Ministry would agree 'to slow down the rate of expansion', and plan to complete its expansion schemes by 1932 rather than 1925. This, he wrote, would afford the Exchequer 'a very great measure of relief'. But he decided not to bring this demand forward until after the Debt settlement. At the same time, he hoped that an imaginative development of air power could provide both a cheaper and a more effective method of defence. On December 12, in a letter to Samuel Hoare, who had become Secretary of State for Air, he suggested, as an example of such a development, that the best way to defend Singapore against attack was by the expansion of aerial defences, rather than by the more expensive method proposed by the Admiralty, of an enlarged submarine defence. The Admiralty's proposal to mount two enormous gun batteries did not appeal to him. Would not 'heavy bombing machines' be a preferable substitute for guns, he wrote; and, if so, 'how much better to have this cost represented in mobile air squadrons rather than tied up forever to one spot on two heavy batteries'. Churchill told Hoare:

I am going to press for a new and detailed examination of methods, stages and rate of construction at Singapore. It seems to me that if this work were completed in fifteen or twenty years, the air should play a far larger part in it than is now contemplated. We ought to arrive at a time table showing exactly what will be done each year in the fifteen or twenty years, and at what period each of the successive methods of defence will come into operation.

'I have had a preliminary talk with Trenchard,' Hoare replied on December 15, 'and, broadly speaking, we are both in entire agreement

---

[1] Hugh Montague Trenchard, 1873–1956. Entered Army, 1893. Active service, South Africa, 1899–1902 (dangerously wounded). Major, 1902. Assistant Commandant, Central Flying School, 1913–14. Lieutenant-Colonel, 1915. General Officer Commanding the Royal Flying Corps in the Field, 1915–17. Major-General, 1916. Knighted, 1918. Chief of the Air Staff, 1918–29. Air-Marshal, 1919. Created Baronet, 1919. Air Chief Marshal, 1922. Marshal of the Royal Air Force, 1927. Created Baron, 1930. Commissioner, Metropolitan Police, 1931–35. Created Viscount, 1936. Trustee of the Imperial War Museum, 1937–45. His elder son, and both his stepsons, were killed in action in the Second World War.

with your views and believe that the substitution of torpedo and bombing squadrons for submarines and heavy guns—the latter in any case
requiring aircraft to "spot" for them—should result in substantial
economy and enhanced efficiency.'

Determined to reduce income tax if possible, on December 2
Churchill instructed Sir Richard Hopkins to draw up a detailed
statistical report. 'Everything turns upon your scales,' he wrote, and on
December 9, while waiting for Hopkins to complete his calculations, he
informed Lord Salisbury[1] that an 'increasing distinction' between
earned and unearned incomes 'might be one solution to raising new
taxes'. But he opposed as 'more trouble than it was worth' any attempt
'to hunt down "the idle rich" '. His letter continued:

The existing system of death duties is a certain corrective against the
development of a race of idle rich. If they are idle they will cease in a few
generations to be rich. Further than that it is not desirable for the legislature
to go. The christian or the moralist alone can pursue an inquisition into what
is 'service' and what is 'idleness'. A dilettante philanthropist wasting money
on ill-judged schemes may be a poorer asset to the State than a man who
having, say, £10,000 a year spends £5,000 selfishly and allows the rest to
accumulate at compound interest increasing funds available for enterprise
and employment.

Again, a man may be a most admirable citizen, spend his whole life in
public and philanthropic service, and yet be accustomed to be maintained
on such a scale and in such a state that a very large number of persons are
kept in unproductive employment serving him.

My maturer views of life lead me to deprecate the personal inquisition,
except when self-instituted, into actions which are within the law. I think
the rich, whether idle or not, are already taxed in this country to the very
highest point compatible with the accumulation of capital for future production.

'The existing capitalist system,' Churchill told Salisbury, 'is the foundation of civilisation and the only means by which great modern populations can be supplied with vital necessaries.'

On December 12 Hopkins submitted the various calculations for
which Churchill had asked. A reduction of super-tax costing £14½
million a year could be largely offset by an increase in Estate duty of
£10 million. A sixpenny reduction of income tax would cost £31½

[1] James Edward Hubert Gascoyne-Cecil, Viscount Cranborne, 1861–1947. Educated at
Eton and University College Oxford. Conservative MP, 1885–92 and 1893–1903. Succeeded
his father (the former Prime Minister) as 4th Marquess of Salisbury, 1903. President of the
Board of Trade, 1905. Lord President of the Council, October 1922–January 1924. Lord
Privy Seal, 1924–29. Leader of the House of Lords, 1925–29.

million. Another of Churchill's schemes, the reintroduction of the penny post, would cost £5 million a year. Writing to Hopkins two days later, Churchill declared: 'I greatly admire the wonderful clearness with which these complicated matters have been examined and unfolded.' His letter continued:

. . . what I am aiming at is a substantial diminution in actual burden on the direct taxpayer. I believe that this burden is at the present time a grave discouragement to enterprise and thrift and a potent factor in the tendency to high profits. I want to make a real impression upon this. For this purpose I am anxious to supplement my modest resources of relief by a direct transfer of the burdens from current taxation to Death Duties. I am sure this is in accordance with modern thought and my instinct is that the change will be welcomed by the classes affected.

Moreover the imposition of the increased Death Duties and the friction that will arise thereupon will assist us in the general presentation of the treatment of the higher class of direct taxpayers. It harmonises with the plan of emphasising the distinction between earned and unearned income in the lower ranges. It is intended to be an encouragement to people to bestir themselves and make more money while they are alive and bring up their heirs to do the same. . . .

Churchill then set out his philosophy of wealth:

The process of the creation of new wealth is beneficial to the whole community. The process of squatting on old wealth though valuable is a far less lively agent. The great bulk of the wealth of the world is created and consumed every year. We shall never shake ourselves clear from the debts of the past and break into a definitely larger period except by the energetic creation of new wealth. A premium on effort is the aim and a penalty on inertia may well be its companion.

In the second week of December Churchill learned that the Admiralty were about to propose a substantial increase in the Naval Estimates, not only for 1925, but for at least three further years. 'We must certainly break into this plan of imminent preparations for a gigantic naval war in the Far East,' he wrote to Sir George Barstow on December 11. The preliminary Admiralty forecast, which Churchill learnt of on December 13, was for an extra ten million pounds for 1925, and a further seventeen and a quarter million for the construction of new ships, to be spent over three years. This projected increase hit directly at Churchill's long-term plans. 'It is no use my trying to take off taxes this year,' he wrote direct to Baldwin that same day, 'in order to have to put them back next year.'

In his letter to Baldwin, Churchill stressed that the estimate for new construction would only be a minimum. The building of new ships, he wrote, 'must carry with it an increase in other Votes', so that the total cost involved was likely to be, not seventeen, but 'at least' twenty-five millions. To accept these armament increases 'is to sterilise and paralyse the whole policy of the Government. There will be nothing for the taxpayer and nothing for social reform. We shall be a Naval Parliament busily preparing our Navy for some great imminent shock. Voilà tout!'

Churchill used three further arguments to impress on Baldwin the folly of any increase in naval expenditure. The first argument combined electoral and international considerations. As he told Baldwin:

We should come up to the Election with these enormous Navy Estimates and nothing else to show. Besides this, we should be accused of starting up the whole armament race all over the world and setting the pace towards a new vast war. I cannot conceive any course more certain to result in a Socialist victory. If the Socialists win in a tremendous economy wave, they will cut down and blot out all these Naval preparations so that in the end the Admiralty will not get the Navy programme for the sake of which your Government will have broken itself.

Churchill's second argument concerned the impossibility of borrowing money in order to finance the naval increases. For more than a year the Governor of the Bank of England, Montagu Norman,[1] had been pressing for a return to the Gold Standard; the sole means, as Norman saw it, of stabilizing the economy. The Treasury officials supported Norman's proposal, which had been delayed only on account of the change of Government. But a return to Gold involved the need for carefully balanced budgets and a more restrictive financial policy. Greatly increased naval estimates could seriously endanger that policy. As Churchill explained to Baldwin: '. . . there is nothing for it, if we accept the armament policy, but to put out of our mind all idea of reduction of taxation and practically all plans of social reform during the whole lifetime of the present Parliament.'

Churchill's third argument concerned the actual need for new warships. 'It seems to me,' he wrote, 'that the Admiralty imagine themselves confronted with the same sort of situation in regard to Japan as we faced against Germany in the ten years before the war.' To meet this danger, Hong Kong was to become a submarine base, Singapore to be developed 'as fast as possible', shipbuilding accelerated

---

[1] Montagu Collet Norman, 1871–1950. Educated at Eton and King's College Cambridge. On active service in South Africa, 1900–01 (despatches). A Director of the Bank of England, 1907–19. Governor of the Bank of England, 1920–44. Privy Councillor, 1923. His brother Ronald was Chairman of the BBC from 1935 to 1939.

and reserve stores and ammunition 'rapidly completed on a large scale'; even merchant ships were to be armed with six-inch guns. 'For what?' Churchill asked. And he continued: 'A war with Japan! But why should there be a war with Japan? I do not believe there is the slightest chance of it in our lifetime.' The Japanese, he wrote, were Britain's allies. America was 'far more likely to quarrel with Japan' than Britain. 'What question is pending between England and Japan?' he asked. 'To what diplomatic combination do either of us belong which could involve us against the other?' There was no analogy, he explained, with the situation before 1914:

Then we were joined with France by a military agreement begun in 1906, France was set against Germany by the terrible quarrels of the past. England, France and Russia formed the counterpoise to the Triple Alliance. Europe was divided into two armed camps. Germany made a bold bid for naval supremacy, and we had to face this mighty power across the narrow North Sea with every feeling that our whole national existence was at stake.

Japan is at the other end of the world. She cannot menace our vital security in any way.

Churchill went on to examine one possible cause of Anglo-Japanese friction:

. . . suppose we had a dispute with Japan about something in China and we declared war upon her, what would happen? We should have to move the best part of our Fleet to Singapore. Hong Kong would of course be taken by Japan in the early days. What should we do then? We should have to send large armies (how we should raise them I do not know) to go and attack Japan in her home waters. The war would last for years. It would cost Japan very little. It would reduce us to bankruptcy. All the time it was on we should be at the mercy at home of every unfriendly power or force hostile to the British Empire. We could never do it. It would never be worth our while to do it.

The only war it would be worth our while to fight with Japan would be to prevent an invasion of Australia, and that I am certain will never happen in any period, even the most remote, which we or our children need foresee.

'I am therefore convinced,' Churchill added, 'that war with Japan is not a possibility any reasonable Government need take into account.'

Churchill then set out for Baldwin what he wanted the Admiralty to do. 'They should be made to recast all their plans and scales and standards,' he wrote, 'on the basis that no naval war against a first class Navy is likely to take place in the next twenty years'; the lives of all ships should therefore be prolonged, and the cost of all replacements should be spread over 'at least three times the period specified'. By such economies, Churchill wrote, by diplomatic efforts to limit world naval construction, and by social reform at home, 'we may be able to secure a second term of power'. Within five to ten years, Churchill concluded, 'by a steady yet moderate maintenance of our armaments the Empire will be in a far stronger position militarily, navally, financially and socially than by any other method'.

Two days later, on December 15, Churchill sent a similar letter to William Bridgeman. 'It is surely worth considering,' he wrote, 'whether a more moderate policy, if persevered in, not for four years but for eight or nine, might not leave us in a stronger naval position.' In 1913, Churchill added, when he himself had been First Lord, he had supplied the Treasury with 'every detail' of proposed naval expenditure. 'I trust therefore you will give directions in accordance with these precedents.' Churchill also wrote to Austen Chamberlain on December 15, enclosing a copy of his letter to Baldwin, and asking Chamberlain, if he 'were so inclined', to allow the subject of Japan to be raised in Cabinet. 'What I seek,' Churchill told Chamberlain, 'is a declaration to the Cabinet by you, ruling out a war with Japan from among the reasonable possibilities to be taken into account in the next 10, 15 or 20 years.'[1]

In a letter to Neville Chamberlain on December 30 Churchill expressed his hope that 'after my talks with the Prime Minister and Austen . . . we may lower the temperature in regard to Japan sufficiently to bring Naval expenses into reasonable relation with our other affairs'. It was therefore essential, he believed, 'to get our teeth into the insurance project', and he was quite prepared to justify 'laying the burden of the new insurance on future Parliaments and Ministries'. In his letter, Churchill set out in detail his hopes for the more extensive state insurance schemes. 'Let us have a talk in the near future,' he added, 'and to tell me how you are viewing all this aspect.' Churchill even thought of enlisting Liberal support, telling Chamberlain:

. . . we do not want to take all this trouble and incur all this expense and have the scheme ungratefully received. I do not think it would be. But it is a point to ponder over. . . .

Ll.G. as the parent of insurance would, I am sure, be with us. Anyhow we do not want them all crabbing it and a little tact should avoid this. It is a fence to jump at a gallop. Once over with acclamation, and people start

---

[1] On 29 December 1924 Churchill tried to reinforce his arguments by circulating to the Cabinet a note drawn up in the Treasury on Japan's economic power. The theme of the note was that Japan was 'a very poor country', mainly agricultural; that industrial productivity was far lower than Britain's; that Japanese industry lacked capital for development; and that compared with Britain Japan collected only a quarter of the income tax, and a fifth of the railway revenue, both evidence 'of the slender resources of the country'.

paying, everything will work out according to the actuaries, and the inestimable blessings which this measure may carry to the whole population
will plead their own cause in every home.

Churchill pressed Neville Chamberlain to begin work on detailed
plans which could be launched in the 1925 budget, rather than delay
until 1926 or 1927. 'Personally, my instinct is all for it,' Churchill
added, 'and it is only experience and disillusionment that make me
cautious.' Chamberlain's instinct was even more cautious. 'In the circumstance,' he wrote to Churchill on 1 January 1925, 'I think I had
better defer comment until I return which will be about the middle of
this month, and this will be all the better because I should like to see
what the Committee have to say before I make up my mind as to the
advisability of proceeding with a scheme.' But Churchill had already,
on December 28, sent details of the widows' pension scheme to Baldwin,
who replied two days later:

My dear Chancellor,
    I have read your letter dated Friday with the keenest interest and pleasure.
You are a Chancellor after my own heart!
    You will observe the present tense. I have every hope that after accomplish-
ing much I shall use the present when our term is completed.

                                                              Yours very sincerely
                                                              Stanley Baldwin

Commenting on Churchill's first seven weeks at the Treasury, on
December 27 Clementine Churchill had written to Professor Lindemann: 'Winston is immersed in thrilling new work with the Treasury
officials whom he says are a wonderful lot of men.'

On January 5 the question of the Naval Estimates was raised at a
meeting of the Committee of Imperial Defence. 'Yesterday I was
vigorously engaged with Winston,' Lord Beatty[1] wrote to his wife on
January 6, 'and I think on the whole got the better of him. I must
say, although I had to say some pretty strong things, he never bears any
malice and was good-humoured throughout the engagement.' During
the meeting, Austen Chamberlain had strongly supported Churchill's
view that the prospect of war with Japan was, as he put it, 'very remote'.
Chamberlain went on to tell his colleagues:

[1] David Beatty, 1871–1936. Entered Navy, 1884. Commanded a gunboat at Omdurman,
where he first met Churchill, 1898. Rear-Admiral, 1910. Churchill's Naval Secretary, 1912.
Commander of the Battle Cruiser Squadron, 1913–16. Knighted, 1914. Vice-Admiral, 1915.
Commander-in-Chief of the Grand Fleet, 1916–19. First Sea Lord, 1919–27. Created Earl,
1919. Admiral of the Fleet, 1919. Order of Merit, 1919.

I cannot conceive it possible that Japan, singlehanded, should seek a conflict with us. The only case in which I think Japan (which is an uneasy and rather restless Power, whose action is not always easy to predict) might become dangerous is after a new regrouping of the European Powers. In other words, unless we see signs of a German-Russo-Japanese Alliance or agreement, I should not anticipate war between ourselves and Japan. I should regard the signs of such an agreement, such a new regrouping of the Powers as being a danger signal which would at once call our attention to the situation and would require that we should review it afresh. Of that regrouping there is at present no sign.

Later in the discussion a former Foreign Secretary, Lord Curzon,[1] also spoke of the unlikelihood of war with Japan; the Japanese, he asserted, were very pro-British, and wanted only to maintain 'intimate and cordial relations' with Britain.

In seeking to resolve the question of inter-Allied war debts, Churchill had to consider the United States' demand that the money owed to her by Britain must be repaid without waiting until Britain had received the money owed to her by France. Churchill wanted all debts settled by a simple plan, whereby Britain would pay America in proportion to receiving money from France. For more than a month he discussed and elaborated on this plan with his advisers. To Sir Otto Niemeyer[2] he had written on December 10 to point out the many ways in which Britain had borne the brunt of war indebtedness: 'we have taxed ourselves far more heavily', he wrote, 'than any other country', a fact which had contributed to the high rate of unemployment. In view of the financial exertions Britain had made, 'We have no need to ask favours from anybody, nor are we under any obligation to give concessions.' Churchill repeated these themes when he spoke during a debate on the Debt in the House of Commons on December 10. Writing to Churchill on December 15, Austen Chamberlain reported Etienne Clémentel's[3]

[1] George Nathaniel Curzon, 1859–1925. Educated at Eton and Balliol College Oxford. President of the Oxford Union, 1880. Conservative MP, 1886–98. Under-Secretary of State for India, 1891–92; for Foreign Affairs, 1895–98. Created Baron, 1898. Viceroy of India, 1898–1905. Created Earl, 1911. Lord Privy Seal, May 1915–December 1916. President of the Air Board, 1916. Member of the War Cabinet, 1916–19. Secretary of State for Foreign Affairs, 1919–24. Created Marquess, 1921. Lord President of the Council, 1924–25.

[2] Otto Ernst Niemeyer, 1883–1971. Educated at St Pauls and Balliol College Oxford. Entered the Treasury, 1906; Controller of Finance, 1922–27. Member of the Financial Committee of the League of Nations, 1922–37. Knighted, 1924. A Director of the Bank for International Settlements, 1931–65, and of the Bank of England, 1938–52. Chairman of the Governors, London School of Economics, 1941–57.

[3] Etienne Clémentel, 1862–1936. Deputy, Puy-de-Dôme, 1898. Occupied several Ministerial posts between 1898 and 1924, including Minister of Colonies, 1898, and Minister of Commerce, 1916–20. Instrumental in establishing the Inter-Allied Wheat Executive, 1916,

suggestion that Churchill, on his visit to Paris for a Finance Conference due to open on January 8, should summon a conference of all the debtor and creditor nations. This Churchill accepted. Chamberlain ended his letter:

> May I add that I was delighted to see from the papers what an outstanding success your first appearance in the House of Commons as Chancellor of the Exchequer had been? I have never doubted that you will greatly enhance your reputation in this post which will give you an opportunity of showing to the country your possession of just those powers which perhaps hitherto have been recognised only by your personal friends.

Replying to Austen Chamberlain on December 30, Churchill set out his views of the inter-allied debts, expressing his total opposition, both in law and in equity, to the American view that all debts must be paid bilaterally, without any *pari passu* arrangements. He was particularly upset by the continuing American pressure on France for a direct debt settlement, and saw his role as that of arbitrator between France and America. 'At the same time,' he wrote, 'both France and ourselves will have to squeeze the Belgians over their abuse of their 100 million priority on reparation.' In urging a general settlement, Churchill added, 'we shall be in a very strong position, being quite independent and committed to no proposition which is not backed with massive arguments'. In explaining his policy to the Cabinet on January 5, Churchill said that he intended 'to hold the British Government free to make any arrangements with France independently in time or terms of America'. At the same time, he intended, he said, to impress upon Clémentel 'that we considered it the duty of France to pay her debt to us'.

On January 6 Churchill left London for Paris, and on the following day, in his opening address to the Conference, he declared: 'Hope flies on wings, and international conferences plod along dusty roads, but still the conviction exists that progress is being made towards the reconstruction of the unity and prosperity of Europe, that the healing process is active and that problems are assuming increasingly simple form'. Churchill added that nothing should be done by the delegates to disappoint that conviction. The overriding need was for 'harmony in mood and for simplicity in method'.

On January 8 Clementine Churchill wrote to her husband of how the newspapers had been full of his departure for Paris, 'illustrated by snapshots of a debonnaire Pig'. Altogether, she noted, 'you are the Pet

---

and the Inter-Allied Maritime Transport Council, 1917. Senator, 1918. President and founder of the International Chamber of Commerce, 1919. Minister of Finance, 1924–25.

of the moment'. On January 10 he sent her an account of what he had
been doing:

I have scarcely moved outside the Embassy except to the series of conferences & discussions & interviews wh have occupied the days. Even meal
times have been devoted to meeting people of consequence. I had an interview with Herriot[1] in his sick room. Poor man—he seemed vy seedy & worn
with worry & phlebitis. We got on well. Tomorrow I am to see President
Doumergue.[2] . . .

I have had tremendous battles with the Yanks, & have beaten them down
inch by inch to a reasonable figure. In the end we were fighting over tripe
like £100,000! However there was never any ill will & I have now made
quite a good arrangement with them wh will be announced on Tuesday with
the rest. I think on the whole I have succeeded. Certainly I have had plenty
of compliments. But that is not a vy trustworthy test.

The course of the Paris negotiations proved a triumph for Churchill's
tact and negotiating skill. After a week of discussions, all the former
Allied powers accepted the principle that Britain's debt payments to
the United States should be accompanied by simultaneous, proportionate payments to Britain by France, Belgium, Italy and Japan, Britain's
principal debtors. Rumania, Serbia, Brazil and Czechoslovakia also
agreed to accept the general plan. This conclusion was strongly to
Britain's advantage: the £1,000 million pounds which Britain owed
America was offset by over £2,000 million which the other former
Allies owed to Britain.

The Press applauded Churchill's success, and was particularly
impressed at his having persuaded the United States to play a more
constructive part in European affairs. He himself recognized and
acknowledged the important work done by his Treasury advisers,
writing to Frederick Leith-Ross[3] when the Conference was ended: 'I

[1] Edouard Herriot, 1872–1957. Mayor of Lyon, 1905–40. Senator, 1912–19. Minister of
Public Works, 1916–17. President of the Radical Party, 1919–40; of the Socialist-Radical
Party, 1945–57. Deputy, 1919–40. Prime Minister, June 1924–April 1925 and July 1926.
Held numerous Ministerial posts, 1926–36. President of the Chamber, 1936–40. Arrested by
the Vichy Government, 1940. Interned near Berlin, 1944–45; liberated by Soviet troops.
President of the National Assembly, 1947–54.

[2] Gaston Doumergue, 1863–1937. Lawyer; magistrate in Indo-China, 1890–92, in Algeria,
1893. Minister of Colonies, 1902–05; of Commerce and Industry, 1906–08; of Public Instruction, 1908–10; of Foreign Affairs, 1913–14; of Colonies, 1914–17. President of the Senate,
1923–24. President of France, 1924–31; Prime Minister, February to November 1934.

[3] Frederick William Leith-Ross, 1887–1968. Educated at Merchant Taylors' School and
Balliol College Oxford. Private Secretary to H. H. Asquith, 1911–13. British Representative on
the Finance Board of the Reparations Commission, 1920–25. Deputy Controller of Finance,
Treasury, 1925–32. Chief Economic Adviser to the Government, 1932–46. Knighted, 1933.
Minister of the British War Debts Mission to Washington, 1933. Negotiated financial arrange-
ments with Germany, October 1934 and with Italy, April 1935. Financial Mission to China,

was deeply impressed by the obvious ascendency of the British experts, headed by yourself, over their foreign colleagues. You seemed to be accepted as trusted guides and exponents. Pray accept my congratulations and thanks.' Congratulations reached Churchill himself from a former Foreign Secretary, Lord Grey of Fallodon, who wrote from Northumberland:

It is a real pleasure to me, who have known the difficulties of such things, to read of so great a success; and when that is due to a man for whom one has feelings of personal friendship, it adds to the happiness of life. I gather from the Times that not only has the Conference been a success, but that your share in bringing that about has been great, & that the recognition of this is due to the spontaneous tribute of the foreigners with whom you have dealt. To uphold the interests of this country & at the same time to secure this recognition from the representatives of other countries is a rare achievement & a great public service. . . .

Churchill returned to London on January 14, and on the following day gave the Cabinet an account of the Paris Conference. According to the official minutes, the Cabinet 'expressed their high appreciation of the success of the Chancellor of the Exchequer's mission, which had resulted not only in clearing up very difficult and complicated financial questions, but also in an improvement of the general political situation'. On January 15 Sir Eric Phipps[1] wrote to Churchill from Paris: 'I hear on all sides nothing but expressions of gratitude by the French for the consideration which you displayed towards them.'

Following his return from Paris, Churchill began to prepare, in detail, his arguments against any increase in naval expenditure. 'Where you are in a particularly strong position,' Sir George Barstow advised him on January 14, 'in which I believe it would have the support of the whole Cabinet, is on the question of high policy. It is precisely on this ground that the Naval Lords will have difficulties in opposing you.' Churchill took this advice. 'The statement of the Foreign Secretary,' he wrote to Bridgeman on January 19, 'upon the improbability of any war with Japan for many years to come should make it possible to slow down

---

1935–36. Chairman of the Economic Committee of the League of Nations, 1936 and 1937. Director-General, Ministry of Economic Warfare, 1939–42. Chairman, Inter-Allied Post-War Requirements Committee, 1941–43. Deputy Director-General of UNRRA, 1944–45. Governor of the National Bank of Egypt, 1946–51. Deputy Chairman, National Provincial Bank, 1951–66.

[1] Eric Clare Edmund Phipps, 1875–1945. Diplomat; Attaché in Paris, 1899; First Secretary in Petrograd, 1912; Counsellor of Embassy in Brussels, 1920–22; Minister in Paris, 1922–28. Knighted, 1927. Minister in Vienna, 1928–33. Privy Councillor, 1933. Ambassador in Berlin, 1933–37; Ambassador in Paris, 1937–39.

the whole process of naval preparation.' Nevertheless, he insisted, the economies should never be at the expense of preparedness. The Admiralty's proposal to arm a hundred merchant ships was one 'with which I fully agree'. He had indeed initiated this very measure before 1914. But he could not see that there was 'the slightest urgency' to complete this programme at once. 'During the next 15 years,' he explained, 'many ships now armed with 6-inch guns will necessarily be scrapped. It would in my opinion be a most prudent measure on the part of the Admiralty to preserve the guns, mountings, and reserve ammunitions of these vessels, and promote their armed merchant cruiser programme gradually by this means.' Churchill went on to suggest that even the surplus 4·7-inch guns might be set aside for the same purpose, thus averting further capital expenditure, but at no loss to preparedness. 'The Treasury,' he wrote, 'will be quite ready to provide for the proper care and maintenance of such weapons as they become available through the scrapping of existing vessels.'

In a letter to the Chancellor of the Duchy of Lancaster, Lord Robert Cecil, on January 20, Churchill gave his view of the Estimates' dispute:

Do you realise that the Navy Estimates are up more than ten millions, and that the new construction programme on which the Admiralty insist will raise them ten millions next year and five millions more on top of that, a total increase of twenty-five million pounds in three years, and an aggregate total of over ninety millions in 1927–28 and following years? This is what I am trying to fight at the present time.

The immediate question is not one of disarmament but of preventing Britain from leading the world in a vast expansion of naval armaments, accompanied to a lesser extent by a development of air power. From the moment these estimates are presented and the Admiralty designs disclosed to Parliament, we shall be irretrievably branded as a Jingo Armaments Administration. . . .

On January 23 Churchill wrote again to Bridgeman, warning that the Navy's requirements 'will absorb the whole available resources of the Exchequer not only this year but for two or three years to come', with the result that there could be neither income tax relief, nor 'any schemes of social betterment'. Having followed since 1908 the movement of naval affairs, Churchill wrote, he was convinced that the expanded naval programme was 'not warranted by any consideration of the safety of the country or of the adequate maintenance of our naval power' and that it would be 'deeply injurious to the political foundations of the State'. On the following day Churchill wrote direct to Baldwin:

I shd be vy grateful for any advice as to how to handle this extremely awkward business. I thought myself that after one or two Cabinets on the main issue, you wd perhaps yrself mention certain figures for the next three years and ask that plans shd be made for working to them by a Cabinet Committee, or by further discussions *on that basis* between the Adm^{lty} and the Exchq^r.

Bridgeman appreciated Churchill's efforts to maintain good personal relations, and understood the reasons for Churchill's search for economy. 'I am sure,' he wrote on January 26, 'the fact that our respective conceptions of our duty have brought us into strong departmental conflict will not impair the friendliest relations between us.' But Beatty, as Bridgeman's senior naval adviser, was determined to carry out the Admiralty's plans, and took a more personal view of the situation, writing to his wife that same day:

That extraordinary fellow Winston has gone mad. Economically mad, and no sacrifice is too great to achieve what in his short-sightedness is the panacea for all evils—to take 1s off the Income Tax. Nobody outside a lunatic asylum expects a shilling off the Income Tax this Budget. But he has made up his mind that it is the only thing he can do to justify his appointment as Chancellor of the Exchequer. The result will be a split in the Conservative Party and nothing else. As we the Admiralty are the principal Spending Department, he attacks us with virulence.

Poor old Bridgeman our 1st Lord takes a very gloomy view and sees his job fading away from him. But I have heartened him up a lot and I think he will stand firm. It's then a case of Winston coming off his perch or a split in the Govt, followed by the resignation of the Board of Admiralty. Every year it is the same struggle. We have won through up to now, but we are up against tougher stuff just now and it requires very careful watching.

On January 27 Bridgeman circulated a memorandum to the Cabinet, defending his estimates. His policy of naval expansion and consolidation, involving an additional expenditure of over £10 million, was based, he wrote, on two decisions taken by Lloyd George's Government, one in November 1921 by the Committee of Imperial Defence, the other in February 1922 by a special Cabinet Committee, presided over by Churchill himself. Two days later Churchill circulated his reply: a six thousand word memorandum reiterating his reasons for rejecting Bridgeman's estimates. Income tax could not be reduced for three years to come, he insisted, nor funds found for social reform, if the naval budgets of the next four years were not curtailed. Were the Government to build five new cruisers and eight submarines, he added, as well as '6 costly depot, repair and victualling ships', it would make it a Government of naval expansion, and would 'excite national and world wide attention'. Churchill added: 'We might even find that building five more cruisers had merely called ten or twelve into existence against us.'

Churchill then repeated his view that the future danger from Japan had been much exaggerated by the Admiralty. Britain alone, he pointed out, possessed 18 battleships, as against 6 Japanese; each had 4 battle-cruisers; Britain had 57 cruisers against only 24 Japanese. It was Japan, he argued, who should take alarm, 'webbed about' as she was by the 'Naval apparatus of the two mighty English-speaking nations'. What would Britain's feeling be, he asked, 'if we saw ourselves being laid hold of by a similar pair of tongs?'

Churchill went on to warn against making the Japanese danger the principal criterion of naval policy. A proper naval policy, he wrote, would be to ensure that the Navy would not be inferior either to the Japanese or United States navies, rather than to seek 'to dominate either of these two powers in their quarter of the globe'. Even the con-struction of the Singapore naval base, he stressed, 'however desirable as a pillar of Imperial communications', had become a peg 'on which to hang the whole vast scheme of scientific naval control of Japan'. The existing international situation, he felt, did not justify 'either the rate or the scale' of the proposed naval activity in the Far East, and he added: 'We are invited to live, perhaps for a quarter of a century, with our pistol at full-cock and our finger on the trigger. I regard this not only as utterly unreasonable but as positively injurious to the main interests of the State.' Churchill then set out his view of how events would develop, and what the guidelines should be for Britain's future defence policy:

During a long peace, such as follows in the wake of great wars, there must inevitably develop gaps in our structure of armaments. We have to select the essential elements of war power from amidst great quantities of ancillary and subsidiary improvements. These gaps can be gradually and unostentatiously filled up if deep international antagonisms, the invariable precursors of great wars, gradually become apparent in the world.

Churchill hoped to persuade Bridgeman to modify his proposals be-fore the matter came before the Cabinet. He hoped too that Baldwin would look sympathetically upon his arguments, and felt he had every chance of success. On January 29 Lord Birkenhead wrote to the Viceroy of India, Lord Reading:[1] 'Winston's position in the Government and

---

[1] Rufus Daniel Isaacs, 1860–1935. Liberal MP, 1904–13. Knighted, 1910. Solicitor-General, 1910. Attorney-General, 1910–13. Entered the Cabinet, 1912. Lord Chief Justice

Cabinet is very strong. He takes infinite trouble with the Prime Minister, who likes him and for whom he feels a very sincere gratitude.'

On January 31 Baldwin went to Chequers to study Churchill's naval memorandum. That same day, in a letter to his wife, Beatty described the memorandum as a bomb which Churchill hoped 'will pulverize us, setting forth the extravagance of our claims'. But, he added, 'Winston and I are very good friends, and there is no malice or bad feeling attached to it.' Within the Treasury, Churchill's position received strong support from Sir George Barstow, who wrote to Sir Warren Fisher on February 3, in the course of a long letter arguing against increased estimates: 'I hope very much that if you consult with Ministers on the subject of Navy Estimates you will drive home one point to which I attach great importance—the immense political value of an announcement that the Govt does not intend to initiate *any* new construction in the coming year.' Of Japan's potential naval power, Barstow wrote: 'I believe our building resources are so much greater than theirs that if it came to a race we could always give them a start & pass them.' Fisher sent Barstow's letter to Baldwin with the comment: 'I commend to your serious notice this most admirable letter.'

On February 3 Churchill informed Beatty that he would not seek an immediate Cabinet decision. It was better, he wrote, 'that the Admiralty and the Treasury should continue discussions between them as far as possible', in the hope of reaching agreement. That same day he and Beatty discussed the estimates together for two and a half hours. 'Winston very amicable and friendly,' Beatty wrote to his wife later that day, 'but he says it is a very difficult position and it is not easy to bring our differences into line.' On February 4 Churchill wrote to Beatty again, sending him a six-page list of suggestions 'in the hope of our being able to come together', and offering to guarantee the Navy 'a steady £60 millions in future years', even though this was 'far more than I had realized would come on the Exchequer'. It included £4 millions more for 1925: a year, Churchill pointed out, 'when everyone was looking for reductions'. This, he added, 'is the absolute limit on which I could agree'.

Churchill's list of suggestions included a stricter limit on the building up of reserves of oil fuel; all new dockyard work at Malta or Devonport to 'stand over' until the existing work was finished; Singapore to be

---

1913–21. Created Baron Reading, 1914. Viscount, 1916; Earl, 1917. Special Ambassador to the USA, 1918. Viceroy of India, 1921–26. Created Marquess, 1926. Secretary of State for Foreign Affairs, 1931.

fully developed 'on a 15 year basis instead of 10 or 12, which is the present tempo'; and a pruning of as much as £750,000 from the Navy's administrative costs. 'It is no good telling me the First Sea Lord cannot do this if he lets it be known that it is his wish,' Churchill wrote. 'Even when First Lord, as you know, I often found this amount and larger amounts in a few mornings with a blue pencil.'

Beatty and Churchill discussed these suggestions together on the evening of February 4. 'It takes a good deal out of me,' Beatty wrote that night to his wife, 'when dealing with a man of his calibre with a very quick brain.' And he added: 'A false step, remark, or even gesture is immediately fastened upon, so I have to keep my wits about me.'

No agreement was reached; on February 5 Churchill wrote to Bridgeman of his 'not only admiration, but warm personal regard' for Beatty. Their conversation, he added, 'could not be unpleasant. It was however utterly unfruitful.' Beatty had seen no way of going below £63½ million, and even this sum included a 'shadow cut' of £2 million which, Churchill wrote, 'is of no value to the Exchequer'. He was very disappointed, also, that Beatty had been unable to accept that the naval construction programme for 1925–9, while remaining intact as far as the actual projects were concerned, should be spread over twice the period: a scheme which Churchill was prepared to finance. There seemed no point, Churchill continued, in further discussions between the Treasury and the Admiralty. 'It is quite clear,' he wrote, 'that the matter must go to the Cabinet.' And he added: 'After all, it is their money, not mine, which has to be distributed. If they like to spend all the available funds in the next few years on Naval development, if they think that necessary to the safety of the country and in accordance with our deepest political and national interests, it is for them to say so.'

Churchill felt that he had been put at a disadvantage during his discussions with Beatty because, when arguing about the Japanese danger, he found that Beatty had seen certain secret telegrams about Japanese intentions which Churchill had not been shown. In December 1924, Churchill had obtained Baldwin's approval to be shown all important intercepted telegrams passing between foreign embassies and foreign capitals. But this had not been done entirely as Churchill had wished. On February 5 he complained to Baldwin:

I still receive from time to time an intercept relating to some money question. But I remain entirely ignorant of the information possessed by the Admiralty and War Office. For instance, last week when I was discussing the great & vital question of the Navy Estimates with the Admiralty representatives they quoted to me freely & extensively the telegrams which have passed between the Japanese Embassy & Government. These telegrams, they said, showed the true intentions & feelings of Japan, particularly in regard to cruisers in the event of another Washington Conference: how they were willing to discuss the maximum size but certainly not to bind themselves about numbers etc.

I concealed my ignorance of these essential matters as well as I could; for I thought it hardly becoming that the Ch of the Exchequer should shew himself at such a disadvantage in secret information with the subordinate representatives of a spending Department. But the unfairness & impropriety of such a situation will, I am sure, appeal to you. How can I conduct the controversies on which the management of our finances depends unless at least I have the same knowledge of secret state affairs freely accessible to the officials of the Admiralty? The words 'monstrous' & 'intolerable' leap readily to my mind. I prefer to bury them in the cooler word 'absurd'.

Baldwin at once agreed to let Churchill see all intercepted telegrams relating to Japan, and on February 7 Churchill circulated a five-page secret memorandum to the Cabinet, casting doubt on the reality of the Japanese threat. If, he wrote, Britain was really in 'mortal peril' from Japan, 'I am sure the sacrifices will be made, and of course the money must be found'. His definition of 'mortal peril' was: 'a physical assault so sudden and so violent as to deprive Great Britain finally of the power to convert to war purposes the latent energy of the Empire'. His memorandum continued:

Great as are the injuries which Japan, if she 'ran amok', could inflict upon our trade in the Northern Pacific, lamentable as would be the initial insults which she might offer to the British flag, I submit that it is beyond the power of Japan, in any period which we need now foresee, to take any action which would prevent the whole might of the British Empire being eventually brought to bear upon her. And I believe that this fact, if true, will exercise a dominating influence on the extremely sane and prudent counsels which we have learned over a long period of time to expect from the Japanese Government.

On receiving Churchill's memorandum, Bridgeman wrote, on February 7: 'I do not see how we can safely go any appreciable distance further to meet you.' A Cabinet discussion, he added, was essential. To this Churchill agreed, and the Cabinet met on February 11. Bridgeman was supported only by Leopold Amery and Lord Robert Cecil.[1] A

[1] On February 12 Cecil explained to Churchill that he had only supported Bridgeman because, with the Cabinet 'practically unanimous against him', he did not want to 'bear too hardly on him'. After all, Cecil added, there was 'no danger of his views being adopted'. On February 13, in a draft reply to Cecil which he decided not to send, Churchill wrote: 'Is it any kindness to a colleague to encourage him in an unwise direction, or ought kindness to come in in matters of such moment.'

majority of Ministers agreed to Churchill's upper limit of £60 millions a year for all naval expenditure for several years. Baldwin sought to assuage Bridgeman's discontent by setting up a special Cabinet Committee under Lord Birkenhead to examine the whole question of future naval construction; but Bridgeman still insisted that no formal decision be reached until his naval advisers had been heard, and later that afternoon, having discussed the proposals with the Admiralty Board, he wrote to Baldwin threatening both his own, and his Board's resignation unless a programme of four new cruisers to be laid down in 1925 were accepted without delay, 'subject to its modification later on'. Should the Board resign, Bridgeman added, 'I believe a very large proportion of our party will sympathise with their attitude'. But when the Cabinet reconvened on the morning of February 12 only Lord Robert Cecil supported Bridgeman's request, and Bridgeman had to agree, reluctantly, not to authorize any new construction 'at this stage', but to abide by the decisions of the proposed Cabinet Committee. He also agreed that the precise sum to be spent on the Navy in 1925–6 should be decided, not by the Cabinet, but by Baldwin, Churchill and himself.

Baldwin, Churchill and Bridgeman met during the afternoon of February 13. Without having obtained Cabinet support for his proposals, Bridgeman's arguments carried little weight, and he finally agreed to limit the 1925–6 Estimates to £60½ million. He also agreed to accept the decision of a special inter-departmental Committee which would examine the question of marriage allowances. For his part, Churchill agreed to make a further £2,000,000 available, if needed, by means of a supplementary estimate, it being understood, as Churchill wrote to Bridgeman that evening, 'that the Admiralty make no undue effort to get rid of their money'. Bridgeman accepted this proviso. 'I assure you we shall do everything we can,' he wrote, 'to avoid having to draw upon the £2 million ... but the matter rests more with the contractors and their workmen than with us.' Bridgeman added: 'You may rely upon my making every endeavour to use the time before us this year in investigating every possible means of economy.' All his advisers, he added, were 'genuinely anxious to avoid any extravagance'. On February 16 Churchill replied: 'Many thanks for your letter and particularly for what you say about the way in which you and your Parliamentary colleagues will try to reduce unnecessary expenditure by a strict overhaul during the year. It is surely in the interests of the Navy to concentrate on the rugged essentials of strength rather than upon a meticulous perfection or a standard of immediate readiness.'

On February 18 Churchill and Bridgeman gave the Cabinet a summary of their conversations, and the Cabinet accepted what had been decided. During the discussion, it was agreed that the Navy's administrative charges were a legitimate matter for Treasury concern, and Baldwin asked Bridgeman to give 'most careful consideration to the question of economy in this respect'.

Beatty and Churchill both believed that they had been successful. For Beatty, the case for increased naval construction could still be made at Lord Birkenhead's Committee; for Churchill, the Admiralty having abandoned its original Naval Estimates for 1925–6, the Budget could go ahead along the lines he wished, dominated by tax relief and social reform.

On February 5, in sending Baldwin a detailed account of the progress of the insurance plans, Churchill wrote: 'It will show you how the Great Design is ripening.' As he went on to explain:

. . . all the benefits we spoke of would be realised for additional contributions of no more from the employer than 2d for men and *nothing* for women; and in the case of workers of no more than 2d for men and 1d for women. The above rates of course only apply to trades within the ambit of Unemployment Insurance. Still that is the bulk. For Agriculture and the rest the rates will be a little stiffer—though much less than was originally thought.

Strong opposition to the scale of Churchill's insurance proposals came from Neville Chamberlain and Sir Horace Wilson,[1] both of whom felt that too large a contribution was being demanded, particularly from the agricultural labourer. On February 9 Chamberlain warned Churchill of the 'political difficulties' involved in asking for an almost doubled contribution from the agricultural labourer, while Sir Horace Wilson proposed postponing the whole scheme for at least a year. But on February 23 the Government Actuary, Sir Alfred Watson,[2] in a strongly worded minute, urged that 'The only prospect of bringing the scheme into existence on a contributory basis seems to me to lie in its early presentation to Parliament.' Watson went on to stress the 'social value' of the benefits, which in his view, outweighed the 'burden' of the

[1] Horace John Wilson, 1882–1972. Entered the Civil Service, 1900; Permanent Secretary, Ministry of Labour, 1921–30. Knighted, 1924. Chief Industrial Adviser to the Government, 1930–39. Seconded to the Treasury for special service with Stanley Baldwin, 1935–37, and with Neville Chamberlain, 1937–40 (when he had a room at 10 Downing Street). Permanent Secretary of the Treasury and Head of the Civil Service, 1939–42.

[2] Alfred William Watson, 1870–1936. Actuary to several Provident Institutions. Chief Actuary to the National Health Insurance Joint Committee, 1912–19. Knighted, 1915. Government Actuary, 1917–36. President of the Institute of Actuaries, 1920–22. Member of the Royal Commissions on Decimal Coinage and National Health Insurance.

contributions which Wilson had stressed. On February 24 Churchill, Chamberlain and Horace Wilson met to discuss the impasse, and, as a result of their discussion, Chamberlain and Wilson agreed to withdraw their objections. But in the months that followed Chamberlain was often to take up with Churchill some small point or other on which he felt that his views were not being adequately consulted, while the disagreements between Churchill and Sir Horace Wilson also continued. On May 12, more than two and a half months after the insurance benefits had been decided on, Sir George Barstow wrote to Churchill: 'I think I am betraying no confidence in saying that Sir Horace Wilson, the Secretary of the Ministry of Labour, is convinced that the present rates of benefit are too high. Not merely do they reduce, as the Labour memorandum points out, the incentive to seek work but, what is still more important, they affect the willingness of bodies of workmen to accept modifications of wages and hours which are desperately badly needed in the present industrial situation.'

Despite the problems created by the Admiralty, the Ministry of Health and the Ministry of Labour, Churchill's work for the Insurance scheme had, in three months, greatly extended its scope and possibilities. His efforts and achievements were recognized outside the Cabinet and administration. On February 11 Asquith had written to a friend: 'he is a Chimborazo or Everest among the sandhills of the Baldwin Cabinet'.

5

Return to the Gold Standard

FROM the moment Churchill became Chancellor of the Exchequer in November 1924, public interest centred on his first Budget, and throughout December it was widely rumoured in the Press that income tax would be reduced. In the public mind, a reduction in income tax represented a return to normalcy; to a period of orderly financing and steady economic progress belonging to the era before 1914, when the piling up of war debts had begun. Churchill understood this popular desire. Many economists were likewise convinced by 1924 that the old economic values could be restored: for them the return to a Gold-based currency was the essential preliminary to such stability.

The Gold Standard itself had been suspended in March 1919; since then both the Cunliffe Committee and the Bank of England had urged the Government to 'return to Gold' as soon as possible, and in March 1924 Churchill's predecessor at the Treasury, Philip Snowden,[1] had told the House of Commons that the Labour Government accepted this advice. Two months later a special Committee on Currency and Banking was set up to examine the question in detail. Austen Chamberlain, a former Chancellor of the Exchequer, was appointed its Chairman. The Governor of the Bank of England, Montagu Norman, was among the witnesses who were called to give evidence to the Committee: all but two recommended a return to Gold.

The two dissident voices were another former Chancellor, Reginald McKenna, and the Cambridge economist, J. M. Keynes.[2] In October

[1] Philip Snowden, 1864–1937. Educated at Board School. Entered the Civil Service, 1886; retired, 1893. Chairman, Independent Labour Party, 1903–06 and 1917–20. Socialist MP for Blackburn, 1906–18; for Colne Valley, 1922–31. Privy Councillor, 1924. Chancellor of the Exchequer, 1924 and 1929–31. Created Viscount, 1931. Lord Privy Seal, 1931–32.

[2] John Maynard Keynes, 1883–1946. Educated at Eton and King's College Cambridge. Economist. Editor of the *Economic Journal*, 1911–44. Served at the India Office, 1906–08; the

1924 the Committee completed its work, but the fall of the Labour Government that same month delayed the decision. A decision, nevertheless, was being pressed for, particularly by Montagu Norman. The fact that the Act of Parliament suspending Gold payments was due to expire at the end of 1925 meant that the Government would either have to return to Gold, or make out a special case for renewing the Act. Norman urged a return, and prepared to go to the United States to seek special credit facilities to help protect the British economy against any ill-effects. On December 15 Churchill wrote to Baldwin:

The Governor of the Bank will, I hope, have told you this weekend about the imminence of our attempt to re-establish the gold standard, in connection with which he is now going to America. It will be easy to attain the gold standard, and indeed almost impossible to avoid taking the decision, but to keep it will require a most strict policy of debt repayment and a high standard of credit. To reach it and have to abandon it, would be disastrous.

Norman reached New York on December 28. Among those he consulted was the Governor of the Federal Bank of New York, Benjamin Strong.[1] According to a note written by Strong on 11 January 1925, all the Americans whom Norman consulted 'were unhesitating in expressing the view that the time for deciding upon a resumption of gold payment by England had arrived'. Not only the United States, but also Germany, had already returned to Gold.

While Norman was still in the United States, Churchill began to formulate a number of questions about the problems involved in a return to Gold. On January 2 he wrote to Sir Otto Niemeyer:

The United States has accumulated the greater part of the gold in the world and is suffering from a serious plethora. Are we sure that in trying to establish the gold standard we shall not be favouring American interests. Shall we not be making their hoard of gold more valuable than it is at present? Shall we not be relieving them from the consequences of their selfish and extortionate policy?

On January 28, after his return to England, Montagu Norman appeared before the Currency and Banking Committee. For him it was not

---

Treasury, 1915–19. Principal Treasury Representative at the Paris Peace Conference, 1919. Created Baron, 1942. Leader of the British Delegation to Washington to negotiate the American Loan, 1945. Among his publications was *The Economic Consequences of the Peace* (1919) and *The Economic Consequences of Mr Churchill* (July 1925).

[1] Benjamin Strong, 1872–1928. Entered banking as a clerk; subsequently Secretary of the Atlantic Trust Corporation, and President of the Bankers Trust Corporation. Governor of the Federal Reserve Bank, New York, from 1914 until his death.

a question of whether or not Britain should return to Gold, but only of when it should be done. 'I am now greatly in favour of a return during this year,' Norman told the Committee, buttressing his view with an account of his American discussions. On February 5 the Committee, now headed by Lord Bradbury,[1] recommended an early return to Gold. Anticipating this conclusion, Churchill had already sent a long memorandum to Montagu Norman, Sir Otto Niemeyer, Lord Bradbury and Ralph Hawtrey[2] on January 29. The memorandum, which was known inside the Treasury as 'Mr Churchill's Exercise', reflected in stronger terms, and at greater length, his questionings of January 2. 'The writer of the memorandum,' Bradbury wrote scathingly to Niemeyer on February 5, 'appears to have his spiritual home in the Keynes–McKenna sanctuary but some of the trimmings of his mantle have been furnished by the Daily Express.'

Churchill's memorandum began with an open challenge. 'If we are to take the very important step of removing the embargo on gold export,' he wrote, 'it is essential that we should be prepared to answer any criticism which may be subsequently made upon our policy. I should like to have set out in writing the counter case to the following arguments.' The arguments were that domestic credit and monetary stability were independent of the Gold Standard; that the Gold Standard itself was a survival 'of rudimentary and transitional stages in the evolution of finance and credit'; that any return to Gold would involve Britain in helping the United States to share the cost of maintaining the value of Gold; and that the value of sterling could be better raised by the simpler expedient of paying off £100 million of Britain's war debt to America with gold from the Bank of England's reserves. One of Churchill's arguments read:

The whole question of a return to the Gold Standard must not be dealt with only upon its financial and currency aspects. The merchant, the manufacturer, the workman and the consumer have interests which, though largely common, do not by any means exactly coincide either with each other or with the financial and currency interests. The maintenance of cheap money is a matter of high consequence.

[1] John Stanwick Bradbury, 1872–1950. Educated at Manchester Grammar and Brasenose College Oxford. An Insurance Commissioner, 1911–13. Knighted, 1913. Joint Permanent Secretary, Treasury, 1913–19. Principal British Delegate, Reparations Commission, Paris, 1919–25. Created Baron, 1925. Chairman of the National Food Council, 1925–29. President, British Bankers' Association, 1929–30 and 1935–36.

[2] Ralph George Hawtrey, 1879–1975. Educated at Eton and Trinity College Cambridge. Civil Servant, Admiralty, 1903–04; Treasury, 1904–45. Director of Financial Enquiries, Treasury, 1919–45. Knighted, 1956. Author and economist.

In his memorandum Churchill argued against a hasty decision. 'What risks shall we run?' he asked, 'what evils shall we encounter? ... why should we not leave well alone, and let events take their course on the present basis?' To go back on Gold, Churchill feared, would enable people to accuse the Government of having 'favoured the special interests of finance at the expense of the interests of production'. Churchill's memorandum ended:

In setting down these ideas and questionings I do not wish it to be inferred that I have arrived at any conclusions adverse to the re-establishment of the Gold Standard. On the contrary I am ready and anxious to be convinced as far as my limited comprehension of these extremely technical matters will permit. But I expect to receive good and effective answers to the kind of case which I have, largely as an exercise, indicated in this note.

Replying on February 2, Sir Otto Niemeyer stressed that previous Governments 'of all political shades' had declared themselves in favour of a return to Gold, and that any hesitation now would convince the world that Britain had never really 'meant business' about the Gold Standard, 'because our nerve had failed when the stage was set'. One immediate result of failing to go back on Gold, would, he wrote, be 'a considerable withdrawal of balances and investment (both foreign *and British*) from London'. Niemeyer also sent Churchill an advance copy of the Currency Committee's Report, advocating a return to Gold. Montagu Norman also replied to Churchill on February 2. There was, he insisted, no alternative to a return to Gold, at least in the opinion 'of educated and reasonable men'. And he added: 'The only practical question is the Date.' Norman's reply continued:

... the Chancellor will surely be charged with a sin of omission or of commission. In the former case (Gold) he will be abused by the ignorant, the gamblers and the antiquated Industrialists; in the latter case (not Gold) he will be abused by the instructed and by posterity.

Plain and solid advantages can be shown to exist which justify—and seem to require—this sacrifice by the Chancellor. He could hardly assume office with Free Gold in one country and watch half-a-dozen others attain Free Gold ... without his own.

Ralph Hawtrey and Lord Bradbury also replied to Churchill's memorandum. Hawtrey, writing on February 2, argued that a return to Gold was the only means of attaining international exchange stability, while Bradbury, writing on February 5, believed that for the foreseeable future gold would be the ultimate means of settlement, nor could he see any real advantage in delaying the decision.

Churchill studied the replies to his memorandum, which were, he wrote to Niemeyer on February 6, 'very able'. He added that the Currency Committee's Report provided 'a solid foundation of argument and authority justifying the action proposed'. But he was still unhappy about the course which his advisers were urging him to take, and told Niemeyer of a conversation with the Chairman of Barclays Bank, F. C. Goodenough,[1] who, while supporting a return to Gold, also had 'private confirmation' that Reginald McKenna, the Chairman of the Midland Bank, 'is personally opposed to the Gold policy and regards it as unnecessary and unwise'.

Churchill also wrote to Austen Chamberlain on February 6, asking for his comments on the Currency Committee's Report. The matter, he wrote, was one 'of considerable urgency, and decision on the question of the Gold Standard cannot long be delayed'. Chamberlain replied two days later, advising Churchill to return to Gold at once. He added:

I feel sure that, if you make your announcement with *decisive confidence* on your own part, the operation will now be found, all things considered, an easy one, and that to delay your decision much longer would be to expose you to a serious risk of a renewed fall in sterling. All the world is now expecting us to return to the gold standard, and has become convinced that we can do it. If we do not do it, we shall not stay where we were, but inevitably *start a retrograde movement*.

The pressure for a return to Gold was considerable; on the day of Chamberlain's reply, Philip Snowden wrote in the *Observer* that the difficulties involved in such a course would be small 'compared with the evils from which the world is suffering as a result of unstable and fluctuating currencies'. But Churchill still hesitated. 'Gold is excessively active and very troublesome,' Niemeyer wrote to Leith-Ross in mid-February. 'None of the witch doctors can see eye to eye and Winston cannot make up his mind from day to day whether he is a gold bug or a pure inflationist.'

On Saturday February 21 J. M. Keynes published an article entitled 'The Return Towards Gold' in the *Nation*. In it he argued against a return to Gold. During the course of his argument Keynes declared:

A gold standard means, in practice, nothing but to have the same price level and the same money rates (broadly speaking) as the United States.

---

[1] Frederick Craufurd Goodenough, 1866–1934. Born in Calcutta. Educated at Charterhouse and Zurich University. A director of Barclay's Bank, 1913; Chairman from 1917 until his death. A Member of the India Council, London, 1918–30. First Chairman of Barclays Bank (Overseas) Ltd, 1922. Member of the Council of Foreign Bondholders, and a pioneer of empire banking.

The whole object is to link *rigidly* the City and Wall Street. I beg the Chancellor of the Exchequer and the Governor of the Bank of England and the nameless others who settle our destiny in secret to reflect that this may be a dangerous proceeding.

The United States lives in a vast and unceasing crescendo. Wide fluctuations, which spell unemployment and misery for us, are swamped for them in the general upward movement. A country, the whole of whose economic activities are expanding, year in, year out, by several per cent per annum, cannot avoid, and at the same time can afford, temporary maladjustments. This was our own state during a considerable part of the nineteenth century. Our rate of progress was so great that stability in detail was neither possible nor essential.

This is not our state now. Our rate of progress is slow at the best, and faults in our economic structure, which we could afford to overlook whilst we were racing forward and which the United States can still afford to overlook, are now fatal. The slump of 1921 was even more violent in the United States than here, but by the end of 1922 recovery was practically complete. We still, in 1925, drag on with a million unemployed. The United States may suffer industrial and financial tempests in the years to come, and they will scarcely matter to her; but we, if we share them, may almost drown.

Churchill was much impressed by Keynes' arguments, which strengthened his own doubts. But Niemeyer immediately set down his counter-arguments, which he sent to Churchill on February 21. The danger of not being linked to gold, he wrote, was a real one. 'How are we,' he asked, 'a great exporting and importing country, to live with an exchange fluctuating with gold, when United States of America, Germany, Austria, Sweden, Holland, Switzerland, the Dominions, probably South Africa, and Japan have a stable gold exchange.' Churchill was still unwilling to defer to the Treasury view, writing to Niemeyer on Sunday February 22:

The Treasury has never, it seems to me, faced the profound significance of what Mr Keynes calls 'the paradox of unemployment amidst dearth'. The Governor shows himself perfectly happy in the spectacle of Britain possessing the finest credit in the world simultaneously with a million and a quarter unemployed. Obviously if these million and a quarter were usefully and economically employed, they would produce at least £100 a year a head, instead of costing us at least £50 a year a head in doles. We should have at least £200 millions a year healthy net increase. These figures are of course purely illustrative. It is impossible not to regard such an object as at least equal, and probably superior, to the other valuable objectives you mention on your last page.

The community lacks goods, and a million and a quarter people lack work. It is certainly one of the highest functions of national finance and credit to bridge the gulf between the two. This is the only country in the world where this condition exists. The Treasury and Bank of England policy has been the only policy consistently pursued. It is a terrible responsibility for those who have shaped it, unless they can be sure that there is no connection between the unique British phenomenon of chronic unemployment and the long, resolute consistency of a particular financial policy. I do not know whether France with her financial embarrassments can be said to be worse off than England with her unemployment. At any rate while that unemployment exists, no one is entitled to plume himself on the financial or credit policy which we have pursued.

Churchill's letter continued:

It may be of course that you will argue that the unemployment would have been much greater but for the financial policy pursued; that there is no sufficient demand for commodities either internally or externally to require the services of this million and a quarter people; that there is nothing for them but to hang like a millstone round the neck of industry and on the public revenue until they become permanently demoralised. You may be right, but if so, it is one of the most sombre conclusions ever reached. On the other hand I do not pretend to see even 'through a glass darkly' how the financial and credit policy of the country could be handled so as to bridge the gap between a dearth of goods and a surplus of labour; and well I realise the danger of experiment to that end. The seas of history are full of famous wrecks. Still if I could see a way, I would far rather follow it than any other. I would rather see Finance less proud and Industry more content.

Although the return to the Gold Standard was widely regarded as a technical matter for the Bank of England and the Treasury experts to decide, Churchill nevertheless had grave doubts. His letter ended:

You and the Governor have managed this affair. Taken together I expect you know more about it than anyone else in the world. At any rate alone in the world you have had an opportunity over a definite period of years of seeing your policy carried out. That it is a great policy, greatly pursued, I have no doubt. But the fact that this island with its enormous extraneous resources is unable to maintain its population is surely a cause for the deepest heart-searching.

'Forgive me, adding to your labours,' Churchill added, 'by these Sunday morning reflections.' Niemeyer replied at once. The alternative to the return to Gold was, he argued, inflation; and with increasing inflation the credit of the country would be destroyed, and money would 'cease to be acceptable as value'. As inflation grew, wage demands would increase, and there would be grave industrial unrest. 'I assume it to be admitted,' he wrote, 'that with Germany and Russia before us we do not think plenty can be found on this path.'

Towards the end of February Lord Beaverbrook invited Churchill to dine with him. Eight months later, on 2 November 1925, Churchill recalled their conversation. '. . . You advised me most strongly against adopting the Gold Standard,' Churchill wrote, 'on which point you used many, if not most, of the arguments which have since been employed by its opponents. I reflected a great deal on what you said, but in the end the counter-arguments prevailed.' These counter-arguments reached their climax during March, when Churchill made one further effort to influence his senior Treasury officials. On March 17 he brought together over dinner the two strongest critics of gold, Keynes and McKenna, and its two principal advocates within the Treasury, Niemeyer and Bradbury. Churchill's Private Secretary P. J. Grigg,[1] who was present during the dinner, later recorded in his memoirs the course of the discussion:

The Symposium lasted till midnight or after. I thought at the time that the ayes had it. Keynes's thesis, which was supported in every particular by McKenna, was that the discrepancy between American and British prices was not $2\frac{1}{2}$ per cent as the exchanges indicated, but 10 per cent. If we went back to gold at the old parity we should therefore have to deflate domestic prices by something of that order. This meant unemployment and downward adjustments of wages and prolonged strikes in some of the heavy industries, at the end of which it would be found that these industries had undergone a permanent contraction. It was much better, therefore, to try to keep domestic prices and nominal wage rates stable and allow the exchanges to fluctuate.

Bradbury made a great point of the fact that the Gold Standard was knave-proof. It could not be rigged for political or even more unworthy reasons. It would prevent our living in a fool's paradise of false prosperity, and would ensure our keeping on a competitive basis in our export business, not by allowing what I believe the economists call the 'terms of trade' to go against us over the whole field, but by a reduction of costs in particular industries. In short, to anticipate a phrase which Winston afterwards used in

---

[1] Percy James Grigg, 1890–1964. Educated at Bournemouth School and St Johns College Cambridge. Entered the Treasury, 1913. Served in the Royal Garrison Artillery, 1915–18. Principal Private Secretary to successive Chancellors of the Exchequer, 1921–30. Chairman, Board of Customs and Excise, 1930; Board of Inland Revenue, 1930–34. Knighted, 1932. Finance Member, Government of India, 1934–39. Elected to the Other Club, 1939. Permanent Under-Secretary of State for War, 1939–42. Secretary of State for War, 1942. Privy Councillor, 1942. National MP, East Cardiff, 1942–45. British Executive Director, International Bank for Reconstruction and Development, 1946–47. Subsequently a director of Imperial Tobacco, the Prudential Assurance Company, and other companies. On 19 May 1930 Churchill wrote to Grigg: 'Your friendship is ever of great consequence to me, and my regard for you is deep. . . . I have the warmest feelings of admiration for your gifts and character.'

answering a sneer about our having shackled ourselves to gold, we should be doing no more than shackling ourselves to reality.

To the suggestion that we should return to gold but at a lower parity, Bradbury's answer was that we were so near the old parity that it was silly to create a shock to confidence and to endanger our international reputation for so small and so ephemeral an easement.

Grigg's account continued:

Having listened to the gloomy prognostications of Keynes and McKenna, Winston turned to the latter and said: 'But this isn't entirely an economic matter; it is a political decision, for it involves proclaiming that we cannot, for the time being at any rate, complete the undertaking which we all acclaimed as necessary in 1918, and introducing legislation accordingly. You have been a politician; indeed you have been Chancellor of the Exchequer. Given the situation as it is, what decision would you take.' McKenna's reply—and I am prepared to swear to the sense of it—was: 'There is no escape; you have got to go back; but it will be hell.'

Montagu Norman was on holiday at the time of this dinner discussion. As soon as he returned to London, he set about obtaining both Churchill's and Baldwin's formal approval for an immediate return to Gold. 'Chancellor for lunch in Downing Street,' he noted in his diary on March 19. 'Gold return to be announced April 6th–8th. Cushion to be meanwhile arranged by Bank. I warn him of 6% Bank rate next month.' And on March 20 he recorded: 'Prime Minister, Chancellor, Austen Chamberlain, Bradbury, Niemeyer at 2.30. Free gold statement to be in Budget about April 28th . . .' On April 23, five days before the Budget, Churchill explained the decision to the King:

Germany and the United States are already on the gold standard. It is believed that Holland will move to a gold basis in conformity with Great Britain. As far as the British Empire is concerned, the step will be taken unitedly. Canada is already on the gold standard, South Africa, Australia and New Zealand only await the British signal. The importance of a uniform standard of value to which all transactions can be referred throughout the British Empire and through a very large part of the world cannot be over-estimated. It benefits all countries, but it benefits no country more than our crowded island with its vast world trade and finance by which it lives.

6

Preparing the 1925 Budget: 'Keeping His Nose to the Grindstone'

THE decision to restore the Gold Standard was only one of the many financial and economic problems with which Churchill was confronted in the three months leading up to his Budget. During March the long-term plans of the Admiralty were under discussion at the Naval Programme Committee, whose task was to indicate a five-year programme for Naval construction. The Committee held its first meeting on March 2, when Lord Beatty gave a detailed account of the Navy's needs, and, according to the lengthy stenographic notes of the meeting—which filled twenty-five printed pages—again stressed the Japanese danger.[1] During Beatty's lengthy exposition, Churchill often interrupted, seeking extra details about Admiralty intentions, and the exchanges between the two men became acrimonious.

Beatty's main point was that the Japanese would be able to launch a surprise attack on points in the British Empire in the Far East at their selected moment, and that the condition of the Royal Navy was such that an attack could not be countered. But Churchill stressed that the Navy could 'afford to wait' at least for two weeks, before engaging the Japanese Fleet. It might, he said, be inconvenient for Britain to avoid

---

[1] As Lord Birkenhead was ill, Lord Salisbury (Lord Privy Seal) took the Chair. The others present were Churchill, Bridgeman, Edward Wood (Minister of Agriculture and Fisheries), Lord Peel (First Commissioner of Works), Lord Beatty and Captain Pound (Director of Plans, Admiralty). On March 1 Churchill had written to Birkenhead (in a note marked 'Secret and Personal'): 'No doubt Beatty will want to make a general statement, and no doubt it should be allowed to him; but I suggest that the questions which are interjected should as far as possible tend to bring out his actual requirements, rather than a general lecture on strategy.'

a naval engagement with the Japanese for the first month or two after a Japanese attack in the Far East, but even then 'the life of the Empire would not be impaired', and in the meantime the outlying cruisers could be brought together 'to make the chance of winning the action much better'.

The Naval Programme Committee held its second meeting on March 5. Lord Birkenhead took the Chair; Sir Roger Keyes stood in for Beatty, who had gone abroad. Churchill opened the proceedings by setting out in copious detail his objections to the naval expansion. 'It is astonishing,' he said at one point, 'that the Japanese are able to preserve vessels which at 26 years of age are a source of anxiety to the Admiralty.' Churchill again challenged Beatty's insistence upon the need to expand and build on the assumption of a war with Japan. Without such an insistence, he said, 'there would be no financial problem that could not be easily solved . . . apart from this great scheme and plan of preparation for a war with Japan in the Pacific, for waging war at the other end of the world—apart from that there would be no difficulty at all about the Navy estimates'. Churchill's argument continued:

This war with Japan depends absolutely upon the creation of a great new Rosyth at Singapore on which the Grand Fleet can be based. It involves, in the second place a decision to move the main British fleet with all its attendant vessels to Singapore at the outbreak of hostilities, or, if possible, during a period of strained relations, and carrying out operations on the largest scale against Japan at this great distance from home.

No such proposal has ever been considered by the Committee of Imperial Defence or by the Cabinet at all. . . .

Churchill warned the Committee that once the demand for matching each new Japanese cruiser construction were met, it would lead to an unending programme of expansion, rather than a parallel programme of replacement. Yet even such a 'gigantic expansion', he said, 'multiplying four or five-fold at the very least the power of the British cruiser fleet', would not act as an adequate security if Japan were really determined to take full advantage of her strength in the Far East and her proximity to Britain's remotest possessions.

Churchill proposed that no British battle fleet should be based on Singapore 'for at least ten years'. Beatty had argued on March 2 that it would need seven or eight years intensive British preparation before the Royal Navy would be ready to face Japan on an equal basis. To this Churchill replied:

All the formidable dangers which the First Sea Lord brought before our eyes when we were last here are already upon us at this time when we sit here, and we have been passing through them quite comfortably for years past. If, however, now that the Japanese see that we are making preparation to carry our main fleet to the other end of the world, if that wicked and sinister people are planning to attack us, these next ten years afford them, according to the Admiralty arguments, their best opportunity.

'If the Admiralty policy of basing our fleet at Singapore in a war with Japan is right and absolutely necessary to us,' Churchill asked, 'why should the Japanese strategists wait until Singapore is completed and we are in a position to attack them?'

In a memorandum written on the same day as the second meeting of the Naval Programme Committee, Bridgeman commented that in the contention that Japan was not intent on war, Churchill 'ignores history, real facts and the psychology of the people'. Japan, he said, had built 'more modern cruisers, destroyers and submarines since the war than the rest of the world put together'. To substantiate his criticisms, Bridgeman circulated a six-page Naval Staff memorandum, in which stress was laid on Japan's sense of mission, and her 'set purpose'. A large body of Japanese opinion, the Naval Staff asserted, 'believes that victory in war is an efficient cause of improvement in National economy'. And they added that 'the need of outlets for the population and for increased commerce and markets, especially new sources of self-supply, will probably be among the most compelling reasons for Japan to push a policy of penetration, expansion and aggression'.

While Churchill was continuing his battle against the Admiralty, Baldwin was persuading the House of Commons not to support a Conservative Private Members' Bill designed to weaken the power of the trade unions. It was essential, he told the Cabinet on March 5, 'to promote peace in the industrial world'. On the following day Baldwin argued the case in the House of Commons. 'The PM jumped his big fence with a foot to spare,' Churchill wrote in a letter to Birkenhead on March 8. 'It was an amazing performance and constitutes a political event of first importance.' To Clementine Churchill he wrote that same day:

Baldwin achieved a most remarkable success on Friday. He made about the only speech which could have restored the situation, and made it in exactly the right way. I had no idea he could show such power. He has never done it before. The whole Conservative Party turned round and obeyed without one single mutineer. Poor Horne, willing to wound and yet afraid to strike, prudently sat mum. As Sieyès said of Napoleon when he and his fellow directors returned to Paris after the eighteenth of Brumaire 'Nous avons un maître'. I cease to be astonished at anything. However this is all to the good.

A strong Conservative Party with an overwhelming majority and a moderate and even progressive leadership is a combination which has never been really tested before. It might well be the fulfilment of all that Dizzy and my father aimed at in their political work.

Churchill added: 'The revenue is coming in well; and if only I can win my battle with the Admiralty, I shall not be left penniless.'

On March 11 Clementine Churchill wrote to her husband from the South of France, urging him to 'stand up to the Admiralty'. Her letter continued: 'don't be fascinated or flattered or cajoled by Beatty. I assure you the Country doesn't care two pins about him. This may be very unfair to our only War Hero, but it's a fact. Of course,' Clementine Churchill added, 'I think it would be not good to score a sensational Winstonian triumph over your former love, but do not get sentimental & too soft hearted. Beatty is a tight little screw & he will bargain with you & cheat you as tho' he were selling you a dud horse which is I fear what the Navy is.'

With Beatty still abroad, the Naval Programme Committee met again on March 12. After a long and detailed argument about the relative state of British and Japanese warships, Churchill offered to give the Admiralty the same amount of money to spend on the repair of destroyers as Japan spent, 'plus 25 per cent'. And he added a few moments later: 'I might go a little higher in the percentage on Monday.' But towards the building of new ships, and the large-scale extension of dock facilities, he remained opposed. On March 15 he wrote to his wife:

The battle with the Admiralty continues ding dong in the Cabinet Committee. F.E. reveals continually his extraordinary mental powers. He sits like a stuck pig, hardly saying a word for hours, until I wondered whether he was really taking these to him unfamiliar topics in at all. But when the time came for him to draw up a series of questions to be remitted to the Committee of Imperial Defence, he showed a mastery and penetration of the difficulty of the argument, and a power of getting to the root of the matter, most profound and astonishing.

When the Cabinet met on March 18, it was agreed, at Churchill's suggestion, that the Committee of Imperial Defence must decide whether Admiralty policy should be based on the likelihood of war with Japan, and, if so, whether Singapore ought to be developed as the base for a British fleet 'at least equal' to the Japanese Navy. Meanwhile, Keyes decided to try to influence Churchill directly. On March 21 he warned Churchill privately of Japan's intention to 'turn Europeans out of China, and, in time, Asia', unless Britain were sufficiently strong 'to make it not worth her while to attempt it'. In his reply on the following day, Churchill wrote:

Your letter distresses me because it shows how very differently we are viewing the position. I do not believe Japan has any idea of attacking the British Empire, or that there is any danger of her doing so for at least a generation to come. If, however, I am wrong and she did attack us 'out of the blue', I do not think there would be any difficulty in defeating her. She would not, as was the case with Germany, have any chance of striking at the heart of the Empire and destroying its power to wage war. We should be put to great annoyance and expense, but in three or four years we could certainly sweep the Japanese from the seas and force them to make peace.

The Naval Programme Committee held its fifth meeting on March 23, but reached no conclusion. Eight days later, on March 31, Churchill set down proposals for a settlement. The Admiralty, he wrote, should plan to have a battle-cruiser squadron at Singapore 'during the period of strained relations, or as soon as may be after War has begun'; such a squadron would 'prove an effectual deterrent against a Japanese attack upon Singapore', but should not attempt any offensive operations in Japanese waters, or sink itself for the defence of Hong Kong. Simultaneously with the declaration of war, 'a preconceived programme of new construction shd be begun', aimed at reinforcing the Singapore squadron, and making it capable of defeating the Japanese in their home waters. Churchill's notes ended:

In the event, which is not admitted as a reasonably probable contingency, of Singapore falling before the forces based on it are capable of delivering decisive battle, our covering forces hitherto based on Singapore should, unless a favourable opportunity has been offered to them, withdraw without being drawn into decisive action at an inferiority to Colombo, to Bombay, or to Aden & the Red Sea, beginning their advance from this point as soon as the Floating Base for the whole fleet has been completed.

Determined to see his views prevail, Churchill prepared to argue them at length, both before both the Naval Programme Committee, and the Committee of Imperial Defence. Meanwhile, as Budget day drew near, many interest groups pressed Churchill to look with favour on their particular needs. On March 2, in a letter to Balfour, he had agreed to a substantial increase in university grants. On March 10 he had received a deputation from the Association of British Chambers of Commerce, urging him to reduce income tax and to restore the Penny Post. On March 8 he had written to his wife:

The work gets heavier every day. All this week I am to have a stream of deputations, and every morning my boxes are full of stiff papers about the Budget. I have decided not to try the third volume and to retire from the literary arena, at any rate for some time to come. I could not do justice to it and my other commitments. Moreover the taxes ate it nearly all.

'I am at work all day long now,' Churchill wrote to his wife again on March 10—from eight in the morning, he explained, to eight at night. 'Today and tomorrow,' he added, 'I am leading the House of Commons in Baldwin's absence. He made a gt point of my doing so. I have not been formally in charge since 1910!' He had lunched the previous day with Lord Rothermere, who said he would support the budget 'what ever it was. If I took off taxes good—if not—then he wd applaud the courage of stern finance.'

On March 15 Churchill dictated a progress report to his wife. He also sent her a more personal covering note:

I am tired & have rather a head at the end of a long week. I do hope you are having rest, peace & sunshine & that you will return really refreshed. I have polished off two more articles to help pay the Income Tax: & perhaps I may get another one out of myself this afternoon or tomorrow morning.

Mary is flourishing. She comes & sits with me in the mornings & is sometimes most gracious. Diana[1] is just back from school & we are all planning to go to see Randolph this afternoon.

When do you think you will return my dear one. Do not abridge yr holiday if it is doing you good—But of course I feel far safer from worry and depression when you are with me & when I can confide in yr sweet soul. It has given me so much joy to see you becoming stronger & settling down in this new abode. Health & nerves are the first requisites of happiness. I *do* think you have made great progress since the year began, in spite of all the work & burdens I have put on you.

The most precious thing I have in life is yr love for me. I reproach myself for many shortcomings. You are a rock & I depend on you & rest on you. Come back to me therefore as soon as you can.

In his report Churchill wrote:

The week has passed in a whirl of deputations, sometimes as many as four a day, and I have had to listen patiently to every kind of request for relief of taxation and to give answers which revealed nothing. I think, however, I have succeeded in making courtesy a substitute for more solid services.

We are still ignorant of what the revenue will be for this year or next. But in a week from now trustworthy figures will be available, and from that

---

[1] Diana Churchill, 1906–1963 Churchill's eldest child. In 1932 she married the eldest son of Sir Abe Bailey, John Milner Bailey (from whom she obtained a divorce in 1935). In 1935 she married Duncan Sandys MP.

moment I must lock every secret in my bosom until the 28th of April; and I weigh and balance all the possibilities of my plan.

In the second week of March Churchill's mother-in-law, Lady Blanche Hozier, fell seriously ill at her home in Dieppe. Clementine Churchill hurried from the south of France to be with her mother. On March 21 she telegraphed to her husband that Lady Blanche was dying. On receiving his wife's telegram, Churchill wrote at once from Chartwell:

Yr Mamma is a gt woman: & her life has been a noble life. When I think of all the courage & tenacity & self denial that she showed during the long hard years when she was fighting to bring up you & Nellie[1] & Bill,[2] I feel what a true mother & grand woman she proved herself, & I am more glad & proud to think her blood flows in the veins of our children.

My darling I grieve for you. An old & failing life going out on the tide, after the allotted span has been spent & after most joys have faded is not a case for human pity. It is only a part of the immense tragedy of our existence here below against wh both hope & faith have rebelled. It is only what we all expect & await—unless cut off untimely. But the loss of a mother severs a chord in the heart and makes life seem lonely & its duration fleeting. I know the sense of amputation from my own experience three years ago.

I deeply sorrow for yr pain. I greatly admired & liked yr mother. She was an ideal mother-in-law. Never shall I allow that relationship to be spoken of with mockery—for her sake. I am pleased to think that perhaps she wd also have given me a good character. At any rate I am sure our marriage & life together were one of the gt satisfactions of her life. . . .

The death of Lord Curzon on March 20 was another break with the past. 'I marched in poor G. Curzon's cortege this morning,' Churchill wrote to his wife on March 25. 'The service was dull and dreary.' And he added: 'He faced his end with fortitude & philosophy. I am vy sorry he is gone. I did not think the tributes were vy generous. I wd not have been grateful for such stuff. But he did not inspire affection, nor represent gt causes.'

Clementine Churchill remained at Dieppe, looking after her dying mother. Churchill frequently telephoned to Dieppe for news. 'The

[1] Nellie Hozier, 1888–1957. Clementine Churchill's sister. Served as a nurse in Belgium, 1914. Captured by the Germans, but released almost immediately. In 1915 she married Colonel Bertram Romilly.

[2] William Ogilvy Hozier, 1888–1921. Clementine Churchill's brother. Entered the Navy, 1904. Lieutenant, 1909. Qualified as a German interpreter, 1910. Commanded the Destroyer *Thorn*, 1914–15. First Lieutenant on board the cruiser *Edgar*, at the Dardanelles, 1915–16. Commanded the *Clematis*, 1916–18. Lieutenant Commander, 1918.

telephone talks are a comfort,' he wrote. On March 29 Lady Blanche Hozier died.

The bulk of Churchill's work and correspondence during March concerned the new insurance scheme. On March 4 he had received a deputation from the National Conference of Employers' Organizations. The spokesman for the deputation, Lord Weir,[1] warned that the incidence of insurance schemes was beginning to 'impair' the national character, undermining thrift and self-reliance. But Churchill still adhered to the views which he had held so strongly more than fifteen years before, telling the deputation:

Personally, I feel that that system of insurance, whatever may be the effects on the self-reliance of the individual, is going to be an absolutely inseparable element in our social life and eventually must have the effect of attaching the mind of the people, although their language and mood in many cases may not seem to indicate it. It must lead to the stability and order of the general structure.

Four days later Weir replied: 'Once again, I plead that employment at decent wages is the most important factor in the security of the worker's home,' while on March 20 Churchill set out his views on some of the details of his scheme in a 'Secret & Personal' letter to Neville Chamberlain:

It is clearly contrary to public policy to allow the present condition to continue under which the dependent and often helpless children of a widow are deprived of the care and attention they ought to have because the mother is compelled to work long hours and laboriously to provide a bare maintenance for them. This then is the foundation on which our treatment of the uncovenanted should be built. . . .

So far as the allowances to children are concerned, I think they should be continued to 14 in all cases, and thereafter to 16 if the child is still attending school. This would put a strong premium on better education and discourage early blind alley occupations. I do not think an allowance ought to be paid in

---

[1] William Douglas Weir, 1877–1959. Shipping contractor; his family won its first Royal Navy contract in 1896. A pioneer motor car manufacturer. Majority shareholder in G. & J. Weir Ltd, manufacturers of machinery for steamships. Scottish Director of Munitions, July 1915–January 1917. Controller of Aeronautical Supplies, and Member of the Air Board 1917. Knighted, 1917. Director-General of Aircraft Production, Ministry of Munitions, 1917–19. Created Baron, 1918. Secretary of State for Air, April–December 1918. Adviser, Air Ministry, 1935–39. Created Viscount, 1938. Director-General of Explosives, Ministry of Supply, 1939. Chairman of the Tank Board, 1942.

respect of a child between 14 and 16 who is withdrawn from school and earning 7/- or 8/- a week running errands.

On March 22 Churchill wrote to his wife from Chartwell: 'I have been working all day (Sunday) at pensions & am vy tired.' Two days later, at 11 Downing Street, he spoke to a deputation of Old Age Pensioners, minuting that same day for his advisers: 'It is when misfortune comes upon the household, when prolonged unemployment, or old age, or sickness, or the death of the breadwinner comes upon this household, that you see how narrow was the margin on which it was apparently living so prosperously, and in a few months the result of the thrift of years may be swept away, and the house broken up.' On April 2 he wrote to the Government Actuary, Sir Alfred Watson, asking if the State could make an additional contribution to unemployment insurance which would benefit both employers and employees, both 'already burdened' by insurance contributions; and in another letter to Neville Chamberlain on April 3 he explained that his aim was that all pensions should begin at 65, and that widows in particular should be provided for 'from the very outset' of the new scheme. Men over 65 should, he wrote, pay £1 a year for three years, as a small contribution towards their pension of £25 a year. 'The whole principle of contribution is valuable,' Churchill wrote, 'it avoids pauperisation and the stigma of doles; it will promote each man's self-respect and make him value his pension the more when he gets it.'

On April 6 the Minister of Labour, Sir Arthur Steel-Maitland, asked Churchill to delay the Insurance Bill until at least the following year. 'Apart from any other reasons,' he wrote, 'benefits are soon forgotten and the nearer this is to the next Election the better.' Steel-Maitland also felt that the Bill should be changed specifically into a children's, rather than a widow's bill. 'Public sentiment is for it,' he explained, 'because of the children *emphatically*, rather than the women.' Churchill had no intention of pandering to purely electoral considerations, replying that same day:

(1) It would fatally derange the balance of the Budget, and I should have to recast every plan if Insurance were postponed.
(2) We are committed to pensions for *Widows*; that is the whole character of the pledges which have been given.
 (*a*) Surely also it would be invidious to leave the Mother with the care of the children without any provision of her own, and solely dependent upon what she could make out of their keep.
 (*b*) There are anomalies in the inauguration of every new plan; but it is

surely an important distinction that the covenanted widow will have paid for her benefits through her husband, and the uncovenanted will not.

(c) A covenanted widow is only very partially 'subsidized'.

(d) The Bill provides 7/6 for the eldest orphan and 6/- each for the rest of the family.

On April 6 Sir Otto Niemeyer explained to Churchill that, as a result of the insurance scheme, there would have to be very strict budgeting in the following years, no further reduction of income tax rates and no bowing to the strong public demand for the re-introduction of the penny post. 'You are introducing a big budget,' Niemeyer wrote, 'taking many risks. In order to achieve large projects, we are counting every penny of possible revenue and leaving ourselves practically no margin . . .' Churchill replied on the following day that he accepted Niemeyer's argument, and agreed with his assessment. 'This is a fine rampart,' he minuted.

On April 8 Sir Alfred Watson suggested that Churchill point out in his Budget speech that for a widow to obtain the equivalent benefit from the £600 capital value of the proposed widows' pension, costing a worker fourpence a week under Churchill's scheme—her husband would have had to set aside four shillings a week under a voluntary life insurance policy. 'Instead of 4/-,' Watson wrote, 'you charge him 4d and his employer 4d. . . . Moreover you give him other benefits if he lives ie the pension at 65 for himself and his wife.' Churchill commented in the margin: 'Wonderful!'

That same day Churchill explained to the House of Commons the progress that had been made in setting up a Reparations pool, whereby Britain would be paid its share in sterling which had been acquired by the sale of German goods in Britain. That evening Baldwin wrote to the King:

Even the Treasury would have found it difficult to present a Minister with a more complicated and technical subject, but Mr Churchill steered a wonderful course through all the shoals and reefs which might have beset him, and gave an illustration of the most lucid exposition which won for him the respectful admiration of the House and must hearten Mr Churchill for the more serious ordeal which awaits him.

On April 9 Parliament rose for the Easter vacation. Budget day was fixed for April 28. On April 11 the *Democrat* noted: 'In these days of national holiday making there is one Minister who is keeping his nose to the grindstone. Winston Churchill will be hard at it whilst others play.' Six days later Churchill wrote to Baldwin: 'Everything is moving "according to plan", and all will be in readiness by zero hour.' He had, he wrote, carried out 'all the negotiations' about the Gold Standard with the Federal Reserve Bank, as approved by both Baldwin and Austen Chamberlain at their conference on March 20. He had also settled, with Neville Chamberlain, all the outstanding details of the insurance scheme. He and Chamberlain had 'worked together in complete harmony', and in consultation with the Ministry of Labour, the Ministry of Agriculture and a small Cabinet Committee set up a month before. Churchill hoped that the full Cabinet would approve the scheme at its meeting on April 22: 'It would of course be disastrous,' he added, 'if hesitation and division arose now that we are so very near to the battlefield.'

At the Cabinet meeting on April 22 there was some disagreement about the insurance scheme. Steel-Maitland in particular felt that the State benefits were too high. But after Neville Chamberlain had explained the scope of the Bill, and Churchill had outlined its financial aspects, Baldwin gave the scheme his strong support, and it was approved.

On April 23 Churchill sent the King a fifteen-page summary of his budget proposals. He had prepared them, he wrote, 'from the first weeks of taking office . . . in the closest accord with the Prime Minister'. At one point in his letter he wrote:

Many years ago immediately after the introduction in 1906 of the original scheme of non-contributory Old Age Pensions, when Mr Churchill was President of the Board of Trade, he was struck by the immense opportunities which the State gift of pensions at 70 offered for a contributory Insurance Scheme for pensions at 65. By providing for people after 70 the State virtually took off all the bad risks, and the actuarial possibilities of a scheme providing for the earlier period become extraordinary. It is strange that this should so long have been neglected. A treasure almost measureless could be made available for the people by contributions which at any rate in the earlier years are comparatively very small.

Nationwide insurance was, Churchill added, a miracle, which gave 'millions of people a stake in the country which they will have created largely by their own contributory efforts'.

The Cabinet met again on Monday April 25, when it approved all Churchill's financial measures, including the decision to return to the Gold Standard. That same day Lord Stamfordham[1] wrote from Buckingham Palace that the King had read Churchill's letter 'with deep interest, and, I may add, much approval', and that he congratulated Churchill on the results 'of your anxious labours of the past five months'.

---

[1] Arthur John Bigge, 1849–1931. Entered Army, 1869. Entered the Royal Household, 1880. Private Secretary to Queen Victoria, 1895–1901; to George V, 1910–31. Created Baron Stamfordham, 1911. His only son was killed in action on 15 May 1915.

7

Churchill's First Budget: 'The Appeasement of Class Bitterness'

CHURCHILL spent the weekend before his first Budget at Chartwell, putting the final touches to his Budget speech. 'Remember that you will have a very friendly house to speak to,' his cousin Frederick Guest wrote to him on April 26. 'It is *almost* the biggest day we have been looking forward to for, now, nearly a generation. There can only be *one* bigger,' and General Seely wrote on April 27: 'One line to wish you all possible success tomorrow in the House of Commons —indeed I am certain that success is assured. But it is such a splendidly romantic episode that you should complete what your Father was robbed of doing that a word of good wishes from your oldest friend may be permitted.'

When Churchill rose to speak, shortly after half past three on April 28, his wife was in the Strangers' Gallery to hear him, together with their son Randolph and their daughter Diana. He spoke for more than two and a half hours. 'No country,' he told the House of Commons, 'had ever made the exertions this country had made since the war to pay its debts and meet all its obligations with strictness and punctuality.' In the previous year £34 million pounds had been repaid, reducing the total debt to £7,646 million. Since he himself had become Chancellor, the interest to be paid on the debt had been reduced by £2½ million; a reduction which could only benefit the taxpayer, and which reduced the annual payments to £67 million a year. A further £12 million had been paid by Germany in the financial year 1924–5 as Reparations.

Churchill then told the House of the Government's decision to return to the Gold Standard. 'No responsible authority,' he declared, 'has advocated any other policy. It has always been a matter of course that we should return to it. . . .' Successive Governments had made it their aim, and the Report of Currency and Banking Committee had been 'unanimous'. At this point a Labour MP, John Jones,[1] called out: 'Prisoner in chains,' but Churchill continued:

We have entered a period on both sides of the Atlantic when political and economic stability seems to be more assured than it has been for some years. If this opportunity were missed, it might not recur soon, and the whole finance of the country would be over clouded for an indefinite period by the fact of uncertainty. 'Now is the appointed time.'

The return to gold, Churchill explained, would not lead to a rush of speculation. Not only had Britain accumulated a gold reserve of £153 million, it had also accumulated over 'many many months' the whole of the £166 million needed to pay the June and December instalments of Britain's debt to the United States. At the same time, he added, the United States had offered Britain credit facilities of not less than $300 million. 'These great credits . . .' Churchill warned, 'have been obtained and built up as a solemn warning to speculators of every kind. . . .'

Churchill then announced the new sources of revenue. There was to be a small duty on hops, to bring in £130,000 in 1925 and £250,000 a year thereafter; a small sum, but, he said, 'I cannot afford to disdain any revenue. Even the most modest contributions are thankfully received.' There were also to be new duties on certain luxuries, and in particular on all raw and artificial silk. 'These duties,' he explained, 'do not fall on the masses of the people. They do not touch the necessaries or interfere with the modest comfort of daily life.' But they would bring in more than £10 million in 1925, and £20 million in 1926. 'To some the imposition of these duties is a relish,' he said, 'to others a target, and to me they are a revenue.' This new revenue represented, he said, 'enormous power' in the hands of the State, and he intended to use it to protect 'the security of the home of the wage earner'. He went on to declare:

The average British workman in good health, full employment and standard wages, does not regard himself and his family as an object of compassion. But when exceptional misfortune descends upon the cottage home with the slender margin upon which it is floated, or there is a year of

---

[1] John Joseph Jones, 1873–1941. Secretary, London Transport Workers Federation District Committee, 1911–13. General Organizer, National Union of General and Municipal Workers. Labour MP for Silvertown, 1918–40.

misfortune, distress, or unemployment, or, above all, the loss of the bread-winner, it leaves this once happy family in the grip of the greatest calamity.

Although the threat of adversity has been active all these years, no effective provision has been made by the great mass of the labouring classes for their widows and families in the event of death. I am not reproaching them, but it is the greatest need at the present time.

If I may change to a military metaphor, it is not the sturdy marching troops that need extra reward and indulgence. It is the stragglers, the exhausted, the weak, the wounded, the veterans, the widows and orphans to whom the ambulances of State aid should be directed.

Churchill then explained the new Insurance scheme in detail. Its origin, he explained, was the Committee appointed by Baldwin in the summer of 1922, when Baldwin himself had been Chancellor of the Exchequer. 'The forethought of the Prime Minister,' he explained, 'has enabled me to make this announcement today.' The Committee's material, he said, had been available to Neville Chamberlain and himself, 'and we have done our best to frame a scheme'. Fifteen million wage-earners would be affected, and with them a further fifteen million dependants. Both employer and employee would contribute. Churchill then explained why the scheme was needed at all:

If everybody in the ambit of Health Insurance had from the age of 16 onwards contributed 4d a week and had 4d a week contributed by their employers, with women at half rates, a self-supporting scheme would now be in operation which would afford 10s a week to widows, with allowances to orphans and ordinary children, and secondly, 10s a week to all married persons and their wives from 65 years onwards.

But such a scheme is not in existence, and the vast majority can never contribute on any scale sufficient to pay for benefits on this scale. If left to its own resources, the scheme could not be brought into full operation for many years, and whole generation of men and women might toil their lives out before the distribution of benefits would be wide enough sensibly to raise the general level of comfort among the masses.

Here, then, is where the State, with its long and stable finance, with its carefully-guarded credit, can march in to fill the immense gap.

Churchill then revealed the full extent of the new pensions. Widows would receive ten shillings a week for life. Eldest children would receive five shillings and other children three shillings until they reached the age of fourteen and a half. Orphan children would receive seven shillings and sixpence a week. More than 200,000 widows and 350,000 children would benefit under the scheme. All other pensions would come into force at the age of 65. At the same time the Government had decided 'to sweep away altogether restrictions, inquisitions, and means test'. After this Act was passed, he said, 'it would be nobody's business what they had or how they employed their time'.

Reflecting on the 'miracle of nation-wide insurance', Churchill told the House of Commons:

I like the association of this new scheme of widows' pensions and earlier old-age pensions with the dying-out of the cost of the war pensions. I like to think that the sufferings, the sacrifices, the sorrow of the war have sown a seed from which a strong tree will grow, under which, perhaps many generations of British people may find shelter against some at least of the storms of life. This is far the finest war memorial you could set up to the men who gave their lives, their limits, or their health, and those who lost their dear ones in the country's cause.

There was still a surplus to be disposed of. The penny post was not to be restored, but for a cost of £1,720,000 a year Churchill had decided to remove all duties on Empire dried fruits, and to give increased preference to Imperial-grown tobacco, wines and sugar. At the same time, super tax would be reduced, to be compensated for by an increase in death duties.

Churchill had kept his most eagerly awaited announcement till last. Only after he had been speaking for more than two hours did he reveal his plans for income tax: it would be reduced, with the greater benefits to the lowest income groups. Earned incomes up to £2,000 would be given a 10% reduction, and the scale of allowances would increasingly help the less well-off. A married man with three children, earning £500 a year, would pay 44½% less. Finally, the standard rate of income tax would be reduced by sixpence in the pound, from four shillings and sixpence to four shillings.

In conclusion, Churchill told the House of Commons that he had tried in the budget 'to balance it fairly in the scale of social justice as between one class and another', and that he intended his scheme to be 'national, and not class or party in its extent or intention'. His speech ended:

I cherish the hope, Sir, that by liberating the production of new wealth from some of the shackles of taxation the Budget may stimulate enterprise and accelerate industrial revival, and that by giving a far greater measure of security to the mass of wage-earners, their wives and children, it may promote contentment and stability, and make our Island more truly a home for all these people.

It was ten past six when Churchill resumed his seat, to much enthusiastic applause. 'I have heard 40 Budget statements exactly,' Lord

Mildmay[1] wrote that evening, '& I have never heard one that kept my unflagging interest all through. I was sitting very near your wife & children, and it made one happy to see *their* happiness in your success.' 'I heard your speech described as Gladstonian,' Churchill's cousin Ivor Wimborne wrote on the following day, 'and I suppose no higher praise could be found for a budget statement: may it lead on to all the greater things that I am sure the future holds for you.' Stanley Baldwin wrote that day to the King:

The general impression was that Mr Churchill rose magnificently to the occasion. His speech was not only a great feat of endurance, lasting as it did for two hours and forty minutes, but was a first-rate example of Mr Churchill's characteristic style. At one moment he would be expounding quietly and lucidly facts and figures relating to the financial position during the past and current years. At another moment, inspired and animated by the old political controversies on the subject of tariff reform, he indulged in witty levity and humour which come as a refreshing relief in the dry atmosphere of a Budget speech. At another moment, when announcing the introduction of a scheme for widows and mothers pensions, he soared into emotional flights of rhetoric in which he has few equals; and throughout the speech he showed that he is not only possessed of consummate ability as a parliamentarian, but also all the versatility of an actor.

Baldwin concluded that Churchill's speech 'was one of the most striking Budget speeches of recent years', and that the widows and orphans pension scheme, 'bold in its character and conception', would establish Churchill's reputation as Chancellor of the Exchequer.

The Budget debate was opened in the House of Commons on April 29. Philip Snowden's remark that it was 'the worst rich man's Budget ever presented' was greeted with derisive laughter from the Conservative benches. During the debate a Liberal MP, Sir Alfred Mond,[2] criticized the return to the Gold Standard, an act, he said, which would 'enslave' Britain to America. On the following day there was further criticism, led by Churchill's electoral opponent of 1923, F. W. Pethick-

---

[1] Francis Bingham Mildmay, 1861–1947. Educated at Eton and Trinity College Cambridge. Unionist MP for Totnes, 1885–1922. On active service in South Africa, 1899–1901 and in Europe, 1914–19 (despatches four times). A Director of the Great Western Railway Company, 1914–45. Privy Councillor, 1916. Created Baron, 1922. President of the National Unionist Association, 1922–23. Lord Lieutenant of Devon, 1928–36.

[2] Alfred Moritz Mond, 1868–1930. A Director of Brunner, Mond & Co, 1895. Created, by 1926, the Imperial Chemical Industries (ICI), with a capital of £95,000,000. Liberal MP 1906–10, 1910–23 and 1924–28. Created Baronet, 1910. First Commissioner of Works, 1916–21. Minister of Health, 1921–22. Joined the Conservative Party, 1926. Created Baron Melchett, 1928.

Lawrence, and one of his former Liberal colleagues, Walter Runciman. But his cousin Frederick Guest announced his intention, together with a small group of other Liberals, to support the Budget as a sincere attempt to institute social reform, while a recently elected Conservative MP, Captain Harold Macmillan,[1] caught, as *The Times* recorded, 'the spirit of audacity' and gave the social reform measures in the Budget his 'undubious and provocative acceptance'.

In his reply to Labour criticisms, Churchill warned that it was in the interest of the trade unions, as well of employers, 'to see that there was not growing up a habit of qualifying for unemployment relief'. His remark caused an immediate uproar. It was, declared George Lansbury,[2] 'an insult to the working classes'. Churchill tried to continue with his remarks, but Labour protests continued, and he could not make himself heard. To Labour shouts of 'Shame' and 'Withdraw' Churchill replied: 'I do not withdraw for one moment. On the contrary, we shall have to probe it.' And he added, amid further Labour cries: 'Are we not to have free speech in this House?' But the interruptions continued, and Churchill remarked defiantly that there was not a single British working man who would allow Labour members to accuse him of a rich man's Budget, and then not allow him to reply. 'Withdraw,' the Labour men shouted. 'I withdraw nothing,' Churchill retorted. 'I would rather never speak another word in this House than withdraw that.' To the accompaniment of further Labour protests, Churchill then sat down, unable to continue with his speech. The next speaker was a Communist member, Mr Saklatvala,[3] who began his speech: 'the Chancellor having created this interruption, it falls upon the

---

[1] Maurice Harold Macmillan, 1894–1986. Educated at Eton and Balliol College Oxford. On active service, Grenadier Guards, 1914–18 (wounded three times). Conservative MP for Stockton-on-Tees, 1924–29, and 1931–45. Author of *Reconstruction: A Plea for a National Policy*, 1933; *Planning for Employment*, 1935; *The Next Five Years*, *The Middle Way*, 1938; and *Economic Aspects of Defence*, 1939. Parliamentary Secretary, Ministry of Supply, 1940–42. Privy Councillor, 1952. Minister Resident, Allied HQ, North-West Africa, 1942–45. Secretary for Air, 1945. Minister of Housing and Local Government, 1951–54. Minister of Defence, 1954–55. Secretary of State for Foreign Affairs, 1955. Chancellor of the Exchequer, 1955–57. Prime Minister, 1957–63. Chancellor of the University of Oxford from 1960. Created Earl of Stockton, 1984.

[2] George Lansbury, 1859–1940. Left school at the age of 14. Was employed unloading coal trucks for the Great Eastern Railway. First attempted to enter Parliament, 1895. Labour MP for Bow and Bromley, 1910–12. Resigned to fight the seat as a supporter of women's suffrage. Not re-elected until 1922. Mayor of Poplar, 1919–20 and 1936–37. Editor of the *Daily Herald*, 1919–25. First Commissioner of Works in the second Labour Government, 1929–31. Leader of the Labour Party, 1931–35.

[3] Shapurji Saklatvala, 1874–1936. A Parsi, born in Bombay. Joined his family firm of Tata and Sons, and helped to establish the Tata Iron and Steel Works in India. Came to England, 1905. Active in the Independent Labour Party from 1910. Communist MP for North Battersea, 1922–23 and 1924–29.

revolutionary Communist to restore order'. A minute later, Churchill left the Chamber.

In describing this 'most deplorable' scene to the King on May 1 Baldwin noted that some Labour MPs:

... resented in particular Mr Churchill's suggestion that some of the unemployment was due to malingering, partly because it came from Mr Churchill, and partly because they must have been only too conscious that the suggestion had some foundation in fact. It was, however, unfortunate that Mr Churchill faced with such a situation, notwithstanding the fact that he was innocent of any guilty intention, did not adopt a more conciliatory attitude. It is true that at this moment and during the scenes which followed, he retained complete control of his temper, but his attitude of bold defiance undoubtedly helped to stimulate the anger of his opponents.

On the afternoon of May 1, at a Primrose League demonstration in the Albert Hall, Churchill described the pensions scheme as 'only the first instalment of the Government's social policy', and he went on to answer Snowden's charge that it was a rich man's Budget:

Let the Socialists go after January 4 next to the 200,000 widows, who, with 350,000 children, will be enjoying their pensions, and let them say to these people—'You are the victims of a rich man's Budget.' Let them go into 6,000,000 homes and tell the wives who will have behind them the guarantee that they will not be left penniless if anything happens to the breadwinner. ... Let them go to the 75,000 veterans, over 70 years of age, who are not allowed to receive their pensions because they are still earning wages by honest work, and who after July 1926, will find all these inquisitions and restrictions and disabilities swept away. Let them say to them—'All this is part of a dodge to enable the Conservative Government to relieve the poor, starving supertax payer'. Let them go in 1928 to the 500,000 men and women of 65 who will march or hobble up to receive their pensions and say—'Comrades, we meant to give you these pensions ourselves. We would have given them to you on a non-contributory basis, but we had to go and help our Russian friends first.'

Writing in the *New Leader*, Arthur Ponsonby[1] remarked: 'His sympathy for the poor was eloquent, his sympathy with the rich was practical.' That same day Neville Chamberlain wrote in his diary:

[1] Arthur Augustus William Harry Ponsonby, 1871–1946. Educated at Eton and Balliol College Oxford. Page of Honour to Queen Victoria, 1882–87. Served in the Diplomatic Service, 1894–1902. Liberal MP for Sterling Burghs, 1908–18. Labour MP for Sheffield Brightside, 1922–30. Under-Secretary of State for Foreign Affairs, 1924. Parliamentary Secretary, Ministry of Transport, 1929–31. Created Baron, 1930. Chancellor of the Duchy of Lancaster, 1931. Leader of the Opposition in the House of Lords, 1931–35.

Winston's exposition of the Budget was a masterly performance, and though my office and some of my colleagues are indignant at his taking to himself the credit for a scheme which belongs to the Ministry of Health, I did not myself think that I had any reason to complain of what he said. In a sense it *is* his scheme. We were pledged to something of the kind, but I don't think we should have done it this year if he had not made it part of his Budget scheme, and in my opinion he does deserve special personal credit for his initiative and drive.

Where the return to Gold was commented on in the Press, it received approval. 'By this bold declaration,' wrote *Time and Tide* on May 1, 'the Government has made a real contribution to the recovery of world stability and confidence.' 'In a careful balancing of all the advantages and disadvantages,' the Labour MP William Graham[1] wrote in the *New Leader* that same day, 'it seems to us to be the only possible course for a country which has much to gain, in the export trade particularly, by an exchange stabilisation,' and in its leading article on May 2, *The Times* declared that it had never doubted 'that the best interests of the country would be served by returning to the gold standard as soon as the course became practicable and safe'.

The Gold Standard Bill was debated in the House of Commons on May 4. Churchill's son Randolph was under the Gallery, and *The Times* reported an 'enormous crowd of members' assembled to hear the debate. Walter Guinness opened the discussion by setting out the Government's case. In reply, Philip Snowden said that although he was not opposed to a return to Gold, he felt that the decision had come too soon, and would continue the too hasty policy of deflation which had 'ruined thousands of businesses'. Another former Chancellor of the Exchequer, Sir Robert Horne, felt that it was best to trust the experts of the Currency Committee. In reply to the debate, Churchill insisted that the Government had only decided 'to shackle themselves to realities', that prices would remain stable, that the value of wages would be preserved, that it was essential to act with the Dominions, and that Britain must always try to act with the United States—'our chief shop and chief customer'. In its report of the debate, *The Times* noted that Churchill's remarks were greeted with 'tremendous cheers'. That same day Lord Beaverbrook wrote to Brendan Bracken: 'I knew from the beginning he would

[1] William Graham, 1887–1932. Junior clerkship, War Office, 1903. Entered Edinburgh University, 1911; MA in economic science, 1915. Labour MP for Edinburgh Central, 1918–31. Member of the Royal Commission on Income Tax, 1919; of the Speaker's Conference on Devolution, 1919–20; of the Royal Commission on the Universities of Oxford and Cambridge, 1920–21. Member of the Medical Research Council, 1920–28. Financial Secretary to the Treasury in the first Labour Government, 1924. Privy Councillor, 1924.

give in to the Bankers on the Gold Standard, which, I think, is the biggest sin in this budget.' Writing to the King on May 5, Baldwin described Churchill's speech as 'the best speech of the sitting', and he added: 'He probably approached the subject with a sense of deep humility, but the eloquence which he brought to bear and the effectiveness of his arguments might have created the impression that he had a complete mastery of the technicalities of the subject. He was not content with walking on a tight-rope: he seemed to revel in the dangers of dancing on it. . . .'

On May 13 Churchill was the guest of the British Bankers' Association at their annual dinner in London. He was not, he said, going to 'eulogize' his budget. 'It must make its own field, it must defend itself entirely by its intrinsic merits,' he said. At the end of his speech he stressed the need for 'a national policy and not a party policy', which would help 'every class and every section', and he added:

That is our aim. The appeasement of class bitterness, the promotion of a spirit of co-operation, the stabilisation of our national life, the building of the financial and social plans upon a three or four years' basis instead of a few months basis, an earnest effort to give the country some period of recuperation after the enormous efforts it has made and the vicissitudes to which it has been subjected. . . .

8

1925: 'Alarm Bells Ringing'

AS he had done throughout Lloyd George's premiership, Churchill continued to maintain his deep interest in foreign policy. On 4 December 1924 the Committee of Imperial Defence met to discuss a League of Nations Protocol on arbitration and disarmament.[1] Churchill argued against Britain undertaking international obligations 'of an unlimited character'. It was better, he suggested, to work 'in stages, by means of regional agreements', and 'by the maintenance of good understanding between various groups of Powers' within the framework of the League. He also favoured the setting up of demilitarized zones in disputed areas. To begin with, he told his colleagues

... such a zone might be drawn up between France and Germany, and various Powers might be induced to guarantee the sanctity of such a zone. Whichever of the two Powers, France or Germany, was the first to violate this zone, that Power would then become 'the aggressor', and would be dealt with as such by the Powers who were signatories to the regional agreement.

As a second stage Churchill suggested that the same scheme could be applied to the Polish side and a demilitarized zone laid down there. He pointed out that all the Powers who were signatories to one agreement might not necessarily be signatories to another. Such schemes might eventually be applied 'to all points of danger in the world. . . .'

The meeting of December 4 decided to reject the Geneva Protocol, but in doing so to put forward some alternative suggestion. While discussions on this continued, Churchill went to France for the debt

---

[1] Nine Cabinet Ministers were present: Baldwin (President), Curzon (Chairman), Churchill, Amery, Worthington-Evans, Lloyd-Greame, Bridgeman, Hoare and Cecil. Among the others present were Earl Balfour, Admiral of the Fleet Earl Beatty, Air Chief Marshal Sir Hugh Trenchard, General the Earl of Cavan, Sir Eyre Crowe and Sir Warren Fisher.

negotiations, and on 10 January 1925 he sent Austen Chamberlain a full account of his conversation with the French President. Doumergue had been anxious to discuss with Churchill the future of Anglo-French relations, believing that throughout the world, 'French and British interests were one', and explaining to Churchill: 'Both were responsible for great Mahometan populations. Both were affected by the rapidly developing propaganda of Bolshevism among the coloured people.' It was essential, he added, for Britain and France to create a unity 'which the Germans would realize was unbreakable'. Churchill replied that Germany 'would perhaps rest content with the arrangement of Versailles', as far as her western frontier was concerned. But as to Germany's Polish frontier, Churchill told Doumergue:

I was personally convinced that she would never acquiesce permanently in the condition of her eastern frontier. This then was the great cause of anxiety which brooded over Europe. The wars of Frederick the Great as well as those of Peter the Great had arisen from deep causes and ambitions which so far from having passed away, were now associated with great historic memories.

Churchill then told Doumergue:

I did not feel that the British position in Asia or Africa was subject to any grave danger at the present time, certainly not to any danger comparable to the awful risk we should run if a continuance of the age-long quarrel between France and Germany led, in some future generation, to our being involved in a renewal of the European war.

I said that of course I was only expressing a personal opinion, but one which I had expressed in public on many occasions, and which it was well known I had held for several years, namely, that the one real security against a renewal of war would be a complete agreement between England, France and Germany. That alone would give the security which all were seeking, and that alone would enable the commerce of Europe to expand to such dimensions that the existing burden of debts and reparations would be supportable and not crushing.

Churchill added that it would be better to try to come to good terms with Germany, and to settle her grievances, than to have a defensive alliance between France and Britain 'while the fundamental antagonism between France and Germany continued unappeased'.

Austen Chamberlain, however, supported by a sub-committee headed by Sir Maurice Hankey, favoured a direct Anglo-French pact, based upon the maintenance of the Versailles Treaty, and guaranteeing France and Belgium's borders, against attack. At a meeting of the Committee of Imperial Defence on February 13, Chamberlain set this

out to his colleagues. During the meeting Churchill spoke strongly
against Chamberlain's proposal for a unilateral British commitment to
defend France against German attack. 'We do not feel we should be
justified,' Churchill said, 'in taking these great burdens upon the country
in the absence of the United States,' and he added that it would be quite
wrong 'to ask the people of this country, at this juncture, to bind themselves to go to war on the side of France without leaving us to a very full
latitude of judging the circumstances and occasion of the quarrel'.
Churchill went on to tell his colleagues:

This war which has occurred between France and Germany several times
has broken up the world. What guarantee have we got while things are going
as they are that we shall not have another war. In fact, it seems as if we were
moving towards it, although it may not be for twenty years, certainly not
until Germany has been able to acquire some methods of waging war,
chemically or otherwise.

It was essential, Churchill continued, for the Versailles Treaty to be
recast as far as Germany's eastern frontier was concerned, and for
Britain to help bring about 'a real peace' between France and Germany,
as well as 'a substantial rectification' of Germany's frontier with Poland.
Only then should England offer guarantees, simultaneously to both
France and Germany, to make a 'real peace'.

Balfour opposed Churchill's suggestion, arguing that any alteration of
the Polish or the Czech frontiers would mean' the tearing up' of the
Versailles Treaty, and ought therefore to be discounted, and at a further
meeting of the Committee of Imperial Defence on February 19, Austen
Chamberlain again argued in favour of an immediate guarantee to
France. Churchill pleaded for delay. 'I think,' he said, 'you may have
France in a much better state of mind in the course of two or three
years'; then there could be 'a better and more general solution'. But, he
warned, a bilateral pact with France would be 'a tremendous risk'.

The disagreement between Austen Chamberlain and Churchill could
not be resolved. When the meeting was over, Churchill began to dictate
a series of notes on the European situation. On February 21 he sent a
copy to Balfour. 'I am sure,' he wrote in his covering letter, 'France will
come to us if we do not offer ourselves to her. . . . What is wanted is a
better atmosphere, and that I believe is slowly coming.' He agreed with
Balfour that it would not be wise to concentrate too much 'upon
"Armageddon No 2"', but in his notes he wrote at length of the dangers
of another war, 'victory in which would compass our ruin scarcely less
surely than defeat'. Such a war could only begin between France and

Germany. His notes continued: 'This antagonism, which has lasted through centuries, is unappeased. All the minor feuds of Europe group themselves around it. Everyone feels that it may lead to another World conflict,' and he pointed out: 'Germany is prostrate. In an age when lethal apparatus is almost everything, she is disarmed. At the worst there is a breathing space, measured by decades. Our problem is how to use this breathing space to end the quarrel. That problem dominates all others.'

Sooner or later, Churchill went on, 'Germany will be rearmed', either with existing weapons, or with new inventions. France might decide to attack Germany before this re-arming process was complete. Britain would then be obliged to support France, possibly even as a result of some German military action elsewhere, such as 'aggression against Poland'. In such a case, although France and Germany were at war, Britain might not feel bound 'by treaty or sentiment' to join in. War would have returned to Europe, and Britain would be powerless to avert it. What, he added, would Britain then do, with Germany in control of the Channel ports? The answer, he said, 'depends on who has the best and most powerful weapons. If in addition to sea superiority we had air supremacy, we might maintain ourselves as we did in the days of Napoleon for indefinite periods, even when all the Channel ports and all the Low Countries were in the hands of a vast hostile military power.' Churchill added: 'It should never be admitted in this argument that England cannot, if the worst comes to the worst, stand alone.'

To stand alone, Churchill believed, although possible, was 'a grim choice'. Far better to take every possible initiative to prevent a renewal of war between France and Germany by influencing France towards concessions and moderation now. Britain, he believed, should say at once to France: 'The better friends you are with Germany, the better friends we shall be with you. The more you can settle your quarrel with Germany, the more ready we shall be to associate ourselves with your fortunes in the event of all your efforts proving unavailing.'

Churchill summarized his arguments in a brief formula: 'When France has made a real peace with Germany, Britain will seal the bond with all her strength,' and on February 23 he sent a copy of his notes to Austen Chamberlain. 'They only represent,' he wrote, ' "a thinking aloud".'

On March 11, while Austen Chamberlain was in Paris negotiating with the French, Baldwin summoned a meeting of eight senior Ministers —Lord Salisbury, Lord Birkenhead, Lord Robert Cecil, Sir Samuel Hoare, Leopold Amery, William Bridgeman, Sir Laming Worthington-

Evans[1] and Churchill, together with the Permanent Under-Secretary of State for the Foreign Office, Sir Eyre Crowe.[2] All the Ministers expressed reluctance to enter into a direct alliance with France. 'It is a terribly trying time for you,' Baldwin wrote to Chamberlain on the following day, and he added: 'We have immense difficulties ahead. . . . But we will win through.' That same day Sir Eyre Crowe wrote to Chamberlain of how, as he was explaining the Foreign Office policy in Cabinet:

I was interrupted, first by one Minister, then another, and a debate was begun which lasted for about $1\frac{1}{2}$ hours, extending over every conceivable point, mostly entirely irrelevant—in fact a discussion as vague and inconclusive and very much on the same lines as that I had listened to some weeks ago in the Defence Committee.

Mr Winston Churchill once more developed the theory on which he had then expatiated, the gist of it being that there was no reason why we should do anything at all; or why we should come to any arrangement with France, who could be left to stew in her own juice without its having any bad effect on anybody or anything; that there was no immediate hurry either to take action or to make any decision; all we had to do was to go our own way and in a few years time we should see France on her knees begging for assistance and allowing us to impose anything whatever on her. . . .

Before the discussion ended, Baldwin asked Crowe to leave. In a private note, Bridgeman recorded their final decision 'to continue the policy of opposing any pact with France . . . unless a quadrilateral arrangement could also be made to include Germany'. Churchill's arguments had prevailed.

Throughout the summer of 1925, during the passage of the Finance Bill through the House of Commons, Churchill was active on several Cabinet committees. Among the subjects with which he was concerned

[1] Laming Evans, 1868–1931. Admitted solicitor, 1890; retired, 1910. Conservative MP for Colchester, 1910–18, 1918–29 and for Westminster St Georges, 1929–31. Inspector of Administrative Services, War Office, 1914–15. Controller, Foreign Trade Department, Foreign Office, 1916. Assumed the prefix surname of Worthington, 1916, and known as 'Worthy'. Created Baronet, 1916. Parliamentary Secretary Ministry of Munitions, 1916–18. Minister of Blockade, 1918. Minister of Pensions, 1919–20. Minister without Portfolio, 1920–21. Secretary of State for War, 1921–22 and 1924–29.

[2] Eyre Alexander Barby Wichart Crowe, 1864–1925. Born in Leipzig; educated at Düsseldorf and Berlin (his mother was German, his father British). Entered Foreign Office as a Junior Clerk, 1906. Knighted, 1911. Assistant Under-Secretary of State, Foreign Office, 1912–19. Attacked by a section of the Press in 1915 for his German origins, his integrity was upheld publicly by Sir Edward Grey. One of the British plenipotentiaries at the Paris Peace Conference, 1919. Permanent Under-Secretary of State, Foreign Office, 1920–25.

were the further working out of the details of the unemployment insurance scheme, electrical development and the effect of death duties on
agricultural interests. He was also confronted with a protest from the
British silk manufacturers, who, in a deputation to the Treasury on
May 14, pressed him to remove the newly imposed silk duties. Churchill
was friendly but firm, telling the deputation: 'You do not imagine I am
putting this tax on for fun, out of mischief?' Silk, he went on to explain,
'is the only commodity I could call a luxury commodity which would
produce sufficient revenue'. He had looked at fur coats and ostrich
feathers, but neither offered enough revenue. Nor did he feel that the
new duties would harm the silk industry in the long term. 'It is just like
putting a stone in a stream,' he said. 'The stream is stopped for a while
but the water rises and flows over it and it makes no difference to the
flow of the stream.' On June 5 Churchill wrote to his wife:

The Bachelors' Party arrive tomorrow, minus, alas, A.J.B. As he was not
coming, I did not ask Lindemann, and now find Mary extremely disappointed
at the non-arrival of the 'Fesser'.

I have had a good deal of work this week, as I am driving forward at
least ten large questions, and many smaller ones all inter-related and
centering on the Budget. So far I am getting my own way in nearly everything. But it is a most laborious business, so many stages having to be gone
through, so many people having to be consulted, and so much detail having
to be mastered or explored in one way or another.

Later in his letter Churchill wrote:

I am seeing a great deal of my colleagues now through the week-end
parties, and also at lunch and dinner in Downing Street. It is really very
necessary, when one has so much controversial business about money matters
with them, to take the edge off things by a little friendly post-prandial talk
across a dining room table.

On June 25 the Budget passed its third reading in the House of
Commons. Four days later Churchill wrote to the chairman of the Board
of Customs and Excise, Sir Horace Hamilton:[1]

Now that the Budget is through the House of Commons, I must send you
my most sincere and heartfelt thanks for the help you gave me. I cannot

[1] Horace Perkins Hamilton, 1880–1971. Educated Tonbridge School and Hertford College
Oxford. Entered the Inland Revenue Department, 1904; transferred to the Treasury, 1911,
Private Secretary to successive Chancellors of the Exchequer, 1912–18. Deputy Chairman,
Board of Inland Revenue, 1918–19. Chairman, Board of Customs and Excise, 1919–27.
Knighted, 1921. Permanent Secretary, Board of Trade, 1927–37. Permanent Under-
Secretary of State for Scotland, 1937–46. Adviser to the Syrian Government on taxation,
1946–47. United Kingdom Member of the Commonwealth Economic Committee, 1947–61.

express too strongly my sense of the ability and resource which you have shown, or your power of continuous hard work in exacting circumstances, and I think myself most fortunate to have had such a Lieutenant.

To Sir Richard Hopkins Churchill wrote that same day: 'No Chancellor could have been better served than I, and I should like everyone to know how much their efforts have been appreciated.' Replying on July 3, Hamilton told Churchill: 'This is by far the most noteworthy Budget that we have had since the war.'

On June 30 Churchill dined with the editor of the *Manchester Guardian*, C. P. Scott.[1] The dinner was arranged by Brendan Bracken, and the Polish Ambassador[2] was also present. A few days later Scott recorded in a private note that Churchill, who sat next to him, 'talked incessantly'. Scott's account continued:

He professed himself entirely at home in the Tory party. In foreign policy it was now a peace party. In home politics he differed from it only on Protection. Its errors on that subject were only small and for his own part he always frankly admitted them. They would not go much further. . . .

Insufficient attention had been paid to his insurance scheme. It was a very big thing and meant great alleviation to the risks and hardships of the working class. It would no doubt have received more notice if brought in as a separate measure, but he was obliged to include it in his Budget because of the costs it involved to the Exchequer. . . .[3]

Discussion of Churchill's budget continued throughout the summer. On July 12 Lord Beaverbrook published a signed article in the *Sunday Express*, criticizing the return to the gold standard, higher taxation and the increased insurance contribution paid by employers. During the course of his article he asked: 'Who is responsible for this strange departure from the policy and traditions of the Conservative Party?'; and he went on to answer his own question: 'The real responsibility for the damage which is injuring the Conservative cause rests on Mr Churchill. He is the influence which dominates the Prime Minister to-day.'

[1] Charles Prestwich Scott, 1846–1932. Editor of the *Manchester Guardian*, 1872–1929. Liberal MP, 1895–1906. A friend of Lloyd George, who often sought his advice.

[2] Konstanty Skirmunt, 1866–1951. Born in Russian Poland; studied law at the University of St Petersburg. A member of the Russian Council of State, 1909–17; of the Polish National Committee, 1918–19; of the Polish Delegation to the Paris Peace Conference, 1919. Minister of Foreign Affairs, Warsaw, 1921–22. Ambassador to London, 1922–34. Polish representative to the League of Nations, 1934–39.

[3] Speaking of Poland, Churchill had 'argued strongly', according to Scott, 'that Poland should by all means cultivate the friendship of Germany. Else, if Germany were driven back on Russian support, Poland in the end would be crushed between them. But the ambassador was not inclined to take so long a view and could only reiterate that Poland was quite ready to be friends with Germany provided only that she was asked to give nothing up.'

Speaking at the Mansion House on July 15, Churchill defended his economic policy. 'The main object of all Governments,' he declared, 'was to effect a continuous rise in the comfort level of the mass of the nation.' One way of reducing unemployment and improving working conditions was to have a vastly expanded programme of house-building. 'Should not those who want work,' he asked, 'build homes for those who want homes?' The Government, he said, would make the most 'persevering search' in this direction. At the end of his speech he argued that the return to prosperity did not depend upon Budgets alone, telling his listeners:

As long as we are in contact with Reality, however stern it may be, we may suffer but we shall live. If we lose contact with Reality, we might quite swiftly get ourselves into a position where recovery would be impossible. As long as we keep on sound lines, we shall have warning of every economic danger. If wages are, or hours of labour are, out of economic relation to our competitors, if employers become slack and unenterprising, if the plant of our industries becomes obsolete, if their organisation is antiquated, if we consume too much or borrow too much or lend too much, all the alarm bells begin to ring immediately. You can hear them now ringing in your ears.

I am glad we can hear the alarm bells ringing. I rejoice that we have not been doped and drugged and stupefied by reckless inflation, by fabricated credits, by unwholesome stimulants; or lulled into a false security. We can see where we are; we can see where we alter our conduct in so far as it may be necessary before it is too late. Work, thrift, enterprise, effort, co-operation, science! We have done it before; we can do it again. In that spirit alone shall we prosper and survive.

Since May, the Cabinet's Naval Programme Committee had been trying to work out the pace and scale of future naval construction. At its meeting on May 11 Beatty expressed his fears that, from the point of view of war readiness, the Royal Navy was in many respects as yet unprepared to meet a sudden threat, and that there was a major deficiency of supply shipping in overseas waters. In reply, Churchill explained that under the proposed extension of the Ten Year Rule ample warning would in fact be given for the Navy to send out supply ships from home waters. Under the Ten Year Rule, Churchill noted:

. . . every year we are to re-examine the question of whether the ten years' period still exists, and if under any one of those examinations we had to say the situation had become very much worse, that would be the moment to make discreet changes in the ships to make them available for the Fleet.

At a three-day conference summoned by Baldwin in July to bring the Naval Estimates dispute to an end, Churchill again argued that the

Admiralty wanted to embark upon too rapid and too costly a programme. On the first day, July 17, Churchill put forward a compromise
suggestion that the Admiralty should build its first four new cruisers over
two years instead of one. But Bridgeman and Beatty would not agree,
nor was Austen Chamberlain able to persuade Bridgeman to accept
Churchill's suggestion. 'Vy many thanks for yr invaluable help this
afternoon. . . .' Churchill wrote to Chamberlain that evening. 'I tried
my best too, but I have now come to the end of my resources,' and he
added: 'I still hope that the compromise will be accepted.' On the
following day Chamberlain wrote to Churchill from the Foreign Office:

My dear Winston,

    I thought your tone & temper in our Friday conference admirable.

    I can & do feel sympathy with both sides, & I want a compromise & tried
to put the case for compromise in a way that might appeal to Beatty. You led
straight up to the same goal.

    As I said in Cabinet the Chancellor often has to play a very lonely hand,
& I felt so much the lack of support by my immediate predecessor[1] when I
was last Chancellor in 1920 that I have tried throughout to help you where I
could.

Yours ever,
Austen Chamberlain

In his postscript Austen Chamberlain added: 'I believe it is the first
time that you & I have signed "Yours ever" to each other. It is a solemn
form of signature, but after so many years of friendship I follow your
example with confidence.'

    While the conference continued, newspaper speculation was rife;
some headlines told of Bridgeman's impending resignation. The Westminster Gazette of July 18 wrote of 'Mr Bridgeman's wish to resign'.
'Will Mr Bridgeman Go?' asked the Weekly Dispatch on July 19, adding
that Asquith had warned of the 'lunacy' of the Admiralty's plans.
Bridgeman was still insisting upon a programme of four new cruisers to
be laid down in 1925–6 and a further three in 1926–7. Such insistence,
Churchill wrote to Austen Chamberlain on July 20, was 'unreasoning
obstinacy'. The conference ended on July 20 without a decision, and on
July 22 the dispute was taken to the Cabinet. Churchill again supported
his arguments with a detailed memorandum, which the Cabinet had
been sent two days before. 'If the Admiralty were able to effect economies,' he wrote, 'it would be possible for them, with Cabinet approval,
in a year or over a series of years to accelerate new construction', but
just as £60½ million had been the upper limit for 1925–6, so in successive

[1] Andrew Bonar Law.

years the limit would have to be £61 million, £61½ million, £64½ million and £66 million, for successive financial years up to 1929–30. All he was asking, he wrote, was for the Admiralty 'to make the moderate sacrifices of reducing some of the excessive costs of their interior administration'.

Baldwin appealed to the Admiralty to agree to a revised timetable of construction, which would delay, but not cut back, the cruiser programme, while at the same time postponing other work. A compromise was essential, he said, particularly 'in view of the threatened industrial crisis'—a threatened coal strike which might weaken still further the economic situation, and force even more drastic economies. Bridgeman accepted Baldwin's proposals: two new cruisers to be laid down in October 1925, a further two in February 1926, two more in October 1926 and one more in February 1927; the bulk of the rest of the Admiralty's programme, including all submarine and destroyer construction, to be deferred for twelve months; savings on all aspects of administration charges, as well as 'further underspending'. Baldwin himself announced these decisions in the House of Commons on July 23.

Although Churchill had accepted Baldwin's final compromise, it went further than he thought was necessary. At the expense of a delay in their timetable, and relatively minor economies elsewhere, the Admiralty had gained their main objective, seven new cruisers by the end of 1927. On July 27 Lord Rothermere wrote to Churchill from the Savoy Hotel:

My dear Winston,
    You are taking life far too seriously.
    We are having the most brilliant summer on record and instead of enjoying this—the Gods' greatest gift—you are fretting and fuming in Downing St. . . .
    I have not altered my belief that the present Administration will come to grief early or later in 1927 and for one who is taking life so hardly as you are this prospect I am sure must be a most welcome one.

During July the crisis in the coal industry became acute. The mine owners announced that they would have to make substantial reductions in wages, and pointed to losses of up to £1 million a month as justification for these reductions. The Miners' Federation, in rejecting wage cuts on July 29, pointed to a total mine owners' profit of more than £58 million between mid-1921 and March 1925. Yet the owners had already refused a Government request for an investigation into the financial, commercial and managerial control of the coal industry, while the miners regarded a complete reorganization of the industry, and a guaranteed national minimum wage, as indispensable.

Both Baldwin and Churchill believed wage cuts could be avoided, and a shut down of the mines prevented, if the Government were to grant a sufficient subsidy to the coal industry to enable wages to be maintained at their existing level until a major reorganization of the industry could be begun, agreed to by both owners and miners. On July 28 Baldwin had appointed Churchill to be Chairman of a special Cabinet Committee[1] to investigate one possibility of a long-term solution, the state control of all mining royalties. This would cost the Government some £100 million. In its report two days later, Churchill's Committee recommended a scheme 'of gradual acquisition of mineral royalties for the State by purchase'. The Committee also suggested that Baldwin should appoint 'an expert Committee' which would 'consider and advise whatever any or what steps can be taken to bring about an improvement in the organisation, development and management of the mining industry'.

The mine owners maintained their intention to cut wages, and during July 30 the Trade Union General Council issued instructions for a nation-wide embargo on the movement of coal. In retaliation, the owners prepared to issue dismissal notices. That afternoon Churchill spent three-quarters of an hour with Baldwin discussing his Cabinet Committee's recommendations, and working out details of the proposed Government subsidy. Thomas Jones, who saw Baldwin immediately afterwards, noted in his diary that the idea was for the subsidy to be spread over nine months 'and to be used to fill such gap as would remain between the terms offered by the owners and the terms which the men were willing to accept'. Baldwin also accepted Churchill's proposal for a Royal Commission, to examine the complete reorganization of the mining industry.

In Cabinet that evening, Baldwin proposed a subsidy, estimated at £10 million, and covering the next nine months. Several Ministers were opposed to such action on the part of a Conservative Government, but Churchill strongly supported Baldwin, and the subsidy was accepted. There was 'a strong feeling', Hankey noted in his diary, 'that the miners have a certain amount of right on their side'. Hankey also reported that Sir Philip Cunliffe-Lister supported the subsidy in order to give the Government time to complete its anti-strike preparations, but for both

---

[1] The other members of the Mining Royalties Committee were Lord Birkenhead, Sir Laming Worthington-Evans, Sir Philip Cunliffe-Lister (formerly Sir Philip Lloyd-Greame), Edward Wood, Sir Douglas Hogg and George Lane-Fox (Secretary for Mines).

Churchill and Baldwin the subsidy offered, in conjunction with the Royal Commission, the possibility of an eventual industrial settlement.

On July 31 Churchill and Baldwin met both mine owners and miners at Montagu House, in London. When the meeting was over, Baldwin was able to announce that the owners had withdrawn their dismissal notices, and that the unions had cancelled their strike instructions. Both sides accepted the idea of a Government subsidy as a satisfactory solution.

The coal subsidy was debated in the House of Commons on August 6, when Baldwin defended it in a major speech, and again on August 7, when Churchill made the closing speech for the Government. In his diary, Thomas Jones described Churchill's speech as 'very deft and, of course, very well phrased', delivered, he added, 'in admirable temper and thoroughly enjoyed in all parts of the House'. Three weeks later, Neville Chamberlain wrote to Baldwin:

Looking back over our first session I think our Chancellor has done very well, all the better because he hasn't been what he was expected to be. He hasn't dominated the Cabinet, though undoubtedly he has influenced it: he hasn't tied us up to pedantic Free Trade, though he is a bit sticky about Safeguarding of Industries. He hasn't intrigued for the leadership, but he has been a tower of debating strength in the House of Commons. And taking him all round, I don't think there can be any dispute but that he has been a source of increased influence and prestige to the Government as a whole.

. . . there is no doubt that you made us both happy, and I for one have never for a moment regretted the decision I made then or envied Winston his pre-eminence. What a brilliant creature he is! But there is somehow a great gulf fixed between him and me which I don't think I shall ever cross. I like him. I like his humour and his vitality. I like his courage. I liked the way he took that—to me—very unexpected line over the coal crisis in Cabinet. But not for all the joys of Paradise would I be a member of his staff! Mercurial! a much abused word, but it is the literal description of his temperament.

During the summer of 1925 Churchill spent most of his time at Chartwell, finishing his dam, supervising the setting out of the garden, painting and entertaining. Among those who came to stay was the Oxford scientist Professor Lindemann, who first arrived at Chartwell on July 27, staying until August 3. Churchill's Private Secretary, Edward Marsh,[1] arrived on August 14; Montagu Norman eight days

[1] Edward Howard Marsh, 1872–1953. Known as 'Eddie'. Educated at Westminster and Trinity College Cambridge. Entered the Colonial Office as a 2nd Class Clerk, 1896. Private Secretary to Churchill, December 1905–November 1915. Assistant Private Secretary to

later, and Lord Birkenhead on September 5. That summer Churchill played his final games of polo. In July he had been in the House of Commons team which played the House of Lords; but, at the age of fifty, he felt that the time had come to give up the game which he had played with such enthusiasm since before the turn of the century. It was a difficult decision for him to make. 'It is dreadful giving it up for ever,' he had written to his brother at the end of 1924.

On August 21, while Churchill was at Chartwell, Baldwin wrote to him from Aix-les-Bains that he had persuaded a senior Liberal politician, Sir Herbert Samuel,[1] to take the Chairmanship of the new Royal Commission on the coal industry. Baldwin told Churchill:

The infant Samuel duly arrived as the clock was striking six on Monday evening.

Cool, competent and precise as when he was first lent to this temporary world by an inscrutable providence, it was the work of a moment for him to grasp our problem in all its manifold implications.

But he would have none of it and for 'worthy reasons', if I may borrow a happy phrase of the Marquess Curzon which he employed in accounting for Sir Laming's adherence to the coalition at the Carlton Club and subsequent acceptance of a modest office. Suddenly conscious of a paranoisia (if I remember that boss word correctly) he substituted 'proper' for 'worthy'. Whether he realised the admirable choice of the first epithet, I shall never know!

To resume. He (the original subject) had been counting the hours until his release from office, hoping to get to work on a monumental volume he wished to write. He had retired into Tirol and had actually started on it. He had already taken his passage to India where he had arranged to study divers aspects of his subject for several months etc. etc. Very strong private reasons with which I sympathise. Would we do our utmost to find a substitute? Until we could assure him we had done so, he couldn't look at it. Hence the fevered telegrams which passed and now all is well.

I think he is quite the best man we could have. The brief talk we had convinced me.

Baldwin's letter ended, on a holiday note:

Asquith, November 1915–December 1916. Private Secretary to Churchill, 1917–22 and 1924–29. Private Secretary to successive Secretaries of State for the Colonies, 1929–36. Elected to the Other Club, 1932. Knighted, 1937.

[1] Herbert Louis Samuel, 1870–1963. Educated at University College School and Balliol College Oxford. Liberal MP, 1902–18; 1929–35. Chancellor of the Duchy of Lancaster, 1909–10. Postmaster-General, 1910–14. President of the Local Government Board, 1914–15. Home Secretary, 1916. Chairman of the Select Committee on National Expenditure, 1917–18. Knighted, 1920. High Commissioner for Palestine, 1920–25. Home Secretary, 1931–32. Leader of the Parliamentary Liberal Party, 1931–35. Created Viscount, 1937.

Aix is very full: so are most of the people here. The hotel buses discharge 'em at the baths and they look, many of them, as if you stuck a fork in them, a rich gravy would burst forth.

But the beauty of the country is unchanged and unchangeable. And there is enough to make everybody happy. For those who would go from the trough to the straw and back again, well, there never were troughs so filled or so often and never straw softer or cleaner.

During the summer of 1925 Churchill's work centred on the question of France's war debt to Britain. On July 17, in a conversation with the French Ambassador, de Fleuriau,[1] he urged France to settle with Britain as soon as possible, and before negotiating with the United States. 'If we reached an agreement here,' Churchill told the Ambassador, 'that could be used as a means of limiting American demands on France,' and he added that the British had shown themselves 'far more ready to consider European difficulties than the United States'.

The French Government responded to Churchill's initiative, and on August 24 proposed to repay £620 million of this sum, and to do so by annual payments to Britain of £10 million a year for sixty-two years, half of which would be dependent on France receiving the money due from Germany. Churchill, however, rejected both the sum itself and the condition attached to it, and at a meeting of the Cabinet on August 26 proposed asking France for sixty-two payments of £12½ million a year, without any link to German payments to France. This would bring Britain a total of £775 million by 1988. The Cabinet agreed with this suggestion, which Churchill then put to the new French Finance Minister, Joseph Caillaux,[2] who had come to London for the negotiations. After three days of negotiations Caillaux accepted Churchill's terms. Their agreement was at once denounced in the United States, to which France owed an almost equally large sum of £650 million, and which the United States Treasury had hoped to recover long before 1988. On September 1 Churchill wrote to Austen Chamberlain: 'I never had the slightest doubt of what the reception of the Anglo-French debt arrangement would be in the United States.' His letter continued: 'Although

---

[1] Aimé Joseph de Fleuriau, 1870–1938. Entered the French Diplomatic Service, 1892. Counsellor of Embassy, London, 1913–20, and close friend of Paul Cambon, the Ambassador. Minister to Peking, 1921–24. Ambassador to London, 1924–33.

[2] Joseph Caillaux, 1862–1944. Born in Le Mans. A Socialist-Radical Deputy from 1898. Minister of Finance, 1899–1902, 1906–09, 1911 and 1913–14. Prime Minister, 1911–12. Arrested for treason on Clemenceau's orders, 1918; sentenced to 3 years in prison and 10 years deprivation of political rights. Amnestied, 1924. Senator, 1925. Minister of Finance, April–October 1925, June–July 1926 and June 1935. In June 1937 he played a major part in the Senate in bringing about the fall of Blum's Government. Chairman for the Commission for Finances, 1937–40.

sunk in selfishness in the present period, the American people have an extremely uncomfortable conscience, and when this conscience is being stirred, as it is now, they are naturally very resentful. I think you will find everything will calm down in a short time, and I am pretty sure that the secondary reaction will not be unfavourable.'

On September 5 Churchill saw Strong of the Federal Reserve Bank, and two days later he was able to report to Chamberlain that Strong not only thought that Britain had 'acted wisely in making a moderate settlement with France', but that he would also use 'all his influence in America to procure a similarly reasonable solution'. Speaking at Birmingham on September 16, Churchill explained the task which he had set himself during the negotiations:

We have not sought to be judged upon this question by our ability to extract the uttermost farthing. We think it our duty to consider not only the capacity of our debtors to pay, but the circumstances in which these debts were incurred. We believe it also to be in the interests of Britain to promote a general appeasement and revival on the Continent of Europe. It is in our moral interests, it is in our material interests.

On October 15 Churchill wrote to Caillaux, who had returned from Washington, asking if they could now begin negotiations on the outstanding details, in order finally to complete a formal debt agreement. 'I hope,' Churchill wrote, 'that despite your many preoccupations, you may find it possible to come to London again in person, as I feel sure that this would be the most satisfactory procedure . . .' Unfortunately, Caillaux fell from office on October 29. On the following day Churchill wrote to him from London:

I have from time to time the melancholy duty of writing valedictory letters to French Ministers of Finance when the political kaleidoscope revolves. But it is in no formal sense that I express to you my regret on personal grounds that our agreeable conversations on disagreeable subjects have been so prematurely interrupted. . . .

But I hope when you next come to England you will let me know; and whether I am at Downing Street or in a humbler abode I should like to gather a small, select and cheerful company to welcome a statesman who faces facts and foes.

Caillaux replied on November 7—his letter translated by Edward Marsh:

Do you know, my dear Mr Churchill, it would be difficult to write a more delicate & charming letter than the one you have sent me? It touched me greatly—it even rather moved me.

Well well! the job of a Finance Minister is complicated in all countries & at all times. It is infinitely difficult for a man who takes upon himself to tell the truth, the whole truth, to a nation which has for a long time been diligently lulled with illusions. It is human nature to dislike the wretch who dispels the delightful mirages, & speaks roughly to the dupes; & sometimes they make haste to show him the door. But pshaw! Talleyrand said that 'in politics one only dies to rise again'. Haven't we both experienced the truth of this maxim?

Of their negotiations together, Caillaux wrote: 'you showed me such courtesy throughout and you received me with so much grace, & had such a happy touch in vivifying & brightening our conversations, that they left me with the impression that we were in complete agreement'.

At the beginning of November, Austen Chamberlain invited the French Foreign Minister, Aristide Briand,[1] to London, to sign the Locarno Pact between France, Germany, Britain, Italy and Belgium. On November 28 a new Finance Minister was appointed, Louis Loucheur.[2] Churchill was pleased to be dealing with a former colleague, with whom as Minister of Munitions in 1917 and 1918 he had worked so closely. But his pleasure was shortlived, for on December 15 Loucheur himself fell from power. On December 18 Churchill sent his friend words both of encouragement and advice. He had looked forward, he wrote, to discussing the French debt with him, believing that their friendship 'extending over so many years, & born amid war-time scenes' would have made even this 'disagreeable topic easy and fruitful'. Churchill ended with words of comfort drawn from his experience:

Political life is full of ups and downs on both sides of the Channel. I have had my share, and as you know I have never accepted a hostile decision without carrying matters forward to fresh battlefields. This is only what will

---

[1] Aristide Briand, 1862–1932. French politician, Minister of Public Instruction and Worship, 1906–09. Prime Minister, 1909–10. Minister of Justice, 1912–13. Prime Minister, January–March 1913. Minister of Justice, 1914. Prime Minister, October 1915–March 1917. Prime Minister and Minister of Foreign Affairs, January 1921–January 1922. Minister of Foreign Affairs, April–July 1925. Prime Minister, November 1925–July 1926. Minister of Foreign Affairs, 1926–32. Awarded the Nobel Peace Prize for his part in the Locarno Agreements, 1926. Prime Minister for the sixth time, July–October 1929.

[2] Louis Loucheur, 1872–1931. Engineer, contractor and munitions manufacturer. One of the first French businessmen to receive political office during the war. Under-Secretary of State at the Ministry of Munitions, December 1916–April 1917. Minister of Munitions, 1917–20. Elected to the Chamber of Deputies, 1919. Helped in the drafting of the economic section of the Treaty of Versailles, 1919. Minister for the Liberated Areas, 1921; Minister of Trade, 1924; Minister of Finance (for seventeen days), 1925; Minister of Trade, 1926; Minister of Labour, 1928. Author of the 'Loucheur Law' of 1928 to help deal with housing crises by building low-priced houses with the help of public funds.

be expected of you by all who knew you & especially by your friends, among whom permit me with kind regards to subscribe myself

Yours very sincerely
Winston S. Churchill

During his first year as Chancellor of the Exchequer, Churchill had established excellent relations with Baldwin. Writing to Baldwin from Chartwell on November 1, he reflected on their work together, and warned against the dangers of introducing a protective tariff on steel.

It is a year almost to a day since you asked me to work with you. We know each other better than we did then, & I have been vy happy under yr leadership. I am sure that you have a winning hand to play if only you have the firmness and patience to play it regularly through. Gradually but surely the nation will revive its strength & be conscious of an increased well being.

Time will vindicate all the principal action we have taken, whether it be yr forbearing attitude on Labour provocations, or the Widows Pensions, or the Gold Standard. The Rothermere Beaverbrook attack will be repulsed, not by speeches, nor by disdain; but by events. What about that Roman Fabius Maximus Cunctator—was there not some famous quotation about him? Did he not give his country a chance to pull round & realise its mighty strength & let the deep long forces work for him—instead of being lured into desperate & premature struggles.

As long as we stick to the platform of the General Election all will be well & we shall wear down all our foes, & what is most important do our duty in securing the country its promised breathing space. But if Amery—who publicly repudiated yr declarations of fiscal policy before the election—is allowed to rush the Conservative party on to the slippery slope of Protection, then friends will be divided and enemies united and all the vultures will gather for the prey.

A general tariff wd encounter no more reproaches of departure from election pledges, & less effectual resistance than an isolated general protection duty on Steel. One is a policy—t'other a meaningless & unrelated episode, the result not of scientific thought on Trade conditions but only of drifting from one half measure & compromise to another. I expect that if these steel men knew that the tariff was off for this Parlt & if you let me get into direct touch with them we cd find a way of helping them to regional concentrations on the most profitable plants. At any rate I wd gladly try.

Baldwin's growing confidence in Churchill's judgement and past experience led him, at the end of November 1925, to entrust Churchill with a complex and potentially dangerous situation which had arisen in Ireland. Following the publication in the *Morning Post* on November 7 of an alleged secret decision of the Irish Boundary Commission, the Free State leaders had become alarmed at the possibility of change in the

Ulster boundary which would favour the North. Regarding this as a grave breach of the Irish Treaty, they were also in an uncompromising mood towards the repayment of the Free State's debt to Britain, a debt calculated on the basis of Britain's loss of revenue and munitions supplies in Southern Ireland, and estimated at £155 million. On December 1 Baldwin asked Churchill to preside over an emergency meeting of the Irish Boundary Commission, and for three days Churchill conducted a series of intense and difficult negotiations with the Northern and Southern leaders, both on the boundary and debt question. Lord Birkenhead, Lord Salisbury and Sir John Anderson helped him to devise an acceptable formula, whereby it was agreed that the boundary would not be changed, and that the debt would be repaid over a period of sixty years. 'I feel it impossible to leave for Ulster,' Sir James Craig[1] wrote to Churchill on December 4, 'without first thanking you most sincerely for the big part you have successfully played in bringing about a settlement.'

From the early summer of 1925 until February 1926 Churchill was busy preparing his second budget. In an attempt both to balance the budget, and to try to avoid an increase in income tax to meet the cost of the coal subsidy, Churchill and his advisers scrutinized the proposed expenditure of each Government department, while at the same time suggesting a wide range of cuts and economies in the existing expenditure. The most important economies were decided upon at the Standing Committee on Expenditure, which had been set up by the Cabinet in April 1925, and of which Baldwin was Chairman. But in a memorandum to his Treasury officials on November 7, Churchill himself established the guidelines which were to be followed. His principal aim, he informed Sir Warren Fisher, Sir Otto Niemeyer and Sir Richard Hopkins, was to have a Budget surplus of between £1 and £2 million, 'apart from the coal subsidy of £17 million, which would constitute the deficit'. To balance the Budget he wanted no new taxation, nor did he see any way of reducing or eliminating the coal subsidy deficit.

---

[1] James Craig, 1871–1940. A Protestant. Born in Dublin, the son of a wealthy distiller. A stockbroker by profession. Served in the South African War, 1899–1902. Unionist MP, 1906–21. A leading opponent of Irish Home Rule before 1914. On active service against the Germans in South-west Africa, 1914–15. Created Baronet, 1918. Parliamentary Secretary, Ministry of Pensions, 1919–20. Financial Secretary, Admiralty, 1920–21. First Prime Minister of Northern Ireland (under the Government of Ireland Act), from June 1921 until his death. Created Viscount Craigavon, 1927.

During a meeting of the Standing Committee on Expenditure on November 17 it was agreed that Churchill should provide £12 million as the Government's insurance contribution for 1,150,000 unemployed. 'Of course the situation would be entirely altered,' Churchill warned, 'if a great labour crisis developed next Spring. This might indeed involve an increase in direct taxation and a return to War budgeting.' This warning cast a shadow over all subsequent discussions, and at a further meeting of the Committee two days later Churchill asked his colleagues to agree not to embark on any new unemployment relief schemes, as, with unemployment rising, their cost would be prohibitive. 'In the view of the Treasury,' he added, 'unemployment is more effectively arrested by National economy than by National expenditure.' The Committee agreed not only that all future relief must be curtailed, but that cuts would have to be made in every branch of Government expenditure. During the meeting, the Minister of Labour, Sir Arthur Steel-Maitland, agreed to reduce expenditure on the training of women for employment from £90,000 to £70,000 and to cut provision for Juvenile Unemployment Centres from £100,000 to £60,000, and the President of the Board of Education, Lord Eustace Percy,[1] was asked to reduce his budget of £40 million by at least £1 million.

On November 20, in a departmental memorandum, Churchill pressed for substantial reductions in the numbers of civil servants employed in the three Service departments, and also in the India Office and the Foreign Office. There must, he wrote, be fewer civil servants employed in 1926 than there had been in 1925, not by sacking, but by refusing any further expansion. The Treasury must give an example to the others. The complexities of the tax system should not be made the occasion for increased staffs, for it was wrong to look upon these complexities 'with the same eye of respect as the bricklayer looks upon the house which he makes his living in building'.

One substantial source of extra revenue which Churchill had decided to tap was the Road Fund. This Fund, built up principally from motor car licence fees, had a surplus of over £8 million, which Churchill wished to incorporate into the general budget. The motor car lobby, however, was vociferous in its opposition to this proposal, and claimed that money obtained from car licences could only be used on projects

---

[1] Lord Eustace Sutherland Campbell Percy, 1887–1958. 7th son of the 7th Duke of Northumberland. Entered the Diplomatic Service, 1909; served in the Foreign Office, 1914–19. Conservative MP for Hastings, 1921–37. Parliamentary Secretary, Board of Education, 1923; Ministry of Health, 1923–24. President of the Board of Education, 1924–29. Minister without Portfolio, 1935–36. Created Baron Percy of Newcastle, 1953. His brother-in-law, Lieutenant-Colonel A. E. Maxwell, was killed in action at Antwerp, 8 October 1914.

directly related to the motorist. On October 16 the Home Secretary, Sir William Joynson-Hicks,[1] had sent Churchill a memorandum warning of 'strong and well-grounded opposition from the whole of the motoring community' to any use of the Road Fund for non-motoring purposes. The motorists regarded the Fund as the private preserve of their particular interest. But, as Sir George Barstow pointed out to Churchill in a minute on October 30, 'The tax is no more voluntary than any other tax. It is imposed by Statute, and what Parliament has done, Parliament can undo.' Barstow went on to propose an additional tax on luxury cars, to produce an extra revenue of £2 million a year. Churchill liked this suggestion. But, he noted on November 2, it was 'of the highest importance that this temptation should not be put before the Cabinet Committee until every possible saving from other sources has been determined upon. It is too easy a way out. We must get the hard work done first.' The motorists, aware of the use Churchill might propose for the Road Fund, continued to argue that its surplus should be used solely for motoring purposes. 'Such contentions,' Churchill minuted on November 22, 'are absurd, and constitute at once an outrage upon the sovereignty of Parliament and upon commonsense.'[2]

On November 26 the Expenditure Committee turned its attention to education, the Air Force and the Navy. Churchill strongly criticized Lord Eustace Percy's request for a year's delay in introducing economies in education. The Air Ministry, he went on, had agreed to cut its budget from £18 to £16 million. Both these reductions had been recommended by the Committee set up seven months earlier, under Lord Colwyn,[3] to make recommendations about defence spending.

[1] William Joynson-Hicks, 1865–1932. Known as 'Jix'. Solicitor. Conservative MP, 1906–29. Created Baronet, 1919. Parliamentary Secretary, Department of Overseas Trade, 1922–23. Postmaster General and Paymaster General, 1923. Entered the Cabinet as Financial Secretary to the Treasury, 1923. Minister of Health, 1923–24. Home Secretary, 1924–29. Created Viscount Brentford, 1929. Chairman of the Automobile Association. Vice-President of the Safety First Council and the Institute of Transport. President of the National Church League. Member of the Joint Select Committee on Indian Affairs, 1933–34.

[2] On 12 February 1926 Churchill sent Sir Horace Hamilton a detailed proposal for the taxation of luxury cars. Churchill's plan was a 5% per annum tax on the purchase price of any car costing more than £1,000. Heavy lorries, too, he believed, should be taxed, their 'weight and road smashing' characteristics being the 'governing factors'. Four days later he wrote to Hamilton again, suggesting a tax on imported American films. 'It would naturally give great pleasure in this country,' he wrote, 'if any revenue could be derived from the profits of American Film Producers.'

[3] Frederick Henry Smith, 1859–1946. India rubber and cotton manufacturer; colliery and railway director. Created Baronet, 1912. High Sheriff of Carnarvonshire, 1917–18. Created Baron Colwyn, 1917. Vice-Chairman of the Post Office Advisory Council, 1921. Chairman of the Government Contracts Committee; the Royal Commission of Income Tax; the Bank Amalgamation Committee and the Defence Spending Committee. Privy Councillor, 1924.

At a meeting of the Expenditure Committee on December 10 Churchill proposed a £4 million reduction in health service expenditure, but Neville Chamberlain spoke strongly against any such reduction, warning the Committee that 'any attack on the Health Service would produce an uproar out of all proportion to the amount of money which could possibly be saved'. Baldwin stated emphatically that the Committee must 'consider the political implications' before coming to a final decision. The Committee met again on December 18, when Churchill pressed for increases in the taxation of luxury cars and heavy commercial vehicles, as well as the introduction of a tax on petrol, both of which were accepted.

On December 22 a deputation of race-horse owners called on Churchill to argue in favour of a betting tax. Churchill had not yet decided what course to adopt. 'In these matters,' he said, 'I speak as a child, and am only seeking information.' His personal instinct, he said, was opposed to a betting tax. 'I am afraid we might get accused . . .' he said, 'of having deliberately spread and multiplied this vice—I won't say vice but evil.' Nevertheless, plans for such a tax went ahead. Churchill had already given Sir Otto Niemeyer and Sir Horace Hamilton his thoughts on the technical aspects of the tax, writing to them on December 12: 'So far as the betting shop is concerned, it would be essential to prohibit any notice, placard, list of betting odds, or other street sign which would flaunt itself before the passer-by. A registered bookmaker would be entitled to transact business behind a plain house front and in a building used for no other purpose.'

Throughout November and December, Churchill had played a leading part in the House of Lords Reform Committee. On November 4 he spoke in favour of a national Referendum in order to determine the public's view of a comprehensive reform scheme, with 'Lords' chosen by a select committee on a rotating basis. Eight days later on November 12, he told the Committee that the future House of Lords must be 'based on and moving with the national will'. Members should be chosen, he said, from a list of 1,200 'notables', including all the hereditary peers, all Privy Councillors, 'all persons who had filled certain important public or municipal offices' such as Lord Mayors and Chairmen of Royal Commissions and all members of the House of Commons 'of 12 years standing'. The new Lords should sit for a period of twelve years, one-third retiring every four years.

Churchill spent both Christmas and the New Year with his family at Chartwell. On 4 January 1926 Professor Lindemann motored from Oxford to join him for a week, and on January 11 Edward Marsh arrived. Throughout his holiday Churchill pressed the Treasury to send him facts and figures on a variety of topics. 'I am much obliged for all the information you are sending me,' he wrote to Sir Horace Hamilton on January 4, 'and I fear that its preparation is putting a heavy strain on the heads of your department.' On learning of an Air Ministry proposal to extend their programme beyond the agreed limit of two experimental airships, he wrote at once to Sir George Barstow, on January 6: 'I do not want to abrogate any right to criticize all this waste of money.' On the following day he wrote to Sir Richard Hopkins of a new and 'extremely revolutionary scheme' which he had devised to separate earned and unearned income from a tax point of view. 'Upon the whole,' he explained, 'the emphasis of favour will be shown to the earned; and the emphasis of burden to the investment.' Churchill suggested a 'National Register' of all taxpayers who received income from investment, and an automatic deduction of tax from each dividend, before it was actually paid over by the company.

On January 14, Churchill began negotiations in London with the Italian Minister of Finance, Count Volpi,[1] aimed at reaching a final settlement of the Italian war debt. Italy owed Britain £592 million, and Churchill hoped to obtain a clear repayment schedule, while at the same time being prepared to accept, as he had done with France, lenient repayment terms over a long period. On January 15 he suggested to Volpi that Italy should defer all payments until 1930, and should then pay £7 million a year until the debt was paid off. The negotiations continued for twelve days. On January 19 the Cabinet gave Churchill a 'free hand' to finalize the agreement, which was signed on January 27. In his speech at the signing, Churchill spoke warmly of the fact that Italy possessed a government, 'under the commanding leadership of Signor Mussolini, which does not shrink from the logical consequences of economic facts'. The best evidence of the fairness of any settlement, he added, 'is the fact that it fully satisfies neither party'. Under the Churchill–Volpi agreement, Italy agreed to complete its payments, and fully repay the debt, by 1988.

On January 20, in a speech at Leeds which was widely reported, Churchill spoke of the industrial situation, contrasting the 'gloom' of the previous year with the growing hope—'Hope for all; hope for the

[1] Giuseppe Volpi, Conte di Misurata, 1877–1947. Born in Venice. Financier and industrialist. Founded the Societa Adriatica di Elettricità, 1905, which established control of the electric energy grid of fifteen Italian provinces. Took part in the Italo–Turkish peace negotiations, 1912. Governor of Tripolitania (Libya), 1921–25. Senator, 1922. Minister of Finance, July 1925–July 1928. Podestà of Venice.

manufacturer; hope for the merchant; hope for the artisan; hope for those who are out of employment. A brightening and a broadening hope.' His speech ended:

Prosperity, that errant daughter of our house who went astray in the Great War, is on our threshold. She has raised her hand to the knocker on the door. What shall we do? Shall we let her in, or shall we drive her away? Shall we welcome her once again to our own fireside settle, or banish her once more to roam about among the nations of the world? That is the choice that will be before the British nation in these next few anxious months. It is a fateful choice, and, like most fateful choices in life, it is a very small choice. And I, for my part, knowing something of the deep sagacity and fundamental good will that underlie our British national life, will never be in a hurry to assume that we shall be found incapable as a people of reaching a successful and practical conclusion of our difficulties.

The impact of Churchill's speech was considerable; indeed, Lord Stamfordham asked Thomas Jones on January 29 if the King could incorporate the last paragraph in a speech of his own, as it 'really expresses what I venture might come from the King's lips', and Baldwin himself approved the King's use of Churchill's peroration.

During the first two weeks of February Churchill completed the details of his budget, writing to Bridgeman on February 5 to confirm that the 1926–7 Naval Estimates were to be limited to £57½ million, as agreed by the Expenditure Committee. 'Thank you once more,' Churchill wrote, 'for all the efforts you have made to assist the Government in its financial difficulties, and with a lively sense of still a few remaining favours to come.' To Sir Arthur Steel-Maitland he wrote on February 9, thanking him for making a reduction of £117,000 on the Ministry of Labour vote: 'If there is a Coal Strike all calculations would be vitiated.' But he added that he had no other option but 'to make our estimates on the basis of industrial peace and not of industrial war'.

On February 9 the Standing Committee on Expenditure circulated its Report to the Cabinet, warning that the coal subsidy would now cost at least £19 million, and would create a £19 million budget deficit. The budget was, otherwise, a balanced one, as a result of the agreement of all Government departments to make substantial cuts in their annual spending—cuts amounting in all to over £15 million.

The coal subsidy had become the largest item of Government expenditure. Yet Churchill still believed that it was essential to provide such a subsidy in order to try to preserve industrial peace. On the day that the Cabinet Committee's Report was shown to the Cabinet, Lord

Beaverbrook reported to the Canadian Prime Minister, Mackenzie King:[1]

Churchill, whom I saw the other night, gave me the impression that he was in favour of renewing the Coal Subsidy when it expires at the end of April. And Churchill practically is the Government. He has got a complete strangle-hold on the younger reactionary Tories, who used to move Baldwin about as they liked, and now keeps the Prime Minister in a padded room of his own. The latter even goes into Churchill's bedroom (for W.C. is a late riser) on the mornings he is leaving for the country, to get the last word.

This is really a wonderful performance on Churchill's part, for so recently as 1923, when Baldwin formed his first administration he would not hear of Churchill's inclusion in any capacity. . . .

On January 31, Clementine Churchill had left England for the South of France. Four days later Churchill sent her an account of his activities during the first week of the new Parliament:

The session opened like a doped lamb. A feeble bleat about the Italians, but no challenge in debate. A much milder Socialist amendt & a half empty H of C. L.G. dined with me à deux on the first night. I found him rather bothered, & quite astonishingly empty of knowledge & ideas, but vy genial and plucky. It surprised me to see how far adrift he was from the actual detailed prospect of Government business. It was vy nice to see him again.

'My big plans,' Churchill added, 'are steadily falling into their combination; & I now see my way through. . . .'

On February 6 Churchill entertained several of his friends at Chartwell, including two Cabinet Ministers, Sir Laming Worthington-Evans and Sir Philip Cunliffe-Lister, and Ronald McNeill.[2] 'The House is vy warm & comfortable,' he reported to his wife on the evening of February 7, '& everything seems to work smoothly & easily.' He had worked all day in the garden, 'fruit trees being planted every quarter of an hour'. He had invited an ever larger number of friends to

[1] William Lyon Mackenzie King, 1874–1950. Born in Ontario, Canada. Fellow in Political Science, Harvard University, 1897–1900. Editor of the *Labour Gazette*, Canada, 1900–08. Liberal MP in the Canadian Parliament, 1908–49. Minister of Labour, 1909–11. Leader of the Liberal Party of Canada, 1919. Leader of the Opposition, 1919–21. Prime Minister of Canada, 1921–26, 1926–30 and 1935–48. Privy Councillor of the United Kingdom, 1922. Secretary of State for External Affairs, 1935–46. Order of Merit, 1947.

[2] Ronald John McNeill, 1861–1936. Educated at Harrow and Christ Church Oxford. Barrister, 1887. Editor of the *St James Gazette*, 1900–04. Assistant Editor, 11th edition of the *Encyclopaedia Britannica*, 1906–11. Conservative MP, 1911–27. Parliamentary Under-Secretary of State for Foreign Affairs, October 1922–January 1924 and November 1924–November 1925. Financial Secretary (to Churchill) at the Treasury, 1925–27. Created Baron Cushendun, 1927. Chancellor of the Duchy of Lancaster, 1927–29.

Chartwell on February 13, including Sir Samuel Hoare, Walter Guinness, Beaverbrook, Lindemann, Philip Sassoon and Lord Hugh Cecil.[1] At the last minute Beaverbrook was unable to go, but on February 15 Hoare sent him an account of the weekend's activities:

> I had never seen Winston before in the role of landed proprietor. Most of Sunday morning we inspected the property, and the engineering works upon which he is engaged. These engineering works consist of making a series of ponds in a valley, and Winston appeared to be a great deal more interested in them than in anything else in the world.
>
> The House struck me as being very comfortable, but rather gaunt to look at from the outside. It certainly has a pleasant situation and Winston seems blissfully happy over it all. He scarcely stopped talking the whole time, though occasionally Hugh Cecil talked at the same time.

Churchill was 'convinced', Hoare added, 'that he is to be the prophet to lead us into the Promised Land in which there will be no income tax and everyone will live happily ever afterwards. The trouble is that he has got so many schemes tumbling over each other in his mind, that I am beginning to wonder whether he will be able to pull any one of them out of the heap.'

---

[1] Lord Hugh Richard Heathcote Gascoyne Cecil, 1869–1956. Known as 'Linky'. Fifth son of the 3rd Marquess of Salisbury. Educated at Eton and University College Oxford. Conservative MP for Greenwich, 1895–1906; for Oxford University, 1910–1937. Provost of Eton, 1936–44. Created Baron Quickswood, 1941. In 1908 he was the 'best man' at Churchill's wedding.

9

The General Strike and the
British Gazette

THROUGHOUT January and February of 1926 the coal industry continued to be riven by discontent, with only the Government's continuing subsidy enabling the coal owners to maintain the existing level of wages. The miners feared that the subsidy would not be renewed, and their wages would fall. They also wanted major improvements in their working conditions. Speaking to the Belfast Chamber of Commerce on March 2, Churchill said he welcomed the coal subsidy if, despite its cost, it allowed both the coal owners and the miners 'to set their house in order', and thus help avert 'a dangerous collapse of national industry'. Churchill was confident that industrial strife could be avoided, telling his audience:

I have never taken the view,' which seems to give so much pleasure to morbid and misanthropic minds, which is spread so widely abroad, and which has apparently been deeply inculcated in the mentality of the United States—the view that Britain is down and out, that the foundations of our commerce and industrial greatness have been sapped; that the stamina of our people is impaired; that our workmen are mutinous and lazy; that our employers are indolent; that our Empire is falling to pieces. I have never been able to take that view.

Self-criticism, no doubt, has a most valuable part to play, but such moods in their extravagant expression, are not only unrelated to truth, but extremely unhelpful to the immediate public interest.

Churchill went on to point out that even 'our much-abused coal miners' hewed more coal per shift than any other miners in the world. It was true, he added, that the coal industry was 'in chaos', steel was 'seriously depressed' and shipbuilding was 'lamentably stagnant'; but things were slowly improving, and he opposed all 'idiotic pessimism'.

On March 10 the Royal Commission headed by Sir Herbert Samuel advocated drastic measures which appealed neither to the mine owners nor to the miners. The owners were told to institute long-term reforms in working conditions. They were also told that there should be an end to the Government subsidy. This, the owners hastened to point out, would lead to an immediate reduction of miners' wages. On March 17 Churchill was appointed a member of a special Cabinet Committee, headed by Baldwin, to discuss the Samuel Report. The other members were Sir Laming Worthington-Evans, Lord Birkenhead, William Bridgeman, Sir Philip Cunliffe-Lister, Sir Arthur Steel-Maitland and Colonel Lane-Fox.[1] On March 19 the Committee agreed to accept the Report, and urged 'the co-operation of all parties', but at subsequent meetings between the miners, the coal owners and the Government, it was clear that a serious crisis could not be avoided. Churchill took no part in these later discussions, which were conducted principally by Baldwin himself, Lord Birkenhead and Sir Horace Wilson.

While the coal negotiations continued between Baldwin and the miners' leaders, Churchill worked at the final details of his second budget and prepared his budget speech. 'I have had a very laborious but quite successful week,' he wrote to his wife on March 20, 'and am now at Chartwell with Jack . . .' His letter continued: 'All is well here. Mary breakfasted & Sarah[2] dined with me. Diana talked quite intelligently about politics & seemed to have a lot of information derived from the newspapers. They are all vy sweet & it is a joy to have them down here.'

The industrial discontent grew rapidly at the beginning of April, when the miners' reluctance to accept a reduction in wages was supported by the Trade Union Congress, which threatened to call a nation-wide general strike to support them. The state of the mining industry gave strength to the miners' complaints. On April 10 Harold Macmillan wrote to Churchill from Stockton of 'the appalling conditions in this area' and went on to comment on how 'the patience and

---

[1] George Richard Lane-Fox, 1870–1940. Educated at Eton and New College Oxford. Barrister, 1896. Conservative MP for Barkston Ash (Yorkshire), 1906–31. Served in the Great War, 1914–17 (wounded). Secretary for Mines, October 1922–January 1924 and November 1924–January 1928. Member of the Indian Statutory Commission, 1928–29. Chairman, Pig Products Commission, 1932; Fat Stock Reorganization Commission, 1933. Created Baron Bingley, 1933. President of the National Union of Conservative and Unionist Associations, 1937. In 1903 he married Mary Wood, 2nd daughter of the 2nd Viscount Halifax and sister of Edward Wood (later Viceroy of India and Foreign Secretary).

[2] Sarah Millicent Hermione Spencer Churchill. Born while her father was returning from the siege of Antwerp, 7 October 1914. Edward Marsh was her godfather. An actress, she published *The Empty Spaces* (poems) in 1966, and *A Thread in the Tapestry* (recollections) in 1967.

endurance of the workers as a whole is really remarkable. Certainly adversity brings out greater virtues than prosperity in all classes, but peculiarly so among the working people.'

On April 15 Baldwin, Steel-Maitland and Lane-Fox met representatives of the Miners' Federation at 10 Downing Street. The miners' leader, Herbert Smith,[1] warned against any attempt to impose local wage agreements, instead of a national minimum wage acceptable to the Federation. 'We shall resist it to the bitter end,' he said. 'It will be a national kick-off if it is to be a kick-off at all.' Six days later, on April 21, Baldwin, Steel-Maitland and Lane-Fox met the mine-owners' representatives, led by Evan Williams.[2]

Baldwin asked Williams if the owners would agree to a national minimum wage, but Williams insisted on each coal owner being able to negotiate his own, local wage rate, while at a further meeting between Baldwin and the miners' leaders on April 23 Herbert Smith reiterated the miners' insistence on a uniform minimum wage, below which no owner would be allowed to go, even by means of freely negotiated local agreements. When Steel-Maitland asked Smith if the miners would accept a general reduction in wages, Smith replied: 'We are not prepared to have our wages reduced under present conditions,' and he added: 'I am compelled to say this because my people are down.' At further meetings with both the TUC and the miners on April 26, and with the mine owners on April 27, Baldwin was unable to break the stalemate.

That same afternoon, April 27, Churchill introduced his second budget, speaking for nearly two hours to a crowded House of Commons. His son Randolph was again among those present. As he had already done at Belfast, Churchill deprecated excessive pessimism. 'The economic picture,' he said, 'is not black; it is not grey; it is piebald, and on the whole the dark patches are less prominent this year than last.' His message was: 'let us persevere'. The overriding needs, he said, were thrift and economy. Luxuries must be taxed, and there would therefore

---

[1] Herbert Smith, 1876–1938. Born in a Lancashire workhouse, the posthumous son of a miner killed in a pit accident. Began work in the mines at the age of ten; Vice-President of the Yorkshire Miners' Association, 1904; President, 1906–38. Frequently led rescue parties down the mines after pit accidents. President of the National Association, 1922–29.

[2] Evan Williams, 1871–1959. Educated at Clare College Cambridge. Coal owner. Chairman of the Monmouth and South Wales Coalowners Association, 1913. President of the Mining Association of Great Britain, 1919–44. President of the National Board for the Coal Mining Industry, 1921–25. President of the National Confederation of Employers Organizations, 1925–26. Chairman of the Joint Standing Consultative Committee for the Coal Mining Industry, 1926–44. Chairman of the Central Council under the Coal Mines Act, 1930–38. Created Baronet, 1935.

be a tax on betting, amounting to 5% on all bets. Income tax, however, would remain unchanged.

Churchill sounded one note of caution; this budget, he said, was based on 'a peace footing', but if there were a coal strike he would have to come before the House again, and ask for powers to levy new taxes, both direct and indirect, on a substantial scale.

On the day after the budget Baldwin again met representatives of both the mine owners and the TUC. The owners were again insisting on an immediate reduction in wages in order to cut their losses, while Sir Adam Nimmo[1] declared that in his district, 'fighting for its life' to break even, a national minimum wage was out of the question. Baldwin suggested that wages might at least be kept at their existing level, if the miners were to agree to work for eight instead of seven hours a day, a proposal the owners agreed to look into. On April 28 the owners provisionally accepted the idea of the eight-hour day, and no wage reductions. But when Baldwin put the same offer to the miners later that day, it was clear that whatever the compromise, the miners were insisting upon a national minimum wage, while the owners still clung to the existing scheme of locally negotiated, varied settlements. The suggestion of longer hours also caused a protest. 'Surely,' Herbert Smith told Baldwin, 'a man working under surface conditions as miners are has got to work less hours.'

The crisis finally broke on Saturday May 1, when the miners rejected outright the owners' insistence on an immediate reduction in wages, and the entire work force of the mines was locked out. That same day the TUC Executive announced that, in support of the miners, a general strike would begin on May 3, at one minute before midnight. At six on the evening of May 1 the telegrams calling for strike action were despatched from TUC headquarters, and the start of the strike was set for 11.59 pm on May 3. The Cabinet were informed of this fact at an emergency meeting on the morning of Sunday May 2. 'This order for a General Strike,' Thomas Jones noted in his diary, 'of course made a deep impression on the Cabinet, and Ministers more than ever felt that the PM was a helpless innocent moving about amid dangers unrealised. Only yesterday the TUC had informed the PM that they had as yet passed no formal resolution in favour of a General Strike.' Throughout the day negotiations continued between the Government and the TUC,

---

[1] Adam Nimmo,   –1939. Coal owner. Chairman of the Fife Coal Co Ltd. President of the Mining Association of Great Britain. Chairman of the Board of Trade Committee on the Coal Trade after the war, and a member of the Coal and Coke Supplies Committee, 1915–18. Knighted, 1918.

the main discussions being held between Lord Birkenhead and J. H. Thomas[1] during the evening. In a memorandum written four days later Birkenhead noted that he had told Thomas 'that further negotiations seemed to me to be useless unless the Trades Unionist leaders were prepared to take the responsibility of advising the Miners that either in the matter of hours or wages there must be a concession whilst the matter of reorganisation was under adjustment'. Birkenhead added that the 'whole course' of his discussion with Thomas 'made it plain that, so far from approaching accommodation, we were drifting from it'. But the Cabinet still hoped, despite the strike notices, that the TUC leaders would be able to influence the miners in favour of compromise. Leopold Amery recorded in his diary:

. . . at 9.30 we assembled in Winston's room and passed the evening as best we could until about 11. Then Stanley came in very tired and threw himself into an armchair leaving it to F.E. to read out as far as they had got with the discussions. . . .

While we were discussing the news arrived that the Daily Mail had been suppressed altogether by the printers because they did not like its leading article. We had already had information that in the Sunday Express and other papers articles had been considerably censored or dropped out. This turned the scale.

Davidson, in a note written ten days later, described the effect of the *Daily Mail* suppression:

Churchill, Neville Chamberlain, Balfour, Bridgeman and Hogg successively made it clear that it must be the result of the General Strike instructions that had already been dispatched, and the Cabinet came to the conclusion that they could no longer negotiate under the threat of a General Strike, particularly now that this had resulted in an action to silence the press.

The negotiations were promptly suspended and the Government demanded the repudiation of the actions that had taken place and an immediate and unconditional withdrawal of the instructions for a General Strike.

It is a point worth making that there was no dissension on this point. It has often been written that the extremists forced Baldwin's hand, but nothing could be further from the truth.

[1] James Henry Thomas, 1874–1949. Began work as an errand boy at the age of nine; subsequently an engine-cleaner, fireman, and engine-driver. Labour MP for Derby, 1910–31; National Labour MP, 1931–36. General Secretary, National Union of Railwaymen, 1918–24, and 1924–31. President of the International Federation of Trade Unions, 1920–24. Vice-Chairman of the Parliamentary Labour Party, 1921. Secretary of State for the Colonies in the first Labour Government, 1924. Elected to the Other Club, 1925, but resigned in 1930. Minister of Employment and Lord Privy Seal, 1929–30. Secretary of State for the Dominions, 1930–35; for the Colonies, 1935–36.

The unanimity of the Cabinet in breaking off negotiations was unknown to the public. Indeed, it was widely believed, especially in Labour circles, that a 'peace party' led by Baldwin, Birkenhead and Steel-Maitland had been defeated by a 'war party', led by Churchill, Neville Chamberlain and Cunliffe-Lister, whose aim was said to have been confrontation and bloodshed. 'There were no divisions among Ministers,' Hoare noted in his diary a few weeks later, 'and it is incorrect to say that a Churchill–Birkenhead section was determined upon a fight to the finish.' Baldwin himself had been determined to uphold parliamentary democracy in the face of what he believed was an unconstitutional attempt to undermine it. Strongly supported by Birkenhead and Horace Wilson, Baldwin saw the strike of the *Daily Mail* compositors as a direct threat to the freedom of the Press. 'In these circumstances,' he told the House of Commons on the following afternoon, 'and with infinite regret, we had to take the stand that we could go no further.'

As soon as the Government broke off negotiations with the TUC there was no further chance of averting the strike, and on Monday May 3 the Government finalized its preparations. Executive authority for all measures in confronting the strikers was given to the Home Secretary, Sir William Joynson-Hicks, who prepared to send troops to wherever they were needed to protect vehicles carrying food and fuel. The country was divided into ten Divisions, each headed by a Civil Commissioner, and Special Constables were recruited from among the civilian population in each Division. All strike-breaking plans were discussed by a special Cabinet Committee, the Supply and Transport Committee, presided over by Joynson-Hicks.

During the morning of May 3, Joynson-Hicks' Committee decided that as the strike was likely to affect all newspapers, the leading newspaper editors should be asked to cooperate in the publication of a single emergency news-sheet, and that Hoare, Amery and Davidson should arrange for its distribution by road and air. At the Committee's request, Churchill prepared a twelve-point programme on the nature of the proposed news-sheet. The Government, he wrote, would 'assume the whole responsibility' for its finances, and would also use its powers of requisition 'as may be thought advisable'. The Air Ministry would 'co-operate in deliveries', and the editorial staff would receive all Government communications through Davidson 'working under direct instructions from the Cabinet'. Under Churchill's plan the staff would not be 'confined' in their production to official communications, but would aim to produce as interesting a publication as possible 'with the object of encouraging and helping the action of all loyal men'.

At midday, Churchill summoned the editors to his room at the Treasury. Two groups were represented at the meeting, the Newspaper Proprietors' Association, for the London Press, and the Newspaper Society, for the Provincial Press. Among those present were Lord Burnham,[1] Lord Riddell, Sir Andrew Caird[2] and Esmond Harmsworth. Churchill opened the meeting by reading his twelve-point note, which contained, he said, 'merely rough ideas' for discussion. Nevertheless, he added, it ought to form the basis of some 'prompt decisions'. The first speaker, Lord Burnham, offered the Government all the assistance it required to produce its own news-sheet, and recommended either an advisory committee of newspaper men, or 'the services of good journalists'. Churchill then set out in greater detail what he had in mind as the aim of this special newspaper. The minutes of the meeting recorded his words:

. . . the essential thing is that we should produce a really powerful readable broadsheet not merely to contain news but in order to relieve the minds of the people. Something must be done to prevent alarming news from being spread about and there is no reason why it should not be done as well as possible. I do not contemplate violent partisanship, but fair, strong encouragement to the great mass of loyal people.

Churchill explained to the editors that the Government intended to produce its news-sheet with volunteer labour. When 'all this is over', he promised, 'if amateurs have been using the machines and damage is done I will be responsible'. Lord Riddell then pressed Churchill to explain 'what sort of comment' would be put in the news-sheet. Would there, he asked, be a leading article, and if so what would be its policy? In answer to these questions Churchill outlined what he considered the news-sheet should consist of, so far as content was concerned:

---

[1] Harry Lawson Webster Levy Lawson, 1862–1933. Educated at Eton and Balliol College Oxford. Conservative MP, 1885–1906 and 1910–16. Mayor of Stepney, 1907–09. President of the Institute of Journalists, 1910. Succeeded his father (the principal proprietor of the *Daily Telegraph*) as 2nd Baron Burnham, 1916. President of the Empire Press Union, 1916–28. Created Viscount, May 1919. President of the International Labour Conference, Geneva, 1921–22 and 1926; of the Press Experts Conference, 1927 and 1929; and of the Public Health Congress, 1924 and 1927.

[2] Andrew Caird, 1870–1956. Educated at Montrose Academy and Dundee University College. Administrator, New York Headquarters, British (Northcliffe) War Mission to the United States, 1917–18. Knighted, 1918. Managing Director of the *Daily Mail*, 1922–26. Chairman and Managing Director of the *Calcutta Statesman*, 1927–28. Unsuccessful Conservative candidate for St Ives, 1928 and 1929.

Obviously mainly of news, speeches, etc, also recruiting going on, anything occurring in the country organisations. But it should have a leading article, not violently partisan, but agreeable to the great majority of the people of our side: Constitutional, the hope for peace, Parliament maintain authority in the country, injury to trade and reputation of the country.

Lord Burnham argued that such a paper 'must be a Government publication'; it would be unfair to make the newspaper proprietors responsible for it. To this Churchill replied: 'I contemplate the whole of the responsibility to any stage you wish. . . .' All the newspaper men present favoured a Government publication. They also realized that to proceed on these lines, the Government would have to requisition a printing press, ink, paper and personnel. 'No office would be aggrieved,' declared Lord Burnham, 'if it were commandeered.'

Among those present at the meeting was the Controller of the Stationery Office, William Codling,[1] who, as soon as the meeting was over, promised Churchill that he could produce 'one million copies of a news-sheet per diem', using the Stationery Office personnel and printing works and staff.

The House of Commons assembled during the afternoon of May 3 to discuss the impending strike. Baldwin, who opened the debate, spoke of how the Government was challenged by an 'alternative Government' which was 'ignorant of the way in which its commands were being carried out, and incapable of arresting disobedience to them'. It was not wages which were imperilled, he warned, 'it is the freedom of our very Constitution'. When Churchill spoke his tone was conciliatory. Commenting on the moderate tone of the Labour MPs who had spoken, and of Ramsay MacDonald in particular, he described it as 'the measure of the deep anxiety and sorrow we all feel at the miserable turn which the fortunes of our country have taken'. Churchill went on to praise the 'efforts for peace' which had been made by the Trade Union leaders throughout the Sunday negotiations. In particular, he said, J. H. Thomas had tried 'with all the compulsive and persuasive powers of his nature and of his experience to bring about a warding-off of this shocking disaster in our national life'.

Churchill pointed out that the Government had sought peace in the coal industry by means of the special subsidy, now totalling £24 million, 'although it ruined and shattered the finances of two successive years'.

1 William Richard Codling, 1879–1947. Educated at Enfield Grammar School and King's College, London. Entered the Stationery Office, 1898; Superintendent of Publications, 1916–17; Deputy Controller, 1917–19; Controller, 1919–42. Knighted, 1935. Member of the Statute Law Committee of the United Kingdom and Northern Ireland.

He had always believed that if common sense had prevailed a settlement could have been obtained. The Trade Union leaders, he said, had likewise sought agreement, but the miners had been obdurate. Now there was nothing in front of them but 'the terrible, blasting, devastating menace of a general strike'. 'Even so,' he said, 'I am not going to use one single provocative word, for, after all, what is the use of provocative words on such an occasion.' As for the Government's position, he added: 'We cannot by any means divest ourselves of the responsibility of maintaining the life of the nation in essential services and public order.'

Pointing out that the miners' strike was a legitimate one, Churchill added: 'But that is an entirely different thing from the concepted, deliberate organized menace of a General Strike in order to compel Parliament to do something which otherwise it would not do.' If fought out to a conclusion the conflict between the strikers and the Government could only end 'in the overthrow of Parliamentary Government or in its decisive victory'. There was no middle course open. 'The Government may be bundled out of the way,' he said, 'but the other forces, enemies to the Parliamentary constitutional system of this country, forces which deserve and require the consistent control of democrats in every land, would emerge and carry on the struggle in infinitely more disastrous and tragical forms than with which we are now threatened.'

Churchill sought to strike a balance between firmness and compromise, telling the House of Commons:

We are seeking peace, we are defending ourselves, we are bound to defend ourselves from the terrible menace which is levied upon us from tomorrow morning, but we are still perfectly unchanged in our attitude as it was last week. The door is always open. . . .

There is no question of there being a gulf across which no negotiator can pass—certainly not . . . it is our duty to parley.

As soon as the TUC withdrew the strike notices, Churchill concluded, 'we shall immediately begin, with the utmost care and patience with them again, the long and laborious task which has been pursued over these many weeks of endeavouring to rebuild on economic foundations the prosperity of the coal trade. That is our position.'

While the House of Commons was sitting, Davidson was discussing with the editor of the *Morning Post*, H. A. Gwynne, the production of a daily four-page strike bulletin on his own newspaper presses in order to avoid having to make use of the Stationery Office's more limited facilities. Early that evening, Gwynne and his senior editorial colleagues drafted a scheme of cooperation between the Government and the *Morning Post*, promising, if their premises were protected against pickets, to produce a daily bulletin with their own staff, under Government direction. Gwynne believed that by the end of the week he could obtain a circulation of up to 400,000.

At 9.45 that evening Churchill called a meeting of Government officials in his room in the House of Commons to discuss Gwynne's scheme, which they accepted. Churchill then instructed all those present, Davidson, Codling, Sir Malcolm Fraser[1] and David Caird,[2] to go to the offices of the *Morning Post*, and to begin work.

On the arrival of Churchill's four emissaries at eleven o'clock that evening, Gwynne agreed to suspend all *Morning Post* operations then in progress, and to do what he could, as editor, to enable the Government paper to appear at the earliest possible moment. Shortly before midnight Churchill himself arrived at the *Morning Post* building, accompanied by Sir Samuel Hoare. The two Ministers stayed there until three in the morning, helping to supervise the transfer. As some of Gwynne's technical staff refused to accept the new arrangement, Sir Malcolm Fraser was busy throughout the night seeking men to replace them. By four in the morning a skeleton staff was ready, supervised by Fraser on the production side, and by David Caird on the editorial. By then, the General Strike had begun.

On the morning of Tuesday May 4, the first day of the strike, Churchill went to 10 Downing Street to inform Baldwin that there now existed a Government newspaper. At Hoare's suggestion, it had been decided to call it the *British Gazette* and the first issue would appear, if all went according to plan, on the following morning. Thomas Jones, who was present when Churchill made his report, recorded in his diary:

I asked both what was to be my line in any private conversations to-day with any of the Labour folk. Winston said 'There are two disputes on: there is the General Strike which is a challenge to the Government and with which we cannot compromise. Strike Notices must be withdrawn unconditionally. There is also a trade dispute in the coal industry: on that we are prepared to take the utmost pains to reach a settlement in the most conciliatory spirit.'

[1] John Malcom Fraser, 1878–1949. Journalist. Adviser on Press matters to the Conservative Party, 1910. Lieutenant, Royal Naval Air Service, 1915; Captain, 1918; Director-General of Airship Production, Admiralty, 1918–19 (when over 100 airships were completed). Knighted 1919. Principal Conservative Agent, 1920–23. Created Baronet, 1921. Editor of the *Evening Standard*; editor-in-chief, *Birmingham Gazette*; Government representative, *British Gazette* 1926. Vice-Chairman of the Conservative Party, 1937–38.

[2] David Caird, 1863–1934. Born in Scotland. Educated at Aberdeen University. Journalist and Congregational Minister. Director of Publicity, National War Savings Committee and Ministry of Munitions, 1916–19. Director of the Information Section, War Office, 1919–21. Transferred, on Churchill's recommendation to the Colonial Office, 1919; retired, 1929.

Churchill returned to the offices of the *Morning Post*. At three o'clock that afternoon the composing room staff, who had agreed to set up the first number of the *British Gazette*, were ordered by their Union, the London Society of Compositors, to stop work. Churchill telephoned at once to Lord Beaverbrook, for help from the now idle *Daily Express*. Beaverbrook invited Churchill and Hoare to Fleet Street, where they approached the night superintendent of the paper, Sydney Long,[1] a master of the technical side of printing, and his two senior engineers. All three agreed to help rescue the *British Gazette*. Two hours later, on reaching the offices of the *Morning Post*, they found that only five of the fourteen columns of the new paper had been set up in type. While they began work on the remaining nine columns, Malcolm Fraser collected further printers from other papers, including the Chief Stereotyper of the *Daily Mail*, Alfred Hawkins. The editorial staff of the *Morning Post*, who had all remained on duty, also agreed to give what help they could on the technical side.

Churchill watched the process of production with fascination and enthusiasm, exhorting the men to greater efforts, while Gwynne remained in the editorial chair, Caird scrutinized the proofs on behalf of the Government, and Fraser attended to every aspect of the production, as well as making arrangements throughout the day for the paper's distribution. Motor cars and vans were obtained, all with volunteer drivers, to distribute the paper in London and the Home Counties. A special motor park was organized in the quadrangle of Somerset House. Aeroplanes were alerted on Hoare's instructions to fly copies to the north, while Churchill himself enlisted the services of a young Conservative MP, Derrick Gunston,[2] to accompany one of the aeroplanes to Newcastle.

By eleven o'clock on the evening of May 4 the *British Gazette* was almost ready to be printed. Churchill sent a message to the Managing Director of the BBC, John Reith,[3] asking him to broadcast the sound of

---

[1] Sydney W. H. Long, 1878–1958. Joined the *Daily Express* as a production worker at the age of 17. Night Production Superintendent, 1926. A director of London Express Newspapers, 1926–57.

[2] Derrick Wellesley Gunston, 1891–1985. Educated at Harrow and Trinity College Cambridge. On active service, 1914–18; second-in-command, 1st Battalion Irish Guards, 1918 (Military Cross). Conservative MP for Thornbury, 1924–45. Parliamentary Private Secretary to Kingsley Wood (Minister of Health), 1926–29; to Neville Chamberlain (Chancellor of the Exchequer), 1931–36; to David Margesson (War Office), 1940–42. Created Baronet, 1938.

[3] John Charles Walsham Reith, 1889–1971. Educated Royal Technical College Glasgow. Engineer's apprentice; then joined S. Pearson & Son Ltd as an engineer, 1913. On active service, Royal Engineers, 1914–15 (seriously wounded in the head). Major, 1915. Mission to America, for munitions contracts, 1916–17. Admiralty Engineer-in-Chief's Department, 1918.

the paper presses. But Reith declined to do so, and the presses began their work unheard by the wireless-owning public. No sooner had the printing begun than Churchill telephoned to P. J. Grigg, asking him to come at once to the *Morning Post* offices. It was nearly midnight. After some search, Grigg later recorded, 'I discovered the great man sitting in solitary contemplation by the rotary presses. With a wave of his arm he directed my attention to the inexorable mechanical power rolling out newspapers which would, a few hours later, be distributed all over the country. . . .'

The presses worked all night; by six o'clock on the morning of May 5 a total of 230,000 copies had been printed, the majority of which were already on their way to news vendors throughout the country.

As a result of the somewhat chaotic nature of its production, the May 5 edition of the *British Gazette* had several defects. Of its four pages, the centre two were blank. Several items on its back page had been culled from the reserve copy of the *Morning Post*, so that neither the 'Zoo Notes' nor the item on 'Ice Hockey in Canada' bore any relation to the gravity of the hour. But apart from this, each of the paper's fourteen columns of print bore the professional look of a well-established paper. The tone of the main article on the front page was optimistic, minimizing the effect of the strike, and describing with enthusiasm the myriad voluntary services that had sprung up. The central column quoted Baldwin's declaration in Parliament warning that the strikers' aim was to replace the existing Constitution by a 'reign of force . . . threatening the basis of ordered government and coming nearer to proclaiming civil war than we have been for centuries past'.

Churchill himself wrote the article, unsigned, which covered the sixth and seventh columns of the first page.[1] If the strike were to succeed, he declared, the Trade Union leaders could become 'masters of the whole country'. This would involve 'the virtual supersession of Parliament and of the representative institutions which we have established in our island after three hundred years of struggle, which we have preserved almost alone among the nations of Europe, and which are the foundation of our democratic freedom'. Later in his article Churchill wrote:

In charge of liquidation of munitions engineering contracts, 1919. First General Manager, BBC, 1922; Managing Director, 1923; Director-General, 1927–38. Knighted, 1927. Chairman, BOAC, 1939–40. Minister of Information, 1939–40. Minister of Transport, 1940. National MP for Southampton, 1940. Created Baron, 1940. Minister of Works, 1940–42. Lieutenant-Commander, RNVR, 1942; Director of Combined Operations, Material Department, Admiralty, 1943–45. Member Commonwealth Telecommunications Board, 1946–50.

[1] As with each of his subsequent unsigned articles, Churchill kept a copy of his original typescript among his private archive.

Nearly all the newspapers have been silenced by violent concerted action. And this great nation, on the whole the strongest community which civilisation can show, is for the moment reduced in this respect to the level of African natives dependent only on the rumours which are carried from place to place. In a few days if this were allowed to continue, rumours would poison the air, raise panics and disorders, inflame fears and passions together, and carry us all to depths which no sane man of any party or class would care even to contemplate.

It was proposed, Churchill added, 'to use the unlimited resources of the State' in order to raise the newspaper's circulation.

That same morning Churchill took steps to increase the staff of the *British Gazette*, telegraphing to Lindemann at Oxford: 'Your volunteers should report to Locker-Lampson's office at St Stephens House where full arrangements can be made to put them up . . .' Churchill added that the fourteen undergraduates Lindemann had collected should report to the Treasury that evening.

On the evening of May 5 the General Council of the TUC published its own strike newspaper, the *British Worker*, which declared in an editorial: 'Never have the workers responded with greater enthusiasm to their leaders.' That evening Joynson-Hicks broadcast an appeal over the wireless for special constables, and declared that by supporting the General Strike, the Trade Union movement was violating law and order. During the day Churchill attended a meeting of Joynson-Hicks' Supply and Transport Committee, but as P. J. Grigg, who accompanied him, later recorded, 'it immediately became evident that little, if anything, had been overlooked, and Winston very soon confined himself to the business of supervising the official newspaper . . .'[1]

By nightfall on May 5 the search for paper had become acute, particularly after the *Daily Herald* had put its own substantial stocks at the disposal of the *British Worker*. 'To defeat this plan,' Sir Malcolm Fraser later recorded in a memorandum for the Cabinet, 'the "British Gazette", on behalf of the Government, commandeered the whole of the "Daily Herald" and "British Worker" paper, and also caused a check in their ink supplies so that the TUC were reduced to producing an insignificant quantity of a small quarto sheet. . . '. Further paper was commandeered from what Fraser described as 'friendly newspapers', although

---

[1] Under Malcolm Fraser's control, the search continued for technical help. During May 5 he sent Churchill a list of those who 'could be used most usefully at the moment': 20 linotype operators, 8 stereotypers and 30 rotary machine mechanics. Churchill approached two of the newspaper men who had been at the meeting on May 3, Sir Andrew Caird and Esmond Harmsworth, both of whom agreed to find men willing to leave the *Evening News* and *Daily Mail* for the duration of the strike, and to work on the *British Gazette*.

the editor of *The Times*, Geoffrey Dawson, resented the move, refused to disclose the size of his stocks, and protested in its own columns at what it regarded as unjust interference. As a gesture of defiance, Dawson, having told Fraser that he only intended to print 80,000 copies of the small format emergency paper still being printed at *The Times*, raised his production to half a million.

The second issue of the *British Gazette*, published on the morning of Thursday May 6, consisted of four pages instead of two. The main article on the front page, which Churchill had written but not signed, admitted that the strike was inflicting 'increasing loss and inconvenience' on all sections of the population, but went on to declare: 'Ample forces are available to maintain order. . . . The supplies of fuel and food are sufficient to maintain the life, though not the prosperity of the country for many weeks to come. . . . The nation remains calm and confident, and the people are bearing with fortitude and good temper the inestimable hardships of a national crisis.' The front page also carried a message from Baldwin, in which he stated: 'The General Strike is a challenge to Parliament and is the road to anarchy and ruin.' A leading article on page three, also written by Churchill but likewise unsigned, warned that there could be 'no question of compromise of any kind', and added: 'either the country will break the General Strike, or the General Strike will break the country'. The article stressed the responsibility of the Trade Union leaders, who bore, Churchill asserted, a 'grievous' responsibility for all that had happened. The well-meaning majority among them, he wrote, had 'drifted weakly forward under the pressure of extreme men', and had yielded themselves to a course of action 'reckless, violent, and, but for the strength and good sense of the British nation, immeasurable in its possibilities'. The Trade Union leaders, he went on, should now reconsider their action. Such would be the 'manly' course. They should realize into what 'deep and deepening waters' the strike was 'daily carrying them'. But whatever the Trade Unions decided, he added: 'the authority of Parliamentary Government over any sectional combination must be vindicated'.

The May 6 issue of the *British Gazette* sold more than half a million copies, twice the sales of the previous day, at a penny each. That morning Sir Philip Sassoon telegraphed to Hoare from Cambridge that the paper 'has impressed & heartened people all over the country enormously'. The extra work required for so rapid an increase in both production and distribution led to strains among the staff, and there was some resentment at Churchill's constant supervision and exhortation. Gwynne wanted the Government's control to come through one source alone, preferably Davidson, and on May 6 he protested to Davidson about the continued division of authority. Davidson at once wrote angrily to Baldwin, explaining the cause of Gwynne's discontent, and criticizing Churchill's activities:

The failure to some extent in the details of distribution of the British Gazette has been due entirely to the fact that the Chancellor occupied the attention of practically the whole of the staff who normally would have been thinking out the details. Of course he was anxious, but it was unfortunate that he tried so persistently to force a scratch staff beyond its capacity.

So long as he does not come to the Morning Post offices again tonight the staff will be able to do what it is there to do, viz organizing the printing, the production and distribution of the Gazette.

I must depend on you, and the staff are relying on me, to find some means of preventing his coming. By all means let him put what pressure he can personally upon Sir Malcolm Fraser, who is in general control, and the Stationery Office, by interview or letter, but the technical staff should be left to do their job. He rattled them badly last night.

He thinks he is Napoleon, but curiously enough the men who have been printing all their life in the various processes happen to know more about their job than he does.

With the circulation of the *British Gazette* soon likely to reach a million copies, the problem of paper became hourly more urgent. By telephone, Sir Malcolm Fraser ordered a shipload of 450 tons of paper from Holland; a load equivalent to thirteen million copies of the four-page newspaper. He then commandeered the Bowater Paper Mill at Northfleet, and, as the mill workers themselves were on strike, collected more than two hundred volunteers to work the machinery. As the local population resented this strike-breaking action, the War Office agreed to send a company of Royal Engineers to the works to protect the volunteers, while the Admiralty sent a naval guard to protect the barges taking the paper to London.

On the morning of May 7 the *British Gazette*'s main article, signed with the words 'by a Cabinet Minister', and in fact written by Churchill, declared that J. H. Thomas had lied when he had told the House of Commons two days earlier that the negotiations between the TUC and the Government had only broken down because the Government had 'taken offence' at the stoppage at the *Daily Mail*. This, Churchill wrote, was untrue. The TUC, by sending out strike instructions on the previous day, had put 'a pistol' at the head of the Cabinet, and it was this 'brutal threat' of a General Strike that had made further negotiations futile; to have given way to such a threat would have left the Government 'bankrupt in public respect'. Writing in his diary later that day, one Union leader, Walter Citrine,[1] described this article as 'a poisonous attempt to bias the public mind'. In Labour circles, it was widely, and correctly believed that Churchill himself was its author.

The May 7 issue contained a second unsigned article by Churchill entitled simply 'Official Communiqué', which stressed the success of the voluntary services in progressively surmounting 'every obstacle'. All attempts to 'impede the free movement' both of the public and its food would, the article declared, 'be methodically and finally repulsed'. The communiqué also gave a guarantee 'that all persons who continue or resume their work in faithful duty to the country will be protected thereafter from reprisals or victimization by the Trade Unions, and the Government will take all necessary steps to secure this'.

During the morning of May 7 Churchill sent a personal letter to Worthington-Evans, warning him that if there were not sufficient special constables by the following week, serious disorders might occur, and it would then be necessary to call in troops from the Territorial Army to protect food convoys from the docks, volunteer bus and train crews, and those factories which were still operating with volunteer labour. 'I am not suggesting that this measure need be decided upon for the next two or three days,' he wrote, 'but only begging you to prepare your mind for it,' and he added:

Do not, I beg you, speaking with the knowledge of so many years of military affairs, be misled by silly War Office objections against this measure. The Territorial Army will recover after the conflict is over, but even if it suffers for some years it will not have suffered in vain. Such an embodiment will immediately give you the necessary mass of men to afford the widespread protection which is essential, and will enable you to keep the regular units concentrated.

'It is far better,' Churchill stressed, 'to take too many precautions than too few.'

Churchill was under no illusion about the efficacy of the strike, despite his efforts in the *British Gazette* to create an optimistic impression: 'All our vaunted railway services,' he told Worthington-Evans, 'do not exceed one-twentieth of the normal.' Remaining at the Treasury, Churchill arranged for a continual supply of strike information which

[1] Walter McLennan Citrine, 1887–1983. Secretary of the Electrical Trades Union, 1914–20; Assistant General Secretary, 1920–23. Assistant Secretary, Trade Union Congress, 1924–25; General Secretary, 1926–46. Director of the *Daily Herald*, 1929–46. Knighted, 1935. Visited Russia, 1936 and 1938. Privy Councillor, 1940. Member of the National Production Advisory Council, 1942–46, and 1949–57. Created Baron, 1946. Member of the National Coal Board, 1946–47. Chairman of the Central Electricity Authority, 1947–57.

he himself sifted to see if it were suitable for publication. The collection of material was organized by P. J. Grigg, who received daily reports of the strike situation from all over Britain; from the railway companies, the police, the Civil Commissioners and private individuals. Churchill's principal instruction to Grigg was to suppress any news that might encourage the strikers, or discourage the volunteers. Thus, on May 7, he marked several items on the Civil Commissioner's secret report No 6: 'not recommended for publication'. These included a report of serious shortages of flour in several London districts, an acute sugar shortage in Leicester and the refusal of petrol drivers employed by Shell to take out their lorries without protection. Churchill also wished to keep out of the *British Gazette* all details of 'rowdyism and intimidation' by the strikers, such as the overturning and stoning of trams by 'a disorderly crowd' at Hammersmith, and the looting of shops in the Old Kent Road, when police had been forced to use their truncheons in order to clear the street.

One account of Churchill's advice in Cabinet, and his relations with his colleagues, was given by Davidson in a letter which he wrote to the new Viceroy of India, Lord Irwin,[1] more than one month later, on June 14. According to Davidson, the 'most striking example of the difference of opinion' was when it was decided to send the first convoy to the docks to bring meat, sugar and other necessities into London. Then, Davidson wrote, 'Winston was all for a tremendous display of force; machine guns hidden but there, should be placed along the route; tanks should be used in addition to armoured cars; and so on.' On that occasion, Davidson added, 'Moderation prevailed,' and he went on to tell Irwin of another incident, in which Baldwin had been the moderating influence: 'The Prime Minister played a very skilful game,' he wrote, 'in postponing a decision by the Cabinet, on the question repeatedly raised by Winston and F.E. of taking over the BBC and running it as a governmental propaganda agency. Winston was very strong in his insistence that the Government ought to assume complete possession. I was equally strong and Jix shared my view that it would be fatal to do so.'

---

[1] Edward Frederick Lindley Wood, 1881–1959. Educated at Eton and Christ Church Oxford. Conservative MP for Ripon, 1910–34. Parliamentary Under-Secretary of State for the Colonies, 1921–22. President of the Board of Education, 1922–24. Minister of Agriculture, 1924–25. Created Baron Irwin, 1925. Viceroy of India, 1926–31. President of the Board of Education, 1931–34. Succeeded his father as 3rd Viscount Halifax, 1934. Secretary of State for War, 1935. Lord Privy Seal, 1935–37. Lord President of the Council, 1937–38. Foreign Secretary, 1938–40. Ambassador in Washington, 1941–46. Order of Merit, 1946. One of his three sons was killed in action in Egypt in October 1942.

At 10 Downing Street on the morning of May 7, Thomas Jones urged
Baldwin to make some conciliatory gesture towards the moderate Trade
Unions. Jones pointed out that an article in the *British Worker* issued the
previous evening had declared 'The General Council is ready at any
moment to resume negotiations for an honourable settlement', without
prior conditions. Baldwin was attracted by Jones' suggestions, but not so
Churchill, as Jones recorded in his diary:

I then hurried to see Winston and had one of the fiercest and hottest
interviews in my life. I put to him the policy I put to the PM a few minutes
earlier, but before I had got any distance with it and when he saw what was
coming, he overwhelmed me with a cataract of boiling eloquence, impossible
to reproduce.

'We were at war. Matters had changed from Sunday morning. We were a
long way from our position then. We must go through with it. You must
have the nerve.'

I shouted back 'I have plenty of moral nerve, but we want something
beside nerve.'

He retorted, 'You have a terrible responsibility in advising a man so
sympathetic like the Prime Minister.'

At the Cabinet meeting that morning, Churchill presented a scheme
for incorporating Territorial troops into the volunteer police services.
Complete units of the Territorial Army, he urged, ought to join a special
volunteer 'Civil Force' which would remain part of the Police Force.
The Cabinet accepted this suggestion, and Baldwin then set up a special
Committee, under Churchill's chairmanship, to work out the details
that same afternoon. The two other members of the Committee were the
Home Secretary, Joynson-Hicks, and the Secretary of State for War,
Worthington-Evans, and its Secretary was an official of the Committee
of Imperial Defence, Major Ismay.[1] In his memoirs Ismay recalled the
scene that afternoon in Churchill's room at the House of Commons:

The Committee duly assembled and Churchill put everyone at their ease
at once. 'I have done your job for four years, Jix, and yours for two, Worthy,
so I had better unfold my plan.' Whereupon he propounded the eminently

[1] Hastings Lionel Ismay, 1887–1965. Educated at Charterhouse and Sandhurst. 2nd Lieutenant, 1905; Captain, 1914. On active service in India, 1908 and the Somaliland, 1914–20
(DSO). Staff College, Quetta, 1922. Assistant Secretary, Committee of Imperial Defence,
1925–30. Military Secretary to the Viceroy of India (Lord Willingdon), 1931–33. Colonel,
1932. Deputy Secretary, Committee of Imperial Defence, 1936–38; Secretary (in succession
to Sir Maurice Hankey), 1938. Major-General, 1939. Chief of Staff to the Minister of Defence
(Churchill), 1940–45. Knighted, 1940. Deputy Secretary (military) to the War Cabinet,
1940–45. Lieutenant-General, 1942. General, 1944. Chief of Staff to the Viceroy of India
(Lord Mountbatten), 1947. Created Baron, 1947. Secretary of State for Commonwealth
Relations, 1951–52. Secretary-General of NATO, 1952–57. He published his memoirs in 1960.

sensible idea of asking territorial battalions, particularly those in London, to volunteer *en bloc* as auxiliary police. They would be paid at military rates, and given a reasonable subsistence allowance in lieu of rations. They would not be used individually, but in formed bodies; and they would have arm-bands instead of uniforms, and truncheons instead of rifles.

Joynson-Hicks intervened to enquire where the money for the extra expenditure was to come from. The Home Office, he said, had no funds available.

'The Exchequer will pay,' retorted Churchill. 'If we start arguing about petty details, we will have a tired-out police force, a dissipated army and bloody revolution.'

The Committee's conclusions, which Churchill himself dictated to Ismay, instructed the Secretary of State for War 'immediately' to order the headquarters of all territorial units to form companies of the Civil Constabulary Reserve, to be 'a paid whole-time force'. In addition, all commanding officers should be ordered 'actively to promote the forma-tion of Civil Reserve Companies'. The aim was to create an unarmed, non-military force from military units which would, wherever possible, be retained as complete units. Baldwin accepted the Committee's scheme.

The policy of commandeering paper for the *British Gazette* led on May 8 to a short but acrimonious clash with *The Times*. On the previous day Geoffrey Dawson had written direct to Baldwin to protest that his own paper was quite capable of adopting a firm pro-Government stance. The task of the regular newspapers struggling to appear in truncated form would be 'greatly simplified', Dawson wrote, if they were not sub-jected by the Government 'to competition for scanty supplies of men and materials, to say nothing of the prospect of their being paralysed alto-gether by the seizure of their stocks'. Baldwin sent Dawson's letter to Churchill on May 8. That same day Churchill explained what had been done, and why, telling Dawson that the urgent shortage of paper had led the Government to make its requisition 'general to all newspapers', but, he added:

It is quite possible, however, that it will not be necessary to put it into effect against any well disposed paper that is actually making an effective production. We shall know in a few days much better how we stand and how the new supplies are coming forward. Meanwhile there is no reason why you should not go on as at present with your most brilliant and courageous effort. . . .

The *British Gazette*, Churchill continued, 'is devouring paper at a terrible rate'; and he went on to explain its aims and importance:

. . . this is the one means which at present exists of holding together, in direct contact with the Executive Government and Parliament, the whole loyal mass of citizens throughout the nation, on which success depends. It is the only vehicle now left for concerting action simultaneously in all parts of the country. I hope you will remember what a frightful task it is to feed all these millions of people in the face not only of desertion, but of widespread obstruction. Any serious breakdown in supplies or vital services might lead to an appalling local catastrophe. We cannot really afford to take needless risks or neglect any possible precaution.

'One of the difficulties of the situation,' Churchill added, 'is that large numbers of working people feel quite detached from the conflict; and they are waiting, as if they were spectators at a football match, to see whether the Government or the Trade Union is the stronger.'

10

'Tonight Surrender:
Tomorrow Magnanimity'

ON May 8 Sir Herbert Samuel, who had returned from abroad, began to act, with the Cabinet's approval, as an independent intermediary. On the Government side the discussions were conducted throughout the day by Baldwin, Birkenhead, Neville Chamberlain and Steel-Maitland. That evening Baldwin broadcast over the BBC. 'No door is closed,' he declared, 'but, on the other hand, while the situation remains what it is, we have no alternative whatever but to go forward unflinchingly and do our duty. . . .' These were Churchill's identical words in his Commons speech on May 3. 'I am longing, and working, and praying for peace,' Baldwin continued, 'But I will not surrender the safety and the security of the British constitution.'

That night a special *Sunday Gazette* was being prepared at the offices of the *Islington Daily Gazette*. It was a small operation, organized by Oliver Locker-Lampson and produced largely by student volunteers. Towards midnight Churchill himself visited the newspaper office, while Lindemann, who had provided many of the students, remained until dawn, when the last copies of the paper were despatched for circulation. The whole edition of the *Sunday Gazette* was sold out by nine o'clock that Sunday morning: nearly 7,500 copies had been printed, bringing in a total of £30.

Sir Herbert Samuel continued his attempts at mediation throughout Sunday May 9. During the day Thomas Jones recorded in his diary the continuing friction at the *British Gazette*, where Monday's issue was being prepared. 'The Private Secretaries at No 10,' he wrote, 'are all trying to get Winston put in charge of Transport. Gwynne of the "Morning Post" has sent several messages begging that Winston should be kept away from that office where the "British Gazette" is being printed. He butts in at the busiest hours and insists on changing commas and full stops until the staff is furious.'

During May 9 Sir Malcolm Fraser warned Churchill that the proprietors of the *Daily Mail* were becoming resentful at the depletion of their own resources involved in helping the *British Gazette*. Sir Andrew Caird felt that by continuing to provide technical experts, the *Daily Mail* were placing their paper at a disadvantage for renewing publication 'unless other Newspaper Owners do the same thing'. For his part, Churchill took immediate steps to try to persuade the still hesitant newspaper proprietors to send help of their own. In a telegram to the four uncooperative proprietors—Lord Burnham, Major Astor, Sir William Berry[1] and Edward Cadbury[2]—he asked for 'any assistance in your power' to enable the *British Gazette* to 'double circulation'. To Lord Beaverbrook, who was anxious to begin printing the *Daily Express* again, and who had threatened to withdraw Sydney Long and his two engineers from the *British Gazette*, Churchill telegraphed on May 9: 'Earnestly request you give any further assistance in your power.'

Churchill's appeals were not entirely successful; most of the newspaper proprietors had begun to resent his activities, fearing that when they were ready to appear, he would use his emergency powers to continue to control newsprint, ink and personnel. Only Cadbury's response was favourable, for on May 10 he telegraphed to Churchill that he was 'encouraging non-technical staff assist any way possible'. As for his technical staff, Cadbury explained, they were all on strike.

On the evening of May 9 Churchill dined at 11 Downing Street with Lord Grey of Fallodon. The two men discussed a draft message to be sent by Grey to the *British Gazette*. 'The issue now,' Grey wrote in his message, 'is not what the wages of miners should be, but whether democratic Parliamentary Government is to be overthrown.' After dinner, John Reith arrived to drive Grey to the BBC, where he was to broadcast. In his memoirs Reith recalled how:

. . . hearing that someone had come for Lord Grey, Churchill came out and invited me to join them for coffee. In due course he enquired if I were

---

[1] William Ewert Berry, 1879–1954. Son of a Merthyr Tydfil Alderman. Founded the *Advertising World*, 1901. Editor-in-Chief of the *Sunday Times*, 1915–36. Created Baronet, 1921. Editor-in-Chief of the *Daily Telegraph* from 1928 until his death. Created Baron Camrose, 1929; Viscount, 1941. Chairman of the Financial Times Ltd and Chairman of the Associated Press. Principal Adviser to the Ministry of Information, 1939.

[2] Edward Cadbury, 1873–1948. Educated at Quaker schools. Director of the British Cocoa and Chocolate Co Ltd. A Life Governor of Birmingham University. Owner, *Daily News*.

connected with the BBC. Yes. In what capacity? Managing director. He swung round in his chair: '*Are you Mr Reith?*' Perhaps I had not come up, or rather down, to what he had been expecting. He said he was greatly interested to meet me; had been trying to do so all week. I replied that I had been on the job every day and most of every night, and would have been very glad to meet him. . . .

He was polite to me; I wished we had had a proper set to at the beginning of the strike. He came to the car with us; said he was very glad to have met me; he had heard I had been badly wounded in the war—'In the head, wasn't it?' I said yes, but that my present attitude was not traceable thereto.

In its issue on the morning of May 10, the *British Gazette* published Lord Grey's message. It also gave prominence to a message from Lord Balfour warning of the dangers of revolution should the strike succeed. In such an event, Balfour wrote, Britain's national heritage would be squandered 'amid incalculable suffering' at the hands of 'violent and irresponsible doctrinaires'. That evening an article in the *British Worker* declared:

Day by day in the Cabinet's newspaper, Mr Churchill, acting as its super-editor, publishes articles by prominent public men. These are suspiciously like one another.

This morning's contribution is signed 'Balfour', but the hand almost all through is the hand of Churchill, who is trying, still, to create panic by representing an industrial dispute about wages as an attempted revolution. . . .

The reference to the Strike being directed by a 'relatively small body of extremists' again betrays Mr Churchill's hand. It is mere violent, headlong, foolish propaganda—foolish because no sensible person will believe it. It is impossible that Lord Balfour can suppose Mr Pugh,[1] Mr Thomas, Mr Bevin[2] and other members of the General Council, who have always been moderate, reasonable men, to have been suddenly transformed into 'extremists' as rash and reckless as Mr Churchill himself.

The threat of revolution, the newspaper added, 'exists nowhere save in Mr Churchill's heated and disorderly imagination'.

[1] Arthur Pugh, 1870–1955. Educated at elementary school. Lost both his parents in infancy. Apprenticed to a farmer and butcher at the age of 13. Took up the trade of a steel smelter in Wales, 1894. Assistant Secretary, British Steel Smelters' Association, 1906. General Secretary of the Iron and Steel Trades Federation, 1917–36. Knighted 1935. Chairman of the General Congress of the Trade Union Congress, 1925.

[2] Ernest Bevin, 1881–1951. National Organizer, Dockers Union, 1910–21. General Secretary, Transport and General Workers' Union, 1921–40. Member of the TUC General Council, 1925–40. Labour MP for Central Wandsworth, 1940–50; for East Woolwich, 1950–51. Minister of Labour and National Service, 1940–45. Privy Councillor, 1940. Secretary of State for Foreign Affairs, 1945–51. Lord Privy Seal, 1951.

During May 10 there had been several Parliamentary questions about the *British Gazette*; 'a number of angry little scenes', as the paper itself described them. Commander Kenworthy[1] asked whether newsprint was being requisitioned by the Government, and if so, whether all newspapers could use it. Churchill replied that 'all available newsprint' was indeed being requisitioned, but that there was no question of it being put at the disposal of any newspapers 'engaged in imperilling the life of the nation'. The Government, he added, 'cannot be impartial as between the State and any section of its subjects with whom it is contending'.

In the early hours of May 11 more than a million copies of the *British Gazette* were printed and distributed. The tone of the articles and news items was optimistic. 'Supplies improving everywhere' read the main headline. According to the reports sifted by Gwynne and Fraser, a fifth of the railway staff were still at work; a record number of special constables had been recruited in London during May 10; and a convoy of 170 lorries, driven by volunteers and escorted by armoured cars, had brought supplies from the London docks without incident. 'Most of the onlookers,' the paper wrote, 'professed a kind of cynical amusement.' At the docks, all the unloading had been done by volunteer labour, much of it by students. It was also announced that several newspapers had begun printing again, and that 'a considerable number' of *Daily Express* employees had applied for reinstatement.

During May 11 Lord Beaverbrook decided to re-start the *Daily Express* as soon as possible, and resisted Churchill's attempts to requisition his newsprint. 'I have in the premises two hundred tons of newsprint,' Beaverbrook wrote to him on May 11. 'It would be necessary to leave us in possession of this supply. Otherwise our plans would be impeded.' To this Churchill replied on the same day:

My dear Max,

We are trying to solve the news-print difficulty as quickly as possible. The rapidly increasing circulation of 'The British Gazette' will make the paper shortage very acute. We are expecting to publish over three millions tonight, and we shall probably have to requisition every scrap of news-print which is available and suitable. I hope, however, that by the middle of next week our supplies will be coming forward well, and I hope it may be possible to help

[1] Joseph Montague Kenworthy, 1886–1953. Entered Royal Navy, 1902. Commanded HMS *Bullfinch*, 1914; HMS *Commonwealth*, 1916. Lieutenant Commander, 1916. Admiralty War Staff, 1917. Assistant Chief of Staff, Gibraltar, 1918. Retired from the Navy, 1920. Liberal MP, 1919–26. Labour MP, 1926–31. Succeeded his father as 10th Baron Strabolgi, 1934. Opposition Chief Whip, House of Lords, 1938–42. President of the United Kingdom Pilots Association, 1922–25. Chairman of the Advisory Committee on Sea Fisheries, 1926–32.

both you and Rothermere to start then. I hope you will not attempt to do so beforehand, as it would then be necessary for me to release all the key-men that Rothermere's people have contributed and this would gravely cripple the Government organ during the days when its influence may be indispensable to the successful termination of the crisis. . . .

I have in confidence told Sir Malcolm Fraser of the position and of your wish, and have asked him to facilitate your resumption on or after Wednesday, the 19th, if the news-print situation can possibly be adjusted. We are also training understudies for all the key-men sent us by 'The Daily Mail', as well as for the three splendid fellows you so kindly lent us at the beginning. . . .

Beaverbrook replied at once, pointing out the extent of the help he had given to the *British Gazette*. 'We have made immense sacrifices at this end,' he wrote, 'and I personally guaranteed the employees of this office who took on the task of producing the "British Gazette", at a time when no other London newspaper, except the "Morning Post" was giving material assistance.' Nevertheless, Beaverbrook added, he would be willing to hand over his final two hundred tons of paper 'if it is absolutely necessary for the Government'.

During the evening of May 11, Churchill learnt that Beaverbrook still intended to start printing both the *Daily Express* and the *Evening Standard* as soon as possible. At a Cabinet meeting that evening Amery also argued in favour of a return to 'normal newspaper publication' for all papers, and an end to the *British Gazette*, recording in his diary:

This let loose Winston in a magnificent tirade on the wonders achieved, the selfishness of the Press in wishing to increase its circulation at expense of others during the crisis, the impossibility of letting go at the moment without unfairness to one or other newspaper and ended with his determination to suppress the Daily Express, if, as they intended, they started an evening paper in the next four days. Against his vigour and enthusiasm nobody except Eustace Percy had the courage to say anything and most of those who for days have been going around and complaining rather left me alone when I belled the cat!

According to the Cabinet minutes, Churchill agreed 'to bring the Gazette to an end as soon as the daily newspapers were in a position to resume normal publication'. The minutes also recorded that 'general appreciation was expressed of the success achieved by the Chancellor of the Exchequer'.

On the morning of May 12 Churchill wrote to Beaverbrook to protest once more. 'The withdrawal of your key men . . .,' he wrote, 'would practically bring us to a standstill.' At the end of his letter Churchill told

Beaverbrook of a sudden change in the strike situation. 'There are persistent rumours,' he wrote, 'that a crisis has been reached in the TUC. Within 48 hours we shall know a great deal more than we know now. Therefore I beg of you to defer, as you have so consistently done hitherto, to my wish in the public interest, and take no fresh departure at any rate until we have had some further conversation.'

The TUC were now anxious to end the strike, and had begun to try to persuade the miners to agree to negotiate with the Government. During May 11 Churchill had dictated a letter for Baldwin, setting out his own views on how the Prime Minister ought to proceed:

Dear PM,

The point to which I wish to draw your mind is that there must be a clear interval between the calling off of the General Strike and the resumption of the coal negotiations. The first tonight—the second to-morrow. But nothing simultaneous and concurrent. That will I am sure be fatal.

No question of subsidy even for a fortnight can be mixed with the withdrawal of the General Strike. To-night surrender. Tomorrow magnanimity. On the interval between these two depends the whole result of this deep national conflict.

On the morning of May 12 the General Council of the TUC decided that it could no longer support the miners in their determination to remain on strike, and shortly after midday they went to see Baldwin at 10 Downing Street. Arthur Pugh, speaking as Chairman of the TUC General Council, informed Baldwin that the TUC had decided to call off the strike notices immediately. Walter Citrine, who had accompanied Pugh to Downing Street, recorded in his diary:

While we were talking, Churchill, Baldwin, and Steel-Maitland were pacing rapidly up and down the garden, talking animatedly. There was no sign of jubilation amongst them, and Pugh muttered to me: 'I saw Churchill a few minutes ago, and he said, "Thank God it is over, Mr Pugh."'

On the afternoon of May 12 Churchill summoned the leading newspaper editors to the Treasury, and it was agreed that the next issue of the *British Gazette* should be its last. 'There was always the possibility,' Churchill warned, 'that a further appearance might have a bad effect on the relations between newspapers and their employees.' As soon as the newspaper editors had gone, Churchill wrote to H. A. Gwynne to thank him for his help in 'a novel and unprecedented crisis', and to describe the cooperation of Gwynne and his staff with Sir Malcolm

Fraser as 'beyond all praise'. In his reply on the morning of May 13, Gwynne reciprocated this praise. 'You have been kind enough to say nice things about our humble efforts here to bring out the BRITISH GAZETTE,' he replied. 'May I lay at your feet my tribute of admiration at your wonderful energy and your marvellous powers of seeing a thing through.'

On Thursday May 13 the final edition of the *British Gazette* announced the end of the strike. One headline declared: 'Surrender received by Premier in Downing Street.' The newspaper also announced its own demise. This final issue of the paper sold 2,209,000 copies, a 'stupendous total', in its own words. An article drafted by Churchill gave the history of the newspaper's eight issues, and ended: 'The *British Gazette* may have had a short life; but it has fulfilled the purpose of living. It becomes a memory; but it remains a monument.' That same day Lord Goschen[1] telegraphed his congratulations on the 'firm stand' taken by the Government throughout the crisis. 'I agree with you,' Churchill replied on May 14, 'that what has happened is a most striking testimony to the stability of the country.'

Contemporary assessments of Churchill and the *British Gazette* varied. Lord Irwin, separated as Viceroy of India from all his former colleagues, received four distinct accounts, the first on May 15 from the Earl of Crawford and Balcarres,[2] who described the newspaper itself as 'extremely serviceable'. But Lane-Fox, writing on May 23, described Churchill as 'most belligerent and troublesome', while Geoffrey Dawson, who had been in dispute with Churchill during the crisis, wrote on June 8 with a hostile and inaccurate account, the content of which was to gain wide acceptance:

Winston seems to have been the only minister who rather lost his head. He was excitable, provocative, and a great trial to his colleagues. They tried to divert his energies at an early stage to the editing of the *British Gazette*, an official propagandist organ, in which capacity he became a similar trial to us. However, all went well in the end, and we bear no malice for his outrageous raid on our paper.

[1] George Joachim Goschen, 1866–1952. Educated at Rugby and Balliol College Oxford. Conservative MP for East Grinstead, 1895–1906. Succeeded his father as 2nd Viscount 1907. Joint Parliamentary Secretary, Board of Agriculture, 1918. Governor of Madras, 1924–29; acting Viceroy of India, June–November 1929. Privy Councillor, 1930.

[2] David Alexander Edward Lindsay, Lord Balniel, 1871–1940. Educated at Eton and Magdalen College Oxford. Conservative MP for Chorley, 1895–1913. Succeeded his father as 27th Earl of Crawford, 1913. Served in the Royal Army Medical Corps, 1915. President of the Board of Agriculture and Fisheries, 1916. Lord Privy Seal, 1916–18. Chancellor of the Duchy of Lancaster, 1919–21. First Commissioner of Works, 1921–22. Minister of Transport, 1922.

The fullest account of Churchill's activities came from Davidson, who had actually seen Churchill at work on the paper from day to day, and who wrote to Irwin on June 14:

Winston is really a most remarkable creature. His energy was boundless and he ran entirely on his own lines. Whether it was right or wrong he desired to produce a newspaper rather than a news sheet. He, in fact, conceived that the *British Gazette* should be a better newspaper than any of the great journals whose operations had been temporarily suspended. . . .

The result was, I think quite good, and the energy and vitality of Winston were very largely responsible for it. He is the sort of man, whom, if I wanted a mountain to be moved, I should send for at once. I think, however, that I should not consult him after he had moved the mountain if I wanted to know where to put it.

From the moment the strike ended, Churchill's part in the Government's policy towards the strikers was singled out, and exaggerated. Within two weeks of the end of the strike, the *New Statesman* set out, in its issue of May 22, a detailed account of the alleged activities of the 'war party' on the night of May 2. According to the paper, Churchill had led this group in the threat of immediate resignation if negotiations with the TUC were continued, and had been throughout that critical day 'in favour of war at all costs'. The newspaper continued: 'Mr Churchill was the villain of the piece. He is reported to have remarked that he thought "a little blood-letting" would be all to the good. Whether he actually used this phrase or not there is no doubt about his tireless efforts to seize the providential opportunity for a fight.'

Outraged by this allegation, Churchill contemplated legal action. 'It is wholly untrue and unfounded,' he wrote to Sir Douglas Hogg from Chartwell on May 26, and he continued:

As you will know, my arguments in Cabinet were all directed to keeping the Military out of the business, and to using, even at great expense, very large numbers of citizens unarmed. I am sure I have never used any language not entirely consistent with this. The charge appears to be a gross libel upon a Minister in the execution of his duty, and I certainly do not feel inclined to allow such a lie to pass into the general currency of Labour incriminations.

Churchill asked Hogg if the allegations in the *New Statesman* made it liable for a criminal prosecution by the Crown. Replying two days later, Hogg agreed that the article could probably be made the subject 'of a criminal prosecution for libel', but he cautioned that any such prosecution would enable the defence to 'discuss in detail' the Cabinet's deliberations. Hogg felt reluctant to advise this, and Churchill agreed to let the matter drop. But his anger was not easily assuaged, and he resented the persistent Labour attempts to portray his actions during the strike as provocative. 'I decline utterly,' he told the House of Commons on July 7, 'to be impartial as between the fire brigade and the fire.'

Several Labour members objected to Churchill's tone, but Churchill was in a teasing mood. In organizing a newspaper, he said, it was essential to decide whether 'to fortify the faithful or to convert the heathen', a remark which caused Labour protests and Conservative laughter. But, as Baldwin wrote to the King:

. . . the climax to it all came in the last sentence of Mr Churchill's speech when he turned his attention to the revolutionary threats uttered by Mr Purcell.[1] Speaking in the most dramatic tones in which defiance and solemnity were mingled and shaking his finger in a threatening manner at the Members of the Opposition, Mr Churchill, in a House that was tense with anticipation, delivered this solemn pronouncement:

'One last word. The Honourable Member for the Forest of Dean has indicated that a time may come when another trial of strength will occur and when something like this will be tried again upon the country or the community. I have no wish to make threats or to use language which would disturb the House and cause bad blood. But this I must say; make your minds perfectly clear that if ever you let loose upon us again a general strike, we will loose upon you—another "British Gazette".'

The anti-climax was perfect. The shouts of angry defiance which were waiting on the lips of the Labour Party gave way to an outburst of unrestrained laughter in which the House was convulsed. Mr Churchill's whole attitude had led the Labour Party to believe that they might expect one of his fulminatory and warlike declarations with reference to tanks, machine-guns and all the armed forces of the State, and the complete bathos contained in his final words was a consummate jest which no one appreciated more than the victims at whose expense it was effected. It was a happy ending to a good humoured debate.

A year later, on 10 June 1927, Churchill wrote to H. A. Gwynne: 'I shall always look back to that extraordinary ten days. They form one of the most vivid experiences of my somewhat variegated life. . . .'

[1] Albert Arthur Purcell, 1872–1935. Secretary, Manchester and Salford Trades Council. Labour MP for Coventry, 1923–24; for the Forest of Dean, 1925–29. President of the International Federation of Trade Unions, 1924–27.

11

The Coal Strike:
The Search for a Settlement

DURING May the Government adhered to its proposed settlement of the Coal Strike, based on an immediate return to work, a reduction of wages and no increase in working hours, and on May 20 Baldwin asked Churchill to be a member of the Cabinet Committee on the Royal Commission on the Coal Industry. At its meeting that day, this 'Coal' Committee learnt that the miners' Executive were 'unable to recommend the miners to accept any reduction in their wages'. The owners also, the minutes recorded, 'were dissatisfied with the Government's proposals and would probably reject them on the following day'. At the meeting Churchill proposed a new settlement, which he drafted with Cunliffe-Lister, and which they both initialled on the following day. If there were to be a reduction in miners' wages, they wrote, there should also be a reduction in owners' profits, 'ie there should be a sacrifice by both parties'. Nor should the minimum wage be set at a figure 'below which on social grounds miners ought not to work'. By May 31 these proposals had been elaborated, put to both the owners and miners, and actually found acceptable in West Yorkshire. During the day Cunliffe-Lister telephoned a message to Baldwin, Churchill and Lane-Fox that the acceptable terms were an 8-hour day, subsistence wages and the owners to 'work without profit' until those wages reached the 1924 level. Outside Yorkshire, however, no such agreement seemed possible.

On May 31 the Government's policy towards the Coal Strike was discussed at an informal meeting between Baldwin, Birkenhead and Churchill. Thomas Jones, who was present, recorded in his diary Churchill's opposition to prolonging the confrontation with the miners:

Winston said it looked like a policy of starvation at a frightful cost to the country. It was not as easy as in 1921 to sit still for a month or two. Public now more excited and exasperated because prosperity seemed not far away. Many railwaymen out, many out on relief. Union funds largely exhausted. Government might not sit still. We ought to legislate at once and say what hours may be worked in any mine in which wages are not below a certain level. That minimum should be one which commends itself to the good sense of the wage-earners. Whether should add limitations of profits was a subsidiary point on which he could not express an opinion. Birkenhead was in general agreement with Winston and wanted the Cabinet called.

The PM resisted. He recalled 1921 and recalled L.G.'s refusal to butt in. He was successful.

Winston: After 12 weeks at frightful cost.

PM: We've got to guard against a settlement which is not a settlement. No time wasted so far. Our proposals turned down ten days ago. There are mutterings in various parts of the country. That process will quicken. I am not clear in my mind on what we should butt in. For tomorrow I see nothing but a stone wall.

On June 3 Churchill was present at another Cabinet Committee, that on Trade Union Legislation, at which proposals were made for stronger anti-Union laws. Churchill urged caution, telling his colleagues that he hoped 'that the contemplated legislation would be confined to declaring general strikes to be illegal, and to secure that no strike should take place unless a majority of those affected was in favour of it. . . . He hoped, however, that the Bill would not attempt to deal with matters such as peaceful picketing or the repeal of any part of the Trade Disputes Act of 1906. He doubted whether any ballot conducted otherwise than on the lines of a Parliamentary Ballot would be satisfactory.'[1]

At a Cabinet meeting on June 9 Churchill warned his colleagues of the 'serious financial position of the country, which was likely to be aggravated by any continuance of the coal strike'. That same day he wrote to Baldwin, reiterating that the Coal Strike was beginning 'to cut deep into our prosperity and finance', and adding:

More than 3 weeks have passed since our talk on the eve of the holidays without any progress except by the slow process of attrition. I believe that if we had legislated on June 1 to the effect that any mine that can pay the

---

[1] At a further meeting of this Cabinet Committee on June 22, Churchill supported the idea of a secret ballot, telling the Committee: 'He was convinced that the majority of working men would adopt a sound and sensible attitude and that a secret ballot would be a most effective method of restricting the influence of the young and extremist members of the Union'.

existing rate (or some lesser quite defensible rate) may work 8 hours during (say) a 3-years period of reorganisation—we should now be nearer to a break away in the coalfields & to a series of district settlements. But if I am wrong how could we be worse off than we are? We are relying solely upon economic pressure administered regardless of cost. That remains after all the final process. We ought to avoid it & save the country & the mines from it, if it be in human power. . . .

The Ministers of Mines & Labour are content to wait on from day to day & week to week in the hopes of the miners' resistance collapsing. But I am bound to point out to you the *terrible* cost to the nation of these time units wh are being so lavishly & passively paid out. The Trade future is being compromised for a whole year in advance. As to Finance conceive the effects upon an Income tax no longer based on the 3 years average.

I feel strongly on this matter & against a policy of continuous waiting from day to day. Even if in a fortnight there is a settlement, I shall still believe that guidance by the Govt & H of C wd have produced it earlier. But if it lasts still longer, as well it may, then a grave injury will be done to us all. Even if Government legislation were rejected by both sides, nothing wd happen worse than that. . . .

At three in the afternoon of June 14 the Coal Committee met to consider the terms it would offer to the owners. These terms were based on the points drawn up earlier by Churchill and Cunliffe-Lister; an extra hour of work with wages to remain substantially the same as for the shorter working day, but with upward revisions of wages to reach a national minimum in districts where wages had already fallen. Churchill then spent two hours with the owners, from 6.30 to 8.30 pm, putting this suggestion to them. An hour and a half later he reported to Baldwin and the Committee that he had told the owners 'that the Government might find themselves driven to legislate over the heads of both parties to the dispute, that the miners would not be willing to lose on both hours and wages, and that some advance on the position hitherto taken up by the owners was most desirable and urgent'. The Committee then decided to go ahead with its proposals for an eight-hour day, with wages at the seven-hour rate, and a minimum wage set within a national framework based on existing rates.

While it was also agreed that a further subsidy was impossible, Churchill told the Committee that he would like to use the money offered by the Government 'to help provide steel houses in mining areas, and for training schemes and other forms of assistance for dis-placed miners'.

On June 15 the Government informed the Commons that it had decided to introduce a Bill legalizing an eight-hour working day in the mines, and that, in return, the mine-owners had promised to put forward definite wage offers in each district within a national framework. But for two weeks the mine-owners refused to put forward the promised proposals, and on June 26, after two further meetings of the Cabinet Committee, Churchill wrote to Baldwin:

. . . I am seriously concerned about the delay in the mine owners' posting the new wage scales on an 8 hours basis at the pits. It was a fortnight last Thursday since we took the decision to introduce the Bill & they for their part assured us of the wage scales they wd offer. We were told they were meeting on the Saturday & that early in the next week the notices wd be issued. Since then nothing has appeared. The miners have been left with nothing but the proposed increase of hours, & yr general statement of the wage position. We were I thought counting on definite wage offers in each district, & in more than half of a satisfactory character to bring about district cleavages. But this process has so far been wholly inoperative, & meanwhile losses and misery are rolling up thicker and thicker. . . .

It seems to me that very good reasons not known wd be required to justify this long & hideously costly delay. If of course you have plans & are in negotiations with which I am not acquainted there is no doubt a perfectly satisfactory explanation; & my misgivings are groundless. But if it is just drift on the part of the Ministry of Labour, then I feel they are taking a good deal of responsibility.

Churchill resented his colleagues' reluctance to act with decision when dealing with the coal-owners. 'Nothing would be easier for me,' he told Baldwin, 'than to leave these events to take their course, & confine my gaze to the depleted Exchequer, & it is only my earnest desire for the success of yr Government wh induces me to write this letter.' But Steel-Maitland and Lane-Fox, who were together conducting the negotiations with the coal-owners, did not share Churchill's sense of frustration. 'I get constant evidence,' Lane-Fox wrote to Thomas Jones on June 26, 'that if an Eight Hours Bill is pushed through the strike may break.' The Bill received its second reading on June 28, its third on July 1. During the debate on the third reading Churchill defended the Bill as one which 'extended the basis' on which the owners and the miners might reach a settlement. Describing the debate to the King on July 2, Baldwin wrote:

. . . The House always crowds in to hear Mr Churchill, who, quite apart from the entertainment which any 'bonny fechter' affords, is always worth hearing as an orator after the old school and of the grand manner. His performance on this occasion was admirable, and although in his exposition he emphasised the facts of the situation—a proceeding which is always repugnant to the feelings of the Opposition—yet his consideration for those feelings and his good humour gave them no opportunity to denounce him as 'provocative'.

He observed that however mild a use might be made of the powers given by these emergency regulations, no responsible person could say that in a stoppage like this they were not necessary or that their necessity did not increase as the continuance of the dispute aggravated conditions in the country. It was easy to criticise the handling of a big dispute. At any stage some other decision might have been taken, and since the dispute continued irresponsible critics could always say that the decision taken was the wrong one. If the Government are firm, they say, 'How stubborn!': if they are conciliatory, 'How weak!': if they act, 'How precipitate!': if they wait, 'How dilatory!'. . . .

The Eight Hours Bill received the Royal Assent on July 8. But the owners still refused to put forward new wage scales for the longer day, and the strike continued. On July 10 the miners' leader, A. J. Cook,[1] announced defiantly: 'Not a penny off the pay, not a second on the day.'

For more than a month the coal negotiations were suspended, and the strike continued. During this period Churchill's work centred on the final settlement of the French war debt. The French Government had already agreed to repay the sum they owed, including interest, in regular instalments. Now they wanted to be protected against having to pay money to Britain in the event of the Germans refusing to pay reparations to them. Churchill was anxious to allay French fears. Negotiations continued throughout June and early July. Then, on July 12, Churchill and Caillaux signed an agreement settling the outstanding questions. On the following day Churchill made a statement in the House of Commons, explaining that Britain had finally agreed that France's discharge of her debt—by means of sixty-two annual payments of £12½ million—depended upon the French receiving the reparation still owed to her by Germany. In the event 'of a complete or very serious failure' of German payments, Churchill explained, France would be entitled to ask for reconsideration of her own debt to Britain. Such a concession by Britain, Churchill added, 'in no way invalidates the responsibility of France'.

[1] Arthur James Cook, 1885–1931. After elementary school, he worked underground as a miner for 21 years. Won a scholarship to the Central Labour College, 1911. Miners' Agent, Rhondda district; imprisoned 1918 and 1921 for taking part in strikes and lock-outs. Member of the Executive of the Miners' Federation of Great Britain, 1918–31; subsequently General Secretary. Member of the General Council of the TUC. Member of the Executive of the Labour Party. Member of the Government Mines Welfare Committee and Advisory Board, 1929–31. A member of the 1917 and Trade Union Clubs.

Churchill's proposals were debated in the Commons on July 19. Among those who defended them was Captain Eden,[1] who rejoiced that 'a source of possible friction between us and France has been removed'. Churchill himself, in what Baldwin described to the King as 'a quiet, logical and reasoning frame of mind', urged patience and tolerance in Britain's attitude to war debts, telling the House that experience and the passage of time would produce 'immense alleviations of the situation which at the present time presses with iron severity on the war-racked nations of Europe'.

On July 21 the Finance Bill passed its Third Reading in the Commons. Debating it in the Lords five days later, Lord Balfour remarked that 'so far as my judgement goes, at a very difficult period, under conditions of unusual difficulty, our finances have been directed by the Chancellor of the Exchequer with singular courage, great caution, great invention and, as I think, great success'. Churchill was delighted by Balfour's accolade, sending him a note across the Cabinet table at 10 Downing Street two days later:

I was so pleased to read yr vy gt compliment of my work at the Exchequer wh you paid me in yr speech in the H of L.

It was like being 'mentioned in despatches'.

During August, with the Coal Strike in its fourth month, all attempts to reconcile the mine-owners and the miners broke down. By mid-August, Baldwin's colleagues felt that he was badly in need of a rest. 'S.B. has suffered most from the strike. . . .' Neville Chamberlain wrote in his diary on August 10, 'he too is worn out, and has no spirit left.' Chamberlain added: 'Winston has decidedly improved his position and is very popular, I believe, with our side, as he really is with the whole House for the wonderful entertainment he gives them.' Writing to Lord Irwin five days later, Chamberlain described Baldwin as 'worn out and almost paralyzed'. As for Churchill he wrote:

Winston constantly improves his position in the House and in the Party. His speeches are extraordinarily brilliant and men flock in to hear him as

[1] Robert Anthony Eden, 1897–1977. Educated at Eton and Christ Church Oxford. Served on the western front, 1915–18, when he was awarded the Military Cross. Conservative MP, 1923–57. Parliamentary Under-Secretary, Foreign Office, 1931–33. Lord Privy Seal, 1934–35. Minister for League of Nations Affairs, 1935. Foreign Secretary, 1935–38, 1940–45 and 1951–55. Knight of the Garter, 1954. Prime Minister, 1955–57. Created Earl of Avon, 1961. One of his brothers was killed in 1916 at the battle of Jutland. His elder son was killed in action in Burma in 1945.

they would to a first class entertainment at the theatre. The best show in London they say, and there is the weak point. So far as I can judge they think of it as a show and they are not prepared at present to trust his character and still less his judgement.

Personally I can't help liking and admiring him more, the more I see of him, but it is always accompanied by a diminution of my intellectual respect for him. I have noticed that in all disputes of a departmental character that I have had with him he has had to give way because his case was not really well founded.

On August 18 Lane-Fox also sent Irwin a character sketch of Churchill. He too had once had his suspicions, but the passage of time and experience of the man himself had begun to allay them:

> Winston seems to me to be playing the game very well, he is an affectionate creature at heart, and I really think he has a deep affection for S.B. I think he feels he owes unexpectedly high office to him, and the possible conspiracy that you and I once dreaded, when Winston and F.E. might rally the Die-hards and break up the Cabinet seems to me more unlikely now, partly because F.E.'s still bibulous and I think Winston would not feel him to be a very reliable ally, but mainly I believe because of Winston's own personal feelings for S.B.

In the third week of August Baldwin suffered a severe attack of lumbago, and was persuaded to go abroad, to Aix-les-Bains. Before leaving, he asked Churchill to take charge of the coal negotiations. 'I am quite happy that S.M. & Winston should deal with coal,' Joynson-Hicks wrote to Baldwin on August 24, and on August 25 Churchill telephoned Thomas Jones, who was serving as Secretary to the Committee, asking him to dine that night at Chartwell to discuss the next day's meeting between the Committee and the miners' leaders. Jones reached Chartwell at 8 in the evening. Professor Lindemann was among the guests. In his diary, Jones gave an account of the dinner:

> Winston plunged into the coal business at once, and I tried in vain to postpone the subject until after dinner when I could have talked in private with my host, but he is the most unsubtle and expansive person. He talked with the greatest freedom and frankness before Lindemann and the rest, making several little speeches in the course of dinner, one especially in defence of a change of opinion which Mrs Churchill alleged against him. The two elder children were with us, Diana about 17, and Randolph about 15. Nothing could be more charming than Winston's handling of the children throughout my short visit.
>
> Lindemann, I quickly discovered, regarded all miners, if not all the working classes, as a species of sub-humans. This drove me to the Extreme Left with Winston at the Right Centre. The ladies left at about 10 pm and

we carried on till past midnight, Randolph being allowed to stay to the end as a special privilege, and his father frequently deferring to him for his opinion on some phase or other of the coal crisis: the boy was extremely intelligent, and obviously under the influence of the Prof (as he was called).

Jones remained at Chartwell overnight, recording in his diary on the following day:

I was out and about before 9.0 am, and found the Chancellor attired in dungarees and high Wellington boots superintending the building of a dam by a dozen navvies. This is the third lake, and the children are wondering what their father will do next year, as there is room for no more lakes.

As I was going away, he told me 'I am very glad you expounded the democratic faith last night, as the small boy does not often hear it, and it will be very good for him.' I agreed, and said that in view of what was likely to happen in the next twenty years it was desirable he should not be unduly Lindemannised. The father agreed but said he was eager that the boy should get a scientific outlook.

During the morning of August 26 Jones returned to London. Churchill's cousin Lord Wimborne, who had been negotiating privately with the miners, reported that their terms for ending the strike remained unchanged: no lengthening of working hours, no reduction of pay, and a renewal of the full Government subsidy. But Cook was still anxious for a meeting between the miners' leaders and the Government, and Churchill, who had meanwhile returned to London, at once agreed.

At four that afternoon, an hour before his meeting with the miners' leaders, Churchill summoned the Cabinet's Coal Committee to a special session. Lord Birkenhead, who was unable to be present, sent a telegram urging the Committee to remind Cook that it was 'his own perverse obstinacy' which made a settlement impossible. During the discussion Churchill spoke sympathetically of the miners' desire for a national wage arrangement, telling the Committee that, as the minutes recorded:

... he had no wish to see the Government assist in breaking up the Miners' Federation. The sound position for the Government was to refuse further financial help. Other aspects of the dispute were on a different plane. If the Miners' leaders attached great importance to a national agreement it was not the business of the Government to oppose, provided there was the necessary elasticity for dealing with exceptional districts. If the men continue unreasonable and break up in the field, there would be district settlements but they were not likely to be permanent.

After the meeting Thomas Jones recorded in his diary: 'The prevailing view at the Committee was that Cook is simply playing for time by keeping up a pretence of negotiations and delaying the break-away of the men. Cook & Co are due here at 5 o'clock and we hear that they will try to prevent a Press report of the meeting being issued tonight and will try to keep up the mystery until Parliament meets on Monday.' The Coal Committee, Jones added, 'will have none of this; they will force the Miners' leaders to state categorically whether they have any new proposals to make which the Government can put before the Owners'.

The meeting between the Coal Committee and the miners' leaders began, at 10 Downing Street, at five o'clock. According to the stenographic notes of the meeting, Churchill declared at the outset: 'we are here to listen to any statement or suggestions which you make', but when Herbert Smith asked for financial help from the Government, Churchill rejected his request at once, telling the miners that the possibility of any further Government subsidy 'has long passed out of the sphere of practical politics', and he continued:

When I last saw Mr Cook I told him that we gave 23 millions to secure nine months in which to try and come to some sort of settlement of this position. It was a very questionable thing for the Government to do to use the taxpayers' money in that way and we had the greatest difficulty in justifying it. That was the end, absolutely the end.

Churchill pointed out that in his April budget he had set aside £3 million to help miners where pits had been closed, but that as a result of the 'tremendous expenses' created by the Coal Strike, that sum was 'entirely withdrawn'. Nevertheless, he added, there could still be a small sum left over for 'aiding the movement of miners from any pits which may be closed'. But that sum might amount only to £1½ million, and once it was used up, 'that is the end'. He continued:

It is not our money: we are answerable to the taxpayers of the country as a whole, and there are 750,000 men out of work who would now be working apart from miners but for this prolonged stoppage. There is an immense amount of suffering throughout the country in many districts particularly in the working class districts in the big basic industries.

The revenue is affected, everything is affected. We made an effort last year to avoid these evils, but now these evils have happened. We could not possibly consider anything in the nature of financial help.

Churchill reiterated that if the miners would put forward some new proposals, he would be prepared to press the owners to make concessions. The Government had no intention, he stressed, 'to humiliate you or the miners. As a Government we have no such idea or feeling in our mind, nothing of the sort. There is nothing we should rejoice in more than that you should make a good working arrangement in the industry.'

As the discussion developed, Cook seemed to favour a more flexible approach than Smith. But the Government's refusal to consider a subsidy united both men in their determination not to give way. 'I want to emphasise this,' Smith told Churchill, 'we are not here to say to you we are beaten . . .,' and Cook added: 'We feel that your reply was rather brutal to us.' A few moments later, addressing himself to Cook, Churchill declared: 'I sympathise with you in your task' and he explained that the Government could only go back to the owners if the miners had new proposals to offer, and he went on: 'I wondered if there was something new on the tip of your tongues except this old demand for a subsidy.'

Replying, the miners spoke bitterly about the profits accruing to the owners, and about the low wages and grim conditions of the men in the pits. The Government, said Tom Richards,[1] 'is indebted to the mining industry, and should not be squeamish about four million pounds to try and put it on its feet'. But Churchill would not give way, and after two hours of discussion, agreement was nowhere in sight. Churchill insisted that the Government's policy was to try to reach an agreement. 'We would rather have a settlement reached by an agreement to which both parties put their names,' he said, 'than by the struggle being fought out to the bitter end.' Smith reacted with scepticism to Churchill's appeal. The Government's offer to help, he said, 'puts me in mind of a man in the river drowning and a man on the bank saying "if you come in to the side and drag yourself out I will wipe your feet" '. Smith added: 'We are not going to settle on any terms. I am going to fight a bit yet. I am nearly 65 and there is a bit of fight in the old dog still.'

The meeting broke up at seven o'clock without any agreement.

[1] Thomas Richards, 1859–1931. Born in Ebbw Vale. Left elementary school at the age of ten to work in the mines. In 1884, while still working at the coal face, he formed the Ebbw Vale Miners' Association. Miners' Agent, Ebbw Vale District, 1888–1901. General Secretary of the South Wales Miners' Federation from 1898 until his death. Labour MP for West Monmouth and Ebbw Vale, 1904–20; resigned to devote his services to the Miners' Federation, of which he became Vice-President (President, 1930–31). Privy Councillor, 1918. Member of the TUC General Council, 1925–31, and of the National Executive of the Labour Party. On 9 November 1931 *The Times* wrote: 'Moderate, cautious, and conciliatory in his counsel to the miners on all occasions, and often dissenting profoundly from the policy they were bent on pursuing, he held their loyalty and confidence by the courage and firmness he displayed when the battle was joined. Beneath his mild and deprecating demeanour there were surprising reserves of strength and determination. He could not be browbeaten. He met intimidation with outspokenness and candour.'

Churchill was disappointed that the miners had brought no new proposals; the miners were angered by the Government's refusal even to consider a possible short-term subsidy. But at a further meeting of the Cabinet's Coal Committee on August 30 the owners' inflexibility was the main point of discussion. Churchill and his colleagues were almost unanimous in wanting to warn the owners that they must either make concessions, or lose the Government's support. Only the Secretary for Mines, Lane-Fox, dissented from this view. Lane-Fox read the Committee a letter which Evan Williams had sent him on the previous day, in which he stated 'that any further meetings between Coalowners and the Miners' Federation on a National basis are absolutely out of the question'. Williams went on to expose what he believed were the real intentions of the miners' leaders, 'working for nationalisation or socialisation by means of the power which national agreements give them to threaten and hold up the whole country and then make an industrial question a political issue'.

Throughout the ensuing discussion, as Thomas Jones recorded in his diary, Churchill remained convinced that it was the owners whose attitude was impeding a settlement, and he argued in favour of warning the owners that if they were 'unreasonable', the Government 'would not shrink from modifying the Eight Hours Act', introducing independent district boards with Government-appointed chairmen, and enforcing a national minimum wage rate. 'The dominant note of this morning,' Jones wrote to Davidson later that day, 'was the desire to retain the Government's reputation for playing fair with both sides.'

On August 31 Churchill explained to the House of Commons that his personal desire was for a fair and just settlement, and that he had no desire to coerce the miners. It was also beyond Parliament's power, he explained, either to coerce the miners or to compel the owners to keep their pits open. As to his own position, he wanted an agreed settlement, and would work hard for one, in spite of rumours to the contrary. 'One set of criticism,' he remarked caustically, 'is that the Prime Minister is always anxious to be very tender-hearted and make peaceful settlements, and that I am the marplot who frequently comes forward and intervenes to obstruct.' As for the miners, he asked: 'Surely there ought to be a little generalship among those who aspire to lead a million men?' At the end of his speech he declared:

Look at the year we have passed through. It has been an utterly wasted year. Business is all disorganised. The trade union masses are lamentably impoverished . . . hideous reciprocal injuries are being inflicted by British hands on British throats. All this year has been squandered in what is the most melancholy and at the same time the most ignominious breakdown of British common sense ever exhibited.

But it is still not too late if we proceed together in a sincere spirit, if we remember that we all have to dwell together in this small island of which it is our bounden duty, whatever our political opinions, to make the best and not, as we are now doing, to make the worst.

Churchill's speech won widespread praise. Writing that same day to Baldwin, Thomas Jones described it as 'a brilliant speech, dignified, conciliatory, and fair', while Joynson-Hicks wrote to the King: 'Mr Churchill's reply could hardly have been excelled. It is almost sufficient to say that he has seldom appeared to better advantage in the House.' Churchill, wrote Joynson-Hicks, 'reviewed the whole problem in the most calm unprovocative and dispassionate manner that was possible. . . . It was a speech of conciliation, reasonableness and good-will which undoubtedly made a considerable impression on Members of the Labour Party.'

On the afternoon of August 31, immediately following his speech, Churchill and his Coal Committee met an owners' delegation led by Evan Williams. According to Jones' letter to Baldwin on the following day, Churchill told the owners 'quite plainly' that if an agreement could be reached on how long the miners should work, and how much they should be paid, the Government 'would not allow' the owners' refusal to accept a national agreement to block a settlement. The owners, however, reiterated their desire to settle with the miners on a district-by-district basis, still hoping to concede less in some districts than a comprehensive national agreement might allow. The owners also pointed out that miners were already drifting back to work in two districts, Nottingham and Derby, and that in their view 'we were in sight of the end, and that other districts would quickly follow'.

Churchill did not accept the owners' arguments. At the same time he persevered with his efforts to persuade the miners to put forward negotiable proposals. When, on September 1, Ramsay MacDonald asked to see him privately, he at once agreed. Before meeting Mac-Donald, Churchill received from Donald Fergusson[1] a secret note of the terms to which, apparently, Cook had already committed himself. These terms, which had been obtained through Thomas Jones, were:

[1] John Donald Balfour Fergusson, 1891–1963. Educated at Berkhamsted School and Magdalen College Oxford. On active service, 1914–18. Entered Treasury, 1919; Private Secretary to successive Chancellors of the Exchequer, 1920–38. Permanent Secretary, Ministry of Agriculture and Fisheries, 1936–45; Ministry of Fuel and Power, 1945–52. Knighted, 1937. One of his three sons was killed on active service in the Second World War.

1. Subsidy abandoned.
2. Government to help with displaced miners.
3. Government to help expedite reorganisation.
4. Settlement by national agreement.
5. A national minimum percentage with district variations.
6. Right of appeal of districts to National Committee on wage rates.
7. National Committee with independent Chairman whose decision shall be final.
8. The National Committee to be authorised to review and fix wages subject to the following conditions: Wage rates and percentage may be fixed for 8 hours, 7½ hours and 7 hours providing that the men shall have the right to accept either.

On the afternoon of September 1 MacDonald was driven to Chart-well, his journey a closely guarded secret. At discussions during the evening, Churchill and MacDonald were joined by Steel-Maitland, Lane-Fox and Sir Ernest Gowers,[1] the latter of whom drafted an account of the conversation. MacDonald stressed that no one knew he had come, but that he had 'much influence' with the miners, and in particular with Herbert Smith. He was prepared to urge them to begin negotia-tions on the question of wages and hours, provided these were really open to negotiation, and that they could be embodied in a compre-hensive national settlement, albeit with district variations. Churchill approved these terms, and suggested inviting both the owners and the miners to a tripartite Conference, at which the Government would act as intermediary. 'It was quite likely,' he told MacDonald, 'that the owners, in view of their present attitude, might refuse to come, or, if they did come, might take a line that would make progress impossible.' If this happened, the Government 'would make no secret of their opinion that they were in the wrong'. But even if this happened, Churchill added, 'the powers of actual coercion that the Government possessed were very limited'.

MacDonald expressed himself content. That evening Churchill telegraphed to Baldwin: 'Things are moving a little favourably but nothing definite yet. Am keeping close touch with George [Lane-Fox]

---

[1] Ernest Arthur Gowers, 1880–1966. Educated at Rugby and Clare College Cambridge. Entered the Inland Revenue, 1903; transferred to the India Office, 1904. Principal Private Secretary to Lloyd George (at the Exchequer), 1911–12. Chief Inspector, National Health Insurance Commission, 1912–17. Secretary, Civil Service Arbitration Board, 1917–19. Director of Production, Coal Mines Department, 1919–20. Permanent Under-Secretary for Mines, 1920–27. Knighted, 1926. Chairman, Board of Inland Revenue, 1927–30. Chairman, Coal Mines Reorganization Commission, 1930–35; the Coal Commission, 1938–46. Chairman of the Royal Commission on Capital Punishment, 1949–53. Author of *Plain Words* (1948).

and Arthur [Steel-Maitland]. Shall know by Saturday and will wire you again. General position quite satisfactory.'

Lane-Fox had wanted Churchill to be much firmer with MacDonald. In a letter to Lord Irwin two weeks later, on September 15, he wrote of how, during the Chartwell discussions, 'Winston became more and more expansive and talked, as you might expect, very rashly; and though I did my best to get the formula made pretty stiff so as to be sure the miners meant business, Winston was very impatient and the others did not back me much. . . .'

Throughout September 2 MacDonald put pressure on the miners to agree to tripartite negotiations, and at four in the afternoon he sent Churchill a message that the preliminaries had gone well. By late afternoon it looked as if the miners' delegates would authorize their Executive to negotiate. 'So far so good,' Thomas Jones wrote during the day to Davidson, who was at Aix with Baldwin. 'If the delegates give the executive plenary powers, negotiations with owners via the Government will start at once and will be pushed forward by the Chancellor of the Exchequer with the utmost vigour.' Churchill himself telegraphed to Baldwin that evening:

We have offered miners to press owners to negotiate in three-cornered conference with Government providing miners assent to our formula involving adjustment of wages and hours to meet immediate economic needs. MacDonald who is helping told me good progress today and probably desire consult me tomorrow. Owners' opposition to national negotiations will be serious and if miners really make honest offer a clash will occur with them. I shall probably have more definite information for you to-morrow or Saturday. Meanwhile everything is well in hand.

In writing again to Davidson on September 2, Thomas Jones commented: 'The Chancellor of the Exchequer is doing excellently,' and he added that there was no need for Baldwin to return until the settlement was ready to be 'sealed & signed'. Asked about Baldwin's possible return, Hankey wrote to Jones on September 3:

The true statesmanship is to get the PM to use his best agent in the matter. Of course I see the danger of Winston's 'reaping the harvest'. But the PM will get more kudos by effecting a settlement through Winston than by 'swapping horses while crossing the stream'. From the point of view of the Government, and even of the head of the Government, the settlement is the thing. . . .

During Friday September 3 the miners agreed to allow their Executive to negotiate with the owners. At three o'clock that afternoon

Ramsay MacDonald held a second secret meeting with Churchill, this time at the private house of Churchill's friend Sir Abe Bailey,[1] in Bryanston Square. The two men, who were alone, discussed what sort of formula the miners should use in writing to the Government. At 4.15 Churchill took the formula to the Treasury, where he examined it with Steel-Maitland, Lane-Fox and Sir Ernest Gowers. Once more, Lane-Fox disapproved of Churchill's compromise, but, as he informed Irwin in his letter of September 15, 'we could not repudiate him'.

Two hours later Churchill and Jones returned to Bryanston Square, where, together with MacDonald and four miners' leaders, including Cook, a final version was worked out. The final formula read: 'We are prepared to enter into negotiations for a new national agreement with a view to a reduction in labour costs to meet the immediate necessities of the industry.' Returning again to the Treasury, Churchill informed Steel-Maitland, Lane-Fox and Gowers that the miners were now willing to break the deadlock. Reflecting on Churchill's actions during the day's discussions, Lane-Fox wrote in his letter to Irwin: 'I have little doubt that seeing conciliation in the air with his usual impulsiveness he said a good deal more to the miners than he ought and raised their hopes of what he was going to do to coerce the owners much too high.'

While these negotiations were proceeding, a telegram from Baldwin, sent from Aix-les-Bains early in the afternoon, arrived for Churchill at 11 Downing Street. In it Baldwin declared:

Assume your conference has object of bringing parties together and not making Government a partner. If district settlements, wages and hours can be included in national agreement well and good. You on the spot can alone judge when to jump in but be careful of Ramsay. Awaiting further news.

Cook's letter, embodying the agreed formula, reached the Treasury early that evening. At 8.15 Churchill, Steel-Maitland, Lane-Fox, Fergusson and Jones dined at the Savoy Grill, where news was brought to them by Ernest Gowers that Evan Williams 'was quite firm', as Jones reported to Baldwin, 'in refusing to enter into a joint conference'. At 9.45 Churchill returned to the Treasury where he spent two hours with Evan Williams. Although the owners were still determined not to enter into negotiations with the miners, they agreed, reluctantly, to meet the Cabinet Coal Committee. According to the minutes, Churchill

---

[1] Abe Bailey, 1863–1940. One of the principal mine-owners of the Transvaal. Knighted, 1911, for his services in promoting South African Union. Served as a Major on the staff of the South African forces which attacked German South-West Africa, 1915. Created Baronet, 1919. His son John married Churchill's eldest daughter, Diana, in 1932 (divorced 1935).

urged Williams in his reply to the Government's invitation to a joint conference 'to avoid closing the door upon further meetings with the Government'. At 11.15 that night Churchill telegraphed the text of the miners' new formula to Baldwin. His telegram continued:

It was clearly understood at informal meeting I had with them and MacDonald that the phrase 'reduction in labour costs' meant hours as well as wages. On this Coal Committee decided that sufficient ground existed for government to request owners to resume negotiation. We all felt that any conference to be useful must be three-cornered with the government presiding. Next step will be refusal of coal owners to negotiate nationally and we shall argue they are already committed by the assurance they gave before you introduced the eight hours. I expect we shall meet them Monday.

Public opinion seems unanimous in approving and even demanding government intervention and its pressure upon coal owners will be very strong. I do not think stoppage will collapse by itself. 2,000 or 3,000 men a day are going back in Midlands but quarrel might easily slough along for many weeks. Earnest efforts on our part even with risk of failure are imperative.

At Aix, Davidson was still concerned about the possibility of a settlement being reached before Baldwin's return to London. On 4 September Sir Patrick Gower[1] tried to put Davidson's mind at rest, writing to him from 10 Downing Street:

Knowing Winston as you do you may entertain fears lest he should use every endeavour in the Prime Minister's absence to effect a settlement of the dispute in order that all the kudos should fall into his lap. You need not, however, worry on this score. Winston has shown a most loyal and sporting attitude and has on many occasions in private conversation expressed a very sincere anxiety lest his activities while the Prime Minister is away should lead people to give him undue credit for anything which he may be able to do. What is more, he has on many occasions expressed his determination to call the Prime Minister home as soon as the necessity arises. It is only fair to Winston to mention this, because otherwise there might be misunderstandings as to his attitude.

In the meantime, I rather gather that Steel-Maitland is a bit disgruntled because he feels that his nose is put out of joint by Winston's predominance in the negotiations. I do not put it higher than that, but the position was not

---

[1] Robert Patrick Malcolm Gower, 1887–1964. Educated at Marlborough and Emmanuel College Cambridge. Entered the Inland Revenue, 1910. Transferred to the Treasury, 1919; Assistant Private Secretary to Bonar Law, 1917–18. Private Secretary to Austen Chamberlain, 1919–22. Private Secretary to successive Prime Ministers (Bonar Law, MacDonald and Baldwin), 1922–28. Knighted, 1924. Chief Publicity Officer, Conservative Central Office, 1929–39.

improved by the fact that Steel-Maitland made a very poor speech on Tuesday while Winston excelled himself.[1]

'I spoke to the Chancellor yesterday quite frankly about the PM's return,' Jones wrote to Hankey on September 4, 'and he was most correct and loyal in every way.'

Churchill decided to put what pressure he could on the owners to look with some understanding at the miners' demands. On September 4 he invited one of the more moderate of the leading owners, Sir David Llewellyn,[2] to dine with him at Chartwell. That same day Jones wrote to Llewellyn: 'The Chancellor feels very strongly that it will neither be right nor possible for the owners to refuse to negotiate nationally and I have told him that you take the same view. I believe the men are in a mood now to go a long way to meet your district requirements and if this can be secured, why not have a peace with some elements of permanence in it?'

On the evening of September 4 Sir David Llewellyn discussed the Coal Strike with Churchill at Chartwell. Churchill's cousin Lord Londonderry, himself a mine-owner, was also present, together with Sir Ernest Gowers and Thomas Jones. Churchill reiterated his view that a tripartite conference could lead to peace in the mines, if the owners would agree to certain concessions. To Baldwin, Churchill telegraphed on the following day:

I am trying to procure a three-cornered conference with representatives of both parties and ministers. Miners have directly asked me to undertake this task. It will certainly be several days before opposition of owners is overcome and perhaps it may never be overcome. Should we however get to three-cornered conference, the first series of important questions to be decided will not be details of wages and hours but procedure to be followed in the negotiations in order to secure earliest possible resumption. It is in this stage that help of the Government is indispensable.

Once agreement has been reached on the broad principles of procedure it would certainly be convenient to substitute one or more independent chairmen for the various committees or sub-committees which will probably be necessary. I certainly do not contemplate myself sitting to fix hours or wage

---

[1] On September 3 Steel-Maitland himself had written to Baldwin: 'Winston you know much better than I, and of course with a beastly complicated thing like this he doesn't know the difficulties, and so his boundings this way & that & impulsiveness are an anxiety. But he made a *very* good speech indeed in the House. And so far I think the right action on the whole has been taken. . . .'

[2] David Richard Llewellyn, 1874–1940. Educated at University College Cardiff. Deputy Chairman of Amalgamated Anthracite Collieries. A Justice of the Peace for Glamorgan, 1920. Created Baronet, 1922.

conditions but only to settle the order and method of dealing with these points, the relation of national to district agreements.

Of course we cannot see very far into the way things may develop and there are so many obstacles that they may not develop at all. It is very important I should know that you approve this procedure.

Without active Government help involving serious risk and labour no progress will be made.

Thomas Jones telegraphed to Baldwin on September 5, supporting Churchill's request. 'Gowers and I agree,' he said, 'that procedure indicated by Chancellor is right in present circumstances.' Baldwin hesitated to commit himself. 'I am a great believer in playing the rope to the last,' he wrote to Churchill that same day; but he added that 'only the man on the spot' could judge 'when the moment is come to jerk it in'. Baldwin wanted the Government's involvement in any settlement to be kept to an absolute minimum, and any agreement made to be made between owners and men, with minimum Government involvement. As he explained in his letter:

The men will be eager to have the government a party to any agreement because (A) if anything goes wrong they can curse 'em and (B) so long as government can be indicated as a partner so long is there a peg for nationalization and all that the dreams of the wild men stand for.

If any declaration of gov^m policy is involved, eg help for displaced men, it should be a separate undertaking.

The worst danger, Baldwin wrote, was a settlement which might fail after a year, and 'fall on us like a load of bricks within a measurable distance of the general election'. Unless a permanent settlement could be reached, he added, 'it is far better not to pursue it'. In his letter Baldwin also praised Churchill's efforts. 'Your speech in the House I thought admirable,' he wrote, 'and I think that you have probably followed the only course available and followed it with skill and success, but it is just at the moment that one seems in a fair way to pass through a difficult channel that one has to look out for sunken rocks.' His letter ended: 'It is a great relief to me to feel what a strong committee I have left in charge to handle this most difficult situation.'

During September 5 Churchill continued with his efforts at Chartwell, pressing both Llewellyn and Londonderry to induce the owners at least to contemplate a compromise. But they could not hold out any serious hopes that the owners would agree to abandon either the eight hours minimum working time, or district agreements. In his diary Thomas Jones recorded the talk and atmosphere at Chartwell. During the discussions with Llewellyn and Londonderry, he wrote, Churchill was ' "humming" with coal all the time—discussing it from every conceivable angle'. Jones noted: 'W. is a most brilliant and incessant talker—his sentences full of colour and alliteration and frequent military metaphor. He is always deploying guns or barrages on the owners or the men.' During the conversation Churchill commented on how rare it was to find statesmen who could be 'defiant in defeat and magnanimous in victory'.

Churchill returned to London on the morning of Monday September 6. The mine-owners having agreed to meet the Coal Committee that afternoon, the Committee members met immediately after lunch to discuss the Government's position. It was agreed to concentrate on a single tactic, an appeal to the owners to agree to negotiate with the men, and Churchill told his colleagues that 'he proposed to press the owners to seek release from the embargo on national negotiations and obtain authority from their constituent bodies to meet in joint conference'. But Steel-Maitland warned 'that according to information which had reached him the owners would not give way'.

The meeting with the owners began at 3.15 pm. 'Ding-dong debate at No 10,' Thomas Jones noted in his diary, 'between Winston and Evan Williams, the verbatim report of which ran into fifty-six foolscap pages.' In opening the discussion, Churchill asked the owners bluntly: 'Is there to be any National Agreement at all or is the industry in future to be regulated purely by District Agreements without any National Wage Negotiating body?' For five years the owners had insisted that any form of National Agreement was wrong. On the eve of the General Strike, when this view had been rejected by the Royal Commission, the owners had agreed, in a public statement on April 13, 'to discuss and arrange' a National Agreement. On May 14, two days after the General Strike had ended, the owners, in 'pressing strongly' for an Eight Hours Bill at an interview with Baldwin, had given no indication that they no longer accepted the idea of a National Agreement. When Baldwin announced the Eight Hours Bill in Parliament, Churchill went on, he had spoken specifically of the owners' willingness to meet the miners' desire 'for a national settlement'. To this the owners had made 'no protest of any kind'. Churchill then told the owners:

I am quite sure of this, that if we had known that following the passage of the Eight Hours Bill into law a new obstacle to a settlement, a new complication, would arise through the closing of one of those doors to peace we never should have passed the Bill or proceeded with it. Therefore if you take up the attitude that you have now no more power to negotiate and that there can be no national negotiations of any kind, if you take up that *non possumus* attitude, while I am not for a moment making a charge of breach of faith I do think you will see that we shall have been placed in a position which is from our point of view at any rate, extremely unfortunate and even, as it might be thought, unfair. . . .

Churchill added: 'If two States are negotiating and then they go to war, it is idle to suppose that negotiations can be taken up after a prolonged campaign at the point at which they left off.' Now the Government was making the owners 'a formal deliberate request' to talk to their men, and to understand their men's insistence upon a National Agreement. The miners, he said, 'were earnestly desirous of making a peaceful and lasting settlement'; there had been in the past few weeks 'a change of heart . . . an earnest wish for peace' which the owners must match. Churchill ended his opening remarks with a direct appeal to the owners:

Will you meet us with the men and let us see what are the practical steps, by national discussion and by district discussion—for both will unquestionably be necessary, to bring this trouble to an end; and on behalf of his Majesty's Government, with whom you have been so long in close and amicable discussion and negotiation, who are after all the trustees of the public as a whole, on their behalf I most earnestly venture to express the hope that you will defer to our wishes.

In his reply, Evan Williams insisted that, 'in the interests of peace and prosperity' in the Coal industry, the owners wanted a return to district negotiations. They were determined, he added, 'that no further national agreements would be entered into on their behalf by any body for them'. Williams then declared that when the Eight Hours Bill became law, there was no suggestion whatsoever from the Government 'that this was conditional upon a National Agreement'. To this Churchill retorted: 'I cannot possibly accept that.' During the passage of the Eight Hours Bill, he pointed out, the owners knew full well that the Government intended it to be coupled with a National Agreement, and yet they had kept silent. 'You singularly failed to undeceive us,' Churchill commented, and he added: 'if we had known that the introduction of the Eight Hours Bill would synchronise with a decision on your part the moment you got it to close the national door, never should we have allowed ourselves to be placed in that position'. Yet the owners, he pointed out, had hidden their opposition to a National Agreement until the third week in August.

Undeterred by Churchill's criticisms, Evan Williams defended the owners' total opposition to a National Agreement, pointing out that in certain areas, under purely district agreements, men were already returning to work. 'There are districts,' he said, 'where the owners' offer has been accepted without reference in any way at all to national agreements. That movement is spreading rapidly.'

Churchill's colleagues then entered the discussion, pressing the owners to abandon their inflexible position. Steel-Maitland, Worthington-Evans, Bridgeman and Lane-Fox each likewise appealed to the owners to adopt a less rigid attitude. But Evan Williams refused to give way. A National Agreement, he insisted, would have a 'cramping effect' upon district agreements, and would enable political considerations to override economic ones. There was, he insisted, not 'a single element of national advantage, of national benefit' in having a National Agreement. To this Churchill was stung to reply: 'Surely it would be an advantage if by national negotiations at the present time we ended this terrible dispute and got the men back to work and the industries of the country going? Surely that is our object? What we are here for is to find a way of ending the dispute.'

As the discussion continued, Churchill's anger with the owners increased. In answer to Williams' insistence that district agreements were the only ones the owners would accept, Churchill replied: 'You may not succeed in making district agreements apart from a national understanding. In June you were confident that district agreements would be made on an eight hours basis, but nothing has occurred . . .' A few moments later he urged Williams 'most earnestly' not to use language which would preclude a tripartite meeting and not to proceed with his threat to leave all future interests of the owners in the hands of the individual owners. In a final appeal Churchill declared:

. . . if it is your view that district settlements are much better than national settlements and that district settlements would remove the necessity for national settlements, surely it is at least your duty to appear in the presence of the other party and to argue your case.

But to take the course of saying, 'we are out of action altogether for the purposes of national negotiations as an Association, and the matter no longer rests with us in any way' is to take a most serious attitude. After all, the question of a national agreement is an industrial issue in the dispute as much as wages and hours, and if the Government thought fit to set up an Industrial Court you would have to attend as a national body before that Court or else see your case go by default. The matter is really not one when a body, which for a whole year has been before the public as the united spokesman of one side in the industry, should suddenly say 'We have dissolved ourselves, our powers have gone, there is nothing but the void to talk to now.'

An attitude of that kind is bound to array against you a mass of public opinion in the country.

If a final decision on your part never to negotiate again with anybody on a national basis, never even to enter into a discussion with anyone on a national basis, was going to be the last word in the matter, if that should unhappily be your position—and I most devoutly and earnestly hope it will not be your decision—if it should be then it seems to me quite clear that we shall have to move forward upon our own course of action in your absence.

Steel-Maitland, writing to Davidson immediately after the meeting, described Churchill's remarks as 'awfully good'. But he also felt that as a result of it the Government had been put 'into an anti-owner position'. Steel-Maitland added: 'He's jolly difficult when he's in a napoleonesque attitude, dictating instructions in military metaphors, and the spotlight full on him.' But in a letter which he sent to Baldwin immediately after the meeting, Churchill was both calm and realistic in his assessment of the situation, and of the effect of the owners' refusal to negotiate on a national basis. 'There is a slight chance this may be modified tomorrow,' he wrote, 'as they have promised to discuss the whole affair with their members. Still, we must count on a final refusal.' His letter continued:

What to do? I should propose in that event going to the miners and sounding them without committing the Government to action on the following proposition: If you will order your men to begin district negotiations and to resume work as and when these negotiations are complete we will amend the Eight Hours Act so as to deny its indulgence to any pit which does not conform to certain conditions. These conditions are being carefully studied by Gowers. They cannot be very drastic or else the Eight Hours Act would remain a dead letter, but they may be sufficient to keep alive the principle of a national structure within which district settlements are comprised. If the miners refuse, then we shall have shown a perfect readiness to implement our undertaking to the very best of our ability and power, and that will be the end of this peace effort. No one will be able to say that we have not tried or that we have not played fair with the men. We shall not be worse off than we are now, which is pretty bad. If on the other hand the miners play up, then I shall have to ask you to come home and convene a Cabinet at which action must be decided. . . .

'As far as I can make out,' Churchill added, 'we have overwhelming public support for the line we are taking, and I think we shall retain that support so long as we act in a straightforward and resolute spirit.'

That evening Churchill dined at the Savoy Grill with Lord Beaverbrook. 'He explained his plans,' Beaverbrook wrote to Lord Derby two weeks later. 'I pointed out to him the Conservatives' objections. He became eloquent and of course would not tolerate any opposition.

However, he did promise me that he would not use any threats. Then he showed me what he had already said that afternoon—full of threats, of course. Yet he was perfectly unaware that he had said anything extreme.'

In sending Baldwin the stenographic notes of the meeting, Patrick Duff[1] wrote in his covering letter to Davidson on September 7: 'Winston, considering the very disingenuous and provocative attitude of the owners, was comparatively restrained, although he always puts his points aggressively and every now and then jumped on Evan Williams'. But, Duff added, 'I don't think Winston's activities are at present beyond what the circumstances of the situation call for, or are actuated by any desire for self-advertisement. . . .'

On September 6 Lord Londonderry had written to Churchill urging him to show as much sympathy towards the owners as he was showing towards the miners. During the course of his letter he wrote:

> We all have our different points of view. You approach it as a Minister, a statesman and as one who naturally wants a settlement for every reason. I approach it as one who is in politics, has a certain experience of conferences and administration etc etc, and also as an owner. Cook and Smith want nationalisation and to save their faces; the owners want to get back to work and make money but are obsessed with the idea that they cannot make money on National lines. They trace all the troubles to the growth of the National idea and the case is a very strong one indeed. The railway arrangement is a failure because the porter at a wayside station gets the same wage as the porter at a big and profitable station.

At a meeting of the Cabinet Coal Committee on September 7, Churchill stated that in the event of the owners 'persisting in their refusal' to come to a tripartite conference, it would be necessary to ask Baldwin to return to England. During the discussion Bridgeman urged caution. There should, he said, 'be no pressure nor threat of legislation at this stage, especially as the Prime Minister was away'. Churchill, Cunliffe-Lister and Gowers then drafted a letter to Evan Williams, explaining that the aim of the tripartite conference was 'to lay down certain broad principles and to recommend practical steps necessary to secure an early and universal resumption of work'. Urging an end to

[1] Charles Patrick Duff, 1889–1972. Educated at Blundell's School and Balliol College Oxford. Entered Board of Trade, 1912. On active service, Gallipoli, France and Mesopotamia, 1914–18 (wounded, despatches twice). Private Secretary to successive Presidents of the Board of Trade, 1919–23; to successive Prime Ministers (Baldwin, MacDonald, Baldwin, MacDonald) 1923–33. Knighted, 1932. Secretary, Ministry of Works and Public Buildings, 1933–41. Deputy High Commissioner, Canada, 1941–44; High Commissioner, New Zealand, 1945–49. A Church Commissioner for England, 1949–54.

further delay, the letter stated bluntly: 'At least 1,700,000 families affected by the dispute are looking for the opportunity of regaining their weekly wages.'

On September 7 Churchill sent Baldwin a full telegraphic account of the situation. He was now prepared, he wrote, to moderate the Eight Hours Act in such a way as to secure 'something of the structure of a national settlement'. In return for amending the Act, and thus making it possible for men to work fewer hours for the same wage, Churchill would ask the men to begin district negotiations within the framework of the amended act, thus effecting a compromise which, if the owners still refused to accept it, the Government could enforce. 'The anxiety throughout the country,' Churchill added, 'is acute.' His own fear, he explained, was that 'both parties will continue unreasonable', and that an early settlement was unlikely.

At ten on the evening of September 7 Churchill had discussed his Committee's draft letter to Evan Williams with three of the miners' leaders, Cook, W. P. Richardson[1] and Smith, at the Treasury, together with Steel-Maitland and Lane-Fox. On the following day Jones wrote to Bridgeman, describing the meeting:

> The Chancellor tabled the draft letter right away, and for 3½ hours it was discussed from every conceivable angle with occasional adjournments for private consultation. The miners were naturally very critical of the frequent emphasis on district agreements in the document, and it was to meet them that we inserted the 'national' paragraph. The Chancellor, as you would expect, was more emphatic than his two colleagues about making the national agreement real and not a mere camouflage, but he carried them with him completely in the draft which was finally tabled. The miners were not asked of course to accept the letter in any sense. The letter was from the Government to the owners. But they did say that the publication of the letter would not be allowed to prevent their attending a joint conference.
>
> At 1.40 am the Chancellor motored Smith and Cook to their hotel whilst Steel-Maitland took Richardson to his—all in a friendly mood.

At midday on September 8 Jones and Gowers drove to see Churchill at Chartwell, to finalize the draft. The letter itself was sent both to Evan Williams and to the Press at five that afternoon. 'The Chancellor is more

---

[1] William Pallister Richardson, 1873–1930. Educated at elementary school. Lost his father in a pit accident in March 1885. Began work in the pits himself in August 1885, at the age of twelve. Worked underground until 1915. Member of the Durham Mining Federation Board, 1912; Miners' Agent, Durham, 1915. Treasurer of the Miners' Federation, 1921–30. An active member of the Independent Labour Party, and a noted advocate of the minimum wage. His brother, T. Richardson, was Labour MP for Whitehaven, 1910–18.

optimistic than the Mines Department,' Jones reported to Baldwin, 'and thinks it is 6 to 4 (as he put it) that the owners will cave in.' In the letter to Williams, Churchill stressed that the aim of any National Agreement would be to 'lay down certain broad principles', which would then be embodied in detailed agreements at a district level. 'We believe,' he wrote, 'that with such national guidance the task of negotiating agreements on wages, hours and other conditions could be undertaken in each district with the assent of both parties.' The Government could not afford 'further delay or long ceremonial procedure'. The dispute could only be resolved, Churchill insisted, if all district agreements were concluded in conformity with 'agreed general principles', and all local decisions of importance would have to be referred 'to the central body' for confirmation, or for reference back to the district concerned.

Some of Churchill's colleagues were disturbed by his firm attitude to the owners. During September 8 Steel-Maitland wrote to Davidson that Churchill's 'impulsiveness and combativeness' were 'an awful danger' in negotiations. According to Steel-Maitland:

One trouble is that we jumped in too soon. The miners were nearly down and out & ready to agree to anything. A few days more and perhaps the Notts and Derby agreement would have clinched it. As it was Winston jumped in too readily and it was impossible to stop. With his impulsiveness he was all over the miners. Cook is able to quote him as ready, with them, to make peace and of course the miners have in turn stiffened a lot. On the other hand, the interview with the owners was lamentable. The strong hand may need to be shown, but not in a way that put all their backs up. If they were in a weak position (as during the passing of the Eight Hours Act) it would be different. But they are not, and coercive measures by the Govt are not at all easy and they probably know it. . . .

What has also put their backs up is that they think W.C. is actuated by political and industrial reasons and of course it is true. He thinks out industrial policy in terms of making a political speech. . . .

Steel-Maitland ended his letter:

I have had to write quickly, and I may have over-emphasised Winston's failings in the present difficulties. I have got along with him all right, and have been determined to do so, though he doesn't like independent advice from another Cabinet Minister when there isn't time to do so very slowly and we aren't old colleagues. He is a most brilliant fellow, but his gifts aren't those of judgement, nor of appreciating industry, nor of a negotiator. Only don't let yourself or the PM get troubled. We have worked along all right.

'Winston is far too optimistic,' Steel-Maitland wrote direct to Baldwin that same day. 'He thinks that because the owners have referred the matter to districts that they will of course come round, and will in any case attend on Monday. It isn't so.' Not only were the owners unhappy about the principle of Churchill's demands, Steel-Maitland added, but they were also 'very sore and angry'. But in his own telegraphic report to Baldwin on September 8, Churchill expressed himself confident that the owners would 'act rightly', and agree to his proposals.

Lane-Fox, who lunched with Evan Williams on September 8, learnt from him that there was no chance whatsoever of the local mine-owners reversing the owners' decision about national negotiations. Reporting this to Churchill later that day, Lane-Fox continued: 'I told him he was laying up a great store of trouble for coalowners—& that we were already starting to draft bills to coerce them.'

Lane-Fox was also worried, however, about giving the miners too strong an impression of Government support—an impression that Ramsay MacDonald had certainly gained two days earlier. In his letter to Churchill, Lane-Fox added:

I hope we shall not get the men's tails up too much. Last night's interview has left me a little troubled—& will have restored their spirits considerably. I think we put rather too much into the national negotiations. They will be much easier to deal with if they remain what they in fact are, a hopelessly defeated body.

Churchill and his colleagues waited throughout September 9 for the owners' reply. 'I fear you are having a very anxious and difficult time,' Clementine Churchill wrote to her husband that same day, and she added: 'The Coal position is hard and cruel.' The miners were desperate to return to work, and increasingly looked to Churchill to arrange a settlement. On September 9, William Brace[1] wrote to Sir Ernest Gowers: 'I find nearly every Miners' Leader in a hopeless frame of mind but trusting greatly to the Chancellor and yourselves discovering a pathway to peace.' But that same day, after Sir Ernest Gowers had spent two hours talking to Evan Williams, it became clear, as Jones wrote to Baldwin on September 10, 'that the owners will not budge'. Jones also warned Baldwin that Churchill's handling of the crisis had begun to rouse strong criticism in the Conservative Press. 'My own view,' Jones wrote, 'is that this is due in large measure to the hostility which

---

[1] William Brace, 1865–1947. Educated, Risca Board School. A working miner; subsequently President of the South Wales Miners' Federation. Labour MP for Glamorgan South, 1906–18; for Abertillery, 1918–20. Parliamentary Under-Secretary of State, Home Department, 1915–18. Privy Councillor, 1916. Chief Labour Adviser, Department of Mines, 1920–27.

the personality of the Chancellor excites. He has hinted at what the Government will do to the owners if they prove obdurate. The newspapers ask: "Is it conceivable that a Conservative Government will coerce the owners, however foolish," and the assumption is, No.'

Jones doubted whether Churchill's plan was feasible. 'What compulsion can the Government put on the owners,' he asked Baldwin, 'assuming the Cabinet agrees to go ahead'. If they were to follow Churchill's approach, the Government might have to undertake to give all local agreements some national character by making them a part of the Eight Hours Act, and by limiting the advantages of the Act to those areas in which the Government was satisfied with the owners' terms. 'You will not like travelling in this region,' Jones warned, 'but the Government cannot recede now without throwing over the Chancellor and his approving colleagues.' The Government's 'way of escape', Jones believed, would probably come 'through the failure of the miners to exploit the situation in their own interest. . . .'

Churchill continued to keep his wife informed of the developments in the crisis. The attitude of the owners, he telegraphed to her on September 10, would lead to 'serious collision, with political reaction next week'. From Scotland, Clementine Churchill sent her husband a word of caution: 'You are having an anxious but a thrilling & engrossing time with power & scope which is what the Pig likes—I suppose Steel-Maitland and Lane-Fox are not often allowed near the trough? I hope you let them have a tit-bit now & again. If the Cat were Minister of Labour or mines she would not give up her place there without a few "miaows".'

During September 10 Churchill sent an account of the crisis to Lord Stamfordham. It was sad, he wrote, 'to see industrial England tearing itself to pieces while the rest of the country is only just about able to keep its head above water'. Churchill ended his letter on a pessimistic note:

I do not see any sign so far of the miners giving in. Less than 50,000 working miners, out of nearly a million, have returned; and with the modern methods of local relief there is no decisive pressure upon them to return. The situation therefore causes me the very greatest anxiety. I was never in the least frightened of the General Strike, and felt sure that, if taken by the throat, it would be speedily broken. But a Coal Strike, prolonged as this has been, is like a ship sinking slowly in a calm sea.

Churchill also sent a full account of the crisis to Baldwin, to whom he wrote on September 10:

My dear Prime Minister,

This should reach you before you start on your homeward journey. I think you must count on a flat refusal by the owners to come to national negotiations and you and the Cabinet will have to decide what measures to take. It would seem quite impossible for us to avow impotency when confronted with recalcitrant owners. We have legislated against the miners, broken the general strike, imported foreign coal, and kept the ring these long five months. We can hardly take the purely class view that owners however unreasonable are sacrosanct and inviolable. This would be contrary to our general position as a Government and especially to your own personal declarations.

I shall therefore urge you strongly to march against the more unreasonable party at the moment. Before doing so however it will be necessary and possible to come to absolute grips with the miners. So far they have risked nothing and though edging ever nearer to the indispensable surrender have put up no definite flag of truce. If as I hope you find yourself in general accord with your committee, a very interesting and by no means unhopeful situation will await you. You will be able to extort from the miners and they will be able to yield more than was ever possible before as the condition for legislating against the owners. And unless the miners toe the line in earnest there will be no need to legislate. But if the miners are willing to take effective steps to end the stoppage by allowing district settlements to be negotiated you will be able to give them their meagre consolation prize through an Act of Parliament modifying the Eight Hours Act in various ways. These are now being explored. Thus we shall acquire power to deal with both sides: the loyalty of the miners and the law against the owners.

And how long can this business continue! The Governor of the Bank spoke with great anxiety to me last night of the effects on next year's trade and exchange, through the immense curtailment of future expectations. The things we ought to sell in April and May are not going through their primary processes. Philip Cunliffe-Lister will tell you about how the difficulties of buying oversea coal increase in the winter weather which aggravates the demand etc. And 1,700,000 families are wageless who otherwise would be employed.

I do hope that a little employers' agitation will not prevent HMG from advancing with courage and conviction against both the obstructors of the public interest.

Two of Churchill's closest friends, Lord Londonderry and Lord Birkenhead, resented his attitude towards the owners, and on September 11 Londonderry wrote to him from Loch Choire Lodge, in Scotland, protesting about Churchill's tone in his meeting with the owners on September 6. 'I know you want to be impartial,' he wrote, 'but you really have come down on the side of Cook and Smith; not on the side of the men nor on the side of the owners.' His letter continued:

You are an optimist and you say that everything produces a vaccine, a reaction, an antidote or whatever you like to call it. I sincerely hope you are right: but I beg of you not to buttress Cook and Smith because you are impatient with the owners. The owners are absolutely right in theory, as a Capitalist State sees the question, but they are bad tacticians. Evan Williams made an excellent statement the other day and without knowing exactly what you were going to say. He showed very clearly how the Association had been forced to take up a position vis à vis the Federation to oblige the Government; and everything they have done, every concession has been used as a jumping off ground by the Federation for demanding more. . . .

Tom Jones is dead against the owners point of view because he is not of your or my political belief; and the Ministry of Mines like many ministries and many people follows the line of what seems to be the least resistance, vide that pitiable bill the re-organization Bill which I had to go into the Government Lobby and support because I am so anxious to support you in public that I accept all you do. You may compel the owners to do what you want and what Cook and Smith want them to do; the Government have invariably gained their point with the owners but invariably attach all the blame to the owners when anything goes wrong.

From Lord Birkenhead, who was then at Biarritz, and who had also read the September 6 transcript, Churchill received a telegram on September 12 which began: 'I am not happy about your attitude,' and which went on to ask: 'Why should we impose upon owners national settlement if they are strong enough to obtain district settlements? Why should we enable men's leaders who have done their best to ruin England to escape without the brand of failure?' Churchill hastened to defend his position, and that of the Coal Committee of which Birkenhead was an absent member. 'All others agreed with steps taken,' he telegraphed back on September 13. 'Your telegram begs question whether owners strong enough win on all points.' That same day, the owners formally rejected Churchill's appeal. According to a letter from Evan Williams to Churchill, twenty-four of the twenty-five local owners' associations had declined 'clearly and emphatically' against a National Agreement. On the following day Churchill wrote tersely to Lord Londonderry:

My dear Charlie,

If the owners had deferred to the Government wish to attend a Conference, it could have been held last Wednesday; and by Thursday last either the men would have shown they were ready to face the economic facts and we should be approaching an end to this disastrous period, or the Conference would have been broken off and a perfectly clear cut situation been established. As it is, there must be a continued uncertainty till the Prime Minister returns, till the Cabinet assembles and action is decided upon. This is certainly detrimental, but I personally accept no responsibility for it. The injury of the stoppage to the nation deepens progressively week by week, and there is no longer any question of a swift recovery.

At a meeting of his Cabinet Committee on September 14 Churchill told his colleagues[1] that it was 'of the utmost importance in the interests of the country's finances to secure a resumption of work in the collieries at the earliest possible moment. It was vital that the situation should be quickly cleared up.' Churchill then proposed a direct Government initiative, beyond anything yet contemplated. In view of the owners' refusal to accept a tripartite conference, he argued, a letter should at once be sent to the Miners' Federation 'the object of which should be to discover what coercive action the miners desired the Government to take, and how far the miners, in return, would be prepared to go in the way of a satisfactory offer on hours, wages and district settlements'. The Cabinet Committee rejected Churchill's appeal for coercion. According to the minutes it was urged 'by the majority of ministers present', that any further action should be postponed until after Baldwin's return.

On September 15 Baldwin returned to England, and, on the following day, at a meeting of the Cabinet Coal Committee at which Baldwin took the chair, Churchill set out for his colleagues the terms of a draft Bill, prepared in the Mines department, the purpose of which was, 'to bring pressure to bear on the owners'. The aim of the Bill was to deny the owners any of the benefits of the Eight Hours Bill unless they were prepared to amend miners' wages in accordance with a Government supervised scheme, whereby all District Board decisions could be reviewed and amended every six months 'by a National Board'.

The main opposition to the Bill came from Cunliffe-Lister, but Churchill stressed that, as the situation stood at that moment, 'the Government had been rebuffed by the Owners'. Baldwin did not speak. Worthington-Evans shared Churchill's view, telling his colleagues that the owners 'should not be allowed to flout the Government'. It was agreed that Churchill and the other Ministers 'immediately concerned' should meet later that afternoon 'to consider the position further'. This they did, reporting to Baldwin that evening that in their view the Government should at once offer the miners, in return for a return to work, a National Arbitration Tribunal, as a review body for all District agreements. As for the owners, they could only benefit from the Eight Hours Bill if they accepted this procedure.

[1] Five Cabinet Ministers were present: Churchill (in the Chair), Sir Laming Worthington-Evans, William Bridgeman, Sir Arthur Steel-Maitland and Colonel Lane-Fox. The civil servants present were Sir Horace Wilson, Sir Ernest Gowers, C. S. Hurst and P. J. Grigg.

On September 17 Churchill drafted a letter which he wanted Baldwin to give to the miners' leaders. 'His Majesty's Government,' the draft read, 'are prepared to secure by legislation the main objects of a national settlement for the Coal Industry.' In return for Government intervention, the miners must, for their part, agree to an immediate return to work, and to negotiate district settlements to that end; settlements which the Government would ensure conformed to an overall and acceptable national agreement. Baldwin endorsed Churchill's suggestion. But Churchill realized that it might not go far enough to meet the miners' full demands. 'The men are undoubtedly prepared to go a considerable distance,' he wrote to H. A. Gwynne on September 20, but, he added, gloomily, 'I do not think they are prepared to go the necessary distance. . . .' It was quite wrong, Churchill added, for the owners to have refused to come to a tripartite conference. This refusal had roused the miners' fears, and strengthened their resolve. 'I am very grateful,' Churchill wrote, 'to the Cabinet and the Prime Minister for endorsing the course which, in the circumstances of the Owners' refusal, I felt bound to recommend. But it is always a mistake for people to refuse to come to a conference, especially people in the responsible position of coal owners.'

Writing to Cook on September 21, Baldwin reiterated the Government's policy, that in return for an eventual national agreement, the miners must agree to 'the immediate opening of negotiations in every district'. That evening one of the miners' economic advisers, R. H. Tawney,[1] wrote to Jones that district negotiations would only be tolerated once there was a national agreement 'defining principles in a broad way'. Tawney feared that the Government was now seeking 'a spectacular victory' over the miners, and he warned: 'The only hope of bringing things to an end is to start with some form of national agreement as promised by the Chancellor.'

At nine-thirty that night the miners' leaders went to 10 Downing Street, where Baldwin read them the final version of the Government's proposals. The miners then withdrew to another room, and Churchill suggested that they should be told either to produce their own proposals, 'or in ten minutes PM's letter goes to the Press'. Thomas Jones recorded the immediate sequel:

---

[1] Richard Henry Tawney, 1880–1962. Educated at Rugby and Balliol College Oxford. Lecturer, author and economic historian. Member of the Executive of the Workers' Educational Association, 1905–47 (President, 1928–44). Member of the Board of Education Consultative Committee, 1912–31. Member of the Coal Industry Commission, 1919. Member of the Cotton Trade Conciliation Commission, 1936–39. Professor of Economic History at the University of London, 1931–49.

11.10 pm: Miners given five more minutes.

11.35 pm: Miners back. Temperature rapidly rising.
Winston: You have not come into the open with anything.

11.50 pm: Herbert Smith begins to approach proposals with much pre-liminary preparation of the ground. . . .

At five minutes to midnight the miners produced their proposals. They would order an immediate return to work, provided that wages were held above the 1921 minimum, and that all district agreements were subject to arbitration by a National Tribunal. When the Coal Committee met at eleven o'clock on the following morning, September 22, Sir Ernest Gowers suggested that the Government could take these terms 'and endeavour to fit them into its own scheme for coercing the owners'. But Baldwin did not take up this suggestion; indeed even Thomas Jones was moved to protest in his diary at the Prime Minister 'doing nothing whatever' to guide the course of the discussion, 'and contributing nothing more than a weary ejaculation to the effect that we seemed deeper in the soup than ever, and that if we coerced the owners they could also refuse to open their pits. . . .' Churchill how-ever, Jones recorded:[1]

. . . as always, was eager to continue negotiating and to put the best face possible on the midnight proposals. He was quite prepared to go to great lengths in the way of legislation on hours, wages and conditions which terrified his colleagues.

Steel-Maitland was sceptical of the men's intentions, and wanted to con-front them plainly with the question, would they discuss the variation of the minimum in the districts? Lane-Fox as usual said hardly anything and Sir Laming on the whole backed Churchill.

By the end of the meeting Churchill was back to his earlier position of giving the men a national facade, ie a body of principles which should guide the district negotiations and these to be given the form and force of law.

Baldwin would still not come to a decision. Instead, he summoned another meeting of the Coal Committee for 3.15 that afternoon, after Sir Horace Wilson and Sir Ernest Gowers had spoken to the miners again, and obtained an elaboration of their proposals. Churchill was angered by such procrastination. Summoning Jones to his room, he expressed without reserve his anger and frustration, telling Jones:

[1] For this meeting of the Coal Committee there were no official minutes. Jones, its Secretary, noted on the official list of those present: 'In view of the secret character of the proceedings, the Prime Minister has given instructions that no Minutes are to be circulated.' These instructions did not deter Jones from keeping his own private account.

... the situation was becoming impossible for him and that he would not come to the 3.15 meeting. It was hopeless exploring one device after another in the confused fashion of the meeting we had just attended with the Prime Minister thoroughly sound at heart and in intention, doing nothing to pilot the discussion, and with Steel-Maitland and Lane-Fox quite futile. 'It is quite easy to understand why the stoppage has lasted all these months. They are now sending Wilson and Gowers to see the miners: they have not the prestige even if they had the knowledge, and they cannot adjust themselves to the course of the talk with the miners, and perhaps get into a new and better position; they will simply come back and report all the difficulties. I wanted the PM to let Worthy and me see them, but that was turned down, so I will clear out of it. I will put down my views in writing. I can do a job of work if it is given to me to do, and I can work with a colleague putting it through, but I can't go meandering all over the place and arrive nowhere in the way we are now doing.'

I said that I thought the bottom fact which paralysed the discussions was that Steel-Maitland, Lane-Fox and Gowers did not believe settlement with the men possible, and there was no settlement which the men would accept which the owners would look at. I then said that if he carried out his threat of not going to the 3.15 meeting it would get about at once, fill the papers, and its importance would be vastly exaggerated; that infinite patience was required at a time like this, especially as the PM himself was suffering from sciatica and obviously did not know which way to turn in the midst of his conflicting advisers.

I gradually calmed him down, and before I came away he had promised to turn up this afternoon.

The afternoon meeting was inconclusive; so also was a further meeting between Churchill and Herbert Smith. The miners wanted to see what sort of legislation the Government was prepared to draft, embodying the proposed National Arbitration Tribunal. But Baldwin was reluctant to take any steps which might further upset the owners, and was strongly supported in this attitude by Lord Birkenhead, who had just returned from Biarritz. On September 23 Birkenhead set out his views in a letter to Lord Irwin. The negotiations between the Government and the miners were a mistake, he wrote. 'If we had not resumed discussion with these dangerous and discredited men,' he added, 'I think that the situation might have been carried to a victorious conclusion.'

The full Cabinet met during the afternoon of September 24. Baldwin expressed his fears that, given the owners' hostile attitude towards any national agreement, the only action the Government could take was compulsory arbitration, 'a very strong measure' which he was reluctant to support. But if the Government took no action, many people would feel, as Jones recorded, 'that the Government has left a mass of miners to be beaten to their knees by the owners'. Evan Williams was reported as saying that the men 'know they are beaten', and that if the Government refrained from action, they would soon accept district agreements, and return to work. The discussion revolved around the question, should the Government act or not? Churchill lamented the refusal of the owners to accept tripartite talks. It was, he said, 'wholly wrong and unreasonable an attitude without precedent in recent times'. They had, he alleged, even influenced the Government Whips, who had 'been at some of the Ministers urging them to do nothing'.

Some Ministers, led by Amery, saw grave danger in any compulsory Government Arbitration Tribunal. 'Suppose Tribunal formulated wage rates,' Jones recorded, 'and Owners refused to open the pits, the result would be a demand for nationalisation. And it would give men right to demand unemployment benefit. Is every industrial dispute to come to PM and to lead ultimately to arbitration?' As the discussion continued it was clear that a majority of the Committee felt that the Government had neither the desire nor the funds to challenge the owners. Amery wrote in his diary of Churchill's proposed Bill on compulsory arbitration on district settlements: 'I championed the extreme opposite view that we ought not only not to take up this scheme but announce definitely that we did not mean to intervene in the matter again believing that the more definite our announcement the quicker the men will come in.'

The discussion was brought to an end by Lord Birkenhead, who felt that it was the most difficult decision 'since the evacuation of the Dardanelles' in the winter of 1915.[1] Nevertheless his view was clear, that the Government should now dissociate itself from the dispute, and leave the owners and miners to fight it out among themselves. This negative conclusion became the formal decision of the Committee. It was now Churchill's task, as Chancellor of the Exchequer, to explain that decision to the House of Commons.

Churchill spent much of September 25 and September 26 preparing his speech. On the morning of September 27 he asked Thomas Jones to read through what he had written. 'He prepares most carefully, well in advance,' Jones noted in his diary, 'and circulates drafts for criticism. Hurst,[2] of the Mines Department, was to read this draft also.' Jones was

[1] Birkenhead (as F. E. Smith) had entered Asquith's Cabinet on 3 November 1915. Churchill (then Chancellor of the Duchy of Lancaster) had left the Cabinet on 12 November 1915. The decision to evacuate the Dardanelles was taken, after much discussion, on 7 December 1915, and the evacuation itself was completed by 9 January 1916.

[2] Christopher Salkeld Hurst, 1886–1963. Educated at Uppingham and Exeter College Oxford. Public Trustee Office, 1910; Ministry of Munitions, 1915; Ministry of Labour, 1919;

worried that Churchill made no mention of the 'national facade' in describing the Government's offer to the men. 'It would be much better to anticipate L.G.,' he told him, 'who is sure to make capital out of this backing out of the Government's offer in their letter to Evan Williams.' Jones then went to see Baldwin, who was to open the debate, but found his proposed speech 'all very colourless and pious. . . . He will leave the tale of recent negotiations to Winston.' While Jones was with Baldwin, Churchill arrived to see the Prime Minister, and to tell him, as Jones noted in his diary, 'that he proposed to use a portion of the letter which he had sent to the PM at Aix which would prove that quite early in September Winston had a clear-cut policy, and had not seriously departed from it'.

The debate began shortly after three o'clock that same afternoon. Baldwin, who was hissed by the Labour benches as he rose to speak, expressed regrets that the owners should have rejected the Tripartite talks. Ramsay MacDonald, who spoke next, preserved the secrecy of his two meetings with Churchill, but derided the Government for its 'impotence' when confronted by the owners. Lloyd George then spoke, critical of the Government's request to ask the men to begin district negotiations before giving them any indication of the national principles by which all district agreements could be tested. As soon as Lloyd George sat down, Thomas Jones felt that Churchill should speak, recording in his diary:

I whispered to Grigg, the Chancellor's Secretary, that Winston ought to rise at once and reply to L.G., but Grigg remarked 'Winston can't do that, hates doing it, he likes an interval to gather his material', so the PM and Winston got up and went together to the Chancellor's room. It was now about 6 pm. The Whips found it difficult to carry on the debate, and in a quarter of an hour or so Winston was back in the House, and on his feet invigorated, I surmise, by a pint of champagne. . . .

Churchill began his speech by defending the Government against charges that if it had not intervened, 'the great bulk of the pits would be at work now and all would be over', and he utterly rejected the claim of coal owners that had the miners not been misled by the Government into hopes of negotiation, the strike would already have ended. Defending his attempts at mediation, he told the Commons:

Coal Control Department, 1919; Mines Department, 1925. Secretary to the Royal Commission on the Coal Industry, 1925. Principal Assistant Secretary, Mines Department, 1930–38, Secretary and Controller, Coal Commission, 1938–47.

In a country like ours—a civilised country, a democratic country, a Christian country—you will not ever have a fierce prolonged distressing struggle of this kind without repeated sincere efforts being made to effect a compromise for a friendly and honourable settlement between both parties. Those who feel that the interests of the country are best served by fighting such matters out to the bitter end ought at any rate to take that fact into their calculations. They have to reckon upon it just as they have to reckon upon the weather. For my own part I do not believe that the peace discussions which have taken place have either abridged or prolonged the conflict.

Churchill went on to explain in detail the process whereby the Government had sought talks, and the owners had rejected them. 'I am not aware of any precedent in recent times,' he said, 'for a body of citizens engaged in an industrial dispute deliberately refusing to come to a conference at the request of the Government of the day.' The owners' claim that a national agreement would involve 'the entangling of the coal industry with politics' was, he added, without foundation; district agreements were, he believed, 'an illusory aim'; there was no possibility of killing the idea of a national organization in the coal mining industry.

Later in his speech, Churchill defended his own attempt, during Baldwin's absence at Aix, to achieve a compromise solution by means of Government action. 'I have always thought,' he said, 'that the 8-hour day afforded the means, if need be, of imposing conditions upon the owners . . .', and he quoted from his letter to Baldwin to show that this had always been his view. This, he said, was still his view, and still Government policy:

We are prepared to amend the 8-Hours Act, to introduce conditions limiting the owners' use of that Act, and to set up an independent tribunal to which district settlements can be subsequently referred. It is a serious step and a step not free from disadvantages. First of all it constitutes another interference by the Government with the coal industry, which in itself must be deprecated; secondly, it introduces an element of uncertainty and provisionalism into any district settlements that may be negotiated in the meanwhile; and thirdly, it erects the principle of compulsory arbitration in a great industry into a statutory form.

It would have been very much better if the owners had obviated the necessity for such a step by coming into conference, out of which either a satisfactory agreement or a clear cut breach would speedily have emerged. We felt, however, that if the men asked for a conference and all conference was refused by the owners, it would be necessary for the Government—if we wished, as we do, to hold the scales even—to take further legislative action and to make sure that, if there could be no national settlement by agreement, there should at any rate be a fair settlement as the result of an independent review of district settlements by a tribunal having the force of law.

Such legislation, Churchill stressed, depended upon the immediate resumption of work by the miners, 'on the basis of district negotiations, pending a national review by a statutory tribunal'. The Labour Party had derided this offer, he said, but he trusted that the miners themselves would not throw it away. 'All experience shows,' he warned, 'that as struggles are prolonged everyone becomes hardened and embittered; and moreover, the resources, national and private, which might have led to a happy settlement are consumed in the sterile and destructive process of mere fighting.'

When, in the course of his speech, Churchill criticized the *Daily Herald*'s articles during the strike, there was, as Baldwin wrote to the King, 'slight uproar for two or three minutes' from the Labour benches, but, Baldwin added:

... when calm had been restored Mr Churchill seized the occasion to administer a sharp and well deserved rebuke to the Labour Party for their general attitude in recent debates. He pointed out that it was a matter of absolute indifference to him whether he was allowed to state his case to the House or not. If it were thought better to pass the remaining seventeen minutes of the debate in howling rather than in arguing, he was perfectly prepared to facilitate the general wish. But if the House was to be allowed a debate, it must also be allowed liberty of debate. It was impossible to conduct parliamentary discussion if the Labour Party continually shouted down and interrupted because Conservative Members made use of expressions which annoyed them. Why, he asked, should the Labour Party be so mealy-mouthed about parliamentary debates? Why should revolutionary and advanced politicians be afraid of hard words?

Churchill went on to appeal for 'an orderly and recognised settlement', telling the House:

The miners' associations in the various districts, keeping in touch with national Federation, have only to enter into discussions with the owners locally. The owners have every inducement to open their pits. They are suffering very heavy and increasing loss. The highest possible reward will come to those districts which open first and reap the cumulative harvest of demand from all industries and from all parts of the country for fuel. Therefore there are the elements of a bargain, and of the best possible bargain in the circumstances, open to the miners in every district.

It does not at all follow that the terms which the owners have posted in the different districts need necessarily be the terms which will emerge from a settlement. Both sides are keen to start work for mutual advantage, and a whole series of arrangements could no doubt be made very quickly if the Miners' Federation removed their present veto on district negotiations. Then after these settlements have been made, they can be reviewed by an independent appeal tribunal in any case where a departure from the old hours is involved.

Thus the principle of a national review and co-ordination of district settlements would have been preserved in spite of the owners' refusal to come to conference, and work can be immediately resumed.

'Do not, I beg you,' Churchill ended, 'throw this chance upon the rubbish heap of so many others.'

'Mr Churchill was in his most robust and spirited vein,' Baldwin reported to the King, and Thomas Jones recorded his impressions of Churchill's speech in his diary: 'He was in splendid form, and though he had his manuscript on the table, he moved quite freely, dealing wittily with interruptions, and by imperceptible stages heightening the Government's policy in favour of the Miners, appealing to them not to turn down the offer of arbitration now made to them.' Jones added: 'In their heart of hearts the Cabinet hate this offer, and are dreadfully afraid it may be accepted. During this brilliant performance, the PM's face was turned towards the Official Gallery, and covered with one of his hands.'

Churchill hoped that his speech would be followed by an early response. In the Strangers' Dining Room that night he urged Jones to 'get busy tomorrow' with the miners' leaders, in order to obtain their acceptance of the Government's offer. Churchill told Jones that he could go 'some distance' to meet the miners on the question of the 'facade', and also on extending the scope of the arbitration 'to include those districts working seven hours'.

When, at midday on September 28, Jones asked the Coal Committee to confirm Churchill's instructions—Churchill himself being at Chartwell—all but Worthington-Evans were 'alarmed' at the idea of the miners accepting the National Tribunal, and thus obliging the Government to carry out its pledge: 'It was going beyond the views of Friday's Cabinet' was the Committee's view of Churchill's speech. Jones had already arranged to explain Churchill's ideas in detail to Cook and Tawney; he at once cancelled his appointment. 'At this moment,' he wrote in his diary, 'Winston came through on the private wire from Chartwell. I told him what had taken place. He boiled up at once, called Steel-Maitland a bloody fool, said they were all afraid of the owners, that he had taken up a public position which he must maintain. . . .'

Churchill demanded another meeting of the Coal Committee that same day, for which he would return at once to London. It was fixed for six o'clock that evening. Jones went to see him a few minutes before the meeting began, recording in his diary that Churchill 'was much quieter than on the telephone at lunch time, and it was possible to reason with him'. According to Jones' account of the meeting:

Winston put his point: he wanted the men to be helped and guided privately; 'I don't like leaving this flapping in the wind; if we are to have legislation there must be a swift surrender and resumption of work. Force the pace, but don't force it unfairly; tell the leaders to-night that the Government's offer is our last friendly gesture, and won't be open beyond this week. Let Wilson or Jones or Gowers tell them they can have the national principles (ratio, subsistence, and minimum) put, not on the face of the Bill, but in a schedule as a guide to the Tribunal.' He produced a letter sent him on the previous day by Steel-Maitland approving of this procedure, and the Minister of Labour, who was so emphatic in his opposition this morning was now silent, and left Bridgeman, Lane-Fox, and the others to oppose the Chancellor.

Winston insisted that he was suggesting nothing which had not been publicly offered, but he was gradually worn down in the course of over an hour's discussion, especially when it came clear that the declaration of national principles to which his colleagues were now willing to assent, were so platitudinous as to be futile. He himself would have put a specific figure for the national minimum in the Bill, while allowing variations in exceptional districts, but this frightened the others.

Churchill's proposals were finally overruled. Baldwin gave his opinion that it was now up to the miners to come to the Government with proposals; that the Government should no longer approach them; and that even the civil servants such as Horace Wilson, Ernest Gowers and Thomas Jones should no longer seek out the miners' leaders and try to work out a compromise with them. Birkenhead supported Baldwin; 'We ought not to go further than we have gone,' he insisted: 'Don't let us go to them, let them come to us.' With this conclusion the Coal Committee concurred. On September 29 Lane-Fox wrote to Irwin that 'most of our Party dislike Government interference, and believe that Winston had started a new and unnecessary stage of interference, and were not at all cordial to him. . . .'

Churchill returned to Chartwell, his new suggestion for encouraging the miners to accept the Government's proposals having been rejected. The return of Baldwin and Birkenhead to the Coal Committee had given courage to those other members whose sympathies were with the owners. 'I cannot conceal from you my own view,' Birkenhead wrote to Irwin on September 30, 'that in all the history of the case the owners are entitled to victory.'

At the Coal Committee on October 5 Churchill wanted the Miners Federation to be 'informed forthwith that, with the absence of acceptance within, say, 48 hours, of the Government's offer of the 17th September, the offer would be withdrawn'. He would, he added, 'enter into no discussions of detail' unless the Federation were prepared to accept the offer in principle 'and without qualification'.

On October 7 the Miners' Federation, feeling cheated of their national minimum wage, rejected the proposed arbitration Tribunal, as Churchill had feared they would. 'Personally,' Birkenhead wrote to Irwin, 'I welcome the death of this particular plan.'

The Coal Strike continued, but 100,000 of the $1\frac{1}{4}$ million miners had already returned to work, driven by poverty and hunger, and the triumph of the owners seemed only a matter of time.

Having gone much further in his efforts at mediation than several of his colleagues wanted, and having exposed himself to their anger, Churchill was disappointed by the miners' refusal to accept his compromise, and became increasingly angry at the attitudes now adopted by both the miners and the owners. Both sides, he believed, had only been prevented from reaching a settlement because of extremists in their ranks. On October 9 a young Conservative MP, Robert Boothby,[1] wrote to him from the Carlton Club, explaining why the miners believed that the Government had let them down. 'It is the impression,' Boothby wrote, 'growing every day, that the Government has now divested itself of all responsibility for the conduct of our national industries in the interest of the country as a whole . . . that despite the promise of the first months, it has become what the people of Scotland have never tolerated, and will never tolerate—a Government of reaction.' Boothby's letter continued:

[1] Robert John Graham Boothby, 1900–1986. Educated at Eton and Magdalen College Oxford. Conservative MP for East Aberdeenshire, 1924–58. Parliamentary Private Secretary to the Chancellor of the Exchequer (Churchill), 1926–29. Elected to the Other Club, 1928. Parliamentary Secretary, Ministry of Food, 1940–41. A British Delegate to the Consultative Assembly, Council of Europe, 1949–57. Knighted, 1953. Created Baron, 1958. President of the Anglo-Israel Association. Rector of St Andrews University, 1958–61. Chairman, Royal Philharmonic Orchestra, 1961–63. Published *The New Economy* (1943), *I Fight to Live* (1947) and *My Yesterday, Your Tomorrow* (1962).

It would be difficult to exaggerate the effect of your vigorous intervention in the mining dispute last month upon the average moderate-minded person in Scotland; or the disappointment which attended the failure of your efforts. There are many who consider (I can really answer for this) that at the time you wrote to the Prime Minister the letter which you quoted in the House of Commons, you were resolved to go forward and to compel the owners (not necessarily the Mining Association) to meet the executive of the Federation using, if necessary, the threat of suspension of the Eight Hours Act; but that you subsequently succumbed to pressure from many quarters.

Moreover the miners' leaders assert in speech after speech that you gave them positive assurances that if they made such an offer as their last one 'the whole force and authority of His Majesty's Government' would be brought into action in their support. This has never been publicly contradicted.

To put it quite frankly, there is a widespread feeling even amongst those who most strongly disapprove of the policy and performances of the Miners' Federation, that you made a great attempt to obtain fair and reasonable peace in the interests of the nation; that the miners went a long way to meet you; but that the owners, supported by a section of the Conservative Party, contemptuously declined even to negotiate, and that you did not feel yourself strong enough to hold on the right course.

Boothby ended with a plea for the miners, whom he described as 'doggedly awaiting their fate. Obstinate, stubborn and stupid. Misled by their leaders, abandoned by the Government, but loyal according to their lights, peaceable, and, despite increasing hunger, resisting (in Scotland almost to a man) what is to them a temptation to return to work.' Churchill replied on October 16:

The Miners get 10½d, out of every shilling of profits calculated on an agreed basis. If this is not good enough for them, they ought to find something else to do. There are twelve hundred thousand living on the same coal-output which sustained a million twenty years ago. There are too many miners. In trying to divide work they have divided wages. The Eight Hours will I hope enable them gradually to reduce numbers and share the wages in a smaller circle. . . . Anyhow the rest of the country is not going to pay a shilling to keep the miners on an artificial level. So much for the economics.

Churchill went on to defend his own part in the negotiations:

I never promised anybody to procure a joint conference or agreement. Such a promise would be inherently impossible and absurd. I always contemplated meeting an Owners' refusal by a conditional amendment of the new Eight Hours Act. The Cabinet supported me in this. 'Twas all I got, 'twas all I asked. I told MacDonald and the Miners at the outset that that was the limit of any coercion we could put on the Owners, and that we would only do that to settle the business promptly. Subsequently the men's leaders went back on lengthening hours, and made other proposals which though a great advance did not bridge the gap.

Now I am afraid it must be fought out. These people think themselves stronger than the state. But that is a mistake. There is a similar attitude among the Owners, as to which I share your feelings; but after all the 10½d in the shilling is a pretty considerable fact. . . .

The issue is not one between Government and Opposition, but what are good laws for the community. Intimidatory picketing, privileged immunity, political levies under pain of boycott, are not—once the issue is raised—compatible with any form of good government. . . .

'I quite understand your pangs and anxieties,' Churchill added, 'but don't let them draw you from a coherent view.'

By mid-October a further 100,000 miners had returned to the pits, and on October 25 a TUC deputation, headed by Arthur Pugh, met Baldwin and Churchill, and begged the Government to intervene once more. Baldwin told Pugh that if the miners would accept the combination offered earlier, of district agreements ratified by a national tribunal, the Government would be willing to seek a settlement. But, he insisted, the miners must give the TUC full powers to negotiate. The TUC at once pressed the miners for a positive response, and at the same time rejected a request from the miners for an embargo on coal imported from abroad. Churchill, meanwhile, in a speaking tour in his constituency, reiterated the views he had expressed to Boothby. 'I am going to tell you a secret,' he told an audience at Royden on October 28. 'I am not in favour of the mine owners *or* the miners. I am against both. They are thoroughly unreasonable in the attitude they have taken from beginning to end.' Speaking of the coal subsidy on November 1 he declared: 'Both sides lapped up the subsidy like cats drinking cream and thought no more of the future than those domestic animals. . . .'

On November 2 Churchill set out his views in a Cabinet memorandum entitled 'The Coal Situation'. Once more, he was critical of both parties to the dispute. He had just learned that the Treasury was paying out almost £250,000 a week for social welfare in the mining districts, and this, he wrote, 'is the explanation of the protraction of the dispute with consequently increasing injuries to the nation'. His memorandum continued:

These reliefs, turned to the best advantage by communal kitchens, enable the married miner to live upon the food of his family. No wonder the struggle continues! It is difficult to see why it should not continue indefinitely, the miners adhering to their principles while subsisting on the outdoor relief of their families and becoming gradually habituated to an indigent idleness.

Churchill's second paragraph was devoted to the owners, towards whom he was equally scathing. They were, he wrote, 'seeking to demonstrate "a principle" which was not asserted when the dispute first began, viz; that there should be no national negotiations or settlement. They have even refused the invitations of the Government to come to a joint conference.' Churchill went on to argue that sooner or later the Government would have to intervene, and he proposed a three-point basis for such intervention. First 'override the owners' by passing a Compulsory Arbitration Bill and setting up an Arbitration Tribunal; second, 'prescribe by law' the interim conditions of a return to work, based on a maximum of $7\frac{1}{2}$ hours a day, except where men had already accepted 8, and with no reduction in wages below the pre-strike level; and third, only allowing the owners to open their pits after they had accepted the arbitration, and cutting off all unemployment relief to any men, and their families, who refused to return to the pits once a national arbitration had been secured.

The Cabinet were still reluctant to coerce the owners in the way Churchill proposed, and his proposals got no further. But the miners were still convinced that their best hope of a fair deal lay with Churchill. On October 19 the *Evening Standard* had reported that both the Trade Union and miners' leaders had expressed 'a marked preference for Mr Churchill as mediator', as opposed to Baldwin.[1] On November 2 Lord Londonderry sent Churchill a long letter of protest against his recent constituency speeches. In fighting the strike, Londonderry insisted, the owners were 'fighting Socialism'; and he warned: 'You will have to fight Socialism in the very near future and the Miners' Federation is one of the powerful army corps in the field against us.' The coal-owners, Londonderry added, 'are one class of the captains of industry, and while you may not desire a victory for the Owners over the men, which really is not the issue at all, we want a victory over the strongest Communistic force in the country'.

Replying to Londonderry on the following day, Churchill wrote, of the owners' refusal to accept a national settlement: 'A national agreement or provision for the review and co-ordination of district settlements is indispensable and ultimately inevitable. Nothing that the Owners can

---

[1] Three weeks later, on November 11, Churchill's cousin Frederick Guest wrote to him: 'I must send you a piece of news that has come to me through my Agent in Bristol. He attended an open-air Socialist Meeting where the coal question was being discussed and the speaker, by no means an irresponsible person, having twice been a Labour Parliamentary candidate, told his audience that if only the matter had been left in your hands some weeks ago it would have been settled and the men would have had a square deal. I think this is good hearing from such a source and is likely to be an indication of a much wider and similar feeling in the country.'

do will destroy a National Federation among the Miners. All other great trades are organised nationally. . . .' Churchill went on to give his personal view of why the negotiations had failed. 'Both sides,' he wrote, 'are represented by their worst and most unreasonable elements and by people selected for their obstinacy and combative qualities. In my opinion they both share the discredit of leading their industry and the country into their present lamentable position.'

Churchill's reply continued with a stern rebuke:

With those parts of your letter which deal with the necessity for combating Bolshevism I am in entire accord. But there could be no worse way of combating Bolshevism than to identify the Conservative Party and His Majesty's Government with the employers, and particularly with a body of employers like those headed by Mr Evan Williams and Sir Adam Nimmo. The duty of the Government is to occupy an impartial position in the interests of the State and of the whole community. . . .

You say that the Owners are fighting Socialism. It is not the business of Coal Owners as Coal Owners to fight Socialism. If they declare it their duty, how can they blame the Miners' Federation for pursuing political ends? The business of the Coal Owners is to manage their industry successfully, to insist upon sound economic conditions as regards hours and wages, and to fight Socialism as citizens and not as owners of a particular class of property.

'I may add,' Churchill ended, 'that by far the greater part of every speech I have made in my constituency on the Coal Dispute has been devoted to showing the unreasonable character of the miners' claims and the wrongfulness of their leaders' conduct. But no-one with the slightest spark of impartiality could avoid reference to the faults and errors of the other party to the dispute.'

Throughout the first ten days of November, the TUC sought to mediate between the miners and the Government. At the Cabinet Coal Committee on November 5, in an attempt to rescue the essential formula of national agreements, Churchill again proposed that all district wage settlements should be reviewed by the Industrial Court. On November 8 the miners insisted that they could accept no settlement which was not based on the seven-hour day. Two days later Churchill pointed out to the Coal Committee the 'serious disadvantages' of the Government's proposals of September 17. 'For example,' he said, 'the tendency under those proposals would be for the owners to offer less than they were really prepared to give, so that in effect a subsequent application to the Tribunal would only result in the men obtaining what the owners would have given in the first instance had there been no appeal to the Tribunal.' It was essential, Churchill believed, to give the owners 'every inducement to offer good terms'.

On November 11, Baldwin, Churchill and the other members of the Coal Committee put their proposals both to the miners' leaders and to the owners. Harold Laski,[1] who accompanied the miners' leaders, sent a description of the meeting to a friend on November 30:

The change in Baldwin since I saw him last was quite tragic. He had become hard and a little cynical and impatient of all criticism. We had some private talk and I found that he was a most curious mixture of the sentimental phrase and the hard act. Churchill who was there was bigger and more skilful in every way—he knew how to negotiate. Baldwin merely blundering uncouthly.

As Churchill now set it out, the Government's position was a clear one: the miners must return to work at once under district agreements and the owners must accept the final arbitration of a Central Tribunal. But Churchill's attitude was still too radical for Lane-Fox, who wrote to Irwin on November 9: 'He ignores that tiresome fact that the pit belongs to the owner, and says this miserable man must conform to the will of Parliament etc etc. The Prime Minister sits dumb and bored while Winston makes flowery speeches to the miners . . .'

On November 12, while the miners were still considering the terms, the owners rejected them. As Churchill wished, the Government at once announced that if the miners accepted the terms, then the Government would proceed with its plans despite the owners, and introduce legislation to set up an independent national Arbitration body. On November 16 the Coal Committee drafted a Bill on these lines, establishing what was described as a National Arbitral Authority. 'This,' Lane-Fox wrote to Irwin on November 18, 'was what we got Winston's unfortunate efforts reduced to.' That same day, the miners voted in their districts against the settlement. Deprived of any hope of an agreement, desperate for wages, caught by the severity of the winter, the men had no alternative but gradually to return to work.

On November 20 the Coal Strike came to an end. The owners' inflexibility had triumphed. Every miner returning to the pits had no alternative but the eight-hour day and such local wage scales as he

[1] Harold Joseph Laski, 1893–1950. Political philosopher and historian; the son of Nathan Laski (an influential member of the Jewish community in North-West Manchester, Churchill's former constituency). Lecturer in History, McGill University, Montreal, 1914–16; Harvard University, 1916–20. Vice-Chairman of the British Institute of Adult Education, 1921–30. Member of the Fabian Society Executive, 1922. Lecturer in Political Science, Magdalene College, Cambridge, 1922–25. Professor of Political Science, London, 1926–50. Member of Executive Committee of Labour Party, 1936–49.

could best obtain at the district level. Despite his repeated criticism of the owners and their tactics, Churchill's final criticism was for the miners; but he reserved his actual condemnation for those whom he believed had pushed them into an inflexible position. Writing to Sir James Hawkey on November 16 he declared:

Although many of the older Trade Union leaders are men of goodwill and patriotism, and although the majority of Trade Unionists wish to be good citizens of the country and Empire, the spirit of faction for political and Party ends pervades and dominates the Trade Union World. The extremists are able on nearly every occasion to force the majority into violent courses, to repulse all efforts at compromise and conciliation and to levy the class war inside the industries in order to procure by an increase of misery the triumph of Socialist or Communist doctrines.

We have seen these extremists sway the miners' Councils to the general misfortune at every critical moment in the ruinous dispute now probably ending. But for that the miners could have obtained seven months ago, and without suffering to themselves or the mass of their fellow-countrymen, terms incomparably better than those which they will now have to accept. Even three months ago they could have had from the Government terms greatly superior to those of which their leaders have now advised acceptance. But the Moscow influence and the Moscow money have been powerful enough to drown the voice of reason and good feeling.

The struggle has been fought to the bitter end. All classes have suffered much; no class has suffered more than the members of the great Trade Unions, and among them the greatest sufferers have been the miners themselves. . . .

The miners ought not to have allowed themselves to be led by the nose in this shocking manner. Anyone can see the reasons for the policy of the Russian Bolsheviks. They argue that the more miserable and impoverished the working classes of Britain become, the better is the chance of a bloody revolution and general collapse which would reduce this country to the social and economical level of the Russian Republic. Besides this they saw the chance of grabbing British markets for their own coal exports. A lot of sensible British workingmen ought not to let themselves be used as pawns in these deep foreign intrigues.

Churchill went on to warn Hawkey, and through him his own constituents, that the immediate threat to the British Empire was not from any 'warlike assault' from abroad, nor from any constitutional dispute between Britain and the Dominions, but from inside Britain itself. His letter ended: 'The attempt to establish in this island a Socialist State in sympathy and alliance with Moscow will be resisted by whatever Constitutional means and measures may be found necessary.'

On December 8 Churchill defended the Government during a Labour motion of Censure on the conduct of the coal negotiations, explaining to a crowded House the part he had played. 'Time after time,' he said, 'terms had been offered and turned down', first by the owners and then by the miners. He was not trying 'to fix all the blame upon the Opposition', he said. But he believed that the Labour Party had 'a very great responsibility' for bringing politics into industry, and industry into politics. His speech, as reported in the Press, continued:

If the industries of this small, over-crowded, over-industrialised, highly artificial island were going to be plunged into the political arena, and if these inherent antagonisms were going to be used as pawns in the party fight, that would not only injure Parliament, but would more gravely strike at the industries upon which the mass of our people depended for their daily bread.

Could they not come to an arrangement as far as possible to declare as a neutral area in their party struggles that the basic industries, on which the great mass of workers depended for a livelihood, would be allowed fair play to do the best they could?

Churchill went on to point out 'the influence of Russia' in aggravating and embittering industrial life. After his return from a visit to the Soviet Union, A. J. Cook had announced that the Russian Trade Unions had given £1,200,000 to the miners' cause, as against £430,000 subscribed by the British Trade Unions. 'Was it not an extraordinary thing,' Churchill asked, 'that these Russian miners, whose wages, he was assured, were one third less than the wages of British miners, should have spontaneously and out of the generosity of their hearts, subscribed two and a half times more than the whole British trade union movement?' At the same time, he pointed out, the miners had received more than £9,000,000 in British social welfare funds. In conclusion, he said:

He did not grudge the miners the relief they had obtained from Russia, which he was told, was one-eighth of what they had received from British boards of guardians. Mr Cook had said, 'Thank God for Russia.' By the same arithmetic they ought to say, 'Thank God for England eight times more.' (Laughter and cheers!) But out of evil might come good. We had learned that neither a general strike nor a prolonged stoppage in the coalfields could break down the life and organization of our country.

Writing to the King on December 9 about Churchill's speech, Baldwin commented: 'It was a debating speech, but a debating speech of such skill and power that it probably could not have been delivered by any other Member in the House', and he added: 'In its orderly array of arguments presented with all Mr Churchill's pugnacity and force, in its well arranged sequence of thought, and, above all, in its Parliamentary strategy, it was a masterpiece of its kind.'

12

'The Smiling Chancellor'

A S soon as the Coal Strike was over, Churchill began two months of intense work, in an attempt to finish the third volume of his war memoirs. He also made plans for a winter holiday, and in a letter to Roger Keyes on November 15 he accepted the Admiral's invitation to join him at Messina on January 6 for a week or ten days cruising in the Mediterranean. 'On leaving you,' Churchill wrote, 'I am going to stay in Rome for a few days to see Mussolini (while he lasts). . . .' Churchill also hoped to play one final game of polo at Malta. 'If I expire on the ground,' he added, 'it will at any rate be a worthy end!'[1] On December 5 Churchill wrote again: 'I greatly look forward to such a complete change from my grind here, and still more to fighting old battles over again in your company.' To his son Randolph, who had also asked him if he could leave Eton before the end of the school year and go to Oxford, Churchill wrote on December 13 to explain that they would be spending Christmas at Chartwell and would then leave together for the Mediterranean. His letter continued:

It was very disappointing to me while arranging this very interesting expedition for you to learn how little you are using your abilities and opportunities at Eton.

You will certainly not go to Oxford unless you show some aptitude and love for learning.

Many thanks for your letter on my birthday and for the cigarettes. It would give me much more pleasure to hear something creditable about you from your masters.[2]

---

[1] Churchill's game of polo at Malta was the last he ever played.

[2] Randolph's housemaster, A. C. Sheepshanks, had written to Churchill on 2 December 1926: 'I have been trying to persuade him not to be so obstinate, and to make him realize that it is essential sometimes to believe that the other person is right although he holds an opinion diametrically opposed to his own. He will never persuade himself that he is wrong, and becomes quite intolerable for everyone.' Randolph was then 15½ years old.

Before leaving for the Mediterranean, Churchill spent a number of evenings with Lord Beaverbrook, with whom his friendship, despite the brief friction over the *British Gazette*, had continued to flourish. On December 28, after an exchange of Christmas gifts, Churchill wrote to Beaverbrook:

My dear Max,

Many thanks for yr letter & the cigars to wh I will do full justice.

I am sincerely glad that the year wh is passing has been one of such pleasant relations between us. I have a vy deep regard for you and feel the full attraction of yr vivid, genial, loyal & dominating personality. I always enjoy myself in yr company & look forward to all our meetings. The difficulty of my being in the centre of a govt to wh you have every right to be opposed, has I rejoice to think ceased to be any obstacle to our personal intimacy. Whatever differences we may have on public matters—& look at the differences I had with Fred[1] for years—we ought to keep our friendship clear & intact. As life flows on one does not make many new friends, or meet many people from whose society real pleasure is to be gained. It is vital to preserve & cherish those associations wh are mellowed by time & by common experiences & adventures. Some day the wheel may turn—it surely will—& political action may superimpose itself on bright companionship. In the main & on the greatest issues I expect we shd be together.

You have had wonderful success in yr eventful life while still quite young, & everything you have touched has prospered. All yr direct & finite ambitions have been attained. What lies before you now, properly understood holds I believe greater possibilities & deeper satisfactions than any you have known —even in the fierce battle-days of youth. The best part of life lies before you: & the hardest & fiercest work. Splendid opportunities will reward the earlier risks & toils. Personally I have so far enjoyed life more every year. But I do not think that wd continue if I felt that the future was closed or cabined. I do not feel that it is—either in my own case or in yours. There are vy great things to be done by those who reach a certain scale of comprehension & of power in their early prime. As long as health & life are ours, we must try to do them—not to be content except with the best & truest solutions—but I am writing a tract & not the New Years' Greeting I set out to pen.

With all good wishes then for that New Year & may we get things going a little better in it.

Believe me

Your sincere friend
Winston S.C.

On 4 January 1927, accompanied by his son Randolph and his brother Jack, Churchill left England for the Mediterranean. After a day

---

[1] Lord Birkenhead, whose friendship with Churchill dated from 1906.

in Paris they took the night train south, reaching Genoa on the following morning. During his day in Genoa Churchill was much struck by the atmosphere of the Fascist state. 'This country gives the impression of discipline, order, goodwill, smiling faces,' he wrote to his wife from on board ship. 'A happy, strict school—no talking among the pupils. Great changes have taken place since you and I disembarked from this ship nearly six years ago.'[1] The Fascists, he added, 'have been saluting in their impressive manner all over the place'.

Churchill's main news was of his book: he had worked on the proofs 'till 2.30 this morning and again from 8 till now'. They were now finished, packed up, and would be posted by the Hotel on the following day 'under threats of vengeance from Mussolini if anything goes wrong'. It was his last day's work on the final chapter of the final volume. 'Thank God the book is over,' he exclaimed. 'It is now off my mind for good or ill for ever. I hope it will secure us an easy two years . . . and by that time I will think of something else.'

On January 7 the Churchills reached Naples by boat from Genoa. Churchill's mind was still on his book. 'I trust I shall not see its face again . . .' he wrote. 'It is an immense relief to have ended my task. I am not going to think any more about it—or the mioulings that will attend its publication.' He also had something to say about his son:

The Rabbit is a very good travelling companion. He curls up in the cabin most silently and tidily. We have played a great deal of chess in which I give him either a Queen or two castles, or even castle, bishop and knight—and still wallop him.

I am shocked to see him wear nothing under his little linen shirts, and to go about without a coat on every occasion. He is *hardy*, but surely a vest is a necessity to white people. I am going to buy him some.

At Naples, Churchill and his son watched an eruption of Vesuvius, and visited the ruins of Pompeii. On January 8 they reached Malta. 'I am having a vy interesting trip,' Churchill wrote to Baldwin from Malta on January 10, '& it is a new pleasure to me to show the world to Randolph. . . . After 12 years it interests me greatly to revive all those topics in wh I used to dwell—& see the ships we planned in the far off, thrilling pre-war days.' In his letter Churchill urged Baldwin to include in the forthcoming Trade Union Bill the right of individual members to contract out of the Union's compulsory Political levy. As he wrote:

---

[1] Six years earlier, this same ship, the *Esperia*, had brought Churchill back from Egypt in his unsuccessful attempt to try to reach London in time to succeed Austen Chamberlain as Chancellor of the Exchequer.

My view is that we are bound to have a Bill, that we *ought* to have a Bill; that any Bill even the most perfunctory will excite united Labour Opposition; that therefore we shd have a real Bill which rallies our own forces for the fight & wh when passed will have cut into the vitals of our enemies, & given them something to cry out for.

To be precise I hold most strongly that the political levy shd be included; & that to leave it out will be to discourage supporters without mitigating the anger of foes.

I do not think that arguments alone—not uniting the moderates & the extremists, not blighting the alleged impending lion-lying-down-with-the-lamb performance—ought to influence action.

Immense injury has been done this year to the whole country, & a deliberate assault made upon its institutions by the forces resting upon the political activities of the TUs. Their activities have been unhealthily developed by privilege legislation. And the privilege in its harmful aspects shd now be removed. I am sure this is an issue wh we ought to face sternly; & that once it is dealt with the path will be clear for soothing processes. I am rather afraid this may not make you relish particularly my eagerness to be present when the issues are decided!

I agree with you vy much that the Bill shd be simple & not loaded up with nagging little points interfering with ordinary TU life. Two or three broad real applications of principle—on wh battle can be joined. I do not believe it will be a vy severe battle.

'These nettles,' Churchill added, 'are best grasped firmly.'

On January 13 Churchill was at Athens, where, as *The Times* reported, he 'expressed his pleasure at the restoration of Parliamentary Government in Greece'. On January 14 he was in Rome, the *Evening Standard* reporting that he had briefly discussed Italy's war debt. 'I am kept apprised of your wanderings by the newspapers,' Clementine Churchill wrote from Chartwell on January 15. While in Rome Churchill spent several hours discussing the Italian debt with Count Volpi, and had two short meetings with Mussolini, one at a Ball, the other after dinner at the British Embassy. 'There was much mutual appreciation,' the British Ambassador, Sir Ronald Graham,[1] reported to Austen Chamberlain on January 21. In a Press statement, Churchill stressed the traditional friendship between Britain and Italy. 'I well remember,' he said, 'the emotion with which in the spring of 1915 I learned of the secret clause in the Treaty of the Triple Alliance, by

[1] Ronald William Graham, 1870–1949. Educated at Eton. Entered the Diplomatic Service, 1892. Second Secretary, St Petersburg, 1899–1903. Councillor of Embassy, Egypt, 1907–10. Adviser to the Egyptian Government, Ministry of the Interior, Cairo, 1910–16. Knighted, 1915. Assistant Under-Secretary of State for Foreign Affairs (London), 1916–19. Minister to Holland, 1919–21. Privy Councillor, 1921. Ambassador to Italy, 1921–33.

which Italy stipulated that in no circumstances should she ever be brought through that Alliance into a war with England. Such memories ought to be cherished and dwelt upon and made familiar to the general public.' As for his interviews with Mussolini and Count Volpi, he said: 'It is a good thing in modern Europe for public men in different countries, who have been a long time connected with affairs, to meet on a friendly and social basis and form personal impressions of one another. It is one of the ways in which international suspicions may be diminished and frank and confident relations maintained.' Commenting on the personal impression which Mussolini had made on him, Churchill told the assembled journalists:

I could not help being charmed, like so many other people have been, by his gentle and simple bearing and by his calm, detached poise in spite of so many burdens and dangers. Secondly, anyone could see that he thought of nothing but the lasting good, as he understood it, of the Italian people, and that no lesser interest was of the slightest consequence to him.

It was, Churchill continued, 'quite absurd to suggest that the Italian Government does not stand upon a popular basis or that it is not upheld by the active and practical assent of the great masses'. No political issue could be judged 'apart from its atmosphere and environment'. As for Fascism, he continued:

If I had been an Italian, I am sure I should have been whole-heartedly with you from the start to finish in your triumphant struggle against the bestial appetites and passions of Leninism. But in England we have not yet had to face this danger in the same deadly form. We have our own way of doing things. But that we shall succeed in grappling with Communism and choking the life out of it—of that I am absolutely sure.

The theme of the dangers of Communism also permeated Churchill's remarks on the international aspect of Fascism. 'Externally,' he said, 'your movement has rendered service to the whole world.'

Churchill's statement caused an uproar in the Labour and Liberal Press. 'We always suspected that Mr Winston Churchill was a Fascist at heart,' declared the *New Leader* on January 28. 'Now he has openly avowed it,' and on February 1 Clementine Churchill wrote to her husband: 'C. P. Scott is I see vexed over your partiality to "Pussolini".'[1]

---

[1] During his visit to Rome Churchill also had an audience with the Pope. Randolph Churchill recorded in his memoirs: 'A lot of careful protocol went into the private audience which my father and I had with Pope Pius. As an important minister serving under a Protestant sovereign my father felt that he ought not to kneel, but everything was arranged very easily. We were told that we should treat His Holiness merely as a temporal sovereign and bow to him three times: once at the door, once halfway and once when we arrived at his

From Rome, Churchill went by train to the South of France, where he spent four days with his wife at Consuelo Balsan's villa, Lou Seuil, at Eze. On his arrival he learnt, from P. J. Grigg, that the Cabinet had decided to send British troops to China, where British lives and property were being threatened by local warlords. British subjects had already been expelled from two Treaty ports, Hankow and Kiukiang, while at Nanking several British traders had been murdered by the mob. Churchill was in no doubt as to what should be done, and had already made his views clear to the Cabinet. Indeed, on January 18 Baldwin had written to Churchill that the Cabinet, 'fired by your statement that we ought to have a policy and recognising that soon we shall have no more cheeks to turn, and taking their courage in both hands' had decided to send at least a Division of British troops to protect the threatened ports. 'Of course there never was such cruel luck as yours,' Grigg wrote to Churchill from the Treasury on January 22, 'first the coal subsidy, then the 7 months' coal strike, and now "heavily armed neutrality" in China'. But in his reply to Baldwin on January 22, Churchill wrote that it had in fact been a 'relief' to him to learn of the Cabinet's decision to send more troops to China, and he added:

Short of being actually conquered, there is no evil worse than submitting to wrong and violence for fear of war. Once you take the position of not being able in any circumstances to defend your rights against the aggression of some particular set of people, there is no end to the demands that will be made or to the humiliations that must be accepted.

On January 25 a British steamship, the *Megantic*, sailed from Liverpool to Shanghai with troops for the Shanghai Defence Force. That same day Churchill wrote to Worthington-Evans from Eze:

. . . my motive in writing is to urge you to send out plenty of Tanks to Shanghai. A dozen of those fast tanks we saw at Aldershot would do more to keep order in a great Chinese city than 20,000 infantry soldiers. Moreover, how are Chinese troops going to resist an attack by tanks? Unless they have really good artillerists—like the German officer who shot six tanks in succession single-handed before being killed[1]—they will be quite helpless against these vehicles.

---

desk. All this passed off very well. The early part of the conversation was a little sticky. Then my father and the Pope got on to the subject of the Bolsheviks and had a jolly half hour saying what they thought of them.'

[1] The officer was Lieutenant Müller of the 108th Regiment. The incident took place on 20 November 1917, during the Battle of Cambrai. According to Sir Douglas Haig's despatch of 20 February 1918: 'Many of the hits on our tanks at Flesquières were obtained by a

I was very glad to see that you had carried your point about Gas. 'Gas for Asia' may be a phrase of great significance. But I believe you will find Tanks even more effective, both for street fighting and operations in open country.

'I hope,' Churchill added, 'that firm action and *adequate forces* will lead to a peaceful solution. But if not, I beseech you at the outset of what may be great responsibilities to use the right tackle.'

Churchill left Eze for Paris on the evening of January 25. On the following day, in Paris, he lunched with Louis Loucheur. Among those present were Aristide Briand, Vincent Auriol,[1] Raoul Peret[2] and, as Churchill wrote to his wife, 'about 15 MP's representing leading elements in all parties. . . . I conducted a general conversation in my best French, & defended Debt demands & Mussolini interviews with some spirit.' From Paris, Churchill travelled to the Duke of Westminster's château at Eu for three days hunting. The object of the chase was the wild boar, which Churchill had nicknamed the 'penwipers'. On January 28 he sent his wife an account of his activities. 'There are plenty of pigs,' he wrote, '& the country people of all classes are enchanted at the hunt & follow it on foot in motors or on any kind of quadruped. They are as eager to kill them as if they were Germans.' That afternoon Churchill motored from Eu to Dieppe, where he laid wreaths on the graves of Clementine Churchill's mother and brother. He also visited the British military cemetery in the same churchyard, where he and the Duke of Westminster were struck, as he wrote to his wife, by the 'orderly lines of tombstones & the high cross of sacrifice'. He added: 'We wandered among them reading the inscriptions wh recall the history we know so well.'

Churchill crossed from Dieppe to Newhaven by the night ferry on

---

German artillery officer who, remaining alone at his battery, served a field gun single-handed until killed at his gun. The great bravery of this officer aroused the admiration of all ranks.' Lieutenant Müller was the only individual German officer ever to be mentioned in British despatches.

[1] Vincent Auriol, 1884–1966. The son of a village baker, he founded a local newspaper, *Le Midi Socialiste* at the age of 21. Elected to the Chamber of Deputies in 1914. General Secretary of the socialist group in the Chamber, 1919–36, and principal financial expert of the Socialist Party. Minister of Finance in Léon Blum's Popular Front Government, 1936. Minister of Justice, 1937. Co-ordinator of the Prime Minister's Department, 1938. One of the few Socialist Deputies to vote against Marshal Pétain, 1940. Imprisoned by the Vichy regime, but escaped. Worked with the Resistance; then joined de Gaulle in London. Vice-Premier in de Gaulle's Provisional Government, 1945. First President of the Fourth Republic, 1947–54. Active in persuading the Socialists to work with de Gaulle in 1958, and a member of de Gaulle's Constitutional Council, 1958–59.

[2] Raoul Peret. French Minister of Finance, March–June 1926. Minister of Justice, March–November 1930.

Saturday January 29, and was driven direct from the coast to Chartwell. Grigg had arranged for a box of Treasury papers to be waiting for him in his car.

On February 7 *The Times* began its daily serialization of Churchill's new volume of *The World Crisis*.[1] From the first day of the serialization, Churchill received many letters of congratulation. The Jutland story, wrote R. D. Blumenfeld[2] on February 11, 'is the best piece of clear, incisive and instructional journalism that I have seen for a long time. You have swept away, irrevocably, a thousand misconceptions. . . .' The volume itself was published on March 3, in two parts. Two days later J. M. Keynes wrote approvingly in the *Nation and Athenaeum* of how Churchill 'pursues no vendettas, and shows no malice'. The volume itself, Keynes wrote, was 'a tractate against war—more effective than the work of a pacifist could be'.

'I have been at a loss which to admire more,' Neville Chamberlain wrote on March 4, 'your command of language, the vividness of the pictures you conjure up, or the interest & originality of the views you have presented so clearly & fortified with such abundant evidence. How you have found time to have put together so vast a work fairly dumbfounds me.' On March 8 Robert Boothby, who had just become Churchill's Parliamentary Private Secretary, and whose cousin Henry Dundas[3] had been killed on the western front, wrote from the Treasury: 'Your book proves that the sacrifice of that generation is not yet forgotten. It rivets attention upon the battlefields of France and those who died there, for all time: and the comfort that this will give to those who have lost everything must be the measure of their gratitude,' and on

---

[1] The volume was also serialized in Canada, France, Germany, Holland, Italy, Greece Hungary and Czechoslovakia. Its success was immediate, bringing Churchill a substantial income. On March 4, the day after publication, he received a £2,000 advance, followed by a thousand dollars for Canadian serialization. Within two months of publication the volume had sold over eleven thousand copies, and Churchill received a further £4,874 in royalties. Only in the United States were the sales disappointing. On March 18 Charles Scribner Junior wrote from New York that although the American reviews 'have treated it as one of the outstanding books of the year', it had sold only a thousand copies.

[2] Ralph D. Blumenfeld, 1864–1948. Born in the United States. Entered journalism as a reporter on the *Chicago Herald*, 1884. London Correspondent of the *New York Herald*, 1887–93. News Editor of the *Daily Mail*, 1900–02. Editor of the *Daily Express*, 1902–32. Founder of the Anti-Socialist Union. Author of several volumes of memoirs, including *All in a Lifetime* (1931). Chairman of the *Daily Express* from 1933 until his death.

[3] Henry Lancaster Neville Dundas, 1897–1918. Son of an Edinburgh solicitor. Oppidan Scholar at Eton; Captain of the Fifteen and Rosebery History Prize. Awarded scholarships at both Christ Church and New College Oxford. 2nd Lieutenant, Scots Guards, 1915. Acting Captain, 1916. Awarded the Military Cross and bar. Killed in action after the capture of the Canal du Nord, 27 September 1918.

March 14 A. S. Le Maitre[1] wrote to Churchill from the Admiralty: 'Aged 19 I went to the Somme & saw my generation destroyed, and to them you have made a memorial not very different from the other about Harry the King. . . . The Somme I expect was a nastier business than Agincourt, but there is something in common. I'm glad that knowledge of the difficulties is hidden from the ordinary folk.'

At the Treasury the first three months of 1927 were dominated by the Budget preparations. Churchill's main task in his third Budget was to make up the £30 million deficit caused by the Coal Strike. To do this, he and Baldwin were agreed that cuts of about 3 per cent ought to be made in all three Service estimates. In January Baldwin himself asked Worthington-Evans to make a 3 per cent cut in Army expenditure, and on February 7 Churchill wrote to him to explain that it was in the realm of cavalry that he felt this cut would best be made. There was, Churchill insisted, only a limited future for mounted cavalry; fast tanks, armoured cars and mechanization were the basis for the army of the future; there was no merit in 'a lengthy overlapping of the new and the old'. On February 14 Churchill discussed the Army Estimates with Worthington-Evans at the Treasury, and, as a result of their meeting, it was agreed to reduce the Estimates from £43,167,000 to £41,565,000, or nearly a million pounds less than the 1926 figures. 'Let me thank you for the efforts you have made to assist me in my task,' Churchill wrote to Worthington-Evans three days later. 'I was very sorry to have to press you so much, for I know how close the Army has been cut and how frugal you are yourself in administration.'[2] A week later William Bridgeman agreed to reduce the Naval Estimates from £61,420,000 to £56,350,000, the figure requested by the Cabinet's Standing Committee on Expenditure.

On January 6 Sir Otto Niemeyer had written to Churchill that the Coal Strike deficit was, in the Treasury view, 'an imaginary evil', as it

---

[1] Alfred Sutherland Le Maitre, 1896–1959. Educated at Fettes and St John's College Cambridge. 2nd Lieutenant, 7th Battalion, Black Watch, 1915–18. On 16 September 1916 he won the Military Cross for bravery during a raid across No-Man's-Land into the German trenches on the Somme. Entered the Admiralty, 1920; Admiralty Delegation to Washington, 1944; Under-Secretary, 1946. Member of the Economic Planning Board, 1947. Controller of Ground Services, Ministry of Transport and Civil Aviation, 1948–57. Knighted, 1951.

[2] At the end of April Churchill saw a War Office proposal to build a new Cavalry barracks and permanent Horse Lines in Cairo. This proposal, he wrote to Worthington-Evans on April 29, ran counter to the War Office agreement in January to reduce Cavalry expenditure, and he added: 'It would be unpardonable to waste the large sum of money involved in constructing Cavalry Lines when probably half a dozen Whippet Tanks or an armoured car detachment would give far greater security to public order in Cairo than a mass of Horse soldiers.' He was totally opposed, he added, to allowing money 'to flow out month after month' for a Cavalry arm that was in the process of being reduced.

could easily be recovered by Government loans. Churchill, however, opposed any such solution, minuting on January 25: 'Why do you call it an "imaginary evil"? Surely having to raise 37m by taxation and repaying it to bondholders in the distant future is as much a real evil as any other onerous obligation.' On the following day he wrote to Niemeyer again: 'the dead hand of the debt will continue to rest for a longer period and with greater weight upon the productive energies of the country', while any increase in long-term indebtedness would constitute 'a heavy fresh burden upon posterity'.

Churchill persevered in his search for economies to enable at least some of the Coal Strike costs to be recovered. On February 9, in a memorandum opposing any Government contribution towards the backlog of distress in the mining industry, he wrote: 'We must harden our hearts,' and on February 10, at a meeting of the Cabinet's Tax Revision Committee,[1] whose aim was to examine tax evasion, he told his colleagues that he wished to distinguish between 'the one man company established legitimately by a land owner to protect his estate, and the one man company created by the financier, the sole purpose of which was to avoid taxation'. A few moments later he observed 'that it would be very much better for the present Government to deal with the more glaring cases of avoidance than to allow the abuse to grow into a public scandal to be dealt with on very drastic lines, possibly by some future Socialist Government. . . .'

Churchill's efforts at economy were successful. On February 11 Sir Philip Sassoon accepted, on behalf of Sir Samuel Hoare, a reduction in the Royal Air Force estimates from £16 million to £15½ million. Hoare had agreed to these cuts two months before on condition that, as he had written to Churchill on 17 December 1926, that there were also 'substantial reductions' in the Army and Navy.[2]

Publicly, as well as in Cabinet, Churchill urged restrictions on spending, and on deficit expansion, telling a deputation of the Federation of British Industries on March 9: 'Every form of borrowing impaired the national credit' and that all projects for fresh borrowing would be 'firmly resisted'. As for the reduction of defence expenditure, he said, Britain 'had disarmed to an extent that no other victorious power had

---

[1] The Tax Revision Committee (Tax Evasion) consisted of Churchill (the Chairman), Lord Salisbury, Sir Laming Worthington-Evans, Walter Bridgeman, Sir Douglas Hogg and Ronald McNeill.

[2] Churchill's principal dispute with Hoare was over the Air Ministry's desire to continue to build airships. On reading Hoare's report of his successful 12,000-mile aeroplane flight from England to India and back (circulated to the Cabinet on 18 February 1927), Churchill noted: '*Moral*. Good: but don't waste money on foolish airships.'

attempted, but there was a point beyond which the cutting down of the defensive services would only create uncertainty and alarm'. To his colleagues in the Cabinet, however, he insisted that this point had not yet been reached. He also continued to press for further cuts in non-Service expenditure. On April 2, only nine days before the Budget was to be introduced, he circulated a stern note urging 'a new effort' for final economies. 'I am sure,' he wrote, 'that Parliament and the country will require a further resolute effort on our part and I ask my colleagues to authorise me to speak in this sense on the Budget.'

The Standing Committee on Expenditure met in Baldwin's room in the House of Commons during the afternoon of April 5.[1] The forthcoming Budget, Churchill told his colleagues, 'would represent the limits of what could be done by way of taxation without checking a trade revival'. Nevertheless, immediate economies were needed to avoid increased taxation in 1928. He therefore proposed to abolish several postwar Ministries—the Ministry of Transport, the Mines Department and the Department of Overseas Trade. As an additional means of reducing Government spending, he wished to cut Civil Service recruitment by 50% for at least three years.

The full Cabinet met to discuss the Budget on April 6. The principal discussion centred on a proposed relaxation of Death Duties. Churchill opposed such a move, despite its obvious popularity in Conservative circles. He had come to the conclusion, he told his colleagues, 'that if he made some concession in regard to the evasion of Death Duties which would benefit the land-owning classes, he would have to give some corresponding concession to other classes of taxpayer'. Any tax concessions, he insisted, were quite 'undesirable' in the existing financial situation.

Churchill had also worked out several means of increasing the revenue, details of which he sent to the King on April 8. A tax on imported tableware pottery would bring in £200,000 in a full year; a duty of 33⅓ per cent on imported motor car tyres, £750,000; a small increase in the tax on matches, £700,000; an increase in duties on imported wines, £1,500,000; and an increase in the tax on tobacco, £3,400,000. Much of this latter sum, Churchill explained, 'will be found from the extraordinary profits of the Imperial Tobacco Company', and not from smokers. A reduction in the credit terms extended to brewers would produce a further £5 million, and a speeding up of the collection of Schedule A taxes on landlords' rents, half of which

[1] The members of the Committee were Baldwin (in the Chair), Lord Salisbury, Lord Birkenhead, Walter Guinness, Churchill, Sir Philip Cunliffe-Lister and Lord Peel. Two other Ministers, Neville Chamberlain and Ronald McNeill, were also present.

landlords could hitherto defer by six months, would produce a further £14,800,000. 'All that will happen,' Churchill explained, 'is that when the world comes to an end, if that date should fall between December and July in any financial year, the Chancellor of the Exchequer of the day, whoever he may be, will be found in possession of one additional instalment of Schedule A.' By such means, Churchill said, it would not be necessary to resort to the 'ugly' alternative of an extra sixpence on the income tax.

'Although, as you will appreciate,' Lord Stamfordham wrote from Windsor Castle that same day, 'His Majesty finds it difficult, without further study, to grasp completely some of the more technical points, he congratulates you upon the ingenious manner in which you have met so formidable an undertaking. . . .'

On April 10 Leopold Amery wrote to Baldwin to protest against Churchill's whole approach to the Budget:

A few hand to mouth dodges for picking up odd windfalls, a hope that better trade and a few millions saved by cheese-paring here and there may tide matters over next year: that is the beginning and end of it. Not the glimmering of an idea how the paralysing burden of our present direct taxation is to be progressively reduced, not a suggestion for helping the productive industries from which the revenue after all is derived, still less any inkling of the difficulties threatened by our growing adverse trade balance and by the repercussion of this on our power of investment overseas, on our bank rate at home, or of the effect of a high bank rate on the recovery of industry and on the possibility of debt conversion.

Amery suggested removing Churchill from the Treasury, and giving him a Cabinet post as coordinator of the Army, Air Force and Navy strategy. But Baldwin had complete confidence in Churchill, and had approved the Budget proposals at every stage.

On the afternoon of April 11 Churchill introduced his third Budget in the House of Commons. Since eight o'clock that morning MPs had been booking their seats on the floor of the House, and long before Churchill entered the Chamber many MPs had to be content with seats in the upstairs galleries. 'The scene was quite sufficient,' Baldwin wrote to the King, 'to show that Mr Churchill as a star turn has a power of attraction which nobody in the House of Commons can excel', and he went on to describe the enthusiastic welcome given to Churchill himself 'when he came into the House beaming with smiles, having apparently filled the role of a Pied Piper of Hamlin from Downing Street to the House of Commons'. Among those who crowded the upper galleries to hear the speech were his wife, his son and the Prince of Wales.

'We are met this afternoon,' Churchill began, 'under the shadow of the disasters of last year.' The Coal Strike had cost the taxpayer £30,000,000. 'It is not the time to bewail the past,' he went on. 'It is the time to pay the bill. It is not for me to apportion the blame. My task is only to apportion the burden. I do not assume the role of the impartial judge: I am only the public executioner.' Despite the strike, Churchill added, there had been no serious weakening of the 'strength and resources' of the nation. 'When we reflect on what happened last year,' he continued, 'the marvel is not that we have suffered so much, but that we have not suffered more. The revenue, though mauled and wounded, has, in the main, survived'. The balance of trade, however, had turned 'still further' against Britain. 'We are clearly not advancing among the people of the world at the pre-war rate,' he warned. But nevertheless 'our fortune is still in our own hands, to make or mar'.

To increase the revenue, Churchill announced the extra taxes which he had already explained to the King, and also a more stringent collection of tax on literary royalties from authors resident abroad.

The heaviest burden on the Exchequer, Churchill pointed out, was Britain's war debt to the United States, amounting in all to over £900 million. Of this £162 million had been paid since 1922. To offset this, Britain would continue to try to collect the sums due to her from the Allies. Since becoming Chancellor, Churchill had secured debt repayment agreements with France, Italy, Rumania, Portugal 'and, I am glad to add, on Saturday last, with Greece'. These agreements had already brought in £10 million, and would bring a further £10 million in 1926–7. The Soviet Union, however, had refused to contemplate any repayment of the Tsarist Russian debt of £757 million. Since the Dawes Plan of 1924, Germany had paid £14½ million, and would pay a further £14½ million in 1926–7. The deficiency between the sums received, and the sum paid, was over £110 million; a deficiency, Churchill pointed out, 'which has had to be borne by the British taxpayer'. Public opinion, he said, had accepted the principle of prompt repayment as in the interests 'of the stabilisation of Europe'. And he added: 'The sacrifice and effort involved are without parallel or precedent.'

Churchill's Budget speech had lasted for almost two and a half hours. 'I never remember a budget speech which kept everyone's attention riveted in all the details so closely as yours did,' wrote Sir Harry Goschen on April 12, and Ronald McNeill declared: 'You seem to me to have increased in brilliancy since you returned from riotous living with the Liberal harlots to your own Spiritual House.'

Reporting to the King, Baldwin described Churchill's speech as 'a masterpiece of cleverness and ingenuity', and during the course of a twelve-page letter expounded both on its virtues and its humour, telling the King: 'There is in Mr Churchill an under current of buoyant mischievousness which frequently makes its appearance on the surface in some picturesque phrase or playful sally at the expense of his opponents.' After commenting on 'a slight appearance of flippancy' in some of Churchill's observations, Baldwin drew attention to Churchill's 'cheerful and buoyant optimism', his sense of the dramatic and his ability to keep MPs 'keyed up to the highest pitch' throughout his speech. These qualities, Baldwin continued:

. . . were merely the ornaments and embellishments which helped to place the speech in the very front rank. The framework of the speech which constituted the background exhibited all the practised skill of the perfect craftsman which is the product of intensive training and hereditary ability.

During the delivery of the statement which lasted for two hours and twenty-five minutes, Members of the House listened quietly and dispassionately. Apart from muttered rumblings from Mr Jack Jones, who was apparently in one of his discontented moods, the Labour Party listened in respectful and appreciative silence. . . .

It was not until the speech was concluded that Members were able fully to realise the marvellous ingenuity of the Budget. The trepidation of the Conservatives rapidly turned into intense rejoicing and intense admiration for the cleverness exhibited by Mr Churchill. . . .

'His enemies will say that this year's budget is a mischievous piece of manipulation and juggling with the country's finance,' Baldwin added, 'but his friends will say that it is a masterpiece of ingenuity.'

Churchill had much enjoyed introducing his Budget, and his enthusiasm communicated itself to the Press. To several cartoonists he had become 'Winsome Winston' and 'the smiling Chancellor'. 'In appearance Mr Churchill is almost jovial,' wrote someone described as 'a close acquaintance' in the *Times of India* on April 11; 'one can imagine him, dressed in a cowl, the incarnation of the jolly monks and friars of centuries ago'. On April 13 Baldwin wrote to the King of the two further days of debate that 'the exceptional dullness of which was a tribute to the success of the Chancellor's budget', while on April 14 he described Churchill as in a 'happy, joyous and extremely effective mood'.

Churchill's own private comment on the Budget, in a letter to Sir Eric Geddes[1] on April 14, was: 'I felt sure it would be accepted as a good escape from very disagreeable alternatives.' Even Lane-Fox, who in a letter to Irwin on April 12 described the Budget as 'a cheap jingle', admitted: 'it has revived the certainly flagging spirit of the Conservative Party', and Lord Winterton,[2] reflecting on the session in a letter to Irwin of June 6, explained the transformation in Churchill, as seen from Westminster:

The great Parliamentary event was Winston's Budget speech, I thought it a masterpiece, and about the best I have ever heard. Winston is a wonderful fellow, I consider that he is head and shoulders above anyone else in the House (not excluding Lloyd George) in Parliamentary position, and both oratorical and debating skill, at the present moment.

The remarkable thing about him is the way in which he has suddenly acquired, quite late in his Parliamentary life, an immense fund of tact, patience, good humour and banter on almost all occasions; no one used to 'suffer fools ungladly' more fully than Winston, now he is friendly and accessible to everyone, both in the House, and in the lobbies, with the result that he has become what he never was before the war, very popular in the House generally—a great accretion to his already formidable parliamentary power.

[1] Eric Campbell Geddes, 1875–1937. An engineer on Indian railways before 1914. Deputy Director-General of Munitions supply, 1915–16. Director-General of Transportation, British Expeditionary Force, France, 1916–17. Director-General of Military Railways and Inspector-General of Transportation, in all theatres of war, 1916–17. Knighted, 1916. Privy Councillor, 1917. Honorary Major-General, and honorary Vice-Admiral, 1917. Conservative MP for Cambridge, 1917–22. First Lord of the Admiralty, 1917–18. Minister Without Portfolio, 1919. Minister of Transport, 1919–21. President of the Federation of British Industries, 1923 and 1924. Chairman of Imperial Airways and of the Dunlop Rubber Company.

[2] Edward Turnour, 1883–1962. Educated at Eton and New College Oxford. Conservative MP, 1904–18, 1918–40 and 1940–51. Succeeded his father as 6th Earl Winterton, 1907. As an Irish peer, he continued to sit in the House of Commons. An original member of the Other Club, 1911. Served at Gallipoli, in Palestine and in Arabia, 1915–18. Under-Secretary of State for India, 1922–24 and 1924–29. Chancellor of the Duchy of Lancaster, 1937–39. Paymaster-General, 1939. Chairman, Inter-Governmental Committee for Refugees, 1938–45.

13

De-Rating:
'A Plan for Prosperity'
1927–1929

FOLLOWING the 1927 Budget, Churchill was much concerned with the problem of how to bring about an economic revival. It was essential, he felt, to devise a comprehensive scheme to encourage industrial expansion. On April 16, only four days after the Budget, he wrote to Sir Otto Niemeyer of how it was essential to devise some drastic means of reducing the debt, other than by taxation. 'In my opinion,' he wrote, 'the Socialists ought to, and easily may, concentrate upon the admitted failure of the Capitalist system and our present policy to deal adequately with the debt and to liberate the country from its thralls.' Rather than wait until a Labour Government were to try to meet 'a public need obvious to all' by a forced loan, a capital levy or super-tax, the Conservatives should reduce the debt by a public loan, at 4 per cent interest, redeemable in 25 or 30 years.

Worried by the scale of Government spending and by the nature of Government financing, Churchill had been angered by a memorandum which Niemeyer sent him on April 28, arguing that the debt was not as burdensome as Churchill believed. Churchill pondered Niemeyer's arguments, and then, replying on May 20, commented bitterly on the Government's policy of the previous decade:

We have assumed since the war, largely under the guidance of the Bank of England, a policy of deflation, debt repayment, high taxation, large sinking funds and Gold Standard. This has raised our credit, restored our exchange and lowered the cost of living. On the other hand it has produced bad trade, hard times, an immense increase in unemployment involving costly and unwise remedial measures, attempts to reduce wages in conformity with the cost of living and so increase the competitive power, fierce labour disputes arising therefrom, with expense to the State and community measured by hundreds of millions. . . .

Churchill saw a bleak future in the economic policies to which the Treasury were committed, telling Niemeyer:

We have to look forward, as a definite part of the Bank of England policy, to an indefinite period of high taxation, of immense repayments and of no progress towards liberation either nominal or real, only a continued enhance-ment of the bondholders' claim. This debt and taxation lie like a vast wet blanket across the whole process of creating new wealth by new enterprise. Moreover, however desirable from many points of view a gradual steady decline in the cost of living may be, it must be recognised that such a process means continuous bad trade. . . .

Troubled by the rising unemployment and falling trade, Churchill tried to express his sense of frustration, declaring emphatically:

. . . the financial policy of Great Britain since the war has been directed by the Governor of the Bank of England and distinguished Treasury per-manent officials who, amid the repeated changes of Government and of Chancellors, have pursued inflexibly a strict, rigid, highly particularist line of action, entirely satisfactory when judged from within the sphere in which they move and for which they are responsible, and almost entirely unsatis-factory in its reactions upon the wider social, industrial and political spheres.

Two of Churchill's three Budgets had been forced to reflect the burdens of war debts, and industrial disruption. Two more years at the Treasury, and two more Budgets, were still in prospect before the next election; years which Churchill was determined to use in a constructive way. During the spring of 1927 a new idea had begun to form itself in his mind, a scheme which he hoped would revive industry, stimulate agriculture, reduce unemployment and lead to a definite increase in both individual and national prosperity. This scheme had first been suggested to him nearly two years before by Harold Macmillan.

On June 4 Churchill set out what he had in mind in a minute to Alfred Hurst.[1] The centre piece of the scheme would be 'an immense reduction in the burden of Local Rates'. By relieving factories and farmers of £30 million in rates, it would be possible for 'the greatest advantage' to be secured in all areas of production. The money itself, Churchill told Hurst, could come partly from further economies in

[1] Alfred William Hurst, 1884–1975. Educated at Emmanuel College Cambridge. Entered the Treasury, 1907 (first place in the Civil Service examination); CB 1926; knighted, 1929; Under-Secretary, 1932. Under-Secretary for Mines, 1940–42, in charge of reconstruction. Member of the Secretariat, War Cabinet, 1942–44.

Government spending, to the extent of £15 million, and partly from new taxation, of which a tax on petrol, he suggested, would alone bring in £12 million. Churchill's letter ended:

Assume therefore that you possess this tremendous leverage of £30 millions a year. Show how it could be used to the greatest advantage. You need not make detailed calculations. At this stage I only want a picture and a desideratum. We have nothing to put before the country next year; and the way is therefore clear for a vast campaign against the Rates with forces large enough to overbear the obstructions fatal to smaller measures. Also suggest me some literature upon the subject.

On June 6, before receiving Hurst's reply, Churchill sent Baldwin an eleven-page outline of what he proposed. 'I have been pondering on our position and prospects,' he wrote, 'and in particular on the great need we have to dominate events lest we be submerged by them.' His letter continued:

Each year it is necessary for a modern British Government to place some large issue or measure before the country, or to be engaged in some struggle which holds the public mind. In our first year we had the Widows' Pensions and Locarno; in our second we gained our victory over the General Strike; this year we have the Trade Unions Bill, Shanghai and the Russian expulsion.[1] All these three have appealed very strongly to our own people, but gain us no support beyond the Party limits. They have enabled us to retain the initiative and keep our forces in good heart. But what are the prospects for next year?

It seems to me that in their present showing they are very bleak. We shall be in our fourth Session; and the Opposition forces will have every inducement to such common action as is possible to them. On the other hand what have we to offer to our supporters or to the wider public with whom the decision rests?

We cannot pretend to have been successful in our treatment of labour. All your efforts have not secured 'peace in our time'. The state of the coal fields is certainly nothing for us to be proud of. We have not succeeded in economising and reducing expenditure. All my efforts, such as they have been, have failed and were, I think, bound to fail. We have no Agricultural policy, and the grumbling of the farmers will certainly continue and grow. What then is to be our new legislation?

---

[1] On May 12 the police had raided the London premises of the Trade Delegation of the USSR in Great Britain, and of Arcos Ltd. On May 24 Baldwin told the House of Commons that Soviet agents in Britain had been trying to obtain by illegal means secret information relating to the armed forces. Two days later, on May 26, the Soviet Chargé d'Affaires was asked to leave Britain, and the Foreign Office announced that 'the existing relations between the two Governments are suspended'. They were not renewed until November 1929, during the second Labour Government.

Churchill then criticized the various legislative proposals for the coming year: a Factory Bill 'made up of a host of minor improvements, but with no great feature or principle on which opinion can be rallied'; a Poor Law Bill 'which will equally fall between two stools, disturbing many things and settling few'; and a Franchise Bill disliked by Conservatives, which nobody wanted and many feared, to give the vote to women between 21 and 30.[1] 'Forgive me for marshalling the disagreeable facts as I see them,' Churchill wrote. 'I do so only to see how they can be overcome.' Some measure was needed, he went on, which would rally Party loyalty and rouse Party enthusiasm for, 'if it seems that our message is exhausted, we may easily find the Session of 1928 unpleasant to ourselves and injurious to the national interests we guard'. Churchill's letter continued:

It is for these reasons that I have been casting about for some large new constructive measure which, by its importance and scope, by its antagonisms as well as by its appeal, will lift us above the ruck of current affairs. I see the plan at present only in the barest outline. To complete it and to achieve it involves an enormous amount of effort; and I inflict this tiresome letter upon you because, unless it commends itself to your judgment, it would be no use wasting time and strength upon it. The plan constitutes the main conception of the Budget of next year, and indeed of the remaining finance of this Parliament.

Churchill then set out the scheme he had already put to Hurst: £30 million to be raised mainly from Ministerial economies 'principally the Navy', and a petrol tax 'not as a substitute for the Motor Licence Duties, but as an additional burden upon the motoring public'. Such a tax was, he believed, a 'just 'one, and he went on to give Baldwin his reasoning:

The motorists are on the whole the most fortunate representatives of every class from the motor bicycle to the Rolls Royce car. They are making an immense demand upon the roads, upon the Police, upon traffic arrangements in London, upon the railways, upon the rural rates, and upon the goodwill of pedestrians. We cannot be overrun with motorists or forced into an expenditure upon roads and bridges, both upon the rates and the taxes, disproportionate to the growth of the national wealth and in striking contrast to the adversity of our basic industries. In spite of this heavy addition to their burdens, motor traffic will still steadily increase. It is so buoyant that in my opinion it will easily support and bear upwards this new charge.

With the extra £30 million, to which the motorist would contribute

[1] The *Representation of the People Act* of 1918 had given the vote to women over 30. The *Equal Franchise Act* of 1928 lowered the voting age for women to 21.

more than a third, 'action on the greatest scale' would be possible. A substantial reduction in the rates would benefit every household, every class and every manufacturer, 'no one would it help more than those very basic industries that employ the greatest mass of labour and have to use the largest quantities of real property', and it would directly influence and reduce 'the cost of living of the masses'. Churchill's letter ended:

£30 millions applied to the Rates would enable us to make Neville Chamberlain's Bill the greatest measure of the Parliament. It would be a steam roller flattening out all the petty interests which have obstructed Block Grants and rating reform. With the power to pay such a price we should not need to be content with anything less than the very best arrangements which can be devised. The relief which the manufacturers would gain would brush away their minor grievances about the Factory Bill. Industry would be stimulated, Agriculture placated, and the immense mass of the ratepayers would be astonished and gratified. Every town and every part of the country, as well as every class, would share the boon. It might even be possible, without starving local services, to shift the basis of assessment from property to profits; and if this could be done, the relief would come with increasing effect to the depressed and struggling industries and factories, with reactions upon our competitive power and upon employment of the utmost benefit.

On June 7, the day after his letter to Baldwin, Churchill sent out a six-page summary of his scheme to Neville Chamberlain. It would be wrong, he wrote, to use the £30 million to reduce income tax, as the non tax-paying public 'would only regard that as class favouritism'. Nor would a reduction in the beer duty be attractive politically once the vote were extended to 'all those millions of women'. But a reduction in rates would help 'every class, all parts of the country, every town, every Constituency'. Mines, railways and shipyards would all benefit. Chamberlain's own Rating Bill, aimed at regularizing Local Government spending, could be much strengthened. 'We should override the petty opposition,' Churchill declared, 'and establish a sound relation between national and local finance, with proper incentive to economy and real responsibility for the local bodies.' Churchill's letter ended:

Of course you will realise what a struggle it will be to gather the £30 millions of revenue. Nevertheless I am sure it can be done, if we have enough resolution. Will you therefore—but without holding me committed—turn the whole matter over in your mind and let me know how such a policy appeals to you. I do not propose at this stage to open it to anyone except yourself and the Prime Minister, and possibly later Walter Guinness; and of course unless there is very earnest support, it would not be worth while embarking on the enterprise.

On June 8, before Chamberlain could reply, Churchill received Hurst's notes. These notes, sixteen pages in all, confirmed Churchill's view of the serious burden which rates imposed on industrial production. The rating system, Hurst wrote, 'operates to crush productive industry', a process that was accelerated 'by the tendency of local rating authorities who have large industrial establishments within their borders, to look upon them as a sort of milch cow to provide revenue for extravagant local schemes'. According to Hurst:

. . . these defects can only be removed by a drastic alteration of the present rating system under which
  (a) productive industry is assessed according to its profits instead of its occupation of rateable hereditaments and
  (b) the rate of levy is no longer dependent on the accidents of local government boundaries, the movements of population and the ups and downs of local politics.

Churchill was delighted by Hurst's notes. 'The principles underlying his paper seem to me incontestable,' he wrote to Sir Richard Hopkins on June 10. That same day Neville Chamberlain replied from Birmingham. His reaction was cautious. 'I don't see why you want as much as thirty millions for your purpose,' he wrote, 'and I am disposed to think at first sight that the disposal of so large a sum would provoke quite as much criticism as approval.' Churchill replied on June 11 that the large scale of his proposal was 'fundamental' to its merits. 'I should take no interest in a petty handling of this subject . . .,' he wrote. 'Thirty millions is, after all, only one-fifth of the total amount of the rates and I cannot believe that any figure less than that would effect a first-class reform of the existing system.'

Throughout the summer Churchill's advisers examined de-rating in all its aspects, spurred on by his own high hopes for it. Statistical tables prepared in the Board of Inland Revenue, and sent to Churchill by Hopkins on June 22, showed that, on average, 7 per cent of the profits of sample trades had been taken in rates.[1] On July 15 Hurst gave Churchill a twenty three page criticism of the existing rating system in which he wrote of 'the most glaring inequalities', and pointed out that where the market price of a product was dependent upon prices abroad, a high

---

[1] Those trades most heavily affected were the Cotton trade which had to pay more than 20% of its profits in rates, Iron and Steel 11·7%, Mines and Quarries 10·8%, Timber and Building 9·7% and Metals 7·9%, Leather 6·8%, Bleaching and Dyeing 6·1% and Food 6%.

level of rates tended 'to hinder successful competition on the markets of the world and so cause unemployment'.

Churchill had become convinced that a major de-rating scheme could bring with it substantial economic benefits for society as a whole. He was also aware of a deep malaise in the public mood. On June 29, during a Cabinet discussion on House of Lords Reform, he noted on a sheet of 10 Downing Street notepaper:

> A wave of negativism.
> People don't want anything done in any direction.
> 'fed-uppism'.

During the summer of 1927 Churchill took a prolonged holiday, spending as much time as possible at Chartwell, where he painted, organized the building of walls, ponds and dams, and entertained his friends. He also began work on a new literary venture, an autobiography, telling the story of his childhood, youth and military career, from 1874 to 1900. On August 10 Victor Cazalet[1] was a guest at Chartwell; 'a wonderful day', he noted in his diary: 'He was in a marvellous mood, and just would not let us go.' Churchill had been reading about India, and, as Cazalet noted, 'admires the book *Mother India* and would have no mercy with the Hindus who marry little girls aged ten'.[2]

For five days, from August 19 to 24, Churchill went as Lord Beaverbrook's guest, on board his private yacht, to Amsterdam. The pleasures of the cruise had been overshadowed by the death of Beaverbrook's mother. On August 7 Churchill had written in condolence: 'My dear Max, I am grieved to learn of the death of yr mother & offer you my deep sympathy. It must have been a gt pleasure in yr life to have had her to watch yr successes & to be able by yr own exertions to make the path of life smooth for her. Eighty-four is a venerable age & no one wd wish to live forever. Nevertheless as I know well the death of one's mother breaks links with the past that can never be revived & without

---

[1] Victor Alexander Cazalet, 1896–1943. Educated at Eton and Christ Church Oxford. Oxford half blue for tennis, racquets and squash, 1915. Served on the western front, 1915–18, when he won the Military Cross. A member of General Knox's Staff in Siberia, 1918–19. Conservative MP for Chippenham from 1924 until his death. Parliamentary Secretary, Board of Trade, 1924–26. Political Liaison Officer to General Sikorski, 1941–43. Killed in the air crash in which Sikorski died.

[2] On 16 August 1927 Lord Irwin wrote to Neville Chamberlain about *Mother India*: 'Miss Mayo has dropped a brick with her book "Mother India". . . . It will make the Hindus of course see red. . . . I think the general effect may be useful if it gives a shock to the unsatisfactory conditions of Hindu thought on many of these subjects.' On 25 September 1927 Lord Lloyd wrote to Irwin: 'I was staying a weekend recently with Winston who was immensely struck with Mother India—Miss Mayo's book. It is all true . . .'.

wh the world is different. I thought you wd not mind my writing these few lines; for I know you will be in the shadows.'

On September 9 Churchill went to Balmoral, where he had several talks with the King, and painted the highland scene from his window. After he had left the castle, the painting was auctioned for £120, and on September 20 Churchill wrote to Lord Stamfordham: 'If I could be sure of equally skilful auctioneering, I really might endeavour to reduce our national liabilities by turning out a few pictures.' His letter continued:

I enjoyed myself very much at Balmoral. It is not often that the paths of duty and enjoyment fall so naturally together. I had a particularly pleasant luncheon with the King when we went out deer driving, and a very good talk about all sorts of things. I am very glad that he did not disapprove of my using the Ministerial room as a studio, and I took particular care to leave no spots on the Victorian tartans.

On his return from Balmoral, Churchill found that his wife had been taken ill. In June she had been knocked down by a bus while shopping in the Brompton Road, and although she had gone straight back to 11 Downing Street by taxi, the shock of the accident had been more severe than was at first realized, and she was ordered to rest by the doctor. It was decided that she would go abroad for six weeks, to Venice, while Churchill remained at Chartwell. To Beaverbrook, Churchill wrote on September 20: 'I shall be here alone all next week. Why do you not come down and spend a night, see my works on construction and discuss the situation at home and abroad over a sound bottle of 1906?'

On September 26 Churchill sent his wife a long account of events at Chartwell: his 'Chartwell Bulletin' as he called it. His account began:

Sickert[1] arrived on Friday night and we worked very hard at various paintings and had many discussions. I am really thrilled by the field he is opening to me. I see my way to paint far better pictures than I ever thought possible before. He is really giving me a new lease of life as a painter.

Jack proposed himself for the week-end, Abe came to lunch on the Sunday. So I had plenty of company. Jack brought with him his portable wireless and we had a wonderful concert each night. I had no idea that they could produce such results; no blare, no clack, just quiet, fine music. We turned out the lights and listened by the hour together. . . .

With four men, he was building a dam, and although 'enormously attracted' by his wife's suggestion that he should join her in Venice, was

---

[1] Walter Richard Sickert, 1860–1942. A friend of Clementine Churchill's mother, Lady Blanche Hozier. Painter. Royal Academy, 1934 (resigned, 1935). He taught Churchill the 'Panafieu technique', of painting in oils on top of a black and white photograph whose image was projected on to a canvas screen. Many of the photographs on which Churchill and Sickert worked were taken by Professor Lindemann.

reluctant to leave Chartwell, telling her: 'every minute of my day here passes delightfully. There are an enormous amount of things I want to do—and there is of course also the expense to consider.' Clementine Churchill was most anxious that her husband should join her, and wrote once more urging him to do so, but first, on September 29, he took the train to Scotland, where he stayed with the Duke of Westminster, hunting stags and fishing. Two days later he wrote to his wife from Lairg: 'Here I am at the North Pole!' Most of his letter was about fishing. 'Last night the fishing was unexpectedly vy good,' he wrote, 'I had connexion with 5 fish in 3 hours, & killed 3 viz: 16, 14 & 12½ lbs . . .' and he added: 'Today the river was "in perfect order": & of course after 6 hours grinding toil (wh has nearly broken my back) not a fish wd bite. Curious creatures of caprice, these salmon! If they don't choose to be killed nothing will persuade them.'

Churchill returned to London on October 4; two days later, accompanied by Lindemann, he left for Venice to join his wife. For ten days he swam, painted and wrote more of his autobiography. On October 17 he and Lindemann returned to England, leaving Clementine Churchill to continue her recuperation in Italy. 'Our journey was uneventful,' Churchill wrote to his wife after his return to Chartwell on October 19, 'and the time passed smoothly and swiftly in the Prof's agreeable and always instructive company'.

During 1927 Churchill's political future, and his relationship with Baldwin, had been the subject of repeated comment. On August 25 Neville Chamberlain wrote to Lord Irwin:

Winston remains the figure most interesting to the general public. I think he has materially improved his position in the party, and it is admitted on all sides that he has no equal in the House of Commons. His manner with the opposition is so good-humoured that although they often interrupt him, they look forward to his speeches as the finest entertainment the House can offer. I watched an excitable creature called Salter[1] recently while Winston was on his feet. His features were distorted by the convulsions of his mirth; at intervals he relieved the overwhelming pressure by a series of resounding slaps on his own thigh. At other times I have seen this man totally unable to control his temper shouting out 'Liar, coward, murderer', and any other similar abuse that entered his mind. I think it was on the third reading of the TU Bill that Winston was much interrupted by an excited opposition in a full house as he neared the end of his peroration. 'Of course it is perfectly possible,' he said, 'for Hon'ble members to prevent my speaking, and indeed

---

[1] Alfred Salter, 1873–1945. A doctor of medicine; Resident Obstetric Physician, Guy's Hospital, 1896. Bacteriologist, British Institute of Preventative Medicine, 1897–1900. Labour MP for West Bermondsey, 1922–23 and 1924–45.

I do not want to cast my pearls before . . .'—he paused and then concluded 'those who do not want them', in a roar of delight that lasted several minutes.

Baldwin himself wrote, in a letter to Irwin on September 15: 'Winston's position is curious. Our people like him. They love listening to him in the House, look on him as a star turn and settle down in the stalls with anticipatory grins. But for the leadership, they would turn him down every time. If anything happened to me, the best men are Neville and Hogg, and I think on the whole the second would be chosen. . . .'

Three weeks later, on October 4, Josiah Wedgwood[1] wrote to Lord Irwin: '. . . Baldwin seems to be getting very much under the influence of Churchill. Perhaps because C. never despairs of the republic. He is as young as ever, and the country and politics are still his game. They say that Baldwin is so tired and, perhaps, ill that he will retire before the election, and advise the King to send for Churchill. . . .'

After nearly four months of thought and study, Churchill had at last made up his mind to go forward with his de-rating scheme. Writing to Sir Richard Hopkins and Alfred Hurst on September 27 he declared: 'The formation of a "mass of manoeuvre" of 30 millions for a vast reduction of rates upon Producers constitutes the budget of 1928.' His letter continued: 'I will see Mr Chamberlain and find out whether he is willing to help. If so, we may aid him in his schemes. If not, we must go on alone. Our plan will then be to take the Producers out of the Mediaeval Rating system.' On October 17, in answer to Churchill's letter, Hurst produced an eleven-page outline of the proposed reforms. In place of rates, producers would pay a tax based on profits 'at a uniform rate over the whole country', but in no case as high as the existing rating system. On the following day Churchill wrote again to Neville Chamberlain, seeking to enlist his support for the new scheme:

Whether it can be achieved or not, I do not yet know. If the money were available, it could be achieved as a mere Budget relief. But the opportunity is too good, and the safeguards are too necessary, for a purely departmental solution on my part.

[1] Josiah Clement Wedgwood, 1872–1943. Naval architect, 1896–1900. On active service in South Africa, 1900. Liberal MP for Newcastle-under-Lyme, 1906–19. Commanded armoured cars in France, Antwerp, Gallipoli and East Africa, 1914–17 (DSO, wounded, despatches twice). Assistant Director, Trench Warfare Department, Ministry of Munitions, 1917. War Office Mission to Siberia, 1918. Granted the Labour Whip, May 1919. Labour MP, 1919–42. Vice-Chairman of the Labour Party, 1921–24. Chancellor of the Duchy of Lancaster, 1924. Created Baron, 1942.

I see no reason why your plans and mine should not be interwoven. All progress has been arrested since the beginning of June, when I first wrote to you, by the fact that our officials have been studying separate aspects of the question: none can be made until a whole-heartedly co-operative exploration is undertaken. I shall therefore rejoice to thrash the matter out with you on your return—as you suggest.

Joint action is indispensable for success. But you really must not expect me to produce 3 or 4 millions a year for a partial scheme of modest dimensions. That would only hurt the Finances without helping the Government. The agencies which we can command are so limited and overstrained that we must utilize them to the highest advantage.

I think I could deal with your 'necessitous areas' in the most economic way—viz by removing the deterrent of high rates which prevents factories from growing up where there is cheap and abundant labour. . . .

On October 19 Churchill and Bridgeman met to discuss the new naval estimates. As part of his search for £30 million for de-rating, it was Churchill's hope that naval expenditure could be curtailed. The meeting, however, was not a success. 'My opening talk with the Admiralty,' he wrote to Baldwin later that day, 'revealed abysmal differences', and on October 22, in a letter to his wife, Churchill reported that he saw 'no likelihood of agreement' without a struggle in Cabinet. But, he added:

I am almost certain that the Cabinet Committee and the Cabinet will endorse my views. There may be a very stiff tension before it is settled, and really I think I am bound to fight this pretty hard. I have been looking deeply into the out-turn of the revenue and expenditure in the first six months and the reports which I called for from the Treasury before I went to Venice are now complete. It looks as if I am going to get through all right but this must not be proclaimed. I have to talk beggary and bankruptcy for the next few months. I have had some awful blows in expense, now from this quarter, now from that. Luckily however there are windfalls[1] and what we lose on the swings we shall perhaps more than recover on the roundabouts. It is really very like our private affairs though on a larger scale. . . .

On October 21 Churchill embarked on a week of country speeches.[2]

---

[1] The principal windfall was the Iveagh death duty. On 7 November 1927 *The Times* announced that estate duty of £4,400,000 had been paid on the property of the 1st Earl of Iveagh, who had died a month before, aged 80, leaving property valued at £11,000,000.

[2] The first of the speeches was at Nottingham on October 21, when Churchill met an old friend of his father's, Sir Lancelot Rolleston. 'He had been wanting to meet me for thirty years,' Churchill wrote to his wife three days later. 'He talked about "Randolph" as one would speak of someone one had seen a week or ten days ago, and all his memories shone across the intervening gulf of years like lights from another world.'

Three days later he spoke at Chingford, in his constituency. 'There must have been more than 2,000 people present,' he told his wife, 'and some offence was given to numbers who had to be turned away.' Nevertheless, as he spoke, he was much impressed by 'the friendly and even delighted attitude of the people'. His letter continued: 'I told them that these last three months had been the first three months of Peace, social and political, domestic and foreign, that England has had since the century began, which is quite true. I look back on three months so utterly undisturbed by action or faction. Pray God it is not a mocking interlude!'

On October 26 Churchill put forward his proposed economies at a meeting of the Cabinet's Standing Committee on Expenditure,[1] telling his colleagues that 'it was imperative that substantial reductions of expenditure must be effected'. He was surprised, he said, to see that Neville Chamberlain had asked for an increase of £2 million for the Ministry of Health, and Lord Eustace Percy an increase of £2½ million for Education. As for the Army, he again pressed most strongly for the speediest possible transformation of cavalry regiments into mechanized units. But it was of naval expenditure that he spoke most sternly. Any increase whatsoever, he said, 'would be a very grave matter'. By abandoning the new cruisers planned for 1927 and 1928, nearly £8 million would be saved. 'No step which the British Government could take,' he told his colleagues, 'would more effectively prevent a renewed naval armament race. . . .' Yet Britain's position was, he said, a strong one; by 1931, even if his economies were agreed to, Britain would have sixteen of the largest type of cruisers, compared with Japan's six and America's five. According to the minutes of the meeting, 'The Chancellor of the Exchequer after pointing out that the figures showed superiority in cruisers such as Great Britain had never before possessed, stated that the Admiralty had urged that in the years following 1931 a very heavy replacement programme would in any case have to be undertaken, but he emphasised the wisdom of building as late as possible and also the financial advantages of postponement.'

On October 27 Churchill discussed the naval estimates with Lord Beatty and Admiral Field.[2] As a result of this discussion he proposed, in

[1] The meeting was held at 10 Downing Street. Seven Ministers were present: Baldwin (in the Chair), Salisbury, Birkenhead, Walter Guinness, Cunliffe-Lister, Lord Peel and Churchill.

[2] Frederick Laurence Field, 1871–1945. Joined Royal Navy, 1884. On active service in China, 1900 (wounded). Captain, 1907. Served at Jutland (despatches). Director of Torpedoes, Admiralty, 1918–20. Rear-Admiral, 1919. Third Sea Lord and Controller of the Navy, 1920–23. Knighted, 1923. Commanded the Battle Cruiser Squadron, 1923. Vice-Admiral, 1924. Deputy Chief of the Naval Staff, 1925–28. Admiral, 1928. Commander-in-Chief, Mediterranean Fleet, 1928–30. First Sea Lord and Chief of the Naval Staff, 1930–33. Admiral of the Fleet, 1933.

a letter to Bridgeman on the following day, to reduce the period during which all naval construction would be halted from 24 to 14 months. 'Financially,' Churchill wrote, 'it will be easier to find the money in 1929 than earlier because of the progressive diminution in debt and war pension charges & the recovery of the Income Tax from the after effects of the Strike', and he added: 'Navally, it is uneconomical to begin ships till the last moment and sacrifice fruitlessly a period of their short lives; and better ships can be built as science advances year by year.'

As a result of his meeting with Beatty and Field, Churchill was hopeful of a rapid solution along the lines he proposed, not only in the naval estimates but elsewhere. 'The battle is joined on the estimates,' he wrote to his wife on October 30. 'No more airships, half the cavalry, and only one-third of the cruisers.' The Admirals, he told her, 'are showing signs of far more reasonableness than ever before'. His sights were set principally on two domestic ministries, Health and Education. 'Neville is costing £2½ millions more[1] and Lord Useless Percy the same figure,' Churchill wrote, 'and we are opening a heavy battery against them this week. It is really intolerable the way these civil departments browse onwards like a horde of injurious locusts.' On the whole, he added, 'we think the finance of this year will hold water, and even perhaps may exactly balance'.

Contrary to Churchill's hopes, the naval estimates question rapidly became acrimonious, and for the whole of November and December plunged him into a controversy with the Admiralty which could not be resolved without repeated recourse to the special Cabinet Committee on the Naval Programme. The dispute began on November 3, when Bridgeman informed Churchill that even the proposed 14 months' delay in shipbuilding would lead to 'very great complaints' from the armament firms already contracted to build the 'definite programme laid down in the White Paper of 1925'. Under this programme there were to be one 8-inch and two 6-inch cruisers begun in 1927, and one 8-inch and two 6-inch in 1928. On these six vessels Bridgeman was insistent. 'I am indeed sorry,' Churchill wrote in a letter to Bridge-

---

[1] Writing to Neville Chamberlain on November 2, Churchill stated that he was 'greatly disturbed' to learn that the Ministry of Health intended to increase its expenditure for 1928 by at least £2 million. Such an increase, Churchill wrote, 'puts me in very great difficulties'. On the following day Chamberlain replied: 'I have not yet had an opportunity of going through my estimates myself,' but that he thought £1½ million would be the maximum likely increase. Meeting on November 8, the two men agreed to let the details be examined by their respective officials.

man on November 4, 'that we shd have failed so utterly. I tried my vy best.'

On November 6 Churchill circulated to the Cabinet a 3,000-word memorandum on the cruiser programme. Were no British cruisers at all to be laid down in 1928, he wrote, Britain would still have, under the programmes agreed to, 62 cruisers in 1930, as against Japan's 28 and the United States' 15. To announce three new ships for 1928, he added, when they can just as easily be begun in 1929, 'combines the loudest noise with the least strength, and raises the greatest antagonisms for the smallest practical result'. If Britain's 'national safety' were involved, Churchill concluded, considerations of world disarmament 'would not count'; but when national safety was not in question, 'as the figures plainly show', then the policy of a year with no new construction 'would be an important contribution to Disarmament, and would put us in a favourable position on that score for the rest of this Parliament'.

At a meeting of the Naval Programme Committee on November 10[1] Bridgeman asked for, and the Committee opposed, the immediate construction of a 6-inch-gun cruiser. To Sir Douglas Hogg, who had spoken in favour of this proposal, Churchill wrote two days later: 'Judged by the test of naval strength, it seems a very great pity to order a vessel definitely weaker than the contemporary type of other Powers', and he added: 'It may be wrong to make weapons of war, but it is certainly stupid deliberately to make weapons which will be out-matched.' Churchill's letter ended: 'It is painful to me to see our hard-earned money invested so unfruitfully.'

In his letter to Hogg, Churchill reiterated his belief that there was no danger to national safety in a year's delay. 'We are able to build war ships faster than anyone else in the world,' he wrote, 'and much faster than the Japanese, consequently it has always paid us to lay back as long as possible and then go one better in design.'

Bridgeman continued to insist on the need for three new cruisers to be laid down at once. The Naval Programme Committee met to discuss this demand on November 18. At the meeting Churchill set out his principal contention. All he asked for was a single year's delay. 'There is nothing to prevent the Admiralty laying down three ships in 1929,' he

---

[1] Seven Ministers were present: Lord Birkenhead (in the Chair), Lord Balfour, William Bridgeman, Lord Peel, Churchill, Neville Chamberlain and Sir Douglas Hogg. Also present were Admiral of the Fleet Sir Charles Madden (the First Sea Lord and Chief of the Naval Staff), Vice-Admiral Sir Frederick Field (Deputy Chief of the Naval Staff), Sir Richard Hopkins (Controller of Finance and Supply Services, Treasury) and Captain W. A. Egerton (Director of Plans, Admiralty).

told a further meeting of the Committee on November 22, 'if at this time next year the Cabinet decide that we ought to have them,' and on November 28 he wrote direct to Bridgeman, stressing that what is necessary for safety in any period has got to be provided when the proper time comes'. Indeed, he added, 'I do not believe Parliament would refuse to make the necessary provision year by year and if a Government fell short for a year or two, the movement of public opinion would grow so strong that the policy would be changed and the arrears made up in good time.'

Despite Churchill's assurances, Bridgeman was still reluctant to agree to his proposals, and it was decided to hold a further meeting of the Committee with neither Churchill nor Bridgeman present. This meeting took place on December 1. The Chairman, Lord Birkenhead, told his five other colleagues—Balfour, Neville Chamberlain, Lord Salisbury, Lord Peel[1] and Sir Douglas Hogg—that 'in the main' he believed that Churchill 'had succeeded in establishing his case for a modification of the programme laid down in 1925, so far as the years 1927, 1928 and 1929 are concerned'. If he thought that Churchill's proposals 'would imperil the security of the country in the slightest degree', Birkenhead added, 'he would not advocate them for a moment. It was because he had satisfied himself that the acceptance of these proposals involved no risk of any sort or kind that he was prepared to recommend their adoption.'

Lord Birkenhead's judgement was supported both by Lord Peel, and also now by Sir Douglas Hogg. But Neville Chamberlain gave his support to the Admiralty's view, telling the Committee that there were economic reasons for 'a continuous steady programme'. According to Chamberlain:

Unless such a programme existed it would be impossible to keep the dock-yards efficient and the skilled men would drift off elsewhere. He was not satisfied that the United States of America did not intend to build a large fleet; if so, there would be a big demand for skilled craftsmen in America, and our best dockyard hands would migrate there and would not return. If this happened our boasted supremacy would have vanished for good.

[1] William Robert Wellesley Peel, 1867–1937. Educated at Harrow and Balliol College Oxford. Conservative MP, 1900–06 and 1909–12. Succeeded his father as Viscount Peel, 1912. Chairman of the London County Council, 1914. Chairman of the Committee on the Detention of Neutral Vessels, 1916. Under-Secretary of State for War, 1919–21. Chancellor of the Duchy of Lancaster and Minister of Transport, 1921–22. Secretary of State for India, 1922–24 and 1928–29. Created Earl, 1929. Lord Privy Seal, 1931. Member of the Indian Round-Table Conference, 1930–31 and of the Joint Select Committee on the Indian Constitution, 1933–34. Chairman of the Burma Round-Table Conference, 1931–32; and of the Palestine Royal Commission, 1936–37.

It had been argued that we could always catch up our rivals in a naval race, and that therefore no risk was involved in the postponement of the construction of cruisers; the Admiralty reply was to the effect that this meant asking some future Government to impose a burden on the taxpayer which he would not face. . . .

The Naval Programme Committee met again on December 12, once more without Churchill or Bridgeman. Birkenhead's support for Churchill was overruled, largely as a result of Neville Chamberlain's insistence, and the Committee's report, signed that same day, recommended one 6-inch-gun cruiser for 1927–8, two 6-inch-gun cruisers for 1928–9 and the original 1925 programme—one 8-inch- and two 6-inch-gun cruisers—for 1929–30.

Churchill had failed to achieve all the naval economies he had hoped for. But he had secured a modification of the 1925 Programme, and would be able to use for his de-rating scheme the £10 million that would otherwise have gone on two 8-inch-gun cruisers (one from 1927–8 and one from 1928–9) and the one 6-inch-gun cruiser saved from the 1927–8 estimates. Any such increase, had it been allowed, would have destroyed any chance of the de-rating scheme. Already, on November 18, Churchill had sent detailed instructions to Hopkins and Hurst about how to proceed, telling them that they should assume 'that £35 millions will be available' for the scheme, and advising them on how to 'work in' with Neville Chamberlain's officials at the Ministry of Health. It was essential, he wrote, to establish 'intimate and comprehending relations with the Ministry of Health and make them feel that our scheme picks up and looks after the points they are keen about'. As to the Board of Education, he wrote, 'let us have alternative plans either to leave them out or take them in. It is better that they should sit up and beg to come in.'

In his letter to Hopkins and Hurst, Churchill also instructed them to work out the details of the two new taxes on which de-rating would depend, a tax on business profits of up to sixpence in the pound, and a petrol tax to bring in a total of £10 million. The motoring public, he wrote, 'constitute the most buoyant feature of our national life'. At a Conference held in the Treasury on December 1 the de-rating scheme was discussed by senior officials from the Treasury, the Ministry of Health and the Board of Inland Revenue. According to the minutes, 'Sir Richard Hopkins stated that the Chancellor of the Exchequer was understood to attach great importance to giving as great relief as possible to the railways, with a view to encouraging them to reduce their charges.'

In order to obtain as much information as possible about the burden of rates on industry, the Treasury had decided to take the Board of Trade into their confidence. On December 5 Churchill also asked Sir Arthur Duckham,[1] who had been on his Munitions Council in 1917, to enter into 'secret consultations' on the scheme. That same evening Churchill discussed de-rating with the President of the Board of Trade, Sir Philip Cunliffe-Lister, reporting on the following day to Sir Richard Hopkins: 'The President is on the whole a strong supporter of the scheme, and I have no doubt will give all possible information.' On the afternoon of December 6 Churchill also took Sir Horace Hamilton into his confidence, and, together with Hopkins and Hurst, the four men discussed in detail the proposed profits tax, aimed at producing £10 million a year by a tax of sixpence in the pound. That same day Churchill wrote to Hopkins:

It is to be noted that the effects of any remission are cumulative, ie a relief of the rates on railways means cheaper freight; and on coal, cheaper coal; and on ore, cheaper ore. All these inure ultimately to steel, in addition to the specific relief which steel receives in respect of its own rates; and the cheaper steel embodying all these advantages again contributes towards cheaper shipbuilding, in addition to the specific relief of the shipyards. You have a virtuous instead of a vicious circle.

On December 9 Churchill informed Baldwin that he would be ready to give the Cabinet outlines of his de-rating scheme in eleven days time. 'These outlines will cover *policy* and aim,' he wrote, 'not detailed method.' This would enable Ministers to 'think over the scheme during the Christmas holidays; and if conclusions were generally favourable, we should be able to come to grips with its many difficulties by the middle of January'. So important were the possibilities of the scheme, Churchill added, that he had cancelled 'the short journey' he had hoped to make to the South of France, in order to be 'continually at work'.

At the end of November Churchill had decided to take Harold Macmillan into his confidence, and on December 11 Macmillan sent Churchill nine pages of notes about the critical questions and their answers. Macmillan's notes contained a series of ten questions and answers. One of them concerned the political aspect:

---

[1] Arthur McDougal Duckham, 1879–1932. Educated at Blackheath School. Engineering apprentice; engineer specializing in furnace work, the carbonization of coal, and chemical engineering. Member of Council, Ministry of Munitions, 1916–17; Member of the Air Council, 1917; Director-General of Aircraft Production, 1917–18. Knighted, 1917.

Will the Socialists raise the cry 'You are letting off the rich employer & doing nothing for the poor working man'? Will this be a dangerous cry?

It will be more dangerous in prosperous areas than in distressed areas. It will be no good in agricultural areas at all.

We can in reply point to
1. Gold standard for the Rentiers.
2. Widows, orphans & old age Pensions Acts for the people.
3. This scheme for depressed Industry. Industry is after all our 'father & mother'. On its prosperity we all ultimately depend.

I am not much afraid of this cry nowadays. It wd have been more dangerous before 1920. But the 'slump' has left its mark & a great number of ordinary folk have begun to learn the lesson, in a hard school, of the mutual interdependence of all classes & interests.

By December 12 Churchill had prepared a six-thousand-word draft memorandum for circulation to the Cabinet. That same day a Board of Inland Revenue memorandum described the proposed profits tax as 'practicable' and set out a working scheme. But two days later Grigg warned Churchill against undue haste. 'Some of your memo must clearly be altered & you dont want to give Neville—who is not over-friendly—a chance of bowling you out at once. Wait at any rate for the first revise, please.' Churchill accepted Grigg's advice, and on December 15 a revised draft was ready. This took into account the advice of a wide range of experts, including Sir Warren Fisher, Sir Richard Hopkins and Alfred Hurst from within the Treasury itself, and officials from the Ministry of Health, the Board of Inland Revenue and the Board of Trade. Both Hopkins and Fisher criticized the scheme because, as Hopkins wrote on December 15, it would deprive the Sinking Fund of those 'assumed future surpluses' on which the Fund depended for its progressive reduction. Some of the criticisms were against the scheme, not in its financial, but in its political aspects. The Ministry of Health, Hurst reported on December 16, 'take the view that the scheme, while attractive in many respects, goes too far and would have undesirable reactions on local government'. Above all, Chamberlain's advisers saw rating relief to industry as simply cutting at industry's contribution to local government funds. 'But there is nothing in this,' Churchill himself noted in the margin of Hurst's report. 'The industry renders a service to the locality.' In his answers to the Ministry of Health's criticisms, Hurst set out his reasons for wanting the local authorities to have the least power possible over local industry. 'From the point of view of local efficiency,' he wrote, 'it is, I think, even more important to secure the extension of the areas of administration than the maintenance of the business elements on local councils. Experience in connection with Parliament would seem to shew that true economy can only be achieved by an administrative machine like the Treasury, well removed and carefully protected from electoral influences. The wider the area of management and the more intricate the task of the Council, the more its affairs tend inevitably to come into the hands of officials.'

During the third week of December Churchill incorporated into his memorandum the technical points raised by his advisers, and was confident that the scheme could be properly financed. 'I count on a progressive improvement in the revenue,' he wrote to Fisher and Hopkins on December 17. 'The Income Tax of 1929 will recover its normal position after the Strike disaster has run off. . . . I have no doubt whatever that, unless there is some great disaster creating a new situation, the revenue from existing taxes will stand in 1931-2 £20 millions above its present figure. I predict it with the confidence born of everything that has happened in the last three unlucky years.' Of course, he wrote, the United States debt, rising from £33 millions a year in 1930 to £38 millions by 1935, might no longer be offset by German reparations, which could easily fail. But, he wrote, 'these two evils share a sphere of their own', which could justifiably be met by an increase in income tax. Financing the de-rating scheme ought not to be looked at in the light of possible events 'so far afield'. Answering the Hopkins-Fisher criticisms about depriving the Sinking Fund of a source of credit, Churchill wrote:

Do not delude yourselves by supposing that our policy of Sinking Funds, Conversions, etc, have in any effectual way met this formidable difficulty. We are making no impression on the Debt at present: in fact rather the contrary. I do not therefore believe that additions of £10 or £15 or £20 millions a year to the true Sinking Fund constitute a means of escape. Either something very much larger—as Mr Snowden seems inclined to propose— or some novel or fortunate scheme of conversion on a great scale will be required to deal with this problem. The mere adding at great inconvenience to the taxpayer and at undue strain upon industry of a few millions a year to the new Sinking Fund is quite irrelevant to any real solution. I have tried it, and it has failed.

Churchill's letter continued:

I must beg you to inscribe hope and confidence in the growing strength of the country upon all your Memoranda. . . .

A steady Government, a firm hand on new expenditure, the lightening and judicious redistribution of burdens will, as the war years recede, bring us into more easy circumstances. Indeed in spite of the follies of the Strike and of many other national errors, we are far stronger financially and economically today than we were only three years ago.

By all means confront me with facts and put the worst complexion on figures, but let this dominant belief subsist between us.

Churchill now felt ready to circulate his memorandum. Its theme was that under the existing rating system 'productive industry of every kind suffers an excessive and injurious oppression'. Drawing on one of the themes of Macmillan's notes he pointed out that by returning to the Gold Standard 'we have helped the merchant and the banker', by taking sixpence off income tax 'we have benefited the general taxpayer and especially the rentier', and by the Widows' and Old Age Pensions Act 'we have given a new and important security to the wage-earner'. Yet so far nothing had been done for the producer, 'on whose continued vitality the heart-beat of the nation depends'. Of £160 million paid in rates each year, between £40 million and £50 million were paid by manufacturing and agricultural producers. To give these producers relief would cost £48 million. To obtain this he proposed, after first balancing the Budget, to introduce a new tax on all imported liquid fuel. 'It is,' he wrote, 'the only simple new indirect tax now available' and could bring in £24 million a year if fixed at fourpence a gallon. 'This tax,' he wrote, 'falls upon the buoyant pleasure motor vehicles of every class,' as well as on commercial transport and private trade oil engines, but so low was the duty that it need not be either 'vexatious or injurious'. In addition, Churchill proposed a profits tax of a shilling in the pound on all profits, to bring in a future £12 million. No one who did not get rating relief would pay the tax. Both the liquid fuel tax and the profits tax would come into force before the de-rating scheme, thus enabling a surplus to be accumulated. As Churchill explained:

In this case the finance of 1929 would be very strong, for in addition to the Suspensory Fund of 1928, it would be armed with a whole year's currency of the two new taxes aggregating £32,000,000 net in 1929 and have only to pay in 1929 a half-year's relief. Moreover the General Revenue of 1929 will have got clear of the Strike period and an increase is to be expected. The passage and bringing into force of the necessary Rating legislation and the life of Parliament are therefore both within our control, and simultaneously affected.

Churchill's memorandum concluded:

The fact that all producers will know that as from April—or at the latest from October 1929, all their rates will be taken over by the Exchequer, will from that moment enable forward contracts to be made upon a greatly improved basis. This on a rising tide of trade will help business and diminish unemployment and all its deleterious reactions on the health and economy of the State. It will hold the political field. The opposing parties will, out of partisanship, attack it to their disadvantage. This is a controversy from which, pushed in every field, we have nothing to fear.

On December 17 Churchill sent his memorandum to Baldwin. 'This draft plan is only a sketch,' he wrote to Baldwin from Chartwell in a covering note. 'A gt deal of work has been & is being done behind it.' His letter continued:

I am sure the policy is practicable.

Is it sufficiently attractive? That is what you must judge.

Do not, I beg you, think that I am asking for this plan to be put through as a treat & favour to me. If it is not thought well of by you or by the Cabinet, the only consequence to me will be the saving of an immense amount of toil, worry & responsibility. I offer it as my best contribution to the successful culmination of yr Government in 1929.

But if you decide that it ought to be tried, then I must ask not for ordinary approval or for Cabinet acquiescence, but for active & concerted aid: & for all yr countenance & authority to make it go.

Churchill accepted that much could be said against the scheme, which was in every way 'a new heavy burden for the Exchequer'. The Treasury officials themselves, he wrote, 'hanker for large Sinking Funds, & hate to see future margins disposed of'. The Ministry of Health, 'while mildly attracted' to the scheme, preferred to embark on 'their own compact little scheme for 2 or 3 millions'. Industrialists would prefer protection. Lord Rothermere 'will crab anything yr Administration proposes'. 'How much easier,' Churchill wrote, 'to slip back into the arm chair, pay our way stolidly, make a few small surpluses for the Sinking Funds, & leave the rest to the effluxion of time & the caprice of the new electorate.' But, he added, 'It is because I believe you will repulse such moods that I send you now My Best Endeavour.'

That same day Churchill also sent his memorandum to Neville Chamberlain and Cunliffe-Lister. 'I need not say how earnestly I desire your aid,' he wrote in his covering letter to Chamberlain. 'Without that aid I do not believe it will be possible to carry this scheme through.' Were that aid not forthcoming, he wrote, 'I shall be saved an immense amount of risk and trouble, and shall have to recast my finance on purely negative but highly orthodox lines'. Churchill's letter ended with the appeal: ' "Think well, think wisely, think not for the moment but for the years to come," before you reject this Bill.' In his letter to Cunliffe-Lister Churchill added, on a more personal note: 'I shall be bitterly disappointed if this plan is knocked on the head, for I am quite sure it carries with it a great hope for the Party, and still more for the country.'

Neville Chamberlain's reply, on December 20, was not encouraging. It was 'only fair', he wrote, 'to say that in its present form I see grave difficulties departmental or administrative, financial and political. . . .' Another criticism came from within the Treasury itself, when Sir Warren Fisher wrote on December 20: 'I hate to appear to you in the role of a Jeremiah, on the other hand I know you expect from me a genuine expression of the views I hold.' Fisher feared that the money needed for the continuing cruiser programme, the expansion of the Air Force, pensions and the war debt would make it impossible to guarantee a sufficient surplus in future years to cover the cost of the scheme, whatever might be its merits in terms of a revived industry. Churchill replied on December 22:

If the proposals I have in mind constituted new expenditure of an irrevocable character, the sort of alarmist forecasts you now put out might have validity. But when these proposals aim purely at a relief of burdens and are in fact a remission of taxation (and a peculiarly injurious form of taxation), other considerations apply. The worst that would happen is that the Fuel Tax and the Profits Tax would have to be increased, or alternatively a portion of the Rates restored. Meanwhile the experiment of relieving industry would have had its chance.

Determined to try to answer all these objections, Churchill continued to seek facts and statistics, modifications and amendments. On December 21 he discussed the scheme with Sir Arthur Duckham, who, a week earlier, had stated in a memorandum that the de-rating proposals were not only 'sound', but would give a greater benefit 'to the Country as a whole' than any other financial scheme of similar scale. Duckham advised, however, against a profits tax, and suggested instead that in the initial relief, a quarter of the rates should remain. Churchill also arranged for copies of the scheme itself, and the comments of his officials, to be sent both to Lord Weir and to Sir Josiah Stamp[1] for their

[1] Josiah Charles Stamp, 1880–1941. Economist and statistician. Entered the Inland Revenue Department 1896; Board of Trade, 1898; resigned from the civil service, 1919. Secretary and Director, Nobel Industries Ltd, 1919–26. Knighted, 1920. Joint Secretary, Royal Statistical Society, 1920–30; President, 1930–32. British Representative on the Reparations Commissions Committees of 1924 (Dawes) and 1929 (Young). Member of the Court of Enquiry, Coal Mining Industry Dispute, 1925. Director of Imperial Chemical Industries, 1927–28. Created Baron, 1930.

opinions. It was essential, Churchill minuted to P. J. Grigg on December 21, that leading industrialists should approve the scheme, as he did not intend 'to take trouble and run risks for people who do not want to be helped, or for people the helping of whom would only cause ill-will among their workmen'.

On December 21 Churchill arranged for Harold Macmillan to be invited to the Treasury to read through the de-rating papers. 'These papers,' he warned Grigg in his minute, 'are not to be shown to any persons other than those specified by me, nor are tales of undue despondency or alarm about the scheme to be countenanced by our representatives in inter-departmental discussions.' His minute ended: 'It is only possible to test the practicality of schemes like this by pushing them vigorously forward in the teeth of obstacles, being quite sure these obstacles are not likely to give way easily to testing pressure.'

At first glance a five-page memorandum from Neville Chamberlain on December 24 offered more hope. 'The main proposition on which the scheme is based,' Chamberlain wrote, 'namely that the contributions to local services exacted from the producer are a hindrance to industry to act unfairly upon one producer as compared with another is sound.' Chamberlain added: 'The present practice of rating industry accords neither with the benefits received nor with ability to pay. A bold and comprehensive plan, which transfers some of this burden to the National Exchequer and places it upon the shoulders of those best able to bear it is undoubtedly attractive.'

'You will see,' Chamberlain wrote in his covering letter, 'that my attitude, though cautious, is not wholly unfriendly.'

Many of the criticisms in Chamberlain's memorandum had already been anticipated, and answered in detail, by Churchill's advisers. But Churchill felt that with rising employment and increasing national prosperity, the cost to the Exchequer would fall, not rise. Chamberlain also feared that once local industry was freed from rates, it would 'cease to have any further financial interest in good administration'. To this very criticism Macmillan had noted in his memorandum of December 11: 'These people will still be to some extent interested as *residential* ratepayers. Moreover, if the fat kine are taken away, the lean kine will have nothing left to devour but their own proletarian hides.'

Chamberlain went on to criticize the proposals from what he called 'the political aspect', telling Churchill:

No doubt relief from rates would be welcomed by any section of the community, but that relief would be a good deal tarnished, if it were accompanied by further taxation, and I fear the feature that would be seized upon would be the addition to the taxpayer's liabilities. The fuel tax would be resented by every motorist, already irritable on the subject of the road fund, and the motorists are now a formidable body. When the General Election arrived, the benefits would have already have been received, and nothing would be left but to pay for them. Past experience shows that political gratitude is confined to the anticipation of favours to come.

In conclusion, Chamberlain apologized for his 'rather formidable list of doubts and difficulties', as he did not wish, he wrote, 'to be considered hostile to the main idea of the proposal'. In particular he felt, as indeed Sir Arthur Duckham had done, that if the exemption for rates were partial instead of total 'many of my objections would be removed'. On Christmas Day, in a long letter to Lord Irwin, Chamberlain had revealed an ambiguous, and at times caustic attitude both towards Churchill and towards the whole de-rating scheme, whose origin, he believed, was to be found in Churchill's search the previous spring 'for some new thing to ornament and illuminate his next budget'. The scheme itself, Chamberlain wrote, was 'characteristic of Winston in its ingenuity, audacity and vagueness'; and when first broached by Churchill 'No details were thought out, that was to be done by his officials and mine'. Chamberlain added:

Winston has been very much excited all summer over his idea which he seems to have imparted to everyone he met; always binding them to secrecy, as no one else knew anything about it. But in the last week or two there has been a perceptible cooling of the fires. First Warren Fisher warned him that its finance was unsound, then I sent him a very chilly letter and now he tells me he has had some very 'knobbly criticism' from certain industrialists whom he had consulted. He doesn't want another Gallipoli, he says, and I am in good hopes that he will have the wisdom to construct his next Budget on more orthodox lines.

Such was Chamberlain's adverse criticism. Yet even Chamberlain was in two minds about the scheme, for he ended his letter to Irwin: 'I have told Stanley that I consider the underlying idea to be sound, and that if we were given time to work it out, it might be made into quite an attractive feature of our election programme.' Two days later, on December 27, Chamberlain expressed his doubts once more, writing to Cunliffe-Lister:

I thought I heard Winston asking for your opinion of his great scheme, and I concluded that he had sent you a copy of that secret print which must now be known to half London. You may like to know that I have sent him a very critical study of it setting out a long list of difficulties. The fact is that I do not believe such a disturbing scheme to be practicable in time for next

Budget. But if he would make his exemption partial (say 50%) instead of total we might make into quite an attractive feature of our election programme.

In a letter to Churchill on December 27 Lord Weir, while approving the scheme itself as 'an amelioration of existing handicaps with quite important psychological influences', was critical of the proposed profits tax as 'a purely opportunist suggestion'. Churchill, recognizing the force of both Weir's and Chamberlain's criticisms, was prepared to moderate the scheme in order to gain their support, and instructed Hopkins and Fergusson to study the Chamberlain and Weir memoranda. In his letter to Fergusson he explained the immediate procedure:

You will realise that I am anxious to revise my own printed paper in the light of all the subsequent information which has come in. The process should be expedited as much as possible. In particular what has happened to Sir Josiah Stamp? You had better ring up Hamilton himself and ask him about the effect of Rates on particular firms and when that is to be expected. I have not yet decided whether to adumbrate my scheme to the Cabinet on the 11th or to put it off a fortnight.

On New Year's Day, 1928, Churchill was sent powerful encouragement for the de-rating scheme, in the form of a twenty-page handwritten letter from Harold Macmillan. Having studied the files in the Treasury, Macmillan felt convinced that the new scheme offered important advantages not merely for industry, but for the whole economic future of the depressed areas. Churchill's memorandum of December 12 was, Macmillan wrote, 'absolutely masterly, and quite unanswerable'. His one area of doubt concerned the profits tax, which he feared would be regarded, not only by those who had to pay it 'as a weapon, forged no doubt honestly for the purpose of financing this great relief to industry, but capable of proving in the hands of a Socialist Government a horrid engine of fiscal extortion'. Better, Macmillan felt, to have to find the money for a partial, or two-thirds remission of rates, rather than for the full £50 million. Of the wider implications of the scheme, Macmillan wrote:

. . . If you can carry through your programme, you will have made the greatest possible contribution in your power to a revival of the great basic industries. The party will have the stimulus of a strenuous 18 months of preliminary & interesting legislation. We shall 'dish the Whigs' & steal their clothes while they are bathing, in the true Disraelian style. We shall stand before the people as the only party capable of combining progress with sanity. That is our political duty & should always be our watchword.

Certainly it is true that if you are beaten in the Cabinet on this matter, it will be a decision with very important repercussions. The Conservative Party will of course go on, whatever Conservative statemen may do to wreck it. There will always be room for it in the body politic. But it will not, alas!, be the party of our dreams. It will become more & more the party of vested interests; of the rentier, not of the producer; of the middleman, not of the manufacturer, be he master or man. If it merely drifts along aimlessly and incoherently it cannot much longer command the support of active and energetic men. It will rather sink to the position of a party dominated by middle-class aspirations, composed of middle-aged personalities, and attractive only to mediocre minds.

'I should like you to know,' Macmillan added, on a personal note, 'how deeply I appreciate the favour of your confidence. You have always been most kind to those of us who are ordinarily classed merely as troublesome young men, & if I can be of any assistance to you at any time in this & similar matters, you have only to command me.'

Over the New Year Churchill examined every facet of the new scheme. 'If the railways are included,' he wrote to Sir Richard Hopkins on January 2, 'it will only be on condition that they pay over the whole relief in improved freights.' Churchill also warned Hopkins, on the basis of Treasury experience so far, and Neville Chamberlain's doubts, that the Ministry of Health 'may continue obstructive and may withhold their indispensable aid. . . .' That same day, in a further letter to Hopkins, Churchill announced that he had decided to drop the profits tax, and to allow a third of the rates to remain in force. The total cost of the remaining two-thirds relief was estimated at £32 million, of which a minimum of £20 million would be raised by a tax on petrol of threepence a gallon 'without exemptions & rebates of any kind'.

On January 4 Churchill sent an eleven-page outline of the revised scheme to Baldwin. His own belief, he explained, was still strongly in favour of the profits tax. In agreeing to Chamberlain's preference for retaining a third of the rate he was, he wrote, 'only bowing to the need of obtaining more general agreement, and defacing the classical purity of the conception for the sake of an easier passage!' Commenting on the political advantage of the scheme Churchill declared:

We are carped at for being unprovided with solutions of current social problems, or even with remedial ideas upon them. These problems are ineffectually attacked by each of the Department Ministers concerned from his separate point of view. Neville has his rating plans to help the necessitous areas and to improve Local Government. Steel-Maitland has had his run on Unemployment Insurance. We are groping for a policy about Coal Mines. The Ministry of Transport have plans about traffic and for allowing the railways to compete with the roads. All these efforts will fail. They will be quite useful; they will cost money; but they will not be related to any design; and they will not be strong enough to produce any appreciable effect. Two things are wanted in peace or in war for a successful assault: first, unity of command; and secondly, heavy artillery. The latter I am trying to provide in spite of the expense; the former rests with you.

'I must point out finally,' Churchill wrote in answer to Chamberlain's anxiety about proceeding so quickly, 'that it is this year or never. I cannot impose the Fuel Tax without unfolding the scheme of relief; and unless I impose the Fuel Tax in the Budget of 1928, no scheme of relief will be possible within the lifetime of the present Parliament.'[1]

Under the revised scheme, instead of remitting the whole of the rates and imposing a profits tax in addition to the other taxes needed, only two-thirds of the rates would be remitted, the cost of this relief to be raised largely by means of a liquid fuel tax. Churchill had decided 'to discard the plan of a Profits Tax' because manufacturers were afraid 'that it might be used in bad hands as a means of extortion'. As Churchill put it: 'We present a somewhat smaller rose, but without a thorn.' To make up the remaining third of the rates a National Rate would be levied on all rateable property, at a standard level for the whole country, at about 5/- in the £, to bring in £13 million a year. The liquid fuel tax of 3d per gallon would bring in £15 millions in 1928, rising to £33 millions by 1933.

On January 5, from Chartwell, Churchill sent Baldwin a copy of Harold Macmillan's notes, which constituted, he wrote, 'the most clear explanation I have seen'. He also sent Baldwin a second memorandum in favour of the scheme, written by Lord Weir on January 3. 'You will do more for the coal industry by this action,' Weir wrote, 'than all the coal commission reports put together.' Writing to Macmillan on January 5 Churchill commented:

It is always pleasant to find someone whose mind grasps the essentials and proportions of a large plan. I made you party to it because I was sure you would enrich its preliminary discussion, and also because—though you may have forgotten it—a chance remark of yours about the rating system, made more than two years ago, first implanted in my mind the seed of what may become a considerable event. . . .

If you will come to the Treasury when next you are in London, my private

---

[1] 'I do not see why more time is needed,' Churchill had written in an unsent letter to Chamberlain over Christmas. 'There are three more months, in fact nearly four before the Budget need be introduced—more time in fact than was needed to prepare the infinitely more complicated Widows' Pension scheme. So far as the Treasury is concerned I see no difficulty at all in having the scheme ready for the Budget.'

office will show you all my papers on this subject and you can read them there. I hope this will not be inconvenient, but it is on general principles better not to circulate secret papers except in locked pouches or boxes.

I am now planning to bring this matter before the Cabinet on the 11th or 12th, and to ask for a Committee of five or six to study it with me. Of course everything in my sphere remains uncertain until the results of the Income Tax this year and of the sample taken to frame the estimates of the next year are to hand. A bad crash therefore would leave me with no strength to spare for other than purely Treasury concerns. I see no reason to suppose that all will not be well.[1]

On January 6 Baldwin wrote to Churchill from Worcestershire that he had read the notes on the revised scheme 'with keen interest', and that he hoped to have a good talk about it as soon as he returned to London. Churchill replied on the following day:

I send you a print of a very fine Memorandum by Hurst on this damnable question of the redistribution of rating relief and generally on the evils of the rating system. It is rather long but if you could find the time to read it, it would repay you.

Churchill's letter continued:

It astounds me that successive Governments have allowed us to drift into this rating muddle, and have produced such forlorn monstrosities as the poverty-stricken suburb which no local authority will include in its boundaries if it can help it, and from which all productive industry is remorselessly driven. Of course I know very little about the rating system. None of my official work has brought me into contact with it. It is almost the only large block of our affairs of which I have no ministerial experience. It is a mass of compromises, makeshifts and anomalies, and perhaps for this reason I find it very difficult to understand. Nevertheless both the need and the possibility of a great reform loom up through the fog. But never will you get that reform except on the flood tide (topical metaphor) of some big financial scheme, such as I am now proposing, which conciliates farmers and manufacturers by a substantial boon, and which at the same time provides a douceur to the local authorities.

'Flood tide' was a reference to the 'Thames flood' of January 1928. Among the victims in London was P. J. Grigg, whose house was made uninhabitable by the water shortly after midnight January 6. In his memoirs he later recalled: 'When it was light I sallied out to buy some food for breakfast and then hurried off to the Treasury to ring up

---

[1] Churchill ended his letter to Macmillan on a domestic note. 'We have been for a spell completely isolated here by quite formidable weather,' he wrote. 'In fact the wireless was our only connection with the outer world; and that can be switched off at will—altogether a most unusual and by no means a disagreeable sensation.'

Winston at Chartwell to ask if we could shelter in No 11 for the next 48 hours. He very readily and hospitably consented.'

On January 9 Churchill left Chartwell for France, crossing with his son from Newhaven to Dieppe, where they were met by the Duke of Westminster. For two days they hunted wild boar in the Forêt d'Eu and the Forêt d'Arques. Three days later the *Daily News* published an account of his holiday activities:

If you want a 'close-up' of the Chancellor just consider him in the light of this adventure of the French forests. He goes to France in a gale, he rises in the dank cold and sets out in the rain over a sodden muddy country. He rides hard for hours, subsisting on sandwiches.

The next day he displays the same Spartan qualities. His son, Randolph enthusiastically follows in his father's adventurous footsteps. He comes back to his hotel and, spurning a night's rest, embarks on a stormy night on his four hours' crossing which will land him home in the grey uncomfortable dawn.

Churchill and his son were back at Chartwell on the morning of January 11. Randolph had invited a friend of his, James Lees-Milne,[1] to spend four days at Chartwell. Forty-seven years later, Lees-Milne recalled, in a letter to the author, how:

One evening we remained at that round table till after midnight. The table cloth had long ago been removed. Mr Churchill spent a blissful two hours demonstrating with decanters and wine glasses how the Battle of Jutland was fought. It was a thrilling experience. He was fascinating. He got worked up like a schoolboy, making barking noises in imitation of gunfire and blowing cigar smoke across the battle scene in imitation of gun smoke.

The other things I remember about him were his pacing overhead during the daytime, dictating. The sounds of footfalls on the boards and his familiar voice were clearly audible. And in the afternoons he was waist deep in waders in the lake. . . . .

---

[1] James Lees-Milne, 1908–   . Educated at Eton and Magdalen College Oxford. Private Secretary to Lord Lloyd, 1931–35. On the staff of Reuters, 1935–36; the National Trust, 1951–66. 2nd Lieutenant, Irish Guards, 1940–41 (invalided). Author; an expert on the Tudor and Baroque periods, and on country houses.

14

The 1928 Budget:
'Everyone But You Is Frightened'

W HEN the Cabinet met on the morning of January 20 to discuss the revised de-rating scheme five Ministers were absent: Austen Chamberlain in Spain, Leopold Amery in Canada, Sir Laming Worthington-Evans in India, Sir Samuel Hoare in Switzerland and Sir William Joynson-Hicks in the South of France. Churchill outlined the scheme and asked the advice of his remaining colleagues 'as to whether the substantial relief it would give to producers would be sufficiently popular to justify the exertions required to finance the scheme'. A majority of those present gave the scheme their full support, beginning with the President of the Board of Trade, Cunliffe-Lister, who declared that he was 'convinced that the benefit to our hard-pressed industries would be so great that the scheme ought to receive the most careful consideration'. Several 'staple industries', he said, would gain particular advantage, including steel, shipbuilding, coal, engineering and textiles. The Minister of Agriculture and Fisheries, Walter Guinness, said that, from the agricultural point of view 'it was impossible to exaggerate the importance of the scheme'. Only Neville Chamberlain was cautious. According to the minutes of the meeting he told his colleagues that:

He doubted if the revenue to be raised from taxation would be sufficient to compensate the Local Authorities for the loss of rates. He viewed with some anxiety the possibility that, when relieved from rates, manufacturers would withdraw from all active participation in local government. And he apprehended that in some districts the Local Authorities would be deprived of so large a proportion of their rateable area as to make it impossible for them to carry out essential improvement schemes, such as water-supply or drainage.

In its conclusion the Cabinet decided to set up a special Policy Committee, headed by Churchill, to consider the technical problem of whether the de-rating scheme could be carried through during the life-time of the current Parliament. Discussion of the political aspects of the scheme, it was agreed, should wait until the Policy Committee had presented its report. That same afternoon Churchill wrote to Lord Balfour, who had been ill for some months:

I unfolded the plan of wh I told you in September to the Cabinet this morning. We only mustered 14—luckily not 13! & the reception, as you will see from the Cabinet papers, was on the whole vy favourable. They seemed a little oppressed with the amount of labour wh wd be involved; but after all, the bulk of this will fall on me,—I am quite ready to undertake it & pretty sure I can produce a satisfactory result.

I send you herewith the first printed copy of the paper I am circulating to the Cabinet—an egg hot from the hen! There are only two points to add to it, (1) the scheme is self-contained financially & does not cost me a groat. Therefore anything I can save or find in '28 & '29 is still free for actual concessions to other tax-payers, & a good Dissolution Budget is in no way compromised. Secondly, we cannot dissolve before the young ladies have reached the register in May; but at any time after that, even tho' the longer Rating Bill was only introduced, we cd go to the country, if convenient, on the issue *inter alia* of these large rate-reductions: therefore we are not fettered in any way. . . .

The Cabinet Policy Committee held its first meeting in the Treasury Board Room on the afternoon of January 25, when Churchill explained that he hoped to see the first rating relief payments in October 1929. Neville Chamberlain felt that April 1930 would be a more realistic date, as there would have to be 'considerable negotiation with the local authorities'. But when the Minister of Education, Lord Eustace Percy, began to criticize the wide scope of the scheme, both Churchill and Chamberlain together, as the minutes recorded, 'emphasised the importance of adopting the scheme as a whole'. A second meeting was held, again at the Treasury, on January 31, with Neville Chamberlain in the chair. Churchill was present only at the end of the meeting. But its conclusion was as he had wished: de-rating was to be a part of the 1928 Budget, was to become law by April 1929, and to come into effect that October. On February 1 Chamberlain himself drafted the form of announcement that was to be made in the King's speech, and this Churchill at once approved. At a meeting of the full Cabinet on February 1, both the timetable and the announcements were accepted, and six Bills dropped to make room for the debating time that the de-rating Bill would demand.

On the evening of February 3, in a speech at Birmingham, Churchill gave the first public intimation of the de-rating scheme. Local rates, he said, were 'a harassing burden upon productive industry and agriculture. . . . They vary capriciously between one part of the country and another. They vary with the results of the local elections. They are constantly changing, and usually rising. Unlike the income tax, they are levied whether there are any profits or not. . . . I will go so far as to say that if I had the money, an advance in this direction would round off with singular completeness the Financial policy of the present Parliament. . . . I say there is no direction in which we ought more readily to advance.'

Churchill had already taken his son into his confidence about his de-rating scheme. But in a letter on February 5 he advised the utmost caution. 'Please do not write any reference to my plans,' he asked, 'as any mention of such topics on paper is dangerous. You will see from what I said at Birmingham that difficulties are gradually being cleared out of the way and that *design* is taking the place of *chaos*. You should read also the King's Speech, which will be published on Tuesday, with an observant eye.'

The prospect of a de-rating Bill was indeed hinted at in the King's Speech, on February 7, and a week later, during the debate on the Address, Churchill again extolled, and elaborated on, its merits. All parties, he said, were agreed on 'the burden' of local rates; all sought to relieve that burden; and he, if the money could be found, would favour such relief. 'Money,' he said, 'was the only power in time of peace available at the disposal of Governments to influence administrative reform. It was the one precious and potent agency. To squander it and fritter it away would be at all times a blunder, and at this time a crime.' If a de-rating scheme were put on the statute book, it must not be 'a mere sop', but a major relief and a major reform.

On February 15 the former Prime Minister, Lord Oxford and Asquith, died at Sutton Courtney, near Oxford. On the following day, as a mark of respect, the Cabinet gathered at 10 Downing Street. 'When Winston came out,' Thomas Jones noted in his diary, 'he started addressing me on the importance of his rating policy.' When Jones began to criticize it, Churchill retorted, of the new rating scheme, 'that it really was the communist principle, from each authority according to its ability, to each authority according to its need, but that we must not shout that from the housetop. . . .'

During February, Clementine Churchill was again taken ill, and

Churchill spent more time at Chartwell than he had intended.[1] From Chartwell he would go up to London for meetings of the Cabinet Policy Committee, and he would invite his Treasury advisers to Chartwell for consultation; among the most frequent of these official visitors was Alfred Hurst, who often stayed overnight.

At Cabinet on February 15, as part of the continuing search for economy, Churchill asked Neville Chamberlain to reduce the Public Health Grants by £150,000. Chamberlain, however, felt unable to offer more than £35,000, and was supported by the Cabinet. Churchill accepted the lower sum; later that day Baldwin wrote to him by hand from 10 Downing Street:

My dear Winston,

I want to thank you warmly for the way in which you met the wish of the Cabinet this morning.

Some of our colleagues have spoken to me already about it and I am sure there is a general feeling that you met them generously and ungrudgingly.

And I felt very sorry that such a worrying matter had to come up at a time when you have burdens enough at home.

Yours ever
S.B.

Churchill replied at once from the Treasury:

My dear PM

You are always vy kind to me. Some one (& you chose me) has to fight all these points. But you know that I always rank the interests of yr Government above any departmental issue, not touching the fundamental interest of the Show.

Unhappily the Treasury has to defend a good many positions wh cannot be reconciled with generosity or gentlemanlike *largesse*. As an ex-Ch of the Exch you know the seamy side; I also, what wd happen if it did not receive constant attention.

Of course I shall present the decision *at its best*.

Yours ever
W.

[1] Clementine Churchill's illness gave Churchill much anxiety. On February 13 he wrote to his son: 'We had a very trying day yesterday. Two separate operations at 2.30 and midnight! Your mother astonished the hardened doctors by her wonderful courage. If you should turn out—as I do not doubt—to be a fearless man, you will know where you got it from. Today the doctors declare themselves entirely satisfied, and I hope and believe the corner is turned. She still however has a good deal of pain and is a little disappointed at its not stopping as she had been encouraged to expect.' Of the doctors, Churchill added: 'Naturally I have cross-questioned them searchingly. And as a result I do not feel particularly anxious at the moment.'

At a further Cabinet on February 17, three more of Churchill's economies were agreed to: £300,000 from the Navy, £100,000 from Overseas Settlement and £500,000 from the Empire Marketing Board. But as a result of a protest from Sir Samuel Hoare, Churchill agreed not to press 'any further' for reductions in the Air Estimates beyond the 6 per cent cuts to which Hoare had already agreed.[1]

The de-rating discussions were to be continued in the first week of March. On March 4 Leopold Amery wrote in his diary: 'It looks as if we may have a real bustle over this as he intends his scheme definitely to bury all questions of safeguarding and preference. I think I have rather riddled his scheme and hope its collapse will pave the way to better things.'

On March 5 a dispute arose between Churchill and Neville Chamberlain at a meeting of the Policy Committee. At the previous meeting, on February 27, Chamberlain had proposed that the rating relief funds should be controlled, not by the Exchequer, but by the local authorities 'by whom it would be levied'. At the meeting of March 5 Cunliffe-Lister, Walter Guinness, Lord Eustace Percy and Wilfrid Ashley[2] each supported Chamberlain. But Churchill fought hard for his scheme. Chamberlain's proposal, he said:

... was open to the very serious practical objection that it would be impossible politically to retain any system under which the Local Authority could only levy a fixed rate of say 5/- in the pound on its industrial property, while the poundage on its residential property was rising to 25/- or even more. In such circumstances there would inevitably arise a strong demand, either for the restoration of the power to rate industry equally with other property, or for the Government to make good the obvious loss of rates. In all probability the second alternative would have to be adopted, and the whole scheme would degenerate into a percentage grant of the Agricultural Rates Act type.

Churchill was 'confident', he told his colleagues, that Chamberlain's proposal 'would involve the Government in very serious embarrassments, that it would spoil the symmetry and prospects of the scheme, and that it would do nobody any good'. For his part, Chamberlain

---

[1] Four of Churchill's five Budgets provided *increased* Air Estimates: £15,513,000 in 1925; £16 million in 1926; £15,550,000 in 1927; £16,250,000 in 1928 and £16,960,000 in 1929.

[2] Wilfred William Ashley, 1867–1939. Educated at Harrow and Magdalen College Oxford. Lieutenant, Grenadier Guards, 1889–98. Conservative MP for Blackpool, 1906–18; for Fylde, 1918–32. A Conservative Whip, 1911–13. Lieutenant-Colonel commanding the 20th Battalion, King's Liverpool Regiment, 1914–15. Under-Secretary of State for War, 1923–24. Privy Councillor, 1924. Minister of Transport, 1924–29. Created Baron Mount Temple, 1932. Chairman of the Anti-Socialist Union. President of the Anglo-German Fellowship.

commented that he 'regretted that the Chancellor had found it necessary to raise such strong objections to the present proposal'.

On March 6, during a discussion on de-rating at the Treasury, there was a brief moment of friction between Churchill and Grigg. Churchill hastened to apologize. 'Always be assured,' he wrote, 'that our friendship is proof ag'st all minor tiffs. But make allowances for the effect of suddenly pulling me up with a round turn, and forcing me to some measure of self-defence—however mild. Cet animal, etc. Yours ever, W.' In his reply, Grigg wrote of his worries at the situation on the Policy Committee; worries which were shared, he said, by Alfred Hurst. Grigg's letter continued:

The plan can be made a success if all your colleagues do their utmost to make it so & throw all their energies into getting it sufficiently forward by Budget day to be sure that it can survive all attacks on it without loss of any essential part of the structure & without ruin to its finance. But, except in Cunliffe Lister, I find no evidence of any disposition to approach the plan in this spirit. Worthy obviously reads the papers for the first time at the meetings & keeps both eyes on Colchester. Gilmour[1] either does not come or says nothing although the application of the plan to Scotland is a considerable problem. Percy does little but make bright & incomprehensible suggestions. But it is Neville who frightens me most. He is rather enigmatic but I should say his attitude is something like this:—he is in a great funk about the scheme & does not at all like his part in it. At the same time he wants it for political reasons as well as a measure of reform. Between the two motives he is sulkily negative & you are getting no help from your chief co-adjutor.

Altogether the Dardanelles situation seems to be re-creating itself. Everybody loves the idea, everyone but you is frightened at its boldness & magnitude. Everybody therefore stands looking on idly—perfectly ready to be pleased if it succeeds & equally ready to say 'I told you so' if it doesn't & to kick you downstairs.

On March 9 Churchill circulated a memorandum to the Policy Committee describing Chamberlain's proposal to transfer control of de-rating to the local authorities as 'dangerous to the Exchequer and subversive of the main principles which should be our guide', that principle being the decision 'to withdraw productive industry entirely from the

[1] John Gilmour, 1876–1940. Educated at Edinburgh University and Trinity Hall Cambridge. Conservative MP for East Renfrewshire, 1910–18; for Glasgow Pollock, 1918–40. On active service in South Africa, 1900–01 (despatches twice), and in France, 1914–18 (despatches, DSO). Scottish Unionist Whip, 1919–22 and 1924. Succeeded his father as 2nd Baronet, 1920. Privy Councillor, 1922. Secretary of State for Scotland, 1926–29. Minister of Agriculture and Fisheries, 1931–32. Home Secretary, 1932–35. Minister of Shipping, 1939–40.

rateable area and to substitute Grants to the Local Authorities from the National Exchequer in lieu thereof'. Compensation to Local Authorities, he added, must be based upon local needs, not upon the variable and debatable amounts which could be raised from local industry. 'I would far rather face a larger fixed, not fluctuating, *douceur*,' he wrote, 'than leave these highways of policy for the jungles and swamps which lie on either side.'

At the fifth meeting of the Policy Committee on March 12, only six weeks before the Budget, Chamberlain expressed his doubts as to whether Churchill realized 'the strength of feeling of Local Authorities' on the subject of not receiving the rate relief funds direct. Churchill could make no headway against Chamberlain's opposition, and agreed to Chamberlain's reiterated proposal that the Local Authorities 'should retain the proceeds of the national rate'. The only definite decision reached, however, was to postpone 'further consideration' of the question for another nine days. The tone of Chamberlain's dissent led Churchill to write to him, on the following day:

My dear Neville,

I was not only concerned but startled by the air of antagonism which you seemed to me to show yesterday morning. . . . Pray dismiss altogether from your mind the idea that I wish to overbear you in the matter, or that I have any feeling apart from making sure we go on the right lines. Obviously if you impose a veto in the way you did yesterday morning, I must after all arguments have been deployed submit to it. I can make no progress in the face of your opposition. You are therefore the master; and my only remedy, if I find the task too hard or too wearisome will be to withdraw the scheme. It will be quite easy to do this, so far as I am concerned, on financial grounds, and by stating that no satisfactory safeguards for the Exchequer could be devised. Indeed, when I see how very great are the difficulties which you apprehend, and how very hard would be the effort I should have to make, I feel at times not so far from taking such a decision.

Do not, I beg you, suppose that I have set my heart upon the project or that you are doing me a personal kindness by assenting to it. I have been actuated solely by a desire to help the Government in the very critical phase now opening by producing a large constructive plan. Of course the Treasury think it quixotic of me to quit the beaten track of economy and debt-repayment. I am sure however that if we show ourselves incapable of offering solutions of any of the three or four large questions involved in this project, and remain in a rut of blank negation, political disaster awaits us next year. Therefore I have tried, and will continue to persevere.

Churchill went on to comment on Chamberlain's continual air of criticism since the scheme had first been mooted nine months before:

I have been puzzled from your first rather chilling letter at the outset down to the present moment that this policy did not more appeal to you. Without it there could be no poor law reform in this Parliament such as I understood you had greatly desired. With it the whole system of Local Government can be the subject of a reform as famous as that of 1834. I always expected that you would be eager for this opportunity, and would supply at least half the driving power. Instead of this, I have felt extremely lonely in the shafts. Without your active aid, not merely acquiescence, I am sure I cannot drag the cart up the hill—nor shall I try.

Chamberlain replied on March 14 from the Ministry of Health:

The 'air of antagonism' with which you reproach me was forced upon me by your own proceedings. If, instead of firing off a memorandum to the Committee, you had spoken to me personally you would have realised that I felt strongly and perhaps we might have agreed to differ privately if no further compromise could have been found. But in the circumstances I had no alternative but to speak plainly.

As I see the position it is I who am in the shafts in this business while you are the leader in the tandem and if we are to work together there must be give and take on both sides. Up to now I have done all the giving but very little weight has been attached to my views if they have differed from yours.

I had a scheme which I believed would reform the Poor Law and deal with the necessitous areas. I could have carried it with your help but you were not satisfied unless you could have something much bigger and incidentally much more difficult from the point of view of Local Government. I am trying now to fall in with your views and have gone a long way further than I should have liked to meet them. Yet you are puzzled that I am not as enthusiastic over your scheme as over my own. Is not that natural and only a reflection of your own case?

On the same day that Chamberlain sent Churchill this letter, Harold Macmillan also wrote to Churchill. He had spent the morning with Robert Boothby at the Treasury, and enclosed a five-page memorandum strongly supporting Churchill's original scheme. His memorandum ended:

. . . if this plan goes awry, we shall see the eventual, and perhaps early dissolution of the Party. If it goes right, it will put new life into the Party. It will provide a constructive policy other than Protection. It will rally the waverers. It will consolidate the moderate vote. It will put fresh hope and enthusiasm into the hearts of all those who have supported the Conservative Party because they honestly believed it to be a Party capable of constructive thought and progressive effort.

The Cabinet Policy Committee met again on March 21, when Chamberlain proposed yet another modification of the scheme, the

P.T.—16

retention of rates for the railways. Once again Churchill was upset by the whittling away of the scheme, writing to Sir John Anderson on March 22 that if the railways had to go on paying rates, not only would their 'helpful co-operation' be lost, but farmers would lose 'the exceptional relief thay are obtaining on the railway traffic'. Such a decision, he wrote, 'would derange entirely the political balances which I have kept in my mind'. To Chamberlain, on March 24, Churchill wrote in protest about the effect of railway rates on industry:

A relief, for instance, of not more than 4/- a ton upon steel will not be very appreciable. It was for this reason that I consider the cumulative effect of the concentrated railway traffic reliefs so important. They raise the relief to steel to something well over 8/- on the average. If the railway reliefs are excluded and nothing substituted in their place, it seems to me very doubtful whether it is worth while going on with the Scheme at all. We shall have all the labours, all the oppositions, all the parochialisms, all the additional expense to the Exchequer, all the friction of a new tax without the strong driving power which would be afforded by a genuine relief to depressed industry.

Churchill was willing, he said, if Chamberlain were in agreement, to accept rating on railways on one condition, that the partial relief on industry, on which Chamberlain had already successfully insisted, be abandoned, and Churchill's scheme for total relief be reinstated. 'But,' he warned, 'if the heavy industries are neither to get total relief from rates nor two-thirds relief from rates plus the railway relief, then I am increasingly inclined to think that we had better leave the handling of these thorny matters to another Parliament, and perhaps to other hands.'

For two weeks the clash between Churchill and Chamberlain dominated all discussion at the Policy Committee, and threatened to undermine the whole de-rating scheme. On March 26 the Committee met without its civil servants, and without even a stenographic account being taken of its deliberations. According to its conclusions it was decided to exclude the railways from the de-rating proposals. At a further meeting on March 28 another of Chamberlain's reservations was taken account of, when the Committee examined proposals 'for giving local authorities some share in future expansion of local industry'. When the Policy Committee reported to the Cabinet on March 29 it stated that all its members were agreed that should the scheme be considered desirable, 'no insuperable obstacles will be encountered in Parliamentary time and procedure, in Local Government legislation or in Finance'. But the report went on to note that a majority of the Committee wanted railways excluded from the scheme, and that Chamberlain, supported by the Secretary of State for Scotland, John Gilmour, was still strongly in favour of the benefits of the scheme going direct to the local authority. Chamberlain and Gilmour were described in the report as 'the two Ministers who are most closely acquainted with the problems of local government and who have the direct responsibility of negotiating with the Local Authorities'. The report, which was signed by Churchill, went on to ask for the 'provisional guidance' of the Cabinet to resolve 'these serious differences'.

The gulf between Churchill and Chamberlain seemed impossible to bridge. On March 28 Chamberlain recorded in his diary that he had told Baldwin: 'I had had an unhappy week, facing up to resignation, and I was determined to go rather than assent to a scheme which I believed to be dangerous to the future of local government.' But Baldwin, while holding himself apart from the actual discussions, encouraged Churchill to persevere. After the *Sunday Times* had published a leading article approving of his previous Budget,[1] Baldwin wrote to him by hand:

My dear Winston,

As you know, I am inclined to be—shall we say phlegmatic where the Press is concerned? but I do congratulate you warmly on the leader in today's Sunday Times. It seems to me to be a very fine appreciation and I hope it has given you pleasure.

Yours ever
S.B.

Within the Cabinet, Chamberlain's position had some sympathizers. 'As you know, we wish to do something with the rates,' Hoare wrote to Irwin on March 30, 'but the difficulty is to decide how much is practicable and whether if we attempt to do a very big thing, we may not be sunk in a mass of details. Neville is very much alive to this danger and is obviously rather nervous of it all.'

When the Cabinet met on the morning of April 2 Chamberlain opposed Churchill's suggestion that, if railways were to get no relief at all, then industry ought to get the full relief, and not merely the two-

---

[1] The *Sunday Times* leader described Churchill as 'a dexterous steward of the national finances' and wrote of his Budget decisions: 'The proof that he chose rightly is in the realised surplus with which the financial year has ended. There were, roughly, two courses open to him. One was to treat the deficit with pedantic purism as an objective for a frontal attack by the big guns of new, heavy and direct taxation. The other was to skirmish round it, and so to speak, sharpshoot it into nothingness. Mr Churchill decided on the more daring and less conventional method. He brought out of the national arsenal a variety of financial weapons, which he fashioned anew and turned one by one upon the enemy.' The article added: 'If one can feel to-day that the outlook for British trade is perceptibly brighter than it was a year ago, Mr Churchill's mercifulness in his last Budget has very largely to be thanked for it. He made better trade possible by refraining from saddling it with a new load of taxation.'

thirds remission to which he had earlier, and reluctantly, agreed. According to the minutes, 'The whole of the morning meeting was taken up by explanations from the Chancellor of the Exchequer and the Minister of Health of their respective points of view.' When the Cabinet resumed that afternoon no further progress was made in reconciling the opposing points of view. During the meeting, Leopold Amery recorded in his diary: 'I came down very strongly on the side of Neville and Jack Gilmour in favour of local contribution and also against derating of railways, the tide flowing pretty definitely in this direction in spite of Philip and Worthy and a majority on Winston's Committee.'

On the morning of April 3 the Cabinet was reconvened without either Churchill or Chamberlain being present. According to the minutes:

While there was a strong body of opinion in favour of proceeding with the Chancellor of the Exchequer's Plan in some shape or form, and while it was felt that in view of tentative announcements already made on the subject action of some kind was essential, there was general agreement that, in order to carry so comprehensive a scheme, a united Cabinet and a united Party was essential, and, above all, that the Minister of Health and the Secretary of State for Scotland, as the Ministers mainly concerned, must be in cordial agreement with the policy.

There was general agreement that, as part of the scheme, Agriculture ought to be entirely de-rated, and that the Railways should be excluded.

The Cabinet Policy Committee met at six that evening in the House of Commons. The basis of a compromise was proposed, not in the discussion itself, but in a pencilled note which Churchill passed across the table to Chamberlain. 'Is it not worth while,' Churchill asked, 'our discussing together a smaller *variable* rate to be justified on preserving contact between local industry & local govt, & without prejudice to the principles of certainty and uniformity instead of the 5/-?'

'I have not asked my people about this,' Churchill added, 'so am not committed.' Chamberlain responded favourably to Churchill's suggestion, returning the note with a pencilled note of his own on the back. 'It seems to me that there is a rather strong body of opinion in the Cabinet in favour of the variable rates,' he wrote, and added: 'If you are prepared to consider a compromise on these lines I should be very ready to discuss it & am inclined to think we might reach agreement.'

The disagreement seemed at last capable of resolution, and the evening's discussion ended with the Policy Committee agreeing unanimously to recommend to the Cabinet a rating subsidy the equivalent of a quarter of the amount levied in any particular area, instead of a fixed national sum. It was also formally agreed to exclude the railways from rating relief. That evening Chamberlain noted in his diary of the evening's discussion: 'Winston began to trim his sails to the wind. He declared it obvious that we must be united; clearly the consent of the Minister of Health who had shown himself such a perfect master of the subject was absolutely vital.'

When the full Cabinet met on April 4 Churchill reported on the agreement that had been reached, and Baldwin, as the minutes recorded, 'congratulated the Policy Committee on the agreement reached, which would enable the Government to proceed with the Chancellor of the Exchequer's plan'. As soon as the Cabinet was over Churchill telegraphed to his wife: 'Finally completed agreement,' and in a letter to her that evening he wrote: 'These last days have been one continuous strain of Cabinets, Committees & personal discussions. But all is settled now: complete agreement and at any rate ¾ of what I was aiming at.'

Churchill's pre-Budget labours were almost over. 'Now I have chucked work,' he added, '& am off to Chartwell for a change. You know all of a sudden you feel you do not want to stay any longer in the same place.' From Chartwell, Churchill wrote again on April 5, sending his wife further details, and reflections, on his battle:

The Cabinets on my big policy were very lengthy and difficult. Neville most obstinate and, I thought, unreasonable. But he made his point a matter of *amour propre* and, as I cared about the scheme much more than he, I had to give way. It was not a very important point, and substantially my plan is intact.

The great advantage is that we are completely united and the whole Cabinet is keen. The PM intervened, quite decisively and declared that we must act and that the Party authorities whom he had consulted were all sure that, with really energetic propaganda, they could make the whole thing go. This is a great relief for me, as it lightens my heavy load of responsibility.

Churchill remained at Chartwell almost without interruption from April 4 to April 23, the day before Budget Day. At Chartwell he played golf with Lindemann and worked on the details of his Budget with P. J. Grigg. 'I am extending my plans in various important directions,' he wrote to his wife on April 8, 'now that I am sure of the united support of the Cabinet & of the party machine. Pray God these plans bring back a little more prosperity to Poor Old England.'

Much of Churchill's news was about his son:

There is no doubt he is developing fast, and in those directions wh will enable him to make his way in the world—by writing & speaking—in politics, at the bar, or in journalism. There are some vy strange & even formidable traits in his character. His mind is free & growing more powerful every day. It is quite startling to hear him argue. His present phase is rabid Agnosticism, & last night in argument with Grigg he more than defended his dismal position. The logical strength of his mind, the courage of his thought, & the brutal & sometimes repulsive character of his rejoinders impressed me vy forcibly. He is far more advanced than I was at his age, & quite out of the common—for good or ill. . . .

While at Chartwell, Churchill decided to make one further effort to include the railways in his de-rating scheme, despite the Policy Committee's adverse decision of April 3. On April 7 he wrote to Cunliffe-Lister, his principal Cabinet ally:

My dear Philip,

I am increasingly indisposed to accept the railway decision as final. All our labour and expense will be lost if we do not bite deep enough to give the basic industries a real jerk. There is no doubt that including the railways would win us a great deal of goodwill from the railwaymen, and even the railway shareholders would see that their interests were far from harmed. The Prime Minister seemed at the Cabinet disposed to make some personal exertion in favour of this section of the plan. At any rate I have decided to bring it up again and leave the Cabinet the responsibility of turning it down if they choose. . . .

'Neville will not be affected by the change,' Churchill added. 'The railways will remain rated as at present. Instead of disturbing the local authorities and the Ministry of Health by first depriving them of their railway rates and then reimbursing them afterwards from the Exchequer, I shall let the railways pay their rates as at present and reimburse *them* direct.' Such, Churchill added, was the result 'of my cogitations in the intervals of building a concrete wall for my new lake. You will see that my mood is robust, and if you are in similar fettle, we will together deliver a vigorous offensive.'

Churchill also wrote to Chamberlain on April 7, declaring bluntly: 'I am in revolt against the Cabinet decision to exclude the railways,' and adding: 'To go half way is to pay the price and miss the prize.' At the Cabinet of April 4, he pointed out, Baldwin had produced 'a very definite view' in favour of railway de-rating, and all he now asked for was a clear ' "Aye" or "No" decision' at the next Cabinet meeting. To Baldwin himself Churchill wrote that same day:

In meditation alone here and in the intervals of building a reinforced concrete dam, my mood has become robust. I am not content to drop the railways out of the original scheme. I am not afraid of any arguments that can be used against 'subsidies' or 'favoured traffics'. I see the target and the bull's eye in the middle of it quite clearly in this country air. To relieve the basic industries in such a manner and on such a scale as will give them a real galvanic jerk is the only thing worth all this trouble and expense. To act by half-measures with a lack of conviction miscalled 'caution', is to run the greatest risks and lose the prize. No, let us be audacious. One does not want to live forever. We have the power: let us take the best measures.

'I shall not interfere with Neville or any agreement with him in any way,' Churchill added, but now that 'all this Ministry of Health rating stuff is settled', the time had come for a decision in isolation on the railway question.

While waiting for the reactions to the new proposal, Churchill continued to work on his Budget speech. 'Your lord and master Winston is now at Chartwell,' Brendan Bracken wrote to Frederick Leith-Ross on April 10, 'charging his rating squib.'

On April 11 Cunliffe-Lister replied to Churchill's appeal of April 7; he was in favour of bringing the railways into the scheme, and prepared to say so in Cabinet. 'I have always held the view,' he wrote, 'that logically, and on merits, complete de-rating of Industry should be the objective, and that this objective should be reached as soon as possible.'

On learning of Churchill's new effort to exclude railways, Chamberlain wrote direct to Baldwin on April 12, complaining of how his 'riverside soliloquies' in Aberdeenshire had been 'broken by the irresponsible Chancellor. . . .' His letter continued:

I know you are in favour of a reduction in railway rates to be effected by a contribution from the taxpayer. On the whole I think I am against it. It seems to me economically unsound & I don't like the possible implications & developments. I might think it politically a good card to play at an election. I doubt its virtue if it is played prematurely. But to tie up a subsidy to the rates seems to me mad.

On April 12 Cunliffe-Lister began to have doubts about the wisdom of proceeding as Churchill proposed, and that same day Churchill learnt, to his deep disappointment, that within the civil service his three senior advisers, Sir John Anderson, Sir Horace Hamilton and Sir Richard Hopkins, all opposed railway relief. 'Therefore,' Churchill wrote to Baldwin on April 12: 'I shall not disturb the Cabinet by raising the topic again,' and he added: 'Thus "The Chartwell hue of resolution is sicklied o'er by the Downing Street cast of thought"!'

Baldwin replied from Downing Street on April 14:

My dear Winston,

You are probably right to bow to the storm and not run the risk of over-loading. Railways may come, and I should have the problem examined in all its aspects in good time before the election.

For a Tory cabinet they have successfully and pretty contentedly swallowed a large morsel and the inevitable cud-chewing must follow before they are ready for more.

Good luck to your hunting!

Yours ever
S.B.

Chamberlain had also written to Churchill about the railway de-rating. In his letter, sent from Scotland on April 12, he deprecated 'tying up the subsidy to the rates'. On April 15 Churchill wrote to Grigg: 'Neville's letter is tyrannical, but let him strut.'

On April 15 Churchill wrote to his wife from Chartwell: 'I shall not go up to London until Tuesday as I can work down here much better than in that centre of effervescence and unrest called Westminster,' and he reported:

All day long I am grappling with the Budget Speech. It will be 15,000 or 16,000 words long and at the rate of the articles would be worth a lot. It is about three-quarters done. But the number of difficult questions that have to be settled precisely—Yes or No is very large; one keeps on balancing and hesitating and turning and twisting for a comfortable place in the bed up to the last few days before the event. But I have now reached the stage where final answers have to be given of great importance. This is tiring and anxious although there is some exhilaration about it.

'I shall put the Budget to the Cabinet on Thursday,' Churchill added, 'but everything of consequence is settled. There only remains to fire the gun. Please God it hits the bull's eye.'

The Cabinet met on April 19, and approved all Churchill's Budget proposals. Asked by Baldwin to explain the situation as far as the exclusion of the railways from the de-rating scheme was concerned, Churchill told the Cabinet that the representatives of the Railway Companies 'had expressed the greatest regret', and he added: 'Although it had been contemplated that the Companies should pass on to other industries the advantages they would receive in the remission of rates, nevertheless they desired to be included in the scheme owing to the immense advantage which they believed would accrue to trade and industry and thus indirectly to the railways from their inclusion.'

Churchill asked the Cabinet if, given the attitude of the railway companies, it would not 'even now be willing to re-examine the question of the inclusion of the railways'. It was decided to resolve this question at a special Cabinet on the following day. Baldwin's attitude would clearly be decisive, and at the special Cabinet of April 20 he did indeed advise the Cabinet 'to give further consideration' to the reinstatement of the railways. 'On the whole,' Amery noted in his diary, 'the Cabinet were prepared, in view of the PM's attitude, to reverse their previous decision.' According to the minutes of the meeting, as the result 'of a long discussion' the Cabinet agreed, '*by a majority*', to include the railways in the de-rating scheme.

Writing on April 22 to the King, Churchill set out the main features of the scheme, its final modifications and its principal advantages:

> The Cabinet, after some very protracted discussions, decided that the relief to industry was to take the form of a ¾ remission of their existing rates, leaving the ¼ to vary with local circumstances and fortune. Mr Churchill was inclined to think that a fixed rate would have been better, but in view of the very large measure of relief which this decision accords to productive industry he does not grieve at the general opinion. A similar proportion of relief will be accorded to the railways, who will pass it on to certain selected heavy traffics likely to benefit the basic industries. Agriculture will be completely relieved of rates, which ought to be an important service to the farmers.

While outlining the rest of the Budget to the King, Churchill commented: 'thanks to the deaths of several of Your Majesty's wealthiest subjects' there would be an unexpected surplus.

On April 23 Churchill returned to Chartwell where, together with Boothby and Hurst, he put the final touches to his Budget speech. On the morning of April 24 he returned to London, and that same afternoon, accompanied by his daughter Diana and Robert Boothby, walked from 11 Downing Street to the House of Commons to deliver his fourth Budget. 'Every public gallery was crammed,' Baldwin wrote to the King, 'while in the Peers' Gallery Their Royal Highnesses the Prince of Wales and the Duke of Gloucester[1] were seen to take their places.'

Churchill referred at the beginning of his speech to two unexpected 'windfalls'—death duties had provided £9½ million more than had been expected, and the Kenya and Palestine administrations had repaid loans totalling £4½ million. At the same time, as part of the Govern-

---

[1] Prince Henry William Frederick Albert, 1900–1974. 3rd son of King George V and Queen Mary. Educated at Eton, the Royal Military College and Trinity College Cambridge. Created Duke of Gloucester, March 1928. Chief Liaison Officer, BEF, 1939–40; Home Forces, 1940–41. His elder son was killed in an aeroplane crash in 1972.

ment's policy of curbing expenditure, new entries into the Civil Service had been severely restricted, and from 1925 to 1927 the total number of civil servants reduced by 7,000. Between 1927 and 1932, Churchill added, it was planned to suppress 11,000 posts.

Churchill then outlined his principal measures. Extra revenue would be found by increasing by 50 per cent the Excise duty on British wines established in his previous Budget. There would be a new duty on cigarette lighters. There would be a Customs duty on buttons, calculated so as to bring in £200,000 a year. All imported fuel oils would also be taxed at the rate of fourpence a gallon, on a gallon costing 1s ½d. Oil used by fishing fleets would be untaxed; oil used by agricultural tractors would be remitted; but petrol used for motor cars must carry the same tax with all other industrial fuels.

The Budget contained two small benefits. The sugar duty was to be reduced to allow the retail price to fall by a farthing, and children's allowances were to go up from £36 to £60 for the first child, and from £27 to £50 for each other child: 'another example', Churchill said, 'of our general policy of helping the producer'.

The main part of Churchill's speech was devoted to his de-rating proposals. 'Under our present arrangement,' he said, 'unemployment, distress, and pauperism increase, and to meet that the rates are raised. Industry flies from these districts or else withers and dies. Who would start a new industry in such a district?' Yet it was in the areas where unemployment was highest that industry, and new industry, was most needed. At present, he said, 'we see industry shifting outside heavily rated areas and starting afresh with needless capital outlay in green meadows without population or communication, and they then demand motor roads to bring at uneconomical expense workmen and to deliver their produce to market. They demand new houses, subsidised by the State, for the new community.' An urgent, and at the same time long-term decision had to be taken to try to revive industry and create new jobs. 'We have to face the fact that unemployment remains obstinately chronic round the dismal figure of 1,000,000,' Churchill declared, 'and all those basic industries which used to be the glory of these islands are under a serious eclipse.' De-rating would relieve industry of a heavy burden. The coal mines, Churchill pointed out, were making a loss, yet having to pay 'millions a year' in rates. Free them from rate charges, and they stood a chance of making a profit; given such a chance, they could expand, building new plant and taking on new men. 'We are sure,' Churchill said, 'that the relief of the rates upon production is the first and most obvious and the most urgent remedy which Parliament can apply.' The scheme, he said, must be accepted or rejected as a whole:

We cannot possibly give the reliefs which are needed to industry, unless in reimbursing the local authorities, we put ourselves, the central Exchequer, in a firm and secure financial position. There can, for instance, be no question of a widespread extension of the Agricultural Rates Act policy. There can be no question of giving large sums of public money to local authorities, except as the counterpart of reforms which will benefit the national economy, and of reliefs to industry which will revive the public revenues. You cannot have the new reliefs without the new taxes and the new reforms. No one can take out of this scheme the parts he likes and reject the parts that do not suit him. Everyone who approves of the general plan must take the rough with the smooth. . . .

If the de-rating scheme were carried into law, Churchill concluded, it would win 'for this present Assembly some honourable distinction among the Parliaments of our time'.

Churchill had spoken for three and a half hours; there was, Baldwin wrote to the King, 'a vein of seriousness which was eminently suited to the introduction of a Budget epoch-making in its effects', and he added: 'The House became intensely interested in watching a master in the art of oratory and of tantalising the imagination unfold his ideas in a speech packed with detail, yet so simple and clear that there could be no possible misunderstanding.' The whole speech, Baldwin ended, would be recognized by the public 'as being almost the most remarkable oratorical achievement of Mr Churchill's career'. There was 'no doubt', Amery wrote in his diary, 'that the first impression was very formidable indeed, and our Party was delighted. . . .' That same evening Lord Derby wrote to Churchill: 'It is not the budget of an electioneer but of a statesman.'

On April 25 Lord Tyrrell described the Budget as 'a great landmark in your career & your certificate of statesmanship to the historians of the future'. That same day Lord Balfour wrote from his sick-bed in Carlton Gardens:

My dear Winston,
    I am not allowed to write—but, doctors or no doctors, I must send you one line of *warmest* congratulations. It is a great moment in the history of British finance and of the Unionist Party;—of your personal fame I will say nothing.
                                                                Yrs aff
                                                                A.J.B.

Churchill replied to Balfour on April 26:

My dear Arthur,

Yr letter gives me the vy greatest pleasure & pride. I value yr approval in public things more than that of anyone else.

The whole policy has gone wonderfully well at the first shock: & as you know, all is long & well prepared behind the lines of battle.

I do hope that you are making good progress.

Yours always
W.

On April 28 Frederick Guest added his voice to the wide chorus of public and private acclaim, writing to his cousin:

Dear Winnie,

You will have had so many letters of congratulations on your performance yesterday that you will hardly want another—but here are mine.

I think it will rank as a 'classic' budget. It has broken new ground. It will be known as 'Winston Industrial life buoy' and *will become a milestone* in the history of Reconstructions.

I think also you have made many thoughtful friends of cross bench mind. . . .

The press tributes are sincere and have a non party atmosphere that I like.

It seems to me that you have taken a sure step towards your future premiership. . . .

Guest added: 'I think the PM welcomes your steady & increasing popularity with the Conservative party—on obvious merits.'

All was set for the forthcoming debate, but on April 28 Churchill was forced to go to bed with a sudden and severe attack of influenza. Not only was he unable to pilot his Budget through the House of Commons, he was even forbidden to receive visitors. 'There is great sympathy with you in yr illness,' Robert Boothby wrote on May 3, '& I have had innumerable enquiries: indeed the widespread and heartfelt anxiety for your return at the earliest possible moment is rather amusing as an indication of the nakedness of the land, & not without significance.' The ten days work leading up to the Budget, Boothby added, and the speech itself, 'must have imposed a strain on you greater than any mortal can sustain'.

15

Towards the Fifth Budget: 'Vy Independent of Them All'

A WEEK after he had been taken ill, Churchill was still confined to bed. But by May 10 he felt well enough to send his Treasury officials a series of notes and exhortations to guide them during his absence. He was still eager to see the fullest details of a possible profits tax, and he wanted the Treasury to cooperate with the Ministry of Health about the Rating Apportionment Bill. 'What is the position of the legislation?' he asked Sir Richard Hopkins, 'when is it going to be introduced?', and he added: '. . . the whole of this field wants careful co-ordination and constant attention. The tendency to lapse into inertia is one of the most dangerous in affairs & the most common.'

On May 13 Churchill wrote to Baldwin from Chartwell:

My dear Prime Minister,

I am much better, and I think in another week I shall be fit for work. I am going to Scotland tonight to stay with Westminster at Loch More. Possibly there will be fishing; but if not, there will be sunshine and a keen air. I am taking full advantage of your generous permission to recuperate thoroughly, and I shall not be attending the Cabinet this week.

I have been thinking a great deal about the Budget position and am very contented with it. The Profits Tax corrector would be altogether logical and just. All the same if we could do without it at any rate for the present, it would be better. I had a message from Rothermere, through Esmond, to say that he had been thinking over the Profits Tax and thought it might cause a lot of uncertainty and anxiety among Chairmen of Companies and other very influential people who would be afraid that it would be put to bad uses later on. This was very much your view; and anyhow I think we shall gain by chewing the cud on this matter for another fortnight.

But what I feel we must do is to bring the Railway Rates business into operation from about October, costing £2 millions in the present year and £2 millions more next year over and above the present bill. . . .

'It is astonishing,' Churchill added, 'what a lack of criticism there has been.' Two days later Baldwin replied from 10 Downing Street:

My dear Winston,

Figure to yourself my feelings! Having still a vivid recollection of that frail invalid in bed and of the enthusiasm with which he welcomed the prospect of a call at Chartwell (somewhere about lunchtime), I telephoned yesterday morning that I would farm out my questions and come down right away.

And then to be told that you had gone to Scotland!

I had not recovered from the shock before your letter was brought to me.

Well, I am delighted that you are better, but I beg you won't hurry back.

I am glad you are very contented with the Budget situation. Keep on with the cud.

And don't worry about Rothermere. He has done you all the service he can for the present, and I think you are a little disposed to overrate his influence in the country.

It is suburban mainly, in a wide sense, but the provincial press is very strong and it is working well for us.

And I want you to consider two points when you think it desirable to bring in some of the benefits at an early date.

A. The carrot side of it. If the carrot is to be served after the election it will be hanging up in sight during the contest and our opponents will have to promise not to interfere with our programme.

If swallowed before it may be more in their stomachs than in their minds.

B. By giving the carrot in instalments, may you not tend to dissipate the effect of the whole?

I know this is Stamp's view and I need not enlarge on it. It also adds to the difficulties on the financial side.

Enough for one day. I go to Manchester to-morrow to address the cotton people in words of one syllable at lunch.

Yours ever
S.B.

On May 13 Churchill travelled by the night express to Scotland, where he recuperated at one of the Duke of Westminster's houses, Rosehall, in Sutherland. His wife remained at Chartwell, likewise recuperating. 'This is a very agreeable house in a highland valley well equipped with salmon trout & snipe . . .,' he wrote to her on May 15. 'The air is most exhilarating, keen & yet caressing. It is quite different to England,' and he added: 'I was somewhat tired by the journey wh was longer than I expected—so I did not fish yesterday but lay about on sofas & read musty books. Today however I must sally forth. But I am vy lazy, &

curiously averse from anything requiring work or exercise physical or mental. . . .'

While he was in Scotland, Churchill read the proofs of Lord Beaverbrook's volume *Politicians and the War*, which described in detail the political intrigues and conflict of policies of the opening months of the war. Thrilled by the volume, he wrote to Beaverbrook on May 21:

My dear Max,

I have now been able to read it all. I think it vy valuable & sincere, recalling the earliest Max I knew,—when he still had worlds to conquer, & kings to captivate.

As for me you have *testified* in a manner far beyond my deserts—with generosity—indeed it has given me gt pleasure to read it. Candour and faithful keeping of confidences are not easy to combine. But you have succeeded. And in addition you have produced a vital—tho limited—too limited—contribution to the slowly emerging truth. 'What happened & Why!' After all that is history or what history ought to be.

But what a tale! Think of all these people—decent, educated, the story of the past laid out before them—What to avoid—what to do etc, patriotic, loyal, clean—trying their utmost—What a ghastly muddle they made of it!

Unteachable from infancy to tomb—There is the first & main characteristic of mankind.

Churchill added at the bottom of his letter: 'No more War'.

After six days in Scotland, Churchill returned to Chartwell to prepare for the forthcoming Budget debate, which was to be opened on June 5 with a motion by Philip Snowden to reject the Finance Bill altogether, and was to be followed on June 6 by the Rates Apportionment Bill. On May 24 Churchill set out his thoughts in a letter to Baldwin. 'I am convinced,' he wrote, 'that a fuller disclosure of our policy, in order to prevent needless misunderstanding, should now be made.' Churchill suggested that Neville Chamberlain should, during the Apportionment Bill debate, 'unfold a coherent and complete explanation of our main plan, of course in general terms, and reserving all details. It may well be that a large part of the Opposition will then be shown to be irrelevant or superfluous.' Baldwin gave this plan his approval, adding, on a personal note: 'You look run down and you want building up again, and the finance bill will want all your vitality.' Two days later Churchill explained his strategy to Neville Chamberlain. He would, he said, during his answer to Snowden on June 5, 'demolish' the criticism that with the de-rating scheme 'we help the rich industries and not the poor'. Churchill added: 'I am most anxious to conform to your wishes; and it would be a great help to me if, after having considered what I have written here, you would put down the principal points you do *not* wish to give away at this stage.'

On June 4, in a further attempt to prevent friction between himself and Neville Chamberlain, Churchill wrote to Baldwin: 'I am very anxious to keep in touch with the rating side of the policy, and equally to associate Neville with the finance. We do not want to get into water-tight compartments on an issue where the consequences of failure or discord would be so serious.'

On June 5 Churchill introduced the Finance Bill to the House of Commons, and did so, Baldwin informed the King, 'in his most entertaining and vigorous manner'. On June 7 Neville Chamberlain introduced the second reading of the Rating and Valuation Bill, which was to transform the de-rating scheme into law. He was, wrote Baldwin to the King on the following day, 'most accurate and steady in his aim and provided an excellent contrast in method to Mr Churchill, who, supported by Sir John Gilmour, may be called upon today to complete the defeat of the Opposition'. Following Churchill's closing speech on June 8 Baldwin wrote again to the King:

. . . he exercised on the whole the greatest restraint and gave the House a close and competent analysis of the benefits which would accrue to depressed basic industries. He showed clearly the fallacies in the various criticisms which had been made by the Opposition Parties.

The Government emerged well satisfied with their scheme. Their faith in the principle is unshaken, and, while much work lies ahead, they see no reason to modify the methods of applying the principle which they have proposed.

Even while the Finance Bill was being debated, Churchill began to make plans for his fifth Budget. Once more, it was the need for a reduction in naval expenditure that most concerned him, both for economic and electoral considerations. Nevertheless, he wrote to William Bridgeman on June 15, 'I share your earnest hope that this last year of our stewardship in the present Parliament may not be disturbed by another tussle.' It was, Churchill added, 'repugnant to me to have to worry the Admiralty and you so much', but it was most important to reduce the 1929 Estimates to 'their lowest point' so that the Government could go to the country 'with a good answer on economy. I am bound to work for this.'

While devising his new budget Churchill also explained to P. J. Grigg why he now felt it was necessary, despite his free trade convictions, to support protective duties in certain specific cases, writing on July 2:

No one could possibly have thought as much about this matter as I have done, with a quarter of a century of reflection and action behind me. It is no use speaking of Free Trade as if it were something more important than England. The question is not what will vindicate Free Trade but what would really be a sensible and helpful thing for England to do. I am always focussing this in my mind's eye. I am pretty sure we should be better off by doing what I have talked about to you and putting the proceeds into further relief of freights. I should not challenge the theoretical argument against it but present it as a practical step necessitated by revenue requirements and likely to be beneficial to trade and employment, without involving any fundamental change in the long-established fiscal policy of the island.

In his letter to Grigg, Churchill also reflected on the policies of the Treasury and Bank of England officials during his three and a half years as Chancellor, policies which were, he wrote, characterized by 'complacency' and 'indifference' to social needs. In his letter he wrote bitterly of the financial experts with whom he had worked, and to whom, over the return to the Gold Standard, he had deferred:

They have caused an immense amount of misery and impoverishment by their rough and pedantic handling of the problem. In ruined homes, in demoralised workmen, in discouraged industry, in embarrassed finances, in inflated debt and cruel taxation we have paid the price. As the ship goes through the seas its smoke and smells drift to leeward. One always hopes one will make the port in good time when the discomforts of the voyage will soon be forgotten.

Churchill reiterated this point in a minute to Sir Richard Hopkins on July 22:

The Niemeyer attitude of letting everything smash into bankruptcy and unemployment in order that reconstruction can be built up upon the ruins, is neither sound economics nor wise policy. Stated shortly his view, and I presume the orthodox Treasury view, is that no aid whatever should be given to industry which should be left to face its own troubles and stand on its own feet. This comfortable Victorian doctrine may have the consequences of throwing scores of thousands of men out of employment and leading to immense expenditure in other directions. What is airily called 'cutting out dead wood' means transferring vast masses of workmen and their families from productive industry to Poor Law, with the results we see around us. I should think on the whole with 300,000 miners unemployed we have cut out enough dead wood for the moment.

On June 15, in order to put the now annual estimates dispute into the wider context of defence policy, Churchill asked his Cabinet colleagues for a firm decision on 'the general assumptions which should now govern our preparations for war'. His own belief, he wrote, was that the principle of the Ten Year Rule should again be confirmed, and 'that it should now be laid down as a standing assumption that at any given date there will be no major war for ten years from that date; and that this should rule unless or until, on the initiative of the Foreign Office or one of the Fighting Services or otherwise, it is decided to alter it'. Should the Ten Year Rule be confirmed, Churchill added, a special Cabinet sub-committee should be asked to consider 'whether the policy of the Admiralty, as embodied in the Navy Estimates, is in conformity with the above assumption. . . .'

A special meeting of the Committee of Imperial Defence met on July 5 to discuss the Ten Year Rule. Churchill proposed that the Ten Year Rule should be renewed, advancing henceforth 'from day to day', but 'reviewed every year' by the Committee of Imperial Defence. Bridgeman expressed his support for Churchill's suggestion, provided that it did not prevent the Admiralty from 'maintaining the One-Power standard', by which the Navy would never fall in strength below that of its nearest single rival—at that time the United States. But Balfour opposed the Ten Year Rule altogether, telling the Committee that he:

. . . was of the opinion that nobody could say that from any one moment war was an impossibility for the next ten years, and that we could not rest in a state of unpreparedness on such an assumption by anybody. To suggest that we could be nine and a half years away from preparedness would be a most dangerous suggestion. We had but a small Army and a Navy that we could hardly reduce. These must be maintained in the highest pitch of perfection. It would be wholly impracticable to suggest a scheme which allowed our arms a period of ten years in which to prepare.

Churchill replied briefly to Balfour's remarks. It was unnecessary, he said, for Britain to be 'at the same concert pitch for any given date now, as we had been prior to the outbreak of hostilities with Germany. To-day there was no likelihood of a great war, and there was therefore no need for us to be in the state of instant readiness which was found necessary in the years prior to 1914.' A few moments later Austen Chamberlain reiterated Churchill's suggestion that the Ten Year Rule should remain in force as at present, but should be brought up for renewal each year 'before the Estimates were made out'. Chamberlain proposed, as an extra precaution, that any Department could express its fears and seek to have the Rule revised 'between each yearly review'.

Speaking for the Air Ministry, Sir Samuel Hoare was worried lest the Ten Year Rule might be used by the Treasury 'to stop necessary developments', but Churchill intervened to assure him that whereas the rule should have the effect of reducing the Estimates generally, it would not 'in any way' hamper the development of ideas, but would merely 'check mass production until the situation demanded it'. In this way Britain would avoid heavy expenditure from year to year on armaments that would be obsolete once war came.

Baldwin then asked Austen Chamberlain to speak about 'the world outlook'. War with France, Chamberlain said, was 'inconceivable'. Not only was Britain's goodwill important to France, but the French 'were not economically in a position to go to war'. The same argument, he said, 'applied both to Germany and Italy', nor could he imagine either of these countries contemplating a war with Britain, 'at any rate for many years to come'. As to the United States, Chamberlain argued that no British Government 'would be mad enough' to provoke hostilities. With regard to Japan, he added, it was no longer the Japan 'of feudal times', but a country 'that had suffered heavily in the earthquake',[1] had just given its population manhood suffrage, and whose public opinion viewed military action such as that in China 'with dislike and alarm'. He would not say that Japan 'would never become a menace' to the Empire, 'but Japan did not constitute such a menace now'. For Chamberlain, the one area of 'uncertainty' was Russia, which had been buying equipment and strengthening her army, but he believed that at present the Russian Army was 'incapable of offensive operations on a large scale'. It was Russia, he concluded, that was 'the greatest danger spot', and but for the uncertainty as to Russia's future policy, 'he would be without any grave doubts that we could reckon on no war of any magnitude occurring during the next 10 years'.

Following Austen Chamberlain's assessment, Baldwin told his colleagues that he assumed that the Ten Year Rule was agreed on, and went on to propose that the annual reconsideration which Churchill had advised at the outset of the discussion should also be accepted. Such a review, he suggested, should be made 'not later than June of each year'. Baldwin added that the Cabinet 'must take every means it can of investigating how it can obtain the greatest amount of defence for the minimum expense'. The Committee of Imperial Defence finally concluded, according to Sir Maurice Hankey's minutes, that 'it should be assumed, for the purpose of framing the Estimates of the Fighting Services, that at any given date there will be no major war for ten years'. It was also agreed that this assumption should be renewed annually, that it was the

[1] During an earthquake on 1 September 1923 more than 180,000 Japanese had been killed in Tokyo and Yokohama.

duty of the Secretary of the Committee of Imperial Defence 'to remind the Prime Minister of this Conclusion at the appropriate moment', and that it was the duty both of any British Department or of any Dominion Government to review the conclusion 'at any other time' if they felt circumstances demanded it.

Balfour's doubts had been outweighed. Baldwin, Austen Chamberlain and Churchill were each convinced that the Ten Year Rule, given the safeguard of yearly scrutiny, would prevent excessive expenditure while ensuring security.

During the summer of 1928 a number of Ministers, led by Leopold Amery and Sir William Joynson-Hicks, began to press Baldwin to commit the Conservative Party once more to the principle of protective tariffs. Both believed that protection should be a basic feature of Conservative policy for the next General Election, and at a meeting of the Cabinet on July 4 Amery advocated protection 'as a remedy for the present difficult unemployment situation, giving our industries some measure of shelter in the home market'. The pressure for Protection increased during the following weeks. But on July 21 Amery expressed in his diary his vexation at 'the whole attitude of the Cabinet under Winston's influence, and the PM's decision not to do anything for iron and steel in the present Parliament'. On July 26 Lane-Fox wrote to Irwin of 'a rather depressing debate' on unemployment during which:

S.B. made a very unimpressive speech, and Winston who is thoroughly tired and nervy did equally badly, ending up by a rather unnecessary and violent defiance of our die-hard safeguarders, who were already indignant at having their proposal for the safeguarding of steel turned down. They [are] now very angry and a lot is going on. It is the first sign of a real party fissure that I have yet seen.

Among those who spoke publicly in favour of Protection, and who criticized Churchill's hostility towards it, were two senior Conservative backbenchers, Brigadier-General Sir Henry Page Croft[1] and Patrick

---

[1] Henry Page Croft, 1881–1947. Educated at Eton, Shrewsbury and Trinity Hall Cambridge. Conservative MP for Christchurch, 1910–18; for Bournemouth, 1918–40. Served in the Great War, 1914–16 (despatches); Brigadier-General, 1916. Member of the Speaker's Conference on the Franchise, 1918; Civil List Committee, 1936; Committee of Privileges, 1939. Created Baronet, 1924; Baron, 1940. Parliamentary Under-Secretary of State for War. 1940–45. Privy Councillor, 1945.

Hannon.[1] Both were veteran opponents of free trade, and both believed that the existing safeguarding measures were merely a sop to Protectionist feeling. Churchill himself, in his progression from Liberal to Conservative during 1924, had regarded Safeguarding as a fair compromise, and one which had enabled several Liberals to transfer their allegiances to the Conservatives without feeling that they had been forced to abandon their Free Trade convictions. In the third week of July he drafted a five-page reply to Page Croft's charges, which had been sent direct to Baldwin. 'Perhaps you will allow me to say,' Churchill wrote, 'that I think it would have been better if you had come to me. After all we are all colleagues working together to win the next election, and it is most important that there should be no misunderstanding between us.' His draft letter continued: 'I am of course most anxious in our general interest that the next election should not drift into a fight between Protection and Free Trade. Probably a million Free Trade votes were cast in 1924 for Conservative candidates, and it is of the highest importance to the Conservative cause that these should not be given away wholesale.'

On July 24 Churchill sent an account of the pressures for Protection to Lord Derby, who replied on the following day: 'I was very much disturbed at what you told me today but you may rely entirely on my support for what it is worth in opposing the Amery-Page Croft gang. I hate the whole lot of them. They ruined our party once and they will ruin it again if they have their way.' Derby added: 'I am not attending any political meetings just at present but if during the autumn you want me to go to any place in Lancashire I can easily get a small meeting arranged and then I should not hesitate to speak out.' Derby ended his letter on a note of caution: 'Take care,' he wrote, 'that there is not an attack on Free Trade disguised under a vendetta against you. Temporize, because I feel sure that the power at the back of the intrigue is not very strong & can be scotched unless the flames are fanned.'

Churchill accepted Derby's advice, and held back his letter to Page Croft. But the Protectionists continued to urge their cause, and on July 28 Joynson-Hicks, in a public speech at Broadlands, insisted that all true Conservatives should follow the Protectionist flag. Speaking in the

---

[1] Patrick Joseph Henry Hannon,   –1963. Educated Royal College of Science and the Royal University of Ireland. Agriculturist. Vice-President, Grand Council of the Tariff Reform League, 1910–14. Member of the General Council of the National Service League, 1911–15. General Secretary of the Navy League, 1911–18. Conservative MP for Birmingham Moseley, 1921–50. President of the Industrial Transport Association, 1927–37; of the Institute of Export, 1939–43. Knighted, 1936. Chairman of the Political Committee of the Carlton Club. Deputy Chairman of the Birmingham Small Arms Group of Companies.

House of Commons two days later, Baldwin himself criticized Joynson-Hicks' speech as one which contained no constructive policies, and could only do harm. That night Randolph Churchill wrote to his father from Eton: 'I am so glad to see in the Evening papers that the PM has come down on your side re Free-Trade.'

In Cabinet on August 1 Baldwin urged his colleagues to stop their pressure for Protection. Amery was angry, writing in his diary that Baldwin's attitude was 'very decidedly negative and dictatorial. It sufficed to bring Jix to his knees with an apology for having said anything indiscreet if he did and promised to be a good boy in the future. . . .' The Cabinet met again on August 2 to discuss the issue in detail. Amery put the case for the maximum increase in Imperial Preference, and in particular for an extension of safeguarding to cover Iron and Steel. He was supported by both Cunliffe-Lister and Neville Chamberlain. Sir Douglas Hogg, while approving of Protection in principle, urged silence on electoral grounds. Churchill, in an attempt to reach a compromise, agreed to the inclusion of Iron and Steel into any safeguarding enquiry. On the following day Baldwin wrote an open letter to the Chief Whip, Commander Eyres-Monsell,[1] stating that there would be no general introduction of Protection. 'The letter looked as if it had been drafted for S.B. by Winston before the Cabinet,' Amery noted in his diary, 'and slightly modified after.' Amery, furious, thought of resigning, but did not do so. On August 4 Beaverbrook wrote to Mackenzie King:

We have had quite a storm here over Protection or Safeguarding this week. After the most obvious contradiction on the public platform between Winston Churchill and Joynson-Hicks—Baldwin gets up and produces the usual formula which appeases all and settles nothing.

But the cat is out of the bag. You cannot put it back. The cat will scratch too, as the next General Election will certainly show. The Tory Party is fundamentally disunited on Protection and the moment the subject is given any prominence the mischief is done. . . .

Baldwin, who was about to go to France, had, Churchill believed, wanted to leave him in charge of the House of Commons. But at the last moment Baldwin asked Hogg to take charge. On August 10 Churchill

---

[1] Bolton Meredith Monsell, 1881–1969. Known as 'Bobby'. Entered HMS *Britannia*, 1894; midshipman, 1896. Torpedo Lieutenant, 1903. Assumed the additional surname of Eyres, 1904. Conservative MP for South Worcestershire, 1910–35. A Conservative Whip, 1911. An original member of the Other Club, 1911. Returned to the Navy, 1914; on active service in Egypt, 1915; Commander, 1917. Treasurer of the Royal Household, 1919. Civil Lord of Admiralty, 1921; Financial Secretary, Admiralty, 1922–23. Privy Councillor, 1923. Chief Conservative Whip, 1923–31. Parliamentary Secretary, Treasury, 1923–24, 1924–29 and 1931. First Lord of the Admiralty, 1931–35. Created Viscount Monsell, 1935. Government Director, Board of British Airways, 1937.

wrote to his wife, who was staying with Lord and Lady Londonderry in Northern Ireland:

All this reveals how serious is the handicap I have had to carry in the party by warning them off the protectionist question. I do not at all regret the steps I took which are only for their good; but of course all the powerful interests who would make money out of Protection keep up a steady pressure and half the Tory party are religiously convinced about tariff.[1] I am glad the Election is coming in nine months time. The situation will then be very interesting; but it is quite impossible beforehand to see how it will develop. Such is life!

In the margin of his letter to his wife Churchill noted: 'Really I feel vy independent of them all.' Not only over Protection and de-rating, but over questions of personality, Churchill's four years at the Treasury had roused strong hostility. Indeed, so great was the gap between him and some of the leaders of the Conservative Party that Neville Chamberlain had been seriously alarmed when Baldwin decided to give Sir Douglas Hogg a peerage, thus ending the possibility of Hogg succeeding Baldwin as Party Leader and Prime Minister. As Chamberlain explained in a letter to Lord Irwin on August 12:

S.B. did not consider the fortunes of the party to be so dependent on D.H. as I did and do. I think he has all the qualities of a great leader and with him available there would have been no question of a possibility which he and I both consider very dangerous, *viz* the acceptance of Winston as leader.

However there it is. Douglas is now out of the running definitely and the future is in the lap of the Gods. Assuming that we come back next year with a diminished majority and stay in the full term, most of us will be a good deal older and a good deal the worse for wear. Probably we should then have several years of Opposition and that would give Winston his chance of establishing himself in the party's favour. . . .

'In opposition,' Chamberlain added, 'his want of judgement and his furious advocacy of half-baked ideas would not matter, while his wonderful debating and oratorical gifts would have free play.'

Chamberlain's hostility to Churchill, and the clash of temperaments from which so much of it sprung, had been deepened with every phase of the de-rating scheme. In his letter to Irwin, Chamberlain reflected on what had been, for him, a painful and embittering confrontation:

[1] On September 17 Page Croft wrote to Baldwin: 'I cannot see any hope of an improved industrial atmosphere unless safeguarding is pushed ahead now. I do not think the Whips ever quite appreciated the strength of feeling in the House of Commons over iron and steel last session. It was only with the greatest difficulty that our people could be restrained from taking Parliamentary action.'

I must tell you something about the rating proposals which have occupied most of my time for the last six months and are likely to do so from now until the election. Their history has been rather a chequered one. In their original form they emanated from a rather clever but somewhat inexperienced Treasury official named Hurst. Hurst at a very early moment got Winston's ear, so much so that the older Treasury men like Barstow were treated with marked discourtesy and eventually resigned. . . .

When these proposals came to me I declared my approval of the principle that industry should be relieved of a part of its rates, but I strongly objected on Local Government grounds to any plan which completely severed all connection between industry and industrial interests and local Government. It appeared to me most dangerous if a large part of the community were given to understand that they were unaffected by any inefficiency, extravagance or corruption in Local Government. Moreover seeing that industry required and is provided with certain costly local services, I thought it inequitable that they should pay nothing for them.

Over this point we had numerous battles. I accused Winston of reckless advocacy of schemes the effects of which he himself did not understand. He accused me of pedantry and of personal jealousy of himself. At times feelings became rather acute. But I had one advantage over Winston of which he was painfully conscious. He could not do without me. Therefore in the end I was the sole judge of how far to go because whenever I put my foot down he was helpless. As a matter of fact I only put it down once and he gave way directly. But it was a very harassing time for me and to tell you the truth, Edward, Winston is a very interesting but a d——d uncomfortable bed fellow. You never get a moment's rest and you never know at what point he'll break out.

Chamberlain's distaste seemed more of Churchill's character than of his scheme. Indeed, in his letter to Irwin he declared of the scheme itself:

. . . its value must not be under-rated even for election purposes. It provides an answer to the criticism so often brought against an ageing Government, that it has exhausted its vitality and its ideas and no longer has a policy. Neither of the other parties has any new ideas for dealing with unemployment. Here is a plan which we can advocate as meeting one of the most generally admitted industrial grievances.

Chamberlain was also critical of those whom Churchill had taken into his confidence, telling Irwin: 'On the backbenches Harold Macmillan speaks often and well. He is patronised by the Chancellor, I think, through the influence of R. Boothby who is the Chancellor's PPS and a friend of Macmillan. But both of them are rather mistrusted by the rank and file. . . .'

Chamberlain went on to reflect on the personalities with whom he had become embroiled during the de-rating discussions. Baldwin, he wrote, 'often vexes me by what seems to me timidity or lethargy when rapid or vigorous action are wanted. But I have an immense respect and affection for him.' Nevertheless, in the House of Commons itself, Baldwin 'fails again and again to make the speech that is wanted'. As for Churchill, Chamberlain's mixed feelings of admiration, resentment and suspicion welled up as he wrote to Irwin:

One doesn't often come across a real man of genius or, perhaps, appreciate him when one does. Winston is such a man and he has *les defauts de ses qualités*. To listen to him on the platform or in the House is sheer delight. The art of the arrangement, the unexpected turn, the master of sparkling humour, and the torrent of picturesque adjectives combine to put his speeches in a class by themselves. Then as you know there is no subject on which he is not prepared to propound some novel theory and to sustain and illustrate his theory with cogent and convincing arguments. So quickly does his mind work in building up a case that it frequently carries him off his own feet.

I have often watched him in Cabinet begin with a casual comment on what has been said, then as an image or simile comes into his mind proceed with great animation, when presently you see his whole face suffused with pink his speech becomes more and more rapid and impetuous till in a few minutes he will not hear of the possibility of opposition to an idea which only occurred to him a few minutes ago.

In the consideration of affairs his decisions are never founded on exact knowledge, nor on careful or prolonged consideration of the pros and cons. He seeks instinctively for the large and preferably the novel idea such as is capable of representation by the broadest brush. Whether the idea is practicable or impracticable, good or bad, provided he can see himself recommending it plausibly and successfully to an enthusiatic audience, it commends itself to him. . . .

Chamberlain ended his letter with a direct comparison between himself and Churchill, telling Irwin: 'There is too deep a difference between our natures for me to feel at home with him or to regard him with affection. He is a brilliant wayward child who compels admiration but who wears out his guardians with the constant strain he puts upon them.'

16

1928–1929: The Last Year of the Baldwin Government

IN March 1928 Churchill had begun work on a further volume of *The World Crisis*, which would tell the story of the Versailles Treaty and the first four post-war years. Among those who helped him to collect material was a near neighbour of his at Chartwell, Major Desmond Morton,[1] who agreed to look through all the documentary material as it arrived, and to suggest how and where it could best be used. Churchill's friendship with Morton, which dated back more than a decade to their first meeting on the western front in 1916, grew swiftly, sustained by increasingly frequent discussions together at Chartwell.

Throughout June and July Churchill was also helped on his new volume by Owen O'Malley,[2] who worked at Chartwell selecting documents from Churchill's own archive, and preparing outlines for each chapter. In his memoirs O'Malley later recalled: '. . . as a man fourteen

---

[1] Desmond Morton, 1891–1971. Second Lieutenant, Royal Artillery, 1911. Converted to Roman Catholicism shortly before the First World War. Shot through the heart while commanding a Field Battery at the Battle of Arras, April 1917, but survived the wound. Later awarded the Military Cross. ADC to Sir Douglas Haig, 1917–18. Seconded to the Foreign Office, 1919. Head of the Committee of Imperial Defence's Industrial Intelligence Centre, January 1929–September 1939; its terms of reference were 'To discover and report the plans for manufacture of armaments and war stores in foreign countries.' A member of the Committee of Imperial Defence sub-committee on Economic Warfare, 1930–39. Principal Assistant Secretary, Ministry of Economic Warfare, 1939. Personal Assistant to Churchill throughout the Second World War. Knighted, 1945. Economic Survey Mission, Middle East, 1949. Seconded to the Ministry of Civil Aviation, 1950–53.

[2] Owen St Clair O'Malley, 1887–1974. Educated at Radley and Magdalen College Oxford. Entered the Foreign Office, 1911. Counsellor in Peking, 1925. Suspended from duties on account of a currency speculation, 1926. Worked as Churchill's research assistant, 1926–27. Reinstated in the Foreign Office, with the rank of Counsellor, 1927. Minister to Mexico, 1937–38. In charge of the British Embassy to Spain (at St Jean de Luz, France), 1938–39. Minister to Hungary, 1939–41; to Poland, 1942–45. Knighted, 1943. Ambassador to Portugal, 1945–47. He published his memoirs, *The Phantom Caravan*, in 1954.

years younger than him I was now inspired to try harder than I had tried before to make of myself a loving husband, tender parent, constant friend, faithful servant, considerate master and magnanimous opponent. So far as devilling for his book was concerned I was ineffective, but it was out of regard for him and for the book that I was not more active to help him. I felt that it was better to do little or nothing as long as the composition of the book was going easily and well; and in fact it went very easily and very well. . . .' On July 22 Churchill instructed O'Malley to discuss all military problems with General Edmonds,[1] and to enlist Edmonds' support in assembling material on all the military episodes referred to in the outlines. As for the general narrative, Churchill wrote: 'I have all that in my head.'

On August 3 Baldwin celebrated his sixty-first birthday. Churchill, who was still at Chartwell, sent him a telegram of good wishes. 'I am touched by your remembering my birthday,' Baldwin replied on August 5, and he added: 'Remember my counsel to you and abide by it! Paints, pens, dams and nought else. Yours ever, S.B.' Churchill abided by Baldwin's advice, writing to his wife on August 7 about his progress. 'Nearly 3,000 words in the last two days!' he exclaimed, and added: 'Certainly nothing will suit me better than to be quiet here and have hardly any visitors. . . .' On August 10 Churchill wrote again. Bernard Baruch[2] had come to lunch on the previous day, 'and sent you ceremonious messages'; Victor Cazalet had come for two days 'and I play bezique with him'. Randolph and Lindemann played golf and tennis. 'I have persuaded the Prof to stay on until Monday,' Churchill added. 'He is a great companion both for me and for Randolph.' As relaxation, Churchill supervised the building of a small cottage for his five-year-old daughter Mary, and from time to time helped with the bricklaying.[3]

---

[1] James Edward Edmonds, 1861–1956. Educated at King's College School London. 2nd Lieutenant, Royal Engineers, 1881; Major, 1899. On active service in South Africa, 1901–02, and on the Western Front, 1914–18. Colonel, 1909. Deputy Engineer-in-Chief, BEF, 1918 (despatches six times). Head of the Military Branch of the Historical Section of the Committee of Imperial Defence, 1919–49. Brigadier-General. Knighted, 1928.

[2] Bernard Mannes Baruch, 1870–1965. Born in New York. Financier. Chairman of the Allied Purchasing Commission, 1917. Commissioner in Charge of Raw Materials, United States War Industries Board, 1917–18. Chairman of the War Industries Board, March 1918–January 1919. Economic Adviser to the American Peace Commission, 1919. Member of the President's Agricultural Conference, 1922. American Representative on the Atomic Energy Commission, 1946.

[3] Churchill's bricklaying activities received much press publicity. When, on September 4, Alderman Lane invited him to join the Amalgamated Union of Building Trade Workers, Churchill was much tempted to accept, and consulted Sir Horace Wilson about the ethics of such a move. 'It would be pleasing to know that you had joined,' Wilson wrote on September 14. 'The trade is well paid and you could always earn a living at it.' Wilson also assured

On August 11 Stanley Baldwin left England for two months at Aix-les-Bains. Before leaving he wrote to Churchill from 10 Downing Street:

My dear Winston,

The car is at the door pawing the ground and I am just leaving. My last words are to you.

Do remember what I said about resting from current problems. Paint, write, play with your dams.

But a big year will soon begin and much depends on our keeping fit. You will have a great deal to do as Chancellor and you need to be at your best, and our combined judgement will have many a test.

I am sure if we keep together and go forward boldly into the New Year we can win a great victory.

Yours ever
S.B.

Churchill replied from Chartwell on September 2:

My dear PM,

Yr very kind letter is greatly valued by me. You may count upon any help I can give in the tussle that is before us. We cannot I think do better than fight it thro' on the lines of your letter to Bobbie.[1] I cannot feel that there is any decisive drift agst us. But Labour will have a heavy class vote; & the Liberals will queer the pitch—(What else *can* they do?) The new Parl^t will certainly be vy different from this.

But what about the team? Austen I fear very serious—a stroke! A.J.B.: S.: Steel M.: Willie B.: P.C-L.:[2] (so he says) all riding at single anchor. F.E. still resolved to go I understand. On the other side Cushendun[3] a real find— but 66. There are others who will stay—but will they help?

You made some fine references to the wealth of young talent wh the Parl^t had produced. But vy little has been done for them. They have just drummed their heels; & some of them if not preserved by office—will not reappear after the fray.

I am for 'The old cause & the new lot'. I am sure it wd be wise to refresh

---

Churchill that he would be within his rights to refuse to contract-in for the Political Levy, and he added: 'What you should do if your Branch nominated you for the TUC can perhaps be left over till the time comes!' On September 23 Churchill wrote to Alderman Lane: 'I may say that I should be very pleased to join the Union, if you are of the opinion that it would not be unwelcome to your members. I take a high view of the dignity both of craftsmanship and manual labour.'

[1] Baldwin's letter to Commander Robert Eyres-Monsell of 3 August 1928, in which Baldwin stated that there would be no general reintroduction of Protection.

[2] A. J. Balfour; Lord Salisbury; Sir Arthur Steel-Maitland; William Bridgeman and Sir Phillip Cunliffe-Lister.

[3] Ronald McNeill, Churchill's former Financial Secretary, who had been created Baron Cushendun in 1927, when he was appointed Chancellor of the Duchy of Lancaster.

the team *before* the match, & not too long before. Painful, worrying but safer. And you must provide for the future of the party. Without a stream of new talent we cannot hold our ascendency. We don't want to be left alone with Jix & Amery!

There is not much in the second line. Walter Elliot[1] is by far the best. It is in the rank & file that the needful new figures can be found. You know them better than I do: but I cd suggest a few names if the occasion arose. Anyhow meet change with forestalling change.

'I have had a delightful month,' Churchill added, 'building a cottage and dictating a book: 200 bricks and 2,000 words a day.'

On September 21 James Scrymgeour-Wedderburn[2] was among the guests at Chartwell invited for the weekend. In his diary he noted:

Winston is building with his own hands a house for his butler, and also a new garden wall. He works at bricklaying four hours a day, and lays 90 bricks an hour, which is a very high output. He also spends a considerable time on the last volume of his war memoirs which he is writing. His ministerial work comes down from the Treasury every day, and he has to give some more hours to that It is a marvel how much time he gives to his guests, talking sometimes for an hour after lunch and much longer after dinner. He is an exceedingly kind and generous host, providing unlimited champagne, cigars and brandy. Even poor old Prof who is really a teetotaller, is compelled to drink ten cubic centimetres of brandy at a time, because he was once rash enough to tell Winston that the average human being could imbibe ten cc of brandy without causing any detectable change in his metabolism.

'This evening,' Scrymgeour-Wedderburn wrote in his diary, 'Winston talked very freely about the USA. He thinks they are arrogant, fundamentally hostile to us, and that they wish to dominate world politics. He thinks their "Big Navy" talk is a bluff which we ought to call. He considers we ought to say firmly that we must decide for ourselves how large a navy we require, and that America must do the same.'

[1] Walter Elliot, 1888–1958. Educated, Glasgow Academy and University. On active service, 1914–18 (Military Cross and bar). Conservative MP for Lanark, 1918–23; for Glasgow Kelvingrove, 1924–45; for the Scottish Universities, 1946–50; for Kelvingrove, 1950–58. Parliamentary Under-Secretary of State for Scotland, 1926–29. Financial Secretary, Treasury, 1931–32. Minister of Agriculture and Fisheries, 1932–36. Privy Councillor, 1932. Elected to the Other Club, 1932. Secretary of State for Scotland, 1936–38. Minister of Health, 1938–40. Director of Public Relations, War Office, 1941–42.

[2] Henry James Scrymgeour-Wedderburn, 1902–83. Educated at Winchester and Balliol College Oxford. President of the Oxford Union, 1924. Succeeded his father as 11th Earl of Dundee, 1924 (claim only admitted by the Committee of Privileges of the House of Lords in 1953). Conservative MP for Renfrew, 1931–45. Parliamentary Under-Secretary of State for Scotland, 1936–39. On active service with the 7th Black Watch, 1939–41. Additional Parliamentary Under-Secretary of State, Scottish Office, 1941–42. Minister without Portfolio, 1958–61. Privy Councillor. Minister of State for Foreign Affairs, 1961–64. Deputy Conservative Leader in the House of Lords, 1962–64.

On September 23 Scrymgeour-Wedderburn wrote in his diary:

Last night I had the great privilege of two hours' conversation with Winston alone, as Lindemann and O'Malley had both left and the ladies had gone to bed. He began by asking how old I was. When I said twenty-six, he replied 'Ah! The age at which Napoleon was given command of the French Army of Italy,' and he then discoursed for some time on the changes in military tactics and strategy since 1795, and stressed the importance of the revolution brought about by the invention of tanks and armoured cars, which were incomparably superior to cavalry for all purposes.

'When he becomes engrossed in his subject,' Scrymgeour-Wedderburn noted, 'he strides up and down the room with his head thrust forward and his thumbs in the armholes of his waistcoat, as if he were trying to keep pace with his own eloquence. If he shows signs of slowing down, all you have to do is to make some moderately intelligent observation, and off he goes again.'

Another young man who visited Chartwell twice during the summer of 1928 was Alan Lennox-Boyd,[1] who had been introduced to Churchill by Lindemann. Later he recalled, in a letter to the author: 'On one of these occasions he said to me—"How old are you?" I told him nearly twenty-five. He said Napoleon had taken Toulon before he was 25. "Quick, quick"—here whipping out his watch—"you have just got time to take Toulon before you are 25—go and take Toulon." I told him my Toulon was a seat in the House of Commons and a little later on, having been adopted for the hopeless seat of Gower in Glamorgan (Polling Day May 30th 1929) I spent a weekend at Chartwell and he gave me much useful information about the effect of his plans as Chancellor on industrial derating on district like Swansea and Llanelly, both adjoining the Gower division.'

On September 24 Churchill went to Balmoral for four days' stag hunting and grouse shooting. Whenever he could find a spare hour, Churchill dictated further sections of his book, for he had taken with

---

[1] Alan Tindal Lennox-Boyd, 1904–83. Educated at Sherborne and Christ Church Oxford; President of the Oxford Union, 1926. Unsuccessful Conservative candidate at Gower, 1929. Conservative MP for mid-Bedfordshire, 1931–60. Joint-Secretary (with Patrick Donner) of the India Defence Committee, 1934–35. Parliamentary Secretary, Ministry of Labour, 1938–39; Ministry of Home Security, 1939; Ministry of Food, 1939–40; Ministry of Aircraft Production, 1943–45. Minister of State for Colonial Affairs, 1951–52; Privy Councillor, 1951. Minister of Transport and Civil Aviation, 1952–54. Secretary of State for the Colonies, 1954–59. Created Viscount Boyd of Merton, 1960. A director of Tate and Lyle, 1966–74. Joint Vice-Chairman, Arthur Guinness, Son & Co Ltd since 1967. His three brothers were all killed: Donald Gray Haig in Germany on 5 April 1939; George Edward in action on 9 November 1943 and Francis Gordon in action in Normandy in 1944.

him both his secretary, Miss Fisher,[1] and a substantial dossier on the Paris Peace Conference which had been prepared for him by Sir James Headlam-Morley.[2] A few hours after Churchill's arrival at Balmoral, he wrote to his wife:

There is no one here at all except the family, the Household & Princess Elizabeth[3]—aged 2. The last is a character. She has an air of authority & reflectiveness astonishing in an infant. . . .

The King is well—but ageing. He no longer stalks but goes out on the hill where the deer are 'moved about for him', & it may be that some loyal stag will do his duty. He & the Q asked much after you.

'I am much looking forward,' Churchill added, 'to my release on Saturday from this honourable & luxurious captivity.'

For some days, Clementine Churchill had been upset about certain domestic problems. In his letter, Churchill sent her a word of caution:

Mind you rest & do not worry about household matters. Let them crash if they will. All will be well. Servants exist to save one trouble, & shd never be allowed to disturb one's inner peace. There will always be food to eat, & sleep will come even if the beds are not made. Nothing is worse than worrying about trifles. The big things do not chafe as much: & if they are rightly settled the rest will fall in its place.

Following Baldwin's return from Aix in the last week of September, the problem of when to call the General Election absorbed much of the Cabinet's time. On October 1 the Chief Whip, Commander Eyres-Monsell, told the Cabinet that all the impending legislation was likely to be passed through Parliament by the end of May, making 30 May 1929 the earliest possible date. Lord Birkenhead cast doubt on so optimistic a view of the speed of Parliamentary legislation. Thomas Jones noted in his diary Churchill's advice: 'Why not have a sudden election and come

[1] Lettice Fisher. A Junior Administrative Assistant at the Treasury; Churchill's secretary and stenographer while he was Chancellor of the Exchequer, 1924–29.

[2] James Wycliffe Headlam-Morley, 1863–1929. Educated at Eton, King's College Cambridge and Berlin University (his mother was German). Professor of Greek and Ancient History, London, 1894–1900. Staff Inspector of Secondary Schools, Board of Education, 1902–20. Assistant Director, Political Intelligence Bureau, Department of Information, 1917–18. Assistant Director of Political Intelligence, Foreign Office, 1918–20. Member of the Political Section, Paris Peace Conference, 1919. Historical Adviser to the Foreign Office, 1920. Diplomatic historian. Knighted, 1929.

[3] Elizabeth Alexandra Mary, elder daughter of the Duke of York (later King George VI). Born on 21 April 1926, she succeeded her father, as Queen Elizabeth II on 6 February 1952.

back and finish off the Bills? The PM could announce policy and give no pledges.' Churchill suggested May 11 as election day; but Baldwin felt this would cut into the Budget debate, and Sir Kingsley Wood insisted that Bills should be taken 'in one jump'. It was finally decided to hold the election on June 4.

During the summer of 1928 there had been much international activity, initiated by the United States, designed to secure the progressive disarmament of the strongest Powers, Britain, France and the United States. 'We always seem to be getting into trouble over these stupid disarmament manoeuvres,' Churchill wrote to Donald Fergusson on September 9, 'and personally I deprecate all these premature attempts to force agreements on disarmament. . . .' Five days later, in a seven-page note to Sir Warren Fisher, he explained his reasons for opposing any pressure on France to disarm:

We are frequently told that Germany would disarm on the understanding that other nations would disarm too, and that further France in particular is bound morally to disarm. However I do not admit that any moral obligation exists. The Germans were prostrate and yielded themselves virtually at discretion. Any undertakings about Allied disarmament were not a matter of bargaining but a voluntary declaration on the part of the Allies.

Since then important changes have taken place in the position of France. She gave up the Rhine frontier in return for a promise by the United States together with Great Britain to come to her aid in the event of German aggression. This American promise has been withdrawn and France has not now the security on which she was induced to abandon the Rhine. The only securities for the defence of France are the French Army and the Locarno Treaties. But the Locarno Treaties depend for their efficiency upon the French Army. As long as that army is strong enough to overpower a German invasion no German invasion will be attempted.

On the other hand, the British undertaking to protect Germany from the misuse of the French Army affords Germany full security, and it is unthinkable that France would attack Germany in defiance of England and Germany together. Thus the strength of the French Army protects us against the most probable danger of our being forced to intervene in Europe, and it is not in our interest at all to press for the whittling down of this force below the point of security. Moreover France will never consent to such a whittling down and all expectations that she will are futile. . . .

Churchill went on to warn against bowing to pressure from the United States for a further reduction in German reparations. 'We have given everything, and paid everything,' he wrote, 'and we cannot make any new sacrifice.' In Cabinet on October 17 Churchill reiterated this view, telling his colleagues that Britain should insist on 'all concessions on our side' being dependent upon 'equivalent concessions by the United States'. Two days later he was in Paris, where he discussed with Raymond Poincaré[1] the forthcoming Reparations Conference. Britain's position, Churchill insisted, remained that of the Balfour Note of 1924, that 'the taxpayers of the United Kingdom . . . should receive from Europe enough to pay America'. But he did see one way of reducing a small portion of the £100 million a year due to the Allies from Germany, of which £32 million a year was paid to Britain. If Britain and France were to end their military occupation of the Rhineland, he explained, 'all the military charges' for the occupation would be ended, thus reducing British and French expenditure by £6½ millions a year.

Returning from the Paris negotiations, Churchill reflected on what he saw as the folly of premature disarmament, and on October 25, during a speech in his constituency, he told what he called a 'disarmament fable'. The tale was as follows:

Once upon a time all the animals in the Zoo decided that they would disarm, and they arranged to have a conference to arrange the matter. So the Rhinoceros said when he opened the proceedings that the use of teeth was barbarous and horrible and ought to be strictly prohibited by general consent. Horns, which were mainly defensive weapons, would, of course, have to be allowed. The Buffalo, the Stag, the Porcupine, and even the little Hedgehog all said they would vote with the Rhino, but the Lion and the Tiger took a different view. They defended teeth and even claws, which they described as honourable weapons of immemorial antiquity. The Panther, the Leopard, the Puma and the whole tribe of small cats all supported the Lion and the Tiger. Then the Bear spoke. He proposed that both teeth and horns should be banned and never used again for fighting by any animal. It would be quite enough if animals were allowed to give each other a good hug when they quarrelled. No one could object to that. It was so fraternal, and that would be a great step towards peace. However, all the other animals were very offended with the Bear, and the Turkey fell into a perfect panic.

The discussion got so hot and angry, and all those animals began thinking so much about horns and teeth and hugging when they argued about the peaceful intentions that had brought them together that they began to look at one another in a very nasty way. Luckily the keepers were able to calm them down and persuade them to go back quietly to their cages, and they began to feel quite friendly with one another again.

---

[1] Raymond Poincaré, 1860–1934. Minister of Public Instruction, 1893 and 1895; of Finance, 1894 and 1906. Prime Minister, 1911–13. President of the French Republic, January 1913–February 1920. Prime Minister and Minister of Foreign Affairs, January 1922–June 1924. Minister of Finance, 1926–28. Prime Minister, 1926–29. Between 1913 and 1934 he published ten volumes of memoirs.

Among those who read Churchill's fable in the Press was Stanley Baldwin, who wrote to him two days later from Downing Street:

My dear Winston,

I have been green with envy for two days because I never thought of the Zoo Allegory. It is just perfect and there is no more to be said.

It ought to give food for thought to any one capable of thinking.

What a whoop you must have given when it came into your head!

On November 5 Churchill was among the guests at Baldwin's eve of session dinner. Amery, who sat next to him, noted in his diary: 'Winston was more forthcoming on safeguarding than I have known him. He tells me that he does a certain amount of work in bed in the morning, spends only twenty minutes in dressing, and keeps two hours free every night for dictating his books.' Two days later Churchill wrote to his wife, who was convalescing from blood poisoning at a nursing home near Northampton:

The session opens super-tame. The PM almost mute—a sort of Coolidge [1] or Hoover.[2] It is astonishing what goes down in these days of mass politics. One thing is as good as another. All the old Parliamentary drama & personal clashes are gone—perhaps for ever.

So Hoover has swept the board—I feel this is not good for us. Poor old England—she is being slowly but surely forced into the shade. . . .

On November 11 Churchill was Beaverbrook's guest at a dinner and film show. Much of the talk was about the coming election. On the following day Beaverbrook wrote to Amery of how Churchill 'put forward the argument that unemployment will not do the Government any widespread damage at the polls'. Bad unemployment, he had asserted, 'was confined to certain areas, which would go against the Government anyhow, but it was not sufficiently spread to have a damaging influence all over the country'. Beaverbrook had disagreed, telling Amery: 'I think unemployment will be the one and only issue which counts.' Churchill also wrote an account of the dinner, in a letter to his wife. Beaverbrook, he wrote, 'declares the Socialists & Libs are coming in. He will not give us any real help. My time wd come, he said, the moment we got into Opposition. I rather agree.'

It was nearly five years since Churchill had entered Baldwin's Cabi-

---

[1] Calvin Coolidge, 1872–1933. Govenor of Massachusetts, 1919 and 1920. Vice-President of the United States, 1920; President, 1923–29.

[2] Herbert Clark Hoover, 1874–1964. Born in Iowa. Graduated from Stanford University, 1895. A mining engineer. Head of the Relief Commission for Belgium, and United States Food Commissioner during the First World War. Secretary of Commerce, 1921. 31st President of the United States, 1929–33. An ardent exponent of private enterprise.

net. 'The time flashes away,' he wrote to his wife on November 15. 'Next year is the unknown.' But two days later, in a letter to Lord Rothermere, who was on holiday in Egypt, he spoke optimistically of the Government's election chances, and advised Rothermere against withdrawing his support. His letter continued:

Of course, if you and Max rock the boat it will do a good deal of harm and I am sure you will be very sorry after the Socialists are returned. Certainly everything you have stood for, friendship with France, breach with Russia, economy in expenditure, reduction of taxation, will be violently overthrown. The addition of 40 or 50 millions to direct taxation would not particularly hurt the rich individuals affected, but I am sure it would be a great injury to the saving power of the nation. Our capital accumulations are horribly depleted by the war and the strikes, and to draw upon that heavily for further social easements would be injurious to all classes. It is not for the sake of the rich people but for the economic strength of the country that I should deprecate this new assault on capital.

However, this is a free country and everyone may try to make his own bed so long as he is ready to lie in it afterwards. . . .

'The times in which we live are very difficult,' Churchill added, 'and might easily become critical, and everyone has a great responsibility, few more than you.' That same day he wrote angrily to his wife: 'Rothermere, having ordered his organs to smash up the de-rating Bill, has gone off to luxuriate in Egypt. The wretched papers loathe doing this sort of work which is against their convictions and sympathies but to which they are forced by an imperious, ill-informed, restless and sore proprietor.' Of the de-rating Bill Churchill wrote: 'We shall drive the Bill through. It is a great piece of social reform and well worth fighting for amid the shallow chatter of these days.'

Churchill was also angered, as his wife had been, by a recent anti-British speech by President Coolidge. 'My blood boiled too. . . .' he wrote. 'Why can't they let us alone? They have exacted every penny owing from Europe; they say they are not going to help; surely they might leave us to manage our own affairs.'

Of his own activities Churchill wrote:

I have had very busy days, trying to push the book forward and at the same time with heaps of engagements and politics. I spent yesterday afternoon preparing a speech on the Safeguarding amendment to the Address but after going through it all with Worthy decided it was better for him to do it, not me. So I handed him over my notes. He is very trustworthy, sound on fiscal matters and a friend. . . .

During November the United States Government continued to press for world naval disarmament. On November 15 Lord Cushendun circulated a note by Robert Craigie,[1] warning of the dangers of ignoring United States opinion, which from President Coolidge downwards was strongly hostile to Britain's refusal to enter negotiations. On November 19, in a Cabinet memorandum on Anglo-American relations, Churchill strongly opposed any such negotiations, informing his colleagues:

I am decidedly of opinion that this would be a great mistake. We shall never agree among ourselves either to abandon our belligerent rights at sea or to cut the British Navy down by treaty to the limits which the United States considers suitable for herself. Any attempt to enforce such an agreement would divide the Conservative Party from end to end on the eve of the Election. There would be a stand-up fight in all the Constituencies on the question of whether British interests had been betrayed to the United States; and there would certainly be enough Conservatives who would sustain that view to destroy us as a political force.

Churchill advised waiting until the inauguration of Herbert Hoover as President. Nothing could be gained by negotiation with Coolidge, whose attitude he described as crude and amateur—'the viewpoint of a New England backwoodsman'. Whatever British Government were in power in 1929, he wrote, 'cannot have a worse, and may conceivably have a better, chance of re-opening the Naval controversy'. Above all, Churchill wrote, 'I deprecate a panic mood in our relations with the United States.' His memorandum continued:

... the only bad thing that has happened in Anglo-American relations is our not being able to agree about cutting our Navy down. We are told that this has wiped out all, or most of, the effects of such great events as the abrogation of the Anglo-Japanese Alliance, the settlement of the Irish question, the Washington Treaty and the Anglo-American debt settlement. If so, it only shows how little advantage is to be gained by making such efforts to conciliate American opinion. Whatever may have been done at enormous cost and sacrifice to keep up friendship is apparently swept away by the smallest little tiff or misunderstanding, and you have to start again and placate the Americans by another batch of substantial or even vital concessions.[2]

---

[1] Robert Leslie Craigie, 1883–1959. Entered the Foreign Office, 1907. British Representative, Inter-Allied Blockade Committee, 1916–18. First Secretary, Washington, 1920–23; transferred to the Foreign Office, 1923; Counsellor, 1928; Assistant Under-Secretary of State, 1934–37. Knighted, 1936. Privy Councillor, 1937. Ambassador to Japan, 1937–41. UK Representative to the United Nations War Crimes Commission, 1945–48.

[2] Churchill's concern for constructive Anglo-American relations affected even his literary work. On December 27 he wrote to W. Lints Smith of *The Times*, about the serialization of the final volume of his war memoirs: 'There are some passages about the United States which are

Throughout November Churchill had worked on his book at Chartwell, where he received Major Morton's comments on the Russian intervention chapters. 'I am most obliged to you,' Churchill wrote on November 20, 'for your most extraordinarily penetrating and helpful criticism, the bulk of which I am incorporating.' Two days later Morton was sent another Russian chapter for his scrutiny. Further copious notes and comments arrived during November from Sir Archibald Sinclair, General Edmonds and Sir John Anderson.

On November 29, on the eve of his fifty-fourth birthday, Churchill dined at the House of Commons with a small group of friends, among them Sir Philip Sassoon, Professor Lindemann, Esmond Harmsworth and Harold Laski. After the dinner, Churchill drove down to Chartwell, in order to be there on his birthday. During the day Baldwin wrote from 10 Downing Street:

My dear Winston,

I woke this morning to find that it is your birthday.

To communicate with No 11 was the work of a moment and I learned that you had already fled overnight to keep the sacred day in your own home.

A brief reference to Dod[1] shews me that you are still a child, so I may say 'Many Happy Returns' and a happy birthday to you to-day.

Yours ever
S.B.

Work on the book continued through December. 'I have been working very hard at my new volume which goes to press in three weeks,' Churchill wrote to Balfour on December 21, 'I really thought the Peace Conference would crush me. I tried to compress it into two or three chapters, but the more one writes about it the more there is to do. . . . I enclose a chapter in case you care to skim over it.'

Churchill spent Christmas at Chartwell with his family, and continued to work on his book. His wife had returned from the convalescent home, and Randolph was on holiday from Eton. On New Year's Eve, Professor Lindemann arrived at Chartwell, where work on the book continued throughout January. Even Churchill's Cabinet colleagues were enlisted to help improve it; both Worthington-Evans and Austen

---

rather critical. If your selection should fall on these, I should have to ask that the counterbalancing passages of a complimentary and soothing nature should have publicity at the same time. . . .'

[1] *Dod's Parliamentary Companion*, published annually, an indispensable source of information about all Members of Parliament and Peers.

Chamberlain were sent chapters to comment on, and to 'improve', and Baldwin himself was pleased to be a critic. 'Your proofs never came,' he wrote to Churchill on January 6, 'but I am greedy for them and hope yet that possibly you can let me have them for an early week end.'

On January 7, in a letter to Baldwin enclosing his proofs, Churchill set out what he felt should be the guidelines for the coming election campaign. 'I am sure,' he wrote, 'that everything should be done to confront the electors with the direct choice between Socialism and modern Conservatism. The more blunt and simple the issue, the better for our cause. The world tides are favourable. They set in every country towards Conservatism, co-operation and continuity of national policy.' Churchill added: 'Women can feel these tide movements by instinct.'

In his letter of January 7 Churchill suggested that the decision to restrict the year's cruiser programme to two ships should be used during the campaign 'as a noticeable sign of peace consolidation, and as the means of a *détente* in Anglo-American relations'. As for the desire of the Postmaster General, Sir William Mitchell-Thomson,[1] to promise the electorate to reintroduce the Penny Post, this, he wrote, was impossible, for, he explained: 'The Rating elephant eats all our buns.'

At the beginning of January, Churchill decided that his son should not return to Eton for his last four months as a schoolboy.[2] Professor Lindemann was able to find a place for Randolph at Christ Church, and indeed he became an undergraduate that same month, in the middle of the academic year, writing to his father from Oxford on January 28:

Dear Papa,
I am so enjoying being here, and I cannot tell you how glad I am that I did not have to return to Eton. There are so many interesting and enjoyable things to be done each day that the time passes very rapidly.

---

[1] William Mitchell-Thomson, 1877–1938. Educated at Winchester and Balliol College Oxford. 2nd Baronet, 1900. Engaged in West India business. Conservative MP, 1906–32. Director of the Restriction of Enemy Supplies Committee, 1916–19. Parliamentary Secretary, Ministry of Food, 1920–21; Board of Trade, 1921–22. Privy Councillor, 1924. Postmaster General and Chief Civil Commissioner, 1924–29. Created Baron Selsdon, 1932. Chairman of the Television Advisory Committee, 1934–38.

[2] On 17 December 1928 one of Randolph's masters, Robert Birley, had written to Churchill that he considered Randolph 'lacking in a sense of duty' and warned: 'If he lets things slide until the big moments he will never really get on.' Randolph's housemaster, A. C. Sheepshanks, was even more critical, having written to Churchill about his son's 'fearful conceit', and adding: 'I have tried to talk to him about all this, but it is almost impossible. He gets so angry and talks so fast and interrupts so much that one cannot get anywhere. Nor does he pay any attention to what one says, when he is angry. He is merely preparing some crushing answer to something said long before. When not angry,' Sheepshanks added, 'he can be very attractive, and would be nicer still if he could learn to take advice now and then.'

My tutor is a very brilliant man called Feiling.[1] He wrote the 'History of the Tory Party', which I believe you have read. . . .

I am so looking forward to seeing you and telling you all about Oxford. I shall be in London on Wednesday for Diana's wedding.[2]

Your very loving son
Randolph

Throughout the second week of January, Churchill received more comments and more material for his book; during the third week of January Beaverbrook, Archibald Sinclair, Desmond Morton and Edward Grigg each sent Churchill further thoughts and suggestions, while from the Foreign Office Robert Vansittart[3] was among those who sent detailed notes and amendments.

When the Cabinet met on the morning of February 7, Churchill informed his colleagues that the Bank of England had decided to increase the Bank Rate by 1 per cent. 'He feared,' the minutes recorded, 'that this would have a chilling effect on trade revival.' The Cabinet were also informed—the minutes do not say by whom—that the problem arose because 'American prosperity was so great that money was being drawn into the United States from all over the world and was being used for purposes of speculation'. It was also emphasized—again by an unnamed Minister—that the Government 'had no responsibility for the movement of the Bank Rate and does not control the policy of the Bank of England'.

The purpose for which the Cabinet had been called was not, however, the Bank Rate, but an 'emergency' matter brought up at Churchill's request. On 19 December 1928, Baldwin recalled, the Cabinet had decided to adhere to the naval construction programme for 1928–9 unless 'some new factor' were to arise during the Recess. The Cabinet's

[1] Keith Grahame Feiling, 1884–1977. Lecturer and historian. Fellow of All Souls, Oxford, 1906–11; tutor at Christ Church, 1911–46. 2nd Lieutenant, Black Watch, 1915. Secretary to the Central Recruiting Board, India, 1917–19. OBE, 1918. University Lecturer in Modern History, Oxford, 1928–36; Chichele Professor of Modern History, 1946–50. Knighted, 1958. His first book, *The History of the Tory Party, 1640–1714*, was published in 1924. In 1946 he published a biography of Neville Chamberlain.

[2] Clementine Churchill's cousin Diana Mitford, who married the Hon Bryan Walter Guinness (later 2nd Baron Moyne) on 30 January 1929. Five years later she obtained a divorce, and in 1936 married Sir Oswald Mosley.

[3] Robert Gilbert Vansittart, 1881–1957. Educated at Eton. Entered the Diplomatic Service, 1902. Assistant Clerk, Foreign Office, 1914; 1st Secretary, 1918; Counsellor, 1920. Secretary to Lord Curzon, 1920–24. Principal Private Secretary to Ramsay MacDonald, 1928–30. Knighted, 1929. Permanent Under-Secretary of State for Foreign Affairs, 1930–38. Elected to the Other Club, 1933. Chief Diplomatic Adviser to the Foreign Secretary, 1938–41. Privy Councillor, 1940. Created Baron, 1941. His autobiography, *The Mist Procession*, was published posthumously, in 1958. His brother Arnold was killed in action in 1915.

fear had been that the United States would accelerate its cruiser programme. That had not happened, but now, Baldwin explained, 'the
Chancellor of the Exchequer had brought to his attention a new factor of
another kind. . . .' Baldwin went on to say that it was 'essential' that the
Cabinet should reach their decision that morning, as a question about
the 1928–9 programme was being asked that afternoon in the House of
Commons by the Member for Devonport, Leslie Hore-Belisha.[1]

Churchill then explained that the cause of his concern was not the
United States, but Germany. A secret memorandum, prepared by
General Gröner,[2] had been obtained and published by a British magazine, the *Review of Reviews*. From this memorandum it was clear that
the Germans were building a new 10,000-ton vessel embodying novel
features. 'By lightening weights and developing a very high horse-power
per ton,' Churchill pointed out, 'they had been able to design a very
remarkable ship.' It would be armed with 11-inch guns, would have 'a
greater radius of action' than the British battle-cruisers, and would fire
a heavier weight of shell per minute than its nearest British rival. In
reply to this sudden German interest in sea power, the French Government had already indicated its intention to build a 15,000- to 16,000-ton
ship. These developments, Churchill warned, 'indicated that Cruiser
design was passing into a phase which would render obsolete our existing Cruisers', and he recalled the superior speed of the German cruisers
during the last war.

Churchill concluded that the 1928–9 cruiser programme was already
out of date; that the two 8-inch-gun 10,000-ton cruisers which the
Cabinet had approved for 1928–9 would quickly be outclassed; and that
the news from Germany illustrated 'the mistake of building prematurely'. He therefore proposed a full year's postponement in the
British cruiser programme, 'in order that they might be introduced in
later years so as to incorporate all the most recent technical improve-

[1] Leslie Hore-Belisha, 1893–1957. His father, an Army officer, died when Hore-Belisha was
nine months old. Known, on account of his Jewish origins, as 'Horeb Elisha'. Educated at
Clifton and St John's College Oxford. On active service in France, 1915–16 and at Salonika,
1916–18. President of the Oxford Union, 1919. Liberal MP for Plymouth Devonport, 1923–42
(National Liberal from 1929; Independent from 1942 to 1945). Parliamentary Secretary,
Board of Trade, 1931–32. Financial Secretary, Treasury, 1932–34. Minister of Transport,
1934–37 (with a seat in the Cabinet from October 1936). Privy Councillor, 1935. Secretary of
State for War, 1937–40 (Member of the War Cabinet, 1939–40). Minister of National
Insurance, 1945. Created Baron, 1954.

[2] Wilhelm Gröner, 1867–1939. Entered the German Army, 1885. Chief of Field-Railway
Transport, 1914–16. In charge of the economic intensification of war production, 1916–17.
First Quarter-Master General to the Kaiser, October 1918. The leading Military supporter
of the Weimar Republic. Minister of Transport, November 1918. Minister of Defence,
January 1928–May 1932; in October 1931 he was also appointed Minister of the Interior.

ments'. By postponement, he added, 'we should get the advantage not only of better ships but also we should show to the world a more pacific policy'. As it was, Churchill continued: 'we were not making the best use of the limited funds available for naval construction, and we were casting away a great opportunity for easing the pressure for armaments all over the world. What he desired was a sounder policy and better ships.'

Bridgeman challenged Churchill's contention. The new British cruisers, he said, would be 'shorter but stouter vessels', in which protection would be more prized than speed. As for the 11-inch gun in the German warship, this, Bridgeman pointed out, 'was debarred to us under the Washington Treaty'. Were the Cabinet to adopt Churchill's plan of postponement now, and acceleration later, Bridgeman added, Britain would be 'taken to task' for too rapid a rearmament both 'at home and at the League of Nations'. The Cabinet supported Bridgeman; the existing cruiser programme, it decided, 'should stand' and Bridgeman should have 'authority to proceed therewith'.

On the evening of February 12 Churchill made his first major pre-election speech, as the guest of honour of the Anti-Socialist and Anti-Communist Union at the Queen's Hall, London. The speech received wide Press coverage, and was published within a few days as a twopenny pamphlet entitled 'Ringing the Alarm'. If Labour came to power, Churchill declared, they would be 'bound to bring back the Russian Bolsheviks, who will immediately get busy in the mines and factories, as well as among the armed forces, planning another general strike'. There was no community in the world, Churchill warned, which could be 'so easily shattered by an internal explosion as the British, and no community which would find it so difficult to recover'. The real danger, he insisted, lay in the sinister forces which a well-meaning Labour Cabinet would be unable to resist. 'If a Socialist Government came into power,' he warned, 'they might well have a facade of well-meaning and respectable Ministers who were moved here and there like marionettes in accordance with the decision of a small secret international junta.' There was no virtue, Churchill continued, in denouncing his remarks as alarmist. 'Better be sure than sorry. Better be warned in time. . . . I am deliberately ringing the alarm bell and ringing it before it is too late.'

These were to be Churchill's themes throughout the election

campaign. His fears of a Labour victory were deep-felt; on 26 December 1928 Lord Beaverbrook had written to Robert Borden:[1] 'Churchill is plunged in despair. He accepts electoral defeat in advance, but then his judgement on such matters is worse than that of any prominent man I know.'

As the election approached, Churchill's political future became the subject of much speculation. On February 25 Baldwin asked Thomas Jones what he thought of the possibility of making Churchill Secretary of State for India, should the Conservatives win the election. Jones replied that he thought it 'a splendid notion'. A week later Baldwin again asked Jones what he thought of the idea and Jones recorded in his diary, on March 5: 'I said I was all for it, that he would rise to the height of a great opportunity, that there was nothing petty about him, that we officials might quarrel and denounce him to his face, but he was not vindictive.'

Churchill's critics used the fact of the impending election to press their demands for his departure from the Exchequer. On February 27 Amery and Neville Chamberlain discussed Churchill's future. They were agreed, Amery noted in his diary, 'that nothing would help the situation more than if he could be moved'. Amery suggested making Churchill Lord President of the Council, with a 'direct mission to co-ordinate the fighting services'. In such a post, Amery noted, he 'would be kept happy and busy planning wars in Afghanistan and elsewhere'. When Amery went on to suggest the possibility of Churchill becoming Foreign Secretary, Chamberlain, as Amery recorded:

thought the PM would not run such a risk and would dread to find himself waking up at nights with a cold sweat at the thought of Winston's indiscretions. I suggested that Winston was not really so rash as picturesque, that there were no really critical situations in foreign policy just now, and that a little colour and vivacity would do no harm and that my experience of Winston as a negotiator with his equals was that he was both skilful and reasonable.

'The essential thing,' Amery wrote to Baldwin on March 11, 'is to move Winston,' and he went on: 'I say this not only because he is fundamentally opposed to all ideas of Empire development and Empire preference, as well as to safeguarding, but because, in spite of all his

---

[1] Robert Laird Borden, 1854–1937. Canadian Prime Minister, 1911–20. Knighted, 1914. First overseas Minister to receive summons to meeting of British Cabinet, 14 July 1915. Representative of Canada at Imperial War Cabinet, 1917–18. Chief Plenipotentiary Delegate of Canada at the Paris Peace Conference, 1919. Represented Canada on Council of League of Nations. Chairman of Sixth Committee of the League Assembly, 1930.

brilliancy and verbal originality, he is entirely lacking in constructive thought and imagination in the economic field.' Amery added: 'He has been, in every direction, a paralysing negative influence, and the Party knows it and would breathe a profound sigh of relief if he were shifted.' At the end of his letter, Amery again suggested making Churchill either Foreign Secretary, or Lord President of the Council. As Churchill's 'obvious successor' as Chancellor, Amery proposed Neville Chamberlain. 'Such a change,' he wrote, 'would be acclaimed with enthusiasm by our Party.' When Amery saw Baldwin on March 4 the Prime Minister suggested sending Churchill to the Foreign Office, 'where', Baldwin remarked, 'he would have a rare chance of spreading himself and giving life and picturesqueness to what Austen has made a deadly dull business'.[1]

With the approach of the election, two separate assaults were launched on Government policy; one by the Labour Party, the other by Lloyd George. The success of these assaults, and their obvious outcome, was foreshadowed during March by five by-elections, two of which the Conservatives lost to the Liberals and one to Labour. The publication by Lloyd George of a Yellow Book on unemployment, proposing a massive Government financial scheme of public works, added to Conservative unease. On March 6 Thomas Jones recorded in his diary a discussion at 10 Downing Street with Churchill, Hailsham, Cunliffe-Lister, Neville Chamberlain, Samuel Hoare and Walter Guinness:

Much speculation about the Election, and general agreement that 'we must get our people properly frightened at the prospect of a Socialist Government'. Winston (more and more voluble as the luncheon proceeded) inclined on the whole to wish Labour could be in for a short spell to allow him to display his powers in Opposition. . . .

'We should not try to compete with L.G.,' urged Winston, 'but take our stand on sound finance. I remember in Gairloch when the unemployed figures were tremendous, we toyed with these big national schemes of artificial employment, but L.G. came down after a few days' reflection solidly against them.'[2]

[1] In an undated letter at this time Clementine Churchill wrote to her husband: 'I think it would be a good idea if you went to the Foreign Office. But I am afraid your known hostility to America might stand in the way. You would have to try & understand & master America & make her like you. It's no use grovelling or even being civil to her. But I think you could do it. Austen is just an animated cardboard marionette.'

[2] On 12 September 1921 Lloyd George had conferred with his principal Cabinet colleagues at Gairloch, in Scotland. During their discussions Churchill had pressed for a positive and imaginative policy towards unemployment. Two weeks later, on 28 September 1921, he had circulated a memorandum on unemployment in which he wrote: 'It is not possible for a civilised State with a large portion of its members living in luxury and the great bulk of its

Hostility towards Churchill among some Conservatives was still strong, and increased as the election drew nearer. On March 6 Davidson lunched with the newspaper proprietor Sir William Berry. 'He is very anti-Lloyd George,' Davidson recorded in his diary, 'and I also suspect very anti-Winston, and is pinning his faith on Neville as the first lieutenant to the Prime Minister. He feels that Jix ought to go, and also Winston from the Exchequer. . . .' Davidson's account continued:

In a little monologue about Winston he put the position exactly as I understand it myself, the main point being that he is not trusted in the party because he is always out for office and never prepared for opposition, and therefore people suspect he is already in negotiation with Lloyd George to secure a post as second man on the new ship if it is ever launched.

Such rumours of Churchill's disloyalty had no foundation in fact; they arose from a meeting between Churchill and Lloyd George at which Lloyd George gave Churchill his terms for supporting a Conservative Government, in the event of the Liberals holding the balance between Labour and Conservatives, as they had done in 1924. Lloyd George wanted electoral reform to help the third party, no tariffs on iron, steel or wool, and certain Cabinet changes. Churchill promised to pass on these conditions to Baldwin.

It was when the question of Baldwin's successor as Party leader was under discussion that the strongest anti-Churchill feeling emerged. This feeling was again revealed in the second week of March, when Baldwin began to talk of reconstructing the Cabinet before the election. On March 11 he went as far as to suggest to Neville Chamberlain that he might like to replace Churchill at the Exchequer. According to Chamberlain's account in his diary, Baldwin told him that it would be 'an extraordinarily popular appointment in the party. For one thing they liked to have the next man to the PM in that office, and they did not want Winston in that position.' The two men then discussed the possibility of a stalemate at the election, with the Lloyd George Liberals hold-

---

members living in comfort to leave a proportion of its citizens with neither work nor maintenance. No doubt the standard of maintenance must vary with the resources of the State, and in hard times it must be reduced to the absolute minimum so as to encourage and, indeed, compel the most earnest efforts to seek economic employment. But we must have some answer to give in regard to every class of workpeople who are affected by the present trade depression. In answer to the question, which can be posed by hundreds of thousands of men to-day: "What am I to do?" we must have an absolutely clear-cut reply. It may not be popular, but it must be comprehensive, and it must be complete.'

ing the balance. Chamberlain's diary recorded: 'S.B. said the King's government must be carried on, but that he personally would not serve with L.G. I said I was in the same position, and S.B. said in that case he supposed the leadership would go to Winston.'

In the first week of March Churchill had sent out more than a hundred personal copies of *The World Crisis: The Aftermath* to his Cabinet colleagues, to Ramsay MacDonald and Philip Snowden, to those who had helped him with material and advice, and to his friends and family circle. 'You have not only a wonderful power of narrative,' Sir Samuel Hoare wrote on March 3, 'but, what is very rare among public men, an equal skill with the written word as with the spoken word,' and Philip Snowden wrote: 'I shall treasure it, not only for its own worth but as a memento of the friendly personal relations which can and do exist between keen political opponents.'

Among those to whom Churchill had sent a copy were three former Prime Ministers, Lord Rosebery, Lord Balfour and Ramsay MacDonald. On March 4, Rosebery wrote from his home at Epsom in a shaky hand: 'My dear Winston, Many thanks. I love these tokens of recollection', while Balfour wrote on March 6:

My dear Winston

The last volume of your great work has safely arrived, and I must send you a line of thanks and admiration. It is a most remarkable performance, and I count myself as fortunate in living long enough to see its accomplishment.

Nobody is better qualified than I to speak of its merits;—not merely on the general grounds that in my own way, and in a very different fashion, I have spent much time in mixing up politics with writing and writing with politics, but that I have had unique opportunities of seeing you at work in both these exacting spheres of activity.

Do you remember my visits to the Admiralty at the beginning of the war when you were good enough to explain all the difficulties and anxieties of a First Lord in a great Naval War dealing with wholly novel problems both of tactics and strategy? That was little more than fourteen years ago. Into those fourteen years you have not only compressed unique experiences in war by sea and land, in diplomacy, in House of Commons' work, and in constructive legislation; but you have contrived to write a book which, both as an original authority and as a most admirable literary performance, will hold a permanent place in the history of our country. During all those years I have been a friend and admirer, and, unless my memory fails me, an occasional opponent. It amuses me to think of this period as beginning with discussions on the defence of our trade routes in the Pacific, and opening its final act with your explanations to me at Whittingehame of your ideas of de-rating,—now in process of being happily embodied in a great legislative effort.

Five volumes of immortal history is a wonderful addition to this great period of administrative activity.

With warmest congratulations,

Believe me
Yrs aff
A.J.B.

All of those who had helped Churchill in the work received signed copies. 'I am more than proud you should have sought my humble opinions in any matter,' Desmond Morton wrote on March 4 and Robert Vansittart wrote two days later: 'It was of great interest to me to be allowed to read it in advance like that, I have to thank you for some very absorbing days and evenings.'[1]

The Aftermath was published on March 7; by the end of the year it had sold over sixteen thousand copies. 'I like it best of them all,' T. E. Lawrence—then 338171 Aircraftman Shaw—wrote from RAF Cattewater, near Plymouth on March 18, and he added: 'If the Gods give you a rest, some day, won't you write a life of the great Duke of Marlborough? About our only international general . . . and so few people seem to see it. He hasn't had a *practical* book written about him: and you are deep enough into affairs to see all round him.'

The published reviews were mostly favourable. 'With what feelings does one lay down Mr Churchill's two-thousandth page?' J. M. Keynes wrote in the *New Republic* on March 28, and he went on: 'Gratitude to one who can write with so much eloquence and feeling of things which are part of the lives of all of us of the war generation, but which he saw and knew much closer and clearer. Admiration for his energies of mind and his intense absorption of intellectual interest and elemental emotion in what is for the moment the matter in hand—which is his best quality. A little envy, perhaps, for his undoubting conviction that frontiers, races, patriotisms, even wars if need be are ultimate verities for mankind,

---

[1] Among those who helped Churchill in preparing *The Aftermath*, and in providing documents and criticisms, were three Foreign Office officials, J.W. Headlam-Morley, Captain W.J. Childs and Robert Vansittart, as well as Lionel Curtis, Lord Cecil of Chelwood, Brigadier-General Edwards, Brigadier-General Aspinall-Oglander, Sir Maurice Hankey, Lloyd George, Sir Archibald Sinclair, Major Desmond Morton, Sir John Shuckburgh, Sir John Anderson and Sir Edward Grigg.

which lends for him a kind of dignity and even nobility to events, which for others are only a nightmare interlude, something to be permanently avoided.'

Churchill expressed his own view of history in a letter to Katherine Asquith[1] on April 5: 'How strange it is that the past is so little understood and so quickly forgotten. We live in the most thoughtless of ages. Every day headlines and short views. I have tried to drag history up a little nearer to our own times in case it should be helpful as a guide in present difficulties.'

T. E. Lawrence had not been alone in urging Churchill to write a life of John, Duke of Marlborough. Following the publication of *The Aftermath* Churchill received several substantial offers, including one of a £6,000 advance from Hodder and Stoughton. For two months he would not commit himself, but when, on April 4, the publisher George Harrap[2] expressed interest in the book, he was at once invited to Chartwell to discuss terms. Within a month, on May 3, Harrap had offered an advance of £10,000, exclusive of serial rights, for publication in Britain and the Empire. News of these negotiations spread rapidly throughout the world of publishing. On May 21 Charles Scribner telegraphed from New York with an offer of £5,000 for the American rights alone; he added the welcome news that the American sales of *The Aftermath* had almost reached 4,000, higher than any of the three previous volumes. Churchill telegraphed his acceptance of Scribner's offer two days later, and on May 27 accepted Harrap's offer for Britain and the British Empire. *Marlborough* was to be in two volumes, each of at least 90,000 words, to be completed within five years. This was the book, which, since the turn of the century, Churchill had always wanted, and intended, to write; a history and a vindication of his famous ancestor. As he had written to his cousin the Duke of Marlborough on 9 June 1926: 'Although the labour will be hard and long, the task is inspiring. To recall from the past this majestic shade and invest it with life and colour for the eyes of the twentieth century, would be a splendid achievement and is even, in a certain sense, a duty.'

---

[1] Katherine Frances Horner. Daughter of Sir John Horner of Mells, Somerset. In 1907 she married Asquith's eldest son Raymond, who was killed in action on the Somme in 1916. Her brother Edward was killed in action in 1917. She herself died in 1976.

[2] George Godfrey Harrap, 1867–1938. Educated at West Ham Model School; left school at the age of 14. In publishing all his life; began publishing modern language and other textbooks, 1901. Managing Director, George G. Harrap and Company Limited. Planned and launched Harrap's Standard French Dictionary, 1919–34. Published Churchill's biography of *Marlborough* (in four volumes 1933–38) and *Arms and the Covenant*, 1938, but declined to publish his *History of the English Speaking Peoples* (which was published by Cassell).

The speculation about Churchill's alleged intrigue with Lloyd George continued throughout the spring of 1929. For his part, Churchill still doubted whether the Conservatives could possibly hold off a combined Liberal and Labour onslaught. On March 26 Lord Beaverbrook wrote to Robert Borden:

Churchill himself appears to be more defeatist than ever. I dined with him last night and I judge he is certain the Government is going out. The Conservative faith in Baldwin as a leader has evaporated.

Churchill has no intention whatever of allying himself with Lloyd George, although rumours to this effect in Conservative circles are doing him a great deal of harm.

In the last week of March, Churchill was at Chartwell working on his next Budget. On March 27 he received a seven-page handwritten note from Harold Macmillan proposing a set of vigorous new policies designed to appeal to the electorate. 'The problem is not so much how to win a clear majority,' Macmillan wrote, 'but how to avoid a debâcle. We may easily drift into the position of 1906.' Macmillan proposed the slogan: 'Modernization at Home, Markets Abroad.' Not tariffs or safe-guarding, Macmillan insisted, but modernization and research, was the key to industrial progress. In the first week of April Churchill gave Macmillan an outline of the main features of his new Budget. Commenting on them in a letter to Churchill on April 8, Macmillan wrote:

I believe you've got an absolutely first-class fighting Budget forming itself into pretty definite shape.
1. *Relief for the Publicans & the Bookies* (say £2 millions)
Two classes which work well for the Tory party & will work for us again (very powerful recruiting agent, esp in the poorer districts).
2. *Removal of Tea Duty* (say £7 millions)
A first class canvassing point. Every house one goes into, one is offered a cup of tea. What a gambit! 'Ah! Tea cheaper now, Mrs Jones. Mr Churchill's cheap tea, I call it.' You don't have to hesitate for an opening; its simply made for you. Every woman likes her tea & thinks of her tea 3, 4, & 5 times a day. (Snowden will gnash his teeth over this.) 1 & 2 are the popular lines; for the man in the street & the woman in the home.
    Then comes—
3. *The Railway Modernisation Stunt*
Capital expenditure at once put in hand of nearly £8 millions.
Industry again; we stand behind the heavies.
    This leads to
4. *The acceleration of De-Rating*
This seems to me ABSOLUTELY BRILLIANT. I'm afraid at first it rather over-whelmed me; but, really, the more I think of it, the better it is

a. It's simple (like most really good ideas).

b. It's arresting.

c. It has the great advantage of bringing back into the limelight the great policy on which we have worked so hard.

d. It avoids the necessity for teaching our people a new part. All our members, candidates, canvassers, speakers, pamphleteers etc have learned it. Now they get a chance to fire it all off again, & with redoubled effect.

3 & 4 are the Grand Policy—the policy we've toiled & slaved & sweated for—and it all fits in with our general scheme & view of the only real cure for unemployment.

Macmillan went on to plead with Churchill for 'something more' at the end of his speech: 'Let's have "The Vision Splendid" and we're home.' By this he meant a combined appeal for industrial modernisation and imperial trade, despite the 'little Englanders' in the Treasury. 'I'm confident,' Macmillan added, 'that the Treasury had the lowest view of Drake, & Clive & Rhodes.'

While Churchill was preparing the final details of his Budget, the Press was filled with speculation about the future of the Cabinet, and in particular of Churchill's future. On March 30 the *Daily News* reported that after the election Neville Chamberlain would 'almost certainly' become Chancellor of the Exchequer, and that Churchill 'will in that case be given a lighter post with the Leadership of the House of Commons as compensation'. 'I am sure,' Lord Irwin had written to Churchill from New Delhi on March 27, 'ingenious minds must be calculating and recalculating every possible permutation of party grouping! I shall watch it with absorbing interest & wish you all the reward that virtue deserves!' Irwin added: 'Good luck, my dear Winston.' Unknown to Churchill, Irwin himself had been asked officially about Churchill's future. On April 13 Thomas Jones, who was with Baldwin at Chequers, recorded in his diary: 'During tea a bag arrived from Town, and in it the expected letter from India to the PM. He read it to me. Irwin was in favour of Ronaldshay,[1] and against Winston for the India Office.' Irwin's letter had been sent from Viceregal Lodge, Delhi, on March 28. In it, despite his friendly letter to

---

[1] Lawrence John Lumley Dundas, 1876–1961. Earl of Ronaldshay. Educated at Harrow and Trinity College Cambridge. ADC to Lord Curzon (when Viceroy) 1900. Conservative MP for Hornsey, 1907–16. Governor of Bengal, 1917–22. Privy Councillor, 1922. Biographer of Lord Curzon (1928) and Lord Cromer (1932). Succeeded his father as 2nd Marquess of Zetland, 1929. President of the Society for the Study of Religions, 1930–51. A member of the Indian Round-Table Conference, 1930–31, and of the Joint Select Committee on India, 1933–34. Secretary of State for India, 1935–40 (and for Burma, 1937–40). Knight of the Garter, 1942. One of his two sons was killed in action in the RAF in February 1942.

Churchill of the previous day, Irwin expressed to Baldwin his doubts as to Churchill's suitability for the post:

> . . . I can very well guess that there might be advantages in substituting Neville for him at the Treasury. And I can also see a great hand for him to play over India with his capacity for seeing the big thing & presenting a broad case. But I think my doubts tend to outweigh my confidence that it would be a good appointment.
>
> Let me try to put some of my feelings—which are more instinctive than rational—on paper.
>
> India today seems to be vy much at a cross ways—and on whether she turns the right road or the wrong, much will depend. She needs the guidance of somebody with courage: and with vision—but with both the courage and he vision of a real desire to help India, and making themselves felt through sympathy with all her difficulties. The 'inferiority complex' is just now very inferior & very complex: & India is very sore. And I am sure that more than half her problems are psychological & of that order of difficulty. How would W.S.C. fit into these necessities? F.E. did an incredible amount of harm here. Not by policy—for that on the whole was good—but by the impression he produced upon sensitive & self important Indians visiting England, whom either he would not see & so mortified: or saw and produced the impression of one out of sympathy & rather disposed to despise.
>
> Frankly I should fear that Winston at bottom would have rather the same point of view & would never be able—as one never can—to conceal it. I remember his attitude of mind vis à vis Indians in Kenya & I doubt.[1] And he has become—or perhaps it's more true to say—has always been, a much more vigorous Imperialist in the 1890–1900 sense of the word than you & me.

'If I thought that Winston would really be interested,' Irwin added, '& would really be liberal minded, about India, I might say different: but I can't bring myself to believe that this is constitutionally likely.'

[1] In 1921, while Churchill was Colonial Secretary, he had supported the right of the East African administration to deny Indians equal rights with Europeans to land purchase. But on 18 May 1921 he wrote to the Secretary of State for India, Edwin Montagu: 'I hope to be able to meet you in regard to segregation by substituting for invidious segregation on race lines, a very strict system of sanitary, social and building regulations which will in fact ensure that the only Indians who will live in the white quarters will be those who really are suited by their mode of living for residence amid a European community.' Following a long and acrimonious correspondence, Montagu wrote to Churchill on 12 October 1921: 'The statement you make that "The Indians in East Africa are mainly of a very low class of coolies, and the idea that they should be put on equality with the Europeans is revolting to every white man through British East Africa", might have been written by a European settler of a most fanatical type. I am trying to get away from a policy in which the Indians in East Africa are treated politically in a special manner because they are Indians. Nobody has suggested doing anything in the way of giving political rights to a low class of coolies.' The Colonial Office representative at the negotiations on this matter was Lord Irwin himself (he being at that time, as Edward Wood, Parliamentary Under-Secretary of State for the Colonies).

During the first two weeks of April Churchill worked at the final details of his Budget. By April 3 he had decided upon the main outlines, writing that day to Baldwin:

I think we ought to meet on Monday. I shall then be ready to tell you what I should like to propose, and also to read the actual text of certain statements of financial policy which require your approval and Cabinet sanction. Could we meet in London on that morning? We shall need some time, as a number of decisions have to be taken.

I should like very much, if you think well, that Neville should be present as he is so long headed and sagacious in counsel. Philip C.L. is staying with me here Friday night, and I shall have thrashed out with him matters affecting the Board of Trade.

After the meeting with Baldwin, only one outstanding point remained, whether to bring forward all the de-rating benefits to April, instead of waiting until October, as planned. Churchill suggested bringing in all the agricultural benefits at once, although even this latter would add £2 million to the Budget outlay. Baldwin decided to put this to the Cabinet on April 11.

Writing to Baldwin on April 10 Churchill explained:

I also propose to remit the whole of the Tea duty, but to leave Coffee, Cocoa & Chicory untouched. Cost 6·2 m, leaving a final prospective surplus of 4·1 or 2·1 according as whether the 2 m of Agric Relief is taken from the Budget or the Suspensory Fund.

I hope the Cabinet will like this arrangement, & that nothing more will be put upon me now. My last few millions of surplus are not quite so robust as the earlier ones and I do not wish to place a real load on their shoulders.

Churchill's letter continued:

. . . you shd promise definitely *if we are returned* to provide a Fund for Imperial development either by direct use or capitalisation: to deal with maternity & to clear or re-condition the slum areas. There is no objection to mentioning figures even, but it shd also be said that 'if responsible we shall in due course make any proposals that may be necessary to supply additional revenue'. I really cannot take any more on the Budget as now constituted.

The Cabinet met on April 11, while Churchill was at Chartwell preparing his Budget speech. Baldwin read out Churchill's letter of April 10, and it was agreed to, subject, as the minutes recorded, 'to an expression of opinion in one point of detail'. As P. J. Grigg explained to Churchill, several Ministers had 'strongly deprecated the reference to the provision of new sources of revenue if necessary!' After the Cabinet, Baldwin sent Grigg a pencilled note, which Grigg sent at once to

Churchill: 'The Cabinet warmly approve the Chancellor's proposal that the derating of industry other than Agriculture should wait until the original appointed date. They feel the 2m for agriculture is a legitimate charge on the suspensory fund and should be so charged.'

On April 13 Churchill sent the King an outline of what had been decided. Among the measures was a further remission of a charge on industry, the £400,000 a year paid by the railways since 1832 as Passenger Duty. As Churchill explained to the King:

The railway companies have pressed continually for this relief and Mr Churchill has now decided to accord it to them on condition that they spend nearly the whole of its capitalised value ie £6½m upon new works designed to make their railways more efficient and more capable of carrying heavier modern waggons. They have agreed to this and considerable activity involving useful employment will shortly follow.

An even older duty which Churchill intended to remove was the tax on tea. 'There has been a tea duty in existence ever since the reign of Queen Elizabeth,' he wrote, 'and Mr Churchill is glad to think that your Gracious Majesty's reign should witness its removal.'

Churchill delivered his Budget on April 15. It was his fifth consecutive Budget, a count reached previously only by Walpole, Pitt, Peel and Gladstone—each of whom were, or were to become, Prime Minister. The *Sunday Times* described the speech as 'the most brilliantly entertaining of modern Budget speeches'. In it Churchill spoke caustically of Lloyd George's Yellow Book proposals on unemployment as 'paying the unemployed to make racing-tracks for well-to-do motorists to make the ordinary pedestrian skip', and as the policy 'of buying a biscuit early in the morning and walking about all day looking for a dog to give it to'. An outburst of road-building such as that proposed by Lloyd George, Churchill added, might exhaust the nation in much the same way as 'an ill-judged spurt' sometimes exhausted a boat-race crew at Hammersmith Bridge.

The Budget's one tax concession was the abolition of the duty on tea: a saving of fourpence a pound to the consumer, at a cost of £6 million a year to the Exchequer. Philip Snowden attacked this welcome measure as 'election bribery', but, as Churchill was quick to point out, a year earlier Snowden himself had described the tea duty as 'crushing the bent backs of the working classes'.

In the face of two years of mounting protests from the racecourse interests, and a declining revenue from the tax itself, Churchill also announced the end of the betting tax: this decision would cost the

Exchequer £1 million a year, but would be offset by a number of smaller duties to be imposed on Bookmakers and Totalisators. New revenue was to come from increased license duties on brewers, distillers and tobacco manufacturers, although retailers of alcoholic drinks were granted tax concessions. Among the smaller measures, motor-cyclists were to pay less duty on their cycles, while more money was to be spent on telephones for the equipment of rural post offices.

Churchill spoke for nearly three hours, holding the attention of the House by his humour, his clear narrative and his easy mastery of the facts. Neville Chamberlain wrote in his diary of how Churchill's speech 'was one of the best he has made and kept the House fascinated and enthralled by its wit, audacity, adroitness and power'. On the morning of April 16 Baldwin wrote to Churchill from 10 Downing Street:

My dear Winston,

Just before I leave for Worcestershire I must send you a line to tell you how it all strikes me after thinking it over in the early morning, the hour (provided it be the beginning and not the end of the day!) in which the eternal verities are stark naked.

I have never heard you speak better, and that's saying a good deal. I hate the word brilliant: it has been to death and is too suggestive of brilliantine: but, if I may use it in its pristine virginity, so to speak, it is the right one.

I congratulate you with both hands.

S.B.

On April 30 Churchill spoke over the radio, as part of the election campaign. 'The political broadcast delivered by Mr Winston Churchill last night,' reported the *Daily Express* on May 1, 'knocked the six preceding broadcasts into a cocked hat . . . as an exhibition of polemical oratory it was superb. His voice was edged alternatively with sarcasm and warning. There was a note in it of extraordinary intimacy with his audience. He began with statistics, merged with derision of his political opponents and ended high on the pinnacle of perfervid patriotism.' During his broadcast Churchill emphasized what he believed were the Conservatives' principal achievements: 'Peace abroad; steady stable government at home; clean, honest, impartial administration; good will in industry between masters and men; public and private thrift.' They had 'lightened the burden of galling rates'. The electorate, he said, must not cast away these benefits, and he warned: 'Avoid chops and changes of policy; avoid thimble-riggers and three-card trick men; avoid all needless borrowings; and above all avoid, as you would the smallpox, class warfare and violent political strife.'

By the end of April Baldwin had decided not to reshuffle his Cabinet before the election, despite the speculation and pressure to do so. Upset by this decision, Amery wrote to Baldwin on April 27, '. . . an announcement that Neville was going to the Exchequer would be worth twenty or thirty seats at least. I don't want to be disloyal or unfriendly to Winston but the fact remains that he is a handicap rather than an asset to us in the eyes of the public.' Amery now suggested the India Office as an alternative. Baldwin did in fact ask Churchill if he would be willing to become Secretary of State for India after the election. In an unpublished note written twenty years later, Churchill explained Baldwin's request, and his refusal. 'The problem of British relations with India had weighed upon our Cabinet,' he wrote and he continued:

A Royal Commission, headed by Sir John Simon, comprising all parties, and including Mr Attlee,[1] had gone out to India in the autumn of 1928. They made an exhaustive tour and study. Their report was impending. Mr Baldwin seemed to feel that as I had carried the Transvaal Constitution through the House in 1906, and the Irish Free State Constitution in 1922, it would be in general harmony with my sentiments and my record to preside over a third great measure of self-government for another part of the Empire. I was not attracted by this plan. My friendship with Lord Birkenhead, then at the India Office, had kept me in close touch with the movement of Indian affairs, and I shared his deep misgivings about that vast sub-continent.

On May 2 Churchill was enlisted to write the 'economy' section of Baldwin's election address. He also embarked upon a series of election speeches, warning, as he had done at the Queen's Hall on February 12, of the sinister dangers of socialism, and praising his colleagues for their moderation and common sense. On May 6 he was in Scotland, where he spoke at both Edinburgh and Glasgow. At Edinburgh he stressed the constructive achievements of five years of Conservative administration.[2] At Glasgow he was more rhetorical. Under Lloyd George's road build-

---

[1] Clement Richard Attlee, 1883–1967. Educated at Haileybury and University College Oxford. Called to the Bar, 1906. Tutor and lecturer, London School of Economics, 1913–23. On active service at Gallipoli, Mesopotamia (wounded) and France, 1914–19; Major, 1917. First Labour Mayor of Stepney, 1919, 1920; Alderman, 1920–27. Labour MP for Limehouse, 1922–50; for West Walthamstow, 1950–55. Parliamentary Private Secretary to Ramsay MacDonald, 1922–24. Under-Secretary of State for War, 1924. Chancellor of the Duchy of Lancaster, 1930–31. Postmaster-General, 1931. Deputy Leader of the Labour Party in the House of Commons 1931–35. Leader of the Opposition, 1935–40. Lord Privy Seal, 1940–42; Deputy Prime Minister, 1942–45. Lord President of the Council, 1943–45. Prime Minister, 1945–51 (Minister of Defence, 1945–46). Leader of the Opposition, 1951–55. Created Earl, 1955.

[2] Between the passing of the Widows', Orphans' and Old Age Contributory Pensions Act of 1925, and January 1928, more than one and a quarter million people had become entitled to benefits under the Act: 236,800 widows, 344,800 children, 227,000 people over seventy and 450,000 people between the ages of sixty-five and seventy.

ing plans, he said, the time would come when Britain would be reduced to 'a few little strips of vegetation and enormous well-tarred motor racing tracks, occupied entirely by the profiteering contractors who have been making the roads'. As for the Russian Government, Churchill declared, 'it never stops by night or day its attacks in every quarter of the globe upon the peace and prosperity of the Empire'.

While Churchill was in Scotland, his wife had taken a house at Epping to serve as a base for their campaign. 'I think you will find this house a snug retreat', she wrote to him on May 6, 'from which to sally forth on the constituency.' She also reported a discussion about Churchill's own political future, telling her husband:

At luncheon yesterday Sir Harry Goschen asked me ('if it is not indiscreet') what office you were going to after the G Election, if the Tories are returned again. I said you would remain where you are & I told him confidentially about your writing to the PM about the newspaper rumours & his assuring you that as long as *he* was PM *you* would be Chancellor—I thought it best to do this as he seemed quite certain you were going to the War Office of all places!

'Darling,' Clementine Churchill ended, 'I do hope you enjoy your Scotch Meetings—I wish I were coming with you. But I think it is wise for me to be here & to start the ball rolling.'

On May 9 Churchill was back in London, where he lunched with Philip Sassoon. Thomas Jones, who was also present, noted in his diary: 'Winston had travelled through the night from two meetings in Scotland, and was very proud to have heard his son address an audience of about 2,000 for 20 minutes without a note, just over 17 years of age. So we all stood up and drank the health of Randolph II. . . .' On May 10 Walter Runciman wrote to Churchill:

It was a real pleasure to see that your bonny son had made his first speech last night and that you and Mrs Churchill had the joy of hearing him. . . .

I trust he will go far in anything he has the aptitude for, which I trust will be politics. No matter what side he is on.

In the two weeks before polling, Churchill campaigned in his constituency, helped both by his wife, and by his son, who spoke at a women's meeting in Wanstead. Because of a shortage of large halls in the constituency, Churchill ordered two large tents, one for Wanstead and one for Woodford, which could hold five times as many people as the largest hall. On May 25, speaking at Wanstead, he hinted at an extension of

State insurance beyond the wage-earning classes. On May 27, speaking at Liverpool, he denounced Ramsay MacDonald's wartime pacifism. 'I do not forget that,' he said, 'nor ought it to be forgotten.' On May 28 he returned to Epping, where, in the evening, he addressed five meetings, reiterating the same themes. At Harlow he declared: 'Victory is in the air. We are on the eve of a decisive manifestation of the steadfastness and perseverance of the nation.'

Polling took place on May 30. That night Churchill joined Baldwin at 10 Downing Street to study the early results as they came in on a tape machine. The scale of the Conservative losses proved even greater than Churchill had expected. Thomas Jones, who was present, recorded in his diary:

. . . at Vansittart's desk, sat the PM with narrow slips of paper on which he inscribed the three lists as they arrived. At Duff's[1] desk sat Winston doing similar lists in red ink, sipping whisky and soda, getting redder and redder, rising and going out often to glare at the machine himself, hunching his shoulders, bowing his head like a bull about to charge. As Labour gain after Labour gain was announced, Winston became more and more flushed with anger, left his seat and confronted the machine in the passage; with his shoulders hunched he glared at the figures, tore the sheets and behaved as though if any more Labour gains came along he would smash the whole apparatus. His ejaculations to the surrounding staff were quite unprintable.

Churchill's own result was announced on the following day. He had been re-elected, but not by a majority of the voters.[2] The national result was a blow to the Conservatives, who won only 260 seats, as against Labour's 288. Two of Churchill's young Conservative friends, Harold Macmillan and Alfred Duff Cooper, were defeated; Robert Boothby was re-elected. The Liberals, with 59 seats, held the balance, but with a clear Labour superiority of 28 over the Conservatives alone. On June 3 the Cabinet discussed what their course should be. Amery noted in his diary that Baldwin proposed immediate resignation, but that Austen Chamberlain, supported by Neville Chamberlain, Joynson-Hicks, Hailsham and Amery himself, suggested that Baldwin should 'stay and definitely fasten on the Liberals the odium of turning us out'. Churchill, however, 'agreed with the PM, more positively because he did not wish to drive the 5 million Liberal voters into the Socialist camp'.

As a result of this discussion, Baldwin decided to resign at once. Three days later Churchill and his colleagues travelled by train to

---

[1] Charles Patrick Duff, Baldwin's Private Secretary (see page 197).

[2] Churchill received 23,972 votes. His Liberal opponent, G. G. Sharp, received 19,005 and the Labour candidate J. T. W. Newbold 6,472: a combined total against him of 25,477.

Windsor to hand back their seals of office to the King. On June 7 the Labour Ministers likewise travelled to Windsor to collect the seals which their opponents had relinquished. Ramsay MacDonald became Prime Minister for the second time. Churchill was once again, but for only the third time in twenty-one years, without political office. 'He's a good fighter,' T. E. Lawrence wrote to Marsh on June 3, 'and will do better out than in, and will come back in a stronger position than before. I want him to be PM somehow.'

Part Three

Warning and Forebodings
1929–1935

17

1929: Travels in the New World

————

WITHIN two weeks of returning his Seal of Office to the King at Windsor, Churchill began work on his biography of the First Duke of Marlborough. Many of the original documents, never before published, were in the muniment room at Blenheim Palace, withheld from other biographers by Churchill's cousin the ninth Duke, specifically for Churchill's biography. In order to piece these documents together, and to relate them to their historical background, Churchill decided to employ a research assistant, and Randolph's tutor, Keith Feiling, suggested a young history graduate, Maurice Ashley.[1] The salary was £300 a year, on a part-time basis. On July 13 Churchill sent Ashley his view of the object of the volume, and of his own plans:

> I have been browsing about among the authorities and have been much stimulated as a result. Broadly speaking my method will probably be not to attempt to 'defend' or 'vindicate' my subject, but to tell the tale with close adherence to chronology in such a way and in such proportions and with such emphasis as will produce upon the mind of the reader the impersonation I wish to give. I have first of all to visualize this extraordinary personality. This I can only do gradually as my knowledge increases.

Churchill went on to explain how he hoped to deal with the controversial aspects of Marlborough's career, telling Ashley: 'One has got to find out what the rules of the age were—there certainly were rules.

[1] Maurice Percy Ashley, 1907-   . Educated at St Paul's School, London and New College Oxford (History Scholar). Historical Research Assistant to Churchill, 1929–33. On the editorial staff of the *Manchester Guardian*, 1933–37; *The Times*, 1937–39. Editor of *Britain Today*, 1939–40. Served in the Army, 1940–45 (Major, Intelligence Corps). Deputy Editor of the *Listener*, 1946–58; Editor, 1958–67. Research Fellow, Loughborough University of Technology, 1968–70. Author of more than twenty-five historical works, many on Cromwellian and Stuart England, including biographies of Cromwell (1937), Marlborough (1939) and Charles II (1971). In 1968 he published *Churchill as Historian*.

Murder plots, for instance, were treated quite differently from treason even in its grossest form.' As for Marlborough's notorious letter to William of Orange, written while James II was still King, Churchill wrote: 'Fancy, living with James all those months, not merely with treason in your heart but with documentary proof and resolute declaration extant.' On July 28 Churchill wrote to Lord Camrose,[1] with whom he was negotiating the serial rights: 'I have no doubt that I shall be able to tell this famous tale from a modern point of view that will rivet attention.'

As well as acquiring his first research assistant, Churchill also took on a new private secretary, Patrick Buchan-Hepburn,[2] who went down for an interview at Chartwell on June 21, and was employed at once. Buchan-Hepburn's task was to help with the political and constituency correspondence, to keep the appointments diary and to take on as best he could the responsibilities which had hitherto devolved upon Edward Marsh, during Churchill's Ministerial years.

During June Churchill made plans for a three-month visit to Canada and the United States. During his visit he hoped to see again the places he had been to in 1900, to see the West Coast for the first time, to help promote the sales of *The Aftermath*, to lecture, and to gather material for a series of articles which Lord Camrose had agreed to publish in the *Daily Telegraph*. On June 28 he wrote to Bernard Baruch, who was then in Paris: 'I want to see the country and to meet the leaders of its fortunes. I have no political mission and no axe to grind,' and on July 29 he wrote to William Randolph Hearst:[3] 'We must discuss the future of the world, even if we cannot decide it.' He would be accompanied, he added, by

---

[1] Formerly Sir William Berry, who, on 19 June 1929, had been raised to the peerage as Baron Camrose.

[2] Patrick George Thomas Buchan-Hepburn, 1901–1974. Educated at Harrow and Trinity College Cambridge. Hon Attaché, Constantinople, 1926–27. Unsuccessful Conservative candidate, 1929. Private Secretary to Churchill, 1929–30. Conservative MP for East Toxteth, 1931–50; for Beckenham, 1950–57. Private Secretary to Oliver Stanley, 1931. A Junior Lord of the Treasury, 1939. Served in the Royal Artillery, 1940–43. A Junior Lord of the Treasury, 1944. Conservative Deputy Chief Whip, 1945–48; Chief Whip, 1948–51. Privy Councillor, 1951. Government Chief Whip, 1951–55. Minister of Works, 1955–57. Created Baron Hailes, 1957. Governor-General of the West Indies, 1958–62. Companion of Honour, 1962. His wife's first husband was killed in action in 1942.

[3] William Randolph Hearst, 1863–1951. Born in San Francisco, the son of a US Senator. Editor and Proprietor of the *New York American*, the *New York Evening Journal*, the *Boston American*, the *Boston Advertiser*, the *Chicago Herald and Examiner*, the *Chicago American*, the *San Francisco Examiner* and the *Los Angeles Examiner*. In 1903 he married Millicent Willson: they had five sons. Unsuccessful candidate for Mayor, New York, 1905. Congressman. Resident at his self-designed castle, the Hearst Ranch, San Simeon, a treasure house of medieval and renaissance European art and furniture.

his son Randolph, his brother Jack, and his nephew Johnny.[1] 'I thought it would be a great thing,' he explained, for these two young boys, who are undergraduates at Oxford, to see these mighty lands at a period in their lives when the proportions of things are established in the mind.'

Before leaving England, Churchill tried to persuade Baldwin to turn the Conservative Party away from Protection, and towards a definite arrangement with the Liberals. To this end he urged Baldwin to seek a direct personal accommodation with Lloyd George, and on June 27, with Baldwin's approval, Churchill himself met Lloyd George privately to discuss a possible compact, limited in the first instance to specific issues as they arose in Parliament. Two days after his meeting with Lloyd George, Churchill wrote to Baldwin: 'He said that he would not disclose either my name or yours, or quote any words as having been uttered by me on your behalf.' Churchill's letter continued:

I am deeply impressed with the critical character of the present situation. Eight million Tories, eight million Labour, five million Liberals! Where will these five million go? If Gretton,[2] Amery & Co have their way and run Protection, or if the anti-Liberal resentments of others have their way, there can be only one result—very likely final for our life time, namely a Lib-Lab block in some form or another and a Conservative Right hopelessly excluded from Power. If the counsels which I offer, and for which I am bound to struggle are followed, swift, certain and long-lasting victory can be achieved. We must recognise the conditions of the new franchise; they are inexorable.

On July 3 the new Chancellor of the Exchequer, Philip Snowden, outlined the Labour Government's plans to relieve unemployment: State aid of £25 million for public works in the distressed mining areas, and further Government encouragement for emigration to the Colonies. Speaking from the front Opposition Bench for the first time since 1917, Churchill approved these proposals, which were, he added, 'taken from the pigeon holes of the late Administration'. During the course of his speech, Churchill re-asserted his complete devotion to Free Trade, tempered by Safeguarding, as the only true path to prosperity. But Churchill's support for Free Trade was challenged within the Conservative Party by Neville Chamberlain, who on July 4 declared his support

---

[1] John George Spencer Churchill, 1910–   . Churchill's nephew; son of Jack and Lady Gwendeline Churchill. Educated at Harrow. Artist and designer of murals; he painted the Marlborough pavilion at Chartwell, 1938. Served in the Royal Engineers, 1939–45; Major, 1945. He published his memoirs, *Crowded Canvas*, in 1960.

[2] John Gretton, 1867–1947. Educated at Harrow. Conservative MP, 1895–1906 and 1907–43. Chairman of Bass, Ratcliff and Gretton Ltd, brewers. Colonel, Territorial Army, 1912. Privy Councillor, 1926. Created Baron, 1944. One of his two brothers, a Captain in the Bedfordshire Regiment, was killed in action at Ypres on 18 December 1915.

for Tariffs, telling members of the Empire Industries Association that the Conservative Party was now free from the conditions it had imposed on itself before the election, and should reformulate its economic policy, not on insular but on imperial lines.

On July 6 Churchill wrote direct to Lord Beaverbrook, firmly rejecting Empire Free Trade and all that it stood for:

I am astonished that with your knowledge of affairs you contemplate any Party going to the vast electorate of consumers with a proposal to tax the basic foods. It is moreover well known that the farmers would scorn a protective duty on foreign food which left them exposed to the equally unbearable competition of Canada and Australia. Any tax which would rally even the traditional protectionist forces would have to be levied upon imported food with a slight duty upon foreign food.

I hope you are not going to devote yourself to a lifetime of strife in such a cause, although it is no doubt an effective way of revenging yourself upon the Conservative Party.

On July 9, at the start of a Commons debate on Empire Trade, Leopold Amery appealed for a comprehensive system of Protection against foreign goods in the interests of Imperial Preference. 'I could feel,' he wrote in his diary, 'the anxiety and horror of our Front Bench at my closing remarks.' On July 11 the Shadow Cabinet met to discuss Amery's challenge. Baldwin began the meeting by 'laying it down', as Amery recorded in his diary, that there could be 'no question' of a reopening of the Party's fiscal policy. But after Austen Chamberlain pointed out that it was important to know 'the main direction in which we were going', Amery put his case once more, and was followed by Neville Chamberlain who, Amery noted, 'made a somewhat half-hearted attempt to back me in a rather confused suggestion that we should get away from safeguarding on to an Imperial policy which however was to exclude definitely the taxation of food'. Amery's diary continued: 'Winston wound up assuring us that he did not mean to go back on our existing safeguarding policy, but that he was definitely for co-operation with the Liberals on the basis of first agreeing with them on the electoral reform committee which is to be set up.'

Throughout the last two weeks of July Churchill was busy making detailed plans for his trans-Atlantic journey, and securing his finances, now that he was without a Ministerial salary. On July 17 Lord Inchcape[1]

[1] James Lyle Mackay, 1852–1932. In India, 1874–93. Knighted, 1894. Member of the Council of India, London, 1897–1911. Created Baron Inchcape, 1911. Shipowner. Chairman of the Governments' Port and Transit Committee, 1915, and several other shipping Committees, 1915–19. In charge of the disposal of the Government's surplus shipping, and all enemy

offered him two directorships, for a total salary of £1,000 a year, which he accepted.[1] The new *Marlborough* volume was also providing economic security, for on August 2 Churchill wrote to Lord Camrose, accepting his offer of £5,000 for the British and Empire serial rights.

Within a week of becoming Prime Minister, Ramsay MacDonald recalled the British High Commissioner in Egypt, Lord Lloyd,[2] and announced the Government's determination to remove all British troops from Egypt, except for the Canal zone. In a note written twenty years later Churchill recalled his reaction to Lloyd's recall, and its ill-effects on his position within the Conservative Party, and with Baldwin —who had sent Lloyd to Cairo in the first place:

I reacted vehemently against this rough and sudden gesture, and hoped the whole Conservative Party would have the same sentiments. But Mr Baldwin, brought up as a business man and certainly a great measurer of public feeling, did not think that this was good ground for a fight with the Government. It would unite the Liberals with them and leave the Conservatives in a marked minority. Lord Lloyd appealed to me to do him justice, and I declared I would confront the Government on the issue, which was one not only of weak policy but of personal ill-usage. Mr Baldwin deprecated any such championship of the High Commissioner; but I persisted. When I rose in my place on the Front Opposition Bench to interrogate the Government, he sat silent and disapproving. I immediately perceived that the Whips had been set to work the night before to make it clear to the Party that their honoured leader did not think this was a good point to press. Murmurs and even cries of dissent from the Conservative benches were added to the hostile Government interruptions, and it was evident I was almost alone in the House.

In his letter to Camrose on August 2, Churchill described the Lloyd debate. 'Our Party,' he wrote, 'had been damped down as much as possible by the Whips,' and he added:

shipping, 1919–21. Member of the National Economy (Geddes) Committee, 1921–22. Chairman of the Indian Retrenchment Committee, 1922–23. Created Viscount, 1924; Earl of Inchcape, 1929. Director of many companies, including several connected with coal.

[1] The companies concerned were R. & J. H. Rea Limited, and Mann George Depots Limited, both of which were involved in the storing and transport of coal.

[2] George Ambrose Lloyd, 1879–1941. Educated at Eton and Cambridge. Travelled widely in the East as a young man. Honorary Attaché, Constantinople Embassy, 1905. Special Trade Commissioner to Turkey, including Mesopotamia, 1907. Conservative MP for West Staffordshire, 1910–18. A director of Lloyds Bank, 1911–18. Captain, 1914. On active service in Gallipoli, Mesopotamia and the Hedjaz; he accompanied T. E. Lawrence on one of his desert raids. Present at the capture of Gaza, 1917. Knighted, 1918. Governor of Bombay, 1918–23. Conservative MP for Eastbourne, 1924–25. Privy Councillor, 1924. Created Baron, 1925. High Commissioner for Egypt and the Sudan, 1925–29. Chairman British Council, 1936.

I do not think Lloyd has been treated at all well. After four years he has left the streets of Cairo as safe as those of London, instead of every European going about armed and in peril of his life.

The removal of the British troops from Cairo to the Canal Zone will strike an immense blow at our prestige throughout the East; and in Egypt this will bring disastrous consequences in its train. The whole quality of Egyptian administration will deteriorate, Cairo will sink into an Oriental slum, and dangerous conflict probably attended by bloodshed, will develop between a crazy Parliament and a despotic King;[1] the protection of minorities and of foreigners will not be effectively discharged, and other Powers will demand or intrigue to fill the gap made by British abdication.

'During the last forty years,' Churchill added, 'everything has turned upon the British garrison in Cairo. With its departure the once glorious episode of England in Egypt comes to an end. It is not without a bitter pang that I contemplate this. My only hope is in the Egyptian extremists who have hitherto broken up every project for an accommodation, however unwise from our point of view it might be.'

On August 3 Churchill left Waterloo Station for Southampton, where, together with his son Randolph, his brother Jack, and his nephew Johnny, he embarked on the *Empress of Australia*. 'What fun it is to get away from England,' he had written to Beaverbrook on July 20, 'and feel one has no responsibility for her exceedingly tiresome and embarrassing affairs.' But his two-month absence from England cut him off, for the first time since he had joined Baldwin's Government in 1924, from all influence over Conservative policy-making, at a time when the Party was having to face new problems and decide on its future course both towards Protection, and towards the Empire. Among those on board ship with him was Leopold Amery himself, with whom Churchill and his party dined on August 5.

The conversation soon turned to Tariffs. In his diary Amery recorded that, after a long argument, he had told Churchill that he had often thought of resigning from the Government during the past year as a result of Baldwin's refusal to accept Imperial Preference, and that whatever happened now he was not going to be 'muzzled' any longer. Churchill replied that he himself would 'retire from politics' if Amery

---

[1] Ahmed Fuad, 1868–1936. A great-grandson of Mehmed Ali. Studied at Geneva, and at the Military Academy of Turin. A Lieutenant in the Italian Army, 1889. Ottoman Military Attaché in Vienna, 1890–92. Khedive of Egypt, 1917; assumed the title of King, February 1922. Gradually increased his autocratic powers during the late 1920s. According to his obituary in *The Times* (29 April 1936): 'Generally speaking, he had no very high opinion of his subjects, and, with a few exceptions, entertained little respect for his Ministers.'

got his way over Tariffs, and that he would then 'devote himself to making money'. Amery's account continued:

He had been all he ever wanted to be, short of the highest post which he saw no prospect of, and anyhow politics were not what they had been. The level was lower; there no longer were great men like Gladstone or Salisbury or Morley or even Harcourt and Hicks Beach. So we branched into a discussion of the Victorians, I asserting that they were relatively small men making a lot of to do about relatively small matters; he admitting the issues were less titanic, but convinced the men were much greater. . . .

On August 6 Amery noted in his diary:

My usual evening talk with Winston turned mainly on the Dardanelles. Talking of the series of mischances which just prevented our getting through he said jestingly that his only consolation was that God wished things to be prolonged in order to sicken mankind of war and that therefore He had interfered with a project which would have brought the war to a speedier conclusion. His other evidence for a Deity was the existence of Lenin and Trotsky for whom a hell was needed.

During August 7 a news telegram arrived from London, stating that Arthur Henderson, the new Labour Foreign Secretary, had embodied the most recent demands of the Egyptian nationalists into a new Anglo-Egyptian Treaty. Churchill was outraged by this, particularly as the Labour Government had denied until that moment that the negotiations were even taking place. Randolph Churchill recorded in his diary that evening: 'Papa called the company at dinner several times to bear record that there would be grave trouble in Egypt. He seemed very upset about this, but some 1865 brandy cheered him up.' On August 8, in a letter to his wife, Churchill explained why he was so angry at the Government's Egyptian policy: 'I predict with certainty,' he wrote, 'that the plan of fortifying ourselves on the canal and leaving Egypt to go to hell will never last, will be followed by disorder and degeneration, and will lead to our resuming an abdicated responsibility, possibly after serious bloodshed.'

Of his own work on board, Churchill wrote to his wife:

I have been reading a good deal on 'Marlborough'. It is a wonderful thing to have all these contracts satisfactorily settled, and to feel that two or three years agreeable work is mapped out and, if completed, will certainly be rewarded. In order to make sure of accomplishing the task within three years instead of leaving it to drag on indefinitely, I am going to spend money with some freedom upon expert assistance.

Churchill ended his letter with some personal news:

I have been trying to enforce discipline upon Randolph, and get him up and to bed at reasonable hours, and to secure a certain amount of reading being done. I have met with partial success. . . .

The wireless is a great boon, and we hear regularly from Vickers[1] about the stock markets. His news has, so far, been entirely satisfactory.

My darling I have been rather sad at times thinking of you in low spirits at home. Do send me some messages. I love you so much & it grieves me to feel you are lonely. . . .

Late on the evening of Friday August 9 the *Empress of Australia* reached Quebec, and on the following day Churchill and his party toured the city. That evening Churchill learnt that Charles Schwab[2] had offered his private railway car for the whole of the journey beyond Vancouver. 'This solves all problems,' he wrote to his wife two days later.

On the morning of Sunday August 11 Churchill spent several hours dictating the speech which he was to make in Montreal on the following Tuesday. Fortunately for his speaking and writing plans, the Canadian Pacific Railroad Company had provided him, not only with a special railway car, but also with a stenographer-typist. That afternoon, Churchill drove in an open motor car some twenty miles into the Quebec countryside, writing to his wife:

I wanted to see the country at close quarters and nibble the grass and champ the branches. We saw hills and forests scarcely trodden by the foot of man, every kind of tree growing in primeval confusion and loveliest Scotch Burns splashing down to rivers. We passed many lakes full of fish. Randolph expressed a desire to buy a piece of land and renounce society and ambition and settle here, building his own house. We have not, however taken any final decision on this pending a view of other sites. We stopped at a little bungalow where four or five motor cars were assembled and found it a

---

[1] Horace Cecil Vickers, 1882–1944. Apprenticed to a firm of stockbrokers as a clerk at the age of 12. Member of the London Stock Exchange, 1904. Founded the firm of Vickers, da Costa, of which he became the Senior Partner, 1917 (his son Ralph Cecil Vickers, MC, became its Chairman in 1972; his daughter, Joan Vickers, was created Baroness in 1974, having been a Conservative MP 1955–74).

[2] Charles Michael Schwab, 1862–1939. President, Carnegie Steel Corporation, 1897–1903. Chairman, Bethlehem Steel Corporation, 1903–39. Coming to England on board the *Olympic* in October 1914, he witnessed the sinking of the *Audacious*; on reaching London he pledged the support of his factories to the allied cause. In 1915, at Churchill's request, he built submarines for the Royal Navy in 5½ months, instead of the usual 14 months; they were assembled in Montreal to avoid breaching the neutrality of the United States. In charge of America's 'Shipbuilding Crusade', 1917–18. Hon Vice-President of the Iron and Steel Institute of Great Britain, 1926–39.

Country Club for fishing with twenty members in modest circumstances—quite Arcadian! Nothing would serve, when I was recognised, but to produce Champagne and the warmest of welcomes. . . .

That night Randolph wrote in his diary: 'From our window we can see at night the Rothermere paper mills all lit up. Papa said apropos of them, "Fancy cutting down those beautiful trees we saw this afternoon to make pulp for those bloody newspapers, and calling it civilisation." '

The size, emptiness and agricultural potential of Canada rapidly impressed themselves on Churchill's mind. 'How silly,' he wrote to his wife, 'for people to live crowded up in particular parts of the empire when there is so much larger and better life open here for millions. Half the effort of the war would have solved all these problems. However, the world is known to be unteachable.'

Shortly before noon on August 12 the train to which their private railway carriage, the *Mount Royal*, was attached left Quebec for Montreal, a journey of 180 miles. During the journey Churchill wrote to his wife:

The car is a wonderful habitation. Jack and I have large cabins with big double beds and private bath rooms. Randolph and Johnnie have something like an ordinary sleeping car compartment. There is a fine parlor with an observation room at the end and a large dining room which I use as the office and in which I am now dictating, together with kitchen and quarters for the staff. The car has a splendid wireless installation, refrigerators, fans, etc. We will certainly need this last. It is about as warm as a very hot English day but the air is cool and personally I do not mind the heat. But I can see that the journey will be laborious, & we shall I expect have enough of our land yachts before we are finished.

At Montreal Churchill made two speeches, one to the Mount Royal club in the evening of August 12, and one to the Canadian Club at a lunch given in his honour on August 13. During his speech to the Canadian Club, Churchill warned against pressure on France to reduce the size of her army, and declared: 'It is so easy for British or Americans dwelling safely as we do under the protection of sea power to raise a finger of reproach about the size and strength of the French Army. But if we were Frenchmen dwelling side by side with a mighty nation whose military manhood was double our own and by whom we had been twice invaded within living memory we should probably not be much impressed by these reproaches, however well intended. . . .' That night the Churchills left Montreal for Ottawa, where they stayed for two nights as the guests of the Governor-General, Lord Willingdon.[1] At midday on August 14 they drove some fifteen miles outside Ottawa, to Kingmere, for lunch with Mackenzie King. It was 'just the sort of place', Churchill wrote to his wife on the following day, 'you would like to buy for me, a tiny bungalow, three hundred acres of hills and forests, with a large lake and Scotch Burns, all just the right size for me'. Mackenzie King intended to construct a number of small dams, on which, Churchill wrote, 'I was able to give most experienced advice'.

At a lunch on August 15 Churchill addressed the Ottawa branch of the Canadian Club, and, in the presence of Willingdon, Borden and Mackenzie King, deprecated all suggestions of Empire Free Trade. That same afternoon he sent his wife a full account of his Montreal and Ottawa speeches:

I took a great deal of time and trouble over them on account of the unfamiliar atmosphere and also because of the delicacy of the topic—The audiences were very large and overflowing and most enthusiastic. I have been everywhere welcomed in the warmest manner. Men whom I have not seen for thirty years, but whom I ran across in my wanderings have come up in twos and threes at every place to shake hands.

Today a former Sergeant of the Engineers, who helped me in 98 make my plans for the battle of Omdurman for the 'River War', held me up in the street, introduced himself and presented me with a box of excellent cigars for use on my journey. He was in quite humble circumstances and I was greatly touched.

Churchill ended his letter on a more personal note: 'Randolph has conducted himself in a most dutiful manner and is an admirable companion. I think he has made a good impression on everybody. He is taking a most intelligent interest in everything, and is a remarkable critic and appreciater of the speeches I make and the people we meet.'

On the morning of August 16 the *Mount Royal* reached Toronto, and at lunch that day Churchill made yet another speech. The meeting was attended, he wrote to his wife six days later, 'by three thousand of the keenest looking fellows I saw'. On the following day Churchill spent the morning at Niagara Falls, before rejoining his train for the journey westward. At Winnipeg, on August 21, he visited the Wheat Exchange, where, as he wrote to his wife two days later, 'frantic dealers screamed

---

[1] Freeman Freeman-Thomas, 1866–1941. Educated at Eton and Trinity College Cambridge. Liberal MP 1900–06 and 1906–10. Junior Lord of the Treasury, 1905–12. Created Baron Willingdon, 1910. Governor of Bombay, 1913–19 and of Madras, 1919–24. Created Viscount, 1924. Governor-General of Canada, 1926–31. Created Earl, 1931. Privy Councillor, 1931. Viceroy of India, 1931–36. Created Marquess, 1936. His elder son, born in 1893, was killed in action on the western front on 14 September 1914.

and gesticulated as the telegrams from all the world recorded the cease-less fluctuations of wheat prices'. From Winnipeg he visited the Lake of the Woods, writing enthusiastically to his wife: 'This was a day you would have really enjoyed. . . . Any one of these islands could be made into a most beautiful summer residence and Randolph and I have given notice of our intention to buy one unless on our journeys we see some-thing we like better. The brilliant aspect of this lake has left a strong impression on my mind and some day I shall have to show it to you.'

From the Lake of the Woods, Churchill returned to Winnipeg, and then proceeded westwards to Regina, where, on August 21, he again spoke on imperial and international affairs. Three days later, after a visit to the Calgary oilfields, Randolph remarked to his father how depressing it was to see so many oil magnates 'pigging up beautiful valleys to make fortunes', yet at the same time being too uncultured to know how to spend their money properly. 'Instantly Papa flared up,' Randolph noted in his diary. 'Cultured people,' his father told him, 'are merely the glittering scum which floats upon the deep river of produc-tion.'

On Sunday August 25 Churchill sent his wife a long description of the Calgary oilfields, and of the natural gas by which the city was heated. 'I went into the whole process in detail,' he wrote, '& could now write a fairly lucid article on it.' From the oilfields the Churchills drove to the Prince of Wales' ranch at High River. That evening Churchill wrote to his wife:

We went for a long ride all morning on sure-footed ponies galloping up and down the hills and obtaining wide views of rolling fertile country on wh every kind of crop & stock can be produced, and under which may lie fiery fortunes. The panorama of the Rocky mountains rises along the Western horizon in endless serrated ridges to grey blue peaks forty miles away, five thousand feet above this place and nine above the sea. In this vast labyrinth of mountains we shall spend the next week and then descend upon the Pacific. Randolph is in the seventh Heaven. . . .

Throughout his visit to each Canadian town, and during the long car journeys to outlying areas, Churchill pressed his hosts to tell him both about local politics and about local business. 'What fun they have in these rising towns and fast developing provinces!' he wrote to his wife in his letter of August 25. 'All the buoyancy of an expanding world and all the keenness of the political game played out with fine Eighteenth Century rigour!' Of one farmer and his wife whom he visited, he wrote: 'It was an abode of toil. However they seemed happy living in this primitive way.'

On Monday August 26 the *Mount Royal* reached Calgary, where Churchill made another speech. On the following day, from Banff, he wrote to his wife: 'We have never ceased travelling, starting, stopping, packing, unpacking, scarcely ever two nights in any one bed except the train; & eight nights running in that. Racket of trains, racket of motor, racket of people, racket of speeches! I have made 9 & have 2 more. It has been a whirl.' After less than three weeks in Canada, Churchill was exhilarated by all that he had seen and heard, telling his wife:

Never in my whole life have I been welcomed with so much genuine interest & admiration as throughout this vast country. All parties & classes have mingled in the welcome. The workmen in the streets, the girls who work the lifts, the ex-service men, the farmers, up to the highest functionaries have shewn such unaffected pleasure to see me & shake hands that I am profoundly touched; & I intend to devote my strength to interpreting Canada to our own people & vice versa; & to bringing about an even closer association between us.

In his letter of August 27, Churchill also wrote at length of his financial situation. Since leaving England less than a month before, his contracts, articles and investments had earned him an extra £5,750.[1] 'I hope,' he added, 'to make some successful investments here & in the US; & am glad to be able to find a little capital for that purpose. So you do not need to worry about money. The more we can save the better, but there is enough for all of us.'

During the journey across Canada, Churchill had reflected on his political position in England. With the emergence of Neville Chamberlain as Baldwin's obvious successor, he realized that the Conservative Party would no longer need his support. To his wife he wrote, in his letter of August 27:

I have made up my mind that if N. Ch. is made leader of the CP or anyone else of that kind, I clear out of politics & see if I cannot make you & the kittens a little more comfortable before I die. Only one goal still attracts me, & if that were barred I shd quit the dreary field for pastures new.

These 'pastures new' were Canada and business. 'Darling,' he wrote, 'I am greatly attracted to this country. Immense developments are

---

[1] While on board ship Churchill had finished two articles, one on Lord Morley for *Nash's Pall Mall Magazine* and the other on 'Will the British Empire Survive' for *Answers*: these would bring him £750. Canadian sales of *The Aftermath* added a further £250. There were share profits of £250 since he had left London, and some investments in electric shares which Sir Harry McGowan had made for him had produced a profit of £2,000. An agreement with Lord Camrose to write a series of ten articles on Canada and the United States for the *Daily Telegraph* would bring him a further £2,500.

going forward. There are fortunes to be made in many directions. The tide is flowing strongly.' However, he added, 'the time to take decisions is not yet'.

Churchill also wrote to his wife about Randolph, whose oratorical skill had much impressed him. 'He speaks so well, so dexterous, cool & finished,' Churchill wrote. As for his son's sleeping habits—ten and sometimes twelve hours a day—'I suppose it is his mind & body growing at the same time. I love him vy much.'

On August 28 the Churchills left Banff for their motor tour of the Rockies, finally reaching Vancouver on the evening of September 1. On the following day Churchill opened an exhibition at the suburb New Westminster, and made the twelfth speech of his tour. On September 3 he spoke again, to the Vancouver branch of the Canadian Club. Then, on September 6 he crossed by boat to Victoria, where he made the last speech of his Canadian tour. That evening Randolph recorded in his diary: 'Papa received a rapturous reception—the best he has had. He made a different speech from his stock one, which was an almost perfect example of his oratorical powers.'

Churchill's Canadian journey was at an end. 'We are now on the ship bound to Seattle, American soil and Prohibition,' Randolph wrote in his diary. 'But we are well-equipped. My big flask is full of whisky and the little one contains brandy. I have reserves of both in medicine bottles. It is almost certain that we shall have no trouble. Still if we do, Papa pays the fine, and I get the publicity.'

The Churchills arrived in Puget Sound, their first port of call in the United States, on Saturday September 7. From Seattle they travelled by the ordinary night train to Grant's Pass, where they were met by the British Consul-General at San Francisco, Gerald Campbell,[1] and set off southwards by car. As Churchill explained to his wife:

We packed our light luggage into the motor car and set off on our six hundred mile journey. The greater part of it lay through the woods with these enormous trees. They are really astonishing. One we saw, the biggest, 380 foot high, three thousand or four thousand or even five thousand years old

---

[1] Gerald Campbell, 1874–1964. Educated Repton and Trinity College Cambridge. Entered the Consular Service, 1907. Consul-General San Francisco, 1922–31; New York, 1931–38. Knighted, 1934. United Kingdom High Commissioner in Canada, 1938–41. Director-General, British Information Services, New York, 1941–42. Minister in Washington, 1942–45.

and it took fourteen of us to join our arms around its stem. The motoring was very long, at least ten hours a day and at first we were crowded. . . .

We slept at two small country hotels, at Crescent City and Willit. Everything very simple, very clean, gushing water and hot baths, no servants and no liquor. However Randolph acts as an unfailing Ganymede. Up to the present I have never been without what was necessary.

On Tuesday September 10 the Churchills reached San Francisco. Two days later they drove sixty miles to the Lick Observatory, situated more than four thousand feet above sea-level. Churchill was amazed by all he saw, telling his wife:

Everything—roof, walls, floor, telescope—moves silently and mysteriously on touching a button. First of all they showed us the planet Saturn. To the naked eye this looks like any other star but when, in the great dark hall, I put my eye to the telescope—an object of sublime beauty was disclosed. I enclose a picture postcard of what I saw but you must imagine this all glowing like a brilliant lamp. This spectacle took my breath away. Although I had often heard of the ring of Saturn, I had no conception of the perfectness and splendor of this orb. Indeed, I thought at first that it was the reflection of a powerful electric light which they had forgotten to turn out and could not realize that I was looking at a world 800,000,000 miles away.

Next we saw the moon—then in her first quarter. She was so bright that one's eyes were temporarily blinded after looking for only a few moments. The dawn was just beginning on the moon and all her great mountain tops were bathed in the light while deep violet shadows spread through the craters and valleys. Being little more than one quarter million of miles away one felt one could almost touch her. The telescope actually brought her to within 800 miles of our eyes. . . .

'It appears,' Churchill added, 'that there are several million universes, each consisting of hundreds of millions of suns equipped with planets which again are attended by moons. After contemplating the heavens for some hours one wonders why one worries about the Epping Division.'

On September 13 the Churchills reached the ranch and mansion of their principal Californian host, William Randolph Hearst. Both father and son were mesmerized by the opulence and eccentricity of Hearst's world. Two weeks later, Churchill wrote to his wife:

Hearst was most interesting to meet, & I got to like him—a grave simple child—with no doubt a nasty temper—playing with the most costly toys. A vast income always overspent: ceaseless building & collecting not vy discriminatingly works of art: two magnificent establishments, two charming wives;[1] complete indifference to public opinion, a strong liberal and demo-

[1] A reference to Mrs Hearst, and Marion Davies (Hearst's mistress).

cratic outlook, a 15 million daily circulation, oriental hospitalities, extreme
personal courtesy (to us at any rate) & the appearance of a Quaker elder—
or perhaps better Mormon elder.

On September 17, after four days at San Simeon, the Churchills
were driven to Santa Barbara, where they were to stay for two days,
and on the following morning they drove into Los Angeles, where
Churchill was the guest of honour at a lunch given in his honour at the
Metro-Goldwyn-Meyer studios. Two days later, while resting at Santa
Barbara, he sent his wife plans for twice-weekly lunches and dinners
after his return for 'colleagues & MPs', as well as 'a few business people
who are of importance', now that 'we are in Opposition', and he added:
'You shd have a staff equal to this.' His principal news was to do with
the 'vy great and extraordinarily good fortune' that had affected his
finances. Since writing to her on August 27 he had earned a further
£16,100, including a £6,000 advance for his *Marlborough* volume,
further share profits of £5,200, royalty payments for *The Aftermath* of
£1,700 and payments of nearly £2,000 for further articles.[1] His letter
ended:

So here we have really recovered in a few weeks a small fortune. And this
with the information I can get & now am free to use may earn further
profits in the future. I am trying to keep £20,000 fluid for investment &
speculation with Vickers da Costa & McGowan.[2] This 'mass of manoeuvre'
is of the utmost importance & must not be frittered away.

But apart from this, there is money enough to make us comfortable & well-
mounted in London this autumn.

On September 20 the Churchills were again entertained in Hollywood, lunching at the Montmartre Club with Hearst and Marion
Davies.[3] After lunch they visited several film studios, before driving to

[1] These articles, written for *Nash's Pall Mall Magazine*, were a series of biographical
essays, including 'Trotsky: The Ogre of Europe', and studies of the Russian revolutionary,
Boris Savinkov, and of Marshal Foch. These articles were subsequently reprinted in Churchill's volume *Great Contemporaries* (first published in 1937).

[2] Harry Duncan McGowan, 1874–1961. Industrialist. Chairman of Imperial Chemical
Industries, of the International Nickel Co of Canada, and of the African Explosives and
Chemical Industries Ltd. Knighted, 1918. Elected to the Other Club, 1930. Created Baron,
1937. His son-in-law D'Arcy Melville Stephens was killed in action on 10 November
1942.

[3] Marion Davies, 1900–1961. Educated at the Sacred Heart Convent, Hastings-on-
Hudson, New York. Began her professional career as a dancer in 'Ziegfeld Follies', 1918. Her
first film appearance was in 'Runaway Romany'; she subsequently appeared in many films,
including 'Blondie of the Follies', 'Cain and Mabel' and 'Ever Since Eve'.

Marion Davies' house where they swam in her heated marble pool, and then dined with some sixty other guests, including Charlie Chaplin.[1] 'Papa & Charlie sat up till about 3,' Randolph noted in his diary. 'Papa wants him to act the young Napoleon and has promised to write the Scenario.' Nine days later Churchill wrote to his wife:

We made gt friends with Charlie Chaplin. You cd not help liking him. The boys were fascinated by him. He is a marvellous comedian—bolshy in politics & delightful in conversation. He acted his new film for us in a wonderful way. It is to be his gt attempt to prove that the silent drama or pantomime is superior to the new talkies. Certainly if patter & wit still count for anything it ought to win an easy victory.

The Churchills spent five nights in Los Angeles, staying at the Biltmore hotel. Although 'the last word in hotels', it had cost them nothing, for, as Churchill explained to his wife, the suite itself, the services of a valet-waiter, the use of a motor car and 'every kind of liquor' had all been paid for by 'a hearty banker', James R. Page.[2] As for his daily life, Churchill wrote:

I met all the leading people & have heard on every side that my speech & talks (to circles of ten or twelve) have given much pleasure. I explained to them all about England & her affairs—showing how splendid & tolerant she was, & how we ought to work together. I gave a dinner & a lunch to the leading men. I liked the best mostly British born, & all keenly pro-England. . . .

On September 22 the Churchills went by yacht to Santa Catalina Island, where they spent an hour fishing for swordfish. 'People go for weeks & months,' Churchill told his wife, 'without catching a swordfish —so they all said it was quite useless my going out in the fishing boat wh had been provided—however I went out & of course I caught a monster in 20 minutes!'

On Thursday September 26 Churchill and his party left Los Angeles

---

[1] Charles Spencer Chaplin, 1889–1977. Born in London. Actor and film producer. Built the Chaplin Studios, Hollywood, 1918. Among his films were *The Gold Rush*, *Modern Times*, *The Great Dictator* and *Limelight* (Oscar, 1973). Knighted, 1975.

[2] James Rathwell Page, 1884–1962. Paymaster of the Los Angeles Gas and Electric Corporation, 1901–12. Entered investment banking, 1914. On active service (First Lieutenant, infantry), 1917–19. Banker and philanthropist. Vice-President of the Los Angeles—First National Bank, 1927–29. President of the California Bank, 1930–34; a partner of Page, Hubbard & Asche, 1936–43. President of the Greenwich Corporation, 1943–52. Trustee of the Huntingdon Library and Art Gallery, 1945–62. Chairman of the Finance Committee of the California Institute of Technology, 1954–62.

by car on their journey eastwards. From the Yosemite valley they continued by train, travelling in a private railway car provided by Charles Schwab, across the Mojave desert to Arizona. Their three weeks in California had been successful as well as enjoyable, for on September 30 the British Consul-General in San Francisco, Gerald Campbell, wrote to Churchill that his visit to Hearst at San Simeon had produced 'wonderful and immediate results amongst those who, up to recent times, have been antagonistic towards us and our interests'.

The Churchills travelled in Schwab's railway car for three more days, stopping briefly to visit the Grand Canyon, and reaching Chicago on the morning of October 2, where they were met by Bernard Baruch. Two days later Churchill spoke to the city's Commercial Club, stressing the need for a final naval agreement between Britain and the United States. Both fleets, he said, if ever used, 'will be together for the preservation of peace', but Britain, 'whose life and daily bread have always depended on the sea', would have to be cautious about binding herself 'to limits of naval strength'. He was pleased, he said, that Ramsay MacDonald was in the United States, as the senior British representative at the Anglo-American naval negotiations, for although MacDonald was a political opponent, it was good for Britain to be represented 'by so experienced a statesman and so distinguished a man'.

On October 5 the Churchills left Chicago for New York, travelling in a private railway car belonging to Bernard Baruch, who journeyed with them. Reaching New York, on the following day, they were Baruch's guests at his house on Fifth Avenue. On October 18, a few hours before leaving New York for Washington to visit the Civil War battlefields, Churchill telegraphed to his wife: 'Am vy remiss writing. Much pressed business. Everything continues satisfactory. Arranged twenty two new articles in weeklies, all maturing before June and usual terms, monthly in addition, all involving heavy work on return.' These articles were to earn him £40,000.

During his visit to the Civil War battlefields, which he described in a series of articles for *Colliers* magazine, Churchill was, as he wrote, 'astonished' by the many traces of the fighting which still remained after more than 70 years. 'The farm-houses and the churches still show the scars of shot and shell; the woods are full of trenches and rifle pits; the larger trees are full of bullets. Before the War Museum in Richmond still flies a tattered rebel flag. If you could read men's hearts, you would find that they, too, bear the marks.'

Churchill returned to New York on October 24 where, for six days, he stayed in the flat of Percy Rockefeller,[1] completing his business arrangements and literary contracts. His return to the city coincided with the sudden collapse of the New York stock market—the 'Black Thursday' which ushered in the great crash. That night Churchill dined with Bernard Baruch on Fifth Avenue. 'He had gathered around his table,' Churchill later wrote, 'forty or more of the leading bankers and financiers of New York, and I remember that when one of them proposed my health he addressed the company as "Friends and *former* millionaires".'

On the following day Churchill witnessed the consequences of the disaster at first hand. 'Under my window,' he wrote, 'a gentleman cast himself down fifteen storeys and was dashed to pieces, causing a wild commotion and the arrival of the fire brigade.' His account continued:

I happened to be walking down Wall Street at the worst moment of the panic, and a perfect stranger who recognised me invited me to enter the gallery of the Stock Exchange. I expected to see pandemonium; but the spectacle that met my eyes was one of surprising calm and orderliness. There are only 1,200 members of the New York Stock Exchange, each of whom has paid over £100,000 for his ticket. These gentlemen are precluded by the strongest rules from running or raising their voices unduly. So there they were, walking to and fro like a slow-motion picture of a disturbed ant heap, offering each other enormous blocks of securities at a third of their old prices and half their present value, and for many minutes together finding no one strong enough to pick up the sure fortunes they were compelled to offer.

It was refreshing to exchange this scene of sombre and for the moment, almost helpless liquidation for a window high in a titanic building. The autumn afternoon was bright and clear, and the noble scene stretched to far horizons. Below lay the Hudson and the North Rivers, dotted with numerous tugs and shipping of all kinds, and traversed by the ocean steamers from all over the world moving in and out of the endless rows of docks. Beyond lay all the cities and workshops of the New Jersey shore, pouring out their clouds of smoke and steam. Around towered the mighty buildings of New York, with here and there glimpses far below of streets swarming with human life.

No one who gazed on such a scene could doubt that this financial disaster, huge as it is, cruel as it is to thousands, is only a passing episode in the march of a valiant and serviceable people who by fierce experiment are hewing new paths for man, and showing to all nations much that they should attempt and much that they should avoid.

[1] Percy Avery Rockefeller, 1876–1934. Son of William Rockefeller, head of the Standard Oil Company of New Jersey. Entered his father's office in 1900, on leaving Yale. A director of numerous mining and public utility corporations, and a member of the New York Stock Exchange. Founder of the American Society for the Relief of French War Orphans.

On October 30 Churchill sailed from New York, reaching England on November 5. Two weeks later the *Daily Telegraph* began publication of a series of twelve weekly articles which he had written on his Canadian and American experiences.[1] Just over three weeks after his return, on November 30, he celebrated his fifty-fifth birthday.

---

[1] Churchill subsequently tried to publish his articles on the United States, and actually set them up in print. The book was to be called *American Impressions*, but neither his London or New York publishers would agree to publish it. Another book that Churchill thought of writing at this time was one on Socialism to be called *The Creed of Failure* for which he outlined the first five chapters, but then abandoned.

18

1929–1930: A Growing Isolation

WHILE Churchill was still in the United States, the Royal Commission headed by Sir John Simon was completing its enquiries in India about the possibility of granting the Indians some measure of self-government, especially at a Provincial level. The Labour Government, however, was anxious to mollify Indian nationalist feeling by announcing, in advance of the Simon report, some more comprehensive offer. MacDonald had in mind the offer of eventual 'Dominion Status', or self-government, at both the Provincial and national level, with British control limited to the Viceregal and military spheres. MacDonald also hoped that Baldwin would agree to make this new policy a bi-partisan one, especially as it was strongly supported by the Viceroy, Lord Irwin, whom Baldwin had himself sent to India in 1926.

At a meeting of the Shadow Cabinet on October 23, while Churchill was still in New York, Baldwin urged his former Cabinet colleagues to commit the Conservative Party to the Labour Party's goal of eventual Dominion Status for India. Only Churchill, Walter Guinness and Lord Cushendun were unable to attend. Five days later, on October 28, Sir Samuel Hoare sent Irwin an account of the meeting, from which it was clear that the Labour Government's proposed statement on Dominion Status, although favoured by Baldwin, had deeply disturbed some of the leading Conservatives. As Hoare wrote:

Before going in I found Willie Peel outside in a great state about your projected statement. I tried to soothe him, though without much effect. We got on to the question after about half an hour and there was a veritable explosion over it. Stanley said very little indeed, confining himself to reading your proposed statement and saying that he had only approved of it in his personal capacity and not as leader carrying the Party with him. As soon as

I could get a word in, which was not for some time, I said that I had seen you just before you went off and that your view was: (1) that the statement went no further than several previous statements on the subject, (2) that you were convinced the statement would be helpful in avoiding a crisis in January and in obtaining a favourable atmosphere for the Simon Report, (3) that Simon had accepted the statement. As to Simon accepting the statement, I am not quite clear what you told me, but the impression that you left upon my mind was that he had accepted it. According, however, to Willie Peel, F.E., Reading and Lloyd George, he now says that he will resign if the statement is made. If this really is so, I suppose that it would be better not to make the statement.

One of those present at the Shadow Cabinet on October 23, Lord Salisbury, had been uneasy at Irwin's own admission that the policy might, in fact, prove impracticable. 'This being my feeling,' he had written to Baldwin immediately after the meeting:

I need not say what a shock it was to learn that the declaration was to be made before anything had been laid before the Country, though we had appointed a Commission for this very purpose. I do not know what arguments were submitted to you in order to secure your assent but it is cold comfort to me to be told that you—most honourably—were careful not to commit any of us. What a dislocation! Poor Conservative Party!

Of course I recognise that you never dreamed that this step was to be taken without Simon's consent. If this last turns out to be true the proposed proceeding would be frankly incredible. But apart from this extreme absurdity I earnestly hope you will be able to stop it, to convince the Govt and to convince Edward that the Party will be shaken to its centre if we were to assent to a declaration anticipating the Simon Report evidently intended to prejudice the issue upon which the Party if not the Country as a whole is profoundly uneasy.

'We must resist it,' Salisbury added. But Baldwin had made up his mind to support MacDonald, and on October 31 Lord Irwin issued a formal Declaration, stating that 'the natural issue of India's constitutional progress', as contemplated since 1917, was 'the attainment of Dominion Status'.

Churchill returned to England on November 5. That same day, in a letter to Lord Dulverton,[1] Irwin explained his reasons for supporting

---

[1] Gilbert Alan Hamilton Wills, 1880–1956. Educated at Magdalen College Oxford. Succeeded his father as Baronet, 1909. Conservative MP for Taunton, 1912–18; for Weston-super-Mare, 1918–22. On active service at Gallipoli, 1915, and in France, 1917–18 (despatches). President of the Imperial Tobacco Company. Created Baron Dulverton, 1929. His nephew Michael (born 1915) was killed in action in North Africa in 1943.

the Declaration, principles on which the Government's India policy was henceforth based. As Irwin wrote:

The principal reality that I see in Indian politics is whether we can, by adroit handling, prevent the extremist political movement going clean off the rails on separatist lines. It is all very well saying that you can keep them in order and rule them by force and the rest of it. So no doubt you can. But the whole of history seems to teach me that, once separatist ideas take firm hold in the heart of an emotional people, they are pretty difficult to eradicate and lead to progressive damage. After all, it seems to me that between the full responsible Government and what we call Dominion Status, there is no distinction in principle, and that what is important is to make perfectly plain to India that the ultimate purpose for her is not one of perpetual subordination in a white Empire.

Writing to Lane-Fox on the following day, Irwin further explained:

I am very sorry to have been the unwilling cause of what seems to be rather a political storm at home. It almost makes one despair to see the gulf that divides opinion in the two countries. The essential root of it is that the Englishman views Dominion Status as an achieved constitutional state, while the Indian regards it as a hall-mark of constitutional promise of growth. Thus the Indian sees no contradiction in terms as we do when he talks about 'Dominion Status with reservations'.

Two days later, in a letter to Hoare, Irwin explained that it had been impossible for him 'at the last moment' either to suspend or delay his Declaration. 'I had communicated the gist of it in advance to the principal politicians here,' he wrote, 'and they would rightly have been suspicious of any eleventh hour delay.'

On November 8 the Labour Government's India policy was debated in Parliament. In the House of Lords, Lord Reading—a former Viceroy —and Lord Birkenhead—a former Secretary of State for India, both spoke forcefully against it. 'I listened to Reading and F.E. from the steps of the throne,' Davidson wrote to Irwin on November 9. 'It was obvious that Reading was frightened, quite genuinely, of the effect of your statement on Indian opinion.' In the House of Commons on November 7 Baldwin had announced that the Conservative Party supported Mac-Donald, while Lloyd George was critical of the declaration. 'Winston,' Davidson informed Irwin, 'had sat through S.B.'s speech glowering and unhappy; he had sat forward during the "Goat's" speech cheering every mischievous passage in it.' According to Davidson, it seemed that 'about one third' of the Conservative MPs, as well as some Liberals, were prepared to vote against the Irwin Declaration, despite Baldwin's support for it. 'The naked truth,' Geoffrey Dawson wrote to Irwin on

November 13, 'is that his speech, to which I listened, was heard in almost icy silence by the House,' and he added: 'You have S.B. very largely to thank for stemming the tide.'

Hoare also sent Irwin an account of the debate on November 7. Of the Irwin Declaration, he wrote: 'It is certainly true that scarcely anyone in the party liked it,' and he added: 'The diehards were much upset and the old coalition element, Austen, F.E., Winston and Worthy, were violently opposed to it. Indeed, I think that of all our people I was about the only supporter of Stanley's attitude.' Hoare's letter ended: 'Throughout the debate Winston was almost demented with fury and since the debate has scarcely spoken to anyone.'

Lane-Fox also wrote to Irwin on November 13. Had the Declaration been put to the vote, he stated, 'we should have had half our Party in each lobby'. But Party loyalties had rallied in the six days since the debate; 'since they have had time to think,' Lane-Fox reported, 'the vast majority of the Conservatives have returned to their loyalty to S.B. and that the debate, instead of—as some of us were afraid—doing him "serious mortal hurt" as Hopey[1] predicted to me, has done him great good. . . .'

From the moment that Baldwin gave his support to MacDonald's India policy, Conservative criticism of that policy became portrayed as disloyalty to the Party. Indeed, during his speech in favour of the Declaration, Baldwin had felt the need to defend Irwin's character and probity in Party terms. 'If ever the day comes,' he declared, 'when the Party which I lead ceases to attract men of the calibre of Edward Wood, then I have finished with my Party.'[2]

On November 16 Churchill made his first public criticism of Dominion Status. Writing in the *Daily Mail*, he described Britain's rule in India

[1] Lord Alexander John Hope, Earl of Hopetoun, 1887–1952. Educated at Eton. Succeeded his father as 2nd Marquess of Linlithgow, 1908. On active service, 1914–18 (despatches). Commanded the Border Armoured Car Company, 1920–26. Civil Lord of Admiralty, 1922–24. Deputy Chairman of the Conservative Party Organization, 1924–26. Chairman, Royal Commission on Indian Agriculture, 1926–28. Chairman, Joint Select Committee on Indian Constitutional Reform, 1933–34. Chairman, Medical Research Council, 1934–36. Privy Councillor, 1935. Viceroy of India, 1936–43. Knight of the Garter, 1943.

[2] On 24 January 1930 J. C. C. Davidson wrote to Irwin, about Baldwin's position in the Party, and how it would be repaired: 'Never has his stock been so low, and, of course, the daily vendetta in the *Daily Mail*, based at the moment mainly on his India speech, is having its effect. . . . This S.B. is going to give the party and the country in about ten day's time, and when he does it and the machine is able to go full steam ahead then I believe myself that the whole situation will be changed, and that S.B.'s stock will go to a premium, and the Party will get the enthusiastic support of the thousands of our rank and file who are waiting for the flag to drop . . .' On 1 February 1930 Lord Winterton wrote to Irwin about Baldwin: 'His hounds trust and like him, and will always come to his voice or horn if he uses either.'

with confidence and pride. 'The rescue of India from ages of barbarism, tyranny, and internecine war,' he wrote, 'and its slow but ceaseless forward march to civilisation constitute upon the whole the finest achievement of our history. This work has been done in four or five generations by the willing sacrifices of the best of our race.' He added:

War has been banished from India; her frontiers have been defended against invasion from the north; famine has been gripped and controlled, and by a patiently evolved and now marvellous organisation the failure of crops in one district is replaced by the surplus of another. Justice has been given—equal between race and race, impartial between man and man. Science, healing or creative, has been harnessed to the service of this immense and, by themselves, helpless population. And by the new streams of health and life and tranquillity which it has been our mission to bring to India, the number of its people has grown even in our own lifetime by scores of millions.

Churchill wrote critically of Hinduism and its influence: 'Progress would have been more swift, health and prosperity more abounding,' he declared, 'if the British civil and technical services in India had not been hampered by the forebearance we promised to observe towards Indian religious and social customs.' Since 1900 there had been two further impediments to progress, 'the growing lack of confidence at home in the reality of our mission', and 'the undermining repercussions of these doubts upon British officials in India'.

Since the war, Churchill continued, it had become 'a declared object' of the British nation 'to aid the peoples of India to become consciously identified with the whole process of their own elevation and advance', and there were no ultimate limits to the assumption by Indians of full responsible Government 'except those limits—hard, physical, obvious, and moral—arising from Time and Facts'. Yet even while waiting for the report of the recently appointed Simon Commission into how this process should be determined, the Labour Government had chosen, 'amid all the Utopian dreams and predatory appetites and subversive movements' which the presence of the Simon Commission in India had excited, to make this new declaration of eventual Dominion Status. Churchill was opposed to any such promise, believing it to be premature, and likely to provoke 'the earnest resistance of the British nation'. He then set out his reasons for rejecting Irwin's declaration as 'criminally mischievous' in the effects it would have, telling his readers:

Dominion status can certainly not be attained by a community which brands and treats sixty millions of its members, fellow human beings, toiling at their side, as 'Untouchables', whose approach is an affront and whose very presence is pollution.

Dominion status can certainly not be attained while India is a prey to fierce racial and religious dissensions and when the withdrawal of British protection would mean the immediate resumption of mediaeval wars.

It cannot be attained while the political classes in India represent only an insignificant fraction of the three hundred and fifty millions for whose welfare we are responsible.

The immediate grant of Dominion Status for India would, Churchill insisted, be a 'crime'; and a crime against which it would be necessary, without delay, 'to marshal the sober and resolute forces of the British Empire, and thus preserve the life and welfare of all the peoples of Hindustan'.

Throughout the ensuing India debates, Churchill never wavered from the views set out in his *Daily Mail* article, that the demand for Dominion Status came from a tiny, disruptive and unrepresentative minority of Indians, and that the rights of sixty million untouchables to a bearable existence would be swept away once Indians became responsible for their own affairs. His unease about the possible effects of the promise of Dominion Status was reinforced on December 23, when an attempt was made to kill Irwin as his train entered Delhi: a bomb placed on the track exploded only a few seconds after the Viceregal carriage had passed over it. That afternoon Irwin received the leading members of the Indian Congress Party, led by Mahatma Gandhi.[1] After expressing concern at the assassination attempt, Gandhi went on to tell Irwin that the promise of eventual Dominion Status must become one of immediate Dominion Status, that it was not the British Parliament but the Indians of India who ought to decide the country's future, that Indians were as capable as Britain of defending India from outside attack, and that he doubted even the Labour Government's sincerity when it said that it would agree to Dominion Status either then or in the future.

As soon as Churchill learnt of the failure of the attempt on Irwin's life he telegraphed his congratulations. 'It is fortunate,' Irwin replied on December 26, 'that the Indians who do these things seem to be less

[1] Mohandas Karamchand Gandhi, 1869–1948. Born in India. Called to the Bar, London, 1889; practised as a barrister in South Africa, 1889–1908; gave up his practice in order to devote himself to championing the rights of Indian settlers in South Africa, 1908; leader of the Passive Resistance Campaign in South Africa, 1908–14; started the Non-Cooperation Movement in India, 1918; given sole authority to lead the national movement by the Indian National Congress, 1921; inaugurated the Civil Disobedience Campaign, 1930; frequently imprisoned; opposed the partition of India into Hindu and Muslim states; severely critical of the Hindu caste-system; assassinated by an orthodox Hindu in 1948, within a year of the creation of India and Pakistan as independent states.

efficient in their execution than in their design.' As for the British protests against his Declaration, Irwin told Churchill:

> Please don't think I am ever likely to forget the sort of point of view that
> you and others have been putting, or indeed that I differ from it. I don't,
> and although the extreme politicians have found it necessary to save their
> faces here, there has never been any serious misunderstanding of the purport
> of what I said. . . .
> Half the problem here is psychological and a case of hurt feelings. I don't
> overrate the politicians, but I do think once Edwin Montagu had set our
> feet upon the present road and unless we are prepared indefinitely to pursue
> methods that I don't think British opinion would long tolerate, you are
> bound to do your utmost to carry some public opinion with you in your task
> of Government.

Irwin's attempt to meet moderate Indian opinion by compromise was
not immediately successful. At the Congress Party meeting in Lahore the
delegates elected as their President a young, outspoken and uncompromising leader, Jawaharlal Nehru;[1] and at midnight on December 31,
by the bank of the Ravi River, the Indian National Congress unfurled
the flag of full Independence, and urged all its members then serving in
Central or Provincial legislatures to resign their seats and to join the
Congress in an all-India campaign of total civil disobedience.

Over the Christmas holidays Churchill had offered Sir John Reith
£100 to be able to broadcast a ten-minute appeal on India. Reith
consulted the Secretary of State for India, Wedgwood Benn,[2] who was,
as Reith later recorded, 'most apprehensive', believing that such a
broadcast 'would do immense harm in India'. Replying to Churchill,
Reith explained that he was unwilling to introduce 'American' methods
into British broadcasting. On January 1 Churchill replied tartly: 'I

---

[1] Jawaharlal Nehru, 1889–1964. Educated at Harrow and Trinity College Cambridge.
Barrister-at-Law, Inner Temple, 1912. Secretary, Home Rule League, Allahabad, 1918.
Member of the All-India Congress Committee, 1918; General Secretary, 1929. Imprisoned
several times. President of the Indian National Congress, 1924, 1936, 1937 and 1946. Chair-
man of the National Planning Committee, 1939. Vice-President, Interim Government of
India, 1946. Prime Minister and Minister for External Affairs from 1947 until his death.

[2] William Wedgwood Benn, 1877–1960. Liberal MP, 1906–27. A Junior Lord of the
Treasury in Asquith's Government, 1910–15. On active service, 1915–19 (Royal Flying Corps,
despatches twice). Joined the Labour Party, 1927. Labour MP, 1928–31 and 1937–42.
Secretary of State for India in Ramsay MacDonald's second Premiership, 1929–31. Created
Viscount Stansgate, 1941. Secretary of State for Air in Clement Attlee's Government, 1945–
46. One of his three sons was killed in action in 1944; another, Anthony Wedgwood Benn,
disclaimed his father's title, and was a member of the Labour Governments of 1964 and
1974.

am sure the American plan would be better than the present British methods of debarring public men from access to a public who wish to hear,' and he added: 'you are certainly obstructing me'.

At the beginning of 1930 the problem of Protection *versus* Free Trade threatened to be as divisive for the Conservatives as India, and Lord Beaverbrook's Empire Free Trade crusade gathered increasing Conservative support. In January Beaverbrook even made an effort to convert Churchill to his cause, and on January 21 Churchill dined with Beaverbrook at Stornoway House in London to discuss the crusade. One of those present was the co-editor of the *Evening Standard*'s Londoner's Diary, Robert Bruce Lockhart,[1] who noted in his own private diary that although Churchill was 'unconvinced', he had given Beaverbrook 'some encouragement'. To Lord Rothermere, who was in New York, Beaverbrook telegraphed on the following day: 'Churchill told me Baldwin has not yet called Shadow Cabinet for purpose of discussing fiscal reforms. He is convinced Baldwin will adopt 1923 programme with vague declarations about Empire development.' Churchill dined again at Stornoway House on January 23, when Bruce Lockhart found him 'very depressed' about his political position. Harold Nicolson,[2] who was also present, noted in his diary:

They talk the whole time about Empire Free Trade. Winston says that he has abandoned all his convictions and clings to the conviction of free trade as the only one which is left to him. But he is clearly disturbed at the effect on the country of Beaverbrook's propaganda. He feels too old to fight it. 'Thirty years ago,' he said, 'I should have welcomed such a combat: now I

---

[1] Robert Bruce Lockhart, 1887–1970. Educated at Fettes College, Berlin and Paris. Entered the Consular Service, 1911; acting Consul General, Moscow, 1915–17. Head of the Special British Mission to the Soviet Government, January 1918; imprisoned for a month, September 1918. Commercial Secretary, Prague, 1919. On private banking business in central Europe, 1922–28. Editorial Staff, *Evening Standard*, 1929–37. Political Intelligence Department, Foreign Office, 1939–40. Director-General of the Political Warfare Executive, 1941–45. Knighted, 1943. Biographer of Jan Masaryk (1951) and author of several volumes of history and memoirs.

[2] Harold George Nicolson, 1886–1968. Son of Sir Arthur Nicolson (1st Baron Carnock). Educated at Wellington and Balliol College Oxford. Entered Foreign Office, 1909; Counsellor, 1925. Served at Teheran, 1925–27 and Berlin, 1927–29. On editorial staff of *Evening Standard*, 1930. National Labour MP for West Leicester, 1935–45. A Governor of the BBC, 1941–46. Joined the Labour Party, 1947. Author and biographer. Knighted, 1953.

dread it.' He seems to think Baldwin absolutely hopeless, and no instructions have been given to the provincial candidates and agents as to the line that decent Conservatives should adopt.

It is quite clear that this Empire Free Trade is going to split the Conservative and possibly the Liberal parties. Winston complains pitiably: 'But Max, Max, you are destroying my party.' Beaverbrook uses every wile to secure if not his support then at least his agreement not to oppose. Winston agrees to the exploitation of the crown colonies and to 'tariffs for negotiation', but he will not agree to anything in the shape of a tax on food. He would prefer freight subsidies.

Beaverbrook's arguments were to no avail. Within a month, on February 19, he sent Lord Rothermere a list of eighteen Conservative MPs who were completely opposed to Empire Free Trade; among them Churchill and Brendan Bracken. Indeed, Churchill went so far as to advise Baldwin to take the initiative against Beaverbrook, for on March 9, Davidson wrote to Lord Tyrrell: 'About a fortnight ago S.B. was pressed very strongly not only by Winston, who was of course the most vocal protagonist, but by all his colleagues to fight . . . by staging a miniature general election in four seats, two in the North, one agricultural and one in or near London.' Churchill was even said to be prepared to allow his own Constituency to be one of the test cases, but Baldwin decided to avoid a direct challenge. 'I am told Winston is denouncing us violently,' Beaverbrook wrote to Rothermere on March 22, 'saying that he is being bullied and dragooned.' Reluctantly, Churchill accepted Baldwin's cautious strategy, but in May an Empire Free Trade candidate, Sir Cyril Cobb,[1] won a by-election at Fulham; a triumph for Beaverbrook and an ominous sign for those like Churchill to whom Protection was anathema. 'Now I suppose the Tory Party will have the millstone of Food Taxes finally clamped round its neck,' Randolph Churchill wrote to his father from Oxford on May 6.[2]

On April 15 Churchill was in the House of Commons to hear his successor Philip Snowden introduce the first Budget of the new Labour Government. Unemployment relief was to rise, and income tax to be increased in order to meet this new charge. Writing in *John Bull* on April 12, Churchill had already denounced 'the Budget of Pains and

---

[1] Cyril Stephen Cobb, 1861–1938. Educated at Newton Abbott College and Merton College Oxford. Barrister. Chairman of the London County Council, 1913–14. Knighted, 1918. Conservative MP for West Fulham, 1918–29, and from 1930 until his death.

[2] Churchill's social relations with Beaverbrook, although curtailed, were not broken off altogether. On July 23 Robert Bruce Lockhart noted in his diary, after dining at Stornoway House: 'Beaverbrook in good form, ragging Winston, who said: "Give me a big navy, and I'll swallow your food taxes." ' On another occasion, asked why he was so friendly towards Beaverbrook, Churchill was said to have replied: 'Some people take drugs. I take Max.'

Penalties which, I fear, lies before us', and had rebuked the Labour Government for its 'new and lavish expenditure' of £20 million on the unemployed. In the Budget debates which ensued, Churchill was the main Conservative speaker.

On June 19 Churchill was the guest of the University of Oxford, where he gave the annual Romanes Lecture. Entitled 'Parliament and the Economic Problem', it was a strong defence of Parliamentary democracy, together with a proposal for a separate Economic Parliament free from political pressures. Churchill told his audience:

I see the Houses of Parliament—and particularly the House of Commons—alone among the senates and chambers of the world a living and ruling entity; the swift vehicle of public opinion; the arena—perhaps fortunately the padded arena—of the inevitable class and social conflict; the College from which the Ministers of State are chosen, and hitherto the solid and unfailing foundation of the executive power.

I regard these parliamentary institutions as precious to us almost beyond compare. They seem to give by far the closest association yet achieved between the life of the people and the action of the state. They possess apparently an unlimited capacity of adaptiveness, and they stand an effective buffer against every form of revolutionary and reactionary violence.

It should be the duty of faithful subjects to preserve these institutions in their healthy vigour, to guard them against the encroachment of external forces, and to revivify them from one generation to another from the springs of national talent, interest, and esteem.[1]

It was in dealing with economic problems, Churchill went on, that Parliament seemed less effective. One may even be pardoned, he said, 'in doubting whether institutions based on adult suffrage could possibly arrive at the right decision upon the intricate propositions of modern business and finance'. Politicians were always looking 'for popular election cries, or the means to work up prejudice against those cries', yet it was now essential to find 'a national policy "to re-invigorate our economic life", and to raise "the material well-being of our whole people" '. Churchill suggested an 'Economic sub-Parliament, debating day after day with fearless detachment from public opinion', and consisting 'of persons of high technical and business qualifications', together with some 100 MPs from the 'political' Parliament, debating as he put it, 'in the open light of day . . . without caring a half-penny who won

---

[1] In a wireless broadcast on 16 January 1934 Churchill argued in favour of a new franchise, which would give a second vote to all heads of households: those people 'who are really bearing the burden and responsibility of our fortunes upon their shoulders, and are pushing and dragging our national barrow up the hill'. This double franchise of several million would, he believed, create a factor for political stability and moderation.

the General Election', and pursuing their task 'day after day without fear, favour or affection'.

On June 20 H. A. L. Fisher[1] wrote to Lord Irwin: 'Winston was down here yesterday, delivering the Romanes lecture. In spite of the fact that he appears to have been speaking for 22 hours on end in the House of Commons, he was as fresh as paint, and gave us an eloquent plea for the establishment of an economic sub-parliament for the solution of our present most urgent problems. He didn't seem to be aware that the Sidney Webbs, Alfred Milner and Arthur Henderson had all been before him in suggesting a measure of this kind.' Fisher added: 'I imagine that he is feeling very uncomfortable as a Free Trader in the Conservative Party, which is now leaning more heavily in the direction of tariffs, and that it would be a great relief to his mind to have the whole economic problem taken out of the political arena and discussed by a body of economic technicians.'

Following his Romanes lecture, Churchill worked at Chartwell on his various literary projects. The main work, the memoirs of his early life, was already partly written in the form of magazine articles, and during April, May and June he had dictated further passages to his new secretary, Mrs Violet Pearman.[2] Henceforth, for nearly nine years, Mrs Pearman was to devote herself to Churchill's work, organising his vast correspondence and making easier his often complicated routine. She also travelled with him during his many working journeys. During July he dictated to her a series of articles which his literary agent Curtis Brown[3]

---

[1] Herbert Albert Laurens Fisher, 1865–1940. Historian. He published his first book, *The Medieval Empire* in 1898, and a further seven books by 1914. Member of the Royal Commission on the Public Services of India, 1912–15 and of the Government Committee on alleged German outrages, 1915. Liberal MP, 1916–18 and 1918–26. President of the Board of Education, 1916–22. A British delegate to the League of Nations Assembly, 1920–22. Warden of New College, Oxford from 1925 until his death. He published his *History of Europe* in 3 volumes in 1935. Governor of the BBC, 1935–39.

[2] Violet Pearman. Served as Churchill's principal secretary from 1929 to 1938. One of those who worked under her, Grace Hamblin, later recalled in a letter to the author: 'In appearance she was tall and striking. She seemed to me to work like a trojan—fast and furious, without stopping. I have never come across anyone who typed so fast! She was always surrounded by papers—a pile of "work to do" on one side and a pile of "work done" on the other. She *ran* up and down stairs. Sir Winston referred to her as "Mrs P." She was devoted to him, and very loyal. She seemed to be in charge of every single thing—not anything special—just *everything*!' In 1938 she was forced by illness to retire, but continued to work for Churchill on a part-time basis at her home near Chartwell until her death in 1941, at the age of 40.

[3] Adam Curtis Brown, 1866–1945. Educated in the United States. Editorial Staff, *Buffalo Express*, 1884–94. *New York Press* Sunday Editor, 1894–98; London correspondent, 1898–1910. Established the International Publishing Bureau, London 1900; Managing Director, 1900–16. Managing Director, Curtis Brown Ltd, Literary Agents, 1916–45.

placed in Britain, the United States, France, Germany, South Africa, Roumania and Poland.

In addition, Churchill had been working since the beginning of the year on a final volume of *The World Crisis*, which would cover the battles of 1914 and 1915 on the Eastern Front—an aspect of the war which he had not dealt with in the five volumes already published. For this new volume General Edmonds provided a series of historical summaries, as well as translations from German histories, maps, and statistical tables, while at the same time Churchill engaged the services of Colonel Charles Hordern[1] for a fee of £500, to collate all the material as it arrived. As a result of his literary activities, Churchill's income for the coming year was likely to exceed £35,000.[2]

On July 5 Churchill and his wife went to Wilton Park, near Salisbury, for the Whitsun weekend. Harold Nicolson, who was also present, recorded in his diary on the following day:

Winston talks long and sadly about Beaverbrook's Empire free trade campaign which he says is ruining the country. He says it will hand over South America to the Yanks, split the Empire for ever, and shatter the Conservative Party into smithereens. He is writing three books: one a last volume of the *World Crisis*; one a life of the Duke of Marlborough; one of reminiscences of his own. He is in gentle and intelligent form.

On August 2 Churchill sent Baldwin the proofs of his memoirs, which he had decided to call *My Early Life*. 'Any comments which occur to you,' he wrote, 'either favourable or unfavourable, or any advice, will always be received by me with customary respect!' But Baldwin had no changes to suggest, writing from Aix-les-Bains on September 4:

I like the part of the chapter on books and your reading them like a young lion tasting meat for the first time: that all helps to explain and illuminate the personality which emerges as quite an engaging one!

[1] Charles Hordern, 1880–1972. 2nd Lieutenant, Royal Engineers, 1899; Captain, 1908; Major, 1915. General Staff Officer, British Force in Italy, 1918. Employed in the Foreign Office, 1920–24. Lieutenant Colonel, 1925. Retired from the Army, 1929. Author of one of the official histories of the First World War, *Military Operations: East Africa*, published in 1941. Re-employed at the War Office, 1941–43.

[2] During July Churchill listed, in a private note, the sums which he expected to receive. These were: £3,000 for his articles in the *Strand Magazine*, £750 in royalties for the volumes of *The World Crisis* already published; £375 from *Colliers Magazine*; £1,000 from shares and investments and £500 from his Parliamentary salary; £1,000 from an abridged, single-volume edition of *The World Crisis* which was about to be published: £4,000 from *My Early Life*; £5,000 from *The Eastern Front*; and as much as £14,000 from the book and serial rights of the Marlborough volume, which he now hoped to complete during 1932. He was also hoping to be paid £2,000 for the serial rights of his memoirs, and £3,500 for a new series of articles being negotiated in the United States with the Hearst group of publishers.

No, my dear Winston, it is a remarkable production and I have read it with real delight. I kept saying 'My wig' or words to that effect 'that is GOOD'.

And it is jolly good. I wish I could do anything half as good. One thing is certain. You will be read, and annotated, and examined and compared, by every one who studies or attempts to write the history of these times, and that will be fun although we shan't be there to see it.

'The public,' Baldwin added, 'will clamour for more,' and three days later Aircraftman Shaw—T. E. Lawrence—wrote from RAF Mount Batten, Plymouth:

A hundred times as I read it I knocked my hands together, saying 'That's himself'. I wonder if those who do not know you (the unfortunate majority today, and all the future) will see the whole Winston in the book, or not? I rather fancy they will. . . .

Another thing I felt as I read it, and that was how past is the epoch of your youth. Nothing of the world, or attitude or society you lived in remains. Not even yourself, for the Winston of today is altogether another man. Part of your excellence lies in that flawless evocation of a temporis acti. It has gone, yet you can bring it to life, just in time. Your book will become a most precious social document.

The ripe & merry wisdom, and the courage and flair and judgment I take rather for granted, having seen you so much in action: but as your current reputation is not all made by your friends, the book will do you good amongst your readers. Not many people could have lived 25 years so without malice. . . .

Beginning on August 30 *My Early Life* was serialized daily in the *News Chronicle*, and the volume itself was published on October 20. 'I am hopeful,' Churchill wrote to Baldwin on September 24, 'that the book will do more than it was originally written to do, namely to pay the Tax Collector. There may even be a small surplus to nourish the author and his family.' The volume spanned in detail his first twenty-six years, carrying his story from his birth in 1874 to the death of Queen Victoria in 1901. 'When I survey this work as a whole,' Churchill wrote in his preface, 'I find I have drawn a picture of a vanished age'; and he continued:

I was a child of the Victorian era, when the structure of our country seemed firmly set, when its position in trade and on the seas was unrivalled, and when the realization of the greatness of our Empire and of our duty to preserve it was ever growing stronger. In those days the dominant forces in Great Britain were very sure of themselves and of their doctrines. They thought they could teach the world the art of government, and the science of economics. They were sure they were supreme at sea and consequently safe at home. They rested therefore sedately under the convictions of power and security. Very different is the aspect of these anxious and dubious times.

Churchill sent out more than a hundred personal copies of *My Early Life* to friends and colleagues. 'I shall recapture some of the magic of those long evenings at Chartwell,' P. J. Grigg wrote on October 18, 'when you were in reminiscent mood & I exceptionally was content to listen in fascinated and happy silence.' On October 20 Ramsay Mac-Donald wrote by hand from 10 Downing Street, thanking him for the volume, and adding: 'When I have the hardihood to put mine in the window you will have a copy in grateful exchange for this. But then, there is no chance of mine ever coming unless some old fishwife turns biographer. You are an interesting cuss—I, a dull dog. May yours bring you both credit & cash.' Two days later G. M. Trevelyan[1] wrote from Cambridge: 'So long as you are with us, it cannot be said that the race of statesmen who are men of letters is extinct.'[2]

After more than a year out of office, Churchill found himself in profound dispute with his fellow Conservative leaders on many issues. Writing to Beaverbrook on September 23, Churchill had contrasted their two situations, and had expressed his own concern. 'No one that I know of,' he wrote, 'has ever risen to the first rank in politics in so short a space. Naturally I regret that the growth of your influence should have been almost exactly proportionate to the diminution of mine. Still I am old enough to take a philosophical view of these things.' It had become a matter of urgency, Churchill added, for the political power of the Press to be exerted 'to help our Island out of the rotten state into which it has now fallen'; and he went on:

When I think of the way in which we poured out blood and money to take Contalmaison or to hold Ypres, I cannot understand why it is we should now throw away our conquests and our inheritance with both hands, through helplessness and pusillanimity. In this disastrous year we have written ourselves down as a second class Naval Power, squandered our authority in

[1] George Macaulay Trevelyan, 1876–1962. Educated at Harrow and Trinity College Cambridge. Historian; author of seven books before 1914, including a trilogy about Garibaldi. Commandant, 1st British Ambulance Unit for Italy, 1915–18. Regius Professor of Modern History at Cambridge, 1927–40. Order of Merit, 1930. Master of Trinity College Cambridge, 1940. Chancellor of Durham University, 1949–57. Among his books was *Blenheim* (1930), and a biography of Sir Edward Grey (1937).

[2] *My Early Life* was an immediate success, and within six weeks of publication had sold over 8,000 copies in Britain and 5,000 in the United States.

Egypt, and brought India to a position when the miserable public take it as an open question whether we should not clear out of the country altogether. Currently with all this, we have so reduced our reputation abroad and among our own dominions, that as you said the other night 'they all think we are down and out'.

My only interest in politics is to see this position retrieved. I am sure it can be retrieved if you will help and be a friend, a guide, and an inspiration to the Conservative Party, instead of a dancing master teaching with much severity a somewhat old-fashioned minuet. . . .

Churchill's letter ended:

Instead of all crabbing each other, we ought to be all helping each other, passing the ball from one to another, everyone helping the other as much as he can. And of course we must gather the Liberals to us. I do not think there will ever be a Government in England capable of restoring the position, which has not got behind it a real majority of the Nation.

19

India and Free Trade, 1930–1931: 'A Real Parting of the Ways'

DURING the summer of 1930 Ramsay MacDonald and Lord Irwin evolved their India policy, to the unease of many Conservatives; the Party, as Lane-Fox wrote to Irwin on June 25, being 'not very comfortable'. On July 2 MacDonald himself pointed out to Irwin how isolated Baldwin had become, and that although he wanted to help the Labour Government's India policy 'he is tied up'. Each of Baldwin's 'immediate counsellors', MacDonald added, 'appears to be opposed to your position'. On July 10 Geoffrey Dawson wrote to Irwin: 'I have been trotting around between Benn, Baldwin, Reading and the rest, and doing what I could to keep them together. *I am sure you underrate the importance of this.* The tide here is running pretty strongly against your ideas, and you cannot hope to carry them out by depending on the Labour Party alone.'

At the end of September the Labour Government announced, with Baldwin's approval, that a Round-Table Conference of British and Indian leaders would be summoned to London in October to discuss India's future. Alarmed at Conservative opposition to Dominion Status, Sir Samuel Hoare was worried about the choice of the Conservative delegates to the conference. On July 15 he had written to Lord Irwin: 'Assuming that it is inevitable, I am sure that you will be wise to say a word, if possible, to Stanley in favour of a very careful selection of the Conservative representatives. If you do not do this, he will take the line of least resistance and put the whole thing into the hands of the elder statesmen, whose names you and I know at once, and who will maintain the kind of position set up by Reading last November. The Conservative Party is obviously very worried about India and is terrified of a repetition of the Irish negotiations . . .' Speaking on August 20 to a Conservative meeting at Lord Carson's house near Thanet, Churchill warned that the promise of eventual Dominion Status had already begun to undermine British authority in India. Afridi tribesmen from the North-West Frontier, he pointed out, had actually attacked Peshawar, a city with a large British garrison. 'Such a lamentable spectacle,' he continued, 'would have been impossible in former times. To go into the mountains to fight an Afridi was like going into the water to fight a shark; but here was the shark coming out on to the beach!' Thirty years ago, when he 'knew something of the Indian frontier, those marauding invaders would have been destroyed or hunted back to their mountains with the heaviest losses'.

The Afridis had only emerged from the hills, Churchill believed, because they had been led to believe 'that Lord Irwin's Government was clearing out of India, and that rich spoils lay open to their raids'. This, he said, was 'the sinister feature of the event', and it had been encouraged by the fact that Irwin, having imprisoned Gandhi for a deliberate breach of the Salt laws, had then allowed him 'to hold Cabinet councils with fellow-conspirators in gaol'—including Jawaharlal Nehru—'while the great governing organism, upon whose calm strength the lives and livelihood of uncounted millions depended, waited cap in hand outside the cell door hoping to wheedle a few kind words out of their prisoner'.[1]

Churchill went on to criticize the Government's decision to exclude Sir John Simon from the Round-Table Conference, despite his three-year study of the Indian constitution. Simon's exclusion, he said, had been decided upon not for constitutional reasons, but in order to try to placate Gandhi—'this malevolent fanatic'—and at the request 'of a handful of disloyal Indian politicians'. Such a decision was, Churchill believed, both 'abject and foolish, reflecting nothing but discredit on those responsible for it, whether here or in India'. The original plan, he stressed, had been to await the Simon Commission report, then to submit it to a Joint Committee of the House of Parliament, and finally to proceed with Parliamentary legislation. All this had been swept aside

---

[1] Irwin had expressed his own view of Gandhi on 6 March 1929, when he wrote privately to Lionel Curtis: 'I am afraid he will never see sense at all, and the truth is that people of his temperament become a public danger when they adopt the role of political leader.' On April 21 Irwin wrote to Dawson, about the Salt march: 'I have no doubt we were right to let him reach the sea, but I have had growing doubts whether we have been right since. The effect has been definitely bad in Gujerat, and I suspect in Bombay, and I also suspect, from what Villiers of the European Association told me today, in Calcutta. If I could have looked with any confidence to getting through this trouble in the near future without taking the step, I should have been glad to do so, for I think the Indian mind does distinguish sharply between this highly irritating saint and the more avowedly political Jawaharlal.'

in favour of 'a large lively circus' of British and Indian delegates. Churchill warned: 'It is very wrong to encourage false hopes in the minds of the Indian political classes. They are only a handful compared to the vast Indian masses for whom we are responsible, but they are entitled to be treated with good faith and sincerity. It would be wrong to lure and coax them over here with vague phrases about Dominion status in their lifetime.'

On the day after Churchill's Thanet speech, Lane-Fox wrote to Irwin that 'a good many Conservatives' believed that Simon had been 'deliberately' excluded from the Round-Table Conference 'in order to make it easier for our recommendations to be ignored'. There was, he wrote, 'a great risk of people like Winston stampeding the Conservatives by the cry that the Socialists are giving India away to the politician minority in India', and his letter continued: 'when the Conference takes place, and the people here realise more fully than they do now, how much Indians are expecting from it, I am afraid there may be a reaction against concession, and that things may be said which may send the Indians back saying that they have been sold again. Winston's latest speech seems deliberately framed to upset Indian opinion, and he uses just the very sort of phrases which we did our best in our Report to avoid.'

During September the civil disobedience campaign launched by Congress led to violence and bloodshed throughout India, mass arrests, and repeated demands for complete independence. On September 24 Churchill wrote to Baldwin from Chartwell:

What times we are in! The most serious of all our problems is India. I am now receiving, in consequence of my speeches, streams of letters from our people in India and the feeling of anxiety that we are being let down, that we are throwing away our position with both our hands, that we are marching up to an impossible solution—is enjoined by all.[1]

I do earnestly hope you will not allow your friendship with Irwin to affect your judgement or the action of your Party upon what, since the War, is probably the greatest question Englishmen have had to settle. Very strong currents of feeling and even passion are moving under the stagnant surface of our affairs, and I must confess myself to care more about this business than anything else in public life.

[1] On September 17 Field Marshal Sir Claud Jacob had sent Churchill a letter from Brigadier Giles of the Indian Cavalry which he described as 'one of the many similar ones I & others have been receiving from India lately', describing the spread of violence and lawlessness in Bombay: 'that such a state of affairs should be possible', Jacob wrote, 'is astounding'. Churchill replied to Jacob on the following day: 'We are galloping downhill.'

Churchill invited Baldwin to Chartwell. 'I have many works of construction to show you,' he wrote. And he added: 'When the sun shines I would rather be here than anywhere in the world.'

On September 28 Churchill issued a brief statement, which was published in the newspapers on the following day, declaring that he had no intention of considering retirement from public life while the question of India was still undecided. 'I am certain that a very stiff fight lies ahead of us,' Lord Burnham wrote to him later that day, 'and the scales are most unfairly weighted against such of us as believe that our betrayal of India would be a crime against civilisation and, for this country, what poor Rosebery once called "the end of all things".' Burnham added: 'F.E.'s illness is a great blow, but all the more do we need a leader who can put the case as trenchantly as you did in a platform speech you made the other day. . . . The real tragedy is that India is crying out to be governed and we refuse to govern. What is lacking on our part is strength and sincerity.'

Churchill had hoped that Lord Birkenhead would join with him in influencing the Conservatives against the new Indian policy. But Birkenhead had been gravely ill for some months, and on September 30 he died. In a tribute to him on October 1 Churchill wrote: 'He was the most faithful, valiant friend any man could have, and a wise, learned, delightful companion. . . . All who knew him well will mourn him and miss him often. But even more is our country the poorer. These are the times when he is needed most.' That same day Churchill wrote to Sir Claud Jacob:[1] 'I am deeply concerned about the folly and weakness which is going to throw India into hideous confusion. It is tragical that F.E. should be taken from us at this period when he would have been of decisive importance.'

On October 11 Sir Mark Hunter[2] sent Churchill details of a new organization, the Indian Empire Society, which had been set up, he explained, in view of 'the perilous situation in India' to warn as widely as possible 'of the dangers which now lie directly ahead of us'. The Society's six-man Executive Committee was made up entirely of

---

[1] Claud William Jacob, 1863–1948. Entered the Army, 1882. Major, Indian Army, 1901. Brigade-Commander, Dehra Dun Brigade, BEF, 1914–15. Divisional Commander, Meerut Division, 1915; 21st Division, 1915–16. Commanded the II Army Corps, 1916–19. Lieutenant-General, 1917. Knighted, 1917. General, 1920. Chief of the General Staff, India, 1920–24. Commander-in-Chief, India, 1925. Field-Marshal, 1926. Secretary of the Military Department, India Office, 1926–30.

[2] John Mark Somers Hunter, 1865–1932. Educated at St Edmund Hall Oxford. Made his career in the Indian Educational Service, being at one time Professor of English at Madras, and subsequently Director of Public Instruction, Burma. Knighted, 1923.

ex-Governors of Indian Provinces, and their manifesto, which Hunter enclosed with his letter, declared adherence to the provision in the Government of India Act of 1919, 'that India should remâin an integral part of the British Empire'; it also reiterated Britain's special responsibility towards those tens of millions of peasants, industrial workers, minorities, untouchables and tribesmen 'who are incapable of protecting their own interests under any elective system'.

Before Churchill could reply to Sir Mark Hunter's invitation to join the Indian Empire Society, the Tariff question underwent a further, and for Churchill unacceptable, development. At the beginning of October Baldwin decided to accept Neville Chamberlain's demand for a specific Conservative pledge on Tariffs at the next election. His decision was set out in a public letter to Chamberlain on October 14, and constituted a formal pledge which could not be reversed. Churchill's immediate reaction was to dissociate himself publicly from the new policy. This he did in a draft letter to Baldwin that same day; a letter which, on reflection, he decided not to issue to the Press, but which expressed his total opposition to Tariffs. 'I refuse categorically,' he wrote, 'to seek a mandate from the electorate to impose taxes upon the staple foods of this overcrowded island. There are perhaps twenty million people alive in Great Britain to-day who would not be in existence but for their power to purchase at world prices world wheat and meat, with neither of which they can ever adequately supply themselves.' Churchill's letter continued:

The electorate has been recently enlarged by the addition of many new millions of consumers. A profound uneasiness will be created throughout the whole mass of the people by vague general declarations of an intention to tax their staple foods. This uneasiness may well rob the Conservative Party of an effective victory at the polls at a time when the installation of a strong and stable government is the first condition of prosperity.

But I by no means base my objections upon mere electioneering, though that is certainly not to be disdained. I hold, as I have held for the last quarter-century, that it would be a disastrous error in Imperial statecraft to try to base the unity of the British Empire upon the protective taxation of staple foods or raw materials. Experience shows that all commodities dependent upon climatic conditions are subject to great variations in price. The imposition of even a small tax on such commodities would be violently resented by the nation as soon as prices began to rise. Prices are now abnormally low; they are bound to rise in future years, and these taxes upon which it is sought to found treaties with the Dominions, will rightly or wrongly be saddled with the whole blame. Not only should we lessen and perhaps destroy our chance of securing a Conservative or non-Socialist government, but we should expose the newly-forged links of Imperial union to the most perilous strains. . . .

Instead of issuing this letter to the Press as he had originally intended, Churchill took it with him when he spoke to Baldwin in person on the morning of October 14, when he declared that he would be unable to support the Conservatives at the next election on a Tariff platform. That same night Baldwin wrote to Churchill:

My dear Winston,

I cannot go to bed to-night without sending you a line, to assure you that if you adhere to what you said this morning there will be no feeling on my part that you have in any way let me down, nothing but profound regret that there is a real parting of the ways and a friendship towards you which has grown up through six years of loyal and strenuous work together. Six years ago, we knew little of each other. We have had good times and bad times and have come through them side by side and the memory of them will abide.

To what your further reflections may lead you, I cannot tell.

But for to-night I still cherish the hope that you may yet see your way to stay with us. Bob Cecil is the only colleague I have lost in seven and a half years: I cannot have many more years before me, and it would be a joy to feel that I had kept the leaders of our party together until the end.

But whatever happens, I am your sincere friend

Stanley Baldwin

Churchill's talk with Baldwin constituted a private, but definite breach between himself and the Conservative leadership. That same day he wrote to Sir Mark Hunter, formally joining the Indian Empire Society, and sending them his subscription. During the day Churchill and Lord Reading discussed the political situation with the Counsellor at the German Embassy, Prince Bismarck,[1] who noted in a secret memorandum of the conversation that Churchill 'expressed extreme concern over Britain's domestic political situation, especially over the present discords within the Conservative Party. Baldwin's position had been made quite impossible by the concentrated attacks of the two press lords, Beaverbrook and Rothermere.' Bismarck added that Churchill 'could not at present see any solution to his party's difficult position. There was no one who could take Baldwin's place.' At the end of the discussion both Churchill and Reading expressed, as Bismarck noted, 'great anxiety over the forthcoming Indian Round Table Conference'.

[1] Prince Otto Christian Archibald von Bismarck, 1897–1976. Grandson of the German Chancellor. On active service, 1915–18 in the Garde du Corps. Studied law at Kiel University, 1919, and subsequently elected to the Reichstag. Served in the German Embassy in London, 1926–39. German Minister in Rome, 1940–43. A member of the Bundestag (Christian Democrat), 1953–65.

2. Churchill and his wife immediately after his defeat at the Abbey by-election, Westminster, 19 March 1924

3. Churchill driving to Buckingham Palace to receive the seal of Chancellor of the Exchequer from King George V, 7 November 1924

4. Austen Chamberlain (Foreign Secretary), Stanley Baldwin (Prime Minister) and Churchill (Chancellor of the Exchequer). A photograph taken in 1925

5. Churchill leaving 11 Downing Street to announce his first
Budget, 28 April 1925

6. Churchill photographed outside 10 Downing Street on 3 May 1926, at the start of the General Strike

7. Randolph Churchill (aged seventeen), Madame Chanel and Churchill at the Duke of Westminster's boarhounds, Dampierre, France, 8 April 1928

8. Sarah (aged thirteen) and Mary (aged five) helping their father to build a cottage at Chartwell, 1928

9. Churchill in Whitehall, on his way from Downing Street to the House of Commons to deliver his 4th Budget, 24 April 1928. With him is Robert Boothby (in top hat), Diana Churchill (aged seventeen) and (on Churchill's left) his plain clothes detective, Sergeant Thompson

10. Churchill leaving Downing Street after a Cabinet meeting: a photograph taken in 1929

11. Sergeant Thompson, Robert Boothby, Churchill, Mrs Churchill, Sarah and Randolph walk down Whitehall to the House of Commons for Churchill's 5th and final Budget, 15 April 1929

12. Churchill and Lord Cushendun at Windsor Station, on their way to surrender their seals of office to the King, 7 June 1929

13. Churchill leaving Southampton for Canada on board the Canadian Pacific Liner 'Empress of Australia', 3 August 1929. With him is his brother Jack, and the captain of the ship, Captain Latts

14. Churchill in Canada, 25 August 1929

15. Churchill and Lloyd George at the memorial service for
Lord Balfour, Westminster Abbey, 22 March 1930

16. Ramsay MacDonald

17. Sir Maurice Hankey

18. Austen Chamberlain, Sir Robert Horne and Churchill after a Conservative Party meeting at Caxton Hall, London, 30 October 1930

19. Churchill about to address the first meeting of the Indian Empire Society, at the Cannon Street Hotel, London, 12 December 1930

20. The Derby Dinner at the Savoy Hotel, London, 25 May 1933. Standing, left to right, Sir Abe Bailey, Churchill, Lord Derby and Lord Camrose

21. Lord Rothermere

22. Frederick Lindemann

23. Brendan Bracken

24. Maurice Ashley, Churchill's research assistant from 1929 to 1933

25. John Wheldon, Churchill's research assistant in 1934 and 1935

26. Hitler proclaimed by his stormtroopers, and by the populace,
Munich, 10 November 1933

27. Hitler at Buckberg, 1934

28. Sir Samuel Hoare and Stanley Baldwin, a photograph taken on 23 July 1935

29. Churchill speaking on 'National and Imperial Defence' at the City Carlton Club, London, 26 September 1935

30. Churchill painting: a photograph taken in France by the painter Paul Maze

Both of them, he added, 'strongly blamed the Viceroy, Lord Irwin, for his policy of appeasement'.

On October 21 Baldwin and Neville Chamberlain decided to issue a further public declaration on Protection, aimed at forestalling further pro-Tariff pressure from Beaverbrook. That same day Baldwin wrote to Churchill: 'From what you said in your letter, I fear this may be the occasion when you feel it necessary to express your dissent. I hope not. But I am confident that nothing will disturb a friendship that I value.' Neville Chamberlain also wrote to Churchill about the new declaration:

I am afraid that you may not like the letter to Beaverbrook which will appear tomorrow although it says nothing that is not implicit in the previous statement. But I hope you will consider the whole situation very carefully before taking any irrevocable step. We have not pledged ourselves to impose taxes on any foreign foodstuff although I have no doubt that such taxes must be involved in any arrangement with the Dominions for mutual preference. But when the position of the staple foods is examined there is at least a strong possibility that taxation may not prove the solution, or if it is required, that it would be on a low scale. . . .

'Whatever you ultimately decide to do,' Chamberlain added, 'I hope we shall not find ourselves driven into opposite camps when there is so much about which we are in agreement.'

Churchill decided not to make any public protest. 'Winston has not yet given tongue to our manifesto,' Davidson wrote to Baldwin on October 23. 'He told Freddie Guest that he was in doubt whether to "lay an egg" or not. To which Freddie replied, "When in doubt whether to lay an egg or not, don't lay it"!'

Not everyone felt that Churchill should remain silent. On October 24 Lord Weir wrote from Glasgow of the existing 'irresolution and nervelessness' of British politics, and added: 'I can well imagine how you feel and how galling it must be to you.' Weir believed that Britain was in need of 'inspiration' and that Churchill could provide it. Nor was he alone in this view. 'Some day you must lead the whole country,' Viscount Knutsford[1] wrote on October 26. 'I look for this.' But Churchill had decided not to try to lead a Conservative break-away faction over Free Trade versus Tariffs, nor did he have the power to do so. 'I propose,' he told Amery early in November, 'to stick to you with all the loyalty of a leech,' and on November 23 Clementine Churchill wrote to

---

[1] Sydney Holland, 1855–1931. Called to the Bar, 1879. Succeeded his father as 2nd Viscount Knutsford, 1914. Director of the Underground Electric Railways Company, and the London and Scottish Life Assurance Company. Chairman of the London Hospital.

her son: 'Politics as you say have taken an orientation not favourable to Papa. Sometimes he is gloomy about this, but fortunately not increasingly so.' And she added: 'The success and praise which have greeted his book counteract his sad moments.'

His great sadness at Lord Birkenhead's death also continued to press upon Churchill during the autumn. On October 30, at a meeting of the Other Club, which he and Birkenhead had founded in 1911, Churchill told those assembled: 'For twenty years we have dined together, but tonight there are more round this board than ever before. That is because tonight we have to mark the loss the Club has sustained in the death of one of its founders and its main support—our dear friend F.E.' Churchill continued:

. . . out of seventy-eight dinners which our small Club has held F.E. attended sixty-eight. We miss his wisdom, his gaiety, the broad human companionship and comradeship which he always displayed and excited from his friends. We admired his grand intellect and massive good sense. He was a rock; a man one could love, a man one could play with, and have happy jolly times. At this narrow table where he sat so often among us, we feel his loss now. He loved this Club. He was always happy here. . . .

I do not think anyone knew him better than I did, and he was, after all, my dearest friend.

Churchill also spoke at the Other Club of 'a loss wider than ours', for, as he explained:

The country is the poorer. Just at the time when we feel that our public men are lacking in the power to dominate events, he has been taken. This was the occasion and these were the very years for the full fruition of his service to our country. He had the calmness of age while still retaining the force and power of his prime, and the questions which are now most grave and urgent are the very ones in which his influence and advice, his experience, his sagacity, his long trained judgment, would have been precious.[1]

---

[1] A few months later Churchill wrote a foreword to a biography of Lord Birkenhead which was being written by his son, the 2nd Earl. In it, Churchill wrote of his friendship with Birkenhead, whom he described as a 'gay, brilliant, lovable, being'. They had been Cabinet colleagues together for nearly ten years, yet Churchill could 'hardly recall any question, certainly none of any importance upon which we were not in hearty and natural agreement'. His tribute continued: 'F.E. was the only one of my contemporaries from conversation with whom I have derived the same pleasure and profit as I got from Balfour, Morley, Asquith, Rosebery and Lloyd George. One did feel after a talk with these men that things were simpler and easier, and that Britain would be strong enough to come through all her troubles. He has gone, and gone when sorely needed.' Churchill added: 'Some men when they die after busy, toilsome, successful lives leave a great stock of scrip and securities, of acres of factories or the goodwill of large undertakings. F.E. banked his treasure in the hearts of his friends, and they will cherish his memory till their time is come.'

As Churchill had feared, Baldwin gave Conservative approval to the Round-Table Conference on India, and selected four Conservative politicians to represent the Party at its deliberations. The Conference opened in London on November 12.[1] Baldwin, who attended the opening session, wrote to Davidson on November 13: 'Our delegation is starting well, but Winston is in the depths of gloom. He wants the Conference to bust up quickly and the Tory party to go back to pre-war and govern with a strong hand. He has become once more the subaltern of hussars of '96.'[2]

Although the Congress Party had boycotted the Round-Table Conference, and both Gandhi and Nehru remained in prison, the Indians present were fully aware of the extent of their power, and pressed for the fullest possible degree of self-government, in the shortest possible time. On December 12 Churchill was the principal speaker at the Cannon Street Hotel, London, to the first public meeting of the Indian Empire Society. During his speech he pointed out that even the moderate Indians at the Round-Table Conference were demanding full Dominion status 'with the right to secede from the British Empire', while the extremists, 'who are, and will remain, the dominant force among the Indian political classes' had already demanded 'absolute' independence.

It was British uncertainty and weakness, Churchill alleged, that had united the conflicting groups inside India: 'On the one hand, you have had the ever-mounting demands; on the other, the ever more apologetic responses.' Hindus and Muslims, Congress and the Princes, upper castes and untouchables, had all been forced to work together on account of 'the weakminded and defeatist tendencies of our present politics', believing that the British regime was coming to an end, and a new authority was 'soon to be erected'. Every Indian group had now to consider what would happen when Britain had gone. 'If the British Raj is to be replaced by the Gandhi Raj, the rulers of the native states must pre-

---

[1] The British Government were represented by three Labour Ministers, four Conservatives and four Liberals. The Labour members were Ramsay MacDonald, Lord Sankey and J. H. Thomas; the Conservatives Sir Samuel Hoare, Lord Peel and Oliver Stanley; the Liberals Sir Robert Hamilton, Lord Reading, Lord Lothian and Isaac Foot. The Indian States were represented by sixteen Princes; and British India by fifty-two Indians, five Englishmen and two more Labour Ministers, Arthur Henderson and Wedgwood Benn.

[2] In a letter to a young Conservative MP, Patrick Donner, on November 29, Neville Chamberlain cast aspersions on Churchill's efforts, warning Donner against those who 'are either hostile to the National Government as a whole, or disposed to join cliques led by men whose motives are much more complicated'. But Chamberlain then went on to express his own doubts about the Government's India policy. 'I, myself', he wrote 'would very much prefer to go much more slowly in the matter of Indian reform, and try a series of cautious experiments, which might perhaps last for fifty years or more, before culminating in a complete system of Central and Provincial self-government'.

pare themselves for a relationship at least as intimate as that which they have had with the old. The same is true of the Muslims. . . . Once the signal of retreat and departure is given, all who are left behind must make terms with the new power,' including the sixty million untouchables, 'denied by the Hindu religion even the semblance of human rights'.

The way to avoid political turmoil in India, Churchill argued, was to concentrate on practical steps 'to advance the material condition of the Indian masses', and to treat with swift severity all extremism and all breaches of the law. The Congress at Lahore, at which the Union Jack had been burnt, ought to have been 'broken up forthwith and its leaders deported'; Gandhi should have been arrested and tried 'as soon as he broke the law'. By firmly asserting 'the will to rule', the British could have avoided the 'immense series of penal measures' which had, in fact, been taken. Churchill added: 'Even now, at any time, the plain assertion of the resolve of Parliament to govern and to guide the destinies of the Indian people in faithful loyalty to Indian interests would in a few years—it might even be in a few months—bring this period of tantalised turmoil to an end.'

Churchill then proposed a solution which would, in his view, halt the strife, and satisfy the political aspirations of the Indian politicians. Each Province should move forward towards 'more real, more intimate, more representative organs of self-government', leaving the central power firmly in British hands, and giving as much autonomy as possible to provincial home rule. Over India as a whole, he believed, all attempts at concessions based on the Montagu–Chelmsford reforms of 1919 had failed. Every service which had been handed over to Indian administration had deteriorated; in particular, Indian agriculture, 'the sole prop of the life of hundreds of millions, has certainly not advanced in accordance with the ever-growing science and organisation of the modern world'. As for the Indians themselves, who were meant to benefit by greater participation at the centre, they had used their new-found political liberties since 1919 'not for the purpose of improving the well-being of India, but merely as convenient tools and processes for political agitation and even sedition'. As a result, there had arisen 'unrest, impoverishment and discontent, drawing with them repressive measures and curtailments of civic liberties, which did not exist before the political liberties were widened'.

Churchill went on to warn that 'the forces of sedition and outrage' could not be satisfied by any decision of the Round-Table Conference, and that any concessions in London would only be 'the starting point for new demands'. He continued: 'The truth is that Gandhi-ism and all it stands for will, sooner or later, have to be grappled with, and finally crushed. It is no use trying to satisfy a tiger by feeding him with cat's-meat. The sooner this is realised, the less trouble and misfortune will there be for all concerned.'

'What a monstrous speech Winston has just made,' Lord Irwin wrote to Geoffrey Dawson on December 13, and in its leading article that same day, *The Times* wrote that Churchill was 'no more representative of the Conservative Party' than 'the assassins of Calcutta' represented the Indians at the Round Table. As for his speech, the paper added, it would have 'just as little influence'.

In the next six months Churchill was to make many speeches on the same themes, hoping thereby to rouse and unite those Conservatives who were already disturbed by their Party's India policy, and to break the informal but strong alliance on Indian policy between Ramsay MacDonald and Stanley Baldwin. But his prospects of success were not thought high. 'I should not be surprised,' Sir Malcolm Hailey[1] wrote to Irwin on December 13, 'if even the general block of Conservatives preferred to follow men like Peel and Sir Samuel Hoare, acting in consultation with Mr Baldwin, than be swayed by the very extreme views of Winston Churchill.' But on December 24, after a series of meetings of Conservative backbenchers, Hailey wrote again to Irwin that 'the influence of Mr Winston Churchill was strong', for, as he went on to explain, 'the general decision took simply the form of stating that in no circumstances would they give any responsible powers to a Central Assembly as now constituted and that they would only agree to giving any extended powers to a federal Government when they were satisfied with the whole scheme of constitution presented . . .' Hailey's letter continued:

One is perhaps beginning to feel that Mr Baldwin may not have been quite correct in believing that he could carry the whole of the Conservative Party in any decision at which he might arrive with the assistance of the Conservative delegates, for it is very clear that there are strong influences on the other side. I understand, for instance, that Mr Winston Churchill openly declared that his first decision was to smash the Conference itself.

[1] William Malcolm Hailey, 1872–1969. Educated Merchant Taylor's School and Corpus Christi College Oxford. Entered the Indian Civil Service, 1895. Chief Commissioner, Delhi, 1912–18. Member of the Viceroy's Executive Council in the Home and Finance Departments, 1919–24. Knighted, 1922. Governor of the Punjab, 1924–28; of the United Provinces, 1928–30 and 1931–34. Member of the Permanent Mandates Commission, League of Nations, 1935–39. Director, African Research Survey, 1935–38. Created Baron, 1936. Chairman, Air Defence Committee, 1937–38. Chairman, Colonial Research Committee, 1943–48. Privy Councillor, 1949. BBC Advisory Council, 1953–56. Order of Merit, 1956.

Even Samuel Hoare was reported to have doubts about the proposed Indian reforms. Writing to Irwin on 2 January 1931, Geoffrey Dawson reported that Hoare 'mellows as each day goes on, but comes back the next morning full of doubts and fears and objections'. In India itself, however, Irwin had decided to embark on the process of conciliation with the extremist Congress leaders, and at the Round-Table Conference it was hoped to attract them to the idea of negotiations and co-operation, through a Federal scheme in which both the Princely States, and the Provinces, would form a single governing instrument at the Centre. On 20 November 1930 the Finance Member of the Viceroy's Council, Sir George Schuster,[1] had written to Irwin of how the idea of an all-India Federation had enabled 'everyone (including our Liberals and Conservatives) to say that the Simon report and the Government of India despatch are both already out of date, because a new situation has arisen since they were written. I should not be surprised to see the Conservatives riding on this excuse and in the end committing themselves to a policy considerably more advanced than that which they have condemned so bitterly when put forward by you . . .'

As the Round-Table Conference continued, a former Viceroy, Lord Reading, who had originally doubted the wisdom of Federation, decided to support it, much to Churchill's distress, and Hoare's position was thereby strengthened. On January 6 Hailey wrote to Irwin of how Hoare was 'quite justifiably keeping his eye on the position which he is creating for himself', and he added: 'If the Conservatives get rid of some of their old diehard elements, such as Lord Brentford,[2] Mr Winston Churchill and the like he would occupy a somewhat important position as being in some ways much more advanced than they but in others not so idealistic as Mr Baldwin himself and some of the younger men like Oliver Stanley.'[3]

[1] George Ernest Schuster, 1881–1982. Educated at Charterhouse and New College Oxford. Barrister, 1905. Director of various companies, 1905–14. On active service in France, 1914–18 and in North Russia, 1919 (Military Cross, despatches four times). Financial Secretary to the Sudan Government, 1922–27. Knighted, 1926. Finance Member of the Viceroy's Executive Council, India, 1928–34. Member of the Colonial Development Advisory Committee, 1936–38. Liberal National MP for Walsall, 1938–45. Treasurer, Medical Research Council, 1947–51. Chairman of the Oxford Regional Hospital Board, 1951–63. One of his two sons was killed in action in 1941.

[2] Sir William Joynson-Hicks, who in 1929 had been created Viscount Brentford.

[3] Oliver Frederick George Stanley, 1896–1950. Son of the 17th Earl of Derby. Educated at Eton. On active service, France, 1914–18 (Military Cross, despatches). Major, 1918. Called to the Bar, 1919. Conservative MP for Westmorland, 1924–45; for Bristol West, 1945–50. Parliamentary Under-Secretary, Home Office, 1931–33. Minister of Transport, 1933–34; of Labour, 1934–35. Privy Councillor, 1934. President of the Board of Education, 1935–37; of the Board of Trade, 1937–40. Secretary of State for War, 1940; for the Colonies, 1942–45.

Churchill was determined to continue with his campaign, and had enlisted Rothermere's support. On January 8, in a letter to his son—who was on a lecture tour in the United States—Churchill explained his own position:

The political situation is increasingly unsatisfactory and my relations with B. are chilly and detached. On the other hand R. and I have come to a definite understanding about India and his papers are all giving me full support. I am going to fight this Indian business à outrance. Perhaps you had a chance of reading my speech in the City in the Morning Post. . . . I am sure that events will justify every word.

On January 30th I am going to speak at Manchester on the same subject. The Indian Empire Society who feed out of my hand, have at my suggestion taken the Free Trade Hall, and the Daily Mail is going to exploit the meeting to the full. We shall see what support we get.

Churchill went on to forecast the eventual collapse of the Labour Government, and the return of Baldwin as Prime Minister. 'He will immediately form a Government and dissolve,' Churchill wrote; but he added:

I have no desire to join such an administration and be saddled with all the burden of whole-hog Protection, plus unlimited doses of Irwinism for India. I shall be much more able to help the country from outside. I feel a great deal stronger since the Indian situation developed, although most people will tell you the opposite. It is a great comfort when one minds the questions one cares about far more than office or party or friendships.

LL.G. has gone definitely to the left and his henchman, Reading, was put up to make a thoroughly defeatist speech on India at the Conference. All this is the effect of the Baldwin, Beaverbrook, Rothermere foolishness during the last year. It will be very difficult indeed to safeguard England's position with the Tories caring very little for else than food taxes, and most of the forces of the centre and left joining up against us. It may well be that the historians of the future will record 'that within a generation of the poor silly people all getting the votes they clamoured for they squandered the treasure which five centuries of wisdom and victory had amassed'.

'I do not know,' Churchill wrote, 'whether you will be able to do anything to stop this. I hope so indeed, but great sacrifices and efforts will be needed, and you should fit yourself constantly for a task which may perhaps be what you have been sent here for.' Churchill's letter ended: 'Very best love my dear Randolph. I pray you may realize all that I hope for you.' Two days later Churchill wrote to his cousin the Duke of Marlborough: 'Politics too foul for written words!' but, he added: 'I am feeling pretty tough and strong.'

On January 19, at the final session of the Indian Round-Table Conference, Ramsay MacDonald declared that although Britain would observe, in framing a constitution for India, 'certain obligations' towards the minorities in order to protect 'their political liberties and rights', nothing would be done to prejudice the advance of India 'to full responsibility for her own government'. The time had come, he said, for 'Indian opinion' to be consulted on the form the constitution should take, and if 'those engaged at present in civil disobedience' were to abandon their campaign of non cooperation, they too would be consulted.

In India itself, Irwin had appealed to the Congress leaders to cooperate in the search for a constitution, but they refused to do so while Gandhi remained in prison. On January 25, in an attempt to break the deadlock, Irwin allowed Gandhi to go free. Before doing so, he had telegraphed to Baldwin on January 23: 'My immediate fear is lest, in the forthcoming debate in Parliament, Winston should make mischief. Do, if you can, get some helpful and cordial speeches made from our side to discount possible bad effect of what he may say. Best of all, speak yourself and send him to Epping for the day.'

Gandhi's release provoked an immediate and widespread protest, both from the British officials in India and from Conservatives in Britain. On the evening of January 26 Churchill spoke in the House of Commons against the course of the Government's India policy and against the proposed Indian constitution. This was his first Parliamentary speech against his own Party's India policy. 'I must, of course, first of all make it clear,' he said, 'that I do not speak for the official Opposition nor for my right hon Friend the Leader of the Opposition. I speak solely as a Member of Parliament, of some service in this House, who holds views upon this matter which might not go unrepresented in this discussion.'

At the outset of his speech Churchill laid great stress on the Government's failure to follow up the report of the Simon Commission, which had been supported by all three political parties, had presented its unanimous report only after 'immense labours, journeys, and studies', and had then had its conclusions 'thrust altogether—though compliments have been paid to it—out of the sequence of events'. He went on to criticize the Irwin Declaration, and to list what he called 'the catalogue of errors and disasters' since it had been issued. The shelving of the Simon report was one; the exclusion of Simon and his fellow Commissioners from the Round-Table Conference was another. 'Our trusted friends,' he said, 'and lawful, formal authoritative advisers were set aside in order to placate those who are the bitterest opponents of British rule in India,' the Congress Party. Yet the Congress leaders had refused to participate in the Conference 'even though it was mutilated . . . to suit their prejudices'. Those Indians who did attend possessed, Churchill declared, 'no power to conclude an agreement and still less any power to enforce it'; yet even these moderate voices had urged 'a responsible Indian Ministry at the summit and centre of Indian affairs', full Dominion status and even the right to secede from the British Empire.

Churchill went on to contrast the promises of self-government put before 'the gleaming eyes of excitable millions' with the 'formidable' powers which Britain would actually retain. He also pointed out that there were sixty thousand Indians in prison for political agitation—'it seems incredible, but it is so'; and the repressive measures and restrictions on civil liberty used to curb political extremism were, he said, 'without precedent in India since the Mutiny, except in some days of the Great War'. The British politicians who welcomed the idea of Indian self-government were, Churchill said, deluding themselves. It was unwise to take comfort, as some had done, from the recent decision of the Indian Princes to accept a future All-India Federal Parliament. This, indeed, was 'the most disquieting feature of all', for, he explained: 'The action of the Princes may well be due to the belief, now spreading so widely throughout the masses of India, that the British Raj will shortly cease to function. . . .'

Churchill argued that the All-India Parliament which was now proposed would quickly be dominated and controlled by Congress, and must inevitably come into rapid and severe conflict with the Viceroy. Yet the Viceroy, in asserting the powers which would still be his, would incur 'all the popular displeasure and odium' of any severe measures. 'We are not relieving ourselves of burdens and responsibilities in India,' Churchill declared, 'we are merely setting the scene for a more complicated controversy, merely creating agencies which will make it more difficult for us to discharge our task.' The All-India Parliament would soon be dominated 'by forces intent on driving us out of the country as quickly as possible'.

Churchill feared a situation where the Viceroy and the Army on the one hand—both to retain wide central powers under Dominion Status—would confront a hostile, extremist-dominated Government, and, in the face of mounting, insatiable hostility, would be forced to use 'that overwhelming physical force which it should be the care and thought of every man wherever he sits never to employ against the natives of India'. Such a confrontation, he believed, would belie the 'one great aim and object' of every British administration in India.

Churchill's final appeal was to the electorate in Britain, and to the British nation. 'For thirty years,' he said, 'I have watched from a central position the manifestations of the will power of Great Britain, and I do not believe our people will consent to be edged, pushed, talked and cozened out of India.' There were, Churchill insisted, 'British rights and interests in India. Two centuries of effort and achievement, lives given on a hundred fields, far more lives given and consumed in faithful and devoted service to the Indian people themselves! All this has earned us rights of our own in India.' His speech ended with a warning that the British public would demand strong action once it saw its women and children 'in hourly peril amidst the Indian multitudes', and that such a confrontation, the worst possible assertion of British rule, was one to which 'step by step and day by day, we are being remorselessly and fatuously conducted'.

It was not Ramsay MacDonald nor Wedgwood Benn, but Stanley Baldwin, who replied to Churchill's speech. In an unqualified defence of the Round-Table Conference, Baldwin pledged both himself and the Conservative Party to 'try to implement' the Indian Constitution which the Conference had outlined, and of which Churchill had been so scathing. Indeed, Baldwin declared, if the Conservatives were returned to power, implementation of that Constitution would become their 'one duty'.

On January 28 Lane-Fox reported to Irwin on the impact of Churchill's speech:

I think our people would have been satisfied to accept the situation as Sam Hoare had left it, that the Conservative Party did not wish to block the Federal solution so much approved by the Conference, but must insist on certain safeguards being real. And when Winston began he had not much support behind him. But I, sitting on the back benches, felt the cleverness of his speech, in the gradual growth of approval among our back benches. They began to feel that this represented their own doubts and what they had been thinking, and gradually quite a number first began to purr and then to cheer.

He was wise enough to say nothing against you, but his speech as you will see was practically an indictment of all advance in India. S.B. very kindly, but very decisively, repudiated his view, but I was conscious that, while S.B. was vigorously cheered by the Socialists, there was an ominous silence on our own benches. And I am afraid this represents the position in our party in many things.

Many think that S.B. is weak and woolly, and is letting the party down, instead of leading it triumphantly against a Government that is manifestly open to easy attack. I am sure he was right in the line that he took, but many of our people are obviously uneasy over his having gone so far, in pledging his party to back the Federal suggestions of the Conference, and to support the policy of this Government.

Lane-Fox went on to comment on Baldwin's response to Churchill's speech:

I don't believe he has ever consulted his colleagues except Sam Hoare with whom he had obviously been dining. And my impression is that he went into that debate without having thought the matter out very carefully, and just drifted on, following his own line of thought. For he told me he was only going to speak for ten minutes and make it clear that he disapproved of Winston. But he spoke for about half an hour—without any notes—and Providence and his own good sense alone were behind him. Good backing, but I think he would have been safer if he had secured the consent of others. For several have suggested to me that his line was a surprise to them, and emanated from himself alone.

Churchill's parliamentary denunciation of the new policy, and Baldwin's immediate defence of it, marked Churchill's final breach with the Conservative Front Bench, on which he had served, first in office and then in opposition, for seven years. On the following day, January 27, he decided that the time had come for him formally to sever his links with the leadership and its policy-making powers. During the day he wrote to Baldwin:

My dear Baldwin,

Now that our divergences of view upon Indian policy have become public, I feel that I ought not any longer to attend the meetings of your 'Business Committee' to which you have hitherto so kindly invited me. I hope and believe that sincere and inevitable differences upon policy will not affect the feelings of friendship which have grown up between us during the last six years. I need scarcely add that I will give you whatever aid is in my power in opposing the Socialist Government in the House of Commons, and I shall do my utmost to secure their defeat at the general election.

Believe me, with the warmest personal regard,

Yours vy sincerely,
Winston S. Churchill

Baldwin accepted Churchill's resignation, replying on January 28:

My dear Winston,

I am grateful to you for your kind letter of yesterday and much as I regret your decision not to attend the meetings, of your old colleagues, I am convinced that your decision is correct in the circumstances.

But I agree with you, gladly and wholeheartedly, that there is nothing in a difference of opinion on a single policy, however important, to prevent our close and loyal co-operation in doing our utmost to turn out the present government.

And with the latter part of your letter I am in complete agreement.

Our friendship is now too deeply rooted to be affected by differences of opinion whether temporary or permanent. We have fought together through testing times: we have learnt to appreciate each other's good qualities and to be kindly indulgent to qualities less good, if indeed they exist, though in many but diverse quarters we are endowed with a double dose of original sin.

With my warm regards,

I am as ever,

Very sincerely,
Stanley Baldwin

For the first time since November 1924 Churchill was cut off from the central workings of the Conservative Party, and from the formulation of its policies. But his discontent at the Party's India policy was widely shared. On January 29 a member of the Simon Commission, Edward Cadogan,[1] wrote to Baldwin: 'No words of mine can possibly describe my feelings as to the way in which the Commission has been treated. What Winston said in his opening remarks upon the subject of the Commission last Monday, blunt and undiplomatic as it was, was perfectly true. . . .' Cadogan's letter continued: 'I cannot vote against my Party, but I certainly should not vote with my Party if it is prepared to go to any further lengths . . . the Conservative Party has only one line to take over this matter, and that is to stand upon the recommendations of the Indian Statutory Commission.'

---

[1] Edward Cecil George Cadogan, 1880–1962. Son of the 5th Earl Cadogan. Educated at Eton and Balliol College Oxford. Barrister, 1905. Secretary to the Speaker of the House of Commons, 1911–21. On active service at the Dardanelles, in Egypt and Palestine (his brother William was killed in action on 12 November 1914). Conservative MP for Reading, 1922–23; Finchley, 1924–35; Bolton, 1940–45. Member of the Indian Statutory Commission, 1927–32; Member of the Joint Select Committee on the Indian Constitution, 1933–35. Knighted, 1939. Royal Air Force Volunteer Reserve, 1939–45. Member of the Committee of Enquiry into the political activities of the Civil Service, 1948. In 1920 his niece Lady Mary Cadogan married Churchill's cousin the Marquess of Blandford (later 10th Duke of Marlborough).

20

India 1931:
'The Conservative Party
Is With Me'

A S soon as Churchill had made his formal break with the Conservative leadership, he embarked on a campaign of public speaking.
His aim was to tell the public of what he believed to be the dangers of
the Government's India policy, as he had expressed them in his Parliamentary speech of January 26. On January 30, only three days after his
formal break, he addressed the second public meeting of the Indian
Empire Society, at the Free Trade Hall, Manchester. So great was the
interest, that several hundred of those who came to hear him were
unable to find room. The object of the meeting, he said, was to 'utter a
solemn warning' against MacDonald's India policy. Churchill was particularly critical of Lord Irwin's negotiations with Gandhi, 'a fanatic and
an ascetic of the fakir type well known in the East', who had rejected
Irwin's overtures 'with contempt'. Irwin's policy, he said, first made
Gandhi 'a martyr in the eyes of his fellows, and then, while he was
actually their captive, solicited his aid. Now that the Round-Table
Constitution has been drafted and sent out to India "on approval",
Gandhi and thirty of his leading fellow-conspirators and revolutionaries
have been set at liberty, unconditionally, in the hopes that they will at
any rate say some kind words about the scheme.'

On February 2 Sir Mark Hunter wrote to congratulate Churchill on
the success of the meeting. 'It was a pity that the speech was not broadcast,' he wrote. 'I did what I could by telephone and letter to persuade
the authorities to broadcast it but without success.'

The Indian Empire Society made immediate plans for a new meeting,
at the Albert Hall. On February 3 Lord Rothermere wrote from San

Remo to encourage Churchill to continue with his speaking campaign. 'Modern electorates forget almost over night,' he wrote. 'Frequent repetition is the only method by which they can be influenced. An occasional article in the Daily Mail does nothing, but repetition does everything.' Rothermere added: 'We have a splendid cause. If India is not held, there is nothing for England but bankruptcy and revolution.'

On February 3, in a letter to Rothermere, Churchill advocated an early party meeting to discuss future India policy, but stressed that it ought to be a meeting at which the question of leadership 'should most carefully be excluded'. Until such time, Churchill wrote, it was essential for the Rothermere press itself to be more helpful. The *Daily Mail*, he pointed out, had given very meagre coverage to his House of Commons and Manchester speeches, and he added:

. . . the speeches I make are the only weapon I have for fighting this battle. They require from me an effort which is equal to that which would enable me to earn £3/400 by writing one of the numerous articles I have on my books. I gladly make this sacrifice for the public cause. As copy, these speeches are just as good reading as any article I write and I should have thought that they would have been no serious drag upon your paper. This week they have been numerous but otherwise they will only occur every fortnight or three weeks. . . .

Unless Rothermere were to give his speeches full coverage, Churchill warned, 'Baldwin with the Times at his back is master of the fate of India'.

Churchill was also critical of Beaverbrook's decision to run Empire Free Trade candidates at by-elections, telling Rothermere:

Merely nagging the party and hampering them at bye-elections unites all its solid loyalties against Max. When all is said and done party is the strongest thing that now survives in Great Britain and almost the only thing that people believe in. Steady working up of a great cause will produce a political situation of deep interest and probably an acute tension. As long as I am fighting a cause I am not afraid of anything. Nor do I weary as the struggle proceeds. You have it in your power to render a great service to the Empire and the motto 'For King and country' which you have printed since the general strike on the head of your paper may well be inscribed on the hearts of millions. Baldwin, the party machine, who gets into office etc etc are mere irrelevances. Policy alone is what counts—win there, win everywhere.

Churchill added that he had found 'remarkable evidence' of support for his views among his fellow backbench Conservatives, but that they were 'all afraid of being labelled "disloyal" '.

Conservative Central Office was determined to prevent Churchill winning backbench support. Under Davidson's guidance a campaign was launched aimed at restoring confidence in Dominion status, and at casting doubt on Churchill's own sincerity. Davidson himself drew up an outline of the methods to be followed, which included correspondence in the Press, weekly talking films, Party vans and 'A close analysis and criticism of Winston's past and present attitude towards India, supported by a picked team of young MPs with the gift of incisive speech'. On February 5, in an attempt to counter these official Conservative activities, and at the same time to widen the basis of his appeal, Churchill asked J. H. Whitley[1] if he could make a wireless broadcast over the BBC. Lord Beaverbrook, he pointed out, had recently been allowed to broadcast on Empire Free Trade, and in both cases 'the views expressed command a large body of public assent not definitely focussed in party organisations'. In addition, his views, like Beaverbrook's on Empire Free Trade, were opposed to those 'of the three official party leaders', while being both controversial, 'and of considerable interest'. The BBC considered Churchill's request for some months, but then turned it down. From the Mediterranean, Lord Rothermere continued to exhort Churchill to greater efforts. 'You have a superb chance,' he telegraphed from San Remo on February 8. 'Be untiring and unfaltering. Chuck holidays and live laborious days.'

Writing to his son, who was then in the United States, on February 8, Churchill had given a full account of his personal situation:

Politics have opened out a great deal for me. I had a famous week of action, two most important speeches in the House of Commons and in the two greatest Lancashire halls—The Free Trade Hall and the Philharmonic Hall which you know. Baldwin's repudiation of me was couched in terms which went far beyond anything the party will agree to about India. There is to be a great gathering of members in the House on Monday to put him on the mat, or even perhaps on the spot. He will of course wriggle back into a more martial position, but I think he has certainly failed to interpret both the wish of the party and the need of the country.

Max is running amok in all directions, but is quite sound on India. He and

---

[1] John Henry Whitley, 1866–1935. Educated at Clifton and London University. Liberal MP for Halifax, 1900–18; Coalition Liberal, 1918–28. A Junior Lord of the Treasury, 1907–10. Deputy Speaker, and Chairman of Ways and Means, House of Commons, 1911–21. Chairman of the Committee on the Relations of Employers and Employed (known as the Whitley Committee), 1917–18. Speaker of the House of Commons, 1921–28. Chairman of the Royal Commission on Labour in India, 1929–31. Chairman of the BBC, 1930–35.

I are independent, but, as I cabled you, converging. Rothermere writes or telegraphs every other day avowing undying fidelity. We are planning a big Albert Hall meeting about the middle of March. At a stroke I have become quite popular in the party and in great demand upon the platform. . . .

Hawkey reports the constituency in a bright flame of enthusiasm, the branches wishing to pass resolutions supporting me against Baldwin etc. I have written to Goschen demanding the vote of the Council of the Association, about 250, on a resolution which will clearly show they support me in my attitude about India, and in my action in withdrawing from the 'Shadow Cabinet'. All these changes would have interested you very greatly.

On February 9 the India Committee of the Conservative Party met, under Baldwin's chairmanship, in the House of Commons. Churchill was not a member of this Committee, but his views were put forward by his friend Lord Lloyd, a former Governor of Bombay. 'Proceedings were opened by a forcible Die-hard speech by George Lloyd,' Amery noted in his diary, 'putting certain very direct questions to S.B. Great enthusiasm from our Die-hard element which was obviously much in the majority.' Among those who supported Lloyd were Lord Burnham, Lord Winterton, Major-General Sir Alfred Knox[1] and Colonel Applin.[2] Lloyd himself, Amery wrote, 'is in a fearful state of mind about India and cannot conceive any other point of view as due to anything but cowardice and time-serving'.

Although Churchill was not present at the India Committee meeting, he was not far off. In his diary Amery recorded:

. . . as we came away heard Winston haranguing a press correspondent in the Lobby to the effect that he was not going to let India be betrayed without telling England all about it.

I am afraid we are in for real difficulties over the India business. Winston has chosen his moment and his excuse for separating with the Party very adroitly. If only S.B. could have been more definite earlier he would have gone on the fiscal question.

Following the meeting of the India Committee, a special session of the Conservative Members Committee met to consider the Indian situation. As Churchill was still a Conservative MP, he attended the meeting, at

[1] Alfred William Fortescue Knox, 1870–1964. 2nd Lieutenant, 1891. ADC to the Viceroy of India (Lord Curzon), 1899–1900 and 1902–03. Lieutenant-Colonel, 1911. Military Attaché, St Petersburg, 1911–18. Major-General, 1918. Chief of the British Military Mission to Siberia, 1918–20. Knighted, 1919. Conservative MP for Wycombe, 1924–45.

[2] Reginald Vincent Kempenfelt Applin, 1869–1957. Entered the British North Borneo Service as a cadet, 1889. On active service in South Africa, 1899–1901. DSO, 1902; and District Commissioner, Bloemfontein. On active service on the western front, including the battles of Messines and Passchendaele, 1917. Brevet Lieutenant-Colonel, 1918. OBE, 1919. Commanded the 14th King's Hussars, 1919–22. Conservative MP for Enfield, 1924–29 and 1931–35. Author of a book on machine-gun tactics.

which Lord Derby's son Oliver Stanley defended the role of the Conservative delegation to the Round-Table Conference. Churchill pressed Stanley to say whether the delegation had 'insisted strongly' on adequate safeguards to ensure the protection of India's minorities, its defence and its foreign affairs. According to a report in the *Daily Telegraph* on February 10: 'Receiving an affirmative reply, Mr Churchill is said to have asserted that the fact was not established sufficiently in the report of the Conference. The answer to his criticism was that the report was not prepared by the Conservative delegation.'

Churchill was more convinced than ever that the Conservative Party was rebelling against Baldwin's Indian policy. 'All is going extremely well,' he telegraphed to Rothermere on February 10. 'B. had bad time with two hundred Conservative members. Is now trying to get under cover.' His own constituents, he added, were 'in excellent form'.

One of those who believed that Churchill had a good chance to win the support of a majority of Conservatives was Brendan Bracken, who wrote to Churchill's son on February 13:

> You ask about your parent's activities with regard to India. Well, I am of opinion that they have been altogether splendid. He has untied himself from Baldwin's apron, rallied all the fighters in the Tory Party, re-established himself as a potential leader & put heart into a great multitude here & in India. By a series of brilliant speeches in the House he has shown the Tories the quality of his genius and the incredible drabness & futility of S.B. The 'boneless wonder' speech is immortal.[1]

'Politics are in an inextricable but deeply interesting tangle,' Bracken wrote. 'One thing is certain—if this Parliament lasts until the winter Baldwin will depart ignominiously. And your father has more than a good chance of succession.'

On February 17 Gandhi met Irwin in Delhi; the first of eight meetings in four weeks. Many Englishmen were outraged that the two men

---

[1] On January 28 Churchill had told the House of Commons, during a debate on the Trade Disputes Act: 'What is the Prime Minister going to do? I spoke the other day, after he had been defeated in an important division about his wonderful skill in falling without hurting himself. He falls, but up he comes again, smiling, a little dishevelled but still smiling. But this is a juncture, a situation, which will try to the fullest the peculiar arts in which he excels. I remember when I was a child, being taken to the celebrated Barnum's Circus which contained an exhibition of freaks and monstrosities, but the exhibit on the programme which I most desired to see was the one described as "The Boneless Wonder". My parents judged that that spectacle would be too revolting and demoralizing for my youthful eyes, and I have waited fifty years to see the boneless wonder sitting on the Treasury Bench.'

met on equal terms. Speaking to the Council of the West Essex Conservative Association on February 23, Churchill denounced the meeting in caustic terms:

It is alarming and also nauseating to see Mr Gandhi, a seditious Middle Temple lawyer, now posing as a fakir of a type well-known in the East, striding half-naked up the steps of the Vice-regal palace, while he is still organising and conducting a defiant campaign of civil disobedience, to parley on equal terms with the representative of the King-Emperor. Such a spectacle can only increase the unrest in India and the danger to which white people there are exposed. It can only encourage all the forces which are hostile to British authority.

What good can possibly come of such extraordinary negotiations? Gandhi has said within the last few weeks that he demands the substance of independence, though he kindly adds that the British may keep the shadow. He declares that the boycott of foreign cloth must be continued until either prohibition or a prohibitive tariff can be put up against it by an Indian national Parliament. This, if accepted, would entail the final ruin of Lancashire. He has also pressed for the repudiation of the Indian loans, and has laid claim to the control of the Army and foreign affairs. These are his well-known aims. Surely they form a strange basis for heart-to-heart discussions—'sweet' we are told they were—between this malignant subversive fanatic and the Viceroy of India.

Churchill's constituents responded favourably to his appeal, and were, he reported to his wife three days later, 'loving, ardent and unanimous'. He added: 'There is no doubt that the whole spirit of the Conservative party is with me, and that much of their dissatisfaction with S.B. turns itself into favour with me.'

On February 24 Churchill had looked in on the quarterly meeting of the National Union of Conservative Associations. In his letter to his wife, he wrote: 'I have never hitherto ventured on to this highly orthodox Central Office ground, and expect six weeks ago I should have had a very cool welcome. As it was they received me with unequalled acclamation, suspended their standing orders and altered their luncheon hour so as to pass unanimously a motion calling for firm government in India. Neville looked very blue, and Maureen[1] who is a vigilant champion of her Oliver's defeatist views tried to prevent the vote being taken by postponing an adjournment until after lunch.' Churchill was also pleased with his Press outlets, telling his wife: 'Rothermere has now, I think, definitely settled down to a solid campaign in my interest. All his

[1] Lady Maureen Helen Vane-Tempest-Stewart, 1900–1942. Eldest daughter of Churchill's cousin the 7th Marquess of Londonderry. She married Oliver Stanley in 1920.

papers in every part of the country are writing eulogistic articles and friendly paragraphs, and the Daily Mail and Evening News are over-doing their support. The verbatim is a great comfort and I am sure these speeches are making many friends.' 'All we want is time,' Churchill added.

The Die-hards, who had not hitherto accepted Churchill's guidance, now turned to him for leadership, and John Gretton agreed to join the platform at his Albert Hall speech. Sir John Simon and Sir Robert Horne had also indicated that they might come. Churchill commented to his wife:

It is astonishing looking back over the last six weeks what a change has been brought in my position. Every speech that I have made, and step that I have taken has been well received beyond all expectation. The turning points were the first Indian speech and my separation from the Shadow Cabinet. Anything may happen now if opinion has time to develop. If not I shall be quite happy.

On February 26 Churchill sent Lindemann a copy of the Round-Table Conference Blue Book, asking him to look at the size of the proposed Indian electorates, and commenting: 'How these great mobs are going to vote in constituencies of four thousand square miles I do not understand. Pray attune your acute mind into analysing this con-stitution, and show up its weak points.' Churchill also asked Lindemann to make a 'scrutiny' of the Congress Party, 'its character, composition and financial resources'.

Within the Conservative Party, Baldwin's support for the Govern-ment's India policy had divided all groups and all constituencies. Although Patrick Buchan-Hepburn had, to Churchill's chagrin, sup-ported Baldwin at his own by-election,[1] the Conservative Central Office was concerned by the growing hostility towards the India proposals. On February 25 the Party's Principal Agent, H. R. Topping,[2] wrote to Neville Chamberlain: 'Many of our supporters are worried about the question of India. They lean much more towards the views of Mr Churchill than to those expressed by Mr Baldwin in the House of

[1] On 8 February 1931 Churchill had written to his son: 'You see Buchan-Hepburn was returned by an enormously increased majority, partly as the result of my advocacy. Bracken got him the seat entirely out of regard for me. I am sorry to say B-H is a very poor spirited creature. All he could do was to profess his undying love and loyalty to Baldwin and to dis-associate himself from my views on India. I do not think we shall see very much more of him.'

[2] Hugh Robert Topping, 1877–1952. Born in Dublin. General Secretary, City of Dublin Unionist Association, 1904–11. Secretary and Agent, South Glamorgan Conservative and Unionist Association, 1911–18; City of Cardiff, 1918–23; Northwich, 1923–24. Conservative Central Office Agent for Lancashire and Cheshire, 1924–28. General Director of the Conser-vative Central Office, and Principal Conservative Party Agent, 1927–45. Knighted, 1934.

Commons. . . .' Topping went on to say that a new Leader was needed, but not Churchill, who could assuage the growing malaise. On March 2 one of the leading figures of the local Conservative Association in Baldwin's own constituency, Sir Richard Brooke,[1] wrote direct to Baldwin himself:

Your speech of Jan 26th has given a very widespread impression that when you are returned to power you will carry on the Socialist Policy which appears to include surrender to sedition and the indignity of conferences with Gandhi. Many of us feel that unless a firm stand is made by the Opposition, matters will have gone too far and the Indian people encouraged to expect more concessions than they can be given. In addition the Prime Minister's 'marching orders' speech indicates that the Socialists are getting encouragement from the lack of protest from the Opposition.

Mr Churchill expressed the views of very many Conservatives in this Constituency with whom I have spoken and as Chairman of the local branch of the Unionist Asstn here I thought it my duty to see that our views should be brought forward.

Churchill himself continued to press his arguments at the Party's Indian Affairs Committee. On March 4 Lane-Fox reported to Irwin:

. . . in our Indian Committee it has taken our Chairman,[2] and a few of the wiser members, all their time to keep George Lloyd, Winston and the red-haired brat (supposed to be his son, and certainly acting now as his jackal— who is member for Paddington—Bracken by name),[3] Alfred Knox, John

[1] Richard Christopher Brooke, 1888–1981. Educated at Eton and Christ Church Oxford. Cheshire Yeomanry, 1908–10; Scots Guards, 1911–18. Succeeded his father as 9th Baronet, 1920. Owner of some 6,500 acres. Elected to the Worcestershire County Council, 1928; served until 1946. High Sheriff of Worcestershire, 1931, and subsequently Chairman of the Worcestershire Conservative Association. Vice-Chairman of the Worcestershire War Emergency Committee for Civil Defence, 1939. Chairman of the Bewdley Division Conservative Association, 1945–46.

[2] John Wardlaw-Milne, 1879–1967. Member of the Bombay Municipal Corporation, 1907–17. A member of the Viceroy's Council, 1915. A Trustee of the Port of Bombay. Lieutenant-Colonel, Indian Defence Force, 1915–19. A Director of the Bank of Bombay. British Government Representative, City of Bombay Improvement Trust. Conservative MP for Kidderminster, 1922–45. Member of the Imperial Economic Committee, 1926–29. Knighted, 1932. Chairman, Conservative Indian Affairs Committee, 1930–35; Foreign Affairs Committee. 1939–45. Chairman, Select Committee on National Expenditure, 1939–45. In 1942 he brought a motion of no-confidence in Churchill's war-time Coalition.

[3] There was no truth in the often-repeated gossip that Brendan Bracken was Churchill's illegitimate son. But he had, by 1931, become an intimate of the Churchill household. Churchill's daughter Sarah later recalled: 'Brendan Bracken was another part of our life at Chartwell. Sunday became know as "Brandon day". He was in complete contrast to the Prof. A red-haired Irishman of booming character and voice, he talked like a fountain without pause, a considerable achievement in our household.'

Gretton, etc quiet. They began by demanding a debate in the House of Commons, and have had to be given a debate on Benn's salary, which at any rate keeps them off legislation and a sequel to the Indian Conference. . . .

Lane-Fox went on to warn Irwin of the extent of Conservative unease. It was 'no use denying', he wrote, that the Government's India policy, and the negotiations with Gandhi, was the one subject 'that for the moment is worrying our best friends terribly', and he continued:

I only hope that the result of the negotiation will turn out to be so completely satisfactory that they will be able to feel it was worth straining a little western principle for it.

The average Conservative was of course rather shocked by the way in which Gandhi was originally allowed to break the law in the matter of his salt campaign and march to the sea. They now say that, while a concession allowing salt to be illicitly made on the seashore probably won't affect the revenue, it is a breach of principle, following on what happened before, which is very deplorable, and could never have been thought of in a western country. The information is not complete and there may be much more than this to say about it, and please don't think that I am trying to express an opinion. I am only trying to give you a description of the sort of view that I find among thoroughly reasonable people.

On the night of March 4 the negotiations between Irwin and Gandhi reached their conclusion. Gandhi agreed to end civil disobedience in all its forms, and to send Congress representatives to a new Round-Table Conference to discuss the future of India within the framework of an All-India Federation. He also accepted continuing British 'safeguards' —unspecified—in the areas of defence, foreign affairs, minority interests and India's overseas debts. In return Irwin agreed to release all those arrested as a result of Gandhi's breach of the salt laws, to remit all fines and to return all confiscated property. The Gandhi–Irwin Pact, as it became known, was made public on March 5. Containing as it did the repeated phrase: 'it has been agreed that', it gave Gandhi the status, not of a subject, but of an equal negotiator. Throughout their discussions, Gandhi had insisted on the right of India to ultimate withdrawal from the British Empire.

As soon as Baldwin announced his support both for the Gandhi–Irwin Pact, and for a second Round-Table Conference, Churchill persuaded Lord Lloyd to challenge Baldwin at the next meeting of the India

Committee. The meeting was held on March 9. Led by Lloyd, the Die-hards dominated the meeting, and passed a disingenuous resolution welcoming 'the decision of Mr Baldwin that the Conservative Party cannot be represented at any further Round-Table Conference to be held in India as now foreshadowed by the Government'. Baldwin was shaken by this challenge to his authority. 'He has been going through great difficulties with his Party,' Dawson wrote to Irwin on March 5. 'Winston has done a good deal to corrupt them, and the people who know better have not done much to help him. Between ourselves, he was pretty near to resigning the Leadership a few days ago. . . .' That same day Colonel Spender-Clay[1] wrote to Irwin:

There is no doubt that yesterday the lobby opinion was that S.B.'s resignation of the leadership could not be postponed for more than a few days, but today his position is far stronger and Winston's is correspondingly lower. Some months ago John Buchan said that God Almighty was so busy looking after Baldwin that He had no time to look after the rest of the world and certainly providence has again intervened.

Don't think that I imagine that Winston could ever be Leader of the Party. I think he would have the shock of his life if his name was put before a party meeting. But S.B. is very far from being an ideal Party leader.

Those who most belittled Churchill's motives, also cast doubts on the seriousness of his support from the Die-hards. On March 6 Davidson wrote to Irwin:

Winston's game, of course, has been very obvious, as it always is. He is not the son of Randolph for nothing, and he must be feeling this morning that the transient contact which he had made with the Die-Hards has done him no good. How Stanley must have chuckled to think that when the door opened and the India Committee entered, as it had done on several occasions, there he saw the same faces that time and again during the last Parliament had come to beg him to get rid of Winston from the Government, and who have recently been acclaiming him as the heaven-born leader of the Party—on, of course, only one subject, namely India.

Churchill was to speak again on India at the Albert Hall on March 18. As there was to be no debate in the House of Commons for Baldwin to make his views public until after Churchill's speech, he asked Ramsay MacDonald if the Supply Debate due a week later could be moved

[1] Herbert Henry Spender-Clay, 1875–1937. Educated at Eton and Sandhurst. Joined the 2nd Life Guards, 1896. On active service in South Africa, 1899–1900 and on the Western Front, 1914–18 (Military Cross, despatches three times). Lieutenant-Colonel, 1910. Conservative MP for Tonbridge from 1910 until his death. Charity Commissioner, 1923–24 and 1924–29. Privy Councillor, 1929.

forward. MacDonald agreed to Baldwin's request, and the debate was set for March 12, six days before Churchill's speech. On the day before the debate Baldwin discussed the situation with Thomas Jones, who kept a note of their conversation. 'I let him realise,' wrote Jones, 'how very strong and general the opposition to him is, and how much I hoped he could go out on a big issue like India,' to which Baldwin replied: 'that is what I propose to do. No Party is so divided as mine. I have done my utmost to keep it together, but it ranges from Imperialists of the Second Jubilee to young advanced Democrats who are all for Irwin's policy.' Baldwin added: 'I am for that policy myself, and mean to say so.' Jones' notes continued:

I begged him to be absolutely frank, and show the country clearly the fissure in his party, and take his stand firmly with Irwin. He might lose his Party and his place, but he would go down with the great mass of the country on his side.

He told me how Sam Hoare was a timid rabbit, Oliver Stanley had cold feet; the Diehards who for the last six years had loathed Winston were now running round him, the silly Burnham had joined them—it was a Party of fools.

I remarked that Winston had been canvassing for the support of the '*Daily Telegraph*' and the '*Sunday Times*'. S.B. knew of this, and went on: 'David[1] has seen Camrose, and *he* is prepared to start at once a London evening paper to counter the '*News*' and '*Standard*'. He can't put all the money into it at present, so David has gone down today to Bristol to ask the Wills' to put in £400,000.'

This news rather made me feel that S.B. was still counting on holding the Leadership. He is convinced that he has the majority of the rank and file of the Party with him. . . .

Baldwin opened the debate on March 12 by quoting the 1917 declaration, in which Britain's aim in India was declared to be 'the granting of self-governing institutions with a view to the progressive realisation of responsible Government in India as an integral part of the British Empire'. This, he said, was still Conservative policy. 'We have impregnated India ourselves with Western ideas,' he said, 'and, for good or for ill, we are reaping the fruits of our own work.' Irwin's talks with Gandhi had, he added, 'definitely enlarged the area of good will and co-operation'. One newspaper had described the pact as a victory for Irwin, another described it as a victory for Gandhi. In his view it was 'a victory of common sense—a victory rare enough in India, and rare enough at home'. It was essential, Baldwin added, 'to keep India out of party politics'. The Conservative Party must find on this question 'the maxi-

---

[1] J. C. C. Davidson (also known as Colin).

mum amount of unity'. The dangers to India came, not from the difficulties of governing the country, but from 'extremists in India and at
home'; and he continued:

I am firmly convinced that such writings as appear in such papers as the
'Daily Mail' will do more to lose India for the British Empire, will do more
to cause a revolutionary spirit, than anything that can be done in any way by
anyone else. . . . Even if the rank and file refuse to face facts, the leader has
to look at them, and he has to warn his people; and they do not like being
warned. It is the supreme duty of a political leader to tell the people of the
country the truth, because truth is greater than tactics. . . .

What is the principal fact that I see in the world today? It is that the
unchanging East has changed. . . .

The Round-Table policy, Baldwin insisted, could not be reversed,
either on the 'simple ground of British Honour', or on the grounds 'of a
sane and wise policy'. He did not believe that 'the bulk' of Conservatives,
either in the House of Commons or in the country, would wish to
reverse that policy. 'I shall carry out that policy,' he declared, 'so long
as I am here. . . . If there are those in our party who approach this
subject in a niggling, grudging spirit, who would have to have forced
out of their reluctant hands one concession after another, if they be a
majority, in God's name let them choose a man to lead them.'

Speaking for the Government, Wedgwood Benn told the House of
Commons that he looked forward 'with confidence' to the participation
of the Congress leaders at the next Round-Table Conference, and
declared: 'If we can come face to face with our Indian friends, if we can
discuss freely our doubts and difficulties, if mischief makers will be
silent, and men will cease to sow tares, then there is a real hope of peace
and understanding.' Churchill, in his speech, repeated each of his earlier
arguments against the Gandhi–Irwin negotiations. 'Nothing,' he went
on, 'could more painfully, and I may say more pitifully, illustrate the
ceaseless descent in British Parliamentary opinion than that these
modest achievements should give so much pleasure, that they should
even be hailed as "a miracle of statecraft". It only shows that we are
becoming accustomed to be thankful for small mercies and glad when
anything is saved from the wreck of our great estates.' But, he warned,
'Although the boycott and civil disobedience have been partially called
off, they remain suspended over us and can be loosed at any moment by
the mere lifting of Mr Gandhi's little finger.'

The sole aim of the Indian Congress, Churchill insisted, was full
independence. All over India, as a result of the Gandhi–Irwin pact,
'expectations, aspirations and appetites have been excited and are

mounting. Already Mr Gandhi moves about surrounded by a circle of wealthy men, who see at their finger-tips the acquisition of the resources of an Empire on cheaper terms than were ever yet offered in the world.'

In answer to the personal charges that had been made against him, Churchill declared:

The Secretary of State for India charges me with being an advocate of violent repression. He says that my policy is the lathi, the bayonet, the machine-gun and artillery. It is easy to say such things, and easy to cheer them when they are repeated, but they are not true, and they are not just. The quotations which my right hon Friend (Mr Baldwin) did me the honour to read from my speech in the Dyer Debate might at least have been borne in mind.[1] I am no advocate of brutal force in India; indeed, I hold that no more physical force is needed in the solution of the Indian question. A tithe of the force and the punitive measures which the Socialist Government and the present Viceroy have vainly employed would have sufficed if they had been part of a firm and coherent policy of the simple maintenance of law and order. . . .

Churchill then compared the riots and lawlessness in Bombay, which had grown stronger in the face of a weak local government, with the situation in Calcutta, where the 'firm, steady guidance' of the Chief of Police, Sir Charles Tegart,[2] had prevented an excess of violence. He was opposed, he said, to any 'pandering to disorder' as had happened in Bombay, and he went on: 'It is my abhorrence of the use of physical force which leads me to resist a policy which will gradually reproduce over large parts of India the lamentable conditions of Bombay, and I say it is not I, but the Secretary of State and those who think with him, who are bringing bloodshed and confusion ever nearer to the masses of Hindustan.'

[1] On 8 July 1921 Churchill (then Secretary of State for the Colonies) defended the Government's censure of General Dyer, whose troops had killed nearly 300 Indians during anti-Government riots and demonstrations at Amritsar. Churchill told the House of Commons: 'Governments who have seized upon power by violence and by usurpation have often resorted to terrorism in their desperate efforts to keep what they have stolen, but the august and venerable structure of the British Empire, where lawful authority descends from hand to hand and generation after generation, does not need such aid. Such ideas are absolutely foreign to the British way of doing things. . . . Our reign in India or anywhere else has never stood on the basis of physical force alone, and it would be fatal to the British Empire if we were to try to base ourselves only upon it.'

[2] Charles Augustus Tegart, 1881–1946. Educated at Trinity College Dublin. Joined the Indian Police, 1901. On active service in France (artillery officer), 1918. Chief of Police, Bombay (retired 1931). Knighted, 1926. Member of the Council of India, London, 1932–36. Government Adviser on Police Organization, Palestine, 1937, where he established the system of strategic fortified police posts known as the 'Tegart Fortresses'. Served with the Ministry of Food, London, 1942–45.

Churchill's speech was punctuated throughout by hostile outbursts, interruptions and expressions of disbelief from Conservative, Liberal and Labour members; but Baldwin's speech, as Thomas Jones wrote to a friend four days later, 'is considered here the speech of his life'. During his speech Baldwin attacked extremists 'at Home and in India', and praised Irwin for having 'definitely enlarged the area of goodwill and cooperation'. On March 13 William Bridgeman wrote to Baldwin: 'Many congratulations on yesterday's triumph—I think it has put you on the top again, and now you must keep there.' The debate, Bridgeman added, had proved 'a damaging touch to Winston & his friends'.

Having, as he saw it, repelled the attack from Churchill and the Die-hards over India, Baldwin moved immediately into battle with Beaver-brook and Rothermere over Free Trade. On March 19 a by-election was to be held at Westminster St George's, in which Alfred Duff Cooper, the official Conservative candidate, was being challenged by an Empire Free Trade nominee, Sir Ernest Petter.[1] The *Daily Mail* and the *Daily Express* both urged the constituency to challenge Baldwin's leadership by voting for Petter and Empire Free Trade. Two days before the poll, on March 17, Baldwin attacked the two Press Lords with fierce invec-tive, denouncing their wrecking tactics in a speech at the Queen's Hall and appealing once more for Conservative unity. 'What the proprietor-ship of these papers is aiming at,' Baldwin declared, 'is power, and power without responsibility—the prerogative of the harlot throughout the ages.'

On the day before the electors of St George's went to the poll Churchill addressed the third public meeting of the Indian Empire Society at the Albert Hall. In his speech he lamented the fact that the 'enormous influence' of the Conservative Party had been cast against Britain's 'vital interests' in India. Bitterly he declared:

The Conservative leaders have decided that we are to work with the Socialists, and that we must make our action conform with theirs. We therefore have against us at the present time the official machinery of all the three great parties in the State. We meet under a ban. Every Member of Parliament or Peer who comes here must face the displeasure of the party Whips. Mr Baldwin has declared that the three-party collusion must continue, and in support of that decision he has appealed to all those sentiments of personal loyalty and partisan feeling which a leader can command. Is it not wonderful

---

[1] Ernest Willoughby Petter, 1873–1954. Mechanical engineer; designed and built (with his brother P. W. Petter) one of the first British motor cars. Unsuccessful Conservative candidate for Bristol North, 1918 and 1923. President of the British Engineers' Association, 1923–25. Knighted, 1925. Contested Westminster St George's as an Independent Conservative, 1931.

in these circumstances, with all this against us, that a few of us should manage to get together here in this hall to-night?

After denouncing Gandhi for seeking 'the substitution of Brahmin domination for British rule', Churchill warned that behind Gandhi were even more disruptive forces. The time would come when Gandhi himself 'would cease to count any more in the Indian situation', and he went on:

Already Nehru, his young rival in the Indian Congress, is preparing to supersede him the moment that he has squeezed his last drop from the British lemon. In running after Gandhi and trying to build on Gandhi, in imagining that Mr Ramsay MacDonald and Mr Gandhi and Lord Irwin are going to bestow peace and progress upon India, we should be committing ourselves to a crazy dream with a terrible awakening.

To keep order in India, Churchill argued, it was not necessary to resort to 'repression and force'. Most of those killed in the past year in India had not been killed in clashes with British troops, but in 'religious fights' between Hindus and Muslims. Experience showed that 'a calm, capable, determined Viceroy properly supported from home could maintain peace and tranquility in India year after year with a tenth of the repressive measures which Lord Irwin in his misguided benevolence has been compelled to employ'. The Indians, Churchill said, should be encouraged to take greater responsibilities at the provincial level. But at the centre, only British rule could provide a 'guarantee of impartiality' between the conflicting races, creeds and classes of India. Provincial self-government, he added, was 'an immense and fertile field', and it should be remembered that the Provinces of India were 'great states and separate nations', each one comparable in size to the leading powers of Europe; the Indians should be content to achieve Provincial self-government, as the Simon Commission had advised.

Churchill forecast grave events if British authority were destroyed. All the medical, legal and administrative services which Britain had created 'would perish with it'; so too would the railway service, irrigation, public works and famine prevention. The Hindus would seek to drive out and destroy the Muslims. Profiteering and corruption would flourish. Indian millionaires, grown rich on sweated labour, would become more powerful, and even richer. All sorts of 'greedy appetites' had already been excited, 'and many itching fingers were stretching and scratching at the vast pillage of a derelict Empire'. Nepotism, graft and corruption would be 'the handmaidens of a Brahmin domination'. Above all, the Hindus would tyrannize the untouchables, and deny them all human rights. These untouchables, Churchill told his audience, were 'A multitude as big as a nation, men, women and children deprived of hope and of the status of humanity. Their plight is worse than that of slaves, because they have been taught to consent not only to a physical but to a psychic servitude and prostration.' Both for the untouchables, and for the five million Indian Christians, it would be 'a sorry day', Churchill declared, 'when the arm of Britain can no longer offer them the protection of an equal law'.

In his final appeal, Churchill denounced the part which the 'official' Conservatives had played in portraying his views, and the views of those who agreed with him, as 'a sort of inferior race, mentally deficient, composed principally of colonels and other undesirables who have fought for Britain'. But, Churchill said, 'we do not depend on colonels—though why Conservatives should sneer at an honoured rank in the British army I cannot tell—we depend on facts. We depend on the private soldiers of the British democracy.'

The political impact of Churchill's speech had been blunted by Baldwin's speech in the House of Commons six days before, and on the following day Baldwin's position in the Party was further strengthened by Duff Cooper's victory at Westminster St George's, with a majority of over five thousand. Churchill was downcast. 'When the sound of battle dies down,' Beaverbrook wrote to J. L. Garvin on March 19, 'he will gather strength again.' Three days later Churchill himself wrote to Sir Mark Hunter: 'I do not think we have been wholly ineffective in our efforts, small though our resources were,' and he advised as the 'next point of attack', a major meeting in Glasgow in the autumn. Meanwhile, on March 21, he had asked Thornton Butterworth to publish his recent India speeches. 'Of course,' he wrote, 'I have taken much more trouble with them than with any book I have ever written.' Two days later Butterworth had agreed to publish this new volume, convinced, as he replied, that it would 'most unquestionably nourish the seed in this country, which you have so carefully sown'.[1]

Searching for further ways of influencing events, Churchill on April 4 asked Brendan Bracken to help the Indian Empire Society put up questions in the House of Commons. Three weeks later he urged the Duke of Marlborough to take part in the next India Debate in the House of Lords. The Conservative front bench had likewise been active in its own

---

[1] Churchill's new volume, entitled *India*, was published by Thornton Butterworth on May 27. Churchill offered his India speeches, he wrote in his introduction 'in sincerity and deep anxiety to those who wish to judge the episodes and events of the immediate future as they unfold or explode upon us'.

defence. On March 20, at Ipswich, Leopold Amery addressed six hundred Party members from all over the Eastern area, and, as he noted in his diary, 'Gave them a good vigorous speech of which twenty minutes was devoted to trouncing Winston.' Four days later Amery lunched with Baldwin 'to meet a number of young men in the Party', and found them 'generally very sympathetic to line I have taken over Winston'. Writing to Irwin on March 24, Churchill himself declared:

I am sure you know that I have no personal feelings of hostility towards you. I feel the deepest sorrow at the course of events in India, and at the impulsion you have given to them. We shall, I fear, be locked in this controversy for several years, and I think it will become the dividing line in England. At any rate you will start with the big battalions on your side.

On March 31 Irwin wrote to Davidson:

Winston's attitude about our affairs seems to me completely and utterly hopeless. It really does mean in effect that you give up the attempt to settle the political problem by agreement, and set out to enforce something by coercive methods. And this I honestly believe will never work. . . .

The day is past when you can make nations live in vacuums. The day is also past in my humble opinion when Winston's possessive instinct can be applied to Empires and the like. That conception of Imperialism is finished, and those who try to revive it are as those who would fly a balloon that won't hold gas. . . .

To Robert Boothby, Churchill wrote on April 2: 'Politics are very interesting. My late colleagues are more interested in doing me in than in any trifling questions connected with India or tariffs. I have a strong feeling they will not succeed, but anyhow my course is clear. . . .'

Events in India seemed to bear out Churchill's warnings. On March 24, at Cawnpore, Muslim traders had refused to close their shops during a period of mourning for a Hindu who had been executed by the British for terrorism and conspiracy.[1] The Muslims' refusal led to an immediate Hindu attack, and three days of murder, arson and looting. By March 26 at least three hundred people had been killed. Speaking to the Constitutional Club on March 26, Churchill declared:

Wednesday's massacres at Cawnpore, a name of evil import, are a portent. Because it is believed that we are about to leave the country, the struggle for power is now beginning between the Moslems and Hindus. A bloody riot

---

[1] The Hindu, Bhagat Singh, had been found guilty of having murdered a police officer, Mr Saunders, at Lahore, in December 1928. He had also taken part in the throwing of bombs into the chamber of the Legislative Assembly in Delhi in April 1929. After sentence had been passed, the Congress Party officially praised Bhagat Singh's bravery and sacrifice. He was executed on the evening of 23 March 1931.

broke out in which more than two hundred people lost their lives with many hundreds wounded, in which women and children were butchered in circumstances of bestial barbarity, their mutilated violated bodies strewing the streets for days. The British troops are now pacifying and calming the terrified and infuriated populace. But the feud is only at its beginning.[1]

The riots at Cawnpore had continued until the end of March, by which time over a thousand Indians were dead, the victims of Hindu–Muslim hatred. Anti-British extremism also flourished, and on April 8 the District Magistrate of Midnapore, James Peddie,[2] was shot dead. Speaking at his Constituency on April 22, to a meeting of the West Essex Divisional Council of the Junior Imperial League, Churchill commented bitterly on the continuing violence in India, on the fact that Gandhi himself had now agreed to come to London for the second Round-Table Conference, and on a recent statement by Irwin that the condition of India was 'sweeter' than before. Speaking in the House of Commons on May 13, Churchill stressed the economic and social arguments against Dominion Status, pointing out that if it came to pass, the Indians would automatically obtain, as had Canada, Australia and New Zealand, full powers to embargo or prohibit British goods, and to discriminate 'to any extent' between Indian producers and British importers. They could even, as South Africa had done, 'favour foreign imports against British imports', a right that was 'inherent' in Dominion Status, but of the utmost danger to Britain if used indiscriminately, or for political ends. That was why, he said, the mill-owners of Bombay and Ahmedabad had given Gandhi their financial support; their profits would be increased, while at the same time no British supervised laws would force them to improve labour conditions in their mills. 'When we put in juxtaposition,' Churchill said, 'the vast profit and grinding conditions, the harsh and wrongful conditions, and when we see that a monopoly is to be given to these people, I do say that we have a right to plead

---

[1] On July 27 the District Judge of Alipore, R. R. Garlick, was shot dead as he sat in court; on December 14 the District Magistrate of Tippera was murdered in his bungalow by two Bengali girl students; and unsuccessful assassination attempts were made on both the Commissioner of Dacca, A. Cassells (August 21), and the District Magistrate of Dacca, L. A. Durno (October 28). On October 29 the President of the European Association, F. Villiers, a merchant, narrowly escaped being shot while sitting in his office. Communal violence also continued: with Hindu–Muslim riots in Srinagar in July and in the Punjab in September.

[2] James Peddie, 1892–1931. Educated at the Bell Baxter School Fife, and St Andrews University. 2nd Lieutenant, Royal Scots Fusiliers, 1914–16; Captain, Northumberland Fusiliers, 1916–17; Major, 1917; acting Lieutenant-Colonel, 1918 (despatches twice). Joined the Indian Civil Service, October 1919. Arrived in India, December 1919. Served at Dacca, 1919; Munshiganj, 1921. Secretary, Police Retrenchment Committee, Calcutta, 1922. Served at Midnapore, 1923. Under-Secretary, Government of Bengal, 1923–24. Magistrate and Collector of Malda, 1924–29; of Midnapore from 1929 until his murder on 8 April 1931.

that it is an Indian interest that they should be prevented from doing this.' The mill-owners, he said, 'are the power behind the boycott'. As for the boycott, whereby Indians were urged not to buy any British manufactured goods, Churchill declared, it was sustained by the tyrannical religious powers of the Congress Hindus, for it was a boycott 'which enriches their wealthy friends, and which ruins Lancashire. . . .' By giving India Dominion Status, Churchill insisted, Britain was thus creating a 'Hindu and a Brahmin movement', whereby superstition and greed would march hand in hand, 'to the spoliation of millions of people'. Another result, he warned, would be to hand over seventy million Muslims to be 'bled and exploited'.

As Churchill's speech progressed, the hostile interruptions increased, but he overcame the barrage of dissent and, addressing the front bench, declared: 'By your actions you have produced misery such as India has not seen for half a century. You have poisoned relations between the Mohammedans and the Hindus.' The photographs he had been sent of the Cawnpore massacre, he said, taken on the spot, were 'so revolting that no paper would be able to publish them'.

After his speech of May 13 Churchill received one letter of support from an Indian member of Council of the Indian Empire Society, Judge Waris Ameer Ali,[1] who wrote to him on May 21: 'Permit me to congratulate you on your speech in the House of Commons last week. If I may say so, your attitude is giving great encouragement to loyalists of all classes in India.'

When the Cawnpore debate took place in the House of Commons on July 9, Lord Winterton blamed the weakness of the India Office in London for the riots, as well as for the anti-British riots which had broken out at Chittagong and Karachi. Wedgwood Benn, defending the Government's policy, argued that, despite the massacre at Cawnpore, India was more peaceful than it had been before the Round-Table Conference; and he reiterated MacDonald's pledge that the minorities of India would receive such safeguards as were required to preserve their existing political rights. Speaking for the Conservatives, Hoare pointed out that the Conservatives attached the utmost importance to

[1] Syed Waris Ameer Ali, 1886–1975. A descendant of the Prophet Mohammed. Son of the Rt Hon Syed Amir Ali, PC, CIE, of Oudh (the first Indian Privy Councillor) and Isabella Konstam of London. Educated at Wellington and Balliol College Oxford. Entered the Indian Civil Service, 1908. Served in the United Provinces, becoming eventually a District and Sessions Judge in Oudh. Retired 1929. Member of the Council, Indian Empire Society, 1930–32. Adviser to the High Commissioner for India in London, 1939–45. CIE, 1942. In 1918 he married Anne Radford; in 1951 (as her fourth husband), Lady Eleanor Dawson, younger daughter of the 3rd Earl of Dartrey. Resident in London from 1929.

these safeguards, which, if not secured, would endanger the Conservative agreement to cooperate with Labour in a non-partisan Indian policy. Churchill, while welcoming Hoare's reservations, poured scorn on the attempt to keep the Indian issue clear of party politics. It was this very effort, he believed, which had led to the weakness of the policy, and the bloodshed at Cawnpore. This bloodshed, he declared; this 'outbreak of primordial fury and savagery', unleashing 'animal and bestial instincts', was only a foretaste of what was going to happen throughout British India, but on a larger scale, when Britain withdrew 'its governing, guiding, and protecting hand'.[1]

Churchill went on to speak of the urgent need for social reform in India. 'If the Viceroys and Governments of India in the past had given half as much attention to dealing with the social conditions of the masses of the Indian people,' he declared, 'instead of concentrating upon political change, how much better for the working folk both of Burnley and Bombay, of Oldham and of Ahmedabad.' The conditions in the Indian mills were 'shocking'. Had successive Viceroys, instead of 'busying themselves with negotiating with unrepresentative leaders', chosen instead to address themselves 'towards the moral and material problems which are at the root of Indian life, I think it would have been very much better'.

Two years of Wedgwood Benn and the Labour Government, Churchill declared, had achieved only four things: the revival of the boycott, the ruin of Lancashire, the broken credit of India and 'the horrors of Cawnpore'. Muslims and Hindus were 'inflamed against one another'. The loyalty of the Princes was 'distracted and confused'. Gandhi and the Congress, who sought nothing less than 'absolute, complete independence', had been 'erected by the Government into a treaty-making power, quite unnecessarily and needlessly'. When deadlock was finally reached, Churchill warned, 'you will have to begin all over again to rebuild in suffering all that you have cast away in folly'.

During the debate, Brendan Bracken, who had been elected for Paddington in 1929, was one of the few Conservatives to support Churchill's stand. At the end of the debate Wedgwood Benn sought to counter the effect of Churchill's speech. Reminding the House of Commons of what he believed to be a historical parallel from the early 1920s, he declared:

... though he entered the Irish Conference with a dripping sword, he emerged with a dripping pen, and I am not without hope that even here, as

[1] In 1947, when India became independent, more than two million Hindus and Moslems were killed during six months of civil war.

he did in the Irish case, he will come in this matter to a better judgement, and that the greatest prophet brought by the King of Moab from afar to curse the chosen people may remain to bless, accompanied by his faithful friend from Paddington.

Despite Churchill's catalogue of the weaknesses and failures of Labour's India policy, Baldwin remained firmly committed to supporting that policy, not only by attending the second Round-Table Conference, but also by accepting the Labour Government's leadership of the India negotiations. The close cooperation between Baldwin and Mac-Donald ensured an overwhelming majority for the Government's India policy from both the Labour and the Conservative Parties, even though the Conservatives were still nominally in opposition. The Conservative leadership, by its appeal to Party loyalty, made Churchill's supporters reluctant to be counted, while at the same time his stand was increasingly portrayed as opportunist, and his arguments belittled and misrepresented. Thus his championing of the Muslim, Christian and Untouchable minorities, and his calls for social reform in India, were ignored; so too was his support for Provincial autonomy, while his forecasts of the grim events that would follow in India when British rule ended were denounced as provocative exaggerations, designed to frighten rather than to warn.

21

The Formation of the Coalition: Churchill's Final Isolation

ALTHOUGH the India controversy dominated the end of 1930 and the first seven months of 1931, Churchill had also become deeply concerned by the rise of National Socialism in Germany, and by reports of Nazi violence which had begun to appear in the Press. On 18 October 1930, after his meeting with Prince Bismarck at the German Embassy, Bismarck noted in a secret memorandum that Churchill had been following newspaper reports of events in Germany 'in detail', that he was 'pleased about the parliamentary victory of the Brüning[1] government', but that he expressed himself 'in cutting terms' on National Socialism. It was the Nazis, Churchill said, who had, under their leader Adolf Hitler,[2] 'contributed towards a considerable deterioration of Germany's external position', particularly towards France. Churchill went on to tell Bismarck that 'France was still afraid of Germany', as she had been five years before, and that it was 'no bad thing for Europe' that France had a strong army, as the French 'were

---

[1] Heinrich Brüning, 1885–1970. Fought in the First World War, winning the Iron Cross second and first class. Served in the Prussian Ministry of Health, 1919–21. Adviser to the German Christian Trade Union Movement, 1922–29. Centre Party Member of the Reichstag, 1924–33. Chancellor of the Reich, 1930–32. Emigrated to the United States, 1934. Research Fellow, Queen's College Oxford, 1937–39. Professor of Government, Harvard University, 1939–52. Returned to Germany as Professor of Political Science, University of Cologne, 1951–55. Died in the United States.

[2] Adolf Hitler, 1889–1945. Born in Austria-Hungary. Served on the western front as a Corporal in the German Army, 1914–18; wounded and gassed; Iron Cross first class. Assumed the Leadership of the National Socialist Workers Party, July 1921. Staged an unsuccessful putsch in Munich, 8 November 1923. Imprisoned in the Landsberg Fortress, January–December 1924. Published *Mein Kampf*, 1925. Chancellor of the German Reich from 30 January 1933, until his death. Chief of State, 2 August 1934. Committed suicide in Berlin, 30 April 1945.

not an aggressive people and would never think of making an un-provoked attack on Germany'. The Maginot Line which the French were building was the 'tangible' expression of French fears. Bismarck's note of Churchill's remarks continued:

Hitler had admittedly declared that he had no intention of waging a war of aggression; he, Churchill, however, was convinced that Hitler or his followers would seize the first available opportunity to resort to armed force.

Churchill went on to defend 'the re-creation of the Polish state' in 1919, and when Prince Bismarck spoke of the 'unsuitability' of the Polish corridor—a source of anger to Germans of all political parties—Churchill refused to agree, insisting 'that Poland must have an outlet to the sea'. Churchill then questioned Bismarck in detail about Germany's rights to cross the corridor, thus linking East Prussia and the rest of Germany, and 'seemed satisfied', as Bismarck reported, 'that railway and freight traffic was able to pass freely through the Polish Corridor'.

Churchill also spoke to Bismarck about post-war reparations, greatly regretting 'that no one had adopted his suggestions, made after the war, that the debtor and creditor nations, including Germany, should unite to form a common front against America'. This opportunity, he said, 'had now gone for ever' and he did not believe that America, 'in her present state, would ever grant Britain any remission'. Bismarck's memorandum was forwarded to the German Foreign Ministry in Berlin on 21 October 1930. In a covering note, the Senior Counsellor at the German Embassy in London, Albrecht Bernstorff,[1] commented: 'Although one should always bear in mind Winston Churchill's very temperamental personality when considering his remarks, they never-theless deserve particular attention,' especially because, 'as far as can be humanly foreseen he will play an influential role in any Conservative government in years to come—however difficult his personal position may be in the Conservative party, where he is mistrusted as an erstwhile Liberal and free-trader.'

At the beginning of 1931 Churchill spent some time writing a series of articles on foreign affairs for Hearst newspapers. These articles were syndicated throughout the United States. 'I have got a good crop of articles for 1931,' he had written to his son on January 8, 'and indeed am quite weighed down with work. But that is much better than being unemployed.' On January 11, in an article entitled 'the United States

[1] Albrecht Graf von Bernstorff, 1890–1945. Secretary to the German Embassy in London, 1923; Counsellor, 1925–30; Senior Counsellor, 1930–33. Left the civil service because of his opposition to Nazism, 1933. An uncompromising opponent of the Nazi regime. Imprisoned in Dachau Concentration Camp, 1940. Murdered by the Gestapo in Berlin, April 1945.

of Europe', Churchill made a bold appeal for European unity, writing optimistically of the benefits which a peacefully united Europe could bring. But these hopes received a sharp setback less than three months later, when, on 23 March 1931, Austria and Germany announced the establishment of a Customs Union. This was not the nature, or the process of unity which Churchill had envisaged. Writing again for the Hearst newspapers eight days later, he warned of the danger to peace in 'a revival of the secret old world diplomacy, supposed to be officially dead and buried'. No other powers had been informed in advance. Austria, despite the economic help she had received from the League of Nations, 'spoke no word of her plans to that kind-hearted body'. Both Arthur Henderson and Aristide Briand had expressed violent indignation at the proposed union. In his article, Churchill examined why they had reacted so critically. 'Beneath the Customs Union,' he wrote, 'lurks the "*Anschluss*" or union between the German mass and the remains of Austria.' Once Germany and Austria were united, Churchill warned, two European States in particular would feel themselves in danger, nor did he belittle the reality of that danger:

France with her dwindling but well-armed population sees the solid German block of seventy millions producing far more than twice her number of military males each year, towering up grim and grisly, luckily as yet largely unarmed. You cannot ask France to treat this as a trivial matter. When you have been three times invaded in a hundred years by Germany and have only escaped destruction the last time because nearly all the other nations of the world came to your aid, which they certainly do not mean to do again, you cannot help feeling anxious about this ponderous mass of Teutonic humanity piling up beyond the frontier.

The second State threatened by the *Anschluss*, Churchill warned, was Czechoslovakia, and he wrote:

Monsieur Masaryk[1] and Monsieur Beneš[2] have refounded an ancient nation. After centuries of 'bondage' they are what they call free. They have

---

[1] Thomas Garrigue Masaryk, 1850–1937. Born in Moravia. Professor at the new Bohemian University in Prague, 1882. A member of the Austro-Hungarian Parliament, 1891–93 and 1907–14. He opposed the encroachment of Germany on Austria, and fled first to Italy, then to Switzerland and finally to London, 1914. Organized the Czechoslovak independence movement, London, the United States and Russia, 1917–18. President of the Czechoslovak Republic, 1918–35.

[2] Eduard Beneš, 1884–1948. Born in Bohemia, the son of a farmer. Educated in Prague, Berlin and London. A leading member of the Czechoslovak National Council, Paris, 1917–18. Czech Minister for Foreign Affairs, 1918–35; Prime Minister, 1921–22. President of the Czechoslovak Republic, 1935–38. In exile, 1939–45; President of the Czechoslovak National Committee in London, 1939–45. Re-elected as President of the Republic, Prague, 1945. Resigned, 1948. Author of many books and pamphlets on the Czech question.

established a strong state on the broad basis of social democracy and anti-communism. They have three million five hundred thousand Austrian-Germans in their midst. These unwilling subjects are a care. But the *Anschluss* means that Czechoslovakia will not only have the indigestible morsel in its interior, but will be surrounded on three sides by other Germans. They will become almost a Bohemian island in a boisterous fierce-lapping ocean of Teutonic manhood and efficiency.

Churchill could see only a single advantage in the Austro-German plan, and that only if it were strictly limited to economic union, without any political links. By such a move, he wrote, the new extremism in Germany might conceivably be controlled. In his article he explained that a success for Brüning's foreign policy could have one important sequel, if it served to rob 'the much more dangerous Hitler movement of its mainspring', and he went on to ask: 'Will not the mastery of Hitler-ism by the constitutional forces in Germany be a real factor in the imme-diate peace of Europe? This also should be weighted.'

On 29 June 1931 Ramsay MacDonald, speaking in the House of Commons on the forthcoming disarmament conference, stated that British disarmament had not only been 'swift, patient and persistent', but that it had gone 'pretty near the limit of example'. His present aim, MacDonald explained, was to seek in Europe an 'all round' reduction of armaments and then to make 'still further reductions' on his return. Speaking after MacDonald, Churchill warned that since the Washing-ton Naval Conference of 1921 Britain had so disarmed as to become 'extremely vulnerable'; her army, 'cut to the bone', was now no more than a 'glorified police force', and her Air Force only an eighth as strong as that of France.[1] He feared a threat from Stalin's Russia, 'incalculable, aloof, malignant and actively preparing for war'. Above all, he feared that if France were forced to disarm, it would have a terrible effect in Eastern Europe, where all the States from the Baltic to the Black Sea looked to France 'for guidance and leadership'.

Churchill went on to oppose any pressure being put on France to disarm, warning the House: 'The sudden disappearance or undue weak-ening of that factor of unquestionable French military superiority may open the floodgates of measureless consequence.' Above all, he warned, Britain herself must be properly armed, and he declared: 'England's hour of weakness is Europe's hour of danger.' In an article for the Hearst

---

[1] Because of the disarmament policies of MacDonald's second Labour Government (1929–31), even the 1923 Air Programme had fallen into arrears, see page 457. Under the Versailles Treaty, Germany was not allowed a military air force.

newspapers on 10 August 1931 he wrote: 'German youth mounting in its broad swelling flood will never accept the conditions and implications of the Treaty of Versailles.'

During the summer of 1931 the economic situation worsened considerably. Following the New York stock market crash, in which Churchill's own United States stocks severely declined in value, unemployment rose in Britain, and all MacDonald's hopes of reviving the economy were shattered. One possible solution seemed to be the formation of an all-Party national Government. The only group that seemed to contemplate Churchill's help was the New Party, led by Sir Oswald Mosley,[1] who had resigned from the Labour Government a year before, but at a meeting with Mosley, Lloyd George, Brendan Bracken, Harold Nicolson and Sir Archibald Sinclair at Sinclair's house in Surrey on July 21, Churchill, though 'brilliant and amusing', as Nicolson recorded in his diary, expressed no interest in these political manoeuvrings, and during the last week of July he remained at Chartwell working on his new volume, the Eastern Front, and pushing forward research on Marlborough with the help of Maurice Ashley and a new research assistance, for naval aspects of the work, Lieutenant-Commander Owen.[2] He also completed the first two articles for a new and lucrative literary contract.[3]

[1] Oswald Ernald Mosley, 1896–1982. Educated at Winchester. Entered Sandhurst, January 1914; commissioned in the 16th Lancers, October 1914; transferred to the Royal Flying Corps, January 1915. Served with the 16th Lancers at Ypres, 1915. Invalided out, 1916. Worked at the Ministry of Munitions, and then the Foreign Office, 1917–18. Conservative MP for Harrow, 1918–22; Independent, 1922–24; Labour, 1924. Labour MP for Smethwick 1926–31. Succeeded his father as 6th Baronet, 1928. Chancellor of the Duchy of Lancaster in the second Labour Government, 1929–30. Elected to the Other Club, 1930. Founded the New Party, 1930; the British Union of Fascists, 1932. Imprisoned under Regulation 18B during the Second World War.

[2] John Hely Owen, 1883–1970. Midshipman, 1907; Lieutenant, 1912. Qualified as a submariner. Served in Submarine H2, 1916–18. Lieutenant-Commander, 1920. Served with the Reserve Fleet Destroyers and Minesweepers at the Nore, 1929–31; with the Naval Intelligence Department, 1931–33. Commander retired, 1934. Naval Intelligence Division, Admiralty 1939. Co-editor of four volumes of the Navy Records Society.

[3] The articles, on H. G. Wells and David Lloyd George, opened a twelve-part series, 'Personalities', published in Lord Rothermere's *Sunday Pictorial* between July 26 and November 15. The others of whom Churchill wrote were Ramsay MacDonald (July 26), Philip Snowden (2 August), Lord Brentford (August 9), Lady Astor and George Bernard Shaw (August 16), Baden-Powell (August 30), Montagu Norman (September 27), J. H. Thomas (October 4), Arthur Henderson (October 11), Sir John Simon (November 1) and Sir Herbert Samuel (November 15). For the twelve articles, Churchill received £2,400.

At the end of July Ashley left for Vienna to study the military archives there, while Churchill's cousin Shane Leslie[1] began a search for further material in the British Museum. At Chartwell, Colonel Hordern took charge of all the checking and final additions for the Eastern Front while Churchill, his wife and son left England for a month's holiday in France, going first to Consuelo Balsan's chateau at Dreux, and then to Biarritz. Churchill also took Mrs Pearman with him to France, as he intended to continue work both on the final proofs of the Eastern Front, and on further chapters of Marlborough. From Biarritz on August 7 he wrote to Edward Marsh, who had just read the Eastern Front in proof:

I am relieved that you take a favourable view of the book. Thank God it is finished. I am longing to get on to Marlborough, and am most interested to hear what you think about the two jumble chapters in which I broke into the subject. I am deeply indebted to you once again for helping me with my proofs. No one is your equal.

Here we have no sun for a whole week. It *is* a shame. I am tired of painting low tone pictures. Everybody I meet seems vaguely alarmed that something terrible is going to happen financially. I hope we shall hang Montagu Norman if it does. I will certainly turn King's evidence against him.

From Biarritz, Churchill, his wife and son travelled by car, first to Carcassonne and then to Avignon, but on August 16 Churchill returned briefly to London, where the Labour Government were facing serious economic difficulties. MacDonald and Snowden both wanted to stabilize the economy by a 10 per cent cut in unemployment benefits, in order to obtain an economy of £12½ million which had been made the condition for an American banking loan. The proposed economies had already divided the Cabinet, and now threatened to destroy the Government altogether. On August 13 MacDonald had approached Baldwin for guidance, and Baldwin had promised Conservative Parliamentary support for any acceptable economic scheme which MacDonald might devise to deal with the crisis. There was much talk of a Labour–Conservative Coalition, but Churchill did not favour it. On August 18 Sir Robert Horne wrote to Neville Chamberlain: 'the more I reflect on the situation, the more "tricky" it seems to me to be. There is

---

[1] John Randolph Shane Leslie, 1885–1971. Son of Sir John Leslie and Leonie Jerome. Churchill's first cousin. Educated at Eton and King's College Cambridge. Author and lecturer. Received into the Catholic Church, 1908. Contested Derry City as an Irish Nationalist, 1910, but defeated. Served in British Intelligence in the United States, 1915–16. Editor of the *Dublin Review*, 1916–25. Succeeded his father as 3rd Baronet, 1944.

a very definite body of Conservative opinion which would prefer us to take no responsibility whatsoever for Government plans. Winston Churchill, who came back last night for forty-eight hours, is aggressively of that view. This perhaps you would expect and discount.'

When Churchill returned to the South of France on August 20, the Labour Government was still intact, and as the crisis within the Cabinet worsened he remained in the South of France. 'I am waiting with great interest,' Colonel Hordern wrote to him on August 23, 'to see whether the present highly interesting political situation brings you back again: for your sake I hope not, though from every other point of view I wish it might.'

On August 23 Churchill went to the Hotel Provençale at Juan-les-Pins, where he painted, relaxed and enjoyed the warmth and sun. He also accepted a contract which Bracken had negotiated on his behalf with the *Daily Mail* whereby he would receive £7,800 for a series of weekly articles over the coming year. Churchill needed the money to help cover his substantial investment losses in the United States stock exchange crash. Nevertheless, he wrote to Bracken on August 23, 'I must reserve liberty to terminate the contract should I be called upon to take Office, and decide to do so.'

That same day, MacDonald's Cabinet met in London. The Trade Unions had already made it clear that they would not accept cuts in unemployment benefits. They were supported by several senior Cabinet Ministers, led by Arthur Henderson. Agreement proving impossible, the Ministers resigned. On August 24, at a Conference held at Buckingham Palace to resolve the crisis, the King asked MacDonald to remain in office at the head of an all-Party National Government. MacDonald accepted this commission, and was supported in his decision by Philip Snowden and J. H. Thomas. Most of his other Labour colleagues refused to serve in a Coalition, but the Conservatives at once agreed to do so. Lloyd George was too ill to play an active part in the crisis; instead Sir Herbert Samuel and Sir John Simon indicated acceptance of coalition on behalf of the Liberals, and MacDonald was able to form an all-Party Government. Churchill was not invited to be a member of the new administration.[1] On August 31 Sir Samuel Hoare wrote to Neville

[1] Of the ten members of MacDonald's Cabinet, four were Conservatives: Baldwin (who became Lord President), Neville Chamberlain (Minister of Health), Sir Samuel Hoare (Secretary of State for India) and Sir Philip Cunliffe-Lister (President of the Board of Trade). The two Liberal members of the new Cabinet were Lord Reading (Foreign Secretary) and Herbert Samuel (Home Secretary). Only three Labour Ministers agreed to serve under MacDonald: Philip Snowden (Chancellor of the Exchequer), J. H. Thomas (Colonial Secretary) and Lord Sankey (Lord Chancellor).

Chamberlain: 'As we have said several times in the last few days, we have had some great good luck in the absence of Winston and L.G.'

On his return from France at the beginning of September, Churchill continued his campaign against the now officially bi-partisan India policy. On September 7, in an article in the *Daily Mail*, he warned that it was important 'that we should not lose sight of India amid the anxieties of the financial crisis and the excitements of a new Government'. Gandhi was even then on his way to Britain for the second Round-Table Conference 'from which', Churchill wrote, 'nothing but further surrenders of British authority can emerge'. Without many more years of British 'guidance and control', such 'pure savagery' as the Hindu–Muslim violence at Cawnpore would continue, supported by the 'whole apparatus' of Hinduism, as seen on the river front at Benares 'with its palaces and temples, its shrines and its burning ghats, its priests and ascetics, its mysterious practices and multiform ritual . . . unchanged through the centuries, untouched by the West'.[1]

On September 8, when the second Round-Table Conference opened at St James's Palace, the British delegates declared that the change of Government would make no difference to the aim of full Dominion status for India. A few days later, Gandhi himself arrived in London for the Conference, to be welcomed personally by Ramsay MacDonald.

Also on September 8, Parliament discussed the emergency measures which were being adopted to alleviate the economic crisis. Following the decision to reduce the dole, the Bank of England had been able to obtain financial credit from the United States, thus staving off the immediate threat of national bankruptcy. Churchill, who spoke during the debate, made a short but fierce attack on the Labour Government's incompetence which had, he insisted, created the crisis. Although it was now the duty of Liberals and Conservatives alike 'to come to the rescue of a Socialist Government reduced to impotence', he said, they should not forget their 'grievous complaints' against MacDonald's previous administration.

[1] Entitled 'India Insistent', Churchill's article was a review of the book *India Insistent* by Sir Harcourt Butler, a former Governor of the United Provinces, who had served in India for thirty-eight years. At the end of his article Churchill wrote: 'By a curious, and it may be a fortunate, coincidence a nephew of Sir Harcourt Butler has been appointed private secretary to the new Secretary of State for India. Let us hope he will lose no time in placing a copy of his uncle's work upon the writing table of Sir Samuel Hoare.' The nephew was the young Conservative MP, R. A. Butler. He was already a staunch supporter of Dominion status. On 13 May 1933, in supporting Sir Harcourt Butler's election to the Other Club, Churchill wrote to Lord Reading: 'Unless he has changed his views since he wrote his book, he should be a valuable corrective to your unhappy propensities.'

On September 10 Philip Snowden introduced the National Government's emergency Budget, raising income and surtax, and increasing the taxes on tobacco, beer and petrol. These stern measures, which would normally have provoked Conservative indignation, were met instead with Conservative cheers. But Churchill was dissatisfied with the scope of the measures. Speaking in his constituency on September 11, he declared that the nature of the taxes imposed followed 'the most vexatious and irritating paths'. He would have preferred, he said, some bold, new scheme; indeed, because of the crisis, he was now prepared to abandon his most cherished economic tenet. Free Trade, he said, was too expensive a luxury for times of extreme economic distress. The urgent need was to limit the importing of foreign goods. Without 'a substantial measure of protection', Britain's balance of payments would never be corrected. The severity of the crisis had been accelerated by the 'excessive importation of unnecessary goods'. Protection, Churchill pointed out, had been urged by Walter Runciman, 'the life-long free-trader', and by Arthur Henderson, 'the leader of the Socialist Party'. Now he too, its opponent for many years, believed it to be essential in this time of crisis.

Churchill reiterated his call for Protection on September 15, during the House of Commons debate on the Budget. It was his 'strong belief', he declared, that a tariff was an absolute necessity 'for dealing with the present emergency'. During the debate, Sir John Simon, another life-long Liberal free-trader, also declared his conviction that tariffs were now essential.

The Government, having decided not to impose tariffs, had other plans to protect the economy; plans which Sir Maurice Hankey referred to in his diary that same Sunday: 'I spent the morning sun-bathing, interrupted by a long harangue on the telephone by Winston Churchill (who has Charlie Chaplin as his guest at Chartwell) on the situation. I could not enlighten him that we were going off the gold standard tomorrow, and had to listen to a torrent of suggestions to deal with a situation that had already passed out of history . . .'. The Gold Standard was formally abandoned on September 21. Thus came to an end the measure against which Churchill had argued seven years before, for which he nevertheless accepted full Ministerial responsibility, and to the workings of which most economists laid the growing unemployment, the industrial weakness and the increasing economic difficulties of the past five years. Another victim of the economic crisis was the Conservative Government's de-rating scheme of 1928, into which Churchill had put so much thought and time and energy. Rates, industrial as well as domestic, became henceforth a permanent feature of the economy, and Churchill's efforts, so successfully guided on to the statute book, and so linked with a vision of national prosperity, were cast aside.

In an article in the *Daily Mail* on October 6, Churchill urged the five million Liberal voters of 1929 to support the National Government in such a way as to make sure that Socialism 'will cease to impede British progress for a good many years to come'.[1] But despite a visit from Mac-Donald, Lloyd George refused to commit the Liberal Party to support the National Government, and MacDonald, after consulting Baldwin, decided to call a General Election without Lloyd George's support. Sufficient Liberals would support the National Government, Mac-Donald believed, to split the Liberal Party, and deprive it of the balancing power which it had wielded both in 1924 and 1929. MacDonald's calculation was correct. On October 5 a senior Liberal politician, Sir John Simon, declared that he was forming a special Liberal organization, the 'Liberal National' Party, to support MacDonald at the polls, and he was at once joined by twenty-three of the fifty-nine Liberal MPs who had been elected to Parliament in 1929.

On October 7, Parliament was dissolved, and the election set for October 27. The campaign was a bitter one, with more than two hundred of the Labour MPs of 1929 rejecting MacDonald's call for unity with the utmost scorn. Throughout his own election campaign at Epping, Churchill urged his constituents to support the National Government. There was, he insisted, no other solution to Britain's ills.[2]

When the election took place on October 27 it proved a triumph for the Conservatives, who won 473 seats. Of the three other supporters of the National Government, National Labour won 13 seats, Liberal National 35 and the Liberals 33. Of the National Government's principal opponents, the Labour Party were reduced to 52 seats, a loss of 236, while the Lloyd George Liberals won only 4 seats. At Epping, Churchill himself greatly increased his majority; in 1929 it had been under 5,000, in 1931 it was nearly 10,000. 'It was certainly a great triumph for you,' Thornton Butterworth wrote to him on November 3, 'and I feel that Mrs

[1] Following the formation of the National Government, more than 250 of the 288 Labour MPs had refused to support MacDonald, and formed an immediate Parliamentary opposition to all his proposed legislation. Thus, on September 29, on the third reading of the National Economy Bill, the main opposition speaker was Sir Stafford Cripps, who had been Solicitor-General in MacDonald's previous Government.

[2] During the election campaign, Churchill had been unable to persuade the BBC to allow him to broadcast. On October 23 he wrote to M. A. Frost, Managing Director of Colonial Radio Programmes Ltd: 'I have long resented the way in which the British Broadcasting Company denies me access to the public.'

Churchill and your family, if not yourself, are overjoyed at the result.'[1]

Despite the Conservative success within the Coalition, Ramsay MacDonald remained Prime Minister, and on November 5 he announced the composition of his new Government. Baldwin remained Lord President of the Council, Neville Chamberlain succeeded Snowden as Chancellor of the Exchequer and Sir Samuel Hoare remained Secretary of State for India. National Labour held only three Cabinet posts and the National Liberals two; the Conservatives held eleven. Baldwin's personal victory was complete; he and his Party had won effective control of the administration, beneath the umbrella of an all-Party Government.[2]

Given the Conservative Party's new and overwhelming dominance, Churchill neither expected nor received an invitation to participate, despite his support for the National Government at the polls. The result of the Election made his opposition to the Government's India policy much more difficult, for, of 615 MPs, only 20 were members of the Indian Empire Society, whereas Baldwin could also rely upon the 81 non-Conservative MPs committed to support the National Government, and who thereby provided him with a virtually unassailable political predominance. After two years out of office, Churchill was more isolated than at any time in his career.

On November 2, between polling day and the formation of the new Government, Churchill's final war volume, *The Eastern Front*, had been published by Thornton Butterworth. Because of the political crisis, it attracted far less attention than its predecessors.[3] One person who appreciated the work was his research assistant, Colonel Hordern, who had written to him on October 8: 'I have lived with the book so much during these last few months that I cannot help feeling an acute sense

---

[1] Churchill's principal opponent had been a Liberal lawyer, A. S. Comyns Carr, KC, who stood as a Free Trader, and also as a critic of the return to the Gold Standard in 1925. At the poll Carr received 15,670 votes, as against Churchill's 35,956.

[2] The list of junior Ministers, issued on November 10, contained 19 Conservatives, 4 Liberals, 3 National Liberals and 4 National Labour members.

[3] On November 19 Thornton Butterworth wrote to Churchill: 'I am sorry to say that "THE EASTERN FRONT" has not done as well as we expected. But I hear the same account all round, particularly in regard to Crewe's "LIFE OF ROSEBERY". However I am sure you will be sorry to hear that we are already about £500 on the wrong side.' Churchill of course, had already received his £2,500 advance for the book, a sum that was non-returnable.

of loss now it is done.' Working on the book, Hordern added, was 'the most congenial task anyone ever had'. Churchill was touched by Hordern's letter, thanking him three days later 'for the friendship it expresses', and adding: 'I am afraid my methods of book-making must have seemed rather rough and ready, however, thanks to you a creditable result has I believe been achieved.'

Without a place in the Government, Churchill remained at Chartwell writing articles. The abuse of wealth and privilege was a regular theme of Churchill's articles. On November 28 he wrote in the *Daily Mail*, in an article on 'the spartan life' in public schools: 'The Public Schools were founded for poor scholars and men of moderate means. To make them the privilege of temporary wealth is an insult to the past and a danger to the future.' Several times during the first week of November Admiral Dewar[1] sent copious corrections for a series of five articles which Churchill had written on the war at sea; and on November 6 Dewar wrote: 'I am very sorry to see that you are not in the new Cabinet. I had hoped that you might have gone to the Admiralty and done very necessary work for the Navy.'[2]

Parliament reassembled on November 10. Churchill now sat below the gangway. On November 11 he made his first contribution to the debate, amusing MPs by 'borrowing' a phrase from the King's speech: 'My relations with foreign powers continue to be friendly'. During his speech, Churchill said of MacDonald that he had rendered the nation an 'inestimable service'; and he added: 'He has destroyed the Socialist Party as a Parliamentary force.' The small Labour opposition deeply resented this remark.

On November 20 the House of Commons debated the Statute of Westminster Bill, whose aim was to determine the constitutional relationship between the different nations of the British Commonwealth. J. H. Thomas explained that the Bill would finally bring to an end the powers of the House of Commons to disallow legislation passed in the various Dominion Parliaments. The Bill was welcomed on behalf of the

[1] Kenneth Gilbert Balmain Dewar, 1879–1964. Entered HMS *Britannia*, 1893. Commander, 1911. Assistant Director, Plans Division, Admiralty Naval Staff, 1917. Deputy Director, Naval Intelligence Division, 1925–27. Commanded HMS *Royal Oak* and *Tiger*, 1924–29. Rear-Admiral, retired, 1929; Vice-Admiral, 1934.

[2] Two days later Admiral Dewar returned the last of Churchill's naval articles with the note that he had corrected several 'serious inaccuracies which would expose you to serious attack'. The articles, which were published in the *Daily Telegraph*, were 'Germany's Desperate U Boat Decision' (November 16); 'Politicians were Right and Admirals Wrong' (November 18); 'Jellicoe's Dramatic Decision at Admiralty' (November 23); 'Triumph of the Convoy System' (November 25) and 'Eleven U-Boats Destroyed in Dover Minefields' (November 30).

Labour Party by Sir Stafford Cripps,[1] as recognizing the stage of evolution now reached by the Empire. Churchill was the first speaker to criticize the proposals. Although he had, in 1926, subscribed to the Imperial Conference Declaration on which the Bill was based, he feared the effect the Bill would have on India. For the first time, the Indians would see set out, in 'cold legal language', the meaning of Dominion status. They would see that it meant much more, in terms of local powers, than it had meant ten years before; and they would see the limitations to the safeguards which Westminster could in reality impose.

Churchill had intended to leave England on December 2 for a three-month lecture tour in the United States. At the last moment, however, learning that there was to be a debate on India on December 3, he postponed his departure. He was determined not to leave without making his views clear in the new Parliament, containing as it did so many newly elected Members, and on December 1, at the Conservative Party Conference, he warned the delegates of the dangers of surrendering Britain's protective power in India, at a time when so many other States were jettisoning democracy. That same day, at the final session of the second Round-Table Conference, Ramsay MacDonald said that despite the deadlock which had been reached on how to safeguard Muslim and other minority rights, the Government were determined to set up as soon as possible a Federal legislature, and to proceed without delay towards the goal of Dominion Status.

On December 3 the House of Commons debated the Government's India policy. MacDonald insisted that the 'political capacity' of the Indian people had much increased since the Simon Commission's recommendations two years earlier. The fact that the Indian communities themselves were in disagreement, he declared, must not lead Britain to hesitate in its aim. Sir Samuel Hoare, as Secretary of State for India, stressed that the Government had no intention of dispensing with the necessary Imperial safeguards, or allowing the ultimate decision to be taken away from Westminster.

Churchill was profoundly dissatisfied by these declarations and assurances. Despite an appeal from MacDonald, he insisted on moving an amendment and thus forcing a vote. In a speech lasting an hour and a half he castigated the Conservative Party for having abandoned its

---

[1] Richard Stafford Cripps, 1889–1952. Educated at Winchester. Barrister, 1913. Red Cross, France, 1914. Assistant Superintendent, Queen's Ferry Munitions Factory, 1915. Labour MP, 1931–50. Solicitor-General, 1930–31. Knighted, 1930. Ambassador to Moscow, 1940–42. Minister of Aircraft Production, 1942–45. President of the Board of Trade, 1945. Minister for Economic Affairs, 1947. Chancellor of the Exchequer, 1947–50.

principles, and for having, in the plenitude of its new power, accepted without dissent the Labour Party's India policy. During his speech he warned that were the Indians allowed to control defence, finance or the police, disaster would follow and he repeated his earlier warnings that Britain's restraining hand would be needed for many years to keep in check the warring passions of Muslim and Hindu, and to protect the Indian minorities.

In answer to Churchill, first Simon, then Austen Chamberlain, and finally Baldwin insisted that the Government's India policy must be followed through. 'Give us our mandate tonight,' Baldwin declared, 'and wish us luck in the most difficult task that anyone in this Empire has ever tried to undertake.'

The Conservative leaders were hopeful that Baldwin's appeal would succeed. 'Of the attitude of the House of Commons I was very nervous,' Hoare wrote to the new Viceroy of India, Lord Willingdon, on December 3. 'The debate is not yet over, but it is clear to me that three quarters of the House at least will accept our position.' Hoare judged the mood correctly. When Churchill's amendment was put to a division it received only 43 votes, as opposed to 369 votes for the Government. Five days later, in the House of Lords, an attempt by Lord Lloyd to challenge the Government's policy was defeated by 106 votes to 58. MacDonald, his policy secured by these results, proceeded at once to set up three Commissions of Inquiry to make detailed proposals. Each Commission was headed by a Conservative or Liberal supporter of the Government's policy.[1]

His protest made, Churchill embarked on the earliest possible liner *en route* for the United States, the German steamship *Europa*, together with his wife, and their daughter Diana.

---

[1] Of the three Commissions sent out to India, the Federal Finance Committee was headed by Lord Eustace Percy, the Indian States Enquiry by J. C. C. Davidson and the Finance Committee by Lord Lothian (formerly Philip Kerr).

22

Visit to the United States:
A Serious Accident

CHURCHILL'S main aim in going to the United States was to regain some of the money he had lost in the New York stock market crash. As he had explained in a letter to Bernard Baruch on November 1, he had contracted to give forty lectures during his visit, for a total guaranteed minimum fee of £10,000. In addition, largely as a result of Brendan Bracken's persistence, the *Daily Mail* was paying him nearly £8,000 for a series of articles whose sale in the United States he was still free to negotiate. Furthermore, Bracken had written to him on August 22, 'as you are going on this hateful American journey you will have time to dictate a number of articles on American and other topics which will give you but little labour & will swell your income'.

Confidence in Britain's future was to be one of the principal themes of Churchill's lectures; the other was the need for closer Anglo-American cooperation. On December 11 the *Europa* reached New York, and on the following day, during the first of his lectures, at Worcester, Massachusetts, he urged such cooperation in a lecture entitled 'Pathway of the English-speaking People'. Five weeks later, in a letter to his son, Churchill wrote: 'It certainly went extremely well. The people were almost reverential in their attitude.'

On December 13 Churchill was back in New York, preparing further lectures. That evening, after he had dined with his wife, Bernard Baruch telephoned to ask him to meet a few mutual friends who had gathered at Baruch's house, further up Fifth Avenue. Churchill at once took a taxi from his hotel, the Waldorf-Astoria, to Baruch's house. But the taxi-driver did not know exactly where it was, nor could Churchill remember the number, nor recognize the house. There followed an hour-long search, during which Churchill grew more and more impatient at the repeated traffic light stops—not having travelled on a road with traffic lights before. Finally, after driving for nearly an hour up and down Fifth Avenue, he told the driver to stop on the Central Park side of the avenue, while he himself crossed the avenue to the houses opposite to see if at last he had arrived at Baruch's, which he was sure he would still recognize from his previous visit two years before. Crossing the road he looked left, saw the headlights of an approaching car more than two hundred yards away and began to cross. Suddenly, from the right, he was struck by an oncoming car and hurled to the ground. The blow was a serious one, both on his forehead and his thighs, for the oncoming car was travelling at between 30 and 35 miles per hour.[1] A crowd rapidly gathered. Churchill, although in great pain, remained conscious, and when a policeman pressed him for details of the accident he insisted that it was entirely his own fault. An ambulance approached, and was stopped by the crowd, which urged its driver to take Churchill to the nearest hospital; but the ambulance already had a serious case on board and had to drive off. Finally a taxi-driver took Churchill to the Lennox Hill Hospital.

As a result of the severe blow which he had sustained, Churchill developed pleurisy, and had to remain in hospital, where he received several thousand telegrams and letters of sympathy from friends and strangers. Clementine Churchill remained at her husband's bedside, telegraphing to Randolph on the morning of December 15: 'Temperature 100.6. Pulse normal. Head scalp wound severe. Two cracked ribs. Simple slight pleural irritation of right side. Generally much bruised. Progress satisfactory.'[2]

It was not until December 21 that Churchill was well enough to leave the hospital and for two more weeks he had to remain in bed at the Waldorf-Astoria. 'I do hope you will get properly rested before you start lecturing again,' Randolph wrote to his father from London on

---

[1] According to legend, Churchill was knocked down by a taxi. But although he had *left* a taxi to cross the road, the car which hit him was a private one. Its driver, Mario Constasino, was a mechanic and truck-driver who had been driving for more than eight years without ever having had an accident. At the time of the accident he had been out of work for two months; his mother having died, he was having to support his father and two sisters. Subsequently he visited Churchill in hospital, and attended Churchill's first New York lecture after his recovery.

[2] On learning from Churchill of his recovery from his accident, Professor Lindemann telegraphed: 'Just received wire. Delighted good news. Collision equivalent falling thirty feet on to pavement. Equal six thousand foot pounds energy. Equivalent stopping ten pound brick dropped six hundred feet or two charges buckshot point-blank range. Rate inversely proportional thickness cushion surrounding skeleton and give of frame. If assume average one inch your body transferred during impact at rate eight thousand horsepower. Congratulations on preparing suitable cushion and skill in bump.'

December 22, 'I feel sure it would be a great mistake to try anything so tiring as lecturing till you have completely got over the shock.' On the political front, Randolph reported, 'David Margesson[1] tells me that the House is not likely to meet again until he has tamed all his forces', and he added: 'Poor Brendan was almost in tears over your accident.' On December 23 Churchill was well enough to dictate a number of replies to the many telegrams he had received. The accident, he informed George Harrap, 'nearly put an end to all possibilities of "The Life of John, Duke of Marlborough"'.

Randolph Churchill continued to telephone his father to find out about his progress. 'Dearest Randolph,' Churchill telegraphed back on December 28, 'I was delighted to hear your voice and to feel your thought for me. You caught me when I was tired and depressed. Am feeling much better today.' Churchill added that he was much looking forward to resuming his lectures after a week's recuperation in the Bahamas, that American opinion and interest were 'admirable', and that all the lectures for January, February and March were already sold out. Of his son's financial problems, he warned: 'Please think of our common interests and your responsibilities.'[2]

On December 28 Churchill telegraphed a full account of the accident to the *Daily Mail*. 'Am now able to crawl around fairly well . . .' he informed Esmond Harmsworth in a covering cable. 'Have had horrible bump. Good wishes for New Year and love to your pets Ramsay and Baldwin.' In his article he wrote:

I certainly suffered every pang, mental and physical, that a street accident or, I suppose, a shell wound can produce. None is unendurable. There is neither the time nor the strength for self-pity. There is no room for remorse or fears. If at any moment in this long series of sensations a grey veil deepen-

---

[1] Henry David Reginald Margesson, 1890–1965. Educated at Harrow and Magdalene College Cambridge. On active service, 1914–18 (Military Cross). Captain, 1918. Conservative MP for Upton, 1922–23; for Rugby, 1924–42. Assistant Government Whip, 1924. Junior Lord of the Treasury, 1926, 1926–29 and 1931. Chief Government Whip, 1931–40. Privy Councillor, 1933. Secretary of State for War, 1940–42. Created Viscount, 1942.

[2] Less than two months earlier, on November 3, Churchill had protested to his son about a debt of £600 which Randolph had incurred in betting on the 1931 election result. In agreeing to pay his son's debt, Churchill had written: 'If you feel yrself able to keep a magnificent motor car & chauffeur at a rate wh must be £700 or nearly £800 a year, you are surely able to pay yr debts of honour yrself. Unless & until you give proof of yr need by ridding yrself of this gross extravagance you have no right to look for aid from me; nor I to bestow it. I have many to look after whom you should not trench upon. I grieve more than is worth setting down to see you with so many gifts & so much good treatment from the world leading the life of a selfish exploiter, borrowing & spending every shilling you can lay yr hands upon, & ever increasing the lavish folly of yr ways. But words are useless.'

ing into blackness had descended upon the sanctum I should have felt or feared nothing additional.

Nature is merciful and does not try her children, man or beast, beyond their compass. It is only where the cruelty of man intervenes that hellish torments appear. For the rest—live dangerously; take things as they come; dread naught, all will be well.[1]

On December 31 Churchill and his wife sailed from New York for Nassau, in the Bahamas. While they were still on board ship, Churchill's article on his accident reached the *Daily Mail*. The article was published in two parts, on January 4 and 5. Syndicated all over the world, it earned Churchill more than £600. 'I rather plume myself,' he wrote to his son from Nassau on January 5, 'upon having had the force to conceive, write and market this article so soon after the crash.' 'I received a great price for it,' Churchill added, 'but find it very dearly bought.'

Still weak from his accident, Churchill decided to prolong his stay in the Caribbean until January 22, and to postpone his American lectures accordingly. 'In spite of all the accident trouble and pain I have had,' he told his son, 'I am very glad to be away from this administration and look forward greatly to being back in my corner seat in the House of Commons.'

For three weeks Churchill remained in the Bahamas, but his recovery was slow. On January 12 Clementine Churchill wrote to her son:

> I am sure he will be again as well as before, but he is terribly depressed at the slowness of his recovery and when he is in low spirits murmurs 'I *wish* it hadn't happened.' He has horrible pains in his arms and shoulders. The doctors call it neuritis but they don't seem to know what to do about it. I think the sunshine and the bathing are doing him good, but of course what is really needed is 3 or 4 months complete relaxation. . . .
>
> Papa is worried about the Lectures and thinks he will not be able to stay the course. . . . I hope however that they may *actually* help his recovery, especially if he starts off with a big success in New York. As for staying the course after he has done, say, 6 or 10 if he is feeling the strain I shall persuade him to cancel the rest and I shall bring him home.
>
> Last night he was very sad and said that he had now in the last 2 years had 3 very heavy blows. First the loss of all that money in the crash, then the loss of his political position in the Conservative Party and now this terrible physical injury. He said he did not think he would ever recover completely from the three events.

[1] On 14 February 1932 Churchill's aunt Lady Leslie, wrote to him: 'Thank goodness you are alright again, and with no tiresome after effects I trust. What an escape and how lucky for you that Clemmy was there. I was in hospital in Dublin myself at the time, and said many a prayer for you as I laid awake at night. Of course you have been spared to still do great things in the future and I mean to live on to see it all!' Lady Leslie died in 1943, aged 83.

You can imagine how anxious I am and I often wish you were here to help and advise me. I had hoped he would paint here but he does not seem to have the strength or energy to start. He bathes every morning and likes that but he stays in only a few minutes in the shallows.

We play a lot of backgammon. He has been reading one or two novels. The climate here is delicious. . . .

On January 13, on Brendan Bracken's initiative, a number of Churchill's friends decided to buy him a car to celebrate his recovery. Their choice was a Daimler, and Churchill was delighted by the gift.[1] He was also slowly recovering, as he wrote to his son on January 20:

You will be glad to hear that during the last week I have made a decided improvement. The neuritis in my arms has diminished and I can move much more freely and sleep in any position. I bathe every day and have a sun bath too whenever there are no clouds. Today I swam about two hundred yards and was up and about from 11 to 5. I am now resting before dinner. The bathing does me any amount of good. The temperature of the water today was 74°, crystal clear, buoyant and delicious. . . .

The days pass very quickly. I wish I had another fortnight here; that, I believe, would make me quite well. However, I expect that the electric atmosphere of New York will act as a tonic itself after this soothing and somewhat enervating climate.

Your Mother and Diana are enjoying themselves very much here and have made many friends. I have never seen your Mother so well or so completely amused. It has done her a power of good and I know she will want to come back here some day. . . .

'I have not felt like opening the paint box,' Churchill added, 'although the seas around these islands are luminous with the most lovely tints of blue and green and purple.'

On January 22 Churchill, his wife and his daughter left Nassau for New York, which they reached on the morning of January 25. For three days Churchill worked at the Waldorf-Astoria on his lectures, the first of which was delivered on January 28 before two thousand people in the Brooklyn Academy of Music. Churchill's theme remained as before the 'Pathway of the English Speaking Peoples', and he repeated it in each of his lectures. The 'great opposing forces in the future', he forecast, would be 'the English-speaking Peoples and Communism'. It would be the duty of Britain and the United States to stand together to protect 'the distracted peoples of Europe' from Communist tyranny. It was absurd, Churchill said, for Britain and America to go on 'gaping at

[1] There were eight donors, Lord Burnham, Sir Harry Goschen, Esmond Harmsworth, Lord Lloyd, Lord Londonderry, Sir Harry McGowan, Sir Archibald Sinclair and Bracken.

each other in this helpless way', and to be ashamed of Anglo-American cooperation 'as if it were a crime'.

On February 1, while still in New York, Churchill wrote to Sir James Hawkey, at Epping: 'I am making steady progress and gaining strength every day. I am, however, still suffering from the after-effects of what was a hideous shock, and I expect it will be some months before I am really myself again.' As for politics in Britain, he wrote: 'I think that the MacDonald–Baldwin combination will last for some time in a sort of amorphous and gelatinous condition, and that gradually the need for more clear-cut solutions will come home to the public.'

Leaving New York, Churchill travelled westwards, lecturing every day in a different city.[1] From Chicago, where he reiterated his plea for the closest possible Anglo-American cooperation, he wrote to Robert Boothby on February 6:

I have had a most strenuous week, travelling every night, lecturing every day, with much weakness caused by my accident and a bad sore throat, but with very fine meetings and very large profits. I am now back in Chicago for a second meeting.

The United States Police have played up wonderfully, and I have been guarded every moment, night and day, by groups of armed plain-clothes men. Detroit and Chicago are both places where Indian trouble was expected, but as they had about two police gun-men along-side every Indian seen no trouble arose.

I have gone the whole hog against gold. To hell with it! It has been used as a vile trap to destroy us. I would pay the rest of the American Debt in gold as long as the gold lasted, and then say—'Hence-forward, we will only pay in goods. Pray specify what goods you desire.'

Surely it will become a public necessity to get rid of Montagu Norman. No man has ever been stultified as he has been in his fourteen years' policy.

I am very glad not to be at home just now. I shall return to find us a tariff country, and I shall accept with simple faith the new dispensation. How glad I am not to be mixed up in this slatternly show!

Churchill went on to suggest to Boothby that they should go together to the Republican and Democratic Conventions that summer. 'We should, of course, see all the politicians of both great Parties,' he wrote, 'and be in the very centre of their affairs.' Churchill would write articles on the Conventions, and Boothby could pay his way either by writing

---

[1] For each of his lectures Churchill received £300; during the first week of February he spoke in Brooklyn, Hartford, St Louis, Chicago, Cleveland, Toledo and Detroit; during the second week in New York, Rochester, Washington and Philadelphia; and in the third week in Baltimore, Atlanta, Grand Rapids, Indianapolis, Cincinnati, Concord, Boston and Ann Arbor. His total earnings exceeded £7,500. A Prime Minister then earned £5,000 a year.

articles of his own, 'or failing that, by helping me with mine'. Churchill added: 'It certainly will be a thing to see. Better than watching the Ramsay–Baldwin performance on the Westminster stage. These two old tired Tims of the Commons have ceased to command my allegiance.'

On February 8 Churchill returned from Chicago to New York, where he addressed a meeting of industrialists, bankers and economists. 'Let us have good courage,' he declared at the end of a long lecture on the causes of the depression. 'Do not add to monetary deflation the hideous deflation of panic and despair.'

Churchill's lectures continued with increasing success. On February 10 the *Daily Telegraph* reported that his tour had developed 'into a triumphal progress', and that at each lecture he was received with a 'tumultuous' welcome, with the entire audience rising to their feet to cheer him. On February 13, during his visit to Washington, he had an interview with President Hoover, and visited the House of Representatives, where the debate was briefly suspended so that members could greet him. On February 28, in a telegram to his son from Indianapolis, Churchill rejoiced that his 'lecture pilgrimage' was 'drawing wearily' to its close. To Esmond Harmsworth he wrote on February 29:

I have been terribly remiss in my articles, but, although I have got several very good ones in my head, I have not had the margin of life and strength to do them while travelling and speaking so many nights in succession. We must talk about it all when I come home, which, I rejoice to say, will be soon.

I am having a very successful tour and am everywhere received if not as well as you were in Hungary,[1] quite well enough for all practical purposes. There is great tension here beneath the surface, and almost everyone and everything in a tight place. One feels, at this distance, the solid enduring strength of England and her institutions.

I have never seen anything like the friendliness of sentiment towards us in any of my former visits. All classes and both Parties are in an entirely favourable mood. . . . In spite of all the humbug that attended the formation of the National Government, one feels the benefit of it abroad. We are a power respected and considered to be revivified. I am very glad to have been away during these months, and look forward to a comfortable Spring and Summer.

During a final week in New York Churchill spent much of his time discussing his future books with Charles Scribner, reviewing his investments with Bernard Baruch, and planning new literary projects with

---

[1] Esmond Harmsworth and his father (Lord Rothermere) were both outspoken critics of the Trianon Peace Treaty, which had transferred large Magyar speaking areas from Hungary to Rumania. At one time, Esmond Harmsworth was even considered as a possible Regent for Hungary.

the editorial staff of *Colliers*. Then, on March 11, he left New York for England, on board the liner *Majestic*. 'I shall not attempt to see you off,' Charles Scribner wrote to him on the day of his departure, 'as you probably will have more friends at the ship than you know what to do with,' and he added: 'I sincerely hope that you made no mistake in trusting your books to us. It is true that they have not yet had the success that we know they merit but we have not lost courage and will continue to back them until they come into their own.'

The *Majestic* docked at Southampton on March 17, where Churchill's friends awaited him with the new Daimler. For two weeks he rested at Chartwell, dictating articles and taking up the threads of his *Marlborough* biography. In his absence, Maurice Ashley had done three-and-a-half months' work in several archives. Writing to Thornton Butterworth on April 1, Churchill commented: 'I am much better, but I feel I need to rest and not to have to drive myself so hard. You have no idea what I have been through.'

23

1932: 'Not Exhibiting This Year'

FOR most of April, Churchill remained at Chartwell. The effects of his New York accident were proving difficult to shake off. 'I am alright,' he wrote to Lord Salisbury on April 2, 'but I get tired more easily than I did; and of course eight nights out of ten in the train and twenty-five harangues in a month were a rough kind of convalescence.' That same day, learning that Edward Marsh had been seriously ill, Churchill wrote to him from Chartwell: 'We shall be down here a great deal now and if you like to come and pay us a visit, pray let us know. You could rest comfortably here. Clemmie says you *must* come. Just vegetate —as I do.'

On April 21 Churchill made his first speech in the House of Commons since his accident. Criticizing the National Government's first Budget, which had been introduced by Neville Chamberlain, he expressed his deep regret that the duty on beer had not been reduced. Much of his speech was in humorous vein; but his concluding theme was a serious one, drawn from his experiences in the United States. During his visit in 1929, he said, the Americans had regarded Britain as decadent and outworn; now she was looked at with admiration and envy. It was up to Britain to exploit this feeling, and to give a lead in Anglo-American cooperation, especially in the economic sphere. 'If tomorrow,' he said, 'the English speaking world were in agreement on its main purpose, France, in spite of her hoarded gold, would seek admission to their Councils on the following day.'

Churchill returned once more to Chartwell, where he worked on *Marlborough* with Maurice Ashley. On April 30 he went up to London to speak at the Royal Academy dinner. His speech was a masterpiece of humour during which, as his notes recorded, he began by speaking of Ramsay MacDonald:

> His works are well-known;
> regret not more of them at home.

Exhibiting so much in foreign galleries,[1]
   that we miss his productions here.

Believe he has several most important masterpieces
   on Continent,
     which are still unfinished;
       look forward hopefully their arrival and his return.

I have watched many years
   his style and methods.

For long time
   thought too much vermillion
     in his pictures

Those lurid sunsets of Empire,
   and capitalist civilisations,
     began to pall on me.

Very glad altered his style so fundamentally.

In all his new pictures
   see use of cobalt, French ultramarine,
     Prussian blue,
       and all other blues,
         especially cerulean—a heavenly colour.

Uses blue now like Sargent,
   not only for atmosphere,
     but even as foundation.

I like his modern style much better
   than his earlier method.

Churchill went on to speak about Baldwin:

If criticised—
   little lacking in colour,
     and in precise definition
       of objects in foreground.

He too has changed in later life
   not only his style but his subjects.

We all miss very much
   those jolly old-English scenes
     he used to paint.

[1] On 21 April 1932 Ramsay MacDonald had travelled to Geneva to take part in the five-Power conversations on disarmament, a part of the World Disarmament Conference. He had remained in Geneva until April 28.

The Worcestershire farm,
    Pigs in clover,
        brocolli in Autumn,

and above all, just now,
    'Brewing the audit ale'.

Still must admit
    something very reposeful
        his twilight studies
            in half-tone.

Finally, Churchill spoke of himself:

But sure you will ask
    why I am not exhibiting this year,
        why no important pictures on the line?

Frankly, differences with the Committee
    and this year
        not submitting any of my works
            for their approval.

Joined the teaching profession—
    a sort of Slade school.

We have a very fine lot of young students,
    and glad to assist them
        in learning some rudiments
            of parliamentary technique.

Still a few things on easel
    which I hope some day
        present to public.

On May 2 Baldwin wrote to Churchill:

My dear Winston,

I am profoundly touched by your generous appreciation of my work as expressed in your speech at the Academy on Saturday night.

There is so much jealousy in the art world that a kind word to the painter from so distinguished an exponent of a far different style shews a breadth of mind as it is delightful.

And I am glad to think that although my own preference is for still life and half-tone, I do enjoy the bright and sometimes fierce lights in which you revel, and no one will be more interested than I when you come to exhibit the work which is still on your easel.

Yours always
S.B.

Churchill, touched by Baldwin's letter, replied from Chartwell on May 3:

My dear S.B.,

I was vy glad that my chaff did not vex you. My shafts though necessarily pointed are never intentionally poisoned. If they cut, I pray they do not fester in the wound.

I am also glad to feel that although we have differences, we have not had any misunderstandings.

It was nice of you to write.

Yours always

W.

On May 8 Churchill made his first radio broadcast to the United States. 'They tell me,' he began, 'I may be speaking to thirty millions of Americans. I am not at all alarmed. On the contrary I feel quite at home. I have often spoken to American audiences before. I know the goodwill and attention with which they listen to fair and plain statements.' His main appeal was, as it had been in the United States, for a joint Anglo-American monetary policy to combat the depression. 'Believe me,' he said, 'no one country, however powerful, can combat this evil alone.'

As Churchill had forecast, the Government's policy of conciliation in India did not go smoothly; indeed, as he had warned on 12 March 1931, the Congress Party decided early in 1932, under Gandhi's leadership, to revive the civil disobedience campaign which had been called off as a result of the Gandhi–Irwin pact. Its reason was the refusal of the new Viceroy, Lord Willingdon, to discuss with Congress his emergency legislation to deal with a series of murderous attacks on British officials in Bengal, the North-West Frontier and the United Provinces. This legislation gave the Government substantial new powers of search and arrest. On January 4, after Gandhi himself had been arrested in Bombay, Churchill had written to his son from America about the Government:

What troubles they have brought upon themselves, the Indians and all of us! However, there seems to be nothing to quarrel with them over now. I predict that the firm handling of the situation and the knowledge throughout India that there is strong United Conservative power in London will soon expose the hollowness of the Congress pretensions and show what lies were told when it was said that many divisions of troops would have to go from

England to restore order. As I have always said an effort of will-power was the main need.

Churchill's approval of Willingdon's measures lessened his hostility to the Government. 'I am not ill-disposed to them now they have begun to act sensibly in India,' he wrote to Robert Boothby on February 6. 'I always said how easy it would be to crush Gandhi and the Congress. You remember how we were told it meant sending an Army and all that! What lies to darken counsel!'

On May 25, at a private meeting of the Indian Empire Society, Churchill warned his listeners that although, since Gandhi's arrest nearly five months earlier, civil disobedience had been met by stern measures, not all these measures had been adequate to counter the force and fury of Indian extremism. The trade of some cities, in particular Bombay, had been repeatedly brought to a complete halt by boycotts and picketing. On February 7 the retiring Governor of Bengal, Churchill's Harrow contemporary Sir Stanley Jackson, had narrowly escaped assassination while addressing the Convocation of Calcutta University, and on April 30 the new District Magistrate of Midnapore, Robert Douglas,[1] had been shot dead during a meeting of his District Board. During the first three weeks of May more than 200 people were killed and 3,000 injured during Hindu–Muslim riots, and more than 30,000 Indians had been convicted of offences against the new regulations.

Churchill reminded his audience of how he had said, a year and a half before: 'Sooner or later we shall have to crush Gandhi and the Congress and all that they stand for,' and he went on:

You will remember how I was abused—practically in every newspaper— for these remarks, as exacerbating racial feeling, and creating an obstacle to progress in India. The 'Times' of course, led the way, but there was some cocoa slop from the Daily News. Now what do we see a year and a half afterwards. This assertion, with which nobody then agreed, except the Indian Empire Society, who placed it in the forefront of their main pronouncement, has been accepted as an integral part of the Government policy. . . .

There was, Churchill insisted, a new danger emerging; the Indian Franchise Committee, established by MacDonald and sup-

---

[1] Robert Douglas, 1889–1932. Educated at George Watson's College and Edinburgh University. Entered the Indian Civil Service, 1914; an Assistant Magistrate and Collector, Bengal, 1915–16. On active service with the Indian Army, 1916–19. Under-Secretary to the Governor of Bengal, Financial Department, 1919. Employed by the Princely State of Bikanir, 1923–24. Deputy Secretary, Financial Department, Bengal, 1924–25; Government of India, 1925. Magistrate and Collector, Burdwan, 1929; Midnapore, 1931. Murdered, 30 April 1932.

ported by Baldwin, had recommended increasing the Indian electorate from 7 millions to 36 millions. 'I know that everybody here agrees with me,' Churchill declared, 'that democracy is totally unsuited to India, and that the Franchise is almost a farce. Instead of conflicting opinions, you have bitter theological hatreds.' It was, he said, 'humiliating to remember that this policy was introduced by a Conservative Government, supported by a Commission which had a Lord[1] at its head'. Those of his listeners who were Members of Parliament, he urged, should refuse to accept these Indian Franchise proposals. In the present Parliament, he declared, 'whatever the press may tell you, we have power'; when that power was asserted, 'Government will obey, and India will be saved'. It was essential, he said, for the Government to go back to the proposals of the Simon Commission, and to limit its commitment to provincial self-government.

Churchill's warnings were not exaggerated. 'The nearer we get to the Bill,' Hoare wrote to Willingdon on May 27, 'the more apprehensive I am becoming of its possible fate. There is no doubt that recent events in India have hardened opinion against many of the constitutional changes we have been discussing.'

In an attempt to assuage Parliamentary discontent, the Government decided to set up a Joint Select Committee, composed of members of both Parties, to examine the Round-Table proposals. The Committee was seen as an impartial body which would sift the conflicting arguments and then report to Parliament. On July 1, after the House of Commons had debated, and approved, the setting up of the Committee, Hoare wrote to MacDonald: 'There is no doubt whatever as to the satisfaction in the House about the policy. The moderate Conservatives are delighted, as our proposal for the Joint Select Committee gives them an answer to Winston's most damaging line of attack, namely that Parliament was going to be edged out of the final settlement.' Hoare's letter continued:

The opposition were extremely mild, and, indeed, Morgan Jones,[2] their chief spokesman, threw me a note across the table saying that he liked a great

---

[1] Philip Henry Kerr, 1882–1940. Educated at the Oratory School Birmingham and New College Oxford. Worked as a civil servant in South Africa, 1905–08. Editor, *The Round Table*, 1910–16. Secretary to Lloyd George, 1916–21. Secretary of the Rhodes Trust, 1925–39. Succeeded his cousin as 11th Marquess of Lothian, 1930. Chancellor of the Duchy of Lancaster, 1931. Chairman of the Indian Franchise Committee, 1932. Ambassador in Washington from 1939 until his death.

[2] Morgan Jones, 1885–1939. Educated at Lewis' School and Reading University College. A trained teacher, 1907. Joined the Independent Labour Party, 1908. Opposed the Great War, 1914. Conscientious objector; imprisoned; deprived of his post as a teacher and refused

deal of the programme. As to Winston, he was completely knocked out. He had got with him sheets of typewritten invective against everybody and everything, and with all his stage army, including Randolph in the gallery, and the Bracken claque carefully dotted about the House. After my speech he did not know whether to make a speech or not. Finally he said that he wished to speak at 10. Not unnaturally Lansbury and the Opposition jibbed and he was told that he must speak at 9.30. . . .

It was not until 10 o'clock, however, that the previous speaker sat down. Then, as Hoare explained to MacDonald:

Lansbury and Winston both got up and Lansbury was, of course, called. As Winston looked as if he was going to hit Lansbury over the head with the Mace, I suggested that if Lansbury sat down before half-past-ten, I would give Winston the intervening time. Lansbury having nothing to say, came to an end about 10.15, and Winston then had to get his forty-five minutes oration into a quarter-of-an-hour. It consisted mainly in a bitter attack upon Lothian's Committee and a mixture of equally offensive compliments and warnings to me. I am sure that, except amongst his own crowd, it went badly and the main body of the House was evidently pleased when I told him that there was a great difference between us and that it was no good pretending that we agreed. The House was remarkably full for an India debate and I think that everything went as well as we could expect.

Simultaneously with the setting up of the Joint Select Committee, Churchill learnt that the BBC would not allow him to broadcast to Paris on British monetary policy. He was furious at the ban, writing to Sir John Simon on July 1: 'Surely such a Government containing so many statesmen, and supported by such overwhelming majorities, has no need to fear independent expressions of opinion upon the controversies of the day.' The ban, however, remained in force.

In May 1932 Randolph Churchill celebrated his twenty-first birthday. He had already decided not to return to Oxford, but to seek a career in journalism. Lord Rothermere had made him a reporter on the *Sunday Graphic*, and his first overseas assignment was to cover the General Election in Germany during July. Before his son left for Germany, Churchill arranged a birthday party for him, inviting many famous men and their sons to dinner at Claridges. 'I've never enjoyed a dinner

---

re-employment. Member of the National Council of the Independent Labour Party, 1920–22. Labour MP for Caerphilly, 1921–39. Labour Whip, 1923–24. Parliamentary Secretary, Board of Education, 1924 and 1929–31. Chairman, Public Accounts Committee, 1931–38. Member of the Joint Select Committee on Indian Constitutional Reform, 1933–34.

more,' Edward Marsh wrote to Clementine Churchill on the following morning, '& *such* good speeches. . . . What a splendid send off for R!'[1] That same day, Oliver Stanley wrote to Churchill that the dinner had been a tribute 'to one man's personal popularity', and that half of those present were people who, like himself, 'sometimes differ from you in politics, without its ever diminishing their admiration of or their affection for you'. Churchill replied on June 21:

I am much touched by your letter. It was awfully nice of you to come and all you say pleases me so much. I do not think we differ at all except in emphasis; and there I think the future rests with my view. The movement of the whole world is to a stronger assertion of sovereignty. You are I believe embarked on a wrong course in an ebb tide but all these things will manifest themselves quite soon.

Churchill was proud that his son's speech at the dinner was so well received. 'Naturally I have high hopes of Randolph,' he wrote to the Earl of Crawford and Balcarres on June 17. 'He has a gift and a power of presentation which I have not seen equalled at his age. Whether he will be noble and diligent has yet to be proved.'

Among those whom Churchill had invited to his son's 'festival', as he called it, was his stockbroker, H. C. Vickers, to whom he wrote on June 21, to suggest the purchase of £12,000 worth of United States stocks while the market was at such a low point. 'I am very much afraid of missing the bus,' he wrote. 'I do not think America is going to smash. On the contrary I believe that they will quite soon begin to recover.' Churchill then explained to Vickers:

. . . As a country descends the ladder of values many grievances arise, bankruptcies and so forth. But one must never forget that at the same time all sorts of correctives are being applied, and adjustments being made by millions of people and thousands of firms. If the whole world except the United States sank under the ocean that community could get its living. They carved it out of the prairie and the forests. They are going to have a strong national resurgence in the near future. Therefore I wish to buy sound low priced stocks. I cannot afford any others. I do not mind whether they pay dividends this year or next year, all I want to know is that they are sound and honest as far as anything is sound and honest.

[1] Among those present were Lord Rothermere with his son Esmond Harmsworth (aged 34), Lord Hailsham and his son Quintin Hogg (aged 24), Lord Camrose and his son Seymour Berry (aged 22), Lord Reading with his son Lord Erleigh (aged 43) and the young Lord Birkenhead (aged 24).

It is only by this method of putting these low priced bargain stocks away that I can hope to recoup myself. . . .[1]

On July 25 Churchill wrote to his United States Lecture agent, Louis Alber,[2] explaining why he did not wish to do a lecture tour in 1933, but expressing his confidence in the future:

In two or three years—perhaps sooner—everything will be booming again. Of this I have no doubt. And then the same number of lectures will be produced with no more effort for at least double what could be secured now. It rests entirely with the *world* whether it smashes or recovers, and I think it has a strong interest in choosing recovery. We are quite unshakable here.

'*The only thing that matters now is to survive*,' Churchill added. 'Those who have come through this pinch will reap the future.'

Throughout July Churchill worked at Chartwell on his Marlborough volume. While Maurice Ashley scrutinized each draft chapter, and provided Churchill with a succession of documentary evidence, a new assistant, Lieutenant-Colonel Pakenham-Walsh,[3] made copious suggestions on all military matters relating to Marlborough's campaigns. Churchill also sought Keith Feiling's expert advice on all

[1] Churchill acted promptly upon his belief, and on June 28 bought £700 worth of Worthington Pump stocks. On July 4 he bought a further £500 worth. Within three weeks the value of Worthington Pumps had risen from nine dollars to fourteen; Churchill promptly sold a quarter of his holding. Four days later, when they reached fifteen dollars, he sold a further quarter. During 1932 his English investments also did well. Early in 1930, at Vickers' instigation, Churchill had purchased £2,969 worth of Marks and Spencer shares. Between June 1930 and May 1932, a time of general economic recession, these shares alone brought him over £100 in dividends, and increased in value by £338.

[2] Louis John Alber, 1879–1962. An organizer of entertainments and lectures from 1900. Editor of the *Lyceum* magazine, 1907–08. President of the Affiliated Lecture and Concert Association Inc, 1909–33; Director of Alber and Wickes Inc, lecture agents. Associate director of the Liberty Loans campaign, 1917–18. Executive Director, National Housing Commission, Washington, 1937–38. Foreign correspondent in Europe for the *Cleveland Plain Dealer*, 1945–47.

[3] Ridley Pakenham Pakenham-Walsh, 1888–1966. Educated at Cheltenham College and the Royal Military Academy, Woolwich. 2nd Lieutenant, Royal Engineers, 1908; on active service at the Dardanelles, 1915, and in France 1916–18 (Military Cross). British Representative, International Commission, Teschen, 1919–20. Instructor in Tactics, School of Military Engineering, 1923–26. General Staff Office Grade Two, War Office, 1934–35. Brigadier-General, General Staff, Eastern Command, 1935–39. Major General, School of Military Engineering, and Inspector, Royal Engineers, 1939. Engineer-in-Chief, British Expeditionary Force, 1939–40 (wounded). General Officer Commanding, Northern Ireland District, 1940–41; Salisbury Plain District, 1942. Lieutenant-General, 1941. Controller-General of Army Provision, 1943–46. Vice-Chairman, Harlow New Town Development Corporation, 1948–49.

matters of historical controversy, and on August 12 Feiling arrived at Chartwell. Forty-two years later he recalled, in a letter to the author:

The background was sometimes sombre, for he was in vehement opposition over India and felt it: very rarely there would be some petulance over trains, cars, or guests, which it seemed to me *she* bore angelically: once an embarassing outcry of hers 'If only you had stuck to the Liberal Party!' Not liked. There seemed a good many telephone calls to Baruch in New York and some sense of financial botherations. . . .

I began as to an undergraduate pupil and after a little grumbling his amazing quickness of intellect—as I thought—would seize the point at issue. After the first day or two he would call in a stenographer and get written down a summary of what he wanted to retain. And very entertaining—and often illuminating—those recordings sometimes were. I remember one very vividly—and my memory is accurate as to the two *names*, though I can only reconstruct the sentences: 'Robert Harley, Leader in the Commons, adept in its moods, intriguing, shifty . . .' Continuing—'square brackets, Baldwin'.

Keith Feiling's first visit to Chartwell lasted for eight days. During his visit, Churchill not only improved the chapters that he had already drafted or put in proof; he also dictated a new and substantial chapter on the Europe of Charles II. During Feiling's visit Churchill made plans to travel, first to Belgium and then to Holland and Germany, in order to see Marlborough's battlefields for himself.

On August 27 Churchill left Dover by car ferry for Calais, together with Lindemann. At Brussels they were joined by Lieutenant-Colonel Pakenham-Walsh, and for two days toured the battlefields of Flanders and the Low Countries; then continued into Germany and to Munich. From Munich, Churchill, Lindemann and Pakenham-Walsh drove to Blenheim, where Churchill studied the course of the battle on the actual spot. Three weeks later, on September 19, he wrote to Keith Feiling: 'The battlefields were wonderful. Pakenham-Walsh presented them admirably, and I was able to re-people them with ghostly but glittering armies. . . . I was deeply moved by all these scenes and feel sure I can interpret them for the *first time*.' To his cousin the Duke of Marlborough Churchill wrote on September 25:

My general staff officer, a most able man, had gone on beforehand and he was able to conduct me to exactly the points where J.D. surveyed the battle scenes and took his decisions at every important moment. The surprising thing is how big these battlefields are, far bigger than Waterloo, about the same size as Gettysburg, and so many more troops were used. These were very fine, far flung and swiftly moving episodes. The barn at Ramilles shows all the marks of cannon and musket. At Malplaquet the peasants showed us cannon balls about the size of cricket balls which they had dug up. Nearly everywhere the ground is almost unchanged. You will be surprised when I tell the story of these actions how splendid they were, full of life and modernity.

Some day I am going to ask you to give me some money £2-300—and I will give half as much as I ask you to give, in order to put up a few granite stones with bronze tablets at Blenheim, Ramilles, Oudenarde and Malplaquet. The governments of these countries would be very willing. It is a shame that these historical fields should have no record upon them. The French have put up a monument at Malplaquet to Villars and Boufflers; but nothing marks the British *victory*. . . .

Of Marlborough's departure from Coblenz to Blenheim Churchill wrote:

. . . none of the hostile watching armies ready to spring, not even our army, was sure where it was going to. They still thought it was a campaign in Alsace; but no, a fortnight later the long scarlet columns swung off to the Danube and the great strategic design which altered the history of Europe became apparent. This marvellous march was distinguished first for its absolute secrecy and mystery—no one knew, not the Queen, not Sarah, not the English government, except Eugene; and secondly for the extra-ordinary elaboration with which every detail was worked out. New boots for the troops were found in Coblenz; food and wine appeared at every camping ground as if by magic; all the soldiers had to do was to pitch the tents and boil their kettles. The army arrived for battle at the Schellenberg as if it had been taken out of a bandbox. Pretty good! These tales have never been told before as I shall tell them.

Immediately afer his visit to Blenheim, Churchill intended to continue southwards to Venice, for a holiday with his wife, his son, his daughter Sarah and Professor Lindemann. But while still in Bavaria he was taken ill with paratyphoid fever. There was no time to bring him back to England; he went instead to a sanatorium in Salzburg. There he lay for two weeks, unable once more to work or travel. On September 16 his brother, a partner of Churchill's stockbroker, H. C. Vickers, wrote to him from London: 'I am very glad your temp is down. You are "quoted" in all the papers. This morning you were 98⅝ and so was conversion 3½%. I have not worked out your parity in London but evidently you are much better.' Jack added: 'There was a rumour you had been poisoned by drinking water! I contradicted this libel at once!'

By September 17 Churchill felt well enough to begin work again, although he was still confined to the sanatorium. His main effort concerned a series of twelve articles which Lord Riddell had persuaded him to write for the *News of the World* entitled 'The World's Great Stories'.

Edward Marsh had agreed to help choose the stories for him, and also to prepare them. One of these reached Churchill at Salzburg, where he worked to polish it. On September 17 he wrote to Marsh: 'I am throwing off this foul attack and planning to travel home Thursday if all well. Shall finish convalescing at Chartwell. . . .' On September 19 Thornton Butterworth wrote to Churchill: 'It seems to me that during the last few years you have had more than your meed in this direction—your operation for appendicitis, your unhappy intercourse with a taxi in New York, and now this unfortunate paratyphoid in the midst of your travels in search of rest and peace!'

Churchill returned to Chartwell on September 25. 'I am back again rather battered,' he wrote to the Duke of Marlborough that same day, but in another week I shall be alright. It was an English bug which I took abroad with me, and no blame rests on the otherwise misguided continent of Europe.' To Pakenham-Walsh he wrote that same day: 'I am quite well though somewhat weakened, but in ten days or so I hope to be okay. Meanwhile I can do a great deal of work. I am longing to get on to your battles. The impressions made by those fields upon me is most vivid.'

While Marsh busied himself with summarizing the world's great stories, Churchill continued with his work on *Marlborough*. 'I am getting very enthusiastic about it all,' he wrote to George Harrap on September 25, 'and am sure that the general design will be large enough and true enough to command the allegiance of my loyal reader.' Churchill asked Harrap if his book could be in two volumes instead of one. Harrap readily agreed. That same day Maurice Ashley arrived at Chartwell to help with the weaving together of the narrative and the documentation. Much of the work had, because of Churchill's illness, to be done in Churchill's bedroom. Ashley would sit in one chair with a file of notes and documents, Mrs Pearman in another with her shorthand pad, while Churchill dictated each chapter. By September 27, a total of 90,000 words had been completed. That day, although he was not fully recovered from his illness, Churchill insisted on getting up; indeed, he began to walk with Ashley to and fro in the garden. But he was still too weak for such activity, and, Ashley later recalled: 'as we were pacing up and down, he got whiter and whiter. Suddenly he collapsed.' It was a recurrence of the paratyphoid. An ambulance was summoned, and Churchill was driven at once to London. That night a statement was issued to the Press, reporting that 'Mr Winston Churchill, having had a relapse, with some haemorrhage, has been removed from Chartwell, Westerham, to a London nursing home. He will be unable to do any public work for several weeks.' Two days later it was revealed that Churchill had suffered a severe haemorrhage from a paratyphoid ulcer.

The Press followed Churchill's illness with much sympathy. On September 28 the *Daily Express* pointed out that he was now unlikely to be able to attend the Conservative Party conference at Blackpool, which was to open on October 6. On September 29 it was announced from the nursing home that he had spent a 'good night, and his condition is satisfactory'. On the following day the *Evening Standard* reported that Churchill had been able at last to take 'a bowl of soup', but that his complete recovery would take 'three or four weeks'. Churchill, however, was determined to be present at the forthcoming Conservative conference, and on October 5 Leopold Amery noted in his diary: 'Dined with Sir J. Hawkey, Winston's Vice Chairman, who had just seen him, very restless and anxious to go to Blackpool in an ambulance!'

No such journey was possible, and Churchill returned to Chartwell from the nursing home to regain his strength. As a result, his resolution criticizing the Government's India policy had to be put forward by others, and debated without him. Even so, its impact was considerable, and the Party leaders had to make a strong effort to defeat it. On October 7 Samuel Hoare sent Ramsay MacDonald an account of how the debate developed. Lord Lloyd, he wrote, 'had a surprisingly good reception and I thought when he sat down most people would have said that he would carry Winston's resolution with a big majority. Fortunately Butler[1] and I had organised a counter-blast.' At the end, Hoare added, 'We had a substantial majority, but it is idle to blink the fact that the sentiment apart from the reasoning of the meeting was on the other side.' Many Conservatives, Hoare noted, were 'genuinely anxious' about the proposed constitutional changes, and unless they were taken along 'quietly', 'they will become mulish and then I do not know what will happen'.

Despite Hoare's success at Blackpool in securing a majority for the India policy, many Conservative MPs were still dubious about the wisdom of so large a measure of self-government, and did not seem dis-

---

[1] Richard Austen Butler, 1902–82. Educated at Marlborough and Pembroke College Cambridge. President of the Union Society, 1924. Conservative MP for Saffron Walden, 1929–65. Under-Secretary of State, India Office, 1932–37. Parliamentary Secretary, Ministry of Labour, 1937–38. Under-Secretary of State for Foreign Affairs, 1938–41. Privy Councillor, 1939. Minister of Education, 1941–45. Minister of Labour, 1945. Chancellor of the Exchequer, 1951–55. Lord Privy Seal, 1955–61. Home Secretary, 1957–62. Deputy Prime Minister, 1962–63. Secretary of State for Foreign Affairs, 1963–64. Created Baron Butler of Saffron Walden, 1965. Master of Trinity College Cambridge since 1965.

posed to trust entirely to the deliberations of the Joint Select Committee. 'At the moment,' Hoare wrote to Sir John Anderson on November 10, 'the majority in the House of Commons are much more suspicious than they have ever been', and to Willingdon he wrote eight days later: '. . . the Conservative rank and file are extremely jumpy and I do not know how I shall get through the next few weeks without embroiling myself either with them or with the Indians'.

Recovering slowly at Chartwell, Churchill continued to dictate passages of *Marlborough* to Mrs Pearman and to scrutinize the proofs as they arrived in batches from the printer. On October 20 Mrs Pearman wrote to Nancy Pearn:[1] 'Mr Churchill is steadily improving, though progress is rather slow, but as usual nothing can keep him from work, and he busies himself a good many hours each day and gets through a lot. It will be some time I think before he really gets as strong as before.' By the end of October Churchill had written half the chapters of the first *Marlborough* volume. At the same time he decided to try to sign a contract as soon as possible for a major book which would ensure him both work and income between 1934—when he hoped to finish *Marlborough*—and 1939. The subject he chose was one he had long contemplated writing, a history of the English-speaking peoples, and on October 28 he spoke about the project to the Managing Director of Cassell & Company, Newman Flower.[2] Two days later he wrote to Flower: 'In broad principle I should be willing to undertake to write "A History of the English Speaking Peoples", their origins, their quarrels, their misfortunes and their reconciliation for the sum of £20,000.' Churchill added: 'It would be necessary for me to set on foot this year the studies and accumulation of material in order that I might begin composition as soon as "Marlborough" was completed. I should suggest that the expenses that I should be put to for assistance for the period of four or five years would certainly not be less than £3,000.'

---

[1] Nancy Pearn. Secretary to A. Curtis Brown before the First World War. Subsequently worked for the Literary Agent, Hughes, Massie. Returned to Curtis Brown shortly after the war, first in charge of the Foreign Rights department, and then of the Magazine and Newspaper Rights departments. In 1935 she was one of the founders of the Literary Agency Pearn, Pollinger and Higham. She died in 1950.

[2] Walter Newman Flower, 1879–1964. Educated at Whitgift School. Joined Cassells, publishers, 1906; purchased the firm in 1927; subsequently its Chairman and President. Knighted, 1938.

Agreement was quickly reached; on December 7 Churchill wrote to Flower accepting in full the detailed terms. He was also to receive at least £2,000 a year for several years from his articles for *Colliers* magazine.

On November 30 Churchill celebrated his fifty-eighth birthday. He also celebrated the engagement of his eldest daughter, Diana, to John Bailey,[1] son of his friend Sir Abe Bailey. At Chartwell, he continued his work on his biography of Marlborough, and on the many newspaper articles which he was contracted to write.[2] Throughout the winter Keith Feiling, Maurice Ashley and Colonel Pakenham-Walsh continued to send him documents and suggestions about Marlborough, but in December a severe chill had forced him once more to relax the pace of his literary activities. Nevertheless, by the end of 1932 his literary, and therefore financial future was secured for several years to come, while *Marlborough*, the *English-Speaking Peoples*, and *Great Contemporaries*, as well as the newspaper and magazine articles, filled his time, engaged the constant efforts of several assistants, many advisers and a full-time secretary.

On December 16 Lindemann arrived to keep Churchill company. More than ten years had passed since they had first met, and their friendship was unbreakable. All those who visited Chartwell were struck by Lindemann's loyalty to Churchill, which Churchill reciprocated. Churchill's nephew Johnny later recalled, in a conversation with the author: 'He swore by Lindemann. Anything that was a query, which Winston did not know he would say "What do you think about that Prof" "What is that about". If Prof said it was all nonsense, Winston believed it was nonsense. He was a loner, Prof—almost an eccentric. He could not bear not to be right. Everything we said Prof pulled to bits.' Churchill's daughter Sarah also recalled her impressions of Lindemann, the most frequent of all her father's guests during the twenties and thirties:

The dear Prof was a vegetarian, a bachelor and a teetotaller, all of which things my father greatly deplored, but which slight imperfections he tolerated because of the value he placed on the Prof's splendid mind and friendship. He was part of our Chartwell life. It is hard to remember an occasion on

---

[1] John Milner Bailey, 1900–1946. Married 1st, in 1932, Diana Churchill (who obtained a divorce in 1935); 2nd, in 1939, Mrs Muriel Mullins (marriage dissolved in 1945); 3rd, in 1945, Stella Chiappini. Succeeded his father as 2nd Baronet, 1940.

[2] The number of Churchill's articles was considerable: six were published in the *Daily Mail* between mid-October and the end of December, one in *Colliers* and one in the *Sunday Dispatch*; a further twelve were being written, based on outlines prepared by Marsh, for the *News of the World*, and three on unemployment, for both *Colliers* and the *Sunday Chronicle*.

which he was not present. His exterior was conventionally forbidding—the domed cranium, the close-cropped-iron-grey hair which had receded as if the brain had pushed it away, the iron-grey moustache, the sallow complexion, the little sniff which took the place of what normally would have been a laugh, yet he could still exude a warmth that made scientific thinking unfrightening.

Prof had the gift of conveying a most complicated subject in simple form. One day at lunch when coffee and brandy were being served my father decided to have a slight 'go' at Prof who had just completed a treatise on the quantum theory. 'Prof' he said, 'tell us in words of one syllable and in no longer than five minutes what is the quantum theory.' My father then placed his large gold watch, known as the 'turnip' on the table. When you consider that Prof must have spent many years working on this subject, it was quite a tall order, however without any hesitation, like quicksilver, he explained the principle and held us all spell-bound. When he had finished we all spontaneously burst into applause.

24

Germany 1932–1933:
'Tell the Truth to the
British People'

D URING the first five months of 1932 Dr Brüning's Government in Germany had been under fierce attack from the extremist parties of both right and left. Churchill's concern about these events had continued throughout 1932, made more acute by the worsening situation. As the German economic crisis intensified, and unemployment rose, Adolf Hitler's following had increased, and by mid-January more than 400,000 men had joined his semi-military 'Stormtroopers', while Nazi Party membership reached two million. The three most strident Nazi demands were an end to the Versailles Treaty, rearmament, and the removal of German Jews from all walks of German life.

On 13 March 1932 Hitler received more than eleven million votes in the first ballot for the Presidential elections, as against more than eighteen million for Hindenburg,[1] and five million for the Communist leader Ernst Thaelmann.[2] In the second ballot, on April 10, Hindenburg received nineteen million votes and was re-elected President. But Hitler's share of the poll rose to nearly thirteen and a half million, almost

[1] Paul von Benckendorff und Hindenburg, 1847–1934. 2nd Lieutenant, 1866. Fought in the Austro-Prussian and Franco-Prussian wars of 1866 and 1870–1. Retired from the Army with the rank of General, 1911. Recalled, 1914. Commander-in-Chief, 7th Army, 1914. In August 1914 he moved German troops rapidly by rail from Gumbinnen, where they had been defeated by the Russians, to Tannenberg, where they were victorious. Marshal and Commander-in-Chief of all German Forces in the East, 1915. Chief of the General Staff, 1916–18. President of the Reich, 1925–34.

[2] Ernst Thaelmann, 1886–1944. Dockworker. A Social Democrat before 1914. Communist Member of the Reichstag, 1924–33, and Leader of the Communist Party. Imprisoned without trial on the Nazi accession to power in January 1933, he died in Buchenwald Concentration Camp on 28 August 1944.

444

40 per cent of the total votes cast. Two months later, on 13 May 1932, the Foreign Secretary, Sir John Simon, urged on the House of Commons the need for further rapid and comprehensive disarmament. Only by reducing the level of arms, he said, could the dangers of a future war be averted; nothing could be worse, than for a disarmed Germany to have to face, and to fear, a well-armed France.

Simon's appeal for disarmament was widely and enthusiastically supported. Churchill, however, sounded a note of alarm, telling the House of Commons:

I should very much regret to see any approximation in military strength between Germany and France. Those who speak of that as though it were right, or even a question of fair dealing, altogether underrate the gravity of the European situation. I would say to those who would like to see Germany and France on an equal footing in armaments: 'Do you wish for war?'

For my part, I earnestly hope that no such approximation will take place during my lifetime or that of my children. . . .

On 26 May 1932, in an article in the *Daily Mail*, Churchill conceded that 'millions of well-meaning English people' hoped that the Disarmament Conference at Geneva would succeed, and he continued: 'There is such a horror of war in the great nations who passed through Armageddon that any declaration or public speech against armaments, although it consisted only of platitudes and unrealities, has always been applauded; and any speech or assertion which set forth the blunt truths has been incontinently relegated to the category of "warmongering".' Churchill went on to point out that at every disarmament conference, each State had sought security for itself by maintaining its existing armaments, while urging all other States to disarm down to the lowest level. But was it likely, he asked, 'that France with less than forty millions, faced by Germany with sixty millions, and double the number of young men coming to military age every year, is going to deprive herself of the mechanical aids and appliances on which she relies to prevent a fourth invasion in little more than a hundred years'? Likewise, could the new states of northern and eastern Europe like Finland, Latvia, Lithuania and Poland be expected not to seek the most effective armaments possible 'to protect themselves from being submerged in a ferocious deluge from Russia'. Churchill's article ended:

The cause of disarmament will not be attained by mush, slush and gush, It will be advanced steadily by the harassing expense of fleets and armies. and by the growth of confidence in a long peace. It will be achieved only when in a favourable atmosphere half a dozen great men, with as many first class powers at their back, are able to lift world affairs out of their present increasing confusion.

On May 30, only four days after Churchill's article was published, Dr Brüning was replaced as German Chancellor by Count von Papen.[1] Although the Nazi leaders were not invited to join the new Government, von Papen hoped that with Hitler's tacit support he could remain in power for several years. On June 19, in the provincial elections at Hesse, the Nazi vote increased from 37 to 44 per cent, making the Nazis the largest single party in the province. Following this electoral success, Nazi bands attacked their Social Democrat and Communist opponents throughout Germany, killing not only political rivals, but also women and children.

A new international conference opened at Lausanne on June 16, aimed at reducing still further, and to a nominal minimum, Germany's outstanding Reparations liability. MacDonald represented Britain and von Papen Germany. On July 9 the Conference accepted all that the Germans had asked, retaining only a nominal demand for 3,000 marks. Two days after the end of the Lausanne Conference Churchill declared that he could not join in the general applause for the end of Reparations, and referred to a statement by Hitler—'who is the moving impulse behind the German Government and may be more than that soon—that the 3,000 marks payable by Germany would only be worth three marks in a few months'. Churchill went on to point out the actual benefits which Germany had gained as a result of the Reparations system, including substantial economic loans from the United States for new industrial machinery, and other aids to production.

The ending of Reparations did not help the moderate elements in Germany. In the streets, Nazi bands continued to demand Germany's release from the 'shackles' of the Versailles Treaty. A General Election was set for the end of July. Randolph Churchill, who had gone to Germany to report on the election campaign, travelled one afternoon in Hitler's aeroplane from meeting to meeting, amazed by the enthusiasm of the crowds for the Nazi leader. The election was held on July 31. The Nazi Party won 230 seats, as against 133 for the Social Democrats, and only 78 for the Communists. That same day Randolph Churchill wrote in the *Sunday Graphic*: 'The success of the Nazi party sooner or later

[1] Franz von Papen, 1879–1969. Cavalry officer, and member of the Westphalian aristocracy. Military Attaché, Washington, 1914–16; expelled from the United States on a charge of sabotage. A leading shareholder in the Centre Party newspaper, *Germania*. Never elected to the Reichstag. Chancellor, June–November 1932. A member of Hitler's Cabinet, 1933–34. German Ambassador to Vienna, 1934–38. Tried at Nuremberg, and acquitted, 1946.

means war.' Hitler's lieutenants, he explained, 'burn for revenge' for the German defeat of 1918. 'They are determined once more to have an army. I am sure that once they have achieved it they will not hesitate to use it.'

With over 13½ million votes, the Nazis were now the largest Party in the State. They had won, however, only 37·1 per cent of the total poll. Von Papen remained Chancellor, and the Nazis were not invited to join his Cabinet.

Hitler's immediate reaction to his exclusion from power was to intensify the terror in the streets. Writing to Sir John Simon on August 4, the British Ambassador to Germany, Sir Horace Rumbold,[1] described how, in the East Prussian capital, Königsberg, 'prominent Socialists and Communists were surprised at night and murdered in their beds or shot down at the doors of their houses. The windows of shops owned by Jews were smashed and their contents looted.' On August 29, bowing to the force of terror, von Papen offered Hitler the post of Vice-Chancellor, but Hitler refused, insisting that his aim was to be offered the Chancellorship itself. It was at this moment that Churchill had left England for his tour of Marlborough's battlefields. His son was eager to introduce him to Hitler, by whose electoral campaign he had been so impressed two months before, and asked one of Hitler's friends, Putzi Hanfstaengel,[2] to try to arrange a meeting. Churchill and Putzi Hanfstaengel dined together at Churchill's hotel in Munich. Fifteen years later Churchill recalled how, during dinner, Hanfstaengel 'gave a most interesting account of Hitler's activities and outlook. He spoke as one under the spell.' Hanfstaengel told Churchill that as Hitler came each afternoon to that same hotel 'nothing would be easier' than for them to meet. Churchill agreed, but according to Hanfstaengel's memoirs, Hitler was nervous of meeting a man 'whom he knew to be his equal in political ability', and when Hanfstaengel pressed him, Hitler remarked: 'In any

[1] Horace Rumbold 1869–1941. Educated at Eton. Entered the Diplomatic Service, 1891. Succeeded his father as 9th Baronet, 1913. Chargé d'Affaires, Berlin, July 1914. Minister in Berne, 1916–19; in Warsaw, 1919–20. High Commissioner, Constantinople, 1920–24. Signed the Lausanne Treaty with Turkey on behalf of the British Empire, 24 July, 1923. Ambassador in Madrid, 1924–28; in Berlin, 1928–33. Vice-Chairman of the Royal Commission on Palestine, 1936–37.

[2] Ernst Hanfstaengel, 1887–1975. Son of a leading Munich art dealer, with a branch business in New York. A Harvard history graduate, he befriended Hitler in 1923, when he lent him the [$1,000 that enabled Hitler to print the *Völkischer Beobachter* as a daily paper. One of Hitler's confidants, in 1933 he became the Nazi Party's official Foreign Press spokesman. In March 1937 he left Germany for the United States, where he acted for a while as an adviser to President Roosevelt (whom he had known at Harvard). Returned to Germany, 1945.

case, they say your Mr Churchill is a rabid Francophile.' Still Hanfstaengel hoped that Hitler, overtaken by curiosity, might decide to join
Churchill's party for coffee. With Churchill were his wife, his daughter
Sarah, Randolph, Lord Camrose and Lindemann. 'I turned up at the
appointed hour,' Hanfstaengel recalled, and his account continued:

We sat down about ten to dinner, with myself on Mrs Churchill's right and
my host on the other side. We talked about this and that, and then Mr
Churchill taxed me about Hitler's anti-Semitic views. I tried to give as mild
an account of the subject as I could, saying that the real problem was the
influx of eastern European Jews and the excessive representation of their
co-religionaries in the professions, to which Churchill listened very carefully,
commenting: 'Tell your boss from me that anti-Semitism may be a good
starter, but it is a bad sticker.'

On the following day Hanfstaengel made one further effort to persuade Hitler to meet Churchill, but in vain. 'In any case,' Hitler asked
him, 'what part does Churchill play? He's in opposition and no one
pays any attention to him,' to which Hanfstaengel retorted: 'People say
the same thing about you.' Two days later the Churchills had left
Munich for Blenheim. Hitler, as Hanfstaengel noted, 'kept away until
they had gone'.

Throughout the summer and early autumn of 1932 von Papen's
Government demanded 'equality of status' for Germany in the matter
of armaments. The new Minister of Defence, General Kurt von
Schleicher,[1] was insistent that Germany must be allowed to rearm. On
September 18 the British Foreign Office issued an official Note, signed
by Sir John Simon, declaring that in Britain's view the disarmament
clauses of the Treaty of Versailles were still binding upon Germany, and
deprecating any attempt by Germany to rearm. As a protest against this
Note, von Papen withdrew Germany from the Disarmament Conference. Churchill, who had only just returned from Germany, supported
the Simon Note, and was shocked to find that many people in Britain
opposed it on the grounds that a disarmed Germany was in an unfair
position of inferiority compared to France. On October 17, in an article
published in the *Daily Mail*, Churchill insisted that Simon's firm stand
had 'done more to consolidate peace in Europe than any words spoken
on behalf of Great Britain for some years'; he had 'raised the hand of

---

[1] Kurt von Schleicher, 1882–1934. Entered the Imperial German Army, 1900. Appointed
to the General Staff, May 1914. Served under Groener, and then Ludendorff, 1914–18.
Organized the military measures against the Communist uprisings in Saxony and Thuringia,
1923. Colonel, 1926; Major-General, 1929. Defence Minister June–December 1932. Chancellor, December 1932–January 1933. Murdered by the Nazis, 30 June 1934.

warning in the interests of peace'. Such firmness, he added, was essential, as every right wing party in Germany was trying to win votes 'by putting up the boldest front against the foreigner'. Hitler, he pointed out, 'has to outdo Papen, and Papen has to go one better than Hitler, and Bruning must hurry or he will be left behind'. His article continued:

General Schleicher, the main repository of force in the new German autocracy, has already declared that whatever the Powers may settle, Germany will do what she thinks fit in rearmament. Very grave dangers lie along these paths, and if Great Britain had encouraged Germany in such adventures, we might in an incredibly short space of time have been plunged in a situation of violent peril.

'It was high time,' Churchill noted, 'in everyone's interest that the Germans of all parties should be apprised and reminded of the realities of the external situation,' and he went on to point out that the aim of France in building up armaments, fortifications and alliances since 1919 had been the belief that these measures would 'effectively shield her from the horrors of war and renewed invasion'. Into Europe's 'highly complicated and electrical situations', Churchill declared, 'our well-meaning but thoughtless and reckless pacifists expect us to plunge with sweeping gestures, encouraged by long distance halloos from the United States'.

On November 6 the Germans held their second General Election within five months. The Nazis retained their position as the largest single Party, with 196 seats, despite a drop in their vote from 37% to 33%. The Social Democrats, with 20%, remained the second largest Party, the Communists third with 17%, a slight increase on July. Once more, von Papen offered Hitler the Vice-Chancellorship, and once more, Hitler refused. Von Papen's Government, deprived of a majority in the Reichstag, negotiated desperately in an attempt to survive, and General Schleicher emerged as the man on whom power might devolve.

On November 10 the House of Commons debated the question of European disarmament. Churchill, still recovering from the lingering effects of paratyphoid, was not well enough to attend. During the debate Sir John Simon stated on behalf of the Government that British policy would henceforth take into account 'the fair meeting of Germany's claim to the principle of equality', while at the same time seeking 'a solemn affirmation' that the European states 'will not in any circumstances attempt to resolve any present or future differences between them by resort to force'. Closing the disarmament debate, Baldwin spoke of 'the terror of the air' telling the House: 'I confess that the more

I have studied this question the more depressed I have been at the perfectly futile attempts that have been made to deal with this problem,' and he warned: 'I think it is well also for the man in the street to realize that there is no power on earth that can protect him from being bombed.'

On November 11 Leopold Amery wrote to Churchill:

I am sure you are wise in not coming back to the House prematurely. But I confess you were badly missed yesterday when the most incredible amount of sloppy nonsense was talked from every quarter of the House about disarmament, ending in a duet by Lansbury and Baldwin, both on almost identical lines. S.B. 'Safety First! No flying!'

'The whole disarmament problem is smothered with hypocrisy,' Churchill replied on the following day, 'each nation trying to score an advantage for itself and put some other nation in the wrong. This is a game which HMG are quite good at playing.'

On November 17, in an article in the *Daily Mail*, Churchill urged the Government to devise a policy capable of protecting Britain should Europe descend once more into conflict. 'If Geneva fails,' he wrote, 'let the National Government propose to Parliament measures necessary to place our Air Force in such a condition of power and efficiency that it will not be worth anyone's while to come here and kill our women and children in the hope that they may blackmail us into surrender.'

The day on which Churchill's article appeared was one of ill omen. Unable to form a Government, von Papen resigned as Chancellor, and two days later, on November 19, President Hindenburg asked Hitler if he would be willing to serve in the Government of von Papen's successor, whoever he might be. Within forty-eight hours Hitler refused, telling Hindenburg that he would only place his movement at the disposal of a Government of which he himself was Chancellor.

On November 23 Churchill explained to the House of Commons his fears for the future. 'He spoke for an hour and a half . . .' Amery noted in his diary, 'a very able and essentially statesmanlike speech which profoundly interested a full house who for the first time heard any sort of reply to the twaddle that has been talked about disarmament of late.' 'I do not know where Germany's Parliamentary system stands today,' Churchill stated, 'but certainly military men are in control of the essentials.' His speech continued: 'I am making no indictment of Germany. I have respect and admiration for the Germans, and desire that we should live on terms of good feeling and fruitful relations with them; but we must look at the fact that every concession which has been made—many concessions have been made, and many more will be made and ought to be made—has been followed immediately by a fresh demand.' Across Europe, Churchill pointed out, France, Belgium, Poland, Rumania, Czechoslovakia and Yugoslavia were all determined both to defend their frontiers 'and to defend their rights'. Although the Germans were only asking for equality of arms with France, this in itself spelt danger for Europe, and he continued:

Do not delude yourselves. Do not let His Majesty's Government believe— I am sure they do not believe—that all that Germany is asking for is equal status. I believe the refined term now is equal qualitative status by indefinitely deferred stages. That is not what Germany is seeking. All these bands of sturdy Teutonic youths, marching through the streets and roads of Germany, with the light of desire in their eyes to suffer for their Fatherland, are not looking for status. They are looking for weapons, and, when they have the weapons, believe me they will then ask for the return of lost territories and lost colonies, and when that demand is made it cannot fail to shake and possibly shatter to their foundations every one of the countries I have mentioned, and some other countries I have not mentioned.

Before each disarmament conference, Churchill told the House of Commons, the 'poor good people of the League of Nations' had clapped their hands for joy; yet as each conference progressed they had been deceived. 'The process is apparently endless,' Churchill declared, 'and so is the pathetic belief with which it is invariably greeted.' He himself was sceptical of these disarmament conferences and pledges. Comparing the situation in 1932 with that of 1925, Churchill warned the House: 'The war mentality is springing up again in certain countries. All over Europe there is hardly a factory which is not prepared for its alternative war service. . . .' Such facts must not be ignored. Ramsay MacDonald's 'noble, if somewhat flocculent eloquence' must be replaced by greater precision. The dangers were too acute to be hidden behind bland platitudes. 'I cannot recall any time,' Churchill said, 'when the gap between the kind of words which statesmen used and what was actually happening in many countries was so great as it is now. The habit of saying smooth things and uttering pious platitudes and sentiments to gain applause, without relation to the underlying facts, is more pronounced now than it has ever been in my experience.' He continued:

Just as the late Lord Birkenhead used to say about India—I think it the beginning and end of wisdom there—'Tell the truth to India,' so I would now say, 'Tell the truth to the British people.' They are a tough people, a robust people. They may be a bit offended at the moment, but if you have told them exactly what is going on you have insured yourself against complaints and reproaches which are very unpleasant when they come home on the morrow of some disillusion.

Churchill went on to express once more his approval of France's military strength. 'They only wish to keep what they have got,' he said, 'and no initiative in making trouble would come from them.' 'I say quite frankly,' he continued, 'though I may shock the House, that I would rather see another ten or twenty years of one-sided peace than see a war between equally well-matched Powers. . . .'

'I am not an alarmist,' Churchill declared. 'I do not believe in the imminence of war in Europe. I believe that with wisdom and with skill we may never see it in our time. To hold any other view would indeed be to despair,' and he then set out what he believed was the only possible way to revive 'the lights of goodwill and reconciliation' which had shone 'so brightly but so briefly' at the time of Locarno. He was eager, he said, to follow 'any real path' which could lead to a 'lasting reconciliation between Germany and her neighbours, but this path could only be found if a principle were followed, and he went on to explain what he advised:

The removal of the just grievances of the vanquished ought to precede the disarmament of the victors. To bring about anything like equality of armaments if it were in our power to do so, which it happily is not, while those grievances remain unredressed, would be almost to appoint the day for another European war—to fix it as if it were a prize-fight. It would be far safer to reopen questions like those of the Dantzig Corridor and Transylvania, with all their delicacy and difficulty, in cold blood and in a calm atmosphere and while the victor nations still have ample superiority, than to wait and drift on, inch by inch and stage by stage, until once again vast combinations, equally matched confront each other face to face.

Churchill ended his speech with a reference to Baldwin's remarks on November 10 about the horrors of air bombardment. That speech, he said, 'had led to no practical conclusion', and he went on: 'It created anxiety, and it created also perplexity. There was a sense of, what shall I say, fatalism, and even perhaps helplessness about it, and I take this opportunity of saying that, as far as this island is concerned, the responsibility of Ministers to guarantee the safety of the country from day to day and from hour to hour is direct and inalienable. . . .'

Churchill's speech was widely reported. 'Mr Churchill is to be praised,' declared the *Morning Post* on November 24, 'for standing up in the House and giving sentimentalism a good, sergeant-major-like "Halt!" ' His appeal for the redress of the grievances of the defeated nations was, wrote the *Daily Mail* on November 24, 'a much more practical policy of appeasement than efforts to secure the world's disarmament'. Writing in the *Sunday Pictorial*, George Ward Price[1] commented on November 27:

... though it was from the unofficial benches of the House that Mr Churchill made his great speech, the Government and the country have none the less had the advantage of his admonition and advice. It is unfortunate for the nation that this statesman of long service and proved courage should have no direct share in the control of our destinies, but it would be a double disaster if those who bear that responsibility were to turn a deaf ear to his plain words of warning.

Sending his personal congratulations on November 23, Major Herbert Noyes[2] told Churchill: 'During your absence there has been no one courageous enough to tell the truth.'

During December the 1922 Committee of Conservative backbenchers asked Churchill to address them. His cousin, Frederick Guest, who believed that he could still emerge as eventual leader of the Conservative Party, in succession to Baldwin, wrote to him on December 20: 'Your speeches have been admirable and not too frequent. Your serious review of international politics delivered on the Address last month was much the best, and has attracted the attention of the rank and file of the Conservative Party to a more real extent than any of the previous ones, with the possible exception of the one you delivered on India a year ago.' Were MacDonald to cease being Prime Minister, Guest believed, the Premiership 'would quite gently fall into Baldwin's lap', and he continued:

My study of Baldwin is that he is once again looking for a righthand man, and that if you gave him a chance he would be quite prepared to trust you

[1] George Ward Price,   –1961. Educated at St Catherine's College Cambridge. *Daily Mail* War Correspondent, in the first Balkan war. Official War Correspondent at the Dardanelles and with the Salonika army. A Director of Associated Newspapers Ltd and special foreign correspondent for the *Daily Mail* between the wars. War Correspondent in France, 1939; in Tunisia, 1943; in France, 1944.

[2] Herbert Noyes. Colonial civil servant in Malaya (4 years), Transvaal and Natal (20 years) and Western Australia (6 years); traveller and naturalist. On active service in South Africa, 1900. Special correspondent of the *Morning Post*, Russo-Japanese war, 1905. Battery Commander, Royal Field Artillery, 1914–18; Major, 1918. Subsequently special correspondent of *The Times* in eastern Africa, and a frequent broadcaster on the BBC on India and Africa. Served with the Central Electricity Board, 1932–40. Lecturer, Ministry of Information, 1941–46.

again as he did in 1924. He needs someone with more fire, polish and debating capacity than any of his present colleagues can provide. I am quite certain that he will hold on forever rather than hand the leadership over to Neville.

Guest then suggested a course of action for Churchill to improve his political standing:

Why do you not reconsider your policy and get back into the hierarchy and continue to develop your popularity with the Conservative Party by sagacity and loyalty to it. Sooner or later a Party Meeting will be held and candidates will be put forward in the proper constitutional way. . . .
I am sure you will produce a hundred arguments against this course and I know that your basic intention is to be either No 1 or no where. I submit however that when you formed this intention eighteen months ago you were not aware of the composition and calibre of the present Conservative Parliamentary Party. There are at least 350 free thinkers, but I can assure you they will do nothing to effect a change in leadership except through the constitutional machinery of the Party which they have joined. The control of the Whips in the Party today is even stronger than in the last Parliament as the old gang of 'Independents' are being replaced by younger men. . . .

Churchill had gone abroad with his wife, for a short holiday at St Saens, in France, when his cousin's letter reached Chartwell. But in the forthcoming months, far from finding his differences with the Conservative Party narrowing, they grew wider, for the disarmament policy of the National Government, which the majority of Conservative back-benchers supported, he believed to be profoundly wrong, nor would he moderate his views in order to stay in favour with the Party leadership. Nor did MacDonald himself intend to give Churchill a chance to return to office, for, as Baldwin wrote to Hoare on December 22: 'I had a long talk with the PM. His firm reaction is the same as mine was. He thinks nothing of W.'s judgement.'

On 30 January 1933 Adolf Hitler became Chancellor of Germany. Although his Cabinet was a Coalition with only two other Nazi members, within less than three weeks he obtained complete control of the State. A 'Law for the Protection of the German People', issued on February 6, enabled him to silence entirely the democratic, Socialist and Communist Press, while anti-semitic violence in the streets became a daily feature of the new regime. During Hitler's first week as Chancellor the semi-independent Prussian Government was abruptly dismissed, the national broadcasting company was taken over by the Nazi Party, and Hermann Goering[1] declared, in a public speech on February 1, that at its very first meeting the new Cabinet had agreed to provide the necessary funds for aviation 'so as to enable it to obtain the status required for the security of the German people as a whole'.

The question of disarmament, which continued to exercise the British Government, was one bedevilled by increasing disagreements between the French and German Governments. The French sought some security arrangement in return for the reduction and limitation of armaments. The British Government's dilemma had been clearly expressed in a Cabinet on February 15. Although the Committee of Imperial Defence had recommended abandoning the Ten Year Rule on 22 March 1932, no scheme for making up the deficiencies of the previous eight years had been put in its place since then. It was the Japanese attacks on northern China that led the Cabinet to review the problem on 15 February 1933, when the First Lord of the Admiralty, Eyres-Monsell, told his colleagues that 'some investigation should be undertaken with a view to making a start in defence preparations next year. He was particularly apprehensive owing to the situation in the Far East.' The Secretary of State for War, Lord Hailsham, and the Secretary of State for Air, Lord Londonderry, 'both called attention to corresponding deficiencies in their respective departments', while Londonderry added that he was worried about the 'coordination of the services'.

In reply to these anxieties, the Chancellor of the Exchequer, Neville Chamberlain, drew attention to a Treasury memorandum that 'today financial and economic risks are by far the most serious and urgent that the country has to face, and that other risks have to be run until the country has had time and opportunity to recuperate and our financial situation to improve'. Ramsay MacDonald, who followed Chamberlain, said that 'at the present moment it would be difficult to find any assumption on which even to base an enquiry', and he added: 'In the financial conditions described by the Chancellor of the Exchequer the

---

[1] Hermann Goering, 1893–1946. Served as a Lieutenant in the German Infantry, 1914. Commander of the Richthofen fighter squadron, 1918. A follower of Hitler from 1923. Wounded during the unsuccessful Munich putsch of November 1923, after which he lived in Austria, Italy and Sweden. Air Adviser in Denmark and Sweden, 1924–28. Returned to Germany, and elected to the Reichstag, 1928. President of the Reichstag, 1932–33. Prime Minister of Prussia, 1933. Commander-in-Chief of the German Air Force, 1933–45. Air Chief Marshal, 1935. Commissioner for the Four-Year Plan, 1936. Field-Marshal, 1938. President of the General Council for the War Economy, 1940. Sentenced to death at Nuremberg, October 1946, but committed suicide the night before his intended execution.

Cabinet would have to take responsibility, as they had done before, for the deficiencies of the Defence Departments.'

The Cabinet of 15 February 1933 had decided to accept Chamberlain's Treasury caution and MacDonald's decision, making themselves 'responsible for the deficiencies in the Defence Service which are imposed by the difficult financial situation of the country at the present time'. As for what should be done in practice, it was agreed to accept the March 1933 recommendation of the Committee of Imperial Defence that 'a start should be made in providing for the commitments that are purely defensive, including defence of bases, first priority being given to requirements in the Far East'.

On February 17 Churchill spoke at the 25th anniversary meeting of the Anti-Socialist and Anti-Communist Union. Commenting on the recent debate in the Oxford Union, at which a majority of the undergraduates present had approved the motion 'That this House refuses in any circumstances to fight for King and Country', Churchill declared: 'That abject, squalid, shameless avowal was made last week by 275 votes to 153 in the debating society of our most famous university. We are told we ought not to treat it seriously. "The Times" talks of the Children's Hour. I disagree. It is a very disquieting and disgusting symptom,' and he went on to explain why it troubled him:

My mind turns across the narrow waters of Channel and the North Sea, where great nations stand determined to defend their national glories or national existence with their lives. I think of Germany, with its splendid clear-eyed youth marching forward on all the roads of the Reich singing their ancient songs, demanding to be conscripted into an army; eagerly seeking the most terrible weapons of war; burning to suffer and die for their fatherland. I think of Italy, with her ardent Fascisti, her renowned Chief, and stern sense of national duty. I think of France, anxious, peace-loving, pacifist to the core, but armed to the teeth and determined to survive as a great nation in the world.[1]

One can almost feel the curl of contempt upon the lips of the manhood of all these peoples when they read this message sent out by Oxford University in the name of young England.[2]

---

[1] On 11 December 1932 France had agreed to accept the principle of German 'equality of rights' in return for discussions on a system 'which would provide security for all nations' This agreement had induced Germany to return to the Disarmament Conference.

[2] Although he was no longer an undergraduate, Randolph Churchill attempted, on March 2, to reverse the Oxford Union verdict, but he was unsuccessful, gaining only 138 votes against 750. On March 11 Churchill wrote to Lord Hugh Cecil: 'He stood a hard test at the Oxford Union. Nothing is so piercing as the hostility of a thousand of your own contemporaries, and he was by no means crushed under it.'

During the course of his speech Churchill praised 'the Roman genius' of Mussolini, whom he described as 'the greatest lawgiver among living men', for his anti-Communist stance, but he rejected Fascism as a model for Britain. 'It is not a sign-post which would direct us here,' he said, 'for I firmly believe that our long experienced democracy will be able to preserve a parliamentary system of government with whatever modifications may be necessary from both extremes of arbitrary rule.' Churchill also referred to the situation in the Far East, where the Japanese army, having occupied Manchuria in 1931, now prepared to extend its conquests to the Chinese province of Jehol. 'I must say something to you which is very unfashionable,' Churchill declared. 'I am going to say one word of sympathy for Japan,' and he added: '. . . I hope we should try in England to understand a little the position of Japan, an ancient state with the highest sense of national honour, and patriotism and with a teeming population and a remarkable energy. On the one side they see the dark menace of Soviet Russia. On the other the chaos of China, four or five provinces of which are actually now being tortured under Communist rule.'

On March 14 the House of Commons debated the Air Estimates. Opening the debate, the Under-Secretary of State for Air, Sir Philip Sassoon, stressed 'the need for economy' and reported a further reduction of £340,000 in addition to the £700,000 reduction of the previous year. These reductions, he explained, had 'only been rendered possible by such drastic measures as the decision to close down one of the four flying training schools', and he went on: 'Risks have had to be taken. As the House will have observed, no new units have been formed either at home or abroad during the last year, and no provision is made for new units in the present estimates'. The Home defence forces now stood at 42 squadrons. Ten more were still needed 'to meet the modest programme which was approved as long ago as 1923, and which is already several years overdue for completion'. Sassoon added: 'The decision to hold this ten-year old programme in suspense for another year is a practical proof of the whole-hearted desire of His Majesty's Government to promote a successful issue of the deliberations of the Disarmament Conference.' Pending the outcome of the Disarmament Conference, Sassoon noted, the Government 'are once again prepared to accept the continuance of the serious existing disparity between the strength of the Royal Air Force and that of the air services of the other great nations'.

In opposing Sassoon's economies, Churchill declared: 'It is no kindness to this country to stir up and pay all this lip-service in the region of unrealities.' Speaking of the strong diplomatic pressure which the

British Government had been putting on France to disarm, Churchill asked: 'In the present temper of Europe can you ever expect that France would halve her air force and then reduce the residue by one-third?'

Only by strengthening their naval and air armaments, Churchill declared, could the British remain 'judges' of their future. Without sufficient means of defence, even neutrality could not be preserved. It was essential to possess the power, particularly in the air, to strike back at an attacking force. 'Not to have an adequate air force in the present state of the world,' he warned, 'is to compromise the foundations of national freedom and independence.' His speech continued:

I regretted very much to hear the Under-Secretary state that we were only the fifth air Power. I regretted very much to hear him say that the ten-year programme was suspended for another year. I was sorry to hear him boast that they had not laid down a single new unit this year. All these ideas are being increasingly stultified by the march of events, and we should be well advised to concentrate upon our air defences with greater vigour.

During his speech, Churchill called for the abandonment of the Ten Year Rule. He also urged the Government, and Baldwin in particular, to stop encouraging 'this helpless, hopeless mood'. There was no need, he said, for Britain to fear a foreign air attack, provided the Government took immediate, comprehensive action. 'There is no reason to suppose that we cannot make machines as good as any country. We have—though it may be thought conceited to say so—a particular vein of talent in air piloting which is in advance of that possessed by other countries.'

The Cabinet discussed the debate on March 15, when Londonderry proposed that MacDonald and Simon, who were already in Geneva for the Disarmament Conference, should be 'given some knowledge of the state of opinion in the House of Commons'. But a Minister not named in the minutes suggested 'that the more important criticisms in the House of Commons were perhaps not wholly disinterested and had been prompted to some extent by political motives'.

On March 16, two days after Churchill's speech, Ramsay Mac-Donald submitted Britain's disarmament proposals to the Disarmament Conference at Geneva. These included specific figures for military and aerial disarmament.[1] A week later, on March 23, following intense Nazi

[1] The main points were: a maximum period of military service in all European armies of eight months; a maximum calibre of 105 millimetres for all mobile land guns manufactured in future; a maximum limit for the weight of tanks of 16 tons unladen weight, 20 tons laden weight; land-armed forces to be restricted numerically (the Soviet Union to have 500,000 soldiers; Germany, France, Italy and Poland to have 200,000 each, and all other European

pressure, the German Reichstag passed an Enabling Bill giving Hitler full dictatorial powers. That afternoon MacDonald described the Government's disarmament plans to the House of Commons. Of the Government's specific proposals he said: 'I cannot pretend that I went through the figures myself,' but the Government intended to give Germany 'equality of status' in the conference. Churchill, answering MacDonald, warned once more of what he believed was the folly of disarmament. 'Our first supreme object,' he said, 'is not to go to war. To that end we must do our best to prevent others from going to war.' But to press France to disarm could only encourage Germany, whose internal policies were increasingly alarming. Churchill continued:

When we read about Germany, when we watch with surprise and distress the tumultuous insurgence of ferocity and war spirit, the pitiless ill-treatment of minorities, the denial of the normal protections of civilized society to large numbers of individuals solely on the ground of race—when we see that occurring in one of the most gifted, learned, scientific and formidable nations in the world, one cannot help feeling glad, that the fierce passions that are raging in Germany have not found, as yet, any other outlet but upon Germans.

The Disarmament Conference was discussing the halving of France's army, and the doubling of the German army, as the first step towards lower, but equal armaments. 'As long as France is strong,' Churchill insisted, 'and Germany is but inadequately armed there is no chance of France being attacked with success, and therefore no obligation will arise under Locarno for us to go to the aid of France.'

Churchill reiterated his plea that before the victors disarm, the grievances of the vanquished should be redressed. MacDonald's four years of control over British foreign policy had failed to redress these grievances; instead, he declared, those four years 'have brought us nearer to war and have made us weaker, poorer, and more defenceless'. The House of Commons was outraged by this accusation, and cries of 'No, no, no' broke out from both the Labour and the Conservative benches. Churchill turned angrily towards those who had interrupted him. 'You say "No",' he retorted. 'You have only to hear what has been said today to know that we have been brought much nearer to war.' 'By whom?' the

States lower figures); the prohibition of aerial bombardment; military aeroplanes limited to 500 for Britain, France, Italy, Japan, Russia and the United States (with the German figure left open); no military aircraft to exceed twelve tons in weight, and all aeroplanes exceeding these numerical and weight limitations to be disposed of, one half by June 1936, the other half by 1939. In addition, all armaments surplus to the scheme were to be destroyed.

Conservatives demanded, to which Churchill replied, of Ramsay MacDonald:

I don't wish to place it on one man. But it seems to me that when a single man has held the whole power of Foreign Affairs for four years and has pursued certain lines of policy which I have indicated, you are making a very profound mistake if you think that the efficiency of your public service will be enhanced by pretending that there is no responsibility to be affixed anywhere.

Churchill ended his speech by warning the House, amid repeated interruptions, that the Disarmament Conference at Geneva had become 'a solemn and prolonged farce'; that the Naval Treaty of London, against which the Conservatives had voted in 1930, was 'cramping and fettering our naval development'; and that the recent visit of MacDonald and Simon to Mussolini in Rome—when Mussolini had proposed a four-power pact between Germany, Italy, France and Britain—was a valueless excursion that should not be treated too seriously. His speech ended with yet a further attack on MacDonald:

We have got our modern Don Quixote home again, with Sancho Panza at his tail, bearing with them these somewhat dubious trophies which they have collected amid the nervous titterings of Europe. Let us hope that now the right hon Gentleman is safely back among us he will, first of all, take a good rest, of which I have no doubt he stands in need, and that afterwards he will devote himself to the urgent domestic tasks which await him here, in this island, and which concern the well-being of millions of his poorer fellow-subjects, and leave the conduct of foreign affairs, at any rate for a little while, to be transacted by competent ambassadors through the normal and regular diplomatic channels.

Many MPs deeply resented the sarcasms which Churchill, not for the first time, had levelled at MacDonald. In the ensuing debate a Liberal MP, Geoffrey Mander,[1] called Churchill's speech 'a disgraceful personal attack on the Prime Minister, and an attempt to drive a wedge into the National Government, that he might enter that Government by the breach', while a Labour MP, David Logan,[2] declared that it was 'mean and contemptible that Mr Churchill should have a personal vendetta against, and insult, one who, whether they agreed with him on other things or not, was a harbinger of peace in Europe'. Another Labour MP,

[1] Geoffrey Le Mesurier Mander, 1882–1962. Educated at Harrow and Trinity College Cambridge. Liberal MP for East Wolverhampton, 1929–45. Parliamentary Private Secretary to Sir Archibald Sinclair (Secretary of State for Air), 1942–45. Knighted, 1945.

[2] David Gilbert Logan, 1871–1964. Justice of the Peace, Liverpool, 1924. City Alderman, 1929–35. Labour MP for the Scotland Division of Liverpool from 1929 until his death.

Sir Stafford Cripps, described Churchill's speech as 'thoroughly mischievous', while a Liberal National MP, John Wallace,[1] insisted that Churchill, in donning 'a jesters cap and bells', had tried 'to poison and vitiate the atmosphere' which MacDonald and Simon had sought to create. 'Mr Churchill's speech,' Wallace added, did not strike him 'as that of a statesman or of a man who was willing to help his country, but as that of a man who had some personal vendetta against the Prime Minister and largely as the speech of a disappointed office-seeker.'

John Wallace's remarks were met by several cries of 'No, No!', for Churchill was supported in the debate by his friend General Spears, by Colonel Gretton and by a Labour MP, Josiah Wedgwood, who regretted that MacDonald had not felt the need to make 'some generous reference to those friends who were now hunted from one prison to another in Germany'; but the majority of the House was against them.

On behalf of the Government, Churchill's speech was answered by the Under-Secretary of State at the Foreign Office, Anthony Eden, who said that it was unfortunate that Churchill had chosen so serious a debate to practise his 'quips and jests'. For Churchill to accuse Mac-Donald of being responsible for the deterioration of international relations, he said, was 'a fantastic absurdity'. The causes of that deterioration 'went back to a time when Mr Churchill himself had a considerable measure of responsibility'. Without French disarmament, Eden insisted, 'they could not secure for Europe that period of appeasement which is needed'. Britain did not wish France to halve her army, as Churchill alleged. 'The reduction was nothing like that,' Eden continued. 'It was 694,000 to 400,000.' As for Germany, they did not wish to double her army, but to change the system 'which was imposed on her at Versailles', replacing a small long-service army by a larger, but short-service militia.

The House of Commons cheered Eden's rebukes. On the following morning the Press were strongly censorious. 'The House was enraged in an ugly mood—towards Mr Churchill,' declared the *Daily Dispatch*; and the *Northern Echo* called Churchill's speech 'vitriolic', 'a furious onslaught' and 'one of the most audacious he has delivered'. That evening, speaking at Birmingham, Neville Chamberlain expressed his sorrow that Churchill 'should have used his talent in order to try apparently to throw suspicion and doubts in the minds of other Governments who have not expressed such feeling for themselves', and he continued: 'We

---

[1] John Wallace, 1868–1949. Educated at Kirkaldy Public School. Coalition Liberal MP for Dunfermline Burghs, 1918–22; Liberal National MP, 1931–35. Parliamentary Secretary to the Paymaster General, 1920–22. Knighted, 1935. Company director.

want to see that other countries do not go to war, not merely because war is wasteful, wasteful in men, wasteful in money, not only because if other nations go to war they thereby destroy the possibility of markets for ourselves, but also because when war starts no one can say where it will end.' Chamberlain added: 'It is our duty by every effort we can make, by every influence we can exert, to compose differences, and to act as mediators to try and devise methods by which other countries may be delivered from this great menace of war.'

Following his speech, Churchill received only one letter of support, from Admiral Sir Reginald Custance,[1] who wrote to him on March 24: 'You were really setting forth the fundamental principle of war and were talking over the heads of your audience who for the most part are quite ignorant of that principle.'

On April 13 Churchill spoke again in the House of Commons on European affairs. Ten days before his speech he was sent a cutting from the Swiss newspaper *La Liberale Suisse*. Wanting to know the paper's background, he sent the cutting to Major Desmond Morton, who had earlier given him much factual help and information on the 'Bolshevik' chapters of *The World Crisis*, and who was still working under the authority of the Committee of Imperial Defence as head of the Industrial Intelligence Centre. Morton reported back to Churchill on April 10, drawing upon his official sources to report on a relatively obscure matter. 'Supports a Liberal democratic continental outlook,' he wrote. 'Foreign politics very friendly towards England and France. Was strongly pro-Ally in war. It is read by a high class population, but only has a comparatively small circulation in French-speaking Switzerland, about 3,500 to 4,000 copies a day. Its reputation financially and morally is excellent.' Morton sent other details about the paper's foreign correspondents and contributors; subsequently Churchill was to send Morton all the material he received from abroad for comment. In the speech itself, Churchill contrasted Hitler's desire for Treaty revision and rearmament with MacDonald's continuing pursuit of disarmament. 'The rise of Germany to anything like military equality with France,' he reiterated, 'or the rise of Germany or some ally or other to anything like military equality with France, Poland or the small states, means a renewal of a general European war.' Churchill also warned of the dangers of the 'odious conditions now ruling in Germany' being

[1] Reginald Neville Custance, 1847–1935. Entered the Navy, 1862. Director of Naval Intelligence, 1899–1902. Rear-Admiral, Mediterranean Fleet, 1902–04. Knighted, 1904. 2nd in command, Channel Fleet, 1907–08. Retired, 1912. Author of *War at Sea: Modern Theory and Ancient Practice* (1919) and *A Study of War* (1924).

extended by conquest to Poland, 'and another persecution and pogrom of Jews begun in this new area'. His speech ended:

What the Prime Minister proposed so recently for the disarmament of Europe seems to move towards German equality in armaments. He is suspected all over the continent of wishing to help Germany at the expense of her neighbours. The other day he spread on the table at Geneva a vast plan for bringing all the armaments down and thus bringing Germany much nearer to equality with her neighbours. He told us an (extraordinary admission) that he had not gone through the figures himself, but he took responsibility for them. It is a very grave responsibility. If ever there was a document upon which its author should have consumed his personal thought and energy it was this immense disarmament proposal. I doubt very much whether even the Committee of Imperial Defence was consulted upon it. We have not been told whether the heads of all our fighting services were consulted upon it. Unknown hands have prepared it and its author tells us that he has not mastered it either in its scope or detail.

I was reading the other day the comments of a Swiss newspaper of respectable standing upon our British plan. They say it is part of a deliberate plot by which the British Prime Minister is pursuing those pro-German sympathies which he has had for so many years. It is devised in order to bring about the defeat or paralysis of France at the hands of Germany and Italy, and so to expose the small nations to the ambition of the Teuton mass. Of course it is not true. I am glad to be able to declare wherever my words will carry that it is not true. But when you see how the small countries work out these proposals, how they say that the naval proposals are the counterpart of the military, and that France would not be able to bring their colonial armies back to France across the Mediterranean against the military and naval combination of Germany and Italy; and the detailed calculations and allegations which they make, one is astonished at the levity, temerity and I might almost say presumption, with which such things are launched upon seas which the hurricane may so easily lash to fury. I repeat and I will continue to repeat again and again as long as I have breath, that we have no right to meddle too closely in Europe.

25

India 1933: A Party Divided

AS well as expressing great concern over disarmament, Churchill
continued to watch the development of the Government's policy
towards India with alarm. On January 2 Lord Sydenham[1] had written
to him: 'I earnestly hope you will return in full vigour. You alone can
now stop this surrender of India with what it means to this Empire &
Foreign Powers.' Five days later Churchill replied: 'We shall now this
year come into our full battle about India,' and he added: 'The position
is even worse than I had apprehended. Irwinism has rotted the soul of
the Tory party and I have no doubt they will vote for any measure,
however disastrous, when the Whips are put on. Still it is our duty to
fight with every scrap of strength we can command, and you may be
sure I will do all I can.'

In Government circles it was realized that opposition to the policy
would be widespread. But Hoare was prepared to continue the battle.
'As to the future,' he wrote to Baldwin on January 9, 'my course is set.
Neither Winston nor George Lloyd will deflect it. Will they sink the
ship? I do not think so, for although my guns may be very light, yours
are very formidable.' On February 3 Hoare wrote to Willingdon: 'My
difficulty will be to keep the Lancashire members quiet,' and he added:
'you can rely on me to be as discreet as possible'. A week later Hoare
wrote again: 'With the reassembling of Parliament it is quite obvious to
me that the extreme right are mobilising an extensive attack upon our
India policy. . . . It will be a great gain when we have got the whole

[1] George Sydenham Clarke, 1848–1933. Joined Royal Engineers, 1868. On Staff of Royal
Indian Engineering College, 1871–80. Secretary to the Colonial Defence Committee, 1885–
92; and to the Royal Commission on Navy and Army Administration, 1892–1900. Knighted,
1893. Governor of Victoria, Australia, 1901–04. Secretary to the Committee of Imperial
Defence, 1904–07. Governor of Bombay, 1907–13. Created Baron Sydenham of Combe, 1913.
Chairman of Central Appeal Tribunal, 1915–16. President, National Council for Combating
Venereal Disease, 1915–20. Member of the Air Board, 1916–17.

question safely into the hands of the Joint Select Committee. . . .' On February 11, the day after Hoare wrote this letter to Willingdon, Churchill received an appeal from Lord Salisbury, who feared that the Joint Select Committee would not be 'fairly chosen' as far as opponents of the Bill were concerned. Salisbury was also critical of the Government's plan 'to admit Indian assessors' to the meetings of the Committee as an 'unprecedented' concept. Churchill replied on February 13:

I imagine HMG intend to do only provincial government now, minus the police, ie less than Simon; but that they will incorporate into their Bill the whole Federal structure. They will assign no date (see Sam Hoare's speech at the third Round Table Conference) to bringing this into effect, and thus make it easy for the House to accept it in principle, as nothing is going to happen for some years.

This seems to be a very deadly and insidious line of attack. The Indian political classes will be kept in continual agitation. Little will have been given them and enormous hopes held out, not by speeches but by statute. The realisation of these hopes will be the only theme in India. . . .

I should have thought it was vital to prevent the formulation of a federal scheme merely as a bait to dangle in the future. Parliament ought to confine itself to the immediate tasks and practical measures and keep itself entirely free to judge further extensions of government when those now to be given are seen at work.

Churchill was also critical of the proposal to allow Indian assessors to be present at the meetings, telling Salisbury:

They will immediately raise the question of their status. It will be held to be a slur upon the people of India if all persons of colour are turned out of the room when the Joint Committee deliberates in secret. Yet surely Englishmen must have the right to deliberate in secret. Powers to consult with them on particular occasions to the utmost extent desired, and of course to summon witnesses, are not only unobjectionable but convenient.

During his speech to the Anti-Socialist and Anti-Communist Union on February 17 Churchill pointed out that the 'whole official power of the Conservative organisation, all the influence of its leaders, all the loyalty and docility of its followers' had combined to support the Government's India policy. Yet it was not too late, he declared, for Conservatives to reverse that policy. 'One deep-throated growl from the National Union of Conservative Associations,' he declared, 'would be enough to stop the rot—to save India from an ordeal as hideous as that of China, to save the British Imperial power from a disastrous eclipse, and to save the character and texture of Toryism from a deed to which it would long look back with shame and sorrow.'

The National Government's India policy depended to a large extent upon the Princes agreeing to join the proposed all-India Federation. Indeed, without the support of the Princes, nearly half of the sub-continent would be excluded from the scheme. Hoare saw clearly the danger of a rejection by the Princes, writing to Willingdon on February 17:

I greatly hope that you will be able to get a pro-Federal resolution out of them. A very formidable attack is being made upon the Government scheme by Salisbury and Winston, and one of the points of which they make the greatest possible play is the allegation that the Federation is a sham Federation and that the Princes are not really coming in. We do, therefore, badly want some outward visible sign that the Princes are not receding from the position that they have hitherto taken up. The further you can get them the easier it will be for us here.

Of the forthcoming India debate in the House of Commons Hoare wrote: 'We are doing everything that we can to ensure a good Government majority, but there is no gainsaying the fact that the Conservative party as a whole is very jumpy in both Houses.' Among those Conservatives who felt uneasy at the Government's India policy was the Duchess of Atholl,[1] who wrote to Baldwin on February 20 'of how much opinion there is against a transfer of responsibility at the centre among men who have held responsible office in the Indian Civil Service'. The Duchess was particularly concerned about the difficulties of retaining adequate and effective powers in the hands of the Viceroy and Provincial Governors to carry out the Government's promise to protect the Muslim and untouchable minorities. Many Indians to whom she had talked shared her view, but were, she wrote, 'afraid to say all they really think before each other'. The Duchess added: 'I am convinced that there is widespread anxiety about India among loyal supporters of the Government.'

Following Churchill's Queen's Hall speech of February 17, many Conservatives appealed to him to join their opposition to the Government's India policy. Several of those who now encouraged him were elderly, die-hard Tories, to whose policies, in the past, he had been strongly opposed, and whose support now discredited him in the eyes of

---

[1] Katharine Marjory Ramsay, 1874–1960. Educated at Wimbledon High School and the Royal College of Music. Married the 8th Duke of Atholl in 1899 (he died in 1942). Commandant, Blair Castle Auxiliary Hospital, 1917–19. DBE, 1918. A leading Scottish educationalist. Conservative MP for Kinross and West Perth, 1923–38. Parliamentary Secretary, Board of Education, 1924–29. Member of the Royal Commission on the Civil Service, 1929–31. Among her publications were *Searchlight on Spain* (1938) and *The Tragedy of Warsaw* (1945). Her husband fought with Churchill at Omdurman in 1898. Her elder brother was killed in action in South Africa in 1899.

many moderates and liberals. On February 18 Lord Carson wrote to him sympathetically: 'I think the Conservative Party are doped over India,' while on February 24 Sir Alfred Knox invited him to a meeting with Sir Henry Page Croft and John Gretton to discuss tactics for the forthcoming meeting of the Conservative Central Council. 'I am more than ever determined,' Knox wrote, 'to fight to the last ditch.'

When the House of Commons debated the India policy on February 22, Page Croft was the main anti-Government speaker, asking the Government to agree to restrict the current reforms in India to Provincial self-government, and to retain the full authority of British rule at the centre. 'He was answered,' Leopold Amery wrote in his diary, 'by Eustace Percy in the best speech I have yet heard him make, which greatly impressed the House and killed the attack at the outset, nor could it be revived as Winston had for once decided not to speak.' Churchill's influence, meanwhile, was being portrayed as a pernicious one by the advocates of Dominion Status. 'There have been a good many alarms and excursions since I wrote last week,' Hoare wrote to Willingdon on February 25, and he continued:

The Winston crowd have been very active with meetings, lunches, and propaganda of every kind. Some of our people got rattled and genuinely feared that we should find in the Page-Croft debate a very awkward situation in which many Conservatives were beginning to move to the extreme right.

We did what we could, and I can say that so far we have had a considerable success. Winston and the Morning Post were convinced that they would get a much better division than they did in December 1931. As it turned out, their number was actually less than it was then.

Nobody here or in India, however, must imagine that things are going to run too smoothly. The attitude of most Conservatives is one of suspended animation. They are waiting to see whether the White Paper really does make the safeguards as effective as possible, and also whether the federation looks really like taking shape. . . .

The vote at the end of the debate was indeed a disappointment for Churchill, 297 votes being cast in favour of Dominion Status and only 42 against. Yet the widespread unease of many Conservative voters was clearly expressed in a resolution which Baldwin's close friend Davidson received on February 28 from his own constituents. This resolution stated that: 'The demand for a central self-government comes not from the peoples of India as a whole, but from a small, noisy minority of townsfolk, whereas 89 per cent of the population are not town dwellers and 66 per cent are rural cultivators. What the great majority of Indians desire is not self-government, but firm and stable rule.' Davidson defended the Government by seeking to cast doubts on Churchill's motives. 'I do most sincerely hope,' he told his constituents, 'that the Conservative Party will not allow itself to be stampeded into ill-considered action by Mr Churchill whose ill-disguised intention is rather the break-up of the National Government than the safety and the welfare of India.'[1]

On February 26 Willingdon warned Hoare that there was strong opposition to the Federal scheme from the Princes, who were proving 'very difficult to get hold of'. For his part, Hoare still feared a growth of Conservative dissent at home, and in a letter to Willingdon on March 3 he described Churchill's success in acting as a focus of discontent on February 28 at a meeting of the Central Council of the National Union of Conservative Associations, where a motion to repudiate the Party's policy was only narrowly defeated, by 189 votes to 165. As Hoare explained to Willingdon:

The National Union is the body to which delegates are sent from every constituency, and unfortunately one of its half-yearly meetings came this week. Winston saw his chance and did everything in his power to carry a resolution against the White Paper policy. Knowing what was up I went to the meeting to answer him. The delegates who attend are, of course, the keen partisans of the Party. None the less it must be remembered that they are most of them the leading Conservatives in the constituencies who take a part in electioneering and the local organisations. It was at once evident to me that they had proved very susceptible to Winston's propaganda, and when Winston spoke it was clear that the hall was full of his partisans and of a great many people who were wobbling towards him.

When I came on at the end of the debate, I think that most people would have said that Winston would carry the vote. He made one of his very effective speeches and certainly made a great impression on the audience. I took the only line that I could, namely not to budge at all and to contradict the many false statements that he made. Fortunately this seemed to impress the meeting and the result was that we just won. But it was a touch and go affair and whatever else it shows, it does prove conclusively the strength of the doubts and suspicions that are in many people's minds. . . .

It was essential, Hoare added, to issue the White Paper 'as soon as possible', and in great detail. 'Any delay or vagueness,' he warned, 'will deliver us into the hands of our enemies here,' and he noted with foreboding: 'I can assure you that there is the making of a first-class crisis

---

[1] A young Conservative MP, Richard Law, later recalled in conversation with the author: 'It was said that Winston was trying to break the Government over India. I have no doubt that this was inspired by the Whips. It was deliberately put about.'

here and a breakaway of three-quarters of the Conservative Party unless we keep to this line.'

During his speech Churchill had again stressed the wisdom of trying to follow up the proposals in the Simon Report. 'What he had always felt about the Simon Report,' he said, 'was that at least it gave to the Provinces a chance to show whether Indians were really capable of governing themselves wisely and incorruptibly, and if they succeeded, then they would establish their case for a further advance. If, however, they failed, the Imperial power at the centre of the Government of India, remaining intact with all its resources, would be able to come to the rescue of any Province in which self-government failed and help to restore law and order.' Praising Hoare's 'patience, force and skill' in restoring order after the arrest of Gandhi and several thousand Congress supporters, Churchill continued:

Yet the Secretary of State was now proposing to hand over the government of India to the very people who had been responsible for these disorders, at the very time when we were faced with the spectre of Ireland and all our unhappy experiences in regard to that country. . . .

The policy seemed to be dictated by the desires of four or five amiable and powerful men in this country who had developed idealist conceptions, and had become profoundly interested in, and fascinated by, the noble art of constitutionmongering.

In his opinion, the present policy of the National Government was nothing but a Socialist policy, and the Conservative Party was failing to exercise its critical faculty with regard to great proposals of constitutional change.

In working out the composition of the Joint Select Committee to study the India Bill, the Government were determined not to put themselves in too weak a position. On March 1, a few days after discussing the Committee's possible membership with the Government Chief Whip, David Margesson, Churchill wrote to him: 'Of course the Government must have an effective majority; but we consider that we represent three-quarters of the Tory party in the constituencies. Anyhow, we can prove half,' and he continued:

It is not surely too much to ask, in the circumstances, that if the Government have twelve all committed to the Round Table plan, we should have eight who are definitely on the other side, ie four from each House. The matter has never yet been thrashed out, and the Joint Committee should furnish the occasion.

I do not think that anyone on either side, however strong may be their prepossession, ought to sit on such a body with closed mind. It would be unfortunate if the Committee seemed to be packed as every other body has been which has examined the question.

Of the Government's decision to include several Indians on the Committee Churchill wrote:

There is also the very difficult question raising several serious constitutional issues of the relation of the Joint Committee to any delegation of Government nominees from India. It would be quite inadmissible that persons having no seats in either Houses of Parliament should sit as assessors on a Joint Committee.

'You are always so courteous and considerate to me,' Churchill added, 'that I venture to write to you thus freely.'

The Government itself were worried about the nature of its forthcoming India White Paper. It was, Hoare told his Cabinet colleagues on March 10, 'not a Bill, but rather a Terms of Reference to the proposed Joint Select Committee ... he would not like to say it was a perfect scheme'; it was, rather, a compromise scheme based upon past promises, and would involve the Federation of 'very incongruous units'. Many Indians would say that the proposed constitution was 'tied up too much' by safeguards; British critics 'would maintain that the safeguards were inadequate'. Other critics would say 'that the constitution was too complicated to work'.

Hoare explained that under the safeguards written into the scheme, the Viceroy would have 'great powers', including 'complete control' over the Foreign Affairs and Defence departments. Even under the All-India Federation proposals, 'there was no great risk of a Congress majority', as the Princely States would have 30 per cent and the Muslims 30 per cent of the votes in the lower chamber, and, Hoare stressed, the whole constitution 'was conditional' on this All-India Federation being a part of it.

In conclusion, Hoare 'admitted that the scheme was complicated and liable to attack'. Lord Hailsham then told his colleagues that 'From the first he had had misgivings as to our Indian policy'. Now he 'violently rejected the suggestion' that the proposed constitution 'was the minimum that was required to satisfy our pledges' and he expressed his doubts 'as to whether the safeguards were effective'. Under the Government's proposals, Hailsham warned, 'India would be run more and more by Indians who were very clever, but not good administrators and often corrupt, as their own religion compelled them to look after their own relations. Justice would be sold, the poor oppressed, and there would be a breakdown in the services.'

Hoare, replying to Hailsham, admitted that he himself 'did not claim to be confident or optimistic and shared many of the doubts of the Secretary of State for War', but, he added, 'every alternative policy appeared to lead to a situation of great danger in which everyone in India might be against us'. The Muslims in particular were 'determined to have provincial autonomy' and he pointed out that 'one of the basic principles in Imperial Policy was agreement, if possible, with the Moslem World'.

The Cabinet agreed to proceed with the All-India Federal scheme, as the basis of the White Paper. Meanwhile, while waiting for the Joint Select Committee to be announced, Churchill attended a meeting, organized by Gretton, Page Croft and Knox, of all those MPs who had hitherto voted against the Government's India policy. The aim of the meeting, Churchill informed Lord Salisbury on March 12, was to establish 'a nucleus in the House of Commons'. The group, which called itself the India Defence Committee, came into formal existence in the third week of March, and consisted of some fifty Conservative MPs. The Government watched these activities with growing alarm, and sought to attribute to Churchill the worst possible motive. Writing to Willingdon on March 17, Hoare set out both his fears for Party unity, and his contempt for what he described as Churchill's purely selfish and wrecking aims:

Winston and his crowd have been very active and completely unscrupulous. They have been making a dead set at the party organisations in the constituencies, with the result that they have seriously disturbed a large number of Conservative MPs and have produced a sheaf of resolutions against the Government programme. . . .

It must, however, be constantly kept in mind that Winston is out chiefly to smash the National Government and that he will stick at nothing to achieve his end. India gives him a good fighting ground as he can play upon the ignorance and the very natural suspicions of some of the most trusted members of the Conservative Party. . . .

No one at present, Hoare believed, could 'assess the strength' of Churchill's forces, but it would be 'a mistake to underrate them', and he added, again deprecatingly:

Winston's idea is to capture the Conservative caucus and to appeal from it over the head of the House of Commons with the object of forcing all of us out of office next autumn. However effective Winston's attack may be, there is a great body of opinion in the country what will never trust him and even the extreme right of the Conservative party, whilst they will use him for their own ends, would never, I believe, take him as their leader.

On March 17 the Government issued its White Paper, setting out its proposals for the new Indian constitution. Each Indian Province was to be granted autonomy, while the previously strict viceregal control at the centre was to be replaced by a Federal Government with substantial Indian participation. From the outset it was clear that the new constitution would be criticized from many different viewpoints. The Princes, Willingdon wrote to Hoare three days later, 'don't like your suggested scheme of representation in the Upper Chamber. . . .'

Four days later the House of Commons began its debate on the Government's proposal to set up a Joint Select Committee to discuss the White Paper proposals 'before Parliament is asked to give a decision'. This form of words, stressing Parliament's ultimate responsibility, had been deliberately chosen to answer Churchill's criticisms that the policies were not being given proper Parliamentary scrutiny. As Hoare explained to Willingdon on March 23: 'We had a good deal of discussion over the form of the resolution for setting up the Committee. A false move might have enabled Winston to gather together a big crowd into the lobby against the Government.' As a result of the form of words used, Hoare added, 'Our own moderates were delighted and Winston, although he is outwardly claiming it as a victory for himself, is really bitterly disappointed.'

Speaking in the House of Commons on March 30, Churchill appealed to the Government not to use the Joint Select Committee as a means of prejudicing in advance the debate which the House of Commons must hold on the future constitution of India. The Montagu–Chelmsford reforms, he said, had failed. 'Every service which has been transferred to Indian hands has deteriorated markedly. Nepotism, corruption, inefficiency, general slackening, a lowering down of the Services has invaded and infected all the departments which have been experimentally handed over. . . .' Later in his speech Churchill alleged that for the previous five years 'the high personnel of India has been arranged, continuously arranged, with a view to securing men who will give a modern and welcome reception' to the Government's proposals, and he added: 'It was one of the greatest evils of the Montagu–Chelmsford reforms that throughout the Service the path of promotion has tended to be more easy for those who readily throw themselves into what are regarded as the irresistible moods of the British nation.' At this point the Chairman of the Conservative India Committee, Sir John Wardlaw-Milne, interrupted, demanding proof of Churchill's charge. When Churchill defended what he had said, Hoare himself rose to protest. 'The right hon Gentleman,' he said, 'has no justification whatever for that statement.'

Churchill's accusation against the Indian Civil Service weakened the reception of his subsequent arguments. His main criticism of the White Paper was that despite the enormous powers which the Viceroy would have over defence, foreign affairs and taxation, he would have no practical authority over the individuals who would have to carry out his orders. He had been instructed to govern by consent with the new legislature, but that consent would not be forthcoming.

'I thought your speech in a cold House was going quite well,' John Gretton wrote on the following day, 'until the entirely unjustifiable interruption by Wardlaw-Milne which had the effect of breaking up the atmosphere of attention to your case which you were carefully building.' For Hoare, the hostile reaction to Churchill's speech was the cause of relief, and even jubilation, and in a letter to Willingdon on March 31 he gave an account of what had happened. He himself, Hoare wrote, was 'purposely as cautious and conciliatory as I could be as it was the sort of occasion when, if I had tried to push the House further than it was ready to go, I should have delivered myself into Winston's hands'. As for Churchill, he wrote:

His much advertised speech was one of the greatest failures of his life, his long prepared invective falling very flat and the speech being much too long. Apart, however, from the make-up of his speech, he fell into the fatal error of making an unjustifiable attack upon the ICS and, still worse, of refusing to withdraw it.

After Wardlaw-Milne and I had interrupted him he never got started again and completely lost the ear of the House. The only thing remaining was for Eddie Winterton to get up and drown him in ridicule to the delight of the House.[1] Altogether it was a most surprising crash. He himself realised it and admitted his failure freely to the Chief Whip and many others in the House.

No doubt he is still far from crushed. But what has happened is that his failure has given heart to the undecided and the waverers to stand up against the extreme right in their constituencies. I think also that the papers that are backing him so strongly will begin to wonder whether he is the divine leader that they had assumed.

[1] During his opening remarks Winterton said, of Churchill, that he 'possesses, like the right hon Gentleman the Member for Carnarvon Boroughs (Mr Lloyd George), oratorical guns of a range and calibre which are unsurpassed by almost anyone else in this House, but those guns are open to attack from the bombs of the records of their own past deeds, the damaging quotation, the devastating parallel. . . . If I may change the metaphor, I will say that with all the experience of my right hon Friend in manual labour, he cannot shovel enough earth over his past to obliterate it from human view. His colourful and arresting personality has been indissolubly bound for the last 25 years with constitutional experiments and evolution in South Africa, in India and in Ireland which whether we like it or not, have left an indelible mark on the situation at present existing in India and affect the means for dealing with it.'

At the end of a three-day debate, the Government's policy was upheld by 475 votes to 42. It was then decided that the Joint Select Committee would have the power to frame proposals for constitutional reform in India within the framework of the White Paper.

Churchill was not entirely surprised by the hostile reception of his protest, writing to Sir Reginald Banks[1] on March 31: 'The House was very leaden, but it listened with attention. The subject is so vast that it is difficult to know where to begin or end.' To Lord Carson he wrote that same day: 'I did my best, as you see. But when one has all the machines of three parties and their hangers-on hostile in the House of Commons it is uphill work. I shall fight this business to the end without the slightest regard to any other considerations. It was very pleasing to me to have your sympathy and approval.' To John Gretton he replied on April 1, 'I ought to have had a shorter and less ambitious speech. One worries so much about this gigantic subject, that the art of selective presentation is little to the onlooker. Better luck next time!'

The realization that he would meet with enormous opposition from the Conservative Party in Parliament did not deflect Churchill from his course; indeed, it strengthened his determination. 'You may be quite sure,' he wrote to Sir Henry Page Croft on March 31, 'that any check or disappointment only makes me fight harder and if we all continue to do our best with no other thought but the public cause, it is by no means certain that we shall not save much from the wreck, if we do not save the ship.'

On March 31 Sir Samuel Hoare wrote to Churchill from the India Office, at Ramsay MacDonald's request, inviting him to join the Joint Select Committee as one of the representatives of the House of Commons. In a personal covering letter, very different in tone to his letter to Willingdon, Hoare expressed his hope that Churchill would agree to serve on the committee. 'I am afraid,' Hoare wrote, 'that in recent months our ways have not so much parted as crossed, and that the differences between us have seemed to be enlarged rather than diminshed.' His letter continued:

Be this as it may, I can honestly say that no such differences of opinion will ever make me think that your unique talents should or could be lost to the service of the State. It is on this account that I am the more hopeful that you

---

[1] Reginald Mitchell Banks, 1880–1940. Educated at Rugby and Christ Church Oxford. Called to the Bar, 1905. Enlisted as a private, 1914; 2nd Lieutenant, 1915. On active service in Mesopotamia, 1915–16. Military Censor, Press Bureau, 1917. Conservative MP for Swindon, 1922–29 and 1931–34. Recorder of Wigan, 1928–34. Knighted, 1928. In 1929 he published *The Conservative Outlook*. A County Court Judge (Circuit No 16), 1934–40.

will take a part in this immensely important investigation. If you are able to accept, I can undertake on my part to see that full and fair consideration shall be given to your point of view.

On the evening of March 31 David Margesson informed Churchill of the composition of the Committee. On the following morning Churchill explained to Lord Salisbury that the names, when added up carefully, constituted twenty-five supporters of the Government's policy against nine. 'I told him,' Churchill added, 'that we had agreed to consult among ourselves before taking any decision as to joining. . . .' That same day Churchill wrote to Hoare, asking for a few more days in which to make up his mind. During the course of his letter he expressed his fears that not only Indian affairs, but also the whole fabric of British political life, was being adversely affected by the Government's India policy:

I have watched with grief and indignation the process by which during the last two and a half years you and Baldwin have turned the whole official power of the Conservative party and of the Government of India to paralysing or overcoming the Conservative resistance at home and loyalist resistance in India in order to bring your scheme into effect. I survey with profound sorrow the injury to Imperial strength and the life of our country which has resulted. Even your own admirable administration has been made the means, by temporarily allaying anxieties, of furthering a disastrous end. All the loyalty of the Conservative party to its leaders added to the drift of Liberal and Socialist opinion make a tide which may well be irresistible. You will probably have your way. But then the consequences will begin both in India and at home.

When the nation realises what it has lost, and the Conservative party realise what they will have done, there will be a sombre reckoning. But these issues—about which of course I may be entirely wrong—are far too wide and majestic for personal feelings, and there are many grounds on which I feel a high regard for you.

Churchill could not decide whether or not to serve on the Committee. Like Lord Lloyd and Sir Henry Page Croft, both of whom had also been invited, he feared that being in a minority, their viewpoint, however forcibly argued, would inevitably be dismissed in the end. But on April 4 H. A. Gwynne wrote to Churchill urging him to serve. 'I feel very strongly,' Gwynne argued, 'that you could produce a minority report that would run up and down the country like a flame in dry grass.' There should also, Gwynne believed, 'be someone on our side in the Committee who will be able to cross-examine and to make the most of our case, and I think that there are few who could do it as well as yourself'. Churchill decided, however, not to serve. On April 5 he wrote to Hoare, explaining the reason for his decision:

I observe that at least three-quarters of the Committee of thirty-four consists of persons of distinction who have already declared themselves in favour of the principle of the abdication at this juncture of British responsibility in the Central government of India. To this I am decidedly opposed. I believe that if the scheme of the White Paper is carried out, it can only lead after some years either to the evacuation or to the re-conquest of India. I do not wish to share the burden for such grievous events. I see no advantage therefore in my joining your Committee merely to be voted down by an overwhelming majority of the eminent persons you have selected. It is better that those who believe in the policy of the White Paper should work it out for themselves in the Joint Committee unhampered by the criticism or protest of those from whom they are unbridgeably divided.

Churchill's letter ended:

I shall no doubt find the opportunity for any advice I may think useful, when the Bill giving effect to your decision is eventually brought before the House of Commons. I can well understand that others who have misgivings about your policy may nevertheless think it right to accept your invitation in order to have the chance of placing their views on record. But I will have neither part nor lot in the deed you seek to do.

Hoare replied on April 6, expressing his 'great regret' at Churchill's decision. He also rejected Churchill's specific arguments, writing in his reply:

I gather from your letter that you conceive the Committee to be divided between those who wish to abdicate in India and those who do not. Let me assure you that if this is your view it is founded upon a complete misconception of the views of those who, like myself, believe that the wisest and surest way to carry out our responsibilities to India is to proceed upon the lines set out in the White Paper.

I note that you will give us the value of your advice when the proposals come before Parliament in the form of a Bill. Naturally we shall always value such advice, but may I suggest that it would have been more helpful if you had been prepared to give us it now at once as a member of the Joint Select Committee.

Writing that same day to Lord Willingdon, Hoare totally misrepresented Churchill's motives and intentions. Churchill, he wrote:

... has convinced himself that he will smash the Government sooner or later and that if he joins the Committee he will be muzzled at any rate for a time. I believe that at the back of his mind he thinks that he will not only smash the Government but that England is going Fascist and that he, or someone like him, will eventually be able to rule India as Mussolini governs north Africa. I believe that he is wrong, but no doubt he sees around him at the moment a good deal of evidence in the break up European governments that gives colour to his thought.

Several of Churchill's friends were surprised by his decision not to participate in the Joint Select Committee. 'Will you let me say that I deeply deplore your refusal to enter the Joint Select Committee,' Lord Burnham wrote on April 7, and he added: 'I shall especially miss your leadership and guidance.' Two days later Churchill replied: 'I am so sorry not to be able to help you, but I feel sure my work lies outside. The way in which the Committee has been picked is a scandal.'

On April 10 Hoare laid before Parliament the list of those who had agreed to serve on the Joint Select Committee[1]. A Conservative member then moved an amendment to remove the six members of the Government who had been selected. Although the amendment was defeated only by 209 votes to 118, this 118 constituted the largest vote recorded in Parliament against the National Government's India policy. Churchill at once issued a statement, which was published in the *Evening News*:

If the House had been given a free vote the Government proposal would probably have been defeated by a majority of the Conservative party. What the Government is trying to do is to get support for its views and not to have an impartial investigation. The Government is not looking for advice but for advertisement. It is not seeking guidance but a guarantee.

Churchill was now determined to lead a public crusade against the Government's India policy. 'We are in for a hard long fight,' he wrote to his friend Commander Diggle[2] on April 14, 'but I do not despair.' Hoare himself was worried both about Churchill's campaign, and about the Joint Select Committee. 'Very rightly,' he wrote to Willingdon on April 28: 'we shall try and keep evidence down to the lowest possible quantity,' and he added: 'After all, evidence has already been taken upon every conceivable question and what with the discussion of the

---

[1] The House of Commons representatives on the Joint Select Committee were twelve National Government supporters: Hoare, Butler, Simon, Davidson, Austen Chamberlain, Eustace Percy, Winterton, Reginald Craddock, Joseph Nall, Edward Cadogan, Mary Pickford, Wardlaw-Milne; one Liberal: Isaac Foot, and three Labour MPs: Attlee, Morgan Jones and Seymour Cocks. Among the Lords' representatives were Sankey, Reading, Lothian, Peel, Snell and Burnham. Of a total of thirty-four members, eight, including Lord Salisbury, were members of the India Defence Committee.

[2] Nestor William Diggle, 1880–1963. Entered the Royal Navy, 1901. Commander, 1913. Served on the China Station, with the Dover Patrol and at the Dardanelles, 1914–18. Assistant Beach Master during the V Beach Landing, Gallipoli, April 1915. Naval Attaché, Rome, 1919–22. CMG, 1919. Employed at the Admiralty, 1922–26. Retired, 1926.

Round Table and the innumerable reports that have resulted from the preparation of the White Paper we really do not want a lot of verbal evidence. Moreover, if we get involved in months of evidence, there will be no chance of getting even Provincial Autonomy working for about three years.' As for Churchill, he wrote: 'His chief ally is the ignorance of ninety nine people out of a hundred. . . . The result will be that he will get a formidable backing in Conservative circles and that he will certainly stir up a great deal of suspicion and irritation in the organisations of many constituencies.'

Hoare's fears of a constituency revolt were borne out on April 28, when the annual meeting of the Horsham and Worthing Conservative Association rejected the Government's White Paper policy by 161 votes to 17, despite the fact that the policy had been defended by the MP who had represented them for twenty-nine years, Lord Winterton. Speaking at Worcester on the following day, Baldwin insisted that the White Paper policy was the only sound one, that it was supported by each of the three post-war Viceroys, by the three Provincial Governors[1] and by the Indian Civil Service in India itself; that it has been supported in the House of Lords by Lord Linlithgow; and that it was the result of long and responsible investigation. Against that policy, he insisted, 'you have a mass of negative criticism, unsupported by responsible opinion in India, and bearing little relation to the developments which have taken place during the last 16 years'. He was 'surprised and disappointed', he said, that Churchill and Lord Lloyd 'and those who support them' had refused to accept a place on the Joint Select Committee; and he declared: 'It is a much easier matter, and means much less hard work, to go about the country trying to split the Conservative Party—a great deal easier.' Yet such action, he warned, could, if successful, destroy national unity, and lead 'to some form of Bolshevism or Fascism'.

Churchill was outraged by this accusation. In his first direct conflict with Baldwin since he had left the Conservative Business Committee three years before, he answered Baldwin's charges in a statement issued from Chartwell on April 30. Who, he asked, was responsible 'for splitting the Conservative Party?' and he answered:

Surely the whole burden rests upon a leader who forces upon his party a policy on which it has never been consulted and which runs directly counter to its deepest instincts and traditions. History has always assigned the responsibility for splitting a party to the leader who proposes the departure.

[1] The three Viceroys were Lord Reading, Lord Irwin and Lord Willingdon; the three Governors were Sir John Anderson (Bengal), Sir Frederick Sykes (Bombay) and Sir George Stanley (Madras).

Churchill went on to set out once more his arguments against the White Paper policy. He was particularly angry that Baldwin had cited Government servants in defence of the policy, for, as he explained, all promotion in India 'rests on the authority of the Secretary of State', while the Viceroy and all the Governors act on the Secretary of State's directions. Churchill went on to ask: 'What would be said if high officials, or still more younger civil servants in India began to express individual opinions hostile to the main policy of the Government of the day? In these circumstances it is improper to cite these officials as supporters of the White Paper. Their lips are sealed; they can neither speak nor answer.'

In fact, Churchill asserted, many of the British officials in India were carrying out the policy 'with serious misgivings'. What was the use, he asked, of Baldwin citing Lord Willingdon in his defence; Willingdon had been appointed by Ramsay MacDonald and Wedgwood Benn 'to carry through the policy of the Round-Table Conference'. Baldwin's speech, he declared, was clear proof 'that the leading men in the present Government, and Mr Baldwin above all, are resolved to force the India abdication policy through at all costs and by every use of party machinery at their disposal'.

Lord Linlithgow, who had just been appointed Chairman of the Joint Select Committee, sought to dissuade Churchill from continuing with his India campaign. In a letter on May 1 Linlithgow gave it as his considered view that 'something like the White Paper scheme is bound to go through', and that the Indian problem 'does *not* interest the mass of voters in this country'. It was against the Government's trade and tariff policy, Linlithgow suggested, that Churchill should concentrate his future opposition. Churchill replied on May 2: 'I am so sorry to see the line you take about India. Curiously enough your remarks to me three or four years ago of the immense deterioration in the agricultural department which has taken place since the Montagu Reforms was one of the facts which played a part in forming my judgment,' and he continued:

Many thanks for your suggestion that it would be better tactics for me to attack the Government upon their trade agreements and let India slide. I do not think I should remain in politics, certainly I should take no active part in them, if it were not for India. I am therefore quite indifferent to any effect which my opposition to the White Paper may produce upon my personal situation. . . .

On May 3 Churchill informed Lord Rothermere that there were now nearly seventy MPs in the India Defence Committee, and that following

Lord Winterton's 'most severe rebuff' in his own constituency 'many Conservative bodies of every kind are pressing resolutions at their meetings against the White Paper'. His letter to Rothermere continued:

I am full of hope that we shall prevent the Bill from passing next year. At any rate we shall fight it inch by inch in both Houses. If the Daily Mail and your other papers go on as they have done, or perhaps even a little more so, the Conservative Associations will continue to respond. You deal with the mass of middle class voters and party men and women. The Morning Post which has taken off its gloves reaches the local swells. Max has been helpful too. So we really have a very formidable press gripping the whole party. Moreover in every constituency there are a large number of intelligent influential Conservatives who have Indian connections or experience and they only require to see that a fight is being put up to lend their aid.

Lord Linlithgow continued to try to convince Churchill that he was mistaken. The Indian Agricultural Service, he wrote on May 4, had been 'marked for 100% Indianisation' since 1924, and the process had been virtually completed without anyone suggesting that it should be reversed. 'If you and those who are with you are able to recreate the India of 1900,' he wrote, 'and—what is a great deal more difficult—fit it with even reasonable success into the world of 1934, I shall be the first to admit my error of judgement, and to rejoice in your strength and wisdom.' Churchill wrote a strong and thoughtful reply, in which he set out his deeper fears for the future:

I think we differ principally in this, that you assume the future is a mere extension of the past whereas I find history full of unexpected turns and retrogressions. The mild and vague Liberalism of the early years of the twentieth century, the surge of fantastic hopes and illusions that followed the armistice of the Great War have already been superseded by a violent reaction against Parliamentary and electioneering procedure and by the establishment of dictatorships real or veiled in almost every country. Moreover the loss of our external connections, the shrinkage in foreign trade and shipping brings the surplus population of Britain within measurable distance of utter ruin. We are entering a period when the struggle for self-preservation is going to present itself with great intenseness to thickly populated industrial countries.

It is unsound reasoning therefore to suppose that England alone among the nations will be willing to part with her control over a great dependency like India. The Dutch will not do it; the French will not do it; the Italians will not do it. As for the Japanese, they are conquering a new empire. All the time you and your friends go on mouthing the bland platitudes of an easy safe triumphant age which has passed away, whereas the tide has turned and you will be engulfed by it.

In my view England is now beginning a new period of struggle and fighting for its life, and the crux of it will be not only the retention of India but a much stronger assertion of commercial rights. As long as we are sure that we press no claim on India which is not in their real interest we are justified in using our undoubted power for their welfare and for our own. Your schemes are twenty years behind the times.

Churchill's reiterated warnings stimulated the Government to urge the Joint Select Committee to move more quickly. 'The more I think of the future,' Hoare wrote to Willingdon on May 5, 'the more sure I am that, unless the Committee hurries through its work and finishes with the Indians by the late summer, the Committee will not be able to finish its work before the end of the session.' The result of this, he added: 'will be that, a Select Committee not being able to continue after a session is ended, it will cease to exist'. As well as seeking a swift end to the Joint Select Committee's deliberations, Hoare was also involved in a scheme to counter Churchill's arguments, telling Willingdon:

We are trying to get up an effective organisation to meet the Winston propaganda in the country. For various reasons it is not an easy task but I hope that we shall get something started in the course of the next fortnight. It looks as if we might want Villiers[1] to play a prominent part in this organisation as he is a very effective speaker in favour of the White Paper programme. That is one of the reasons why I telegraphed to you about getting him a Knighthood. I think it would have helped us a good deal in getting the most out of him. . . .[2]

Churchill and those who felt as he did were determined to press their challenge to the Party leaders still further. On May 13 Churchill wrote to Lord Salisbury that the India Defence Committee in the House of Commons had decided to widen its scope, uniting a similar body from the House of Lords and the Indian Empire Society into a single organization, the India Defence League. 'We have already taken offices,' Churchill explained, 'and are appointing secretaries and officers.' Conservative Associations throughout the country would be invited to affiliate themselves to this League 'upon a quite simple and short declaration of our views' on Indian policy. 'We shall certainly continue the

[1] Francis Edward Earle Villiers, 1889–1967. Educated at Eton and Christ Church Oxford. Served in the Royal Flying Corps, 1915–18; in the Royal Air Force, Afghan War, 1919. Member of the Bengal Legislative Council, 1924–26. President of the European Association of India, 1931 and 1932. Vice-Chairman, Union of Britain and India, 1933–35. Knighted, 1936. Director New World Pictures Ltd. Served in the Films Department, Ministry of Information, 1940–45.

[2] On 15 May 1933 Willingdon wrote to Hoare: 'If you make good use of Villiers, of course I will be very glad to consider him for an honour in the future. . . .'

fight in Parliament and in the country by every means in our power,' Churchill added, 'and I hope and trust that although you are a member of the Joint Committee, we still have your sympathy and may count on your aid.'

For Hoare, Churchill's efforts were a source of continual anxiety. Writing to Willingdon on May 19 he warned of 'the magnitude of the task that faces us of getting a Bill of about two hundred clauses through Parliament with half the Conservatives in the House of Commons doubtful or hostile', and he added: 'Churchill thinks that by that time he will have captured most of the Conservative organisations. I think myself that he is overbidding his market and that there will probably be a reaction in our favour.'

On May 19 Lord Linlithgow made a third and final attempt to persuade Churchill of the wrongness of his course. 'You envisage,' he wrote, 'as I think I discern, an approaching period of red tooth and claw, a struggle for the means to live. I doubt it, Winston!' Linlithgow foresaw instead an increasing interdependence of trade and distribution, with economic negotiations replacing military adventures, and economic integration replacing racial and imperial conflicts. Such integration, the sole path to increased prosperity, postulated 'enhanced goodwill between nations and races'; such would be the world of the future. Linlithgow's letter ended:

I hope, my dear Winston, that I am never impertinent to anyone. Forgive me, then, if I say that it is not, it seems to me, so much I who am 'mouthing the bland platitudes of an age that has passed away, twenty years behind the times', but rather *you* who are hanging, hairy, from a branch, while you splutter the atavistic shibboleths of an age destined very soon to retreat into the forgotten past.

In conclusion, let me as one Tory to another, beseech you to see in time the errors of your mind, and to retract them, lest irretrievably you miss the bus. All this in fun as well as in seriousness.

The Conservative Central Council[1] was to discuss India at a special meeting summoned for June 28. Well in advance, on June 8, *The Times* devoted its main leader to what it called 'The Conservative Choice'. The article was outspoken in its condemnation of Churchill's attack. Any 'ill-judged' step would, it warned seriously—'perhaps irrevocably'—

---

[1] Known also by its fuller title: the Council of the National Union of Conservative and Unionist Associations.

weaken the Conservative Party. The leader insisted that whatever might be the Parliamentary view of the detailed India proposals 'there can be no permanent reversal of the broad lines of policy which it represents'. But if the Conservatives were to follow Churchill's lead, *The Times* warned, and reverse that policy, 'Mr Baldwin might think it necessary to withdraw from the leadership of the party, or even from public life', bringing Churchill 'greater prominence', and Baldwin 'undisturbed repose'. Such a Churchill victory, *The Times* declared, would not only stimulate Indian extremism; it might bring down the National Government. Yet if an Administration were then formed to reverse the India policy 'its life at the best would be a matter of weeks or months; and there would be no certainty that its successor, inevitably recoiling much farther to the Left, would devote to the Indian problem the same anxious scrutiny that is being bestowed on it at the moment'. Of course, *The Times* added, Churchill himself had never envisaged 'so glittering a climax' to the forthcoming Conservative confrontation.

The Conservative Central Council met at Friends' House, Euston Road, on Wednesday June 28. More than 1,200 Conservatives were present. The meeting was opened by Baldwin, who spoke of the dangers 'if you get a great Imperial interest into the party arena', and defended the White Paper policy. Four speakers challenged him: Churchill, Lord Lloyd, Sir Henry Page Croft and Lord Carson, who warned that the proposed safeguards for India would surely prove as valueless as those for Ireland had been. Churchill, whose speech was continually interrupted, declared with bitterness that he was being made 'the victim of a personal campaign', but even this assertion was derided. During his speech there were continued angry outbursts from the delegates and he was unable to finish most of his sentences. Finally, in an almost totally hostile atmosphere, he exclaimed: 'It is no good being angry with me because I have to put the case . . . we have an absolute duty to justify on this occasion our true opinions.' But the mood of the meeting had turned against him, and after trying, in vain, to set out his reasons for opposing the Federal scheme he exclaimed angrily: 'It is easy to run propaganda to victimize a particular man.' Even this appeal to the audience to listen to him was greeted, as the *Yorkshire Post* reported, by 'Cries of dissent and laughter'. Amid further interruptions, Churchill pleaded that no plan of federal self-government should be tried until the provincial autonomy advocated by the Simon Commission had first been put to the test. Only then, he said, would it be seen whether or not Indian politicians could rule justly, without prejudice to their own minorities, and with loyalty to the Crown.

The dispute was finally put to a vote, on a resolution of Lord Lloyd expressing 'grave anxiety' over the proposed transfer of the central government, the judicial system and the police to the hands of ministers responsible to elected provincial assemblies. The resolution was defeated by 838 votes to 356, the largest Party vote so far recorded against Baldwin's policies. Yet it was also a victory for Baldwin both politically and personally; his India policy, which had been under constant attack for three years, was upheld by nearly 70 per cent of those present. Churchill's campaign had faltered amid the uncompromising obloquy of Conservative Party workers and constituency leaders. Henceforth, Baldwin's support for Indian self-government at the centre could not easily be undermined within the Party itself, and only Parliament could now reverse the course upon which the National Government had embarked; and it was to this most difficult task that Churchill intended to devote himself. Isolated from all his former Cabinet colleagues, rejected by a definite majority within the Conservative Party, only the strength of Churchill's convictions drove him forward, and sustained him, in his much-derided course. Nor did he have any doubts that his chosen course could only weaken still further his political position, and possibly destroy altogether his chance of future political office.

26

Germany 1933:
'There Is No Time to Lose'

CHURCHILL'S warning to Linlithgow on May 4 that Parliamentary democracy was threatened by 'dictatorship real or veiled in almost every country' and that England was now beginning a new period of struggle and fighting for its life, sprang from his vigilant scrutiny of developments in Europe. In Germany, following a special Enabling Law passed by the Reichstag on March 23, liberty had been extinguished and terror extended. During the last week of March all Jews in public office had been systematically removed from their posts, and a Nazi manifesto instructed local organizations throughout Germany 'to carry on anti-Jewish propaganda among the people'. On April 3 control of all youth clubs was transferred to the Ministry of Labour; these clubs had already, with General Schleicher's encouragement, taken on a semi-military training, and other groups intended to give only purely athletic and even religious training to boys under sixteen became subjected to military discipline. At the same time, duelling and corporal punishment were reintroduced. On April 5 Sir Horace Rumbold reported to Sir John Simon: 'Large concentration camps are being established in various parts of the country, one near Munich being sufficiently large to hold 5,000 prisoners.'[1]

On April 7 Hitler formally imposed Nazi rule on each of the German States, ending their much-prized autonomy, and appointing himself Governor of Prussia, ousting von Papen. Six days later, on April 13, a law came into effect officially barring all Jews from national, local and municipal office. That same day during a debate in the House of Commons, many MPs, including Austen Chamberlain, spoke angrily

[1] This was Dachau concentration camp, ten miles north-west of Munich.

of the Nazi persecution of the Jews, and warned of the dangers of German rearmament. Churchill took the opportunity to warn the Government once more of the dangers involved in a militarized Germany, telling the House of Commons that 'one of the things which we were told after the Great War would be a security for us was that Germany would be a democracy with Parliamentary institutions. All that has been swept away. You have dictatorship—most grim dictatorship.' Churchill went on to comment on several frightening aspects of the German dictatorship: militarism, appeals 'to every form of fighting spirit', the reintroduction of duelling in the universities and the persecution of the Jews. Commenting on these things, Churchill continued, 'I cannot help rejoicing that the Germans have not got the heavy cannon, the thousands of military aeroplanes and the tanks of various sizes for which they have been pressing in order that their status may be equal to that of other countries.'

Much of Churchill's speech consisted of an attack on Ramsay MacDonald for agreeing to Mussolini's plan for a Four-Power Pact. Such a Pact, he felt, could only raise grave fears in the small States excluded from it. Nothing could be worse for European security than 'a threatened overlordship of the four Great Powers'.

The Nazis were angered by Churchill's speech, and in particular by his censure of their domestic policies. On April 19 a correspondent of the *Birmingham Post* reported from Berlin: 'Today newspapers are full with "sharp warnings" for England, introduced by headlines about Sir Austen Chamberlain's "lies" and Mr Winston Churchill's "impudence".'

On April 24, St George's Day, Churchill spoke at the annual meeting of the Royal Society of St George. In his speech, which was broadcast, he took the opportunity to reassert his faith in the British way of life, and in the parliamentary system. And yet, he added, Britain's difficulties always arose from 'the mood of unwarrantable self-abasement into which we have been cast by a powerful section of our own intellectuals'. These 'defeatist doctrines', he went on, had been accepted by a large proportion of politicians. But, he asked, 'what have they to offer but a vague internationalism, a squalid materialism, and the promise of impossible Utopias?' His speech continued:

Nothing can save England if she will not save herself. If we lose faith in ourselves, in our capacity to guide and govern, if we lose our will to live, then indeed our story is told. If, while on all sides foreign nations are everyday asserting a more aggressive and militant nationalism by arms and trade, we remain paralysed by our own theoretical doctrines or plunged into the stupor of after-war exhaustion, then indeed all that the croakers predict will come true, and our ruin will be swift and final. . . .

Although the Disarmament Conference continued at Geneva, the gulf between France and Germany had widened. On May 5 Anthony Eden told the Cabinet: 'The main difficulty was that Germany had rejected the proposals for the standardisation of Continental Armies, to which the French attached the utmost importance.' Five days later Sir John Simon told his Cabinet colleagues that the Germans now wanted to rearm up to 'qualitative equality'; for example, 'in the Air, as the French air force was brought down the German would rise. . . .' One French desire, the regular inspection and supervision of armaments was disliked both by Germany and by Britain. On May 31 the Cabinet was told that the three Service departments were against regular inspection because it would 'expose to the world our grave shortage of war supplies, and we should have to spend many millions in correcting the position in this and other respects'.

Throughout the summer of 1933 the news from Germany continued to bode ill for European peace, and for civilized life. On May 10 the Nazis organized a mass public bonfire of books of which they disapproved: books by Socialists, Communists, Liberals and Jews, books on philosophy and psychology, books of protest and dissent. That same month, all Trade Unions were banned, and Trade Union leaders sent to prison and concentration camps. On July 1 German aeroplanes flew on the first of a series of propaganda raids across the border into Austria, where they dropped leaflets extolling Nazism and abusing the Austrian Government. On July 15 a special decree established the Nazi Party as the sole legal German political party, the Coalition of January 1933 was formally ended, and Hitler ruled supreme, terror in the streets providing a continual and fearful stimulant to obedience. Leading German politicians of the Weimar republic were arrested, marched through the streets and sent off to concentration camps; all property and funds of the former political parties were confiscated; civilian outrages against Jews were encouraged and condoned.

The British Foreign Office were kept fully informed of all developments in Germany, as well as of a secret and ominous development. On June 21 the British Air Attaché in Berlin, Group Captain Herring,[1]

[1] Justin Howard Herring, 1889–   . A tea planter in Ceylon, 1912–14. Joined the Royal Flying Corps, 1915. Served on the Western Front, Mesopotamia and Salonika, 1915–18;

wrote a secret memorandum giving clear evidence that Germany had
begun to build military aircraft in violation of the Treaty of Versailles.
According to Herring, the Nazis had put all private and civilian air
activities under the direct control of the Air Ministry, and throughout
Germany 'a process of mobilisation is in progress'. Herring had been
told by a high official at the German Air Ministry that 'the German
Government were already engaged in building a military air force'.
Herring added: 'When the attendant organisation is over it may be
anticipated that all German aviation will remain a Government controlled branch of public life so long as the Nazi regime lasts. . . . This
machinery and its production capacity will, therefore, always have to
be taken into account when attempting to assess Germany's strength
in the air.' Herring's memorandum of June 21 was one of several pieces
of evidence of German rearmament which Sir Robert Vansittart
printed for distribution to the Cabinet on July 14. Twelve days later
the Cabinet discussed these reports, Neville Chamberlain stating that
'France ought not to be pushed by us into a position of weakness', more
particularly as he felt misgivings as to the attitude of Germany, and it
was decided to express official concern 'at the indications of German
rearmament'.

On August 12 Churchill spoke to his constituents in Theydon Bois,
telling them that Europe lay under an 'evil and dangerous' storm cloud,
and he warned:

Nobody can watch the events which are taking place in Germany without
increasing anxiety about what their outcome will be. At present Germany is
only partly armed and most of her fury is turned upon herself. But already her
smaller neighbours, Austria, Switzerland, Belgium, and Denmark, feel a deep
disquietude. There is grave reason to believe that Germany is arming herself,
or seeking to arm herself, contrary to the solemn treaties exacted from her in
her hour of defeat.

Alarmed by Germany's secret rearmament, Churchill declared:

I hope our National Government, and especially the Cabinet Ministers in
charge of the Navy and Army and Air Force, will realize how grave is their

---

awarded the Military Cross (1916) and DSO (1917). Commanded No 4 School of Navigation
and Bomb Dropping, 1918–19. Commanded the Aerial Committee of Control, Munich,
1919–21, and the Guarantee Committee, Berlin, 1922–26. Wing-Commander, 1923. Commanded No 2 Flying Training Command, 1927–29. Air Attaché, Berlin, 1931–34. Acting
Group Captain, 1932; Group Captain, 1935. Invented the 'Harwell Box' to give wireless
operators ground training in Wireless Telegraphy, 1939. Training air crews for heavy bombers,
1940. President of the Aviation Candidate Selection Board, Air Ministry, 1942.

responsibility. They are responsible, like the Ministers before the War, for our essential safety.

I trust they will make sure that the forces of the Crown are kept in a proper state of efficiency, with the supplies and munition factories which they require, and that they will be strong enough to enable us to count for something when we work for peace, and strong enough if war should come in Europe to maintain our effective neutrality, unless we should decide of our own free will to the contrary.

In the second week of September Churchill received private confirmation of his fears about Germany from Duff Cooper, who had been on holiday in Austria, only a few miles from the German border, and who wrote to Churchill on September 8:

We are living here on the frontier of Austria and the inhabitants are nervous of invasion. We motored through the centre of Germany and it was a remarkable sight. Everywhere and at all times of the day and night there were troops marching, drilling and singing. Hitlerite uniform is an exceptionally unpleasant shade of khaki and one sees as much of it in Germany now as one did of khaki in England, in 1918. This is not an exaggeration. They are preparing for war with more general enthusiasm than a whole nation has ever before put into such preparation. Meanwhile I read in the 'Times' that a special meeting of our Cabinet has been discussing disarmament. . . .

'Thank you so much for your most interesting letter,' Churchill replied on September 13. 'No one can help being very anxious at what is happening all over Europe and in the Far East.'

On September 5 Sir John Simon had told his Cabinet colleagues that the French were now 'eager for a Disarmament convention' on the basis of a trial period with 'some system of supervision', but he doubted if Germany would accept this 'in her present mood'. At an emergency meeting of the Cabinet on September 20 Eden confirmed the French desire for a disarmament convention, based on a four year trial, with no new weapons built which ultimately were to be prohibited, an all round reduction in armed strength, and automatic and regular inspection. Simon warned that if a breakdown were to occur in the disarmament talks, British public opinion would be upset, and Germany 'would rearm as and when she liked'. Nevertheless, Simon added, if other powers would not reduce their armaments as the French proposed, 'Germany would have to be allowed some increase of hers'. Worried about the implications of a breakdown of the talks, Lord Hailsham warned that Britain could not agree to an Italian suggestion that the present level of land and air armament expenditure should not be exceeded, and he continued:

We had already disarmed to a degree that rendered our position most perilous if there were any risk of war within the next few years. . . .

Our ports were almost undefended, and our anti-aircraft defences were totally inadequate. He did not think anyone was prepared to allow that state of affairs to continue. Everyone must agree that some increase in expenditure on armaments would be required within the next few years. He thought this probably referred to the Royal Air Force, also.

The Cabinet conclusions reflected Hailsham's worries by stating that if Germany were to rearm, and the Disarmament conference collapse, the other states were 'absolved from their obligations' in the matter of disarmament, but at the same time the conclusions emphasized that as far as any German rearmament was concerned 'we could accept no new responsibilities in the matter of sanctions'.

Speaking at the Conservative Party Conference at Birmingham on October 6, Baldwin echoed Hailsham's argument in favour of a possible British rearmament up to the level of the well-armed powers, but within the general framework of a continuing world effort at disarmament, urging on his audience the need for a Disarmament convention, and adding:

When I speak of a Disarmament convention I do not mean disarmament on the part of this country and not on the part of any other. I mean the limitation of armaments as a real limitation, such a one that is real by the gestures made for disarmament, and if we find ourselves on some lower rating and that some other country has higher figures, that country has to come down and we go up until we meet.

Churchill, speaking after Baldwin, supported a motion by Lord Lloyd expressing 'grave anxiety' about the inadequate state of British defences, telling the Conference: 'The moment has come when it is indispensable that this conference should give a strong indication to the Government that a change must be made and we must not continue long on the course in which we alone are growing weaker, while every other nation is growing stronger.' Lloyd's motion was passed unanimously.

Three days after the Birmingham conference, the Cabinet discussed the German attitude to disarmament, Simon explaining that Germany 'cannot accept the period of probation', nor any numerical prohibition on weapons—'that is to say', he added, they wished for 'naked rearmament'. MacDonald suggested a warning to Germany, but this was rejected on the grounds that 'we would be revealing our intentions to the Germans, who might find means to forestall us, and thus avoid having to face up to the situation at Geneva'. There was also some criticism of Baldwin's speech at Birmingham, as the minutes recorded:

It was pointed out also that the Lord President's speech at Birmingham on Friday, October 6th, had, abroad as well as at home, been interpreted as a warning to Germany. It was further suggested that there was some danger in warnings unless we knew our minds in case those warnings were dis-regarded and Germany re-armed—but the Cabinet did not wish to pursue this aspect at the meeting.

On October 14 Hitler announced Germany's withdrawal not only from the Disarmament Conference, but also from the League of Nations itself. The British Cabinet's reaction was to seek to preserve the Conference. Indeed, on October 18 it was proposed to press the French Minister of War, Edouard Daladier,[1] to make 'some concessions' on the question of sample weapons. This reaction was confirmed at a further Cabinet of October 23, when the whole discussion was concerned with how to restore the broken-off disarmament negotiations. It was again suggested that Daladier 'should be encouraged' to embark on conversations with Germany with a view to some compromise on sample weapons. Lord Hailsham suggested pressing for 'qualitative disarmament', under which, he explained, the British, French and Italian Governments 'should agree to dispense with certain of the heavier classes of weapons now as a first step towards disarmament, but with a provision making it subject to other nations coming in'. Once qualitative disarmament were 'achieved', Hailsham added, 'the question of quantative disarmament might be tackled in the same way'. The Cabinet concluded: 'Our policy is still to seek by international co-operation the limitation and reduction of world armaments, as our obligations under the Covenant and as the only means to prevent a race in armaments.'

In a Cabinet memorandum written on October 24, Lord Londonderry explained that Britain's air production had been halted in 1932 as a result of 'the Armament Truce' of November 1931. Although this truce had ended in February 1933, Londonderry added, 'as a further earnest of His Majesty's Government's desire to promote the work of the Disarmament Conference, the standstill was voluntarily extended to the

[1] Edouard Daladier, 1884–1970. Mayor of Carpentras, 1912–58. Member of the Chamber of Deputies, 1919. Minister of Colonies, 1924. Minister of War, 1933. Minister of Foreign Affairs, 1934. Minister of War and Defence, 1936–38. Prime Minister, April 1938–March 1940; also Minister of War and Defence. For his part in the Munich Conference he received the Grand Cross of the Order of St Michael and St George (GCMG).

current year in spite of marked inferiority in air strength as compared with other great powers'. It was therefore necessary, Londonderry explained, to postpone completion of the 1923 Programme from 1936 to 1940. The 1933 air construction, he added, of less than thirty new machines, was 'comfortably within' the Foreign Office's proposed draft Disarmament convention. Londonderry added, with reference to the public's anxieties following Germany's withdrawal from the League, that he had indeed 'hesitated as to whether it is not my duty to put before my colleagues a much more substantial increase, which would I believe, command widespread support both in Parliament and in the country at large. . . .' He would not propose an increase, however, as 'we must still hope that a one-power standard will be achieved in the main by a reduction of foreign air forces to the British level, rather than by our being compelled to build up to theirs'.

The Cabinet's decision of October 23 to continue to seek 'the limitation and reduction of world armaments' had been taken two days before a by-election at East Fulham, where the National Government candidate lost to an independent Socialist, John Wilmot,[1] whose platform included a plea for continued and more rapid disarmament. He was supported by the East Fulham Liberal Association, which had issued a statement to the Press on October 19 recommending 'all Liberal voters to give Mr John Wilmot their support, if on no other grounds than the question of disarmament alone'. When the result was declared, Wilmot told the electors 'that the British Government shall give a lead to the whole world by initiating immediately a policy of general disarmament'.

In the House of Commons on November 7 Sir John Simon spoke of the 'vehement resentment' of the Germans at the failure of the allied powers to disarm after 1919, and urged the need for 'international agreement on disarmament'. He then explained that the Government's policy was to work for a reduction of existing armies, under supervision, followed by 'substantial disarmament by the heavily armed powers, involving the complete abandonment of types of specially offensive weapons by everyone'. In his speech, Churchill first challenged Lloyd George's view that Germany was the aggrieved and threatened power, weakened by the Allies at Versailles and surrounded by the heavily

---

[1] John Wilmot, 1895–1964. Served as a clerk, Royal Air Force, 1918–19. Unsuccessful Labour candidate, 1924, and 1931. Labour MP for East Fulham, 1933–35; for Kennington, 1939–45; for Deptford, 1945–50. Parliamentary Private Secretary to the Minister of Economic Warfare, 1940–42; to the President of the Board of Trade, 1942–44. Joint Parliamentary Secretary, Ministry of Supply, 1944–45. Privy Councillor, 1945. Minister of Supply, 1945–47. Created Baron Wilmot of Selmeston, 1950.

armed forces of France, Poland and Czechoslovakia. 'If I could believe that picture,' he said, 'I should feel much comforted, but I cannot,' and he added:

The great dominant fact is that Germany has already begun to rearm. We read of importations quite out of the ordinary of scrap iron and nickel and war metals. I have no sources of information but the public Press, but we read of the military spirit which is rife throughout the country; we see that the philosophy of blood lust is being inculcated into their youth in a manner unparalleled since the days of barbarism.

Churchill went on to say that he was glad that 'a period of probation' had been introduced 'into this dangerous process of disarmament in Europe', but he criticized MacDonald's plan for reducing the level of armies and air forces because it 'never had the slightest chance of being accepted' by the French. He then asked: 'How could you expect those countries that feel themselves in so great a danger to make the very large reductions which were asked for in their armaments, their air forces and their armies, while at the same time substantial increases were offered to the Germany with which we are now confronted?'

'How lucky it is,' Churchill declared, 'that the French did not take the advice that we have been tendering them in the last few years, or advice which the United States has given them—advice rendered from a safe position 3,000 miles across the ocean! If they had accepted it, the war would be much nearer. . . .' Churchill then set out what he felt were the true guidelines for Britain's future policy, the uniting of the small and threatened States under the protection of the League:

Whatever way we turn there is risk. But the least risk and the greatest help will be found in re-creating the Concert of Europe through the League of Nations, not for the purpose of fiercely quarrelling and haggling about the details of disarmament, but in an attempt to address Germany collectively, so that there may be some redress of the grievances of the German nation and that that may be effected before this peril of rearmament reaches a point which may endanger the peace of the world.

It was already certain, Churchill warned, that Britain had already disarmed 'to the verge of risk—nay, well into the gulf of risk'. A very great responsibility therefore rested on the three Defence Ministers 'to assure us that adequate provision is made for our safety, and for having the power and the time, if necessary, to realize the whole latent strength of our country'.

On November 12 Sir Ian Hamilton wrote to Churchill: 'How pleased

& amused the Ghost of your Great Ancestor must be to see you fighting your lone hand with all his own spirit.'

Speaking to his constituents at Chingford on November 13, Churchill linked his attitudes towards India and Europe in a fierce attack on the socialist forces inside the National Government. During his speech he told his constituents:

The Socialist foreign policy, always associated with Mr Ramsay MacDonald, of interfering on the Continent and trying to weaken France and strengthen Germany, and above all of disarming Britain, had already been carried a long way. The Socialist policy about India and the Round Table Conference and the White Paper were steadily marching forward, and Mr Baldwin used all the power of the Conservative Party, all its social influence, and that of the Party Whips and the Central Office to crush down resistance. Well might Sir John Simon exclaim at the luncheon to the three leaders of the National Government 'We are all Socialists now'.

By mid-November in Germany, there were at least 100,000 opponents of the Nazi regime in concentration camps, and more than 50,000 Germans had fled abroad in search of refuge. On November 12 a General Election was held at which only the Nazi Party was allowed to canvass, with the result that it secured 95% of the vote. Returning briefly to London during his constituency tour, Churchill spoke at the Devonshire Club on November 14, at Thornton Butterworth's invitation. It was the Nazis, he said, 'who declare that war is glorious, who inculcate a form of blood lust in their children extraordinary without parallel as an education since Barbarian and Pagan times. It is they who have laid down the doctrine that every frontier must be made the starting point of an invasion.' Disarmament, Churchill continued, would no more bring peace 'than an umbrella would prevent rain'. Yet he did believe that peace might still be preserved, telling his audience: 'You have heard me described as a war monger. That is a lie. I have laboured for peace before the Great War, and if the naval holiday which I advised and suggested had been adopted the course of history might have been different.' Churchill's speech continued: 'There is no time to lose. Here is a practical step to take. Wipe up this Disarmament Conference, sweep away the rubbish and litter of the eight years of nagging and folly and hypocrisy and fraud, and let us go to Geneva, to the other part of Geneva—to the League of Nations.' 'Everyone was enthusiastic about your speech,' Thornton Butterworth wrote to Churchill on November 16. 'You secured a hundred per cent vote at the dinner.'

Churchill's concern about disarmament led him to make two more

public speeches before the end of the year, one at Harlow, in his constituency, on November 14, and the other at the opening of Parliament on
November 21. His theme was the danger of German rearmament.
During his speech at Harlow he spoke of Ramsay MacDonald's 'mania
for conferences', and warned that there would be no disarmament in
Europe while Germany was busy spending the money 'she has been let
off in reparations', in buying on the international market 'the means of
rearming and making cannon contrary to the solemn treaties of peace'.

On November 15, following their annual review of Imperial Defence
policy, the Cabinet asked the Chiefs of Staff sub-committee to prepare
a programme 'for meeting our worst deficiencies'.[1] At a further Cabinet
on November 29, in anticipation of a motion to be brought by Captain
Sueter[2] in the House of Commons expressing 'grave disquiet at the
present inadequacy of the provision made for air defence', Sir John
Simon 'raised doubts as to whether it was desirable at this moment to
accept a resolution which would not help forward that urge towards
disarmament which the Government's policy necessitated'. Lord
Londonderry, in agreeing to base his reply on Baldwin's Birmingham
speech of October 6, told his colleagues: 'we should admit that we
had disarmed to the edge of risk and had done it deliberately in pursuit
of a policy of disarmament'. Londonderry added that he had hoped to
have been able to announce a decision about completing the 1923
programme, 'but had not had one'. A few moments later Baldwin told
his colleagues:

> If we had no hope of achieving any limitation of armaments we should
> have every right to feel disquietude as to the situation not only so far as
> concerns the Air Force, but also the Army and Navy. Let us, however,
> examine what would be the effect of a Resolution of that kind. Here, in the
> House of Commons, everyone knew the right meaning to attach to it. Abroad,
> however, it would be taken as a decision by the Government to rearm.

'At present however,' Baldwin pointed out, 'we were using every possible effort to bring about a scheme of disarmament which would
include Germany.' If Germany saw the House of Commons pass an air
rearmament motion 'the effect on her would be serious'.

---

[1] This sub-committee, for which Sir Maurice Hankey took the chair, was subsequently
known as the Defence Requirements Committee.

[2] Murray Fraser Sueter, 1872–1960. Entered Navy, 1886. Assistant Director of Naval
Ordnance at the Admiralty, 1903–05. Member, Advisory Committee in Aeronautics, 1908–17.
Captain, 1909. Director of the Air Division at the Admiralty, 1911–15. Superintendent of
Aircraft Construction, 1915–17. Commanded Royal Naval Air Service units, Southern
Italy, 1917–18. Rear-Admiral, 1920. Conservative MP, 1921–45. Knighted, 1934.

27

1933–1934: Authorship, India and Rearmament

SINCE the beginning of 1933 Churchill had spent as much time as possible at Chartwell, finishing his first Marlborough volume and weaving in the historical materials which Maurice Ashley had collected. Entitled *Marlborough: His Life and Times*, the first volume was published on 6 October 1933. Churchill sent out more than a hundred and twenty personal copies, and received over two hundred letters of congratulation, several from former colleagues. Baldwin himself wrote on October 7:

> You really are an amazing man! I look sometimes at that row of volumes in my little library, and I cannot think how you can have found the mere time to have got through the physical labour alone of writing them. This last book would mean years of work even for a man whose sole occupation was writing history. Well, there is the miracle. . . .

'I am very grateful for the pleasure which I shall get from reading it,' Neville Chamberlain wrote on October 9, 'not less so from the fact that you have not yet cut me out of your beneficiaries.' That same day P. J. Grigg wrote: 'I cannot tell you how touched I am that you should continue to send me your books as they appear. Of all my masters you have been much the most generous to me personally,' and he added: 'How are you? Pretty sick at heart, I dare say, both at what is and what is not happening.'

Writing on October 18, Lord Riddell also referred to contemporary events. 'From the horrible state of affairs,' he wrote, 'it looks as if someone in the near future will have the task of writing the history of the

496

Second Great War—that is if any inhabitants of Europe are left to purchase the book.'[1]

During the summer and autumn of 1933 Churchill, Salisbury and Austen Chamberlain had each expressed their dislike of the proposed All-India Federation, believing it to be a mere device whereby the Government would appear to bring in the Princes as a balance to the Congress Party. On August 2, after a series of questions in the House of Commons when the nature of the Federation was under scrutiny, Hoare wrote to Sir John Anderson to tell him of the situation, and to enlist his help: 'I was able to get away with it for the moment by implying that I should be able to tell the Committee more in the autumn. It seems to me quite essential now, unless we are to give people like Austen the impression that the federation is nothing more than a shadow, that we should bring the question of grouping to a definite issue with the Princes,' and Hoare went on to ask: 'Would it be a good thing to bring strong pressure to bear upon the more important of them in their states themselves?'

In the first three weeks of October Churchill prepared his evidence for the Joint Select Committee on India. On October 22 all members of the Committee received a copy of a memorandum which he had written setting out his opposition to the proposed Federal system, which he believed was a device which would neither satisfy extremist Indian aspirations, nor protect the proposed Viceregal powers from attack and erosion. On October 24 he underwent what he described to Maurice Ashley as 'a long day of examination' by the Committee, and was questioned in detail about his views, in particular about his assertion that adequate powers must be retained by the Centre to enable the Viceroy to supervise effectively the work of the Provincial departments, unhampered by pressure from the Federal Assembly.

On October 27 the Duchess of Atholl wrote to Churchill from Scotland that she was 'amazed' at the ignorance of Hoare during the questioning. Her letter continued:

I notice that the Committee pressed you for more evidence in regard to deterioration of the departments already transferred. I have been finding out

[1] Financially, the publication of *Marlborough* was a boon to Churchill. A month earlier, in mid-September, his bank overdraft had stood at £9,500. Sir Abe Bailey had reduced it to £6,000 by buying some of Churchill's shares on September 20, and the salary from his two coal directorships brought it down to £5,500 on September 28, but it was only with the publishers' payment of £5,000 on October 6 that the overdraft was effectively dismantled. By October 12 the volume had sold 8,500 copies.

what I cld about Health and Education, & enclose you an article which summarises very briefly the evidence I know about on this subject. . . .

You will see that I emphasise that the Simon Commission wanted more central guidance for Education, & more *control* of epidemic diseases! But the most amusing thing is to see how much of both Lord Linlithgow's Commission on Agriculture wanted!

On October 28 Churchill received a letter of congratulation and encouragement from Waris Ameer Ali, who wrote from his flat in London that Churchill's evidence 'ought to have a great effect in assisting the cause you have at heart', and added:

Nothing will placate the implacable, or mollify the terrorist. But however much the ordinary Indian politicians may grumble & protest, after the manner of the bazaar folk from whom many of them are sprung, they will be in the main delighted at the new openings given to them.

Far better to disappoint some of their expectations than to risk the ruin of the social order by the collapse of the law courts & and police; the loss of confidence in the even-handed justice of the Raj, by the masses; & their uprising by the hundred million. . . .

Speaking in the House of Commons on November 22, Churchill reiterated his view that the Joint Select Committee had no purpose, as the Government had already made up its mind to legislate on the basis of the White Paper. 'If the Secretary of State,' he said, 'had shown a larger sense of tolerance and of fair play, and a greater detachment from his own schemes, I believe that he could have created a body whose labours would have been a real help in solving these profound Indian problems, or might, at any rate have made some valuable contribution thereto. It was a great chance which my right hon Friend threw away through being too greedy.' Churchill went on to argue that·the proposed All-India Federation would never work, as the Congress Party and the Princes had no real common ground for the required cooperation. He was supported in the debate by Josiah Wedgwood. Writing of this joint criticism, Hoare informed Willingdon three days later: 'I am still recovering from the heated debate that took place in the House of Commons on Wednesday. Wedgwood and Churchill could not have been more mischievous and the only thing for me to do was to attack them both as hard as I could. They and their friends will, no doubt, feel a considerable resentment.' Hoare added: 'It was very important to give our own supporters as much encouragement as I could.'

On November 30 Churchill celebrated his fifty-ninth birthday. During the winter he remained as much as possible at Chartwell, working with Ashley on the second volume of *Marlborough*, and planning two further volumes. By New Year's eve, with Parliament in recess, Stanley Baldwin had made progress in reading volume one, writing that evening from his home at Astley Hall:

My dear Winston,

I haven't enjoyed anything more in years than your Marlborough. I am about a third through it, savouring it as an epicure, and I shall finish it this week.

It is A1.

If I had—which God forbid—to deliver an address on you, I should say Read Marlborough and you may then picture yourself listening to Winston as he paced up and down the Cabinet room with a glass of water in his hand and a long cigar in the corner of his mouth.

I can hear your chuckles as I read it.

I feel now quite eager to go to Blenheim!

All good wishes for the New Year. . . .

On 3 January 1934 Churchill replied:

My dear S.B.,

Your letter gave me so much pleasure. I am vy glad you are reading Marlborough, & still have a kindly feeling for me. It is good of you to find the time amid so many cares to express it.

It must be a gt comfort to you to find the Unemployment figures & the Finances now definitely coming round. I trust indeed the coming year will see a continual improvement, & will win a fair recognition from the public for the measures and restraints which have contributed towards the national recovery. India apart—you have my earnest good wishes; and I shall try to say something about it when I broadcast on the 16th.

But after all it is the European quarrel that will shape our lives. There indeed you must feel the burden press.

I have decided to write two more volumes on M. The second will cover Blenheim and end with 1705, during which year the Tory Diehards or 'High fliers' were decisively defeated by the two great National Statesmen Marlborough and Godolphin! But I hope you will remember when you read it, that all this took place more than two hundred years ago.

I am working all day long at it & expect it will be ready in the Summer. With every good wish for the New Year (West of Suez). . . .

Throughout January and early February, Churchill worked at Chartwell on his next two volumes, both of which were dominated by Marlborough's military campaigns. 'I am now living in the wars of Marlborough,' he wrote to General Edmonds on January 5, and added:

It is extraordinary how modern Marlborough's military conceptions were. He saw all that Napoleon saw, but being only a servant in a liquid age, instead of a sovereign in a molten one, he could only occasionally give effect to his genius. Napoleon could order, but Marlborough could never do more than persuade or cajole. It is hard to win battles on that basis.

As work progressed Churchill once more enlisted the help of Commander Owen on naval strategy, while Ashley continued to seek out documents on the political and diplomatic side. To Owen, Churchill wrote on January 6: 'Any specific details which are novel would be welcomed by me, but in the main it is the broad picture I should like to draw. I think it reasonable to claim that British control of the Mediterranean, which still endures, is the outcome of Marlborough's mind.'

During February Churchill took on a resident research assistant to help with the great mass of material which had to be read and sorted. His name was John Wheldon.[1] 'I think he is going to be very helpful indeed,' Churchill wrote to Ashley on February 11. 'I am very pleased with what I have seen of his work.'

Forty years later Wheldon recalled how he and Churchill used to work. After dinner Churchill would dictate until two or three o'clock in the morning and begin work at about seven, sometimes even earlier, seldom sleeping more than four and a half hours. 'In those days rural post was very early indeed,' Wheldon recalled, 'the house domestics used to bring the early post up to him. It included proofs etc—he liked these—he required this as a kind of check on anything being done inside his office without his knowledge. He would sit up in bed reading it.' Of the literary work in the evening Wheldon recalled: 'The great man dictated, no-one was allowed to contribute a creative word.' The typescripts were then scrutinized by himself, Owen and Edmonds. 'He always took criticism very, very meekly,' Wheldon added. 'One could say exactly what one liked in the way of criticism. This was partly because he knew he was not fully educated in the ordinary academic

---

[1] John Wheldon, 1911–   . Educated at Sedbergh and Balliol College Oxford. Studied for nine months in Germany, 1930. Traffic Apprentice, London, Midland and Scottish Railway, 1933–34. Resident Research Assistant at Chartwell, 1934–35. Lecturer in Modern History at Balliol, 1935–36. Started the Tariffs and Quota Section, Courtaulds Limited, 1936. 2nd Lieutenant, June 1939. Posted to France, October 1939. Wounded during the Dunkirk evacuation, 1940. Headquarters Staff, Medium Artillery, 8 Corps, 1940–41 (served in artillery liaison with beach defences). Captain, Special Operations Executive, 1941–44. Intelligence Officer attached to General Montgomery's staff during the Normandy landings, 1944. Major, 1944. Intelligence Officer on General Eisenhower's Staff, Versailles and Frankfurt, 1944–45. Second Secretary, Board of Trade, 1945. Member of the Allied Control Commission for Germany, 1945 (Press and Public Relations Officer). Rejoined Courtaulds, 1945; Director of their main export subsidiary, 1952–60.

sense, partly it was temperament. He wanted the full critical value from subordinates.'

Churchill also asked Lewis Namier[1] for his comments on the first volume. Namier replied on February 14 praising the book as 'a work of art and at the same time a masterly analysis of the historical material'. But he was critical of the amount of space which Churchill had devoted to answering Macaulay's accusations: 'by paying too much attention to him in the body of your book, you have impaired your own picture of Marlborough, whom you seldom discuss without turning aside and engaging in an argument calculated to expose the caricature which Macaulay had drawn of him. As a result, having finished reading your book, I am fully convinced that Macaulay's account of him is wrong, but I have nothing to put in its place. . . .'

Namier was also critical of Churchill's frequent 'imaginary pictures of what *may* have happened or what some people *must* have felt', telling Churchill:

. . . such imaginary accounts always throw me into opposition. Our conjectures must always be rational, whereas neither men nor events are rational, and there is seldom a real correlation between a so-called historic moment and what people feel or do on the occasion. I think the most ridiculous and most disappointing moment in the life of every man must be his death.

Namier went on to advise Churchill to make more use of his own personal experiences:

There is no-one alive engaged on history work with your experience of politics, government, and war. Please do not try to write history as other historians do, but do it in your own way. Tell us more how various transactions strike you, and what associations they evoke in your mind. When studying the detail of government at that distant period of almost 250 years ago, many comparisons must have occurred to you, which you seem to have suppressed. . . .

'I do hope,' Namier ended, 'you will let your own experiences bear stronger and more visibly on your account of past transactions.'

[1] Lewis Bernstein Namier, 1888–1960. Born Ludwik Bernsztajn, in Galicia. Historian. Educated at Balliol College Oxford. Private, 20th Royal Fusiliers, 1914–15. Worked in the Propaganda Department, London, 1915–17; the Department of Information, 1917–18; the Political Intelligence Department of the Foreign Office, 1918–20. Lecturer in Modern History, Balliol College, 1920–21. In business, 1921–23. Engaged in historical research, 1923–29. Political Secretary of the Jewish Agency for Palestine, 1929–31. Professor of Modern History at Manchester, 1931–53. Knighted, 1952. Converted to Catholicism shortly before his death.

Churchill replied to Namier's criticisms on February 18:

Very many thanks for your letter and for its cogent comments. It is not possible to defend effectively Marlborough's early career except by contrasting the true facts with the odious accusations which have so long reigned. Hence the importance of Macaulay to the structure.

I agree with you about the imaginary conversations. I felt at the time they were a weak indulgence on my part, but they sometimes make the ordinary reader realise the position. I hope to avoid them altogether in Volume II.

As to Namier's third point, Churchill wrote:

I certainly propose to apply my experience in military and political affairs to the episodes. One of the most misleading factors in history is the practice of historians to build a story exclusively out of the records which have come down to them. These records in many cases are a very small part of what took place, and to fill in the picture one has to visualise the daily life—the constant discussions between ministers, the friendly dinners, the many days when nothing happened worthy of record, but during which events were nevertheless proceeding.

During 1934 Churchill wrote fifty articles for the Press, and made more than twenty important political speeches in Parliament and in the country. The nature of Nazi tyranny, the dangers of continuing disarmament and British policy in India were his three main themes. On February 7, in a speech in the House of Commons, he criticized the Government's White Paper on disarmament, issued a week earlier, which reiterated the MacDonald–Baldwin commitment to continuing European arms limitation. This would mean, Churchill insisted, more pressure on France to disarm, while German rearmament would continue unchecked. Again, for the second year running, he pressed the Government to abandon the Ten Year Rule, telling the House of Commons that with the Locarno Pact of 1925 'and the more mellow light which shone on the world at that time, with the hopes that were then very high, it was probably right to take that principle as a guide from day to day, and from year to year'. This could be done no longer, he said:

No one could take that principle as a guide today. No Cabinet, however pacific and peace-loving, could base their naval and military organisation upon such an assumption as that. A new situation has been created, mainly in the last three or four years, by rubbing this sore of the Disarmament Conference until it has become a cancer, and also by the sudden uprush of

Nazi-ism in Germany, with the tremendous covert armaments which are proceeding there to-day. Everyone sitting on the Government Bench knows how seriously the position has been changed.

Speaking of Baldwin's Birmingham speech of October 6, Churchill said that in discussing Britain's ability to carry out any European commitments 'we must consider our military, naval and aviation defence', and he went on:

We are engaged in demanding equality for armies, in imposing equality for armies as far as we can, upon the nations of the Continent—France, Germany, Poland and Italy. Suppose it is asked in a few years that there should be equality for navies too? When the Government are asked about this, they say, 'Oh no, that would not apply; we should not agree to that.' Suppose we are asked some time in the future to restore colonies for which we hold a mandate the Government would say, 'certainly not, we should not open the question in any way. . . .'

What do we back our opinions with; what arrangements and force have we to summon behind these serious issues of opinion on which we declare our will and right?

Churchill went on to warn that unless Britain was in 'a proper state of security', a diplomatic crisis would arise—'within a measurable time, in the lifetime of those who are here'—when threats would be made, and pressure applied, and within a few hours 'the crash of bombs exploding in London and cataracts of masonry and fire and smoke will apprise us of any inadequacy which has been permitted in our aerial defences'. Churchill advised the Government to prepare the nation so that if war came it would be able to face it, and hope that the very act of preparation would deter a would-be enemy. 'We ought,' he said, 'to begin the reorganisation of our civil factories so they can be turned over rapidly to war purposes.' Every factory in Europe, he said, was being prepared so that it could be turned over quickly to war production, in order to produce material 'for the deplorable and melancholy business of slaughter'; and he asked: 'What have we done? There is not an hour to lose.' As for air power, he declared: 'I cannot conceive how, in the present state of Europe and of our position in Europe, we can delay in establishing the principle of having an air force at least as strong as that of any Power that can get at us.' To have an air force as strong as the air force of France or Germany, whichever were the stronger, ought, he said, 'to be the decision which Parliament should take, and which the National Government should proclaim'.

There would be 'grave harm', Churchill said, if the Government waited for the answers to their White Paper proposals before the provision of security at home' was ensured, and he criticized the Government for arguing that 'they have to wait for public opinion', that the public did not wish for rearmament, and that the politicians of all three parties must bow to this pacifist, or peace-craving sentiment. 'The responsibility of His Majesty's Government is grave indeed,' he said, 'and there is this which makes it all the graver; it is a responsibility which they have no difficulty in discharging if they choose.' His argument continued:

The Government command overwhelming majorities in both branches of the Legislature. Nothing that they ask will be denied to them. They have only to make their proposals, and they will be supported in them. Let them not suppose that if they make proposals, with confidence and conviction, for the safety of the country, their countrymen will not support them. Why take so poor a view of the patriotic support which this nation gives to those who it feels are doing their duty by it?

Replying to Churchill, Baldwin, after commenting on Churchill's 'eloquent' and 'picturesque' language, and on his position 'of greater freedom and less responsibility', told the House: 'We are trying to get an ordered armament limitation.' With equality of arms, he said, 'there should be, for everybody's sake, a much better chance of getting what we all want'. But he went on to tell the House that if the Disarmament Conference failed 'the Government will feel that their duty is to look after the interests of this country first and quickly'. As for the future, Baldwin added, 'I do not think we are at all bound to have a war.'

Baldwin described Churchill's speech as 'of great interest, of excellent temper and full of sound sense', but Sir Herbert Samuel characterized it differently, telling the House that Churchill's policy was 'Long live anarchy, and let us all go rattling down to ruin together.'

On February 23 Churchill was the guest of the Oxford University Conservative Association. The meeting was held at the Oxford Union, and more than five hundred undergraduates were present. Instead of making a formal speech, Churchill agreed to answer in detail twelve questions which had been prepared in advance, printed and distributed to the audience. One of the questioners was a German Rhodes scholar, Adolf Schlepegrell,[1] who asked Churchill whether it would not be

---

[1] Adolf Frederick Karl Schlepegrell, 1912–   . Born in Hamburg. Educated at schools in Berlin and Hamburg. Studied law at Hamburg and Freiburg Universities, 1929–31. Rhodes Scholar, University College Oxford, 1931–34. Elected Secretary to the Oxford Union a few days after his confrontation with Churchill. After leaving Oxford he found himself not admissible to State law examinations in Germany because of a Jewish maternal grandmother. Naturalized as a British citizen, 1938. Served in the Political Intelligence Department of the

advisable for the Allies, in the interest of better relations with Germany, to evacuate the Saar at once, without waiting for the plebiscite which was to take place in 1935. Churchill rejected this idea, declaring that the German people, who had started the war, must abide by the terms of the Versailles Treaty. Schlepegrell then pleaded for some 'magnanimous gesture' to undo the Treaty's mistakes, but again Churchill defended the Treaty and repeated that it was the Germans who had played a leading part 'in plunging the whole world to ruins'. To this Schlepegrell asked: 'Does Mr Churchill believe that the German people, the men and women who live in Germany today, are responsible for the war? Would he please answer "yes" or "no".'

In a tense atmosphere Churchill went up to the despatch box and looking straight at the questioner replied: 'yes'. At this point Schlepegrell bowed to Churchill and without saying another word walked out through the middle of the audience, amid a tremendous uproar of applause and disapproval from both sides. The German newspapers were delighted by Schlepegrell's gesture, as were many of the undergraduates present.

A second incident further marred Churchill's visit to Oxford. As one of the undergraduates present, Michael Hutchison,[1] recorded in his diary, Churchill's references to Britain's need for rearmament 'in order for us to be "safe in our Island Home" evoked laughter, which annoyed Winston, who repeated the phrase'. Churchill was not to forget this laughter.

On February 28 the Cabinet accepted the 1934 Air Estimates, which were £1 million lower than those of 1931. These estimates involved continuing to work towards the 1923 programme. However, Lord Londonderry pointed out to his colleagues, 'other Powers, almost without exception, were pursuing a far more active policy of air development', and he went on to express his 'grave perturbation'. Nevertheless, he concluded, 'with the fate of the Disarmament Conven-

---

Foreign Office, 1942–46. Acquired Canadian citizenship, 1948. Served in the Allied Control Commission for Germany (in Frankfurt), 1948–51. On the staff of the Secretariat of the Organization for Economic Co-operation and Development (OECD), Paris, since 1953.

[1] Michael Hutchison, 1912–   . Educated at Eton, and at Magdalen College Oxford, 1931–35. Admitted as a solicitor, 1939. Served in the King's Royal Rifles (in England), 1939–45. Joined the Allied Commission for Austria, May 1945. Lieutenant-Colonel, 1946. Worked in the Department of the Director of Public Prosecutions, 1946–72.

tion still undecided it would not be advisable to consider any more extensive measures in the coming year'.[1]

Throughout February and March the unrest in Europe continued. Street violence in Austria and France seemed to threaten democracy.[2] In Germany, the grip of Nazi tyranny over the German people was complete. Parallel with the ruthless suppression of dissent, Germany's rearmament made continual progress; and the Versailles Treaty's limit of 100,000 soldiers was surpassed.

On February 28, the same day that the Cabinet had ignored Londonderry's warning of the dangers of German air rearmament, the Defence Requirements Committee presented its report to the Cabinet. One of its assumptions was that Germany would not soon have an air force sufficient to challenge Britain; and that 20 new squadrons would be an adequate defence, together with a defence expenditure for all services of £70 million over five years. On March 2 Sir Robert Vansittart, himself a member of the Committee, sent Hankey a letter of dissent. Germany, he wrote, 'will not be inferior to us in the air for any appreciable time'; this was clear 'to all who study Germany closely'. Vansittart was supported in his appeal by Sir Warren Fisher, but three days later Hankey replied: 'I do not accept this view. In a few years' time Germany might have as many first-line aeroplanes and pilots as we have; but pilots and aeroplanes do not make an Air Force. It takes years of intensive effort and training to build up an air force to a state of efficiency comparable with the RAF with its unique experience under what are often practically war conditions in many parts of the world.'

On March 4 the British Government published its White Paper on defence. In the event of disarmament negotiations failing—as Churchill believed they would—the Government now pledged themselves to increase Britain's air strength.

On March 8 Sir Philip Sassoon told the House of Commons that there

---

[1] The Cabinet of February 28 also agreed to the sale of 118 aero engines to Germany. Although intended for civilian use, these engines, the Cabinet noted, 'could be used in small fighter planes'.

[2] On February 6, during riots in Paris near the Chamber of Deputies, fifteen people had been killed and several hundred wounded. On the following day the Prime Minister, Edouard Daladier, had resigned, despite a 343 to 237 vote of confidence. Further riots took place in Paris on February 7 and February 9. On February 9 a Cabinet of National Union was formed under Gaston Doumergue, a retired former President, with General Pétain as Minister of War. In Austria, Fascist groups attacked the working-class districts of Vienna on February 12 supported by the army, and in four days more than a thousand people had been killed on both sides. The socialist leaders accepted an amnesty on February 16, after which Dr Dollfuss' Government sent many of them to prison without trial, dismissed them from public office and confiscated their private property.

was to be an increase of four new squadrons, of which two were for home defence, one Fleet Air Arm and one flying boat squadron. This estimate, Sassoon told the House, had been devised 'out of our desire to pursue disarmament and to study economy on the one hand', but also from 'our reluctant conviction that the policy of postponement cannot be continued'. Britain, he added, did not wish to fire a 'starting gun for a race in air armaments'.

Even this limited pledge provoked an immediate and widespread protest. On behalf of the Labour Opposition, Clement Attlee declared: 'We deny the need for increased air arms. We deny the proposition that an increased British Air Force will make for the peace of the world, and we reject altogether the claim of parity.' Another Labour spokesman, Sir Stafford Cripps, charged that: 'the Government has had its hands forced by the wild men like Mr Churchill', and even Churchill's friend Sir Archibald Sinclair, speaking for the Liberal Party, denounced 'the folly, danger and wastefulness of this steady accumulation of armaments'.

In his speech, Churchill told the House of his fears. We had, he said, 'reached a turning point in our affairs'. Germany 'is arming fast', he went on, 'and no one is going to stop her.' No one, he pointed out, was proposing 'a preventative war' to stop her breaking the Versailles Treaty', and he went on:

I have not any knowledge of the details, but people are well aware that those very gifted people, with their science and with their factories, with what they call their 'Air Sport', are capable of developing with great rapidity a most powerful air force for all purposes, offensive and defensive, within a very short period of time.

'I dread the day,' Churchill added, 'when the means of threatening the heart of the British Empire should pass into the hands of the present rulers of Germany.' That day 'is not perhaps far distant. It is perhaps only a year, or perhaps 18 months distant.' Churchill continued: 'There is still time to take the necessary measures. We do not want this paragraph in the White Paper. We want the measures. It is no good writing that first paragraph and then producing £130,000. We want the measures to achieve parity.'

It was Baldwin, Churchill added, who 'has the power' to do what was needed: 'There need be no talk of working up public opinion. You must not go and ask the public what they think about this. Parliament and the Cabinet have to decide.' Replying, Baldwin said he 'valued the moderation' of Churchill's speech, and continued: 'I have by no means given up the hope yet of a convention, something on our lines, that will give that equality in air strength which I believe to be the first requisite in avoiding danger.'

To Sir Samuel Hoare, who in 1924 had been Secretary of State for Air when Churchill had been Chancellor of the Exchequer, Churchill wrote on March 11: 'You and I are in the same boat in this past matter. But the situation has changed entirely, and no time should be lost in doubling the Air Force.'

On March 14 there was a further debate on foreign affairs, when Churchill spoke of the 'illusions' of seeking an arms limitation agreement, and commented:

Why, it is only a little while ago that I heard Ministers say and read diplomatic documents which said that rearmament was unthinkable— 'whatever happens we cannot have that. Rearmament is unthinkable.' Now all our hope is to regulate the unthinkable. Regulated unthinkability, that is what is the proposal now; and very soon it will be a question of making up our minds to unregulate unthinkability.

'I honour the French,' Churchill added, 'for their resolute determination to preserve the freedom and security of their country from invasion of any kind; I earnestly hope that we, in arranging our forces, will not fall below their example, so far as the freedom and independence of this country are concerned.' Speaking of Baldwin's pledge during the air debate of March 8, Churchill declared:

I accept a statement of that kind in absolute good faith, because I am certain that with his reputation and with his responsibility my right hon Friend would not have made such a statement if he had intended merely to use it to get round a Parliamentary corner on a particular occasion, or to stave off the fulfilment of his undertaking by dilatory processes.

While accepting the 'parity' pledge, Churchill went on to warn that Baldwin's concept of an air convention would be 'very dangerous indeed' if it delayed a review of Britain's defences. His idea had been for a limitation not on the number, but on the use of air weapons. This would involve no delay in production, but would allow, if the other powers agreed, the restriction of air warfare 'as far as you can to the zones of the armies or military objectives'.

Churchill's arguments were challenged by Sir John Simon, who told the House, of Churchill:

He is a vehement opponent of the disarmament discussions. He does not believe in and therefore he does not want regulated armaments . . . those who reject, with the great vehemence and positiveness that he rejects, the idea of disarmament conventions and regulated armaments doing any good, must be prepared to face the alternative ... unregulated competition in armaments throughout the world.

'That,' Simon added, 'is an appalling prospect.'

That same day, when the Cabinet discussed the report of the Defence Requirements Committee, Sir John Simon proposed 'further concession' to Germany and 'additional undertakings' to France, in order to keep the Disarmament Conference in being, and to avoid 'the return to pre-war conditions of competitive rearmament'. In explaining the Defence Requirements report, Hankey explained that its aim was to provide 'a nucleus of strength sufficient to safeguard our responsibilities in any theatre of war until any necessary expansion can be carried out'. Given this limited aim, and 'on the understanding that there was no intention to incur expenditure on measures of defence required to provide exclusively against attack by the United States, France or Italy', the Cabinet accepted that the report's criteria were valid. A further discussion took place on March 19, on whether, as the report suggested, Germany was 'the ultimate potential enemy against whom our long range defence policy must be directed'. Sir John Simon felt that 'a German menace, if it developed, was more likely to be in the east and south than the west. Austria, Danzig, Memel, appeared to be principally menaced'. Neville Chamberlain felt that 'when confronted by an expenditure of over £70,000,000 in five years' the Cabinet were 'bound to consider whether there was no alternative', and that if Britain could arrange her defence requirements under 'some general scheme' of arms limitation under the aegis of the Disarmament Conference, the cost might be found to 'come to less than the figure suggested in this Report'. Londonderry told his colleagues:

Excuses might be found for delaying the decision indefinitely. If there was much delay in taking decisions on our armaments policy he thought a serious situation might arise in the country. He was being pressed very hard about our air position. The question he asked was when we should begin to lay the foundations of our future policy on air armaments.

The Cabinet concluded that in view of the fact that Germany's power 'may soon be great enough to make her a potential source of danger to others', the Government should 'consider' two possible courses: 'joining in arranging to provide further security against breach of the peace' and 'facing further heavy expenditure on armaments'.

Three days later, during a speech on March 21 Churchill urged the gradual creation of a Ministry of Defence which would put Army, Navy and Air Force coordination under the control of a single Minister.

Although the Secretary of State for Air, Lord Londonderry, had already rejected such a plan as impracticable, Churchill persisted in his arguments. The principle of a unified Ministry of Defence, he said, should be accepted at once, even if the fusion itself were to take place over several years, and he went on to warn that without a carefully coordinated defence plan there could be no way of averting, or being able to face with confidence, a German threat. But in official circles the idea of a Minister of Defence was not welcomed. 'I do not see how even a superman will be able to carry that burden,' the Secretary to the War Office, Sir Herbert Creedy,[1] had written to Sir Maurice Hankey on March 8, and he added: 'Winston found it more than he could manage to give full attention to the War Office and the Air Ministry when he was Secretary of State for both,' to which Hankey replied on the following day: 'I agree with the point you make about the difficulty of finding super men.'

Although the Government rejected Churchill's advice, the House of Commons listened with attention to what he had to say, and many critics recognized the sincerity of his views. On March 28 Lord Beaverbrook wrote to Sir Robert Borden: 'Churchill, now that he seems to have reconciled himself to the part of a farewell tour of politics, speaks better than for years past. He has cut the rhetoric and gained dignity.'

---

[1] Herbert James Creedy, 1878–1973. Joined the War Office as a Clerk, 1901. Private Secretary to successive Secretaries of State for War (including Churchill), 1913–20. Knighted, 1919. Secretary of the War Office, 1920–24. Permanent Under-Secretary of State for War, 1924–39.

28

India 1934:
The Committee of Privileges

DURING the last two weeks of March 1934 rumours circulated in London that a serious impropriety had been perpetrated during the previous year, at the time when the Manchester Chamber of Commerce had given evidence before the Joint Select Committee on Indian Constitutional Reform. At a meeting of the Committee on 3 November 1933, the senior official representative of the Chamber of Commerce, Harold Rodier,[1] had been asked whether Manchester had any alterations to suggest in the Government's India White Paper. He had answered, succinctly, 'No', and had repeated his 'No' when the question had been put a second time. According to the rumours, however, this answer had not been a true guide to Manchester opinion. Indeed, it was being alleged that there had been an earlier Chamber of Commerce submission, prepared during May and June of 1933, which had contained substantial arguments, expressed in forceful terms, to the effect that the proposed India constitution would be detrimental to Lancashire. According to this original submission, it was argued that the White Paper proposals would give an Indian finance minister, at the centre, power to penalize imports of cotton goods from Lancashire in order to further the interests of the Indian mill-owners of Bombay and Ahmedabad. This original Manchester submission had apparently detailed four distinct areas in which the Lancashire cotton manufacturers sought specific safeguards to protect their trade and livelihood. But, according to rumour, pressure had been put on the Chamber of

---

[1] J. Harold Rodier,   –1965. Textile manufacturer. Appointed a Director of the Manchester Chamber of Commerce in 1923, and Chairman of the India Section, 1923–33. Chairman of the Lancashire textile delegation to the Ottawa Conference, 1932. Treasurer of the Manchester Chamber of Commerce, 1937 and 1938.

Commerce to change their submission; pressure, not from a neutral or outside source, but from two of the most senior members of the Joint Select Committee itself, Lord Derby—Lancashire's representative on the Committee—and Sir Samuel Hoare, the Secretary of State for India.

Churchill was first sent details of these allegations by a director of Associated Newspapers Ltd, William McWhirter,[1] who wrote to him from the offices of the *Sunday Dispatch* on Sunday March 31: 'Lord Rothermere has asked me to send on the enclosed news article dealing with the suppression of Lancashire views on India.' The article gave further details of 'the almost incredible story' of how the Manchester Chamber of Commerce evidence 'was returned to its authors with a demand for drastic amendment'. These allegations were then published, on Rothermere's responsibility, in the *Daily Mail* of April 1.

Churchill decided to seek further details for himself, and on the morning of April 3 he discussed the allegations on the telephone with the Foreign Editor of the *Daily Mail*, Douglas Crawford.[2] Churchill asked Crawford if he could study the documents on which the charges were based, and Crawford sent him the documents that same day, adding in a covering letter: 'Round about the time the evidence was prepared, Lord Derby was apparently busy in Manchester. He conferred with Thomas Barlow,[3] manufacturer and a leading member of the Chamber of Commerce, and others, and we understand Barlow forced the revision on the Indian section by threatening to resign.' Barlow was subsequently

---

[1] William Allan McWhirter,   –1955. Educated at Glasgow High School. Associated with Lord Rothermere (then Harold Harmsworth) from 1907. On active service in Egypt and the Balkans, 1915–18. Editor of the *Sunday Pictorial*, 1921–24 and 1928–30. Managing Director of Associate Newspapers, 1930. Chairman of the Hull and Grimsby Newspapers Ltd, and Gloucestershire Newspapers Ltd.

[2] Douglas Crawford, 1883–1943. Born in Arbroath; worked on the *Manchester Courier* as a young man. Subsequently private secretary to Lord Northcliffe, first Editor of the *Continental Daily Mail* in Paris, and Night Editor of *The Times*. War Correspondent, 1914–18 (when he was 'taken prisoner' by the French during the Battle of the Marne). Foreign Editor (the first ever appointed) of the *Daily Mail*, 1921–36. A friend of Vansittart, who in 1936 discussed with him the organization of a news agency for British counter-propaganda (never started through lack of funds). Did publicity for the Red Cross, 1939–40. Press Officer to General de Gaulle, in charge of publicity for the Free French Movement in both Britain and the United States, from 1940 until his death.

[3] Thomas Dalmahoy Barlow, 1883–1964. Educated at Marlborough and Trinity College Cambridge. Director (later Chairman) of Barlow and Jones Ltd, Manchester. President of the Joint Committee of the Cotton Trades Organizations, 1931–33 and of the Manchester Chamber of Commerce, 1931–33. Chairman of the Lancashire Development Council, 1931–34. Knighted, 1934. Director-General of Civilian Clothing, 1941–45. Chairman of the District Bank (retired, 1960).

a member of the five-man official delegation to the Joint Select Committee on November 3.

On reading the documents which Crawford had sent him, Churchill was convinced that a grave injustice had been done; and that the pressure which seemed clearly to have been exerted by two members of the Joint Select Committee to persuade the Manchester Chamber of Commerce to alter its evidence in advance of the hearing constituted a definite and serious breach of the Privileges of Parliament. Churchill believed the evidence to be incontrovertible. He therefore asked Crawford if he could meet the men who had provided it. On Rothermere's initiative, the meeting between Churchill and the Manchester informants took place at the Savoy Hotel on the afternoon of April 8. Churchill was accompanied by Brendan Bracken. The senior of the two Manchester representatives present was H. Y. Robinson,[1] who produced further items of evidence which Churchill read.

Among the documents Robinson showed Churchill was the original evidence of the Manchester Chamber of Commerce. On 21 June 1933, after this evidence had been unanimously approved by the Chamber of Commerce's Board of Directors, of which Thomas Barlow was a member, a hundred printed copies had been sent to the Joint Select Committee in London. Robinson then explained that six days later, on 27 June 1933, Lord Derby had given a dinner at which Sir Samuel Hoare had been present, together with the members of the India section of the Chamber of Commerce. A Chamber of Commerce delegation had then gone out to India to examine the situation on the spot. But after Lord Derby had again discussed the matter in Manchester, a telegram had gone out, under his name, asking the delegation in India if they wished to modify the evidence already submitted, and stressing the urgency of a swift reply. The delegation replied that the original evidence had to stand, although a supplementary note could, if agreed, be added to it. Their reply was ignored. Instead the original evidence was called back from London on October 25, and redrafted with all criticisms of the White Paper either deleted altogether or severely modified. Commenting on this, Robinson told Churchill: 'Lord Derby's friends say openly he has stopped Lancashire making a fool of herself.'

The notes of the Savoy Hotel conversation record Churchill's view that 'the time was ripe' to bring the matter forward in Parliament.

[1] Harold Yorke Robinson. A Manchester businessman; Director of a textile exporting firm of Indian shippers, Oliver, Barrett & Robinson. Prominent in the Cotton Trade League, formed to defend the Lancashire textile trade against Japanese competition. Member of the India Section of the Manchester Chamber of Commerce.

Bracken added that 'nothing can prevent it being brought out'. The notes continued:

Mr Churchill in answer to questions said that he thought the best procedure to adopt was to raise the matter as a question of privilege. The fact was that the evidence presented by Lancashire had been altered from the form in which it was originally submitted to the India Office for circulation to the Committee.

Then the next point to make is that evidence has been placed before Mr Churchill that a member of the committee was concerned in inducing this withdrawal of the original evidence and the substitution of the new evidence.

The third point, of course, was that the India Office acquiesced—appeared to have acquiesced to the substitution of the one set of evidence for the other.

'Once the secret is out by a Question in the House,' Churchill added, 'the press will immediately take it up, and keep on with it. What will then happen will be an uproar.'

Towards the end of the discussion, Bracken pressed Robinson to produce as much documentation as possible, which Robinson promised to do. But, he warned, 'everyone would hedge and be on their guard once the matter really came to a head in public'.

As a result of his meeting with Robinson, Churchill was convinced that Derby, himself a member of the Joint Select Committee, had used his immense influence in Lancashire to put pressure on the Manchester Chamber of Commerce, and to suppress evidence which he and Hoare were duty bound to allow to go forward. Churchill decided to submit the documents to the Speaker[1] of the House of Commons, and to ask that a Committee of Privileges examine the whole question. On April 10 he wrote to Lloyd George, the senior Privy Councillor in the House of Commons, enclosing copies of the documents, and commenting on the advice of the Manchester delegation that had been in India: 'It is very remarkable that these people who have everything at stake and were actually in India, did not think it advisable to give in.'

Unknown to Churchill, further documents already existed which bore out his suspicions even more clearly. During the subsequent year of intense controversy, however, none of these essential documents came to light, and the precise nature of Hoare's involvement remained hidden,

---

[1] Edward Algernon Fitzroy, 1869–1943. Son of the 3rd Baron Southampton. Educated at Eton and Sandhurst. A page of honour to Queen Victoria. Conservative MP for Daventry, 1900–06 and 1910–43. Captain, 1st Life Guards, 1914 (wounded at the first battle of Ypres). Commanded the mounted troops of the Guards Division, 1915–16. Deputy Chairman of Committees, House of Commons, 1922–28. Privy Councillor, 1924. Speaker of the House of Commons from 1928 until his death. His widow was created Viscountess Daventry in 1943. Their son Michael (born 1895) was killed in action on 15 April 1915.

even from a full Parliamentary enquiry. On 6 April 1933 Hoare had written to Willingdon: 'There was also some talk as to the question of British trade, and the cotton trade in particular, coming before the Joint Select Committee. I think it is inevitable that this question should be raised in some form though whether it will be advisable for the Lancashire people to appear in evidence I am not sure.' Hoare continued: 'It might be better that their interests should be watched and looked after by a member of the Committee, Derby for example, who carries great weight in Lancashire and whose services I am glad to say we have secured.' A month later, on 3 May 1933, Willingdon had written to Hoare warning that he would be unable to obtain any Indian agreement to safeguards for Lancashire, and that the Lancashire interests must therefore reconcile themselves to the inevitable. Writing to Hoare again, on June 12, Willingdon added: 'I do wish we could induce our Manchester friends to keep their mouths shut. . . .' On July 7 Hoare sought to put Willingdon's mind at rest. 'Derby is being very helpful about bringing together Lancashire and Indian representatives,' he wrote. 'He has already had one dinner for this purpose and is going to have another. . . .' Hoare added: 'If only we could get a better feeling in Lancashire, a great deal of the really formidable opposition to the White Paper would fizzle out. . . .'

On October 20 Hoare wrote again to Willingdon, to report what he had been obliged to do, and was still doing, in an attempt to obtain Manchester's acquiescence in the White Paper terms which would enable the India mill-owners to impose their own protective tariffs:

I have been doing my best to stave off the evidence of the Manchester Chamber of Commerce. As you know, it is likely to be of a threatening and provocative character and I have been nervous of it embarrassing the trade discussions in India. . . .

I intend to have another word with the Chairman to see whether we can postpone it. . . .

Writing to Hoare from New Delhi on October 23, Willingdon stressed 'the difficulty with the Lancashire people'—the Lancashire delegation then in India—and added: 'it is going to be extraordinarily difficult for them to stem the tide of complete opposition to the White Paper on the part of all the Lancashire constituencies'. No economic concessions could be made to Lancashire without offending Indian sentiment and aspirations. But Hoare was still not deterred, and on November 3 informed Willingdon that he need fear no more:

Derby has been exceedingly good with the Manchester Chamber of Commerce. He has induced them to withdraw a dangerous and aggressive memorandum that they had sent in to the Committee and that fortunately I had prevented from being circulated. They have now substituted a very harmless document that ought not to bring them into serious conflict with the Indians. . . .

Derby's efforts as revealed in this letter remained a secret. So too did Hoare's direct part in them. But on April 11 Robinson informed Churchill that it was only after a 'heated debate' in the India section in October 1933 that 'the altered evidence was approved by a small majority'. As for the 'unaltered evidence' of June 21, this, Robinson believed, had definitely reached the India Office 'prior to the critical Dinner'.[1] During April 11 Churchill sent copies of the documents at his disposal to Lord Salisbury, the member of the Joint Select Committee most opposed to the White Paper. As a result of Hoare's direct intervention, Salisbury, in common with his other Committee members, had not been shown the original printed evidence sent to the Committee from Manchester on 21 June 1933. Nor did he know anything of what Hoare and Derby had done to obtain the new submission. In his covering letter to Salisbury, Churchill wrote of how individual members of the Manchester Chamber of Commerce 'in their anger at the way they have been treated', had sent him this material. Churchill added:

The dinner of the 27th is the only contact which can be proved, but there is no doubt that Lord Derby was continually in close touch with Messrs Barlow and Rodier, and details of his visit to Manchester are being ascertained. Moreover I know from a private and unquotable source that he takes credit to himself for having 'prevented Lancashire making a fool of herself'. I cannot conceive that he would deny, if challenged, that he had advised the Manchester Chamber of Commerce to modify their evidence.

That is not to make any charge involving dishonour against him. His action was certainly well-intentioned, and many people will argue that it was wise, but there is a prima facie case that the House of Commons Sessional Order No 4 which forbids 'tampering with witnesses or evidence to be offered to any committee' has been infringed. To tamper means to meddle and does not imply corruption, which of course is not in question.

However the fact that a member of the Joint Committee sitting in a quasi judicial capacity has meddled with the evidence to be offered by a very

[1] In point of fact, the Secretary to the Lancashire Chamber of Commerce, Raymond Streat, had sent the final draft evidence to Lord Derby on 23 June 1933, and, to the suggestion that a copy should also be sent in advance of the dinner of June 27 to Sir Samuel Hoare, Streat had written to Derby on June 24: 'I am in rather a delicate position inasmuch as after the most tremendous difficulty the evidence has been unanimously supported by the whole of Lancashire. I suppose constitutionally it ought not to be seen by anybody until the copies are distributed by the Secretary of the Joint Select Committee. I have already committed one indiscretion by sending copies to you and Sir Joseph Nall.'

important body, and has used his great personal and local influence with the evident connivance of the Secretary of State to induce them to alter their evidence, is highly objectionable. I cannot conceive that any fairminded man would approve such behaviour.

Lord Salisbury replied on April 12. He had himself been uneasy ever since the Manchester delegation had appeared before the Joint Select Committee on November 3, informing Churchill:

Of course it was at once evident when the Manchester witnesses appeared before us that they had been got at. I was profoundly disgusted. It was useless to put any questions, but I hope I showed, and I think I did, what I thought about them. Clearly the business of a Committee is to get at the truth, and equally clearly what the papers which you send me disclose made it impossible for the Committee to get at the truth in this particular.

Salisbury commented that he was 'very dissatisfied' with the Government's attitude towards the Joint Select Committee, and he added: 'I do not doubt that all sorts of pressure has been applied to different people in India and here in order to back up the White Paper.'

Encouraged by Salisbury's letter, Churchill persevered in his course of action, fully aware of the gravity of accusing a member of a Parliamentary Committee of acting in an unconstitutional manner. As he saw it, the evidence was such that the Committee of Privilege of the House of Commons could not fail to uphold the charge. On April 13 another document came to light, forwarded by Robinson to Crawford, and from Crawford to Churchill. This was a letter from Sir Samuel Hoare to the President of the Manchester Chamber of Commerce, Richard Bond.[1] It had been sent from London on 5 May 1933—before the India section had finalized its original evidence—informing Bond that it would not be possible for the Government to include in the Indian constitution any provision for restricting the powers of an Indian legislature to impose tariffs on British goods. Bond had at once protested at this limitation on what had yet to be decided; a limitation, he wrote, which was tantamount to abandoning in advance the vital commercial interests of Britain. With his reply, Bond also sent Hoare a draft outline of the Chamber of Commerce's proposed evidence to the Joint Select Committee. It was thus evident to Churchill that Hoare himself was aware, well before Lord Derby's dinner of June 27, that the Manchester merchants were about to put in a strong plea for economic safeguards at the

---

[1] Richard Bond, 1875–1951. Born in Nottingham. Began work at the age of fifteen in the wholesale textile trade, with Marshall and Aston of Manchester; subsequently Chairman of the company. President (for two years instead of the usual one) of the Manchester Chamber of Commerce. A Justice of the Peace.

centre, to protect the mills of Lancashire against politically inspired tariffs, imposed by Indian politicians on behalf of Bombay and Ahmedabad. Churchill himself had pointed out several times during 1933 that it was these very mill-owners who, while imposing harsh conditions on their workers, were making substantial financial contributions to the Congress Party, the resolute aim of which was complete independence from Britain.

Several other documents were forwarded by Robinson on April 13. Among them was a copy of the minutes of a meeting of the India section on 28 July 1933, at which it had been decided 'in view of a report that pressure might be brought to bear', that no change should be made in their original evidence.

Churchill decided that there was already sufficient evidence to make out a well-documented case, and on April 15 he wrote to the Speaker, stating that he would raise the issue of privilege in the House on the following day, and setting out the case he intended to make. In the course of his letter Churchill declared:

... the members of the Joint Select Committee sit in a judicial capacity, and we have been continually assured of this and of their impartiality. Everyone has been asked to await their verdict. In fact however, two of the members of the Joint Select Committee—to wit Sir Samuel Hoare and Lord Derby—have been jointly and severally concerned in procuring a complete alteration of the evidence tendered by the Manchester Chamber of Commerce. Their action was no doubt well-intentioned, but it is grossly irregular and highly objectionable for a member or members of a Joint Select Committee to bring influence to bear upon witnesses to induce them to alter the evidence which they have actually handed in officially to the Secretary of a Joint Select Committee.

Sessional Order No 4 shows how serious is the view which has always been taken by Parliament of attempts to meddle with witnesses or procure the alteration or suppression of the evidence which they wish to tender.

Still more marked is the case when evidence which had actually come into the possession of a Joint Select Committee through its Secretary has been withdrawn and fundamentally transformed, without (incidentally) other members of the Committee being made aware of the transaction.

Most of all is it repugnant to the proprieties of public business and to the dignity and authority of the Joint Select Committee that one or more of its members should be active agents in such a process. Although, of course, neither malice nor corruption is imputed, the irregularity and impropriety is so gross and grave as to constitute a case of breach of privilege.

Churchill went on to inform the Speaker that he was in possession of documentary evidence 'which cannot be challenged', and which proved that outside pressure had been applied. It was his intention, he wrote, to submit this evidence to the Committee of Privileges 'in order to substantiate the statements which to my very great regret (especially on personal grounds) I conceive it to be my duty as a member of the House of Commons to make'. He had, he added, sent notice of his intention to Hoare 'in order that he may be in his place and able to deal with the matter if he desires to do so'.

In his letter to Hoare on April 15, Churchill described the pressure that he believed had been put on the Manchester Chamber of Commerce as 'most irregular and regrettable'. Writing that same day to Lord Derby he declared: 'I am forced to complain of your action while a member of the Joint Select Committee sitting in a judicial capacity. . . . I shall of course make it clear that in challenging your action as most irregular, I make no reflection either upon motives or character. Nevertheless it is with keen sorrow that I find myself after all these years drawn into a direct public controversy with you.' Derby replied on April 16, commenting on Churchill's 'incomplete knowledge' of the facts, and adding:

No alteration whatever in the evidence was made by me. I do not wish you to suppose by that I am pretending ignorance of what was going on at the time. As you know, I am always in close touch with my Lancashire friends and I was aware of the alterations which they were debating amongst themselves, but the actual evidence was dealt with by a Special Committee of the Manchester Chamber of Commerce who did alter their original report largely as a result of information which reached them from their Mission in India.

But I want you to clearly understand that the evidence given before the Select Committee is the evidence passed by the Special Committee of the Manchester Chamber of Commerce untouched by me.

Churchill was not convinced by Derby's defence. He knew, for example, that the Chamber of Commerce's Mission in India had not advocated any change in the body of the original evidence, but only the addition of a supplementary note. Indeed the telegram from the Mission, which was then in Simla, had reached Manchester on 23 October 1933, arriving while the India Section of the Chamber of Commerce was actually in session discussing whether or not to change their original evidence. Of this original evidence the telegram from the Mission stated: 'We have not suggested withdrawal at any stage, and do not understand whence your reference to withdrawal arises.'[1]

---

[1] One of the Manchester witnesses, R. M. Downie, wrote to Churchill on 11 June 1934: 'I cannot understand how, with all the evidence they had before them, the Committee of Privileges

Immediately after Question Time on April 16 Churchill was called upon by the Speaker to put his charges. 'On personal grounds,' he began, 'I raise this question with the greatest reluctance, but I do so with the conviction that I have no other choice.' He then set out the facts as he saw them, stressing that from the moment of Lord Derby's dinner pressure had been applied on the Manchester Chamber of Commerce 'to procure a fundamental alteration' in their evidence. That pressure, he said, came 'primarily' from Sir Samuel Hoare, 'through all the channels which His Majesty's Government can command, direct and indirect', and in particular through Lord Derby, who had travelled to Manchester in September 1933, had interviewed members of the Chamber of Commerce, and 'sought to persuade them and to counsel them to alter their evidence'. A month later, he said, on 24 October 1933, 'as a result of this continuous pervasive pressure', the India section of the Chamber of Commerce had agreed to 'substantial and indeed fundamental alterations' in their original evidence of the previous June. Churchill's speech continued:

A new statement of evidence was printed. This was but a ghost of the original evidence—(cheers)—a poor, shrunken, emasculated thing—(laughter)—an acceptance of what might be thought to be an inevitable drift of events that was but a ghost of the original evidence that Manchester wished to give and had actually deposited.

This in due course was presented to the Joint Select Committee, and heard by them at their session on November 3, the vast bulk of the members being in total ignorance that all this had been going on behind the scenes before they were at last allowed to hear the opinions of the Manchester Chamber of Commerce. (Hear, hear.)

I must make it clear, because I have to make out the points as I go, that I am prepared to prove, although I am not going to quote any secret documents at this moment, that the differences between the original evidence and the evidence which was tendered eventually are of a decisive character and not small alterations or emendations or tonings down.

I place these facts before the House, and I wish now to point my claim that a breach of privilege has been committed.

---

could come to the conclusion that the Executive's evidence was altered to meet the views of the Indian Mission. The Indian Mission had nothing to do with our evidence. It is true they wanted it delayed as they had an idea of creating a "favourable atmosphere". . . . The pressure to alter the evidence was put on Messrs Barlow and Rodier by the "responsible persons" in London and this pressure was passed on to the Executive in such emphatic terms that unfortunately it induced a majority of the Executive Committee to agree to alter a very excellent statement of what we required to one which was of no value at all.'

Churchill pointed out that the issue before the House of Commons was solely one of wrongful pressure. 'I do not argue on the merits of the question,' he said. 'Many may think that the advice tendered was wise. That is not the question which the House of Commons has to settle this afternoon.' The only issue before them was whether or not it was, as Churchill believed, 'grossly irregular and highly objectionable' for members of a Joint Select Committee to bring pressure to bear upon witnesses 'to induce them to alter evidence which they naturally would have wished to tender (cheers), to suppress the truth as they wish to tell it, and which they have officially placed in the possession of the secretary of the Joint Select Committee'. Churchill went on to ask the House, amid further cheers:

What would be said if a tribunal of Judges were trying a case about which there was a keen public controversy and on which very large issues, immeasurable issues, depended; and if one or more of the Judges, hearing from the Government that inconvenient evidence was likely to be tendered by important witnesses, sought them out, got into touch with them, invited them to dinner, induced them to transform their evidence, induced them to alter the evidence which they had already manifested their intention to submit to the Court—what would be thought of that?

Although he had known Derby for more than thirty years, Churchill said, he could not condone 'so monstrous a confusion of functions' as Derby had exercised while seeking to replace one set of evidence which was to be put before him by 'a weak, meaningless, and colourless testimony', and he continued:

These are not the days, I think, when Parliament can afford to be too lax and easy-going on the assertion of its rights and responsibilities. (Cheers.) Things cannot be done in such an easy, quiet, good-natured manner. There must be firm assertion of principle and of decorum. Personal considerations must not affect the faithful and uncompromising discharge of public duty by members of the House, even if private friendships have to suffer thereby.

Persons, however elevated, however virtuous, must be made to understand and to respect the proper limits of the various functions they discharge. No man can be cited before all the country as an independent and impartial arbiter, and then at the same time go round and manage and whittle down the evidence which is going to be presented to his colleagues and fellow-judges. The two roles are absolutely irreconcilable.

In appealing to the Speaker to lay the whole case before the Committee of Privileges, Churchill declared: 'I have not sought this information; it has been volunteered to me; and what course have I, as a member of Parliament, but the course which I ask the House, subject to your ruling,

Sir, to allow me to take?' In reply, Captain Fitzroy gave as his ruling that Churchill had indeed 'made out a case for a breach of privilege'. Hoare rose at once to accept an enquiry by the Committee of Privileges, telling the House:

I welcome the chance of proving, as I know I shall prove, that practically every one of those things just urged as facts by my right hon friend are without substantial foundation. (Hear, hear.) My right hon friend, in the motion he has just made, has asked for an impartial investigation. I wish he had shown a little more care and impartiality in the charges he has just hurled at my head.

Hoare went on to deny that he had ever sought to exert an improper influence on the Manchester Chamber of Commerce. But, he added, 'certain passages' in their original memorandum had seemed to him at the time 'likely to destroy any chance of negotiation'. He added, however, that Lord Derby's dinner of June 27 had taken place before, and not after, he had first seen the original Manchester memorandum. There followed an acrimonious exchange between Churchill and Hoare:

Mr CHURCHILL.—Does my right hon friend mean to convey to the House that differences between him and the Manchester Chamber of Commerce upon the subject of the evidence they were to give had not developed before the end of June and before this dinner?
SIR S. HOARE.—I will give the dates, and in giving the dates I will answer the right hon gentleman's question. The dinner took place—so I find by referring to my engagement book—on June 27. The Committee did not receive the evidence until June 30. I myself did not know that they put in any memorandum at all until the end of the first week of July. (Ministerial cheers.)

Mr CHURCHILL.—I shall submit to the Committee of Privileges proof that the right hon gentleman on May 5 wrote his first letter to the Manchester Chamber of Commerce warning them of the kind of evidence they should not give, that their protest was made on May 23, and that in that letter of protest by the president of the Chamber of Commerce were included the heads of the evidence to be offered before the Joint Select Committee.
SIR S. HOARE.—I should like to refresh my memory.
Mr CHURCHILL.—Yes; the right hon gentleman had better.

Hoare ended his remarks by welcoming the chance of proving to the House 'once again' that Churchill had found 'another mare's nest'.

The Deputy Leader of the Opposition, Clement Attlee, supported Churchill's motion that the matter should go to the Committee of Privileges; so also did the Liberal spokesman Sir Herbert Samuel and the Prime Minister, Ramsay MacDonald. The last speaker was Samuel Hammersley,[1] a Conservative MP who had been a member of the Lancashire Mission to India in the autumn of 1933, and who supported Churchill's contention that the Mission had not been responsible—despite what both Derby and Hoare alleged—for the alterations in the original evidence, but that it had, in fact, repeatedly urged 'that the essential safeguards should be included'. To say that pressure had been put by the Mission to alter the evidence would, Hammersley insisted, 'not be true'.

The House of Commons agreed to submit Churchill's complaint to the Committee of Privileges. No sooner had it done so than further materials and documentation which it was thought Churchill might need were sent in to him from Douglas Crawford at the *Daily Mail*, from H. J. Wilson[2] at the *Morning Post*, from Sir Henry Page Croft and from the Duchess of Atholl. It was from H. Y. Robinson that Churchill received an example of the hostile feelings which he had aroused within the Conservative Party, writing from Manchester on April 19:

I have heard this afternoon that J. P. Morris,[3] MP is endeavouring to persuade Members of Parliament to sign a petition condemning your action in bringing up the matter of the Evidence, and I am doing my utmost to circumvent this by acquainting the leading industrialists in the North with the true state of affairs, so that whatever may happen in regard to the verdict of the Committee, the fact that undue pressure has been brought to bear will at least be known in the North.

Robinson went on to express his own appreciation of Churchill's action:

I cannot conclude without conveying my deepest thanks for your courageous action in bringing this matter before the House of Commons, and at the same time congratulate you for the masterly way in which this difficult subject was tackled.

Believe me Lancashire is deeply indebted and I am sure that when this has

[1] Samuel Schofield Hammersley, 1892–1965. Son of a Lancashire cotton spinner. Educated King's College Cambridge. Served as a 2nd Lieutenant at Gallipoli 1915, and as a Captain in the Tank Corps, France, 1916–18. Conservative MP for Stockport, 1924–35; for East Willesden, 1938–45. Parliamentary Private Secretary to the Financial Secretary, Treasury, 1927. Member of the Textile Mission to India, 1933. Tank Adviser, Ministry of Supply, 1940–43. Chairman of the Parliamentary Palestine Committee, 1943–45. Executive Chairman, Anglo-Israel Association, 1951–63. Chairman of several cotton-spinning companies.

[2] Harold J. Wilson, 1905– . Lobby correspondent of the *Morning Post*, 1934.

[3] John Patrick Morris, 1894–1962. Educated at the Municipal Secondary School, Bolton. On active service, 1914–18 (Lieutenant, Royal Engineers, despatches). A member of the London Stock Exchange. Conservative MP for Salford North (where he defeated the Labour leader Ben Tillett), 1931–45. On active service 1939–45 (including the Burma campaign).

been thrashed out there will be a new spirit and probably more action from this part of the world.

On April 19 Churchill lunched with Lloyd George and Sir Robert Horne to discuss his evidence with them. Frances Stevenson[1] recorded in her diary that Lloyd George thought Churchill 'has a very strong case'. Lloyd George also reported to her that 'Winston was very excited and excitable'.

When Hoare wrote to Willingdon on April 20, it was clear that the Government's attitude towards Churchill was one of suspicion and sarcasm. 'This Winston business,' Hoare wrote, 'is really one of the most unscrupulous affairs that there has been in politics for a hundred and fifty years,' and he added:

Apparently he and his friends have been secretly collecting material from the discontented elements in Lancashire for months past. Having got it and having sat on it for weeks they seem to think that now was the psychological moment when they could discredit the Joint Select Committee before its report came out.[2] I had no word of warning until late on Sunday night when Winston sent me a letter saying that he was going to raise a question of privilege on the following day in the House. You will have seen the way he did it next day. I might have been a traitor being arraigned by the Star Chamber in the sixteenth century, or Warren Hastings being attacked by Sir Philip Francis. All this was made a thousand times worse by the fact that I had sat next to Winston at luncheon with Philip Sassoon on the previous Thursday, when he had behaved as the best of old friends and colleagues. The very next night he was dining with Lloyd George and Horne for the purpose of arranging an attack, and the following day he was trying to bring the leader of the Labour party and the Liberal party into it on his side. Can you imagine a more treacherous way of treating not only two former colleagues in various Governments, but two prominent people in his own party.

I now hear that he is mobilizing a terrific case with solicitors, counsel and dozens of witnesses and he intends to turn the whole business into something in the nature of an impeachment. I should hope that every decent person greatly resents all this.[3]

[1] Frances Louise Stevenson, 1888–1972. Schoolteacher. Private Secretary to Lloyd George, 1913–43. She married Lloyd George in 1943. Countess Lloyd-George of Dwyfor, 1945. She published her memoirs, *The Years That Are Past*, in 1967. Her brother, P. W. J. Stevenson, was killed in action on the western front in May 1915.

[2] In fact, Churchill first learnt of the allegations, in outline, on April 1; received copies of the actual documents from Manchester in four sections, on April 3, 8, 11 and 13; and informed both the Speaker and Hoare of his charges on April 15.

[3] In his reply Willingdon wrote: 'You can rest assured that you have everyone's sympathy regarding this monstrous attack of Winston's upon you and Derby. It seems unthinkable that a former colleague in the Cabinet should make such a designed attack of this kind and mobilise solicitors, counsels, and witnesses in the way that he has done. My feeling is that

At eleven o'clock on the morning of Monday April 23 Churchill was summoned before the Committee of Privileges at a committee room in the House of Commons. Ramsay MacDonald was in the Chair, and there were nine other Committee members, including Clement Attlee, Stanley Baldwin, Lord Hugh Cecil, Sir Herbert Samuel, Austen Chamberlain and the Attorney-General, Sir Thomas Inskip.[1] 'We will not examine you in a formal way,' MacDonald began; 'we would like you, if you would, just to tell us your story.'

Churchill began by stressing the duty of every member of the House of Commons, once he has received information suggesting a breach of privilege, 'to probe it and to pursue it, and, if a prima facie case is shown, to expose it'. He continued:

I do not come before you as a witness, according to my conception of my position here. There is nothing I can testify to at first hand. I come before you as a Member of the House of Commons, into whose hands information of a breach of privilege has come, and who has had to act promptly upon it under the Rules. I am sure that the very fact (I hope I may be permitted to say this) that this Committee consists in the main of my political opponents and of Ministers of the Crown, whose respected colleague is attacked, will be sufficient to secure me all fair and reasonable consideration and facilities.

Churchill then explained how the documents had been 'spontaneously produced to me'—without mentioning Lord Rothermere or his newspapers; and he then handed copies of all the documents to MacDonald. In addition to these documents, he said, there were clearly others which must exist, and which the Committee ought to 'use its powers to discover'; he had listed them in a letter which he proposed to hand to MacDonald after the session. They include all the minutes of the India section of the Manchester Chamber of Commerce during 1933, and all communications 'which passed between the Chamber or the India section of the Chamber and Lord Derby', together with the draft memoranda of evidence containing Derby's 'suggested alterations'.

---

every decent minded person resents this unscrupulous attack which savours of the middle ages. It looks as if Winston & Co with their great obsession about India have become orientalised, as I can quite imagine a bitter, disgruntled Oriental taking up this line . . .'

[1] Thomas Walker Hobart Inskip, 1876–1947. Educated at Clifton and King's College Cambridge. Barrister, 1899. Served in the Naval Intelligence Division, Admiralty, 1915–18. Conservative MP for Central Bristol, 1918–29 and for Fareham, 1931–39. Knighted, 1922. Solicitor-General, October 1922–January 1924, November 1924–March 1928 and September 1931–January 1932. Attorney-General, 1928–29 and 1932–36. Minister for the Co-ordination of Defence, 1936–39. Secretary of State for Dominion Affairs, January–September 1939 and May–October 1940. Lord Chancellor, September 1939–May 1940. Created Viscount Caldecote, 1939. Lord Chief Justice, 1940–46.

Before Churchill began to give his evidence, one of his particular requests was overruled; he was not to have the right to cross-examine or to question other witnesses. 'I must point out,' he commented, 'that if I am to have no facilities for putting what I will call awkward questions to important witnesses, I am, at any rate, relieved of a good deal of responsibility in this matter, and it passes to the Committee.'

Churchill then set out his case in detail, quoting from each of the documents in his possession. He also quoted from Sir Samuel Hoare's speech of the previous Monday, April 16. During his speech Hoare had said, of the original Manchester memorandum of June 1933:

Certain passages of the original memorandum of the Chamber of Commerce seemed to me to be likely to destroy any chance of negotiation. I felt bound to have this brought to the notice of the Chamber. My responsibilities as Secretary of State for India comprise much more than a defence of the White Paper, and so far from apologising for what I did, I should have been guilty of a breach of my duty if I had refrained from doing anything in my power which would promote so important an agreement.

To this Churchill commented:

. . . when the Secretary of State claims that, in discharge of his duty as Secretary of State, he is entitled to do anything in his power to promote a trade agreement, and with that end in view, is entitled to procure, or try to procure, the withdrawal of certain passages of the original memorandum of the Chamber of Commerce, he admits to tampering with evidence to be presented to the Committee set up by Parliament. I therefore claim, upon the facts, the decision of the Committee that a breach of privilege has occurred. The question of motive does not arise. We are concerned with fact and with action.

Document by document, Churchill led the Committee through the narrative which he had pieced together. During the discussion of what Sir Samuel Hoare had said at Lord Derby's dinner, Churchill commented on the position of members of the Joint Select Committee:

It is perfectly legitimate for them to express their opinions in cross-examining witnesses before the Committee and eliciting information from their own point of view, but what I think is very objectionable is their going outside the Committee, summoning the witnesses who are actually preparing the evidence and then discussing very fully with them so many points and aspects; I think that is very much to be deprecated.

It is undoubted that a dinner of this kind tended to exercise an influence from London upon these Manchester men; that it created an atmosphere, and that it brought into being new special contacts which followed on steadily as the weeks and months passed.

Churchill urged the Committee of Privileges to study carefully the documents in which members of the Chamber of Commerce spoke of 'pressure'. They were, he said, 'very conscious of what was going on'. All should be examined, and examined impartially. 'Nothing would be worse,' he believed, 'than that some witnesses should be called as Churchill witnesses and others as Government witnesses: they would greatly resent that.'

The meeting adjourned at one o'clock, and reassembled on the following afternoon, Tuesday April 24. Sir Thomas Inskip pressed Churchill to reveal how he had first heard of the rumours of impropriety, but Churchill refused to do so. 'If I were to repeat gossip,' he said, 'I could say a great many things, and produce people to swear to what they said, but I am not allowed to do that. There is nothing I have said that I cannot prove, as I believe, by documents of a *quasi* public or at any rate of an official character.' Sir Thomas Inskip rephrased his question. Had Churchill invited someone to come to see him, he asked, to report or confirm the gossip, or had somebody approached Churchill 'in the first instance'. Churchill replied: 'Somebody approached me in the first instance. I was told that this gentleman was anxious to give me information upon what was widely spread talk in London.' In a letter that morning he had already given the Committee H. Y. Robinson's name.

During his evidence, Churchill stressed the importance of the omissions in the revised Manchester memorandum, 'whatever one's view of the merits of the White Paper policy'. In its first submission the Chamber of Commerce had sought serious safeguards in relation to the policy. In its second, it had abandoned all reference to safeguards, or to reservations. At the same time, he pointed out, the telegrams from the Mission in India made it clear that Hoare had been wrong to say, in his speech in the House of Commons on April 16, that the first submission had been withdrawn because of the advice of that Mission. It was Churchill's belief that Lord Derby had been the prime mover behind the change of documents. On 3 November 1933, when the revised document was finally discussed by the Joint Select Committee, the situation, Churchill declared, was as follows:

Two of the Members of the Joint Select Committee, we know, who heard these declarations were well aware of all that had led up to them, but little did the other 30 guess, and little does the country know or Lancashire know, that up till 10 days before these statements, these answers to [the original] Questions . . . had rested in the strong boxes of the Secretary of the Joint Select Committee, long prepared, solidly adhered to, reluctantly abandoned, which was the direct contrary of these manipulated declarations.

Churchill appealed to the Committee to compare the documents he had put before them with Hoare's statement of the previous week, and then 'to pronounce upon these conflicting accounts'. He also urged them to do their utmost to procure all the 'other relevent documents' which must exist. Sir Herbert Samuel asked Churchill whether his principal complaint was solely that evidence had been tampered with, or that it had been tampered with specifically by two members of the Joint Select Committee. Churchill agreed that all tampering was wrong, but he added:

... one must select from many laxities which occur in our lives the most heinous examples of breaches which occur, and although it is not essential to my argument about privilege that they should have been Members of the Committee, the fact that they were Members of the Committee invested their action with a significance which made it necessary for me to draw the attention of Parliament to it. . . .

You must judge what a man does. If a man, who is not a Member of a Committee takes a very outrageous action to alter evidence, that might constitute a case with which you might trouble Parliament; but much more strictly must be judged the action of those who have accepted this special obligation.

'I only wish,' Churchill commented, 'I had equally good information about the influences which have been applied over the vast and valuable areas of our Indian Empire . . . but I have no evidence upon that.'

During his evidence, Churchill had been involved in several acrimonious exchanges, including one in which Sir Thomas Inskip had urged him to answer the questions 'without rhetoric', and he felt acutely what he believed to be a basic hostility of the Committee of Privileges. But on April 25 one of his legal advisers, Cyril Asquith,[1] wrote to him that the transcript of his evidence showed clearly 'that they were not able to blanket or obstruct your full statement of your case, as far as it can be made at this stage'. Asquith warned, however, that 'the predominant element' on the Committee 'will of course stress *opinion* as opposed to fact, *advice* as opposed to pressure, and so on, inclining within each

---

[1] Cyril Asquith, 1890–1954. 4th son of H. H. Asquith. Educated at Winchester and Balliol College Oxford. Captain, Queen's Westminster Rifles, 1914–19. Called to the Bar 1920. Member of the Lord Chancellor's Law Revision Committee, 1934–52; the Law Reform Committee 1952–54. King's Counsel, 1936. Recorder of Salisbury, 1937–38. Knighted, 1938. Elected to the Other Club, 1938. Judge of the High Court of Justice, 1938–46. Privy Councillor 1946. A Lord Justice of Appeal, 1946–51. Created Baron Asquith of Bishopstone, 1951. A Lord of Appeal in Ordinary, 1951–54. Chairman of the Political Honours (Scrutiny) Committee, 1952–54.

distinction, to the extreme which makes for innocence (or extenuation) as against full culpability'.

The daily work of the Committee of Privileges did not encourage Churchill to believe that his charges would be dealt with in as thorough a manner as he had hoped. On April 25 he learnt officially that the Committee did not intend to ask for the further documents which he had requested. He also learnt that although witnesses would be called, no witness would have facilities 'to examine or cross-examine another witness'. Two days later Churchill asked the Committee if he could have more than one printed copy of the evidence as it was given, but this was refused that same day. On April 26 Churchill drafted a strong protest against each of these decisions, but on April 27 his principal legal adviser, Sir Terence O'Connor,[1] cautioned him against sending this protest. 'You might be told,' he warned, 'that you were seeking to dictate to the Committee how they are to discharge their functions or that you were trying yourself to usurp those functions.' Churchill accepted this advice, with which Cyril Asquith concurred.

Unknown to Churchill and his advisers, Sir Samuel Hoare had discussed his evidence with Lord Hailsham on April 26, at the India Office. During the course of the discussion, it was decided not to let the Committee of Privileges see certain documents. According to the transcript, which was sent to Lord Derby from the India Office:

Sir Samuel Hoare referred to the difficulty of putting in all copies of the correspondence and some reference was made in particular to the letters between Lord Derby and Sir Louis Kershaw[2] which might be considered to raise a point of some difficulty. It was suggested that departmental privilege might be claimed as to such production, but the point of whether it should be definitely claimed or not was left open. . . .

So far as Lord Derby's personal position is concerned, it was felt that he might be pressed to explain the discrepancy between his opinion expressed at an earlier stage in a Memorandum that the evidence was satisfactory and his subsequent action in suggesting alterations. It was also felt that his

[1] Terence James O'Connor, 1891–1940. On active service, 1914–18, with the Highland Light Infantry and the West African Frontier Force. Barrister, 1919. Conservative MP for Luton, 1924–29; for Central Nottingham, 1930–39. King's Counsel, 1929. Elected to the Other Club, 1933. Knighted, 1936. Solicitor-General, 1936–40. He died on 8 May 1940, two days before Churchill became Prime Minister.

[2] Louis James Kershaw, 1869–1947. Educated at Belfast Methodist College and Trinity College Dublin. Entered the Indian Civil Service 1890; Secretary, India Revenue, and Agriculture Department, 1914. India Office London, 1915; Paris Peace Conference, 1919. Knighted, 1921. Representative of India on the International Labour Organization, 1923–26. Assistant Under-Secretary of State, India Office, 1924–33; Deputy Under-Secretary, 1933–34.

correspondence with Sir Louis Kershaw if disclosed might be another point upon which he would be exposed to cross-examination.

The letter which Derby had written to Kershaw was never produced in evidence before the Select Committee. A copy of it survives in Lord Derby's archive. It was dated 26 July 1933. In it Derby wrote to Kershaw:

I find it very difficult to redraft a memorandum and I wish I could persuade the Manchester people to withdraw it altogether but I fear to attempt to do that would only create a great deal of trouble.

The points I thought of raising with them are contained in the enclosed memorandum. It would be very good of you if you would look through it; just see if you agree with what I say and also if there is any other point which you think I ought to take up.

I have to be a little careful as to how I go in this matter as I know I have got Sir Joseph Nall[1] opposed to me over it and as he is always in Manchester he could very easily get up an agitation which would undo any good that I have been able so far to do in the matter of conciliation. I think probably too that by the time their memorandum is published and circulated the Committee will have got to work in India and that even the hot heads will see that we ought not to publish anything which might inflame Indian public feeling against us.

On July 31 Kershaw had replied from the India Office: 'Like you, I deplore that the memorandum cannot be entirely rewritten,' and he sent Derby four pages of proposed alterations.

Equally unknown either to Churchill or to the Committee of Privileges was the full correspondence between Lord Derby and the Secretary to the Chamber of Commerce, Raymond Streat.[2] On July 23 Derby had written to Streat, of the Manchester evidence, that he was 'in thorough accord that it is an excellent and moderate statement of the position'. But three days later he had written again, telling Streat of the need for 'somewhat radical changes' in the memorandum. To this

[1] Joseph Nall, 1887–1958. Director of several transport companies. On active service at Gallipoli and in France, 1914–18 (wounded, despatches, DSO). Conservative MP, Hulme Division of Manchester, 1918–29, and 1931–45. Knighted, 1924. President of the Institute of Transport, 1925–26. Created Baronet, 1954.

[2] Edward Raymond Streat, 1897–1979. Educated at Manchester Grammar School. On active service, 1915–18. Director and Secretary, Manchester Chamber of Commerce, 1920–40. Director, Lancashire Industrial Development Council, 1931–40. President, Manchester Statistical Society, 1936–38. Chairman, the Cotton Board, Manchester, 1940–57. Secretary, Export Council, Board of Trade, 1940. Knighted, 1942. Member, Advisory Council, Department of Scientific and Industrial Research, 1942–47. President of the Textile Institute, 1946–48. Member of the BBC General Advisory Council, 1947–52. One of his three sons died of wounds received in action in 1944.

Streat had replied on July 31: 'if the Lancashire interest was abandoned to the needs of a purely political situation the resultant storm would be very severe'. But Derby had already persevered in his efforts, writing to Streat again on July 28, of the evidence: 'There are many things in it that I do not like and that I am sure can be altered without in any way diminishing the force of the evidence, but of course it would mean to a certain extent rewriting it and that might be difficult for you to get passed.'

The Committee of Privileges continued to examine witnesses for more than a month, to the annoyance of both Hoare and Baldwin. 'Whether or not Winston succeeds in his Committee upon the point of privilege,' Hoare wrote to Willingdon on April 27, 'he will have succeeded in adding an enormous burden of work to my shoulders. . . . I have to spend practically the whole of my time going through endless files and letters as to what happened on this or that day during the last year and a half.' Writing in his diary for April 28, Thomas Jones recorded a conversation with Baldwin:

T.J.: 'I suppose you are wasting a lot of time over Winston's Committee of Privileges?'
S.B.: 'Yes—meeting after meeting this week and next. They are all die-hards who'll stop at nothing to bring the Government down.'[1]

Throughout May Churchill continued to seek further evidence from the Manchester Chamber of Commerce, and from members of the India Defence League. On May 7 he discussed privately with MacDonald the eventual publication of the evidence on which the charges were based. Churchill favoured the fullest possible publication, as he had at the time of the Dardanelles Commission of Enquiry nearly twenty years before. Full publication, he wrote to MacDonald that same day, 'seems to me very important as justifying the course which I thought it my duty to take'. MacDonald pointed out, however, and Churchill accepted, that if published some of the Manchester Chamber of Commerce's views might 'provoke reactions detrimental to the public interest', especially towards the commercial relations between Manchester and India.

During the first and second weeks of May Churchill prepared an even more detailed memorandum setting out his charges. At their meeting on May 7, MacDonald had tried to persuade him not to submit this

---

[1] On April 30 the Governor of Bombay, Lord Brabourne, wrote to Hoare: 'I want to write you a personal line, which you can destroy, to tell you how indignant Doreen and I are at Winston's latest dirty attack on you. That you will win hands down I have no doubt at all but I do think it is such a filthy trick to play on you . . . All your Indian friends merely express their disgust with W.S.C. & their belief that you will defeat him, as usual.'

memorandum, or at least to delay submission, but when Churchill put the gist of their conversation in writing MacDonald urged him, on May 8, to 'substitute another letter containing no reference to our private conversation'. In reply, Churchill told MacDonald that he would go ahead with his memorandum, and would reserve 'the fullest freedom to claim the faithful and substantial publication of the evidence'. On May 11, four days after Churchill's meeting with MacDonald, Churchill described the dispute to Lloyd George, whose Secretary, Frances Stevenson, recorded in her diary:

Ramsay has sent for Winston & harangued him on the duty of everybody to pull together, at a time when the position here & in Europe, & in the East, is getting worse & worse, (according to Ramsay). He added that the position in the Dominions was also getting worse, & suggested that the Government were thinking of asking someone of good standing, & a knowledge of the Dominions, to go and talk to them. Winston, scenting a trap, said: 'If you are going to suggest that I should suppress the result of my inquiry, I tell you frankly that nothing will persuade me to do so.' Of course Ramsay protested that he meant nothing of the sort—what they wanted most of all was to have the actual facts, & to have them published, without bias one way or the other.

Helped by his son Randolph, and advised by Terence O'Connor and Cyril Asquith, Churchill redrafted his memorandum several times, seeking to present the evidence in the most telling form, and on May 10 he sent the Committee of Privileges twenty printed copies of the final draft. 'Whether the verdict is 100% the way we should desire or not,' H. Y. Robinson wrote on May 10, 'it does not matter because even though the whitewash brush may be used in certain directions, the fact remains that Lancashire is seething with indignation at events which have taken place.'

Among the materials which Churchill had been sent after his original submission of evidence, and which he included in his final memorandum, were some of the letters exchanged between Derby and Streat. These letters had been shown to Churchill in confidence by the Committee of Privileges, and seemed to him to substantiate his case. In his memorandum he pointed out that on July 17, three weeks after Derby's dinner, Hoare had written to Derby that 'if you agree with me in feeling, as I feel very strongly, that the line which the Lancashire people are taking will injure their chance of doing a deal with the Indians, then I hope you will use your great influence with them to look into the matter from the point of view which I have described. . . .' In his letter Hoare asked Derby for his help 'as mediator' over specific points in the original Manchester evidence. Churchill's memorandum continued:

Immediately upon receipt of Sir Samuel Hoare's letter of July 17, Lord Derby wrote on July 19 to Mr Streat, the Secretary of the Manchester Chamber of Commerce a letter which urged the alteration of the Manchester evidence. It reproduced almost textually the points conveyed to him by the Secretary of State. In fact, as can be seen by comparing the letters, he copied out word for word, for five or six lines at a time, the operative passages in Sir Samuel Hoare's letter, and sent them forward with all the weight of his own influence. The fact that he marked this letter 'Private and Confidential' detracts nothing from its public importance.

Negotiations to alter evidence would naturally be so marked. If no other evidence existed, the Breach of Privilege would be proved by these two letters of Sir Samuel Hoare to Lord Derby of July 17 and of Lord Derby to Mr Streat of July 19—alone.

Churchill then pointed out that the Derby–Streat correspondence had continued beyond this exchange. On July 31 Streat had written again, pointing out how difficult it would be to alter the evidence, in view of the strong opinions in Lancashire. But on August 9 Derby had written to Streat:

I send you a copy of the suggestions for alteration of the draft [ie the original memorandum of evidence]. I must tell you how they have come about. I was, as you know, disturbed about some of the wording of the memorandum and I had a long talk with Sir Louis Kershaw on the subject, whom I know was equally disturbed. After that conversation I went carefully through the memorandum and jotted down various suggestions that I should make, in the way of alteration, for him to consider. The notes I send you are really therefore the joint efforts of himself and myself, and you are at liberty to show them to anybody you like. I do not think they alter the sense of the memorandum but put it in slightly different language. . . .

In his own memorandum Churchill declared:

Thus it is proved that Lord Derby was 'using his great influence' upon the Manchester Chamber of Commerce through its Secretary in direct fulfilment of the wishes of the Secretary of State, and that he was in close contact with the India Office. He was in fact concerting his action with Sir Louis Kershaw, who was giving him the views of the India Office. It is difficult to believe that the Secretary of State did not approve of the action of Sir Louis Kershaw or that his subordinate acted contrary to his wishes and policy. Sir Samuel Hoare and the India Office are thus shown to be in continuous association with the Manchester Chamber of Commerce through the medium of Lord Derby, who was exerting his influence in accordance with their wishes to induce the Chamber to modify its views so that they might accord with their own.

Churchill knew nothing of the earlier Derby–Kershaw correspondence, of July 1933, which neither Derby nor the India Office chose to submit to the Committee of Privileges, and which would further have strengthened his charges. But he had seen, and referred to, Thomas Barlow's threat to resign if the first Manchester evidence were not withdrawn. This threat had been made at the Chamber of Commerce on October 23, and recorded in the Minutes on the following day. Churchill commented on Barlow's threat:

He struck this blow for the alteration of the evidence (in the sense desired by the Secretary of State in his letter of May 5, and by Lord Derby in his suggestions of July and August) on October 23 and 24. On January 1 he received the honour of knighthood in the New Year's List. It must, however, be remembered that coincidence may afford a perfectly innocent explanation for his actions.

Churchill's memorandum concluded:

The actual decision to alter the evidence was taken on October 23rd after the expression by the delegation in India of a desire to delay the hearing of the evidence and to avoid publicity until their negotiations were completed. A decisive contributory factor in this resolve was the influence of Mr Barlow and Mr Rodier carrying out the views which they had formed with Lord Derby during the consultations of July, and especially by Mr (now Sir Thomas) Barlow's disclosures at the critical moment of his long-conceived intention not to be personally responsible for presenting the evidence in its original form. That all these factors were present in the final decision is apparent, from the evidence and from the documents. The Committee of Privileges must assign the relative weight which should be attached to each or any of them in order to decide whether the admitted influence, or pressure, exercised by Sir Samuel Hoare and Lord Derby, played a major or only a minor part in the final result.

Cyril Asquith read Churchill's memorandum on May 10. 'With the reinforcements of the uncirculated Derby–Streat letters,' he wrote, 'it seems to me powerful & damning beyond our original hopes.' Asquith also passed on to Churchill some disturbing news: the man who was drafting the Report of the Committee of Privileges was Sir Maurice Gwyer,[1] who had earlier drafted the India White Paper. 'A parental

[1] Maurice Linford Gwyer, 1878–1952. Educated at Westminster and Christ Church Oxford; Fellow of All Souls, 1902–16. Lecturer in Private International Law, Oxford, 1912–15. Legal Adviser to the Ministry of Shipping, 1917–19; to the Ministry of Health, 1919–26. Solicitor to the Treasury, 1926–33. Knighted, 1928. Member of the Indian States Inquiry Committee, 1932. First Parliamentary Counsel to the Treasury, 1934–37. Chief Justice of India, 1937–43. Vice-Chancellor of Delhi University, 1938–50.

bias in favour of the WP,' Asquith wrote, 'might I imagine communicate itself not only to the form but to the substance of the Report he is drafting.' On the following day Hoare wrote to Derby's brother, Sir George Stanley,[1] who was acting Viceroy during Willingdon's leave: 'My enemies have stuck at nothing in recent months. They have evidently got it into their heads that if somehow or other they can get me out of the Government, the White Paper will end in smoke and the National Government probably come to an end. There has been nothing like the ruthlessness of the campaign for generations.' Later in his letter Hoare told Stanley:

As a result of these outrageous proceedings my office, myself and three prominent members of the Government have been doing nothing but dealing with Winston's preposterous charges. All this has entailed an enormous amount of useless work upon me, for dealing with this kind of crowd one can take nothing for granted and one has to work up every conceivable detail. Whatever the result of the Committee may be, I am certain that I have smashed Winston's case to pieces. So far all the gossip goes to show that Winston's case has worn very thin.

Churchill showed Lloyd George his deposition on May 11. That evening Frances Stevenson recorded in her diary Lloyd George's view that 'this document is a very powerful one'. Four days later Churchill wrote to the Committee of Privileges, asking them to include in their Report the whole of his final memorandum, pointing out that the Derby–Streat letters constituted 'material documents of the highest consequence', proving conclusively, as he believed, 'the association between Sir Samuel Hoare and Lord Derby, and between the India Office and Lord Derby to bring Lord Derby's great influence to bear through its leading official to procure the alteration in the evidence'. But Hoare was still confident that Churchill's charges would be dismissed, writing on May 17 to Sir George Stanley:

The proceedings have been carried out with the greatest secrecy and it is impossible for anyone to say what the report will contain. I would, however, be very much surprised if it did not repudiate Winston's charges and criticise directly or indirectly his general behaviour. Quite apart from personal reasons, I greatly hope that this will be the result. If Winston were

[1] George Frederick Stanley, 1872–1938. Sixth son of the 16th Earl of Derby. 2nd Lieutenant, Royal Horse Artillery, 1893; Captain, 1900; on active service in South Africa and during the European war (despatches twice). Conservative MP for Preston, 1910–22; for Willesden East, 1924–29. Opposition Chief Whip, 1913–14. Financial Secretary, War Office, 1921–22. Parliamentary Under-Secretary at the Home Office, 1922–23; at the Ministry of Pensions, 1924–29. Privy Councillor, 1927. Knighted, 1929. Governor of Madras, 1929–34; and acting Viceroy of India, May–August 1934.

to get away with the report, the effect would be very damaging to the whole Government. . . .

You cannot imagine what a nuisance it has been. The whole affair created a most unpleasant atmosphere of suspicion, mystery and intrigue and put an immense amount of additional work upon me and my office. I hope that Eddie[1] and the family will never forgive Winston. I certainly shall not. Winston and his friends are completely unscrupulous. They stick at nothing. They misrepresent everything that is said and spread about all kinds of groundless charges and baseless rumours. I do not think that I have ever seen a more unscupulous and relentless propaganda.

On May 22 Hoare wrote again to Stanley, of the White Paper itself:

Very much between you and me I don't think that Willingdon or any of his advisers realize in the least the tremendous difficulties that exist here over the reforms. The Conservatives are getting into the same mood into which they got at the end of the L.G. Coalition, and a Government of India Bill will not only drive some of them into open opposition, but, however necessary it may be, is regarded by all of them as an unpopular nuisance. Unless, there-fore, independent leaders like Eddie and Austen back us, neither the Govern-ment nor the Bill will survive.

The Report of the Committee of Privileges was due to be printed on June 6. Five days earlier, on June 1, Hoare wrote maliciously to Stanley: 'I do not know which is the more offensive or more mis-chievous, Winston or his son. Rumour, however, goes that they fight like cats with each other and chiefly agree in the prodigious amount of champagne that each of them drinks each night.'

On June 4 Terence O'Connor had discussed with Churchill what his course of action should be once the Committee of Privileges had reported, and on June 5 he wrote to warn Churchill of the likelihood of the Committee deciding that no breach of privilege had occurred, and recommending 'that no further action be taken'. O'Connor's letter continued:

The innate Conservatism of public opinion will be loth to reject or assail conclusions which have been reached after patient inquiry by a Committee drawn from all political parties. I do not think your criticism of pro-white-paper bias by the majority of Members of the Committee will carry con-viction. People will be most reluctant to conclude that Members of different political parties meeting together to investigate a subject which is essentially different from the pro's and con's of the white paper are unable to leave their white paper beliefs behind and act in a judicial spirit. For these reasons I think you should carefully avoid any challenge of the Committee's findings

---

[1] Lord Derby.

on the ground of the composition of the Committee. You should, I think, even disown any such charge, if it is voiced by your supporters.

O'Connor sought to guide Churchill's thoughts towards his speech in answer to the report. He should seek to 'catalogue the salient features of the evidence', including any evidence which had emerged during the hearings, but which might not be published in the Report. O'Connor advised Churchill not to speak at the beginning of the debate, but only at 'a comparatively late stage', and he added:

You should, I think, avoid giving the impression that you are merely attempting to obtain, on appeal, so to speak, a conviction which you have failed to get at first instance. It would be disastrous if you gave the impression that your only object was to demolish the white paper procedure. Make it plain that your aim is to preserve intact the privilege of Parliament. Your slogan 'Publish the Evidence' (if in fact it has not been published) is the right one, and you might express your confidence that full publication would support up to the hilt the charges which you have made; always of course carefully disclaiming any suggestion of corrupt motive on the part of Hoare.

The above observations show that I have cast for you a judicial role in this matter which may not be very much to your liking. They are intentionally based upon the most pessimistic prognosis of the Committee's findings; not because I hold a pessimistic view but because that is I think the only contingency for which you can with advantage prepare yourself in advance. Whatever view you take of them, I hope you will not consider them impertinent in face of a sphere of action in which you have much more experience than I have, and that you will believe that they are put forward with the single aim of keeping unimpaired the position which you hold in public opinion. If I venture to formulate them in the noxious shape of a corrective, it is because I know that your buoyant personality will supply its own antitoxin, and also because I know that there are plenty of your followers who will be prepared to urge you to a more spectacular course than, in your interests, I should care to advise.

As O'Connor had forecast, the Report of the Committee of Privileges did not uphold Churchill's charges. Printed on June 6, and made public on June 9, it came to the unanimous conclusion that there had been 'no breach of privilege' by Hoare or Derby. According to the Report, the Joint Select Committee was 'not in the ordinary sense a judicial body', so that the ordinary rules applied to tribunals 'engaged in administering justice' did not apply to it. There was thus no legal basis for accusing members of the Committee of applying 'wrongful pressure'. In any case, according to the Report, 'What was called pressure was no more than advice or persuasion.' In conclusion, the Report stated that none of the actual documents involved would be published, as many of them were of a 'confidential nature', the publication of which, so the Committee wished to state 'unanimously and emphatically', would be 'harmful to the public interest'.

On June 7 Hoare wrote scornfully to George Stanley: 'Mrs Winston, by the way, is going about London saying that Winston was most reluctant to raise the question in the House and that he only did so because he was impelled by his great sense of public duty.' But Churchill's friends and acquaintances hastened to console him. On June 8 one of the *Daily Mail* journalists who had originally pieced together the story, R. A. Cannell,[1] wrote to Churchill from Manchester:

I am taking the liberty of writing to you to express my deep disappointment at the cleverly constructed report from the Committee of Privileges. Though we in Manchester hardly imagined a favourable outcome as even possible, we hoped for some tangible recognition that our fears, which you voiced so clearly and so eloquently, were well founded.

Still, the battle for India has only now been joined in real earnest and we shall keep on fighting in Lancashire so long as we have spokesmen of your calibre at Westminster. . . .

Please forgive me so lengthy a trespass on your generosity. But to see so strenuously-conceived work treated so cavalierly is bitter. Your own disappointment must be keener felt.

The debate on the Committee of Privileges Report was fixed for June 13. Two days before the debate, Major Henry Lygon[2] wrote sarcastically to Churchill: 'The report is a wonderful document. Persuasion was pardonable, because most of the Committee had already made up their minds. Then why trouble to examine witnesses from Manchester or anywhere else?' Lygon added: 'More power to yr elbow.' Lord Halsbury[3] wrote that same day:

This is the opinion I heard given by one of whom I think greatly. (He is also a member of the Carlton Club).

[1] Robert Cannell, 1908–1965. Joined the *Daily Mail* staff in Manchester in 1929; transferred to London, 1938; acting Night News Editor, 1940–50. A pioneer in the field of television news coverage. From 1950 until his death he was Radio and Television Correspondent of the *Daily Express*.

[2] Henry Lygon, 1884–1936. 4th son of the 6th Earl Beauchamp. Educated at Eton and Magdalen College Oxford. President of the Oxford Union, 1906. On active service, 1914–18. (Intelligence Corps, Royal Flying Corps, wounded.) Four times unsuccessful Conservative candidate for Parliament. He lived at 90 Piccadilly, London. His half-brother Edward was killed in action in South Africa in 1900.

[3] Hardinge Goulburn Giffard, 1880–1943. Educated at Eton and New College Oxford. Barrister, 1906. Unsuccessful Conservative candidate, 1910. Major, RAF, 1918. Succeeded his father as 2nd Earl of Halsbury, 1921. Recorder of Carmarthen, 1923–25. King's Counsel 1923. He died in an internment camp in France on 15 September 1943.

'I do not care what the evidence was; the report is contemptible. We did not need a Committee to tell us that version No 2 was agreed. Obviously it must have been or it would not have been given as evidence. The point is how did it come to be agreed. The Committee say by persuasion—persuasion by a Secretary of State for India!, and they approve it! It is peaceful picketing pure and simple.'

The term 'peaceful picketing' struck me at once as likely to be very adhesive if it were ever mentioned and for that reason I am passing it on to you.

On June 12 Baldwin discussed the situation with Thomas Jones, who recorded in his diary: 'He told me that Inskip had drawn up the report against Churchill for the Committee of Privileges. . . .'

On the afternoon of Wednesday June 13 the House of Commons debated the Committee of Privileges Report. Opening the debate, Ramsay MacDonald asked the House to accept the Report. In his speech, MacDonald described the individual documents which Churchill had presented as having 'very little meaning or very little significance'. The Committee had tried to relate these documents to 'the long stream of events' between April and November 1933, and had concluded that neither Hoare nor Derby had committed a breach of privilege. MacDonald appealed to the House to uphold this conclusion, and then to support the Committee's 'unanimous and emphatic' recommendation that none of the documents should be published.

Despite O'Connor's advice to the contrary, Churchill rose immediately after MacDonald, and spoke for an hour, with great anger and sarcasm, about the work and findings of the Committee. He began by setting out the essential difference between the Lancashire mill-owners and Hoare. They had wanted specific safeguards in the forthcoming India Constitution so that the full tariff autonomy granted by Britain to India would not be used 'arbitrarily or capriciously' by the Indian politicians at the Centre in order to ruin Britain's trading interests. Such safeguards, they believed, should be 'brought into review' during any discussion of the new India Constitution Bill. But Hoare had believed that to insist on safeguards would be to alienate Indian opinion, 'and that our only hope is to trust to good will and trade negotiations'. Churchill continued:

This is a grave controversy, and, of course, there are two opinions about it. I myself hold that it is a controversy which lies at the root of the whole of this discussion, all that runs through the report turns upon that issue, and, therefore, it is not a small thing, a little thing, no light matter, about which we are fighting as we are. It is a matter of such grave consequences to our country that in serving that cause one might well sacrifice personal friendships or anything else which may be necessary for the purpose.

This was the issue which the Manchester Chamber of Commerce wished to raise in their evidence before the Joint Select Committee, and this was the issue which the Secretary of State for India wished to deter them from raising. Obviously, he had—not a strong personal interest, there is no such idea— a strong personal political interest in doing so, because if Lancashire had brought this claim into the full light of day before the Joint Select Committee there would undoubtedly have been considerable alignment to that opinion of all Lancashire members in opposition to the policy which the Secretary of State was conducting.

The claim of Lancashire, Churchill asserted, 'has never been brought before the Joint Select Committee in the full light of day'; indeed, as a result of the pressures which he was convinced had been applied between April and November 1933, the Joint Select Committee had concluded their hearings 'in complete ignorance of the fact that Lancashire desires to raise this question'. He then went on to defend his action in raising once again all the dates and details of his charges, telling a predominantly hostile House of Commons:

. . . it is my duty to justify the course I have taken in invoking this grave, formidable procedure of Privilege which is the power and glory of the House of Commons and which, in this country, as in no other country in the world, enables a private Member of this House to hold the whole machinery of the State up to accountability—a procedure which has come down from our ancestors.

In any other country in the world, I suppose, I should be put in a concentration camp and visited by a party of overgrown schoolboys. But here one has this right, and I would regard it as most dishonourable to have invoked this procedure unless I could offer solid reasons of duty and fact as a justification for taking that course.

Churchill then drew the House's attention to the Hoare–Derby and Derby–Streat correspondence—documents which the Committee of Privileges had decided not to publish in full, but to which they had referred, and from which they had quoted extracts. 'I claim,' said Churchill, 'that the report has established that the Secretary of State and Lord Derby, jointly and severally, from the best of motives, and in a perfectly honourable manner, endeavoured to deter Manchester witnesses from presenting evidence they desired to present.' But the Committee's report, he added, gave no fair picture of what had happened. It was 'jumbled both in topics and chronology'. Reference to 'salient facts' was so obscure as to fail to convey either a clear, or even an intelligible

impression of many of the details. It was not an adequate account of the
events, of the evidence, 'and still less of the documents'. In a letter to
MacDonald that morning he had stated, he said, that he intended to
raise the question of 'certain points where, I think the Committee have
made a mistake, or committed an oversight, or not given an adequate or
a true account—I do not mean in any offensive sense—of particular
documents they have cited, summarised or quoted fully'; in particular
Hoare's letter to Bond of July 7, in which—ten days before enlisting
Derby's help as a mediator—Hoare had told Bond that it would not be
'appropriate' to discuss Lancashire's objections, in view of the fact that
'the whole matter so far as the Constitution is concerned, is now in the
hands of the Joint Select Committee'.

Churchill's speech was then interrupted by both MacDonald and
Hoare, who argued against the omitted sentence being read out. They
were supported by the Speaker, Captain Fitzroy. But Inskip admitted
that Churchill was, in law, 'at liberty' to read it out. Having done so,
Churchill declared—contrasting Hoare's letter to Bond with his subsequent letter to Derby:

Why was it appropriate, I want to know, for the Secretary of State to ask
Lord Derby, a fellow member of the Joint Select Committee, to use his great
influence with the Manchester Chamber of Commerce, when at the same
time he himself knew that it was inappropriate for him to do it any further?

I am entitled to ask these questions. These matters do not turn, thank God,
in this country upon any hideous scandals, but they do turn upon nice points
of Parliamentary conduct which the House is perfectly capable of deciding. I
say that this account of this letter is most unsatisfactory. Part of it is contained
in one part of the document and part in another, but the letter is a most
important document.

The letter of the Secretary of State to Lord Derby of the 17th July has
already been half, or rather quarter, published here, and summarised in a
manner that is colourless and bald, so that no one can see the significance of
it. It was the letter in which the Secretary of State urged Lord Derby to do
what he himself did not feel he ought to continue to do, and it puts, in the
most categorical manner, the great alterations of principle which he wished to
have induced in the Manchester evidence.

At this point Sir Samuel Hoare indicated his disagreement. Churchill
continued:

My right hon Friend the Secretary of State—I hope he will allow me to
continue to call him so—shakes his head. I am not going to ask for further
quotations in this matter, but because I have opened a point on which I have
been denied, I say that the Government ought themselves to publish the

exact requests for the alteration of the evidence on the great fundamental points which the Secretary of State made to Lord Derby and which he asked him to use his influence to procure. We ought to have that. What do we read in the very next line? What I can only call a complete misstatement.

Sir PERCY HARRIS:[1] Is that an attack on the Committee of Privileges?

Mr CHURCHILL: It is an attack on the report. Why is it brought before the House if we are not allowed to quote it? In the very next line of the quotation of this letter of the 17th is a statement about the letter which Lord Derby wrote in consequence of that letter, and this is the statement:

'As the result of this suggestion the Earl of Derby wrote to the Secretary of the Manchester Chamber of Commerce on 19th July urging re-consideration of the wording of certain clauses in the memorandum.'

That is quite untrue. I do not mean that it is not true—he may have said it was the wording—but it is quite untrue that what he asked was re-consideration of the wording, and if the letter were published, everybody would see that that could not hold water for a moment.

Great and fundamental changes were demanded by the Secretary of State. Lord Derby copied out these changes and sent them forward, line after line, with all his influence, to his friend the Secretary of the Manchester Chamber of Commerce, and yet the Committee comes before the House and writes on the face of the report the statement that this is only a matter of wording. I deny it altogether, and I say that that is a complete misrepresentation of the facts.[2]

Summaries and paraphrases of documents, Churchill warned, gave no real impression of the documents themselves. Yet the House of Commons, having set up the Committee of Privileges as its 'instrument' to examine Churchill's charges, was now being asked to decide on a Report 'without seeing the documents'. Churchill then listed the documents he believed should be published: the Hoare–Bond letters of May 5, May 23 and July 7; the Hoare–Derby letter of July 17; and the Derby–Streat exchange of July 19 and August 9. By basing itself on the summaries alone, Churchill argued, the House was in no position 'to judge fairly what those documents convey'.[3]

---

[1] Percy Alfred Harris, 1876–1952. Educated at Harrow and Trinity Hall Cambridge. Barrister, 1899. Member of the London County Council, 1907; Deputy Chairman, 1915–16. Assistant Director Volunteer Services, War Office, 1916. Liberal MP for Harborough, 1916–18; for South-West Bethnal Green, 1922–45. Created Baronet, 1932. Chief Whip of the Liberal Parliamentary Party, 1935–45; Deputy Liberal Leader, 1940–45.

[2] That Churchill was correct in his charge is clear from Hoare's private letter to Willingdon of 3 November 1933, not known to Churchill, and not produced in evidence, in which Hoare had written of how the original 'dangerous and aggressive memorandum' had become 'a very harmless document' (quoted on pages 515–16).

[3] Churchill elaborated on these arguments on 7 March 1935, when he gave evidence before the Select Committee on Witnesses, to whom he said: 'I had always pressed that the cor-

Churchill's final point of complaint was a constitutional one. In paragraph 21 of its Report, the Committee of Privileges had decided that as the Joint Select Committee was 'not in the ordinary sense a judicial body', that the ordinary rules which applied to tribunals 'engaged in administering justice' did not apply to it, and that there was therefore no legal basis for accusing members of the Committee of applying wrongful pressure or giving unlawful advice. And yet, Churchill pointed out, Baldwin himself, on 29 June 1933, at the Friend's House meeting of the Conservative Party, in explaining why he would not discuss the merits of the Government's India policy had declared, as his reason: 'Its merits are under semi-judicial consideration of the Joint Select Committee.' Churchill continued: 'I give you the "semi"; I do not wish to be at all captious about that. . . . I suppose it is judicial one way and not judicial the other,' and he added:

Again and again we have been exhorted in these matters—I could multiply them with quotations—to wait while this question is sub judice. We have been invited time and time again to admire the restraint of the Secretary of State and other members of the Committee who are supporters of the Government in remaining silent on the public platforms and not embarking in public discussions, but apparently this prohibition only extends to their public activities.

There is a charter for everyone to do what he likes to carry on the good work behind the scenes so long as he marks it 'Private and confidential'. Nothing that is dishonourable and criminal can be done in those circumstances. These liberties are not only extended to the right hon Gentleman in his dual capacity, which argument has not been pressed at all because he sought it himself, but are offered freely, as far as I gather, to all members of the Committee.

The Report's ruling laid it open, Churchill stressed:

. . . for any member of the Joint Select Committee to do anything in his power to endeavour to deter any witness from presenting evidence as he wished to present it; to do this without informing other members of the Joint Select Committee; and to sit still while those witnesses are giving evidence contrary to what it was known was their original wish to give without informing the other members of the Committee.

---

respondence should be published, but the Committee decided to suppress that altogether with the rest of the evidence. A lawyer can properly advise his client as to the line he should take or the case he should set up in judicial proceedings. But for jurymen to leave the box, or judges the bench, and give similar advice, is obviously improper. More objectionable still is such a course when pursued by one or two members of a tribunal only, who thereby prevent or attempt to prevent the witnesses' original and uninfluenced opinion from ever being known to their colleagues.'

As I say, these rulings are authoritative. We shall have to recognise them as the conditions which will govern us and the working of our committees in future. I do not wonder that before the Committee of Privileges and the leader of the Conservative party could have brought themselves to such decisions, they thought it necessary to explore every other avenue before they broke their way out through this emergency exit.

Churchill continued his speech with a bitter denunciation of the Committee of Privileges' attempt to seek a special, non-judicial status for the Joint Select Committee, a status which would in his view permanently alter the procedure and solemnity of Parliamentary Committees, and 'cast a slur' upon future relations between Committee Members and witnesses. 'Many here,' he said, 'may live to regret that the custodians of the rights and privileges of the House of Commons have decided to meet a temporary difficulty by taking that course.' Churchill went on to refer once more to Baldwin's speech at Friends' House:

I have no doubt that when he spoke as he did at the Friends' House a year ago, he believed what he said, and he meant what he said; and many people have noticed that on frequent occasions the right hon Gentleman—what is quite rare in our public life—is found to be keeping his word even in his own dispute.

I am sure that that was what he meant when he made that speech, and I ask him whether this account set forth in this report is really the way which Parliament meant and expected this great inquiry by the Joint Select Committee to be conducted. Is it really the way which he as leader of the Conservative party meant it to be conducted?

Churchill ended his speech with a series of further questions and warnings:

Are these the methods, quite blameless in personal honour, these methods of management and organising, to be approved indiscriminately and even applauded? Are they to be our guide in the future? Are they to be applied in every direction?

We have seen this Lancashire case to a certain extent explored, and we see all there is behind it; but let the House imagine what would happen or may have happened when such processes are applied over the whole vast field of the Indian case. Apply it to the evidence of the Rajahs and the European associations in India. Apply it to the formation and expression of opinion throughout the Civil Service.

The noble Lord the right hon Member for Oxford University (Lord H. Cecil) used a searching phrase when he spoke of witnesses being marshalled as if they were an orchestra under the baton of a conductor. In this Indian sphere, it is the rod of the ruler which would be applied. I ask the House to pause long and to think deeply before they blindly apply to the methods revealed in this report the seal of Parliamentary approbation.

Churchill's speech provoked fierce anger among many Conservatives. Leopold Amery, who spoke immediately after him, commented derisively on Churchill's 'unique achievement of disclosing a mare's nest within a mare's nest'. Churchill's aim, Amery asserted, was to stir up a crisis sufficient 'to force' Hoare's resignation, to dislocate 'for months' the work of the Joint Select Committee and to create a situation 'which would have shattered the Conservative Party'. All this, Amery declared, proved that Churchill wished at all costs to be true to 'his chosen motto', *Fiat justitia ruat caelum*'. Unwarily, Churchill called out 'Translate it,' to which Amery replied, amid much laughter: 'If I can trip up Sam, the Government's bust.'

Amery's charge was widely believed. Churchill, he went on, had built upon certain documents 'a structure of inference, of surmise, of innuendo which the searching investigation of the Committee of Privileges has tumbled down like a house of cards'. Following Amery, first Lord Hugh Cecil and then Clement Attlee defended the Report of the Committee. Next, on behalf of the Liberal Party, Churchill's friend Sir Archibald Sinclair welcomed the Report. As the debate continued, the Report was criticized by Sir Henry Page Croft, the Duchess of Atholl, Samuel Hammersley and Robert Boothby.[1] It was then defended by Sir John Simon, who stated that as a result of Churchill's efforts since the beginning of April, Hoare had been subjected to 'this grievous charge and this great worry', designed to bring 'ruin' upon him—and then by J. P. Morris, who made a vicious personal attack on Churchill's past career and future prospects:

. . . I would like to make a few observations upon the conduct of my right hon Friend the Member for Epping in the matter which we are now discussing. A man who for so many years has been a Member of this House, who has occupied so many high positions of State, but who, in the course of fighting a losing battle, tries for a knock-out blow by questionable tactics, raises the question of his fitness to be selected for any responsible post in any Administration in the future.

All his political life has been notorious for changing opinions, just like the weathercock, which vacillates and gyrates with the changing winds. . . .

---

[1] Boothby had put down an amendment urging the fuller definition of the status and procedure of Committees of the House of Commons. During his speech he said: 'I know that some of my hon Friends think that I put that Amendment down because of my association and friendship with the right hon Gentleman the Member for Epping (Mr Churchill). It is not so.' His sole motive, he said, was to ensure that the House of Commons was not 'careless of its privileges'.

It is about time this House took notice of this menace. If he were an ordinary human mortal, such chameleon-like performances would pass unnoticed, but he is not an ordinary human mortal. He is an extraordinary human being, with such power that he constitutes a definite menace to the peaceful solution of the many problems with which this country is confronted at the present time. The power of that menace is not decreasing; it is increasing in geometrical progression downwards. It has now become atavistic. . . .

A high proportion of the debate consisted of personal attacks on Churchill's motives. Sir Thomas Inskip, in the concluding speech, declared that Churchill himself, in criticizing the Joint Select Committee in a speech in the House on 29 March 1933, had derided their impartiality, and 'scandalized the judges'. When the debate was over, Churchill's friends hastened to comfort and to congratulate him. Lord Wolmer[1] wrote that same day: 'The Joint Committee never was judicial! S.B. has tricked his Party into muzzling itself. The evidence has been "staged". Back stairs intrigues are rife.' That evening Frances Stevenson wrote in her diary:

Winston has been unlucky again. The Report of the Committee of Privileges went unanimously against him. The Debate today, while not being exactly a triumph for the Gov was not exactly a triumph for Winston. He is unpopular in the House. Nevertheless the Gov must feel the backwash, Baldwin having been forced to say that the India Committee is not a judicial one.

On June 14 Oliver Locker Lampson telegraphed to Churchill: 'I marvel at your courage and success in very adverse circumstances.' A former Conservative MP, James Rankin,[2] wrote that same day: 'I write merely as an obscure individual moved by the injustice of last night's debate. . . . I think you would be cheered to know how many there are of us ordinary folk who are not lacking in loyalty to you in the appreciation of what you have done, not only in this, but on many other occasions.' Cyril Asquith also wrote to Churchill on June 14, remarking that it was a 'fine speech and good to listen to'. Of course, Asquith wrote,

---

[1] Roundell Cecil Palmer, Viscount Wolmer, 1887–1971. Known as 'Top'. Eldest son of the 2nd Earl of Selborne and a grandson of the 3rd Marquess of Salisbury. Educated at Winchester and University College Oxford. In 1910 he married Churchill's cousin, Grace Ridley daughter of the 1st Viscount Ridley. Conservative MP for Newton, Lancashire, 1910–18; and for Aldershot, 1918–40. Assistant-Director, War Trade Department, 1917–18. Parliamentary Secretary, Board of Trade, 1922–24. Assistant Postmaster-General, 1924–29. Succeeded his father as 3rd Earl, 1942. Minister of Economic Warfare, 1942–45. President of the Church Army, 1949–61. His brother Robert was killed in action in Mesopotamia in 1916. His eldest son was killed accidentally by a shell while on active service in 1942.

[2] James Stuart Rankin, 1880–1960. Educated at Sedbergh and University College Oxford. Captain, Royal Field Artillery, France and Mesopotamia, 1914–18. Conservative MP for East Toxteth, 1916–24.

'with a packed C^{tee} and a packed House you couldn't expect proper recognition of its merit'; and he added:

Dialectically, the things that irritated me most were (1) the tacit assumption that because the C^{tee} had arrived at certain conclusions, those conclusions must be right (on which the whole of Simon's very adroit speech was founded). (2) the refusal (also tacit) to publish such parts of the evidence as could not be shown to be witheld in the public interest. Inskip's was the only presentable attempt to justify this. (3) the slight bathos created (in minds uninformed as to its context and significance) by the word 'inappropriate' (an intrinsically mild expression).

This bathos is as good an illustration as can be imagined of the effect of not publishing letters.

'I think,' Churchill replied to Cyril Asquith on June 18, 'the ultimate political reaction will be very favourable to the purpose I am pursuing and I do not at all regret the course I took.' But the public criticisms were intense, *The Times* being especially censorious of Churchill's actions. 'I believe you have done great good,' Sir Alfred Knox wrote on June 19, 'in spite of that horrible "Times".' On June 18 Sir Archibald Sinclair, Churchill's close friend for nearly twenty years, sent him a summary of Parliamentary opinion. It was not encouraging; Lord Reading had 'strongly condemned' Churchill's action as 'mischievous' and Sir John Simon 'considered that it could do nothing but harm alike to your own and to the public interest'. Sinclair added that he had gained the impression from his conversation with Simon 'that he regarded your agitation as mischievous in method and premature in time, but a good deal more formidable than he would have cared to admit'. Sinclair had one further piece of news to report: 'when I called in on your old enemy Snowden' all of a sudden he declared 'quite of his own accord' that he thought that Churchill 'had had a pretty rough deal from the Committee of Privileges'. Snowden had made it clear to Sinclair that although he was still a convinced supporter of the White Paper 'he agreed that the course of the debate had been most unlucky for you and he saw clearly that the House had failed to appreciate the significance that a breach of privilege had been committed'.

Hoare was delighted at the result of the debate, writing to George Stanley on June 15:

The debate itself ended about 8.30 in a unanimous House with Winston's friends greatly discomforted and discredited. I do hope that the result will have a lasting effect upon the situation. If it has cramped the style of the die-hards and weakened the unscrupulous and violent propaganda that they have been carrying on in almost every constituency, all the worry and trouble through which we have passed will have been worth while. . . .

However much Churchill's motives were questioned and his methods derided by his political opponents, he did receive some encouragement from both friends and strangers. On June 26 Lady Lambton[1] wrote from Zurich:

. . . I admire you *quite enormously*, for your action in recent events. And I like to think there is a bright spot in England still, which won't bow the knee to insolent might. When I met the stalwarts of the other side last week, I asked has Winston failed in his case, they said 'completely'. I then asked 'under the same circumstances would Hoare and Derby do what they did again'. They looked uncomfortable and I knew my point was gained. And so I said how can you say he failed. He has made a standard & upheld a principle which will last longer than a momentary Parliamentary success, & which makes me and all the other lovers of England say 'Thank God for Winston'.

On June 27 H. Y. Robinson issued a public statement explaining the action he had taken in sending Churchill the Chamber of Commerce documents. Given such action on his part, Robinson wrote, 'Mr Churchill had no option but to take the course he did'; and he added: 'The courage and ability he has displayed in fighting this battle for Lancashire will, I am sure, go down in history as one of the finest examples of British Statesmanship.'

Four months later Churchill sent several friends copies of his Committee of Privileges memorandum. It was, wrote Lord Wolmer on October 30, 'a masterly document', and Lord Lloyd wrote that same day: 'I always thought you had a strong case: I had never, however, realised till I read this document how overwhelmingly strong the case was and I cannot, having read it, see how the Committee could bring itself, in the circumstances, to come to the conclusion they did.'

---

[1] Lady Katherine de Vere Somerset, daughter of the 10th Duke of St Albans. In 1921 she married the sixth son of the 2nd Earl of Durham, Major-General Sir William Lambton (who died in 1936).

29

1934: Armaments, 'Sounding a Warning'

REBUFFED by the Committee of Privileges, and distressed by the hostility of the Conservative Party hierarchy, Churchill continued to assert the primacy of the Parliamentary process, and to warn against all attempts to weaken, to belittle or to replace the Parliamentary system. He made his views public in a series of magazine articles during the spring and summer of 1934, insisting above all on the need to tolerate, and to take seriously, the opinions of those who, although without a powerful organization to back them, spoke with concern about current problems. The need for independent views to be heard was even more urgent, he believed, at a time of National Government, when party differences had been muted, and political issues blurred. Writing in *Answers* on March 31 he argued that in the modern age of great combinations both of labour and of capital 'the individual must be all the more our care', and that this was of particular importance in the political sphere. It was quite wrong, he insisted, to regard the few independent Members of Parliament as a 'public nuisance', or to resent their 'awkward way of thinking things out for themselves'.

During June Churchill worked to finish his second *Marlborough* volume, helped by John Wheldon at Chartwell, while Colonel Pakenham-Walsh and Commander Owen continued to send material on the military and naval aspects. On June 30 while in the midst of his work, Churchill was greatly saddened by the death of his cousin 'Sunny', the 9th Duke of Marlborough, with whom since his childhood he had been on terms of intimate friendship. 'I think much of you in your sorrow at losing so suddenly a friend & kinsman who was so dear to you,' Sir Archibald Sinclair wrote to Churchill on July 21, and he recalled also Lord Birkenhead's death. 'You are surrounded,' he wrote, 'by devoted friends but none, I know, can replace the two whom you have so recently lost.'

The death of his cousin provoked Churchill to sombre reflections, but his friends tried to cheer him. '*Please* don't talk of yourself as a very old man,' Lady Lambton wrote during June. 'You are letting us *all* down by doing so. To me you are still a promising lad.'

During 1934 Churchill began to concentrate his attentions on exposing the weakness of Britain's air policy, and seeking to create public concern at Germany's growing air strength. His speeches and articles on the themes of air defence and air power gained him the serious attention of a wide public. On May 30 a leading London businessman, Sir Stanley Machin,[1] asked him to speak to the City Carlton Club. 'While any subject you might choose would create great interest,' Machin wrote, 'it appears to me that a speech from a high authority to a representative City audience on what, in my opinion, is a deplorable weakness in defence (especially in the air) would be of great value and might go far.' As the summer progressed Churchill continued in his outspoken criticisms of Britain's air defence. This he did without fear of the political consequences for himself. 'I am happily in an independent position,' he wrote in the *Sunday Dispatch* on June 29, 'having had all the public office any man could want.' On July 7 he spoke at Wanstead, in his constituency, about the slow pace of Britain's air preparations. It was true that Baldwin had told the House of Commons that the plans were being made, but, Churchill insisted, 'All that ought to have been done long ago. We ought to have a large vote of credit to double our Air Force; we ought to have it now, and a larger vote of credit as soon as possible to redouble the Air Force.'

On July 9 the *Daily Mail* published a long article by Churchill in which he wrote: 'I marvel at the complacency of Ministers in the face of the frightful experiences through which we have all so newly passed. I look with wonder upon our thoughtless crowds disporting themselves in the summer sunshine, and upon this unheeding House of Commons, which seems to have no higher function than to cheer a Minister'; and all the while, across the North Sea, 'a terrible process is astir. *Germany is arming.*'

[1] Stanley Machin, 1861–1939. Member of the Council of Foreign Bondholders. President of the London Chamber of Commerce, 1920–22. President of the Association of British Chambers of Commerce, 1924–25. Knighted, 1926. A member of the Junior Carlton and City Carlton Clubs.

Discussions on the Defence Requirements Committee report had been going on at Cabinet level for nearly four months. On April 30 Lord Londonderry had told his colleagues: 'There was strong public pressure to increase our air force, and it was time the Cabinet made up its mind definitely and told the country the truth.' Such proposals, MacDonald commented, 'were not going to be popular', but Lord Hailsham stated that 'he had never been under the delusion that the proposals would be popular. He urged, however, that whatever decision was reached it was essential to announce it, as the responsibility of the National Government for the safety of the country was involved.' On May 3 Hailsham pointed out to his colleagues that in asking for further expenditure up to £70,000,000 in five years 'the departments were not asking for anything new or for any rearmament', but only to reach an 'effective strength' which had already been approved. Nevertheless, on June 25, Neville Chamberlain spoke of the economic problems: 'to put it bluntly', he had written in a memorandum for their consideration, 'we are presented with proposals impossible to carry out'. Chamberlain commented: 'it was necessary to cut our coat according to the cloth', and he went on to oppose a suggestion by Baldwin for a defence loan 'as he regarded that as the broad road that led to destruction'.

Chamberlain argued for 'considerations of priority', and suggested concentrating first on the Air Force. This was accepted on July 2, when Baldwin told his colleagues on the Cabinet Committee that the Defence Requirement Committee's recommendations were 'a counsel of perfection' that could not be achieved. To this Lord Hailsham had pointed out that 'it was an estimate of our worst deficiencies', but his protest was to no avail.

As a result of the Ministerial decision of July 2, to focus first on air force needs, the problem of German and British air rearmament was being discussed by a Cabinet sub-committee on the Allocation of Air Forces. At the sub-committee's meeting on July 5 the Chief of the Air Staff, Sir Edward Ellington,[1] pointed out that the capacity of the British aircraft industry was already greater than the calls being made upon it. Four days later Ellington circulated a memorandum showing the Air Ministry's plans to prepare the Royal Air Force for a war in

[1] Edward Leonard Ellington, 1877–1967. 2nd Lieutenant, Royal Artillery, 1897; Major, 1914. Deputy Assistant Quartermaster-General, 1914–15. Lieutenant-Colonel, 1915. Major-General, Royal Air Force, 1918. Appointed by Churchill Director General of Aircraft Production (later Supply) and Research, Air Ministry, 1919–21. Knighted, 1920. Air Vice-Marshal, Commanding the Royal Air Force, Middle East, 1922–23; India, 1923–26; Iraq, 1926–28. Air Officer Commanding-in-Chief, Air Defence of Britain, 1929–31. Chief of the Air Staff, 1933–37. Inspector General, Royal Air Force, 1937–40.

Europe 'in about eight years time', that is, in about 1942. At a Cabinet sub-committee on July 6 Ellington pointed out that the Defence Requirements Committee had suggested that any adequate air programme would have to include 100% reserves, thereby adding £10 million to the £20 million already requested. But speaking for Neville Chamberlain and the Treasury, Sir Richard Hopkins said that as 'only a limited sum' was available for all three Services, 'the Chancellor had suggested dispensing with reserves'. This, Ellington stressed, 'was a big risk', but he went on to state that as far as the German Air Force's capacity to make war, 'he considered that it would really be about eight years before it became a truly formidable weapon'.

At a further Cabinet sub-committee on July 10 the German air potential was put at 48 squadrons by 1935, 82 by 1939 and 123 by 1942. The provision of forty more British squadrons by March 1939, Cunliffe-Lister insisted, 'would be a great deterrent to war and would discourage Germany in time of peace'. But Ellington pointed out that 'at present' only five squadrons had war reserves. Cunliffe-Lister commented that 'there was no necessity to inform the House of Commons what the actual state of the war reserves was'. But in its report the sub-committee stressed that without a further £10 million for reserves the Air Force 'would not be capable of operating on a war footing for more than a week or two'.

Speaking in the House of Commons on July 13, Churchill commented with approval on the change that was slowly taking place in Parliamentary opinion. Earlier in the debate the leader of the Opposition, George Lansbury, had spoken, he said, 'in a courageous manner' in stating that the Labour Party's 'abhorrence of war' did not extend 'to passive recognition of flagrant wrongdoing'. Sir Herbert Samuel, he said, was likewise to be congratulated for abandoning his long-held view that it was French armaments and French militarism that were the main barrier to European reconciliation. Churchill again urged the need for a strong, united League of Nations, and stressed the 'dominant fact' of German rearmament, especially in the air. He went on to warn that Britain's air strength was, in his view, too low. In 1914 Britain possessed 'a supreme fleet'; now she was without the modern equivalent, an adequate air force. On this topic he answered Sir Herbert Samuel who, during the debate, had described Churchill's plea at Wanstead for a doubled and then redoubled air force as 'rather the language of a Malay running amok than of a responsible British statesman'. Churchill's language, Samuel had added, was that 'of blind and causeless panic'. In replying to this charge Churchill said that the existing situation 'is in many ways more dangerous' than 1914, when he and Samuel had been

Cabinet colleagues. But Anthony Eden told the House: 'where I differ, with respect, from my Right hon Friend the Member for Epping, is that he seems to conceive that in order to have an effective world consultative system nations have to be heavily armed. I do not agree. . . . General disarmament must continue to be the ultimate aim.'

During the debate Clement Attlee also questioned the need for re-armament, and said, of Hitler: 'I think we can generally say today that his dictatorship is gradually falling down.'

On July 16, in a secret note for the Cabinet, Sir Maurice Hankey reiterated that the Chief of Staff's Annual Review for 1933 had disclosed 'considerable deficiencies in our Defence Forces', due largely to the Government's policy in connection with the 'disarmament question' since 1929. On the following day, in a private letter to Baldwin, Lord Londonderry warned that 'a weak air force' would be neither a deterrent to aggression, nor an adequate defence. 'In the absence of proper defences,' Londonderry added, 'there would be nothing to stop the enemy concentrating his maximum bombing force against London and continuing to bombard it until he had achieved his aim.' The Cabinet accepted the plan for forty new squadrons on July 18. It was also decided that this plan, costing £20 million, should be spread over five years. This Cabinet decision was made in spite of Ellington's two warnings, of July 6 and July 10, about the plan's lack of adequate reserves. Under this new scheme, known as Scheme A, Britain's first line air strength was intended by March 1939 to reach 84 squadrons (960 aeroplanes) for home defence, 27 squadrons (292 aeroplanes) for overseas and 16½ squadrons (213 aeroplanes) for the Fleet Air Arm, a total of 1,465 aeroplanes.[1]

---

[1] As a result of Chamberlain's insistence, the defence expenditure proposed in the Defence Requirements Committee report was scaled down substantially, from £76 million to £50 million. Within this reduced scale, priority was given to air force expansion, which was actually raised by £10 million at the expense of the Royal Navy and the Army, both of whose proposed increases were halved. The Army regarded this decision as an unfair one; on July 30 the Military Assistant Secretary to the Committee of Imperial Defence, Colonel Pownall, wrote in his diary: 'It is extraordinary the effect of (so-called) public opinion, the press and the Lord Lloyd–Churchill group on the minds of Ministers. It is slow working perhaps, but if continued it has inevitable effects.' Pownall believed the decision to be 'actuated by Air Panic'. At a meeting of the Cabinet on July 31 the Secretary of State for War 'took this opportunity', the minutes recorded, 'to warn the Cabinet that the Army was not in a condition to fight at the present time, and that under the programme now proposed it would not be in readiness until some unspecified date after 1938, when the deficiencies had been made good. The reason for this was that the Chancellor of the Exchequer could not provide the money, so that the five-year programme had had to be cut down from £40,000,000 to £20,000,000. The Cabinet would have to take the responsibility for that, though of course he took his share. He was anxious that his colleagues should be under no misapprehension on the subject.'

Churchill's warnings on air weakness, and the coming Defence debate in the House of Commons, prompted a retired Air Commodore, Peregrine Fellowes,[1] to write to him on July 21, stressing the danger of an air policy devised 'by those who are out of touch with practical flying conditions, a state of affairs which all important countries but ourselves have adjusted'. This question, wrote Fellowes, ought to be raised by someone 'to whom the country will listen', and he offered to call on Churchill in order to put him 'in possession of the facts'. On July 24 Churchill asked Fellowes to send him a detailed note of what he had in mind, and two days later he received a six-page memorandum, in the course of which Fellowes wrote of the serious lack of 'practical knowledge of flying' among senior officers at the Air Ministry. 'Many senior officers,' he wrote, 'seldom flew even as passengers.' In Germany, Fellowes pointed out, 'civil aviation is under the direction of real flying men who are competent and knowledgeable'.

A debate on Britain's air policy was to be held on July 30. On behalf of the Labour Party, Attlee had brought a motion of censure against the Government for having announced an increase—albeit a small one—in Britain's air construction. The Liberals, led by Sir Herbert Samuel, supported the censure motion. During the debate, Baldwin explained that the 52 squadrons laid down in 1923 had been 10 short of completion in 1932, at the opening of the Disarmament Conference. For the two years since no squadrons had been added. The 'sole reason' for the delay, he said, was to 'set an example to other countries'. All other countries had moved far ahead, so that what the British had been doing in effect was 'practising unilateral disarmament'. The new programme was intended to raise the total number of British aircraft both at home and overseas from 844 to 1,465 by 1939. In defending the policy of greater air strength, Baldwin pointed out that 'when you think of the defence of England you no longer think of the chalk cliffs of Dover; you think of the Rhine. That is where the frontier lies.'

Churchill, who spoke in support of the Government, again sought an assurance that Britain would never be allowed to fall behind Germany in air strength. Much of his information had been provided by his friend Desmond Morton, the head of the Government's Industrial Intelligence Centre, who set out on a single sheet of paper the facts which Churchill

---

[1] Peregrine Forbes Morant Fellowes, 1883–1955. Educated at Winchester and HMS *Britannia*. On active service 1914–18 (wounded, DSO and bar, prisoner-of-war, 1918). Director of Airship Development, Air Ministry, 1924–29. Retired with the rank of Air Commodore, 1933. Leader of the Mount Everest Air Expedition, 1933.

then added to his speech notes.[1] According to Morton's figures, even on existing first-line strength Britain, with 910 aeroplanes, came sixth after France (1,650), the USSR (1,500), Japan (1,385), the USA (1,100) and Italy (1,000). Under present plans, Britain would have 1,304 by 1939. But Germany, according to Morton, would have 500 by the end of 1935, with a subsequent capacity, beginning in 1936, of a further thousand a year. 'At the present time,' Churchill told the House of Commons, 'we are the fifth or sixth air Power in the world,' and at the existing rate of building 'would find ourselves worse off in 1939 relatively than we are now—and it is relativity that counts. By that time France, Soviet Russia, Japan, the United States, and Italy, if they carry out their present intentions, will be farther ahead of us than they are now'; so too would Germany.

Churchill noted that even for the existing 'tiny, timid, tentative, tardy' increase in air strength for which the Government had asked 'they are to be censured by the whole united forces of the Socialist and Liberal parties. . . .' He opposed the vote of censure, telling the House that while he disliked the 'apologies and soothing procedures' adopted by the Government, he feared even more the Opposition's refusal to face the facts.

Churchill went on to set out 'some broad facts' which in his view could not be contradicted, and ought to be countered by immediate British air force expansion on a substantial and decisive scale:

I first assert that Germany has already, in violation of the Treaty, created a military air force which is now nearly two-thirds as strong as our present home defence air force. That is the first statement which I put before the

---

[1] In his war memoirs Churchill stated that Morton had received from Ramsay MacDonald 'permission to talk freely to me and keep me well informed'. Several authors have stated that this permission was given in writing, and that it was renewed by both Baldwin (in 1935) and Chamberlain (in 1937). No evidence has been found for any of these assertions; indeed, as the reader will see, much of the factual and statistical information which Morton gave Churchill about German rearmament enabled Churchill to intensify his criticisms of respective Governments, and to do so making use of intelligence materials which those Governments repeatedly stressed (in rejecting Churchill's arguments) that Churchill could not know about. In fact, Morton gave Churchill this secret information, and many critical assessments of the Government's policies over several years, because he was convinced that German rearmament was 'not as fully realised as it should be' (letter to Churchill of 17 August 1934, quoted on page 558). Furthermore, the Government decided at a Cabinet meeting on 25 November 1934, to tell the House of Commons that Churchill's figures were exaggerated; not something they could have done if he had received those figures with their frequent approval, and the charge was made by Baldwin himself three days later and often repeated. A possible cause of the misunderstanding was MacDonald's offer to Lord Londonderry on 13 April 1935 to supply Churchill with 'all the real figures', to which Churchill replied: 'I thought my own were better' (see page 635 of this volume).

Government for their consideration. The second is that Germany is rapidly increasing this air force, not only by large sums of money which figure in her estimates, but also by public subscriptions—very often almost forced subscriptions—which are in progress and have been in progress for some time all over Germany.

By the end of 1935 the German air force will be nearly equal in numbers and efficiency—and after all no one must underrate German efficiency, because there could be no more deadly mistake than that—it will be nearly equal, as I say, to our home defence air force at that date even if the Government's present proposals are carried out.

The third statement is that if Germany continues this expansion and if we continue to carry out our scheme, then some time in 1936 Germany will be definitely and substantially stronger in the air than Great Britain. Fourthly, and this is the point which is causing anxiety, once they have got that lead we may never be able to overtake them.[1]

There were other facts which Churchill believed to be of importance. German civil aviation was three times the size of its British counterpart, and at the same time was designed in such a way as to be easily converted for military purposes. Indeed, the whole scheme of conversion 'has been prepared and organised with minute and earnest forethought'. The same was true of civil and amateur pilots; Germany had 500 qualified glider pilots as against 50 in Britain. Yet even these pilots had 'air sense', and could quickly be trained for military aviation. Weakness in the air, Churchill warned, 'has a very direct bearing on the foreign situation'. Only if Britain were strong could her air force, in conjunction with that of France, act as 'a deterrent' against German aggression. As for the Labour Party, they were 'the driving force' behind the public demand for caution and disarmament, and he regretted that so much attention was paid 'to these evil counsels'.

Replying to Churchill, Simon stated that he could not give any 'guarantee' that Germany was observing her obligations under the Treaty of Versailles, and he added: 'I am free to say that Germany's interest in air development is very marked.' During the debate, several speakers had poured scorn on Churchill and his arguments. According to Sir Herbert Samuel: 'It would seem as if he were engaged not in giving sound, sane advice to the country but as if he were engaged in a

[1] A secret Air Ministry memorandum written in May 1938 showed that although the Air Ministry had, in 1935, hoped to reach parity with Germany by 1937, this aim had been abandoned, and that the estimated 3,240 German first-line planes by the end of 1939 were to be met instead by a British expansion scheme of only 2,373 planes by 1940. On 25 October 1938 the then Secretary of State for Air, Sir Kingsley Wood, told the Cabinet that the new estimate for 1 August 1939 was 1,890 first-line and 1,502 reserves for Britain (a total of 3,392) as against 4,030 first-line and 3,000 reserves for Germany (a total of 7,030).

reckless game of bridge, doubling and redoubling and for terribly high stakes. All these formulas are dangerous.' According to James Maxton:[1]

I found something very terrifying in the speech of the right hon member for Epping. The Right Hon Gentleman the member for Epping must remember from his position of relative irresponsibility below the Gangway that his name is still a big name in international affairs . . . his cynical, sarcastic words in this House are taken much more seriously abroad than he takes them himself.

Sir Stafford Cripps remarked:

As the Right Hon member for Epping stood in his place declaiming, one could picture him as some old baron in the Middle Ages who is laughing at the idea of the possibility of disarmament in the baronies of this country and pointing out that the only way in which he and his feudal followers could maintain their safety and their cows was by having as strong an armament as possible.

The Labour vote of censure was defeated by 404 votes to 60. Among those who congratulated Churchill on his speech was Sir Terence O'Connor, who wrote on July 31:

I hope that you are as happy as I am at the realisation that all our 'privilege' disappointment has failed to lessen the position you hold in the House & in public opinion. It was a gallant speech yesterday & outshone all else in the debate & the obvious impression which it made on the House showed that au fond there is no lessening of your hold on affairs.

On August 1 Lord Rothermere wrote to Churchill, telling him that he was underestimating Germany's air potential. 'What is your information,' he asked, 'which leads you to suppose that Germany, at the end of next year, will have only a few hundred aeroplanes.' According to Rothermere, the Germans would have as many as 20,000 aeroplanes by the end of 1935, and he went on to ask: 'Is everybody in this country blind?' Churchill showed Rothermere's letter to Desmond Morton for his comments, before replying, on August 6:

My information comes from a source which ought to be well informed, and which I have found trustworthy. It is to the effect that the Germans have *now* a regular military air force, in violation of the treaty, of three hundred aeroplanes fully organised, as against our home defence force of five hundred and fifty aeroplanes. The Germans are increasing this by two hundred organised military aeroplanes to a total of five hundred by the end of 1935, by

---

[1] James Maxton, 1885–1946. Known as 'Jimmy'. Educated at Glasgow University. A teacher; Scottish Organizer of the Glasgow Federation of the Independent Labour Party, 1919–22. Labour MP for Glasgow Bridgeton, 1922–46. Chairman of the Independent Labour Party, 1931 and 1934–39. Biographer of Lenin.

which time we shall have fifty more under the Government scheme, or six hundred in all at home apart from the Navy. This of course takes no account of the German civil aviation which is certainly five times as great as ours, and a large part of which is rapidly convertible into war machines.

I said all this in my speech, of which I send you a Hansard. These statements which the Government virtually admitted are quite sufficient to convict their scheme of hopeless inadequacy. My informant to whom I shewed your letter is sure that your figure of twenty thousand can have no reality. He says that if now the Germans began manufacturing on a war basis with three shifts in their factories, and turning over all the emergency factories now engaged on civil production, they could by the end of next year develop a manufacturing capacity in the twelve months following, of twenty thousand aeroplanes. This compares with the twenty-four thousand a year I was making for you and Weir at the end of the war.

Churchill went on to warn Rothermere strongly against exaggeration:

I think it is wise not to overstate the case when enough is indisputable to justify much greater action. If what you say is true and were believed, many weak brethren would regard the task as hopeless and we should defeat our own object. I prefer to err in these circumstances, on the side of understatement. If I can get further information I can easily increase my figures without any reproach.

In his letter, Churchill told Rothermere that he intended, in November, to initiate a debate on air defence by moving an amendment to the address. To this end he would continue to assemble the facts, and during the debate he would seek to 'extort more vigorous action' from the Government. 'Whether it will be too little or too late,' he added, 'is a matter upon which I am glad not to have the responsibility. I feel a deep and increasing sense of anxiety.'

Rothermere was not convinced, and in a further letter on August 10 he insisted that the existing German air preparations 'far exceed anything that was accomplished by any of the belligerents during the war'. On August 11 he wrote again. 'All my information,' he insisted, 'corroborates my belief that Germany is building aeroplanes in series just like sewing machines or motor cars.' Anxious neither to understate nor to magnify German air strength, Churchill sent Rothermere's second and third letters to Desmond Morton, again seeking his comments. Replying to Churchill on August 17, Morton wrote:

Whereas I am all for continuing the battle for an adequate Air Force in this country, in view of a German development which is sufficiently disturbing, and which I am persuaded is not as fully realised as it should be, I think it would be the gravest pity to spoil a good case by anything which might later be revealed to be gross or even ludicrous exaggeration.

It is therefore vital that any new information, greatly at variance with the mass of information from all other quarters, should be meticulously examined before too much weight is rested upon it. . . .

R. has misunderstood what 'your informant' said about the size of the German Air Force. 'Your informant' did not say it would number 500 machines by the end of next year, but that some time next year Germany would have a first-line air strength of 500 aircraft in the balanced proportion of types, with a corresponding completely organised ground staff, aerodromes and proportionate reserves of aircraft and pilots. Your references to the same matter were correct. No one has supposed that you consider Germany would only possess 500 aircraft in 1935. Your insinuations were very much more alarming.

Morton added that he had heard rumours that the Germans hoped to attain by about 1939 a first-line air strength of between 1,500 and 1,800 aircraft. This, he pointed out, was three times what the Germans would have by the end of 1935, and twice what Britain expected to have in 1939. Yet on August 23 Sir Maurice Hankey wrote to Baldwin, in a letter marked 'Private & Personal', that in his opinion 'the Cabinet are over-rating the *imminence* of the German peril. The peril is there all right, but will take much more than 5 years to develop in the military and air sense.'

In the second week of August Churchill left England for a three-week working holiday in France, where he and his son, and Lindemann, were the guests of Maxine Elliot[1] in her villa, the Château de L'Horizon, at Golfe-Juan. Mrs Pearman, who also travelled with them, continued to take dictation both for volume three of *Marlborough* and for general correspondence. On August 16 Churchill wrote to his wife, who had remained at Chartwell, with news of his progress on *Marlborough*. 'I have had to work nearly all day at the proofs,' he wrote. 'A very strange way to earn a living!'[2] he commented. On August 22 he wrote again:

I was disgusted by the DM [Daily Mail]'s boosting of Hitler. R. [Rothermere] is sincerely pacifist. He wants us to be vy strongly armed & frightfully

---

[1] Jessie Dermot, 1868–1940. Born in Maine, USA. She adopted the name 'Maxine Elliot' for her stage career. In 1914 she organized a Belgian Relief Barge, from which in fifteen months, she fed and clothed some 350,000 refugees.

[2] In February 1933 Churchill had received £2,000 from the *News of the World* for a series of twelve articles entitled 'The World's Great Stories', including Ben-Hur, Ivanhoe, Jane Eyre and Don Quixote; but that same month he had paid £1,600 of debts incurred by his son.

obsequious at the same time. Thus he hopes to avoid seeing another war. Anyhow it is a more practical attitude than our socialist politicians. They wish us to remain disarmed & exceedingly abusive.

I was glad so many had the courage to vote against making that gangster autocrat for life.

On August 20 Lord Riddell had asked Churchill to write a new series of twelve articles for the *News of the World* on his life story. 'The matter would have to be popular,' Riddell wrote, 'not too much politics.' The last article, Churchill wrote to Riddell on August 25 from Golfe Juan, would be called 'Conclusion (but not I hope Finis)'. The first of these articles was published on 13 January 1935, the last, entitled 'Rise and Fall of Parties and politicians', two and a half months later. The whole series was called 'My Life', and earned Churchill £4,200. During August, five of Churchill's articles, written in July, were published in Britain and the United States.[1]

On August 27 Churchill wrote again to his wife: 'Tomorrow at nine we start in two cars—one the Prof's—for Grenoble along Napoleon's route,' and he added: 'I really must try to write a Napoleon before I die. But the work piles up ahead & I wonder whether I shall have the time & strength.'[2]

Churchill, his son and Lindemann returned slowly from the South of France to Chartwell, stopping briefly at Aix-les-Bains, where they saw Stanley Baldwin, and discussed with him the need for a more active air defence policy, both in research and in preparation.[3]

On August 29, while Churchill was still in France, the Director of Talks at the BBC, Charles Siepmann,[4] asked Churchill to broadcast in a

---

[1] On September 30 Josiah Wedgwood tried to persuade Churchill to write the most modern of the volumes of the newly planned History of Parliament. There would, he wrote, be £2,000 for research 'by devils' for the period 1885 to 1918, and he added: 'It must be started directly ... because the war record of the House must be done before it grows dim. Those 26 who died were your friends and mine, and the chapter in the war record of that great House can only be done by you.' Churchill, however, was forced because of his other commitments to turn down this request.

[2] Three months earlier, on May 14, Baldwin had visited Avallon, where Napoleon had stayed on his return from Elba in March 1815. This fact was printed at the bottom of the postcard which Baldwin, remembering Churchill's ambition to write a life of Napoleon, had sent him on May 14. 'Read below,' Baldwin wrote, 'and admit that I have gone one better than you! You will have to put in a night here when you begin the Life!'

[3] On August 8, in a letter to *The Times*, Lindemann had attacked the 'defeatist attitude' of those who said, as Baldwin had done, that 'the bomber will always get through' and had called for a concerted scientific effort to meet the challenge of aerial attack.

[4] Charles Arthur Siepmann, 1899–1985. Educated at Clifton. On active service in Europe, 1917–18 (Military Cross, Italy, June 1918). Keble College Oxford, 1919–21. Education Officer, HM Borstal Institutions, Feltham and Rochester, 1924–27. Joined the BBC, 1927; Director

forthcoming 'causes of war' series. 'Would you be prepared,' Siepmann wrote, 'to contribute a talk to the series, sounding a warning note against unpreparedness and developing your own point of view on the subject, both in general terms and with particular reference to this country?' Churchill welcomed this opportunity; Siepmann's letter was yet another sign that his views on Foreign Affairs were becoming more widely listened to, and respected.

During September 1934 Alexander Korda[1] asked Churchill to write a full-length film script on the reign of George V, for the Silver Jubilee in 1936. Randolph agreed to help with the planning and research, and Korda offered Churchill £10,000 for the completed script. Churchill accepted, writing to Korda on September 24: 'I am going to begin this scenario immediately and side track all my other work. I hope to send you in a week or ten days a preliminary outline of my scheme in such a form that you can immediately put one of your best technicians on to it. . . .' On the following day Churchill and his wife left Chartwell for a month's holiday in the eastern Mediterranean, where they were to be the guests of Lord Moyne[2] on board his yacht, *Rosaura*. While Churchill was abroad John Wheldon assembled the materials for the third *Marlborough* volume, and Keith Feiling began work on the multi-volume *History of the English-Speaking Peoples*, which Churchill hoped to finish by 1939. On September 22 Churchill wrote to Feiling:

As you know, I wish to give special prominence in the first section of the work to the origin and growth of those institutions, laws and customs and national characteristics which are the common inheritance, or supposed to be, of the English speaking world. Language and literature play a large part, and indeed these studies would be as it were threaded together by a vivid narrative picking up the dramatic and dominant episodes and by no means undertaking a complete account.

Churchill asked Feiling to prepare a rough scheme of the chapters of the whole work, as well as a list of books 'which I should read' covering

---

of Talks, 1923–35; of Regional Relations, 1935–36; of Programme Planning, 1936–39. University Lecturer at Harvard, 1939–42. Office of War Information, San Francisco, 1942–45. Professor of Education, New York University, 1946–67. A pioneer in the teaching of the use of broadcasting in schools, and adviser to the Ford Foundation on educational television.

[1] Alexander Korda, 1893–1956. Born in Hungary. Educated at Budapest University. Film producer in Budapest, Vienna, Berlin, Hollywood and Paris. Founder and Chairman of London Film Productions Ltd, 1932. Became a British subject, 1936. Founded Alexander Korda Productions, 1939. Made 112 films, including *The Scarlet Pimpernel* (1935), *The Third Man* (1950) and *Richard III* (1955). Knighted, 1942.

[2] Churchill's friend, and former Financial Secretary to the Treasury, Walter Guinness, who in 1932 had been created Baron Moyne.

each of the periods: hopefully 'three or four first rate authorities for each period'. 'There is of course no question of research of any kind,' he added, 'but of course we should base ourselves wherever possible upon the original sources.'

Travelling overnight from Paris on September 25, Churchill and his wife reached Marseilles on the morning of September 26, where they joined the *Rosaura*. Six days later they reached Athens. During the journey Churchill worked on the text of his film script. From Athens, on October 3, he wrote to Korda with his ideas on the actual film-making process:

Suppose we took one of the innumerable excellent photographs of three or four pre-war Cabinet ministers, or of some pre-war scene with a group of people in it. Starting from the original photographs could not these figures be made to move on the Micky Mouse plan? Even if they only moved for a few seconds it would just enable the necessary points to be made.

For instance, after the Irish Treaty in 1922 the King received all his Ministers who had signed it at Buckingham Palace and had a photograph taken, which was published. If this static picture could just be made to move only for ten seconds, it would solve the point. . . .

Churchill also suggested re-filming the old flickering newsreels to get 'a greater smoothness', possibly throwing 'a spotlight impression upon the parts of each old picture that you wish to illustrate'. Churchill then discussed the problems of music and sound, telling Korda:

There should be an underlying accompaniment of music throughout the film. Sometimes it rises to dominate, as in the surge and chorus of a patriotic tune —sometimes it is barely perceptible. Sometimes it should express a rising storm and stress of events, and then can fall into a lull. And ever and anon there should be a lilt, almost like an echo, of the well-known popular airs of those days which illustrate the theme.

About the talkie aspect. I think we should have no rule except to use everything unhesitatingly which best conveys the meaning. I contemplate that I should speak some passages myself, like a Greek chorus, and thus put points that can be put in no other way. Certainly I contemplate a few sentences of peroration near the end. But side by side with this, some of our characters in certain passages, and in certain passages only, will talk to each other. In addition where convenient we will readily use written captions. The rise and fall of the music should be made to balance this, so that on the whole there is an even catering to eye and ear.

The story, Churchill added, should be based in the first instance 'upon most serious lines', dominated by unemployment insurance, old age pensions and the other social advances of the pre-war years. It should then be 'buoyed up by the patriotic sentiment of the British Empire and the British people', culminating in the war itself. Once the main story had been settled, there would still be time to consider some 'lighter relief', but, he added, 'on the whole the less of this the better'.[1]

From Athens the *Rosaura* sailed eastwards, to Cyprus and the southern coast of Turkey. Churchill swam, painted and worked on his film script. On October 6 the yacht reached Beirut. 'Trust collection old news reels ready October 22,' he telegraphed that day to Korda. 'Sure we have unrivalled opportunity.' From Beirut, Churchill and his wife drove inland to the ruins of Palmyra, and thence to Damascus. On October 9 Churchill and his wife drove from Damascus to Nazareth, where they spent the night.[2] From Nazareth they drove on October 10 first to Nablus, and then to Jerusalem, where they joined Lord Moyne at the King David Hotel. That night they were entertained by the acting High Commissioner, John Hathorn Hall,[3] who later recalled, in a letter to the author:

I managed to rush up from Cairo some splendid old Napoleon brandy & there was plenty of champagne; and I instructed my head suggragi (waiter) to keep Churchill's glass always filled. Churchill started rather morose, and monosyllabic, & was not very responsive while the women were there. But when the women withdrew, & he had sunk a couple of brandies, he really got going & was positively coruscating. I acted as a 'feeder', raising all sorts of controversial political & international issues and wild theories for him to demolish, which he did with devastating wit & in superb prose. He simply scintillated for the rest of the evening. . . .

When I saw him to his car he said to me 'I know that you don't really believe those things that you were saying, I knew what you were doing, my boy.'

[1] Another film project which was put to Churchill during 1934 came from the Managing Director of British National Films, John Corfield. On October 26 Corfield wrote to Churchill, asking if he would consider writing the original screen story for a film on Cecil Rhodes. 'It is common knowledge that you are a great admirer of Rhodes and his work,' Corfield wrote. But Churchill's contract with Korda precluded any such commitment.

[2] The *Palestine Post* reported on October 11: 'The visit of Mr Winston Churchill to Palestine has been marred by the distressing news of the double assassination in Marseilles which he received through the Palestine Post on Tuesday night, while at Nazareth. Mr Churchill kept in close touch with the office of this newspaper by telephone and showed the deepest anxiety lest this tragedy lead to a European complication.'

[3] John Hathorn Hall, 1894–1979. Educated at St Paul's and Lincoln College Oxford. On active service, 1914–18; awarded the Military Cross and the Belgian Croix de Guerre. Entered the Egyptian Civil Service (Ministry of Finance), 1919–20. Assistant Principal, Colonial Office (Middle East Department), 1921; Principal, 1927. Chief Secretary to the Government of Palestine, 1933–37. British Resident, Zanzibar, 1937–40. Governor and Commander-in-Chief, Aden, 1940–44. Knighted, 1944. Governor and Commander-in-Chief Uganda, 1944–51.

From Jerusalem Churchill and his wife drove by car to Jericho, from where they flew to Amman, and then to Petra where they spent the night. Then they continued by air to Akaba, and thence across the Sinai desert to Cairo.

After two days in Cairo, and painting at the pyramids, the Churchills sailed from Alexandria on board the *Rosaura* to Naples on October 18, then took the train to Paris. From Paris, on October 21, they returned by air to Croydon. From Chartwell, on the following day, Churchill wrote to Sir Eric Geddes, inviting him to stay the night, and adding: 'I am sure we must do more to support civil aviation in view of the enormous preponderance of German machines and their convertability for war purposes.'

On October 6, while Churchill had been at Beirut, the second volume of his *Marlborough* was published in London. As soon as he returned to England, Churchill sent out eighty inscribed copies to friends and former colleagues. On October 24 General Edmonds wrote to thank him for his 'never forgotten memories of my association with genius for once in my life'. Two days later Stanley Baldwin wrote from 11 Downing Street:

My dear Winston,

I am again beholden to your generosity and I have turned out two or three small volumes to make room for the Marlborough. . . . There is much in it that I particularly enjoyed. Those pages contrasting the responsibilities of the C/in-Chief through the ages with his function to-day are illuminating as a search light. . . .

'I have not yet read it all,' Desmond Morton wrote from Crockham Hill on October 26, 'but it is making me neglect my work and giving me indigestion at meals since I find it impossible to put it down for long.'

In the last week of October, while Churchill discussed the groundwork of his new 'English Speaking Peoples' volumes with Keith Feiling at Chartwell, he continued to receive letters about his books and articles. 'What an amazing man you are,' Sir Harry McGowan wrote on October 29. 'What a prodigious worker. It is given to few to fill such a position in Public Affairs and to write so wonderfully and so prolifically. You are indeed an example and so worthy of emulation.' Five days later, on November 3, a businessman who had fought at Gallipoli in 1915, Major William Darling,[1] wrote to Churchill from Edinburgh:

---

[1] William Young Darling, 1885–1962. Educated at Edinburgh University. Worked in business in Ceylon and Australia, 1905–13. Private, Black Watch, 1914. 2nd Lieutenant, Royal Scots, 1915. Served at Gallipoli, Salonika and Egypt, 1915–17; on the western front, 1917–18 (Military Cross and bar); in Ireland, 1920–22. Member of the Edinburgh Town

In these confused and confusing days I doubt if you know how frequently in ordinary experience men seem to turn half expectantly to you. Your detachment from politics recently, the compelling merit of what you have written, added to your own signal achievements prior and during the last war have created an expectancy and only last week I said to Boothby, whom I met casually—when was something going to emerge?

How pitiable it is, our necessity for leadership, but after all, pity is akin to love.

Hitler had continued to consolidate his power in Germany throughout the spring and summer of 1934, and on June 30 most of his Nazi Party rivals had been killed in a night of butchery. That same night several former political leaders had also been killed, including General Schleicher and a number of prominent Catholics. 'I was deeply affected by the episode,' Churchill later recalled in a draft note, 'and the whole process of German rearmament, of which there was now overwhelming evidence, seemed to me invested with a ruthless, lurid tinge.'

A month after the murders, on August 1, President Hindenburg had died, at the age of eighty-seven, and on the following day Hitler had united under his personal leadership the offices of Chancellor and President. That same day the German armed forces swore an oath of 'unconditional obedience' to Hitler himself, as their new Commander-in-Chief.

During the autumn the militarization of Germany continued without pause. 'I suppose you have read "Berlin Diaries",' Sir Reginald Barnes[1] wrote to Churchill on October 25. 'It is an illuminating book, & even if not entirely true, it has quite convinced me that Germany is preparing hard, & only waiting until she is ready to play hell again. I only hope our Ramsays and Baldwins are alive to it all.'[2]

Council, 1933–37. City Treasurer, Edinburgh, 1937–40. Lord Provost of Edinburgh, 1941–44. Director of the Royal Bank of Scotland, 1942–47. Knighted, 1943. Conservative MP for South Edinburgh, 1945–57.

[1] Reginald Walter Ralph Barnes, 1871–1946. Entered Army, 1890. Lieutenant, 4th Hussars, 1894, and one of Churchill's close Army friends. Went with Churchill to Cuba, 1895. Captain, 1901. Lieutenant-Colonel commanding the 10th Hussars, 1911–15. Colonel, 1914. Brigadier-General, commanding the 116th Infantry Brigade, and the 14th Infantry Brigade, 1915–16. Commanded the 32nd Division, 1916–17 and the 57th Division, 1917–19. Major-General, 1918. Knighted, 1919.

[2] The Berlin Diaries, edited by Dr Helmut Klotz and published by Jarrolds. Other books on Nazi Germany published in 1934 were Dorothy Woodman's edition Hitler Rearms and a picture book entitled Heil, both published by Lane. On September 8 the Daily Mail had

In the third week of November Churchill made his BBC broadcast in their series on the causes of war. Anxious to work as closely as possible with the Foreign Office, he had offered to show it to Sir Robert Vansittart; but Vansittart suggested that it should be read by Orme Sargent.[1] Churchill sent his draft to Sargent, who replied from the Foreign Office on November 13:

I return the draft, having ventured to query a few passages which appear to suggest that Germany is plotting a war of aggression in the immediate future, thus constituting herself the sole and direct 'cause of war' at the present time. I am inclined to doubt whether this is Hitler's purpose.

Sargent believed that Hitler's aim was to achieve his purpose, not by force, but by the threat of force, 'playing off one power against the other', and isolating each power in its turn. As for Britain, Sargent wrote, it would 'probably be the last Power to be dealt with but its turn will come'.

Churchill made his broadcast on November 16. German domestic policy, he said, had brought back 'the most brutish methods of ancient barbarism, namely the possibility of compelling the submission of races by terrorising and torturing their civil population'. Although, he said, disarmament was 'the shrill cry of the hour', it would not prevent war, but encourage the potential aggressor. Nor could Britain 'detach' herself from Europe. His broadcast continued:

I am afraid that if you look intently at what is moving towards Great Britain, you will see that the only choice open is the old grim choice our forbears had to face, namely, whether we shall submit or whether we shall prepare. Whether we shall submit to the will of a stronger nation or whether we shall prepare to defend our rights, our liberties and indeed our lives.

If we submit, our submission should be timely. If we prepare, our preparations should not be too late. Submission will entail at the very least the passing and distribution of the British Empire and the acceptance by our

---

published an article by George Ward Price, which Churchill read, describing how the Germans were undertaking 'a systematic transformation of their national character. Individual ambition is to give place to the idea of being a unit in a mighty state.' Ward Price reported that there were already six million boys and girls in the Hitler youth movement, and that those who thought Nazism a passing phenomenon 'have not reckoned with the permanence of the impression which it is making on the responsible mind of German youth'.

[1] Orme Garton Sargent, 1884–1962. Educated at Radley. Entered Foreign Office, 1906. Second Secretary, Berne, 1917; 1st Secretary, 1919. At the Paris Peace Conference, 1919. Counsellor, Foreign Office, 1926. Head of the Central Department of the Foreign Office, 1928–33. Assistant Under-Secretary of State for Foreign Affairs, 1933. Knighted, 1937. Deputy Under-Secretary of State, 1939; Permanent Under-Secretary, 1946–49.

people of whatever future may be in store for small countries like Norway, Sweden, Denmark, Holland, Belgium and Switzerland, within and under a Teutonic domination of Europe.

Preparation, Churchill pointed out, 'involves statesmanship, expense and exertion', and he ended:

Peace must be founded upon preponderance. There is safety in numbers. If there were five or six on each side there might well be a frightful trial of strength. But if there were eight or ten on one side, and only one or two upon the other, and if the collective armed forces of one side were three or four times as large as those of the other, then there will be no war. . . .

If the first stage of such a structure could be built up by the League of Nations at the present time—and there may still be time—it would, I believe, enable us to get through the next ten years without a horrible and fatal catastrophe, and in that interval, in that blessed breathing space, we might be able to reconstruct the life of Europe and reunite in justice and goodwill our sundered and quaking civilisation. May God protect us all!

Churchill's broadcast was heard by tens of thousands of people who could never hear his Parliamentary speeches, and provoked an immediate response. 'I can't go to bed tonight,' wrote Filson Young,[1] 'without sending you a word of homage and gratitude for your splendid talk. . . . To me your words opened a clear line of sanity and hope because I felt that those who heard them *must* be convinced by what you so nobly and so infinitely wisely said.' Filson Young added: 'I am simply aching for the day (which if you keep your health will come) when you will have the power to implement your convictions. When that day comes you will have a following that will astound the scaremongers and isolationists. But oh, the wasted days and years!'

A young Conservative backbencher, Captain Harold Balfour,[2] wrote from the London Clinic:

[1] Alexander Bell Filson Young, 1877–1938. Special Correspondent of the *Manchester Guardian* in South Africa, 1900. Served on the staff of Admiral Beatty, HMS *Lion*, 1914–15. Correspondent with the BEF in France, 1916. Special Correspondent of *The Times* in Spain and Portugal, 1917–19. Editor of the *Saturday Review*, 1921–24. An active broadcaster and deviser of music programmes for the BBC in the 1930s.

[2] Harold Harington Balfour, 1897–   . A great-grandson of Field Marshal Lord Napier of Magdala. Educated Royal Naval College Osborne. Joined 60th Rifles, 1914; Royal Flying Corps, 1915–17 (Military Cross and bar). Served in the Royal Air Force, 1918–23. Conservative MP for the Isle of Thanet, 1929–45. Parliamentary Under-Secretary of State for Air, 1938–44. Privy Councillor, 1941. Minister Resident in West Africa, 1944–5. Created Baron Balfour of Inchrye, 1945. A member of the Board of British European Airways, 1955–66. Chairman, BEA Helicopters Ltd. He published *An Airman Marches* in 1935 and *Wings Over Westminster* in 1973. His elder brother, a Lieutenant-Commander, Royal Navy, was killed on active service in 1941.

My dear Churchill,

Lying helpless from an appendicitis operation, tonight I listened to your broadcast. Solemn, clear, logical and impressive, it was the finest wireless address I have ever heard.

That it will sway opinion and impress those whom it should is the sincere wish

of your colleague
Harold Balfour

'I have just heard you on the wireless,' wrote Esmond Harmsworth that same night. 'It was quite excellent and I was greatly impressed. Some more speeches of equal vigour given over the ether and you would be living in 10 Downing Street.'

Unknown to Churchill, both Lord Londonderry and Sir Samuel Hoare were themselves uneasy about the Government's defence policy. On November 13 Londonderry had written to Ramsay MacDonald that while Germany was rearming so rapidly 'it is quite impossible for the rest of the world to discuss disarmament'. Moreover, he added, it was essential to make it 'clear to the rest of the world' that the danger of German rearmament 'does exist and that it will be well for all of us to take some steps to meet the consequences which must ensue'. Six days later, on November 19, Hoare, in a personal letter to Baldwin from the India Office, urged that in the coming debate the Government must make 'a frank and careful statement about the German menace, for after all the German menace is the justification for the expansion and it is the German menace that is stirring up the grave anxiety in the minds of most of our supporters'.

On November 21 Londonderry circulated to the Cabinet a memorandum on German rearmament, in which the Committee of Imperial Defence estimated that within two years, and no later than October 1936, the German Air Force would have 3,264 aircraft 'for service purposes', of which 1,296 would be first line, and a further 1,296 would be 'immediate reserves for first line aircraft'. That same day the Cabinet were told, by a Minister who was not named in the minutes, that 'all the available evidence showed that the German rearmament had reached a very formidable stage' and that there was every reason to believe 'that in a year's time she would have as large an air force as the United Kingdom'.

For the debate on the address, Churchill had decided to put forward an amendment criticizing Britain's air defences as 'no longer adequate to secure the peace, safety and freedom of Your Majesty's faithful subjects'. Five Conservative MPs agreed to sign: a former Chancellor of the Exchequer, Sir Robert Horne; a former Air Minister, Frederick Guest; a former First Lord of the Admiralty, Leopold Amery; a former Under-Secretary of State for India, Lord Winterton; and Robert Boothby.

At a further Cabinet meeting on November 22, MacDonald told his colleagues he feared 'that we should only get into trouble if we said that we were expanding the Royal Air Force to meet Germany's expansion in the air'. But Sir John Simon, in an attempt to persuade MacDonald of the need for a full statement of British policy, referred, as the minutes recorded:

. . . to the speech made by Mr Winston Churchill in the House of Commons on 30th July last, and in particular to the series of questions which Mr Churchill had then asked in regard to German rearmament and more especially to her air rearmament. He (the Secretary of State) in winding up the Debate had evaded these questions, but Mr Churchill had made it clear that he proposed to revive the subject next week and on this occasion he would, no doubt, press for specific replies to his questions. Were the Government prepared to state in the Debate as a fact that the Treaty of Versailles is not being complied with? If so, they must also be prepared to state what further steps they contemplated.

Ramsay MacDonald agreed that 'hard though it was for us to say so, Germany had become war minded again', and was already producing the physical means which would enable them 'to take the offensive against their neighbours'.

While preparing his speech, Churchill was again provided with the basic facts by Desmond Morton, who had informed him on November 20 that Germany might well have between 750 and 1,000 aeroplanes by 1935, 'instead of the 600 we had hitherto considered'. The new German bombers, Morton added, had a 'sphere of action' of about 950 miles, starting with a full load of petrol and bombs'—an effective range of 500 miles from their point of departure. On November 22 Morton wrote again:

I hope you saw the statement made by Denain [1] (French Air Minister) in the Chamber of Deputies yesterday. He said that the Germans have now 1,100 aeroplanes capable of immediate use or rapid conversion as Service

[1] Victor Denain, 1880–1952. Entered the French Army, 1901. Transferred to the Air Force, 1915. Commanded the Allied Air Forces in the Balkans, 1916–18, and the French Air Force in Syria, 1918–23. Head of the French Military Mission to Poland, 1924–31; Head of the General Air Staff, 1933. Air Minister, February 1934–January 1936; during his tenure of office he inaugurated a complete re-equipment of the Air Force. Inspector-General of all French Overseas Air Forces, 1936–37.

aircraft. This is an important complementary statement to Archambaud's[1] and balances it. The French official opinion evidently is that the Germans have between 3,500 and 4,000 fully qualified pilots and 1,100 military aircraft.

My estimate is slightly below that. I would say they will have, by the 1st January next, about 1,000 military aircraft and something over 3,000 pilots. However, for practical purposes, there is no grave difference in our estimates.

Either estimate means that, at the present moment, Germany can lay hands on more Service types of aircraft than we can in this country, and has a larger reserve of pilots. On the other hand, of course, the German Air Force is not yet organised to perfection, as I hope ours is!

Churchill received further information about the inadequacies of existing air defence plans from Professor Lindemann, who wrote from Oxford on November 25 that although he did not believe that the Germans had 'any great surprises up their sleeves' as far as the quality of their material was concerned, unfortunately 'no improvement of quality is needed to enable bombing aeroplanes to dominate England if available in sufficient quantities'. That same day Desmond Morton sent Churchill a three-page analysis of German air plans. The figures which he gave were again based upon intelligence to which he had access as Director of the Industrial Intelligence Centre of the Committee of Imperial Defence.[2] Churchill had no intention of quoting these figures directly, but they served as the basis for his argument, and increased his concern. These facts were of course even more readily available to the Government, for whose intelligence service Morton worked. In his note, Morton stated that the existing German first-line strength was between 800 and 900 planes. He based this figure on military aircraft, complete with machine-guns and bomb racks, plus civil aircraft 'capable of conversion to military use as above in a few hours'. By the autumn of 1935, he wrote, his figure would have risen to 1,200 first-line and first-

---

[1] On November 20 *The Times* reported that the French rapporteur Archambaud, in giving the Chamber of Deputies a report on France's war budget, stated that 'next year' Germany would possess between 3,500 and 4,000 'fully trained pilots equipped with the necessary machines'. Archambaud also gave Germany's military and para-military forces as made up of 600,000 standing army; 400,000 Reichswehr; 100,000 police; 100,000 auxiliaries; 2,100,000 ex-Service men reserves, and labour corps; and 2,800,000 para-military personnel including SS and SA, making a total of men available for military and para-military service as over six million.

[2] Of the visits made by Desmond Morton to Chartwell at this time, John Wheldon later recalled: 'he was there quite often. He was not at meals, he dropped in. I was always mystified by his total indiscretion. I was there when he purveyed secret intelligence reports almost verbatim to Churchill. He was incredibly courageous in his continuous, wholehearted breach of the Official Secrets Act. I was impressed by his sincerity and total patriotism.'

reserve aircraft, and eventually to a total of 3,000. '*When will this be achieved?*' Morton asked rhetorically, and then gave as his answer that the Germans 'are believed to wish to reach the above state by the autumn of 1939'. Morton added: 'They should be able to do this at the present rate of expansion of industry,' but could, if they desired to speed up production, 'reach the final stage in my opinion by 1937'.[1]

On November 24 Churchill sent Baldwin a précis of what he intended to say during the debate. He also informed Baldwin that he had done the same for Lloyd George before the Secret Session debate in May 1917. It appeared, Churchill wrote to Lloyd George on November 24, 'that my amendment has caused much disturbance in Government circles. The facts set out in the precis cannot I think be controverted and the Cabinet have woken up to the fact that they are "caught short" in this very grave matter.' Churchill added that the obstacles to greater air production 'seem to come from the Air Ministry rather than the Cabinet'.

The question of what the Government should say in the debate was still not resolved, but at a further Cabinet on November 25 Sir Samuel Hoare expressed the view that 'in the Debate, it was most important to show the world that the Government had just as much and more information than Mr Churchill. . . .' Sir John Simon added that he wished to explain to the German Ambassador[2] that it was 'impossible' for the Government to avoid the debate, and that he himself was very worried about what Churchill might say. Later in the discussion Hoare stressed that it was important 'to make it clear that Mr Churchill's charges were exaggerated and that we were going to be stronger than

---

[1] According to an Air Ministry memorandum of November 21, Germany would not have 1,300 first line aircraft until the autumn of 1936. But a Foreign Office memorandum, drafted by Ralph Wigram on November 24, citing this figure pointed out that 'considerable attention should also be given to the industrial and commercial aspects of the matter', and pointed out that a 'danger point' would be reached when Germany 'feels herself sufficiently armed to secure compliance with the sort of demand which she is likely to wish to make upon individual powers without risk of retaliation or resistance'. Morton's estimate of the German air capacity was correct. On 25 October 1938 the Cabinet were informed that the existing German first-line strength had reached 3,200, with 2,400 in reserve.

[2] Leopold von Hoesch, 1881–1936. Grandson of a prominent Ruhr industrialist. Entered the Imperial German Diplomatic Service, 1907. Third Secretary, London, 1912–14. Served in Sofia, 1915, Constantinople, 1916 and Oslo, 1918. Counsellor in Paris, 1921–24; Ambassador in Paris, 1924–34. Appointed Ambassador in London (in succession to von Neurath), June 1932. He died in London while still Ambassador, on 10 April 1936. In its obituary on the following day *The Times* wrote: 'It may be doubted whether Germany possesses any diplomatist of more exceptional gifts, riper knowledge and experience, or more attractive personality. His influence on the international events of the post-War period was far-reaching, more particularly on the course of his country's relations with France and England; he did much to promote closer collaboration between the three countries.'

Germany for the next eighteen months. . . .' The Cabinet finally agreed, largely along the lines of Hoare's suggestions, that Baldwin should speak immediately after Churchill, and that his statement should be 'confined to German rearmament making clear Mr Churchill's charges are exaggerated. Our statement to be bold showing we are determined to have a strong Air Force. Make point no panic, but we have a definite programme for a large expansion.' It was also agreed that Baldwin should show that the Government was 'fully alive to situation, but do not want discuss future while purely hypothetical', and that in addition 'no attempt should be made to visualise at the moment the consequences of the action we are proposing. We must wait to see how the situation develops.'

At a further Cabinet meeting on November 26 it was suggested by the Air Staff that the whole of the new air programme should be accelerated, so that all the aeroplanes involved in Scheme A should be completed by the end of 1936, rather than by March 1939. Neville Chamberlain spoke against this suggestion, telling his colleagues 'that there was nothing in our information in regard to German preparedness to justify the proposed acceleration'. The existing programme, he said, 'was as much as could be accomplished efficiently and without waste of money or effort'. The economic situation, Chamberlain added, 'was a serious one and he felt bound to warn the Cabinet against incurring any fresh commitments'. In conclusion, the Cabinet agreed that only 22 of the 40 new squadrons should be completed by the end of 1936.

On November 27 Simon telegraphed to Sir Eric Phipps, explaining that on the following day, as a result of Churchill's amendment, the Government would have to make 'a parliamentary declaration' on armaments, and that the debate 'could neither be postponed or evaded'. The British Government wished, Simon instructed Phipps, 'to inform the German Government in advance of our intention and of the general tenor of what we might say'.

Churchill's speech of November 28 marked a climax in his campaign for a more active Government policy towards defence and foreign affairs. 'To urge preparation of defence,' he began, 'is not to assert the imminence of war. On the contrary, if war was imminent preparations for defence would be too late.' War, he continued, was neither imminent nor inevitable. But unless Britain took immediate steps to make herself secure 'it will soon be beyond our power to do so'. German rearmament threw all other issues into the background. German youth was being taught 'the most extreme patriotic, nationalistic, and militaristic conceptions'. Germany was building up a powerful, well-equipped army—'though little is said about it in public'—with factory production geared increasingly to war material. Much of this was in violation of the Treaty of Versailles.

It was in German aerial rearmament, Churchill declared, that the danger was greatest. 'However calmly surveyed,' he said, 'the danger of an attack from the air must appear most formidable.' He did not wish to exaggerate, or to accept 'the sweeping claim' that extreme alarmists put forward. Nevertheless, he believed, in a week or ten days' intensive bombing of London, one could hardly expect 'that less than 30,000 or 40,000 people would be killed or maimed', and with the use of incendiary bombs the situation could be even worse. As a result of 'such a dreadful act of power and terror', in which bombs could go through a series of floors 'igniting each one simultaneously', as he had been assured 'by persons who are acquainted with the science', grave panic would affect the civilian population, three or four million of whom would be 'driven out into the open country'.

Churchill went on to warn that it was not London alone that would be at risk from aerial bombardment; Birmingham, Sheffield and 'the great manufacturing towns' would likewise be the targets of bombing raids in the event of war. All dockyards and oil storage depots would be at risk. It was therefore essential to devise means to 'mitigate and minimize' the effects of such attacks. Merely to disperse industries would not be enough. One must remember 'the enormous range' of foreign aeroplanes, flying at 200, 230 and 240 miles an hour. 'The flying peril,' he said, 'is not a peril from which one can fly. It is necessary to face it where we stand. We cannot possibly retreat. We cannot move London. We cannot move the vast population which is dependent on the estuary of the Thames.' His speech continued with a warning to the Government not to neglect 'the scientific side of defence against aircraft attack —the purely defensive attitude against aircraft attack', and he went on to say that he had already heard 'many suggestions' that ought to be explored 'with all the force of the Government behind the examination'. Churchill continued: 'I hope that there will be no danger of service routine or prejudices, or anything like that, preventing new ideas from being studied, and that they will not be hampered by long delays such as we suffered in the case of the tanks and other new ideas during the Great War.'

There was, Churchill told the House of Commons, another aspect to the question of defence which must not be overlooked. The 'only direct measure of defence on a great scale' was to possess the power to inflict 'simultaneously upon the enemy' as much damage as he himself could inflict. He went on to explain why he thought it necessary to double or even treble the money being spent on air force expansion, telling the House:

I believe that if we maintain at all times in the future an air power sufficient to enable us to inflict as much damage upon the most probable assailant, upon the most likely potential aggressor, as he can inflict upon us, we may shield our people effectually in our own times from all those horrors which I have ventured to describe. If that be so, what are £50,000,000 or a £100,000,000 raised by tax or by loan compared with an immunity like that? Never has there been so fertile and so blessed an insurance which might be procurable so cheaply.

Complete air mastery by one power over another, Churchill warned, would lead to the 'absolute subjugation' of the weaker power, which would have 'no opportunity of recovery', and he added: 'That is the odious new factor which has been forced upon our life in this twentieth century of Christian civilisation.' He therefore proposed:

. . . that we ought to decide now to maintain at all costs in the next 10 years an air force substantially stronger than that of Germany, and that it should be considered a high crime against the State, whatever Government is in power, if that force is allowed to fall substantially below, even for a month, the potential force which may be possessed by that country abroad.

The time had come, Churchill insisted, when the 'mystery' surrounding German rearmament should be cleared up: 'We must know where we are.' Germany's illegal air force was, he declared, 'rapidly approaching equality with our own'. It was for Baldwin to produce the facts. Taking the 'first line of forces', and assuming that both sides continued 'with their existing programmes', in 1937 the German Air Force would, he believed, be 'nearly double' the size of the Royal Air Force;[1] nor did this estimate take into account Germany's ability to convert, 'in a few hours', 200 or 300 long-range civilian mail planes 'into long-distance bombers of the highest efficiency'. He went on to explain:

All that is necessary is to remove some parts of the passenger accommodation and fit in bomb racks. Those bomb racks, I told the House five months ago, are already made and kept in close proximity to the machines. By this time next year the number will have risen at least to 400 of these machines, which in the case of war will be a striking addition to the German military air force.

[1] On 12 October 1937 the then Secretary of State for Air, Lord Swinton, pointed out to his Cabinet colleagues that Britain was 'in a position of grave inferiority to Germany in effective air strength'. A year later, on 25 October 1938, Swinton's successor, Sir Kingsley Wood revealed to the Cabinet a German superiority of nearly treble: contrasting as he did Britain's 2,018 first-line and reserve strength with a similar German strength of 5,600.

Against that we can set nothing that is in the slightest degree comparable or available for military purposes; indeed, it has been the custom of Ministers and others to boast of this as an indication of our pacific intentions if indeed proof were needed. We have built for comfort and for safety and without the slightest contemplation of convertibility.

Churchill went on to urge the Government to give immediate attention to the 'proper protection of our aerodromes'. Could not some 20,000 or 30,000 unemployed, he asked, be taken from unessential relief works and given 'good wages' to construct the earthworks needed for aerodrome defence. Such schemes ought constantly to be in the Government's mind. But they must also be aware of 'another cause of anxiety', which Churchill then explained:

So far I have dealt with what I believe is the known, but beyond the known there is also the unknown. We hear from all sides of an air development in Germany far in excess of anything which I have stated to-day. As to that all I would say is 'Beware'! Germany is a country fertile in military surprises. . . .

It is never worth while to underrate the military qualities of this most remarkable and gifted people, nor to underrate the dangers that may be brought against us. . . .

It sounds absurd to talk about 10,000 aeroplanes and so on, but, after all, the reserves of mass production are very great, and I remember when the War came to an end the organization over which I presided at the Ministry of Munitions was actually making aeroplanes at the rate of 24,000 a year and planning a very much larger programme for 1919. Of course, such numbers of aeroplanes could never be placed in the air at any one moment, nor a tenth of them, but the figures give one an idea of the scale to which manufacture might easily assume if long preparations have been made beforehand and a great programme of production is launched.

Churchill went on to recall that during the Air debate in March Baldwin had said, 'If you are not satisfied, you can go to a Division.' But what was the point, Churchill asked, in dividing the House and calling for votes. 'You might walk a majority round and round these lobbies for a year,' he said, 'and not alter the facts by which we are confronted.'

Although in July the Government had announced that 42 new squadrons would be added to the Air Force by 1939, the programme was such, Churchill pointed out, that only 50 new machines would be in full service by March 1936. Despite the details of rapidly growing German air strength which had emerged since July, this programme had not been accelerated. Were this 'dilatory process' to continue even for only a few months, he declared, it would deprive Britain of the power 'ever to overtake the German air effort'. Churchill ended his speech by an appeal to the Labour and Liberal Oppositions, who had shown themselves the severest critics 'of the existing German regime', not to 'cover with contumely and mockery everyone and every policy which comes forward to secure most effective and reasonable defence to maintain the safety of the country', and he declared: 'Let the House do its duty. Let the Government give the lead, and the nation will not fail in the hour of need.'

Frances Stevenson recorded in her diary on November 30 that when Churchill sat down he had 'almost an ovation', and she added: 'I did not consider that he spoke as well as usual. But I suppose it was the *matter* of the speech that was more important than the delivery. . . . There was imagination in it too, coupled with a patriotism that was almost imperialistic.'

Replying to Churchill's speech, Baldwin told the House of Commons that he had not 'given up hope either for the limitation or for the restriction of some kind of arms'. But it was 'extraordinarily difficult', he went on, to give accurate figures of German air strength; it was 'a dark continent' from that point of view. 'Possibly,' he said, 'my right hon friend has many sources of information: probably they are all different, and probably not one who gives it can guarantee the accuracy of the information he has brought home.' Baldwin then gave certain tentative figures. The German Air Force, he said, had probably between 600 and 1,000 military aircraft. Britain's first-line strength was 880 aircraft, including the Fleet Air Arm, of which 560 were stationed at home. There were also 127 aeroplanes of the auxiliary Air Force and special reserve squadrons, making just under 690 aircraft stationed in Britain. Behind this was 'a far larger number' held in reserve. There was therefore 'no ground at this moment for undue alarm and still less for panic. There is no immediate menace confronting us or anyone in Europe at this moment—no actual emergency.' But, Baldwin added, in looking ahead 'there is ground for very grave anxiety'. Britain would watch for the signs, and would not be caught unprepared. He therefore proposed to build by the end of 1936 some 300 first-line aircraft above the existing figures. There would also be eleven new aerodromes, and twice the number of pilots and mechanics. As to Churchill's comparative figures, Baldwin was sceptical. It was 'not the case', he said, that the German Air Force was 'rapidly approaching equality with us'. It was in fact 'not 50%' of the British air strength. Indeed, he added, by the end of 1935 Britain would still have 'a margin of nearly 50 per cent' in Europe. As for

Churchill's forecasts, Baldwin declared: 'I cannot look further forward than the next two years. My right hon friend speaks of what may happen in 1937. Such investigations as I have been able to make lead me to believe that his figures are considerably exaggerated.'

Following this denial of all Churchill's claims, Baldwin made a formal pledge to the House of Commons and to the nation. 'His Majesty's Government,' he declared, 'are determined in no condition to accept any position of inferiority with regard to what air force may be raised in Germany in the future.'

During the debate that followed Morgan Jones, on behalf of the Labour Party, moved a counter amendment expressing regret at the Government's policy of 'increased armaments', which could only be ascribed, 'to a renewal of international rivalry'. The Opposition, he said, questioned whether Churchill's proposals were the best method 'of safeguarding the peace, safety and security of our people'. For the Liberal Party, Archibald Sinclair associated himself with Churchill's protest against the Government's sloth in solving the problem of the defence of civilians against air attack, but he went on to oppose Churchill's 'dangerous argument' that so much more money should be spent on the air arm 'in view of the financial condition of the country and the intolerable burdens of our National Debt and taxation'.

Later in the debate Lloyd George warned of the dangers of treating Germany 'as a pariah'. She was 'a revolutionary country', he said, which had been 'driven into revolution' by the formidable rearmament of her neighbours. 'This must be put right,' he insisted; and he added that in two or three years time 'the conservative forces' in Britain would be looking to Germany as a bulwark against Communism. 'If Germany broke down,' he said, 'and was seized by the Communists, Europe would follow.'

At the end of the debate Churchill withdrew his amendment. The House then divided on the Labour amendment, criticizing the existing rearmament plans, and this was defeated by 276 votes to 35.

On November 29 Desmond Morton wrote to Churchill: 'Your magnificent exposition of the situation last night has undoubtedly gone far to achieve the object in view. At any rate we have a declaration from S.B. that this Government is pledged not to allow the strength of the British Air Force to fall below that of Germany.' Only Churchill's speech, Morton added, 'was clear, straightforward, and utterly lacking in equivocation . . . a masterly pronouncement on the part of a genuine statesman'. Morton went on to analyse the figures Baldwin had given. Even these figures, he said, did not at all bear out Baldwin's assertion that Britain had a 50% superiority. After listing in detail the respective air strengths, Morton continued:

S.B. was evidently confused when saying the figures given him varied between 600 & 1,000. They did not. The figures given him were as above ie 600 Military planes & something under 400 dual purpose aircraft. = Total; something under 1,000 aircraft capable of immediate use as service aircraft.

Britain's maximum strength, as given by Baldwin, came to 1,247 aeroplanes: a first-line strength of 560, with 560 reserves, and 127 auxiliary forces. Under this calculation the first-line strength included the Fleet Air Arm, some of which were seaplanes restricted in their war uses. The German minimum strength, including 350 'dual purpose' civil aircraft that were quickly convertible to war uses, came to 950—French estimates 1,100. 'How on earth,' Morton wrote, '950 aircraft can be expressed as less than 50% of 1,247 beats me!'

Morton sent Churchill a further memorandum after the speech, in which he asked rhetorically whether Baldwin had 'any information which would lead him to suppose that Germany is now going to rest content with her Air Force of 600 first line? And if not, that Germany, who has built up such an Air Force in two years from nothing, will not be able, and does not intend, to double that Air Force in another two years?'. Lindemann also sent Churchill a comment on one of Baldwin's statements in the debate, to the effect that there was no possible defence against night bombing. 'But why,' he asked, 'should one adopt this defeatist attitude? To every mode of attack an antidote has been found; why should this be the sole exception?' Lindemann's note continued: 'I believe a committee is charged with the duty of considering these problems. But how much has it done? How many thousand pounds, how many man-hours have been devoted to research and investigation of this supremely important issue?' The 'menace from the air', Lindemann believed, could be combated only if a 'small but vigorous committee under an independent chairman containing scientists as well as service representatives, should be charged with the duty to discover some form of protection and given facilities to carry out any experiments required'. His note ended:

What are a few hundred thousands spent for such a purpose? It is a cause of national, even international concern. And what answer will the Government give to the enraged remnants of a decimated population if it has failed to make every effort to safeguard our people?

On November 29 Colin Coote[1] wrote to Churchill from Printing House Square, offering his 'private congratulations upon your most timely and admirable speech on national defence'. Coote added that the 'only disquieting point' in Baldwin's reply was his avoidance of any reference to the German civil aircraft that could be converted into military aircraft without delay. He disliked also, he said, 'the easy assumption that it takes months to turn a civil pilot into a military pilot and believe it to be the professional bunkum to which regular officers are all too prone'. Coote was himself hopeful that once Germany had completed 'a substantial measure of secret rearmament', and obtained back the Saar, as a result of the forthcoming plebiscite, she would then 'come out into the open, rejoin the League, and talk sense'. Four days later Churchill replied: 'More disquieting than the point you mention about the Air Debate was the anxiety of the Government to fill their shop window with the 127 territorial Air Force machines which everyone knows are the oldest, have no reserves and only weekend pilots. To class those with our best front line machines is quite indefensible.'

Commenting on the debate in a letter to Lord Willingdon, Hoare belittled Churchill's motives, which were, he said, an attempt 'to bring on to the centre of the stage and to gather round him the very many people who are worried about German rearmament and what they believe to be the weakness of the Air Force'. But Hoare went on to admit that had the Cabinet decided to 'let the Departmental Ministers answer him upon technical service questions' then Churchill 'would have scored heavily'.

On November 30 Churchill celebrated his sixtieth birthday. To mark the occasion, his son had arranged a dinner dance at the Ritz for the previous night. 'There never was a party that went with such a swing from first to last,' Randolph's aunt, Nellie Romilly, wrote to him on

[1] Colin Reith Coote, 1893–1979. Educated at Rugby and Balliol College, Oxford. On active service in France and Italy, 1914–18 (wounded and gassed). Coalition Liberal MP for the Isle of Ely, 1917–22. On the staff of *The Times*, 1923–42. Elected to the Other Club, 1933 (and author of its history, 1971). Joined the staff of the *Daily Telegraph*, 1942; Deputy Editor, 1945–50; Managing Editor, 1950–64. Knighted, 1962. Biographer of Walter Elliot (1965). Edited Churchill's *Maxims and Reflections* (1947). Published his own memoirs *Editorial* (1965). Coote later recalled, to the author, how he was 'reproached' by several friends for not resigning from *The Times*, and he added: 'I went to Winston and asked him, "should I resign". He urged me not to, telling me: "I should very much like to have a friend in the enemy's camp."'

December 1. 'Your speech was delightful. The whole Churchill family was resplendent, & beautiful & dearest & noblest of all, your beloved Papa, who certainly didn't look sixty.'

Churchill returned to Chartwell during the morning of November 30. His friends and colleagues hastened to send him birthday greetings; on December 1 Colonel Pakenham-Walsh sent his 'very best wishes for the years to come—May they be many, and if possible, even more distinguished than those that are past. I have been following with great interest your efforts to obtain recognition for our state of defensive unpreparedness in a combustible world.' Yet despite such enthusiasm, Churchill was still prone to pessimism about his own political future. His friends, however, continued to encourage him. 'In spite of what I hear you say,' Sir Almeric Fitzroy[1] wrote on December 1, 'you have yet a great life before you. . . .'

Although sixty, Churchill was seven years younger than Baldwin and five years younger than Neville Chamberlain. His admirers were convinced that the day would yet come when his qualities and experience would be made use of. 'You fill a place in many people's lives,' Terence O'Connor had written on July 28, 'and your own fortunes & happiness are the concern of more people than you can guess.'

[1] Almeric William Fitzroy, 1851–1935. Grandson of the 3rd Duke of Grafton. Educated at Balliol College Oxford. Clerk of the Privy Council, 1898–1923. Knighted, 1911.

30

India 1934–1935:
'A Very Stern Fight Before Us'

THROUGHOUT the second half of 1934 Churchill continued with his campaign to secure adequate safeguards for Lancashire, and for the Indian minorities, in the proposed Indian constitution. On June 26 he had spoken at the Free Trade Hall in Manchester on the subject of Lancashire and India. Although, as some newspapers had forecast, none of the local Conservative MPs agreed to appear on the platform with him, the meeting itself had been well attended, and on June 29 a young Conservative MP, Patrick Donner,[1] wrote to him: 'May I take this opportunity of saying how delighted I was to hear of your success at Manchester and to learn that people in the North responded with such enthusiasm to the stand you have made . . . even though local members of Parliament failed for reasons of mugwumpery to emerge from their lairs.'

Encouraged by Lancashire's concern, on July 1 Churchill published in the *Sunday Dispatch* an attack on Lord Derby and the suppression of the Manchester demand for safeguards. Derby asked Baldwin if he could read out to a Lancashire audience a letter rebutting Churchill's charges that the request for safeguards had been withdrawn only under pressure, but on July 3 Baldwin tried to dissuade him. 'I think it would be unwise to read the letter,' he wrote. 'We are in a strong position now vis-à-vis our enemies and we must not risk weakening it by a false step.' Derby

---

[1] Patrick William Donner, 1904–88. Son of Ossian Donner, Finnish diplomat and first Finnish Minister to London, 1919. Educated at Exeter College Oxford. Conservative MP for West Islington, 1931–35; for Basingstoke, 1935–55. Honorary Secretary, India Defence League, 1933–35. Member of the Advisory Committee on Education in the Colonies, 1939–41. Parliamentary Private Secretary to Sir Samuel Hoare at the Home Office, 1939; to Oliver Stanley at the Colonial Office, 1944. Royal Air Force Volunteer Reserve, 1939. Acting Squadron-Leader, 1941. Knighted, 1953. High Sheriff of Hampshire, 1967–8.

accepted Baldwin's advice, but, he wrote on July 4, 'I should have liked to read the letter because I think it would be a knock-out blow for Winston, who I am sorry to say has still got a big following in Lancashire. I do not think it will last, but at the same time it is for the moment doing mischief.' To George Stanley, Hoare wrote on July 6: 'Winston is once again on the ramp, this time in Lancashire. He and his crowd are arranging a series of mill meetings at which they hope to stir up trouble.' Derby, he wrote, was worried about this development, but Hoare himself believed 'that Winston will not do more than stir up again the discontent that already exists, and will not add to his own following'.

For some months Churchill's cause had been vigorously supported by his son Randolph. On May 6, at the annual conference of the Junior Imperial League, Randolph had brought a motion opposing the White Paper policy. His motion had been defeated by the narrow margin of 210 votes to 159. On July 2 he had begun a speaking campaign throughout Lancashire, where he denounced the Government's India policy to mill-workers and businessmen. Churchill had followed his son's campaign with close attention, and encouraged him to persevere in it; 'I have talked to Rothermere,' he wrote to Randolph on July 12, 'and told him the pressure should be kept up till the meeting.' Churchill added:

All these speeches you have been making to working-class audiences ought to be most valuable and give you a sympathetic insight into their affairs and ways of thinking. If you could get in touch with the Trade Union leaders that would be most advantageous. You could point out to them how every other industry is getting large favours and help from the Government, and can they really afford to let their case go without even being considered.

'One can hardly ever afford,' Churchill commented, 'not to be present upon a battle ground.'

In attempting to persuade the Manchester Chamber of Commerce to raise again the question of safeguards, Churchill appealed to them in the *Sunday Dispatch* on July 21 'to tell the truth as they see it or believe it'. On the following day he wrote to James Watts[1] that the 'capture' of the Chamber of Commerce 'by live people determined to give the cotton trade a fighting chance of survival is the greatest prize that could be won'. 'On the other hand,' his letter continued, 'defeat must be doggedly borne.'

---

[1] James Watts, 1903–1961. Educated at Shrewsbury and New College Oxford. Worked in his family's textile firm, S. and J. Watts, Manchester. A nephew of Agatha Christie. Treasurer of the Manchester Conservative Association, 1933–51; Chairman, 1951–53. Elected to the Manchester City Council, 1933. Resigned, 1939, to join the Cheshire Regiment. On active service in France, Iraq and Persia, 1939–45. Conservative MP for Moss Side, 1959–61.

On July 23 Sir Henry Page Croft wrote to Churchill that 'a considerable section of people in Lancashire have been very much stirred at last by this India issue', and that Randolph's speeches had done 'quite a lot to shake up all the big towns radiating from Manchester'. At the Chamber of Commerce meeting that day, the original demand for safeguards was reaffirmed. That evening Watts sent Churchill an account of the meeting. 'All our thanks are due to you,' he wrote. 'You are the only man to help us among the 615 MPs with the exception of Page Croft, Wolmer & Hartington.'[1] Writing to James Watts on the following day, Churchill expressed his gratitude 'for all your exertions in the public cause'. It was essential, now, he said, to work for '*effective* safeguards', ideally within an Indian constitution which set up, as he himself had argued before the Joint Select Committee, 'provincial Home Rule only'.

Hoare's reaction was to belittle Churchill's achievement, writing to George Stanley on July 27:

Upon the whole we are satisfied with the result of the meeting of the Manchester Chamber of Commerce. Winston and his friends did a great deal of propaganda with the result that a good many people were nervous as to what would happen. It seems that the moderates had to make some move to meet this attack and it was no doubt this necessity that accounts for the curious passage in the resolution about the imperative need for safeguards for the cotton trade. I understand, however, that this reference is not intended to mean more than the special safeguards against penal discrimination that they discussed with the Committee in the autumn and that the delegates went some way to accept in principle.

Winston is of course, claiming the resolution as a victory for himself. No one who knows anything about it takes this claim seriously.

Eager to encourage his Manchester supporters to remain on their guard, Churchill wrote to Alan Chorlton[2] on August 8:

At the present time everyone on the Government's side is trying to temporize. But this cannot last much longer. In October we shall have the

---

[1] Edward William Spencer Cavendish, Marquess of Hartington, 1895–1950. Educated at Eton and Trinity College Cambridge. On active service at the Dardanelles and in France, 1915–18. Conservative MP for Western Derbyshire, 1923–38. Succeeded his father as 10th Duke of Devonshire, 1938. Parliamentary Under-Secretary of State for Dominion Affairs, 1936–40; for India and Burma, 1940–42; for the Colonies, 1942–45. His sister Lady Dorothy Cavendish married Harold Macmillan in 1920. His elder son (who married Joseph Kennedy's daughter Kathleen in May 1944) was killed in action in Belgium on 9 September 1944.

[2] Alan Ernest Leofric Chorlton, 1874–1946. Educated at Manchester Technical College and Victoria University, Manchester. A constructional engineer. A director of Smethwick Drop Forgings. Chairman of the Manchester and Lancashire Dynamo Company. CBE, 1917. President of the Institute of Mechanical Engineers. Conservative MP for Manchester Platting 1931–35; for Bury, 1935–45.

report of the Joint Select Committee and the question of commercial safe-guards will be one of the vital issues to be submitted first to the National Union of Conservative Associations, and next year the Parliament.

I expect that the White Flaggers in the Chamber are not only playing with words themselves, but being played with by the adroit and quite unscrupulous Sir Samuel Hoare. Two separate layers of humbug will be presented to the Lancashire folk. This is what we must get ready to expose. . . .

'Tenacity is what tells in these long delayed fights,' Churchill added. 'Meanwhile there is nothing to be done except to gather privately important friends.'

Churchill had no illusions about the strength of official Conservative policy, or the lengths to which the Government might go to weaken and undermine his efforts. On August 8, in a letter to Cyril Asquith, he reflected on the procedure and Report of the Committee of Privileges:

I do not mind confessing to you that I sustained a very evil impression of the treatment I received and some day I hope to nail this bad behaviour up upon a board, as stoats and weasels are nailed up by gamekeepers. The matter has now, of course, an academic interest. I consider that the summarizing of the important documents was a masterpiece in the arts of suppressio veri and suggestio falsi. Some of them are dirty dogs and their day will come; though I thank God I am not a vindictive man.

It made him 'very indignant', Churchill wrote to his cousin Captain George Spencer-Churchill[1] on August 11, to see how the power of the Empire 'is used with such great effect to undermine its own foundations. It is an odious spectacle to watch.'

As the publication of the Joint Select Committee Report drew nearer, Churchill's optimism returned. 'I have good hopes,' he wrote to Sir William Ray[2] on September 21, 'that we shall persuade the Government to confine the experiment to the provinces in the first instance and thus preserve the unity of the party.' But Hoare had plans to extend the range of his active supporters, writing to Willingdon in his letter of September 14: 'Neville Chamberlain, who has a greater influence with the caucus than anyone else, is taking a personal interest himself in the position. As he is coming here next week, we shall have a chance of

---

[1] Edward George Spencer-Churchill, 1876–1964. A grandson of the 6th Duke of Marlborough (Churchill's great-grandfather). Educated at Eton and Magdalen College, Oxford. 2nd Lieutenant, Grenadier Guards, 1899. On active service in South Africa and the Great War (twice wounded, Military Cross, Croix de Guerre with palm); Captain, 1918. Unsuccessful Conservative candidate, 1906 and 1910. Landowner, he lived at Northwick Park, Blockley, Gloucestershire. High Sheriff of Gloucestershire, 1924.

[2] William Ray, 1876–1937. Army Remount Service, 1914–18. Alderman, Hackney Borough Council, 1918–34. Knighted, 1929. Conservative MP for Richmond, 1932–37.

getting the position as safe as we can.' Others were less confident that the Government's policy would succeed; on October 5 Willingdon wrote to Lord Reading: 'the Diehards have evidently made a very good showing and must have given the official people in the Conservative Party a considerable shock . . . it may be quite conceivable that the Tories may give up the Bill'.

It was while Churchill was on his way from Athens to Beirut that the Conservative Party Conference had met to discuss, among other topics, the Government's India policy. 'I believe the White Paper had not a score of real friends in the Hall,' Sir Henry Page Croft wrote to him on October 8, 'and the majority was most clearly composed entirely of Ministers, Private Secretaries and Officials assembled on the platform.'[1] One new development had been the support of 'the Beaverbrook press'.

On October 30, following his return from the eastern Mediterranean, Churchill gave a dinner for several of those who would be prepared to oppose the report of the Joint Select Committee, both at Westminster and in the provinces. Among the guests were Page Croft, James Watts, Commander Diggle, Ian Colvin[2] and Sir Michael O'Dwyer.[3] On November 1 Diggle wrote to Churchill: 'I did so enjoy it, and came away from it feeling very much "heartened" for the coming big fight.' He wished also to thank Churchill 'for the splendid leadership which you are giving us'. Churchill realized the difficulties of his position. On November 3 he wrote to Ian Colvin:

We have a very stern fight before us and in the House of Commons it will be particularly up-hill work. All the forces of the Government and their Whips, backed by all the partisanship of the Socialist and Liberal parties,

---

[1] Among the Indian Civil Service in India itself, the White Paper's friends were also dwindling. On October 16 Lord Brabourne wrote direct to Baldwin from Bombay: 'I have taken great pains to find out what the ICS & Police Officers in this Presidency *really* think of the White Paper proposals & in nearly every case their attitude can be summed up as a dislike of the whole thing but a firm conviction that it is much too late to go back now. Some of the younger Policemen are strongly against the whole Policy . . .'

[2] Ian Duncan Colvin, 1877–1938. Educated at Inverness College and Edinburgh University. A journalist, he began work on the *Inverness Courier*. Subsequently he was on the staff of the *Allahabad Pioneer*, 1900–03 and served as Assistant Editor of the *Cape Times*, 1903–07. Leader writer of the *Morning Post* from 1909 until his death. Biographer of General Dyer (1929) and Lord Carson (1934 and 1936).

[3] Michael Francis O'Dwyer, 1864–1940. Born in County Tipperary. Entered the Indian Civil Service, 1885. Revenue Commissioner, North-West Frontier, 1901–8. Acting Resident Hyderabad, 1908–09. Viceroy's Agent in Central India, 1910–12. Knighted, 1913. Lieutenant-Governor of the Punjab, 1913–19. He published *India as I knew It* in 1925.

make an audience not merely unfavourable and forbidding and I fear quite ready to be unfair. We have none of the facilities even of a small party in debate. We cannot even sit together. We must always expect about three speeches to every one and all the best occasions of debate will be monopolised by the three front benches. We shall I presume not even be allowed to wind up on important questions.

I write this not because it will make the slightest difference to the course which we shall take, but in order that you may make all allowances for the difficulties which confront us.

It was of the utmost importance, Churchill wrote to Lord Wolmer that same day, 'to make clear that we are not to be cowed or browbeaten'.

On November 21 Page Croft himself warned Churchill against a premature attack on Baldwin's position. 'The Conservative Party,' he wrote, 'are curious people, and loyalties are very deep-seated.' A further letter of warning—six pages long—was sent to him on November 22 by Lord Melchett,[1] who wrote, on reading the long-awaited report of the Joint Select Committee:

I must say at once that I feel the Joint Select Committee has gone a very long way indeed to meet the objections that I had to the proposals in the White Paper. In fact, were I a supporter of the White Paper (which person I believe, like Mrs Harris, never really existed) I should complain that the White Paper had been completely emasculated, so far as I can see by the present proposals. I think that in the course of its passage through the House the Bill will strengthen rather than weaken this aspect of the question.

The Governor-General and the Governors have powers to step in and take over any or every service of the State which in their judgment is not being properly administered. In other words, the principle is to set up a form of benevolent sovereignty in the provinces and at the Centre, which will allow the local Parliaments to run things as long as they do it properly, and leave the Governors absolutely free to take over the whole or any part of the administration themselves should the machine not function properly.

As these benevolent tyrants will be Englishmen, or I daresay in some cases very reliable Indians, at any rate appointed by the Imperial Authority, it seems to me that the Members of the Committee have produced a constitution which, while it is likely to work with some difficulty, will be about as good and as reasonable as can be expected. . . .

Melchett advised Churchill against an attack on Baldwin at the Party meeting, which was to be held on December 4. For Churchill to aban-

---

[1] Henry Ludwig Mond, 1898–1949. Educated at Winchester. On active service in France, 1915–18 (wounded, 1916). Liberal MP, Isle of Ely, 1923–24; East Toxteth, 1929–30. Succeeded his father as 2nd Baron Melchett, 1930. Deputy Chairman, Imperial Chemical Industries, 1940–47. Director of the International Nickel Company of Canada. His elder son was killed in a flying accident at sea in April 1945.

don his opposition to the White Paper would be seen, Melchett added, as 'an act of great magnanimity and statesmanship', and accepted as such 'by people at large', as well as by the House of Commons.

The Government realized that it was the maintenance of adequate safeguards—whether in matters of defence or minorities—that would determine whether the report would be accepted or not. Hoare was determined to introduce sufficient safeguards, many along the lines Churchill had intended, to save the Bill, writing to Lord Brabourne[1] on November 28:

I am quite sure that we have taken the Conservative Party up to the utmost limit of their endurance. . . .

Many of the doubters have been satisfied because they think that the safeguards are now effective. If there was any whittling down of them, we should see a great accession of strength to Winston's army and almost insuperable obstacles put in the way of the passage of the Bill. As things are now I am more hopeful about the Parliamentary position. . . .

Without the safeguards being maintained, Hoare added, 'I see before me a prospect of death either at the hands of the die-hards or from exhaustion in a war of attrition.'

Meanwhile, the opportunities for sustained opposition were rapidly being closed. On December 4, at the Conservative Party's National Union Council meeting at the Queen's Hall, Baldwin made a strong and successful defence of the Joint Select Committee report, the acceptance of which was then moved by Leopold Amery. As the senior spokesman of the India Defence League interest, Lord Salisbury moved an amendment favouring Provincial self-government, but opposing central responsible government. Churchill was among those who spoke in support of the amendment, but Austen Chamberlain, the elder states-man of the Party, supported Baldwin, and the amendment was deci-sively defeated by 1,102 votes to 390. On December 5 Hoare wrote to Brabourne: 'I took great trouble with our speakers and between you and me had to deal with them as if they had been prima donnas at Covent Garden.' Hoare added: 'Already there are signs of defection from Winston's camp and accessions to ours, . . .'

On December 12, during the debate on the Report in the House of

[1] Michael Herbert Rudolf Knatchbull, 1895–1939. Educated at Wellington and the Royal Military Academy, Woolwich. On active service, 1915–18 (Military Cross, despatches twice). Conservative MP for Ashford, 1931–33. Parliamentary Private Secretary to Sir Samuel Hoare, 1932–33. Succeeded his father as 5th Baron Brabourne, 1933. Governor of Bombay, 1933–37. His cousin, the 3rd Baron (born 1885) had been killed in action on 11 March 1915. His son the 6th Baron (born 1922) was shot by the Germans in North Italy on 15 September 1943, having earlier escaped from a prison train, and been recaptured.

Commons, Churchill objected to the guillotine procedure being used as 'an excrescence on the traditional procedure of the House of Commons'. Under the Provincial scheme there was no true provision for discharging Britain's responsibility 'for the mass of the Indian people'. The safe-guards would prove inadequate. 'A lot of this talk about liberty for India', he warned, 'only means liberty for one set of Indians to exploit another'. The Federal scheme, paraded by the Government as 'grand and magnanimous', had already been rejected by the Congress.

The unity of India, Churchill said 'is not the end in itself, the welfare of India is the end. The only unity left when your rule has sunk will be the hatred of all foreigners, particularly the foreigners with whom they have been brought into close contact'. The Government would have won the right 'to impose upon India a system wholly unsuited to the welfare of its people and abhorrent to all who speak in their name'; they would 'have plunged vast areas into prolonged political agitation and disputation which will proceed, not only in every Province, but also at the centre and summit of the Government of India'. As for the effect of the Government's policy on the Conservative party in Britain: 'you will have injured, baffled, discouraged and divided the great political force and party which in a world of gathering fears, must remain one of the chief instruments of British strength, and more important than any question of party. You will have depressed the vital heart beat of Britain all over the globe.'[1]

At the end of the Debate an anti-Government amendment was re-jected by 410 votes to 127, of whom 75 were Conservative and 53 were Labour MPs. As soon as the debate was over, Churchill asked Patrick Donner to prepare a list of those who had voted in favour of the amend-ment. There had been fifty-eight members of the India Defence Group's Parliamentary Committee, Donner replied on December 14, and nine-teen 'unattached Conservatives'. To their chagrin, five members of their India Defence Committee had abstained, and six had actually voted with the Government.

On December 15 Lord Salisbury moved a further anti-Government amendment in the Lords, and was strongly supported in his opposition to central responsible government by Lloyd. But Reading, speaking with the authority of a former Viceroy and Cabinet Minister, urged accept-

---

[1] Churchill's own speech was regarded as a triumph. 'The best speech I've heard in my life,' Terence O'Connor wrote that same day, and the lobby correspondent Robert George Emery wrote: 'It was a magnificent effort. Many of the older men in the Gallery said it would rank among the *most* memorable of your speeches.' On December 19 Desmond Morton wrote to Churchill: 'India in the Commons was a great triumph for you.'

ance of the report, and the amendment was defeated by 239 votes to 62. On December 26 Neville Chamberlain sent Hoare a note of encouragement. 'But,' he added, 'you have had to contend at the same time with the most wearing of all criticism, the criticism which comes from your own side,—and it has been bitter, relentless, and often unscrupulous.'

Churchill spent New Year's Eve alone at Chartwell, his wife having left two weeks earlier on a six-month cruise to the Dutch East Indies and Australia on Lord Moyne's yacht *Rosaura*. 'I was sitting down last night to eat my New Year's dinner as I thought in solitude,' Churchill wrote to her on 1 January 1935, 'and in marched Diana looking absolutely lovely. She had come down on her own to keep me company. . . .' On New Year's Day Professor Lindemann arrived for a two-day visit. Churchill began work on his third *Marlborough* volume, writing to his wife about Marlborough:

What a downy bird he was. He will always stoop to conquer. His long apprenticeship as a courtier had taught him to bow and scrape and to put up with the second or third best if he could get no better. He had far less pride than the average man. This greatly helped his world schemes and in raising England to the heights she has never since lost.

But when he fell into evil days and was stripped of power, it is rather pitiful to find him asking the sovereigns he had defeated and well nigh ruined to help him keep his private property. There never was anyone so perfectly shaped for the purpose for which he was required than this valiant, proud, benignant, patient and if necessary grovelling dare-devil and hero. It is only on the field and in his love for Sarah that he rises to the sublime. Still Mars and Venus are two of the most important deities in the classical heaven.

Churchill, encouraged by Korda, also worked during January on his Jubilee film script, hoping to make at least £10,000 from it. On January 14 he completed the script, but on January 30 his career as a script writer came to an abrupt end. 'We have had a great blow about the film,' he wrote to his wife on January 21, and he went on to explain:

It appears that an Act of Parliament says that a film which does not consist wholly or mainly of topical news reels, and which is longer than two reels, must be provisionally released six months before it can be finally released. The Board of Trade's solicitors have now expressed the opinion that this would bar our films until November, when of course it would be much too late for the Jubilee and not worth doing. . . .

Churchill went on to lament the fact that 'all my labours, which have been arduous, will be wasted'.[1]

In his letter of January 1 to his wife, who had just left Madras, Churchill wrote: 'I expect you will now not be far from the toe of the great Indian peninsula. I am very glad you are not going to Ceylon. Owing to their rash experiments in Home Rule they have let down all their sanitary arrangements and so have the plague. Imagine what will happen to India when sagacious, scientific, incorruptible direction is withdrawn!'

Despite the setbacks to their cause in December, at least eighty Conservative MPs, all members of the India Defence Committee, were prepared to vote against their Party's policy on each reading of the Bill. On the evening of January 2 Churchill issued a statement to the Press Association, commenting on a radio broadcast in which Hoare had deprecated spending too much Parliamentary time discussing the India Bill, and had urged Parliament to return to discussions of British domestic policies. 'Such a procedure,' Churchill declared, 'would no doubt be agreeable to the Socialist party who would find it very easy to nationalize the banks or carry out their revolutionary changes once they could be free from the restraints of detailed Parliamentary supervision.' But, he went on, such 'tyrannical abuses' should be avoided in England, if she wished to avoid the fate of Russia and Germany. It was essential to have 'the freest possible discussion', in order that 'all differences may have expression and all weak points in the legislation brought to light'. His statement continued: 'I regard the fight to save India and the British Empire from a great misfortune as only now beginning to come to close quarters. Sir Samuel Hoare already proclaims his victory, but we shall know more about that by the end of the year.'

On January 4, a former Viceroy of India, Lord Hardinge,[2] who had also been a member of the Joint Select Committee, denounced Chur-

---

[1] Two days later, on January 23, Korda himself wrote to confirm that the film would not go on, and Churchill agreed to accept a final payment of £2,750 bringing his total income from the venture to £4,000. Korda also agreed to pay Churchill £2,000 a year to write such scripts as might be needed for any short films on which Korda decided to embark; together with a separate fee of £1,000 for writing the script of a film to be called 'The Conquest of the Air'. Churchill also earned £2,500 from the *Daily Mail* for a series of articles on the Silver Jubilee; articles which he based almost entirely upon the discarded film script. This brought his total 'film script' earnings to over £10,000.

[2] Charles Hardinge, 1858–1944. Educated at Harrow and Trinity College Cambridge. Entered the Foreign Office, 1880. Knighted, 1904. Ambassador at St Petersburg, 1904–06. Permanent Under-Secretary of State for Foreign Affairs, 1906–10. Created Baron Hardinge of Penshurst, 1910. Viceroy of India, 1910–16. Reappointed Permanent Under-Secretary of State for Foreign Affairs, 1916–20. Ambassador to Paris, 1920–22. His elder son, Lieutenant Edward Charles Hardinge, died of wounds received in action, December 1914.

chill's opposition to the Government at a Conservative meeting in Tunbridge Wells. Such were Churchill's powers of speech, Hardinge asserted, that he was able 'to make right look wrong and wrong look right'. Hardinge added: 'It is far easier and far more spectacular to criticise than to create.' Speaking at the end of the meeting, Colonel Spender-Clay declared: 'As for Mr Winston Churchill, I am certain that he has only to walk up and down the room with a cigar in his mouth and he can persuade himself by his own eloquence that black is white.'

Churchill did not allow such comments to deter him. He was convinced that whereas Provincial Home Rule was in principal a workable solution for India, the Federal Home Rule favoured by the Government would fail, whatever safeguards might be devised initially. Even provincial self-government ought, in his view, to exclude, at least temporarily, the handing over to Indian politicians of control over the police and judiciary. On January 13 he wrote to Lord Rothermere that if the Government were prepared to go ahead with a Bill limited to provincial self-government, there would still be serious debates on points of detail, but 'no party rift'.

Sir Samuel Hoare had no intention of reducing the scope of the India Bill; he and Baldwin were confident that a substantial majority of Conservative MPs would support the Bill as it stood. Indeed, on January 3 Hoare had written to Willingdon of his broadcast: 'I made an appeal to Winston, at the end of it, to drop his opposition. He is not in the least likely to pay any attention to anything that I say, but my words may have an influence with the Conservatives who are opposed to our policy but who nonetheless do not wish the whole time of the session taken up with an India Bill.'

On January 19 the *Evening News* announced a surprise development in the India controversy. Randolph Churchill had decided to stand as an anti-India Bill Conservative candidate at the forthcoming Wavertree by-election, even though an official Conservative candidate[1] had

---

[1] The Conservative candidate was James Platt; it was the only time he stood for Parliament. Randolph Churchill was only 23 years old at the time of the Wavertree election. Two years earlier, in June 1933, he had been invited by a group of Lancashire businessmen to contest Altrincham against Sir Edward Grigg, the official Conservative candidate; but he had decided not to contest the seat after Grigg had given certain assurances about the need for pro-Lancashire safeguards in any future India Bill.

already been selected by Central Office. Churchill, caught unawares by his son's decision, wrote to his wife on the following day:

This is a most rash and unconsidered plunge. At the moment Randolph and his three or four Manchester friends, including Mr Watts who has sub-scribed £200 to the expenses, are sitting in the Adelphi Hotel at Liverpool without one single supporter in the constituency whom they know of—high or low.

Randolph is to hold his first meeting tomorrow. Of course with the power-ful support of the local 'Daily Mail' and the 'Sunday Dispatch' and with the cause, which is a good one, and with his personality and political flair he will undoubtedly make a stir. But in all probability all that he will do is to take enough votes from the Conservatives to let the Socialist in.

All together I am vexed and worried about it. It is nothing like the Westminster Election where we had the local Tories split from top to bottom and where we developed quite rapidly a brilliant organisation. Randolph has no experience of electioneering and does not seem to want advice, and the whole thing is amateurish in the last degree. To have a hurroosh in the streets and publicity in the newspapers for three weeks and then to have a miserable vote and lose the election to the Socialist will do no end of harm.

Within a few hours of the announcement of Randolph's candidature, Churchill issued a Press Association statement in which he declared that his son had decided to fight the by-election 'upon his own responsibility and without consulting me'. His son's cause, he wrote, was 'a worthy and a vital one', and he added: 'I should be less than human if in all the circumstances of these critical times I did not wish him success.'[1]

Writing to his wife on January 21, Churchill reported that their son's campaign was to open in Wavertree that evening; that although he had 'no friends or supporters' in the constituency itself, Lord Rothermere was already giving 'tremendous support' through all his papers; and that the Duke of Westminster had subscribed £500, and John Watts a further £200 to the campaign. Churchill's letter continued:

I am producing £200. I do not doubt Rothermere will provide the rest. The total expenditure is limited to £1,200, so that is all right. Much depends on whether this meeting goes well tonight and the impression Randolph makes. Of course in action of this kind he has a commanding and dominating personality, and there is a great feeling that Lancashire needs someone of vigour and quality.

Already the election has become a national fight. I shall know at ten

[1] On 1 March 1935 Churchill wrote to Dr O. C. Pickhardt, MD, of his son's candidature: 'he did not consult me about it beforehand and indeed dragged us all in at his tail. However, he is full of life and energy and will-power and will certainly push a lot of people about as he runs his course.'

o'clock tonight how he gets on. Incidentally before he decided to plunge into the election he wrote a very provocative series of paragraphs about 'a deal in municipal honours' in Liverpool in his weekly letter in the Sunday Dispatch. This coupled with the election excitement has led Sir Thomas White,[1] the Liverpool 'boss' who was reflected on in these paragraphs, to issue a writ for libel against the Sunday Dispatch, and I believe Randolph personally. The contest will therefore not be lacking in bitterness. . . .

'Sarah and Diana both gone Liverpool help Randolph,' Churchill telegraphed to his wife that same day. 'Thus he has already two supporters,' and on January 23 he telegraphed again: 'Randolph making progress. Great local enthusiasm. India Defence League decided give full support, therefore many good speakers. I go eve poll.' That same day Churchill sent his wife a full account of their son's progress, and of the Defence League's decision to support him:

Randolph had a great success at his opening meeting. He took the local Wavertree Town Hall holding about five hundred. He did not know half an hour beforehand whether he would have a large or small attendance, or whether they would be friends or foes. He had no supporters and decided to go without a chairman, standing alone on his platform. However when he got there the hall was packed and the streets outside crowded. The platform also was blocked by enthusiastic people standing there to support him. He made a brilliant speech. Then he went to an overflow almost as packed as the first, and finally more than a hundred walked a mile and a half to the committee rooms to give in their names as helpers.

The Daily Mail and the Morning Post played this up in their front pages and even the enemy papers admitted the enthusiasm shown and the reality of the candidature. On this the India Defence League Executive decided on Tuesday to go all out for Randolph. Although angry at not being consulted they felt they had no choice but to fight with what strength they have.

Churchill's letter continued:

This is the first time we have definitely opposed a Government candidate at a bye-election and it may be we shall lose some of our members for the decision. They even seemed to think that perhaps the Government would refuse the Whip to all members of the League. I do not believe they dare do that. Anyhow all were resolved to go forth, so Randolph will have all our circus at his disposal including Lloyd, Wolmer, Roger Keyes, the D of A! and last but not least Papa. I have promised him to wind up his campaign in the Sun Hall on February 5.

[1] Thomas White, 1876–1938. Brewer; Chairman of Bents' Brewery, Liverpool. Member of the Liverpool City Council. Chairman of the Central Valuation Committee for England and Wales. Knighted, 1928. Chairman of the Mersey Tunnel Joint Committee, 1929–38.

Needless to say this election will cause much heat and bitterness. On the other hand it arouses enthusiasm and will be a national fight. Good judges in the constituency tell me that Randolph will certainly beat the official Tory and that the fight lies between him and the Socialist, who will probably win. In this case the National Government candidate will be at the bottom of the poll. A nasty jar for Ramsay and Baldwin and general anger.

As a result of the India Defence League's decision, Randolph was to have at least two MPs each evening supporting him on his platform. Churchill's letter ended:

Well, there it lies tonight, and it must run its course. You will see that I am much more easy in my mind about it than I was at first sight. Randolph of course is in the seventh heaven. This is exactly the kind of thing he revels in and for which his gifts are particularly suited. He is reported to be rather tired and no wonder considering his excitement and exertions. I am counselling him bed at eleven and great attention to his vocal chords.

Throughout January 24 Churchill despatched telegrams enlisting support for his son's campaign. 'Randolph would greatly welcome letter from you,' he telegraphed to Lord Carson, 'as his grandfather's old friend.' That same day Churchill sought to defend his son against misrepresentation, telegraphing to Duff Cooper, who had become Financial Secretary to the Treasury six months before: 'Randolph did not apply word "toad" to Baldwin but to party bosses.' Duff Cooper replied that same day from Treasury Chambers: 'I am very sorry if I misrepresented Randolph. I had clearly understood from more than one report that Ramsay and S.B. were the two toads on the lion's nostrils.'

Churchill's own anti-India Bill efforts continued simultaneously with his son's campaign. Speaking in Bristol on January 25 he declared: 'My hope is that we shall so handle this India Home Rule Bill in the House of Commons as to prevent an irrevocable abdication of British sovereignty over India.' The Indian Princes, he pointed out, were reluctant to have anything to do with the proposed Federal system, despite 'every kind of pressure' being exerted upon them by the Government.[1] As for his son's campaign, he said:

[1] Six months earlier, in July 1934, Churchill had been among the signatories of an India Defence League letter to the Maharaja of Patiala, in which the Princes were informed that if they were to 'make it clear that they are against the scheme', its promoters would be 'bound by their own pledges to withdraw it'. The letter continued: 'We can well understand the sort of pressure which is brought to bear upon you and your colleagues; but we venture to assure you that whereas, if you yield your destruction is certain; if you stand firm you have nothing to fear. We have no hesitation in assuring you of the strong and increasing opposition to the White Paper in this country. Already the best part of the Conservative Party, which maintains the Government in power, is either openly opposed or secretly critical of the scheme.'

... what a spectacle is presented to the nation of the Conservative machine working frantically, night and day, its wealth, its wire-pulling, Ministers of the Crown in shoals, agents by the dozen, all employed to prevent a young man of 23 making his way as a Conservative into Parliament, where for so many generations his forbears have borne their part.

I think it is a pitiful spectacle, humiliating to the present leaders of the National Government. . . .

Returning from Bristol to Chartwell on January 27, Churchill entertained several leading members of the India Defence Committee, discussing with them the tactics they would adopt in opposing the India Bill. Those present were Lord Lloyd, Sir Henry Page Croft, Lord Wolmer, Patrick Donner and Sir Nairne Sandeman.[1] 'He taught us all the elements of politics by his methods,' Patrick Donner later recalled, in a conversation with the author, and he added:

From the tremendous pressures on us there grew enormous feelings of fellowship—we were a real band of brothers. At the Committee Stage the Government planned a thirty days debate. It was clear that they had only to sit it out to have their way. Many of us wanted to refuse to accept the timetable and to obstruct all business. We had Winston against us. He refused to support wrecking tactics. We had quite a fierce discussion. He thought quite genuinely that thirty days was so much more than any known Bill had ever had that we could shatter it in debate, by force of argument. But it was not argument that counted at the end of the day, it was votes.

On January 28 Churchill wrote to his wife: 'I am now about to begin vy hard fight in the House about India. The odds are vy heavy against us. But I feel a strong sense that I am doing my duty, & expressing my sincere convictions.'

On January 29 Churchill broadcast on India over the BBC, telling his listeners:

Sir Samuel Hoare has thrust upon Parliament the most bulky Bill ever known. If it was as luminous as it is voluminous, it would indeed command respect. But what is this India Home Rule Bill? I will tell you. It is a gigantic quilt of jumbled crochet work. There is no theme; there is no pattern; there is no agreement; there is no conviction; there is no simplicity; there is no courage. It is a monstrous monument of shame built by the pygmies.

India is to be subjected to a double simultaneous convulsion in the Provinces and at the Centre by a crazy attempt to create a Federal system, before the units which compose it have even been formed. The wall before the bricks are made; the faggot before the stakes are cut!

---

[1] Nairne Stewart Sandeman, 1876–1940. Jute and cotton manufacturer, Dundee. Conservative MP for Middleton and Prestwich, Lancashire, from 1923 until his death.

The faithful, trustworthy Indian police, the mainstay of peace and order, are to be disturbed and harassed by divided allegiances arising from unsure, irrational compromise.

The supreme government of India is to be racked by dyarchy—rival authorities clutching at the levers of power. In a period of severe economic and financial stress India is to be launched upon another ten years of furious, costly, sterile political struggles fought out in the heart and brain of the Central Government, as well as in those of the Provincial Administration.

As for the proposed safeguards, Churchill continued:

There are to be eleven Governors armed with dictatorial powers if they dare to use them: that is to say, eleven potential kings of the seventeenth-century type. There are to be eleven actual parliaments on the twentieth-century model.

And these two opposite forces are to begin a wearing struggle with one another which will plunge India into deepening confusion and will impose upon these helpless millions, and hundreds of millions, living as they do already on the very margin of existence, a cruel new burden of taxation and misgovernment.

The Labour Party, Churchill insisted, saw the India Bill only as a stepping stone 'for a further downward leap'. The Conservative Party 'loathe it, and fear it in their hearts'. The friendly countries of Europe— France, Holland and Italy—stood amazed 'at British folly'. There was, he said, one more question to be asked, a question which linked the Government's India proposals with the threat of German rearmament. 'The storm clouds are gathering over the European scene,' he warned. 'Our defences have been neglected. Danger is in the air . . . yes, I say in the air. The mighty discontented nations are reaching out with the strong hands to regain what they have lost; nay, to gain a predominance which they have never had,' and he went on to ask: 'Is this, then, the time to plunge our vast dependency of India into the melting-pot? Is this the time fatally to dishearten by such a policy all those strong clean forces at home upon which the strength and future of Britain depends?'

The Indian people themselves, Churchill warned, were to be delivered by the proposed Bill 'to inefficiency, nepotism and corruption'. As a result of the Bill, power in India would be transferred, not to the masses, but to 'the most narrow, bitter and squalid vested interests and super-stitions'.

Churchill's broadcast had been planned several months earlier; but to his critics it seemed as if it had been deliberately timed to coincide with his son's campaign at Wavertree. Speaking in the constituency on the evening of January 30, the Attorney-General, Sir Thomas Inskip, declared:

It was not quite fair of Mr Winston Churchill to make an election speech on the wireless and to call this proposal 'a monstrous Bill erected by pygmies'. He meant that he was the giant and the Government were the pygmies. Mr Churchill was too much in the habit of representing himself to be the big man, the first class brain, and everybody else insignificant duffers. He regarded him as the gentleman who wanted his epitaph inscribed in stone while he was still alive with the words 'he was believed by everybody'. Mr Churchill was writing as his own epitaph 'He was admired by everybody'. Unfortunately for people who thought they had all the brains and wisdom in the world it was usually not true.

Writing privately to Willingdon on January 31, Hoare expressed his own view of Churchill's broadcast:

I listened to Winston on the wireless. As you will have seen he made the most extreme speech that he has hitherto made. I hope that it was too extreme for the BBC hearers who are on the whole rather a quiet lot. In any case it shows that he is as truculent as ever. It is, therefore, greatly to be hoped that Randolph does really badly and that the effect of his failure will depress Winston before the Committee stage comes on.

According to the gossip, Randolph is not doing well. Sightseers crowd to his meetings as they would to a new film, but most of them come from outside the constituency and as far as one can judge, there has been no serious movement of real conservatives to him. . . .

Churchill continued with his efforts to help his son's campaign. On January 30 he urged the Duke of Westminster to use some of his 'large resources' to help obtain canvassers and motor cars. 'I hope,' he added, 'you are going to bring your local lords to sit on the platform at the big meeting. It occurs to me that on your estate and among your friends there must be people who know some of the well to do folk in the Wavertree Division.' Official Conservative unity was, he believed, 'beginning to crack' in the constituency, 'and even a few prominent individuals detached may start a slide'. Writing to his wife on January 31, Churchill described the state of the campaign:

The important decision was taken by the India Defence League executive to support Randolph and this action was endorsed by our committee of Members of the House of Commons at a meeting where about thirty-five were present. Rumours that the Government would deprive all Members who supported Randolph of the Whip did not deter anyone from going to Wavertree. Sir Robert Horne made a threatening speech to the Government saying that if there was any intolerance of that kind he would himself refuse the Whip.

About twenty-five Members have already sent assurances of their sympathy to Randolph and he has all the speakers that he wants. Fitzalan[1] and Carson have appealed to the Catholic and Orange voters respectively. Whatever resources we can command are being used. Both the cars go up on Tuesday for the poll, and Brendan, Oliver Locker Lampson, Westminster and others are helping in this way too. . . .

He has made a wonderful impression and excites tremendous enthusiasm. All his meetings are crowded out. He has at least five a day. Yesterday he had one on my advice for the business men at the centre of the city where he spoke for about fifty minutes in a most admirable manner, being completely master of all the subjects with which he dealt, and speaking without the slightest note and never at a loss. The Daily Mail rampages away behind him, covering the constituency with placards and making every possible point in his favour. I believe he will beat Platt, in which case the responsibility for losing the seat is thrown upon the weaker candidate. It will be Platt who has split Randolph's vote and not vice versa. More than that I dare not hope, and yet the surge of what is undoubtedly a great wave of local opinion may produce results beyond any on which one would dare to reckon. There is no doubt he will emerge from this election a public figure of unquestioned importance and will be greatly esteemed throughout the unhappy county of Lancashire.

Commenting on the wider issues, Churchill wrote:

The Indian assembly at Delhi has been very helpful in rejecting the trade pact upon which Sam Hoare and Derby were basing their case. This is a foretaste of the kind of terms British trade will get when we have put these gentlemen in the place of power in India. Nothing can more completely stultify the Government's case in Lancashire than this spiteful gesture. Argumentatively Platt has not a leg to stand on, for he has really committed himself to a complete throwing-up of the Lancashire case.

Churchill told his wife that he planned to speak twice on Randolph's behalf, at lunch and on the evening of February 5. More than seven thousand tickets had already been issued for the meetings. 'The demand is extraordinary,' he wrote, 'and there is no doubt both these "Father and Son" meetings will be crowded out.' His letter continued:

All the underlings of the Government have been up, but last night the Attorney General Inskip had his second meeting only half filled. But they have crowded in agents from every part of the north country.

[1] Lord Edmund Bernard Fitzalan Howard, 1855–1947. 3rd son of the 14th Duke of Norfolk. Educated at the Oratory School, Edgbaston. Assumed the name of Talbot, 1876. Adjutant, Middlesex Yeomanry, 1883–8; Lieutenant-Colonel, South Africa, 1900 (despatches). Conservative MP for Chichester, 1894–1921. A Junior Lord of the Treasury, 1905. Chief Unionist Whip, 1913–21. Parliamentary Under-Secretary, Treasury, 1915–21. Privy Councillor, 1918. Created Viscount FitzAlan of Derwent, 1921. Lord Lieutenant of Ireland, 1921–2.

It is the machine against popular enthusiasm, and you know what the machine is. However, as I have said, anything may happen especially as quite a number of Liberals have come over to us. Long before you get this letter you will have heard the news. If Randolph polls eight or nine thousand, we shall not have suffered a rebuff. If he beats Platt, it is a victory. If he is elected, it is a portent.

Of the Prime Minister, Churchill wrote:

Ramsay sinks lower and lower in the mud, and I do not think the poor devil can last much longer. Buchanan,[1] the Clydesider in the House of Commons called him a 'cur', a 'swine' and 'one who should be horsewhipped'. These brutal insults were allowed to pass by the Chair and no single member of this great majority—no Minister on the Treasury Bench, no Whip rose to claim a breach of order. Buchanan got off without withdrawing. If I had been there I would certainly have risen to protect this wretched man from such a Parliamentary outrage. What utterly demoralised worms his colleagues and their hangers on must be to allow their Prime Minister to be insulted in this way in breach of every Parliamentary rule without anyone daring to stir on his behalf.

Churchill was surprised to find that his repeated attacks on Government policy over India had not totally destroyed his personal relations with members of the Government. As he wrote to his wife in his letter of January 31:

Oddly enough, in spite of all this fighting (perhaps because of it) Ministers are extremely civil. I am dining tomorrow night at the Foreign Office to meet Flandin[2] and Co for whom there is a banquet, and last night I gave a dinner

---

[1] George Buchanan, 1890–1955. Educated at Camden Street School, Glasgow. Member of the Independent Labour Party. Glasgow Town Councillor, 1918–23. Labour MP for the Gorbals, Glasgow, 1922–48. Minister of Pensions, 1947–48. Privy Councillor, 1948. Chairman of the National Assistance Board, 1948–53

[2] Pierre Etienne Flandin, 1889–1958. Chef de Cabinet to the Prime Minister (Millerand) 1913–14. Entered the Chamber of Deputies, 1914. Director of the Allied Aeronautical Service, 1917. Under-Secretary for Air, 1920. President of the First International Conference on Aerial Navigation, 1921. Minister for Commerce, June 1924, November 1929 and March 1930. After 1930 he suffered constant pain from a broken arm which never properly healed. Minister for Finance, 1931 and 1932. Leader of the Right Centre group of Deputies, 1932. Prime Minister, November 1934–June 1935. Minister for Foreign Affairs, January–June 1936. After his visit to Germany in 1937, Blum's Government issued a communiqué declaring that he went as a private individual only. Arrested by the Allies in North Africa, 1943. Tried by the French Government, 1946, but acquitted on the charge of collaboration with the Germans (Randolph Churchill spoke in Flandin's defence at the trial, on his father's behalf). Following the trial Flandin was declared ineligible for Parliament.

at Claridges for the Portuguese Ambassador[1] at which Cunliffe-Lister and others were present. You would never have supposed there was the slightest difference between us. They see the terrible difficulties into which they are plunging.

On February 2 Churchill tried to deter his son from spreading his attack beyond the India issue to the National Government as such. 'Grievous mistake,' Churchill telegraphed from Chartwell on February 2, 'to broaden issue about India and against Ramsay now by substituting Conservative versus National Government. . . . Regret any tendency widen issue. Mass party rightly favour real National Government.' Churchill warned his son that if he began to denounce the whole idea of Conservatives cooperating with the National Government, this would cause serious embarrassment in the Parliamentary party and 'probably individual repudiations on eve poll'. Churchill added: 'Pray consider my position if you want me to speak Tuesday night.'

As the campaign entered its final week, Churchill was excited by the thought of his son's possible success, telegraphing to his wife on February 2: 'Tremendous enthusiasm. Magnificent fight against Government and machine. Chances like Abbey election.' Three days later, at Wavertree, Churchill made his eve of poll speech, urging support for his son's candidature. 'If you put him in as the Conservative candidate . . .' he said, 'not only will you make a great sensation, but you will have taken part in a decisive political event.' Speaking of India, Churchill warned in apocalyptic terms of the dangers to Britain if Indian self-government were to become a reality:

I have lived the greater part of my grown up life at the centre and near the summit of our affairs. I have had a prolonged education. There are times when I cannot help feeling the very deepest anxiety and distress about our country and its future. There are times when I, and many of you, must feel it may be impossible to stem the adverse tide; but then there always comes back across our minds a surge of strong and unquenchable faith that we can do it if we try, the confidence that our destiny is still in our own hands, and the consolation that if we do our best while life and strength remain we shall be guiltless before history of a catastrophe which will shake the world. . . .

Churchill went on to tell the voters of Wavertree that in view of the serious issues at stake it would be wrong to put 'loyalty to a party, to a

---

[1] Ruy Ennes Ulrich, 1883–1966. Professor of Law, Coimbra University, 1907–14. Director of the Bank of Portugal, 1914–27. Chairman of the Mozambique Company, 1923–33. President of Portuguese Railways, 1925–32. Ambassador in London, 1933–35. Director of the Faculty of Law, Lisbon University, 1936–51. Chairman of the National Navigation Company, 1936–50. Ambassador in London for a second time, 1950–53.

local organization, to a Government, to a leader like Mr Baldwin, to a leader like Mr MacDonald' before a firm proclamation 'of Britain's will to survive as a great nation among men'.

Voting took place at Wavertree on February 6. Late that night, when the results were declared, it was clear that Randolph Churchill's intervention had split the Conservative vote, and the Labour Party candidate, J. J. Cleary,[1] was elected on a minority vote of 15,611. The official Conservative, James Platt, received 13,771 votes, and Randolph Churchill 10,575; a total Conservative poll of 24,346. On the day after the poll Hoare wrote to Willingdon: 'that little brute Randolph has done a lot of mischief. . . . The fact that he kept our man out will undoubtedly do both Winston and him a good deal of harm in the party. The fact, however, that he got more votes than we expected is disquieting. It shows that there is a great deal of inflammable material about and it makes me nervous of future explosions. . . .'

On February 8 *The Times* denounced both Churchills for their part in creating a Labour victory, stating in its main leading article that the only possible result 'of several hundred Wavertrees' would be Labour rule and a policy for India as advocated by the Labour Opposition, whereby 'the "jungle" would indeed be let in upon India'. *The Times* went on to point out that 'less than one-quarter' of the votes cast at Wavertree were in support of the India Defence League's policies, and it continued: 'India played no real part whatever in the election. It is significant that Mr Randolph Churchill, especially during the latter stages of his campaign, widened the front of his assault to attack the whole policy and system of National Government.' *The Times* concluded: 'The Wavertree election shows nothing more clearly than the fact that those who, in obedience to short-sighted or personal views seek to destroy the system of National Government, may indeed achieve success, but only the success of suicide.'

---

[1] Joseph Jackson Cleary, 1902– . Educated at Skerry's College, Liverpool. Liverpool City Councillor, 1927, and member of the Finance Committee. Unsuccessful Labour candidate at East Toxteth, 1929; unsuccessful candidate at West Derby, 1931. Elected for Wavertree, February 1935; but defeated eight months later in the General Election, and did not stand again for Parliament. Lecture tour to the forces, Middle East, 1945. Lord Mayor of Liverpool, 1949–50. Knighted, 1965.

31

India 1935:
The Final Challenge

ON February 6, during the second reading of the India Bill in the House of Commons, there was much Conservative hostility to the continuing opposition of the India Defence Committee and to Churchill's leading part in that opposition. Opening the debate, Hoare defended the Bill with skill and denounced its critics with acerbity, while the Liberal leader, Sir Herbert Samuel, was particularly scathing about Churchill himself. Had Churchill been born an Indian, he said, 'he would have been a Congress man of a type compared to which Mr Gandhi would be as a dove to a tiger'. That weekend, at Chartwell, Churchill entertained three of the most active members of the India Defence League's Parliamentary Committee, Sir Michael O'Dwyer, Patrick Donner and Charles Emmott,[1] and with them discussed how best to coordinate their opposition to the Bill.

Between January and June 1935 Churchill was host at Chartwell to several meetings of the leading members of the India Defence Committee, and, throughout the various stages of the India Bill they worked out, at Chartwell, their Parliamentary strategy, and discussed Churchill's own speeches. One of those who was most frequently at Chartwell at this time, Patrick Donner, later recalled, in conversation with the author, the pattern of these visits:

We all went down on the Friday in time for a bath before dinner. After dinner, at about 10.30, he would read out the various sections of his speech paragraph by paragraph. Wearing his carpet slippers he would pace up and

---

[1] Charles Ernest George Campbell Emmott, 1898–1953. Educated at Lancing and Christ Church Oxford. Royal Field Artillery, France, 1917–19. Barrister, 1924. Unsuccessful Conservative candidate, 1929; MP for Glasgow Springburn, 1931–35; for Eastern Surrey 1935–45. Served with the RAF, 1939–45. Received into the Roman Catholic Church, 1948.

down and then go into a corner and mumble alternative phrases to himself. Then he would produce an improved paragraph, summon a secretary who would take it down, go out with it and then bring it back retyped. He would then read it out again and ask us if we agreed. If we said no, pointed out an error, something that was not, say, in accord with the Simon report he would ring the bell and tell the secretary to bring in the Simon report and check. God help you if you were wrong. But if you were right he would adjust the paragraph accordingly.

That was part of his greatness and his charm, the continuous adjustment to new facts or to new information. He steeped himself in India. He had a lot of people who really knew. You could not have had a more elastic mind, or a more unbiased mind. He was always adjusting to the truth. That was why we spent so many hours—until three in the morning—every night of the weekend going through the speech word by word. 'How long does a forty-five minute Commons speech take you to prepare?' I asked him. 'Eighteen hours' he said.

We had three hours in bed—not necessarily three hours sleep. When we came down to breakfast every newspaper under the sun was laid out in the sitting-room. He had read them all. I used to arrive back in London on Monday morning completely exhausted.

On February 11, at the close of the second reading of the Bill, Churchill made the final opposition speech, warning that to give India self-government at the centre would give Indians the power to whittle away all trading safeguards, and to hold Lancashire 'as hostages', and would enable a small group of politically motivated men to trample on the rights of millions of inarticulate and ill-represented minorities. Those who would speak against the Bill at each of its stages, he said, hoped 'to kill the idea that the British in India are aliens moving out of the country as soon as they have been able to set up any kind of governing organism to take their place'. Instead, they wished to establish the idea 'that we are there for ever', as 'honoured partners with our Indian fellow-subjects whom we invite in all faithfulness to join with us in the highest functions of Government and administration for their lasting benefit and for our own'.

Hansard recorded the cheers at the end of Churchill's speech. But after Baldwin had wound up the debate on behalf of the Government, declaring that 'the rule of law and order' which Britain had established would 'go on' under Indian supervision, the Bill passed its second reading by 404 votes to 133, on a Labour amendment urging explicit Dominion Status. Among those voting against the Government were 84 Conservatives.

The Committee Stage of the India Bill opened on February 19. For thirty days Churchill and his colleagues in the India Defence Committee challenged successive clauses of the Bill, and sought by detailed argument to amend them. Each division was preceded by serious debate, but in none of them could the Bill's opponents muster more than ninety Conservative votes. On February 21 Churchill supported an amendment, the aim of which was to replace the proposed Federal scheme of responsible Government at the centre by an All-India Advisory Council, in which the British vote would predominate. But the amendment was defeated by 308 votes to 50. Two days later Churchill wrote to his wife, who had reached New Zealand on her eastern cruise:

We do very well in the debate but the Government have mobilised two hundred and fifty of their followers who do not trouble to listen to the debates but march in solidly and vote us down, by large majorities, usually swelled by the Socialists and always by the Liberals. It is going to be a long wearing business.

I think our best reply to these tactics is to avoid divisions, allowing the different questions to be negatived by mere voices, and only now and again having to vote. By this means we compel them to keep these enormous forces constantly at Westminster, without giving their members the satisfaction of divisions, which they wish to score.

Hoare was far from uneasy about Churchill's tactics. The 'most satisfactory' feature of the debates, he wrote to Willingdon on February 22, 'has been the poor attendance of Winston's followers in the division. He is, of course, both active and vocal, so also have been half a dozen of his chief supporters. I greatly hope, however, that unless they get better support from their rank and file they will find it difficult to maintain their activities.' Hoare's main fear was over Federation, and the attitude of the Princes towards it, and he went on to explain that Churchill, who was 'of course, out to make all the trouble that he can', was now saying that Federation was 'a disreputable intrigue between a few Princes, whom we are bribing, and ourselves'. Hoare continued:

I hope and believe that the Princes understand his machinations. If, however, you have a chance of emphasising to any of them the real state of affairs, I suggest that it might be helpful. . . .

I very much hope that the Princes will not embroil the situation in their meeting at Bombay. I can control the situation here as long as there are no bolts from the Indian blue. If, however, the Princes raise new issues and give the impression that they are edging out, the position here will become extremely difficult. I know that you are doing your utmost to avoid this danger and there is nothing more that I can say about it except that it is a real one.

On February 25, while the India Bill was still under scrutiny in Committee, the Indian Princes, meeting in Bombay, passed a resolution expressing strong dissatisfaction with the Federal scheme. On February 26, encouraged by the Princes' decision, Churchill argued in Committee that it had become useless to proceed with the Bill; but in his reply Sir Samuel Hoare insisted that the Princes must accept the scheme as it stood. The issue was put to the vote; but Churchill's motion was defeated by 283 votes to 89. Numerically, this was the largest opposition he and the India Defence League were able to muster. When the discussion continued on February 27, Hoare was the main defender of the Federal scheme, supported by his Under-Secretary, R. A. Butler. Churchill was still optimistic about the chances of altering the policy. 'This is not going to be fought out by numbers,' he said. 'It is going to be fought out by the force of events and by the decisions which are being taken in the minds of men outside this House. Never have I felt more hopeful than tonight.' Writing to Willingdon on March 1, Hoare warned that with the sudden opposition of the Princes 'and the leakage of their foolish speeches', even his colleagues in the Cabinet were asking 'whether it was worth going on with the Bill at all'. His letter continued:

Outside the Cabinet friends like Austen Chamberlain were horrified at the state of affairs. He in particular insisted that we were getting little or no help from your end and that whilst the die-hards were kept fully informed as to what was happening and were daily using great influence with their friends amongst the Princes, we appear to be inert and helpless. Others are freely saying that the Government of India is lukewarm about Federation and that there is no one on your Council who is taking any active interest in it. . . .

I feel sure that you will wish me to tell you about these reactions. They could not have been more serious and it is most fortunate that we have been able to surmount what looked like a first-class Parliamentary crisis. As things turned out, we got away with a big majority in the Commons. But the edge was very thin and we might just as well have had it against us.

Within a few hours of the Princes' meeting, Hoare pointed out, Churchill was able to quote in the House of Commons several extracts from their speeches. 'The House was not unnaturally astonished,' he added, 'that whilst he seemed to know everything that was happening, I seemed to know nothing.' Hoare went on to warn Willingdon: 'If the Princes or any other section of Indian opinion makes us drop the Bill, there is not the least chance of our introducing another. Certainly I myself would have nothing to do with any such expedient. The dropping of the Bill might very well mean the fall of the Government, but it would certainly mean the end of Indian legislation for this Parliament and probably for many years to come.'

On March 2, Churchill wrote to his wife explaining the effect of these developments both for himself, and for the whole Indian debate:

The India Bill is now in Committee and I am in the House all day long two or three days a week speaking three or four times a day. I have been making short speeches of five, ten and fifteen minutes, sometimes half an hour, always without notes, and I have I think got the House fairly subordinate. I am acquiring a freedom and facility I never before possessed, and I seem to be able to hold my own and indeed knock the Government about to almost any extent.

The Government supporters are cowed, resentful and sullen. They keep 250 waiting about in the libraries and smoking rooms to vote us down on every amendment, and we have a fighting force of about 50 which holds together with increasing loyalty and conviction. I have led the opposition with considerable success so far as the debates are concerned. The divisions go the other way, but we mock at them for being lackeys and slaves.

All this would count for nothing but for a great and surprising fact—the Indian Princes have definitely decided not to come into this scheme of federation! This has been the event of the last week, as you will see from the papers and also from the reports of my speeches which I enclose. The cause of this volte-face is that the Indian political classes, not only the Congress but practically the whole lot, have rejected the Government plan. Whereas four years ago the Indian politicians asked the Princes to come in and help in the federal scheme, and the foolish Government embarked upon their course on this basis. Now these same Indian political classes are threatening the Princes with bitter hostility if they associate themselves with this plan, and make it possible. It is a striking sign of Indian national hostility from the highest princes to the most extreme agitator.

The Government still profess to have hopes of meeting the Princes' objections by amendments. But these objections were not taken (in my judgment) for bargaining purposes but only to have definite grounds for refusal. Unless I am entirely wrong they have made up their minds to stand out. This is a political fact of capital importance. It wrecks the federal scheme against which I have been fighting so long. It may also lead to the withdrawal of the whole Government policy. You will see that the reactions of this upon the general political situation will be far-reaching.

Churchill then told his wife of his lack of confidence in the Government itself, and in particular of his despair at the behaviour of its leaders:

The Government stock is very low. They are like a great iceberg which has drifted into warm seas and whose base is being swiftly melted away, so that it must topple over. They are a really bad government in spite of their able members. The reason is there is no head and commanding mind ranging over the whole field of public affairs.

You cannot run the British Cabinet system without an effective Prime Minister. The wretched Ramsay is almost a mental case—'he'd be far better off in a Home'. Baldwin is crafty, patient and also amazingly lazy, sterile and inefficient where public business is concerned.

Almost wherever they put their foot they blunder. Cabinet Ministers can only hold a meeting in any part of the country with elaborate police arrangements and party caucus arrangements to secure them an uninterrupted hearing. It is quite certain that things cannot last.

Lloyd George of course would like to come in and join them and reconstitute a kind of War Cabinet Government, in which I daresay I should be offered a place. But I am very disinclined to associate myself with any administration this side of the General Election.

At the height of the Committee Stage debates, Churchill's son announced yet again his intention to challenge the Government's India policy at a by-election. His plan was to put up a candidate of his own at the South London constituency of Norwood. 'He has acted entirely against my wishes,' Churchill wrote to his wife in his letter of February 23, 'and left my table three days ago in violent anger . . . he is quite beyond reason or even parley; and I am leaving him alone.' In a further letter to his wife that same day, Churchill wrote of how his son was now 'quite uncontrollable', and he added: 'He does not seem to wish to consider any other interests but his own and we have had sharp words upon the subject.'

Although Churchill still hoped that his son would 'defer' to his advice, Randolph was determined to secure the defeat of the official Conservative candidate, Duncan Sandys.[1] In his letter of March 2 Churchill again referred to his son's impetuous action:

The Norwood by election, of which I wrote you in my last letter, has absorbed all the children except Mary. Randolph seems to have got a

[1] Duncan Edwin Sandys, 1908–87. Educated at Eton and Magdalen College Oxford. 3rd Secretary, British Embassy, Berlin, 1930. Conservative MP for Norwood, 1935–45; for Streatham, 1950–74. Political columnist, *Sunday Chronicle*, 1937–39. Member of the National Executive of the Conservative Party, 1938–39. Elected to the Other Club, 1939. On active service in Norway, 1940 (disabled, Lieutenant-Colonel, 1941). Financial Secretary, War Office, 1941–43. Chairman, War Cabinet Committee for defence against flying bombs and rockets, 1943–45. Privy Councillor, 1944. Minister of Works, 1944–45; of Supply, 1951–54; of Housing and Local Government, 1954–57; of Defence, 1957–59; of Aviation, 1959–60. Secretary of State for Commonwealth Relations, 1960–64 (and for Colonies, 1962–64). Created Baron Duncan-Sandys, 1974. In 1935 he married Churchill's daughter Diana (Marriage dissolved, 1960).

considerable fund through Lady Houston[1] and appears disposed to form an organisation to run candidates not only at by elections, but against Government supporters at the general election. His programme seems to be to put Socialists in everywhere he can in order to smash up MacDonald and Baldwin.

I need not enlarge upon the fury this will cause and its unfavourable reactions upon my affairs. Norwood is the first of these essays and certainly no ground could have been more ill chosen. I told you how he quitted my table ten days ago in a rage because I expressed my strong and vehement protest against his disregarding everybody's opinion and interest except his own. Since then I have not seen or heard from him. He has for his candidate at Norwood nothing of the powerful support I was able to bring him at Wavertree. Not a single Member of Parliament will, I expect, appear on his platform. The India Defence League will leave him severely alone, and now the *Evening News* whose aid Rothermere had promised him, has made it clear that they will go no further. . . .

Now that the Rothermere press has deserted him, it seems to me that he is in for a thoroughly bad flop which will strip him of any prestige he gained at Wavertree. This will probably do him a lot of good and reduce his pretensions to some kind of reason. In every other direction, especially in mine, it will do harm.

The nominations are on Monday. Great efforts have been made to try to induce him to withdraw his candidate who is an ex-Fascist airman, Findlay by name[2] (not much good). Max returned yesterday from Brazil and used all his influence and argumentative power upon Randolph without making the slightest impression. He (R.) knows he is onto a thoroughly bad thing, but means to brazen it out. I shall of course have nothing to do with it, except to bear a good deal of the blame.

I merely record these facts dispassionately because when one cannot control, there is not use worrying. Baldwin said to me in the Lobby two days ago that Mrs B. had said to him 'One's children are like a lot of live bombs. One never knows when they will go off, or in what direction.' I suppose this must be the attitude of parents towards the new generation, who will make the world as they choose and not as we choose.

For the Government, the course of the India Bill debate was still worrying. Writing to Willingdon on March 8, Hoare reported that

---

[1] Fanny Lucy Radnall, 1857–1936. Married, 1901, the 9th Baron Byron (who died in 1917); 1924, Sir Robert Houston (who died in 1926). A keen suffragist. Founded and administered the first Rest Home for Tired Nurses, 1914–18; DBE, 1917. Gave £100,000 for the Schneider Air Trophy Contest, 1931. Helped to finance aircraft and air experiments.

[2] Richard J. Findlay. An Observer in the Royal Air Force; Lieutenant, 1918. A strong anti-communist, he joined the British Union of Fascists in 1934, but left it almost immediately on account of its anti-semitism. A supporter of General Franco in the Spanish Civil War, but visited both sides. Arrested under Regulation 18b, June 1940, and imprisoned, 1940–41. Interned in the Isle of Man, 1941; Camp Leader of his internment camp, where he called himself, and was known as, 'Squadron Leader' Findlay.

'many of our own supporters are seriously asking whether it is worth going on with the Bill', and that if the Princes were to reject Federation 'there may well be a landslide against us'. Later in his letter he warned Willingdon that the 'big majorities I have had behind me in the debates are no guarantee of the position. If it looked as if I was withholding information from the House or misleading them upon essential matters, the Conservatives would go against me almost en masse.'

Writing to his wife on March 8, Churchill again reflected on his personal position in the continuing India debate:

I should have felt very solitary but for the fact that the India Bill and Parliament have taken up so much of my time. The great event is that it is now in my opinion practically certain that the Princes have made up their minds not to accept this scheme. I talked last night to Ormsby-Gore[1] and J. C. Davidson and found them both pianissimo. They frankly admit that if the Princes will not come in they themselves would have the gravest apprehensions of going on with the Bill. If they put it on the Statute Book, as no doubt they can by August, and the Princes do not come in and we lost the election, it would be quite easy for the Socialists by very short amendments to the Bill, to make an India constitution which would destroy all the safeguards to which these poor Government folk are clinging. I do not think it at all impossible in the circumstances that they may drop the Bill altogether. If not this wearing struggle will continue with growing loss to all our common interests.

The Morning Post have procured, no doubt through the connivance of one of the Rajahs, a verbatim account of the whole of their secret meeting. They have published in the Morning Post two long column verbatim reports of all the speeches which were delivered by Bikanir, Bhopal, and the great ministers Akbar Hydari and Ramaswami Aiyar.[2] No one can read these statements

---

[1] William George Arthur Ormsby-Gore, 1885–1965. Educated at Eton and New College Oxford. Conservative MP, 1910–38. Intelligence Officer, Arab Bureau, Cairo, 1916. Assistant Secretary, War Cabinet, 1917–18. Member of the British Delegation (Middle East Section) to the Paris Peace Conference, 1919. British Official Representative on the Permanent Mandates Commission of the League of Nations, 1920. Under-Secretary of State for the Colonies, 1922–24, and 1924–29. Privy Councillor, 1927. First Commissioner of Works, 1932–36. Secretary of State for the Colonies, 1936–38. Succeeded his father as 4th Baron Harlech, 1938. High Commissioner, South Africa, 1941–44. Chairman of both the Midland Bank, and the Bank of West Africa. A Trustee of both the Tate and National Galleries.

[2] *The Maharaja of Bikaner*, 1880–1943. Assumed full ruling powers, 1898. Member of the Indian States delegation to the Round Table Conferences of 1930 and 1931. Chancellor of Benares Hindu University from 1929. *The Ruler of Bhopal*, 1894–1960. Succeeded his mother as ruler, 1926. Chancellor of the Muslim University at Aligarh, 1930–35. Chancellor of the Chamber of Indian Princes, 1931–32 and 1944–47. Honorary Air Vice-Marshal, RAF. *Akbar Hydari*, 1869–1942. A leading Hyderabad politician and administrator. Knighted, 1928. Head of the Hyderabad Delegation to the Round Table Conferences, and to the Joint Select

without seeing the resolve is not to settle. I have therefore good hopes of a successful outcome.

We are to have our annual General Meeting of the West Essex Association on the 29th, and I shall demand a vote of confidence in my Indian policy, and allow of no amendment. I hope for a four or five to one majority. If by any chance this vote were refused me, I should resign and fight a by-election. It is nothing to me whether I am in Parliament or not, if I cannot defend the causes in which I believe.

There was, Churchill added, no 'serious danger' that his constituency would reject him. Indeed, he was also able to help a young neighbouring MP, Victor Raikes,[1] to win a vote of confidence in South-West Essex in support of his opposition to the India Bill. At Raikes' meeting, Churchill wrote to his wife on March 10, six hundred members of the association attended, 'and when he entered the hall they received him with wild enthusiasm, howled down the hostile chairman and officials of the Association, and carried a resolution of confidence in him by no less than 594 to 6'. This result, Churchill believed, 'will have a very good effect on Epping, and indeed throughout the whole of our eighty members. Every one of them will feel a sense of security.' This, Churchill added, 'will put an effective stop on the intrigues of the Central Office'.

The Norwood by-election was held on March 14. Randolph's candidate, Richard Findlay, came bottom of the poll with only 2,698 votes, and Duncan Sandys was elected as the Conservative candidate with a majority of 3,348, defeating the Labour candidate. As soon as the result was known, Churchill wrote to his wife:

Randolph's candidate thus forfeited his deposit. I do not think the 2,700 votes was so bad considering that no one gave him the slightest support, and Randolph virtually had to fight alone, carrying everything on his shoulders, managing the organisation, making the speeches, answering the questions, writing the election address, interviewing the press etc.

He has now been electioneering for two months continuously but does not seem to be nearly so tired as he was during the Wavertree contest. This result is of course a set back to him and should teach him prudence, and to

Committee, 1933. President of the Hyderabad State Executive Council, 1937–41. Member of the Viceroy's Executive Council, 1941–42. *Ramaswami Aiyar*, 1879–1966. Advocate General for Madras, 1920. Knighted, 1925. Acting Law Member, Government India, 1931. Delegate to the Round Table Conference. Drafted the Kashmir Constitution, 1934. Dewan of Travancore, 1936–48.

[1] Henry Victor Alpin MacKinnon Raikes, 1901–86. Educated at Westminster School and Trinity College Cambridge. Called to the Bar, 1924. Conservative MP for Ilkeston, 1931–45; for Wavertree, 1945–50; for Garston, 1950–57. Flight-Lieutenant, Royal Air Force Volunteer Reserve, 1940–42. Knighted, 1953.

work with others without at the same time daunting him. He is now off to Wavertree to form his own independent Conservative Association there. . . .

'I do not think the result has done me any serious harm,' Churchill added. 'The fact that the India Defence League stood out of it of course acquits us formally.'

The Government was now seriously concerned about the future of the India Bill. In a letter to Willingdon on March 15 Hoare expressed his worries, and also his personal hostilities, telling the Viceroy:

. . . so far as the Princes' Resolution goes we are still walking on a volcano. Winston and his friends are honestly convinced that they have destroyed Federation and their joy over it is really repulsive. They intend to launch their big offensive next Wednesday when we return to the discussion of the Bill. Of course we are mobilising our forces and will do our utmost to repel the attack. There is, however, no good denying the fact that the position is uncomfortable. We had a long discussion about it all in the Cabinet. Whilst my colleagues were prepared to take my advice as to going on with the Bill, they were obviously disquieted by the recent developments.

'We held it all right this week,' Hoare reported to Willingdon on March 22, 'but I doubt very much whether we can hold it again if there is a repetition of the trouble we have had with the Princes.' His letter continued: 'We took as many precautions as we could over the debate knowing that Winston and his friends believed that they had all the cards in their hands. Our press was very helpful and it was a great advantage to have the united front of the Conservative and Liberal Members of the Joint Select Committee. Winston never does so well when he thinks he has an easy wicket and I feel pretty sure that he and his friends will have been disappointed by the result.'

The India Bill debates continued in the last week of March, when its more technical provisions were discussed. 'Winston has been very little in the House,' Hoare reported to Willingdon on March 29, 'and one or two more of the die-hard critics seem to be growing weary of the protracted discussions. . . . It has become a war of attrition and what the effects of eight continuous days in the next fortnight will be upon us all no one can say.'

On April 5 Churchill sent his wife news of the continuing India debate. 'I have had a very hard time with the India Bill,' he wrote. 'They have taken it four days this week, and there are to be four days next week. I have to be there practically all the time and the only time I was away the Government got sixty clauses through in a twinkling.' His letter continued:

We are keeping our end up very well. I think the Government are absolutely shaken in argument and the Bill utterly discredited, everyone being against it in India and no one wanting it here except its authors. But they will drive it through like a steam-roller and then hope we shall all kiss and make friends. I do not know at all how this will work.

On April 13 Churchill sent his wife a letter, which he hoped would greet her when her ship reached Egypt. Of Chartwell he wrote:

I sleep here almost every night so as to play in the mornings. But sometimes I am so tired after H of C that I just drop into the flat,[1] wh is always ready. Really the combination of these two dwellings is most convenient. . . .

I have been sometimes a little depressed about politics and would have liked to be comforted by you. But I feel this has been a gt experience and adventure to you, & that it has introduced a new background to yr life, & a larger proportion; & so I have not grudged you yr long excursion; but now I do want you back. . . .

On April 13 Churchill wrote to his wife again: his last letter of her cruise, sent to meet her at Marseilles. In it he sent her news of Randolph, who had been suffering from a severe attack of jaundice, but was now 'decisively better'. As Churchill wrote: 'He is in great good spirits and is visited by youth and beauty', and he added: 'He has grown a beard which makes him look to me perfectly revolting. He declares he looks like Christ. Certainly on the contrary he looks very like my poor father in the last phase of his illness. The shape of the head with the beard is almost identical.'[2] Of politics Churchill wrote: 'All the talk here is about reconstruction as soon as the India Bill is through. Whether that process will lead to my receiving an invitation I cannot tell, and I say most truthfully I do not care.' His letter continued:

Of course the Government will get their beastly Bill through, but as the Princes will not come in, all the parts I have objected to will remain a dead

---

[1] 11 Morpeth Mansions, a flat on two floors, near Westminster Cathedral, Pimlico, where Churchill lived and worked when he was in London. He took the lease at the beginning of 1935, and kept it until the outbreak of war in 1939.

[2] In the same letter, Churchill wrote of the mysterious nature of his son's illness: 'Three days ago two specialists were called in, in an effort to diagnose the disease. They were inclined to pronounce it "sewerman's" disease, which is a very rare and new form of infection derived from the baccili in the urine of rats, and consequently contracted by sewermen. But Randolph could not recall having encountered any rats—except Buchan Hepburn! Guinea pigs were inoculated from his water and highly complicated tests are now being made. This disease is endemic in Europe, but hitherto has hardly appeared in England. Yesterday the head of the Tropical School of Medicine arrived, and after seeing Randolph, and how well he was considering he had had a fortnight of temperatures, pronounced himself certain that it was not this extraordinary disease. This was a great relief . . .' Apparently Randolph had caught an infection 'which cannot be diagnosed'. It was probably glandular fever.

letter. India has been thrown into the greatest muddle and in the upshot mocked. The machinery of government there will be far worse when this Bill is passed than before. The Indians will be even more discontented and will I expect in practice have even less power.

Meanwhile Baldwin remains with all his cards in his hands, a power-miser I am going to call him. With the utmost skill and industry, and self-repression, he gathers together all the power counters without the slightest wish to use them or the slightest knowledge how! Ramsay continues to decompose in public.

On a personal note Churchill told his wife:

At sixty I am altering my method of speaking, largely under Randolph's tuition, and now talk to the House of Commons with garrulous unpremeditated flow. They seem delighted. But what a mystery the art of public speaking is! It all consists in my (mature) judgment of assembling three or four absolutely sound arguments and putting these in the most conversational manner possible. There is apparently nothing in the literary effect I have sought for forty years!

Between April and August 1935 the India Bill controversy went through its final convulsions. At no point during the long series of debates did Churchill or the India Defence League give up their attempts to challenge the Federal scheme. But despite the deep unease within the Conservative Party at the Government's India policy, actual opposition in the many Parliamentary divisions never exceeded 90, out of a total Conservative vote of 473. During April, Patrick Donner was taken ill with appendicitis. In his absence Alan Lennox-Boyd was in charge of the Parliamentary organization of the Defence League. On April 20, in thanking Churchill for the flowers which had arrived at the nursing home, Donner wrote: 'I should like you to know what a grand thing I count it *and how much it has meant to me* to be allowed to do battle on your side and in your company. I'm not so sure the Defence League is beaten yet, but if we are I would so much sooner lose a battle in your ranks than win one on the side of the yes-men battalions.'

The Committee stage of the India Bill continued until May 15. Churchill was a frequent speaker, whose arguments were countered by several Government speakers, in particular Hoare, Butler, Inskip and Sir Donald Somervell.[1] To help him with his own speeches, Churchill

---

[1] Donald Bradley Somervell, 1889–1960. Educated at Harrow and Magdalen College Oxford. Fellow of All Souls College Oxford. On active service, 1914–18. King's Counsel, 1929. Conservative MP for Crewe, 1931–45. Knighted, 1933. Solicitor-General, 1933–36. Attorney-General, 1936–45. Privy Councillor, 1938. Home Secretary, 1945. A Lord Justice of Appeal, 1946–54. Created Baron Somervell of Harrow, 1954. A Lord of Appeal in Ordinary, 1954–60.

received a series of memoranda and suggestions from the India Defence League supporters, including the Duchess of Atholl, Lord Wolmer and Sir Michael O'Dwyer. But despite the force of many of Churchill's criticisms, the Government persevered in its efforts, and by one skilful concession averted an increase of opposition among the backbenchers. On May 16 Hoare explained to Willingdon: 'Butler, Inskip and Somervell have from all accounts conducted the Bill with great tact and ability,' but he went on to explain the one area where a concession had been made:

Over Excluded Areas the technical position was more difficult. Several Conservative Members who are not die-hards have made a special study of the backward tracts and upon all sides of the House, including Labour, there have emerged signs of great anxiety over their future. Even the members of the Joint Select Committee who had themselves recommended the proposals set out in the Bill went over to the critics. The result was that we could not have carried the Schedule without creating a very awkward situation and risking a great reduction in our vote at the eleventh hour of the Committee Stage. When, therefore, I discussed the question on the telephone with Butler and the Office I took the view that it was essential to maintain to the end of the Committee Stage our very remarkable record so far as the Government majorities and the general opinion of the House have been concerned. . . .

I do not think that you need be anxious about the concession. You will have seen that Inskip made it very clear that it did not mean any change of policy or large alteration in the actual Schedule. What we shall have to do in due course is to give the House a good deal more information on the subject in the form of a White Paper. When they have this information I do not myself contemplate any serious difficulty with the Order in Council.

On May 31, on the eve of the third reading of the Bill, Churchill gave a dinner at Claridges for many of those who intended to speak against the Bill yet again, including twelve Peers and forty-one MPs. Among those present were Lord Rothermere, Lord Salisbury and Sir Henry Page Croft, and several young MPs, Brendan Bracken, Victor Raikes, Alan Lennox-Boyd, Charles Taylor[1] and Patrick Donner. 'I must drop you a line . . .' Sir Henry Page Croft wrote on June 1, 'to congratulate you on a really remarkable dinner which will help not only to steady the troops for next week, but to form a rallying point for Conservative and Imperial thought.'

---

[1] Charles Stuart Taylor, 1910–   . Educated at Epsom College and Trinity College Cambridge (BA 1932). Conservative MP for Eastbourne, 1935–74. Captain, Royal Artillery, 1939; temporary Major, 1941. Managing Director of Unigate & Cow & Gate Ltd. President of the Residential Hotels Association of Great Britain. President of Grosvenor House (Park Lane) Ltd. Knighted, 1954.

The third reading of the India Bill opened in the House of Commons on June 4. In the opening speech, Hoare upheld the three principles of All-India Federation, Provincial Autonomy and Responsible Central Government with safeguards. Churchill spoke on June 5. 'It has been a long fight,' he said. 'It has also been a very uneven fight. Immense powers have been deployed against us—all the resources of what is called a National Government. . . . All the power of the Conservative party machine used against itself, & its traditions, used against its instincts with cold-blooded calculation.' Both Liberals and Socialists had likewise wanted the Bill, 'except that they wish to go further'. Against the Bill, in addition, were 'all the social influences and political patronage', not only of the British Government but also of the Government of India—'A vast majority,' Churchill described it, 'collected under pressure of emergency and used in directions opposite from what the voters expected or wished.'

During his speech Churchill reiterated that in India responsible Government at the centre would lead to 'a poorer administrative service', that it would be detrimental to the rights of minorities, that it would lead to social injustice, and 'an inferior form of Government, federal and provincial', which would encounter 'almost universal reprobation'. His speech was bitter and outspoken. 'In the name of Liberty,' he said, 'you have done what Liberty disowns. In the name of theoretical progress you have opened the door to practical retrogression. In the name of appeasement and the popular will you have prescribed a course of endless irritation.' He ended with a direct attack on Hoare:

He has won his victory; he has won the victory for which he has fought hard, and long and adroitly; but it is not a victory in our opinion for the interests of this country nor a victory for the welfare of the peoples of India, and in the crashing cheers which will no doubt hail his majority tonight, we pray there may not mingle the knell of the British Empire in the East.[1]

A former Labour Minister, Christopher Addison,[2] wrote to Churchill immediately after his speech: 'I cannot refrain from paying a tribute to

[1] As soon as Churchill's speech was over, several hundred MPs hurried to leave the Chamber: they had only stayed thus far in the debate to hear Churchill speak. Leopold Amery, who spoke immediately after Churchill, began his speech with the scathing words: 'Here endeth the last verse of the last chapter of the Book of Jeremiah,' at which point a member called out: 'Followed, oddly enough, by Exodus.'

[2] Christopher Addison, 1869–1951. Hunterian Professor of Anatomy, Cambridge, 1901. Liberal MP for Hoxton, 1910–22. Parliamentary Secretary to the Board of Education, 1914–15. Parliamentary Secretary, Ministry of Munitions, 1915–16. Minister of Munitions, 1916–17. Minister in Charge of Reconstruction, 1917. President of the Local Government Board, 1919. Minister of Health, 1919–21. Minister without Portfolio, 1921. Labour MP for Swindon,

your masterly performance. That sequence of sentences in which you summarized your case, a few minutes before the end, may well become an example of superb composition and splendid eloquence that will be quoted as a classic of parliamentary oratory.'

Even with Labour Party support, the opponents of the India Bill were able to muster only 122 votes, of whom 84 were Conservatives. The Government secured 386 votes in favour of the Bill, a majority of 264. Churchill's mood was one of reluctant acceptance, and of foreboding. 'We must now look forward and not back,' he wrote to Professor Morgan [1] on July 2. 'No one feels this a greater effort than I do. I am sure the day is gone by when the many tricks and shifts of Sam Hoare about the India Constitution Bill can be brought to book in Parliament. We must now await the melancholy course of events comforted only by the fact that we have done our utmost to avert them.'

As soon as the India Bill was passed, Churchill sought to make his peace with the Conservative Party leaders, convinced that the European situation demanded a lessening of the bitterness which the India debates had created. On July 20, in a public letter to R. A. Butler—one of his leading Parliamentary adversaries throughout the India Bill debates—he wrote:

I wish you all success in your great Essex rally of Conservative and National forces. Mr Baldwin commands a wider measure of public confidence and good-will throughout this island than any other statesman. Whatever our differences we must all support him in his efforts to secure a sane and stable Parliament for the anxious, fateful years that lie ahead. . . .

A Socialist victory, Churchill added, would 'endanger peace' in Europe, 'both through the neglect of our defences and by meddling too much in foreign quarrels which it is beyond our power to heal'.

1929–31; 1934–35. Minister of Agriculture and Fisheries, 1930–31. Created Baron, 1937; Viscount, 1945. Secretary of State for Commonwealth Relations, 1945–47. Paymaster-General, 1948–49. Lord Privy Seal, 1947–51.

[1] John Hartman Morgan, 1876–1955. Educated at Oxford, Berlin and London. Joined the *Daily Chronicle*, 1901; leader writer, *Manchester Guardian*, 1904–05. Unsuccessful Liberal candidate, 1910 (twice). Home Office Commissioner with the BEF, 1914–15. Staff Captain, Adjutant General's Staff, 1915. Adjutant General's Office, Paris Peace Conference, 1919; Inter Allied Military Mission of Control, Germany, 1919–23. Brigadier-General, 1923. King's Counsel, 1926. Reader in Constitutional Law, Inns of Court, 1926–36. Counsel to the India Defence League, 1933–34; to the Indian Chamber of Princes, 1934–37; to the State of Gwalior and the Central Indian States, 1939–45; to the Parliamentary Post-War Policy Group, 1942–45. Adviser to the United States War Crimes Commission at Nuremberg, 1947–49.

In the first week of August Lord Linlithgow was appointed Viceroy of India, in succession to Lord Willingdon. Of all Churchill's friends, he had been the most outspoken in his criticism of the India Defence League. On August 8 Churchill sent him a private letter of congratulation in which he wrote:

I am very glad indeed at your appointment to this splendid office; and I am sure you are the man. Also you have helped to make the bed in which you will lie. If anyone could bring the new constitution into effect without a disaster, you are the one. We apprehend increasing communal ill-will, and steady deterioration in all services; and that the Imperial Power will be blamed for the downward trend. I hope indeed we may be wrong. Anyhow we regard the question settled by the Royal Assent, and we shall await the future without needless controversy. As long as the Princes are not nagged and bullied to come into Federation, you need not expect anything but silence or help from us. We shall count more in the new Parliament than in this fat thing.

You have on every ground, especially personal grounds, my fervent wishes for success in the task you have so bravely accepted.

On August 25 Churchill addressed an open letter to his constituents, urging an end to the India controversy. 'We have done our best and we have done our duty,' he wrote: 'We cannot do more.' His warnings about what would happen in India remained, and if the disasters he predicted did come about he would feel 'free to comment upon them', but, he continued:

I am reminded of the words which the late Lord Salisbury, then Lord Cranborne, used after the fierce and bitter controversy about the Reform Bill of 1867. He said—'It is the duty of every Englishman, and of every English party to accept a political defeat cordially, and to lend their best endeavours to secure the success, or to neutralise the evil, of the principles to which they have been forced to succumb.'

'We have no wish,' Churchill commented, 'to be unfaithful to so wholesome a tradition.'

As a gesture of conciliation Churchill invited one of Gandhi's leading supporters, G. D. Birla,[1] to lunch with him. Their meeting was amicable,

[1] Ghanshyam Das Birla, 1894–1983. Industrialist. President of the Indian Chamber of Commerce, 1924. Member of the Bengal Legislative Council Fiscal Committee. Member of the Indian Legislative Assembly (he resigned in protest against legislation favouring imperial preference, 1930). Unofficial adviser to the Government of India on Indo-British trade negotiations, 1936–37. Member of a family of wealthy financiers and a personal friend of Gandhi; throughout the 1930s he paid monthly allowances to many leading members of the Indian National Congress. Subsequently one of the principal financiers of the Congress Party, and a donor of large sums for charitable and educational purposes.

and when it was over Birla sent a full account of it to Gandhi. Mr Churchill, Birla wrote, 'had been one of my most pleasant experiences' in Britain. On arriving at Chartwell Birla had found Churchill in the garden wearing 'a workman's apron which he did not change at lunch'; after lunch Churchill had shown him the buildings he had built and the bricks he had laid. In talking about India, Churchill had shown 'great emotion' and, as Birla reported, 'took great pride in calling himself a die-hard'. Birla's letter continued:

He asked what Mr Gandhi was doing. I explained. He was immensely interested and said 'Mr Gandhi has gone very high in my esteem since he stood up for the untouchables.' He wanted to know in detail about the untouchability work. I explained. He was glad that I was the President of the Anti-Untouchability League.

Then he asked about Mr Gandhi's village work. I explained. 'Why has the Indian agriculturist deteriorated in his method of cultivation?' This he said was the opinion of Lord Linlithgow. I said, 'Because he has been neglected all along.' 'Well you have the opportunity now. I do not like the Bill but it is now on the Statute Book. I am not going to bother any more, but do not give us a chance to say that we anticipated a breakdown. The die-hards would be pleased if there was a breakdown. You have got immense powers. Theoretically the Governors have all the powers, but in practice they have none. The King has all the powers in theory but none in practice. Socialists here had all the powers when they come into office, but they did not do anything radical. The Governors will never use the safeguards. So make it a success.'

I said, 'What is your test of success?' He said, 'My test is improvement in the lot of the masses, morally as well as materially. I do not care whether you are more or less loyal to Great Britain. I do not mind about education, but give the masses more butter. I stand for butter. As the French King said "fowl in the pot". Oh yes, I am every time for butter. Reduce the number of cows but improve their breed. Make every tiller of the soil his own landlord. Stop the best breed from being slaughtered. Provide a good bull for every village. You have a good Viceroy. Tell Mr Gandhi to use the powers that are offered and make the thing a success. I did not meet Mr Gandhi when he was in England. It was then rather awkward. My son, though met him. But I should like to meet him now. I would love to go to India before I die. If I went there I would stay for six months.'

Churchill went on to ask Birla whether he would be well received in India. Birla hastened to assure him that he would be. He would wait, he said, until Willingdon had left India 'but he would love to go after that'. Churchill's final words to Birla were:

I am genuinely sympathetic towards India. I have got real fears about the future. India, I feel is a burden on us. We have to maintain an army and for the sake of India we have to maintain Singapore and Near East strength. If India could look after herself we would be delighted. After all, the span of life is very small and I would not be too selfish. I would be only too delighted if the Reforms are a success. I have all along felt that there are fifty Indias. But you have got the things now; make it a success and if you do I will advocate your getting much more.

On September 23, after his return to Delhi, Birla wrote to Churchill:

Immediately after my arrival in India I met Mr Gandhi and told him of my impression and the conversation with you and other friends. He was very much interested to hear specially of my interview with you and remarked, 'I have got a good recollection of Mr Churchill when he was in the Colonial Office[1] and somehow or other since then I have held the opinion that I can always rely on his sympathy and goodwill.'

I was very much delighted to read your public interview as regards your Indian attitude in future. Since my talk with you, this did not come to me as a surprise but I was delighted that what you said to me in private conversation was subsequently expressed publicly. This, I think, will have a good effect.

Birla ended his letter with a reference to the European situation. 'This may find you in a turmoil of European crisis,' he wrote. 'I am rather anxious.' This was also Churchill's main concern. In his letter to his constituents of August 25 he had followed up his appeal for an end to the Indian controversy by pointing to dangers 'larger and nearer than Indian dangers', which made it necessary for a national concentration on new and urgent tasks. 'We have to provide for the defence and safety of the country and the Empire which depends on it. . . .' he wrote. 'We have to play our part with other nations in maintaining the peace of the world.'

---

[1] Churchill and Gandhi had met in London in 1908, when Churchill was Under-Secretary of State for the Colonies, and Gandhi a leading member of a delegation of Indians from South Africa protesting at anti-Indian discrimination. Churchill had been sympathetic towards their problem. He and Gandhi did not meet again.

Part Four

'The Prophet of Truth'
1935–1939

32

German Air Strength: 'We Can Never Catch Up'

FOLLOWING the Defence debate of 28 November 1934, the Government had tried to redefine its policy towards Germany's air strength. On December 11 Ramsay MacDonald had told the Cabinet that he 'attached much importance to saying that we recognized, although we did not legalise, German rearmament', while two days later Simon told his colleagues: 'If we were going to permit Germany to rearm in the air, we must somehow make it clear to her that she could not use Holland as a base.'

On 1 January 1935 Churchill wrote to Lord Londonderry, inviting him to Chartwell. 'I shall be paying a great deal of attention to the Air debates in the forthcoming session,' he wrote, 'so you must not tell me anything you do not want me to know. Nevertheless there may be points on which a discussion would be useful and harmless.' Writing to G. M. Trevelyan two days later, about Sir Edward Grey's foreign policy in 1914, Churchill commented: 'If England had not resisted German militarism, in my view the German hegemony of Europe would have been established and our island would have had to face a united Continental army. It is the same old story from the days of Marlborough and Napoleon. . . .'

On January 7 Professor Lindemann sent Churchill a copy of a note that he had written for Ramsay MacDonald, urging an enquiry into defence against air attack. That same day Lindemann wrote to Londonderry that he and his 'friends' would feel obliged 'to continue to press for more vigorous action . . .' This took the form of a letter, drafted by Lindemann and signed jointly by Austen Chamberlain and Churchill, which they sent to Ramsay MacDonald to urge a full Committee of Imperial Defence inquiry. Replying on January 10 MacDonald agreed, but then found out there was already a departmental committee headed by Henry Tizard,[1] which was dealing with this specific question of air defence. MacDonald therefore wrote to Austen Chamberlain on January 15 explaining that he had learnt of the existence of the Tizard Committee. Three days later Lindemann wrote to Churchill from Oxford: 'It is really hopeless the way Ramsay chops and changes. I gather from an Air Ministry man, who was here last night that that department is determined to do everything to inhibit action of the sort we want. I have just had Ormsby-Gore staying and he is very well disposed and promises to do what he can.'

'I quite agree,' Churchill replied to Lindemann on January 21, 'it is most unsatisfactory. The man is a hopeless twister and the only thing now is to have a debate.' Of the existing committee to examine air defence research, Lindemann wrote to Churchill on the following day that its terms of reference were in his view 'totally inadequate', and he went on to criticize 'its complete lack of status and power'. As he explained to Churchill:

What we want is a committee with instructions to find new methods of air defence with power to carry out the necessary experiments and develop the new technique. A committee 'to consider how far recent advances in scientific and technical knowledge can be used to strengthen the present methods of defence' is a mere waste of time. Even if it should exceed its terms of reference and come to a view contrary to that held by the Air Ministry, which selected and instructed it, it would have no power to proceed with experiments.

On February 14 Churchill, Austen Chamberlain and Lindemann went to see MacDonald, and received from him a promise that he would look into the possibility of setting up a special sub-committee of the Committee of Imperial Defence to deal with air defence research.

Speaking on February 22 at Loughton, in his constituency, Churchill warned of the 'great fact' of German rearmament, and urged his constituents to demand that the Government fulfil its promise to create an air force as strong as that of Germany. It was his belief, he added, that the

[1] Henry Thomas Tizard, 1885–1959. Educated at Westminster School, Magdalen College Oxford and Imperial College. Lecturer in Natural Science, Oxford, 1911–21. Royal Garrison Artillery, 1914; Royal Flying Corps, 1915–18. Lieutenant-Colonel, and Assistant Controller of Experiments and Research, RAF, 1918–19. Permanent Secretary, Department of Scientific and Industrial Research, 1927–29. Rector of Imperial College, 1929–42. Chairman, Aeronautical Research Committee, 1933–43. Knighted, 1937. Member of Council, Ministry of Aircraft Production, 1941–43. President of Magdalen College Oxford, 1942–46. Chairman, Advisory Council on Scientific Policy and Defence Research Policy, 1946–52.

German air force would soon be 'substantially stronger' than Britain's. During the course of his speech he pointed out that 'Even at the height of war we had never allowed ourselves to be dominated by such a passion of national exclusiveness as was exhibited by Germany to-day.'

For some months Churchill had been discussing his concerns about German air strength and intentions with the Permanent Under-Secretary of State at the Foreign Office, Sir Robert Vansittart, with whom he had been on terms of close friendship for many years, and who in 1933 had been elected to the Other Club. 'At first,' Vansittart later recalled in his memoirs, 'he only telephoned to my house in Park Street to test parts of speeches on me. Then he would come there after hours, and that was all right too. It was not all right when he took to striding into my room at the Foreign Office, and turned our connivance into an open secret. He cost me more than he knew.' Yet Vansittart was pleased to have found someone of authority who shared his fears, and pointed out to Churchill that although he 'chafed at inaction', even as a member of the Cabinet he would not be able to change the policy. 'He suited me much better outside,' Vansittart recalled, 'for my information on German trends would at least be voiced.'

On March 4, the Government published its Defence White Paper, in which it referred to 'serious deficiencies in all of the Defence Services', and announced that an extra £10 million was to be spent on defence in the coming year. The Germans were angered by MacDonald's decision, and postponed the planned visit to Berlin of Sir John Simon. Hitler's anger was commented on in the Foreign Office by a friend of Vansittart's, the head of the Central Department, Ralph Wigram,[1] who minuted: 'One wonders if in this "rage" there is not also a design to make things difficult for the Govt here, so as to make it more difficult to challenge the German rearmament.' That, Wigram added, 'would be entirely in the tradition of German diplomacy'. Vansittart minuted on March 7: 'All this is a far more overt German interference in British internal politics than anything the Soviets have done. The desire to feed the opposition & weaken the present Govt—on very thin pretexts—is plain to all with open eyes. How far it will succeed will depend upon the Govt's firmness and outspokeness on Monday,' a reference to the forth-

[1] Ralph Follett Wigram, 1890–1936. Educated at Eton and University College Oxford. Temporary Secretary, British Embassy, Washington, 1916–19. 3rd Secretary, Foreign Office, 1919; 2nd Secretary, 1920. 1st Secretary, British Embassy, Paris, 1924–33. CMG, 1933. A Counsellor in the Foreign Office, 1934, and head of the Central Department (among those who worked under him were Duncan Sandys, Michael Creswell and Anthony Rumbold). In 1925 he married Ava, daughter of J. E. C. Bodley (she married again, in 1941, John Anderson, 1st Viscount Waverley).

coming debate of March 10. Churchill himself was fully aware of the seriousness of these developments, explaining to his wife on March 8 that one of his reasons for fearing that their son might split the Conservative vote at Norwood was because 'the Socialist woman candidate[1] is fighting the election on pacifist lines', whereas the Government, 'tardily, timidly and inadequately have at last woken up to the rapidly increasing German peril'. Churchill went on to explain:

The German situation is increasingly sombre. Owing to the Government having said that their increase of ten million in armaments is due to Germany rearming, Hitler flew into a violent rage and refused to receive Simon who was about to visit him in Berlin. He alleged he had a cold but this was an obvious pretext. This gesture of spurning the British Foreign Secretary from the gates of Berlin is a significant measure of the conviction which Hitler has of the strength of the German Air Force and Army. Owing to the severity of their counter-espionage (you saw they beheaded two women with mediaeval gruesomeness last week) it is very difficult to know exactly what they have prepared, but that danger gathers apace is indisputable. All the frightened nations are at last beginning to huddle together. We are sending Anthony Eden to Moscow and I cannot disapprove. The Russians, like the French and ourselves, want to be let alone and the nations who want to be let alone to live in peace must join together for mutual security. There is safety in numbers. There is only safety in numbers.

If the Great War were resumed—for that is what it would mean in two or three years' time or even earlier—it will be the end of the world. How I hope and pray we may be spared such senseless horrors. I send you a copy of MacDonald's memorandum. That such a statement should have been wrung from such a man with such a past is a measure of the situation.[2]

On March 11 the House of Commons debated a Labour Party motion of censure against the Government's proposed increase of £10 million in defence spending. During the debate Clement Attlee deplored the

---

[1] Mrs B. A. Gould, who secured 40% of the Poll (as against 51% for Sandys).

[2] A week earlier, on February 26, Sir Warren Fisher had written to Baldwin: 'The consideration which principally influenced those of us who were responsible for suggesting to the Cabinet the idea of a White Paper was that our own British public should be educated as to the vital necessity of putting our defences in order. Our draft, therefore, was addressed to our own people, and if it were taken in any foreign country as a cause of annoyance, that surely would be a very important element in its justification. We are so convinced (a) of the reality of the danger of war, (b) of the profound ignorance of our own people, (c) of the degree to which they have been misled by so called pacifist propaganda, that we felt that if any document is to serve a useful purpose it must be downright in its expression, and avoid all half-hearted or unconvincing phraseology. Any document whatsoever, however mealy mouthed, if it contains one scintilla of truth cannot fail to tickle up the Germans, who, as we know perfectly well, are set on making themselves the most powerfully armed European state, and are in this mood not for mere display but for action when they think the time has arrived . . .'

policy of any increase in air armaments, telling the House: 'We are back in a pre-war atmosphere, we are back in the system of alliances and rivalries and an armaments race.' Britain could not avert the coming dangers, he warned, 'by national defence', but 'only by moving forward to a new world—a world of law, the abolition of national armaments with a world force and world economic system'. Running through the Defence White Paper, Attlee added, were 'nationalist and imperialist delusions . . . far more wild than any idealist dreams of the future that we hold'. At the end of the debate a Labour vote of censure was defeated by 424 votes to 79, with Churchill voting for the Government. Churchill reserved his own attack on the Government's air policy for the Air Estimates debate of March 19.

On March 16, in yet a further defiance of Germany's Treaty obligations, Hitler announced the reintroduction of compulsory military service throughout Germany. As a result of his decision, the permitted army of 300,000 could be doubled or even trebled without difficulty. Indeed, Hitler declared, he already had 500,000 men under arms.

On March 19, during the Air debate in the House of Commons, the Under-Secretary of State for Air, Sir Philip Sassoon, announced a further increase of 41½ squadrons in the next four years. He also declared: 'A great many inaccurate figures have been bandied about and an unduly black picture has been painted of our weakness in the air.' Nevertheless, he added, 'our numerical weakness is serious and cannot be allowed to continue'. Of Baldwin's pledge of November 1934, Sassoon stated:

We thought we might have at the end of this year, as the Lord President said, a 50 per cent superiority over Germany. From that point of view the situation has deteriorated. There has been a great acceleration, as far as we know, in the manufacture of aircraft in Germany, but still, in spite of that, at the end of this year we shall have a margin, though I do not say a margin of 50 per cent.

Speaking later in the debate Churchill again raised the question of the relative air strength of Britain and Germany. Baldwin had stated three and half months earlier that Germany's 'real strength' in the air was less than 50 per cent of Britain's. This statement, Churchill pointed out, was now admitted to have been untrue; Baldwin had been 'misled' in the figures he had given to the House. The Government's present figures showed the two Air Forces 'virtually on an equality, neck and neck'. Churchill expressed his grave concern at these admissions, telling the House of Commons:

I am certain that Germany's preparations are infinitely more far-reaching than our own. So that you have not only equality at the moment, but the great output which I have described, and you have behind that this enormous power to turn over, on the outbreak of war, the whole force of German industry. . . .

The next point is a matter of geography. The frontiers of Germany are very much nearer to London than the sea-coasts of this island are to Berlin, and whereas practically the whole of the German bombing air force can reach London with an effective load, very few, if any, of our aeroplanes can reach Berlin with any appreciable load of bombs. That must be considered as one of the factors in judging between the two countries. We only wish to live quietly and to be left alone.

Churchill was afraid that the time had already passed when relatively easy steps could have been taken to give Britain a secure margin of air superiority, telling the House:

If the necessary preparations had been made two years ago when the danger was clear and apparent, the last year would have seen a substantial advance, and this year would have seen a very great advance. Even at this time last year, if a resolve had been taken, as I urged, to double and redouble the British Air Force as soon as possible—Sir Herbert Samuel described me as a Malay run amok because I made such a suggestion—very much better results would have been yielded in 1935, and we should not find ourselves in our present extremely dangerous position.

Churchill then commented on Sassoon's earlier statement that 151 aircraft would be added to the British front line during the coming year. The Germans, he pointed out, were adding at least 100 or 150 a month, machines which 'are being turned into squadrons for which long-trained, ardent personnel are already assembled', and aerodromes prepared. He went on: 'Therefore, at the end of this year, when we were to have had a 50 per cent superiority over Germany, they will be at least, between three and four times as strong as we.' Britain, he added, had 'lost air parity already both in the number of machines and in their quality'. Churchill's speech continued:

Everyone sees now that we have entered a period of peril. . . . From being the least vulnerable of all nations we have, through developments in the air, become the most vulnerable, and yet, even now, we are not taking the measures which would be in true proportion to our needs.

Churchill ended his speech by urging the Government not to be deflected from its new policy by ill-informed public criticism, telling the House of Commons:

The Government have proposed these increases. They must face the storm. They will have to encounter every form of unfair attack. Their motives will be misrepresented. They will be calumniated and called war-mongers. Every kind of attack will be made upon them by many powerful, numerous and extremely vocal forces in this country. They are going to get it anyway. Why, then, not insist that the provision for the Air Force should be adequate, and then, however severe may be the censure and however strident the abuse which they have to face, at any rate there will be this satisfactory result— that His Majesty's Government will be able to feel that in this, of all matters the prime responsibility of a Government, they have done their duty.

Following Churchill's speech, a Labour MP, William Cove,[1] spoke scathingly of 'the scaremongering speech of the Rt Hon Member for Epping who endeavoured to make our flesh creep'. Of Churchill's defence demands Cove asked: 'Was there ever such a mad policy put before the House of Commons? Was there ever such a policy enunciated, pregnant with bankruptcy for civilization and indeed with terrible and drastic danger for this country? There was no thought or consideration in that speech for the terrible cost involved—cost in money, cost in trade, cost in human life. . . .'

At the end of the debate Sassoon spoke again, commenting on Churchill's speech: 'I do not think I can follow him into a morass of figures which must be, after all, very largely conjectural.' Sassoon continued:

We have every reason to think that we are today still stronger than Germany. . . . It is also not correct to say that at the end of the present Calendar year the German Air Force will be 50 per cent stronger than ours either on the basis of first-line strength or on the basis of total number of aircraft. So far as we can at present estimate, we shall still, at the end of this year, possess a margin of superiority.

During the coming year, Sassoon told the House, a further 151 aircraft would be added to Britain's first-line strength. For 1934, Sassoon said, Britain's first-line strength was 690 aircraft.[2]

On March 25, within a week of the Air debate, Hitler told Sir John Simon and Anthony Eden, who had finally been received in Berlin, that Germany 'had reached parity with Great Britain' as far as their

---

[1] William George Cove, 1888–1963. Educated at University College Exeter. President of the National Union of Teachers, 1922. Labour MP for Wellingborough, 1923–29; for Aberavon, 1929–59. Chairman of the Welsh Labour Parliamentary Group.

[2] Sassoon had included in his figure the Auxiliary Units and Fleet Air Arm squadrons. The actual British first-line strength as accepted by the Air Ministry was, however, only 453 first-line aircraft (see Sir Christopher Bullock's official letter of 5 April 1935, quoted on pages 632–3).

respective Air Forces were concerned. According to Hitler, Britain had 1,045 first-line machines, to which Simon replied that he 'thought we had 690 first line machines'. Hitler went on to tell Simon that Germany's air power was intended as a bulwark against the Soviet Union. He 'saw the Russian danger', Hitler declared, though he felt himself 'to be a solitary prophet in the desert. But, later, people would find out that he had been right.'[1]

In an article in the *Daily Mail* on April 4, Churchill urged that the Government should regard rearmament as the first priority.[2] 'Preparations should, of course, be made,' he wrote, 'to convert the whole of our industry, should it become necessary, to various forms of munition production. This has already been completed by every other country in the world to an extent and with a refinement which is at once astounding and alarming.' To his wife, Churchill wrote on the following day:

The political sensation of course is the statement by Hitler that his air force is already as strong as ours. This completely stultifies everything that Baldwin has said and incidentally vindicates all the assertions that I have made. I expect in fact he is really much stronger than we are. Certainly they will soon be at least two times greater than we are so that Baldwin's terms that we should not be less than any other country is going to be falsified.

Fancy if our Liberal Government had let the country down in this way before the Great War! I hope to press this matter hard in the next month and a good many of those who have opposed me on India now promise support on this.

On Sunday April 7 Ralph Wigram went to Chartwell to tell Churchill of the strong concern within the Foreign Office at Germany's growing air strength. Wigram stayed overnight. He was, Vansittart later recalled, 'made desperate by our danger'. The story he had to tell was one of increasing conflict between the facts as known to the Departments, and the use made of them by the Government. In a secret

---

[1] On March 22 Sir Eric Phipps telegraphed to the Foreign Office from Berlin: 'From equally reliable sources I learn Chancellor talks not only about Russia but also about Czechoslovakia whose existence he considers a regrettable smudge on the map of Europe. The German minorities numbering 3,000,000 must be restored to the Reich when Austria joins Germany. The problem of disposing of the Czechs is exercising him.'

[2] On April 2 Arthur Leslie Cranfield, managing editor of the *Daily Mail*, had written to Churchill to explain that they were holding back his article 'because it has been decided, for the time being, to keep our leader page articles and our main news page as clear as possible of armaments and the more belligerent phases of international affairs . . .' Cranfield added: 'The article itself is certainly a very powerful exposition of Britain's grave situation . . .'

memorandum of February 27, a member of the Central Department, M. J. Creswell,[1] had noted that on the basis of Air Ministry intelligence, German superiority over both France and Britain in respect of aircraft production 'is immeasurably great, as the German factories are already practically organised on an emergency war-time footing'. Creswell's memorandum also noted that the Air Ministry and the Foreign Office were agreed that this productive capacity 'was the real criterion of strength in the air', rather than any specific figures of first-line or reserve strength. 'This capacity,' Creswell emphasized, 'will determine the output of aircraft in the vital period between the destruction of the original air fleet in the first few weeks of war, and the moment, possibly several months after the outbreak of war, when the factories, reorganised on a war footing, will be able to produce an emergency output.' His memorandum continued:

The figures for first line, and service type aircraft, show that, if present tendencies continue unchecked, the German air force will have a larger number of machines in each category than either our Home Defence air force or the French metropolitan forces, before October 1936. Indeed it seems probable that they will surpass both the figures for our own home-stationed air force towards the end of the present year. . . . They will have the additional advantage of possessing entirely new material throughout. This programme once realised, the Air Ministry believe that the Germans will then begin a further expansion programme, to culminate in 1939.

In an annex to his memorandum, Creswell set out in tabulated form the figures provided by the Air Ministry for relative strengths. These showed, for October 1936, a projected British first-line strength of 710 aeroplanes, compared with a German first-line strength of 1,296. Commenting on Creswell's memorandum on March 8, Wigram himself had minuted: 'The state of affairs which it discloses is to me most alarming,' and he went on to ask: 'if this memorandum is correct, what becomes of Mr Baldwin's statement of last November that we would in no circumstances accept inferiority to Germany in the air—by which I have always understood inferiority in the Home Defence figures'. The new

---

[1] Michael Justin Creswell, 1909–86. Educated at Rugby and New College Oxford. Served in the Foreign Office, 1933–35; 3rd Secretary, Berlin, 1935–38; 2nd Secretary, Madrid, 1939–44; Athens, 1944. Counsellor, Teheran, 1947–49; Singapore, 1949–51. Minister to Cairo, 1951–54. Ambassador to Finland, 1954–58. Senior Civilian Instructor, Imperial Defence College, 1958–60. Knighted, 1960. Ambassador to Yugoslavia, 1960–64. Ambassador to the Argentine, 1964–69. On 8 June 1935 Sir Robert Vansittart wrote of how Creswell 'has greatly distinguished himself during his time in the FO by his papers on aviation, and is himself a very competent aviator'.

German figures, Wigram noted, 'throw a sharp light too on the seem-ingly extravagant German designs in many parts of Europe and with regard to the Colonies . . .' On March 11 Creswell noted that although his figures had come from the Air Ministry, it had 'proved impossible' for him to obtain any opinion from the Air Ministry about his memor-andum. A week later Wigram minuted: 'I do not believe that British people will not defend themselves at whatever inconvenience or danger if they realise the necessity. The problem is surely to make them realise —and there we have to grapple with 15 years of "unreality" brought on by the apparent weakness of Germany.'

Wigram had planned to go to Chartwell on March 24, but had been unable to get away. His wife, however, had gone, and had written, after her visit, that the 'things I told you at Chartwell were for yourself alone'. On the following day the unease within the Foreign Office had been accentuated by a report from the British Embassy in Berlin, sent by the Air Attaché, Group Captain Don,[1] which showed an 'immense factory activity' which would enable Germany to maintain not only her enor-mously increased first-line programme, but also her reserve strength 'on the 50 per cent principle'. Commenting on Don's report, a copy of which was also sent to Desmond Morton, Creswell minuted on April 3: 'the position in the German factories disclosed by this & other papers is a hundred times more disturbing than the position of the German flying fields. Is *this* just to advance the "moral rehabilitation" of the German people?' On April 4 Wigram noted:

This is a very important report, for the replacement of wastage is the decisive factor. As I minuted on another paper, this is a proof that in material as in effectives, equality for Germany means superiority over the so-called 'equals'.

This doesn't necessarily mean Germany is going to make war, but it does mean that—unless we look out—she is going to dictate her wishes to all of us.

On April 5 the Secretary to the Air Ministry, Sir Christopher Bullock,[2] informed the Foreign Office of the Air Ministry's most recent

[1] Francis Percival Don, 1886–1964. Educated at Rugby and Trinity College Cambridge. Qualified as an engineer; in business 1906–14. On active service at Gallipoli, 1915. Royal Flying Corps, 1916. Served in Egypt, 1916 and France, 1916–17 (wounded, prisoner of war). After the war he commanded the Cambridge University Air Squadron. Air Attaché, Berlin, 1934–37. Head of Mission to the French Air Forces in the Field, 1939. Air Officer in charge of Administration, British Forces in France, 1940. Senior Air Staff Officer, Ferry Command, Canada, 1941–42. Retired as Air Vice-Marshal, 1942. Regional Air Liaison Officer, Northern Region Civil Defence, 1943–45.

[2] Christopher Llewellyn Bullock, 1891–1972. Educated at Rugby and Trinity College Cambridge. Entered the Indian Civil Service, 1915. Captain, Rifle Brigade, France, 1915. Royal Flying Corps, Egypt, 1916 (wounded, despatches). On the Staff of the Air Ministry,

estimate of air strengths. His figures bore out in full the fears which Creswell, Wigram, Vansittart and Simon had expressed. Britain's existing first-line Home strength in the air was no more than 453 aircraft. More than 230 of the aeroplanes which Simon told Hitler were Britain's first-line strength were, in fact, Fleet Air Arm and Auxiliary Units. Of the former, amounting to 110 aircraft, 'there is no assurance that they would even be in home waters in an emergency', while the 127 Auxiliary Units 'correspond to "Territorial" and not to regular forces'. This figure of 453 first-line aircraft corresponded with the Air Ministry figure of 850 German first-line and 'Immediate Reserve' aircraft for February 1935. In his letter Bullock confirmed Group Captain Don's report on German factory organization, informing the Foreign Office:

Careful preparations have been made in Germany to organize her aircraft and aero-engine industry for mass production methods. Immense efforts have been made to ensure that the industry can change from a peace to a war footing with the minimum delay. These preparations imply that Germany might accept a lower peace-time figure for her air force than would be the case if her aircraft industry was not so highly organized; since by changing from peace to war production without delay she can make good her initial losses in a much shorter space of time than can countries whose industry is less well organized. In effect, this means that Germany, after the first clash and consequent losses, would be in a stronger position than her opponents during the period in which they were organizing their aircraft industry to meet war wastage.

Sir Robert Vansittart commented, on April 6: 'These figures should be known to every member of His Majesty's Government. I beg the Secretary of State to ensure that they are thus known.' It was quite clear, Vansittart added, 'that the number of service aircraft in Germany is already *greater* than (not equal to) the number in the UK'. Three days later Sir John Simon noted that Don's conclusion as to factory output 'is as serious as can be'.

It was because he was alarmed by these facts, and by all that they implied of a British weakness in the air, that Wigram visited Chartwell on April 7, strongly encouraged to do so by his wife, and discussed the problem in detail with Churchill. Two days later a telegram from Sir Eric Phipps in Berlin reached the Foreign Office, with confirmation that the German first-line strength was between 800 and 850 aero-

1917–18. Major, 1919. Principal Private Secretary to Churchill (when Secretary of State for Air), 1919, and to successive Secretaries of State, 1923–30. Permanent Secretary, Air Ministry, and Member of the Air Council, 1931–36. Knighted, 1932.

planes. The contrast between this figure, and the 453 British first-line strength admitted by the Air Ministry, caused Creswell to note that same day that Germany now had 'a 55% superiority over our home defence squadrons', even with the addition of the Auxiliary squadrons in the British figure, while Wigram minuted with consternation:

These are grave and terrible facts for those who are charged with the defence of this country. Not for nearly 300 years has any British Govt allowed this country to be exposed to such a threat from a Continental Power.

What steps will be taken to remedy this position? This is a question upon the answer of which depends not only our foreign policy but our whole existence.

Is it too much to expect that its study will now be taken out of the hands of the Air Ministry and considered by the Government as a whole with all the issues exposed?

Henceforth, Wigram was to be in constant communication with Churchill, both in correspondence, and in discussion in their respective homes, and was to provide Churchill with detailed documentary evidence, most of it secret, on Germany's strength and intentions. He also encouraged Churchill to talk to the French Prime Minister, Flandin, who agreed to send Churchill the French intelligence estimates of German air strength. In his war memoirs Churchill wrote, of Wigram:

He was a charming and fearless man, and his convictions, based upon profound knowledge and study, dominated his being. He saw as clearly as I did, but with more certain information, the awful peril which was closing in upon us. This drew us together. Often we met at his little house in North Street, and he and Mrs Wigram came to stay with us at Chartwell. Like other officials of high rank, he spoke to me with complete confidence. All this helped me to form and fortify my opinion about the Hitler Movement. For my part, with the many connections which I now had in France, in Germany and other countries, I had been able to send him a certain amount of information which we examined together.

The impact of the new disclosures of German strength led Sir John Simon to inform Ramsay MacDonald on April 10 of the whole situation and to bring it to the attention of the Committee of Imperial Defence. Basing himself largely on Creswell's minutes and Wigram's comments, Simon warned of 'the rapid growth of the German Air Force', and of '*the speed at which these aeroplanes are being manufactured*'. The danger, Simon concluded, was 'graver every day and one may have considerable doubts whether once left behind by Germany in the air, we shall ever be able to obtain a level of parity with her again'. On April 11 Churchill wrote to his wife:

My statements about the air last November are being proved true, and Baldwin's contradictions are completely falsified. There is no doubt that the Germans are already substantially superior to us in the air, and that they are manufacturing at such a rate that we cannot catch them up.[1] How discreditable for the Government to have been misled, and to have misled Parliament upon a matter involving the safety of the country.

On April 13 Churchill wrote to his wife again:

Charlie Londonderry rang up tonight in much earnestness with the evident hope of dissuading me from raising the question of air strength in the debate on Thursday. Considering how completely they have misled the country, I told him that no confidence could deter me from my public duty. Ha ha! He told me Ramsay had said he could tell me all the real figures. I said I thought my own were better. However I have agreed to ask him to luncheon at the flat on Tuesday. It is a shocking thing when a Government openly commits itself to statements on a matter affecting the public safety which are bound to be flagrantly disproved by events.

Churchill's letter continued:

You will no doubt have seen by now all the agitations there have been about the foreign situation. The Government have most foolishly flapped and buzzed about in aeroplanes all over Europe on what they call 'exploratory' missions, without learning anything that could not have been told them by ambassadors.

Poor Anthony Eden has suffered a very serious physical set back. He left Prague in an aeroplane to fly to England. They never told him there was bad weather ahead. But passing over the mountains they were enveloped in terrible snowstorms. Hurled about this way and that, he was frightfully seasick and all of a sudden a stabbing pain at his heart, after which he practically lost consciousness. The pilot managed to claw the machine down to ground near Cologne and German doctors forbad him to continue his journey.

---

[1] Churchill's forecast of German air development was correct, for despite the revised British air expansion schemes, on the outbreak of war in September 1939 the German *minimum* first-line air strength was 4,300 mobilizable aircraft, the *maximum* British first-line mobilizable strength was under 2,000. This was an even greater German lead than at the time of the Munich Conference in September 1938, when the *maximum* first-line British air strength was 1,606 (not all of them mobilizable), the *minimum* first-line German strength 3,200. The British figures were provided for Churchill after the war by the RAF Historian, Denis Richards (on 21 September 1947); the German figures by the Commanding General of the US Army Air Forces, Carl Spaatz (on 17 July 1947). These German figures were taken from the files of the Luftwaffe Quartermaster by Royal Air Force Intelligence agencies, and given to the USAAF (reference number ADI(K)352/1945).

But however the next day he managed to get back to England. He has now retired to bed. A small blood vessel in his heart burst, so no doubt there is a clot in a very dangerous place. He must remain quite quiet and still be in bed for what they tell him is six weeks. Evidently there must be danger in his condition. I am so sorry because we have so few new figures even of second rank, although our problems continually increase in size.

Churchill ended:

On the whole since you have been away the only great thing that has happened has been that Germany is now the greatest armed power in Europe. But I think the allies are all banking up against her and then I hope she will be kept in her place and not attempt to plunge into a terrible contest.

Rothermere rings me up every day. His anxiety is pitiful. He thinks the Germans are all powerful and that the French are corrupt and useless, and the English hopeless and doomed. He proposes to meet this situation by grovelling to Germany. 'Dear Germany, do destroy us last!' I endeavour to inculcate a more robust attitude.

On April 15 Lord Londonderry circulated the Cabinet with a memorandum deprecating 'panic' over German air strength, but seeking authority for a further expansion of the Royal Air Force. He enclosed a memorandum by the Chief of the Air Staff, Sir Edward Ellington, setting out proposals for this expansion.

Wigram had arranged to see Churchill once more, but on April 16 he wrote 'I was kept in a meeting and could not go out.' His letter went on: 'I was so very sorry as I wanted to tell you about what we talked about the other Sunday evening—but there have been developments today, and it looks as if at last the matter was going to be taken up seriously. Perhaps after Easter you will let me come and have another talk.'

Under the new Air Ministry plan, to which Wigram was referring, Britain would not achieve parity with Germany until 1942. By April 1940, under the Ellington scheme, Germany would possess 1,512 first-line aeroplanes, and Britain 1,174. The Foreign Office had not been asked for their opinion on this scheme in advance, and when they saw its details were appalled by it. On April 16 Creswell noted that 'the German superiority of 2 to 1 over our home stationed regular forces' would be maintained 'till after April 1937 even under the proposed new programme'. On April 23 Vansittart sent Simon a memorandum drafted by Creswell and Wigram, pointing out that the 1942 date was 'getting near the recently discarded assumption of the 10 years' immunity from any major war. The Foreign Office cannot concur in such a speculation which is shared by no one else in Europe.' Vansittart added: 'Once allow the Germans over a period of years to grow used to a lead in the air, and they will hang on to it.' Angered by the Air Ministry's tacit acceptance of inferiority in the air for at least five years, Vansittart's memorandum continued:

In recent years our foreign policy has been heavily handicapped by our loss of material weight. This is a view which has been uncomfortably confirmed from many foreign sources. To impose upon us inferiority till 1939 will confirm it still further. Apart from the visibly growing German menace, any continued inferiority in the air will weaken our influence throughout Europe. We are already considered to need more support than we can give. It will increase the difficulty of conducting an independent and effective foreign policy if this foreign estimate of us is to continue. . . .

If a clear foreign policy is adequately backed, there need be no fear of the future. There is much to fear if this is not the case; and it cannot be the case on these dates and figures. Foreign policy and air policy are necessarily complimentary.

On Sunday April 21 Churchill was at Chartwell, where he drafted a memorandum on the air situation. In it, the effect of his discussion with Wigram, and his knowledge of the Foreign Office attitude, was clearly apparent. The memorandum began by pointing out the repeated discrepancies in the Government's public statements, going back to his own warnings of March 1933. In particular, Churchill drew attention to his dispute with Baldwin during the previous November, when Churchill had asserted in the House of Commons that the German Air Force 'was rapidly approaching equality with our own'. Churchill's memorandum continued:

The Lord President [Stanley Baldwin] strenuously denied this. He declared—I presume on figures supplied by the Air Ministry—that the German Air Force on that date (ie November 1934) was not 'rapidly approaching equality with our own', but was in fact not 50% (ie not half) our own. He stated further 'that by this time next year' (ie November 1935) 'we should still have a 50% superiority' (ie three to two) over Germany. These statements were wrong, but they were everywhere accepted as most reassuring by the British public.

Drawing entirely upon the Government's own public statement Churchill continued:

In November 1934 the Lord President stated the British first-line strength for home defence at 880, including the auxiliary squadrons (127) and the Fleet Air Arm (about 100). He also suggested that remarkably large reserves of aircraft existed behind our first line strength which it was not in the public interest to disclose.

In March 1935, the last debate upon the subject, the Under Secretary of State corrected the Lord President's figure of the strength of the British home defence Air Force from 880 to 690, including the auxiliary squadrons and Fleet Air Arm. . . .

If the Fleet Air Arm and Auxiliary squadrons were excluded, Churchill pointed out, the total British first-line strength would be shown to be 'not 880, as stated by the Lord President, but under 460, or little more than half his figure'. Commenting on Hitler's statement that he now had parity in the air with Britain, Churchill wrote:

If it should prove that Herr Hitler was basing himself upon the Lord President's assertion of November (viz a first-line strength of 880 machines), and that he claims to have equality with that at the present time, then it is certain that he has not merely equality, but a very large superiority at the present time over our first-line with its Home Defence strength of under 460. This fact would show how far astray were the statements of the Lord President in November 1934 and of the Under Secretary of State in March 1935.

Churchill went on to stress that in Germany itself the air force had long been regarded 'as the instrument by which Germany will regain dominance in Europe'. Behind the air figures themselves was the industry of Germany 'organized for immediate transition to war and capable of producing under war conditions a steady mass production of aeroplanes and engines. . . .' Churchill's memorandum ended:

The conclusions which cannot be avoided are that the Government have allowed themselves to be mistaken in their estimate of British and German strength at particular dates; and that the statements made by Ministers in Parliament are wrong, are admitted to be wrong, and will be proved still more grievously wrong with every month that passes. The German superiority, already large, will now grow upon all counts with progressive speed, to an extent determinable only by the decisions of the German Government.

The declaration and promise made by the Lord President to Parliament in March 1934 that His Majesty's Government would maintain an Air Force equal to that of any power within striking distance of our shores, is not being made good. We are in a position of perilous weakness compared to Germany at a time when we are involved by our existing commitments in the European situation, and when that situation is degenerating. The realisation of these facts explains the confident attitude which Herr Hitler, no doubt with the assent of the German General Staff, permits himself to adopt not only to all the neighbours of Germany, but to the League of Nations.

On April 26 the *Daily Telegraph* published an article by their unnamed 'Diplomatic Correspondent'[1] on German air strength. The German Air Force was already equipped, the article declared, 'with practically double the number of first-line military aircraft available in this country at any given moment for purposes of home defence'. The British figure, according to the paper, was 480 first-line aeroplanes for home defence, and 1,020 world-wide. Four days later Creswell minuted: 'The figures are wrong: 1020 should be 880, and 480 either 453 or 580 according to whether or not the auxiliary squadrons are included; but in the main, the newspaper's argument is correct, and these points will no doubt be eloquently made by Mr Churchill and Ld Winterton and others in the next House of Commons Debate.'

Churchill telegraphed to several politicians and friends on the day of the *Daily Telegraph* article, urging them to read it.[2] In thanking him for the telegram, Page Croft replied on April 27: 'I had already read the Daily Telegraph, which is a complete vindication of the warnings which you have given with regard to German air preparations. I congratulate you on your triumph although I wish the facts were not so grave and that you had proved pessimist indeed.'[3]

On April 28 Ralph Wigram and his wife were again at Chartwell, where they stayed the night. During the day Churchill wrote to Lord Tyrrell: 'There seems to be now the kind of crisis that there was in 1911, with the difference that we then had three years to put the fleet in readiness whereas I greatly fear that modern conditions will allow us only a much shorter interval in the Air.' That same day Churchill sent out several copies of his air memorandum, writing to Ramsay Mac-Donald to ask that armaments, 'which are as you have pointed out, at the present moment unhappily at the core of the situation', should be discussed in the next foreign policy debate. In sending a copy of his memorandum to Baldwin, Churchill wrote:

I send you a copy of a memorandum which sets forth the main outline of the case which I propose to unfold to the House when the promised debate on

---

[1] Victor Charles Hugh Gordon-Lennox, 1897–1968. A grandson of the 6th Duke of Richmond and Gordon. Educated privately and at Trinity College Cambridge. Captain, Grenadier Guards, 1915–18 (wounded). Military Secretary to General Haking, Danzig, 1919–20. Political correspondent of the *Daily Mail*, 1923–29. Diplomatic correspondent of the *Daily Telegraph*, 1934–42. Editor of the weekly *Whitehall Letter*. A member of the Carlton Club.

[2] In all, nine telegrams were despatched: to Sir Robert Horne, Sir Austen Chamberlain, Lord Winterton, Lord Wolmer, Sir Henry Page Croft, General Seely, Lloyd George, Sir Archibald Sinclair and Frederick Guest.

[3] During May the Cabinet called for an analysis of the *Daily Telegraph* article. According to the article, Britain would have 1,460 aeroplanes by April 1937; the Cabinet figure was 1,512. The article wrote of 498 first-line machines; the Cabinet figure was 580.

the Air Estimates takes place in the early part of May. I have also sent a copy to Londonderry who had expressed a wish to talk over facts and figures with me. The disclosures in Friday's Daily Telegraph which I have only just seen, and which evidently come from some official source,[1] confirm a great deal of my paper written last Sunday. No one will be better pleased than I shall be if any of the essential facts can be upset. I fear they have got ahead of us not only in actual power but even more in the momentum which their air industry has now acquired.

Londonderry wrote to Churchill on April 30: 'I recognize very clearly the determination of Germany to make themselves powerful enough to challenge the rest of the world as soon as possible, and probably the only difference between us is as to the date when they can achieve this result.' The Air Ministry's 'paramount duty', Londonderry added, was to 'accelerate our rate of development', and he was 'leaving no stone unturned to carry this policy into effect'.

As well as seeking to establish the true facts, Churchill continued to deprecate alarmist talk, and was much angered when the *Daily Mail* not only gave credence to a German air strength figure of 20,000, which he was convinced was grossly exaggerated, but also announced its support for the National Government.[2] On April 29 he wrote in protest to Lord Rothermere:

I find it very difficult to follow the line you are now taking. For two years or more you have shown the danger of the German air power. Now when it is admitted, and when the country is bound to realise how frightfully they have been let down, you come out with fulsome praise of the Ministers responsible and declare that the Government could be in no way better. At the same time you continue to quote figures about the air which are so fantastic that they simply deprive you of the enormous credit which otherwise would have been due to your foresight and vigilance.

On April 30 Ramsay MacDonald presided over a meeting of the Ministerial Committee on Defence Requirements, at which Baldwin, Halifax,[3] Londonderry, Neville Chamberlain and Simon were among

---

[1] Possibly the Foreign Office: in his memoirs Vansittart recalled that Ralph Wigram had 'asked leave to leak some of my figures to selected publicists. I pondered and agreed.'

[2] The *Daily Mail* article was based on a memorandum by Captain Norman Macmillan MC, AFC. Lord Rothermere sent Churchill the memorandum itself on May 5. Churchill at once sent it on to Desmond Morton, who replied on May 13 that much of it was 'of a somewhat speculative nature'.

[3] Formerly Lord Irwin, Viceroy of India. In 1934 he succeeded his father as 3rd Viscount Halifax. In June 1932 he had been appointed President of the Board of Education.

those present. Simon pointed out that the new Air Ministry scheme assumed that the German first-line strength, once it reached 1,512 aeroplanes, would remain at that figure, which he doubted would be the case. But even if it were, Ellington's figures made it 'quite clear that we were not keeping our pledge of parity with the German Air Force'. Speaking for the Air Ministry, Londonderry stated that the Air Ministry 'did not wish to embark on a very rapid programme of expansion and be faced at the end of the period with a position in which they would have a large number of obsolescent aircraft on their hands'. To this Simon retorted that Baldwin had, in the previous November, pledged the Government to keep British air strength higher than that of any country within striking distance, and he went on: 'That statement did not say that on some future date we should be equal to a potentially hostile country, but, on the contrary, it implied that *at no time* should we have an inferior force.' The Air Ministry's proposals, Simon insisted, 'did not fulfil the pledge which had been given'.

A few moments later the First Commissioner of Works, William Ormsby-Gore, pressed Londonderry to say when parity would be achieved, and quoted Vansittart's criticism of the Air Ministry view that Germany would not be ready for war until 1942. Ormsby-Gore pointed out to his colleagues that Vansittart believed Germany would be ready for war not later than early 1938. But Londonderry replied 'that this statement in Sir Robert Vansittart's Paper was the non-professional point of view and it did not take into account considerations which the professional had to assess'.

During the meeting Sir John Simon pointed out what he called a 'rather curious feature' of the Air Staff Paper, telling his colleagues:

The revised British plans showed a slower rate of acceleration than the German plans. Our figures were: for April 1935, 453; for April 1936, 576; and for April 1937, 740; whereas Germany, in April 1935, would have 250 more than us and 382 more next year, and the longer the expansion went on, the farther ahead would Germany get.

MacDonald told the Cabinet that by April 1937 'Germany would have 1,512 aircraft, and we should have 740', and he went on to ask whether this was 'a situation that the Government could explain and defend in the House?' For his part, Neville Chamberlain felt that the Government was 'bound to maintain the position' as represented in Baldwin's pledge; not to do so 'would be to give Germany the impression that we were frightened'. Chamberlain then proposed the formula which was finally adopted, telling his colleagues that in his view 'the Government were entitled to put their own construction on the Lord President's statement and that it was not necessary to state the number of aeroplanes but to deal with the matter in terms of air power and air strength'.

Londonderry accepted this suggestion, and went on to stress that as the German pilot training 'was inferior to ours', it was incorrect to state, despite the actual aeroplane situation, 'that Germany was stronger'.[1] The mood of the discussion became one of relief that a way could be found to tell the House of Commons that parity had not in fact been lost, although both the Air Ministry figures, and the Foreign Office interpretation of them made it clear, not only that the gap between the two air forces would continue to grow in Germany's favour, but that German foreign policy would be able to exploit this ever widening gap at least until 1942, when the Air Ministry hoped to close the gap, provided German expansion came to an end by the spring of 1937.

A long discussion followed on whether it would be possible to expand the air programme further. Ellington explained the difficulties of any expansion, a major difficulty being the labour shortage. He added, with reference to MacDonald's earlier disarmament policy, 'that the two or three years during which the armaments truce had been in force had prevented us from doing anything at all, but, at the same time, had allowed Germany to prepare for the expansion which she was now making'. It was clear from the discussion that it would be very difficult to raise Britain's proposed 740 first-line air strength to 1,200. Walter Elliot warned his colleagues 'that the Government might be going to make a pledge in the House which they might subsequently find they would be unable to fulfil for practical reasons and that this might create a rather serious situation'. It was finally decided to set up a small subcommittee, of Cunliffe-Lister, Runciman and Ormsby-Gore, 'to recommend what steps should be taken' actually to fulfil the Air Parity pledge in the future. For the purpose of the debate itself, although all Ministers accepted that Baldwin's pledge was at present not being fulfilled, it was agreed, on Neville Chamberlain's suggestion, that an official statement should be made 'that the Government intended to maintain the position as stated by the Lord President, and were taking the necessary steps to this end'.

[1] On September 20 the Parliamentary Under-Secretary of State for Foreign Affairs, Lord Stanhope, noted: 'The Air Ministry base their claims to our superior position largely to our training—particularly I believe in "formation flying". I believe that the younger airmen say that the speed of modern aircraft [and] their enhanced performance has made this out of date. So Germany may be less behind in training and in equipment than the air ministry is prepared to admit.'

On May 2 Ava Wigram wrote to Churchill to thank him for having seen them. 'I do not know how to express to you my gratitude for your kindness to me & Ralph,' she wrote warmly, on the day of the defence debate. 'It has been a very real joy to us to go and see you at Chartwell & to talk things over with you. Thank you with all my heart.' That same day in Paris, France and the Soviet Union signed a pact of mutual cooperation. In the House of Commons, Ramsay MacDonald gave a survey of European affairs. On February 3, he pointed out, the European Governments had signed the London Declaration aimed at 'a freely negotiated armament pact with Germany and the other Powers, which would take the place of the military clauses of Part V of the Treaty of Versailles'. If this pact were to work, 'the greater part of our immediate European dangers would disappear'. It was therefore 'greatly to be deplored', he said, that Germany had chosen this moment to impose conscription, raise its peacetime army to 550,000 men, and 'create a military air force'. MacDonald stressed that in their anxiety 'to advance the prospects of the Disarmament Conference' successive British Governments had for several years 'deliberately allowed the defences to become weakened'. Now, he said, it was clear from Hitler's statement that Germany had reached parity with Britain, and that the German air force had been expanded 'to a point considerably in excess of the estimates which we were able to place before the House last year'. And yet, he added, the outlook—'and I say this with great conviction and considerable intimacy of knowledge'—still possessed 'chances of appeasement as well as palpable danger'.

Churchill spoke, with appreciation, of France's 'self-restraint and courage'. He also expressed his 'general agreement' with British policy at Stresa, where, on April 12, Britain, France and Italy had agreed to cooperate to maintain the independence of Austria. His fear was that these two measures came too late:

. . . if only Great Britain, France and Italy had pledged themselves two or three years ago to work in association for maintaining peace and collective security, how different might have been our position. Indeed, it is possible that the dangers into which we are steadily advancing would never have arisen. But the world and the Parliaments and public opinion would have none of that in those days.

When the situation was manageable it was neglected, and now that it is thoroughly out of hand we apply too late the remedies which then might have effected a cure.

There is nothing new in the story. It is as old as the sibylline books. It falls into that long, dismal catalogue of the fruitlessness of experience and the confirmed unteachability of mankind. Want of foresight, unwillingness to act when action would be simple and effective, lack of clear thinking, confusion of counsel until the emergency comes, until self-preservation strikes its jarring gong—these are the features which constitute the endless repetition of history.

Britain's foreign policy, Churchill insisted, would depend henceforth on the state of her armaments. The German design was to develop such air, land and sea forces as would enable them to 'dominate all Europe'. Germany's air ascendancy was 'already a fact', her military ascendancy was 'far advanced' and even her naval power was on the increase. Baldwin's assurance in November 1934 that Germany's 'real strength' in the air was less than 50% of Britain's had been proved a false assurance. Sir Philip Sassoon's statement in March 1935 that Britain would still have a superiority by the end of 1935 had likewise been proved false. Churchill's speech continued:

Is there a Member of the Government who will get up now and say that in November next we shall still have a 50 per cent superiority over Germany? Is there a member of the Government who will still assert that in March last, six weeks ago, we had a substantial superiority, or that we have a superiority to-day? No, Sir. The whole of these assertions, made in the most sweeping manner and on the highest authority, are now admitted to be entirely wrong.

Churchill went on to speak of a German air superiority of 'between three and four times' that of Britain by the end of the year, and he added:

It is very dangerous to underrate German efficiency in any military matter. All my experience has taught me to think that any such supposition would be most imprudent. Anyhow, now that the Germans are openly marshalling and exercising their squadrons and forming them with great rapidity, we may take it that six months of this summer and autumn will amply give them the combined training which they require, having regard to the long, careful individual preparations which have been made. Therefore, any superiority which we may at this moment possess in personnel and in formation flying and in air manoeuvring is a wasting asset, and will be gone by the end of the autumn, having regard to the enormously increased German air strength and the superiority of their machines.[1]

---

[1] Churchill's apprehensions were well-founded. By October 1935 the British first-line strength did not exceed 800 aircraft (including reserves) while there were already 2,400 German military aircraft available for first-line service. (Source: Graph of 'Comparative Output of 1st Line Aircraft', prepared during 1948 by Lieutenant-General Sir Henry Pownall on figures provided by the Air Ministry Historical Section, from captured German records.) In a letter to Churchill on 30 September 1935 (see page 671) Desmond Morton explained that there had been 'a slowing down' in the creation of new German squadrons, but that the training of pilots and the actual manufacture of military aircraft had not slowed

There was, Churchill believed, still a possibility of preserving peace. 'Never must we despair,' he said, 'never must we give in, but we must face facts and draw true conclusions from them.' The only solution that now remained lay, he was convinced, in collective European security. The policy of detachment, or isolation, 'about which we have heard so much and which in many ways is so attractive' was no longer open. 'Such a policy,' he added, 'does not close the door upon a revision of the Treaties, but it procures a sense of stability, and an adequate gathering together of all reasonable Powers for self-defence, before any inquiry of that character can be entered upon.' It was now essential for Britain to retrieve 'the woeful miscalculations of which we are at present the dupes, and of which, unless we take warning in time, we may some day be the victims'.

After Churchill had spoken, a Conservative MP, Colonel Moore,[1] told the House: 'Although one hates to criticise anyone in the evening of his days, nothing can excuse the right hon Member for Epping (Mr Churchill) for having permeated his entire speech with the atmosphere that Germany is arming for war.' But on May 3 Ralph Wigram wrote to Churchill: 'I read your speech of yesterday with the greatest pleasure, and I am sure it will have a great effect in Parliament and the Country— and I hope that it will make the Government push on all the faster with the air programme.' Wigram added: 'I hope very much you will speak again in the same style when the defence debate comes on.' That same day Sir Maurice Hankey wrote to Ramsay MacDonald that the atmosphere of recent debates revealed 'that Parliament considers us to be in something approximating to a state of emergency in Defence matters', and that Churchill, Austen Chamberlain 'and a number of lesser lights' would expect 'some sort of pronouncement'. Hankey suggested a special Cabinet Committee to serve as the nucleus of a War Cabinet, which should include two Ministers without departmental responsibili-

---

down. Morton also noted that the mere counting of first-line aircraft gave a false picture of German strength. To obtain a true picture, he stressed, all military type machines (not just those organized in squadrons), together with the potential of German industry, should be taken into account. Churchill's forecast incorporated these criteria. Because Churchill based his calculations on Morton's definition of German air power, he was not taken by surprise by the rapid expansion of the German first-line forces during 1937 and 1938.

[1] Thomas Cecil Russell Moore, 1886–1971. Educated at Trinity College Dublin. Entered the Army, 1908. On active service in France, 1914–15. General Headquarters, Ireland, 1916–18. On active service in Russia, 1918–20; Ireland, 1920–23 (OBE, 1918, CBE, 1919, despatches twice). Retired with the rank of Lieutenant-Colonel, 1925. Conservative MP for Ayr Burgh, 1925–50; Ayr, 1950–64. Knighted, 1937. Created Baronet, 1956.

ties, and would be instructed to conduct 'an intensive inquiry to tune up our arrangements', taking up weak points 'one by one'.

On May 3 the *Daily Express*, in its Opinion column, apologized to Churchill for having 'ignored' his air warnings of six months before. 'The reaction of the British public to the Nazi rearmament,' it asserted, 'will be plain and positive.' But Churchill himself was still uneasy about the slow response to his warnings. On May 3 he wrote to Lord Camrose:

I am sure you will feel, as I do, grave continuing anxiety at the disclosure of the way in which the Germans have turned the tables upon us in the air. Air parity can never be attained by England alone. We must do our best and hope that in close concert with France, which is now tardily making great exertions, we shall be able to preserve our safety. I do trust you will continue to watch with vigilance the development of this lamentable affair.

Churchill reiterated his worries two days later when he wrote to Colonel Pakenham-Walsh:

I am astounded at the indifference with which the press and public seem to view the fact that the Government have been utterly wrong about the German air strength, and that we are now substantially outnumbered and must continue to fall further and further behind for at least two years, in fact we can never catch up unless they wish it.

33

The Need for War Preparations: 'Every Day Counts'

ON May 8 the sub-committee on Air Parity reported to the Cabinet's Defence Requirements Committee. According to the sub-committee's report, it was now virtually 'unavoidable' that in a year's time, by April 1936, the 'relative numerical position' between the British and German first-line air strengths would be 'even more unfavourable' to Britain. For Britain to reach 1,500 first-line aircraft by April 1937, a total of 3,800 aircraft of all types would have to be produced within the next two years. Yet this figure was 1,400 above the 'existing approved programme'. The additional figure could, the sub-committee believed, be reached without 'the reorganisation of industry', although 'vigorous publicity' would be needed to launch a recruiting drive for pilots and labour.

On May 10 a meeting of the Cabinet's Defence Requirements Committee discussed the sub-committee's report. During the discussion Cunliffe-Lister pointed out, as the minutes recorded, 'that it was a cause for anxiety that in heavy bombers Germany was ahead of us in speed, range and load', and that the 'future German air force' was likely to reach 1,500 first-line aeroplanes. Cunliffe-Lister added that 'it was well within German manufacturing capacity to exceed that figure if they wished to do so'.

Lord Londonderry explained that in Britain 'matters have come to a standstill in the development of bombing aircraft because of the Disarmament Conference'. The discussion came to an end with a statement by the Chief of the Imperial General Staff, Sir Archibald Montgomery Massingbird,[1] who declared:

[1] Archibald Armar Montgomery-Massingbird, 1871–1947. Educated at Charterhouse and the Royal Military Academy Woolwich. On active service in South Africa, 1899–1902

647

. . . by aiming at parity with the German Air Force we were issuing a new challenge to Germany in a form of warfare in which we were most vulnerable. Germany was better placed than we were, not only geographically. Everything was in Germany's favour and they had a greater capacity to expand their Air Force than we possessed. We were challenging Germany to a race in air armament and in such a race, Germany was bound to win. Germany had three great advantages. She had conscription, we had not, and this counted for much, especially as her population was 66 million to our 44 million. Germany's preparations for industrial mobilisation were infinitely better than ours. Lastly, Germany could devote all her efforts to her home Army and Air Force; we had world-wide commitments, naval, military and air.

The Defence Requirements Committee concluded 'that the Air Ministry should be authorised to proceed' with the revised programme 'so far as it referred to fighter and light bomber aircraft'; and that this was to be put to the Cabinet on May 21.

On May 8 Lord Rothermere had sent Churchill a copy of a letter he had received from Hitler. In his letter, which Hitler had sent from Berlin on May 3, he assured Rothermere that for fifteen years he had stood for Anglo-German understanding, that it was still his aim, that the 1914–18 war could have been avoided, and had been disastrous both to Britain and to Germany, and that it was essential for both nations to 'bury the hatchet together'. Hitler's letter continued:

All the so-called mutual-assistance pacts which are being hatched today will subserve discord rather than peace. An Anglo-German understanding would form in Europe a force for peace and reason of 120 million people of the highest type. The historically unique colonial ability and sea-power of England would be united to one of the greatest soldier-races of the world. Were this understanding extended by the joining-up of the American nation, then it would, indeed, be hard to see who in the world could disturb peace without wilfully and consciously neglecting the interests of the White race. . . .

Churchill replied to Lord Rothermere on May 12: 'If his proposal means that we should come to an understanding with Germany to dominate Europe I think this would be contrary to the whole of our history,' and he added:

You know the old fable of the jackal who went hunting with the tiger and what happened after the hunt was over. Thus Elizabeth resisted Philip II of

---

(wounded) and in France, 1914–18 (despatches nine times). Major-General, 1918. Knighted, 1919. Lieutenant-General, 1926; General, 1930. Adjutant-General to the Forces, 1931–33. Chief of the Imperial General Staff 1933–36. Field-Marshal, 1935.

Spain. Thus William III and Marlborough resisted Louis XIV. Thus Pitt resisted Napoleon, and thus we all resisted William II of Germany. Only by taking this path and effort have we preserved ourselves and our liberties, and reached our present position. I see no reason myself to change from this traditional view.

However I think a reasonable answer to Hitler would be that his plans of an Anglo-German understanding would be most agreeable provided they included France and gave fair consideration to Italy. Perhaps you will consider this.

Lord Rothermere shared Churchill's apprehensions. 'I do not trust Hitler as a statesman,' he replied on May 13. 'I am quite sure that his group harbour the most ambitious designs. They have the full intention of making Germany *the* world power.' On May 14 Lord Camrose, in his reply to Churchill, showed that he too had no illusions. 'You can rely on us,' Camrose wrote, 'to do all we can in regard to Air parity.' On the following day, H. A. Gwynne wrote from the offices of the *Morning Post* that although he believed Churchill's estimate of German air strength was exaggerated, 'you may rest assured I shall not cease from urging on the Government the creation of an Air Force superior to that of Germany'. On May 16 Churchill replied:

There is no doubt that the German air force is already substantially superior to the British air force at home, and that we shall fall further and further behind with every month that passes for a long time to come.

I do not myself make use of the expression 'first line aeroplane'. I use the following terminology (1) first line air strength and (2) military machines. 'First line air strength' means a military machine formed in a squadron with its pilot, ground services and at least one other serviceable machine in reserve. Our home strength in this respect is today about 460, not including the Fleet Air Arm (110) or the Auxiliary Squadron (127). . . .

The term 'military machine' means a fighting or bombing service aeroplane not used for training purposes. By both these tests the German strength in numbers and still more in modernity is already greater than ours.

Commenting on the proposed air expansion, Ralph Wigram minuted for Sir John Simon on May 14: 'No progress will be made towards catching up the overwhelming German lead in the potentiality of war expansion,' and stressed that the question of Britain's building capacity should be brought before the Cabinet. M. J. Creswell minuted on the following day: 'it is much to be hoped that a more determined attempt than is suggested by this request will be made to reorganise the British aircraft industry so that it can compete with that of Germany for immediate expansion in time of war'.

On May 21 the Cabinet accepted the new air programme, known as Scheme C, whereby Britain's first-line home strength would be 1,512 aeroplanes by 31 March 1937. Yet Cunliffe-Lister had explained to the Defence Requirements Committee on May 10 that the German first-line strength by March 1937 could, if Germany wished, be even higher. Nor was there any discussion of the need to reorganize the British industry, along the lines indicated by Wigram and Creswell, for a further expansion if needed.[1]

In the first week of May, in preparation for the forthcoming defence debate, Churchill had visited Wigram at his home in North Street. 'We so much enjoyed the talk with you here,' Ava Wigram wrote on May 10. Ten days later, at Wigram's suggestion, Churchill saw Lord Tyrrell, and gave him a copy of his air memorandum of April 21. On the following day Tyrrell wrote to Churchill: 'Thank you for letting me see enclosed. It entirely confirms the information in my possession & yet I was told today by a Minister that at present we could beat the German air force. I defied him to make that statement in tomorrow's debate. I don't think he will.' Tyrrell added: 'Thank you also for a delightful evening. Listening to you is a tonic! Your love of country & courage are exceedingly refreshing, though perhaps "démodé"!'

On May 22 during the long-awaited defence debate, Baldwin told the House of Commons that during his speech the previous November he had been 'completely wrong' in his estimate of future German air strength. Baldwin added: 'I tell the House so frankly, because neither I nor my advisers, from whom we could get accurate information, had any idea of the exact rate at which production was being, could be, and actually was being speeded up in Germany in the six months between November and now. We were completely misled on that subject. I will not say we had not rumours. There was a great deal of hearsay, but we could get no facts. . . .' During his speech Baldwin revealed that the Government were now aiming for a first-line air strength of about 1,500. To this figure, he said, 'we intend to proceed with all the speed that we can'. Towards the end of his speech Baldwin declared:

I would only like to say, in concluding this part of my speech, and I think that it is only due to say it, that there has been a great deal of criticism, both in the Press and verbally, about the Air Ministry as though they were responsible for possibly an inadequate programme, for not having gone ahead faster, and for many other things. I only want to repeat that whatever

---

[1] In addition, Scheme C included 204 regular and 120 non-regular light bombers which by February 1936 were considered to have too short a range and too small a bomb load, and had subsequently to be converted to medium bombers.

responsibility there may be—and we are perfectly ready to meet criticism—that responsibility is not that of any single Ministry; it is the responsibility of the Government as a whole, and we are all responsible and we are all to blame.

Later in the debate Churchill repeated his warnings about German air strength, and reiterated his conviction that the Government had no excuse for not having rearmed sooner: 'I have been told that the reason for the Government not having acted before was that public opinion was not ripe for rearmament,' he said. 'I hope that we shall never accept such a reason as that. The Government have been in control of overwhelming majorities in both Houses of Parliament. There is no Vote they could not have proposed for the national defence which would not have been accepted and, if the case was made out to the general satisfaction, as it is now, probably without serious opposition of any kind.' As for the British public, Churchill added, 'nothing that has ever happened in this country could lead Ministers of the Crown to suppose that when a serious case of public danger is put to them they will not respond to any request'.

Churchill suggested that the House of Commons should revert to the precedent of 1917, and hold a secret Session on the subject of British and German air strength. It would be of great advantage to the evolution of a sound policy, he believed, 'if we could discuss some of these technical points without our conversation being heard by all Europe'. Baldwin did not respond to this suggestion. 'Speech successful,' Churchill telegraphed to his son on May 23, 'but Government escaped as usual.' To Lady Houston he wrote two days later: 'I am pleased to have played a useful part in warning the Government of the growth of the German air force, though very sorry that they did not take my advice in time.'

On May 30, in preparation for the following day's debate in the House of Commons, Ralph Wigram sent Churchill a twelve-page Foreign Office memorandum on Hitler's claims and allegations. Commenting on Hitler's claim that before 1933 Germany had disarmed in accordance with the Treaty of Versailles, the memorandum pointed out that there was 'from 1927 onwards an accumulating mass of evidence which tended to show that Germany was even at that date actively laying the foundations of her rearmament'. Evidence was also quoted, some of it from Hitler's own speeches, to show that Germany 'did not intend indefinitely to admit the Treaty clauses dealing with her eastern frontiers or with the independence of Austria'.

On May 31 Churchill spoke again in the House of Commons of the European situation, and of Hitler's appeal of May 21 that all air bombing should be outlawed, and that Germany had no wish to 'interfere' in the affairs of Austria. Many speakers, including Eden and Attlee, had welcomed Hitler's appeal, and were hopeful that it could lead to what Sir Herbert Samuel described as 'an appeasement in Western Europe'. Churchill agreed that Hitler's offer should not be treated 'with blank distrust', and he welcomed the Air Locarno as 'an eminently desirable objective towards which we should work'. But, he warned, 'do not let us underrate the difficulties which attach to them', and he added:

One would imagine, sitting in this House to-day, that the dangers were in process of abating. I believe that the exact contrary is the truth—that they are steadily advancing upon us, and that no one can be certain that a time may not be reached, or when it will be reached, when events may have passed altogether out of control. We must look at the facts. Nourish your hopes, but do not overlook realities.

Churchill went on to speak of the many dangers which Hitler's conciliatory words should not, in his view, be allowed to mask. German arms manufacture, he pointed out, now had the 'first claim' on all German industry. Beginning with schoolchildren, a 'tremendous propaganda' was at work throughout Germany, 'enforced by the most vigorous and harsh sanctions at every stage'. Psychologically, materially and technically, German 'war power' was being built up without respite, 'and with ever-increasing momentum'. In Czechoslovakia, a new Nazi-type Party had been created among the Sudeten Germans, and had begun to flourish. Poland continued politically 'in the German system'. Not only Austria, but Hungary, Bulgaria and even Yugoslavia, were each beginning to look to Germany with admiration; so also was Japan. France was under stress. Italy was preoccupied with Abyssinia. It was therefore easy, Churchill said, for Hitler and his Government to pursue what had been called by some 'power diplomacy', and he pointed out that two or three years before it had been considered 'sentimental' to urge the redress of German grievances. 'Now we see them with their grievances unredressed,' he continued, 'with all their ambitions unsatisfied, continuing from strength to strength, and the whole world waits from week to week to hear what are the words which will fall from the heads of the German nation. It is a woeful transformation which has taken place.' Churchill ended:

By all means follow your lines of hope and your paths of peace, but do not close your eyes to the fact that we are entering a corridor of deepening and darkening danger and that we shall have to move along it for many months and possibly for years to come . . .

'You alone,' Desmond Morton wrote to Churchill that same day, 'seem to have galvanised the House . . . the summaries show it was, if possible, even above the level of your usual magnificent handling of these subjects.'

During the first week of June it became clear that Baldwin was about to become Prime Minister. But Churchill realized that there would be no place for him in the new Cabinet. 'Reconstruction purely conventional,' he telegraphed to his son on June 3. Two days later Ramsay MacDonald presided over his last Cabinet, and on June 7 the new Cabinet was announced. Baldwin thus became Prime Minister for the third time, with Sir Samuel Hoare replacing Sir John Simon as Foreign Secretary, and Sir Philip Cunliffe-Lister replacing Lord Londonderry as Secretary of State for Air.[1]

On June 7, during the debate on the adjournment, Churchill spoke to an attentive House of his dissatisfaction at the slow pace of air defence research. During his speech he pointed out that, in answer to a question he had asked two days earlier, it had been admitted by the Government that the Committee of Imperial Defence's special sub-committee on Air Defence Research had met only twice in the three months since it had been set up. His speech continued: 'Really the whole story is another slow-motion picture,' and he added: 'If a really scientific Committee had been set to work and funds provided, twenty important experiments would be under way by now, any one of which might yield results decisive on the whole of our defence problem.' He was only raising the matter in public, Churchill told the House, 'with a view to stimulating and spurring on' the work of the Committee.

Towards the end of June Churchill tried to set up, for Defence, a Conservative backbench organization similar to that which had existed during the India Bill controversy. 'Not only the bulk of the members of the India Parliamentary Committee,' he explained to Sir Robert Horne

[1] The Marquess of Zetland succeeded Hoare at the India Office. Neville Chamberlain remained Chancellor of the Exchequer and Sir John Simon went to the Home Office. There were two newcomers to the Cabinet: Anthony Eden, aged 38, was appointed to the newly created post of Minister without Portfolio for League of Nations Affairs, and Malcolm MacDonald, four years Eden's junior, became Secretary of State for the Colonies and Dominions. Churchill was not invited to join the new administration. When one of the directors of the British General Press, Allan J. Eidenow, asked him to write an article about the personalities of the National Government he replied, on June 7: 'they are pretty small people though called upon to deal with momentous issues and play large parts'.

on June 29, but also a number of other members 'who are strong supporters of the Government' would agree to join. The objects of the new
organization, he wrote, would be:

1. To watch vigilantly the position of national Defence and to use all
   parliamentary opportunities to procure the necessary action from His
   Majesty's Government.
2. To arouse the country to the peril in which we stand and to combat the
   prevailing apathy and defeatism.
3. To render mutual assistance to Conservative Members and candidates
   who belong to the proposed association:
   (a) by having a concerted policy,
   (b) by speakers,
       and,
   (c) if possible and where needed by funds.

Churchill envisaged, within the Conservative Party in Parliament, 'a
strong core of members accustomed to act together on the great Imperial issues of Defence', but no such organization came into being.
Meanwhile, Churchill's worries about German policy were acute. 'I
think things are going from bad to worse in Europe,' he wrote to Ava
Wigram on July 2, 'and I feel the greatest anxiety about them.'

At the beginning of July the new Secretary of State for Air, Sir Philip
Cunliffe-Lister, asked Baldwin if Churchill could join the Air Defence
Research sub-committee of the Committee of Imperial Defence. Bald-
win agreed, and Hankey was at once deputed to tell Churchill about it.
On July 6 Churchill wrote to Baldwin from Chartwell:

My dear Prime Minister,

I asked Hankey to come over here this morning & tell me about the
Committee & its work. It is as I thought highly technical in character &
quite non-controversial. If you think I can be of any use upon it, I shall be
vy glad to serve. None of this subject is suited to Parly discussion. I have a
few ideas wh, if of any value, would be quite unfit for publication. But I
should be glad to put them into the common stock.

I must remain free to debate all the general issues of Air strength, Air
Policy, Air Programmes. . . .

Two days later Baldwin replied:

I am glad, and I think you may be of real help in a most important
investigation.

Of course, you are free as air (the correct expression in this case!) to
debate the general issues of policy, programmes, and all else connected with
the Air Services.

My invitation was not intended as a muzzle, but as a gesture of friendliness to an old colleague.

Churchill replied from Chartwell on July 9: 'Believe me, I recognise and value the "gesture of friendliness"—especially considering our disputes about various things,' and he added:

You have gathered to yourself a fund of personal good will and public confidence which is indispensable to our safety at the present time. But there lies before us a period of strain and peril which I do not think has been equalled—no, not even in the Great War, certainly not in the years preceding it. Naturally this will never fail to govern my action.

On July 11, in his first speech as Foreign Secretary, Sir Samuel Hoare criticized those people who, he said, 'seem to take a morbid delight in alarms and excursions, in a psychology, shall I say, of fear, perhaps even of brutality', and he continued:

Only yesterday I heard of a small child, a child of one of my friends, who was found surrounded by a number of air balloons, and her nurse said to her, 'Why is it that you have so many air balloons?' The child answered, 'I like to make myself afraid by popping.' That may be a harmless habit in the case of a child, but it is a dangerous habit in the case of the many alarm-mongers and scaremongers who now seem to take this delight in creating crises, and, if there be crises, in making the crises worse than they otherwise would be.

During his speech, Hoare praised the recently-signed Anglo-German Naval Agreement. It was, he said, 'an agreement profitable alike to peace and to the taxpayer'.[1]

Speaking after Hoare, Churchill denounced the Anglo-German Naval Agreement, whereby, he said, 'we have condoned, and even praised, the German treaty-breaking in fleet-building'; an action, he warned, which had weakened the League of Nations and impaired the principle of collective security. Ralph Wigram, who supported the Anglo-German Naval Agreement, had written to Churchill from the Foreign Office on June 18: 'I think anything that will help to extricate us from the disarmament muddle is to be welcomed—and that in the end the French will not regret that we cut the Gordian Knot for them. And after all we are the people who bear the brunt on the sea.' But Churchill was not influenced by his friend's argument, telling the House of Commons on July 11: 'I cannot feel that this German Naval

---

[1] Under the Anglo-German Naval Agreement, which was signed on 18 June 1935, the Versailles Treaty restrictions on German shipbuilding were abolished (without France having been consulted), and Germany was allowed to build at once, from scratch, a fleet of up to 35% the size of the British fleet.

Agreement is at all a matter for rejoicing. I remain still under this impression, that the one great fear of Europe is the power and might of the rearmed strength of Germany, and that the one great hope is the gathering together of Powers who are conscious of that fear.' Without collective security, Churchill added, the 'tremendous process' of German rearmament would inevitably lead to a 'lamentable breakdown of peace'.

On July 12 Desmond Morton sent Churchill his 'humble and profound admiration' for all he had said. During the course of his letter he wrote:

... you made every unanswerable point of criticism of the Government's actions and you cleared the air by recalling attention to the fact that Germany remains the true menace to European peace.

In this last connection, I fear something very odd has come over all the Departments of State. Perhaps it is the heat. If not pro-German propaganda is having considerable success.

Curiously enough Ministers hitherto in mild opposition to their Departments *anti-German* attitude have reversed their position. . . . On Thursday morning Walter Elliot said to me: 'We shall soon be debating these questions under the shadow of the guns'!!

At the end of his letter, Morton told Churchill: 'I am sorry to have inflicted this outburst on you, but the magnificent clarity of your ideas last night have burst the dykes of "pent up feeling".'

'I fear greatly the dangers which menace both our countries,' Churchill wrote to Flandin on July 23, 'and indeed what is still called civilisation. But I cannot shake off that feeling which I have always had for the last quarter of a century, namely that England and France will somehow or other come through together.'

On July 23 Churchill completed a lengthy and detailed memorandum on air strategy and defence. Written for the Air Defence Research subcommittee, it warned of the 'ugly possibility' that the Germans might by air power be able 'to beat a nation to its knees in a very few months, or even weeks, by violent aerial mass attack'. If Britain were separated from France, Churchill wrote, she would be 'a potentially apt victim for this form of aggression'. It was therefore not enough, he argued, to locate enemy aircraft before they reached the coast; it was essential also to intercept and track them. Churchill proposed experiments with single seater aeroplanes 'of the highest possible speed', fitted with wireless, which would be alerted as soon as the enemy aircraft had been spotted, and sent 'to join the raiders while they are crossing the sea at some distance from our coasts'. These aeroplanes would be designed to keep contact with the raiders and to report to ground wireless stations on 'the direction and strength of the raiding force'. Churchill proposed calling the intercepting aircraft 'the Lambs', for, as he explained: 'everywhere that Mary went the Lamb was sure to go'.

Churchill went on to demand vastly accelerated research on every potential anti-aircraft device, including 'imparting power to the Lambs to gain and hold contact and report or signal continuously'. His memorandum ended: 'I trust that at least the whole process of research and experiment will be pursued at exactly the same rate as it would have been by the Ministry of Munitions in 1917 and 1918, and that neither waste of money nor disappointment will slacken our search'.

'Every day counts,' Churchill wrote to Philip Cunliffe-Lister, on August 8, and he went on:

The Germans are spending £1,000 *millions* this year on military preparations direct and indirect. Can you doubt what this portends? Their lead in the Air is growing hourly greater. For eighteen months or more we shall only be falling further behind the Air Parity we were assured would be maintained, and was necessary for our safety. We are moving into dangers greater than any I have seen in my lifetime; and it may be that fearful experiences lie before us.

I wonder that you do not institute a 'Following-up' branch. I found this invaluable in the Ministry of Munitions. If, say, a decision was taken on Monday, on Thursday this branch would ask 'Where is the paper? What has been done about it, etc'. If any hold-up was detected, the Follow-up branch went to that point and had full power to refer at once to high authority. Thus everything rolled forward, faster than any Minister however energetic could make it.

Churchill ended his letter on a personal note of anxiety and alarm:

Time may be so short; and when I think of our position before the war, and the intense efforts made, and our great naval preponderance, I cannot help feeling very anxious about our present leisurely procedure, and woeful inferiority. No one wishes you better than I do in the key office you have undertaken, and that is why I write this word of alarm. Pray do not resent it from an aged counsellor.

Replying on August 12, Cunliffe-Lister stressed that the efforts already being made were substantial. A weekly meeting of the Air Council, he wrote, served as 'what you call a follow-up system', and every item of air policy was under regular scrutiny. 'We are I hope improving all the time,' he wrote. 'But the organisation, the plan, the industrial structure are right and the machine is working at full pressure.' Cunliffe-Lister added: 'I want you to have the whole picture;

and there is a lot of detail I should like you to know, which I can tell you about when we meet.' In his letter, Cunliffe-Lister also informed Churchill about the 'industrial organisation for war', but he revealed that all such planning was still subject to a serious limitation, telling Churchill:

You don't want to divert civil industry in advance, more than you need; but you do want the machine to be ready. A great deal of preliminary work has been done, and improvements in the organisation are now being made. I have made proposals myself; and so have others. Frankly I should myself like to see the whole of this planning, which is the industrial counterpart of the man-power organisation, put under the control of a special minister. It wants the maximum of concentrated effort.

Cunliffe-Lister ended by a description of the work and problems of the Air Defence Research sub-committee, of which Churchill was now a member, of whose secret discoveries he was already being officially and fully informed, and to which he had made his own contribution. As Cunliffe-Lister wrote in his letter of August 12:

The work is of supreme importance; and I agree we want as many experiments as possible carried on concurrently. The key is detection and location. Here by good fortune we have made a tremendous advance. The wireless detection experiments were put in hand very rapidly; they are going on continuously: and they have already yielded results so definite that we know we have got the right line. Then you come along and hit on exactly what is needed as the complement to this. I hope you will go to Orfordness and see the apparatus at work. . . .

Churchill had attended his first meeting of the Air Defence Research sub-committee on July 25, when Sir Henry Tizard reported on the success of experiments, actually completed only on the previous day, by Robert Watson-Watt [1] for locating aircraft by radio-location methods. It was agreed that these experiments, conducted at Orfordness, had already produced results 'sufficient to justify executive action',

---

[1] Robert Watson-Watt, 1892–1973. Engineer and inventor. Educated at St Andrews and Dundee Universities. Joined the staff of the Metereological Office, London, 1915, where he did successful research into the radio location of thunderstorms. Superintendent of the radio research stations at Aldershot and Slough, 1921; subsequently Superintendent of the radio department of the National Physical Laboratory. His radio wave experiments for detecting aircraft were sponsored by the Air Ministry in 1935. Superintendent at Bawdsey, 1936–38. Director of Communications Development, Air Ministry, 1938–40. After Pearl Harbor (December 1941) he advised the United States on radar defence. Knighted, 1942. After the war he received £50,000 for his contribution to radar development.

and on September 16 the sub-committee agreed to establish 'a chain of stations' and to acquire Bawdsey Manor 'as a centre of research work and Head Quarters of the Organisation'. In December Treasury authority was given to build four stations for the new discovery.[1]

From the moment Churchill became a member of the Air Defence Research sub-committee he worked with an ever-present sense of emergency and concern.

Having read an article in *The Times* on August 17, on infra-red detection, Churchill discussed the subject that very same day with Colonel Pownall,[2] and was also sent later in the day a detailed account of the possibilities of infra-red detection from the Joint Secretary of the Sub-Committee, A. P. Rowe.[3] For the next four years, Churchill was to conduct many similar exchanges on detailed technical matters relating to anti-aircraft defence, and was to press continually for vigilance and speed. Each of his letters and suggestions was examined in the department concerned, often with agreement.

On August 22, Lord Weir sent Cunliffe-Lister a five-page commentary on Churchill's letter of August 8, during which he wrote: 'I agree with Winston that the chasing and follow-up must be energetically done,' and he went on to ask:

Are we doing all we ought to to anticipate by proper planning and arrangement the grave delays which were the feature of our almost fatal unpreparedness in 1914? More than that, and apart from mere paper planning, have we anticipated our definite weakness in our facilities for producing war material which undoubtedly exists, and are we taking rapid steps to strengthen these

---

[1] Originally known as Radio Direction Finding, or RDF, the existence of 'radar' was not publicly acknowledged until 1941, when it was referred to as 'Radiolocation'. The name 'radar' an American term (derived from 'Radio Direction and Ranging'), was adopted in 1943 as part of the effort to establish a joint Anglo-American nomenclature.

[2] Henry Royds Pownall, 1887–1961. Educated at Rugby and the Royal Military Academy, Woolwich. Royal Field Artillery, 1906–14. On active service in France, 1914–19 (DSO, Military Cross). Brigade Major, Royal Artillery 17th Division, 1917–19. Brigade Major, School of Artillery, 1924–25. Military Assistant Secretary, Committee of Imperial Defence, 1933–35; Deputy Secretary, 1936. Commandant, School of Artillery, 1936–38. Director of Military Operations and Intelligence, War Office, 1938–39. Chief of General Staff, British Expeditionary Force, 1939–40. Knighted, 1940. Inspector-General of Home Guard, 1940. Vice-Chief of the Imperial General Staff, 1941. Commander-in-Chief, Far East, 1941–42; GOC, Ceylon, 1942–43; C-in-C, Persia and Iraq, 1943; Chief of Staff to the Supreme Allied Commander South East Asia, 1943–44. One of Churchill's principal assistants on his war memoirs, 1946.

[3] Albert Percival Rowe, 1898–1976. Joint Secretary of the Air Defence Research sub-committee, Committee of Imperial Defence, 1935–38. Chief Superintendent, Telecommunications Research Establishment, 1938–45. Deputy Controller of Research and Development, Admiralty, 1946–47. Defence Scientific Adviser to the Australian Government, 1947–48. Vice-Chancellor of the University of Adelaide, 1948–58.

by definite and corrective action? It is my clear impression that we have not done and are not doing this, and in this problem I am in full sympathy with Winston's view.

On August 16 Churchill had drafted a further seven-page letter to Cunliffe-Lister, in which he warned of the dangers of any delays in experimental work, and went on to insist that the Government's policy of aircraft construction was still inadequate. In his draft he wrote:

Your policy is to produce a 1,500 first line Air strength as soon as possible under peace conditions, and at the same time to prepare the factories for the gt supply to be required from them in war time. The Germans have already done this last, and will have a first line air strength equal to the French long before we can achieve this. The French IL air strength is 2,000 not the 1,500 announced to Parliament by S.B.

The French having been greatly alarmed in January by the lamentable condition of their Air Force voted 21 millions sterling supplementary estimates, & since then another supplementary of £26 million, of which a large portion goes to the Air. This shows the rate at wh they are endeavouring to repair their neglect. Moreover they have already the cadres, aerodromes etc on the scale of a 2,000 IL force. Thus these gt additional new sums go mainly to the improvement of their fighting strength. We on the other hand are spending £5 millions supplementary only altho much of this must go into bricks & mortar, land etc.

What is Germany spending on the Air alone this year? I suppose much more than £100 millions sterling.

Besides this scale of expenditure, Churchill added, British expenditure 'seems Lilliputian', and he continued:

We ought forthwith to develop our air force in a war time atmosphere not hesitating where necessary to interrupt or deflect normal industry.

The entire capacity of the existing private firms should be commandeered for British production. Not until the danger period is passed should sales of surplus production to foreign countries be allowed, unless it can be shown conclusively that such sales in no way reduce capacity to manufacture for our own requirements. But you ought to suck it all up like a sponge.

Of course we have to utilise the services of the private firms to the utmost, and there can be no question of substituting national for private manufacture. But I hold strongly that apart from the entire maximum output of the British private aeroplane industry, a national assembling plant should be set up at once upon a very great scale capable of producing by the assembly of major components at least 500 aeroplanes a month from say the eighteenth month of initiation. This plant should be devised to be complementary to rather than competitive with the private firms.[1]

Churchill went on to stress that private and state manufacture were needed, 'both at the maximum', and that in Britain's 'present backward condition' there would be no danger of overproduction. An increase in 'high class military pilots' was also essential, and both the Army and the Navy should be used as sources of recruits. As for the senior Air Ministry personnel, Churchill wrote:

I wonder whether the existing brain power of the Royal Air Force is at all adequate to its staff work as one of the three defence services, or to the study of the decisive strategic problems involved. They are a new service, largely headed by the young aviators I knew a quarter of a century ago when military and naval flying were in their infancy. I say not a word against them. But that they require strong reinforcement from the Staff Officers of the Army, and I wish I could say of the Navy, seems certain.

At the moment, Churchill added, 'I find it difficult to believe that the Royal Air Force can do their share in thinking out the problems of defence in a manner comparable to the two older Services.'

Churchill's final plea was for an aerodrome expansion plan in excess of the existing one, which was, he wrote, 'far below war needs', and he went on to ask: 'why should not say fifty additional aerodromes to those you are planning, with their hangars properly earthed-in be constructed in the best sites for safety and convenience on the western side of the island'. These, Churchill wrote, 'would be alternative refuges for our expansion programme squadrons, even if they were not required for the much larger programme of expansion which emergency will require'.

Before sending this letter, Churchill showed it to Desmond Morton for his comments. Morton suggested several points which Churchill incorporated. Among these points were three which Churchill was to stress repeatedly in his secret correspondence with the Air Ministry. In his letter, of August 23, Morton wrote:

Not only is the German Aircraft Industry capable of very *large* emergency expansion, but through the application of mass production methods, for which preparations have already been made, it is capable of very *rapid* expansion. . . .

In recommending the setting up of a National Assembly Plant, would you

[1] Churchill's suggestion was not taken up. But in Germany, using similar methods, there was a regular output by December 1937 of 500 air frames and 1,010 aero engines a month (Industrial Intelligence Centre, memorandum on the German aircraft industry, 28 January 1938). Comparative British production was 118 air frames and 250 engines a month (Committee of Imperial Defence discussion, 31 March 1938).

agree to add anything suggesting that that plant be laid out on lines suitable for the assembly into aircraft of whole wings, tail pieces, engines, fuselages, engine nacelles and other large components manufactured complete by privately owned firms other than those already normally engaged in aircraft manufacture? This is the German method of attaining rapid mass production in emergency.

I have another idea which you may care to consider for the training of pilots.

The Government subsidises Imperial Airways. Why should not the latter be called upon to do what the German Lufthansa does in return for the German Government subsidy, namely carry on their flights an extra special pilot under training as a military pilot? By this method a reserve is built up of men who are not only trained to fly, but trained to fly heavy aircraft long distances and to find their way to the chief centres of foreign countries under all conditions of light and weather; that is, they are trained as reserve leaders for bombing squadrons.

Henceforth, until the outbreak of war, Morton continued to supply Churchill with detailed information about the development of German military preparedness in all its aspects, and to ensure that Churchill was as well-informed, not only about specific problems, but about all organizational, financial and planning aspects of German policy, as only a Cabinet Minister could be. This advantage, combined with the information on British policy which he received both officially and secretly from the Ministers themselves, together with his work on the Air Defence Research sub-committee, gave Churchill a unique position in British public life for someone without Cabinet office.

During August, Mussolini threatened to invade Abyssinia as soon as the rainy season ended in October, and as proof that he was in earnest broke off negotiations with Britain and France. On August 21 Churchill discussed Mussolini's move with the new Foreign Secretary, Sir Samuel Hoare, and with Anthony Eden, who had become Minister for League of Nations Affairs. According to Hoare's own secret record of the conversation, Churchill 'showed himself deeply incensed at the Italian action and more than once pressed strongly for the reinforcement of the Mediterranean Fleet. In his view, the situation was mainly due to our naval weakness in the Mediterranean.' Churchill then urged the need for 'collective' action. Pressed to explain, he told Hoare and Eden, as the note continued:

that he meant principally Anglo-French co-operation. Should we, we asked him, use every possible pressure with the French to bring them up to the application of sanctions? His answer was that we must realise the extremely difficult position of France and must not make impossible requests to M Laval.[1] He himself was doubtful whether in the last resort the French Government would go as far as economic sanctions, but that was no reason why we should not urge them upon the French. It was most important in his view that at the right time we should make it perfectly clear to the world that as far as we are concerned we are prepared to carry out our League obligations even to the point of war with all our military resources, provided that other members of the League are prepared to take the same action. . . .

Churchill went on to tell Hoare and Eden 'that his main interest in the League was as a defence against Germany', and he added:

If the League now collapsed in ignominy, it meant the destruction of the bond that united British and French policy and of the instrument that might in the future be chiefly effective as a deterrent to German aggression.

Mr Churchill assured us that he would support the Government on these lines, and added that as he now regarded the Indian chapter as closed, he was anxious to co-operate with us.

On August 24 the British Government declared publicly that if Italy attacked Abyssinia, Britain would uphold its obligations under the Covenant of the League of Nations. Churchill was still worried that the naval preparations were not sufficient to sustain the policy. On August 25 he discussed this lack of preparedness with George Lloyd, who encouraged him to put his fears directly to the Ministers concerned. That same day Churchill wrote to Hoare: 'I am sure you will be on your guard against the capital fault of letting diplomacy get ahead of naval preparedness. We took care about this in 1914.' He went on to ask: 'Where are the fleets? Are they in good order? Are they adequate? Are they capable of rapid and complete concentration? Are they safe? Have they been formally warned to take precautions? Remember you are putting extreme pressure upon a Dictator who may get into desperate straits. He may well measure your corn by his bushel. He may at any moment in the next fortnight credit you with designs far beyond what the Cabinet at present harbour. While you are talking judicious, nicely-guarded formulas, he may act with violence.' Churchill went on to

[1] Pierre Laval, 1883–1945. A Socialist Deputy from 1914. Minister of Public Works, 1925; of Justice, 1926; of Labour, 1930 and 1932. Prime Minister and Foreign Minister, January 1931–February 1932. Minister of Colonies, 1934. Foreign Minister October 1934–December 1935. Prime Minister June 1935–January 1936. Deputy Prime Minister and Minister of Information, 1940. Foreign Minister, October–December 1940 and April 1941–November 1943. Minister of the Interior (and of Information and Propaganda), 1942. Deputy Head of State (to Pétain), April 1942–August 1944. Forced by the Germans to move his Government to Germany, August 1944. Escaped first to Switzerland, then to Spain, following Germany's defeat. Tried for treason in France, 1945, and executed.

warn, in detail, of Britain's naval weakness in the Mediterranean. 'I spent some time today,' he wrote, 'looking up the cruiser and flotilla construction of the two countries since the war. It seems to me you have not half the strength of Italy in modern cruisers and destroyers, and still less in modern submarines.' Churchill added that George Lloyd, who was with him, 'thinks I ought to send you this letter in view of the hazards of the situation. I do not ask you for a detailed answer; but we should like your assurance that you have been satisfied with the Admiralty dispositions.'

'Please have no hesitation,' Hoare replied to Churchill on August 27, 'in sending me any suggestions or warnings that you think necessary. You know as well as anyone the risks of a situation such as this, and you also know as well as anyone at least outside the Government the present state of our Imperial Defence.' On August 29 Churchill wrote again, raising with Hoare the question of the location and movement of several individual ships, and urging a proper concentration of forces in the eastern Mediterranean. His letter ended:

I do hope the Admiralty will not despise the Italians and believe they will never dare to put to and face us. Mussolini's Italy may be quite different to that of the Great War. The only safe ruling is to provide superior material forces easily concentratable and if our sailors are better that is a make-weight. I do not like the idea of our Mediterranean Fleet taking refuge in the Suez Canal or the Red Sea. But that would be much better than running any risks of being 'Port-Arthured'. The entry of the Grand Fleet into the Mediterranean would restore the situation. But practically the whole Navy would have to go.

'I need not say,' Churchill added, 'that I write this not to bring about a war but only to warn against the kind of temptations and "trailing the coat" dispositions which are an additional source of danger, and may provide the spark for the explosion.'

On September 1 Churchill left England for a short holiday at Maxine Elliot's villa in the South of France. On his way to Paris by train he found Sir Robert Horne among the other passengers, and they drove together from the Gare du Nord to the Ritz Hotel. 'He had seen Baldwin at Aix,' Churchill reported to his wife that same day, '& says B. does not mean on any account to get into war. Rather it seems they will use the humiliation to rebuild the Fleet & Air F.'

While he was in the South of France Churchill continued to receive letters from those who believed that he should be brought back to the Cabinet. On September 3 the editor of the *Observer*, J. L. Garvin, wrote of how, three months earlier, 'I gave Baldwin a terse memorandum urging him to make you the creator of Air Parity which by a grand effort—with our financial resources not unemployed—could be done in a year, giving us time to make the rest secure and to remake the Navy.' Garvin also reported to Churchill on a visit to Neville Chamberlain, in which he had urged Chamberlain to work with Churchill. 'On India,' Garvin wrote, 'you couldn't have more than $\frac{1}{4}$ of the Unionist Party with you. On Defence you can have $\frac{3}{4}$ of it at least with you for good and change all—by stating the case as you alone can state it. I can see no other hope.' Garvin's letter ended: 'Neville is sound in heart and character but has never had the chance to master these matters of *haute politik* which have engaged you and me all our lives. I have been labouring night and day since June to grip every aspect. Useless to say more until we can talk. Your greatest hour is yours now for the taking.'

Among the guests at Maxine Elliot's villa was a young American writer, Vincent Sheean,[1] who later recalled:

Winston in such a society was slightly out of place—more so even than Maxine—but he never noticed. He went to the South of France for a holiday and he proposed to take it as it happened, accepting whatever company there was, amiably bent upon making the best of everything. Nobody ever had such a lordly way of disregarding what seemed trivial or without significance. He could sit through a whole conversation on some subject that held no interest for him and not a word of it would penetrate. When he was ready to speak he would speak, but on his own subject. . . .

When Churchill did speak, Sheean recalled, it was about the European situation. Suddenly, Sheean wrote, 'he was off, talking about Ethiopia, Mussolini, German rearmament, the character of Hitler, the nature of the Nazi movement. He took it for granted that the company followed what he was saying, although I am quite certain some of them understood next to nothing and regarded him as a bore.'

Churchill remained in the South of France for the first two weeks of September. He was much enjoying his painting, he explained to his wife on September 11, and also 'the general optimism and contentment engendered by old Brandy after luncheon here alone with Maxine. . . .' Commenting on the death of Huey Long,[2] he wrote:

---

[1] James Vincent Sheean, 1899–1975. Born in Illinois. Educated at the University of Chicago. Foreign correspondent in Europe and Asia, 1922–27. Author, essayist and reviewer. He described his prewar meetings with Churchill in his book *Between The Thunder and The Sun*, published in 1943. Biographer of Nehru, 1959.

[2] Huey Pierce Long, 1893–1935. Known as the 'Kingfish'. Born in Louisiana. A travelling salesman at the age of 19. Barrister. Member of the Louisiana State Railway Commission at the age of 25. Elected Governor of Louisiana, 1928. Governed dictatorially, and by means of the State Bureau of Criminal Investigation and the State Militia. Built 5000 miles of roads, and

The Louisiana Dictator has met his fate. '*Sic semper tyrannis*', wh means so perish all who do the like again. This was the most clownish of the Dictator tribe. Let us hope that more serious tyrants will also lose their sway. I do feel that if the L of Nations pull this off & *stop* the Abyssinia subjugation, we should all be stronger & safer for many a long day.

On the night of September 11 Churchill gave a dinner at the Casino, at which the new Minister of Transport, Leslie Hore-Belisha, was among the guests. Churchill wrote to his wife of Hore-Belisha: 'He is an affable & able fellow. How irritating it must be to be in a Govt & know absolutely nothing of what is the policy!' Churchill added, of his own holiday: 'Really I have been utterly careless of the time, & have painted ferociously both out of doors & in my bedroom. There is a time for everything!'

Despite the holiday atmosphere, Churchill continued to worry about European affairs, as Vincent Sheean recorded:

He had a distinction which he tried to bring out in every talk about Ethiopia just then: it seemed to him very important. 'It's not the *thing* we object to,' he would say, 'it's the *kind* of thing.' I had not then succumbed as much to his genial charm as I did later, and I could not quite accept this. I mentioned the Red Sea, the route to India, the importance of Aden. Mr Churchill brushed all that aside: 'We don't need to worry about the Italians,' he said. 'It isn't that at all. It isn't the thing. It's the *kind* of thing. . . .'

Mr Churchill was pinned down firmly one day by an elegant lady, Mme Lepelletier, who said that an objection to the *thing* might be practical and necessary, but that England had no historical right to object to the *kind* of thing. England had too often profited by 'the kind of thing'.

'Ah, but you see, all that belongs to the unregenerate past, is locked away in the limbo of the old, the wicked days,' Mr Churchill said, smiling benevolently upon her across the luncheon-table. 'The world progresses. We have endeavoured, by means of the League of Nations and the whole fabric of international law, to make it impossible for nations nowadays to infringe upon each other's rights. In trying to upset the empire of Ethiopia, Mussolini is making a most dangerous and foolhardy attack upon the whole established structure, and the results of such an attack are quite incalculable. Who is to say what will come of it in a year, or two, or three? With Germany arming at breakneck speed, England lost in a pacifist dream, France corrupt and torn by dissension, America remote and indifferent—madame, my dear lady, do you not tremble for your children?'

---

relieved 70% of Louisiana's population of direct taxation. Planned to abolish poverty by granting 'every deserving family' $5,000 unencumbered by debt, and limiting all personal fortunes to $3 million. Shot dead in the State House, Baton Rouge, 30 August 1935.

Churchill was back at Chartwell in the third week of September, and on September 20 he received a delegation from his constituency, led by Sir James Hawkey, to discuss the Abyssinian crisis. The delegation included one of Churchill's keenest younger supporters, Colin Thornton-Kemsley,[1] who noted in his diary:

Found Churchill in blue overalls painting in his studio and in very grim mood. He was receiving frequent reports of Stock Exchange prices in London and New York—his secretary brought one in while we were at tea; said markets were very depressed owing to the political tension.

He thought the British public had no idea of the gravity of the situation. Thinks the Italians mean to take us all on if any interference with their Abyssinian policy. Mussolini desperately in earnest—no question of bluff. It is indicative of his intentions that he has moved 6 submarines through Suez to the Red Sea and that he has now 50,000 troops in Libya. Would these be able to cross the 200 miles of desert for an Egyptian campaign? . . .

On larger question of policy C. thinks it damnable that for 6 years we should have had to disarm and on the seventh are likely to have to go to war. . . .

He is sorry for 'poor little Italy' which has with such great exertion raised herself to the status of 'a poor sort of first-class power' and is now to face an opposition against which she has no hope at all.

Italy's financial position is, of course, extremely serious, but Germany, whilst refusing to meet her obligations to us, is supplying large quantities of goods and material on credit.

Of course Germany is the real trouble. She imagines, perhaps with justification, that she has only to sit tight and we will be ready to give her back her Colonies if she keeps out of trouble. 'We seem to be very free with these things now,' he said, 'and it appears to have been mooted that we should give away not only the Colonies we took from Germany after the war, but others too.'

On September 21 Churchill sent the First Sea Lord, Sir Ernle Chatfield,[2] a memorandum based on an idea of Lindemann's for spotting

---

[1] Colin Norman Thornton-Kemsley, 1903–77. Educated at Chigwell School and Wadham College Oxford. A chartered surveyor. Active in local politics at Epping, 1925–39; Honorary Treasurer, Essex and Middlesex Provincial Area, National Union of Conservative and Unionist Associations, 1938–43. Conservative MP for Kincardine and West Aberdeenshire, 1939–50; for North Angus and Mearns, 1950–64. Served in the Royal Artillery, 1939–45. Vice-Chairman, Conservative Parliamentary Committee for Agriculture and Food, 1950–53. Member of the Public Accounts Committee, 1955–64. Chairman, Scottish Unionist Members Committee, 1957–58. Knighted, 1958.

[2] Alfred Ernle Montacute Chatfield, 1873–1967. Entered Navy, 1886. Served at the battles of Heligoland (1914), Dogger Bank (1915) and Jutland (1916). Fourth Sea Lord, 1919–20. Knighted, 1919. Rear-Admiral, 1920. Assistant Chief of the Naval Staff, 1920–22. Third Sea Lord, 1925–28. Vice-Admiral, 1930. C-in-C Mediterranean, 1931–2. First Sea Lord,

submarines from the air while they were still under water. The idea had first been mooted in 1917. 'The information I expect is on your files,' Churchill wrote, 'but may have been lost sight of in the last twenty years.' Churchill also saw Chatfield in person, to discuss the general naval situation, and the continuing Italian activity in the eastern Mediterranean. 'I had a good talk with Chatfield,' Churchill wrote to Sir Roger Keyes on September 24, 'and I have a feeling that the Navy is quite capable of looking after itself in view of the precautions so rightly taken. . . . Chatfield strikes me as a very fine fellow. I have known him a long time and he gives me a good feeling to talk to.' Having sent his thoughts on air defence to Sir Philip Cunliffe-Lister at the end of August, Churchill also sent a copy to Baldwin, who responded in a conciliatory way:

My dear Winston,

Thank you for your letter and for sending me a copy of the letter you sent to Philip.

I will study it with care.

Yes, I had a broken holiday—very good what I did have—and here I am again in an atmosphere that no one could have foreseen a year ago.

'It was the riding did it' observed that famous sportsman, Mr Palmer of Rugeley when he was sentenced to death, and we need some pretty riding both at home and abroad to win through.

On September 26 Churchill was in London to address the City Carlton Club. His speech ranged over every aspect of national security, and he urged a more rapid shipbuilding programme. His main concern was the speed and scale of German rearmament. 'German finance is a perpetual war budget,' he told the crowded gathering of Conservative businessmen. 'Internal borrowings for military purposes have already devoured the normal revenues of two or three years ahead.' In contrast, he insisted, the British Government was not doing enough for air re-armament and the House of Commons was being 'kept in the dark'. Nothing that had happened in the previous two months, he stated, could in any way 'diminish our anxiety'. His speech continued: 'On the contrary everything is worse and it is very wrong for public men to close their eyes to the sombre procession of facts.'

Churchill then spoke of the 'impending war' between Italy and Abyssinia. The whole country, he said, would support the Government

1933–38. Admiral of the Fleet, 1935. Created Baron, 1937. Elected to the Other Club, 1937. Privy Councillor, 1939. Minister for Co-ordination of Defence, 1939–40 (with a seat in the War Cabinet). Chairman, Civil Defence Honours Committee, 1940–46.

'in making their contribution to the authority of the League of Nations';
it was both Britain's duty, and her 'vital interest in peace' that made it
essential to support any international action 'which seeks to establish
the reign of law among nations and ward off the measureless perils of
another world struggle'. Later in his speech he warned Mussolini not to
sacrifice both his own army, and European peace, in a hopeless endeavour.

At the end of his speech Churchill repeated his warnings that in the
air, 'So far from being half as strong again as Germany, so far from
making up lee-way, we are already greatly inferior in numbers and
falling further and further behind every month.' His intention, he said,
was to publicize the dangers, and he told his listeners:

No doubt it is not popular to say these things, but I am accustomed to
abuse and I expect to have a great deal more of it before I have finished.
Somebody has to state the truth. There ought to be a few members of the
House of Commons who are in a sufficiently independent position to confront
both Ministers and electors with unpalatable truths. We do not wish our
ancient freedom and the decent tolerant civilisation we have preserved in
this island to hang upon a rotten thread.

Churchill's warnings had begun to win wide support. 'I entirely
agree with your speech as reported in yesterday's *Times*,' Austen
Chamberlain wrote on September 28, 'and was glad to see the line you
took.' Had the Cabinet adopted Churchill's suggestions three months
ago, Sir Harry McGowan wrote to him that same day, 'Mussolini
would have paused in his isolated action.' And he added: 'Why in
God's name you are not in the Cabinet, and Minister of Defence, beats
me and many others.'

One of those who wrote to congratulate Churchill was a former and
severe critic of his anti-Bolshevik speeches of 1919, Osbert Sitwell,[1] who
wrote: 'This letter is more to gratify myself for stupidity in the past,
than to tell you, what you must already know, that you have spoken for
numberless people.' Among the Conservatives who sent him congratulations was a Conservative MP, Arthur Bateman,[2] who had spent the

[1] Osbert Sitwell, 1892–1969. Educated 'during the holidays from Eton' (*Who's Who*). 2nd
Lieutenant, Grenadier Guards, 1912. On active service in France, 1914–18. Author, poet and
essayist, he published his first volume of poetry in 1916. *The Winstonburg Line* (an attack on
Churchill's part in the anti-Bolshevik intervention in Russia) was published in 1919. Suc-
ceeded his father as 5th Baronet, 1943. Chairman of the Management Committee, Society of
Authors, 1944–48 and 1951–52. A Trustee of the Tate Gallery, 1951–58.

[2] Arthur Leonard Bateman, 1879–1957. Councillor, Borough of Camberwell, 1922–31;
also Mayor of Camberwell. Conservative MP for North Camberwell, 1931–35.

day of Churchill's speech in his constituency, celebrating its new royal charter. Although, as Bateman wrote, the occasion was one at which many distinguished figures of London's municipal Government had gathered together:

. . . you were talked about in all the Hotels and hostels here last evening, with even more enthusiasm than the Civic day, all words came of admiration for your good self, some of the comments would make—even you—embarrassed, in the same words they are sarcastic on the names of L.G. and S.B. & Ram McD.

It would do the three gentlemen good to get about amongst the people and hear the comments, but they are words that it is, for the moment, only the privilege of back benchers like myself to hear, who move daily amongst the masses.

On September 28, two days after his speech, Churchill saw the Italian Ambassador, Count Grandi,[1] to whom he reiterated his warnings about the danger of an aggressive Italian policy. On September 28 he sent Sir Robert Vansittart a full account of the conversation. All the British political parties, Churchill told Grandi, would regard the League of Nations as 'the most powerful protection against all future dangers wherever they might arise'. The threat to Abyssinia, Churchill insisted, had brought about a definite change in British public opinion, and were Italy to bombard Abyssinian towns 'an almost measureless rise in the temperature must be expected'. On October 1 Vansittart replied from the Foreign Office: 'I think, if I may say so, that you spoke very wisely to Grandi, and I hope your words will have as good an effect as your speech. Of the latter I have heard nothing but praise, right, left and centre.' Unknown to all but his intimates, Churchill was himself somewhat unhappy about the Government's denunciations of Italian policy, believing that it was against the German danger that all Britain's emotional, as well as material energies should be focused. On October 1 he replied to Austen Chamberlain's letter of congratulation:

I am glad you agree with the line I took about Abyssinia, but I am very unhappy. It would be a terrible deed to smash up Italy, and it will cost us

---

[1] Dino Grandi, 1895–1988. Born at Mordano (Bologna). On active service, 1915–18 (three military crosses for valour). Graduated in law, Bologna University, 1919. Journalist and political organizer; led the Fascist movement in the north of Italy, 1920–21. Chief of the Fascist Fascist General Staff, 1921. Elected to the Chamber of Deputies, 1921; Deputy President of the Chamber, 1924. Under-Secretary of State for Foreign Affairs, 1925–29. Foreign Minister, 1929–32. Italian Ambassador in London, 1932–39. Member of the Fascist Grand Council. Created Count, 1937. A member of several London Clubs, including the St James's, the Athenaeum and the Travellers. President of the Chamber of Fasci and Corporazioni, Italy, 1939–43. Minister of Justice, Rome, 1939–43.

dear. How strange it is that after all these years of begging France to make it up with Italy, we are now forcing her to choose between Italy and ourselves. I do not think we ought to have taken the lead in such a vehement way. If we had felt so strongly on the subject we should have warned Mussolini two months before. The sensible course would have been gradually to strengthen the Fleet in the Mediterranean, during the early summer, and so let him see how grave the matter was. Now what can he do?

At a dinner with Sir Robert Vansittart and Alfred Duff Cooper, the Financial Secretary to the Treasury, Churchill discussed the dangers to Europe if Mussolini were to launch an Italian invasion of Abyssinia. In an unpublished note written twelve years later he recalled how: 'The project was mooted of some of us going out' to see Mussolini 'in order to explain the inevitable course of events once he had launched his invasion. Nothing came of this and I doubt very much whether we could have enlightened him. He was convinced that Britain was rotten to the core.' Churchill added: 'Mussolini, like Hitler, regarded Britannia as a frightened, flabby old woman, who at the worst would only bluster, and was anyhow incapable of making war. She certainly looked the part.'

Churchill's overriding concern about Germany, and about Britain's weakness in the air, was shared by several senior Conservative back-benchers. On September 26 Lord Winterton wrote to Churchill:

I had a long talk with Horne yesterday (I also saw Amery earlier in the day) who gave me some most disquieting news about the Air Force pro-gramme. It seems that the 'havering' and incapacity among the Officials at the Ministry is just as bad as it was under the former Minister. There is still indecision about the types of machines and so on. I have heard this partially confirmed from other sources.

Do you not think it would be a good thing if you, Horne, Amery, Freddie G. and I (ie the supporters of the original resolution in the House) asked to see the PM *alone* and asked him if he would personally investigate the truth of the persistent rumours about the state of the Ministry. . . .

On September 30 Desmond Morton sent Churchill a series of notes 'for his private guidance' to help him prepare his reply to an Air Ministry Paper circulated on 19 September 1935 by Cunliffe-Lister. This Paper, which Churchill had received as a member of the Air Defence Research sub-committee, gave the comparative British and German first-line air figures. In his notes, Morton stressed that a count of first-line aircraft did not provide an adequate measure of comparative air strengths. Morton went on to explain that the number of military aircraft in each Air Force was 'about the same'; but one had, in forming a view, to remember 'that *all* the German aircraft are new'. Germany's first-line strength was 'about 850' aeroplanes, including the training schools, compared with 800 in Britain, if the Fleet Air Arm were included. But Germany's first-line strength, Morton stressed, 'is now misleading'. Although there had been a substantial 'slowing down' in Germany of the creation of new squadrons, there had at the same time been 'no slowing down of training of pilots or manufacture of military aircraft'. Morton continued:

To obtain a fair comparison of the air strength of the two countries one must quote comparative figures for at least:

(i) 1st Line Strength
(ii) No of Pilots in & out of Air Force
(iii) No of military type machines
(iv) No of convertible machines
(v) Rate of output of industry
(vi) Capacity rate of output of industry.

'Only by such fair and frank disclosures,' Morton added, 'can an honest comparison be made.'[1]

Replying to Winterton on September 30, Churchill wrote: 'The Germans are spending four times as much this year upon air as we are, and I contend that they are already substantially stronger. How then can it be pretended that we are overtaking? That race has not yet begun. On the contrary we are falling ever more behind and this will continue certainly to the end of the calendar year 1936.' Churchill added:

With regard to the Navy, we must rebuild the fleet. But that I believe is generally conceded, though I suppose there will be endless procrastination.[2]

---

[1] On October 1 Morton sent Churchill portions of a secret memorandum he had written for the Joint Planning Committee on 'the effects of the modern system of armament supply on the war potential of a number of European countries'. The section on Germany anticipated no shortage of manpower 'either for industry or for the armed forces'. Germany's industrial capacity, second only to that of the USA, was 'carefully planned for expansion to meet war needs. By 1943, its strength may suffice to maintain at least 100 divisions in the field and an air strength of 2,000 first line or more, leaving reserve power wherewith to maintain a strong fleet in the Baltic'.

[2] In a secret report of 28 September 1939, the Admiralty informed Churchill (who had then become First Lord) that the 1936 battleship programme had fallen seriously into arrears, with a result that four of the battleships which were meant to have been completed by the end of 1939 would not be ready for at least a further five or six months. The report also pointed out that there had been a similar delay in cruiser construction—for example the *Dido*, contracted to be finished in June 1939, would not now be offered to the Admiralty until August 1940. Churchill minuted on 8 October 1939: 'These are the ships we want to fight the war with and it is lamentable that they should all be breaking down on contract dates.'

With the army it is mainly a question of preparing civil industry for conversion to war purposes. A certain amount of progress has been made in this, but only on paper, and of course we are immeasurably behind every other country. Nothing in the way of making jigs and gauges for mass production or the accumulation of stores of tools has been done. It must be remembered that some of the essential tools take as much as three years to make.

The Government seem to me very complacent and thinking much more about how not to offend left-wing sentiment than to provide the necessary security.

That same day, with Morton's comments in mind, Churchill replied to the Air Ministry Paper, stressing that the Air Ministry were not taking into account what Germany was capable of doing by 1937, given the existing number of machines and pilots, and the German industrial capacity. By October 1, according to the Air Staff's own figures, Churchill pointed out, 'apparently Germany, with 1,870 militarily trained pilots and 2,150 service military machines, only produces a first-line air strength of 594 *ie* they have three times as many military pilots and three and a half times as many machines as they have first-line air strength'. Churchill continued by showing that the Air Ministry themselves had revealed that Germany did not need reserves on the British scale because of their factory capacity. He continued:

The figure 594 may correspond to some conventional classification of first-line air strength in vogue at the Air Ministry which was perhaps the basis of statements made to Parliament, and must therefore be preserved. It has no relation to the true military air power of Germany at the present time. It would be misleading to use the figure 594 without at the same time stating that in the formations which have not yet been included in that total there are admittedly 1,275 trained pilots and 1,556 military machines in a different phase of organisation.

Churchill went on to argue that a 'conservative estimate' based even on the Air Staff's figures of pilots and machines in general would produce the figure of a minimum first-line strength of 1,100, 'increasing by 110 pilots and machines every month'. If German expansion continued 'at the present rate', Churchill added, 'the elements will exist for a German first-line air strength of over 2,000', completely operational, and with 'full factory capacity for full-time maintenance' by October 1936.

Churchill concluded this part of the paper by saying that any estimate of German first-line strength in October 1937 would be 'purely speculative', but that the Germans would 'have it in their power to maintain at least 3,000 first-line aircraft if they choose to devote so large a proportion of their national preparation-effort to this purpose'. Churchill also pointed out that in giving Britain's first-line strength as 1,015, and contrasting it with a figure of 594 for Germany, the Air Ministry were not comparing 'like with like', as the British figures were for world-wide strength, whereas the Government had already stated in Parliament that the home defence figures, including the Auxiliary Air Force, 'should be 690'.

Another Air Ministry comparison which Churchill believed to be misleading was that of the respective number of pilots. According to the Air Staff, 1,870 German pilots were at present paralleled by a British figure of 3,101 'general duties personnel'. But, Churchill asked:

What is the difference between *pilots* and '*general duties personnel*'? We have a full account of how the German pilots are trained and the numbers issuing from the schools at every stage. Some much fuller explanation of '*general duties personnel*' seems to be necessary to make comparison possible.

It is also stated that 'on completion of the expansion programme of 1935 the number of general duties personnel "required" will be 5,020'. But no date is assigned for this.

Later in his paper Churchill wrote: 'Another test is the money that is being spent. We are only spending this year, 26 millions; the French over 70 millions, and the Germans over 100 millions sterling. How then can it be believed that we are maintaining a larger air force than Germany and increasing our lead over them . . .?' Yet this was the Air Staff's contention.

Churchill concluded his paper: 'These discrepancies illustrate a process of cumulative minimizings of each successive factor in German air strength, and it would be dangerous to trust to conclusions so founded.'

In his covering letter to Cunliffe-Lister, Churchill wrote that he was 'very much distressed' by the Air Staff's figures of relative British and German air strength, and he added: 'I earnestly hope you will not allow yourself to adopt them without the most searching cross-check. I am sure they are wrong and utterly misleading and it would be disastrous if you commited yourself to them publicly.'

The Air Staff answered Churchill's memorandum five weeks later, on November 5, dismissing his concern for the as yet not organized squadrons, and commenting caustically that assumptions had been made in their own paper 'which may not find ready acceptance by those to whom the mass of intelligence data is not accessible'. The Air Staff based its interpretation of the intelligence data on two factors; the experience of 'our own Air Force during the past 15 years' and the experience 'of other foreign Air Forces who have had to overcome "teething troubles" such as the Germans may be expected to have'. There was, they added, 'nothing unusual' in the discrepancy between total service aircraft and the first-line strength, as the term first-line included only those combatant units for which pilots were available 'without measures of mobilization' and that therefore no training school or administrative machines could be counted. In Germany, they wrote, an 'abnormally large proportion' of aircraft were in fact being employed for headquarters' flights, training schools, communications services, experimental units and even 'stored reserve'. On a political note, the Air Staff argued that if it were made clear to Germany that France had no intention of building as many as 2,000 first-line aircraft, 'there is no reason why Germany, on her declared policy and intentions, should herself go higher than 1,500. . . .'

While waiting for the Air Ministry's reply, Churchill had continued with his public campaign for a more active defence policy. The detailed figures he restricted, for reasons of security, and so as not to cause alarm, to his secret memoranda, which were only seen by the Committee of Imperial Defence.

The Conservative Party Conference had opened on October 4, the day on which Mussolini launched his attack on Abyssinia. At the Conference Sir Edward Grigg brought forward a motion urging the Government to provide adequate air, sea and land forces both to safeguard Britain's trade and territory, and to enable Britain to carry out its international obligations. To this motion, Churchill moved a substantial amendment pledging the Conservative Party to organize British industry 'for speedy conversion to defence purposes, if need be'; to make 'a renewed effort' to establish air parity with Germany; to 'rebuild' the Royal Navy; and to support any financial measures which might be necessary for the national safety, 'no matter how great the sacrifices might be'. Grigg's motion and Churchill's amendment were both carried unanimously. 'The great need now,' Churchill wrote to Keith Feiling on October 5, 'is to rearm while time remains.'

During his speech to the Conservative Party Conference on October 4, Churchill had provoked a burst of cheering when he described Baldwin as 'a statesman who has gathered to himself a greater volume of confidence and goodwill than any public man I recollect in my long career'. Baldwin replied that same day, telling the Conference: 'I rejoice to think that whatever differences have existed among us during the past two years, these differences are at an end—and I welcome especially the generous references made to me by Mr Churchill yesterday.' These remarks were punctuated by cheers.

On October 5 *The Times* commented with approval on the fact that Churchill had paid 'his refound leader' a generous but not unmerited compliment; and on October 6 Baldwin sent Churchill a private note from 10 Downing Street:

My dear Winston,

What you were good enough to say about me at Bournemouth gave me great pleasure. I thank you most sincerely.

I was delighted to hear what an excellent conference it was.

Yours very sincerely,
Stanley Baldwin

Churchill replied from Chartwell on October 7:

My dear S.B.,

What I said was no more than the truth; and I am vy glad that it is the truth: because things are in such a state that it is a blessing to have at the head of affairs a man whom people will rally round. But if your power is great, so also are yr burdens—and yr opportunities.

I think you ought to go to the country at the earliest moment, & I hope you will do so. I do not elaborate the many reasons, because no doubt they are weighing with you at this time.

I will abide with you in this election, & do what little I can to help in the most serviceable way. With many thanks for the kindness of yr letter,

Believe me
Yours vy sincerely,
Winston S. Churchill

Baldwin had still not decided whether to hold the election that winter or not. Meanwhile, Churchill's speeches, while continuing to demand the most vigorous possible policy of rearmament and vigilance, contained none of the fierce denunciations of the Conservative leadership that had characterized them in the past two years. It was increasingly felt that once Baldwin had been returned to power, Churchill would receive high office. 'Good luck to you,' Consuelo Balsan wrote from Paris on October 12, '& may you soon be Minister of Defence to preserve the peace.' On the following day Sir Archibald Sinclair wrote from Caithness: 'I have read your speeches not with complete agreement but with immense admiration and with whole-hearted delight at seeing your stock *soaring*!'

34

The 1935 Election:
No Place for Churchill

ON October 12 Churchill offered the Conservative Central Office his services during the election campaign, and suggested certain dates on which he was free to speak outside his constituency. His offer was accepted. 'May I add how grateful we all are to you,' Miss Maxse[1] wrote on October 18, 'for your great kindness in giving us these dates.'

Speaking in the House of Commons on October 24, Churchill forcefully reiterated his earlier warnings that the whole of Germany had become 'an armed camp' and that the whole German population was being 'trained from childhood for war'. Germany, he insisted, was of all the nations of Europe the one most likely first to become 'most completely ready for war'. There could be no anxieties 'comparable to the anxiety caused by German rearmament', and he added: 'We cannot afford to see Nazidom in its present phase of cruelty and intolerance, with all its hatreds and all its gleaming weapons, paramount in Europe.' Churchill went on to argue that the Italian attack on Abyssinia was 'a very small matter' compared to the German danger. Yet it was essential, he added, for Britain to support the League of Nations in the economic sanctions it had imposed against Italy, for the League was 'fighting for all our lives'.

Two days later Desmond Morton wrote to congratulate Churchill on his speech. 'The effect in all quarters—perfect,' he declared. The appeal for action within the League, together with the building-up of Britain's

---

[1] Marjorie Maxse, 1891–1975. Chief Organization Officer, Conservative Central Office, 1921–39. Director of the Children's Overseas Reception Board, and Vice-Chairman of the Women's Voluntary Services, 1940–44. Vice-Chairman of the Conservative Party Organization, 1944–51. Created Dame Commander of the British Empire, 1952.

own strength, was, Morton wrote, 'more of a foundation of a future foreign policy than anything suggested elsewhere'; and he added:

Germany did not like it—but resentfully admires it in private. It is right that Germany should realise that we are not all lulled into weak-livered complacency. They only understand a strong but just & clear line. Like Slavs and orientals they confuse compromise with weakness. I see clearly now that of course we must go on supporting the League so long as we are only called upon to pay a price we are prepared and able to afford. But in case the League prove in practice to be but a cardboard shield, we must back it with our own steel.[1]

Parliament was dissolved on October 25, and the General Election was set for November 14. In his letter of October 26 Morton sent Churchill his good wishes for polling day, 'and my prayers that S.B. will invite you to collaborate with him in the new Government'. That same day Churchill told Morton that he did not intend to wait about for office after the election but, tired by his efforts and wanting a break, he would leave England before the opening of the new Parliament for a six weeks holiday in the sun. Morton wrote to Churchill that evening:

Dear Winston,

I do think that your decision to go away at once for a little while is very wise. Thank you also for telling me.

If S.B. reforms his Cabinet after the new year and offers you anything sufficiently attractive you will have, meanwhile, done nothing to render his or your position difficult. If no offer is made to you, your personal position, far from being impaired, will be the stronger and you can take up any individual line you see fit, with added force. The results of the Naval Conference will be known; there will be a month or two, in which the Government's true Defence Policy will have been to some extent unveiled. If you consider it unsatisfactory you can attack it accordingly without risk of being accused of prejudice.

Your position reminds me greatly and rather bitterly of the fighting services themselves, hailed as saviours in time of danger and, as the old tag has it, as brutal & licencious soldiery when the Public *believe* the danger to be far off. Before the last election it was on everyone's lips: 'We must have Winston in the Cabinet to act as a driving force.' Lulled by the false security of a 250 Conservative majority for four or five years it is: 'Now everything is alright, we don't want a firebrand upsetting things.'

Nevertheless the Public do not realise the true strain of the situation and, unless I am very mistaken, they will not do so for a month or two. Then the word may again go round: 'Oh Lord! make haste to help us.'

[1] On October 15, in preparation for Churchill's speech, Morton had provided him with a map of Abyssinia. 'I hope it may be of some use,' he wrote. 'It is the best the War Office can produce.'

May it be so and meanwhile I do hope you will have a happy holiday painting. . . .

As election day drew near, rumours about Churchill's future proliferated. On October 25 the British Ambassador in Berlin, Sir Eric Phipps, telegraphed to the Foreign Office of the prominence that had been given to Churchill's House of Commons speech. 'Some newspapers,' Phipps reported, 'point out that the speech has special importance in view of Mr Churchill's almost certain inclusion in the next Cabinet.' Phipps continued:

The London correspondent of the 'Völkischer Beobachter' telegraphs that as soon as Mr Churchill opens his mouth, it is safe to bet that an attack on Germany will emerge. He is one of the most unscrupulous political intriguers in England. His friendship with the American Jewish millionaire Baruch leads him to expend all his remaining force and authority in directing England's action against Germany. 'This is the man whom the government are apparently thinking of including in the Cabinet as first lord of the Admiralty merely because he is a first-class speaker and they hope to satisfy the reactionary wing of the Conservative Party.'

On October 28 the British Naval Attaché in Berlin, Captain Muirhead-Gould,[1] wrote to Churchill from Warsaw: 'Magnificent! I had to wait until I left Germany to write & say how wonderful I thought your speech—as the Germans are so annoyed with you for telling the truth that no letters addressed to you would ever have got out of the country.' Churchill had last spoken to Muirhead-Gould in the spring of 1933, when he had been on his way to take up his duties in Berlin. 'I have never forgotten what you said then,' he wrote. 'Two & a half years in Berlin has shown that everything you said then is true today,' and he added:

The Germans have only learnt one thing from the War—& that is *never* to go to war again until they are absolutely ready, & certain, of victory. No chances next time!

The Germans fear, and I hope, you WILL be 1st Lord—or Minister of Defence!

Please don't give me away.

[1] Gerald Charles Muirhead-Gould, 1889–1945. Midshipman, 1905; Lieutenant, 1911; DSC, 1918 (for services in the Mediterranean); Lieutenant Commander, 1918. On intelligence duties, 1920–23. Captain, 1931. Naval Attaché, Berlin, July 1933–November 1936. Commanded HMS *Devonshire*, 1936–37. Went to Australia, 1940; Captain-in-Charge at Sydney, 1941. Flag Officer-in-Command, Sydney, 1941–44; acting Rear-Admiral, 1944. Flag Officer-in-Charge, Western Germany, 1944–45; received the surrender of Heligoland, 1945.

The hostile German reaction to Churchill's speech of October 24 continued for several days. 'Oh Winston!' wrote his aunt Leonie Leslie[1] on October 28, 'What a grand speech and *how* I am enjoying the rage and the abuse from Germany which I hear on the wireless!' At the Foreign Office, in a minute of October 29, Ralph Wigram recorded a further German protest, against an article by Churchill which had just appeared in the November issue of the *Strand* magazine, and that same day Sir Eric Phipps telegraphed to the Foreign Office from Berlin:

I learn that the Ministry of Foreign Affairs have instructed German Ambassador in London to lodge a strong protest against the personal attack on the Head of the German State made in an article by Mr Winston Churchill in the Strand Magazine.[2]

The tone of his article is much resented here. The Magazine will be prohibited and the press will probably be allowed to publish no more than a bald statement to the effect that a protest has been lodged.

'Mr Churchill is making himself very unpopular in Germany,' Wigram noted on October 30.

In his *Strand* article Churchill wrote of how Hitler's success since 1932 had only been made possible by 'the lethargy and folly of the French and British Governments since the War', in not seeking to redress Germany's grievances during the days of her moderate Governments. Now 'the personal exertions and life-thrust of a single man' had completely turned the tables on the 'complacent, feckless, and purblind' victors. His article continued:

Hitherto, Hitler's triumphant career has been borne onwards, not only by a passionate love of Germany, but by currents of hatred so intense as to sear the souls of those who swim upon them. Hatred of the French is the first of these currents, and we have only to read Hitler's book, *Mein Kampf*, to see that the French are not the only foreign nation against whom the anger of rearmed Germany may be turned.

---

[1] Leonie Blanche Jerome, 1859–1943. Sister of Lady Randolph Churchill. She married Colonel John Leslie in 1884. Their younger son Norman was killed in action on 18 October 1914.

[2] Churchill had begun work on this article during June. On June 26 Desmond Morton had written to him: 'I take it you wanted me to comment on your draft about Hitler chiefly from a special point of view. In that connection there is one passage which accidentally reproduces a paragraph from one of Phipps' recent despatches. I have marked it in red'. Commenting on Churchill's sentence about secret German rearmament beginning in 1930 and 1931, Morton noted that it was 'not strictly correct', and added: 'The great plans were being formulated years before and had reached completion as plans under the Brüning Govt. The affair dates from Walter Rathenau who said "They have taken away our weapons. We must forge a new one out of Industry." Alas! I have used that quotation so frequently in official papers and seen it nowhere else so must ask you to refrain from it unless you can trace the original. . . .'

But the internal stresses are even more striking. The Jews, supposed to have contributed, by a disloyal and pacifist influence, to the collapse of Germany at the end of the Great War, were also deemed to be the main prop of communism and the authors of defeatist doctrines in every form. Therefore, the Jews of Germany, a community numbered by many hundreds of thousands, were to be stripped of all power, driven from every position in public and social life, expelled from the professions, silenced in the Press, and declared a foul and odious race.

The twentieth century has witnessed with surprise, not merely the promulgation of these ferocious doctrines, but their enforcement with brutal vigour by the Government and by the populace. No past services, no proved patriotism, even wounds sustained in war, could procure immunity for persons whose only crime was that their parents had brought them into the world. Every kind of persecution, grave or petty, upon the world-famous scientists, writers, and composers at the top down to the wretched little Jewish children in the national schools, was practised, was glorified, and is still being practised and glorified.

A similar proscription fell upon socialists and communists of every hue. The Trade Unionists and liberal intelligentsia are equally smitten. The slightest criticism is an offence against the State. The courts of justice, though allowed to function in ordinary cases, are superseded for every form of political offence by so-called people's courts composed of ardent Nazis.

Side by side with the training grounds of the new armies and the great aerodromes, the concentration camps pock-mark the German soil. In these thousands of Germans are coerced and cowed into submission to the irresistible power of the Totalitarian State.

Churchill went on to ask whether Hitler shared the passions he had evoked. 'Does he,' he asked, 'in the full sunlight of worldly triumph, at the head of the great nation he has raised from the dust, still feel racked by the hatreds and antagonisms of his desperate struggle; or will they be discarded like the armour and the cruel weapons of strife under the mellowing influences of success?' Churchill could give no definite answer. Those who had met Hitler, he wrote, had found him 'a highly competent, cool, well-informed functionary with an agreeable manner. . . .' The world still hoped that 'the worst' might be over, 'and that we may yet live to see Hitler a gentler figure in a happier age'. And yet, he added, while Hitler now spoke 'words of reassurance', in Germany itself 'the great wheels revolve; the rifles, the cannon, the tanks, the shot and shell, the air-bombs, the poison-gas cylinders, the aeroplanes, the submarines, and now the beginnings of a fleet flow in ever-broadening streams from the already largely war-mobilized arsenals and factories of Germany'.

Sir Eric Phipps reported once more, on October 31, the Nazi complaints of Churchill's 'insult' to Hitler in his article, which was, they declared, 'hardly to be exceeded for odiousness'. On November 2 Phipps reported that Hitler himself was said to have commented on Churchill's article: 'What is to be the fate of the Anglo-German naval agreement if the writer of this article is to be the Minister of the British Navy?' If Churchill knew that Hitler had said this, Wigram minuted within the Foreign Office on November 5, 'he might well say that it was only another proof of the necessity of strong armaments—otherwise we shall have the Germans telling us who shall & not be in office in this country'.

Among those who visited Hitler at the time of Churchill's article was Lord Beaverbrook. On December 11 Randolph Churchill wrote to his father: 'He was very reticent about his conversation, but someone who had a first-hand account of it from him tells me that Hitler expressed himself as most alarmed at the idea of your being in the Cabinet. Hitler's information apparently was that this was a foregone conclusion. He was very angry and said it would be most unfriendly. Max, of course, reassured him and told him there was no possible chance of it.'

Despite the German protests, Churchill reiterated his fears of German methods and intentions in each of his election speeches. His only worry was that people would not fully recognize the dangers. 'I think we ought to pull off a satisfactory majority,' he wrote to Abe Bailey on October 31, 'but it is a fearsome thing to cast the whole future of this Empire on the franchise of so many simple folk.'

Churchill received many letters of good wishes as the election approached, and many invitations to speak. 'I see a good deal of the people here,' Bonar Law's son Richard[1] wrote from Hull on November 4, '& your recent speeches have made a terrific impression. If you *cd* manage it, it wd be an enormous help to me & to the other candidates up here.' A note from Conservative Central Office informed Churchill that the Hull Conservatives were 'so anxious that you should speak that the whole meeting will be cancelled if you cannot do so'. Churchill agreed, and spoke at Hull on November 5. 'Do not let us go into col-

---

[1] Richard Kidston Law, 1901–80. Youngest son of Andrew Bonar Law (two of his brothers were killed in action on the western front). Editorial Staff, *Morning Post*, 1927; *New York Herald-Tribune*, 1928. Conservative MP for Hull South-West, 1931–45; for South Kensington, 1945–50; for Haltemprice, 1950–54. Elected to the Other Club, 1936. Member of the Medical Research Council, 1936–40. Financial Secretary, War Office, 1940–41; Parliamentary Under-Secretary of State, Foreign Office, 1941–43. Privy Councillor, 1943. Minister of State, 1943–45. Minister of Education, 1945. Created Baron Coleraine, 1954. Chairman, National Youth Employment Council, 1955–62.

lective security as beggars,' he declared, 'but as champions. We are solvent. Now let us make ourselves safe.' After the meeting Richard Law wrote to Churchill: 'You have worked a mighty change in the atmosphere here. All my canvassers are fired with new enthusiasm, all the long faces have gone and they feel that they have the tide under them. The enemy are badly shaken, too. If I hold this seat, as I hope to do, it will be your doing.'

On October 25 another young Conservative MP, Alan Lennox-Boyd, asked Churchill to speak for him in his constituency, Biggleswade. 'It is going to be a hard task here,' Lennox-Boyd wrote, 'successfully to put the case for rearmament. I did it last time but there were so many other issues then. It could be done again successfully if I could have your help if only for an hour.' Another persistent advocate of rearmament was Churchill's son, who was standing as the official Conservative candidate at West Toxteth, helped by two of his sisters, Diana and Sarah.

In the two weeks leading up to the election Churchill continued to collect information about German rearmament. On November 1 a friend of Brendan Bracken, Sir Henry Strakosch,[1] sent him details of German raw material imports. 'It is really very good of you,' Churchill wrote on November 2, 'to send me such a weighty, lucid paper.' As was now his normal practice, Churchill at once sent Strakosch's figures to Desmond Morton for his comments, and Morton submitted them in his turn both to the Treasury and to the Board of Trade. There was no doubt, Morton wrote to Churchill from the Committee of Imperial Defence on November 4, that even funds originally set aside for unemployment relief were being spent on armaments; and he believed that Strakosch's estimate of a minimum of £1,600 million spent by Hitler on armaments since July 1933 was 'not far out'.

On November 7 Morton wrote again. The Treasury, he said, believed that Strakosch's figures for German rearmament were 'overestimates'. But, Morton continued:

For your private information, I can tell you that the present Reich requirements for financing unemployment and armaments is about 500 million RMs a month, or at a rate of exchange of a little over 12 RMs to the

---

[1] Henry Strakosch, 1871–1943. Entered banking in the City of London, 1891; closely connected with South African industrial development and gold mining from 1895; Chairman of the Union Corporation Ltd. Author of the South African Currency and Banking Act, 1920. Knighted, 1921. Represented South Africa at the Genoa Conference, the League of Nations Assembly, and the Imperial Conference, 1923. Member of the Royal Commission on Indian Currency and Finance, 1925–26. Member of the Council of India, 1930–37. Delegate of India, Imperial Economic Conference, Ottawa, 1932. Adviser to the Secretary of State for India, 1937–42. Elected to the Other Club, 1939.

£, something just short of £500 million sterling per annum. This figure would compare with Sir Henry's estimate of the average expenditure for the last 28 months at the rate of £800 million sterling per annum.

During the election campaign Baldwin effectively dashed Churchill's hopes that rearmament would become a leading Conservative election cry. In its own Manifesto, the Labour Party had accused the Conservative Party of endangering world peace by 'planning a vast and expensive rearmament programme'. Speaking to the Peace Society on October 31, Baldwin answered this accusation by declaring: 'I give you my word there will be no great armaments.' There would be some rearmament, Baldwin explained, but it would be 'spending not a penny more on our defence forces than is necessary for the safety of our people'. Baldwin also spoke in veiled but hopeful terms about Germany, telling his audience:

There may be Governments deliberately planning the future, leading reluctant or unsuspecting people into the shambles. It sometimes looks as if it were so. I confess that in my own political experience I have not encountered Governments possessed of all these malevolent qualities. Most Governments seem not much better or worse than the people they govern. Nor am I on the whole disposed to conclude that the people are such a helpless ineffective flock of sheep as those who claim to speak in their name often imply. They have, in fact, a way of making their opinions known and heard when they feel deeply. . . .

Churchill, however, throughout his campaign at Epping, and at Hull and Biggleswade, continued to press for much greater rearmament, and to warn of the aggressive nature of Nazism. Writing in the *Daily Mail* on November 12, two days before the poll, Churchill declared, in contrast to Baldwin's view: 'Terrible preparations are being made on all sides for war,' and he added: 'I do not feel that people realise at all how near and how grave are the dangers of a world explosion. Some regard the scene with perfect equanimity; many gape stolidly upon it, some are angry to be disturbed by such thoughts in their daily routine and pleasures.'

On November 13 a long despatch from Sir Eric Phipps to Sir Samuel Hoare emphasized the military preparations by which Germany was gripped. 'The armed forces,' Phipps wrote, 'and their creator, Herr Hitler, are the heroes of the day.' His despatch continued:

Germans complain that English public men, in particular Mr Winston Churchill, are apt to concentrate their attention exclusively on German rearmament. They never, it is said, refer to the social achievements of the

German Government, to the reduction of unemployment, for example, or to the improvement in labour conditions or to the work of the 'Kraft durch Freude' organisation. To depict the German Government as engaged solely in rearmament shows a lack of balance and sense of proportion. The error, if error it be, is one of which the Nazi leaders are almost equally guilty. Since March of this year the members of the Government have not ceased to exploit to the full the enthusiasm of the people for their new toy. Relatively little has been heard of social policy; the trump card has always been the crowning mercy of German rearmament . . .

Phipps's despatch led Vansittart to minute, on November 19: 'there is not a week to lose in our own measures. With every new despatch that Sir E. Phipps writes the warning—which all can or should see—grows yet clearer.' At Vansittart's suggestion, Hoare circulated a set of Phipps's despatches to the Cabinet. At the same time, Ralph Wigram gave Churchill a set, under seal of secrecy.[1]

The General Election was held on November 14. Churchill was returned with an increased majority, his son was defeated. The Conservatives won 432 seats, the Labour Party 154, the Liberals 21. In an unpublished note written twelve years later, Churchill recalled the night when the poll was declared:

I went to the Albert Hall to see the results shown upon the screen. It was clear that a sweeping Conservative victory would be won. After an hour or two I went on to Stornaway House where Lord Beaverbrook had a large party to see the results as they came out. When he greeted me he said: 'Well, you're finished now. Baldwin has so good a majority that he will be able to do without you.' I was taken aback and offended by this. I thought to myself that this was a kind of Canadian outlook on British politics. A man like Mr Baldwin, having spoken as he did about me before the Election and having written to me thanking me for my offer of support, would not be influenced in his decision about my joining the Government by the size of his majority.

---

[1] On December 4 Hoare told the Cabinet that Phipps' despatches 'fully justified the warnings of the Foreign Office as to Germany's tremendous preparations, and he thought they would convince the Cabinet that there was no time to lose in the preparation and completion of our own defensive arrangements . . . He was somewhat depressed at the slowness with which progress was being made, as exemplified by the case of the production of anti-aircraft ammunition. If that were so in a matter which had priority in a time of urgency, what would be the position in the general reconditioning of the Services? . . . He could not urge on the Cabinet too strongly the importance of pressing ahead with our own measures. Germany, even if not completely ready, might easily take some action if satisfied that the defences of other countries were even further behindhand.'

Churchill wanted to return to the Admiralty as First Lord, and for six days he waited at Chartwell for a letter or telephone call. But it did not come. 'There are not likely to be many changes in the Cabinet,' Thomas Jones wrote in his diary on November 17. 'Lord Halifax wants to go home to look after his estate in Yorkshire and hunt the fox. Duff Cooper is due for promotion and may go to the War Office. Winston will be kept out, I think.' That same day Nancy Astor [1] wrote direct to Baldwin: 'Don't put Winston in the Government—It will mean war at home and abroad. I know the depths of Winston's disloyalty—and you can't think how he is distrusted by *all* the electors of the country.'

'I hope Baldwin will have the wisdom to persuade you to look after defence,' Sir Roger Keyes wrote to Churchill on November 18. But three days later Harold Nicolson wrote in his diary: 'Clemmie tells me that Winston has not yet been approached. It looks as if he were going to be left out till February. He wants the Admiralty. But he has got tickets for Bali, where, if not offered a Cabinet job, he proposes to spend the winter.'

When the first list of new Ministers was announced, Churchill's name was not on it. 'This was to me a pang,' Churchill wrote in an unpublished note twelve years later, 'and, in a way, an insult. There was much mockery in the Press. I do not pretend that, thirsting to get things on the move, I was not distressed. Lots of people have gone through this before, and will again.'

Churchill's friends were puzzled and disappointed that he had not been given office. 'I hoped to see you back at the Admiralty,' General Bridges [2] wrote on November 23, 'but perhaps that will come. I sincerely hope so.' 'I had expected to see your name in the list of Cabinet changes,' Sir William Graham Greene wrote on November 24, 'but those announced are presumably not final! The country is in need of strong experienced men at the head!' 'I am still hoping to see your name in the cabinet,' his cousin George Spencer-Churchill wrote on November 27, 'possibly as Defence Minister.'

---

[1] Nancy Witcher Langhorne, 1879–1964. Born in Virginia. Married first, in 1897, Robert Gould Shaw (divorced, 1903); second, in 1906, the 2nd Viscount Astor. Conservative MP for Plymouth Sutton, 1919–45 (the first woman to take her seat in the Westminster Parliament). Companion of Honour, 1937.

[2] George Tom Molesworth Bridges, 1871–1939. Entered Royal Artillery, 1892. Lieutenant-Colonel 4th Hussars, 1914. Head of British Military Mission, Belgian Field Army, 1914–16. Major-General commanding the 19th Division, 1916–17. Wounded five times; lost a leg at Passchendaele. Head of British War Mission, USA, 1918. Head of British Mission, Allied Armies of the Orient, 1918–20. Knighted, 1919. Governor of South Australia, 1922–27. He published his memoirs, *Alarms & Excursions*, in 1938 (with a Foreword by Churchill).

Churchill realized at once that there was to be no place for him, writing to Flandin on November 26: 'The full composition of the new Ministry is not yet determined, but I do not think it likely that Mr Baldwin will require my help now he has got so good a majority. I think I can perhaps do some useful work from my corner seat below the gangway and am very content with that position.'

Writing in his diary on November 17, Thomas Jones had praised Baldwin for having 'avoided all trace of the Daily Mail's lust to arm the nation to the teeth'. He had also, Jones wrote, 'kept clear of Winston's enthusiasm for ships and guns'. In a letter to Davidson, Baldwin gave his own comment on Churchill's exclusion. 'I feel we should not give him a post at this stage,' Baldwin wrote. 'Anything he undertakes he puts his heart and soul into. If there is going to be war—and no one can say that there is not—we must keep him fresh to be our war Prime Minister.' Yet throughout December there was speculation about Churchill's possible return to the Cabinet. 'I hope you will have a lovely holiday,' Frederick Guest wrote to him on December 5, 'and come back as Minister of Defence,' and twelve days later Sir Hugh Tudor[1] wrote from the Army and Navy Club: 'The opinion is universal that you are the obvious man.'

With his Mediterranean holiday planned to last for at least six weeks, Churchill had decided even before the election to take up once more his work on the third volume of *Marlborough*, and Commander Owen began work at once, checking Churchill's new draft chapters, and assembling material for those yet to be done. Throughout 1935 Keith Feiling had been working in Oxford on the draft chapters of the *History of the English-Speaking Peoples*, and by the end of November he had sent Churchill fourteen chapters in outline, together with the documents and materials on which they had been based. But on November 19 Feiling wrote to say that the pressure of his Oxford work made it impossible for him to continue after the following May, and he offered to help Churchill find someone who would not only take over the research on

---

[1] Henry Hugh Tudor, 1871–1965. 2nd Lieutenant, Royal Artillery, 1890. On active service in South Africa, 1899–1902. Brigadier-General commanding the Artillery of the 9th (Scottish) Division, 1916–18. Major-General commanding the 9th Division, 21 to 24 March 1918. Major-General commanding the Irregular Forces in Ireland (the 'Black and Tans') 1920–21. General Officer Commanding the special gendarmerie in Palestine (known as 'Tudor's lambs'), 1922, with the rank of Air Vice-Marshal. Knighted, 1923. Retired, 1923, and lived in Newfoundland. In 1959 he published his first war diaries, entitled *The Fog of War*.

the *English-Speaking Peoples*, but also succeed John Wheldon as the principal assistant on *Marlborough*. On December 2 Feiling wrote to Churchill from Christ Church, suggesting one of his own pupils, Bill Deakin,[1] whom he described as a person of 'Great spirit and courage'. Churchill replied on December 8:

> I should like very mu h to see the young man you mention when I return at the end of Janua. y. I think there is very little doubt I shall engage him for a month on probation, but I would rather not take this decision, nor any upon the details, until I return. The future is still very uncertain for me, indeed if the truth were realised, for all of us.

'I am hoping,' Churchill added, 'to master Oudenarde and Lille during my month at Majorca.'

Churchill had intended to leave England for his holiday on December 7. But on December 1 he decided to postpone his departure for three days, in order to attend a meeting of the Committee of Imperial Defence sub-committee on Air Defence Research, which had been called for December 9. At the meeting Churchill reiterated the arguments of his memorandum of September 30, fortified by the information which Sir Henry Strakosch had sent him on German military expenditure, and confident in the scrutiny which Desmond Morton had given to the conflicting or disputed statistics. In a series of notes written for the meeting, and subsequently circulated to the Committee of Imperial Defence, Churchill replied to the Air Staff memorandum of November 5:

> I cannot personally accept the figure 594 as representing German first line air strength on the date mentioned. It is said that this figure is based 'on information received from *most reliable sources*', and from the digestion of a 'mass of information received from a large variety of sources', including 'some thousands of reports examined annually'. When one considers the admittedly conventional and necessarily arbitrary definitions assigned to 'first line air strength' in the two countries, together with the digestion of this mass of secret information, the selection of the exact figure 594 appears to lie in the region of the occult. It is to be hoped, however, that this figure will not be

---

[1] Frederick William Dampier Deakin, 1913–   . Educated at Westminster School, 1926–30. Studied for six months at the Sorbonne, 1931, then at Christ Church Oxford, 1931–34, where he took a 1st class Honours degree in modern history. Teaching in Germany, 1934–35. Fellow and lecturer at Wadham College, Oxford, 1936–49. Research Assistant to Churchill 1936–39. Churchill described him in a private letter on 15 February 1939 as 'a young man of great historical distinction', and wrote of him on 29 April 1939: 'I can say from my own intimate knowledge of him for several years that he is in every way fitted to make an excellent officer.' Served with the Queen's Own Oxfordshire Hussars, 1939–41; Special Operations, War Office, 1941; British Military Mission to Tito, 1943. DSO, 1943. Lieutenant-Colonel. First Secretary, British Embassy, Belgrade, 1945–46. Director of Researches for Churchill, 1946–49. Warden of St Antony's College Oxford, 1950–58. Historian. Knighted, 1975.

made public, as it would certainly give rise to misunderstanding and challenge.

Churchill submitted two full pages of notes, reiterating his own points and conclusions. Even his figures, of 2,000 war planes by the end of 1936, might, he wrote, be 'grievously exceeded'. Commenting on the Air Staff argument that German expansion could be restricted by the French making it clear that they themselves would aim at 'a comparatively low first-line strength', Churchill wrote:

To rely upon such an argument shows an undue belief in the innocence of Germany's intentions. That a nation which has just repudiated its solemn treaty undertaking not to build any air force at all should allow itself to be bound by a casual statement that it was aiming at parity with France and that it should expand or contract its programme religiously to fit the expansions or contractions real or nominal of the French programme seems highly improbable.

Of the Air Staff comment on the discrepancy between German total production and first-line machines, Churchill wrote:

The fact that Germany possesses at least 2150 military machines makes one doubt that there are no more than 594 in the first line, however reliable the sources of information. If it is true however, it only emphasises the danger of estimating relative military air strength of two countries merely by comparing their first-line air strength.

The dispute between Churchill and the Air Staff was commented on within the Foreign Office. On December 19 V. J. Lawford[1] minuted, of the Air Staff's attitude to Churchill's paper: 'one cannot help being struck by the fact that they are above all intent upon minimizing the dangers of the situation'. In a further minute that same day Ralph Wigram pointed out, in further support of Churchill, that discussion of first-line strength was 'not only endless but meaningless', and he went on to explain that:

The real test—and the only real test is the capacity to manufacture machines and to train pilots in emergency. What progress has been made in this matter within the last 9 months (eg since the scare of the spring)? Practically none, I am confident. For the Air Ministry (under the lead of their *civil* staff) have not yet adopted a wide policy of 'educational' orders—but

[1] Valentine George Lawford, 1911–   . Educated at Repton and Corpus Christi Cambridge. 3rd Secretary, Foreign Office, October 1934. Transferred to Paris, March 1937. Returned to the Foreign Office, September 1939; Second Secretary, October 1939; acting First Secretary, August 1944. Private Secretary to Anthony Eden, 1940–45. A member of the United Kingdom Delegation to the United Nations, 1946–47. Counsellor, Teheran, 1949–50.

have almost entirely confined their orders for 1935 & 36 programmes to some 15 firms, who have, I believe, been very chary of expanding their plant, as they don't know what will happen after the beginning of '37.

If anyone doubts these statements, let him ask the Secretary of State for Air to contradict them. . . .

On December 10 Churchill left England for his long-awaited winter holiday. His hopes of Cabinet office had been frustrated, his warnings of the German danger still not accepted by the Government. In demanding interference with normal trade, he had diverged far from Government thinking. Indeed, his repeated criticism of Hitler during the election campaign had publicly accentuated this difference of approach. Although this divergence effectively ensured Churchill's continued exclusion from Baldwin's Cabinet, it was this very same frankness that had begun to win for him an ever-widening public support, and which drew towards him the confidence of officials who were certain that Hitler would soon be able to dictate European policy unless the full-scale rearmament Churchill demanded were put in hand at once.

35

Winter 1935–1936:
Hoping for a Cabinet Post

O N December 10 Churchill and his wife flew from London to
Paris, where they lunched with Flandin. From Paris they took
the train to Barcelona, and from there continued by boat to Majorca.
While they were still travelling, a startling diplomatic event was taking
place in Paris and London. On December 6, in Paris, the British and
French Foreign Ministers, Samuel Hoare and Pierre Laval, with the
approval of their senior advisers, including Sir Robert Vansittart, had
agreed on the basis for a compromise solution for the Abyssinian conflict. News of their compromise had been leaked in Paris on December 9,
and seemed in direct and immoral contrast to Britain's earlier policy of
support for the League of Nations, and sanctions against the Italian
aggressor. That same day, however, in London, the terms of the compromise were agreed by the Cabinet, despite a strong protest by
Anthony Eden, who was almost provoked to resignation. When Parliament met on December 10, Clement Attlee asked Baldwin to reveal the
terms of the compromise, but Baldwin insisted that no agreed basis had
yet been submitted either to Italy or to Abyssinia. On December 11
Randolph Churchill wrote to his father: 'Baldwin seems to have put his
foot in it properly over the Laval–Hoare peace plan. His use of the word
"leakage" gave everyone to understand that the terms printed in the
papers are accurate. Nearly everyone seems very shocked by the proposals.'

The text of the Hoare–Laval proposals was put before the League of
Nations on December 9. They entailed, as the Press leak had correctly
forecast, the surrender by Abyssinia of 20 per cent of her territory.
Churchill was in Majorca when the details reached him, and could not
decide whether to return at once to England. Instead, he left Majorca

for Barcelona, where he painted and worked on volume three of his *Marlborough*. He was still in Barcelona when, on December 16, his son telegraphed to say that Baldwin was 'standing firm' on the Hoare–Laval proposals, that Austen Chamberlain had been 'squared' and that the Government were bound to obtain a 'reasonable majority' in the debate which had been fixed for December 19. Randolph's telegram continued: 'Though Government will get away with it prestige fatally ruined in country. Heavy rearmament inevitable and this your best re-entry card.' Randolph Churchill's advice was that his father should not return to England prematurely. This course, he added, was 'emphatic-ally recommended' by Brendan Bracken, Lindemann and Boothby.

Churchill received his son's telegram on December 17, and agreed with him. That evening Randolph wrote again:

My dear Papa,

I am sure you have taken a wise decision in not coming home. The more I think and hear about Thursday's debate the more certain I am that Baldwin will get away with it. There will be a very large number of abstentions but few Conservatives will go into the Lobby against the Government.

From what I hear, Baldwin, Hoare and Vansittart who planned this shameful surrender, are extraordinarily confident of the outcome. They are going to raise the cry that they have saved the country from war, and to make it worse from our point of view they are going to suggest that it would have been a war which we might have lost.

The average private Member has an absurd idea that the defeat of the Government would involve a new election. It is very hard to break down this fallacy which the Whips are fostering as hard as they can. . . .

All the disgruntled elements in the Cabinet will wish for your inclusion as an offset to Baldwin.

The agitation about the peace proposals will last for many months and you will be in a unique position of strength since you will neither have supported the Government, compromised yourself by hostility, nor taken the negative though semi-hostile line of abstention. Your return and your first pronounce-ments on the subject are sure to be awaited with the liveliest interest, and if you choose the right moment I am sure a considerable situation will at once be opened up.

Randolph Churchill told his father that 'hundreds of Tory MPs' would gladly pay £100 for as good an excuse as Churchill for their absence. 'Poor Brendan,' he added, 'is torn between his desire to see sanctions terminated and Baldwin exterminated.'

The Cabinet met on December 18. Bowing to public protest, and reversing the conclusion of December 9, Baldwin was forced by his colleagues to abandon the proposed agreement. Hoare at once resigned, and on December 19, during the debate in the House of Commons, Baldwin admitted that when the conscience of a nation had been roused, no Government could stand against it. 'The League of Nations,' he promised, 'will remain as heretofore the keystone of British foreign policy.' Austen Chamberlain then told the House that as a result of Baldwin's decision to drop the proposals, he had decided to support the Government in the division. When the vote was taken, 397 MPs voted for the Government, and only 165 against. It was widely believed that Hoare would be succeeded at the Foreign Office by Austen Chamberlain; but on December 23 it was announced that Anthony Eden would be his successor.

On December 20 Desmond Morton sent Churchill a full account of the crisis and its effect. His own view, he wrote, was that the proposals were 'fundamentally sound' because 'remembering Germany, we want Italy as a friend and not an enemy'. But, Morton continued:

Baldwin has completely lost every shred of confidence. He is believed to have sacrificed his friend, not because that friend made an error in method, but because he believed it was the only hope of saving his own skin. At that he was wrong, since even if half his Cabinet had resigned and he had faced the storm with a bold avowal that although his Foreign Secretary had rushed things, the policy was one which he approved and which Hoare had every right to consider was in agreement with his private views, he would have been hailed as the greatest political leader this country has known in modern times. . . .

To-day the name of S.B. is mud. Worse than that, there is an astonishing reaction in certain quarters against all politics and politicians. Were we at all inclined to Fascism, now would be the time for a march on London.

As for the reaction in Germany; a country that was beginning to be very respectful and even alarmed at the resurrection of a forceful, united, purposeful British Nation, and was beginning to believe, with no little apprehension, that it had wholly miscalculated the incalculable English, now looks on us as slightly more futile and decadent than the Portuguese.

Morton believed that on balance it was good that Churchill had been abroad. 'It is certain,' he wrote, 'that in due time the fact that you were not here and had no part, either in the superficial mess or the suspected intrigues behind the scenes, will be an excellent thing in the future. The man in the street does not look on this business as a great national crisis, but as a very nasty stink.'

Churchill neither criticized nor defended the Hoare–Laval proposals. But writing twelve years later, specifically of Sir Robert Vansittart's part in them, he stressed that Vansittart thought continuously of the German threat, and wished to have Britain and France organized at their strongest to face this major danger, 'with Italy in their rear a friend and not a foe'.

On December 20 Churchill left Barcelona by boat for Tangier, accompanied by Professor Lindemann, who had come out to join him. Clementine Churchill returned to England to spend Christmas at Blenheim. Churchill himself spent Christmas at Tangier, where he had found several friends, including Lord Rothermere and George Ward Price, and hoped to relax and paint. But after a few days of incessant rain, during which time he worked on volume three of his *Marlborough*, he and Rothermere decided to leave Tangier for Marrakesh, where Lloyd George was on holiday.

On reaching Rabat on December 26, *en route* to Marrakesh, Churchill wrote again, not only of his journey and of his children, but also of the political events which he had watched from afar, and of Baldwin, Eden and Austen Chamberlain, telling his wife:

I too thought B.'s speech most damaging to his position & repute. Eden's appointment does not inspire me with confidence. I expect the greatness of his office will find him out. Austen wd have been far better; & I wonder why he was overlooked. Poor man, he always plays the game & never wins it. . . .

Ending his letter, Churchill described himself as 'your wandering, sun-seeking, rotten, disconsolate W.'

Churchill, while not hopeful of being offered a Cabinet post, still did not wish to jeopardize his chances by embarking upon, or condoning, any attack on the leading Government personalities. In a letter to his son, sent from Rabat on December 26, he wrote: 'It would in my belief by vy injurious to me at this junction if you publish articles attacking the motives & character of Ministers, especially Baldwin & Eden. I hope therefore you will make sure this does not happen. If not, I shall not be able to feel confidence in yr loyalty & affection for me.'

Earlier that same day, while still in Tangier, Churchill had written to Sir Samuel Hoare:

My dear Sam,
I must venture to write you a few lines to congratulate you on the dignity of yr speech of resignation, & to tell you how vy sorry I am at what has happened. It can only mean a brief interruption in yr career, and after so much work & worry I daresay the breathing space will be welcome.
We are moving into a year of measureless perils.

On December 30, after spending four days with Lloyd George, Churchill wrote to his wife from the Hotel Mamounia, Marrakesh: 'What a fool Baldwin is, with this terrible situation on his hands, not to gather his resources & experiences to the public service.' Of his holiday relaxation Churchill wrote: 'I am painting a picture from the balcony, because although the native city is full of attractive spots, the crowds, the smells and the general discomfort for painting have repelled me.' Of the effects of the Hoare–Laval drama, he told his wife:

There is no doubt we are in it up to our necks. Owing to this vigorous manifestation from the depths of British public opinion, the French have come a long way with us against Mussolini and they will expect a similar service when the far greater peril of Hitler becomes active. We are getting into the most terrible position, involved definitely by honour & by contract in almost any quarrel that can break out in Europe, our defences neglected, our Government less capable a machine for conducting affairs that I have ever seen. The Baldwin–MacDonald regime has hit this country very hard indeed, and may well be the end of its glories.

Now the one thing that matters seems to be to try and find seats for those two ragamuffin MacDonalds![1] Luckily I have plenty of things to do to keep me from chewing the cud too much.

From Marrakesh, on New Year's Eve, Churchill spoke to his wife by telephone. Later that night he wrote to her with family news, both personal and political:

Rothermere offered me 2 bets. First £2,000 if I went teetotal in 1936. I refused as I think life wd not be worth living, but 2,000 free of tax is nearly 3,500 & then the saving of liquor 500 = 4,000. It was a fine offer. I have however accepted his second bet of £600 not to drink any brandy or un-diluted spirits in 1936. So tonight is my last sip of brandy. . . .

I have been idle today. No Marl, only a little daub & a little bezique. Randolph is of course wanting to fight Malcom M but he won't be able to—because it would put a spoke in my wheel & do nothing good for him. I do not think he would really when it came to the point.

On 7 January 1936, while Churchill was still at Marrakesh, his wife replied to his letter of December 30. 'The political situation at home is depressing,' she wrote. 'I really would not like you to serve under Baldwin, unless he really gave you a great deal of power and you were able

---

[1] In the 1935 General Election both Ramsay MacDonald and his son Malcolm had been defeated by Labour Party candidates. Ramsay MacDonald, who had been defeated at Seaham by Emanuel Shinwell, was elected on 31 January 1936 for the Combined Scottish Universities (where his Scottish National Party opponent was Churchill's former battalion adjutant, Andrew Dewar Gibb). Malcolm MacDonald, who had been defeated at Bassetlaw, was later elected for Ross and Cromarty.

to inspire and vivify the Government.' A week earlier P. J. Grigg had written to Churchill from India: 'Is there any chance of that whited sepulchre Baldwin clearing out and allowing the country to be run by somebody with the normal number of faculties?' On January 8 Churchill wrote to his wife:

The world seems to be divided between the confident nations who behave harshly, and the nations who have lost confidence in themselves and behave fatuously. Mussolini is failing more and more in his Italian campaign. What I told you about the Italians being no good at fighting is being painfully proved. They are throwing away their wealth and their poor wedding rings on an absolutely shameful adventure. How it will end no one can tell.

I am very sorry Austen was not made Foreign Secretary. I think you will now see what a light-weight Eden is. The League of Nations Union send me heaps of letters from the constituency clamouring for extreme measures, they having previously disarmed us, so that we are an easy prey!

Churchill's new son-in-law, Duncan Sandys, had come to join him at the Mamounia. 'The more I see of him,' Churchill wrote, 'the better I like him.' His own work had flourished: several newspaper articles[1] dictated to Mrs Pearman, three draft chapters of *Marlborough* sent back to England with Lindemann, seven paintings completed, much 'brilliant sunshine, translucent air', and 'swarms of picturesque inhabitants, every one of whom is a picture'. Churchill's main news concerned their son, who had left Casablanca by air that morning, following the request of the local Unionist Association of Ross and Cromarty to stand as the Conservative candidate against Malcolm MacDonald.[2] Because MacDonald was a Cabinet Minister in the National Government, he could count on the support of his fellow Cabinet Ministers, Conservative and Liberal. Churchill, who still hoped to be invited into the Cabinet, was

[1] Beginning on January 12, the *News of the World* began printing each Sunday a biographical essay by Churchill on the 'Great Men' he had known. The thirteen essays had continued until April 5. During February the *Daily Mail* published two more of his articles, one on his impressions of Morocco, the other on the need for a Channel Tunnel. In the May issue of the *Strand* magazine he published an article on the *Queen Mary*, which was to begin its maiden voyage to the United States on May 27. 'Never in the whole history of Atlantic travel,' he wrote, 'has so lavish provision been made for those who travel tourist.'

[2] Malcolm John MacDonald, 1901–81. Son of Ramsay MacDonald. Educated at Bedales and Queen's College Oxford. Labour MP for Bassetlaw, 1929–31 (National Labour 1931–35); for Ross and Cromarty, 1936–45. Parliamentary Under-Secretary, Dominions Office, 1931–35. Privy Councillor, 1935. Secretary of State for Dominion Affairs, 1935–38 and 1938–39; Colonial Secretary, 1935 and 1938–40. Minister of Health, 1940–41. High Commissioner, Canada, 1941–46. Governor-General of Malaya, Singapore and British Borneo 1946–48. Commissioner General for South-East Asia, 1948–55. High Commissioner, India, 1955–60. Governor-General of Kenya, 1963–64; High Commissioner, 1964–65. British Special Representative in East and Central Africa, 1965–66; in Africa, 1966–69.

appalled by the action of the local Conservatives in enlisting his son, telling his wife:

The stubborn and spontaneous character of this invitation, and the refusal even to hear Malcolm MacDonald, are remarkable facts. You will see how unfortunate and inconvenient such a fight is to me. 'Churchill v MacDonald.' If they get in, it would seem very difficult for Baldwin to invite me to take the Admiralty or the co-ordinating job, and sit cheek by jowl with these wretched people. I therefore would greatly have preferred Randolph to damp it all down. Instead of this he has had his agent up there feeling around.

Quite apart from this, there is no doubt the thoughts of all Conservatives in the constituency turn naturally to him. It is a great insult to a Scottish constituency to be used as a mere utensil for Baldwin's purposes. Moreover this National Labour business is humbug. Here are these two MacDonalds, whom we are told must be elected, in order that the Labour element should be represented in a National Government, otherwise it cannot be called 'National'. . . .[1]

Rothermere is sending Oliver Baldwin[2] to write up Randolph, which he is apparently ready to do, and to write down Malcolm, which of course is what all other Socialists revel in. So we shall have Ramsay's son, Baldwin's son and my son—all mauling each other in this remote constituency. . . .

When the contest gets a little further developed, I propose to utter the following 'piece'. 'I wish Mr Baldwin would tell me the secret by which he keeps his son Oliver in such good order.' However for the present I am completely mum.

Churchill was distressed that his son should have agreed to stand, fearing, as he wrote to his wife, that Baldwin might regard it 'as a definite declaration of war by me', even though Randolph was acting 'entirely on his own'. But, as he wrote to his wife, 'with Rothermere, Beaverbrook and Lloyd George all goading him on, I cannot really blame him. . . .' Churchill added, with a thought for his own future:

I was reading what Marlborough wrote in 1708—'As I think most things are settled by destiny, when one has done one's best, the only thing is to await the result with patience.'

[1] Of the eight National Labour MPs elected in 1935, three received Ministerial office, Malcolm MacDonald as Dominions Secretary, Kenneth Lindsay as Civil Lord of the Admiralty and Earl De la Warr as Parliamentary Secretary at the Ministry of Education. These eight MPs were all that remained in Parliament of the Labour supporters of the National Government, which nevertheless retained its 'National' name.

[2] Oliver Ridsdale Baldwin, 1899–1958. Elder son of Stanley Baldwin. Educated at Eton. On active service in France, 1916–18. Vice-Consul, Boulogne, 1919. Fought in the Armeno-Turkish and Armeno-Russian wars, 1920 and 1921; imprisoned by both Bolsheviks and Turks, 1921. Parliamentary Labour candidate, 1924. Labour MP for Dudley, 1929–31; for Paisley, 1945–47. Succeeded his father as 2nd Earl, 1947. Governor of the Leeward Islands, 1948–50.

I think the Government greatly weakened by what has occurred over the Hoare-Laval agreement, and Baldwin greatly weakened too. Therefore I expect that either Baldwin will be looking for a chance to clear out, or he will want a strong reconstruction.

The Naval Conference is breaking down and Monsell will soon be going.[1] Thus everything comes to a head at once, and Destiny will decide.

On January 14 Churchill left Marrakesh for Meknes, when, together with Lloyd George, he was the guest at two Arab banquets. 'I hope my last for a long time,' he wrote to his wife after the second, on January 15. At the second banquet there had also been a dance by as many as a hundred women 'all in their best silks and finery'. The dance, Churchill wrote, 'consisted of droning chants to kettle drums with rhythmic motions of the hands. Personally my taste is more attuned to the Russian ballet, but the natives seem to have been thrilled by this for thousands of years.' There was also further news of their son's candidature:

Today he telegraphs that an unimportant Scottish paper alleges I am wholeheartedly supporting his candidature. I am reluctant to disavow him and have let things drift. Rothermere however is arranging for Oliver Baldwin to write an article examining the relations of fathers and sons in politics and pointing out that sons must take their own line and their fathers cannot be held responsible.

I shall not make up my mind upon the matter further until I get home, but I should think that any question of my joining the Government was closed by the hostility which Randolph's campaign must excite. Kismet!

While at Meknes, Churchill reflected continuously on his son's action. Unexpected though it had been, foolish though it seemed, and harmful though it might prove, he could not bring himself to denounce it. 'Modern ideas,' he reflected in a note for Lord Rothermere, 'contemplate freedom of action on their own responsibility for grown sons. It follows that parents have no responsibility for action taken by sons.' And he added: 'Political divergences between fathers and sons no bar to affection and sympathy.'

At midnight on January 17 Churchill returned by train from Meknes to Marrakesh, reaching the Mamounia hotel at noon. During the journey he wrote to his wife of his plans to stay in Morocco until January 25, and then to go to France for a week. It would, he wrote, be 'convenient' for him to stay away from England as long as possible, as it emphasized 'without any positive declaration that I am taking no part in Randolph's campaign'. Returning to Marrakesh, Churchill received

---

[1] Viscount Monsell did not leave the Admiralty until June, when he was succeeded by Sir Samuel Hoare.

a gloomy telegram from Brendan Bracken, who declared: 'Randolph's prospects very doubtful. Socialist win probable. More stags than Tories in Cromarty.'

In his letter of January 17 to his wife, Churchill wrote of the political situation in England:

Evidently there is a deep division in the Cabinet between the Hoares and the anti-Hoares or Edens. The Edens pushed on by the febrile League of Nations Union and balloteers want oil sanctions and us to take a lead in them. They will be strengthened if things go worse with the Abyssinians than they have done so far. The other lot headed I suppose by Neville and Runciman, with Vansittart in the background, are determined to play for safety.

I fear they have some grave news about Germany and her aggressive intentions. Certainly our Ambassador at Berlin found a very rough Hitler when he went to talk about an air pact. They are getting stronger every moment. They have chosen to make their Press demonstrate vehemently against the Anglo-French military and naval conversations which were necessary upon the Italian danger.

Churchill had begun to work out what Hitler's next moves in Europe were likely to be, believing that he would soon test his strength by sending German troops into the Rhineland, a province of Germany from which all German troops and fortifications had been banned seventeen years before, under the Treaty of Versailles. Commenting on the German denunciations of the Anglo-French discussions, Churchill told his wife:

Rothermere who has long letters and telegrams from Hitler and is in close touch with him, believes that on the 24th or it may be the 21st, Hitler is going to make a most important announcement. This may well be that Germany will violate Articles 46 and 47 of the Treaty and reoccupy the neutral zone with troops and forts.

This would immediately raise a very grave European issue, and no one can tell what would come of it. Certainly the League of Nations would be obliged to declare the Germans guilty of 'aggression', and the French would be in a position to demand our specific aid in enforcing sanctions. So the League of Nations Union folk who have done their best to get us disarmed may find themselves confronted by terrible consequences. Baldwin and Ramsay, guilty of neglecting our defences in spite of every warning, may well feel anxious not only for the public but for their own personal skins.

In the Far East, the Japanese Government had begun once more to assert formidable military pressure on China, and Japanese troops were even involved in clashes with Soviet troops along the Soviet–Manchukuo border. On January 15 the Japanese delegates had withdrawn from the London Naval Disarmament Conference, refusing thereby to accept any upper limit to the size of their navy. Ten years earlier, Churchill had foreseen no danger from Japan. But under the new world conditions created by the successes of Fascist Italy and Nazi Germany, his optimism had now gone. So too had his new found hope that Britain might take effective, if belated, action. In his letter to his wife of January 17 he wrote:

The Naval Conference has of course collapsed. Japan has ruptured it. The good thing is that we and the United States are working hand in glove and will encourage each other to strengthen the navies. Meanwhile Japan is seeking more provinces of China. Already more than half of their whole budget is spent upon armaments. Those figures I quoted about German expenditure on armaments are being admitted in the press to be only too true.

One must consider these two predatory military dictatorship nations, Germany and Japan, as working in accord. No wonder the Russian bear is quaking for his skin and seeking protectors among the capitalist powers he deserted in the war and sought to destroy at the close of it. What—to quote a famous phrase—'What a fearful concatenation of circumstances.'

How melancholy that we have this helpless Baldwin and his valets in absolute possession of all power. I suppose now that the Naval Conference is over, Monsell will be going and it seems not at all unlikely to me that they may get Sam Hoare back as First Lord. Evidently the reason why he made no complaint of his treatment was because of some promise of early reinstatement.

I doubt whether they will take any effective action however about coordinating the defence measures. Very likely some Minister without Portfolio may be assigned some of the duties in this respect. But all the three service Ministers will be very much against any higher control.

Churchill's friends still hoped that he might be given a Cabinet post. 'I wish you were in the Govt now,' Sir Reginald Barnes wrote to him on January 19, 'as they look like wanting you. I had quite settled it for them that you would be First Lord of the Admiralty, and only hope that you will be so when the present stop-gap goes.'

On January 20, while Churchill was still in Morocco, King George V died at Sandringham. During January 21 Churchill received a telegram from Sir Emsley Carr,[1] asking him to write an article on the late King

[1] Emsley Carr, 1867–1941. Newspaper proprietor; director of George Newnes Ltd; Chairman of the *News of the World*; Vice-Chairman of the *Western Mail*, Cardiff, the *South Wales Echo*, and the Cardiff *Evening Express*. Knighted, 1918. Delegate to the Imperial Press Conference, Canada, 1925; Australia, 1930. Chairman of the Press Gallery of the House of Commons, 1929–30. President of the Institute of Journalists, 1932 and 1933. Chairman of the Newspaper Press Fund, 1936, and the Printers' Pension Corporation, 1939. High Sheriff of Glamorgan, 1938.

for publication in the *News of the World* the following Sunday, January 26. Churchill was at that moment preparing to leave Marrakesh for Tangier. He at once began to dictate the article to Mrs Pearman, who had then to type it out during the train journey to the coast. As soon as they reached Tangier, Churchill telegraphed the article, via Paris, to London, where it arrived on January 24, only four days after the death of the King. That same day, Churchill was invited to be present in the House of Commons on January 27, in order to present the Address of the House to the new King, Edward VIII. He therefore decided to break off his holiday, and to return at once to England.

On January 26 Churchill reached Chartwell from Marrakesh. 'Randolph seems to be enjoying himself amid the snows of Cromarty,' he wrote that same day to Reginald Barnes, and added: 'I have no idea what the future holds in store for me, but you will find me vigorously advocating our rearmament while time remains by every channel that is open.' Three days later, on January 29, with reference to Churchill's earlier correspondence with Cunliffe-Lister, Sir Maurice Hankey wrote to Churchill to ask 'whether you are prepared to communicate in confidence any special sources of intelligence on which your information is based'. Churchill drafted a long reply on January 30, but then decided not to send it in full. In his original draft he had intended to remind Hankey of his previous successful experiences in forecasting military events. His draft began by describing his figures as entirely his own—'the fruits of my judgment'—but he went on:

I hope however that though I cannot claim to possess 'any special sources of intelligence', you will not neglect my judgment, but weigh it carefully with the other opinions at your disposal. I would remind you that on August 13 1911 I wrote a paper for the CID which predicted accurately the exact course on land of the first two months of a possible war between France and Germany, and that I even specified the twentieth day of mobilisation as the date by which the French armies would be in full retreat by the frontiers upon Paris, and the period after the fortieth day of mobilisation as that in which an effective counter-stroke might be expected. Those dates were in fact borne out almost to the day by the event. In forming this conclusion I was running counter to the opinions of the General Staff and Henry Wilson,[1] with whom

---

[1] Henry Hughes Wilson, 1864–1922. Entered Army, 1884. Director of Military Operations, War Office, 1910–14. Lieutenant-General, 1914. Chief liaison officer with the French Army, January 1915. Knighted, 1915. Commanded the 4th Corps, 1916. Chief of the Imperial General Staff, 1918–22. Field Marshal, July 1919. Created Baronet, August 1919, when he received the thanks of Parliament and a grant of £10,000 for his contribution to the war. Ulster Unionist MP, 1922. Shot dead by two Sinn Feiners on the steps of his London house.

I was in very close touch, who taught us to expect a successful French offensive in the first instance. I do not mention this to claim daemonic powers for myself, but only to remind you of the very long and careful thought I have given to these questions, and that it has sometimes been vindicated by the results.

Another instance occurred last year in November 1934 when I drew attention to the secret growth of the German military air force, and made certain statements about its strength relative to our own. These statements were disputed by Mr Baldwin, who I presume after full consideration of all the Intelligence information at the disposal of the Air Ministry, put forward other statements. But only a few months later in the Spring Mr Baldwin was forced to confess in the House of Commons that the Government with their official information were wrong, adding 'we were all in it'. Here then was a case in which an independent outside judgment was proved to be nearer the truth than the estimate from the Government based on all their secret sources.

'For these reasons,' Churchill added, 'I hope you will not brush aside my minimum estimates, although they have no other foundation than my own judgement.' He had only written to Cunliffe-Lister, he stressed, because it seemed to him 'that the Government were allowing themselves to be misled even at this late hour . . .'.

The letter which Churchill finally sent on January 31 simply stated: 'I cannot claim any "special sources of intelligence" for the figures given in my second memorandum. They are simply my personal estimate based on such study as I have been able to make of the problem in the last three or four years. I must however emphasise that they are only minimum figures, and that the real position is probably far more serious.'

On January 27 Randolph sent his father a four-page account of his activities at Ross and Cromarty. 'I was not invited to come here,' he wrote, 'because of my reputation as a specialist in wrecking (as you suggested) but solely on account of you. They are all mystified and puzzled as to why you are not in the Government, and think it an abuse and a scandal.'

Churchill made no plans to help his son publicly. 'Winston is in some doubt,' Beaverbrook wrote to Hoare on January 31. 'He evidently wants to speak for Randolph. Bracken advises against it.' But although

Churchill took no direct part in his son's campaign, he did draft two paragraphs for the Press in which he expressed his personal view of his son's intervention. 'Parliamentary government is under grievous challenge in the present age,' he wrote. 'We see all around us on the Continent the lamentable results of mass psychology and forceful wire-pulling. According to every convention of British public life undue pressure should not be put by the Central Government upon a free choice of the constituency.'

It was widely believed that Churchill had been behind his son's action, and in Conservative circles this belief added to the distrust of him. On February 2 Churchill wrote to Major John Astor, the owner of *The Times* and a fellow Conservative MP:

> I was surprised to read in the leading article of Saturday's 'Times' on the Ross and Cromarty By Election, an insinuation that I had prompted my Son's candidature. As a matter of fact, I strongly advised him to have nothing to do with it. Naturally as a Father, I cannot watch his fight, now that it has begun, without sympathy; but I am taking no part in it, though much pressed to do so by the local people. In these circumstances the innuendo of your leading article is neither true nor fair.[1]

The by-election was held on February 10. Malcolm MacDonald was elected, and returned to Westminster as Secretary of State for the Dominions.[2] 'I am sorry about Randolph,' Robert Boothby wrote on February 12, 'although I feel that a little chastening at this particular juncture will not necessarily be to his ultimate disadvantage.' Boothby added: 'There is more sympathy & friendly feeling for him than he suspects. But, my God, you don't challenge that machine with impunity.' According to a leading article in the *Edinburgh Evening News* on February 13: 'By emphasizing the unpopularity of the Churchillians' attitude, the decisive defeat of Mr Randolph Churchill in Ross and Cromarty seems to be regarded as another nail into the political coffin of Mr Winston Churchill, either as a candidate for the Admiralty or Cabinet Minister charged with the co-ordination of Defence Services.'

---

[1] John Astor replied on 5 February 1936: 'I am sorry that you should have detected an insinuation in our Saturday's leading article on the Ross and Cromarty by-election. None I am assured was intended. Since you wrote you will have noticed that we gave your son quite a large amount of space in which to state that you, among others, had not prompted his candidature. I hope, therefore, that we are forgiven.'

[2] The Ross and Cromarty result was: MacDonald (National Government), 8,949; H. McNeil (Labour), 5,967; Randolph Churchill (Conservative), 2,427; and Russell Thomas (Liberal), 738: a majority for MacDonald of 2,982. Randolph Churchill kept his deposit.

Throughout February, Churchill continued to receive information on the state and scale of European rearmament. On February 10 Desmond Morton sent him two documents, one of which was, he explained, 'based on secret information', setting out details of a recent German decision to maintain the high rate of arms production, and even to sell arms abroad. These documents had been prepared by Morton for circulation to the principal Departments of State, as well as to the Committee of Imperial Defence and MI5, and gave evidence of German arms negotiations in Afghanistan, Uruguay, Siam, Greece and Turkey.

Churchill was also well informed about the internal situation in Germany. Three months earlier, on 10 December 1935, at Churchill's own request, L. G. Montefiore [1] had sent him a full translation not only of the Nuremberg Laws, under which the Jews of Germany had been deprived of their basic rights as citizens, but also of the detailed administrative regulations, whereby those Laws were to be put into force. On March 10 the Duchess of Atholl sent him two copies of Hitler's *Mein Kampf*, the original German edition and the English translation. She also sent copies of those passages which had been expurgated in the translation. 'Sometimes,' she wrote, 'the warlike character of the original is concealed by mistranslating.' In one of the expurgated passages Hitler advocated a German alliance with Italy and Britain, in order to isolate France. In another he described France as 'our bitterest enemy', and in a third he declared: 'the life of a people will be secured not by national grace, but by the strength of a victorious sword'. The Duchess of Atholl also sent Churchill extracts from Hitler's speeches with copies of those more extreme paragraphs which had not been circulated to the foreign press.

During January and February a Government committee on Defence Policy and Requirements, headed by Baldwin, discussed a report of 21 November 1935, signed by Hankey, Chatfield, Vansittart, Ellington, Warren Fisher and Montgomery-Massingbird, which recommended, in the light of the international situation, 'a far more effective standard' of defence preparedness. Their recommendations covered increased expenditure for the Army, Navy and Air Force, up to an additional

---

[1] Leonard Nathaniel Goldsmid Montefiore, 1889–1961. Educated at Clifton and Balliol College Oxford. On graduation, he did welfare work at Toynbee Hall, in the east end of London. On active service, 1914–19. Chairman of the Industrial Committee of the Jewish Board of Guardians. President of the Anglo-Jewish Association, 1926–39, and Chairman of the Association's Joint Foreign Committee, which published a series of pamphlets on the conditions of German Jewry. An active member of the Central British Fund, set up to help German Jewry after 1933. President of the Associated Reform Synagogues in Great Britain.

£417½ million, over five years, but they concluded that to organize for war in peacetime 'is unthinkable in a democratic country like ours'. Instead, they proposed the development of a 'Shadow Armament Industry', but without any interference with normal trade. The Defence Policy and Requirements Committee endorsed this view. Any such interference, it reported on February 6, would 'adversely affect the prosperity of the country', and would 'attract Parliamentary criticism'. On February 25, the Cabinet accepted the principal proposals for increased defence measures, but, by the economy of postponing the modernization of 12 divisions of the Territorial Army, reduced the recommended extra expenditure from £417½ million to £394 million.

On February 10, as part of these discussions, Lord Swinton[1] had circulated a memorandum pointing out the disadvantages of the existing Scheme C, the light bombers of which had a 'strictly limited range', but which had formed more than 20 per cent of the scheme. Swinton suggested abandoning the light-bomber programme altogether, and planning a new first-line 'striking force' of 1,022 bombers, to replace the 840 envisaged by Scheme C. On February 25, Lord Swinton put his detailed proposals for the new air programme, Scheme F, before the Cabinet. The 1,512 first-line aeroplanes of Scheme C were to be increased by an additional 224 aeroplanes to a total of 1,736 by 1939. 'It was now possible,' he told his colleagues, 'during the longer period up to 1939 to organize a much more effective air striking force than had been approved last year.'

The Cabinet approved the new Scheme F. Meanwhile, in the second week of February several MPs, led by Austen Chamberlain, urged Baldwin to set up a special Ministry of Defence, to coordinate and unify the work of the three Service Ministries.[2] On February 11, three days before this proposal was debated in the House of Commons, the First Commissioner of Works, William Ormsby-Gore, commenting on

---

[1] Formerly Sir Philip Cunliffe-Lister; he had been created Viscount Swinton in November 1935.

[2] The campaign for a Ministry of Defence had been launched by a leader in *The Times* on December 2. The author of the leader, Captain Basil Liddell Hart, inclined to favour Churchill for the post, but found that both Geoffrey Dawson and Barrington-Ward preferred Amery, while Duff Cooper was also sceptical. In his diary for January 18 Liddell Hart wrote of how Duff Cooper 'went on to remark that though Winston is one of his greatest friends he doubted his suitability—he would be all for the Navy at one time and all for the Air at another. His enthusiasms carried him away. Moreover, he was not so quick as he had been in grasping points.' Liddell Hart added that Duff Cooper 'went on to reflect that one would have thought that at Winston's present age, and after holding so many high offices, he would have been content to settle down philosophically to become an elder statesman and to devote himself to letters.'

the growing demand for a Minister of Defence, had informed Baldwin: 'I hope you will not under-rate the very strong feeling there is among many well-informed people that some drastic improvement of the existing organisation is needed.'

The motion calling for a special Ministry of Defence was brought by two of Churchill's former Admiralty colleagues, Sir Murray Sueter and George Lambert, but after the debate, in order not to divide the House, the motion itself was withdrawn. There was no doubting, however, the strength of Parliamentary feeling. 'After today's debate,' Sir Maurice Hankey wrote to Sir Warren Fisher, 'I am afraid we have got to make some concession for a Minister of Defence. What I want is something that will work and not upset the psychology of the whole machine.' Both Hankey and Warren Fisher—the two most senior civil servants—were determined that the new Minister should not be a disruptive influence. 'The Minister should be a disinterested type of man,' Warren Fisher wrote to Neville Chamberlain on February 15, 'with no axe to grind or desire to make a place for himself.' Fisher suggested that Lord Halifax would fit the position. That same day Austen Chamberlain wrote to his sister Hilda:

If there is any truth in the rumour—I don't believe there is—that he proposes to hand over Defence to Ramsay MacDonald there will be a howl of indignation & a vote of no confidence, nor is Eustace Percy the man for that job. In my view there is only one man who by his studies & his special abilities & aptitudes is marked out for it, & that man is Winston Churchill! I don't suppose that S.B. will offer it to him & I don't think that Neville would wish to have him back, but they are both wrong. He is the right man for that post, & these are such dangerous times that consideration ought to be decisive.

On February 17 Austen Chamberlain wrote to Duncan Sandys about the debate of February 14: 'I thought that Baldwin had become too complacent and needed convincing that the situation was regarded by his friends as serious, and I chose the occasion of Friday's debate because it was conducted entirely on non-party lines and could not be perverted in any way to the purpose of a Vote of Censure.' He was 'anxious', Chamberlain added, 'lest Baldwin's selection for the post should not be adequate'. On February 21 Thomas Jones, who understood Baldwin's thinking, wrote to Lady Grigg[1]: 'Those who desired Winston will be disappointed.'

---

[1] Gertrude Charlotte Hough, daughter of the Rev G. F. Hough. She married P. J. Grigg in 1919.

Churchill was himself aware that his chance of being made Minister of Defence was small. 'There is no change,' he wrote to his wife on February 21, 'in the uncertainty about my affairs. Evidently B. desires above all things to avoid bringing me in. This I must now recognize. But his own position is much shaken, & the storm clouds gather.' Clementine Churchill replied six days later: 'My darling, Baldwin must be mad not to ask you to help him. Perhaps it is a case of "Those whom the Gods wish to destroy. . . ."'

In the third week of February Baldwin discussed the forthcoming Cabinet changes with Sir Samuel Hoare. Baldwin suggested appointing Hoare to the Ministry of Defence or the Admiralty—'He hoped,' Hoare wrote to Neville Chamberlain on February 23, 'it would be Defence.' Hoare added: 'On no account would he contemplate the possibility of Winston in the Cabinet for several obvious reasons, but chiefly for the risk that would be involved by having him in the Cabinet when the question of his (S.B.'s) successor became imminent.'

On February 25 T. E. Lawrence visited Chartwell for the weekend, one of the several visits which Churchill's children, and those who worked for him, used later to recall. On this occasion Churchill's daughter Diana, Sir Archibald and Lady Sinclair, and Colonel Pakenham-Walsh were among the guests. One of Clementine Churchill's cousins, Sylvia Henley,[1] who was also at Chartwell that weekend, remembered vividly this particular visit when Churchill himself, 'rather out of the blue at luncheon', as she later recalled to the author, asked Lawrence: 'In the event of an air attack what would be our best defence,' to which Lawrence replied: 'multiple air-force defence stations to intercept'. Churchill, she added, 'seemed satisfied' by Lawrence's reply.[2]

On February 28 Sir Roger Keyes sent Churchill an account of a short discussion he had had with Baldwin in one of the corridors in the House of Commons on the previous day. Baldwin had asked Keyes whether the new Ministry of Defence really would be worthwhile. As Keyes wrote:

---

[1] Sylvia Laura Stanley, 1882–   . Daughter of the 4th Baron Stanley of Alderley. In 1906 she married Brigadier-General Anthony Morton Henley (who died in 1925). From 1915 to 1918 she was in charge of the catering for a group of munitions factories in north-west London; MBE, 1919.

[2] Churchill's daughter, Sarah, later recalled of Lawrence: 'He would arrive on his motor-bicycle from a nearby Air Force station on Sunday afternoons for tea. He never announced his arrival. He was a small, slight man, and his fine head looked almost out of proportion. He had a very soft voice and we noisy, extroverted Churchills were silenced by his quiet personality, and we would all listen in pin-drop silence to what he had to say. I remember my father sitting back watching him with a half smile, and letting him run the conversation.'

I said 'Of course it all depends on the personality of the man you choose for the new post.' He said 'of course I know who you want'. I said 'Well it would be a very good appointment both in your interests and those of the Country.' He said 'I cannot only think of my interests. I have to think of the smooth working of the machine.'

In the last week of February there seemed to be growing support for Churchill to be appointed. On February 29 the magazine *Cavalcade* reflected the general view when it reported that even 'left-wing Conservatives, who were hostile to Winston over the India question, now take the line that if there must be a defence minister Winston Churchill is the man'; and the magazine added that both Harold Macmillan and Lord Castlereagh [1] had 'whispered to the Whips that Winston Churchill is the man'. Another of the young Conservative MPs who felt that Churchill ought to be made Minister of Defence was Anthony Crossley,[2] who wrote a poem parodying the Cabinet's arguments against choosing Churchill:

> But Winston were worst, with his logic accursed
>   For he'll scorn our impartial endeavour.
> He'll make up his mind, right or wrong, with the first,
>   And how should we temporise ever?
> Let's have soldier or sailor or peer or civilian,
>   Whatever his faults, so they be not Churchillian.

'I hope it is true that you are to tackle Defence!' Sir Leo Chiozza Money[3] wrote to Churchill on March 3. That same day Churchill wrote to his wife:

The Defence business is at its height. Baldwin is still undecided. His own choice was Swinton (Cunliffe Lloyd Lister Greame). But a really ugly snarl from the Commons has I believe scared him from appointing a Peer. On Saturday Bendor came out of the blue to luncheon at Chartwell, being much

---

[1] Edward Charles Stewart Robert Vane-Tempest-Stewart, Viscount Castlereagh, 1902–1955. Only son of the 7th Marquis of Londonderry. Educated at Eton and Christ Church Oxford. Unionist MP for County Down, 1931–35. Assistant Managing Director of Londonderry Collieries Ltd. Served in the Royal Artillery, 1939–45 (Middle East, 1941–42). Succeeded his father as 8th Marquis of Londonderry, 1949. Member of the Church Assembly.

[2] Anthony Crommelin Crossley, 1903–1939. Educated at Eton and Magdalen College Oxford. Published three volumes of poetry, 1929, 1931 and 1935. Conservative MP for Oldham, 1931–35 and for Stretford, 1935–39. Parliamentary Secretary, Ministry of Transport, 1932–38. Killed in a civilian aeroplane crash on 15 August 1939.

[3] Leo George Chiozza Money, 1870–1944. Born in Genoa. Economist, author and journalist. Managing editor, *Commercial Intelligence*, 1898–1903. Liberal MP, Paddington North, 1906–10; East Northants, 1910–18. Member, Restriction of Enemy's Supplies Committee, 1914–15; War Trade Advisory Committee, 1915–18. Knighted, 1915. Parliamentary Private Secretary to Lloyd George, 1915–16; to the Ministry of Shipping, 1916–18. Unsuccessful Labour candidate, 1918. Member of the Royal Commission on the Coal Industry, 1919.

worked up on my behalf. He asked Gwynne of the MP [the *Morning Post*] about it, who said 'there was reason to believe matters wd be settled as he wished'. Now this morning the DT [*Daily Telegraph*] comes out as the enclosed,[1] wh is the most positive statement yet & the latest—& from a normally well-informed quarter. Anyhow I seem to be still *en jeu*.

I suppose that today or tomorrow it must be settled. Betty Cranborne[2] (whom I met at Jack & Goonie's dining last night) told me that Neville Ch. said to her last week 'Of course if it is a question of military efficiency, Winston is no doubt the man.' Every other possible alternative is being considered & blown upon. Hoare because of his FO position & Hoare–Laval pact, Swinton & Hankey & Weir because Peers: Ramsay because of himself & his size: Neville because he sees the PM'ship not far off. K. Wood[3] because he hopes to be Ch of Exch then, & anyhow does not know a Lieutenant General from a Whitehead torpedo: Horne because he will not give up his £25,000 a year directorship etc.

So at the end it may all come back to your poor [sketch of pig]. I do not mean to break my heart whatever happens. Destiny plays her part.

If I get it, I will work faithfully before God & man for *Peace*, & not allow pride or excitement to sway my spirit.

If I am not wanted, we have many things to make us happy. . . .

'It wd be the heaviest burden yet,' Churchill added. 'They are *terribly* behindhand.'

That same day, March 3, before the decision was made about the new Minister, the Government issued a new Defence White Paper. In view of 'the present state of the world', it declared, Britain's defences were to be reviewed, and the 'necessary means' provided both for home defence and for joint international action abroad. Two new battleships would be laid down; so also would be a new aircraft carrier. The Army would be increased by four new battalions. The Air Force would be expanded by 250 machines to an eventual total of 1,750 first-line aircraft for home defence. Munitions factories would be extended, and civilian industry organized in such a way that it could readily be turned over to war

---

[1] On March 3 the *Daily Telegraph* stated that Churchill's name was 'now prominently mentioned' as the new Minister.

[2] Elizabeth Vere Cavendish, 1897–1982. Granddaughter of the 8th Duke of Devonshire. She married Lord Cranborne (later 5th Marquess of Salisbury), in 1915.

[3] Kingsley Wood, 1881–1943. Member of the London County Council, 1911–19. Chairman, London Insurance Committee, 1917–18. Conservative MP for Woolwich West, 1918–43. Knighted, 1918. Parliamentary Private Secretary to the Minister of Health, 1919–22. Parliamentary Secretary, Ministry of Health, 1924–29 (when Neville Chamberlain was Minister); Board of Education, 1931. Privy Councillor, 1928. Chairman, Executive Committee of the National Conservative and Unionist Association, 1930–32. Postmaster General, 1931–35. Minister of Health, 1935–38. Secretary of State for Air, 1938–40. Lord Privy Seal, April–May 1940. Chancellor of the Exchequer from May 1940 until his death.

production. But, commenting on the Air Ministry's estimate of German air production reaching 1,500 by April 1937 and 2,000 at some later date, Swinton minuted on March 4: 'I feel bound to express a personal anxiety which I feel with regard to estimates of this nature, however carefully prepared. German capacity to produce aeroplanes is enormous.'

That same week, grave events were taking place in Europe. On March 7 Hitler ordered German troops to cross into the demilitarized zone of Germany. Within hours, the Rhineland, whose demilitarized status had since 1919 provided France and western Europe with at least the illusion of security, became the potential starting point for any German aggressive action westwards. Two days after the remilitarization of the Rhineland, the House of Commons debated the Defence White Paper. For the Labour Party, Clement Attlee moved the rejection of the Government's proposals on the grounds that they were too bellicose, and would contribute to world unrest. Sir Archibald Sinclair expressed Liberal concern about how the increases were to be financed. Speaking on March 10, Churchill spoke of the need for industry to be prepared for war production:

The whole industry of a country is prepared in time of peace for an alternative form of manufacture. Even the smallest workshops play their part in making components. Assembly centres are provided where the components can be fitted together. Thus the whole industry is ready to turn over from peace to war conditions on the pressing of a button.

Great stores of reserves of material were not needed; only enough to bridge the period of 'transition from peace to war . . . tools must be to hand, and everything planned in detail, together with the assembly of skilled and unskilled labour and the co-ordination of power and transport'. All this should be prepared in detail, 'and with preparations which have their reflections in the actual stocks of firms throughout the country'. Other nations had achieved this already; it was 'a kind of territorial force for industry'.

Churchill went on to say that he regretted that so much time had already been lost in making the necessary preparations. 'Why,' he said, 'if you had begun this only three years ago, when the danger first made itself so plain, you would be possessed of a reserve power today which could spring at any moment into full preparatory activity,' and it would then have been possible to avoid 'two horrible years of hiatus', when Britain's military and industrial strength was not sufficient to join effectively any collective action by the League of Nations. Meanwhile, he continued, Germany's arms expenditure and war preparations were facts 'unprecedented, unparalleled, and immeasurable in their consequences'.

Churchill then suggested that the Government should at once establish a 'skeleton Ministry of Munitions, with a Munitions Council of ten or a dozen selected businessmen who would serve as before in an honorary capacity'. Referring to the decision announced in a sentence of the White Paper 'that it was not possible' to recondition the Territorial Army, Churchill pointed out that the Regular and Territorial armies combined were only 250,000 men, and he continued:

. . . we are told that this British industry, this vast, flexible, buoyant, rich, fertile, adaptable British industry, is incapable of conducting the equipment of these two comparatively small forces simultaneously.

I refuse to believe such a thing. What is it they are needing? It is not weapons—the weapons they have—which are to be delayed, but the equipment. I suppose waggons, and appliances of various kinds, field cookers, and all the different appliances which the territorials require. These are the things which, we are told, cannot be made by industry in Britain.

Do you want anything other than this tell-tale sentence to prove that industry has not been organized? And what a discouragement to the Territorial Force, which we must exert ourselves in every way to recruit from the gallant and patriotic youth of this country, who have taken this burden on themselves, when they see that a long interval must elapse, even in times like this, before it will be possible to recondition them.

During his speech Churchill praised the Defence White Paper as a step, albeit belated, in the right direction, and approved Neville Chamberlain's decision to set up a special financial Committee to make sure that the money was spent wisely. 'When things are left so late as this,' Churchill said, 'no high economy is possible. That is the part of the price nations pay for being caught short. All the more must every effort be made to prevent actual waste.' Churchill went on to warn that even under the increased armaments of the new White Paper, Britain was not truly safe because she lacked 'the expansive power of the industrial plant', and he added:

. . . it will not be possible for us to overtake Germany and achieve air parity, as was so solemnly promised, unless and until Germany herself decides to slow down or arrest her air expansion. Clearly a saturation point would be reached when Germany will have created as great an air power as she thinks wise, having regard to the other demands upon her war-like energies. If then we continue our development, we shall ultimately achieve air parity. But this day will be fixed by Germany and not by us, whatever we do.

Let us however see what we are doing. There is a general impression that we are overhauling Germany now. We started late but we are making up for lost time, and every month our relative position will improve. That is a delusion. The contrary is true. All this year and probably for many months next year Germany will be outstripping us more and more.

Even if our new programmes are punctually executed, we shall be relatively much worse off at the end of this year than we are now, in spite of our utmost exertions. The explanation of this grievous fact lies in the past.

'I should like to thank you again for the speech you made last night,' wrote Lord Melchett on March 11. 'In many ways I think it was the greatest speech I have ever heard you make, and I was very delighted in the way the House received it. . . . We must hope for the best, and that the period of "pussyfoot" will not last for ever.'

At a Cabinet meeting on March 11 Baldwin warned his colleagues against acceptance of the French demands for action within the League. According to the minutes: 'The Prime Minister thought at some stage it would be necessary to point out to the French that the action they proposed would not result only in letting loose another great war in Europe. They might succeed in crushing Germany with the use of Russia, but it would probably only result in Germany going Bolshevik. . . .' Eden, however, expressed his agreement with the French that Germany would be ready to make war on France by 1939, and pointed out that, in the French and Belgian view, 'if Germany was allowed to remain unmolested in military occupation of the Rhineland, war in two years time was a certainty and would be fought under very unfavourable conditions . . .' Duff Cooper, who had become Secretary of State for War in November, warned his Cabinet colleagues 'that in three years' time, though we should have reconditioned at any rate to some extent our small forces, yet by that time Germany would have 100 divisions and a powerful fleet. We should not relatively, therefore, be in a better position.' Yet not all observers saw the remilitarization of the Rhineland as a pointer to war. To *The Times* it appeared to offer, as one headline declared, 'A Chance to Rebuild'.

The French Government, agitated by the thought of no action being taken, sought to summon a meeting of the League of Nations in Paris, and Anthony Eden, accompanied by both Halifax and Wigram, had gone to Paris on March 9. Two days later, on Eden's authority Wigram urged Flandin to hold the meeting of the League in England in order to try to get more effective support from Britain. On returning to London on March 11 Wigram went at once to see Churchill, and to tell him

the whole story. Early on the following morning Flandin himself went
to Churchill's flat at Morpeth Mansions. As Churchill later recorded in
his memoirs:

He told me that he proposed to demand from the British Government
simultaneous mobilisation of the land, sea and air forces of both countries,
and that he had received assurances of support from all the nations of the
'Little Entente' and from other States. He read out an impressive list of the
replies received. There was no doubt that superior strength still lay with the
Allies of the former war. They had only to act to win. Although we did not
know what was passing between Hitler and his generals, it was evident that
overwhelming force lay on our side. There was little I could do in my
detached private position, but I wished our visitor all success in bringing
matters to a head and promised any assistance that was in my power. I
gathered my principal associates at dinner that night to hear M. Flandin's
exhortations.

On March 12 Churchill spoke at a meeting of the House of Commons
Foreign Affairs Committee, urging that 'we must fulfil our obligations
under the Covenant and follow the procedure it enjoins—it is unthinkable that we should repudiate our signature of Locarno'. According to
Lord Dunglass,[1] who took the official notes of the meeting, Churchill
then drew 'a dramatic picture of all the countries of Europe hurrying
to assist France and ourselves against Germany, but said nothing about
their military preparedness'. Speaking after Churchill, Sir Samuel
Hoare stressed this aspect. 'As regards Winston's reference to all the
nations of Europe coming to our aid,' he said, 'he could only say that in
his (Sir S.H.'s) estimate these nations were totally unprepared from a
military point of view.' Dunglass noted that whereas at the start of the
meeting 'a substantial proportion' of the Committee had seemed
inclined 'not to stop short of being prepared to see this country go to
war', Hoare's speech had 'definitely sobered them down'.

At a conference held in London on March 13, the German delegate, Joachim von Ribbentrop,[2] declared that the German people

[1] Alexander Frederick Douglas-Home, Lord Dunglass, 1903–   . Educated at Eton and
Christ Church Oxford. Conservative MP for South Lanark, 1931–45; for Lanark, 1950–51.
Parliamentary Private Secretary to Neville Chamberlain, 1937–40. 14th Earl of Home, 1951.
Secretary of State for Commonwealth Relations, 1955–60; for Foreign Affairs, 1960–63.
Disclaimed his peerage, 1963. Prime Minister, 1963–64. Leader of the Opposition, 1964–
65. Secretary of State for Foreign and Commonwealth Affairs, 1970–74. Created Baron, 1975.
[2] Joachim von Ribbentrop, 1893–1946. Champagne salesman in Canada, 1910–14.
Lieutenant, Western Front, 1914–18, when he was wounded, and won the Iron Cross, first
class. Aide-de-Camp to the German peace delegation in Paris, 1919. Head of a wine import-
export business in Berlin, 1920–33. A National Socialist Deputy in the Reichstag, 1933.
Ambassador to London, 1936–38. SS-Gruppenführer, 1936. Foreign Minister, 1938–45.
Sentenced to death by the Allied Military Tribunal, Nuremberg, and hanged.

desired henceforth to cooperate in building up a real European solid-arity. On behalf of the British Government, Eden welcomed this declaration, and offered British help in the work of reconstruction.

That same day, Churchill gave his opinion of the situation in an article in the *Evening Standard*. With the remilitarization of the Rhineland, he wrote, Europe was presented simultaneously with 'Hope and Peril'. Were the League of Nations to seize the opportunity to re-establish 'a reign of law' in Europe, then it might still be possible to stop 'the horrible, dull, remorseless drift to war in 1937 or 1938', and bring to an end the 'preparatory piling up' of armaments in every European country. France had appealed to the League of Nations. It was essential for the League to give her justice and 'satisfaction'. If the League proved powerless to act, if no means 'of patient, lawful redress' could be found to put at rest the fears not only of France but also of Belgium, 'the whole doctrine of international law and co-operation, upon which the hopes of the future are based, would lapse ignominiously'. There was only one way to preserve peace: 'the assembly of overwhelming force, moral and physical, in support of international law'. His article ended: 'The fateful moment has arrived for choice between the New Age and the Old.'

On March 14 it was announced in London that instead of the much-expected Minister of Defence, another post, that of Minister for Co-ordination of Defence would be established, and conferred, not on Churchill, but on the Attorney-General, Sir Thomas Inskip.[1] 'Let me say how disgusted I am that the PM has not asked you to take the Defence Ministry,' wrote Sir Leo Chiozza Money. 'To me it is another glaring instance of the stupidity of party politics, which always denies a nation the services of most of its best men.' From Monte Carlo, a young Conservative MP, Charles Taylor, sent Churchill a telegram of 'profound regret'; from Mimizan the Duke of Westminster telegraphed: 'My word I never thought that would be their choice'; and Anthony Crossley added yet another verse to his bitter parody:

> Did you dare, Father Churchill, did you dare to expect
>   A summons to council again,
> In face of the feeling that haunts the elect
>   That they scoffed at your warnings in vain?

[1] This was a compromise suggested by Swinton, and accepted by the Cabinet on February 24, whereby the Prime Minister would retain the Chairmanship of the Committee of Imperial Defence, but that a Deputy should preside over both the CID and the Defence Policy Requirements Committee, and also over the Chiefs of Staff Committee when requested to do so. This Deputy was to be Minister of Coordination of Defence.

> You're polite to the small and you're rude to the great,
>   Your opinions are bolder and surer
> Than is seemly today in an office of state—
>   You've even insulted the Führer.

In his diary on March 11, Chamberlain had commented that the militarization of the Rhineland had 'afforded an excellent reason for discarding both Winston and Sam since both had European reputations which might make it dangerous to add them to the Cabinet at a critical moment. Inskip would create no jealousies. He would excite no enthusiasm but he would involve us in no fresh perplexities.'

Churchill received many letters commiserating with him at this moment of supreme disappointment. Admiral Sir William Goodenough[1] wrote on March 14:

That, after all the labour, this great mountain shd give birth to such a small mouse as announced this morning is deeply disappointing. It is enraging that we seem unable to get away from that safe, smug course of action or inaction that besets us. I had—we all had—hoped for someone who wd carry a torch to lead & light us on our way. The problem is essentially one to be solved by executive action. DAMN.

One of the most sympathetic, and at the same time perceptive letters which Churchill was sent on March 14 came from Desmond Morton, who wrote from his nearby cottage:

I hardly need to write to let you know how sorry I am that, after all the tension of waiting, we are so disappointed in our hope that you would be now co-ordinating Defence. I feel, too, that you must have undergone no little strain. It is a horrible job awaiting the uncertain, as you and I learnt to recognise during the war.

Nevertheless, I really believe you are well out of it, as things stand. You have a great work to perform now. You have begun it without delay, I see and hear. Still, from my parochial point of view, I do regret what appears to me to be the intention of the Government once more to shelve really effective Defence measures. What else are we to read into the appointment of Inskip? It is a little unfair to criticise without giving him a chance to prove what he is capable of doing, but there is a feeling abroad little short of dismay.

Apart from what is publicly known, I hear from legal friends of his, that he is bad at conducting Crown cases in the Courts, that he revokes at Bridge

---

[1] William Edmund Goodenough, 1867–1945. A cousin by marriage of Clementine Churchill. Went to sea, 1882. Captain, 1905. Commanded the 2nd Light Cruiser Squadron, battles of Heligoland Bight, 1914; Dogger Bank, 1915; Jutland, 1916. Superintendent, Chatham Dockyard, 1918–20. Knighted, 1919. Vice-Admiral, 1920. Commanded the Africa Station, 1920–22; the Reserve Fleet, 1923–24; the Nore, 1924–27. Admiral, 1925. Retired list, 1930.

more frequently than any other professed player of the game. The Navy as a whole, with whom, according to the Press, he might be supposed to have some support, is dumbfounded. . . .

Morton went on to give Churchill his own forecast of the next few years:

I think that very big movements are gaining momentum in the political world. At present the country will not shew any real enthusiasm for resisting German frightfulness and consequently appears to approve the apparent attitude of HMG, but a slow current is setting in in the contrary direction. If this current gains momentum it is all up with the present PM whatever he does. If he resists it, it will sweep him away; if he swims with it, he will be looked upon as a time-server and, so soon as the world situation clears, public opinion will be too strong for him.

On March 25 Lord Lloyd informed his son of Professor Lindemann's comment on Inskip's appointment. It was, Lindemann had told him, 'the most cynical thing that has been done since Caligula appointed his horse as consul'.

36

Turning to Churchill

BEGINNING on March 13, the *Evening Standard* published the first of a series of fortnightly articles by Churchill on current affairs. '*Do* write to the papers all you can,' his friend the painter Paul Maze[1] had urged him on the day on which the first of these articles appeared. 'The German propaganda spread about is most harmful especially in Mayfair society! Half England is hardly aware of the situation.'[2] But Baldwin and his Cabinet still believed that they could turn the Rhineland crisis offer to good effect. According to the official Cabinet minutes of March 17, 'our own attitude had been governed by the desire to utilise Herr Hitler's offers in order to obtain a permanent settlement'. Ten days later, on March 27, following a weekend visit to Chartwell, during which he, Churchill and Lindemann discussed Nazi policy in detail, Ralph Wigram sent Churchill a substantial portfolio of documents and material on Hitler and the Nazis. Among the documents were Hitler's twenty-five points of October 1930, Wigram's own notes on Hitler's speech of May 1935, the Government's White Papers on Disarmament, 'in case you haven't got them all', and a copy of Sir Horace Rumbold's despatch from Berlin, sent to Sir John Simon on 26 April 1933, and known within the Foreign Office as the *Mein Kampf* despatch. On the outside of this despatch Wigram warned Churchill:

[1] Paul Lucien Maze, 1887–1979. Born in Havre, Painter. On active service, 1914–18 (DCM, MM and Bar, Légion d'Honneur, Croix de Guerre). He first met Churchill in 1916, on the western front, and subsequently encouraged him with his painting. Churchill wrote the preface to Maze's war memoirs, *A Frenchman in Khaki*, published in 1934. Left France after the German invasion, 1940; subsequently resident in England. Served with the Home Guard, and then with the RAF (intelligence), 1940–45.

[2] For the next three and a half years Churchill's *Evening Standard* articles were syndicated throughout the world. During 1936 different ones were published at different times in the United States, Canada, France, Holland, Denmark, Sweden, Norway, Greece, Czechoslovakia, Switzerland and Luxemburg. These syndications were largely negotiated by H. W. Shirley Long, Manager of the Magazine and Newspaper Department of Curtis Brown Ltd.

'SECRET, but you can use references from Mein Kampf.'[1] His visit to Chartwell, he added, had made both him and his wife 'feel much better in every way', and he added: 'It is such a privilege and encouragement to me to hear your views. I wish and wish they were the views of the Government.'

On March 26 Churchill spoke in the House of Commons of the strength of German propaganda, and of the need to 'confront' the public with the realities of the European situation. The remilitarization of the Rhineland was, he said, 'Hitler's triumph'. It followed on several Nazi successes: the introduction of conscription, the Saar plebiscite and the Anglo-German Naval Treaty. Would Austria be next, he asked, and went on to urge an 'effective union' of all States alarmed by Germany, for mutual aid within the Covenant of the League of Nations. His aim, he said, was not the encirclement of Germany, but of any power that sought to impose its will by aggression. Anthony Eden welcomed Churchill's comments, writing to him from the Foreign Office on April 4 'to say "thank you" to you for all your help & kindness to me in recent debates & during a critical period'.

During March, Churchill's debate with the Air Staff had continued, and at the end of the month Sir Maurice Hankey had authorized one of his assistants, Wing-Commander Warburton,[2] to check some figures of British and German air strength which Churchill wished to use in a confidential memorandum for the Committee of Imperial Defence. Warburton had done so, writing direct to Churchill on March 27 that Churchill's comparison of 1,210 German first-line aeroplanes to 785 British was 'based upon a fallacy'. This fallacy was, according to Warburton, Churchill's inclusion of 360 German aircraft which the Air Ministry counted as second-line. After stressing the high rate of German aeroplane and pilot wastage, and the falling off of German aircraft production, Warburton added:

---

[1] The other Foreign Office documents which Wigram sent Churchill on March 26 were a twenty-four-page memorandum on the aims of the Nazi Party (written in October 1930), a memorandum on Germany's claim for equality of arms status (dated 15 September 1932), a despatch by Basil Newton (sent from Berlin on 22 October 1932), a note communicated by Ribbentrop (on 24 March 1936), and a series of printed extracts from speeches by Hitler, Goering, Goebbels and Hess (the most recent dated 30 January 1936).

[2] Peter Warburton 1897–1950. Educated at Radley College. Lieutenant, Royal Garrison Artillery, 1915–17; transferred to the Royal Flying Corps, 1917 (MBE military, 1919). Flight Lieutenant RAF, 1922; Squadron Leader 1929. Air Adviser to the Iraq Government 1930. Air Adviser to the Committee of Imperial Defence, 1934–37. Wing-Commander, 1936. Air Commodore, 1937. Air Raid Precautions Department, Home Office, 1937–42; RAF, 1942–45; UNRRA, 1945–48. Both his sons were killed in action in the RAF in the Second World War.

I recollect your (of course) correct contention that one should not under-rate one's enemy, but I understand that the Air Staff have every reason to believe that the Germans are suffering very seriously from the absence of a basic training system and an adequate supply of experienced instructors, and the many other disadvantages of trying to build up an air force quickly without a foundation such as we have been able to establish during the past sixteen years.

Churchill was still uneasy; 'I have a feeling,' he wrote to Desmond Morton on March 31, 'they still woefully underrate the German power,' and to Warburton he wrote that same day: 'I am greatly obliged to you for the trouble you have taken to give me this most valuable critique. I will study it at leisure with the closest attention. I trust indeed you may be right. I cannot help being impressed by your supreme confidence when danger may be so near, and I wish I could feel convinced.'

Morton was also not convinced by Warburton's assessment, and on April 3, having scrutinized his figures, wrote to Churchill emphatically:

... you may still calculate the British Metropolitan first line strength at 785, while the Air Ministry estimate of the German first line strength is 850, the French being 900. In respect of first line, therefore, the Germans are now stronger than we are. It is admitted elsewhere that Germany is also stronger than us in both actual production and capacity production of aircraft. It seems difficult, therefore, to contend that Great Britain is stronger in the air than Germany if the Metropolitan Air Forces are considered ...

Warburton says, in fact, that the apparent increase of ten squadrons in the German first line in the two months December 1935 and January 1936 was due to the unexpected discovery of their existence by the British Air Ministry, and there is no proof that they were only formed in those two months. Does Warburton not lay himself open to an enquiry as to whether there may not be more German squadrons in existence which the Air Ministry have not yet discovered?

Later in his letter Morton wrote:

I suggest you are trying to show what number of aircraft Germany might put in the air now if she went 'mad dog', and determined to try and make war according to Goering's theory, ie that the striking of a maximum blow from the air in the first two or three days of war might end the war. Warburton appears to be leaving this out of account and presuming that Germany's future action will develop along the lines laid down by the British Air Ministry. Of course he may be right.

In his conclusion Morton echoed Churchill's own doubts, insisting that the Air Ministry 'are too complacent in their figures and calculations'.

At the end of March both Churchill and Austen Chamberlain

addressed a meeting of backbench MPs concerned with foreign affairs. Churchill's main theme, the need for Britain to support France, did not meet with complete approval. On April 4 Thomas Jones wrote to Lady Grigg of how at the meeting itself the general view was 'on the whole pro-French; but two or three days later opinion had swung round to a majority of perhaps 5 to 4 for Germany'. Part of the opposition to France, Jones noted, was influenced 'by the fear of our being drawn in on the side of Russia'. Churchill himself, however, with Vansittart's approval and encouragement, had begun to see the Russian Ambassador, Ivan Maisky,[1] who lunched with him at the beginning of April, and who, on April 3, sent Churchill a copy of a recent speech which he had made about Russia's desire to participate in the upholding of peace in Europe.

On April 6 the House of Commons debated the question of whether or not to continue the economic sanctions against Italy. Churchill spoke critically of sanctions; they had failed to save Abyssinia, now being destroyed and subjugated; they had roused the antagonism of Italy, so that in future years Britain would need to maintain larger forces throughout the Mediterranean; and they had involved costly naval expenditure. But the policy of sanctions obscured, in his view, 'a graver matter still', the German threat to Europe. 'Herr Hitler has torn up all the Treaties,' he said, 'and garrisoned the Rhineland. His troops are there, and there they are going to stay.' In six months time the line of new fortifications in the Rhineland would enable the German Army to attack France through Belgium and Holland. Yet once these two North Sea countries passed 'under German domination', Britain's own security would be at risk. That danger, Churchill said, 'is brought very much nearer to this island by the erection of the German fortress line'.

Once Germany felt strong enough to challenge France, Churchill warned, the position of the Baltic States, Poland, Czechoslovakia, Yugoslavia, Rumania and Austria would be 'profoundly altered'. Several of these States would feel obliged to commit themselves to the German system. Others would be incorporated by force. 'Where shall we be

---

[1] Ivan Mikhailovich Maisky, 1884–1975. Born in Omsk, the son of a Jewish doctor and a non-Jewish mother. A Menshevik, he was exiled by the Tsarist regime to Siberia, but escaped to Germany, and took a degree in economics at Munich University. Lived in London, 1912–17. Returned to Russia during the revolution. Became a Bolshevik, 1922. Counsellor at the Soviet Embassy in London, 1925–27. Soviet Ambassador to Britain, 1932–43. A Deputy Foreign Minister, 1943–45. Soviet member of the Reparations Committee, 1945–48. Arrested during one of Stalin's anti-Jewish purges, 1949. Imprisoned, 1949–53. Released from prison 1953. Worked at the Soviet Academy of Sciences from 1957 until his death, writing his memoirs, and preparing various historical studies.

then?' he asked, and went on to warn against any attempt by Britain to negotiate with Germany 'on behalf of Europe'. Eden and Ribbentrop should give up all attempts to settle it together. 'We have not the solidarity of conviction,' he said, 'nor the national defences fit for such a dominant role.' All negotiations with Hitler should be through the League of Nations, which contained 'a large number of smaller States who individually are helpless, but who collectively are very powerful, and who feel their existence threatened'. The League States, Churchill said, should 'address Germany collectively' about her armaments and her intentions; but at the same time they should invite her 'to state her grievances and her legitimate aspirations', so that, under the authority of the League, 'justice may be done and peace preserved'.

On reading Churchill's speech of April 6 Sir Clive Morrison-Bell[1] wrote to Churchill: 'It is quite one of your best I think. You are so right about not being mealy-mouthed just now; the tone everywhere is far too apologetic, and you seem to be almost the only person who ever speaks out.'

Churchill's repeated arguments in favour of the League of Nations, and particularly his speech of April 6, encouraged Viscount Cecil of Chelwood—the former Lord Robert Cecil—to approach him on behalf of the League of Nations Union. His support had also been sought by the Anti-Nazi Council. Both groups planned meetings at the Albert Hall, where they wanted him to speak; both had memberships which cut across party lines, and included many Labour voters. For the first time in his three-year campaign Churchill found himself appealed to as a national figure, irrespective of party loyalties. These appeals came from within the Conservative, Liberal and Labour Parties, and from many people who had no particular party allegiance. Replying to Cecil on April 9 Churchill wrote:

I think we are in pretty good agreement on several big things. There is a great danger that the Parliamentary nations and merciful, tolerant forces in the world will be knocked out quite soon by the heavily armed, unmoral dictatorships. But I believe there is still time to organise a European mass, and perhaps a world mass which would confront them, overawe them, and perhaps let their peoples loose upon them. Once you and your friends have formulated your principles you must face 'ways and means'. You need a secular arm. I might help in this.

[1] Arthur Clive Morrison-Bell, 1871–1956. Educated at Eton and Sandhurst. Scots Guards, 1890; on active service in South Africa, 1899–1900. ADC to the Governor-General of Canada (Lord Minto) 1900–04. Conservative MP for Honiton, 1910–31. Parliamentary Private Secretary, Admiralty, 1919–22; Colonial Office, 1922–23; to Churchill at the Exchequer, 1924–26. Created Baronet, 1923. A director of the Holmside and South Moor Collieries Ltd.

Churchill's letter continued:

It seems a mad business to confront these dictators without weapons or military force, and at the same time to try to tame and cow the spirit of our people with peace films, anti-recruiting propaganda and resistance to defence measures. Unless the free and law-respecting nations are prepared to organise, arm and combine, they are going to be smashed up. This is going to happen quite soon. But I believe we still have a year to combine and marshal superior forces in defence of the League and its Covenant.

In his reply, Cecil wrote: 'we must unhappily increase our armaments'. But he made no reference to the peace-films of the League of Nations Union which Churchill believed were as damaging to national morale as the anti-rearmament philosophy of the Labour Party. Yet even within the Labour Party, Churchill's arguments were beginning to be taken seriously, and one Independent MP, Eleanor Rathbone,[1] had actually quoted Churchill's figures to help substantiate her arguments in favour of rearmament. On April 13 Churchill wrote to her from Chartwell:

Having seen your letter in the *Manchester Guardian*, in which you have been tackled for adopting my figures, I send you in confidence a memorandum upon the subject prepared for me by Sir Henry Strakosch (who does not desire his name to be mentioned). There are some points in this memorandum which have not stood the test of the examination to which I have had it subjected in various instructed quarters. Nevertheless, its main conclusion is true and the figures which I quoted are well within the limits of the facts so far as I can ascertain. Furthermore, it was not upon this memorandum that I first made the statement about Germany having spent eight hundred millions in a single year. This I obtained from other and even more confidential sources. . . .

I hope you will believe that I do not make any of my assertions without taking the very greatest pains to find out the truth, and the trouble I had to find out about the air danger two years ago was very considerable.

Will you kindly send me back the memorandum when you have digested it; and I am sure that without going into details you are thoroughly justified in standing to your guns.

We are really in great danger.[2]

[1] Eleanor Rathbone, 1872–1946. Educated Kensington High School and Somerville College Oxford. The first woman member of the Liverpool City Council, 1909–34. Independent MP for the Combined English Universities, 1929–46. Chairman, Children's Nutrition Council and National Joint Committee for Spanish Relief. Secretary, Parliamentary Committee for Refugees. Vice-Chairman, National Committee for Rescue from Nazi Terror.

[2] Three months later, at an Independent Labour Party summer school, Eleanor Rathbone declared: 'I have described Winston Churchill as a new recruit to pro-League forces. Watch that man carefully. You may feel distrustful. So did I. I'm not certain yet. But I ask you to

On Sunday April 19 Sir Maurice Hankey dined with Churchill at Chartwell. 'I do not usually make a note of private conversations,' Hankey wrote to Inskip, 'but some points arose which gave an indication of the line which Mr Churchill is likely to take in forthcoming debates in Parliament.' Hankey's note continued:

As regards the Minister for Defence Co-Ordination Mr Churchill's main criticism was on his assumption of the Chair at the Principal Supply Officers Sub-Committee. When I asked him what role he would have contemplated for the Minister, he said he should be confined to questions of general policy, such as bombs versus battleships, the value of Russia as an ally, and so forth.

As regards the supply side, Mr Churchill takes a strong view that we ought to create a Ministry of Supply or Ministry of Munitions at once, and that a Minister of Munitions should be appointed. He went out of his way to explain that he did not want the job for himself. He had already held that post in war and would not touch it again. Sir Kingsley Wood was his nominee!

Hankey then commented that after 1918 Churchill himself had argued in favour of abolishing the Ministry of Munitions but, as Churchill had pointed out to him, 'times had changed'. Hankey added: 'He favours continued support of the League, and was very down on Conservative Members of Parliament who he said were widely criticising our League policy. He himself of course had no illusions about the weakness of the League, but sees that the British people will not take re-armament seriously except as part of the League policy. . . .'

Hankey also told Inskip of a 'fantastic plan' which Churchill had explained to him in detail for sending part of the British Fleet to the Baltic 'to ensure superiority over Germany in that sea. It would stay there permanently, based on a Russian port of which we should obtain the use under this plan.' All this, Hankey commented, seemed 'to ignore many realities, some of which I mentioned to him. . . .'

Churchill's final concern was whether Russia could be relied upon as an ally, despite the new Franco-Soviet Treaty, which he supported. Hankey's note recorded:

In view of the danger from Germany he has buried his violent anti-Russian complex of former days and is apparently a bosom friend of M Maisky. Until quite recently he has been inclined to believe in the strength

---

dispel prejudice and consider facts. Churchill for three years has pointed out extensive German rearmaments. Later facts have justified his estimates. He was always in theory a pro-League man; but only recently has his imagination clearly been captivated by the potentialities of collective security through the League.'

of Russia. He has, however, been seriously shaken in this by reading a book with the curious title of 'Uncle give us Bread', which he urged me to read. This book has awakened in his mind most serious misgivings of Russia, and he has evidently got the impression that Russia may perhaps present only a facade with nothing behind.

He suggested that Sir Thomas Inskip ought to collect all the evidence official and otherwise that there is about Russia in order to determine whether she is an ally worth having or not, and that in particular we ought to ascertain from the French Government the detailed views of their General Staffs on Russia's naval, military and air strength, since it must have been on such views that the French Government based its decision to enter into the Treaty.

On April 21, two days after Hankey's visit to Chartwell, Churchill received a secret and official letter from a senior Foreign Office official, Reginald Leeper,[1] who wrote to him from the Foreign Office:

Sir Robert Vansittart has asked me to write to you about a matter which he considers of national importance & which is closely concerned with the work of the Foreign Office. He has told me to ask you whether you would give me an appointment so that I might explain to you what this matter is in which he hopes very much to enlist your interest. He would himself like to discuss it with you personally after I have explained to you the general scheme on which I have been engaged myself for some time in the FO.

On January 1 Leeper had written a memorandum for Eden and Vansittart warning of the urgent need 'to discover on what basis public opinion can best be guided in its support of the League', and he pointed out that the League 'is not to be tested by a sensational success in one issue, but rather by shaping events in such a way that the nations of Europe may regain confidence and security'. Public opinion must also be made aware that a 'breach' between France and England 'would not only break the League, but would imperil Europe'; that 'the danger can only come from Germany'; and that it was 'idle to suppose that Germany will be restrained by any consideration save that her own strength is unequal to the strength to which she may be opposed'. Replying to Leeper on January 4, Vansittart had himself stressed the need 'to educate our own people', and he added: 'we have only a very little while ahead of us in which to re-educate the men in many streets'.

---

[1] Reginald Wildig Allen Leeper, 1888–1968. Born in Australia. Educated in Australia, and at New College Oxford. Intelligence Bureau, Department of Information, 1917. Entered the Foreign Office, 1918; Political Intelligence Department, 1918–24. First Secretary, Warsaw, 1924; Riga, 1924; Constantinople, 1925; Warsaw, 1927–29. Transferred to the Foreign Office, 1929; Counsellor, 1933. Assistant Under-Secretary of State for Foreign Affairs, 1940–42. Ambassador to Greece, 1943–48. Knighted 1945. Ambassador to the Argentine, 1946–48.

On January 27 Leeper set out his specific proposals. 'We are approaching a stage in international relations,' he noted in a further memorandum 'when the people of this country will have to be brought face to face with realities in a way that has not happened since the last war. We have to rearm our people not only materially but morally.' In contrast to Germany, where the guiding philosophy was one of racialism, 'our people are being given little or no guidance, and yet time presses and we cannot afford to wait'. Not propaganda, but education was needed. Competition with Germany 'purely on the basis of armaments' was not possible. 'We must therefore concentrate not only on our own rearmament, but on instilling in them such confidence in our leadership and determination that they too will rearm and abandon an attitude of defeatism *vis à vis* Germany.' Leeper continued:

But if we are to inspire them with this confidence, education must begin at home. We have no time to lose. We must be swift, bold and persistent. It is insufficient to make a few public speeches or for the News Department of the Foreign Office to make points with the press. I suggest that the whole programme must be conceived on wider and bolder lines if it is to bear fruit and to bear fruit quickly.

Leeper went on to warn that the Government had 'not yet grasped the importance of educating our own public, or the public of other countries about ourselves'. He wanted to mobilize 'the press, the BBC, the League of Nations Union, and perhaps the Churches, in an educative campaign', and would himself 'undertake to see' that public speakers were properly reported. 'But if we are to succeed,' he wrote, these speeches 'must be bold and frank speeches, not hesitating to call a spade a spade and not shirking unpleasant truths.'

Vansittart approved Leeper's proposal. 'The need for action is urgent,' he minuted on February 1, and he added:

I think the educational appeal should be something even more fundamental than the League, though the League shd of course be 'featured'. But the League includes all sorts of systems, some of them pretty putrid. What is really and ultimately at issue in the world is dictatorship or democracy, liberty or the man-machine.

There need not be war 'at all', Vansittart wrote, 'if democracy will show plainly that it can and will look after itself *in the League*. . . . Meanwhile the people of this country are receiving no adequate education—indeed practically no concerted education at all—against the impending tests. In this, as in every other sphere, it must be repeated again and again that there is no time to lose. There is indeed a grave danger that we shall be too late.'

Churchill shared these beliefs, and after Leeper had visited him at Chartwell on April 24, he agreed to try to help in bringing together, using his personal influence and prestige, the many groups and individuals, of all political Parties, organizations and professions, who were already concerned about the growing German danger and the threat to democracy, but who had no forum or focus to bring them together. Sharing the sense of urgency voiced by Leeper and Vansittart, and working under the aegis of the Anti-Nazi Council in close cooperation with its Organizing Secretary, A. H. Richards,[1] Churchill began the task of enabling scattered and seemingly disparate forces to work out a common approach to the growing dangers.

Leeper himself was convinced that Churchill ought to be in the Government; four months later, on August 17, Robert Bruce Lockhart wrote in his diary: 'Rex Leeper, who admires him greatly, and thinks that he is the man we need, lunched with him the other day,' and he added: 'Rex thinks he will come back.'

On April 23 Churchill made a major speech in the House of Commons, criticizing Inskip's appointment as Minister for Coordination of Defence, and urging speedier rearmament. The occasion was the debate on Neville Chamberlain's Budget proposals, and Churchill was particularly critical of what he regarded as the continuing atmosphere of sloth in matters of defence, telling the House of Commons:

I read in a paper to-day that no meeting had yet taken place between the Government and trade unions in regard to questions of apprenticeship and dilution and transference, without settling which you cannot possibly expand your munitions production. You cannot do anything without a working arrangement with the trade unions and here we are on this 23rd day of April, 1936, and it is said that no meeting has yet taken place upon that matter.

Nor had anything 'effective' been done about profiteering, Churchill said, and he warned: 'You will not get the effective co-operation of the

[1] A. H. Richards. General Organizing Secretary of the Anti-Nazi Council, to combat Nazi propaganda and to help its victims, 1936–39. Worked at the Ministry of Information, 1940–41. Active in charitable work for the British and Allied forces. The Anti-Nazi Council's full name was: 'British Non-Sectarian Anti-Nazi Council to Champion Human Rights.' Its President was the Trade Union leader, Sir Walter Citrine. Its Vice-Presidents included Sir Norman Angell, Sylvia Pankhurst and Eleanor Rathbone. On its notepaper were the slogans: 'Nazi Germany is the Enemy of Civilization' and 'Refuse to Trade with the Enemy'.

working people unless you can make sure that there are not a lot of greedy fingers having a rake-off. We are still drifting and dawdling as the precious months flow out.'

Churchill then spoke in detail of Germany's arms expenditure. In the twenty-seven months between March 1933 and June 1935 this had amounted to a minimum of £1,000 million. But even this figure, he said, did not include such major items of expenditure as the preparation 'of those great military roads where four columns of troops may march abreast, which may play a greater part in a future war than the fortifications that are being built'. A few moments later he declared: 'Europe is approaching a climax. I believe that that climax will be reached in the lifetime of the present Parliament.'

At the end of his speech Churchill called for a Ministry of Supply, or a Ministry of Munitions, to provide the necessary armaments in good time. As he told the House of Commons:

Surely, the question whether we should be working under peace conditions depends upon whether working under those conditions will give us the necessary deliveries of our munitions—upon whether the gun plants and the shell plants and, above all, the aeroplane factories, can fulfil the need in time. If they can do so, then peace conditions are no doubt very convenient; but if not, then we must substitute other conditions—not necessarily war conditions, but conditions which would impinge upon the ordinary daily life and business life of this country. There are many conditions apart from war conditions—preparatory conditions, precautionary conditions, emergency conditions,—and these must be established in this country if progress is to be made, and if Parliament and the nation are not to find themselves deluded in the future by mere paper programmes and promises which in the result will be found to be utterly unfulfilled.

'None of us mind praise,' Margot Asquith wrote two days later, 'so I must congratulate you on yr *wonderful* speech of Thursday. Duffy & Diana also G. Dawson (The Times) & others, who lunched here yesterday were full of praise! It relieved the general depression wh *all* of us feel, & is terribly *true*. We are at the parting of the ways between War, & Peace.' In congratulating Churchill 'warmly and sincerely' on his speech, Desmond Morton wrote, on April 24:

You may be interested to hear that it seems to have had a profound effect in the City. Bodies like Lloyds and the Stock Exchange could do little to-day save talk about it. Curiously enough, I wonder why. Although your speech was one of your masterpieces, the City did not hear you deliver it, and the facts you presented about German re-armament included little if anything that you have not already told them in other words. You will understand that in saying this, I intend no detraction whatever from my admiration for the speech itself. Somehow, this time, it appears to have 'got right across'. . . .

Of the Government, Morton wrote:

I rather think they would be very apprehensive of an informed attack by you on the new Minister. After all, you *know*, and I am afraid he has, at best got to *learn*. Again, the appointment was clearly a fake; made in the hope that the international situation would so right itself that there would be no need for any hurry to rearm, or perhaps even to rearm at all. Recent events have destroyed this hope.

Morton's conclusion favoured Churchill's thesis, for, as he wrote, the Government were persisting in making Britain's weapons expensive 'works of art', rather than cheap and mass-produced on the German plan. Morton noted: 'I do not agree with that policy. The old, old argument applies; on which side would you rather be? The side which can discharge a thousand projectiles of which 100% will be effective, or the side which can discharge a million, of which 50% will be effective?'

According to Morton, Churchill's figures for German expenditure were too high. There was 'much speculation', he wrote, as to Churchill's sources, and he added: 'I don't know, and I don't want to, but with the best will in the world and with the honest help of the Treasury, I cannot make the probable figure more than about half yours over the last three years. God knows that is alarming enough when compared with our own expenditure.' Churchill stood by the accuracy of his figures, writing on April 29 to Sir Henry Strakosch, who had provided them: 'I am deeply indebted to your for the massive, cogent arguments with which you have supplied me. As you will see on Friday I have assumed responsibility for them, and put them forth in the series of articles I am now writing for the Evening Standard and other papers throughout the length and breadth of the land. I thought this was the best way of making an impression.' Churchill also told Strakosch that Chamberlain had refused to refute his figures: '. . . before I quoted your figures in the House, I told Neville what I meant to assert, the main fact of £800,000,000 in 1935, and that I would invite him to contradict me. He replied he would certainly not contradict me. So that I think we have done a public service in establishing a certain basis.'

One barrier to meeting the German rearmament programme was the British Government's reluctance to put even a part of the economy on a war, or semi-war footing, as Churchill had suggested. On April 28 Lord Weir, who was the adviser on industrial production and supply to the Secretary of State for Air, wrote to Churchill praising his Budget speech, which ought, he felt, to serve 'as a perfect lesson to all who can understand the things that matter'. But, Weir added: 'Late in the speech when you come to the key question of the moment, the degree of gravity and the consequent action covering definite interference with our existing industrial situation, I confess my inability to weigh up the pros and cons with your confidence.'[1]

At a meeting of the Cabinet on April 29 Sir Thomas Inskip spoke in the sense of Churchill's arguments, warning his colleagues of 'the urgency and the difficulty of the re-equipment programme'. He had, he said, 'been considering how far the assumption of "peace conditions" on which our present preparations were based, were comparable with the growing anxieties of the international situation'. The minutes recorded that Inskip then 'warned the Cabinet that he might have to ask for authority to adopt more drastic measures such, for example, as would enable manufacturers to give priority to Government orders in connection with the Defence Requirements Programme, and to postpone commercial orders whether for home or foreign account'. But Chamberlain suggested that the question be deferred 'until after decisions had been reached on the major policy of the Government', and no steps were taken to follow up Inskip's warning.

Amid all his preoccupations with defence and foreign affairs, Churchill still found time to work on the third volume of his life of Marlborough. Early in April his new research assistant, Bill Deakin, arrived at Chartwell for the first time. At lunch, Deakin later recalled: 'He hardly spoke at all. There was something else on his mind, as there often was.' Deakin, who quickly won Churchill's confidence, was again at Chartwell on April 25, when the other guests were all members of Churchill's inner circle—Archibald Sinclair, Edward Marsh and Professor Lindemann. 'I like Mr Deakin very much,' Churchill wrote to Keith Feiling on May 6, and within a short time Deakin became part of life at Chartwell. Forty years later, in a conversation with the author, Deakin recalled Churchill's routine: 'the ruthless partition of the day, the planning of things all to time. There was never a wasted moment. He had intense control.' At first, Deakin added, 'I felt very shy and nervous, but once he accepted you he was very considerate, of course he

---

[1] In Lord Weir's archive is an envelope on the back of which Churchill had written, in pencil, after a conversation with Weir in March: 'You musn't mind my talking bluntly. The hour of mere compliments is past.'

expected you to be as tough and concentrated as he was—he rather accepted that.' Deakin continued:

The activities seemed to stimulate him. I never saw him tired. He was absolutely totally organised, almost like a clock. He knew how to husband his energy, he knew how to expend it. His routine was absolutely dictatorial. He set himself a ruthless timetable every day and would get very agitated and cross if it was broken.

He would start the day at eight o'clock in bed, reading things, reading proofs. Then he started with his mail, which he would clear fairly rapidly before going back to whatever interested him. He would get back to his reading or his proofs and say to me: 'Look this up,' 'Find out about this.' If there was something he wanted to hear about I sat at the desk in his library and read to him. At luncheon he did not come downstairs until the guests were there—he would never greet them at the door.

His lunchtime conversation was quite magnificent. It was absolutely free for all. He did not restrain himself. After lunch if people were there he would shut off completely from politics, from writing. If he had guests he would take them around the garden. If there were no guests he would potter off into his room. He never had exactly a siesta. Sometimes he would lie down for a few minutes. Between five and 7 he would clear the mail he had dictated in the morning and sign letters but still there would be no work. He might play cards with his wife or Randolph. At seven he would bath and change for dinner.

Dinner at 8.30 was the event of the day. In very good form he could hold forth on any subject—memories of Harrow, or the western front—depending on the guests. After the ladies had left he might sit up with his male guests until midnight. He seldom talked about the work he was doing, though he might bring out something that had interested him.

At midnight, when the guests left, *then* he would start work. Work on Marlborough would go on to three or four in the morning. One felt so exhilarated. Part of the secret was his phenomenal power to concentrate— the fantastic power of concentrating on what he was doing—which he communicated. You were absolutely a part of it—swept into it.

Deakin ended:

Nothing was allowed to interfere with the night work. While he worked he would call up a secretary and start to dictate. I might have given him some memorandum before dinner, four or five hours before. Now he would walk up and down the room dictating. My facts were there, but he had seen it as a politician. My memorandum was a frame. It set him off, it set off his imagination.

With a research assistant working once more on *Marlborough* Churchill planned to have volume three ready for serialization in the

Sunday Times on July 19, and for publication in October. His other
literary activities also flourished. During May the *Evening Standard*
published three of his articles: 'How Germany is Arming', 'Our Navy
Must be Stronger' and 'Organise our Supplies'. The first of these,
published on May 1, made full use of Strakosch's figures. In it Churchill
asked: 'What is it all for? Certainly it is not all for fun. Something
quite extraordinary is afoot. All the signals are set for danger. The red
lights flash through the gloom. Let peaceful folk beware. It is a time to
pay attention and to be well prepared.' While work on *Marlborough*
proceeded, Desmond Morton continued to call, usually two evenings a
week, to discuss defence problems; his cottage at Earlylands was only
ten minutes walk from Chartwell. Sometimes his visits would last from
dinner to dawn. Keith Feiling, who continued to advise on the literary
side of Churchill's work, later recalled, in a letter to the author:

> The only habitué I saw much of then was Desmond Morton and very much
> liked: W.'s solicitude for him was remarkable—I remember his crying out in
> horror at seeing M. winding up his car handle (he had been shot through the
> heart, had he not?).
> It was on one of the early morning or dawn hours on his quarter-deck that,
> waving his glass towards Morton, myself & one other I can't remember, that
> he quoted Q Anne's famous sentence 'we four must never part till death
> mows us down with his impartial hand'.

During 1936 several of Churchill's closest friends tried to persuade
him to change his mind about Germany. Lord Rothermere, the Duke of
Westminster, Sir Ian Hamilton and his cousin Lord Londonderry had
each in their different ways been impressed by Hitler and his regime. On
May 4 Lord Londonderry, who had recently been in Berlin, wrote
urging him 'to consider the German situation from a different angle'.
Londonderry went on to explain in some detail what he believed to be
the realities of the situation:

> . . . the Germans cannot risk a war for the best part of four years and it seems
> to me that our duty in those four years is to do everything in our power to
> create a situation in which war can be eliminated or at all events, postponed
> for a number of years. I never could convince you or Rothermere that there
> was no imminence of an invasion of Great Britain by Germany from the air.
> You have both been responsible by your speeches and writings for changing
> the attitude of the Government towards our defences and I certainly feel
> that we all owe you a debt of gratitude, but your success was due to your
> being able to frighten the people of this country by giving them wholly
> exaggerated figures. . . .

Londonderry urged Churchill to visit Germany, and to see for himself how, within six years, Germany would become 'the most powerful nation in the world'. His letter continued:

> I am bound to say however, that I regret what I may call the 'defeatist' attitude of this country in assuming that nothing can be done to avert hostilities between this country and Germany. When I saw Hitler in the course of a two hours' interview he spoke chiefly of the Communistic menace and I found myself in agreement with a great deal of what he said. . . .
>
> We in this country, owing to the fact that Communism is non-existent, take the view that Germany is exaggerating the Communistic danger, but I am quite sure that they are doing nothing of the kind and I deeply regret first of all, the Alliance which the French were forced to make with Russia owing to our foolish policy with regard to Sanctions, and the manner in which Russian influences are exercising their power over our Government. . . .

Londonderry's letter ended: 'I should like to get out of your mind what appears to be a strong anti-German obsession because all these great countries are required in the political settlement of the future and Great Britain can play a leading part if only we are not forced into ridiculous positions by people like Baldwin and Anthony Eden.'

In his answer to Londonderry on May 6 Churchill wrote:

> I certainly do not take the view that a war between England and Germany is inevitable. I fear very gravely however unless something happens to the Nazi regime in Germany there will be a devastating war in Europe, and it may come earlier than you expect. The only chance of stopping it is to have a union of nations, all well-armed and bound to defend each other, and thus confront the Nazi aggression with over-whelming force. In this way there is the best chance that an internal revolution rather than an external explosion may avert an ever-growing danger.
>
> My figures about German rearmament have been collected by high authorities and they are not in principle contested by the Government. I have no doubt they will be contradicted, as German propaganda in this country is very strong.
>
> About the air. You ought not to confuse the moderate and precise figures given by me two years ago, and now proved to be understatements, with the extravagant figures which the Daily Mail published. You are, I am sure, wrong in supposing that anything I say, or said, made the slightest difference to the purblind complacency of the Government. What woke them up was a series of horrible shocks, and Intelligence from every quarter streaming in.
>
> You are also mistaken in supposing that I have an anti-German obsession. British policy for four hundred years has been to oppose the strongest power in Europe by weaving together a combination of other countries strong enough

to face the bully. Sometimes it is Spain, sometimes the French monarchy, sometimes the French Empire, sometimes Germany. I have no doubt who it is now. But if France set up to claim the over-lordship of Europe, I should equally endeavour to oppose them. It is thus through the centuries we have kept our liberties and maintained our life and power.

I hope you will not become too prominently identified with the pro-German view. If I read the future aright Hitler's government will confront Europe with a series of outrageous events and ever-growing military might. It is events which will show our dangers, though for some the lesson will come too late.

Churchill ended his letter with a reflection on Baldwin: 'Considering his very mediocre intellect,' he wrote, 'he has had a very fair run. I do not suppose it will last much longer. Arthur Balfour used to say, "This is a singularly ill-contrived world, but not so ill-contrived as that." '

Evidence of Britain's lack of preparedness continued to reach Churchill with almost every post. Throughout the spring he had received detailed comparisons of British and German naval strengths from the Navy League, of which Lord Lloyd was President, while in February one of the principal Government armament contractors, Sir John Thornycroft,[1] had sent him an account of developments in aircraft carrier construction, together with his comments on the use of destroyers and torpedo boats, and his fears about the continual drain of skilled men from shipbuilding to aircraft construction. In April a senior naval officer, Captain Boucher,[2] had sent him a seven-page note on the working of the Fleet Air Arm, and its problems. Boucher stressed the lack of training facilities at aerodromes, the dislike of RAF officers at serving afloat and the disruptive effect of the conflicting systems of naval and air force discipline, and the Air Ministry's failure to supply the Fleet Air Arm with adequate aircraft, the poor performance of the aircraft and the 'dangerously slow' machinery of joint Admiralty and

---

[1] John Edward Thornycroft, 1872–1960. President of J. I. Thornycroft & Co Ltd. Knighted, 1918. President of the Institute of Civil Engineers. Vice-President of the Royal Institute of Naval Architects. A director of the Southern Railway. Member of the Junior Carlton Club.

[2] Maitland Walter Sabine Boucher, 1888–1963. Entered the Navy as a cadet, 1904. On active service, 1914–18 (wounded). Served in the Operations Division, Admiralty, 1923–24. Qualified as a pilot, 1925. Directorate of Training, Air Ministry, 1929–31; Naval Air Division, Admiralty, 1933–34. Captain, 1930. Commanded HMS *Courageous*, 1935–37. Director of Air Materiel, Admiralty, 1938. Second Naval Member, Australian Naval Board, 1939–40. Rear-Admiral, 1941. Commodore, Royal Naval Reserve, in command of convoys, 1943–45. His only son, a Captain in the Royal Artillery, was killed in action in 1945.

Air Ministry control. Further information about the Fleet Air Arm was sent to Churchill, officially, on May 1, by the Third Sea Lord, Vice-Admiral Sir Reginald Henderson,[1] and on the following day by the Assistant Director of the Naval Air Division, Reginald Portal.[2]

Churchill made full use of Boucher's notes during a debate in the House of Commons on May 4. 'I do not pose as an expert on these matters,' he said, 'but as one who is accustomed to judge the opinion of experts.' In his speech Churchill urged that the problems of the Fleet Air Arm could best be resolved by making it the sole responsibility of the Admiralty. Such a move, he argued, must be made at once. His appeal was supported publicly by Air Vice-Marshal Oliver Swann,[3] who wrote to *The Times* on May 5 that the dual-control system 'will not stand the test of war'. That same day the First Sea Lord, Sir Ernle Chatfield, wrote to Churchill privately from the Admiralty:

I hope you will not mind my writing you a line of gratitude for your magnificent speech in the House about the Fleet Air Arm, a speech which will not only be the greatest help to the Admiralty in this tiresome and difficult question, but one that will give the greatest happiness to the whole Navy. To have found a real champion of our cause, which we have been fighting for so many years in the House of Commons, and one whom, if I may say so with due respect, carries such tremendous weight in the country on such matters is something for which we have long hoped, but for so long hoped in vain.

Sir Roger Keyes has done his best for us but your advocacy is on an entirely different plane and I think will compel the Government to hear the Admiralty case, which so far they have absolutely refused to do.

[1] Reginald Guy Hannam Henderson, 1881–1939. Entered the Royal Navy, 1896. Naval Mission to Greece, 1913. On active service, 1914–19 (despatches). Commanded the aircraft carrier HMS *Furious*, 1926–28. Rear-Admiral commanding Aircraft Carriers, 1931–33. Vice-Admiral, 1933. Third Sea Lord and Controller of the Navy, 1934–39. Knighted, 1936. Admiral, 1939. Churchill wrote in an unpublished draft of his second war memoirs: 'I also had a long and old friendship with Admiral Henderson, the Comptroller. He was one of our finest gunnery experts in 1912, and as I always used to go out and see the initial firings of battleships before their gun-mountings were accepted from the contractors, I was able to form a very high opinion of his work.'

[2] Reginald Henry Portal, 1894–1983. On active service, Royal Navy and Royal Naval Air Service, 1914–18 (DSC, 1916). Assistant Director, Naval Air Division, 1936. Commanded HMS *York*, 1939–41; HMS *Royal Sovereign*, 1941–42. Assistant Chief of the Naval Staff (Air), 1943–44. Flag Officer, Naval Air Stations, Australia, 1945. Naval Representative, Australian Joint Chiefs of Staff Committee, 1946–47. Flag Officer, Air (Home), 1947–51. Knighted, 1949.

[3] Oliver Swann, 1878–1948. Entered the Royal Navy, 1891; Port Captain, 1914. Commanded the Fleet aircraft carrier HMS *Campania*, 1915–17. Transferred to the RAF, 1919. Air Member for Personnel, Air Ministry, 1922. Air Officer Commanding Middle East, 1924. Knighted, 1924. Retired, 1926. Air Officer Commanding Halton, 1939. Air Liaison Officer, North Midland Region, 1940–43.

Chatfield himself then proceeded to set out for Churchill a number of serious problems affecting the Royal Navy, and especially anti-aircraft defence. 'We have years of arrears to overtake,' Chatfield wrote. 'Anti-aircraft guns and anti-aircraft ships cannot be immediately produced by voting money and for the next three or four years we are bound to be undergoing horrible risks. . . .'

Henceforth, Chatfield sent Churchill regular and substantial accounts of the Navy's work and problems. Other sources were likewise active as May proceeded. After Churchill's speech on May 4 a Conservative MP, Herbert Williams,[1] who had worked under him at the Ministry of Munitions, spoke to him in the Lobby about German munitions production. Williams told Churchill of his talk with the joint managing-director of Plessey, A. G. Clark,[2] with whom he had dined that same evening. On the following day Williams wrote to Churchill:

Mr Clark is a Contractor to the War Office, and I think the other two Defence Departments, for shells bombs etc. He recently had an opportunity of visiting some munition factories in Germany and from what he told me last night of the rate of output which the Germans are obtaining with the use of new methods I thought you would find it of very great interest to get Mr Clark to come and see you. He would be very willing to give you any information.

Churchill saw Allen Clark, who gave him detailed information about German rearmament, and about the long delays in the War Office contracts with his own firm. Unknown either to Clark or Churchill, on May 5 a disturbing memorandum was circulated by Duff Cooper to the Committee of Imperial Defence, listing War Office deficiencies. These included 8 million shells, 1,400 tanks and 400 field and anti-aircraft guns needed by the regular army. The War Office memorandum went on to state that forty firms earmarked for production had not yet even

[1] Herbert Geraint Williams, 1884–1954. Educated at the University of Liverpool. Electrical and Marine Engineer. Secretary, Machine Tool Trades Association, 1911–28. Secretary, Machine Tool Department, Ministry of Munitions, 1917–18. Conservative MP for Reading, 1924–29; for South Croydon, 1932–45; for Croydon East, 1950–54. Parliamentary Secretary, Board of Trade, 1928–29. Knighted, 1939. Member of the House of Commons Select Committee on Expenditure, 1939–44. Chairman, London Conservative Union, 1939–48; National Union of Conservatives and Unionist Associations, 1948. Created Baronet, 1953.

[2] Allen George Clark, 1898–1962. Known as 'A.G.'. Educated at Felsted School Essex. Volunteered for service in France before his seventeenth birthday; wounded at Cambrai; 2nd Lieutenant, Royal Flying Corps, 1918. Established the Plessey Company, a small contract shop with a staff of six, in 1920, and built it up into a substantial manufacturer of radios, telephones and electronic equipment, with 40,000 employees; Joint Managing Director, 1925; Chairman and Managing Director from 1946 until his death. Member of Council, Society of British Aircraft Constructors, 1960. Knighted, 1961.

been approached, while in the case of many of the armaments required 'design is not yet sufficiently firm to go into production'. In addition, the supplies of explosives were 'totally inadequate for war', and the one new factory being built, which would not be completed for another six months, would, when ready, be insufficient to supply the War Office, Admiralty and Air Ministry requirements. To Lord Weir, to whom a copy of this alarming memorandum was sent, Churchill himself made a personal appeal on May 6:

> You are being laden with vast responsibilities. Everywhere use is being made of your name. Ministers quote it in public and in private. Are you quite sure you are right in lending all your reputation to keeping this country in a state of comfortable peace routine?
>
> All I hear makes me believe that the whole life and industry of Germany is organised for war preparation. Our efforts compared to theirs are puny. As to the Air, you know my views. As to the Army, we have none; and can get neither men nor, except very slowly, weapons. Even the Fleet, if there is more delay, may reach a relative position where the future will lie with the enormous gun-and-armour plants of Germany. . . .

Churchill's letter ended:

> I know how invaluable and disinterested you are in all your work for the Government. Would it not be a melancholy thing if in a year you felt that its main results had been to delay and paralyse till too late the supreme effort which is needed. At present you seem to me to have major responsibilities, no doubt with a great deal of influence, but without power. This is not fair to yourself and to your friends, or to your country. However, if you are contented to bear this load, I can only hope and pray that your judgment has not been deflected by detail and good nature from the true proportion of affairs.

Weir was still not convinced, replying to Churchill a week later:

> 'The true proportion of affairs'—that is the real problem. Are we to take 'the whole life and industry of this nation and organise it for war preparation'? If I was completely confident that this was essential, I would not only advise it but push it hard in spite of its grave effects and dislocations. That is one extreme.
>
> The other extreme is your reference to our comfortable peace routine. Frankly, that is not the case in regard to action in Air supply. As to the Army, I agree that existing action is inadequate and have said so. . . .

On May 9 Desmond Morton sent Churchill more information, telling him that British naval armour-plate was believed to be much inferior to the German plate. 'There is a story,' Morton wrote, 'of three armour-plates being subjected to test under identical conditions by the Dutch not so long ago. The plate from Vickers was smashed. The Dutch plate from Siderius was badly damaged but the Bofors-Krupp plate was undamaged.' On a personal note Morton added: 'The changed attitude of the Press which now reports you at considerable length is satisfactory & significant.'

From both strangers and friends came a continual stream of encouragement, stimulated by the Press reports of each speech Churchill made. On May 9 Eric Long[1] wrote to Churchill:

> Please forgive me for wasting a few moments of your time, but I *just must* write to offer you my humble congratulations on the superb effort you are making to maintain intact this dear old Empire of ours.
>
> Whatever may be the outcome (& one prays daily for your success) of your fight, there will be thousands who will bless the name of *Winston Churchill* & our debt to you, we can never repay in kind, except to rally round you whenever we can. . . .

Working mostly at Chartwell, Churchill sent his warnings to those former colleagues who had themselves expressed concern at Britain's weakness. To Austen Chamberlain, who, with Sir Edward Grigg, had already visited him at Chartwell to discuss defence problems, he wrote on May 10: 'Lindemann is with me here, and he is preparing the case against the slow progress of all the experiments he wishes to have made for our defence against Aircraft.' As for the slow pace of rearmament, he added: 'I have prepared a sheaf of questions which touch a number of crucial points which might be attacked from day to day.' Churchill's letter ended: 'If no satisfaction is given, it will be necessary to bring things to a head, both from within and without.' Austen Chamberlain shared Churchill's worries. 'The evidence which you have accumulated,' he replied on May 11, 'is profoundly disturbing.' So disturbed was Churchill at Germany's growing strength that he now took steps to impress upon the Russians the need for their direct participation in the affairs of Europe. Twice during May he again saw the Soviet Ambassador, Ivan Maisky, on whom he urged the need for Russian support of the League of Nations Covenant.

---

[1] Richard Eric Onslow Long, 1892–1967. Son of the 1st Viscount Long (Walter Long). Educated at Harrow. In business in the City, 1911–14. On active service in France and at the Dardanelles (despatches). Major, 1923. A Member of the London Stock Exchange. Conservative MP for Westbury, 1927–31. President, West Wiltshire Constitutional Association, 1927–33, and 1948. Officer Commanding the 75th Searchlight Regiment, Royal Artillery, 1939–43. His only brother was killed in action on 27 January 1917. His elder son, Lieutenant Walter Reginald Basil Long, was drowned while on active service in Greece, 28 April 1944, aged 22. His nephew (whom he succeeded as third Viscount) was killed in action in northwest Europe on 23 September 1944.

On May 12 Ralph Wigram sent Churchill further Foreign Office extracts from *Mein Kampf*, pointing out two particular sentences which had been deleted from the British translation. In these sentences Hitler wrote: 'if one tells big lies, people will always believe a part' and: 'something always remains of the most impudent lies'.

Churchill took all these indications seriously. On May 13 *The Times* published a long and somewhat bantering letter from him concerning the views of his former best man, Lord Hugh Cecil, who wanted Russia, and all the other dictator powers, excluded from any British-organized alliance system, and who was also distrustful of any British alignment with France, or with Italy. 'It must be very painful to a man of Lord Hugh Cecil's natural benevolence and human charity,' Churchill wrote, 'to find so many of God's children wandering simultaneously so far astray,' and he added:

In these circumstances I would venture to suggest to my noble friend, whose gifts and virtues I have all my life admired, that some further refinement is needed in the catholicity of his condemnation. It might be a good thing, for instance, for him to put his censures down in order of priority, and then try to think a little less severely of the two least bad, or least likely to endanger our own safety. The problem would then simplify itself; and the picture would acquire the charm of light and shade.

On reading Churchill's letter, Robert Vansittart wrote from the Foreign Office: 'My dear Winston, Quite perfect. Nothing could be more timely or more complete than your letter. It gave great joy to yours ever Van.'

On May 15, in preparation for his next Parliamentary speech on Defence, Churchill wrote to Flandin to ask for details of French air force expenditure, and the 'latest French estimate' of German air strength. His own figures, Churchill wrote, 'drawn from a variety of sources', were a present strength of 1,200 first-line machines, 1,500 by June, and 2,000 by the end of 1936. 'In their scientifically prepared industry,' he added, 'they have of course an almost indefinite power of expansion as far as *material* is concerned.' Flandin replied on May 16, sending a two-page statistical summary of French air force expenditure, and adding in a covering note: 'I follow, from afar, your energetic and courageous action.' Flandin also sent Churchill the French estimates of German first-line air strength: 1,236 existing aircraft and 120 Lufthansa auxiliaries; 2,000 by the end of 1936; and 2,800 by the end of 1937, with 1,500 reserves.

On May 19 Churchill attended the first of the private luncheons given by the Anti-Nazi Council, at the Hotel Victoria in Northumberland Avenue, organized by A. H. Richards. Four leading Labour personalities were present, Sir Walter Citrine, Sir Norman Angell,[1] Margaret Bondfield[2] and Hugh Dalton.[3] During the course of a short speech, Churchill urged all those 'so oppositely situated in politics' to find common ground in upholding the ideals in which they all believed, to combat tyranny by upholding those ideals, and to prepare themselves for the time when 'suddenly the tension may rise and we may feel that we could go all lengths together'. It would not be enough, in time of danger, to feel 'an intense emotion, coupled with complete impotence', and he continued: 'That is why we ought to keep a little in touch with one another. That is why we ought to keep some opportunity to proclaim that there are men of all classes, all sorts and conditions, all grades of human forces, from the humblest workman to the most bellicose colonel, who occupy a common ground in resisting dangers and aggressive tyranny.'

Immediately after this lunch-time meeting, a small sub-committee began to examine the possibility of a manifesto to which the public might subscribe. But there was some confusion as to what its theme should be. That evening Lady Violet Bonham Carter wrote to Churchill:

Dearest Winston,

Arising out of our luncheon to-day, the following considerations occur to me.

---

[1] Ralph Norman Angell Lane, 1874–1967. Educated in France and Switzerland. Worked as a rancher, prospector and journalist in California, 1894–98. Using the name Norman Angell, he published in 1910 *The Great Illusion*, which warned of the economic catastrophies even of a victorious war. Henceforth known as Norman Angell. General Manager of the *Paris Daily Mail*, 1905–14. Editor, *Foreign Affairs*, 1928–31. Labour MP for North Bradford, 1929–31. Knighted, 1931. Nobel Peace Prize, 1933.

[2] Margaret Grace Bondfield, 1873–1953. Apprentice shop girl, 1887; Assistant Secretary, Shop Assistants Union, 1898–1908. Member of the TUC General Council, 1918–24 and 1926–29. A British TUC delegate to Russia, 1920. Labour MP for Northampton, 1923–24; for Wallsend, 1926–31. Parliamentary Secretary, Ministry of Labour, 1924. Minister of Labour, 1929–31. Privy Councillor, 1920 (the first woman Privy Councillor and the first woman Cabinet Minister in Britain). Chairman, Women's Group on Public Welfare, 1939–49.

[3] Edward Hugh John Neale Dalton, 1887–1962. Educated at Eton and King's College Cambridge. Barrister, 1914. On active service in France and Italy 1914–18. Lecturer, London School of Economics, 1919. Reader in Commerce, University of London, 1920–25; Reader in Economics, 1925–26. Labour MP for Camberwell, 1924–29; for Bishop Auckland, 1929–31 and 1935–59. Parliamentary Under-Secretary, Foreign Office, 1929–31. Chairman, National Executive of the Labour Party, 1936–37. Minister of Economic Warfare, 1940–42. President of the Board of Trade, 1942–45. Chancellor of the Exchequer, 1945–47; resigned over a Budget leak, 1947. Minister of Town and Country Planning, 1950–51. Created Baron, 1960.

'Pointing the finger at Hitler,' (advocated by Dr Dalton) is a futile policy. We have 'pointed the finger at Mussolini'—& it has done him no harm. Admonitory fingers do not deter dictators.

There are only two policies to be adopted towards Hitler: to hold out the hand or to clench the fist. The country at the moment is unwilling to do either.

If we advocate the second what does it amount to? Re-armament against —& virtual encirclement of—Germany. . . .

Replying to Violet Bonham Carter on May 25, Churchill stressed that it was towards Nazi Germany that public attention should be focused, and he set out a detailed plan of action, including a Mediterranean pact 'for mutual protection against further aggression'. Churchill added:

. . . if Mussolini enters the regional pact having agreed to the terms prescribed, the League of Nations would then be strong enough to face the Hitler problem upon its present basis. I would then proceed by very similar methods under the authority of the League of Nations and by, means of regional pacts linked together to make the strongest and closest encirclement of Nazidom which is possible.

I would marshal all the countries including Soviet Russia from the Baltic southward right round to the Belgian coast, all agreeing to stand by any victim of unprovoked aggression. I would put combined pressure upon every country neighbouring to Germany to subscribe to this and to guarantee a quota of armed force for the purpose.

I would of course offer Germany the right to enter this system, in which case she would receive from all these countries their guarantee pro tanto of support in the event of her becoming a victim of unprovoked aggression from any quarter. This I believe would ensure either the peace of the world or an overwhelming deterrent against aggression.

If on the other hand Mussolini refused to work with us and leaves the League of Nations, then I would say sorrowfully and openly that nothing remains for us but to provide for our own interests and security. This would be done by a strictly limited regional pact among the Western States, Holland, Belgium, France and Britain for mutual aid in the event of unprovoked attack, and for keeping in being a force great enough to deter Germany from making such an attack.

Churchill's letter ended on a personal note: 'There my dear Violet, I have set forth my thought with every feeling of humility before such grievous and giant events.'

The Anti-Nazi Council continued its work with Churchill's active encouragement. Under Richards' guidance a number of private luncheons and meetings were organized at which a plan of action acceptable to the different groups was devised.

In his public speeches, Churchill continued to press for a more vigorous approach to defence policy. On May 21 he told the House of Commons that it was essential to set up a special Ministry of Supply, to coordinate the arms purchases of all three Service Ministries, and to plan service expansion on a war basis. This did not mean that he was 'in favour of war'; that, he said, was a 'foul charge'. And he went on to ask: 'Is there a man in this House who would not sacrifice his right hand here and now for the assurance that there would be no war in Europe for twenty years?'

In spite of the trust that Churchill was now inspiring in ever-widening circles, Baldwin had convinced himself of Churchill's lack of judgement. On May 22 he discussed Churchill with Thomas Jones, who recorded Baldwin's words in his diary:

One of these days I'll make a few casual remarks about Winston. Not a speech—no oratory—just a few words in passing. I've got it all ready. I am going to say that when Winston was born lots of fairies swooped down on his cradle gifts—imagination, eloquence, industry, ability, and then came a fairy who said 'No one person has a right to so many gifts,' picked him up and gave him such a shake and twist that with all these gifts he was denied judgment and wisdom. And that is why while we delight to listen to him in this House we do not take his advice.

Despite Baldwin's private strictures, Churchill's fears and warnings were increasingly shared by others. Indeed, Hankey, with his inside knowledge, was pressing the Government about these same deficiencies, writing to Inskip on May 22: 'I feel constrained to submit to you my concern as to the rate at which our defence programmes are proceeding. . . . An examination of the timetable since the process of reconditioning our Defence Services was first started a year ago is not very flattering to efficiency. This time-table tends to show that at all stages we have been rather slow.' Hankey added that in his view it should be emphasized 'that the circumstances are such that questions connected with the Defence Programme might, administratively, need to be dealt with on a war basis'.

On May 25 Churchill was back at Chartwell. There, in a letter from Desmond Morton, he learnt that the figures on French air force expenditure which Flandin had sent him 'coincide with those the Air Ministry already possess'. That evening a new and quite unexpected source of secret information was added to Churchill's already substantial range of sources. Five days earlier, on May 20, he had received a telephone message from Mrs Pearman, to say that, in his absence, a serving Air Force officer had asked for 'a talk with you very soon'. Her note continued:

As a Service officer you would appreciate his position. He did not wish to write, but thought a talk was better. Would you speak to him tomorrow, if possible? He would come to the flat or the House. He mentioned that he was Director of the Training School, and he would confidently say you would be much interested in what he had to say. When can he come to see you? His number is at the Air Ministry, Holborn 3434 (Extension 673).

At seven on the evening of May 25 Squadron Leader Anderson[1] presented himself at Morpeth Mansions. He brought with him charts and statistics which made clear that too few observer-navigators were being trained, that educational standards were falling and that current plans were inadequate to provide the number of observers needed to confront Germany in 1937, 1938 or 1939.

At their meeting, Anderson gave Churchill a seventeen-page foolscap memorandum, the theme of which was that not enough was being done 'to fit the RAF for War'. He also produced fourteen pages of statistical information setting out the RAF programme in both personnel and aircraft.

---

[1] Charles Torr Anderson, 1896–1981. Grandson of a former Chief Constable of Staffordshire. His father died when Anderson was seven. Educated at Christ's Hospital. A brewer's pupil, 1914. 2nd Lieutenant, 10th North Staffordshire Regiment, 1915. Badly wounded on the western front, 1916, after which he spent a year in hospital. Transferred to the Royal Flying Corps, 1917. Distinguished Flying Cross, 1918. Permament commission, 1919; served subsequently in India and Australia, where he was severely injured in an air crash. Commanded No 504 Bomber Squadron, 1931–34. Director of Training, Air Ministry, 1934–36. Commanded RAF Hucknall, 1936–37. Commanded No 1 Armament Training, Catfoss, Yorkshire, 1938–39. Senior Personal Staff Officer, Headquarters No 5 Group, 1939–40. Group Captain, 1940. Commanded two operational bomber squadrons at Waddington, Lincolnshire, 1940. Personal Assistant and Air Adviser to Lord Beaverbrook, 1940–42, when he helped to establish the Lancaster bomber on a proper production basis. Invalided out of the RAF, 1942. Joined the staff of Bass, Ratcliff and Gretton, 1944. Retired, 1959.

Churchill, meanwhile, continued his correspondence about the Air Defence Research sub-committee, writing to Sir Thomas Inskip on May 25. 'Of course you realise that it is my task and duty, as I conceive it, to arouse the Government and the country to the sense of the dangers by which we are being encompassed, but I shall always be ready to assist you in any way that you may at any time suggest.' His letter continued:

At the 1922 Committee you referred to me (without mentioning my name) about the progress made by the Committee on defence against air attack. You seem to have been led to believe that some very valuable discovery has been made which will improve our defence in the near future. It is true that some wonderful scientific progress has been made for locating hostile aircraft, but this is not likely to be perfected for a long time, and even when it is, the more difficult question arises of how to destroy the hostile plane when detected and located. On this no progress worth speaking of has been made. In fact the main conclusion reached after eight months that I have been on the Committee is that anti-aircraft guns are practically useless with their present shells, except when concentrated for the defence of the Fleet or some special point.

They are now all turning to the kite balloon, and I agree with this. But you will be shocked to see how slow, timid and insignificant is the progress made. I was astonished that Swinton in the Lords four months ago should have referred to the work of this Committee in such glowing terms. It is a very good Committee; it works most agreeably together; it has many bright ideas; but action and progress, except in the one respect I mentioned, are pitiful.

Accustomed as I was to see how things were done in the war, and how orders can be given for large scale experiment and supply, I have been deeply pained by the dilettante futility which has marked our action. The delays are dreadful. Lindemann whom you know and who is on the scientific committee, has been struggling vainly for eight months for certain not very costly experiments to be made. From time to time some little thing is done, and then another month before a variant is attempted, and so on. I have had, and am still having, a great deal of difficulty to prevent Lindemann from resigning.

If you wish to confirm what I have said on this matter you might have a talk with Sir F. E. Smith.[1] I have never discussed it privately with him, nor indeed ever seen him except on the Committee, but I have very little doubt

[1] Frank Edward Smith, 1879–1970. Educated at the Royal College of Science. Superintendent, Electrical Department, National Physical Laboratory, 1901–20. Fellow of the Royal Society, 1918. Director of Scientific Research at the Admiralty, 1920–29. Secretary, Department of Scientific and Industrial Research, 1929–39. Knighted, 1931. Director of Instrument Production, and Controller of Bearings Production, Ministry of Supply 1939–42. Director of Research, Anglo-Iranian Oil Company, 1939–55. Controller of Telecommunications Equipment, Ministry of Aircraft Production, 1940–42. Chairman of the Technical Defence Committee, MI5, 1940–46; of the Scientific Advisory Council, Ministry of Supply, 1941–47. Chairman of the Road Research and Safety Research Board, 1945–54.

that he will tell you that what I have written is true. What Hopkinson [1] said about our having already some means which in the immediate future would spread a reign of terror among hostile aircraft, is utter rubbish. I do not doubt that ultimately the aeroplane will be conquered from the ground, but at the present rate of progress this will certainly not be in the next ten years. Much may happen in these ten years. In the meantime there is nothing at home except retaliation as a deterrent.

'Believe me,' Inskip replied four days later, 'I shall always value your help and shall not resent your criticisms. I am naturally concerned at what you say of the scientific work. . . .' In his letter, Inskip specifically asked Churchill to send him a memorandum on the dangers of invasion by airborne troops; and on June 3 he asked Churchill to talk to him 'about your idea of a Ministry of Supply', adding that it was 'obviously in my own personal interest to pass on this part of my duties to someone else'.

As well as writing to Inskip about the Air Defence Research sub-committee, on May 27 Churchill had taken up the Plessey Company's complaint direct with the War Office, writing to Allen Clark on the following day:

I asked Sir Hugh Elles [2] to come to see me yesterday, and having obtained from his assurance that you and your firm would be in no way prejudiced by the steps you have taken in coming to me, I told him the substance of what you had said and showed him your report. He seemed to be already well informed upon the subject and said at once 'No doubt it is the Plessey Company.' He expressed himself greatly obliged by the action I had taken, and promised to give his personal attention to the matter, which as I have said, had already come to his notice. . . .

'I am sure in these circumstances,' Churchill added, 'the right course will be taken.' But, as Elles himself wrote to Churchill on June 4: 'The matter is far from being an easy one, especially in the processes of peace administration.' On June 3 Churchill sent Weir and Inskip a copy of Clark's account of his recent visit to Germany, telling Inskip in his

---

[1] Austin Hopkinson, 1879–1962. On active service in South Africa, 1900. 2nd Lieutenant, The Royal Dragoons, 1914–16; Private, 1918. Independent MP for Mossley, 1918–29 and 1931–45; a frequent speaker on air matters. Lieutenant, Fleet Air Arm, 1940.

[2] Hugh Jamieson Elles, 1880–1945. Entered Royal Engineers, 1899. Served in the South African War, 1901–02. Deputy Assistant Quartermaster-general, 4th Division, 1914. Brigade Major, 10th Division, 1915. Wounded in action, 1915. Lieutenant-Colonel commanding the Tank Corps in France, 1916–19. Promoted Brigadier-General, 1917; Major-General, 1918. Knighted, 1919. Commandant of the Tank Corps Training Centre, 1919–23. Director of Military Training, War Office, 1930–33. Master General of Ordnance, War Office, 1934–37. General, 1938. Regional Commissioner for South-West England, 1939–45.

covering note: 'I thought the report of this German visit so interesting, and I may add so disturbing, that I asked permission to show it to you and to Weir. Not only is the scale of German war production at least ten times ours, but the pace and method of production are far superior.'

On May 29 Churchill sent Lord Swinton a copy of Flandin's 'latest estimate of the strength of the German Air Force', telling Swinton 'that he believed it was his duty to send it'. His letter continued: 'You will see that their current estimate corresponds very closely, indeed almost exactly, to the figures which I gave in December, and which you somewhat unkindly characterised as "a guess". . . .' Churchill asked Swinton, and also Hankey, not to let the French know that he had passed on these figures. Replying on May 29, Hankey promised secrecy, and added, encouragingly: 'My personal impression is that their [the Air Staff's] latest information from the French does not differ materially from yours—though I am not quite certain.' Swinton had agreed, Hankey added, 'that nothing should be done to interrupt your contact with the French'. But on June 9 Swinton wrote to Hankey that as the French figures included the 'immediate reserve' in German first-line strength, a 'fair standard' of comparison would be to write them down by 30 per cent. Swinton added: 'As I told you, I very much dislike carrying on secret correspondence with Churchill.'

Although no decision had yet been made about a Ministry of Supply, it was now taken for granted that Churchill would not be invited to join the Government in any capacity. *The Times* was particularly hostile to Churchill's inclusion. 'Do not, my dear Abe, suppose that I mind,' Churchill wrote to Abe Bailey on June 3. 'In the present posture of affairs I have no wish whatever for office. I would not join any Government which I did not feel was resolved to lift National Defence to an altogether different plane, nor would I join any Government in which I had not a real share of power for such a purpose'. Churchill added: 'If all our fears are groundless and everything passes off smoothly in the next few years, as pray God indeed it may, obviously there is no need for me. If on the other hand the very dangerous times arise, I may be forced to take a part. Only in those conditions have I any desire to serve.'

Desmond Morton, who wanted a Ministry of Supply, wrote bitterly to Churchill on June 3: 'we have deluded ourselves into believing that war-time practice is only to be used in war'. His letter continued:

Given time, we shall make the stuff that is *now* so urgently required, and shall 'muddle through' somehow. After that—always provided we are given the time—we shall sit back with complacency and say: 'There you are. After all the fuss Winston made, we are all right after all'; quite forgetting that although we have somehow produced what we urgently require, these slipshod methods will never do if war actually comes.

On June 3 Sir Thomas Inskip wrote to Churchill, seeking his advice on how he should delegate the supply aspect of his Ministry: 'My difficulty,' Inskip wrote, 'is in seeing what such a step involves and what advantage will be gained,' and he added: 'It is here that you can help me if you will.' Churchill replied on June 5:

Your job, like Gaul, seems divided into three parts.
(i) Co-ordinating strategy and settling quarrels between the Services.
(ii) Making sure the goods are delivered under the various programmes and
(iii) Creating the structure of War industry and its organisation.

These last two lie together. If you are going to be responsible for them, you will surely need a powerful machine which will grow from month to month and handle increasingly larger blocks of business as its strength and efficiency develop. The successive steps by which this machinery should be formed, and procuring of the necessary powers from Parliament, and the taking over by instalments all the Service Supply Departments require to be scheduled. Wide powers should be taken in the act and applied in stages by Orders in Council as they are required, and as they can be used.

Until you have got a fairly strong machine you cannot take over the work, and it would be most imprudent to accept the responsibility for the punctual execution of the programmes. This business is vast and complex, and no man can manage it without the necessary apparatus.

A Prime Minister may rightly hope for peace and resolve upon a policy of peace. But a Defence Minister must always contemplate the possibility of war at various dates in the future, and must plan accordingly. If, for instance, war comes in 1937, everyone will expect that a complete organisation of our industry for war purposes and a good system of control will be actually in being. It was my experience that while people oppose all precautions in time of peace, the very same people turn round within a fortnight of war and are furious about every shortcoming. I hope it may not be yours.

'Personally,' Churchill added, 'I sympathise with you very much in your task. I would never have undertaken such a task knowing from experience how fierce opinions become upon these subjects once the nation is alarmed.' And he commented: 'It is an awful thing to take over masses of loosely defined responsibilities.'

On June 8 Inskip and Churchill discussed in detail the problems of, and the need for, a Minister of Supply. Churchill suggested setting up a body, similar to the War Priorities Committee of 1917, with power to allocate materials to the service departments. But in a departmental note later that same day Inskip recorded that he had told Churchill that there were already '7 Supply Committees' doing the supply work of the three service departments, and that he did not feel that an overall supervisory body was needed. Nevertheless, at a meeting of the Cabinet's Defence Policy and Requirements Committee on June 11 Inskip expressed his own worries about the supply situation, believing that the period of 3 to 5 years laid down by the Cabinet as the years of preparation was too long and that 'the urgency of the situation might require us to alter the date, and to take new powers', such as making Austin turn their whole factory to war production. Vansittart, who was present at the meeting, agreed with Inskip that peace in Europe could not be guaranteed 'for the next five or even 3 years' and drew the Cabinet's attention to 'a marked change in the tone of Germany which was becoming distinctly sharper'. But Neville Chamberlain, as the minutes recorded, 'suggested that Germany's next forward step might not necessarily lead us into war'. Vansittart disagreed, warning that Germany's next forward move 'would probably be against Czechoslovakia'.

Both Inskip and Swinton argued in favour of emergency powers, but Sir Samuel Hoare opposed them. 'Such powers,' Hoare said, 'might come as a great shock to the country and result in an upheaval of industry.' This was also Neville Chamberlain's view, for, as he explained, 'The disturbance of industry produced by acceleration might result in grave consequences, financial, economic etc, and any alteration could only be justified by over-powering conditions.'

At the end of the meeting Vansittart stated that there would not be 'any more marked symptoms of the foreign situation' than already existed. But Chamberlain insisted that only when 'the situation deteriorated' still further would there be sufficient 'accumulation of symptoms' to persuade public opinion to accept 'a more drastic move'.

In the first week of June Churchill was asked to accept the Presidency of the British section of the New Commonwealth Society. This Society had been formed in 1932 to promote the maintenance of international law and order, 'through the creation of an Equity Tribunal and an International Police Force'. It also favoured the creation, under the League of Nations, of an International Air Police. The members of the Society regarded Churchill as the leading public figure sympathetic to their basic principles, and forty-one MPs, members of the Society's

Parliamentary Group, urged him to accept. The Group included several of his friends, including General Spears, Robert Boothby and Josiah Wedgwood, and cut across all party boundaries. On June 5 Churchill accepted their invitation. 'The fact that you should consider these efforts of mine no barrier,' he wrote to the Chairman, Lord Davies,[1] 'but indeed rather an aid to the cause which you have so much at heart, makes me feel that there is a broad understanding across the gulfs of party both of the dangers in which we lie, and of the bold measures of thought and action which the crisis demands. . . .' Churchill added: 'The task which you have set yourselves, and in which I am willing to bear my part, is beset with every kind of difficulty and exposed to mockery and misunderstanding. But that we should persevere in it with faith, and practical measures, is surely a simple obligation.'

Churchill felt it necessary to explain his decision to join the New Commonwealth Society to his constituents. 'I had a talk with Neville Chamberlain before accepting,' he wrote to Sir James Hawkey on June 8, 'and he told me he had subscribed and was a Member, and he thought that as the ultimate goal this was the right thing.' Churchill added: 'I feel so strongly one ought to do all one can to get this country rearmed and to relieve people from feeling that re-armament means war. In my belief it is one of the few chances of peace.'

Churchill's friends continued to give him information and encouragement. On June 12 General Tudor wrote to him:

I gather from serving officers that the army is in a bad way for men. It seems to me that the nation must be got out of this false pacifism mood, and made to realise that if our forces are reasonably strong & capable of rapid expansion in case of need, we are hardly likely to be attacked. I loved your letter in the Times about Hugh Cecil about a fortnight ago.

I had a letter from Darling,[2] whom you will remember. He said that it was grotesque that the ablest mind in politics should be outside the government, & any little he could do would be done to increase the demand for your inclusion.

It is obvious to everybody I meet that the Defence job should have been given to you.

---

[1] David Davies, 1880–1944. Landed proprietor. Liberal MP for Montgomeryshire, 1906–29. Commanded the 14th Battalion, Royal Welch Fusiliers, in France, 1915–16. Parliamentary Private Secretary to Lloyd George, 1916–22. Created Baron, 1932. Director of several colliery and railway companies. Founder and Chairman of the New Commonwealth Society.

[2] Charles John Darling, 1849–1936. Barrister, 1874. Queen's Counsel, 1887. Conservative MP for Deptford, 1888–97. Knighted, 1897. Judge of the Queen's Bench Division of the High Court of Justice, 1897–1923. An original member of the Other Club, 1911. Chairman of the Committee on Courts Martial, 1919. Created Baron, 1924.

Also on June 12, Ralph Wigram sent Churchill copies of three further
Foreign Office despatches dealing with different aspects of Nazism.
'Will you kindly destroy them when you have read them,' he added. 'I
have marked the important passages.'[1] Six days later the Duchess of
Atholl sent Churchill the transcript of a speech Hitler had made to the
League of German Maidens. One paragraph, she pointed out, had been
deleted in the broadcast version. In it Hitler had said that if war came 'I
should fall upon my enemy suddenly, like lightning striking out of the
night.'

---

[1] The first despatch of six typed papers had been sent from Berlin by Sir Eric Phipps on
June 6, and concerned Press reports denying the existence of 'the German danger of which Mr
Winston Churchill was always speaking'. The second despatch contained a report from the
British Consul-General in Munich, D. St. Clair Gainer, dated 18 May 1936. The third des-
patch, sent by Phipps on June 3, analysed in five pages a new book on the German claim
for the return of Colonies lost by Germany in 1918 and given by the League of Nations as
Mandates to Britain, France, Australia, New Zealand, South Africa and Japan.

37

Defence Preparations:
'A Remorseless Pressure'

ON June 10 Churchill was caught up in a fierce dispute between
Professor Lindemann and Sir Henry Tizard. The latter was
Chairman of the Tizard Committee, a body which worked under the
Air Defence Research sub-committee, and of which Lindemann had been
made a member at Churchill's suggestion. Friction between Lindemann
and Tizard arose from Lindemann's continual pressure for speedier
action, and was accentuated by Tizard's scepticism towards many of the
ideas which Lindemann put forward in rapid succession, among them
the need for night operations, aerial mines to be dropped in the path of
incoming bombers, infra-red detection of night-flying aircraft and the
placing of 'a cloud of substance' in the path of an aeroplane 'to produce
detonation'.

On June 2 Churchill had circulated a paper to the Air Defence
Research sub-committee, criticizing the Tizard Committee's failure to
give priority to experiments with the aerial mine. On June 10 Tizard
complained to Swinton, through Wing-Commander Warburton, that it
was quite wrong for Lindemann to have enlisted the support of 'an
outside individual, however eminent he might be'. On June 12 Tizard
wrote direct to Swinton, to say that either Lindemann must be removed
from his Committee, or he himself would resign. That same day Tizard
circulated a memorandum criticizing Churchill's paper, in which he
wrote that the aerial mine experiments had in fact been begun even
before Lindemann joined the Committee, and had subsequently continued without any untoward delay.

It was not only the aerial mine experiments that were causing
Churcill and Lindemann concern. On June 12 Watson-Watt himself
saw Churchill privately, and sought to enlist his help on the future of

radar experiments, as a matter of urgency. 'I very much appreciated the privilege of meeting you yesterday,' Watson-Watt wrote on June 13, 'and am much encouraged by your generous interest in our work'. Watson-Watt explained that although there were no financial limits to his radar experiments, he felt that 'emergency machinery' was needed, as the normal Air Ministry machinery 'had held down' his rate of advance. Thirteen weeks earlier, he pointed out, it had been recommended that he coordinate all the research connected with the interception of located aircraft, and also the location of aircraft at night. But three months had passed without the Air Ministry putting this recommendation into effect, and Watson-Watt had become desperate at what he described as 'the Air Ministry's unwillingness to take emergency measures'; indeed, 'urgent action', he wrote, was now needed not only for radar, which had itself never been tested 'in conditions at all comparable to war conditions', but also for acoustic detection, and for ground communications between aircraft and the Observer Corps.

On June 22 Churchill set out his worries about the progress of research into air defence in a strongly-worded letter to Swinton:

What surprises and grieves me is your attitude, and that you should be apparently contented with the way this work is going. We are at present entirely defenceless from the ground (except for a few vulnerable points where batteries are massed) against any attack from the air: and it must be at least more than a year before anything practical can be done. During the ten months I have sat upon the Committee I have been shocked at the slowness with which every investigation proceeds. I well know that this branch is a very small part of your labours. All the more therefore I should have thought you would welcome the assistance of others in trying to get things done.

The differences upon the Scientific Committee are not as you suggest of a technical or abstruse character. They are differences about the method and procedure to be used in testing certain ideas, which if found sound would open a new domain to anti-aircraft artillery, as well as helping in other ways known to you. The experiments are neither large nor expensive, but they must be numerous, and can only advance by repeated trial and error.

Churchill then gave a specific example of his concern, the aerial mine, the value of which had still not been determined. 'If this enquiry had been entrusted to a private firm,' he wrote, 'it could have been completed in two or three months at the outside at a cost I should suppose of less than £1,000.' Churchill added:

Apart from knowing that a very modest explosive charge will suffice to do serious damage, we have not made any progress. I certainly thought that an idea like this if adopted provisionally would be tested day in, day out, until it would either be proved sound or futile.

But if these small experiments are to be agreed to one by one, and then fitted in with the mass of important experimental work being discharged at Shoeburyness and elsewhere, with reports in each case back to the Committee which meets about once a month, and with no one person given the means to pursue the quest, then it is certain that nothing will result before the period of maximum danger for Europe and our country has come.

Churchill's letter ended:

It is always difficult to have a public controversy about unmentionable topics. I am however quite sure that if instead of serving on your Committee Lindemann and I had pressed our points by all the various methods and channels open to us, these ideas would have had better treatment than they have received.

I have dwelt upon this particular act of experiments because I have followed them more closely. But I fear that a similar slowness and intermittance characterises other lines of research in this field.

I hope you will weigh what I write without resentment or prejudice.

In his reply three days later, Swinton denied that there was any slowness in defence experiments, but assured Churchill that he would still welcome criticisms. 'I am trying to give of my best,' he added, 'and I know all my people are; and I am sure it is up to all of us to do the same.'

On June 25 Lindemann explained his point of view in a letter to Tizard. 'The point on which we seem to be in complete disagreement,' he wrote, 'is the different urgency which we attach to our endeavour to find some method to deal with air attack. Your procedure would no doubt be excellent if we had ten or fifteen years time. I believe that the period available is to be measured in months.' On July 5 Tizard repeated to Swinton that unless Lindemann were removed he would resign, and ten days later he did in fact resign. But within three months he was back at the head of his Committee, and it was Lindemann who was in fact formally dismissed on November 2.

On June 12 Churchill had written another criticism of British air policy for the Air Defence Research sub-committee. In the third week of June this paper was prepared by Hankey for circulation to the Committee of Imperial Defence, and a copy was shown to Swinton. Quoting entirely from the official documents which he had received as a member of the sub-committee, Churchill challenged the Government's view that Britain's air strength was still adequate in relation to Germany.

Churchill's assessment centred on the much disputed question of how, precisely, to calculate the first-line strength of the German Air Force. Both he, and the Air Staff in their reply of June 26, were in agreement on the total number 'of military aircraft available in Germany' at that time, Churchill giving a total of 3,200, and the Air Staff 3,115. The dispute arose over the calculation of what percentage of this total constituted the first line, and what percentage the reserve. The Air Staff believed that only 920 of these were first line, a further 920 reserve and 1,275 used in the training schools. Churchill, however, interpreted the figures differently. 'After all,' he wrote in his memorandum, 'what we really want to know is the number at given dates of German war planes simultaneously available for service and capable of indefinite maintenance'. His memorandum continued:

We know from previous Air Staff papers that there is a very large surplus of German war-planes and pilots who have passed through the training schools available after the existing squadron formations have been filled. Why then should these three Immediate Reserve trained pilots and war planes in each squadron not be counted? In what respect do they differ from the other nine in each squadron? Unless there is some important difference it would surely be prudent to count them as the French do 'en ligne', and not rule them out as not according to our conventions. At any rate, 330 military aircraft incorporated with their squadrons, manned by pilots who have passed through the official training schools, is not a negligible factor in computing the danger we have to face. It would raise the German effective strength to 1,236 aeroplanes on the 1st May, 1936, to which one monthly increment of 60 has probably been added, making a total of 1,296 exclusive of the Lufthansa, which the French put at 120 and the Air Staff at 72.

In studying these figures, Churchill was trying to take into account the atmosphere of war production prevailing in Germany, and also to be prepared for the least favourable situation that might arise, should the Germans be able to fulfil their production, organizational and training facilities to a maximum. As he wrote: 'It may be, unfortunately, that we are still seriously underestimating the number of German machines formed into squadrons.'

Churchill was convinced that 360 training school aeroplanes, together with their pilots, should be included in the first-line strength. The Air Staff insisted that these aeroplanes were strictly limited to a training role, and that as many as 750 pilots, out of whose number the 360 training school planes would have to be flown, were in fact grounded as far as first-line duties were concerned, manning instead 'the experimental stations, recruit depots, aircraft parks, staff college, Air Ministry and the instructional posts. . . .' Churchill, on the other hand, was more convinced about the possibilities of surprise in the German organizational framework. Commenting on the 1,200 machines and 1,114 pilots for whom the Air Staff had located no specific squadron and only non-first-line duties, he wrote:

This would be amply sufficient to duplicate every one of the 88 squadrons now believed to have been identified. When we remember the fondness evinced by Germany in history for this particular form of surprise, and note the large number of machines and pilots which seem to have vanished into thin air and the hundred odd aerodromes which have been constructed, this possibility cannot be excluded.

In their answer to Churchill's questioning, the Air Staff, while doubting his assessment of German methods, went on, in their own memorandum, to point out yet another source for future German front-line strength, noting:

The Air Staff fully share Mr Churchill's apprehensions as regards German ability to spring a surprise on their enemy on the outbreak of war by some unexpected manoeuvre. They do not, however, feel that the method envisaged by Mr Churchill would be employed since the execution of such a plan would not be in keeping with Germany's well-known love of method and organisation and would be contrary to the first and main principle of sound Air Force organisation.

The Air Staff, however, would again draw attention to the creation of the Air Force reserve (Luftwaffe) through the medium of the DLV (Air Sports Association), mentioned in paragraphs 21–23 of CID Paper No 1216-B, dated the 4th March, 1936.

It is felt that any unexpected addition to first line strength on the outbreak of war will be found by this organisation which is now constituted on a military basis. Admittedly the growth within the framework is to-day a negligible quantity because it would be an impossible feat to form a regular air force and an air force reserve 'ab initio' simultaneously.

In 18 months or two years' time, however, when the framework has been filled out and many of the personnel are trained officers and airmen who have completed their short-term engagements in the regular air force it may be a force seriously to be reckoned with and trained to a standard not far short of the regular air force.

It was clear from these paragraphs that the Air Staff shared Churchill's concern for a substantial future increase in German front-line strength.

Churchill's final concern was for the rate of production of air frames.

The Air Staff had already calculated that, working only one shift in three, the German aircraft factories could produce 270 air frames and 640 engines a month. On this Churchill commented:

We can hardly assume that the German Government has erected three times as many factories as it is able to staff, and we must therefore count upon these factories in the event of war being utilised to their full capacity, giving a monthly output of perhaps a thousand machines. I do not know what is the comparable British output, but I should be relieved to learn that it exceeds 300 to 350 machines a month.

If we assume a war wastage of 80 per cent a month, which is, I believe, the French estimate, this output (350) is not even sufficient to maintain our first line Metropolitan Air strength at its present number of 785 machines. Even if we have one machine in reserve for each first line aeroplane, the number of machines which we can keep in commission will drop below 500 at the end of the fourth month. The German Air Force, on the other hand, with its war-time output of a thousand per month, would be able to maintain a first line strength of 1,200–1,500 machines for an indefinite period.

Thus at the end of the fourth month the British Air Force would be nearer one-third than one-half of the German.

Churchill believed that 350 machines a month was the actual British maximum figure, and in their memorandum of June 26, the Air Staff confirmed this figure. They also confirmed Churchill's wider concern. 'As regards output of airframes and engines it may be said that Germany at present is ahead of us in her organisation for war production.'

The Air Staff answered Churchill's point about the fourth month of the war by arguing that Britain would have 'sufficient reserves' during that period to 'make good war wastage during the period when factories are turning from peace to war production'. But by transferring his calculation to the German figures, the German reserves could in fact already be counted as first line—as Churchill argued—since the German factories were already prepared for war production. This significant factor was noted in a Foreign Office minute on July 8 by Wigram, who wrote:

The Air Ministry explanation is that the peace reserve is intended to be adequate to cover the war wastage during the period after the outbreak of war prior to the completion of the change over of industry from a peace to a war basis. As the Germans are ahead of us in the organisation of industry, the change over will take a shorter period for them; and therefore, as I understand it, our peace-time reserve has to be larger than theirs.

Churchill's assessment of German first-line strength had also been confirmed by a most secret note sent to the Air Ministry from one of the best British observers, Colonel Christie,[1] who had informed them two months earlier: 'Members of the German Air Staff amongst themselves definitely reckon *all* machines housed with the Squadron in peacetime, ie nine "Frontstrength" aeroplanes plus six reserve aeroplanes, as being in the first line (Flugzeuge erster Linie), whereas you appear to limit "First Line Strength" to the nine machines of the "Frontstärke". Obviously therefore your conception of "First Line Strength" in the RAF is equivalent to the German "Frontstrength", but not to the German "Flugzeuge erster Linie".' As for Churchill's concern about British aircraft production, even within the Air Ministry the delays were much commented on. Indeed, on May 11 the Director of Production, Colonel Disney,[2] had minuted to the Air Staff: 'I cannot impress upon you too emphatically that I see no hope of obtaining the output we require unless and until the price question is settled, thus restoring confidence and trust in the Air Ministry on the part of aircraft manufacturers.'

Churchill had sent his memorandum of June 12, and the Air Staff reply, to Desmond Morton, who commented on July 10 that he did not see why the official posts in the German air parks, recruit depots and experimental stations should all be filled, as the Air Staff believed, by trained pilots, even if this was 'in accordance with our own procedure', and he also noted: 'There is still no desire on the part of the Air Staff to estimate the total number of German aircraft that might take the air on the first day of the war.' Morton suggested that Churchill should now reserve his energies 'for an inquiry into our own air rearmament, and as to whether it has proceeded satisfactorily along the lines promised in Parliament'.

On June 26, having read Churchill's memorandum of June 12, Swinton wrote to Hankey, not taking up Churchill's specific arguments, but angered by what he now regarded as interference:

[1] Malcolm Grahame Christie, 1881–1971. An engineer; and graduate of Aachen University. General Manager of the Otto Cokeoven Company of Leeds and President of the Otto Coking Corporation of New York. Served in the Royal Flying Corps, 1914–18, and in the Royal Air Force, 1919–30. Air Attaché, Washington, 1922–26; Berlin, 1927–30. A friend of Göring's, he worked closely with Sir Robert Vansittart in obtaining information about the German air force, and about German military plans, while on business journeys inside Germany between 1930 and 1938.

[2] Henry Anthony Patrick Disney, 1893–1974. Educated Marlborough and Caius College Cambridge, 2nd Lieutenant, Cambridgeshire Regiment, 1914; on active service in Italy; pilot, Royal Flying Corps; Wing-Commander, 1918. A director of several telegraph, telephone and cable companies, 1919–32. Director of Aeronautical Production, Air Ministry, 1936–38; Director of Armament and Equipment Production, 1938–40. Pilot Officer, RAF, 1940; served in India, 1943–45; Group Captain, 1944. Director, British Export Trade Research Organization, 1945–49. One of his four sons was killed in the Second World War.

I return Churchill's further paper about air strength, together with the comments of the Air Staff. I have no objection at all to both these being circulated to the CID; indeed, I think it would be a good thing to do so. But a question of principle arises here on which I think we should have Inskip's ruling. The Air Research Committee of the CID is concerned with research, and only indirectly with general policy. It is the object of the Air Research Committee to explore and undertake any useful research and experimental work in connection with air defence. It is not the business of that Committee to discuss German air strength, except insofar as an appreciation of probable German air strength affords us a test of the magnitude and character of the problem of air defence. Still less is it the business of that Committee to consider or advise upon the strength of the British Air Force. That is the function of the CID and the Cabinet.

In accordance with this obvious principle, all papers relating to German air strength and manufacturing capacity go direct to the CID, and are considered by them. The Prime Minister decided a good while ago that it would be reasonable to let the members of the Air Defence Research Committee have these papers. The reason for this was that Churchill was constantly propounding fallacious statements about German strength, and that as he was a member of the CID Sub-Committee on Air Defence Research, it would be a good thing to let him see the appreciations (which of course represent the combined work of the Air Staff, the Board of Trade Intelligence, and the Secret Service) on which the CID works. But that is a very different matter from discussing these questions on the ADR Sub-Committee. If an attempt is made to do so, I suggest that Inskip, as Deputy Chairman of the CID, must take the line that that would be quite out of order. Moreover, in view of recent events, it is for consideration how far these secret papers should any longer be given to Mr Churchill. . . .

Swinton went on to remind Hankey of 'the great undesirability of my supplying secret information to Churchill in any other way except by a CID paper'.

On June 29 Hankey sent a copy of Swinton's letter to Inskip. It was hoped, he wrote, that the Air Staff's reply to Churchill's memorandum of June 12 was so decisive that 'the matter will automatically come to an end'. He added: 'Wing Commander Warburton assures me that it is very convincing—but of course Mr Churchill does not want to be convinced!'

Hankey shared Swinton's annoyance that the subject of air strength, on which Churchill had obtained official information from the CID papers, was 'not really a subject for the Air Defence Research Committee', and he advised Inskip that if Churchill were to send in another reply of his own on the question of air strength 'the best plan would be for us to try and close the correspondence'. Inskip accepted Hankey's advice, minuting on June 30: 'I should be inclined to let the matter drop whether or not Mr Churchill accepts the last reply of the Air Staff. If he sends a controversial reply, the best answer is that the S/S for Air will take care to put Mr Churchill's comments and information before the CID.'

Churchill knew nothing of the extent to which he had aroused the disapproval of Swinton, Inskip and Hankey, and saw no reason either to hold back his questions, or to stop raising them confidentially with the Ministers concerned. Nor were his actual criticisms the cause of their disapproval. In official circles, at the very centre, there was a growing and acute concern about delays both in production and in experimental work, the two points on which Churchill had been pressing so hard. On June 29 Hankey wrote a note for Baldwin in which he echoed all Churchill's fears, with similar supporting evidence to that which Churchill had acquired. According to Hankey:

I have received a certain amount of evidence that the push and drive required in connection with the Defence Requirements programme—or perhaps I should say the realisation of the need for push and drive—has not penetrated very far below those who hold immediate responsibility. In particular, it has been suggested that it does not extend to establishments maintained by the services.

I have been told that some of those establishments are still being run very much on peace-time lines: that for relatively small and approved expenditure, authority has to be obtained from the Headquarter Department and tenders calling for contracts passed by Directors of Contracts.

The result, if my information is correct, is interminable delays involved by the bandying about of minutes and correspondence between the Service Departments and Technical experts on specifications. This was given to me as one of the causes of noticeable delays in experimental work.

At the end of June Churchill continued his correspondence with Inskip. 'I can't help being sorry,' Inskip wrote to him on June 24, 'that I should be supposed to be unwilling to "disturb the peace-time atmosphere of normal production". That is exactly what I *am* doing,' to which Churchill replied that same day:

I can of course only base myself upon your public statements. You declared a few days after taking office that you must observe the limitations not to disturb the normal course of trade, and you have argued in Parliament against emergency measures. No one would be more pleased than I to learn by some public statement of yours that you have freed yourself from these restrictions. Nothing that you have said to me even in private has led me to believe that you have reached any such decision.

Churchill also raised with Inskip the possibility of an invasion by airborne troops, once Germany had achieved total air mastery. After discussing Churchill's point with the Chiefs of Staff, Inskip replied that their view was that if the Germans were to achieve air mastery, they were more likely to increase the scale 'of bombing attacks against vulnerable points' than to try to launch a full-scale airborne invasion. Were there to be such an invasion, Inskip wrote, the Territorial Force 'would be ready to move quickly to any threatened point'. Inskip encouraged Churchill to express his fears. 'I have found some of your suggestions helpful,' he wrote in a second letter that same day, 'and I welcome any stimulus that you can apply to me.' Churchill replied on June 29, warning that the Territorials would be quite inadequate in the circumstances which Inskip envisaged:

Surely four Territorial Divisions in their present state of training and equipment could not make head against a quarter their number of trained Regular storm troops. If they were raised to full strength and given at least three months training in each year, and mechanised to a high degree, they would be an effective deterrent. Under present conditions it would be most unwise to count upon them until they had been three or four months mobilised.

In the political sphere Churchill received a word of warning, from his cousin Frederick Guest, who wrote to him on June 19:

It seems to me and to many other friends that you have in the House of Commons, particularly the new Members since 1935, that you have a God-given chance of coming straight to the top of the great Conservative Party. . . .

The rank and file know quite well that Baldwin is tired and that you could do it much better than anyone else and with the greatest ease. On the other hand they will not see the old man bullied as they are intensely and pathetically loyal to him.

I need not say any more, but this is the advice from someone who has been trying to help you one way and another for nearly thirty years.

I am convinced that this is the psychological moment in your career. On the other hand if you drive out or break down S.B. the party will simply & immediately crown N.C.

'You can lead the Conservative party,' Guest added, 'but you cannot break the Party machine.'

Churchill did not take his cousin's advice. Speaking in his constituency on June 20 he made one of his most outspoken public attacks on the Government's policy. 'Half-measures and procrastinations are the order of the day,' he declared. Leadership 'at the summit' was entirely lacking. He grieved to see Britain still remaining 'weak, careless and seemingly incapable of realising the awful degeneration which is taking place around her'. The country's defences had been allowed to fall into 'lamentable weakness', and the Government was responsible for this 'improvident neglect'. His speech continued:

At any rate my conscience is clear. I have done my best during the last three years and more to give timely warning of what was happening abroad, and of the dangerous plight into which we were being led or lulled. It has not been a pleasant task. It has certainly been a very thankless task. It has brought me into conflict with many former friends and colleagues. I have been mocked and censured as a scare-monger and even as a warmonger, by those whose complacency and inertia have brought us all nearer to war and war nearer to us all.

But I have the comfort of knowing that I have spoken the truth and done my duty, and as long as I have your unflinching support I am content with that. Indeed I am more proud of the long series of speeches which I have made on defence and foreign policy in the last four years, than of anything I have ever been able to do, in all my forty years of public life.

Churchill's friends continued to encourage him. 'You must not be afraid to speak out,' Abe Bailey wrote to him on June 21.

Another of Churchill's persistent concerns during 1936 was German arms expenditure on which Sir Henry Strakosch had sent him frequent and copious information. On June 25 the *Morning Post* had declared its support for Churchill's claim that since coming to power three years before, the Nazi regime had spent £1,240 million on armaments.

On June 30 a senior Treasury official, S. D. Waley,[1] noted in a departmental minute: 'Dr Schacht[2] told Mr Pinsent[3] recently that the

---

[1] Sigismund David Schloss, 1887–1962. Educated at Rugby and Balliol College Oxford. Entered the Treasury, 1910. Assumed the name of Waley (his mother's surname) in 1914. On active service, 1916–18 (Military Cross, 1917). Assistant Secretary, Treasury, 1924; Principal Assistant Secretary, 1931; Third Secretary, 1946–47. Knighted, 1943. Chairman of the Furniture Development Council, 1949–57. Chairman of Sadler's Wells Trust, 1957–62.

[2] Hjalmar Horace Greely Schacht, 1877–1970. Economist and banker. Assistant Manager, Dresdner Bank, 1908–15. Managing Partner, National Bank of Germany, 1915–22. Senior Partner, Schacht & Co., Bankers, of Düsseldorff. Reich Currency Commissioner, 1923. President of the Reichsbank, 1924–30; reappointed by Hitler, March 1933. Minister of Economics, 1934–37. Tried by the Nuremberg War Crimes Tribunal, 1946, but acquitted.

[3] Gerald Hume Saverie Pinsent, 1888–1976. Educated at King's School Canterbury and Trinity College Cambridge. Entered the Treasury, 1911; Assistant Secretary, 1931. Financial Adviser, British Embassy, Berlin, 1932–39; Washington 1939–41. British Food Mission, Ottawa, 1942–43. Principal Assistant Secretary, Board of Trade, 1943; Treasury, 1944. Comptroller-General, National Debt Office, 1946–51.

figures used by Mr Churchill were remarkably accurate and only slightly exaggerated.' That same day, in a Foreign Office minute, Wigram noted:

It seems to me that it is very important to let the country know the gigantic sums which the Germans are spending on armaments. The information in our possession, which generally coincides with that given by Mr Churchill and the 'Morning Post', shows that in 1935 the Germans spent on armaments a sum about equivalent to the whole of the British Budget, ie about £800 million; and are likely to spend as much, if not more this year.

Surely some means ought to be found of making people here realise this.

Churchill could not free himself from a sense of foreboding. 'I fear,' he wrote to Reginald Purbrick [1] on July 2, 'that by the summer of next year the Germans will be so strong as to dominate all our thoughts,' and on the following day, in a letter to Austen Chamberlain, Churchill supported Chamberlain's idea of a Secret Session of the House of Commons to examine 'the state of the nation'. As Churchill wrote: 'We do not wish to know all the secrets of defence. Indeed all that I want is to be able to debate the defence position with the same freedom as was possible in less dangerous years, and to receive answers from the Government which they would certainly give in ordinary times.' His letter went on: 'I think I could make a considerable case that a secret non-reported session would enable a far more searching debate to take place upon defence, particularly air defence, than is possible in public, and that little more would be known than what is current talk in the Smoking Room and the Lobbies.'

In Cabinet on July 6 Ramsay MacDonald, who had succeeded Baldwin as Lord President of the Council, asked whether his colleagues 'would welcome the prospect of having to face Mr Churchill's criticisms in Parliament'. If not, MacDonald added, 'one method that had occurred to him for meeting the difficulty was by inviting influential members of Parliament to a meeting of the Committee of Imperial Defence. . . .' Lord Swinton stated that at the Air Defence Research sub-committee Churchill's attitude 'had throughout been unhelpful. Instead of confining himself to the research question he had raised wider issues.' Inskip, on a more constructive note, reported on what Churchill had recently told him in the House of Commons Library about a Ministry of Supply. As Inskip explained: 'Mr Churchill's ultimate idea appeared to be to create a great office supervised by business men with a

---

[1] Reginald Purbrick, 1877–1950. Educated in Melbourne. Amateur boxing and walking champion, Australia. In commerce, 1900–21. Conservative MP for the Walton Division of Liverpool, 1929–45.

total staff of a thousand, and at a given moment, so to speak, to pull the lever and switch the whole of the munitions supply over to this new department.'

Churchill's opponents continued both to belittle his suggestions and raise doubts about his motives. On July 7 Thomas Jones recorded in his diary a comment by Baldwin, that to both Lloyd George and Churchill the Parliamentary battle 'is all part of a game'. But on the following day a former Conservative MP, Arthur Bateman, wrote to Churchill from Beckenham, in Kent: 'The same feeling exists in every Club and hotel I travel round, they would like to see you *PM* and it gains ground.'

Churchill persevered throughout July with his public campaign to rouse national opinion. Speaking at Birchington on July 10 he told his Kent audience: 'People must not allow themselves to be lulled into a sense of false security by the large sums of money now being spent. After the General Election there was much talk about the expenditure of £300,000,000 to put our defences in order. Actually the Supplementary Estimates over and above the Regular Estimates amount to about £30,000,000.' Churchill then referred to a recent speech by the Minister for the Coordination of Defence, in which Inskip had said: 'We have now reached the planning stage.' Churchill commented: 'Germany however has finished her planning stage three years ago, and her whole industry has long been adapted on an unexampled scale for war,' and he added: 'I regard it as my duty to keep up a remorseless pressure upon the Government to face the realities of the position, and to make exertions appropriate to our needs.'

On July 7 the Air Ministry circulated to senior officers a comprehensive chart of past expansion schemes, together with Scheme F, which the Cabinet had accepted on February 25, and by which Britain was to have 1,736 first-line aeroplanes for Home Defence by March 1939. Wing-Commander Anderson gave his charts to Churchill, who henceforth was able to calculate in detail the precise British air figures, and to use them confidentially in his correspondence and discussions with Cabinet Ministers.

During July Churchill was again in correspondence with Admiral Henderson. This time their correspondence was of an unofficial status. On July 13 Henderson sent Churchill details of bomb and shell experiments designed to test the impact of armour-piercing bombs dropped on ships from the air. Henderson noted: 'The striking energy of a 15 inch shell at 20,000 yards, however, is, as you estimate, almost exactly ten times that of a 500 lb bomb dropped from 12,000 feet.' Later in the year, on December 28, Churchill wrote to Hankey: 'My dear Maurice,

Included among the file I sent you a few days ago, was a letter from Admiral Henderson. Please treat this as absolutely private and do not mention or quote him to anyone. The point upon which I consulted him was one on which it was quite proper that he should express a purely scientific opinion; but I do not think he would expect his opinions to be cited. May I have your assurance therefore that all will be well?' Hankey replied that same day: 'My dear Winston, I have taken steps to withdraw Henderson's letter from the file, and, in reproducing, to eliminate all reference to the letter. I will treat it as absolutely private. . . .'

By the summer of 1936 the influence of Nazism had begun to penetrate beyond the German frontiers. Throughout western Poland, Nazi organizations were active, stirring the discontent of the local German minority. The Free City of Danzig, established as such by the League of Nations, was falling rapidly under Nazi control. In May a Fascist plot had been discovered in Estonia. With Mussolini drawing closer to Hitler, German pressure on Austria had begun anew. 'Everything is getting steadily worse upon the continent,' Churchill wrote to General Tudor on July 11. 'A good deal of work is of course going on here, but all about two years behind. What will these two years bring forth?'

On July 15, at the first meeting of the New Commonwealth since he had become its President, Churchill commented on his 'profound and gnawing anxiety' at the European situation, and spoke with grim foreboding of recent events, and of the immediate future:

The Austro-German agreement reported over the week end marks the end of the effort to prevent the addition of Austria to the mighty Nazi power. The progress of German fortifications in the Rhineland cuts off the small states of eastern and central Europe from the possibility of effective French assistance. The understanding established between Hitler and Mussolini about Austria frees German policy from immediate anxiety in that direction. The east and south of Europe therefore lie open, in a manner inconceivable a year ago, to the Nazi power animated by Prussian military efficiency and war spirit.

This cutting off of the east and centre of Europe from any possible assistance from the west, seems to me to portend further action by Germany in the near future. . . .

Very soon you may see such a vast gathering of countries from the Baltic to the Black Sea under German authority as would almost constitute a new and warlike League of Nations larger and far more heavily armed than what will be left at Geneva.

'Through our own folly and refusal to face realities and deal with evil tendencies while they were yet controllable,' Churchill added, 'we have allowed brutal and intolerant forces to gain almost unchallenged supremacy in Europe and have placed ourselves in a position of weakness and peril, the like of which our history does not record for two and a half centuries.'

Churchill repeated his warnings at a meeting of the Foreign Affairs Committee in the House of Commons on July 16. But Harold Nicolson, who was present, recorded in his diary: 'the majority of the National Party are at heart anti-League and anti-Russian', and that 'what they would really like would be a firm agreement with Germany and possibly Italy by which we could purchase peace at the expense of the smaller States'. Nicolson added: 'This purely selfish policy would to my mind make an Anglo-German war quite certain within twenty years. I do not believe that this mood will last, and I think that eventually Winston will be able to get a solid block for his League of restricted commitments and unlimited liabilities.'

Speaking in the House of Commons on July 20, Inskip gave an account of the progress of the defence programmes, in which he spoke of 'a swelling tide of production'. Churchill challenged this account as being 'based on a larger measure of anticipation than of reality'. But in his speech Churchill held back the points of detail which had been troubling him. 'I do not feel,' he said, 'that here today, in open debate in this Chamber, I should like the case which I feel capable of stating to be stated.' Later in his speech he declared: 'We have statements to make which we should like to have answered, but not before all the world. The times have waxed too dangerous for that.' Churchill pointed out to the House of Commons that Neville Chamberlain now accepted as reasonable his assertions, which had been supported by the *Morning Post*, that the Germans had spent £800 million on military production during 1935 alone, and he went on to contrast the German expenditure on new construction of £500 million with the parallel British figure of £75 million. His speech continued:

We are going away on our holidays. Jaded Ministers, anxious but impotent Members of Parliament, a public whose opinion is more bewildered and more expressionless than anything I can recall in my life—all will seek the illusion of rest and peace.

We are told, 'Trust the National Government. Have confidence in the Prime Minister, with the Lord President of the Council at his side. Do not worry. Do not get alarmed. A great deal is being done. No one could do more.' And the influence of the Conservative party machine is being used through a thousand channels to spread this soporific upon Parliament and the nation. But, I am bound to ask, has not confidence been shaken by various things that have happened, and are still happening?

Churchill told the House of Commons that he did not ask for the establishment of 'war conditions' for munitions production. That, he said, 'would not be necessary or helpful'. But he did plead for 'an intermediate stage between ordinary peace-time and actual war', whereby 'the whole spirit and atmosphere of our rearmament should be raised to a higher pitch', even though this would mean making inroads into civilian industry, and laying aside 'a good deal of the comfort and smoothness of our ordinary life'. Pointing out that the Government would probably refuse Austen Chamberlain's call for a Secret Session, he asked that at least they would agree to a 'small deputation' to discuss privately, with the Senior Ministers and the Prime Minister, their specific points of concern.

Outside Parliament, Churchill's speech provoked a serious and sympathetic response. 'If Mr Churchill's prophesies on these points ever prove accurate,' *The Times* first leader declared on July 21, 'the present practices can and must be changed,' but the *Daily Telegraph* noted: 'The breach between Mr Churchill and the Government was certainly not narrowed by his speech last night.' On July 21 Oliver Locker-Lampson telegraphed to Churchill: 'Your speech last night and the reactions in today's Press mark a peak point in your national importance.' That same day Churchill wrote to Lord Rothermere: 'As you will see I keep on trying my best. If as you say we are going to be vassals of Germany, I can only hope I shall not live to see it!' Churchill added: 'My information tallies with yours that Czecho-Slovakia will soon be in the news.'

After the debate, Desmond Morton prepared a memorandum for Churchill, commenting on sixteen specific points which Inskip had raised in his Commons speech. The first point to which Morton drew attention was Inskip's claim that the Supplementary Estimates constituted evidence of 'a swelling tide of production'. Morton pointed out that they were in fact 'nothing of the kind', being evidence only that steps were being taken 'to get industry into a condition *eventually* to produce what was required'. Morton's points continued:

2. The Minister stated that regular sources of supply are being used to their utmost capacity.

This means very little, since it is well known that the regular sources of supply have nowadays an insignificant capacity relative to what is required, either to make up the deficiencies in reserves, or to arm the nation's forces in war.

3. The Minister confessed that new firms, by which it is clear that he means all firms other than those referred to above as the regular sources of supply, have to be inspected, or classified etc and then have to learn a new technique of armament production.

This is ample evidence of the long delay that must ensue before output is reached.

4. The Minister said that the preliminary stages have been passed.

This however only applies to 52 firms of which only 14 have accepted definite contracts. The suggestion in the statement that the preliminary stage has been passed is therefore unacceptable. It has only been passed in the case of these 52 firms. How foreign countries must laugh when they learn that 52 firms—or in point of fact only 14—are the total now accepted upon which we can draw for armament manufacture! while the United States has inspected and planned several thousand firms, Germany is known to be employing at the moment several hundred firms in the manufacture of projectiles alone, and all other first class powers have at least planned on the same scale.

5. The Minister said that when all 52 firms are in production seven-eighths of the total requirements of the Government in shells and fuses and cartridge cases will have been provided.

Presumably this refers to the provision of ammunition to make up past deficiencies. Certainly the qualifying phrase that they have entered into production is therefore necessary, since apparently none of the 52, not even the 14 who have accepted firm contracts, have yet entered into production. Later in his speech the Minister admits that new firms have to be supplied with additional plant and machinery. Moreover, then, when that has been supplied and set up in the new factories, output cannot be reached for some further considerable time.

Even if these facts mean that in a year or so deficiencies in reserves of ammunition will have been made good, what steps have yet been taken to ensure an adequate supply in war?

6. The Minister admits that firms do not yet possess the necessary jigs to perform their contract.

How then can they enter into production?

Among two more of Morton's points were:

12. Forty new aerodromes have been or are being acquired.

It is a pity that the Minister found it impossible to say that the whole 40 had not only been acquired, but were in process of transformation into aerodromes. Like factories and industrial production it is quite inadequate to buy a piece of ground and then call it an aerodrome. In this present case it appears that an unknown proportion of the forty pieces of ground have not yet even been acquired.

This piece of information is valueless, unless it be known how many new aerodromes in all it is considered necessary for our defence to set up, and what proportion of these are emergency landing grounds, and what proportion aerodromes at which units will be stationed.

13. The Minister stated that in April, May and June of this year about three and a half times as many air frames, and twice as many engines had been delivered, as in the same months of the previous year.

Surely this confession betrays absolutely an unbalanced production. What is the good of an air frame without an engine? Seeing that a large proportion of air frames require, or should require if they are to be bombers, more than one engine, it is really necessary for at least one spare engine to be manufactured for every engine used in a machine. The engine proportion in this country appears to be hopelessly inadequate, relatively, to airframe production—which we know to be only too small.

Morton also pointed out the heavy reliance on imported machine tools, the admission that up to two years must elapse before the proposed new shell filling factories could start work, and that Inskip's 'hope and trust' to obtain sufficient skilled labour was not enough to ensure it. Morton's analysis ended:

The Minister states that we are still having a very careful examination of war material requirements in the event of war.

What a confession of slackness in the past, that this essential enquiry should not have been completed years ago, and in addition definite arrangements made for the supply of these raw materials should war come, and a reserve already collected of those raw materials the supply of which in war may be unduly difficult or delayed.

Morton's detailed criticisms, as expressed to Churchill, were reflected on July 23 at a meeting of the Cabinet's Defence and Policy Requirements Committee, when Swinton told his colleagues that the production of heavy bombers was falling 'below the numbers promised by the firms', while at a meeting of the full Cabinet on July 29 he explained that air deliveries for the whole programme 'were not up to 100% on promises; perhaps they were rather less than four-fifths'. At the same meeting Inskip again asked for special powers, as the shortage of building labour was 'threatening to hold up the reconditioning programme of the Services', but no such powers were granted.

38

July 1936: The Defence Deputation

FOLLOWING the debate of July 20, Baldwin refused a Secret Session, but agreed to receive a Parliamentary deputation, and to listen to its arguments. The deputation was to be led by Austen Chamberlain, Lord Salisbury and Churchill. Writing to Austen Chamberlain on July 21, Churchill strongly advised making it an all-party deputation and proposed the inclusion of Lloyd George and Archibald Sinclair for the Liberals, and Clement Attlee for the Labour Party. The first to refuse was Attlee, who wrote to Churchill that same day: 'I have considered the matter with my friends and I do not think it would be desirable for His Majesty's Opposition to follow this procedure at this juncture.' No further explanation was forthcoming. Later that day both Lloyd George and Sinclair also declined to join.

Speaking at Horsham on July 23, Churchill warned the Labour Party of the folly of its refusal to support rearmament. Socialists and Trade Unionists would be the largest group whom the Nazis, in their triumph, 'would chastise and discipline'. His speech continued:

I can well imagine some circles of smart society, some groups of wealthy financiers, and the elements in this country which are attracted by the idea of a Government strong enough to keep the working classes in order; people who hate democracy and freedom, I can well imagine such people accommodating themselves fairly easily to Nazi domination. But the Trade Unionists of Britain, the intellectuals of Socialism and Radicalism, they could no more bear it than the ordinary British Tory. It would be intolerable. . . .

Churchill went on to point out that although the official Labour, opposition still mocked at 'the most modest and reasonable precautions' there had grown up 'an increasing body of intelligentsia of the Left wing' who saw the need for strong defence measures both to defend Britain and also to uphold 'the cause of freedom'.

On the day after his Horsham speech Churchill gave a lunch at his London flat to ten senior members of the Anti-Nazi Council, including two influential Labour Party supporters, Sir Walter Citrine and Sir Norman Angell.[1] During the discussion, Churchill and Citrine both stressed the need 'for the enlightenment of public opinion', and a special research section was set up under the supervision of Henry Wickham Steed.[2]

In preparation for the Parliamentary deputation on July 28, Churchill, helped by Morton and Anderson, drafted a substantial statement. Baldwin, who turned to Hankey for guidance, himself received several pages of notes on what he should say. 'It is just possible,' Hankey wrote on July 24, 'that if the deputation is tiresome you may want to deal rather sharply with them, and I have tried to give you some material to meet that contingency.' In particular, Hankey gave Baldwin material on Churchill's part in the evolution of the Ten Year Rule, to enable him 'to speak rather pointedly about it'. Of course, Hankey added, 'in the presence of that particular deputation, you cannot say in so many words that Mr Churchill has a heavy responsibility in the matter'. Hankey advised Baldwin to say to the deputation: 'If some of my Right Hon friends search their memories, and still more if they refresh their memories from the records—as I myself have done—they will find that their responsibility for the "Ten Year Rule", perhaps the root cause of our accumulation of deficiencies, is very great indeed.'

Although in his notes Hankey sought to implicate Churchill for the Ten Year Rule deficiencies, he had to admit, and indeed to stress, the part played by the Labour Government of 1929 and the National Government of 1931. Of the Labour Government of 1929 he wrote: 'when a new Government came into office it was extremely difficult for it to reverse the decision of its predecessor', and yet, he pointed out, the Rule was actually re-examined every year 'and sometimes even more often', with a view to revision. It was, Hankey noted, 'not until 1932 that the Government of the day decided to cancel it', but, he added:

---

[1] The others present were Sir Robert Mond, Lady Violet Bonham Carter, Oliver Locker-Lampson, Duncan Sandys, Wickham Steed, Philip Guedalla and A. H. Richards.

[2] Henry Wickham Steed, 1871–1956. Educated at Sudbury Grammar School; Jena, Berlin and Paris. Joined *The Times*, as acting correspondent, Berlin, 1896; correspondent, Rome, 1897–1902; Vienna, 1902–13. Foreign Editor of *The Times*, 1914–19. Editor of *The Times*, February 1919 to November 1922. Proprietor and Editor of the *Review of Reviews*, 1923–30. Broadcaster on World Affairs for the Overseas Service of the BBC, 1937–47. Author of twenty volumes of history and current affairs.

'Even then it was extremely difficult to embark on any considerable expenditure on armaments, in the first place because the national crisis had brought the National Government into existence, with the rehabilitation of our finances as its first and paramount task; and, second, because the Disarmament Conference had begun work and a temporary truce in armaments had been agreed to.'

In another note for Baldwin, Hankey dealt with Churchill's estimate of the number of German aircraft. 'The deductions of a single individual,' Hankey wrote, 'however brilliant he may be, are less likely to provide a correct basis of calculation than those of the Government Department with their infinitely larger sources of information.' Hankey also advised Baldwin on how to answer Lord Trenchard, who had become critical of the Government's air planning procedure. The plans of 1914, Hankey wrote, were 'extremely defective'; Trenchard himself, 'was not particularly helpful in the matter of planning, and it might even be worth while to ask him how much planning he initiated in his time'. Hankey gave·Baldwin a further theme for possible argument:

It might, however, be as well to indicate that a point may easily be reached at which the concern of Members may become an embarrassment rather than a help. . . . The Deputation might be asked to bear in mind that, whatever may be the size of the staffs concerned, all these Debates and Questions and Inquiries fall, in the last resort, on Ministers and their senior officials, to the detriment of the insistent and exacting work of supervising the rehabilitation of the services.

Copies of Hankey's notes were sent to Lord Swinton and Neville Chamberlain. Hankey also supported Baldwin's view that none of the three Service Ministers, Swinton, Hoare and Duff Cooper, should be present at the meeting. 'I think what is in his mind,' Hankey wrote to Swinton on July 24, 'is that to do so would lend too much importance to the proceedings and might also render it more difficult to avoid answering questions put by the Deputation.'

The deputation met Baldwin on July 28, and again on July 29. As Hankey had suggested, none of the Service Ministers were present. At the first meeting Baldwin was accompanied by Sir Thomas Inskip and Lord Halifax, at the second by Inskip. The verbatim record of their discussion, and the documents submitted, covered forty printed pages.[1]

---

[1] The thirteen MPs on the deputation were Austen Chamberlain, Churchill, Sir Robert Horne, L. S. Amery, Sir John Gilmour, Captain Guest, Earl Winterton, Sir Henry Page Croft, Sir Edward Grigg, Viscount Wolmer, Lieutenant-Colonel Moore-Brabazon, Sir Roger Keyes and Sir Hugh O'Neill. The five Members of the House of Lords were the Marquess of Salisbury, Lord Trenchard, Lord Milne, Lord Lloyd and Viscount FitzAlan.

The meeting opened with a statement by Austen Chamberlain expressing 'grave anxiety and doubts' about the adequacy of Britain's defence programme. Lord Salisbury then commented on Britain's 'want of promptness' in responding to what had 'taken place abroad', and expressed his concern that even now the Government might not have either the necessary war materials 'to make head against those who might be our opponents', or have thought out 'the military policy which they would pursue in the various events which might take place'.

Churchill was the third speaker for the deputation. He began by giving full details of the French estimate of German air strength, a possible 2,000 first-line aeroplanes by the end of 1936. 'The Air Staff thought the French estimate too high,' he said. 'Personally, I think it is too low. . . . Moreover, there is no reason to assume that they mean to stop at 2,000.' He went on to contrast the war-making capacity of British and German industry, declaring that a three-fold increase in British preparations seemed 'urgent in the highest degree'. Modern war, he said, 'is based upon wholesale mass production rather than upon the superfine'.

Speaking of the relative air strengths of Britain and Germany, Churchill stressed the enormous efforts being made in Germany to train pilots and to practise 'night-flying under war conditions'. He then criticized Britain's air training facilities, basing himself on material which he had received from Wing-Commander Anderson. The educational standard, he said, 'is by no means high'. There was too great a stress on the Short-Service Entry. No doubt it would improve with time, he said, and he went on to ask: 'Shall we have time?' Far better, he said, to encourage longer-term engagements and higher educational standards. 'Everything turns,' he said, 'on the intelligence, daring, the spirit and firmness of character of the Air pilots.' There should be more permanent commissions, and more university candidates should be admitted. To date, only fifty were allowed to be commissioned each year.

Churchill went on to make one point on which Anderson had been most insistent, that observer-navigators must also be trained in much larger numbers, and with a much higher standard of education and intelligence. 'To use pilots as observers,' he said, 'is almost to halve your pilot strength.' Churchill then asked whether all the squadrons in the Air Force list were up to full strength. 'I have heard of one,' he said, 'that had only 30 airmen instead of 140.' And he continued:

When such strict interpretations are put forward of first-line air strength for the purpose of comparison with Germany, it is disconcerting to hear that many of our regular squadrons, not new ones in process of formation, but regular long-formed squadrons, are far below their strength, and have a large proportion, if not the whole, of their reserve aircraft either taken away for service in the Flying training schools or unprovided with the necessary equipment or even, in some cases, without engines. . . .

Other worries were also on Churchill's mind; the gap between the planning of an aircraft and its actual delivery, the need to manufacture in time sufficient armament for aeroplanes which each carried eight machine-guns, and the delay in providing spare parts in adequate numbers. 'I may emphasise the fact,' he said, 'that in this superfine sphere of the air, an aeroplane without everything is for all practical purposes an aeroplane with nothing. It may figure on your lists. It will not be a factor in actual fighting.'

Churchill then spoke of the German power to bomb London, and the lack of any real power on Britain's part either to bomb Germany, or to defend the British cities. The Germans, he said, could send a fleet of bombing planes to London capable of dropping 500 tons of bombs on a single journey; in 1918 one ton of bombs had been enough to kill 10 people and do £50,000 worth of damage to property. But the British bombing capacity alarmed him. 'The great bulk of our new heavy and medium bombers—even when they are produced—cannot do much more than reach the coasts of Germany from this island,' he said. 'Only the nearest German cities would be within their reach. In fact, the retaliation of which we should be capable this time next year from this Island would be puerile judged by the weight of explosive dropped, and would be limited only to the fringes of Germany.'

Churchill went on to ask what arrangements had been made to import food through 'subsidiary channels' once 'the feeding ports' of London, Southampton, Liverpool and Bristol had been bombed, and what plans existed to set up 'an alternative centre of Government' if London were to be 'thrown into confusion'. No doubt, Churchill said, 'there has been a discussion of this on paper', but had anything been done, he asked, 'to provide one or two alternative centres of command with adequate deep-laid telephone connections, and wireless from which the necessary orders can be given by some coherent thinking mechanism to the vast panic-stricken or infuriated population with whom we may have to deal'.

A few moments later, outlining the defensive measures which he believed were needed to protect Britain's oil fuel from attack, Churchill suggested underground storage tanks, and went on to ask 'Has this been

31. Major Desmond Morton

32. Wing-Commander Torr Anderson

33. Churchill at Chartwell with Ralph Wigram, a photograph taken by Ava Wigram in 1935

34. Sir Robert Vansittart, a photograph taken in 1934

35. Lord Londonderry and Joachim von Ribbentrop, a photograph
taken in 1936

36. Lord Swinton

37. Sir Thomas Inskip, a photograph taken on the morning of 14 March 1936, his first full day as Minister for Co-ordination of Defence

38. Sir Kingsley Wood, a photograph taken in 1938, shortly after he became Secretary of State for Air

39. Lord Beaverbrook, a photograph taken in 1938

40. Churchill at French military manoeuvres, Aix-en-Provence, 9–10 September 1936

41. At manoeuvres, Aix-en-Provence

42. The Château de l'Horizon, Maxine Elliot's villa at Golfe Juan, South of France. Churchill was a frequent visitor; it was here that he wrote many of his books and articles

43. Violet Pearman, Churchill's Private Secretary for nine years, from 1929 to 1938. She is seen here on board Lord Moyne's yacht 'Rosaura', during Mr and Mrs Churchill's visit to the eastern Mediterranean in 1934. During the journey Churchill dictated to Mrs Pearman his film scenario, 'The Reign of King George V'

44. Churchill and his son Randolph at Chartwell, a photograph taken by Ava Wigram in 1935

45. Churchill leaving 10 Downing Street during the Czechoslovak crisis, 10 September 1938

46. Churchill at Le Bourget airport during the Czechoslovak crisis, 21 September 1938. With him is his European Literary Agent, Emery Revesz

47. Lord Halifax, Georges Bonnet and Neville Chamberlain in Paris, 24 November 1938

48. Léon Blum and Churchill, a photograph taken at Chartwell on 10 May 1938

49. Churchill at Chartwell, a photograph taken in February 1939

50. Bill Deakin, Churchill's research assistant from 1936 to 1939.

51. Churchill at work on his history of the English-speaking Peoples, a photograph taken at Chartwell, and published in 'Picture Post' on 25 February 1939

52. Churchill at Chartwell, March 1939. With him is Stefan Lorant, editor of 'Picture Post'.

53. Churchill and Stefan Lorant at Chartwell, March 1939

54. Churchill fishing at Consuelo Balsan's house near Paris, St Georges Motel, a photograph taken by Paul Maze in the third week of August 1939; Churchill returned to London on August 23

55. A poster in the Strand, London, photographed on 24 July 1939

The TATLER

Vol. CLIII. No. 1993. London, September 6, 1939   POSTAGE Inland 1½d.; Canada and Newfoundland 1½d., Foreign 1d.   Price One Shilling

NOT A CABINET PORTRAIT.—UNFORTUNATELY

Just a snap of Mr. Winston Churchill and Major Anthony Eden walking to the House of Commons for one of last week's momentous debates. They represent, in their political life, the fighting spirit which any act of injustice arouses in the breast of the average Briton. Soldiers both—and neither of them able to spell the word " fear." If we are to have an Inner War Cabinet, it is difficult to see how either of them can be left out of it

56. Churchill and Anthony Eden on their way to the House of Commons for the recall of Parliament on 29 August 1939. This photograph was published on the front page of 'The Tatler' on 6 September 1939

57. Churchill leaving Morpeth Mansions, London, for the House of Commons, on the outbreak of war, 3 September 1939. Carrying his despatch box is Kathleen Hill, his Private Secretary from 1938 to 1946

done?', giving his own answer: 'I say it has not been done. It may have been talked of, but it has not been begun.'[1]

Churchill's next area of questioning was that of the work being done to destroy raiding aeroplanes from the ground. The practical results of the Air Defence Research sub-committee, he said, 'have been almost entirely negative'. Even radar, the one 'potent discovery', would not be ready in 1937, or even in 1938 or 1939. 'I have been disappointed in the rate of progress,' he said, 'and in the reluctance to make large-scale experiments in rapid succession'. Despite the setting up of anti-aircraft batteries in the hands of Territorials, London remained 'highly vulnerable' against day-time raids, and 'completely defenceless' against night bombing.

In his concluding remarks Churchill set out his priorities, and expressed his deepest fears:

. . . ought we not to increase the development of our Air power in priority over every other consideration? At all costs we must draw the flower of our youth into piloting aeroplanes and observing from them. We must draw from every source by every means. We must accelerate and simplify our aeroplane production and push it to the largest scale, and not hesitate to make contracts with the United States and elsewhere for the largest possible quantities of aviation material and equipment of all kinds.

I say there is a state of emergency. We are in danger as we have never been in danger before—no, not in the height of the submarine campaign. I will return to this to-morrow in connection with the supply of munitions and equipment.

Meanwhile, permit me to end upon this thought which preys upon me. The months slip by rapidly. If we delay too long in repairing our defences, we may be forbidden by superior power to complete the process.

Churchill was followed by each of the remaining members of the deputation. 'All subsequent speeches,' Thomas Jones noted, 'were an anti-climax.' Nevertheless, they constituted a formidable array of suggestions and criticisms. Lord Trenchard supported Churchill's arguments about the need for a higher standard of Air Force recruitment, and the harmful effects on morale of the bombing of British cities. Sir Edward Grigg spoke of serious production difficulties in the aircraft industry, and of the continuing reluctance of factory directors to incur capital expenditure on new plant, floor space and personnel. Frederick Guest wanted the higher echelons of the Air Force to be

---

[1] On the outbreak of war in September 1939 there were seven million tons of fuel oil in store for Naval requirements. Yet under the existing pre-war plans only 380,000 tons (1/18th of the total stock) could be protected underground, while a further million tons allocated for protection could not be put underground until the end of 1941.

strengthened by emergency appointments from the other Services, as most of the senior officers had, he said, been either 'superannuated or retired', and the 'whole burden' had fallen on young and inexperienced officers. Leopold Amery proposed 'some form of national organisation' to unite not only the Ambulance, Fire and Fighting services, but also all factory, railway and dockyard workers with 'the very maximum of enthusiasm'.

Speaking for a second time, Sir Edward Grigg said that many of his former military colleagues, some now in high commands, were 'profoundly anxious' about the state of recruiting, training and equipment in the Army, and of the 'entirely inadequate' reserves. Grigg elaborated his criticisms with much technical detail. He was followed by Sir Henry Page Croft, who also warned of the lack of public interest in recruitment, and of 'the danger to Home Defence' if such an attitude were allowed to continue. Lord Winterton spoke likewise of the need for greater Government action to stimulate the recruitment of Territorials. Baldwin himself, Winterton urged, should warn the people that unless they were prepared to defend their country, they would lose it.

When the deputation reassembled on the following day Austen Chamberlain asked both Churchill and Sir Robert Horne to speak about the munitions situation. Churchill first reviewed Germany's progress since January 1933 in 'transferring industry to war', and then spoke at length of the problems which had beset British industry since the first few military orders had been given to civil industry in May 1936, incorporating the detailed arguments which Desmond Morton had sent him after Inskip's speech of July 20. Compared to what had been done in Germany, Churchill insisted, 'Britain's efforts were still on a minute scale', and he continued, with a reference to 1914: 'Whether your army is to be one million or two millions or only 500,000 or 600,000 an enormous plant will be needed because you will have, as we had in those days, millions of people volunteering, clamouring to be given weapons, and there were then no weapons except for our Regular Forces.'

Churchill went on to speak of many specific items, including ammunition, tanks, lorries and armoured cars, for which, he argued, 'our industry, which is so comprehensive and variegated', should be made to contribute on a substantial scale. He was worried also about the shortage of machine-guns, bombs, poison-gas, gas-masks, searchlights, trench mortars and grenades. The Admiralty was also dependent on the War Office for such items, he pointed out, and a shortage of any one of them 'would cause grave injury to the Navy'. Churchill went on to ask:

'What is the conclusion? It is that we are separated by at least two years from any appreciable improvement in the material processes of national defence so far as concerns the volume of supplies for which the War Office has hitherto been responsible, with all the reactions which that entails on the Navy and War Office, but on the scale on which we are now acting even at the end of two years the supply will be petty compared to the needs of a national war, and melancholy compared to what others have already secured in time of peace. . . .'

Churchill continued:

Complaint is made that the nation is unresponsive to the national needs, that Trade Unions are unhelpful, that recruiting for the Army and Territorial Forces is very slow, and even obstructed by certain elements of public opinion. We see the Socialists even voting against the Estimates, and so forth.

As long as they are assured by the Government that there is no emergency those obstacles will continue, but I believe they will all disappear if the true position about foreign armaments is set before the public and if the true position about our own condition is placed before them, placed before them not by words, not by confessions, but placed before them by actions which speak louder than words, measures of State ordering this, that and the other, by events, by facts which would make themselves felt when people see this was happening here and that happening there. . . .

'I do not at all ask that we should proceed to turn ourselves into a country under war conditions,' Churchill ended, 'but I believe that to carry forward our progress of munitions we ought not to hesitate to impinge to a certain percentage—25 per cent, 30 per cent—upon the ordinary industries of the country, and force them and ourselves to that sacrifice at this time.'

After Sir Robert Horne had supported Churchill's appeal, Baldwin addressed the deputation, telling them at the outset: 'I cannot attempt to deal in detail with the many points that have been raised.' There was also to be borne in mind, he said, 'the temper of our people'; the moment war ended in 1919 they thought there would 'never be another one'. In addition, he said, Britain had 'suffered' from the Ten Year Rule, and from the earlier economies of the immediate post-war years which had affected all three Service departments. Referring to Churchill's two years as Secretary of State for War, in 1919 and 1920, Baldwin declared: 'Partly owing to the admirable management of the then Secretary of State, I think probably the War Office was skinned more than any of them.' Baldwin then touched on the electoral considerations which had hampered Government action in 1933, 1934 and the first half of 1935, telling the deputation:

Most of you sit for safe seats. You do not represent industrial constituencies; at least, not many of you. There was a very strong, I do not know about pacifist, but pacific feeling in the country after the war. They all wanted to have nothing more to do with it, and the League of Nations Union have done a great deal of their propaganda in making people believe they could rely upon collective security, and it was a question in 1934 whether if you tried to do much you might not have imperilled and more than imperilled, you might have lost the General Election when it came.

I personally felt very strongly, and the one thing in my mind was the necessity of winning an election as soon as you could and getting a perfectly free hand with arms. That was the first thing to do in a democracy, the first thing to do, and I think we took it at the first moment possible.

For some time a great many powerful influences were against me on that. They wanted to postpone the election until 1936, and I think the Central Office was against me, as we are all Tories here together, but it was wrong. We took it at the first moment we could and we had two elements with us, and I think we used them to the full. The first was people had begun to realise what Hitler meant, and, secondly, that time coincided with a great wave of feeling for what they called collective security.

As a result of the election victory in 1935, Baldwin added, 'you had the support of the democracy for your armaments'. But, he said, 'people will only learn, unfortunately, in a democracy by butting their heads against a brick wall'. He then spoke of the effect on trade of turning the peace-time economy even half-way towards war conditions. 'That is a question which I have thought about a great deal,' he said. He had discussed it 'mainly' with the Chancellor of the Exchequer, Neville Chamberlain. Both of them had felt that to disturb peace-time production 'might throw back the ordinary trade of the country perhaps for many years. It has never been done in peace time, throw it back for many years and damage very seriously at a time when we might want all our credit, the credit of the country.'

Baldwin went on to raise doubts about 'the peril itself', and in particular about the possibility of a war between Britain and 'Germany alone'. He asked the deputation if they were really prepared to warn people that Germany 'is arming to fight us', and he added:

It is not easy when you get on a platform to tell people what the dangers are. I have not dotted the i's and crossed the t's, but I have often spoken of the danger to democracy from dictators which I think is the one line whereby you can get people to sit up in this country, if they think dictators are likely to attack them. I think that is so, and I have always found it, but I have never quite seen the clear line by which you can approach people to scare them but not scare them into fits.

Speaking of Hitler, Baldwin told the deputation: 'none of us know what goes on in that strange man's mind', and he added: 'We all know the German desire, and he has come out with it in his book, to move East, and if he should move East I should not break my heart. . . . I do not believe she wants to move West because West would be a difficult programme for her. . . .' Baldwin's statement ended:

I am not going to get this country into a war with anybody for the League of Nations or anybody else or for anything else. There is one danger, of course, which has probably been in all your minds—supposing the Russians and Germans got fighting and the French went in as the allies of Russia owing to that appalling pact they made, you would not feel you were obliged to go and help France, would you? If there is any fighting in Europe to be done, I should like to see the Bolshies and the Nazis doing it.

Sir Thomas Inskip then promised the deputation that everything that had been said would be 'studied and checked and considered'. Nor did he feel justified, he said, in criticizing Churchill's statement 'so far as German capacity and output in munitions is concerned'. He agreed also that, whatever the precise figures of aircraft might be, Germany had clearly made herself 'supremely strong' in the air. 'It does not seem to me,' he said, 'to matter very much whether it is 2000 or 3000 or 5000 aeroplanes. . . .' Inskip went on to agree with a suggestion that Churchill had made, to purchase aircraft abroad. As for the need to anticipate the bombing of London, he said, 'We have prepared in detail, with the co-operation of the Railways, a cut and dried plan, not merely pigeon-holed but cut and dried, with the organisation for the evacuation of half the population of London.' As for the training of Air Force personnel, he said, 'the numbers are better than Mr Churchill gave. . . . I think they are a good deal better.' The quality of the Short-Service personnel was, he insisted, 'quite first-class', even though the applicants did not come 'from what might be called the first-class public schools'.

When the meetings were over, Baldwin submitted the transcript of what had been said to the Air Ministry, the Admiralty and the War Office. 'I understand there is no great urgency for this examination,' Hankey wrote to Swinton, Hoare and Duff Cooper on July 30. 'It is the facts and not an answer for public consumption that the Prime Minister has asked for.' Each of the Service Ministries completed their memoranda by mid-September; the Air Ministry's filled eighteen printed pages, the War Office's nineteen and the Admiralty's fourteen. Every point raised by Churchill and his colleagues was examined, some in detail, some cursorily. While considering the answers for the War Office, Military Intelligence sought the help of the Industrial Intelligence Centre, and on August 24 Desmond Morton sent its answers to Colonel Ismay. Morton's comments included the declaration that: 'The statement that Germany was planning the mobilisation of industry with a view to rearmament for some years before the National Socialist Government came to power, is correct.' Defending another of Churchill's points, Morton informed the War Office: 'The idea conveyed that the Germans do not hesitate to scrap accumulated armament stores in the event of the discovery and acceptance of definitely improved types, is correct. Incidentally, this is one of the more striking features of the present German rearmament policy.'

Among the points made in the Air Ministry memorandum were some which supported Churchill's allegations, and some that did not. In their reply the Air Ministry stressed that although it might not yet be possible to bomb Berlin, as Churchill had stated, the more important targets of the Ruhr and the Saar could already be attacked, and by July 1937 there would be new aircraft capable of bombing even Berlin. As for Churchill's claim that by the end of 1937 the German air preponderance would be increased, this was 'in the region of speculation'.[1] Nor did they agree with Churchill's view of German air efficiency, stating that German training, organization and equipment all laboured under 'the deficiencies which are to be expected from an attempt to produce a large air force in a very short space of time'. Of Churchill's criticism that there had been no increase in pilot recruitment, the Air Ministry countered by pointing out that there had been a 50 per cent increase in permanent commissions entry, that is to say the university entry had risen from 15 pilots to 25 a year, and the school entry from 53 to 75 pilots. The quality, they added, 'has been as high or higher than before'.

Among Churchill's points which the Air Ministry supported were the following:

It is agreed that the potential war output of the British aircraft industry is not equal to that of the Germans. The efforts of the Air Ministry have been concentrated on the immediate exigencies of the expansion programme, and steps have not yet been taken to deal with the question of war supply.

[1] Churchill's warnings about the unrecognized German Air Force potential, although dismissed, were well-founded. By October 1937 the Air Ministry had finally come to recognize that the preponderance of the German Air Force was on the scale he had consistently forecast for more than three years. On 12 October 1937 Lord Swinton referred to Britain's position of 'grave inferiority to Germany in effective air strength' (see page 881).

Mr Churchill is probably correct when he says that the German plan of production is on the basis of widespread manufacture of components, fitted together in large assembling plants. As far as is known at present, however, this plan of production has only been put into practice by the Junkers firm, and, possibly, by the Heinkel firm. It may be extended to other firms in due course, but it is known that in May 1936 it had not been so extended.

It is agreed that so far as airframes and engines are concerned, the German aircraft industry is running 'easy', and have a very considerable power of rapidly increasing its output.

Mr Churchill suggests that in numbers of aircraft the programme will not be completed by the appointed date. It is admitted that there will be a delay of approximately three months in the completion of the 1937 programme. The principal reason for this is the failure of the aircraft industry to keep to the delivery programme.

Among the points which the Air Ministry challenged was Churchill's demand that industry should be asked, and if necessary compelled, to undertake substantial defence contracts. In its memorandum the Air Ministry noted that in arranging their programme it had been considered 'essential to do everything possible to allow the firms concerned to carry on with their export and civil work, and so create revenue for the country and themselves'.

The War Office memorandum agreed with most of Churchill's contentions in the military and industrial sphere, which it described as 'perfectly correct'. Of the problems of Home Defence, the War Office agreed 'that the present situation is unsatisfactory', and on another point it commented:

Mr Winston Churchill has given his opinion that Germany's enormous war preparation will enable her to launch her first offensive on a 1918 scale; that this may prevent a stalemate of trench warfare; and that, therefore, we shall have no breathing space in which to organise the nation, as we did in 1915. Although no one can say whether or not this prophecy will be fulfilled, the danger that it may be fulfilled is sufficiently great to be taken into serious account.

The Admiralty memorandum likewise concentrated on Churchill's charges and suggestions, and sought to show 'that the problems to which Mr Churchill has referred are engaging close attention'. This was indeed so; Churchill's long campaign to draw attention to the many deficiencies had undoubtedly contributed to the greater alertness with which each problem was being dealt. But politically there was still no intention of following Churchill's appeal for an emergency programme of defence preparation, and this attitude affected the Government's response. No urgency was seen in examining the deputation's arguments, and on September 11, while the various departmental comments were being completed, Hankey wrote to Orme Sargent: 'I am rather reluctant to call for a new review of the strategical situation.' Four days later, at a meeting of the Cabinet's Joint Planning Committee, it was decided that 'in no circumstances' should the departmental comments be shown to Churchill, or to any other member of the deputation. 'The inevitable result of such a step,' Swinton told his colleagues, 'would be a counterblast from the Deputation, with all the waste of time which this would involve.'

39

Foreign Affairs:
Towards France or Germany?

DURING July civil war broke out in Spain, where a group of military leaders, having first established a base in Spanish Morocco, embarked in Spain itself upon a concerted attempt to destroy the Republican Government. On July 30 the 'insurgents', as they were first called, set up a Government of their own at Burgos, but in Madrid and Barcelona the revolt was crushed, and elsewhere in Spain committees of anti-Fascist militia, supported by the Spanish Communists, were set up to defend the Republic.[1]

In Britain, as in France, the outbreak of the Spanish civil war divided opinion, and the conflict, quickly simplified in people's minds to one of Fascism versus Communism, seemed to mirror Europe's growing divisions. When Hitler and Mussolini declared their support for the insurgents, and Stalin expressed his support for the Republic, those divisions seemed even clearer. There was much talk of Republican France helping the Spanish Republicans, and of Fascist Italy helping the insurgents. Churchill deprecated any such developments, writing to the French Ambassador, Charles Corbin,[2] on July 31:

I think I ought to let you know that in my judgment the great bulk of the Conservative Party are very much inclined to cheer the so-called Spanish rebels. One of the greatest difficulties I meet with in trying to hold on to the old position is the German talk that the anti-Communist countries should stand together. I am sure if France sent aeroplanes etc to the present Madrid

[1] In contemporary letters and documents the 'insurgents' were also referred to as the 'rebels', 'patriots', 'nationalists', 'fascists' and 'anti-reds'. The Republican Government was likewise variously described as 'the government', the Republicans', 'the Communists' and 'the Reds'.

[2] André Charles Corbin, 1881–1970. Attaché, 1906; Chief of the Press Service, French Foreign Office, 1920. French Ambassador to Madrid, 1929–31; to Brussels, 1931–33; to London, 1933–40. Honorary knighthood, 1938.

Government, and the Germans and Italians pushed in from the other angle, the dominant forces here would be pleased with Germany and Italy, and estranged from France. I hope you will not mind my writing this, which I do of course entirely on my own account. I do not like to hear people talking of England, Germany and Italy forming up against European Communism. It is too easy to be good.

Churchill ended with his own suggestion as to how the other European powers should behave. 'I am sure,' he wrote, 'that an absolutely rigid neutrality with the strongest protest against any breach of it is the only correct and safe course at the present time. A day may come if there is a stalemate, when the League of Nations may intervene to wind up the horrors. But even that is very doubtful.' On August 7 Churchill wrote to Anthony Eden at the Foreign Office:

This Spanish business cuts across my thoughts. It seems to me most important to make Blum[1] stay with us strictly neutral, even if Germany and Italy continue to back the rebels and Russia sends money to the government. If the French government take sides against the rebels it will be a god-send to the Germans and pro-Germans.

Churchill asked Eden, if he could 'spare a moment', to read his forthcoming article on Spain in the *Evening Standard*. The article was published on August 10. In it Churchill described the Spanish civil war as 'a sinister and, perhaps, a fatal milestone on the downward path of Europe'. Both sides were desperate. Both were resorting to 'cruelties and ruthless executions'. The victory of either side could only be followed by 'a prolonged period of iron rule'. Meanwhile, Churchill urged, Britain and France should not only observe 'the strictest neutrality' themselves, but should encourage other powers likewise to remain neutral. If France were to support the Spanish Communists, or Britain to support the rebels, it might 'injure profoundly the bonds which unite the British Empire and the French Republic'.

'I was most interested to read your article in the Evening Standard,' Anthony Eden wrote on August 12. It was, he said, 'timely and helpful', and while he did not agree with every sentence, 'I do agree emphatically with its concluding paragraphs.' Collective neutrality, Eden added, was clearly the right policy to work from even though it was more

---

[1] Léon Blum, 1872–1950. Born in Paris, of Jewish parents. Chef du Cabinet, Minister of Public Works, 1914. Deputy for Paris, 1919. Prime Minister, June 1936–June 1937. Vice-President of the Cabinet, 1937–38. Prime Minister and Finance Minister, March–April 1938. Interned in Germany, 1941–45. Prime Minister and Foreign Minister, December 1946–January 1947. President of the French Socialist Party.

difficult for Blum—with his Popular Front government which included Communists—than for Britain.

On August 21, in a further article in the *Evening Standard*, Churchill referred to the viciousness of the war in Spain. The cruelties of the 'violent Reds' were, he wrote, 'matched by equally bloody and sense-less retaliation'. The rage of the contestants had become 'sub-human', effacing not only every rule of civilized society, but also 'the calculations of common prudence'. However the Spanish civil war might end, Churchill wrote, both Britain and France would be seriously weakened, and 'the growing ascendancy of Nazism' proportionately accelerated.[1]

During August Churchill took little part in public controversy, although he protested privately to Anthony Eden about the proposed Anglo-Egyptian Treaty. 'I am personally deeply disturbed,' he wrote on August 22, 'about what is being done without Parliament having any inkling. No doubt with the aid of the Socialists, the Government will be able to carry anything of this kind.' Churchill's main effort during August was devoted to finishing his third *Marlborough* volume. Throughout the month, C. C. Wood[2] despatched the page proofs from Harraps, while Pakenham-Walsh completed the sixty-seven maps which were a striking feature of the volume, and Deakin scrutinized the final proofs. Sending the proofs of the last chapter to Deakin in Oxford on August 14, Churchill wrote: 'I think the chapter requires to be enriched at various points and clamped together. Pray study the points marked and bring this back with you on Monday.'

On August 24 Churchill left England for France, spending a few days painting at Consuelo Balsan's château near Dreux. He had been suffer-ing for some months from severe indigestion, and found that he could only paint in comfort standing up. 'Of course painting always tries me highly,' he wrote to Dr Thomas Hunt[3] on August 28, 'but I cannot give

---

[1] Churchill also gave personal advice to the Nationalists. After an interview with the Marques del Moral—who had brought evidence of Communist atrocities in Spain—Churchill 'stressed to him the extreme importance of the victors showing mercy to the rank and file' (as Mrs Pearman wrote on October 31 to Anthony Eden's Private Secretary).

[2] Charles Carlisle Wood,   –1959. Elder brother of Robert Wood, the 'Camden Town Murderer', aquitted in 1907 after a famous trial involving Marshall Hall. Joined the pub-lishing firm of Harrap in 1912; subsequently Head of the Editorial Department. Retired, 1940, but continued to proof-read for Churchill. At Chartwell, proof-reading was known as 'wooding'.

[3] Thomas Cecil Hunt, 1901–1980. Educated at St Paul's School and Magdalen College Oxford. Scholarship in anatomy, 1922; in pathology, 1924. Medical Registrar, St Mary's

it up on my holidays. It is the mental concentration which seems to affect the stomach.'

On August 30 Churchill was in Paris, where he stayed at the Ritz. While in Paris he lunched with the French politician Georges Mandel.[1] Deakin, who had been summoned by telegram in order to collect the final *Marlborough* proofs, joined them at lunch. Later he recalled how Mandel 'gave Winston a long lecture explaining that the British and French had lost everything. We had given it all away. We were going to lose Eastern Europe and the Balkans.' It was, Deakin recalled, 'a most depressing lunch', as Mandel continued to list the catalogue of disasters, telling Churchill: ' "It's finished. We're going to be at a disadvantage. There is a total breakdown of the balance of power in Europe"—he spat it out.'

While still in Paris, Churchill and Deakin also saw General Georges,[2] who reiterated Mandel's warning 'that too much had been given away'. Churchill accepted Georges' invitation to attend the military manoeuvres near Aix-en-Provence on September 9, and then, five days later, to inspect the Maginot Line.

On the evening of September 1 Churchill left Paris by train for Cannes, reaching Maxine Elliot's Château de l'Horizon on the following day. There he painted and recuperated from the political strains of the past months. 'I have been painting all day and every day,' he wrote to his wife on September 5. 'I have found a beautiful clear river—the Loup—& a quiet wild spot, & I study the clear water. I have done two variants which I hope you will admire as much as I do!' Churchill had also begun writing a series of thirteen articles on 'Great Events of Our Time' for the *News of the World*. 'I mean to do at least three before I

Hospital, Paddington, 1928–30; subsequently Consulting Physician. An authority on peptic ulcers and digestive diseases. President of the British Society of Gastro-enterology. Lieutenant-Colonel, Royal Army Medical Corps, 1940–44, West and North Africa; Brigadier, 1944–45, Persia and Iraq.

[1] Jeroboam Rothchild, 1885–1944. Of Jewish parentage, born near Paris. Took the name of Georges Mandel. Joined Clemenceau's Staff on *L'Aurore*, 1903. Chef de Cabinet to Clemenceau, 1906–09 and 1917–19 (during Clemenceau's two premierships). In charge of the trials dealing with treason and defeatism, 1917–18. Elected to the Chamber of Deputies, 1920. Minister of Colonies, April 1938–May 1940. Minister of the Interior, May–June 1940, when he arrested many Nazi sympathizers. Assassinated by Vichy militia, 1944.

[2] Joseph Géorges, 1875–1951. Entered the French Infantry, 1897. Chief of Staff to Marshal Foch, 1918. Head of the French Economic Service in the Ruhr, 1923. Chief of Staff to Marshal Pétain, 1925–26. Chef de Cabinet in the Maginot Government, 1929. Commanded the 19th Corps in Algeria, 1931. Wounded in Marseilles at the time of the assassination of King Alexander of Yugoslavia, 1934. Created Generalissimo, 1934. Commander of the Forces and Operations in the North East, 1939–40. A member of the French Committee of National Liberation, 1943.

leave,' he told his wife. 'They are vy lucrative. It wd be folly not to work them off in view of many uncertainties.'[1] Churchill also commented on events in Spain. 'I am thankful the Spanish Nationalists are making progress,' he told his wife. 'They are the only ones who have the power of attack. The others can only die sitting. Horrible! But better for the safety of all if the Communists are crushed.'

On September 8 Churchill travelled from Cannes to Aix-en-Provence. That day Ava Wigram wrote to him about the visit she and her husband had made to Germany. The purpose of the journey had been to inspect the British Consulates. Each Consul, she wrote, had shared their own view about Germany. 'It is only the visitors who go there for a few days,' she wrote, 'who come away with a false impression.' Four days earlier, on September 4, Lloyd George had visited Hitler at Berchtesgaden. Both men had agreed on the dangers of a Communist victory in Spain. At a second meeting on September 5 Lloyd George called Hitler 'the greatest German of the age', who had restored Germany's honour and made the whole world acknowledge 'her equality of rights'.

Throughout September 9 Churchill followed the French Army manoeuvres, accompanying the senior officers on their tour of the battlefield. 'I have had a most interesting day with General Gamelin[2] at the manoeuvres,' Churchill wrote to Léon Blum that evening. 'I was very pleased with all I saw,' and on the morning of September 10 he followed the manoeuvres in their final phase, before returning to the Château de l'Horizon. On his way back to the château, on September

---

[1] By 28 December 1936 Churchill had contracted for a total income for 1937 of £13,630 from his books and articles alone: £2,880 from the *Evening Standard*, £4,200 from the *News of the World*, £3,500 for *Marlborough* Volume IV, £1,250 for a series of articles on the Coronation and £1,800 for six articles in *Colliers* magazine. A further £3,000 was due as Parliamentary salary, share income and sundry fees. From this total sum of £16,630 he had to pay £4,400 for income tax and super tax for the previous tax year 1935–36. Professor Lindemann provided detailed notes for the scientific articles, and Marshall Diston prepared for Churchill a set of extracts and materials from Churchill's own books and speeches for the historical ones.

[2] Maurice Gustave Gamelin, 1872–1958. Born in Paris. 2nd Lieutenant, 1893. Lieutenant-Colonel, 1914. Served on General Joffre's Staff, 1911–17; drafted the principal directives at the battle of the Marne, 1914. Commanded a brigade during the battle of the Somme, 1916. Commanded the 9th Infantry Division, 1917–18. Military Assistant to the Syrian High Commissioner, 1925–28, when he defeated the Druse rebellion. Commanded the 20th Army Corps (Nancy), 1929. Army Chief of Staff, 1931. Inspector-General of the Army and Vice-President of the War Council, 1935–37. Chief of the General Staff of National Defence, January 1938–September 1939. Honorary knighthood, 1938. Generalissimo, commanding the French Land Forces, September 1939–May 1940, when he was superseded and interned by the Vichy regime. Tried for having 'weakened the spirit of the French armies', 1941. Deported to Buchenwald Concentration Camp, 1943–45. Liberated by American troops, May 1945.

12, he lunched with General Gamelin at Brignoles, and was introduced to several senior French officers. On the following day he sent his wife an account of what he had seen at the manoeuvres:

I drove about all day with General Gamelin the Generalissimo, who was communicative on serious topics. There was nothing to see, as all the troops were hidden in holes or under bushes. But to anyone with military knowledge it was most instructive. The officers of the French army are impressive by their gravity & competence. One feels the strength of the nation resides in its army.

While at the Château de l'Horizon Churchill dictated to Mrs Pearman a further article for the *Evening Standard*, entitled 'A Testing Time for France'. In it he deprecated the current 'alarming talk' about the disintegration of French society under the Popular Front, and pointed out that all political parties in France supported the existing two years' compulsory military service, a symbol 'of national comradeship and unity'.

On September 12 Churchill was at Toulon, where he dined with Mrs Goldschmidt-Rothschild.[1] 'She was pathetic about the treatment of Jews in Germany,' he told his wife in his letter of September 13. 'They have a terrible time.' From Toulon he took the night train to Dijon, and was then driven nearly a hundred miles to Flandin's house at Domecy-sur-Cure. There, as Churchill reported to his wife, he and Flandin discussed the civil war in Spain, where, he wrote, 'Everything gets worse, except that the Nationalists (as they insist on being called) are winning.'

On September 14 Churchill travelled from Domecy to Paris, where he dined and slept at the British Embassy. From there he travelled on September 15 to Verdun, Metz and the Maginot Line. Unlike his appearance at the manoeuvres, this visit was not made known to the Press. For two days, accompanied both by the British Military Attaché to France, Colonel Beaumont-Nesbitt,[2] and by Lord Lloyd, Churchill was shown the fortifications which were intended to prevent any future

---

[1] Marie-Anne Friedländer-Fuld, 1892–1973. The only daughter of a German coal magnate, Herr von Friedländer-Fuld, of Berlin, who died in 1916, leaving her coal mines worth £5 million. In January 1914 she married Clementine Churchill's cousin, Jack Mitford, son of the first Baron Redesdale; the marriage was annulled later in the same year, and she subsequently married Baron Rudolph de Goldschmidt-Rothschild, a cousin of James de Rothschild, MP. In May 1940 she fled to the United States. On learning of the liberation of Paris in August 1944 she donated Van Gogh's *L'Arlesienne* to the Louvre.

[2] Frederick George Beaumont-Nesbitt, 1893–1971. Educated at Eton and Sandhurst. 2nd Lieutenant, Grenadier Guards, 1912. On active service, 1914–18 (Military Cross). Commanded the 2nd Battalion, Grenadier Guards, 1932–35. Military Attaché, Paris, 1936–38. Deputy Director of Military Intelligence, 1938–39; Director, 1939–40. Military Attaché, Washington, 1941. Major-General, General Staff, 1941–45.

German breakthrough into France. From Metz he returned first to Paris, and then to London. 'It was a great pleasure to me to make your acquaintance,' he wrote to Beaumont-Nesbitt two weeks later, 'and I do not think our journeys together have done any harm.'

After his return to Chartwell, Churchill worked on a speech which he was to give in Paris on September 24. He had been encouraged to speak by the Press Attaché at the Paris Embassy, Sir Charles Mendl, who was directly responsible to Leeper's News Department at the Foreign Office.[1] On September 22 Churchill sent a copy of the first draft to Geoffrey Dawson at *The Times*. 'I should be very glad to know how it strikes you,' he wrote, and on the following day he sent Dawson a revised version' Dawson being away, his deputy, R. M. Barrington-Ward,[2] wrote to Churchill on September 23 to put a different viewpoint:

. . . *the Times* has always held that this country should most firmly decline to take part in the formation of 'fronts' until or unless the choice of a 'front' is positively forced upon us. However alien to our way of thinking may be the governing philosophies of other countries, we feel that the only safe and impartial test to apply to them is whether or not they are ready for practical collaboration, political and economic. We should, for example, certainly be against premature abandonment of the hope, supported by many authoritative pronouncements on the German side, that Germany is prepared to reach a general understanding and settlement with the British Empire.

Barrington-Ward added that he hoped Churchill would guard against making any appeal for Franco-British collaboration that might lead to 'misunderstanding and controversy'.

On the morning of September 24 Churchill and his wife flew from London to Paris, arriving in time for lunch with several senior French politicians, including President Herriot, Pierre Etienne Flandin and Paul Reynaud.[3] That evening he made his speech, in English, at the Théâtre des Ambassadeurs. The speech was a clarion call in defence

---

[1] Charles Mendl, 1871–1958. Educated at Harrow. On active service with the 25th Infantry Brigade, 1914–15 (invalided out). Worked for the Admiralty, 1918; for the Foreign Office News Department, 1920–25. Knighted, 1924. Press Attaché, British Embassy, Paris, 1926–40. Subsequently resident in California.

[2] Robert McGowan Barrington-Ward, 1891–1948. Educated at Westminster and Balliol College Oxford. President, Oxford Union Society, 1911. On active service, 1914–18 (Military Cross, DSO, despatches twice). Assistant Editor, the *Observer*, 1919–27; *The Times*, 1927–41. Editor of *The Times*, 1941–48.

[3] Paul Reynaud, 1878–1966. Entered the Chamber of Deputies, 1919. Minister of Colonies, 1931–32. Minister of Justice, April–November 1938. Minister of Finance, 1930, and November 1938–March 1940. Prime Minister March–June 1940. Foreign Minister, March and June 1940. Arrested by the Vichy Government, September 1940. Deported to Germany, 1943–45. Released, 1945. Minister of Finance, 1948. Deputy Prime Minister, 1953.

of parliamentary democracy, liberal civilization and the closest possible Anglo-French cooperation. Churchill also explained why the democracies could never submit to Nazi or Communist rule, asking his audience:

> How could we bear, nursed as we have been in a free atmosphere, to be gagged and muzzled; to have spies, eavesdroppers and delators at every corner; to have even private conversation caught up and used against us by the Secret Police and all their agents and creatures; to be arrested and interned without trial; or to be tried by political or Party courts for crimes hitherto unknown to civil law.
>
> How could we bear to be treated like schoolboys when we are grown-up men; to be turned out on parade by tens of thousands to march and cheer for this slogan or for that; to see philosophers, teachers and authors bullied and toiled to death in concentration camps; to be forced every hour to conceal the natural workings of the human intellect and the pulsations of the human heart? Why, I say that rather than submit to such oppression, there is no length we would not go to. . . .

There were still some people, Churchill continued, who believed that the only choice for Europe was between 'two violent extremes'. This was not his view. 'Between the doctrines of Comrade Trotsky and those of Dr Goebbels[1] there ought to be room for you and me, and a few others, to cultivate opinions of our own.' No aggression, he warned, from wherever it came, could be condoned. All aggressive action must be judged, not from the standpoint of Right and Left, but of 'right or wrong', and he declared: 'We are in the midst of dangers so great and increasing, we are the guardians of causes so precious to the world that we must, as the Bible says, "Lay aside every impediment" and prepare ourselves night and day to be worthy of the Faith that is in us.'

Churchill's speech was widely reported in both the British and the French press, and widely praised. 'You have never done anything better,' a former Cabinet colleague, H. A. L. Fisher, wrote on the following day, while the Civil Lord of the Admiralty, Kenneth Lindsay,[2] wrote on

---

[1] Joseph Goebbels, 1897–1945. Rejected for military service because of a deformed foot. Doctor of Philosophy at Heidelberg, 1921. Unsuccessful playwright. Joined the Hitler movement in 1922. Appointed by Hitler to be Gauleiter of Berlin, 1926. Founder of *Der Angriff* ('The Attack'), a Berlin Nazi newspaper, 1927. Elected to the Reichstag, 1929. Propaganda Leader of the Nazi Party, 1929. Minister of Enlightenment and Propaganda, 1933–45. Committed suicide in Berlin, after poisoning his six children, 1 May 1945.

[2] Kenneth Lindsay, 1897–   . Educated at St Olave's school. On active service, 1916–18. At Worcester College Oxford, 1921–22; President of the Oxford Union, 1922. Secretary, Political and Economic Planning (PEP), 1931–35. Independent National MP for Kilmarnock Burghs, 1933–45; Independent MP for the Combined English Universities, 1945–50. Civil

September 25: 'At last it would seem one heard the authentic note struck, with authority & dignity.' The *Star* commented on the evening of September 25: 'It was a magnificent defence of democracy. . . . Those who listened to that speech must have been very conscious of the great heritage of European civilisation. To compare Mr Churchill at Paris with Dr Goebbels at Nuremberg is to measure the chasm between culture and the new barbarism.' The *Star* added: 'After Paris the wonder grows that the Government should fail to find employment for the cleverest brain and most eloquent tongue on their side of politics. We should like to hear Mr Churchill's defence of democracy reverberate from the sounding board of high office.'

Churchill's political future was a constant topic of conversation. After talking to Reginald Leeper on September 24, Robert Bruce Lockhart recorded in his diary: 'Rex says Winston is making great recovery in the Conservative Party. Many regard him as only "PM" in a crisis.'

On October 3 Churchill was present at the Oxford High School for Boys, for the unveiling of a memorial to T. E. Lawrence, who had been killed in a motor cycle accident in May 1935. 'All feel the poorer that he has gone from us,' Churchill said. 'In these days dangers and difficulties gather upon Britain and her Empire, and we are also conscious of a lack of outstanding figures with which to overcome them.' That night Churchill dined at All Souls, and on October 8 he wrote to Abe Bailey: 'Geoffrey Dawson came down and dined at All Souls to meet me and we had a friendly talk. The Times have done me all the harm they can. Whether they will come round or not I do not know.' Churchill added: 'Things are going from bad to worse abroad, and Baldwin is perfectly incompetent at home.'

Speaking at a private lunch of the Anti-Nazi Council on October 15, Churchill praised the recent initiative of the Trades Union Congress to demand that the Labour Party support the principle of necessary rearmament 'in order that free countries should not be trampled down'. This decision, he said, 'shows that Labour is more alive than many of the Conservatives'. Two days later, at Churchill's request, Desmond Morton sent him an assessment of Baldwin's political position and policies. 'The opinion of the Carlton Club,' Morton wrote, was that

---

Lord of the Admiralty, 1935–37. Parliamentary Secretary, Board of Education, 1937–40. Director of the Anglo-Israel Association, 1962–73. A Vice-President of the Educational Interchange Council (sometime Chairman), 1968–73.

Baldwin would remain Prime Minister 'until death or the Coronation'. His letter continued:

There is trouble brewing about Eden, however. The FO is singularly united in a desire to curtail his activities as a peripatetic ambassador à la Ribbentrop and seem to be hammering out a line of policy for the approval of the Cabinet; briefly that until rearmament is real we must avoid commitments at all costs.

According to my information rearmament is now progressing at last, though it cannot be anything like adequate for at least another three years unless steps are taken really to prefer the claims of the country's defences before those of ordinary trade and commerce.

In the Air, greater success has been realised than was anticipated in the sphere of material; personnel is a different matter. The Navy is reasonably content with proposals and progress. In other spheres—Army, Coast Defences and Anti-Aircraft Defences the situation is bad.

If only Britain were strong, Morton added, and would give a lead, 'there is no nation of the world or combination of nations which would not scurry, however grudgingly, to do our bidding. Not that we may rule the world for the gratification of a common will to power, but that we may compel the world to peace and law and order.'

Speaking at Chingford on October 19,[1] Churchill warned that 1936 'might well be the last year' in which a real collective security system could be built up to prevent Europe 'from falling under the domination of ruthless might'. At the moment, he said, Britain and France together were 'probably at least as strong as Germany in their physical force', and he went on to warn: 'Next year, when the German armies were preponderant, it would be too late.'

Churchill's Chingford speech prompted a Conservative MP, Vyvyan Adams,[2] to write to him on October 20: 'I have been apprehensive for some time—and so have many of my friends—that the Government may be contemplating some kind of an accommodation with Germany which leaves her free to attack Eastwards or Southwards. Your speech precisely exposes the dangers which would accompany any such policy.'

---

[1] As part of a constituency speaking tour; he also spoke about defence and collective security at Woodford on October 14, at Aldersbrook on October 16, and at Netteswell on October 20.

[2] Samuel Vyvyan Trerice Adams, 1900–1951. Educated at Haileybury and King's College Cambridge. Called to the Bar, 1927. Conservative MP for West Leeds, 1931–45. Member of the Executive of the League of Nation's Union, 1933–46. On active service, 1939–45 (Major, Duke of Cornwall's Light Infantry). In 1940, under the pen name 'Watchman', he published *Churchill: Architect of Victory*. Political researcher, 1946–51.

Two days later Sir Eric Phipps telegraphed from Berlin to say that Churchill's constituency speeches had been sharply attacked on the previous day in the *Deutsche diplomatisch-politische Korrespondenz*, which had accused him of trying 'to camouflage personal dislike of Germany under the appearance of practical reasoning'. Churchill, the paper declared, was in favour 'of the encirclement and oppression of Germany'. Churchill himself replied to this attack in a statement to the Press on October 24, where he pointed out that unless Germany herself contemplated aggression, 'it is idle to talk of encirclement or oppression' on the part of the democracies. On the previous day Charles Peake[1] had written from the British Embassy in Paris: 'Your last speech at Chingford was much admired here and has fluttered the dove cotes at Berlin considerably which is an excellent thing in the circumstances. It is good that the Germans shd realize that there is one English statesman, who instead of apologizing for democracy stands up for it.'

On October 23 volume three of Churchill's *Marlborough* was published. Two days before publication he had sent out seventy-one personal copies to his friends. On October 25 Neville Chamberlain wrote from 11 Downing Street: 'I remember your speaking to me of the parallel you had found with current affairs and this will give the volume special piquancy.' Two of those who wrote to Churchill to thank him for his book referred also to a personal worry that had clouded many of his hours during the spring and summer of 1936: the intention of his daughter Sarah to marry the music hall comedian Vic Oliver,[2] and their sudden departure to the United States, where eventually they were married. The Press had made much of the elopement, to Churchill's distress. 'We both sympathise so much with you two,' Sir Maurice Hankey wrote on October 25, 'over the way those cursed newspapers gassed about Sarah,' and Stanley Baldwin, who was resting at Longleat on doctor's orders, wrote on October 9: 'I nearly wrote you a line last month and then I hesitated. But I do want you to know that I felt with you from my

---

[1] Charles Brinsley Pemberton Peake, 1897–1958. Educated at Wyggeston School and Magdalen College Oxford. On active service, 1914–18 (Military Cross, despatches). Captain, 1918. Entered Diplomatic Service, 1922. 1st Secretary Paris, 1936–38; Counsellor of Embassy 1939. Head of the News Department, Foreign Office, 1939. Chief Press Adviser, Ministry of Information, 1940. British Representative to the French National Committee, 1942–44. Political adviser to General Eisenhower, 1944–45. Consul-General, Tangier, 1945–46. Ambassador to Belgrade, 1946–51; to Athens, 1951–57. Knighted, 1948.

[2] Victor Samek, 1898–1964. Born in Austria, the son of Baron Victor von Samek. Educated at the University of Vienna. Relinquished his father's title, 1922. A concert pianist, he worked in the United States from 1933 to 1935 under the stage name Vic Oliver; subsequently he worked on the stage and in revues in Britain and America. Married Sarah Churchill, 1936 (from whom he obtained a divorce in 1945).

heart when I read in the papers of certain domestic anxieties that must have caused you pain. I know you well enough to realize how closely these things touch you.'

On November 7 King Edward VIII opened the new session of Parliament. That same day the Cabinet discussed their policy towards Germany, and towards Britain's own defence preparations. Inskip remarked that it was difficult to know 'what our policy was and what kind of policy our defensive preparations were intended to meet'. Collective security, he pointed out, 'had disappeared and nothing had been substituted for it'. Perhaps a policy aimed at 'the appeasement of Germany's economic conditions' would be one 'for which there was some hope'.[1] An unnamed Minister commented that the British refusal to discuss Germany's colonial demands was 'rather too stiff' an attitude to adopt. Inskip then told his colleagues that if he were to work 'for readiness for war in June 1937' he would need emergency powers the equivalent of putting the country 'practically on a war footing', nor did he, even at that moment, have sufficient spare time 'for consideration of large questions' in the supply field. Sir Samuel Hoare opposed such emergency powers, which would, he said, not only cause 'an immense upheaval', but would also 'prejudice the future'. After both Eden and Duff Cooper stressed the existing weakness in defence preparations, Hoare stated that it would be 'necessary to assume for a long time that we should be unprepared', and that as a result Britain's foreign policy 'would have to proceed very quietly'. According to Ormsby-Gore there was a feeling in Britain 'that we were tied up too much with France and that that prevented us getting on terms with the dictator powers', while Neville Chamberlain stressed the economic aspects of defence policy, telling his colleagues that:

. . . he was getting concerned at the mounting cost of the programme. It was difficult for him to take up a line in opposition in this matter of national

[1] On October 9 Sir Maurice Hankey had written to Sir Eric Phipps: 'Personally I have never despaired of coming to terms with Germany one day. The more I examine the possibilities of war between the two countries—and it is my business to examine them very closely indeed—the more silly a business does it seem . . .' After a prolonged war, Hankey added: 'We should probably become a prey to Bolshevism, the very thing Hitler most fears . . . In fact, all the evidence I have seen is that he does not want it, and that whatever he may be he is not an ass. All the same I can see Hitler must prepare his defences, and for all I know he may have designs eastward, as suggested in his book. If he is strong we must be strong so a race in armaments seems inevitable. Nevertheless I do not in the least see why the race should end in a war so far as we are concerned, if we keep our heads cool.'

safety, but he wanted the Cabinet to realise that the cost was mounting at a giddy rate. The original estimate of £400,000,000 was already far exceeded and programmes were constantly increasing. Before long he thought people would be talking about an unbalanced Budget, and we might find that our credit was not so good as it was a few years ago. He said this because while recognising that national safety came first our resources were not unlimited and we were putting burdens on future generations; also because while assuming that what was essential when the existence of the nation was at stake, he wanted Government departments not to think that because a heavy expenditure was being incurred, this was a time to slip in developments of convenience which had been refused in the past.

On the following day Churchill spoke in the House of Commons about the need for a precise plan in foreign policy. 'The repeated chops and changes,' he said, 'hot fits and cold fits, with which even the last melancholy twelve months have acquainted us, have sensibly diminished our influence and augmented the dangers which menace us and others.' Anglo-French cooperation was essential: 'Together they will be very dangerous to attack. Together they will be very hard to destroy.' No nation sought to encircle Germany. All legitimate grievances were capable of peaceful resolution. And he continued:

It is said that there must not be a front against any nation, against Germany. All I can say is that unless there is a front against potential aggression there will be no settlement. All the nations of Europe will just be driven helter-skelter across the diplomatic chessboard until the limits of retreat are exhausted, and then out of desperation, perhaps in some most unlikely quarter, the explosion of war will take place, probably under conditions not very favourable to those who have been engaged in this long retreat.

Churchill's speech prompted one unexpected and entirely favourable response. 'That is to say "Thank-you" for your speech last Thursday,' Anthony Eden wrote from the Foreign Office on November 9. 'You will probably have seen that the reaction of the whole debate in Europe has been good, & the effect steadying. A very large measure of this we owe to you.'

40

'The Illusion of Security'

DURING the autumn of 1936 Churchill's sources of information on defence were widened. On October 21 A. P. Herbert[1] asked him to meet 'my friend Brigadier P. C. S. Hobart DSO,[2] who is top dog, I think, (or very nearly so) of Tanks, and has lots of interesting things he wants to say to someone like you who knows about Defence'. Six days later Churchill met Hobart at Morpeth Mansions. On October 26, the day before Churchill and Hobart discussed the tank situation, a Royal Air Force pilot, Squadron-Leader H. V. Rowley,[3] who had just returned from a visit to Germany, wrote to Wing-Commander Anderson of all that he had seen while he was the guest of the German Air Ministry. 'The development of air power in Germany,' he wrote, 'has left me in a somewhat dazed condition but with one fact firmly in my mind and

[1] Alan Patrick Herbert, 1890–1971. Educated at Winchester and New College Oxford. Humorist; began writing for *Punch*, 1910. On active service with the Royal Naval Division, Antwerp, Gallipoli and France (wounded), 1914–18. Called to the Bar, 1918. Joined the staff of *Punch* 1924. Independent MP for Oxford University, 1935–50 (when the University seats were abolished). Petty Officer, River Thames Naval Auxiliary Patrol, June 1940. Knighted, 1945. A Trustee of the National Maritime Museum, 1947–53. Author of more than sixty works of prose and verse, including a novel about Gallipoli, *The Secret Battle*.

[2] Percy Cleghorn Stanley Hobart, 1885–1957. Joined the Royal Engineers 1904. Served on the North-West Frontier of India, 1908. On active service on the western front, 1915, and in Mesopotamia, 1916–18, when he was wounded, and taken prisoner. MC, DSO (1916) and OBE (1918). Served in Palestine, 1918; in Waziristan, 1921. Joined the Royal Tank Corps, 1923; Inspector, Royal Tank Corps, 1933–36. Commander, Tank Brigade, 1934–37. Deputy Director of Staff Duties, War Office, 1937. Major-General, 1937. Director of Military Training, War Office, 1937–38. Raised the 7th Armoured Division, Egypt, 1938–39; the 11th Armoured Division, 1941–42; the 79th Armoured Division, 1942 (commanding it in north-west Europe, 1944–45). Knighted, 1943.

[3] Herbert Victor Rowley, 1898–1966. Commissioned into the Royal Naval Air Service, April 1916; into the Royal Air Force, April 1918. Squadron-Leader, 1930. Wing-Commander, 1937, at the Air Ministry, Directorate of Operations and Intelligence where, under Group-Captain R. D. Oxland, he was responsible for policy regarding new aircraft. Air Commodore, 1941. Served in Fighter Command, 1939–41; South-East Asia Command, 1942–45.

that fact is that they are *now* stronger in the air than England and France combined.' Anderson at once sent Rowley's letter to Churchill. Among the other materials which Wing-Commander Anderson had sent Churchill in preparation for the next defence debate was a 'Diagram Showing Peace Organisation of the Royal Air Force', marked 'For Official Use Only' and dated 6 October 1936. The diagram showed the exact location of all operational, training and administrative units, and the chain of command.

On November 4, in a letter to Baldwin, Churchill urged the Prime Minister to allow a full two-day debate on defence. 'There are so many who wish to speak,' he wrote, 'that one day's treatment would be very inconvenient.'

The debate was finally set for November 11 and 12. Opening the debate on November 11, Inskip stated that Britain now possessed 80 aeroplane squadrons, making a total of 960 aeroplanes, available for Home Defence, and insisted that all was proceeding well in defence preparations. Churchill spoke on November 12, moving an amendment identical to that of two years earlier, in which he stated that Britain's defences, particularly in the air, were 'no longer adequate' for the peace, safety and freedom of the British people. The amendment stood, as before, in the names of Churchill, Horne, Amery, Guest and Winterton. As Boothby was abroad, his place was taken by Colonel Gretton. There would be 'a great increase in the adverse factors' in 1937, Churchill warned, and only 'intense efforts' could counteract them. And yet, he said, there were still serious deficiencies in the strength and weapons, of many elements in the national defence, including the Territorial Army, the Regular Army and the Royal Air Force. He then set out his charges in detail, telling the House at one point in his speech:

In the manoeuvres of the Regular Army many of the most important new weapons have to be represented by flags and discs. When we remember how small our land forces are—altogether only a few hundred thousand men—it seems incredible that the very flexible industry of Britain, if properly handled, could not supply them with their modest requirements. . . .

The Army lacks almost every weapon which is required for the latest form of modern war. Where are the anti-tank guns, where are the short-distance wireless sets, where the field anti-aircraft guns against low-flying armoured aeroplanes? . . .

Churchill went on to speak about the Tank Corps, and about the use of the tank as a weapon of war:

This idea, which has revolutionised the conditions of modern war, was a British idea forced on the War Office by outsiders. Let me say they would have just as hard work to-day to force a new idea on it. I speak from what I know.

During the War we had almost a monopoly, let alone the leadership, in tank warfare, and for several years afterwards we held the foremost place. To England all eyes were turned. All that has gone now. Nothing has been done in 'the years that the locust hath eaten' to equip the Tank Corps with new machines. The medium tank which they possess, which in its day was the best in the world, is now long obsolete. Not only in numbers—for there we have never tried to compete with other countries—but in quality these British weapons are now surpassed by those of Germany, Russia, Italy and the United States. All the shell plants and gun plants in the Army, apart from the very small peace-time services, are in an elementary stage.

Of the general attitude towards munition supplies, Churchill warned the House: 'A very long period must intervene before any effectual flow of munitions can be expected, even for the small forces of which we dispose. Still we are told there is no necessity for a Ministry of Supply, no emergency which should induce us to impinge on the normal course of trade'.

Churchill's speech was a sustained and detailed attack on the Government's policy over the past three years. Of the Government's arguments for the delays in embarking upon a rearmament programme between 1933 and 1935 he declared:

I have heard it said that the Government had no mandate for rearmament until the General Election. Such a doctrine is wholly inadmissible. The responsibility of Ministers for the public safety is absolute and requires no mandate. It is in fact the prime object for which Governments come into existence.

The Prime Minister had the command of enormous majorities in both Houses of Parliament ready to vote for any necessary measures of defence. The country has never yet failed to do its duty when the true facts have been put before it, and I cannot see where there is a defence for this delay.

Churchill went on to stress the urgent need for a Ministry of Supply. 'Some interference with the normal trade of the country would be inevitable,' he said, yet Government spokesmen continued to assert the dangers of turning the country 'into one vast munitions camp'. Churchill deprecated such exaggeration, and he added:

The First Lord of the Admiralty in his speech the other night went even further. He said, 'We are always reviewing the position.' Everything, he assured us, is entirely fluid. I am sure that that is true. Anyone can see what the position is. The Government simply cannot make up their mind, or they cannot get the Prime Minister to make up his mind.

So they go on in strange paradox, decided only to be undecided, resolved to be irresolute, adamant for drift, solid for fluidity, all powerful to be impotent. So we go on preparing more months and years—precious, perhaps vital, to the greatness of Britain—for the locusts to eat.

They will say to me, 'A Minister of Supply is not necessary, for all is going well.' I deny it. 'The position is satisfactory.' It is not true. 'All is proceeding according to plan.' We know what that means.

Churchill's main area of concern was still the Air Force, which remained, he said, inferior to that of Germany, and could boast only 960 first-line aeroplanes as against at least 1,500 German planes. 'It must also be remembered,' he said, 'that Germany has specialised in long-distance bombing aeroplanes and that her preponderance in that respect is far greater than any of these figures would suggest.' Churchill ended his catalogue of criticisms on a personal note, telling his fellow MPs:

I have been staggered by the failure of the House of Commons to react effectively against those dangers. That, I am bound to say, I never expected. I never would have believed that we should have been allowed to go on getting into this plight, month by month and year by year, and that even the Government's own confessions of error would have produced no concentration of Parliamentary opinion and force capable of lifting our efforts to the level of emergency.

I say that unless the House resolves to find out the truth for itself it will have committed an act of abdication of duty without parallel in its long history.

In his diary Harold Nicolson noted of Churchill's speech: 'His style is more considered and slower than usual, but he drives his points home with a sledgehammer.' It was Baldwin himself who replied, seeking to explain why he had not rearmed more forcefully between the autumn of 1933 and the General Election in the summer of 1935, and telling the House of Commons:

I would remind the House that not once but on many occasions in speeches and in various places, when I have been speaking and advocating as far as I am able the democratic principles, I have stated that a democracy is always two years behind the dictator. I believe that to be true. It has been true in this case.

I put before the whole House my own views with an appalling frankness. You will remember at that time the Disarmament Conference was sitting in Geneva. You will remember at that time there was probably a stronger pacifist feeling running through this country than at any time since the War. You will remember the election at Fulham in the autumn of 1933, when a seat which the National Government held was lost by about 7000 votes on no issue but the pacifist. . . .

My position as the leader of a great party was not altogether a comfortable one. I asked myself what chance was there—when that feeling that was given expression to in Fulham was common throughout the country—what chance was there within the next year or two of that feeling being so changed that the country would give a mandate for rearmament?

Supposing I had gone to the country and said that Germany was rearming and that we must rearm, does anybody think that this pacific democracy would have rallied to that cry at that moment? I cannot think of anything that would have made the loss of the election from my point of view more certain.

Later in his speech Baldwin explained why there was no need for a Ministry of Supply because there were no 'conflicting demands on the part of the Service Departments', The real conflict, he said, was between 'the demands of private industry and the demands of the Service Departments as a whole'. In such cases, he believed, the right course was to seek the help of the trades concerned on a voluntary basis which, 'while they will give us as far as possible what we need for defence . . . with a minimum of dislocation of our ordinary and particiularly of our export trade'. Baldwin added: 'We do not need a Minister of Supply for that,' and he continued: 'Our method may be described as one of voluntary co-operation between all concerned, while co-ordinating our efforts and interfering as little as possible with normal industry.'

'You cannot do it in fragments,' Baldwin continued. 'It must extend to industry as a whole,' and he added: 'What I fear, in fact what I feel confident of, is that if that were done now, it would create such uncertainty and uneasiness throughout the whole trade of the country that it would check the development of enterprise and stop the trade expansion and I hardly dare to reckon how it might react on finance.'

During his speech Baldwin also attacked Churchill's air figures, telling the House: 'I am in a position to say that my right hon Friend's estimate of the German metropolitan first-line air strength is definitely too high. That is the best information we have. I regret that I cannot give exact figures.'

The contrast between Churchill's charges and Baldwin's explanation provoked much comment. 'I cannot recall seeing the House *as a whole* so uneasy,' Patrick Donner wrote on November 15. *The Times*, so often hostile to Churchill in the past, described his speech as 'brilliant'. Commenting on Baldwin's speech, Lord Londonderry wrote to Churchill on November 13: 'We told him and Neville of the risks, but they were too much frightened of losing bye elections. Neville was really the villain of the piece, because he as Chancellor blocked everything on the grounds of finances.' From the Carlton Club, Sir Archibald Boyd-Carpenter[1] wrote to Churchill that same day: 'I must send you a few words of congratulations on your wonderful & inspiring speech yesterday. I said to myself "Thank God someone has courage" & I feel it all the more after the pathetic effort of S.B. which makes one feel almost ill.' Churchill replied that same day: 'Thank you so much for your most kind letter. I have never heard such a squalid confession from a public man as Baldwin offered us yesterday.'

At their meeting on October 15, the Anti-Nazi Council had decided to set up a 'Defence of Freedom and Peace' movement whose aim was to uphold 'democratic government and public law', to resist all attacks on this freedom 'by violence at home or attack from abroad', and to join with other threatened nations 'in preserving peace and withstanding armed aggression'. Churchill had told those present 'we will make every effort in our power to rally around that Covenant all the effective aid that we can get from any quarter without respect to party or nation', and he added: 'We have the means of being the spear-point of all this vast mass of opinion which guards our rights'.

The first public meeting of the new organization was to be held at the Albert Hall, under the public auspices of the League of Nations Union, and was intended to bring together, on a single platform, all those organizations which favoured collective security and rearmament. Thus the idea put forward by Vansittart and Leeper at the beginning of the year became a reality. On October 21 Churchill explained to A. H. Richards: 'I do not contemplate the building up of a new and rival society, but only a welding together of those organisations and galvanising them into effective use'. Five days later Churchill wrote to Richards again: 'In my view we are a focus bringing together all these various forces'. Of his Labour colleagues Churchill had written to Austen Chamberlain on October 17: 'I have been surprised to find the resolution and clarity of thought which has prevailed among them, and the profound sense of approaching danger'.

[1] Archibald Boyd-Carpenter, 1873–1937. One of Churchill's contemporaries at Harrow. Son of the Rt Rev Boyd-Carpenter, Bishop of Ripon and Canon of Westminster. President of the Oxford Union. Served as a Staff Captain in South Africa, 1901–02, and as a Major in the European War, 1914–19. Conservative MP for North Bradford, 1918–23, for Coventry, 1924–29 and for Chertsey, 1931–37. Parliamentary Secretary, Ministry of Labour, November 1922–March 1923. Financial Secretary to the Treasury, 1923; to the Admiralty, 1923–24. Paymaster General, 1923 and 1924. Knighted, 1926.

The Albert Hall meeting was to be held on December 3. In preparation for it, Churchill exhorted his friends and correspondents to give it their support. 'I am trying to marshal all the forces I can,' he wrote to Sir Guy Fleetwood Wilson[1] on November 13, 'to prevent this coming war, and to strengthen Britain.' To his son Randolph, who was in the United States, he wrote that same day: 'All the left wing intelligentsia are coming to look to me for protection, and I will give it whole heartedly in return for their aid in the rearmament of Britain.' His letter continued:

> The basis of the Anti Nazi League is of course Jewish resentment at their abominable persecution. But we are now taking broader ground rather on the lines of my Paris speech which perhaps you read. A Peace with Freedom committee has been formed. I enclose a copy of the formula at length adopted. This committee aims at focussing and concentrating the efforts of all the Peace societies like the New Commonwealth and the League of Nations Union in so far as they are prepared to support genuine military action to resist tyranny or aggression.

From the moment of the defence debate of November 11, Baldwin had been pressed to receive a second Parliamentary delegation to raise the growing defence concerns of MPs and Peers. Baldwin agreed to receive a second deputation on November 23. Churchill concentrated all his energies on preparing for the new deputation, declining all other requests for speeches or meetings. On November 14, in thanking Lord Wolmer for a memorandum on unemployment, he wrote: 'I have been so pressed with my speech on Defence that I have not had a moment to read it, nor indeed the spare capacity to take it in.'

It had become clear to Churchill that should war be a possibility either in 1937 or 1938, Britain would not have sufficient air defence, or air power, to resist successfully a major attack, or to counter-attack. In the five days leading up to the deputation of November 23 his principal source of new information was again Wing-Commander Anderson, who in a series of notes set out the precise state of Air Force construction under the current expansion scheme. In the first of these notes, dictated

---

[1] Guy Douglas Arthur Fleetwood Wilson, 1850–1940. A Clerk in the Paymaster General's Office, 1870. Private Secretary to Gladstone, 1886; to Campbell-Bannerman, 1892–93. Financial Adviser to Kitchener in South Africa, 1901. Knighted, 1902. Privy Councillor, 1904. Director-General of Army Finance, 1904–08. Finance Member of the Supreme Council of India, 1908–13. Vice-President of the Legislative Council of India, 1911–13. Commissioner, Special Government Enquiry, Dublin 1916. Chairman of the Financial Committee, Flying Corps, 1917. Member of the High Court Tribunal for Naval Prize, 1918–28.

to Mrs Pearman on November 18, Anderson listed in one column the total number of bombers in existence, as stated by Inskip, in a second column the actual mobilization strength, as of June 1937, and in a third column the planned mobilization situation in March 1939. Extant bombers amounted to 744; actual mobilization strength, 372; and in March 1939, the prospective mobilization strength 990. The first column, Anderson added, 'is "shop window dressing" for Parliament'. Among the other points of concern in Anderson's note were:

The number of squadrons promised to Parliament by 1st April 1937 will be deficient by 23. Parliament is going to be openly informed of this. The reason is lack of equipment and the failure on the part of manufacturers to supply. Should Parliament bring pressure to bear, then further shop window dressing will take place, and squadrons which have at present two flights, will be split up into an additional squadron of one flight, to operate from the same aerodrome. . . .

The CID have recommended that we should hold 34,000 tons of petrol. The Air Staff consider the minimum should be 60,000 tons. There is no underground storage, and it has been agreed that a portion of this petrol should be stored in open tanks in the Western counties. . . .

The Battle and Blenheim have only 800 miles of safe range owing to the consumption of petrol and sensitivity of the throttle.

The mobilisation orders for the Air Force are in preparation, and it is agreed that it would take between 3 to 6 days to mobilise, whereas the Metropolitan Air Force should always be mobilised and ready to strike immediately.

On November 19 Anderson saw Mrs Pearman, to whom he dictated two further notes, one on the state of British service aircraft, the other on German air and pilot strength. It was impossible, Anderson stated in his first note, to give the exact strength of British bombers and fighters 'as numbers vary daily owing to crashed and unserviceability etc'. But, he warned:

. . . the approximate number including all types of bombers fighters and army co-operation is 600, of which 66% are bombers and 34% are fighters. The types are of course obsolescent and we should have to operate from France. If we required to mobilise and to use our squadrons as efficient instruments of war in tactical formation, and maintain a force for say four days, the number 600 would have to be halved.

Plans state that the expected output of new aircraft when deliveries commence will be approximately 5 complete aeroplanes and engines per week per factory.

Anderson went on to point out that 'the present output of obsolescent aircraft is approximately two aeroplanes a day'. As for the variable-pitch propeller, he wrote, this was 'now regarded by the USA as obsolete and they have completely gone over to the constant pitch propeller'. Yet the Air Ministry, he noted, 'are still purchasing Wrights and experimenting and giving orders for large quantities of the obsolete variable pitch propeller'.

In his second note on November 19, Anderson passed on to Churchill information which he had received, for a lecture he was giving, from the head of the Air Ministry German Intelligence Section, Wing-Commander Goddard.[1] According to Goddard, the Chief of the Air Staff, Ellington, would only accept German first-line air strength at 550 bombers and 250 fighters, a total of 800. Yet in addition, Goddard had pointed out, both the bomber and the fighter squadrons of the German force 'have 100% reserve in aircraft'. Goddard's information showed both the strengths and the weakness of the German situation. 'Their accepted pilot strength is *8,500*,' Goddard had reported. 'It is agreed that few of these have been fully trained in the full arts of applied flying, ie bombing, gunnery etc. But they are capable nevertheless of piloting an aeroplane and dropping bombs over a target, such as London. These reports are obtained direct from the Secret Service through agents. . . .' Goddard's information added: 'The German squadrons are faced with a shortage of trained personnel ie fitters and riggers, and many civilians are seen working in the squadrons.'

Goddard also gave the estimated German first-line strength for May 1937: 800 bombers and 250 fighters 'again with 100% reserves'. On the question of comparative strengths Anderson's note continued, quoting Goddard:

The Chief of Air Staff will not accept the principle of the Germans using training aircraft for offensive operations, although he realises that such aircraft have the necessary radius of action capable of reaching this country. He considers that if such is the case, when war is likely to take place, our own training aircraft could do likewise.

From these figures it was clear that even in Goddard's estimate the 372 British bombers which would be fully operational in June 1937 would have to be the comparable figure to the German 800, quite apart from

---

[1] Robert Victor Goddard, 1897–1987. On active service with the Royal Navy, Royal Naval Air Service, Royal Flying Corps and Royal Air Force, 1914–19. Air Ministry, 1919; Deputy-Director of Intelligence, 1938–39; Director of Military Co-operation, 1940–41. Chief of the Air Staff, New Zealand, 1941–43. Air Officer in charge of administration, Air Command, South East Asia, 1943–46. RAF Representative, Washington, 1946–48. Knighted, 1947. Member of the Air Council for Technical Services, 1948–51.

the question of how far the 800 German reserve bombers could also be counted as first-line.

On November 20, having given his Air Force lecture, Anderson spoke once more to Mrs Pearman, telling her of his fears, which she passed on to Churchill:

Comdr Anderson told me very seriously that he had never been frightened in his life before, but he is of this, ie that the fact of the vast number of German pilots may come out. IT MUST NOT BE DIVULGED OPENLY as it would implicate not only him, but Wing Commander Goddard, whom he must not harm. The number must be camouflaged. Nothing that can recoil on Cmdr Goddard must come out.

After the lectures they seemed curious to know why Cmdr Anderson should wish to know about the pilots. He does not know whether they are suspicious of him, and may try to trace him. The figures are accurate, and so accurate and staggering, that he thinks this is the reason those who know are frightened of facts coming out.

He has gone back to Hucknall, and hopes that his help has been of real use to you.

On November 20, only three days before the defence deputation was to see Baldwin, another person with access to classified material, Major G. P. Myers,[1] wrote in confidence to Churchill:

General Aircraft Ltd; (Hanworth Aerodrome, Feltham) in October 1935, had a contract placed with them by the Air Ministry for 89 Hawker 'FURY' aeroplanes. Up to the 13th: of the present month only 23 machines of this contract had been delivered, 23 machines in more than twelve months.

The 'FURY' is of course a modified type of the original 'FURY' which dates I think from about 1930 and it can hardly be described as the latest type of 'fighter'.

'May I ask you to note,' Myers added, 'that I am an employee of General Aircraft Ltd: and as such would lose my position were the source of this information disclosed by some mischance.'

On November 23 the second Parliamentary deputation called on Baldwin to discuss the state of Britain's defences. Once again, although Inskip was present, none of the three Service Ministers, Hoare, Swinton and Duff Cooper, were at the meeting to hear the criticisms of their departments, or to question the critics face to face. Baldwin was accompanied by Neville Chamberlain and Lord Halifax; the deputation, as

[1] Gilbert Percival Louis Myers, 1881–   . 2nd Lieutenant, 1900; Lieutenant, 1904–7 (when he resigned). Captain, Machine Gun Corps, 1915; Major, 1916. Instructor in Gunnery, Royal Flying Corps, 1917–18. Mentioned in despatches, 1917. Retired, 1919. Subsequently an employee of General Aircraft Limited.

before, was led by Sir Austen Chamberlain and Lord Salisbury.[1] Baldwin opened the discussion by pointing out that all the speeches made by members of the first deputation had been carefully examined. 'It has taken an immense amount of time,' he said, 'and you will not misunderstand me when I say time on the part of very busy men.' He added: 'We can point to some things which I think are better than you feared; we have spots about which we are anxious; we are all aware of them and are anxious and willing to remedy them. . . .'

Basing himself upon the Service answers, Inskip then dealt point by point with the criticisms that had been made. It was over the question of German air strength that the principal cause for dispute had arisen. Inskip told the meeting: 'The Prime Minister stated in the Debate on the Address that Mr Churchill's estimate of German strength on the 1st of November was too high. I repeat that statement'. Austen Chamberlain then pointed out that if it were a question of interpretation, he himself would, for defence purposes, 'be disposed to base an estimate on the calculation most unfavourable to us'. Churchill then told the meeting:

. . . one of the principal points is that the Air Staff will not accept the same method of calculation as the French: they count the German squadrons as 9 only, whereas the French count them as 12. When you get to 120 or 130 squadrons, it is obvious that a matter of 400 machines is in question.

I personally should be prepared to argue and to submit that from all points of reality and effective strength, these 3 additional machines which the Air Ministry will not recognise and which the French do, are every whit as good—pilots, crews to keep them in order, superiority of machines—every whit as good as the 9 which you count; and it seems to me very odd, purely for purposes of estimate and figures, to rule out as many as 400 machines manned by the best pilots in Germany, interchangeable with all the others, with the very best kind of machines and with the rigging parties all ready standing by them.

Of course, you can rule them out and say 'We do not count them'; but they are there all the same from every point of view.

Churchill then gave the meeting the 'latest' French figures of German air strength. Although he did not say so, he had received them from Léon Blum, who had decided to allow Churchill the same privileges as far as secret French information was concerned as Flandin had given

[1] The members of the deputation were: (House of Commons): Austen Chamberlain, Churchill, Sir Robert Horne, L. S. Amery, Sir John Gilmour, Frederick Guest, Earl Winterton, Sir Henry Page Croft, Sir Edward Grigg, Viscount Wolmer, Lieutenant-Colonel J. T. C. Moore-Brabazon, Sir Roger Keyes, Sir Hugh O'Neill and (House of Lords): the Marquess of Salisbury, Viscount FitzAlan, Viscount Trenchard, Lord Lloyd and Lord Milne.

him earlier. According to the French, Germany's first-line strength would have increased from 1,356 in May 1936 to an estimated 1,964 in January 1937. Churchill added:

If you take 1,964 at 12 in a squadron, you knock off 450 which brings the figure probably near, we should not be very much out, but you are knocking off 450 live things, things which can absolutely work and are of the highest quality. You can knock them off, but you must put them down somewhere.

Inskip, impressed by Churchill's sources, offered an 'exchange of documents' in order to resolve the difference of interpretation, and to this Churchill readily agreed.

As the discussion continued, it was clear that many of Churchill's fears, and public protests, had been fully justified. Two and a half years had passed since the 1935 election, yet the scale of arms production was still not adequate to meet a German threat in 1937 or 1938. Explaining why there could still be no rapid expansion of the Territorials for the defence of London, Inskip told the deputation: 'At present there is undoubtedly a shortage of equipment.' Inskip then rejected the suggestion that all anti-aircraft defences should come under a single Ministry, the Air Ministry.

The discussion of November 23, the record of which filled fifty-eight printed foolscap pages, was dominated by Churchill's continuing questioning of the state of affairs which Inskip had revealed. Following a long discussion initiated by Sir Edward Grigg, on the scale and rate of the delivery of the newly designed heavy bombers, the following altercation took place:

MR CHURCHILL: Do you mean by the 31st March, 1937 there will be a large and substantial amount of aeroplanes delivered which are of the new superior very fast type?

SIR THOMAS INSKIP: No, not of what have been called the new heavy type.

Some minutes later Churchill added:

MR CHURCHILL: I doubt very much whether by this time next year we shall have thirty squadrons equipped with the new type.

SIR THOMAS INSKIP: I am not in a position to say about thirty squadrons. The production of these new heavy squadrons is beginning in driblets, and I hope by the summer of next year it will be not in floods, but greater than driblets. . . .

With Anderson's notes in mind, Churchill pressed for further details about the readiness of the existing squadrons:

MR CHURCHILL: How many squadrons have got their proper supply of aeroplanes and how many have their proper reserves and are up to strength? November Air List only thinks it worth while to mention fifty squadrons, the others being in a rudimentary condition. . . .

SIR THOMAS INSKIP: . . . Eighty is right. They have not all their full complement because it has not been thought right to keep back the formation of squadrons because they cannot have their full personnel. But I am not able to answer the question as to the extent to which they are equipped.

MR CHURCHILL: I am sure a very large number of them have not got half their establishment strength; and I am taking it at twelve, because there is a theoretical establishment strength of eighteen, which is not approached anywhere.

Confident that the materials he had been sent were both accurate and comprehensive, Churchill continued: 'I could certainly name the number of a dozen squadrons which have nothing like their proper outfit of aeroplanes. Others, where there are a great number of pilots but so few aeroplanes for them that the pilots cannot go on with their training. I have also heard 150 at a time are to go to Uxbridge for physical training, so that they do not get toned down and slipshod, and so forth.' Churchill's remarks continued:

I do suggest that if the Minister could for his own satisfaction have a most strict 'field state' made of the strength of the different squadrons on a given day, because your case is you have not only aeroplanes that go into action, behind them you have six per squadron in immediate reserve; behind them again are to be the one hundred per cent stored reserve that is what you call a First Line aeroplane, and that is what you judge the German scale so strictly about. But if you looked you would find hardly half of your own status was achieved.

The fact remained, Churchill charged, 'that we have not got eighty effective Metropolitan Squadrons, or anything like that to guard us in the coming year', to which Inskip replied: 'If the emphasis is on "effective", I agree. . . .'

The deputation of November 23 did not receive the assurances it had hoped for; indeed, Churchill's persistent questioning had revealed important new areas for doubt and concern. Within a month, on December 20, Churchill drew up for the Committee of Imperial Defence a succinct, two-page analysis of the Air Staff's figures for German air strength, the French figures, German statements, and his own deductions. It was the last in a series of papers which he had been allowed to circulate, and in which he had consistently challenged the official

Government estimates of Germany's first-line capacity.[1] Basing himself entirely upon the figures produced in two previous Air Staff papers, 1216B and 1264B, Churchill wrote:

We therefore have on the Air Staff's own figures over 4,000 modern military machines constructed within the last 3 years, and over 3,200 fully trained pilots at the disposal of the German Government to-day. Yet we are asked in CID Paper No 1216B to believe that their front-line strength should be reckoned at no more than 810 machines (ie 90 squadrons of 9 each). In other words, only 20 per cent of the machines and 25 per cent of the fully-trained pilots known to be available are to be reckoned in the German front line. . . .

In Paper No ADR 52, paragraph 3, we are told that on that date 90 squadrons had been identified, so that we must conclude, if the Air Staff information is correct, that between the 1st June and the 1st September, ie in 3 months, not one single squadron has been added to the German Air Force. In fact, if we take the German official figure of 88 squadrons, 2 squadrons have been removed—an unexpected gesture of disarmament. . . .

Churchill's memorandum ended:

A point of some interest is that the French Government believes the German first-line strength to have risen from 1,356 machines at the beginning of May to 1,964 at the end of December ie, 608 machines, or, in their mode of counting, over 50 squadrons. This is, of course, in flagrant contradiction with the Air Staff view that the present strength is only 90 squadrons which had already been identified on the 31st May, ie, that no increase has occurred in the last six months.

On November 25 Churchill learnt of a breakthrough in his efforts to win Labour Party support in his campaign, for on that day Frederick Guest wrote to him, succinctly: 'Attlee will support you on any re-armament programme. He admires & likes you. The door is open if you want to talk to him.'

On November 30 Churchill was at Chartwell, where he celebrated his sixty-second birthday, and prepared his Albert Hall speech. This speech, which he gave on December 3, marked a culmination of his efforts to unite all those who believed in collective security, irrespective

[1] Churchill's memorandum was registered at the Committee of Imperial Defence as paper 1295–B, 'Most Secret'. It was circulated to the CID on Lord Swinton's instructions on 11 January 1937.

of the political party to which they belonged. Sir Walter Citrine presided. A former conscientious objector, Lord Allen of Hurtwood,[1] was among those on the platform, as were Lord Wolmer, Lord Melchett and Sir Archibald Sinclair. Among the messages of support that were read out before Churchill's speech was one from Austen Chamberlain, one from Sir Herbert Samuel and one from J. R. Clynes.[2]

There was, said Churchill in his opening remarks, only a single object in their meeting together—to stop the war of which they had heard 'so much talk'. He then set out the different errors which they sought to avoid, above all those of Sir Oswald Mosley and his followers, 'fascinated by the spectacle of brutal power', and of the Communists 'whose sole aim is to throw the world into one supreme convulsion'. Mosley's followers, Churchill warned, 'grovelled to Nazi dictatorship in order that they could make people in their turn grovel to them'. As for the pacifists like George Lansbury, they were indeed 'pious men', Churchill said, 'but they would lead the country to ruin, even more surely than all the others'. Churchill then set out what he believed to be the duty of 'the whole masses of the people' in all democracies to join together in voluntary and spontaneous comradeship, and even to accept 'a measure of self-imposed discipline'.

The past failures of the League must not dishearten them, Churchill continued. Its great days were still to come. It would be 'madness in the present years of peril' to discard the one potential for salvation. The strongly armed nations should be rallied under the League, and Germany invited 'to take her part among us'; this development alone could ward off from the whole world 'calamities and horrors the end of which no man can foresee'.

[1] Reginald Clifford Allen, 1889–1939. Educated at Berkhamsted, University College Bristol, and Peterhouse Cambridge. Secretary and General Manager of the *Daily Citizen*, 1911–15. Chairman of the No-Conscription Fellowship, 1915–19. Imprisoned three times for refusing military service, 1917–19. A Labour Party delegate to Russia, 1920. Treasurer and Chairman of the Independent Labour Party, 1922–26. Chairman, the *New Leader*, 1922–26. Director of the *Daily Herald*, 1925–30. Created Baron Allen of Hurtwood, 1932. A leading advocate of conciliation with Germany, 1933–37, when he twice visited Hitler.

[2] John Robert Clynes, 1869–1949. Labour MP, Manchester Platting, 1906–31; 1935–45. President, National Union of General and Municipal Workers. Parliamentary Secretary, Ministry of Food, 1917–18. Privy Councillor, 1918. Food Controller, 1918–19. Chairman, Parliamentary Labour Party, 1921–22. Lord Privy Seal, 1924. Home Secretary, 1929–31.

41

The Abdication

AS a senior Privy Councillor, Churchill had been present at the various official ceremonies held to mark the accession of Edward VIII, and on 2 February 1936 he had written to the new King:

> I could not let these memorable days pass away without venturing to write how deeply I have felt for Your Majesty in the sorrow of a father's death, and in the ordeal of mounting a Throne.
>
> I have many memories of the Prince of Wales since the Investiture at Caernarvon Castle twenty-five years ago, which are joyous and gay in my mind, and also above all I have the sense of a friendship with which I was honoured.
>
> Now I address myself to the King; and offer dutifully yet in no formal sense my faithful service and my heartfelt wishes that a reign which has been so nobly begun may be blessed with peace and true glory; and that in the long swing of events Your Majesty's name will shine in history as the bravest and best beloved of all the sovereigns who have worn the island Crown.

Almost from the moment of the King's accession, gossip alleged that he intended to marry his American friend, Wallis Simpson,[1] with whom he was deeply in love. Mrs Simpson, who had been twice married, was hoping shortly to divorce her second husband on the grounds of his adultery. Many people were horrified at the thought of the King marrying an American divorcée, and rumours abounded that he would not, in fact, be allowed by the Government to proceed with such a marriage. Churchill had heard these rumours, and was himself perturbed by the idea of such a marriage, but as a friend of the King, he

[1] Wallis Warfield, 1896–1986. Daughter of Teakle Wallis Warfield of Baltimore, Maryland. She married Edward, Duke of Windsor (as her third husband) on 3 June 1937. Resident in the Bahamas, 1940–45; in France from 1945.

had great sympathy with him in his dilemma. In a short narrative of events which he compiled at the end of December he wrote:

Upon the King's coming to the Throne, it was known through wide circles of politics and society that he had formed a deep attachment for Mrs Simpson. He delighted in her company, and found in her qualities as necessary to his happiness as the air he breathed. Those who knew him well and watched him closely noticed that many little tricks and fidgetings of nervousness fell away from him. He was a completed being instead of a sick and harassed soul. This experience which happens to a great many people in the flower of their youth, came late in life to him, and was all the more precious and compulsive from that fact; the association was psychical rather than sexual, and certainly not sensual except incidentally.

Although branded with the stigma of a guilty love, no companionship could have appeared more natural, more free from impropriety or grossness. Both were forty-two years old. While profoundly interested in all his duties as King, and discharging with dignity and punctilio the laborious regal routine, Edward VIII found in his mature paramour a joy and a comfort without which his life and burden seemed insupportable.

Churchill knew something of the King's burden, and had sometimes helped him. Twice during July he had drafted speeches for him, one on the occasion of presenting Colours to three senior Guards regiments, the other for a broadcast to Canada during a ceremony at Vimy ridge before 6,000 Canadian soldiers. Churchill's narrative continued:

For twenty-five years as Prince of Wales he had faithfully and diligently discharged public duties of a ceremonial character most serviceable to all sorts and conditions of people in all parts of British dominions, but most wearing and exhausting to himself. 'How would you like' he exclaimed once to the present writer, 'to have to make a thousand speeches, and never once to be allowed to say what you think yourself?'

The sense of unreality, of discharging a function which though blatant to the world, must always be kept clear of controversy of any kind, cast its shadows upon the servant of constitutional requirements. To have to seek harmony and reality in his private life such as is granted to the vast masses of men and women the world over, was an intense desire, and might at any moment become an abnormal obsession.

A life of glittering public pomp without a home and some human comfort in the background would not be endurable to the vast majority of men. One must have something real somewhere. Otherwise far better die.

At the beginning of July the King's legal adviser, Walter Monckton,[1] had sought Churchill's advice, and on July 7 Churchill received him at Morpeth Mansions. In his narrative of events Churchill recorded:

He told me that Mrs Simpson was contemplating divorcing her husband who was more than ready to comply as he was already living with someone else. Mr Monckton assured me that the King had no thought of marrying Mrs Simpson, but would be glad to see her free, as his 'possessive sense' was strong. What did I think about this? He also enquired what I thought about Mrs Simpson being invited to Balmoral.

In reply I said that such a divorce would be most dangerous; that people were free to believe or ignore gossip as they chose; but that court proceedings were in another sphere. If any judgement was given in court against Mr Simpson it would be open to any Minister of Religion to say from the pulpit that an innocent man had allowed himself to be divorced on account of the King's intimacies with his wife. I urged most strongly that every effort should be made to prevent such a suit.

About Balmoral: I deprecated strongly Mrs Simpson going to such a highly official place upon which the eyes of Scotland were concentrated and which was already sacred to the memories of Queen Victoria and John Brown.[2] What I said as reported was not at all pleasing to Mrs Simpson and I heard that she had expressed herself with surprise that I should have shown myself to be 'against her'.

Churchill's opposition to the Simpson divorce, and his reluctance to see Mrs Simpson being invited to Balmoral, were decisive; he was not consulted again on the question of how the King ought to proceed. On October 27 Mrs Simpson was awarded a decree nisi at the Suffolk Assizes in Ipswich. The way was open for the King to marry her, once the decree had been made absolute. The British Press was silent, but in the United States there was public speculation as to when the royal marriage would take place. Nor was such speculation fanciful; on November 16, only three weeks after the decree nisi, the King informed Baldwin of his determination to marry Mrs Simpson. Baldwin, while sympathetic to the King's dilemma, was totally opposed to the marriage.

---

[1] Walter Turner Monckton, 1891–1965. Educated at Harrow and Balliol College Oxford. President of the Oxford Union Society, 1913. On active service, 1915–19 (Military Cross). Called to the Bar, 1919. King's Counsel, 1930. Attorney-General to the Prince of Wales, 1932–36. Knighted, 1937. Director-General of the Press and Censorship Bureau, 1939–40. Director-General, Ministry of Information, 1940–41; of British Propaganda and Information Services, Cairo, 1941–42. Solicitor General, 1945. Conservative MP for Bristol West, 1951–57. Minister of Labour and National Service, 1951–55. Minister of Defence, 1955–56. Paymaster General, 1956–57. Created Viscount, 1957.

[2] Queen Victoria's favourite Highland servant. In 1901, as soon as Edward VII ascended the throne, he ordered the immediate destruction or removal of all the statues, busts and other memorials which the Queen had put up to Brown after his death.

The Cabinet shared his opposition, as did a small deputation of senior parliamentarians, led by Lord Salisbury, who called on Baldwin on November 17. Churchill had declined to join this deputation, and at a private meeting in the House of Lords had given his reasons. Two and a half weeks later, in a letter to Churchill on December 5, Lord Salisbury recalled Churchill's attitude at that time:

... you intimated that while you shared our views you would by joining this deputation lose all influence over the King, that he was sure to consult you and that you wanted to say to him that just as you and others had made every sacrifice in the War (so I understood), so he must now be willing to make every sacrifice for his Country.

Churchill was convinced that in order to remain on the throne, the King should at once give up all idea of marrying Mrs Simpson. On the morning of November 25 he joined the two Opposition Party leaders, Clement Attlee and Archibald Sinclair, who had been invited by Baldwin to 10 Downing Street to discuss the crisis. Baldwin told them that he envisaged a moment when, the King having refused to abandon his idea of marriage, the Government would then resign. Both Attlee and Sinclair agreed that in such an event neither the Labour nor Liberal Parties would agree to form an alternative administration. According to Neville Chamberlain's account of the meeting, Churchill told Baldwin that although his attitude was 'a little difficult', he too 'would certainly support the Government'. Chamberlain, however, was suspicious of this assurance, believing that Churchill was 'moving mysteriously in the background and, it is suggested, expressing willingness to form a Government if there should be any refusal on our part to agree'. In fact, Churchill did support the pressure that was being put on Mrs Simpson to bring matters to a conclusion by action of her own. As he recorded in his narrative of events:

... I was aware that very strenuous efforts were being made by Lord Beaverbrook through Lord Brownlow[1] to induce Mrs Simpson who was at Cannes to renounce all idea of marriage, morganatic or otherwise, with the King. This could have been rendered decisive at any moment by withdrawing her petition for divorce upon which she had obtained the decree nisi. It is my belief that if this had been obtained, the intense pressure then

[1] Peregrine Francis Adelbert Cust, 1899–1978. Educated at Eton and Sandhurst. 2nd Lieutenant, Grenadier Guards 1918; Adjutant, 3rd Battalion, 1923–26. Succeeded his father as 6th Baron Brownlow, 1927. Lord in Waiting to King Edward VIII, 1936. Flight Lieutenant, RAF Volunteer Reserve, 1939. Parliamentary Private Secretary to Lord Beaverbrook (Minister of Aircraft Production), 1940. Attached to Bomber Command, 1941. Staff Officer, Air Staff, 1942; attached to US Air Force Staff, 1943. Squadron Leader, 1944.

at work both upon His Majesty and Mrs Simpson would have resulted in her taking this step and thus ending the crisis.

Mrs Simpson knew that the King was determined to marry her, and refused to renounce the idea of marriage. Rumour had it that the King might even abdicate in order to marry Mrs Simpson. Churchill, fearing that pressure or haste might lead to wrong decisions, wanted the King to have plenty of time to decide what to do. But at a meeting of the Cabinet on Wednesday December 2, only Duff Cooper pleaded, in vain, for delay, arguing that the King should be crowned as planned in May 1937, and the marriage question be only then brought forward. That same day Churchill lunched with Sir Walter Citrine, who later recalled how:

> . . . Winston fell to talking about the King and Mrs Simpson. He was very concerned about what might happen. He stressed that the King was deeply in love with her and would not give her up. I then disclosed to him the nature of the conversation I had had with Baldwin and concluded by saying that I had no doubt whatever that the trade union movement would back the Government even if it came to the King's abdicating. Winston seemed perturbed at this and urged me to go to see the King. 'Why should I do that?' I retorted. 'If he wants to see me, of course I will go. Then I will tell him what I told Baldwin.'
>
> Winston then remarked very quietly: 'I will defend him. I think it is my duty.'
>
> 'What?' I said. 'Irrespective of what he has done?'
>
> Winston looked grave, and, putting his hands on his breast, he said with emotion, 'He feels it here. . . .'

On the evening of December 2, the King told Baldwin that nothing could induce him not to marry Mrs Simpson. Baldwin at once made it clear that any such marriage would be unacceptable to the Government, even if Mrs Simpson were to remain a private citizen. On the following morning *The Times*, in its leading article, referred obliquely but censoriously to 'a marriage incompatible with the Throne'. That same day, at Question Time in the House of Commons, Churchill asked for an assurance that 'no irrevocable step' would be taken about the King before Parliament had been informed. His question was met with a hostile murmur. Later that afternoon Churchill went to Stornoway House, where he discussed the King's position with Lord Beaverbrook, and with the King's solicitor, George Allen.[1] All three favoured the King's own preference for making a broadcast in

---

[1] Albert George Allen, 1888–1956. Solicitor. On active service in France, 1914–18 (Military Cross, DSO, despatches twice). Private solicitor to Edward VIII, 1936. Knighted, 1952.

which he would win public support. But that same evening, at Buckingham Palace, Baldwin told the King that such a broadcast would be 'thoroughly unconstitutional. To broadcast would be to go over the heads of your Ministers and speak to the people,' and Baldwin added: 'You may, by speaking, divide opinion; but you will certainly harden it. The Churches are straining at the leash. Only three papers would be on your side, the *News Chronicle*, the *Daily Mail*, and the *Daily Express*.'

It was becoming clear that an increasingly hostile body of opinion was forming against allowing the King to marry Mrs Simpson and at the same time to remain King. In his diary that evening Harold Nicolson noted: 'I do not find people angry with Mrs Simpson, but I do find a deep and enraged fury against the King himself.'

At the end of his interview with Baldwin on the evening of December 3, the King had asked if he could see Churchill, as 'an old friend with whom he could talk freely'. Baldwin agreed, and on the afternoon of Friday December 4 Churchill was invited to dine at Fort Belvedere.

Once more, at Question Time in the House of Commons on December 4, Churchill asked for Parliament to be kept properly informed of the course of events. This time his question was received with cheers, and David Margesson reported to Baldwin that there was a growing support for Churchill's view, which was shared by at least forty MPs.

Early that evening Baldwin informed the King, at Fort Belvedere, that the Cabinet had rejected his request to broadcast. Baldwin added that he would like a decision about Mrs Simpson without delay; if possible during the weekend, and even, perhaps, that same evening. To this request for speed the King replied: 'You will not have to wait much longer. . . .'

Churchill reached Fort Belvedere later that evening. In his narrative of events he recalled:

I saw the King at once. HM was most gay and debonair for the first quarter of an hour, and no one would have thought him in a serious crisis. But after this effort it was obvious that the personal strain he had been so long under, and which was now at its climax had exhausted him to a most painful degree.

On the way down I had made up my mind that never having been consulted at all for so many months, I would not advise on any point except one, viz: time. He must have full time for his decision. During the course of a long evening I confined myself strictly to this point.

The King told me that he had said to Mr Baldwin, '*You* can see anyone you like. You can send for anyone you like. You can consult with any number of people. You can arrange with the newspapers and with the Church; you can bring the Dominion High Commissioners together; you can set the Whips to work upon the MP's. But I cannot see anyone except those you send me, like the Archbishop of Canterbury[1] or Mr Geoffrey Dawson of the "Times". I want to see Mr Churchill.' Mr Baldwin had replied 'Certainly.'

The King also said 'I have not abdicated. I never used the word abdication in my conversation with the Prime Minister. I had Monckton in the room with his permission all the time and he will bear me out.'

HM told me that he had desired to issue a broadcast message to his peoples and that his Ministers had forbidden him, but had told him that there would be no objection if he had abdicated. Then he would speak as a private person and not 'on advice'. Meanwhile if he desired the Government would make a statement on his behalf, and Mr Baldwin would bring him this tomorrow (Saturday) evening.

The King went on 'I am sure that in this statement they will insert a declaration that I have renounced the Throne.' He was evidently most strongly averse from this. He said he wanted a fortnight to weigh the whole matter. He felt himself a prisoner in the Fort. If he could go to Switzerland with a couple of equerries he would be able to think out his decisions without undue pressure. He asked me what would happen if he made this request to Mr Baldwin when he saw him the next day. Did I think that the Ministers would resign unless he immediately consented to abdication.

In reply as the conversation proceeded, I said 'Your Majesty need not have the slightest fear about time. If you require time there is no force in this country which would or could deny it you. Mr Baldwin would certainly not resist you. If he did you could remind him that he himself took nearly three months rest in order to recover from the strain of the session. Your strain was far more intense and prolonged. Mr Baldwin is a fatherly man and nothing would induce him to treat you harshly in such a matter. Ministers could not possibly resign on such an issue as your request for time.'

To avoid any misunderstanding, Churchill dictated the substance of his advice to a shorthand writer, in the King's presence. He also added two extra pieces of advice:

First that he should not on any account leave the country. That would produce the worst possible impression. Everyone would say that he had gone

[1] Cosmo Gordon Lang, 1864–1945. Educated at Glasgow University and Balliol College Oxford; Fellow of All Souls, 1889–93. Dean of Divinity, Magdalen College Oxford, 1893–96. Honorary Chaplain to Queen Victoria. Bishop of Stepney, 1901–08. Archbishop of York, 1908–28. Privy Councillor, 1909. Archbishop of Canterbury, 1928–42. Knighted, 1937. Created Baron, 1942. In a broadcast on Sunday 13 December 1936 he criticized Edward VIII for having 'sought his happiness in a manner inconsistent with the Christian principles of marriage, and within a social circle whose standard and way of life are alien to all the best instincts and traditions of his people. Let those who belong to this circle know that today they stand rebuked by the judgment of the nation which had loved King Edward'.

to meet Mrs Simpson (then at Cannes). His Majesty demurred to this; said he had no intention of seeing her, but that a complete change in the Alps was what he required.

Secondly I urged him strongly to send for Lord Dawson[1] and Sir Thomas Horder.[2] I was sure that he was in no condition to take so grave a decision as that which lay upon him. He twice in my presence completely lost the thread of what he was saying, and appeared to me driven to the last extremity of endurance.

The King himself later recalled several other aspects of the evening's discussion. 'When Mr Baldwin had talked to me about the Monarchy,' he wrote in his memoirs, 'it had seemed a dry and lifeless thing. But when Mr Churchill spoke it lived, it grew, it became suffused with light.' The King's account continued:

Mr Churchill was particularly outraged by Mr Baldwin's action in securing from the leaders of the Opposition parties, namely Mr Clement Attlee of the Labour Party and Sir Archibald Sinclair of the Liberals, a promise not to participate in the formation of a new Government were he to resign and were I to ask them to form another in its place. The practical effect of this *modus vivendi*, he insisted, was to confront the Sovereign with an ultimatum.

Whatever else might happen, he argued, the hereditary principle must not be left to the mercy of politicians trimming their doctrines 'to the varying hour'.

As is usual with Mr Churchill, there was a practical plan behind the fine words. If the Prime Minister persisted with his importunities he suggested that I should claim a respite from strain, adding half whimsically that I should retire to Windsor Castle and close the gates, stationing at one my father's old doctor, Lord Dawson of Penn, and at the other my recently appointed Physician-in-Ordinary, Lord Horder.

Mr Churchill informed us of his own intentions. First, he proposed to despatch on the morrow a private letter to the Prime Minister warning him and his Cabinet colleagues of the disaster that would ensue if they persisted in hurrying the King. At the same time, he would issue a statement to the Press bringing forward all the compelling arguments for delay. His parting words, as he left us well after midnight, were: 'Sir, it is a time for reflection. You

---

[1] Bertrand Dawson, 1864–1945. Physician, 1906. Physician-in-ordinary to King Edward VII, 1906–10; to King George V, 1910–36; to the Prince of Wales (later Edward VIII), 1929–36. Knighted, 1911; Created Baron, 1920; Viscount, 1936. Chairman, Army Medical Advisory Board, 1936–45.

[2] Thomas Jeeves Horder, 1871–1955. Physician to the Prince of Wales (later Edward VIII), 1911–36 and to King George VI, 1936–52. Knighted, 1918. Created Baronet, 1923. Created Baron, 1933. Chairman of the British Empire Cancer Campaign, Wireless for the Bedridden, Mobile Physiotheraphy and the Noise Abatement League.

must allow time for the battalions to march.' Then he set off for London, to Max Beaverbrook.

On the morning of Saturday December 5 Churchill sent Baldwin a full account of his conversation with the King, and of the King's 'mental exhaustion'. The combination of public and private stresses, he pointed out, 'is the hardest of all to endure'. Churchill added:

I told the King that if he appealed to you to allow him time to recover himself and to consider now that things have reached this chaos the grave issues constitutional and personal with which you have found it your duty to confront him, you would I was sure not fail in kindness and consideration. It would be most cruel and wrong to extort a decision from him in his present state.

Churchill was confident that Baldwin would allow the King at least a month in which to decide on what course to take. He was also anxious to encourage the King to avoid all mistakes and to gather as much support as possible. That evening he wrote to the King from Morpeth Mansions:

Sir,

News from all fronts! No pistol to be held at the King's head. No doubt that this request for time will be granted. Therefore no final decision or Bill till after Christmas—probably February or March.

2. *On no account must the King leave the country*. Windsor Castle is his battle station (poste de commandment). When so much is at stake, no minor inclinations can be indulged. It would be far better for Mrs Simpson to return to England for a day or two, than for the King to go abroad now. Please let me talk to you about this if there is any doubt. (This would at any rate show she had not been driven out of the country). But of course better still if she preferred to remain where she is for this critical time.

3. Lord Craigavon, Prime Minister of Northern Ireland is deeply moved by loyalty to the King, and all for time. Could not he be invited to luncheon tomorrow? He has a constitutional right of access (I think) & anyhow there could be no objection. His visit should be made public. He shares my hopes such as they are of an ultimate happy ending. Its a long way to Tipperary.

4. Max. The King brought him back across the world. He is a tiger to fight. I gave him the King's message &—please telephone or write—better telephone. I cannot see it would do harm to see him if it could be arranged. Important however to make contact with him. A *devoted* tiger! Very scarce breed. . . .

For forty-eight hours Churchill had been seeking, as the King had asked him, to obtain support for a short delay in the King's decision. Several senior Conservatives viewed the prospect of any such delay with alarm. On December 5 Lord Salisbury wrote to Churchill from Hatfield House, to remind him of his earlier private declaration, in mid-November, that the King must be prepared to make sacrifices for the sake of his country. Salisbury's letter continued:

I did not press you then, but I am watching your attitude now with great anxiety. If your purpose now is the same as it was in our conversation and you are still intent upon persuading him to make every sacrifice of his personal interests and desires for his Country it would enable us to be less anxious.

It does not shock me that a man should want to marry his mistress nor worry me that a man should be willing to marry a woman who has two other living husbands, but it is very different that a man born to sublime responsibilities should be ready to jeopardise them, as it seems, in order to gratify his passion for a woman of any sort.

Churchill's statement was published in the Press on Sunday December 6. 'I plead for time and patience,' he began, and added: 'The nation must realise the character of the constitutional issue. There is no question of any conflict between the King and Parliament. Parliament has not been consulted in any way, nor allowed to express any opinion. The question is whether the King is to abdicate upon the advice of the Ministry of the day.' Churchill continued:

This is not a case where differences have arisen between the Sovereign and his Ministers on any particular measure. These could certainly be resolved by normal processes of Parliament or dissolution. In this case we are in presence of a wish expressed by the Sovereign to perform an act which in no circumstances can be accomplished for nearly five months, and may conceivably for various reasons never be accomplished at all. That on such a hypothetical and suppositious basis the supreme sacrifice of abdication and potential exile of the Sovereign should be demanded, finds no support whatever in the British constitution. . . .

In his statement Churchill went on to insist that a precipitate abdication could only weaken the constitutional position of the monarchy 'irrespective of the existing occupant of the Throne'. It was essential for Parliament to ensure that such an event as the signing of an abdication was not carried out in such a way as to enable the process to be repeated 'with equal uncanny facility at no distant date in unforeseen circumstances'. Time was needed for 'searching constitutional debate'. His statement continued: 'If the King refuses to take the advice of his Ministers they are of course free to resign. They have no right whatever to put pressure upon him to accept their advice by soliciting beforehand assurances from the Leader of the Opposition that he will not form an alternative administration in the event of their resignation, and thus confronting the King with an ultimatum.' Churchill's statement went on:

Why cannot time be granted? The fact that it is beyond the King's power to accomplish the purpose which Ministers oppose until the end of April, surely strips the matter of constitutional urgency. There may be some inconvenience, but that inconvenience stands on a different plane altogether from the grave constitutional issues I have set forth. National and Imperial considerations alike require that before such a dread step as a demand for abdication is taken, not only should the constitutional position be newly defined by Parliament, but that every method should be exhausted which gives the hope of a happier solution.

Churchill then raised what he called the 'human and personal aspect'. For many weeks the King had been under 'the greatest strain, moral and mental, that can fall upon a man'. And he went on: 'Not only has he been inevitably subjected to the extreme stress of his public duty, but also to the agony of his own personal feelings.'

Churchill's statement ended with a strong criticism of the power of the Cabinet, and of the dangers involved in their exercise of that power:

The King has no means of personal access to his Parliament or his people. Between him and them stand in their office the Ministers of the Crown. If they thought it their duty to engage all their power and influence against him, still he must remain silent.

All the more must they be careful not to be the judge in their own case, and to show a loyal and Christian patience even at some political embarrassment to themselves. . . .

Churchill's statement provoked a mixed response. 'How can you suggest,' J. A. Spender[1] wrote on December 6, 'that the present state of things should be prolonged for five months—five months of raging & tearing controversy, quite possibly a King's party being formed against the Government, the Crown a centre of schism tearing Country and Commonwealth to pieces & all this at this moment in world affairs!' It was, Spender added, 'a grotesque situation for the British Constitution & Monarchy & will set all the Agitators jeering, if it is allowed to go on. The danger of its going on is that the K may suppose

---

[1] John Alfred Spender, 1862–1942. Educated at Balliol College Oxford. Entered journalism, 1886. Editor of the *Westminster Gazette*, 1896–1922. A friend of Asquith's, and a staunch Asquithian Liberal. Co-author of *The Life of Lord Oxford and Asquith* (1932), and of seventeen other volumes, including a memoir, *Life, Journalism and Politics* (1927).

that he will have the backing of influential people like yourself in fighting the Government & damning the consequences & I am sure you can't mean that.'

One close friend who approved of Churchill's statement was Desmond Morton, who wrote on December 6:

Pray God, you may be successful. As you know better than I, there is an overwhelming desire in the country that he should remain our King. Persons of all classes to whom I have spoken, are unanimous in that. True, I find that they cannot acclimatise themselves to Mrs S. as Queen, and I think that the great majority would be very much distressed were she his wife, without the Royal dignity.

If, however, he can by any means give her up, his popularity would be so great that he could make himself Dictator of England, if so he chose. . . .

Baldwin was determined upon an immediate decision, and told a meeting of senior Ministers on the morning of Sunday December 6: 'This matter must be finished before Christmas.' According to Walter Monckton, who was present at the meeting, Neville Chamberlain had argued that to wait even that long—less than three weeks—was impossible, as the continued uncertainty was hurting the Christmas trade.

Despite Churchill's plea on his behalf, the King himself was increasingly disposed to give up the struggle, to abdicate, to make his broadcast as a private person, to go abroad, and to marry Mrs Simpson as soon as her divorce was made absolute. As Beaverbrook had told Churchill on the telephone on the previous day: 'Our cock won't fight.' But while Beaverbrook saw the futility of continuing to press for time, Churchill failed to see that the King had changed his mind since asking for his help on this very matter two days before.

During Sunday December 6 Churchill was at Chartwell, discussing with friends a possible formula to which they hoped the King would subscribe. Among those friends were Archibald Sinclair and Robert Boothby. The best course to avoid abdication seemed to them to be a public statement by the King, in which he would agree to accept the Cabinet's advice as to the possibility of his marriage, as and when the situation were to arise. As Mrs Simpson's divorce would not become absolute until April, the Cabinet's involvement would, by this device, be postponed for more than four months, and its decision, accepted in advance, would enable the King to retain his throne. Churchill put forward this possible solution in a draft letter which his friends asked him to send to the King; a letter which represented the outcome of the Chartwell discussions:

Sir,

You kindly said I might write to your Majesty about the opinion I encounter.

The only possibility of your Majesty remaining on the Throne is if you could subscribe to some such Declaration as the following:—

'The King will not enter into any contract of marriage contrary to the advice of His Ministers.'

I forbear to use any arguments because all that will be apparent to your Majesty.

Sir I cannot claim any authority behind this suggestion except my own belief. But I earnestly hope it may be considered.

With my humble duty

Your Majesty's most faithful servant & subject
Winston S. Churchill

This formula was put to the King in full on the morning of Monday December 7, both Sinclair and Churchill being specifically named as its authors. But, as Churchill wrote to Boothby four days later, when finally he had discovered what had happened to the formula:

. . . he turned it aside on the grounds that it would not be honourable to play for time when his fundamental resolve was unchanged, and as he declared unchangeable. It was certainly this very strict point of honour which cost him his Crown. Whether I could have prevailed upon him personally, I do not know. It is however certain that I should not have been allowed access to him, as the Ministers were already angry with Baldwin for having given him permission to see me on Friday, and he had been made aware of this fact.

From that moment, Churchill added, 'no human effort could have altered the course of events'.

Before he had learned of the King's attitude and of his determination to abdicate, Churchill decided to repeat, and defend, his plea for time in the House of Commons that Monday. At noon, before doing so, he was one of the principal guests at the Anglo-French Luncheon Club, where he spoke of the need for the 'closest possible accord and co-operation between Britain and France'. Paul Reynaud, the principal French guest, spoke approvingly of these sentiments. At the lunch Churchill was photographed grim faced and sombre. Then he went down to the House of Commons, where Baldwin was answering questions about the crisis, and telling the House that no decision had been reached, but that the King was still making up his mind. Churchill, in his letter to Boothby of December 11, explained what happened:

I reached the House on Monday rather prepared in my mind to be attacked for what I had written over the weekend, and, addressing myself too attentively to that possibility, I did not sufficiently realise how far the Prime

Minister had gone to meet the views I had expressed. I ought of course to have welcomed what he said. . . .

On reaching the Chamber, Churchill rose for the third time in four days to demand that 'no irrevocable step will be taken before the House had received a full statement', and began to elaborate and defend his own Press Statement of the previous day. The House reacted with immediate fury and indignation, howling at Churchill with derision. Cries of 'Drop it' and 'Twister' came from all sides. 'He was completely staggered,' Amery noted in his diary, 'by the unanimous hostility of the House.'

Churchill remained standing, trying despite the uproar to make his point about the need for time and patience. But the shouts from both sides of the House remained at a crescendo and then, to Churchill's intense surprise, the Speaker ruled him out of order: he could not make a speech at Question Time.

Angered and flushed, Churchill shouted at Baldwin—according to Lord Beaverbrook's account—'You won't be satisfied until you've broken him, will you?' and then walked out of the Chamber, followed by Brendan Bracken. A few moments later, in the corridor off the Lobby, Davidson was reading the ticker-tapes when Churchill came up to glance at them. 'He said that his political career was finished,' Davidson later recalled.

The extent of the Common's hostility momentarily shook Churchill's confidence. It was, Lord Winterton later wrote, 'one of the angriest manifestations I have ever heard directed against any man in the House of Commons'. Four days later Boothby wrote to Churchill of how, going to the smoking-room immediately after Churchill's sudden exit, 'I found several members of that particular group you always imagine are your most loyal supporters, roundly abusing you, & accusing you of playing for your own hands'. Even his own mood, Boothby wrote, was made up of 'a ferment of indignation and disappointment'.

During the afternoon of December 7, within an hour of the hostile outburst, Boothby himself wrote to Churchill from the House of Commons:

Dear Winston,

I understood last night that we had *agreed* upon a formula, and a course, designed to save the King from abdication, if that is possible. I thought you were going to use all your powers—decisive, as I believe, in the present circumstances—to secure a happy issue, on the lines that were suggested.

But this afternoon you have delivered a blow to the King, both in the

House and in the country, far harder than any that Baldwin ever conceived of.

You have reduced the number of potential supporters to the minimum possible—I shd think now about seven in all.

And you have done it without any consultation with your best friends and supporters. I have never said anything to you that I did not sincerely believe. And I never will.

What happened this afternoon makes me feel that it is almost impossible for those who are most devoted to you personally, to follow you blindly (as they wd like to do) in politics. Because they cannot be sure where the hell they are going to be landed next.

I'm afraid this letter will make you very angry. But not, I hope, irretrievably angry. I could not leave what I feel unsaid.

> Yrs ever
> Bob

That evening Boothby showed Walter Monckton the Chartwell formula. Monckton, who had not seen the formula before, became 'quite excited', Boothby wrote to Churchill four days later, 'and telephoned the King in the middle of dinner asking him to hold his hand, as he had a new suggestion to make. The King agreed; and Walter left for Fort Belvedere immediately after dinner, saying there was hope once more.'

One person who disapproved of Churchill's action in pleading for the King was his friend Commander Diggle, who had supported him throughout the India Bill controversy, and who now accused him of disloyal conduct. On December 8 Churchill wrote to Diggle:

According to my belief an Act of Abdication will produce a profound lesion in the unity of this country, with parallel degeneration in the Dominions. I am still of opinion that given time and patience this disaster will be averted and the news recently received from Cannes seems to indicate increasingly hopeful possibilities. . . .

If in a few days we find that a happy solution has been achieved in which this disastrous marriage has been renounced and abdication avoided, I shall expect you to make your amends to me, for I have never diverged by a hair's breadth from the path of loyalty and honour.

On the morning of December 8 *The Times* published a report by its Parliamentary correspondent, Alan Robbins.[1] 'Members were frankly amazed,' he wrote, 'that Mr Churchill had allowed himself to be placed

---

[1] Alan Pitt Robbins, 1888–1967. Educated City of London School. Reporter, *Yorkshire Post*, 1904–08. Editorial Staff of *The Times*, 1909–53; Parliamentary correspondent, 1923–38, and News Editor, 1938–53. Chairman of the Parliamentary Lobby Journalists, 1932. Chairman of the Newspaper Press Fund. Secretary, General Council of the Press, 1954–60.

in a position in which he experienced the most striking rebuff of modern parliamentary history.' According to the correspondent the only regret was that Churchill had not moved an adjournment, as 'The House of Commons would have been able to see for the first time the insignificant size of the section which is following Mr Churchill.' MPs had already been 'irritated' by Churchill's question on Friday. 'Yesterday there was a wave of real anger when he returned to the point and the protest against him came from Conservative, Liberal, and Labour members alike.'

Throughout Tuesday December 8, Churchill's friends and colleagues speculated on the effect which the unprecedented outburst in the House of Commons would have upon his career. 'The House of Commons has stood firm,' Thomas Jones wrote to Lady Grigg on December 8, 'and of course Winston has sent S.B.'s stock up by his misguided and persistent questioning about the "irrevocable step". . . .' That same day Harold Nicolson wrote in his diary: 'He has undone in five minutes the patient reconstruction work of two years.' This view was widely shared. On December 11 the *Spectator* declared in its editorial column: 'He has utterly misjudged the temper of the country and the temper of the House, and the reputation which he was beginning to shake off of a wayward genius unserviceable in council has settled firmly on his shoulders again.'

In his letter to Churchill on December 11, Robert Boothby expressed these same feelings. 'One thing I regret,' he wrote, 'is that your intervention at question-time last Monday may have temporarily diminished your power and authority in the House, which prior to that had seldom been greater, and certainly had never been so necessary for the country.' Boothby added, still in an angry mood:

For ten years, as one of your most devoted followers, I have fought a losing battle against the influence of the Die-hards, the Press Lords, and Brendan.

Because I believe that the Die-hards are not fundamentally loyal to you, that the Press Lords, (and especially one of them) are your most dangerous enemies, and that Brendan is the best friend and the worst counsellor in the world (for instance, only this morning Clive Baillieu[1] told me he thanked God he had refused to send a series of cables to friends of his in the Australian

---

[1] Clive Latham Baillieu, 1889–1967. Educated at Melbourne University and Magdalen College Oxford. On active service 1915–18. An Australian Representative on the Imperial Economic Committee, 1930–47. Knighted, 1938. Director-General, British Purchasing Commission, Washington, 1941–42. Member of the British Supply Council in North America, 1941–43. Chairman, Fairey Aviation Company, 1943–45. Chairman of the English Speaking Union, 1951–65. Created Baron 1953. Company Director. First President of the British Institute of Management, 1959.

Government at Brendan's instigation, but under the aegis of your authority—which were not only wild and mischievous, but bore no relation to any of the facts which had since been made public).

All these people give you advice which is immediately the most alluring, and ultimately the most fatal. And I cannot help feeling that one of them got at you last Monday morning.

It is only when you rely on the power of clear disinterested argument, based on your unrivalled intellect and experience, with *the solid central mass of the House of Commons*, that you rise to the position of commanding authority which you should always occupy.

You have done it during recent weeks & months. You can and must do it again.

I believe, passionately, that you are the only man who can save this country, and the world, during the next two critical years.

On Wednesday December 9, at Morpeth Mansions, Churchill had dictated replies to all those who had written to him after his Sunday statement. 'I have never thought of such a thing as five months raging propaganda,' he wrote to J. A. Spender, 'but I have asked for ten days or a fortnight. Also that before the irrevocable act of abdication is accomplished, Parliament should examine the matter and also the consequences.' To Lord Salisbury he wrote under seal of secrecy of how, at his meeting with the King, on December 4, he had assured him 'that he had only to ask for a reasonable period of time and no Minister could deny him', and he noted:

. . . the pressure which the Government put upon the King and the Press campaign directed against him with so much brutality by the Times, together with the personal strain to which he was inevitably subjected, might well have led to his abdication any day last week. In fact the Deeds were all drawn up and in my view the Government expected to announce the abdication on Monday.

My main difference with the Government has consisted in the fact that I regarded abdication as a far greater disaster than they did, and I would have put up with the disadvantages and dangers of a prolongation of the controversy within moderate limits, in the hope, which may yet be justified, that the weakest link would snap.

'What has impressed me most during this crisis,' Churchill added, 'has been the King's virtues of courage, manliness and honour; and of his loyalty to his Ministers and respect for the Constitution.'

In his letter to Commander Diggle on December 8, and in his letter to Lord Salisbury on December 9, Churchill had reiterated his hope that the King might still agree to accept the Cabinet's verdict on his intended marriage, and if asked to do so, would give up altogether his intention of marrying Mrs Simpson. This hope, however, was unrealistic in the light of the King's own strong feelings. While Baldwin was aware throughout the crisis of the King's determination to marry, Churchill believed that the King's decision had still not been finalized.

Throughout December 9, not knowing that the King had made up his mind to abdicate, Churchill clung to his belief that a compromise could still be reached, based on the Chartwell formula, that the King would not enter into marriage against the advice of his Ministers. But the King had no intention of giving up Mrs Simpson in order to retain the throne. After spending seven hours at Fort Belvedere on December 8, Baldwin had recognized the King's complete determination to marry Mrs Simpson, even though she herself sent a message from Cannes on the morning of December 9, to the effect that she would be willing to withdraw her petition for divorce, and do 'anything to prevent the King from abdicating'. Were the divorce petition to be withdrawn as she offered, no question of marriage could possibly arise. But Mrs Simpson was no more able to change the King's mind than Baldwin had been, and a day later, on the morning of Thursday December 10, the King signed a Deed of Abdication. That same afternoon Baldwin brought the Deed to the House of Commons, together with a message from the King, asking the Commons to approve his decision. 'No more grave message has ever been received by Parliament,' Baldwin declared, 'and no more difficult, I may almost say repugnant, task has ever been imposed upon a Minister.'

During the course of his speech Baldwin stressed the King's strong personal determination to abdicate, and his reluctance throughout the crisis to seek any compromise which might in any way affect his intention to marry Mrs Simpson. 'I am convinced,' Baldwin told the House, 'that where I failed no one could have succeeded. His mind was made up, and those who know his Majesty best will know what that means.'

The House adjourned for an hour and a half. Churchill himself wrote of Baldwin's speech in the *Evening Standard* of December 28: 'He has never spoken with more force or more Parliamentary skill.' In the Lobby, while waiting for the House to reassemble, Baldwin discussed Churchill's attitude with Harold Nicolson who recorded Baldwin's words in his diary: 'Do you know, my dear Nicolson, I think Winston is the most suspicious man I know. Just now I said that the King had said to me, "Let this be settled between you and me alone. I don't want outside interference." I meant to indicate by that the reasons why I had not made it a Cabinet question from the start. But Winston thought it was a thrust aimed at him, and has been at my Private Secretary within the last five minutes. What can one do with a man like that?'

The House reassembled at six o'clock. The two Opposition Party leaders, Attlee and Sinclair, both spoke sympathetically of the King's decision to abdicate. Churchill, who spoke next, stressed the danger of any further 'recrimination or controversy' now that the abdication was a fact, telling those who three days earlier had shouted him down: 'What is done is done. What has been done or left undone belongs to history, and to history, so far as I am concerned, it shall be left.'

Leopold Amery noted in his diary: 'Winston rose in face of a hostile House and in an admirably phrased little speech executed a strategical retreat.' During his speech Churchill told the House:

Supporting the Leader of the Liberal Party, I venture to say that no Sovereign has ever conformed more strictly or more faithfully to the letter and spirit of the Constitution than his present Majesty. In fact, he has voluntarily made sacrifices for the peace and strength of his realm which go far beyond the bounds required by the law and the Constitution.

Of his own insistence for time, Churchill declared:

It was essential that there should be no room for assertions after the event that the King had been hurried in his decision. I believe that if this decision had been taken last week it could not have been declared that it was an unhurried decision, so far as the King himself was concerned, but now I accept wholeheartedly what the Prime Minister has proved—namely, that the decision taken this week has been taken by His Majesty freely, voluntarily, spontaneously, in his own time and in his own way.

As I have been looking at this matter, as is well known, from an angle different from that of most hon members, I have thought it my duty to place this fact also upon record.

Having accepted Baldwin's assurances, and deprecated further controversy, Churchill then spoke of how, for more than half a century, the King had honoured him with his personal friendship. 'I should have been ashamed,' he added, 'if, in my independent and unofficial position, I had not cast about for every lawful means, even the most forlorn, to keep him on the Throne of his fathers, to which he had only just succeeded amid the hopes and prayers of all.'

The House of Commons listened sympathetically to what Churchill had to say. The bitterness of feeling which had erupted three days earlier seemed to have dissolved now that the abdication was an established fact. Of Edward himself Churchill told the Commons, amid repeated cheers:

In this Prince there was discerned qualities of courage, of simplicity, of sympathy, and, above all, of sincerity rare and precious, which might have made his reign glorious in the annals of this ancient Monarchy. It is the acme of tragedy that those very virtues should in the private sphere have led only to this melancholy and bitter conclusion. (Hear, hear).

But although our hopes today lie withered, still I would assert that his personality will not go down uncherished to future ages—(hear, hear)—that it will be particularly remembered in the homes of his poorer subjects—(Cheers)—and that they will ever wish from the bottom of their hearts for his private peace and happiness and for the happiness of those who are dear to him.

Churchill went on to urge all those 'afflicted' by what had occurred to look to the future, and above all to Europe. His speech ended:

Danger gathers upon our path. We cannot afford—we have no right—to look back. We must look forward; we must obey the exhortation of the Prime Minister to look forward. The stronger the advocate of monarchical principle a man may be, the more zealously must he now endeavour to fortify the Throne and to give to his Majesty's successor[1] that strength which can only come from the love of a united nation and Empire.

Churchill's remarks were greeted by what *Hansard* described as 'Loud cheers'. That same day Philip Guedalla[2] wrote to him: 'I have never felt so much respect for anyone as for you and for the stand which you have made in the past week,' and on December 11 Geoffrey Dawson wrote from Printing House Square: 'I am bound to say that your speech of yesterday, which I have just been reading, seems to me to present a thoroughly sound, constitutional point of view.' Churchill's feelings for the King were intense and sentimental; that evening, at Morpeth Mansions, he told Wing-Commander Anderson: 'Poor little lamb, he was treated worse than any air mechanic, and he took it lying down.'

On Friday December 11, Churchill lunched with the former King at Fort Belvedere. It was their third meeting since the crisis had

[1] Albert Frederick Arthur George, 1895–1952. Second son of King George V. Educated at the Royal Naval Colleges Osborne and Dartmouth; Lieutenant, 1918. Succeeded his brother as king, December 1936. Crowned (as George VI), May 1937.

[2] Philip Guedalla, 1889–1944. Educated at Rugby and Balliol College Oxford. President of the Oxford Union, 1911. Barrister, 1913. Legal Adviser, Contracts Department, War Office and Ministry of Munitions, 1915–17. Organizer and Secretary, Flax Control Board, 1917–20. A friend of Lloyd George. Unsuccessful Liberal candidate, 1922, 1923, 1924, 1929 and 1931. Historian; author of *Mr Churchill: A Portrait*, 1941. Squadron-Leader, RAF, 1943.

broken eight days before. 'His mettle was marvellous,' Churchill wrote to Josiah Wedgwood on the following day. He also wrote that day his letter of explanation to Robert Boothby, during which he commented:

The only thing now to do is to make it easy for him to live in this country quietly as a private gentleman as soon as possible and to that we must bend our efforts by discouraging noisy controversy and (apart from quasi historical investigation) refusing to take part in it. The more firmly the new King is established, the more easy it will be for the old one to come back to his house.

Of Boothby's angry letter of December 7 Churchill wrote: 'Even if you had not written it our old relations would have been unchanged.'

While at Fort Belvedere, Churchill had gone over the text of a radio broadcast, drafted by Walter Monckton, which Edward was to make that same afternoon. Churchill added several phrases to the speech, among them: 'bred in the constitutional tradition by my Father' and: 'one matchless blessing, enjoyed by so many of you and not bestowed on me—a happy home with his wife and children'.

In his memoirs Edward recalled how, while he was lunching with Churchill, 'I ceased to be King,' and he added:

As I saw Mr Churchill off, there were tears in his eyes. I can still see him standing at the door; hat in one hand, stick in the other. Something must have stirred in his mind; tapping out the solemn measure with his walking-stick, he began to recite, as if to himself:

'He nothing common did or mean
Upon that memorable scene.'

His resonant voice seemed to give an especial poignancy to those lines from the ode by Andrew Marvell, on the beheading of Charles I.

Edward's[1] broadcast caught the imagination of listeners all over the world. Churchill, listening to it at Chartwell with Deakin, was in tears. That same evening, the final stages of the Abdication Act having been completed, Edward left England as a private citizen to await Mrs Simpson in a castle in Austria. Before leaving he telegraphed to

[1] Sir John Reith had intended to introduce the former King to his listeners as 'Mr Windsor'. But Edward pointed out that he was still a Royal Prince, and he was introduced as 'His Royal Highness Prince Edward'. On the following day, December 12, at the Accession Council at St James's Palace—at which Churchill was present—the new King, George VI, announced that his first act was to confer a Dukedom on the late King, who would henceforth be known as 'His Royal Highness the Duke of Windsor'.

Churchill: 'Thank you again for all great help and understanding. Au Revoir. Edward.' Four days later Churchill replied from Morpeth Mansions: 'From all accounts the broadcast was successful, and all over the world people were deeply moved; millions wept. The Government were grateful. They certainly ought to be.'

In his letter of December 15 Churchill also sent Edward an account of some of the efforts he had been making on his behalf:

> I went to see Sam Hoare yesterday and had an hour with him. I am sure Your RH can count on him as a friend and a friend in a very important position. He promised to keep in touch with me in order to watch over your interests so far as Parliament and the Cabinet are concerned.
>
> From some words I had with Neville when we went to present the Commons' Address I gathered that what he attached great importance to was your living absolutely separate until everything is settled and the new Civil List is voted. He was rather grim and bleak, but I am sure he is right on this point.
>
> There is an enormous amount of sympathy and goodwill towards you here, and many people are quite stunned. Feeling rather battered myself I am off to Palm Beach on Tuesday where I shall get some peace and sunshine with Consuelo Balsan.[1]

Following the Duke of Windsor's departure from England, Churchill reflected continuously on the crisis, and on his own part in it. To Geoffrey Dawson he wrote on December 12: 'Nothing that was written about me caused me pain, because I have had forty years of such buffetings,' and he went on to explain that it was only 'the sledgehammer blows' which *The Times* had dealt 'the late King' that had angered him. Now, he added, 'the dust of controversy must be laid, and the new reign established on unshakable foundations'.

In several of the letters which he wrote after the abdication, Churchill reflected his distress at what had occurred. 'It is extraordinary,' he wrote to the Duke of Westminster on December 16, 'how Baldwin gets stronger every time he knocks out someone or something important to our country. I greatly fear the dangers of 1937.' To the editor of the

---

[1] Consuelo Balsan had a house, Casa Alva, at Palm Beach in Florida. During November, Churchill had made plans for this visit to the United States. His sole purpose was financial: to earn by a month's lecturing enough money to pay his £6,000 income and super tax demand for the coming year. On November 27 he wrote to his wife: 'I am disappointed not to be with you all at Christmas: I don't know how I shall spend my poor Christmas day. But everything is so uncertain (except taxation) that it would be wise to have this large sum safely banked in US. I have always hitherto managed to provide the necessaries, and I feel that this particular toil is a measure of prudence.'

Morning Post, Ian Colvin, he also wrote on December 17: 'Avoidable havoc is what I call it,' and to Lloyd George, who was on holiday in the West Indies, he wrote on Christmas Day:

It has been a terrible time here, and I am profoundly grieved at what has happened. I believe the Abdication to have been altogether premature and probably quite unnecessary. However, the vast majority is on the other side.

You have done well to be out of it.

42

January–June 1937: 'Everything Is Very Black'

MANY of Churchill's contemporaries cited his intervention in the House of Commons on the afternoon of December 7 as proof of his lack of judgement. But the effect of that intervention did not in fact lessen his influence. Indeed, when he spoke that very evening on defence to the 1922 Committee of Conservative backbenchers, the impact of his remarks was considerable. 'Your speech,' Frederick Guest wrote to Churchill on December 9, 'was admirable, and very well received.' One of those present, Captain Russell,[1] sent a confidential report of what Churchill had said to Sir Thomas Inskip. 'Little applause was forthcoming while Mr Churchill spoke,' Russell wrote, but: 'The general impression, however, was that it was a good speech and it was well received. The remarks about the British Air Force have been the subject of some considerable discussion, and while some frankly feel that he has exaggerated his case, yet at the same time there are, in my opinion, many people who are genuinely disturbed on this account, and Mr Churchill's speech of last night has certainly done nothing to allay their anxieties.' Another of those at the meeting, Adrian Moreing,[2] said that he too had received 'much information of a disquieting nature', which showed that the Air Ministry 'was not only not getting value for money expended but also that there was complete and utter confusion with reference to the placing of orders and contracts'. This applied,

[1] Stuart Hugh Minto Russell, 1909–1943. Educated at Rugby and Trinity College Cambridge. Conservative MP for Darwen, 1935–43. Parliamentary Private Secretary to Sir Philip Sassoon (Under-Secretary of State for Air), 1936–37. Parliamentary Private Secretary to Sir John Simon (Chancellor of the Exchequer), 1937–38. Captain, Coldstream Guards.

[2] Adrian Charles Moreing, 1892–1940. Educated at Winchester and Trinity College Cambridge. Partner in his family firm of mining engineers. Conservative MP for Preston from 1931 until his death. Following Moreing's death, Churchill's son Randolph was elected, unopposed, for the Preston seat (and defeated by the Labour candidate in the 1945 election).

Moreing said, to all the Defence Department, and he added: 'Enquiry from the Department always elicited the reply that all was going well. The facts however, belied the assurances which were given.'

As reported by Captain Russell, Churchill's remarks at the 1922 Committee had covered many aspects of defence. Speaking of the Army, Churchill had insisted 'that we had lost our supremacy in the manufacture of tanks. The quality did not come up to that obtained by foreign powers.' As for medium tanks, he warned, 'we were deplorably short in numbers, and a long time would have to elapse before this could be rectified'. Russell's account continued:

Mr Churchill concluded his speech by saying that 1937 would be the most critical and mournful year we had ever approached. We had no choice in the matter. If we did not keep in with the French republic we should be doomed. Such a policy was vital and essential, and he was proud to think that, together with Sir Austen Chamberlain, he had put pressure on a certain French statesman a very short time ago which might at any rate have been partly responsible for the clear policy recently enunciated by Mr Delbos with reference to the explicit assurances given to this country by France in the event of unprovoked attack.

Reflecting on his own situation as a result of the abdication crisis, Churchill wrote to Bernard Baruch on New Year's Day, 1937:

I do not feel that my own political position is much affected by the line I took; but even if it were, I should not wish to have acted otherwise. As you know in politics I always prefer to accept the guidance of my heart to calculations of public feeling. Baldwin has got a new lease of life. Indeed he throve on the job. He is practically sure now to hang on till after the Coronation.[1]

In the last week of December, in view of the European situation, Churchill cancelled the plans he had made to go to the United States, and instead spent New Year's Day, 1937, with Sir Philip Sassoon at Trent Park. Clementine Churchill, and their youngest daughter Mary, had gone to the Austrian alps to ski. While Churchill was still at Trent Park on January 2, he learnt of the sudden death of Ralph Wigram, at the age of forty. 'I was deeply shocked & grieved to learn from Vansittart by chance on the telephone that poor Ralph Wigram died suddenly on New Year's eve in his wife's arms,' Churchill wrote to his wife on January 2. 'I thought him a grand fellow. Brendan & I are going on Monday to the funeral. . . . Poor little Ava is all adrift now. She

---

[1] On 25 January 1937 Churchill wrote to P. J. Grigg: 'Baldwin flourishes like the green baytree. He has risen somewhat like the Phoenix (though not quite on all fours like that animal) from the pyre upon which the late monarch committed suicide.'

cherished him & kept him alive. He was her contact with gt affairs.' During the day Churchill wrote to Wigram's widow:

I admired always so much his courage, integrity of purpose, high comprehending vision. He was one of those—how few—who guard the life of Britain. Now he is gone—and on the eve of this fateful year. Indeed it is a blow to England and to all the best that England means. It is only a week or so that he rang me up to speak about the late King. I can hear his voice in my memory. And you? What must be your loss? But you still will have a right to dwell on all that you did for him. You shielded that bright steady flame that burned in the broken lamp. But for you it would long ago have been extinguished, and its light would not have guided us thus far upon our journey.

'He adored you so,' Ava Wigram wrote to Churchill shortly before the funeral, '& always said you were the greatest Englishman alive.'

On January 4 Churchill drove to Uckfield for Wigram's funeral. 'The widow was ravaged with grief,' he wrote to his wife three days later, '& it was a harrowing experience. . . . There appears to be no pension or anything for Foreign Office widows: but she says she can manage on her own resources. Her future seems blank & restricted. A sombre world!' After the funeral Churchill gave a small luncheon at Chartwell for the mourners, including Sir Robert Vansittart. Clementine Churchill realized how much Wigram's death had saddened her husband. 'He was a true friend of yours,' she wrote from Switzerland on January 5, '& in his eye you could see the spark which showed an inner light was burning.' Four days later she wrote again: 'I felt Mr Wigram's death would make you unhappy. I'm afraid you will miss him very much.'[1]

Churchill remained at Chartwell for most of January, working with as few interruptions as possible on the fourth and final volume of his *Marlborough*. 'Deakin has been here 4 days & has helped me a lot,'

---

[1] Another friend at whose death Churchill was much saddened was Lord Islington, who had died on December 6. On January 16 he wrote to Lady Islington: 'My dear Anne, I have thought so much about you and your gt sorrow during these last weeks. . . . My mind is full of memories of all those old days at Hartham. What jolly times we had when our world was young! And then politics—so fierce and active. Do you remember the meeting outside the station when trains made such a noise—and that other meeting interrupted by the Tory trumpeter? Jack enjoyed it all, from the day of Mr Brodrick's Army Corps—& the Free Trade Split. He had a vy full & fine life. I was so glad to find we were together in opinion on India & some other things in these last years.' Churchill added: 'As one gets old—the scene contracts, and the colours fade. Dear Anne I hope & pray that there will still be some mellow sunshine left for you, & that you will think kindly of your sincere friend Winston.'

Churchill wrote to his wife on January 7. 'He shows more quality & serviceableness than any of the others,' and he added: 'We have reached definite conclusions about the abortive Peace negotiations of 1709. They are a terrible tangle, & have never been satisfactorily or even intelligibly explained, before. It is quite an effort to keep all the points of this argument in one's mind when so much else is afoot.'

For relaxation Churchill painted, setting up his easel indoors because of the heavy rain. He had, he told his wife, 'been using one end of the drawing room—with a dust sheet'. He added: 'The days pass quickly for I have so much to do. Marlborough alone is a crusher—then there are always articles to boil the pot!'[1]

On January 7, while Churchill was at Chartwell, he received a letter from Lord Davies urging him to take a further lead in stimulating public support for the League of Nations Union and the New Commonwealth. Davies proposed that the objectives of the New Commonwealth 'might become the vehicle in which you could ride to power as the first Minister in this country: I believe it is the only vehicle. Honestly, I prefer to see you in the wilderness than play the part of second, third, or any other kind of Minister.' Later in his letter Davies wrote: 'Recognition of your leadership will come when public opinion demands that you assume the office of Prime Minister. But what I venture to suggest is that you will not win that recognition unless you go all out to get it, and lay your plans accordingly.' Davies suggested that Churchill embark on a six- or twelve-months speaking campaign, using the New Commonwealth, or the Defence of Freedom and Peace Council, or the League of Nations Union 'as a vehicle'. But Churchill was sceptical of Davies' suggestion. In his reply six days later he urged Davies not to 'overrate the value of public meetings', and added:

At the present time non-official personages count for very little. One poor wretch may easily exhaust himself without his even making a ripple upon the current of opinion. If we could get access to the broadcast some progress could be made. All that is very carefully sewn up over here.[2]

[1] Churchill's literary earnings since 1929 were, before tax: £10,695 (1929–30), £12,883 (1930–31), £15,240 (1931–32), £13,981 (1932–33), £6,572 (1933–34), £13,505 (1934–35), £16,312 (1935–36) and £12,914 (1936–37): a total of over £100,000 in eight years. During the tax year 1936–37 the upkeep of Chartwell and Morpeth Mansions, and the general living expenses, had cost Churchill more than £10,000. On 8 April 1937 he drew up a budget whereby the expenditure for 1937–38 was to be reduced to £6,000. 'This cannot on any account be exceeded,' he wrote to his wife.

[2] Unknown to Churchill, on 30 March 1936 a special Cabinet Committee had discussed the BBC's plan for a series of broadcasts on European affairs. According to the official minutes of the meeting, it was decided to ask the BBC to refrain from arranging for independent

On the other hand I do not think you should be at all despondent. There is no doubt that the balance of European opinion is tilting heavily against Germany, and that the idea of strong confederations of armed nations to resist an Aggressor is moving steadily in a concrete and practical way towards reality.

On January 14 Churchill wrote to Inskip from Chartwell about what he feared was the Government's dilatory policy towards machine tool orders: 'In my view it is proof of a serious lack of organisation that when the British Government put out an order for say, gun lathes, they do not know what the consequential reactions of that order are upon industry, nor where nor how it will in fact be executed.' Churchill's letter continued:

With a proper system of control the whole capacity of British industry could be brought in review, and the Government then, when placing the order abroad, would have warned the British firm producing one vital part, that their services would be required, and they would not then be bespoken by the German Government. . . .

You say that it is the Government policy not to interfere with normal trade. It may be Government policy and yet not be right. You are under a misapprehension when you suggest that I wish you to ask the machine tool industry 'to abandon *all* their ordinary trade'. I should be quite content if instead of 'all' were written 'all the Government requires'. . . .

Churchill went on to tell Inskip that he had been assured that the British armament programme was falling 'ever more into arrears', and that Britain's relative weakness in the air, compared to Germany, was 'marked and deplorable'.

Churchill ended his letter to Inskip on a personal note: 'I postponed writing this letter to you until I was delighted to hear you were rapidly recovering from your influenza. I am telling your secretary not to show it to you till you are quite restored. Grave as are the times, I hope you will make sure you have the necessary period of convalescence. All my household has been down with this minor scourge, and a certain number of days of complete relief from work of any kind is absolutely necessary for perfect recovery. So far I have survived and if I escape altogether I shall attribute it to a good conscience as well as a good constitution.'

On January 15 Lord Rothermere wrote to Churchill from the South

---

expression of views on the situation'. The only Minister to speak against this decision was Duff Cooper, the Secretary of State for War, who told his colleagues that he did not think that independent broadcasts could do 'much harm'.

of France, warning that 'even without a great war Britain and France will be practically vassal states before the end of the present decade. The idea that we cannot fight is spreading all over England.' Rothermere, who had been staying with Hitler at Berchtesgaden, informed Churchill: 'I am told I am the only foreigner who has ever stayed with him. He and his entourage communicate an impression of complete assurance. He told me the German Army was better today than in 1914 and that the German Air Force was quite the best in the whole world. He professes great friendship for England but it will be friendship on his terms and not ours.'

Churchill's anxieties were increased, and his detailed knowledge of the state of Britain's defences augmented, by a continued stream of letters and information from a wide and impressive variety of sources. On January 9 Sir Philip Gibbs[1] had written to him of 'the alarming inefficiency and most dangerous condition of the Royal Air Force', and four days later, at lunch at Chartwell, Gibbs had explained his fears in detail. On January 12 Sir Eustace Tennyson-d'Eyncourt[2] had written to say how 'disturbed' he was about the state of tank design and construction; he too had been invited to lunch, at Morpeth Mansions, to explain his concerns in detail, and the meeting took place on February 1. No sooner had Tennyson-d'Eyncourt left the flat than Sir William Beveridge[3] arrived, having sent Churchill on the previous day twenty-seven pages of notes on the problems of the Home Front in wartime—covering such topics as transport, food control and safeguarding the civilian population against attack.

Throughout 1937 Wing-Commander Anderson continued to send

---

[1] Philip Gibbs, 1877–1962. An editor at Cassell and Company, publishers, 1898. Entered journalism, 1902; Literary editor, the *Daily Mail*. War correspondent for the *Daily Chronicle* in the Balkans, 1912, and on the western front, 1914–18. Author of over fifty novels and a further twenty-five historical works, including *Realities of War* (1920). Knighted, 1920.

[2] Eustace Henry William Tennyson-d'Eyncourt, 1868–1951. A naval architect, 1898–1912. Director of Naval Construction and Chief Technical Adviser at the Admiralty, 1912–23. President of the Landships Committee of the Admiralty, 1915–16. Knighted, 1917. Vice-President of the Tank Board, 1918. Managing Director of Armstrong Whitworth's shipyards at Newcastle, 1924–28. Director of the Parsons Marine Steam Turbine Company, 1928–48. Created Baronet, 1930. One of the principal inventors of the Tank.

[3] William Henry Beveridge, 1879–1963. Educated at Charterhouse and Balliol College Oxford. Civil servant at the Board of Trade, 1908–16; Ministry of Munitions, 1915–16; Ministry of Food, 1917–18 (Permanent Secretary, 1919). A pioneer of state insurance. Knighted, 1919. Director of the London School of Economics and Political Science, 1919–37. Member of the Royal Commission on the Coal Industry, 1925. Master of University College Oxford, 1937–45. Chairman, Interdepartmental Committee on Social Insurance, 1941–42. Liberal MP, 1944–45. Baron, 1946. Author of more than twenty books on politics and political science.

Churchill documents and memoranda relating to the state of Air Force training, machines and personnel, and frequently visited him both at Morpeth Mansions and at Chartwell. Anderson later recalled, in conversation with the author:

You would give Churchill a new idea, he would say nothing. Two hours later, while feeding the gold fish he would come out with the flaw in what you said. He had the power to use the unconscious mind.

He said to me once speaking of Britain, and, as it were *to* Britain: 'You came into big things as an accident of naval power when you are an island. The world had confidence in you. You became the workshop of the world. You populated the island beyond its capacity. Through an accident of air power you will probably cease to exist.'

Churchill brought me into the family life at Chartwell. He did it to protect me. He could then say—he is a member of the family.

One day when he was in bed he said to me: 'I know what is troubling you. It is loyalty to the Service and loyalty to the State. You must realise that loyalty to the State *must* come before loyalty to the Service.'

Anderson drew his materials from many sources. On January 29 he sent Churchill an eight-page memorandum written by Group Captain Lachlan MacLean,[1] critical of many aspects of Air Force development, including long-distance navigation, maintenance work and pilot training. 'Lacking modern aeroplanes and adequate equipment,' MacLean wrote, 'not only are we not ready for War, but our whole training for War must wait on the provision of such aircraft and equipment.' Were war to come in the next three, or even five years, he added, 'we shall be powerless to retaliate, at any rate in the air. . . .' MacLean later recalled in a letter to the author, that he had not known at the time that Anderson had sent his memorandum to Churchill, but that his argument had at once 'impressed the latter and he expressed a wish to meet me'. Of the meeting itself MacLean wrote:

Accompanying Anderson I was introduced to Winston in his flat in Westminster and he congratulated me on the paper and we discussed the air rearmament. Subsequently, from time to time, Anderson would ask me

---

[1] Lachlan Loudoun Maclean, 1890–1979. 2nd Lieutenant, Indian Army, 1911; Captain, Gurkha Rifles, 1915; wounded, western front. Royal Flying Corps, 1916. Served in the Middle East, 1916–18 (despatches); Flight Commander, 1917. Subsequently British Air Representative at the League of Nations, and Senior Air Staff Officer, Headquarters No 3 (Bomber) Group; acting officer commanding at the time of the Munich agreement, 1938. Resigned from the RAF, January 1939; recalled, August 1939. Air Commodore, 1939–44 (despatches twice). Commanded Heavy Bomber Group, Middle East, 1940–42; formed the Operational Training Group, Canada, 1943.

to write a short paper on some point that Winston wished to make in a letter to the Prime Minister or in a speech in the House and I would let him have these papers and would perhaps go to Churchill's flat for a discussion. . . .

'This situation gradually developed,' MacLean added, 'into my sending to Winston's personal secretary, Mrs Pearman, papers on the more significant events in the air rearmament.'[1]

At the end of January, Anderson sent Churchill a detailed four-page memorandum of his own, the theme of which was that the standard of pilots under training was 'definitely below average', and that the facilities provided at Air Force camps, as a result of the continual search for economy, were so bad that they could only 'hit back on the esprit de corps and efficiency of the future Air Force'.[2]

On January 7 the Air Staff sent Inskip their reply to Churchill's memorandum of December 20. Churchill's December 20 comments, Inskip noted on January 11, 'are ingenious, weighty & of course picturesque in their presentation'. But the Air Staff memorandum did agree that 'an Air Force with a strong industry can afford to do with less reserves than one with a weak industry or none at all'; thus Churchill's criticism of their underrating of the German reserves remained valid, and on January 20 a Foreign Office official, C. J. W. Torr,[3] minuted:

The Air Staff seem to have disposed of Mr Churchill pretty thoroughly but there is one point on which their explanation does not seem to be quite satisfactory. It is in paragraph 7. They there state that 'the British and

[1] In 1937 Maclean also expressed his anxieties to Clement Attlee and Hugh Dalton, whom he helped to prepare a dossier on air defence. After he resigned from the RAF in 1939 he published his criticisms of air preparedness in four articles in the *Evening Standard*, 1–4 February 1939. Two final articles were suppressed by the authorities. On 17 December 1938 Churchill wrote to Sir Kingsley Wood: 'This officer is a friend of mine, and he strikes me as being one of the ablest men I have met in the Air Force. I would have thought that you could ill afford, at the present juncture, to lose the services of a highly competent technical and military officer in the very prime of his faculties. I am sure he would greatly impress you if you met him.'

[2] During the first six months of 1937 Anderson continued to send Churchill letters he had received from serving officers and trainees, including Air Commodore Tedder (Air Officer Commanding, Singapore); Aircraftman P. J. W. Rowell (a pilot trainee at RAF Halton); and Air Vice-Marshal P. H. L. Playfair (Commanding No 3 Bomber Group). Anderson also sent Churchill a 31-page report by Squadron Leader H. V. Rowley and Flight Lieutenant R. L. Atcherley on a visit they had made to Germany in October 1936, and made available to him a large number of official Air Ministry circulars, instructions and memoranda dealing with questions of training, accidents, equipment, personnel and tactics.

[3] Cyril James Wenceslas Torr, 1896–1940. Entered the Foreign Office, 1920; Second Secretary, 1923; First Secretary, 1932. Transferred to Riga, 1934. Returned to the Foreign Office, 1936. Chargé d'Affaires, Vatican, 1937–38; Berne, 1939–40.

German Air Forces have immediate reserves on the same scale'. Yet when in July (C 4922/G) the Air Ministry sought to dispose of Mr Churchill's previous memorandum they stated that 'we consider that our reserves should be on a higher scale than that adopted by the Germans'; and they went on to explain that the size of the reserve must depend on the country's industrial production-capacity and on the rapidity with which industry could turn over from peace time to war time production. Unless, therefore, our industry is now equal to the German in these respects it would seem that we are falling behind in the matter of reserves.

At the end of February, Hankey protested to Baldwin, Inskip, Neville Chamberlain and Swinton about Churchill receiving copies of the Air Staff answers to his critical memoranda. 'So far as I can see,' Hankey wrote in a confidential memorandum to Baldwin and Inskip on March 1, 'there is no advantage in continuing this controversy with Mr Churchill.' When Churchill had telephoned him at his home on Sunday, February 28, Hankey wrote, 'His manner was irritable,' for he wanted to know why he had not been sent the Air Staff's reply to his memorandum of December 20. Were he not to receive these comments, Churchill told Hankey, 'he would consider himself free to circulate his own memorandum to any of his friends whom he might think fit'.

Swinton agreed to let Churchill see the Air Staff comments on his memorandum of December 20. Churchill showed their comments to Lindemann, who dictated four pages of his own thoughts on March 12. These read, in part:

(a) It is stated that an Air Force with a strong industry can afford to do with less reserves than one with a weak industry. Our industry is incomparably weaker than the German, consequently we ought to have a much greater reserve. The contrary seems to be more than probable. (b) Quite apart from any question of immediate reserves, the Air Force memorandum gives rise to the following disquieting conclusion. Whereas according to paragraph 4 the number of machines in the first line in Germany is in excess of the number arrived at by multiplying the number of formed squadrons by 9, the number of machines in the first line in Great Britain is less than the number of squadrons multiplied by 9.

Lindemann added: 'when people are frightened some of them say the enemy is big but inefficient, and others say he is not as big as he looks. The Air Staff would like to have the best of both worlds.'

A clear indication of the seriousness of Britain's air position was revealed to the Cabinet on January 14, when Lord Swinton circulated a 'Most Secret' Air Ministry memorandum, pointing out in his covering note that under the existing Scheme F, Britain's first-line strength at home by April 1939 would be 1,736 aircraft, of which 1,022 would be bombers, whereas the most recent Air Staff estimate of German air strength by April 1939 was 2,500 aircraft, of which 1,700 would be bombers.

The Cabinet having already decided not to adopt any new programme which would interfere with industry's peace-time production, Swinton had devised a new scheme which would not be based 'on the production of a larger number of aircraft by April 1939'. Under this proposed new scheme, H, the Air Ministry proposed to increase the striking force to 1,631 aircraft by April 1939, by means both of drawing on the reserves and retaining at home ten of the twelve new overseas squadrons being built under Scheme F. The first-line would, by this plan, reach 2,422 machines by April 1939. It was hoped subsequently to 're-create' a 'proper scale' of reserves and overseas squadrons 'by the end of 1940–41'.

In the Air Ministry's view, even the new bomber force of Scheme H 'would not be numerically equal' to that of the Germans, but 'taking all factors into account', should provide 'an adequate deterrent against the risk of air attack by Germany in 1939'. These measures, the Air Ministry added, 'would only be a temporary expedient to meet a transient situation'.

Scheme F was estimated to cost £375,000,000. The proposed Scheme H would cost £425,000,000 to which would have to be added £8,000,000 carried forward 'on works and buildings' into 1941 and 1942, and £15,000,000 a year 'Recurrent expenditure' after March 1941. Much of this extra cost was caused by the need to provide thirteen new operational stations to house the extra twenty-six squadrons which the complete scheme would bring into existence.

The Cabinet discussed Scheme H, and the problem of air parity, on January 27. During the discussion, as the minutes recorded, both Chamberlain and Swinton thought that it was necessary 'to try to get rid of the idea of the mere counting of machines as being the interpretation of parity'. Chamberlain added 'that at present we were a long way behind Germany numerically'. Swinton, while admitting that Britain was 'somewhat behind on a purely numerical calculation', insisted that this did not apply 'to comparative strength'. Baldwin, however, suggested to his Cabinet that they might 'with advantage' remind MPs in the forthcoming debate 'of the danger of referring directly to Germany at a time when we were trying to get on terms with that country'. The Cabinet decided that Scheme H was too costly, and referred it to its committee on Defence Policy and Requirements. As a result of this the scheme was recast in a less expensive, and less effective form.

Speaking in the air debate on January 27, Inskip defended the current air programme. At least 120 of the promised 124 squadrons would be completed by July 1938, he said, 'though not all brought up to their complement'. Churchill, speaking after Inskip, reiterated the various points that Inskip himself had made, stressing the salient fact that of the 124 squadrons promised by March 31, only 100 would actually be ready. But even of these hundred, 22 were single-flight squadrons, and therefore 'cannot bear their part as complete squadrons. They are not in a condition to take part in fighting. They are only nuclei around which are built up new drafts and semi-trained personnel.' This left only 78 squadrons instead of the promised 124, a shortage of 46. 'Therefore,' Churchill added, 'I say that we have not got the parity which we were promised. We have not nearly got it, we have not nearly approached it. Nor shall we get it during the whole of 1937, and I doubt whether we shall have it or anything approaching it during 1938.'

Churchill went on to refer to the German air strength, now believed to be 150 squadrons, or 1,800 first-line machines, counting twelve machines in each squadron, as he had explained when on the defence deputation on 23 November 1936. Together with the Lufthansa aeroplanes, which were convertible to war purposes, this made a total of 2,000 aircraft. 'Therefore,' Churchill added, 'when I said in November last that we had not got two-thirds of their strength, I made, as I have always done on these occasions a very deliberate understatement'. Churchill also pointed out, as far as heavy bombers were concerned: 'If that were to be adopted as the test, then the question of parity would recede to a very remote distance because there is no branch of our service in which the relative comparison is more unfavourable to us.'

At a further Cabinet on February 3 Chamberlain warned his colleagues that 'even the present programmes were placing a heavy strain on our resources', and that any additional expenditure 'might put our present programmes in jeopardy'. Swinton then produced new, secret figures, provided by the German Air Minister, General Milch.[1] To match the 810 German heavy bombers which Milch said would be ready by the autumn of 1938, Britain would have only 240 under the existing

---

[1] Erhard Milch, 1892–1972. Born at Wilhelmshaven. Served as a pilot, 1909–20. Head of the air traffic department of Junkers, 1920–23. Board member of Lufthansa, 1923–26; head of the Lufthansa Finance Department, 1928–33; President of Lufthansa, 1942. Secretary of State for Aviation, 1933–44. General, 1936. Inspector General of the Air Force, 1938–45. Sentenced to life imprisonment at the Nuremberg trials, 1947; released, 1954.

programme, but the two totals were put at 1,755 for Germany and 1,736 for Britain. 'There was no doubt,' Swinton warned, that the Germans 'could increase their output rapidly, if necessary, as they possessed factories for this purpose, to say nothing of the discarded machines', so that by 1939 'they would possess the necessary reserves for expansion'.[1] At the same Cabinet, during a discussion of the Army Programme, Neville Chamberlain again spoke of 'the dangers of overloading the programmes beyond the material capacity of the country', and he asked his colleagues: 'Was it really necessary to stick rigidly to a date in 1939 for completion of our programme?'

As a result of the sense of relief created by General Milch's figures, the expansions called for in Scheme H were no longer considered necessary, and on February 24 the Cabinet accepted a revised Scheme F. Under this scheme, as Swinton had explained in a Cabinet memorandum on February 11, recruitment of pilots and skilled tradesmen would be increased, but no new aircraft would be ordered, and while the land needed for the thirteen new operational stations would be bought and levelled, 'no buildings would be erected'.

The Cabinet discussed the revised Scheme F on February 24. 'Comment was directed,' the minutes recorded, 'mainly to the very large advantage in long-range bombers which Germany would have over this country in May 1937.' Swinton pointed out that the revised Scheme F 'was the utmost that could be accomplished' in first-line strength, 'leaving the reserves to be completed in 1938 and 1939'.

On February 2 Churchill had informed his wife that Baldwin was likely to give up the premiership immediately after the Coronation, in May, and that Neville Chamberlain, who was 'already in fact doing the work, will without any doubt or question succeed him'. It would, Churchill wrote, 'be a great relief and simplification of our affairs to

---

[1] The true situation was, however, more serious than the Government believed. On 8 October 1937 an Air Staff memorandum noted: 'In January 1937, General Milch informed the Deputy Chief of the Air Staff in confidence that Germany intended to build up an Air Force of 180 squadrons (excluding coastal units) to be completed by the autumn of 1938. This was equivalent to only 1,620 first-line aircraft, and was therefore a surprisingly modest aim. General Milch, however, qualified his statement by adding that the German plan might of course be accelerated or expanded further if the political situation so required.' In April 1937 the Air Staff learned through their Intelligence that the 1,620 aircraft would in fact be ready a year earlier, by October 1937. On October 27 Lord Swinton wrote: 'Events have shown that General Milch was not in fact telling the truth.'

have all uncertainty cleared up at that date one way or the other. I really do not care very much which.' His own plans had been helped by a meeting a few days before with Frederick Leathers,[1] as he explained to his wife:

If I am not required for public work he gives me great expectations of important business administrative employment. Then I should be able to do my books more slowly and not have to face the truly stupendous task like Marlborough Vol IV being finished in 4 or 5 months, simply for current expenses. For 1938–9 we have the History of the English-speaking Peoples, worth £16,000, but entailing an immense amount of reading and solitary reflection if justice is to be done to so tremendous a topic.

Churchill's worries about finance were not easily assuaged. On February 2 he wrote to Newman Flower, at Cassells, asking for his fifth and final £1,000 advance for the *History of the English-Speaking Peoples*, which he hoped to begin 'in earnest' that autumn. Even the chance of selling Chartwell seemed worth exploring. 'If I could see £25,000 I should close with it,' he wrote to his wife in his letter of February 2, and he added: 'If we do not get a good price we can quite well carry on for a year or two more. But no good offer should be refused, having regard to the fact that our children are almost all flown, and my life is probably in its closing decade.'

On February 2 Churchill and his son flew from London to Paris, staying two nights at the Ritz before travelling by train to the South of France, where they were the guests of Lord Rothermere at his villa, La Dragonnière, at Cap Martin, before going on to St Moritz to spend a few days with Clementine Churchill and Mary. Churchill took Mrs Pearman with him on the first lap of his journey, in order to dictate further chapters of *Marlborough*, and several more newspaper articles. On February 13, while he was still abroad, Churchill dined with Anthony Eden at Beaulieu. Still intensely worried about Britain's air preparations, he showed Eden, without revealing his source, the critical memorandum by Captain MacLean, which Wing-Commander Anderson had sent him on January 29. Then, on February 16, he lunched with Flandin in Paris, before flying back to London that same afternoon.

---

[1] Frederick James Leathers, 1883–1965. Shipowner and company director. Served at the Ministry of Shipping, 1915–18. Chairman of William Cory and Son Ltd; Mann, George and Co Ltd; R. and J. H. Rea Ltd; and the Steamship Owners' Coal Association Ltd. A director of several steamship companies. Adviser to the Ministry of Shipping on all matters relating to Coal, 1940–41. Created Baron, 1941. Minister of War Transport, 1941–45. Secretary of State for the Co-ordination of Transport, Fuel and Power, 1951–53. Created Viscount, 1954.

On February 16 the Government published a new White Paper, envisaging a total defence expenditure of £1,500 million between 1937 and 1942. Five days later Churchill wrote to Lord Rothermere of how, following this announcement, there was 'an overwhelming wave of optimism and confidence about our position in Parliament'. But, he added, the real effect of the announcement:

. . . has been largely to paralyse criticism at home. People say 'What is the use of crabbing them when they are doing all you wish.' I know too much to feel easier about it all. But there is no doubt that the effect upon the Empire is beneficial and that the Dominions in their own way will gradually get on the move. Moreover the effect, in my point of view, in Europe will be salutary as a declaration of the general military revival of Britain.

'The danger is,' Churchill concluded, 'that something will happen in the meanwhile.'

By the end of February Churchill sensed a growing lethargy. 'Parliament is dead as mutton,' he wrote to Lord Rothermere on March 1, 'and the Tory party feel that everything is being done for the best and the country is perfectly safe.' On the following day he wrote to Reeves Shaw[1] of the *Strand* magazine, who had asked him to write about the senior Army, Navy and Air Force commanders: 'Some pretty good duds are in the big positions. In these circumstances I should clearly not like to commit myself to writing them up.'

On March 4, during the debate on the new Defence White Paper, Churchill spoke of his continued unease at the state of the nation's defences. But he was also worried about causing alarm by revealing in detail the weaknesses of which he knew so much. 'When the perils are distant,' he said, 'it is right then to sound the alarm and to try, even by frantic exertions, to arouse somnolent authority to novel dangers; but once we are in a danger zone, and everybody can see that we are marching through that long dark valley of which I spoke to the House two years ago, then a mood of coolness and calmness is enjoined.' Churchill went on to warn the House of Commons of the need to transform the plans into realities. 'Mere declarations of readiness to spend money over a five-year period,' he said, 'do not affect the realities through which we shall have to live in 1937, 1938, and 1939.' Earlier in the debate Inskip had described several important defence projects which were being planned or put into operation, in the sphere of food

---

[1] Reeves Shaw, 1886–1952. Educated at Brighton Grammar School. Entered journal publishing, 1903. Editor of the *Captain*, 1910–22; the *Humorist*, 1922–40; the *Strand Magazine*, 1931–41. A frequent contributor of short stories to other magazines.

supply, accumulation of raw materials, production of cannon and preparations for air defence. But, Churchill commented:

. . . nowhere was there any quantitative statement, nowhere was there any date given by which particular progress-points were to be reached. Nowhere was there any distinction drawn between the paper plans of committees and the elaborate organization of personnel required to make them work—nowhere any assurance that the programmes would be carried out punctually, or in good time. How could there be when, except for the air programme, no dates for the completion have been assigned to any of the numerous programmes, nor even in most cases their dimensions?

Churchill then spoke of several specific areas of military and defence planning in which he believed insufficient progress was being made, in particular the provision of anti-aircraft guns with trained crews, and the re-equipment of the Territorials. 'I must say that I am astounded,' he said, 'at the wave of optimism, of confidence, and even of complacency, which has swept over Parliament and over public opinion. There is a veritable tide of feeling that all is well, that everything is being done in the right way, in the right measure and in the right time,' and he went on:

When a whole Continent is arming feverishly, when mighty nations are laying aside every form of ease and comfort, when scores of millions of men and weapons are being prepared for war, when whole populations are being led forward or driven forward under conditions of exceptional overstrain, when the finances of the proudest dictators are in the most desperate condition, can you be sure that all your programmes so tardily adopted will, in fact, be executed in time?

Hitler and Mussolini, Churchill continued, were 'wielding entire nations into war-making machines', and doing so 'at the cost of the sternest repression of all the amenities and indulgences of human existence'. Such fanatical efforts could not be combated 'merely by going along in the present comfortable manner without any decisive impingement upon private trade or profit-making or demanding any temporary sacrifices of comfort and changes in our way of living. . . .' Financial sacrifices were not enough; 'the whole nation must pull together'.

Churchill ended his speech by appealing for a genuine British commitment both to the military potential of the League of Nations, and to the moral forces which it embodied. Of those moral forces he declared:

Do not let us mock at them for they are surely on our side. Do not mock at them, for this may well be a time when the highest idealism is not divorced from strategic prudence. Do not mock at them, for these may be years, strange as it may seem, when Right may walk hand in hand with Might.

Following the outbreak of an Arab revolt in Palestine, intended by the Palestinian Arab leaders to halt all further Jewish immigration and to bring British rule to an end, the British Government appointed a Royal Commission, headed by Lord Peel, to examine the future of Britain's Palestine Mandate. Churchill was summoned as a witness before the Commissioners on March 12. As Colonial Secretary in 1922 he had been responsible for the original administration of the Mandate, and was closely questioned about his intentions at that time. In answer to a question from Lord Peel, he declared that the Jewish right to immigration ought not to be curtailed by the 'economic absorptive capacity' of Palestine, and he spoke of 'the good faith of England to the Jews'. This arose, he said 'because we gained great advantages in the War. We did not adopt Zionism entirely out of altruistic love of starting a Zionist colony: it was a matter of great importance to this country. It was a potent factor on public opinion in America and we are bound by honour, and I think upon the merits, to push this thing as far as we can. . . .' The British Government had certainly committed itself, he went on, 'to the idea that some day, somehow, far off in the future, subject to justice and economic convenience, there might well be a great Jewish State there, numbered by millions, far exceeding the present inhabitants of the country. . . . We never committed ourselves to making Palestine a Jewish State . . . but if more and more Jews gather to that Home and all is worked from age to age, from generation to generation, with justice and fair consideration to those displaced and so forth, certainly it was contemplated and intended that they might in the course of time become an overwhelmingly Jewish State.'

The deputy chairman of the Commission, Sir Horace Rumbold, took up the questioning. Was there not, he asked, 'harsh injustice' to the Arabs if Palestine attracted too many Jews from outside. Churchill replied that even when the Jewish Home 'will become all Palestine', as it eventually would, there was no injustice. 'Why,' he asked, 'is there harsh injustice done if people come in and make a livelihood for more, and make the desert into palm groves and orange groves? Why is it injustice because there is more work and wealth for everybody? There is no injustice. The injustice is when those who live in the country leave it to be desert for thousands of years.'

When Rumbold pointed out the danger to British troops of the 'periodical disturbances' in Palestine, Churchill replied that the idea of creating a National Home for the Jews was 'the prime and dominating pledge upon which Britain must act'. If Britain became weak, 'somebody else might have to take it on', but while Britain remained in Palestine 'that is what we are undoubtedly pledged to'. Rumbold spoke up for the Arabs, who were, he said, 'the indigenous population', subjected in 1918 'to the invasion of a foreign race'. Churchill objected to the phrase 'foreign race'. The Arabs, he said, had come in after the Jews. It was the 'great hordes of Islam' who 'smashed' Palestine up. 'You have seen the terraces on the hills which used to be cultivated,' he told Rumbold, 'which under Arab rule have remained a desert.' Rumbold insisted that the backwardness of Palestine was the result of Turkish rule, but Churchill insisted that 'where the Arab goes it is often desert'. When Rumbold spoke of the Arab civilization in Spain, Churchill retorted: 'I am glad they were thrown out.' It was 'for the good of the world', he told Lord Peel a few moments later, 'that the place should be cultivated, and it never will be cultivated by the Arabs'.

Towards the end of the session, Rumbold asked Churchill when he would consider the Jewish Home to be established, and Britain's undertaking fulfilled. 'At what point?' Rumbold asked; to which Churchill replied: 'when it was quite clear the Jewish preponderance in Palestine was very marked, decisive, and when we were satisfied that we had no further duties to discharge to the Arab population, the Arab minority'.

None of Churchill's evidence was included in the Commission's Report. He was even reluctant to have it printed secretly. 'There are a few references to nationalities,' he wrote to Lord Peel on March 16, 'which would not be suited to appear in a permanent record.'

The Peel Commission decided to partition Palestine into two separate states, one Arab and one Jewish, reserving Jerusalem and a corridor to the sea as part of a permanent British controlled enclave. Churchill opposed this decision, believing that it was a breach of Britain's pledge to the Jews to enable them to establish a Jewish National Home throughout the original area of the Mandate, from the Mediterranean Sea to the River Jordan. On June 9 he met one of the leading Palestine Zionists, David Ben Gurion,[1] who recorded in his diary:

Right away Churchill jumped up and said: Our entire tragedy is that we have a weak government. The Baldwins are idiots, totally lacking in talent,

---

[1] David Green, 1886–1974. Born in Russia. Emigrated to Palestine, 1906. Agricultural worker and watchman in various agricultural settlements. A leading advocate of Hebrew as the sole language of Jewish public life. Took the name 'Ben-Gurion' in 1910, while on the

etc. If England is to be dependent on them, she is lost. They are concerned only with deposing and crowning kings, while Germany is arming and growing stronger, and we are slipping lower and lower. But this situation will not last long. England will wake up and defeat Mussolini and Hitler, and then your hour will also come.

During 1937 Churchill sought to extend the European circulation of his articles, many of which were already much sought after by foreign newspapers, especially in France. On February 25 he met for the first time the head of a leading European Press Service, Dr Emery Revesz,[1] who offered to place his articles far more widely than hitherto, and for a guaranteed minimum of £25 for the foreign language rights of each individual article. In return for 40 per cent of the proceeds, Revesz offered a remarkable range of newspaper outlets. In June, Churchill accepted Revesz's services, and within six months Revesz had managed to place Churchill's articles in twenty-six cities.[2] In one of the articles, published in the *Evening Standard* on February 5, Churchill pointed out that Czechoslovakia, with its 15 million inhabitants, was now living 'under the fear of violent invasion, with iron conquest in its

---

editorial staff of *Ahdut* ('Unity') in Jerusalem. Studied law in Salonika, 1912–14, and Constantinople, 1915. Accused by the Turks of conspiring to create a Jewish state, and exiled to Egypt, 1915. Served in the Jewish Legion of the British Army (39th Battalion, Royal Fusiliers), 1918. Secretary-General of the Jewish Labour Union in Palestine (Histadrut), 1921. Member of the Jewish Agency Executive, Jerusalem, 1933; Chairman, 1935–48. Prime Minister of Israel, 1948–53, and 1955–63.

[1] Emery Revesz (later Reves), 1904–81. Born in southern Hungary. Studied at the universities of Berlin and Paris. Doctorate in political economics, Zurich, 1926. Founded the Co-Operation Press Service for International Understanding, 1930, and syndicated articles by public figures in some 400 newspapers in 60 countries. By 1935, when he first met Churchill, his authors included Austen Chamberlain, Clement Attlee, Anthony Eden, Leon Blum, Paul Reynaud, Eduard Beneš and Einstein. In February 1940 Revesz became a British subject. Concerned with propaganda to the USA and neutral countries, June–December 1940. Severely wounded by a bomb during the London blitz, December 1940. In January 1941 he went to New York, where he published several important anti-Nazi works, including two books of his own, *A Democratic Manifesto* (1942) and *The Anatomy of Peace* (1945). Helped to negotiate the American rights of Churchill's war memoirs, 1946. He himself purchased all the foreign language rights to the war memoirs, as well as to the *History of the English-Speaking Peoples*. Churchill was a frequent guest at his home in the South of France, La Pausa, between 1956 and 1960.

[2] Including Prague, Warsaw, Belgrade, Budapest, Bucharest, Helsinki, Riga, and Buenos Aires. By means of this new arrangement, Churchill's views were made widely known, not only in the capitals of Europe and South America, but also in many provincial towns, in over twenty countries. Financially, also, Revesz improved Churchill's literary position. The fortnightly *Evening Standard* articles brought in an average of £60 each.

wake', and he went on: 'At any moment a quarrel may be picked with them by a mighty neighbour. Already they see the directions given to the enregimented German Press to write them down, to accuse them of being Communists, and, in particular, of preparing their airports for a Russian assault upon Germany. Vain to protest their innocence, vain to offer every facility for Germany or neutral inspection of their arrangements. The hate-culture continues, fostered by printing-press and broadcast—the very instruments, in fact, which philosophers might have hoped would liberate mankind from such perils. . . .' German propaganda, Churchill added, might just as easily turn against Belgium, Holland, Sweden, Switzerland or even Britain.

On March 5, in answer to the mounting support for some major gesture towards Germany, Churchill wrote in the *Evening Standard* of the dangers involved in the German claim for a return of its pre-war colonies. 'If,' he wrote, 'a flamboyant and machine-made propaganda is set on foot among the German people upon this issue, it cannot fail to foster the same kind of slow latent antagonism as was created by the growth of the German Navy before the Great War.' But on March 14, writing in the *Observer*, J. L. Garvin supported the German view of the need for a German economic federation that would embrace all the states of Central Europe, from the Baltic to the Black Sea; such a plea, Sir Norman Angell wrote to Churchill on March 15, was typical of a widespread Conservative desire to see 'a surrender to the German hegemony' in Central Europe. Angell's letter continued: 'while the nation is making immense sacrifices for defence on its military and material side, that defence is in fact being neutralised (betrayed?) on its political side'. The only alternative to surrender, Angell stressed, was Churchill's own plan of an alliance of the Western democracies, and Russia, based on 'the nucleus of a firm Anglo-French alliance'.

Angell urged Churchill to use his influence to start some 'process of education' among Conservatives. But the barriers to such a process were substantial. Two months later, on May 23, the editor of *The Times*, Geoffrey Dawson, wrote to Lord Lothian: 'I should like to get going with the Germans. I simply cannot understand why they should apparently be so much annoyed with *The Times* at this moment. I spend my nights in taking out anything which I think will hurt their susceptibilities and in dropping little things which are intended to soothe them.'

On March 16 Austen Chamberlain died; his friendship with Churchill dated back to the turn of the century. Although they had often disagreed, they had as Cabinet colleagues been in frequent harmony, and in the four years since Hitler had come to power in Germany their views of the German danger had been closely linked. On March 18 Churchill wrote to Chamberlain's widow of how he had been 'shocked and shaken to the depths' when he had gone to the Foreign Office that morning, and learned the news from Anthony Eden. 'I pray indeed,' he wrote, 'that you may find the resources in your spirit to enable you to bear this supreme stroke.' Churchill's letter continued:

Nothing can soften the loneliness or fill the void. Great happiness long enjoyed, casts its own shadow. All his friends of whom I am proud to be one will miss him painfully. In this last year I have seen more of him & worked more closely with him than at any time in a political & personal association of vy nearly forty years. I feel that almost the one remaining link with the old days indeed the great days has snapped.

'I know that you loved Austen,' Lady Chamberlain replied on March 20, '& will feel his loss greatly. He always had a great affection & admiration for you even when you did not agree!'

Towards the end of March Churchill raised with Sir Thomas Inskip the problem of Britain's first-line strength in the air, a problem which he had again discussed with Wing-Commander Anderson at Chartwell on March 21. On March 22 Inskip informed the House of Commons that as from April 1 there would be 103 squadrons based in the United Kingdom. But to Churchill himself, Inskip wrote privately on March 23 to explain that, unfortunately, ten of the squadrons would be under strength in aircraft 'pending the delivery of further machines', and that some of the recently formed Auxiliary Air Squadrons would likewise 'not be up to establishment'. Inskip added: 'I feel justified in giving you, as a Privy Councillor, this further confidential information, especially as you have already had so much secret information in this connection.'[1]

Churchill replied to Inskip on March 26, accepting that there must be 'a great deal of reorganisation and weakness during a period of

[1] A year later, on 7 March 1938, Sir Thomas Inskip told the House of Commons that the aircraft that had been promised for July 1938 were in fact 'not the modern machines', and that the full 1,750 programme of modern machines would only be completed by March 1939. Ten weeks after the outbreak of war, on 16 October 1939, Churchill, then a member of the War Cabinet, circulated a memorandum in which he wrote: 'We were told in 1937 that there would be 1,750 First-line aircraft modernly equipped by April 1 1938 (see Sir Thomas Inskip's speeches). However the House of Commons was content with the statement that this position had in fact been realised by April 1 1939. We were throughout assured that reserves far above the German scale were the feature of the British system. We now have apparently about 1500 first-line aircraft with good reserves ready for action. On mobilisation the 123 squadrons of April 1 1939 shrank to 96.'

rapid expansion', and sending him 'in personal confidence' a memorandom on air squadron deficiencies by 'a Staff Officer of the Air Force'.[1] Churchill went on to give Inskip his own views on how these deficiencies should be tackled:

I wonder you do not get a list made out of everything that a regular Air Squadron should have—pilots, machines, spare engines, spare parts, machine guns, bombing sights etc together with the reserves of all kinds which should be kept at the station. And then, armed with this, go down accompanied by three or four competent persons to visit, quite by chance, some Air Squadron by surprise. If then during the course of a whole day your people went through the list while you cross-examined the officers, you would have some information on which you could rest with some security.

It must never be forgotten that the structure of the Air Force both civil and military, is very much weaker, slighter and newer than that of the Army or the Navy. On the other hand a strain has been thrown upon them incomparably more severe than either of the two older services are bearing.

'The reason why I am not dwelling upon these matters in public,' Churchill explained, 'is because of the fear I have of exposing our weakness even more than is already known abroad.'

In his letter to Inskip Churchill wrote that he was sending 'in a separate envelope' a memorandum on the Fleet Air Arm. The memorandum had been sent to him by a member of the Naval Air Division at the Admiralty, Commander Lord Louis Mountbatten,[2] who had written in his covering letter on March 25:

As promised over the telephone I am sending you some arguments in favour of placing all craft concerned in the defence of trade, be they warships, flying boats or specialised shore-based aircraft under the control of a single service. The enclosed memorandum has been prepared by officers who have had more experience of air operations over the sea than any other officers on the active list.

Mountbatten realized, he wrote, that it was 'inevitable' that Churchill would wish for even more information; he therefore recommended

[1] The memorandum had been written by Captain Lachlan MacLean, whose name Churchill did not reveal. Returning it on April 8, Inskip noted: 'It is undesirable that it should be among my papers in view of your wish that I should treat it as very confidential.'
[2] Prince Louis Francis Albert Victor Nicholas of Battenberg, 1900–   . Second son of Prince Louis of Battenberg. A Naval Cadet, 1913–15. Midshipman, 1916. Assumed the surname of Mountbatten in 1917. Married Sir Ernest Cassel's granddaughter, Edwina, in July 1922. Commander, 1932. Naval Air Division, Admiralty, 1936. Captain, 1937. Commanded HMS *Kelly* 1939 (despatches twice). Chief of Combined Operations, 1942–43. Supreme Allied Commander, South-East Asia, 1943–46. Created Viscount Mountbatten of Burma, 1946. Viceroy of India, 1947. Created Earl, 1947. Governor-General of India, 1947–48. First Sea Lord, 1955–59. Admiral of the Fleet, 1956. Chief of the Defence Staff, 1959–65.

him to contact the Deputy Director of the Naval Air Division, Captain Graham,[1] who lived near Chartwell, and would be pleased 'to answer any further questions you wished to put, either over the telephone or in person'. Indeed, Mountbatten added, Graham would be willing to 'drive over at any time to see you'; of course his views would not necessarily coincide 'with any of the "high-up" views, which you may have had put before you'.

The Fleet Air Arm memorandum forwarded by Mountbatten consisted of several separate notes, eleven pages in all. Its argument was that the Admiralty should have plenary control of the Fleet Air Arm, and should provide its entire personnel who, trained by the Air Force, would then join the shore establishments of the Admiralty, and depend upon the Admiralty for discipline and advancement. Churchill sent the notes to Desmond Morton, who amalgamated them into a terse, six-page memorandum, making clear that under the proposed scheme the Air Force would still control absolutely all anti-aircraft defence by means of a special department made up of representatives from all three fighting services. In his covering letter of April 14 Morton wrote: 'As often before, I am astonished at your knowledge of detail on Defence matters.'[2]

At midday on March 27 Churchill left England for a nine-day holiday at Cap Martin, flying from Croydon to Paris and taking the night train from Paris to the South of France. He remained at Cap Martin until April 5. 'The weather here is brilliant but cold,' he wrote to the Duke of Windsor on April 1. 'I paint all day, and so far as my means go, gamble after dark.' On April 5 he took the night train to Paris, flying back to Croydon on the afternoon of April 6, and on the following evening, at Morpeth Mansions, he discussed with Wing-Commander Anderson the state of Air Force training and offensive preparations, and received from him further evidence of neglect and delay.[3]

---

[1] Cosmo Moray Graham, 1887–1946. Lieutenant, Royal Navy, 1909. Served on the destroyer *Nubian* in 1911, while Churchill was First Lord. On active service, 1914–18; as Commander of an aircraft carrier, he was the first commander to learn to fly under the dual control scheme. Captain, 1930. Deputy Director of the Naval Air Division, 1936–39. Commanded HMS *Shoreham*, 1939–41. Rear-Admiral, 1941, and Flag Officer Commanding the Humber Area. He lived at Wadhurst, twenty-two miles from Chartwell.

[2] On July 30, when the Government announced its decision to place the Fleet Air Arm under Admiralty control, Churchill issued a public statement approving the decision. But he commented: 'It is a great pity that this decision was not taken eighteen months ago. I have been pressing for it all this time. There really is no excuse for it not having been settled earlier.'

[3] Three weeks earlier, on March 16, Anderson had sent Churchill a three-page memorandum on the Royal Air Force Volunteer Reserve, which had been created as 'a matter of

On April 14 Churchill spoke in the House of Commons about the European situation, and in a forceful speech urged Britain's continued neutrality towards Spain. 'I refuse to become the partisan of either side,' he declared. 'I will not pretend that, if I had to choose between Communism and Nazi-ism, I would choose Communism,' and he added: 'I hope not to be called upon to survive in the world under a Government of either of these dispensations.' His speech continued: 'I cannot feel any enthusiasm for these rival creeds. I feel unbounded sorrow and sympathy for the victims.'

The Labour Party had brought a motion condemning Britain's refusal to give naval aid to British ships trying to take food to the Republicans at Bilbao, pointing out that while Britain and France adhered to the non-intervention agreement, Germany and Italy ignored it. To cries of dissent from the Labour benches, Churchill then spoke in support of Eden's contention that non-intervention must continue, telling the House:

Is it not an encouraging fact that German, French, Russian, Italian and British naval officers are officially acting together, however crankily, in something which represents, albeit feebly, the concert of Europe, and affords, if it is only a pale, misshapen shadow, some idea of those conceptions of the reign of law and of collective authority which many of us regard as of vital importance?

Churchill ended his speech with an appeal for one final effort by all the outside powers to abandon conflict and seek reconciliation, telling the House:

We seem to be moving, drifting, steadily, against our will, against the will of every race and every people and every class, towards some hideous catastrophe. Everybody wishes to stop it, but they do not know how. We have talks of Eastern and Western Pacts, but they make no greater security.

---

urgent necessity' twelve months before, to train pilots, air observers and aircraftmen. Anderson himself had been personally responsible at the Air Ministry for the 'initiation' of this policy, but had, he wrote, been frustrated in his efforts to set up suitable centres by the Director of Contracts at the Air Ministry, Mr Meadowcraft, who wished to restrict the location of new Schools to those centres 'already in existence and allied with the Ring of Aircraft Constructors and Manufacturers.' Anderson added: 'I realise how difficult it is for anyone to talk about Contracts without creating an ulterior feeling that such a person must have some financial interest, but, as you know I am unbuyable; money means nothing to me; but I hate to see efficiency sacrificed to enable a Ring of Contractors to get their own way. I can prove that, in quoting for previous prices, luncheons and dinners were held in London by Blackburnes and Air Service Training Avros, and including Clydesdale, in order that prices could be fixed. The only honest man who would not agree to these Ring prices was Reid, from Desford.'

Armaments and counter-armaments proceed apace, and we must find something new. . . .

Churchill's speech of April 14 was recognized even by his critics as being of great merit. One of those critics, the Conservative MP Henry Channon,[1] who was still not reconciled to the idea of Churchill being brought into the Government, wrote in his diary:

Winston Churchill made a terrific speech, brilliant, convincing, unanswerable and his 'stock' has soared, and today people are buying 'Churchills', and saying once more that he ought to be in the government, and that it is too bad to keep so brilliant a man out of office; but were he to be given office, what would it mean? An explosion of foolishness after a short time? War with Germany? a seat for Randolph?

Writing to Churchill from the Foreign Office on April 16, Anthony Eden thanked him for his words of support during the debate. 'I can assure you they were appreciated by the occupant of this anxious office,' and he added: 'May I also say how very good I thought your speech as a whole; indeed I heard many opinions that the speech must be ranked among your very best. It was difficult to make with the House in that tempestuous and unreasoning mood, and you contrived to sober them and cause them to reflect.'

Returning to Chartwell after the debate, Churchill spent four days working on *Marlborough*. On April 16 Captain Graham arrived for tea to discuss the Fleet Air Arm, and on the following day Deakin arrived for a weekend of work on *Marlborough*. Churchill also decided that as *Marlborough* would not be finished until the following year, his volume of biographical essays, *Great Contemporaries*, should be published later in 1937.

For several months Churchill had been saddened by the serious illness of his cousin Frederick Guest. 'I fear he will not be with us for long,' he had written to Lord Rothermere on March 1. 'He is very calm and courageous, but does not know how bad he is. We play a little backgammon together each day. Not a very brilliant world is it?' In his letter to the Duke of Windsor on March 24 Churchill had written:

I am sure Your Royal Highness will be grieved to hear that poor Freddie Guest has cancer and that no operation is possible. He insisted upon knowing the whole truth, and has now gone to Brussels where there is a Belgian doctor

---

[1] Henry Channon, 1897–1958. Educated at Christ Church Oxford. Conservative MP for Southend, 1935–50; Southend, West, 1950–58. Parliamentary Private Secretary to the Under-Secretary of State for Foreign Affairs (R. A. Butler), 1938–41. Knighted, 1957.

who holds out some hopes of a cure. They are, I fear, very slender hopes. Nothing could be more admirable than the gallant manner in which he faces this melancholy ordeal. I know he would value immensely a message from you now that polo days are over for him once and for all.

Frederick Guest died on April 28, at the age of sixty-one. He was six months Churchill's junior. The two men had been on terms of intimate personal friendship all their lives. Guest had been for thirty years a convinced believer in Churchill's qualities of leadership, and had sought consistently to guide him towards the Premiership itself. On April 30 Churchill wrote to Sir Edward Marsh:

Freddie's death was a great blow to me. We were very fond of each other. But the pain of his loss is lessened when I knew about two months ago that he had cancer in a hopeless form, and it is a relief that he should have had so painless an end. I have never seen anyone show such a complete contempt of death and make so little fuss about it.

Speaking at Bewdley on April 11 Stanley Baldwin had announced his decision to retire from the premiership immediately after the Coronation of King George VI in a month's time. With Baldwin's imminent departure, Churchill's political future was again a matter of speculation. On April 30, in declining an invitation to visit the Duke of Windsor in France during May, he wrote: 'I do not think it would be wise for me to leave the country till after Whitsuntide. The Government will all be in process of reconstruction, and although I am not very keen upon office, I should like to help in defence.' That same day Churchill wrote direct to Neville Chamberlain, offering advice on how best to organize the National Defence Contribution, a new tax which Chamberlain had announced in his Budget speech on April 20.

A sense of impending calamity was ever-present in Churchill's mind. 'Do not make the mistake,' he wrote to Abe Bailey on May 17, 'of supposing that we have got over our dangers. On the contrary 1937 and 1938 are years of our maximum weakness, and it is not until after that that we begin to improve our position relatively to Germany.' Churchill added: 'I am very glad Baldwin is going. I think we shall come to some real and straightforward politics now he is out of the way.'

Amid his preoccupations about defence, Churchill continued 'toiling', as he wrote to Colonel Pakenham-Walsh on May 7, on his final *Marlborough* volume. Deakin was now frequently at Chartwell, assembling the documents and preparing the draft sections. Mrs Pearman, helped by Miss Hamblin, took turns in working the late-night shifts.

As Miss Hamblin[1] later recalled:

My Senior and myself worked alternately with him long into the night. He would come from the dining room at about 10 o'clock—refreshed and often jovial. It was very obvious that this was his best time for working and that he enjoyed these hours. He would become entirely immersed, and would dictate, until 2 or 3 in the morning: sometimes very slowly, and always weighing every word, and murmuring sentences to himself until he was satisfied with them—then bringing them forth, often with tremendous force, and glaring at the poor secretary when driving home a point. Often one of his 'young men'—a literary assistant—or sometimes a friend—Professor Lindemann or Mr Bracken—would be present during these sessions, and I am sure he liked to have human company at these times—if there were two of us so much the better.

Miss Hamblin added:

There is no doubt he was a very hard taskmaster. He drove us. And he rarely gave praise. But he had subtle ways of showing his approval, and we wouldn't have had it otherwise. He worked so hard himself and was so absolutely dedicated to the task in hand that he expected the same from others. He accepted it as his right. And in time we who worked for him realised that in full return for the stress and strain, we had the rare privilege of getting to know the beauty of his dynamic, but gentle character.

May 1937 saw the death of one more of Churchill's contemporaries, Lord Snowden. On May 20, after Churchill had written an obituary tribute to his former rival, Lady Snowden[2] wrote to him:

I am writing to thank you for your beautiful article on my husband. It is the finest thing which has appeared and bears the brand of sincerity. I am deeply grateful to you, and touched by your kindness beyond the power of adequate expression.

Your generosity to a political opponent marks you for ever in my eyes the 'great gentleman' I have always thought you. Had I been in trouble which I could not control myself, there is none to whom I should have felt I could come with more confidence that I should be gently treated.

[1] Grace Hamblin, 1908–   . Born in London. Educated at Crockham Hill Church of England school, near Chartwell, and at Secretarial Training College. Began secretarial work for Churchill in 1932. Worked as No 2 to Mrs Pearman from 1932 to 1938. Secretary to Mrs Churchill from 1939–66. In charge of the secretarial and accounts side at Chartwell, 1945–65. OBE, 1965. Administrator at Chartwell for the National Trust, 1965–73. Secretary to the Churchill Centenary Exhibition in London, 1974.

[2] Ethel Annakin, 1881–1951. Married Snowden in 1905. An active advocate of women's suffrage, and temperance. Member of the Labour Commission of Enquiry to Russia, 1920, and author of *Through Bolshevik Russia*, critical of Bolshevism. Member of the Royal Commission on Food Prices, 1925. Member of the first Board of Governors of the BBC, 1927–33.

'He had always an affection for yourself,' Lady Snowden added. 'We often spoke of you. And when I told him of our meeting at the Czech luncheon and that you had sent him messages, his face lit up with pleasure.'

On May 26 Neville Chamberlain became Prime Minister, in succession to Baldwin.

On the following night, at Rhodes House, Oxford, Churchill was one of the speakers at a Ralegh Club dinner, telling students and dons: 'When I came to Oxford to make a speech five years ago, I said you must re-arm. I was laughed at. I said we must make ourselves safe in our island home, and then laughter arose. I hope you have learned wisdom now.'

Lord Derby now asked Churchill if he would be willing to second a motion nominating Chamberlain as Leader of the Conservative Party. Churchill agreed to do so. On May 29, while he was preparing his speech, the new Cabinet appointments were announced. 'Heartiest congratulations on your great promotion,' he telegraphed that day to Duff Cooper, who had been made First Lord of the Admiralty, and was succeeded at the War Office by Hore-Belisha. Inskip remained Minister for the Coordination of Defence and Hoare went to the Home Office. No post was offered to Churchill. One young backbencher who was given a junior Government post was Robert Bernays,[1] who had since the 1935 election sat near Churchill below the gangway. 'Many congratulations,' Churchill telegraphed on learning of his appointment as Parliamentary Secretary at the Ministry of Health. Bernays replied on May 31:

I have only one regret—and that is that I am now removed too far to hear your whispered and pungent comments on the passing Parliamentary scene—which were always so exhilarating.

I shall always be grateful—as must be every young man in the House to-day—for the way in which you continually demonstrate to what heights the arts of Parliamentary debate can be made to attain.

Disappointed at not receiving any place in the new administration, Churchill nevertheless spoke as he had offered to do at the Caxton

---

[1] Robert Hamilton Bernays, 1902–1945. Educated at Rossall and Worcester College Oxford. President, Oxford Union, 1925. *News Chronicle* leader-writer, 1925; correspondent in India, 1931; in Germany and Austria, 1934. Liberal MP for Bristol North, 1931–45 (Liberal National after 1936). Parliamentary Secretary, Ministry of Health, 1937–39; Ministry of Transport, 1939–40. Sapper, Royal Engineers, 1942; Captain, 1944. Killed in an aeroplane accident while flying from Italy to Greece, March 1945.

Hall meeting at noon on May 31. In his diary Henry Channon described Churchill's speech as 'an able, fiery speech not untouched by bitterness'. It was his duty, Churchill told the assembled MPs, Peers and prospective candidates, as the senior Conservative Privy Councillor in the House of Commons, to second the resolution nominating Chamberlain to the party leadership. After recalling Chamberlain's 'memorable achievement' as Chancellor of the Exchequer in restoring Britain's financial credit and stimulating foreign trade, Churchill told the meeting that the leadership of the party had never been interpreted 'in a dictatorial or despotic sense', and he appealed for the continued recognition of the rights of those who disagreed with party policy: 'The House of Commons,' he said, 'still survives as the arena of free debate. We feel sure that the leader we are about to choose will, as a distinguished Parliamentarian and a House of Commons man, not resent honest differences of opinion arising between those who mean the same thing, and that party opinion will not be denied its subordinate but still rightful place in his mind.'

Neville Chamberlain would not need to call a General Election until 1940, nor, having inherited Baldwin's enormous majority, did he need to fear Churchill's opposition in debate. Indeed, for the next eight months Churchill confined his major criticisms to private correspondence with Ministers. Speaking during the Budget debate on June 1 he set out his objections to the method of raising the proposed National Defence Contribution, a method which he believed would be 'a check to enterprise' and not help the revenue. In a powerful but good-humoured speech he urged Chamberlain to drop the scheme. His speech was successful. 'One of your best ever,' Lord Melchett wrote on June 2, 'and I believe it was due to the facts you presented, to the tactful manner in which you handled the Prime Minister—grave and gay—that you gave him the courage to abandon NDC.' Melchett added: 'You are indeed a *very* great man, and God knows why you are not in the Cabinet to guide this old country in the difficult times we are going through.' But to Nathan Laski,[1] who had written to Churchill on June 2 to say

---

[1] Nathan Laski, 1863–1941. A Manchester merchant, trading with India for more than fifty years. Chairman of the Manchester Jewish Hospital and of the Jewish Board of Guardians. From 1904–1908 he was one of Churchill's principal supporters at Manchester North-West. Member of the War Pensions Committee. Retired, 1930, to devote himself to social work. Author of *A Week in Palestine* (1924) and *India As I Know It* (1928). On 31 October 1941 Churchill wrote to Laski's son Harold: 'I know how much you and your brother will feel his loss. It is for you the severance of a link with childhood which can never be replaced. He was a very good man whose heart overflowed with human feeling and whose energies were tirelessly used for other people and large causes. I feel I have lost a friend, and all my memories of Manchester and Cheetham are veiled in mourning'.

how great was his support in the country, Churchill replied on the following day: 'I am not anxious to join the Government unless there is some real task they want me to do. They are very pleased with themselves at present.'

Churchill's successful criticisms, made only four days after Chamberlain had become Prime Minister, caused resentment among those who, unlike Melchett, were suspicious of Churchill's motives. On June 14 Thomas Jones recorded in his diary Lloyd George's view, that Churchill's Budget speech 'was a bid for office, but every day lost made his return now more difficult. Every member would vote to keep him out because of his dominating intellectual force and his experience.'

Shortly after Chamberlain had become Prime Minister, Cecil Roberts visited Chartwell. In his memoirs he recalled: 'Chamberlain, like Baldwin, had by-passed him and the House was hostile. . . . "There's no plan of any kind for anything. It is no good. They walk in a fog. Everything is very black, very black," he said, looking at his black swans on the lake. I wondered if they had given him the adjective. Here was the best man in Britain excluded from office.'

Throughout the spring and summer of 1937, Churchill continued to receive information about defence, and to mould it into a coherent picture. His concern for Britain's security was now so well known that many strangers wrote to him, offering to put their knowledge and expertise at his disposal. 'I have first hand information,' wrote Rear-Admiral Bertram Ramsay[1] from Scotland on May 18, 'regarding certain proceedings in the Fleet which would interest you, information which I think you should possess, whether you make use of it or not!' and by return telegram Ramsay was invited to tea at Morpeth Mansions during his next visit to London. On May 21 Churchill received a further document from Wing-Commander Anderson—a six-page letter from Lachlan MacLean to Anderson about the state of the Air Force. 'When Germany is ready in 1938,' MacLean concluded, 'we shall be at

---

[1] Bertram Home Ramsay, 1883–1945. Entered the Royal Navy, 1898; commanded Monitor 25, Dover Patrol, 1915; HMS *Broke*, 1916–18. Chief of Staff, China Station, 1929–31. On the Staff of the Imperial Defence College, 1931–33. Commanded HMS *Royal Sovereign*, 1933–35. Rear-Admiral and Chief of Staff, Home Fleet, 1935. Retired, 1938. Recalled, 1939. Flag Officer, Dover, 1939–42. Knighted, 1940. Naval Commander, Eastern Task Force, Mediterranean, 1943. Allied Naval Commander-in-Chief, Expeditionary Force, 1944–45. Killed in an aeroplane accident in France, January 1945.

the peak of our chaos, with neither the means of offence or defence or any *logical plan of war*.' MacLean enclosed a three-page memorandum on the staff organization of the Air Force, noting that every case 'of misunderstanding, delay and overlap, and there have been many, which have recurred since the new organisation was introduced, can be directly attributed to the lack of a corresponding branch at each Headquarters'.

On May 26, in asking Churchill to talk to an anti-aircraft expert, Colonel Hill,[1] a Conservative MP, Colonel John Sandeman Allen,[2] wrote: 'I feel that with the possession of the facts something must be done and I am afraid I do not quite know how to handle it myself. Your advice and assistance would be invaluable.' Churchill suggested that Hill should discuss the matter with Professor Lindemann. On May 26 the Chief of the Imperial General Staff himself, Sir Cyril Deverell,[3] sent Churchill a memorandum on the tank programme, in order to assure him 'that the best is being done'. Churchill showed the memorandum to Desmond Morton and then, on June 2, replied to Deverell:

I have no doubt the general process of training which you are carrying out is the best that can be advised. It is very disheartening for regiments like my old regiment, the 4th Hussars, to be for a whole year without horses or mechanized vehicles except those for training.

I am not of course apprised of all the later developments in tanks. I have no doubt that the Cavalry light tank regiments will be incomparably stronger than the ordinary horse regiment for every purpose, offensive and defensive, except in very exceptional country. On the other hand I wonder whether all small tanks will not be powerless against a properly dug ditch.

It seems very alarming that no medium tank is now in production. I have heard that the design has not even yet been approved. The original tank was

---

[1] Henry Warburton Hill, 1877–1951. A grandson of Sir Rowland Hill, inventor of the penny post. Educated at Bradfield and Woolwich. On active service in South Africa, 1900 (despatches). Artillery experimental work, 1906–09. On active service in Flanders, 1914–18 (wounded at Ypres, despatches thrice, CMG, DSO, Croix de Guerre). Commandant, Anti-Aircraft Defence School, 1925–29. Commander of the 26th (London) Air Defence Brigade, 1929–33. Retired, 1934.

[2] John Sandeman Allen, 1892–1949. On active service, 1914–18. Chairman of the Liverpool Chamber of Commerce, 1922–26. Chairman of Technical and Commercial Education, Liverpool, 1924–28. Conservative MP for Birkenhead West, 1931–45. Chairman of the Commercial Committee of the House of Commons; of the Coastal Trade Development Council; Beach defence, 1940–42; staff officer, movements, 1942–5.

[3] Cyril John Deverell, 1874–1947. 2nd Lieutenant, 1892; Major, General Staff, India, 1913–14. On active service in France, 1914–18; promoted Major-General for distinguished service in the field (despatches seven times). In India, 1921–31; knighted, 1926; Quartermaster-General, 1927–30; General, 1933; Field-Marshal, 1936. Chief of the Imperial General Staff, 1936–37. Retired (aged 63) in 1937.

devised for the purpose of crossing trenches, and these are certain to be encountered at an early stage in a European war.

On May 3 Churchill had received the French Minister for Air, Pierre Cot,[1] at Chartwell. Following their talk, Cot had sent Churchill a secret, nineteen-page memorandum on German military strength. On June 2, in sending Churchill a note on this memorandum, Desmond Morton went on to point out the 'desperate position' in the French aircraft industry as a result of recent socialist legislation, for which Cot was responsible, nationalizing the industry and imposing a 40-hour week. 'At the moment,' Morton wrote, 'the result is chaos.' On June 9 Churchill wrote direct to Cot: 'I do not feel at all happy about the relative Anglo-French air strength compared to Germany in 1938. Not only do these misgivings apply to the actual formations, but even more to what we call "the war potential of production". I am told the German peace time monthly output is in the neighbourhood of 400.' Two days later Churchill spoke at the annual dinner of the Australia Club. Once more his theme was the link between the preservation of democracy and the maintenance of an adequate defence. 'Lots of people fight for hearth and home,' he said. 'Even sheep bleat at the approach of the wolf.'

On June 14 Churchill gave a further luncheon to the Anti-Nazi Council. Eugen Spier,[2] who was present, later recalled Churchill's remarks to him about his own position. 'I become ever more convinced,' Churchill declared, 'that the Government is greatly under-rating the seriousness of the situation,' and he added:

I feel our country's safety is fatally imperilled both by its lack of arms and by the Government's attitude towards the Nazi gangsters. It is fostering in them the dangerous belief that they need not fear interference by us whatever they do. That can only encourage those savages to acts of aggression and violence of every kind. I have, therefore, chosen to go my own way and to act independently in order to further the safety of our country and of the civilisation without which we cannot survive as a nation.

[1] Pierre Cot, 1895–1977. Elected to the Chamber of Deputies, 1919. Under Secretary for Foreign Affairs, 1932. Air Minister in successive Governments, 1933–37. A pilot himself, he headed several flights to Russia. Reorganized French civil aviation under a single company, Air France. Urged Daladier to take emergency powers to deal with the rioters in Paris, 1934. In political eclipse after January 1938.

[2] Eugen Spier, a German subject and a Jew, he came to Britain in 1922. Helped to organize and finance the Focus, 1935–39. Arrested, 1 September 1939, interned as an enemy alien, and deported to Canada. Released from internment in 1941. Became a British citizen after 1945. Resident in London until his death in 1971. In 1963 he published Focus, an account of his work, and of his meetings with Churchill.

On June 19 Churchill received a long and detailed letter from one of his wife's cousins, Shiela Grant Duff,[1] a journalist then working in Czechoslovakia. In her letter she warned Churchill of the growing German pressures inside Czechoslovakia. As France and Russia could not be relied on, she wrote, the only protection left for Czechoslovakia was 'the moral support of England'. Her letter continued: 'Information has reached this country that our foreign office is hesitating. I am writing to you to ask you to do everything in your power to make our attitude firm and unfaltering. The crisis has never been so great and I am convinced that only a stand on our part can overcome it. Czechoslovakia is, for the moment, almost entirely dependent on us.'

Churchill encouraged Shiela Grant Duff to write to him, and at regular intervals she sent him up-to-date information which made clear the extent of German activity and subversion within Czechoslovakia.[2]

On June 14, in an attempt to influence senior members of the Conservative Party of the continuing weakness of Britain's air defences, Churchill sent Group Captain MacLean's January memorandum on air deficiencies to Lord Salisbury. He had already sent this memorandum to both Inskip and Chamberlain. In a covering letter to Salisbury, Churchill wrote: 'Inskip made the observation that things had improved since then. No doubt this is true to a small extent. I therefore two months ago asked the officer to write another impression bringing his view up to date. I will send you this from Chartwell tomorrow. . . .'

In his second memorandum, which MacLean delivered to Anderson on June 22, and which Anderson forwarded to Chartwell two days later, MacLean wrote: 'At least 100 squadrons of 124 are equipped with obsolete aircraft, and some of the new squadrons being formed even on

[1] Shiela Grant Duff, 1913–   . A granddaughter of Lady Avebury and cousin of Clementine Churchill. Her father, Lieutenant-Colonel Adrian Grant Duff, was killed in action on the western front on 14 September 1914. An undergraduate at Oxford, 1931–34, when she visited Germany (1932) and Sub-Carpathian Ruthenia (Eastern Czechoslovakia, 1933). Graduated, 1934. Worked in Paris for the *Chicago Daily News*, 1934. Covered the Saar Plebiscite for the *Observer*, 1935. Secretary to Hugh Dalton, 1935, and to Jawaharlal Nehru. Lived in Prague, 1936–37, as correspondent of the *Observer*. Resigned, June 1937; worked subsequently for the *Manchester Guardian* and *Spectator*, 1937–38. In Prague at the time of the Anschluss (March 1938), Published *Europe and the Czechs* (a Penguin special), 1938. Travelled in Germany and the Balkans, 1938. Helped Vernon Bartlett and the Duchess of Atholl in their by-elections, 1938. Czechoslovak editor at the BBC Overseas Service, 1940–42; worked on 'London Calling Europe', 1943–44. Published the *Czech Protectorate*, 1941.

[2] Not all Churchill's friends approved of Shiela Grant Duff or of the Czechs. On July 19 Sir Ian Hamilton wrote to Churchill: 'I am rather glad I missed Miss Grant Duff because I should have differed from her too violently. Except the Masaryks there are no distinguished persons amongst the Czechs. They are, in fact, a most harsh and disagreeable lot and to put those 3,000,000 *Sudeten* Germans under them has been a very bad business indeed.'

a one-flight basis are being equipped with training type aircraft only. . . .' In a covering letter to Anderson, written from RAF Mildenhall on June 22, and also forwarded to Churchill, MacLean wrote: 'Under the very suggestion of the menace we have hastily adopted a defeatist policy which is inevitably foredoomed to failure without even putting up the semblance of a good fight.' Churchill discussed these problems with Anderson on June 27. Two days later Lord Salisbury wrote to Churchill:

Of course things may be as bad as you make out (I don't doubt you have access to first-rate information), but it is curiously different from what I hear from Ministers when I talk to them privately. I don't mean to say that they are satisfied, but their attitude is quite different from the sort of acute apprehension which they had a year ago; and you will notice that in Inskip's speech reported this morning his line is optimistic. No doubt his optimism is exaggerated: I wish it were not. I think it a great mistake this Ministerial pose of self satisfaction; but apparently it cannot be avoided. All Ministers do it in all Governments. Nevertheless by making a certain discount one ought to arrive at something like the truth and it does not seem to agree with the papers you sent me and which I return herewith.

On June 28 the Supply Committee of the Committee of Imperial Defence had discussed the state of defence preparedness. Unknown to Churchill, its conclusions bore out all his fears. During the discussion, the Committee's Chairman, Sir Arthur Robinson,[1] pointed out that the continuous absence of firm War Office orders meant that 'the supply work as a whole could not proceed effectively towards a conclusion'. The Air Ministry, Robinson added, had also disclosed 'a huge gap' between the supplies being manufactured 'and the needed war potential'. After a long discussion of the Air Ministry's refusal to work out its exact priorities, and of the resultant lack of firm orders, the Supply Committee recommended 'that the attention of the Committee of Imperial Defence be drawn to the fact that, on present lines, it will not be possible for supply preparations to be completed by November, 1939'.

At Chartwell, Churchill's literary work continued throughout June and July. On June 16 he wrote to Newman Flower that he hoped to

[1] William Arthur Robinson, 1874–1950. Educated at Appleby School and Queen's College Oxford. Entered Colonial Office, 1897 (first place in Civil Service Examination). Permanent Secretary, Air Ministry, 1917–20. Knighted, 1919. Secretary to the Ministry of Health, 1920–35. Chairman of the Supply Board, Committee of Imperial Defence, 1935–39. Secretary to the Ministry of Supply, 1939–40.

finish *A History of the English-Speaking Peoples* by December 1939, but it was work on *Marlborough* which took up most of his time, and on which Deakin found himself more and more frequently summoned to Chartwell. On June 30 Churchill wrote to George Harrap: 'I am working very hard at Marlborough now, night and day in fact,' and on August 3 he wrote to his wife, who was still in Austria: 'Deakin arrives this evening so the pace will not slacken.'

During July Churchill had sent out copies of individual essays for his other new book, *Great Contemporaries*, to people whose comments he believed would be of value. On July 2 he sent a copy of his Hitler article, which had been first published in the *Strand* magazine in 1935, to Sir Robert Vansittart at the Foreign Office. As Vansittart was on leave, the article was read by Clifford Norton,[1] who wrote to Mrs Pearman on July 7:

... it is hardly to be thought that this article would be at all palatable to the powers that be in Germany. In the present rather delicate state of our relations with that country, when one does not know which way the cat will jump, it might therefore be questioned whether republication just now was advisable.

Mrs Pearman replied on July 8 that Churchill had agreed to certain deletions which would 'take the sting out of the article', but that he would cut out nothing that he was accustomed to say 'on public platforms'.

On July 6 the first resident secretary began work at Chartwell, Kathleen Hill.[2] She too became engrossed at once by the diverse work involved in correspondence, speeches, articles and books. Mrs Hill later recalled, in a conversation with the author:

I was the first resident secretary. I was engaged to do literary work for him at night. Sometimes he would dismiss me at two or even three in the morning.

---

[1] Clifford John Norton, 1891– . Educated at Rugby and Queen's College Oxford. On active service at Gallipoli, 1915 and in Palestine, 1916–18. Political Officer, Damascus, Deraa and Haifa, 1919–20. Entered the Diplomatic Service, 1921. Private Secretary to Sir Robert Vansittart, 1930–37. Counsellor, British Embassy, Warsaw, 1937–39. Minister to Switzerland, Berne, 1942–46. Knighted, 1946. Ambassador in Athens, 1946–51.

[2] Rose Ethel Kathleen Hill, 1900– . Chief Clerk, Automobile Association and Motor Union Insurance Company, Portsmouth, 1917–24, and a member of the Portsmouth Philharmonic Society (first violins), 1918–24. District Commissioner of Girl Guides, Bengal-Nagpur Railway, 1928–30. Secretary to the Chief Commissioner of Girl Guides for All-India, 1930–32. Broadcast as a solo violinist, Calcutta, Bombay and Delhi, 1935–36. Returned to England, 1937. Churchill's first Residential Secretary, July 1937; lived at Chartwell from July 1937 to September 1939. Churchill's Personal Private Secretary from 1939 to 1946. MBE, 1941. Curator of Chequers, 1946–69.

The idea was that I would get a rest in the afternoon. It hardly ever happened. I had never been in a house like that before. It was alive, restless. When he was away it was as still as a mouse. When he was there it was vibrating. So much happened that I, with my small brain, I was bewildered by it all. He could be very ruthless. He used to get impatient of delays. He was a disappointed man waiting for the call to serve his country.

Mrs Hill added:

When he was bricklaying we used to take our notebooks and mount the ladder—even there he would dictate but not at length. If it was a long letter he would come down.

Often we would dash up to the House of Commons, he dictating as we drove, and then we would type it out in the Commons. Sometimes we would pass the sheets in as he was speaking.

I had originally hoped to find a post in a school combining school work with music supervision, and I remember thinking when he was in good dictational form—well, I have lost the music but I have got the music of words.

Mrs Hill arrived during a week when Churchill was busy with constituency duties. On July 6 he had spoken at Wanstead on the destructive role of Italy and Germany in the Spanish conflict. During his speech he also criticized Mussolini for the anti-British propaganda which he was then spreading by wireless 'throughout the Middle East'. At Harlow on July 7 he appealed to whatever side might be victorious in Spain to show mercy to the defeated; Britain, he said, must do everything possible 'to avert a terrible vengeance being wreaked'.

On July 9, with Lord Swinton's approval, Churchill visited the RAF station at Biggin Hill to watch an interception exercise. Still a member of the Air Defence Research sub-committee, he studied these developments with care, writing to Swinton two months later:

I visited the Biggin Hill Aerodrome as you authorised, and was much interested by the demonstration which they gave of interception methods. I had not realised the vital important change which has been made in effecting contact with the enemy from the ground, instead of leaving the squadron leader in the air to find them for himself. The officers assured me that provided 'Cuckoo' was accurate, the percentage of interception was extraordinarily high. This had greatly affected my thought upon the subject, and I think of writing a short paper for our Committee upon the tactical aspects, so far as they affect design. . . .

On July 15, and again on July 19, Churchill spoke in the House of Commons on foreign affairs. On July 20 he spoke in the debate on the Royal Navy, and on July 21 he made a critical speech on the Government's Palestine policy, opposing the plan to partition Palestine into a Jewish and an Arab state. The scheme was as yet too vague to be voted on, he said, and more important still, it pitted the Jewish area—'a rich and small state more crowded than Germany'—against vast Arab regions 'stretching up to Bagdad', and he went on to warn of 'this great Arab area confronting this new Jewish State'. On July 25 he wrote to his wife:

My darling Clemmie,

I am overwhelmed with work. Three days H of C last week: the new book in its final birth throes: articles, & always Marlborough: & now ahead on Tuesday next another debate on Inskip's salary. I really don't know how I find all that I need, but the well flows freely: only the time is needed to draw the water from it. . . .

Wing-Commander Anderson continued to send Churchill material throughout the summer and autumn; much of it from Lachlan Mac-Lean. Both were concerned about the slow pace of recruitment and the lack of trained pilots. During July Anderson sent Churchill a letter from MacLean, in which he wrote of the high casualty lists among pilots, and added:

The situation as regards Flight Lieutenants, the back bone of the flying branch is a fair indication of the whole state on that side. We complained that out of an establishment of 42 flight lieutenants, we had 5 in the group. The Air Ministry replied on July 21st 'the marked shortage of flight lieutenants is fully appreciated & is not confined to any particular group'. . . .

'No wonder,' MacLean ended, 'we are beginning to have casualty lists like the attached & we have not started re-equipping with the fast aeroplane on any scale yet.'

On August 1 Anderson took MacLean to Chartwell; four days later Anderson wrote to Churchill from RAF Hucknall:

In all sincerity I was very impressed by that incident in the life of the Duke of Marlborough which you read, and by your conclusion as to the power of personal example and inspiration. It is just that influence which is so disastrously absent from the Air Force at this moment. We are, as a Service, peculiarly dependent on, and susceptible to, the genuine inspiration of leadership, far more so than either the Navy or the Army, since in War work is mainly done as individuals and not in groups or companies.

Anderson added: 'I do hope that a real effort will be made to draw from Parliament that the RAF expansion is permanent; this will give a feeling of security and stability which is so desperately needed to the Service and the Aircraft Industry.'

MacLean continued to send Churchill regular reports on Air Force training, equipment and tactics. At Churchill's suggestion, both he and Anderson also discussed their technical ideas with Professor Lindemann. Anderson also introduced Churchill to Squadron-Leader Rowley, who shared the Wing-Commander's anxieties about the slow pace and poor state of Britain's air preparations.[1]

Since becoming Prime Minister in March 1937 Neville Chamberlain had tried to improve Britain's relations with Italy. But his efforts had been brought to a halt by Italian naval action off the Spanish coast, during the course of which several British merchant ships taking food to Republican-held ports had been attacked by Italian submarines. On August 31 Britain and France decided to call a conference of Mediterranean powers to combat this naval piracy, but Germany and Italy refused to attend. It was decided, however, that the Conference should go ahead, at Nyon, near Geneva, and ten powers agreed to attend: Britain, France, Greece, Yugoslavia, Turkey, Egypt, Albania, Russia, Rumania and Bulgaria. Writing to Eden on September 3, Churchill warned against accepting too great an involvement. The British, he wrote, ought not to make themselves responsible 'for ships which are only nominally British, being chartered and manned by Greeks, Spaniards etc, and run simply to make a profit out of the war. The stakes are now becoming too high for us to take on any burden beyond our own absolute duty.'

Churchill told Eden that he was also worried about the future of submarine warfare. 'It seems to me very important,' he wrote, 'to find out now whether the Admiralty can really find and kill submarines as they declare so confidently. . . . A great deal of our safety, and of your policy, depends upon whether the Admiralty are right in their belief that they have the submarines beaten.'

Eden at once passed on Churchill's suggestions to the Admiralty. Six

---

[1] Throughout 1937 and 1938 Churchill was also sent details of many technical proposals and inventions in the realm of defence. He passed them all to the Committee of Imperial Defence. Among the schemes was one sent from Prague in December 1937 for a more effective method of torpedo detonation, several schemes for new types of anti-aircraft shells, a plan for the safer storage of petrol, and an idea for barrage balloons to help intercept incoming hostile aircraft by means of television-style cameras suspended underneath them which would transmit the picture to screens below.

days later Churchill wrote again. He had discussed the crisis with Lloyd George, and on the eve of Eden's departure for Nyon, sent him their considered views. 'This is the moment,' Churchill wrote, 'to rally Italy to her international duty.' A show of strength would, he believed, dissuade Italy from further naval activity without harming the future of Anglo-Italian relations. His letter continued: 'It is not believed that Germany is ready for a major war this year, and if it is hoped to have good relations with Italy in the future, matters should be brought to a head now. The danger from which we suffer is that Mussolini thinks all can be carried off by bluff and bullying, and that in the end we shall only blether and withdraw.'

The Nyon Conference opened on September 11. It was agreed to set up a joint Anglo-French anti-submarine patrol of the Mediterranean. Writing from Geneva on September 14, Eden sent Churchill a confidential account of what he believed had been achieved. 'The really important fact,' he wrote, 'is that we have emphasised that co-operation between Britain and France can be effective, and that the two Western democracies can still play a decisive role in European affairs.' Eden added: 'It is all the more satisfactory that we have been able to do this without having to call for the active co-operation of the Soviet Government.'

The Nyon Conference, Eden believed, had done something to put Britain 'on the map again', and he added: 'At least it has heartened the French and ourselves to tackle one immensely formidable task together.' Churchill replied on September 20:

It was very good of you, when so busy, to write to me. Indeed I congratulate you on a very considerable achievement. It is only rarely that an opportunity comes when stern and effective measures can be brought to bear upon an evil doer, without incurring the risk of war. I have no doubt that the House of Commons will be very much pleased with the result.

I was very glad to see that Neville has been backing you up, and not, as represented by the Popular Press, held you back by the coat-tails. My hope is that the advantages you have gained will be firmly held on to. Mussolini only understands superior force, such as he is now confronted with in the Mediterranean.

'There is plenty of trouble ahead,' Eden replied from the Foreign Office on September 25, 'and we are not yet, of course, anything like as strong in the military sense as I would wish. . . .'

On September 17, in an article in the *Evening Standard*, Churchill appealed to Hitler to abandon the persecution of Jews, Protestants and Catholics. At present, he wrote, there could be no question of returning

Germany's colonies to her, or of giving her any financial help. But he ended his article on what he hoped would be a note of hope and re-conciliation. 'One may dislike Hitler's system,' he wrote, 'and yet admire his patriotic achievement. If our country were defeated I hope we should find a champion as indomitable to restore our courage and lead us back to our place among the nations.' Churchill went on: 'I have on more than one occasion made my appeal in public that the Führer of Germany should now become the Hitler of peace. When a man is fighting in a desperate conflict he may have to grind his teeth and flash his eyes. Anger and hatred nerve the arm of strife. But success should bring a mellow, genial air and, by altering the mood to suit the new circumstances, preserve and consolidate in tolerance and goodwill what has been gained by conflict.'

Churchill's private correspondence revealed how unlikely he thought it was that Hitler would mellow, and how serious he believed the situation to be. Writing from Chartwell on September 23, he told Lord Linlithgow that everyone was 'united in dealing with our deficiencies as fast as possible without interfering with the ordinary life of the country. This is a serious limitation.' Although the Navy was 'overwhelmingly strong', and its lead increasing, 'The Air Force, alas is but a fraction of the German, and I do not think we shall catch up. On the contrary it would seem that 1938 will see Germany relatively stronger to the British Air Force and the French Army than now.' Churchill ended his letter with a forecast. 'I do not believe in a major war this year,' he wrote, 'because the French army at present is as large as that of Germany and far more mature. But next year and the year after may carry these Dictator-ridden countries to the climax of their armament and of their domestic embarrassments. We shall certainly need to be ready by then.' As for himself, Churchill ended, 'I have been living a perfectly placid life here painting and working at Marlborough, in fact I have hardly moved outside the garden since Parliament rose.'

On October 3 Churchill invited Anthony Eden to lunch at the Savoy with his Freedom and Peace group. Many of their supporters were in-fluential in Labour and Liberal circles, 'but of course', Churchill wrote, 'we always have a proportion of live Conservatives as well', and he added: 'Without the support of the Trade Unions our munition pro-gramme cannot be properly executed. This aspect is of real public im-portance. It may well be in the future that the Trade Unionists will detach themselves from particular political parties.' This, Churchill believed, 'would be a gain enormous to our political life'.

Eden accepted Churchill's invitation. At the same time, Churchill began to write and speak about the need for United States' participation in European affairs, another matter on which Eden and he were in agreement. But to Marshall Diston[1] he wrote on October 3: 'Although the ideals of the two countries are similar, their interests are in many ways divergent. Don't let us merely repeat our wishes in the form of platitudes. Face the real facts.'

Churchill's fears about the increasing German superiority in the air were confirmed and heightened during the second week of October, when he received from Wing Commander Anderson a copy of a letter sent from the Chief Engineer of the Bristol Aeroplane Company, Roy Fedden[2] on October 5. Fedden had twice visited Germany that summer first in June and then in September under what he described as 'the official aegis of my friend, General Milch', and had inspected the latest German aero engine and aircraft plans. 'I am absolutely shattered,' Fedden wrote, 'at the tremendous progress of aircraft and engine production in Germany, not from the technical aspect so much as in quantity and organisation. What they are doing is quite astounding.'

Fedden sent a full report of what he had seen in Germany to the Air Ministry, but this report was never circulated to the Cabinet or to the Committee of Imperial Defence. Anderson however made sure that Churchill received a copy, which Churchill at once passed on to Desmond Morton, who was at that very moment preparing a memorandum for the Foreign Office on the German aircraft industry. Morton brought

[1] Adam Marshall Diston, 1893–1956. Born in Scotland. Served in a Highland Regiment, 1914–18. Joined the staff of Amalgamated Press after the war; subsequently Assistant Editor of *Answers*, and acting Editor (1934). An officer of the Trade and Periodical Branch of the National Union of Journalists. A socialist, he joined Sir Oswald Mosley's New Party in 1931. Unsuccessful New Party candidate for Wandsworth Central in the 1931 election (where he polled only 424 votes out of a total of 11,647, and lost his deposit); he never stood for Parliament again. In 1935 he tried in vain, to be adopted as prospective Labour candidate for Aylesbury. Began helping Churchill (by correspondence only) in 1935; several of Churchill's published articles (none of them quoted in this volume) were written in their entirety by Diston. 'I hope you find my notes on the amusement article a help,' Churchill wrote to Diston on 10 October 1937. 'Do not let them cramp your style or feel any obligation to use them.'

[2] Alfred Hubert Roy Fedden, 1885–1973. Educated at Clifton and Bristol Technical College. Works Manager and Chief Engineer, Brazil Straker & Co, Bristol (manufacturing aero engines and shells), 1909–20. Founded the Engine Department Bristol Aeroplane Co. 1920; Chief Engineer, 1920–42. President of the Royal Aeronautical Society, 1938, 1939 and 1945. Knighted, 1942. Special Technical Adviser, Ministry of Aircraft Production, 1942–45. Research Work, Ministry of Supply, 1945–47. Aeronautical Adviser to NATO, 1952–53.

the report to the attention of J. W. Nicholls[1] at the Foreign Office, who noted, on 9 February 1938: 'Mr Morton learnt by chance of the existence of this report, (which was not circulated, I understand, by the Air Ministry) and managed to obtain a copy *for his own use.* He has offered to let me read it, provided that the Air Ministry are not told!' According to the figures Morton had assembled, which were supported by Fedden's evidence, the monthly output of German planes was 500 air frames and 1,010 aero engines, compared with the earlier German figure of 445 frames and 890 engines in April 1937. Sir Robert Vansittart noted on February 27, of Fedden: 'He is a most able man—the best I have yet come across,' and he added: 'I still think that we needn't have allowed Germany to get away with so great a superiority in the air.'

On October 4 Churchill's new volume, *Great Contemporaries*, was published by Thornton Butterworth. Each of its twenty-one essays had previously appeared in magazine or newspaper form, dating back to 1929. 'Though they are only biographical portraits,' G. M. Trevelyan wrote from Cambridge on October 10, 'there is profundity of political and historical wisdom, perfectly expressed. I wish I had your gift of historical writing.' On October 4 Neville Chamberlain had written from 10 Downing Street:

My dear Winston,

I was very delighted to find on my table yesterday a copy of your new book, inscribed in your own hand.

How you can go on throwing off these sparkling sketches with such apparent ease & such sustained brilliance, in the midst of all your other occupations is a constant source of wonder to me. But the result is to give great pleasure and entertainment to your numerous admirers, of whom not the least sincere is

Yours very gratefully
Neville Chamberlain

On October 6 Churchill left London for the Conservative Party Conference at Scarborough. Speaking to the Conference on the following day, he praised Anthony Eden's achievement at Nyon in setting up a firm Anglo-French resistance to Italian naval piracy. 'The Tories re-

---

[1] John Walter Nicholls, 1909–1970. Educated at Malvern and Pembroke College Cambridge. Entered the Foreign Office, 1932; Second Secretary, 1937; First Secretary, 1942; Counsellor, 1946; Assistant Under-Secretary of State, 1951. Ambassador to Israel, 1954–57; to Yugoslavia, 1957–60; to Belgium, 1960–63. Knighted, 1956. Deputy Under-Secretary of State, Foreign Office, 1963–66. Ambassador to South Africa, 1966–69.

ceived me very well. . . .' Churchill wrote to Beaverbrook on October 20, 'and I do not feel my pilgrimage was in vain.' On the day of Churchill's Party Conference speech, Lord Londonderry wrote to him: 'I want to avoid war, but I think our Government whose actions you praised at Scarboro' are heading straight for one. . . .' Londonderry added: 'I wish N.C. had made you Minister of Defence. I feel you would have liked it and you could have co-ordinated contending forces and developed the strength which is vitally necessary. Our friends here have never known how to control Hitler and Mussolini and they never will. . . .' Londonderry believed Anglo-German friendship was still possible, even with a Nazi regime in Germany. But Churchill replied on October 23:

You cannot expect English people to be attracted by the brutal intolerances of Nazidom, though these may fade with time. On the other hand, we all wish to live on friendly terms with Germany. We know that the best Germans are ashamed of the Nazi excesses, and recoil from the paganism on which they are based.

We certainly do not wish to pursue a policy inimical to the legitimate interests of Germany, but you must surely be aware that when the German Government speaks of friendship with England, what they mean is that we shall give them back their former Colonies, and also agree to their having a free hand so far as we are concerned in Central and Southern Europe. This means that they would devour Austria and Czecho-Slovakia as a preliminary to making a gigantic middle Europe-block. It would certainly not be in our interests to connive at such policies of aggression.

It would be wrong and cynical in the last degree to buy immunity for ourselves at the expense of the smaller countries of Central Europe. It would be contrary to the whole tide of British and United States opinion for us to facilitate the spread of Nazi tyranny over countries which now have a considerable measure of democratic freedom. . . .

At present, Churchill continued, Germany seemed intent upon a policy which would lead her 'to invade her smaller neighbours, slay them and take their farms and houses for themselves'. This was not an idea he had 'been brought up to admire'. All that Germany had to do in order to win British goodwill, Churchill wrote, was 'not to commit crimes', and he added: 'One must hope that in the passage of years, these Dictators will disappear like other ugly creatures of the aftermath.'

43

'Information in the Public Interest'

BY the autumn of 1937 Churchill's sources of information on defence had become widespread, regular and of high quality. During the previous twelve months he had received technical information from many experts who shared his fears, including Sir Robert Vansittart, Sir Philip Gibbs, Sir Eustace Tennyson d'Eyncourt, Sir William Beveridge and Colonel Hill. He had also corresponded in detail on confidential and secret matters with several members of the Government, including Swinton, Inskip and Eden, and with several senior officers who had been authorized to answer his questions, including Vice-Admiral Sir Reginald Henderson and Field Marshal Sir Cyril Deverell. He had also received much secret information from serving officers and Government officials who had contacted him on their own initiative, among them Brigadier Hobart, Rear-Admiral Ramsay, Major Desmond Morton, Captain Lachlan MacLean, Squadron-Leader Rowley, Commander Lord Louis Mountbatten, Captain Graham and Wing-Commander Anderson. In the autumn of 1937, when the problems of air defence became more urgent, Anderson had sought Churchill's advice about a possible ally in their efforts. As Mrs Pearman explained to Churchill on September 23:

A nearby neighbour of his, Lord Addison (who used to be Dr Christopher Addison) came to see his cottage which was up for sale. He stayed and had tea with him and chatted. He told Cmdr that he viewed with much anxiety what was coming in the future, and appeared to hold much the same views as him. Cmdr A. says that he was very discreet in what he said, and thought you would like to know he called, as he seemed quite a good ally in the large common cause. Is this so?

'Yes,' Churchill noted, and encouraged Anderson to persevere with his efforts. On Saturday October 2, after Anderson had lunched with Churchill at Chartwell, he sent by post five foolscap pages of closely typed criticism of the Air Force organization for Home Commands; a scheme, he wrote, which had 'bewildered' the Commanders.

Sir Maurice Hankey, who had continued to hear Churchill's criticisms at meetings of the Air Defence Research sub-committee, was unaware of the exact nature or the frequency of his contacts. On Sunday October 3 he wrote to Churchill from his house nearby:

My dear Winston,

Many thanks indeed for 'Great Contemporaries'—a most valuable contribution to history, as I have already discovered. Someone ought to add to the list by writing a sketch of the author, and he would have to cover a lot of ground!

I spent my leave 'nosing' about in a small car in Italy and France and gathering impressions. I was surprised to find how popular we seem to be with all classes in Italy—but I did not get anywhere near the official crowd in Rome.

Since my return I have had a run round some of the new aircraft factories in the Midlands. It was heartening to find half a dozen huge factories, covering acres of ground (27 acres in Austin's case), full of the most modern machine tools, and carrying on large-scale production, in places where twelve months ago there was nothing but rolling, unlevelled grassland.

We shall meet soon at our Committee. There is good progress but heaps to be done yet. . . .

In his postscript Hankey wrote: 'On the whole my spirits are rising.' Churchill, however, felt no such confidence. On October 12 Wing-Commander Anderson had sent him yet another letter from Lachlan MacLean, in which he commented on the forthcoming visit of a German Air Mission to Britain; a mission led by the German Air Minister, General Milch, and which contained 'a particularly astute and highly trained technical observer', Colonel Udet,[1] the Member for Research and Development on the German Air Staff. MacLean's letter continued:

How we have been let in for this visitation at the present moment is beyond imagination.

The attached notes are a pretty incisive commentary on our state of preparedness to receive such a mission. Every one concerned must realize that the impression created on these people now, must inevitably influence German policy with regard to us & foreign policy generally.

[1] Ernst Udet, 1896–1941. Born in Frankfurt-am-Main. As a fighter pilot from 1915 to 1918 he shot down 62 enemy aeroplanes. After 1918, a stunt pilot and electrical engineer. Director of the Technical Department of the German Air Ministry, 1936. Member for Research and Development, German Air Staff, 1937. Major-General, 1937. Master of the Ordnance (Generalluftzeugleiter), 1938–40. Committed suicide in Berlin, 1941.

At present we are bluffing with the sky as the limit, without holding a single card & we have then invited our opponents to come round & see what cards we hold, trusting to sleight of hand to put across a second bluff—

We know that Milch heads the group which suspects the real state of affairs & that the mission is out to find confirmation of their suspicions.

I suppose this is simply the culminating instance of being caught in the net which we ourselves have woven. Having gone on reiterating that expansion is beyond our most sanguine hopes, & re-equipment were up to expectation— no one dare now call a halt, & disclose the real situation. So the wholesale deceptions & deceits that have been practised, are to continue in order to prevent a disclosure of the past—even at the risk of wrecking civilization in order to ensure that our various nabobs at any cost hold their jobs & continue with the havoc that they have wrought.

Not a day passes, that the situation does not deteriorate.

MacLean also sent Churchill the official notes of all that the Germans were to be shown. These notes included the remark by Air Marshal Sir Edgar Ludlow-Hewitt[1] 'that we should have to comb the country in order to produce sufficient aircraft to get up any sort of show'.

It had been decided to allow the German mission to inspect, on the ground, one example of each modern type—a Wellesley, a Blenheim, a Harrow, a Battle and a Whitley. As none of these aeroplanes was as yet completely equipped either with blind flying panels or gun turrets, arrangements were being made by the Air Ministry, first to provide a fully equipped example of each type, and then to train special pilots in a simple formation fly-past. MacLean noted: 'This is a fair commentary on the state of equipment *and* the state of training!!!'[2]

On October 12, at the Trinity House dinner, Churchill privately expressed his unease at the general lack of air preparedness. Hankey, who was also present at the dinner, wrote to Inskip two days later: 'From some views which I heard Mr Winston Churchill declaiming to

[1] Edgar Rainey Ludlow-Hewitt, 1886–1973. 2nd Lieutenant, Royal Irish Rifles, 1905. Transferred to the Royal Flying Corps, 1914. Major, 1915. Commanded the 10th Brigade, Royal Air Force, 1918. Awarded the DSO and the MC. Chief Staff Officer, Royal Air Force Headquarters, France, 1918–19. Group Captain, 1919. Private Secretary to the Secretary of State for Air, 1919–21. Commandant, Royal Air Force Staff College, 1926–30. Air Officer Commanding, Iraq, 1930–32. Knighted, 1933. Elected to the Other Club, 1933. Director of Operations and Intelligence, Air Ministry, 1933–35. Commanded RAF India, 1935–37. Commander-in-Chief, Bomber Command, 1937–40. Inspector-General of the RAF, 1940–45.

[2] On October 20 Churchill himself dined privately with the German Air Mission at Brooks's Club, as the guest of Lord Trenchard. Camrose, Weir and Amery were also present. A month later on November 16 a member of the British Embassy in Berlin, Ivone Kirkpatrick, reported to London on the Mission's reaction to Churchill: 'He made the impression of a great personality, but it was clear that he was an implacable enemy of German aspirations. On this account, I gathered, the mission had not really taken to him.' On the other hand, Kirkpatrick noted, 'Lord Swinton's charm delighted them.'

a group at the Trinity House Dinner I should judge that he has a pretty shrewd knowledge of the situation, though he told me afterwards that he could not use his information in Parliament in the present dangerous world situation.' Privately, Hankey shared Churchill's anxieties, and believed that a more vigorous defence programme was essential, telling Inskip that while he did not feel competent to judge the political aspect of the question, nevertheless:

I can well believe that if Parliament and the nation—already considerably stirred on the matter of defence—came to believe that the scale of our preparations is insufficient to provide for national security, the Government may well be forced to undertake late in the day panic measures; in a word I submit that it would be better for the Government to lead the public and to ask them for further sacrifices.

In a postscript Hankey wrote: 'if you are as uneasy as I am, I see no reason why you should not make a move yourself'.

Churchill knew nothing of Hankey's letter to Inskip. But on October 16, encouraged by Hankey's interest at the Trinity House dinner, he sent him a copy of Lachlan MacLean's letter. In his letter he described MacLean as 'a high Staff Officer of the RAF', but did not name him. Churchill's letter, marked 'Secret and Personal', read:

As one small instalment of the alarming accounts I have received of the state of the RAF, I send you the enclosed. It is for your own personal information, and I trust to our friendship and your honour that its origin is not probed. But look at the facts! We have invited the German Mission over—why I cannot tell. Highly competent men are coming. A desperate effort is now being made to present a sham-show. A power-driven turret is to be shown, as if it was the kind of thing we are doing in the regular way. Ought it to be shown at all? You will see that a special telegram has to be sent to fetch one of the only men acquainted with this turret to give a demonstration. You will also see the feelings of some of the high officers concerned. You will also see from the statement, made by the Air Officer Commanding-in-Chief Bomber Command (paper C marked in red), Ludlow-Hewitt, how he is forced to address himself to the task of making a show; and what exertions are necessary to put little more than a hundred bombers in the air—the great majority of which (as the Germans will readily see) can barely reach the coast of Germany with a bomb load. . . .

Churchill then appealed to Hankey, on personal grounds, for his reaction, telling him:

I remember how you played an essential part in saving the country over the convoy system, and how when young officers came to you and told you the truth, against Service rules, you saw that the seed did not fall on stony ground. If I had opportunity I could unfold a most shocking state of affairs in the Air Force, and no one would be more pleased than I if I could be refuted categorically. But you have a great responsibility—perhaps on the whole second to none—and therefore I leave the matter for the moment in your hands.

As he was writing this letter, Churchill decided to ask Hankey a few more questions that were on his mind:

Is it credible that we are sending fifty or sixty Gladiators to China while our own squadrons have to carry on with an even less up-to-date machine? Is it true that a great many of the 3 inch AA guns have been sold to foreign countries, or given away, although the new pattern has not yet begun to come into production. Is it true that there are under twenty AA guns at Malta and these only of an old pattern? But I forbear.

Please send me the stuff back when you have done with it, for I am much inclined to make a Memorial to the Prime Minister upon the whole position. Obviously it cannot be dealt with in public.

Although Hankey was himself concerned about deficiencies in the rearmament programme, he was very angry that such secret information should have been given to Churchill. His reply, sent on October 19, was an eight-page rebuke. He would not, he wrote, 'on the present occasion', probe the origin of Churchill's information, but he could not conceal 'that I am a good deal troubled by the fact of your receiving so many confidences of this kind'. His letter continued:

You and I are very old friends who have hunted together in circumstances of supreme danger and difficulty. I have always valued your friendship. The frequent conmendation of one for whom I have an immense admiration has been, and remains, a tremendous encouragement, especially in the parlous times through which we are passing. I feel, therefore, that I can open my mind quite frankly to you on the subject.

It shocks me not a little that high Officers in disciplined Forces should be in direct conmunication with a leading Statesman who, though notoriously patriotic beyond criticism, is nevertheless in popular estimation regarded as a critic of the Departments under whom these Officers serve.

I do not question the motives of these Officers. They can only be of the highest, for the reason that they have personally nothing to gain from their supposed revelations. On the contrary, they jeopardise their official careers by their action, for a slip might prove disastrous to them, and even though they escape this possibility, it may all come out years after and damage their reputations before posterity. . . .

Hankey noted that Field Marshal Sir Henry Wilson's reputation had been 'seriously' damaged when, after his death, his own published diary revealed 'his trafficking with the Opposition leaders before the War', and he went on:

I am prepared to admit also that it is a very difficult position for an Officer who honestly believes (though he is usually in ignorance of the wider factors that control national policy) that his superiors are not doing their job properly. He has, of course, official channels, eg, his official superiors, Inspecting Officers, even an approach to his Government Department, or, in the last resort, to its political Head. But he may be inexperienced or may shrink from representations that might result in his being marked down as a litigious person or a bore by some red-tapy official superior. So he turns to some unofficial channel.

Nevertheless I feel in my bones that these unofficial communications are all wrong, that the thing is infectious, and subversive to discipline and that the damage done to the Services far outweighs any advantage that may accrue— especially as, when the matters in question are investigated, there is almost invariably a perfectly sound explanation forthcoming. . . .

Hankey continued with a warning about Churchill's own part in the matter:

The position of the recipient of such illicit information is also embarrassing. As you may imagine, I am not without experience in the matter. I have sometimes been the recipient of embarrassing confidences of the kind which you enclose. The course which I seek to follow is to try and contrive a way in which the giver of the information can himself get it into the official channel in a perfectly above-board manner and without risk to himself. If, from the circumstances of the case, this is impossible and *prima facie* the matter seems to need probing, I go direct to the Minister or to some friendly official in the Department concerned and put the case before him. That, however, is a delicate matter, as he may demand the source. I am certain that if I had come to you, when you were First Lord of the Admiralty before the War, with material comparable to that with which you have furnished me, you would have turned on me pretty hard. You might well have demanded a searching Inquiry, in which both my informant and I should have found ourselves up against Official Regulations. . . .

Such 'backstairs' information, Hankey argued, could only breed distrust, and have 'a disintegrating effect on the discipline of the Services', and he advised Churchill to give his informants 'friendly counsel', in the interest first of the Service and second of their own 'careers and reputations', that they should speak, not to him, but to 'their Commanding Officers', or a 'friend' in the Air Department. Hankey then defended the existing air policy:

We have to remember that everyone is now working under the greatest difficulties, and this applies especially to the RAF in the expansion period.

New squadrons are being formed. As the butter of experience gets spread more thinly over a greatly enlarged Air Force, senior personnel are no doubt constantly being pulled out of their present posts either to join a new squadron or to undergo some course to fit them for specialist activity. All this is happening at a time when new machines, perhaps harder to fly than the old ones, and a new personnel are coming in. The new machines require, no doubt, new tactics, longer flights, and new apparatus, all of which means more intensive training. Probably also all sorts of annoying things happen. Arrivals of machines and their equipment may not synchronise. All this sort of thing must be very harassing, and the tendency must be rather to set people on edge. Although this will rectify itself in the later stages of the expansion, one has to make allowances.

One has also to make allowances for those responsible in the Air Ministry. They are all very hard driven. They, again, must meet with many exasperations, such as delays due to contractors' failures; or, maybe, unavoidable alterations in designs, machines or apparatus that on trial do not come up to expectations.

If they were not doing their best, or were not doing it competently, there would be a case for appropriate action by the Government or, if they do not realise the position, from outside. That is not true at the present time of the Air Ministry. I believe there is tremendous enthusiasm and competence in the face of a very difficult problem. I believe we are aware of our deficiencies (which do not necessarily arise from incompetence) and that every effort is being made to rectify them.

In a reference to the two defence deputations of 1936, in which Churchill had taken the leading part, Hankey wrote:

I have seen something myself of the immense effort which is involved in answering long strings of questions. They put an extra load on an over-burdened machine, and especially on to those at the top, through whom the replies must necessarily pass, with the consequence that again and again I have seen more harm than good result from that procedure.

Hankey continued his letter with a paragraph of personal advice for Churchill. 'I should like to see you using your great influence,' he wrote, 'to get all concerned to appreciate each other's point of view and difficulties, and thus to strengthen mutual trust and confidence. As a nation we need "jollying" along rather than frightening, and I think in recent writings you have recognised this.'

Hankey ended his letter by commenting on Churchill's reference to his own responsibility. 'I do not shirk whatever responsibility is mine,' he wrote. 'I felt it even more keenly than I do now in the days of the disarmament era, and I did my utmost again and again to bring out the dangers of our course.' Since the advent of the rearmament period,

Hankey added, 'I am happier in the ceaseless activity it entails.' He added: 'I shall continue to devote my utmost energies to the discharge of my responsibilities, and I hope that I shall continue to have your goodwill.'

Churchill's reply to Hankey was brief:

My dear Maurice,

I certainly did not expect to receive from you a lengthy lecture when I went out of my way to give you, in strict confidence, information in the public interest. I thank you for sending me the papers back, and you may be sure I shall not trouble you again in such matters.

Yours vy sincerely,
Winston S. Churchill

Churchill sent his reply to Hankey on October 21. Nine days earlier, on October 12, a secret document, of which Churchill knew nothing, justified his warnings about lack of preparedness, and about the effect of the deficiencies on Britain's stature in Europe. The document, an Air Staff memorandum circulated to the Cabinet by Lord Swinton, stated that by December 1939 Germany would have a total first-line strength of 3,240 as against Britain's total of only 1,736. Britain's present air power, Swinton wrote, represented 'little more than the facade of our projected structure of air defence', as the planned 1,736 first-line aircraft, although the target for Scheme F, did not yet include the 100 per cent reserves envisaged under that scheme. Moreover, Swinton added, 'our anti-aircraft artillery and searchlight defences will admittedly not even be within sight of completion to the approved scale until 1941'. Even the approved scale, he wrote, 'does not provide sufficient security' according to the Home Defence sub-committee. Swinton concluded:

It is clear, therefore, that while we are to-day in a position of grave inferiority to Germany in effective air strength, the completion of our present programme will not provide an adequate remedy, and that by 1939 we shall still have failed to achieve that equality in air striking power with Germany which represents the policy of His Majesty's Government and the subject of Mr Baldwin's pledge to the country.

The Air Staff recommended yet another scheme, J, 'for our minimum requirements for security' to create a total of 2,331 first-line aircraft, including 1,442 bombers, which should be provided 'by the summer of 1941'. This was still 900 less than the estimated German strength in December 1939. Without Scheme J, the Air Ministry had written in a memorandum of October 8:

It is difficult, indeed, to see (even assuming the most drastic degree of State intervention and control) how a standard of air strength, as expressed particularly in terms of aircraft and other forms of material which would be necessary to provide any adequate military deterrent against the risk of attack by Germany, could be attained as early as 1939, by which year it is assumed that Germany might be in a position to strike. But this fact affords no reason for our failing to take every possible further measure to bridge this gap, and the Air Staff strongly represent the desirability of the larger programme being approved, and of every effort being made to complete it as soon after 1939 as possible.

On October 27 Swinton wrote, in a further Cabinet memorandum, that Scheme J's production by 1941 was based 'on the assumption that it will remain the policy of the Government to avoid the control of industry and interference with normal production to meet civil requirements'. Despite Swinton's sense of urgency, the decision was delayed until December.

Swinton's knowledge of Britain's air weakness extended to all the areas of air production about which Churchill had expressed concern. In a letter to Inskip on October 22, Swinton gave the Air Ministry's answer to the question, 'what would be the condition of the Air Force in January 1938'. Its conclusions, together with the Air Staff memorandum of October 12, entirely vindicated all that Churchill had been saying for more than three years, and made it clear, within the secrecy of the Cabinet, that his warnings about Britain's comparative weakness in the air in 1937 and 1938 had been fully justified. Among the Air Ministry's conclusions were:

Due to the present lack of aircraft depots in the United Kingdom, the repair organisation is totally inadequate for war. Should it be necessary to dispatch a contingent to the Continent, the efficiency of any repair and maintenance organisation accompanying it will be of a low order.

Many of the facilities required for the proper distribution of ammunition in war will still be under construction at the date in question. The initial supply of bombs and ammunition to stations, and its maintenance if hostilities started before the necessary construction is completed, would therefore be a difficult problem. . . .

The inevitable result of an expansion which has practically trebled the size of the Metropolitan Air Force concurrently with complete re-equipment and re-organisation, has been very seriously to lower the standard of operational efficiency. Service squadrons previously existing had to be stripped of the majority of their trained personnel in order to form the new squadrons and man the many newly formed flying training schools. . . .

Of Bomber Command, the Air Ministry wrote:

In addition to the shortage of Flight Lieutenants and Flying Officers already mentioned, the position is almost as acute as regards experienced technical NCOs, wireless operators, air gunners and air observers. The situation will improve with time, but the Command will in no way be fit for war as early as January 1st.

The light bombers are reasonably well trained, but the technical limitations of these obsolete aircraft are such that their operational value in modern conditions is very low.

The medium bombers will not have been in service sufficiently long for the squadrons to have reached operational efficiency, except possibly for four or five squadrons. Night flying training is still in an elementary stage, and squadrons will have had little practice in night operations.

The heavy bomber situation is even less satisfactory. Out of a total of 239 pilots in No 3 (B) Group, only 78 have qualified as 'ist Pilots Night' and only 7 as full operational pilots. As most of the effort is perforce having to be devoted to individual training, no great improvement is likely before January 1st. Shortage of turrets and guns is also serious.

'Bomber Command,' the Air Ministry concluded, 'can in no way be said to be ready for war.'

Churchill continued to welcome all the material which Anderson and MacLean could send him. On November 16 MacLean sent him a closely typed three-page foolscap criticism of the visit of the German Air Mission, giving in detail the effect of the visit at his own air station at Mildenhall. That same day, Anderson telephoned an anxious Mrs Pearman, who noted for Churchill:

He said he was not 'huffy' at all, only a little worried. He is too devoted to you to think of being offended over trifles. He says that the conference, about which he had been speaking to you, has gone all in his favour, and that everything will be all right. But please do *not* use what he gave you on Sunday. Bear the fact in mind, and say if you like that it had come to your ear, but do not show the copies to anyone.

He said *himself* that you were *not* to think he was not 'balanced', because he was so pessimistic. I explained that I had said this was because he brooded too much owing to his lonely life, therefore being thrown back into his thoughts and worries, and he agreed that this was so.

He is 'lying low' after this conference for some time, and asks that you do not do anything with anything he has given you, for the present at any rate.

On December 5 MacLean wrote again to Churchill enclosing several documents which dealt with the problems of formation flying, night flying, anti-ice protection, aircraft range, direction finding and other technical matters on which he was critical of current planning.

On November 2 Anderson had sent Churchill a detailed letter, about the 'large number of officers', especially young pilots, who were in the hands of money lenders. Among the documents were a letter and a contract sent out by one of the money-lending companies, The Increased Power Company Limited of Southampton Row, London. Undeterred by Hankey's rebuke, on November 18 Churchill sent Anderson's letter, and the documents, direct to Lord Swinton. 'Money may be needed which your authority alone could procure,' he wrote, 'to pull these young fellows out of their scrapes,' and he added:

If you find the facts are substantiated, it certainly is a great argument for increasing the proportion of senior officers from other Services, so as to give a stronger framework to all this flood of new young pilots necessitated by the rapid expansion. You can certainly rely on my support in the House of Commons for any steps you may take in this direction, unpopular as they will be.

Pray make your own enquiries now from this, and let our correspondence remain entirely secret and personal.

Replying in a long and detailed letter on November 29, Swinton agreed that he too would like to see the initial pilots' pay raised. But, he added: 'As an old Chancellor, you will realize all the difficulties in this, particularly the reactions on other Services.' On December 1 Churchill wrote to Swinton again, thanking him for giving the matter his 'personal attention', and adding his further thoughts and suggestions.

Although, in accusing Churchill of impropriety, Hankey had raised a serious issue, he himself had not denied that Churchill possessed what he had called 'a pretty shrewd knowledge of the situation', nor that the situation itself was a serious one. Nor did Churchill himself have any doubt in his own mind that it was his duty to use the information he acquired to spur on the Government on questions of defence. For their part, serving officers and senior civil servants felt driven to seek him out, knowing full well that it was a breach of the Official Secrets Act to do so, but confident that their secrets would be safe in his hands, and that he would use them in what he and they regarded as the national interest.

Churchill had long warned that 1938 would be the year when Hitler could do what he wanted, unless there were a radical change of attitude and planning in Whitehall. These changes had not taken place. On the contrary, even though the Cabinet knew that the current Air Force expansion scheme was inadequate, and in disarray, they had failed to adopt more vigorous measures, or a new scheme. On every major issue of defence, Churchill's facts had been proved accurate, and his persistent warnings vindicated.

44

Eden's Resignation:
'The Vision of Death'

THROUGHOUT 1937, in his Parliamentary speeches, in after-dinner talks, at private luncheons and in frequent articles Churchill reiterated the twin themes of national preparedness and collective security. Among the English-language newspapers which published his articles during 1937 were the *Evening Standard, Collier's*, the *Sunday Chronicle* and the *News of the World*. On November 3 he wrote to Sir Emsley Carr, one of the owners of the *News of the World*: 'It is indeed a wonderful platform from which to address the stable, sagacious, good-humoured, kind-hearted central mass of the British nation, and I value the opportunity of doing so, quite apart from the handsome payments which you make.' Three weeks later Churchill received a cheque for £4,500 for a series of sixteen articles which he had agreed to write for the *News of the World* in 1938.

By means of the Freedom and Peace luncheons, Churchill also extended the range of his contacts, both inside the Labour movement, and among his fellow Conservatives. On November 2 he brought together as his guests at the Savoy Hotel, the Foreign Secretary, Anthony Eden, and the Socialist Mayor of Manchester, Joseph Toole.[1] Even Lord Derby, his fiercest enemy during the India controversy, was drawn into these gatherings. Churchill had explained to him on October 23: 'We have a small "focus" which aims at gathering support from all Parties, especially those of the "left", for British rearmament, for the association of the two Western democracies (France and Britain), and

[1] Joseph Toole, 1887–1945. Educated at Mount Carmel Roman Catholic School, Salford. Worked first as a newsboy, then as a labourer in an iron foundry and in electrical shops. Labour MP for Salford, 1923–24 and 1929–31. Lord Mayor of Manchester, 1936–37.

for the maintenance of peace through British strength.' Derby replied on October 26: 'Nothing will give me greater pleasure than to attend . . .'

In a letter to Lord Linlithgow on November 3 Churchill described his fears as he watched the growing strength and activities of the dictator States throughout the world: 'the concourse of events is increasingly grim', he wrote, and added: 'The peace of Europe dwells under the shield of the French Army. But in a few years the German Army will be much larger than the French and increasingly its equal in maturity. The deadly years of our policy were 1934 and 1935. "The years that the locusts have eaten." I expect we shall experience the consequences of these years in the near future.' Churchill did not, however, intend to give way to despair, telling Linlithgow: 'Meanwhile our people are united and healthy. The spirit of Britain is reviving. The working people are ready to defend the cause of Liberty with their lives. The United States signals encouragement to us, for what that is worth. We must all fight our corners as well as we can, each in his station great or small.' Churchill then reflected on his personal philosophy:

I have come to think myself in the last lap of life that one should always look back upon the history of the past, study it and meditate upon it. Thus one learns the main line of advance. On the other hand it is wrong to be bound by the events and commitments of the last few years, unless these are sound and compatible with the main historic line. I am sure the right course is to know as much as possible about all that has happened in the world, and then to act entirely upon the merits from day to day.

'Of course,' Churchill told Linlithgow, 'my ideal is narrow and limited. I want to see the British Empire preserved for a few more generations in its strength and splendour.' And he added: 'Only the most prodigious exertions of British genius will achieve this result.'

On November 15 Lord Halifax left England for Berlin at the invitation of General Goering, in order to hunt in East Prussia, and to meet Hitler. On the following day Churchill spoke in the House of Commons in support of the Government's Air Raid Precautions Bill, which had been introduced by the Home Secretary, Sir Samuel Hoare. Stressing the long delays, and the constant official hesitations which had dogged the introduction of the ARP Bill, Churchill commented: 'I do not like to think how the advocates of totalitarian dictatorships will grin when they read this sad story.' During his speech Churchill said: 'I was very glad to hear from the Home Secretary that he is alive to the danger of incendiary bombs. He said yesterday: "I am inclined to think that in the past we have not given sufficient attention to the dangers of the incendiary bomb..that is to say, the small bomb that can start a very large number of fires." I hope my right hon Friend will forgive me if I turn to the records of the House. Exactly three years ago, in November 1934, in the Debate on the Address I said: "The most dangerous form of air attack is the attack by incendiary bombs. Such an attack was planned by the Germans for the summer of 1918, I think for the time of the harvest moon. The argument in favour of such an attack was that if in any great city there are, we will say, fifty fire brigades, and you start simultaneously one hundred fires and the wind is high, an almost incalculable conflagration may result." '

On December 1 Churchill dined with Anthony Eden. Both were agreed that the renewed Japanese aggression against China must not deflect them from their European concerns. 'This Far Eastern question is very anxious,' Eden wrote to Churchill on December 3, 'but we must keep calm & above all avoid ineffective actions.' On the following day Churchill visited Houghton Hall, in Norfolk,[1] and while there he asked the Commander-in-Chief of Eastern Command, General Ironside,[2] if they could have a talk together. Ironside drove over to see him on Sunday December 5. 'I told him that the whole future of the Army was in the melting pot,' Ironside recorded in his diary. 'That neither the Cabinet nor Belisha had any idea what the Army was wanted for. That they were groping about for a solution and hadn't even begun to formulate a policy.' Churchill told Ironside that he ought to 'lead the Army' in the event of war, and urged him not to despair, and not to go abroad, trying to boost Ironside's morale by giving him the example of Sir John French in 1914:

How he had been thrown out at the critical moment over politics. Chiefly Ulster. How he had come on the Admiralty yacht with Winston a broken man. And within a fortnight he was the Commander-in-Chief of the greatest Army we had ever put in the field. A dramatic turn of fortune.

[1] Where he and his wife were the guests of the Marquess and Marchioness of Cholmondeley.
[2] William Edmund Ironside, 1880–1959. 2nd Lieutenant, Royal Artillery, 1899. On active service in South Africa, 1899–1902. Major, 1914. Staff Officer, 4th Canadian Division, 1916–17. Took part in the battles for Vimy Ridge and Passchendaele. Commandant of the Machine Gun Corps School, France, 1918. Brigadier-General commanding the 99th Infantry Brigade, 1918. Major-General commanding the Allied Troops, Archangel, October 1918–October 1919. Knighted, 1919. Head of the British Military Mission to Hungary, 1920. Commanded the Ismid Force, Turkey, 1920; the North Persian Force, 1920–1. Lieutenant-General, 1931. Quartermaster-General, India, 1933–36. General, 1935. Governor and Commander-in-Chief, Gibraltar, 1938–39. Head of the British Military Mission to Poland, August 1939. Chief of the Imperial General Staff, 1939–40. Commander-in-Chief, Home Forces, May 1940. Field-Marshal, 1940. Created Baron, 1941. On 4 July 1938 Churchill wrote of Ironside, to Sir Abe Bailey: 'He is the finest military brain in the Army at the present time.'

He then agreed with me that things were 'written'. They may or may not be 'written' for you, he said, but you must do nothing to prevent the fulfilment. I told him that I had never influenced my career in one single way by asking or intriguing for things. He told me that he had not either, and added 'I have had my ups and downs.'

Churchill then gave Ironside a survey of the military situation in Europe, setting it out with what Ironside described as 'blistering clearness'. In his diary, which he wrote up on the following day, Ironside recorded the main gist of Churchill's remarks:

He thought the French Army an incomparable machine at the moment. It would be so during 1938 and 1939. Unassailable. But from then on he thought the Germans would have caught up the French and out-distanced them. He catechized me over the Germans as to their lack of training, lack of staff and lack of leading experience. An Army in the making. But by 1940 the annual contingent in Germany would be double that of France. He said that the power of France to defend herself was terrific. . . .

He was in agreement with me that 1940 was a very bad time for us.[1]

Talking of Air Force expansion, Churchill told Ironside that 'it was not going as well as it should', and was behindhand 'in many ways'. Ironside was much impressed by Churchill: 'He ought to be the Minister of Supply if we are in for a crisis,' he wrote and added: 'His energy and fiery brain seem unimpaired with age. He is certainly not dismayed by our difficulties. He says that our rulers are now beginning to get frightened. . . . He said that sometimes he couldn't sleep at night thinking of our dangers, how all this wonderful Empire which had been built up so slowly and so steadily might all be dissipated in a minute.'

Merely talking to Churchill, Ironside wrote to a friend a few days later, had done something 'to dispel the anger and disgust which had invaded me at the way things were being mishandled'. Ironside's fears were well-founded. On December 8, three days after Ironside's meeting with Churchill in Norfolk, Neville Chamberlain was telling the Cabinet in London that, as the official minutes recorded, 'our Naval, Military and Air forces, in their present stage of development, are still far from sufficient to meet our defensive commitments'.

On November 24, Lord Halifax had reported to the Cabinet on his conversation with Hitler. The subsequent discussion was recorded in a 'Most Secret' annex to the Cabinet minutes. Halifax reported that 'he had encountered friendliness and a desire for good relations', although

---

[1] On 21 April 1938 Churchill wrote to the editor of *Colliers*, William L. Chenery: 'Never forget that the Germans are adding an army corps of three divisions to their already vast army every six weeks; and that by 1940 they will soon be double the strength of the French.'

his judgement might be wrong. The Germans, he added, 'had no policy of immediate adventure', and all would be well with Czechoslovakia if she treated 'the Germans living within her borders well'. In conclusion, Halifax told his colleagues that he would expect 'a beaver-like persistence' on the part of Germany 'in pressing their aims in Central Europe, but not in a form to give others cause—or probably occasion—to interfere'. Halifax also pointed out that Hitler 'had suggested an advance towards disarmament' and that he had also 'strongly criticised widespread talk of an imminent catastrophe and did not consider that the world was in a dangerous state'.

Commenting on Halifax's visit, Neville Chamberlain told the Cabinet that as a result of what Hitler had said, 'the most hopeful prospect' for disarmament 'was in a qualitative rather than a quantitative direction; that is to say, some limitation of the size and power of weapons such as guns, tanks or aeroplanes, following the precedent of the Naval Treaty of 1936. That might save a great deal of expenditure.' As to the League of Nations, Chamberlain added, he 'took the same view as Herr Hitler. At present it was largely a sham, owing more particularly to the idea that it could impose its views by force.'

Halifax's visit to Hitler was the subject of much discussion on December 21, during a foreign policy debate in the House of Commons. During the debate Chamberlain expressed his regret that the debate was taking place at all. 'It is so difficult to say anything that can do good,' he commented, 'and so easy to say much that might do harm,' and he added: 'A china shop is not the best or the safest place for a fencing match, and if, in my reply to the right hon Gentleman, I am not altogether as informative as he would like me to be, it must be remembered that even if the opposition do not feel any responsibility for the safety of the crockery, certainly His Majesty's Government do.'

Churchill, in his speech, spoke of the persecution of the Jews in Germany: 'it is a horrible thing', he said, 'that a race of people should be attempted to be blotted out of the society in which they have been born', and he went on to express his unease about Lord Halifax's visit to Berlin. 'We must remember,' he said, 'how very sharp the European situation is at the present time,' and he continued:

If it were thought that we were making terms for ourselves at the expense either of small nations or of large conceptions which are dear, not only to many nations, but to millions of people in every nation, a knell of despair would resound through many parts of Europe.

It was for this reason that Lord Halifax's journey caused widespread commotion, as everyone saw, in all sorts of countries to whom we have no commitments other than the commitments involved in the Covenant of the League. . . .

It would be wrong, Churchill told the House, for any nation to give up 'a scrap of territory to keep the Nazi kettle boiling', and he went on to reiterate his theme of continual close relations with France as the keystone to British security. 'These relations,' he said, 'are founded upon the power of the French Army and the power of the British fleet.' Britain and France together, he believed, 'with all their world-wide connections, in spite of their tardiness in making air preparations, constitute so vast and formidable a body that they will very likely be left alone undisturbed, at any rate for some time to come'.

Towards the end of his speech Churchill told the House of Commons that it would be wrong to ignore 'the moral forces involved' in public opinion, and he added: 'For five years I have been asking the House and the Government to make armaments—guns, aeroplanes, munitions—but I am quite sure that British armaments alone will never protect us in the times through which we may have to pass.'

Many congratulations reached Churchill when his speech was published in the Press. Desmond Morton, Sir Roger Keyes, Duncan Sandys and Ava Wigram were among those who hastened to send him their praise. 'How wonderful it was, and how necessary,' Ava Wigram wrote on December 22, 'I wish Ralph could have known about it.' Desmond Morton wrote that same day: 'Warmest congratulations on your brilliant speech last night which I have read with the greatest pleasure and profit. . . . The view I have heard expressed is that your speech alone gave a clear indication of a line of policy.'

Churchill's speech of December 21 prompted yet another Government official to make direct contact with him. On December 22 M. J. Creswell wrote from the St James Club:

I have recently been at the Embassy in Berlin—for two and a half years—and am now, since the beginning of this month, in the Southern Dept of the FO (Austria and Czechoslovakia).

Before going to Berlin, though I never had the honour to meet you personally, I became familiar with your views when I was working under Wigram on the question of the German Air Force, and if I may say so I much admired your speeches on that subject.

When listening to your speech yesterday from the gallery I noticed a remark you made about the strength of the German Army which is at variance with most of the information I have on the subject, and the purpose of this letter is to ask you if you would be good enough to receive me (some evening after 7 pm) to enable me to discuss this point with you.

I would be grateful if your Secretary would send me a reply to this address and not to the Foreign Office.[1]

On December 15 Sir Thomas Inskip circulated to the Cabinet his survey on defence expenditure, in which he reviewed all the defence programmes.[2] Whether in peace or war, he insisted, the maintenance of credit facilities, 'and our general balance of trade', was of vital importance. 'Seen in its true perspective,' he continued, 'the maintenance of our economic stability would more accurately be described as an essential element in our defence system; one which could properly be regarded as a fourth arm in defence, alongside the three Defence Services without which purely military effort would be of no avail.' Economic stability was essential, not merely in war, but also as a means of averting war. As Inskip explained:

Nothing operates more strongly to deter a potential aggressor from attacking this country than our stability, and the power which this nation has so often shown of overcoming its difficulties without violent change, and without damage to its inherent strength. This reputation stands us in good stead, and causes other countries to rate our powers of resistance at something far more formidable than is implied merely by the number of men of war, aeroplanes and battalions which we should have at our disposal immediately on the outbreak of war. But were other countries to detect in us signs of strain, this deterrent would at once be lost.

Another reason for not increasing defence expenditure was that Britain's 'long term' foreign policy aimed at 'changing the present assumption as to our potential enemies'. This would involve planning or expenditure on the basis of no continental role for the Army, whose 'primary role' would be anti-aircraft defence at home and Imperial defence overseas. In addition, Inskip wrote, 'Germany has guaranteed

---

[1] In the last three months of 1937 the Foreign Office had received a continual flow of evidence about the strength of the German army. On October 12 General Hotblack, who had attended German manoeuvres, reported that the Germany army was being prepared for 'attack rather than defence, and upon speed and ruthlessness of execution' and based not upon stalemate or trench warfare, but upon the 'complete destruction of opposing forces'. Six days later Anthony Rumbold minuted: 'Great strides are being made in mechanisation, even at the expense of great casualties' and the German army was 'being prepared to deliver a knock-out blow in any direction that may be required.' On November 11 Victor Mallet reported the serious doubts of the Chief of the General Staff, Sir Cyril Deverell, 'about the ability of the Maginot Line to resist increasingly renewed attacks'.

[2] On June 30 the Cabinet had decided that the three Service Departments should be asked to produce their estimates for scrutiny so that the Treasury could in future fix a maximum for each Department. On October 27 the Cabinet decided that Inskip would examine these estimates, together with 'a panel of officials, such as Sir Maurice Hankey, Sir Arthur Robinson, Sir Horace Wilson and four representatives of the Treasury.' On the 'military side' Inskip could 'consult with' the Service Ministers.

the inviolability and integrity of Belgian territory, and there seems good reason for thinking that it would be in Germany's interest to honour this agreement.' Inskip added, that in the event of France being overrun by land armies, Britain would have to improvise an army and 'the Government of the day would most certainly be criticised for having neglected to provide against so obvious a contingency'. Nevertheless, he concluded that there was 'no alternative but to adopt the more limited role of the Army'.

At the end of his survey, which covered fifteen closely-printed pages, Inskip said that he was 'not wholly convinced' by the Air Ministry's argument in favour of Scheme J. He recognized Britain's weakness in the air relative to Germany, but he added that as far as Baldwin's pledge of air parity was concerned, 'I should not regard the statements made as in any way compelling us to base either the numbers or the types of our aeroplanes on the numbers and types of a potential enemy.' For this reason Inskip recommended the acceptance of Scheme J's fighter squadrons, and some 'increase' in the present first-line bomber strength 'with reduced provision for reserves'. Instead of actually building the required bombers, the Air Ministry should make 'improved arrangements for war potential'.

The Cabinet discussed Inskip's survey, and Swinton's request for Scheme J, on December 22, when Swinton pressed the Cabinet to accept Scheme J, and explained the Air Ministry's view that an 'inferior force of bombers would not meet our public declarations and would have a defeatist appearance'. Swinton also explained, in answer to Inskip's point about parity, that the Air Staff had 'not based their proposals on a mere mathematical comparison', nor upon a purely defensive strategy, but on a carefully worked out plan aimed at reducing Germany's power of attack 'by bombing his aerodromes, factories etc'. Because of this, Swinton warned the Cabinet, they 'could not tell the Air Staff that it was providing an adequate force when the Air Staff knew that this was not the case'. Swinton then urged both the new expansion scheme, and a far more rapid recruitment campaign. The Government, he said, could not accept less than Scheme J 'without a complete reversal of policy'. Sir John Simon, however, spoke against putting any money into an 'exaggerated production of reserves'.

Chamberlain supported Inskip, stating that he did not accept that parity was still essential, and explaining to his Cabinet that 'no pledge can last for ever'. He was, he said, prepared 'to defend a departure from earlier pledges', and did not accept Scheme J as it stood. Scheme J was therefore to be rethought and reduced. Halifax commented that as a result of this discussion he felt 'that it was of great importance to make further progress in improving relations with Germany'.

At the end of December Churchill asked Desmond Morton to explain to him the meaning of recent administrative changes at the War Office, where Admiral Brown[1] had been appointed Member of Supply on the Army Council. Morton, replying on December 31, pointed out that the appointment 'entirely fails to tackle the real problem', first, because the Supply section had been almost entirely separated from the Design section, and second, because a 'military man' would know far less about industrial production than an industrialist would know about warfare. 'Many industrialists,' Morton added, 'have been military men, no military man has been a practical Industrialist.' Morton continued: 'I can see no really sound solution outside of a Ministry of Supply, though it would not be impossible to camouflage such a Ministry in peace-time under other titles,' and his letter continued:

The chief cause of failure in this country to turn out armament stores and aircraft (I exclude warships, since the Navy have long adopted a procedure which conforms to the essential principle) must lie at the door of the military man. He has failed because he has interfered in the Industrialist's job. He has not made up his mind what types of armaments he requires. Having apparently done so, he has constantly changed detail of design, quite oblivious of the effect of such action on eventual production. He has constantly demanded the impossible, namely the marriage of highly complicated design with rapid output.

Morton ended:

In modern warfare there are four arms of Defence; Industry taking its place along side the three Fighting Forces. Until the Military man recognises this fact in deed as well as in words, we shall continue to fail to make adequate preparations to defend the Empire against aggression.

Throughout November and December Churchill had worked at Chartwell on the fourth, and last, volume of his *Marlborough* biography.

[1] Harold Arthur Brown, 1878–1968. Educated at the Royal Naval Engineers College. Entered Navy, 1894. In 1912, when Churchill was First Lord of the Admiralty, Brown was the Engineer-Lieutenant on board the destroyer *Cameleon*. Vice-Admiral, 1932. Engineer-in-Chief of the Fleet, Admiralty, 1932–36. Knighted, 1934. Retired, 1936. Director-General of Munitions Production, Army Council, 1937–39. Director-General of Munitions Production, Ministry of Supply, 1939–40. Controller-General of Munitions Production, 1941–42. Chairman of the Armament Development Board, Ministry of Supply, 1942–46. Chairman of the Fuel Research Board, 1947–50.

As each chapter was scrutinized by Edward Marsh and Maurice Ashley, Deakin incorporated their points into the narrative. While Clementine Churchill recuperated in Austria from illness, Churchill went to Blenheim for Christmas and the New Year. He had already decided to spend the whole of January 1938 in the South of France, resting from his exertions of the previous months, and putting the finishing touches to his book, and on December 29 he wrote to Sir Eric Phipps, who had suggested that he meet certain leading French politicians on his way south:

I shall be much interested to meet Léger[1] and Daladier if they are available at this holiday moment. I should particularly like to meet Blum, with whom I established pleasant relations when he was Premier. I am anxious to persuade him to pay us a visit over here and I would give him a luncheon at our 'focus' of which I will tell you more when I come. Also I would give a dinner in the House for him to meet MPs. I talked to Anthony about this and he seemed to think well of the project of Blum coming over, so very likely the FO would do something too. Anyhow if I meet him this would be the topic I should ventilate.

I warned Blum two years ago that French aviation was falling far behind but alas I could not alarm him sufficiently.

On 2 January 1938 Churchill left England for a month's holiday in Maxine Elliot's villa at Golfe Juan. 'He came away on the 2nd,' Mrs Pearman wrote to A. H. Richards six days later, 'not before he needed it, as he looked very tired.' On his way through Paris, Churchill stayed for two nights at the British Embassy, where he learnt the news of Sir Robert Vansittart's replacement as Permanent Under-Secretary of State for Foreign Affairs by Sir Alexander Cadogan.[2] Vansittart was given a newly invented sinecure, that of Chief Diplomatic Adviser to the Government. Churchill was appalled, and, as Phipps reported to Hankey on January 9, 'could hardly talk of anything else'. Churchill told Phipps: 'that he thought Van's displacement was a very dangerous thing, that it would be represented as a victory for the pro-Germans in England, that it would arouse the suspicions of the French, etc, etc'.

---

[1] Marie-René Alexis Saint-Léger Léger, 1887–1975. Poet, writing under the pseudonym St-John Perse. Joined the French Foreign Service, 1914. Secretary, Peking, 1916–21. Chef de Cabinet, Ministry of Foreign Affairs, 1925–32; Secretary-General, 1933–40. Left France for the United States, 1940. Consultant on French Literature to the Library of Congress, 1941–45.

[2] Alexander George Montagu Cadogan, 1884–1968. Younger son of the 5th Earl Cadogan. Educated at Eton and Balliol College Oxford. Attaché Diplomatic Service, 1908. British Minister to China, 1933–35; Ambassador, 1935–36. Knighted, 1934. Deputy Under-Secretary of State for Foreign Affairs, 1936–37; Permanent Under-Secretary, January 1938–February 1946. Permament British Representative at the United Nations, 1946–50. Government Director, Suez Canal Company, 1951–57. Chairman of the BBC, 1952–57.

On January 15 Chamberlain was informed that the Chancellor of the Exchequer, Sir John Simon, would be asking for reductions in all three Service estimates: cuts of £6 million from the Navy, £4 million from the Army and £2 million from the Air Force. 'My principal aim,' Simon wrote to Chamberlain that day, 'has been to avoid allowing departments to embark on expenditure which would prejudice the review of our defence programmes now being carried out by Sir Thomas Inskip.' Two days later, on January 17, the Secretary of State for India, Lord Zetland, wrote to the Viceroy, Lord Linlithgow: 'so staggering is the present estimated cost of the schemes already elaborated by the Service Departments that the Cabinet as a whole are, I think, convinced that the ideal from the defence point of view is not attainable, and the view which has been held by some for some little time past that we have neither the man power nor the money under a voluntary system to provide an army for continental warfare, is now I think tacitly accepted'. Zetland added: 'All this is germane to our special problem, because it has arisen out of the warnings given us by the Chancellor of the Exchequer that we are running up bills which even with the borrowings contemplated we shall not be able to pay.'

On January 21, in a 'Most Secret' report, the Air Ministry put forward a new scheme, K, noting 'that for financial reasons', they were being asked to modify substantially their schemes to make the Air Force capable of war by the end of 1938. At the same time they admitted that the first-line strength of each German squadron was based, not on nine aeroplanes as they had previously believed, but on twelve, as Churchill had repeatedly insisted. The Air Ministry report also noted that in order to devise a new programme which was not beyond the 'financial capabilities' laid down by the Treasury, 'nothing but an arbitrary cut on war reserves will suffice', and they noted:

The arbitrary cut imposed in the present revised programme is a general scaling down of war reserves which in the case of operational squadrons (other than fighter squadrons, for which the full scale of reserves has been retained) involves a reduction of a 16 weeks reserve to a reserve of approximately 9 weeks, and in the case of war training units must react adversely on our capacity to produce trained pilots and crews in war. This of course is a most drastic step.

'The scale of reserves now contemplated,' the Air Staff wrote, 'is inadequate to maintain an offensive which they believe would be comparable to that of the enemy.'

The policy of cutting back arms expenditure went hand in hand with the search for new and better relations with Germany, and drew its inspiration from Neville Chamberlain. On January 30 Chamberlain wrote to his sister from Chequers of how he had been reading a strongly anti-Nazi book, *The House that Hitler Built*, by Professor Roberts[1]—'an extremely clever and well informed but very pessimistic book'. His letter continued: 'If I accepted the author's conclusions I should despair, but I don't and won't. Fortunately I have recently had a "scintillation" on the subject of German negotiations. It has been accepted promptly and even enthusiastically by all to whom I have broached it and we have sent for Henderson[2] to come and talk it over with us.'

Chamberlain had explained his new idea to the Cabinet's Foreign Policy Committee on January 27. His aim was an agreement with Germany to open 'an entirely new chapter in the history of African colonial development' whereby Germany 'would be brought into the arrangement by becoming one of the African Colonial Powers . . . by being given certain territories to administer'.

Such hopes and plans had strong supporters. 'There has been & still is a great deal of personal depression,' Sir Horace Wilson wrote to P. J. Grigg on January 31, 'the result of the war talk, and it would make a good deal of difference if the idea got about that the outlook was less dangerous. . . . We begin tomorrow a long stretch of Parliamentary hard labour, with very few apples in our basket, but there is no sign of a major crisis. W.S.C. has been very quiet for 8 months, which is rather a long time for him.'

Churchill's letters, forwarded regularly to France from Chartwell and Morpeth Mansions, continued to bring disturbing news. Writing from Berlin on January 4, Ian Colvin[3] informed him that a German plan

---

[1] Stephen Henry Roberts, 1901–1971. Born in Australia. Research Fellow, Melbourne University, 1920–25. Researched into political systems in France, 1929–35, and in Germany, 1935–37. He published *The House That Hitler Built* in 1937. Vice-Chancellor and Principal, University of Sydney, 1947–67. Knighted, 1965.

[2] Nevile Meyrick Henderson, 1882–1942. Educated at Eton. Entered the Diplomatic Service, 1905. 3rd Secretary, Tokyo, 1909–11. Counsellor, Constantinople, 1921–24. Minister at Belgrade, 1929–35. Knighted, 1932. Ambassador at Buenos Aires, 1935–37; at Berlin, 1937–39. He published an account of his Berlin Embassy, *Failure of a Mission*, in 1940.

[3] Ian Goodhope Colvin, 1913–1975. Son of Ian D. Colvin, the journalist and editor. Joined the *Morning Post* as a reporter, 1932. Transferred to Reuters, 1933. *News Chronicle* correspondent in Berlin, 1938–39. Served in the News Department of the Foreign Office, 1939–40; in the Royal Marines and at Combined Operation's Headquarters, 1940–45. Landing craft Flotilla Commander, 1944–45. On the staff of Kemsley newspapers, 1946–52; Foreign Editor of the *Sunday Express*, 1953–55. Leader writer and foreign correspondent on the *Daily Telegraph* from 1955 to his death, specializing in African affairs. Of Colvin's work in Berlin, Churchill wrote in his war memoirs: 'He plunged very deeply into German politics

to mobilize three Army Corps, and to occupy Czechoslovakia, would probably be put into operation in two or three months time. On January 5 Shiela Grant Duff sent him a long account of her travels in Central Europe, and of the desperate attempt of all the small States not 'to provoke Germany'. As for the Germans themselves, she wrote: 'They are convinced that we would be neutral if they attacked Czechoslovakia.' Through Mrs Pearman, Wing-Commander Anderson kept Churchill informed of Air Force problems. On January 7, enclosing details of accidents caused by the inexperience of pilots, maintenance failures and lack of practice, he wrote to Mrs Pearman: 'Will you give the attached papers to Papa. He asked for them to be sent on. . . .'[1]

On January 8 Mrs Pearman sent Lindemann a progress report of the holiday. 'Mr Churchill looks better even for this short change,' she wrote, 'but the sunshine he expected has, alas, sadly disappointed him.' Her report continued: 'He is working very, very hard on his book and has not had time to paint. I am so glad he has come away at last, because I think he would have tired himself out at Chartwell. Contrary to our expectations he has not lost a single thing on his journeyings alone, and is very pleased.'

On January 14, while Churchill was still in the South of France, he lunched with Lloyd George and Eden. In his memoirs Eden recalled how, at the point during the luncheon: 'We spoke of the United States. I gave an account of the efforts I had been making to encourage American co-operation and was gratified to find them apparently impressed with the progress we had made.' On January 17 Churchill again lunched with Lloyd George, to celebrate his friend's seventy-fifth birthday. 'It has been very peaceful out here,' he wrote to his son two days later, 'but I have not painted at all. I have spent all the mornings in bed correcting proofs, and doing nothing of a strenuous character.'

Churchill returned to England in the second week of February. 'I do not know when I have had such a peaceful pleasant month,' he wrote to Maxine Elliot from Chartwell on February 8. 'I found a great deal of work awaiting me here, but am addressing myself to it with a vigour

---

and established contacts of a most secret character with some of the important German generals and also with independent men of character and quality in Germany who saw in the Hitler movement the approaching ruin of their native land.'

[1] On January 16 Anderson wrote again, sending Churchill details of British and German aircraft production for December 1937. These amounted to 600 air frames for Germany as compared with 200 for Britain during the same single month. (On February 16 the Cabinet were given the figures Germany 500, Italy 300, Britain 200 and France 40.)

renewed by the first really good rest I have had for a long time.' His letter continued:

I do not find things any better. On the contrary the latest convulsion in Germany has undoubtedly increased the danger of war.[1] One has always hitherto had the feeling that the Generals, oddly enough, had the power to restrain the Nazi violence. Now the whole place is in the hands of violent men, and I fear very much lest something should happen in Central Europe.

'I am toiling away at Marlborough IV,' Churchill added, 'and am determined to get it finished by the end of the month. I am therefore not paying much attention to the House of Commons, at which I expect the Ministers will not be at all vexed!'

In January Leslie Hore-Belisha had visited Chartwell, his second visit in six months,[2] and in February Churchill sent him a small gift. One evening this friendly gesture was the subject of a quarrel at dinner between Churchill and his son. Churchill had been criticizing Hore-Belisha quite sharply when his son, by way of riposte, reminded him of the gift, and suggested ironically that, in view of his father's criticisms of the Minister, it could only have been given to curry favour. Churchill was so outraged at this suggestion that he refused to speak to his son for the rest of the meal. 'An expression of surprise at my clumsiness would have been quite enough to have brought from me an apology for my stupidity,' Randolph wrote on the following day, and he added: 'When two people know each other as well as we do, it ought to be possible to solve misunderstandings other than by relapsing into moody silence.' Churchill replied on February 14:

My dear Randolph,
    I thought yr remark singularly unkind, offensive, & untrue; & I am sure no son shd have made it to his father. Your letter in no way removes the pain it caused me, not only on my own account but on yours, & also on account of our relationship. I was about to write to you to ask you to excuse me from

---

[1] On February 4, following the resignation of the Commander-in-Chief of the German Army, Field-Marshal von Blomberg, Hitler formally declared himself Commander-in-Chief. Also on February 4 the Foreign Minister, Baron von Neurath, resigned, and was replaced by Hitler's personal nominee, Joachim von Ribbentrop.

[2] On 26 July 1938 Hore-Belisha wrote to Clementine Churchill: 'Although the recollection of my pleasant visit to Chartwell has not been absent from my thought, I suddenly remembered that I had not written to thank you. Do forgive me for this. The omission is all the greater on my part because I was, as a bachelor, so wistfully impressed by the happiness of your home. You have all my good wishes for the perpetual lasting of your happiness. Please apologize to your daughter for my failure on this occasion either to play tennis or swim. Another delinquency of mine was to find that I had misappropriated that wonderful eye-lotion which Winston lent me!'

coming to luncheon with you on Thursday, as I really cannot run the risk of such insults being offered to me, & do not feel I want to see you at the present time.

> Your loving Father,
> Winston S. Churchill

Randolph was deeply upset by his father's attitude. 'I took the earliest opportunity of writing to you,' he replied on February 15, 'to explain that it was only an inept jest and to apologize for it. I don't see what more I can do'. His words, he said, had not intended to be 'unkind or offensive'; indeed, they had only been provoked 'by a violence of your own language'. They were, however, 'words unbecoming in a Son', and he again apologized for them. Churchill was not mollified, replying on February 16:

My dear Randolph,

I do not understand how what you said could be looked upon as 'jocular' or ironic. It was grossly rude, & as such wounded me deeply. It is not enough when you have insulted someone to say it was a joke & to reproach them with attaching importance to small things. If, as you protest, you did not mean to be offensive, surely when you saw that I was hurt, you cd have said 'I am sorry. I ought not to have said such a thing.' Instead you complain in yr first letter that I did not continue to converse with you as if nothing had happened. I really did not & do not want such a thing to happen again. I do not see why at my age I shd be subjected to such taunts from a son I have tried to do my best for.

It was a vy base thing for you to suggest that the small gift I gave was given to curry favour presumably in the hopes of gaining political or personal advantage. It was given out of kindness of heart, & of some pity wh I felt, for a man I do not much like, but who had appealed to me for advice & spoken much of his loneliness etc. I wonder you are not even now ashamed that such a thought shd have sprung so readily to yr mind and yr lips. I have not deserved it of you.

There is no question of my 'owing you a grudge'. I shall always do my best to help you, and I have no doubt the extremely unpleasant impression wh I sustained will wear out and pass away in a little while. Meantime you are welcome to yr own self-justifications wh appear to be in your eyes complete.

> Your loving Father
> Winston S. Churchill

The dispute over Hore-Belisha opened many wounds, and severely exacerbated the relationship between father and son. On several occasions in the ensuing weeks there were painful incidents and harsh words. On March 1 Randolph wrote to his father: 'I should have thought a sensitive man like yourself could easily envisage the deep humiliation I feel when my discretion is repeatedly called in question by you in front of hacks like David Margesson and Victor Warrender[1] and that amiable flibbertigibbet, Brendan,' and he added: 'I do not see why you should not show the same marks of friendship & respect to me that you show to Brendan—to put it at its lowest. I do not think you will find me a less reliable friend than him. . . .'

As soon as he had returned to Chartwell from the South of France, Churchill found an important air force document awaiting him from Group Captain MacLean. It was a secret six-page report by Sir Edgar Ludlow-Hewitt on the training difficulties experienced by Bomber Command during 1937. The report had been circulated to senior Air Force personnel on February 4, and listed the 'principal impediments' to flying training on the new type of aircraft. These included not only a lack of both 'experienced instructors' and 'skilled maintenance personnel', but also a high incidence 'of unserviceability of aircraft'. Churchill was disturbed by the weaknesses which this report confirmed. A second letter awaiting him opened up yet another potential source of information on air matters. On January 31 Lord Munster[2] had written to him:

I have a cousin of mine—Frank Don—by name who will be staying here for the week-end of Feb 19th and I should so like to bring him to see you *on Sunday 20th.*

He has just returned from 3½ years as British Air Attaché in Berlin and although he is still in the RAF I know he would much like to see you. He has, of course, to be careful what he repeats but I know if you would care to meet him he would like to come and see you.

[1] Victor Alexander George Anthony Warrender, 1899– . Queen Victoria's last godchild. Educated at Eton. On active service with the Grenadier Guards, 1917–18 (Military Cross, 1918). Conservative MP for Grantham, 1932–42. An Assistant Whip, 1928–31. A Junior Lord of the Treasury, 1931–32. Vice-Chamberlain of HM Household, 1932–35. Financial Secretary, War Office, 1935–40. Parliamentary and Financial Secretary, Admiralty, 1940–42; Parliamentary Secretary, Admiralty, 1942–45. Created Baron Bruntisfield, 1942.
[2] Geoffrey William Richard Hugh Fitz Clarence, 1906–1975. Succeeded his uncle as 5th Earl of Munster, 1928. Member of the LCC for North Paddington, 1931–37. A Lord-in Waiting to the King, 1932–39. Paymaster-General, June 1938—January 1939. Parliamentary Under-Secretary of State for War, February–September 1939. ADC and Military Secretary to Lord Gort, 1939–41. Parliamentary Under-Secretary of State for India and Burma, 1943–44; at the Home Office, 1944–45; at the Colonial Office, 1951–54. Minister without Portfolio 1954–57. Privy Councillor 1954. Among his cousins, Charles FitzClarence (related by marriage to Churchill), was killed in action in France in November 1914; Edward Fitz-Clarence was killed in action in the Sudan in 1897.

Churchill arranged to see Group Captain Don on Sunday February 20.

The fears which Churchill had expressed in his letter to Maxine Elliot on February 8, that something unpleasant would soon happen in Central Europe, were quickly realized. On February 12 Hitler summoned the Austrian Chancellor, Kurt von Schuschnigg,[1] to Berchtesgaden, and made a series of demands—including full liberty of movement for the Nazi Party in Austria—which Schuschnigg was forced to accept. On February 16, at Hitler's insistence, the Austrian Cabinet was reshuffled, and the Ministry of the Interior, vital to the nation's security, transferred to an Austrian Nazi, Artur von Seyss-Inquart.[2] Henceforth, the independence of Austria was in grave danger.

Four days earlier, on February 8, Sir Thomas Inskip had presented the Cabinet with his second report on defence expenditure. The Air Ministry's new Scheme K, costing £567½ millions over five years, would contribute, he wrote, to bringing the total defence expenditure nearer to £2,000 millions than the £1,500 millions to which the Cabinet had instructed him to work. Such extra money, he warned, would have to come, according to the Treasury, from 'an increase in the level of taxation', and he added: 'the effects of greatly increased taxation upon public confidence and upon the attitude of the people of this country to the defence programmes, are matters which deserve the most serious consideration'. The Government was faced with a dilemma; either to accept increased defence spending and risk another economic crisis 'or a long and painful period of bad trade', or to limit defence spending to the existing £1,500 millions 'which might react upon the prospect of successful negotiations and might therefore be fraught with the danger of war'. Another argument against any increase, Inskip wrote, was that the necessary industrial compulsion would not only be 'most difficult politically' but would threaten national 'stability'.

In spite of the 'relatively favourable revenue position', Inskip advised

[1] Kurt von Schuschnigg, 1897–1977. On active service in the First World War (several times decorated). Elected to the Austrian Parliament, 1927. Minister of Justice, 1932; of Justice and Education, 1933–34. Chancellor of Austria, 1934–38. Imprisoned by the German Government after the Anschluss, 1938, and held in prison until 1945. Professor of Government at St Louis (USA), 1948.

[2] Artur von Seyss-Inquart, 1892–1946. Born in Moravia. A lawyer, he entered the Austrian Ministry of the Interior in 1937. Minister of the Interior, 1938. Chancellor of Austria, March 1938. Governor of the Austrian Province of Germany, 'Ostmark', March 1938–September 1939. Deputy Governor-General of the Polish General-Government, October 1939–May 1940. Reich's Commissioner in the Netherlands, May 1940–May 1945; responsible for the deportation of 5 million Dutchmen as workers to Germany, and for the deportation of 117,000 of the 140,000 Dutch Jews to extermination camps. Arrested by Canadian troops, May 1945. Found guilty of war crimes at the Nuremberg Tribunal, 1946, and executed.

delaying any increase in defence spending for two years. This would enable a further review to be made 'in the light of improvements in the international situation which it is the object of our foreign policy to bring about'. At such a point 'the need for great armaments' might disappear. Inskip's survey concluded:

. . . the burden in peace-time of taking the steps which we are advised—I believe rightly—are prudent and indeed necessary in present circumstances, is too great for us. I therefore repeat with fresh emphasis the opinion which I have already expressed as to the importance of reducing the scale of our commitments and the number of our potential enemies.

On February 16, the day on which the Austrian Cabinet was remodelled to suit Hitler's demands, the British Cabinet met to discuss defence spending. Inskip urged a cutting back of Scheme K to meet the general guidelines of his survey, urging no spending beyond £1,500 million for defence spending. Sir John Simon warned that although the 'financial prospects' for the immediate future 'were good enough, he was fearful for the future', and worried that Britain could not reach 1942 'with the present standard of financial prosperity'. Simon added: 'Whenever we tried to revise expenditure it went up. It could be a most serious matter if, when the examination was made in 1939, the expenditure went up again, as by that time taxation prospects would be worse.' The most he would agree to was £1,570 million for the period 1937 to 1941. Swinton, however, in pressing for the full £567½ millions for Scheme K, warned that the scheme 'was not what the Air Staff thought ought to be done, but what they thought would be the best value that could be got for this sum'. He also pointed out that even this scheme involved, as the Air Ministry had written on January 21, 'an arbitrary cut on war reserves' from sixteen weeks to nine. Swinton added that an increase in 'war potential', such as Inskip had advised on December 15, could not offset this 'most drastic step', and that even Scheme K, 'to speak quite frankly, was inadequate *vis à vis* Germany'.

Despite Swinton's warning, Chamberlain strongly supported Simon's request to restrict defence spending to a maximum of £1,570 million up to 1941, and the Cabinet gave its approval to this sum.

During the Cabinet of February 16 it became clear that in his insistence on a firmer attitude towards Italy, Eden did not have Chamberlain's support. The seriousness of these disagreements was known to many MPs, and came to a climax at a meeting of the Foreign Affairs Committee on February 17. The Chairman of the Committee, Paul

Emrys-Evans,[1] wanted to issue a communiqué supporting Eden's firm stand towards Italy, and rejecting Chamberlain's wish to secure Anglo-Italian friendship by recognizing *de jure* the Italian conquest of Abyssinia. The Chief Whip, Captain Margesson, put pressure on Emrys-Evans to modify his communiqué. Churchill, who was present at the meeting, was angered by the Government's action, and urged support for Eden's policy. Among the others who spoke in Eden's support was Harold Nicolson, who recorded in his diary that he concluded:

... by suggesting that we should keep a stiff upper lip, not throw sops or slops about, wait, and, above all, arm. There is a good attendance and my speech goes well. Winston Churchill who is sitting next to me, says, 'A very good speech: a very good speech indeed.' He himself takes a far more truculent attitude than I do. We must call a halt.

The whole feeling of the meeting is very different from that of a year ago. They no longer believe that we can buy Germany off with concessions.

Eden learnt of the support of the Foreign Affairs Committee on the morning of February 18. Churchill, he later wrote, had urged the Committee 'to rally behind me at a difficult time', and had told his fellow MPs 'that if we were weak now, the risk of war would inevitably be greater in the future'.

Neville Chamberlain was not to be deflected in his search for Italian friendship. He therefore decided to open direct negotiations with the Italian Government. Isolated in Cabinet and frustrated in his desire to face the Italian dictator with firmness, Eden resigned. That day Churchill was at Chartwell, where he was seeing Group Captain Don, when the news of Eden's resignation was telegraphed to him. 'I must confess,' he later wrote, 'that my heart sank, and for a while the dark waters of despair overwhelmed me.' His account continued:

From midnight till dawn I lay in my bed consumed by emotions of sorrow and fear. There seemed one strong young figure standing up against long, dismal, drawling tides of drift and surrender, of wrong measurements and feeble impulses. My conduct of affairs would have been different from his in various ways; but he seemed to me at this moment to embody the life-hope of the British nation, the grand old British race that had done so much for men, and had yet some more to give. Now he was gone. I watched the daylight slowly creep in through the windows, and saw before me in mental gaze the vision of Death.

[1] Paul Vychan Emrys-Evans, 1894–1964. Educated at Harrow and King's College Cambridge. Lieutenant, Suffolk Regiment, 1914–17 (wounded in France, 1916). Foreign Office, 1917–23. Unsuccessful Conservative candidate, 1929. Conservative MP for South Derbyshire, 1931–45. Parliamentary Private Secretary, War Office, 1940; Dominion Affairs, 1940–41. Parliamentary Under-Secretary of State for Dominion Affairs, 1941–45.

On February 21 Eden made his resignation speech in the House of Commons. During the ensuing debate Churchill received several hundred telegrams, most of them from total strangers, urging him to speak out at the first possible opportunity. These were passed along the benches to him tied in bundles. One of the messages he received read: 'Vital necessity support Eden,' another 'Do not support proposed Chamberlain Italian conversations,' and another 'Essential you protest against Eden's resignation.' One telegram, from 'six Leeds Tories', exhorted him to 'Lash Italophile Cowards'.

A few hours before Eden made his resignation speech, Churchill sent him a private note of advice:

My dear Anthony,
Forgive me for intruding upon yr immediate preoccuptns.

It seems to me vital that you shd not allow your personal feelings of friendship to yr late colleagues to hamper you in doing full justice to yr case and above all you shd not say anything that fetters yr action in the future. You owe this not only to yrself which you no doubt feel the least part of the event —but to yr cause wh is also the cause of England.

Yours ever
W.S.C.

As a postscript Churchill added a Boer saying which he had often heard during the South African war: 'Alle zoll recht Kommen'—all will come right in the end.

During his speech Eden explained that in his view the time had not yet come for Britain to open negotiations with Italy. Italian propaganda against Britain was rife throughout the world. Italian troops were still fighting alongside the nationalists in Spain. The moment had come, he said, 'for this country to stand firm'. There could be no constructive appeasement in Europe 'if we allow the impression to gain currency abroad that we yield to constant pressure'. But Chamberlain replied that the cause of peace demanded that Britain should lose no opportunity of entering into conversations both with Italy and with Germany.

That evening Sir Maurice Hankey wrote to Sir Eric Phipps to explain the cause and background to Eden's resignation: 'When the present Prime Minister came into office he was determined to try and improve relations with Italy and if possible, with Germany—in each case, of course, without weakening our friendship with France. In each case his motive was that he felt there was a drift going on towards war. . . .' Not only was Britain 'unprepared for war', Hankey explained, but also France 'at any rate in the air'. Hankey's letter went on to describe

Eden's persistent refusal to agree to conversations with Italy, and he added:

Anyhow, he has gone. Fond as I am of him on personal grounds, I woke this morning with a strange feeling of relief. I am sorry to say that generally I wake on a thought of how we are to provide for some horror in the next war. Today I felt there was just a possibility of peace. I only hope I am right. Strange to say, a Cabinet Minister whom I asked as to his opinion had had almost exactly the same experience!

Two days later Chamberlain's wife wrote to her sister-in-law: 'Maurice Hankey whom we met in the Park yesterday said his relief was so intense that he was sleeping until the morning & that Tom Inskip had told him that he also was not waking till 8 instead of lying awake with anxiety.'

On February 22 the Labour Opposition brought forward a motion of censure 'deploring the circumstances' of Eden's resignation. Chamberlain spoke again, amid increasing uproar, arguing that the League of Nations could no longer ensure collective security 'for anybody', and that it would be wrong 'to delude small, weak nations into thinking that they will be protected by the League against aggression'. Churchill spoke vehemently in Eden's defence. Since May 1937, he said, he had tried to give Chamberlain his 'disinterested and independent support'. He had sympathized with his difficulties. He had known him to be well aware of the dangers 'by which we are encompassed'. But he could no longer 'sit here silent'. It would be wrong for Britain to rush into talks with Italy at a time when 'the Dictator powers in Europe are striding on from strength to strength, and from stroke to stroke, and the Parliamentary democracies are retreating abashed and confused'. His speech continued:

This has been a good week for Dictators. It is one of the best they have ever had. The German Dictator has laid his heavy hand upon a small but historic country, and the Italian Dictator has carried his vendetta to a victorious conclusion against my right Hon friend the late Foreign Secretary.

The conflict between the Italian Dictator and my right Hon friend has been a long one. There can be no doubt, however, who has won. Signor Mussolini has won. All the might, majesty, dominion and power of the British Empire was no protection to my right Hon friend. Signor Mussolini has got his scalp.

'What price have we all to pay for this?' Churchill asked. 'No one can compute it. Small countries in Europe will take their cue to move to the side of power and resolution.'

Churchill forecast that Eden's resignation might well constitute a milestone in history, when Britain's foreign policy became that of coming to terms with the totalitarian powers 'in the hope that by great and far-reaching acts of submission, not merely in sentiment and pride, but in material matters, that peace may be preserved'. Austria, he pointed out, had already been 'laid in thrall, and we do not know whether Czechoslovakia will not suffer a similar attack'. His speech ended: 'I predict that the day will come when, at some point or other, on some issue or other, you will have to make a stand and I pray to God that, when that day comes, we may not find through an unwise policy, that we have to make that stand alone.'

When the Labour motion of censure was put to the vote, it was supported by a single Conservative MP, Vyvyan Adams. But twenty-one other Conservatives, including Churchill, indicated their distaste for Chamberlain's policy by abstaining, and the motion of censure was defeated by only 330 votes to 168, a far narrower margin than during any previous foreign affairs debate since the formation of the National Government in 1931.[1] In the Press the protest was much commented on. On February 23 the Conservative *Yorkshire Post* told its readers: 'Mr Churchill voiced yesterday, as on many other occasions, the widespread sentiments of anxiety and perplexity in the country.' But Lord Beaverbrook's *Daily Express* was hostile, declaring in its leading article on February 25 that Churchill was 'unwittingly lending himself to the most violent, foolish, and dangerous campaign to drive this country into war since he drove us into it himself against Russia in 1919'.

The backbench Foreign Affairs Committee met again on February 28. Those who had abstained in the Eden resignation debate were confronted by great hostility. One of the dissenters, Harold Nicolson, noted in his diary:

Several people got up quite shamelessly and suggested that we should not resign at once but merely do so later when feeling had diminished. At this Winston in all his majesty rose and said that they were being mean and petty. They were not treating us fairly and he must insist on a vote, either Yes or No.

They then voted. Those in favour of our not resigning were unanimous except for one little vicious hand against. That hand was the hand of Nancy Astor.

---

[1] Among the other Conservatives who abstained were General Spears, Anthony Crossley, Derrick Gunston, Harold Macmillan, Ronald Cartland and Paul Emrys-Evans. In numbers they constituted only a quater of the equivalent dissenting vote during the India Bill debates.

On February 26 Chamberlain appointed Lord Halifax as Eden's successor. Two days later Churchill described the appointment as 'derogatory' to the House of Commons; it was the first time a Foreign Secretary had been in the House of Lords—apart from Lord Reading's ten-week tenure in 1931—since Lord Curzon fifteen years before.

Churchill remained convinced that the Government's new policy of negotiating with the Dictators was bound to fail, and that by seeking to meet their wishes Britain would abandon her principles and lose her friends. On March 1, at a luncheon of the Focus Group of the Freedom and Peace movement, he spoke, as Harold Nicolson wrote to his wife on the following day, 'of this great country nosing from door to door like a cow that has lost its calf, mooing dolefully now in Berlin, and now in Rome—when all the time the tiger and the alligator wait for its undoing'.

Impressive though Churchill's warnings and oratory were, his active supporters in Parliament were still few. Even Nicolson added, in his letter to his wife, the cautionary sentences: 'Don't be worried, my darling, I am not going to become one of the Winston brigade.' His 'leaders', he explained, were Anthony Eden and Malcolm MacDonald. Even Eden did not look upon Churchill as a leader to be followed, but rather as elder statesman whose support might at times be useful. As a group, the Conservative backbenchers were in fact far less willing to follow Churchill over rearmament and foreign affairs than they had been over India. Churchill was himself aware of the reservations of those Conservatives who were critical of the Government, as well as of the hostility of the Party as a whole. Writing to Keith Feiling on February 26 about the politics of his final *Marlborough* volume, he commented: 'How like the Tory party of those days our present lot is! I wish I had studied history at the beginning of my life, instead of at the end.'

45

The German Annexation
of Austria:
'Surrendering the Future'

FACED with growing German pressure on Austria, and confronted by the increasing strength of the Austrian Nazis, not only
in his country but also in his Cabinet, Kurt von Schuschnigg sought to
encourage his people not to allow their independence to be subverted.
Broadcasting on February 24 he defended the right of Austria to
nationhood, but at Graz local Nazis forced the town officials to stop
the broadcast as soon as Schuschnigg mentioned the word independence. When Dr Seyss-Inquart visited Graz on March 1 he was
welcomed by a Nazi torchlight procession, while even the streets of
Vienna echoed with Nazi slogans.

On March 4, in one of his fortnightly articles in the *Evening Standard*,
Churchill estimated that as many as two-thirds of the people of Austria
were prepared to defend the independence of their State. 'They could
now probably face a plebiscite,' he wrote, provided it were conducted
'under fair conditions without fear'. But Churchill also saw the dangers
of calling for a national vote. No one could tell, he added, 'what the
reactions in Nazi Germany will be, or what new shattering blows
impend upon a small unhappy State'.

On March 5, Clementine Churchill's cousin Unity Mitford,[1] who had
just returned from Austria, wrote to Churchill to insist that the Austrians

---

[1] Unity Valkyrie Mitford, 1914–1948. Daughter of the 2nd Baron Redesdale; sister of
Diana, Nancy and Jessica Mitford. From 1933, as an admirer of Hitler and the Nazi regime,
she was frequently in Hitler's company, and on the outbreak of war in 1939, while still in
Germany, she tried to commit suicide. The Germans arranged for her to be sent back to
Britain. Her brother Tom died of wounds received in action in Burma in March 1945. Her
brother-in-law Esmond Romilly was killed in action in November 1941.

were 'happy & full of hope' at the idea of union with Germany. 'In Graz, Linz and Vienna,' she wrote, 'I witnessed demonstrations in which the population went mad with joy, and one could not move in the streets for people shouting "Heil Hitler! Anschluss!" & waving Swastika flags. By night, the hills around Vienna were ablaze with bonfires in the shape of Swastikas.' Most Austrians, she added, 'had no doubt at all that a free plebiscite would result in *at least* 80% for the Nazis'.

Churchill decided to seek further information before replying to Miss Mitford. 'This letter,' he wrote to the Austrian Ambassador, Georg Franckenstein,[1] on March 7, 'is from one of the young ladies who have been so attractive to Herr Hitler. Perhaps you will give me a little material from which to answer her. Naturally it will never appear to have come from you.' Franckenstein replied on March 9, telling Churchill that it was well known 'that by means of great activity and noisy demonstrations the National Socialists are trying to create the impression that they are the most powerful factor in Austria and that their followers form the majority in the country. Their tactics have apparently been most successful in the case of your correspondent.' As for the 'rejoicing' in Austria, Franckenstein agreed 'that there was much jubilation among the National Socialists after Hitler's speech'. But, he added, the 'tremendous enthusiasm aroused in other sections of the population by Dr Schuschnigg's speech on February 24th must not be overlooked'.

Franckenstein told Churchill that the 'objectively minded and well informed' people to whom he had spoken estimated that between 25 per cent and 35 per cent of the population supported *Anschluss*, 'but all were agreed that the majority in the country is in favour of an independent Austria'. Franckenstein went on to point out that there were 'great numbers' of people in Austria who belonged to no political grouping, but who were vigorously opposed to having a regime forced upon them which was 'alien in aims and methods to Austrian traditions'. As for a possible plebiscite, he added, this would only provoke Germany to throw 'all her political and financial strength on the scales', thus enabling the Nazis 'to intimidate the rest of the population into voting as they wished them to do'.

---

[1] Georg Franckenstein, 1878–1953. Before 1914, served in the Austro-Hungarian embassies in Washington, St Petersburg, Rome, Tokyo and London. Member of the Austrian Peace Delegation, Paris, 1919. Austrian Minister to London, 1920–38. Knight Grand Cross of the Royal Victorian Order, 1937. Became a British subject, 1938. He published *Facts and Features of My Life* in 1939.

Schuschnigg knew well the dangers that a plebiscite might bring, but, as he watched his own powers being daily undermined by Nazi agitation, as well as by the police forces of the Ministry of the Interior under Seyss-Inquart, he decided to take the risk of a plebiscite, hoping to secure a substantial vote in favour of independence. In the postscript to his letter to Churchill of March 9, Franckenstein wrote: 'We have just been informed by Reuters that a plebiscite will be held in Austria next Sunday. If this news is true it will decide that "American duel" between Miss Unity Mitford and myself.'

Fearing that the plebiscite would result in a majority for Austrian independence, Hitler at once gave secret orders for his army to prepare 'Case Otto'—Germany's long-studied plan for the military occupation of Austria. That same day, in France, a political crisis was at its height; during the day Camille Chautemps[1] resigned as Prime Minister and France was without a Government, or a policy, for three days. During those three days, events in Austria reached a cruel climax. As soon as it was announced that there was to be a plebiscite, the German Press and radio turned viciously against Schuschnigg. 'The horizon has not lightened in the last few months,' Churchill told an audience at Manchester on the evening of March 10, 'or in the last few hours.'

On the morning of Friday March 11 the Germans demanded Schuschnigg's resignation, in favour of Seyss-Inquart. If he did not resign within two hours, Goering threatened, 'the German invasion of Austria will follow'. While Schuschnigg was considering this ultimatum, Churchill was present at 10 Downing Street, as a guest at Chamberlain's farewell lunch to Ribbentrop. During the lunch, a telegram was brought in to Chamberlain, stating that German troop movements near the Austrian border did not, according to Berlin, constitute any threat to Austria, but were probably 'spring training'. In his memoirs Churchill recalled how a kind 'of general restlessness pervaded the company, and everyone stood about ready to say good-bye to the guests of honour. However Herr von Ribbentrop and his wife did not seem at all conscious of this atmosphere. On the contrary, they tarried for nearly half-an-hour engaging their host and hostess in voluble conversation.' At one moment, Churchill recalled, 'I came in contact

[1] Camille Chautemps, 1885–1963. A lawyer, son of a former Minister of the Colonies. Elected as a Socialist Radical Deputy, 1919. Minister of the Interior, 1924; of Justice, 1925; of the Interior, 1925 and 1926. Prime Minister for three days in 1930. Minister of the Interior, 1932 and 1933. Prime Minister, November 1933–January 1934. Mayor of Tours, and a leading French freemason. Minister of Public Works, January, 1936; Minister of State, June 1936; Prime Minister, June 1937–March 1938. Honorary knighthood, 1938. A member of the Reynaud Cabinet, 1940, he was the first Minister to resign from Pétain's Cabinet, July 1940.

with Frau von Ribbentrop, and in a valedictory vein I said, "I hope England and Germany will preserve their friendship." "Be careful you don't spoil it," was her graceful rejoinder.'

That afternoon Halifax telegraphed to Vienna that he could not 'take the responsibility' of advising Schuschnigg to take any action 'which might expose his country to dangers against which His Majesty's Government are unable to guarantee protection'. For its part, the Italian Government announced that it would do nothing to intervene, while the lack of any Government at all in Paris made it impossible for France to act. Unable to obtain any international support, Schuschnigg resigned, and was at once succeeded as Chancellor by Seyss-Inquart. At ten o'clock that evening, at Seyss-Inquart's 'invitation', German mechanized units began to cross into Austria.

On the evening of Saturday March 12 Hitler himself crossed the Austrian border at Linz, where he told an ecstatic crowd of Austrian Nazis:

When I first set out from this town I felt in the depth of my soul that it was my vocation and my mission given to me by destiny that I should bring my home country back to the great German Reich. I have believed in this mission and I have fulfilled it.

That same day, Churchill sent his answer to Unity Mitford:

There can be no doubt that a fair plebiscite would have shown that a large majority of the people of Austria loathe the idea of coming under Nazi rule. It was because Herr Hitler feared the free expression of opinion that we are compelled to witness the present dastardly outrage.

Within twenty-four hours of the German invasion of Austria, all the brutal apparatus of Nazi tyranny was put into effect. Throughout Sunday March 13, and in the days and weeks that followed, all those suspected of hostility to the new order were arrested and sent to concentration camps. Many hundreds were shot. Others, fearful of Nazi terror, committed suicide. Tens of thousands of liberals, democrats, socialists and Jews sought to flee the country. But Austria's three neighbours, Czechoslovakia, Hungary and Poland, were reluctant to receive these refugees, and many were turned back to face immediate capture, imprisonment and death.

On March 12 the Cabinet discussed the forthcoming Defence Estimates, in the light of the annexation of Austria. Two days earlier Sir Horace Wilson had written to Chamberlain that it was anticipated that Churchill would repeat a recent Labour Party call for an air defence enquiry. Wilson noted: 'The Prime Minister decided that an enquiry should be refused and should be refused flatly and firmly, the decision to be adhered to notwithstanding any criticisms that may be raised during the debate.' It was agreed by Wilson and Chamberlain that Inskip, in winding up the debate, would repeat that Chamberlain's decision 'is to hold good in spite of anything which Mr Churchill may say'. Commenting on this decision the Chief Whip, David Margesson, 'did not think that Mr Churchill is getting, or is likely to get much support for his request for an enquiry'. During the Cabinet meeting on March 12, Ministers were informed, according to the official minutes:

. . . that the Right Hon Winston Churchill was intending to attack the Government on the ground of the inadequacy of their Air Force Programme, and to support the motion of the Opposition for an enquiry into the Air Ministry. It was suggested that a speech belittling our efforts might have a very adverse effect on the international position just now when the only hope of saving Czechoslovakia from the German menace was by creating an impression of force.

In preparation for the Cabinet of March 12 Swinton had circulated to the Cabinet a secret nineteen-page memorandum on British air strength, pressing for the immediate adoption of Scheme K, which, he repeated, provided that 'minimum first line strength which the Air Staff regard as necessary to meet known German intentions'. Even so, Swinton pointed out, Scheme K did not in the view of the Air Staff provide 'adequate reserve or war potential'. Nevertheless in his memorandum Swinton urged the immediate adoption of Scheme K as the Government's expansion programme. 'It would be impossible,' he warned, 'for the Air Ministry to accelerate their programme in a year or eighteen months time when the review takes place unless they lay the foundation of that larger programme now.'

At the Cabinet, Swinton asked his colleagues to authorize the 'preliminary steps' for Scheme K, as this 'would enable the Government to say that they were taking all the steps necessary for further expansion'. But Chamberlain 'warned the Cabinet', as the minutes recorded, 'against giving the impression that the country was faced with the prospect of war within a few weeks'. Although the announcement of 'an increase' in air construction should be made, as 'this would enable them to approach Mr Churchill with better prospects of success', Chamberlain added that 'he did not think it would be wise to announce that commercial work was to be interfered with'. Yet Swinton and the Air Staff had made it clear that unless trade were to be interfered with, and double shift working made obligatory, even Scheme K could not be fulfilled.

At a further Cabinet on March 14, Swinton again urged the immediate adoption of Scheme K. By the expenditure of £657 million, the setting up of double shifts and civilian repair shops, and the procurement of extra labour 'this arrangement might give an increase in aggregate output of something like one third, commencing at the end of three months'. Under the scheme there would be 1,320 first-line bombers and 544 fighters by March 1939, plus full reserves by March 1940, a year earlier than contemplated under the existing schemes. Hoare spoke in favour both of air and naval increases, but Sir John Simon opposed Scheme K, arguing that he wished 'to avoid any public impression of the increase being a panic decision'. The maximum he wished to authorize for the expenditure of all three Services remained £1,570 million, whereas Swinton's minimum estimate for Scheme K would raise the total defence expenditure to £1,735 million. During the discussion, Simon warned his colleagues: 'The danger was we might knock our finances to pieces prematurely.' But Swinton warned that Scheme K was 'below what the Air Staff regarded as the minimum insurance'.

Inskip, reporting the views of a director of the Employers' National Federation, Sir Alexander Ramsay,[1] warned the Cabinet that if the Trade Unions were brought in to discuss such emergency measures as dilution and compulsion there would be certain dangers. The minutes recorded: 'The sort of difficulty he anticipated from the Trade Unions was that they would make conditions: eg they might demand that the Government should undertake to use the arms in support of Czecho-Slovakia or insist on the question being dealt with by the League of Nations.'

Only Winterton and Duff Cooper spoke in Swinton's favour. The minutes recorded Winterton's comment that he 'had had exceptional opportunities for knowing Mr Winston Churchill's views', and that since joining the Cabinet 'and having access to Cabinet documents, he was deeply concerned at our inability to fulfil the pledges of the late Prime Minister'. Duff Cooper then told his colleagues:

> He hoped the Cabinet were under no illusions as to the extent of our ability to defend ourselves from the air. . . . At present we were trying to carry through our Programme without any interference with trade against a power that was concentrating every effort on armaments. We ought, therefore,

---

[1] Alexander Ramsay, 1887–1969. Engineer; member of the Lincoln Corporation, 1916–19. OBE, 1920. A Director of Ruston & Hornsby Ltd, and Chairman of the Enfield Cycle Co Ltd. Conservative MP for West Bromwich, 1931–35. A Director of the Engineering and Allied Employers' National Federation. Knighted, 1938.

to consider a great intensification of our efforts. It was all very well to have a five years' Programme but we should not have five years for it.

It was clear that Germany meant business.

The Cabinet reached no conclusion, except, as the minutes recorded, to 'adjourn the discussion', and to instruct Inskip to 'further investigate' Swinton's proposals.

In preparation for the defence debate, Churchill himself had prepared a substantial memorandum on air deficiencies. On March 4 Wing-Commander Anderson had sent him a note on the thirty fighter squadrons, only one of which was equipped with the latest Hurricanes. 'The remaining 29,' he wrote, 'are equipped with Furies, Gauntlets and Gladiators, all designed before 1932.' On March 9 Anderson sent Churchill the secret Annual Training Report of Bomber Command, written by Air Chief Marshal Sir Edgar Ludlow-Hewitt, which concluded:

When taken from a training point of view the past year cannot be regarded with much satisfaction for although all concerned have worked under high pressure and done their utmost the year closes with the Command still far from attaining operational efficiency and readiness for war. . . .

In conclusion I must repeat that particularly in view of the unsettled international situation I cannot but regard the present low level of operational efficiency generally prevailing throughout the Command with concern and anxiety.

On March 10 Anderson wrote again, with evidence to show that the Air Force lacked sufficient mechanics to service the new aircraft, and that the 600 wireless operator mechanics 'deficient now' could not be trained and ready for their work 'for another 18 months or so'. He also gave Churchill copies of the Air Force Intelligence Summaries for January and February.

On March 11 Desmond Morton sent Churchill a series of notes on Churchill's draft air memorandum. 'I expect you would be prepared to recognise that the *very latest* types of British aircraft are superior to the very *latest types* of German aircraft,' he wrote, 'but whereas there may be several hundred of the latter in use, the number of the former in service can be counted on the fingers of both hands.'

Churchill completed his memorandum on March 12—the day of the annexation of Austria. In it he pointed out that of the 123 squadrons available for Home Defence, 'more than half are still armed with obsolete types', and that of the 1,500 to 1,700 machines, at least 850 consisted of Hinds, Harts, Heyfords and Gauntlets, 'the design of which are in most cases more than ten years old'. His memorandum continued:

Such new machines as have reached the squadrons mostly lack essential armament and equipment, namely, Browning guns, turrets, sights and modern blind-flying equipment. Without these elements the machines have no war value and even training is obstructed. The number of Metropolitan first-line aircraft of a relatively modern type which could go into action to-day properly equipped in all respects and be so maintained is certainly less than 700.

As for the rate of delivery of new aeroplanes and armaments, this, in the third year of rearmament, was 'astonishing', for the monthly output of aeroplanes, some 200, was only a third of the German output 'although the latter are not pressing their factories'. Churchill added: 'Since less than one-half of the Regular squadrons have received their outfit of new machines, it would seem to follow that there are no reserves of new machines available. Thus the picture of "British first line aircraft" with 100 per cent reserves behind it is an illusion.'

Churchill went on to refer, without naming his source, to Wing-Commander Anderson's figures for crashed aeroplanes, figures which, he wrote, 'although operative mainly over old machines, are grievous subtractions from the new deliveries, already so meagre', and he went on to ask:

What of the new types with which we are assured the 123 squadrons will be fully equipped by March 31, 1939? Owing to the slow production some of these types are already becoming outclassed. For instance the Hurricane fighter of which a dozen or two have been delivered, was ordered by the Air Ministry in 1935, and a specimen was actually available at the end of 1936. It is only now being delivered at a present rate of perhaps 200 a year.

Meanwhile it can hardly be doubted that the Germans have laid new types of fighters and bombers dating from 1936 and 1937 upon their mass production plants. As they order wholesale from a unified industry, full supplies of these should be available on March 31, 1939. It is not therefore true that we are overtaking them in the quality of the machines which will be in general use in the regular squadrons by that date.

'The idea that the expanded Air Force is upon a temporary basis,' Churchill urged, 'should be discarded. A far larger proportion of wholetime careers should be offered to proved men.'

The House of Commons debated the German annexation of Austria on Monday March 14. Opening the debate, Chamberlain announced his 'severest condemnation' of the methods used during the crisis. He also promised a 'fresh review' of Britain's defence programmes, and he added that 'in due course we shall announce what further steps we may think it necessary to take'. Churchill welcomed this promise, but in his speech he warned that in a year's time it would be no easier 'to face the problems with which we are confronted'. Were resistance to be delayed for too long, he said, a point might well be reached 'where continued resistance and true collective security would become impossible'. His speech continued:

The gravity of the event of the 11th of March cannot be exaggerated. Europe is confronted with a programme of aggression, nicely calculated and timed, unfolding stage by stage, and there is only one choice open, not only to us, but to other countries who are unfortunately concerned—either to submit, like Austria, or else to take effective measures while time remains to ward off the danger and, if it cannot be warded off, to cope with it.

Churchill went on to ask what would become of Britain by 1940, when the German Army 'will certainly be much larger than the French Army', and when all the small nations of Europe would have abandoned the League of Nations 'to pay homage to the ever-waxing power of the Nazi system, and to make the best terms they can for themselves'. He then spoke of the State which was likely to be threatened next, Czechoslovakia. This State, he said, manufactured the munitions on which both Rumania and Yugoslavia depended for their defence. Yet she had been isolated politically and economically as a result of Hitler's annexation of Austria. Surrounded now on three sides by German-controlled borders, her communications and her trade were both suddenly in jeopardy. 'To English ears,' he said, 'the name of Czechoslovakia sounds outlandish,' and he continued: 'No doubt they are only a small democratic State, no doubt they have an army only two or three times as large as ours, no doubt they have a munitions supply only three times as great as that of Italy, but still they are a virile people; they have their treaty rights, they have a line of fortresses, and they have a strongly manifested will to live freely.'

Churchill feared that Chamberlain's promise to accelerate rearmament would not, in itself, be enough to preserve peace. The small states of Europe had to be brought in to a system of collective defence; had to feel that they could rely upon Britain's word, and he continued, addressing the Conservative benches:

I know that some of my hon Friends on this side of the House will laugh when I offer them this advice. I say, 'Laugh, but listen.' I affirm that the Government should express in the strongest terms our adherence to the Covenant of the League of Nations and our resolve to procure by international action the reign of law in Europe.

'The matter,' he said, 'has an importance in this country. There must be a moral basis for British rearmament and British foreign policy,' and a 'common cause in self-defence' with France. 'But why stop there?' he asked, and went on: 'Why be edged and pushed farther down the slope in a disorderly expostulating crowd of embarrassed States? Why not make a stand while there is still a good company of united, very powerful countries that share our dangers and aspirations?'

There was, Churchill believed, little time in which to act, yet he was convinced that constructive action was still possible, telling the House of Commons that there should be 'a solemn treaty for mutual defence against aggression', organized by Britain and France, 'in what you may call a Grand Alliance', and he added:

. . . if they had their Staff arrangements concerted; if all this rested, as it can honourably rest, upon the Covenant of the League of Nations, in pursuance of all the purposes and ideals of the League of Nations; if that were sustained, as it would be, by the moral sense of the world; and if it were done in the year 1938—and, believe me, it may be the last chance there will be for doing it—then I say that you might even now arrest this approaching war.

Churchill ended with a solemn warning, telling the House of Commons: 'Before we cast away this hope, this cause and this plan, which I do not at all disguise has an element of risk, let those who wish to reject it ponder well and earnestly upon what will happen to us if, when all else has been thrown to the wolves, we are left to face our fate alone.'

'Winston makes the speech of his life in favour of the League,' Harold Nicolson noted in his diary, and on March 15 the *Star* declared, in its leading article: 'We are grateful that one man spoke out in Parliament last night, and made a speech which fitted the hour.'

On March 16 Lord Halifax reminded the Cabinet 'that public opinion was moving fast in the direction of placing the defences of the country more nearly on a war footing', but Chamberlain, while accepting that this was the public view, and that some announcement was needed, added that 'at the moment, he himself did not feel clear how far they were to go or in what direction'.

Churchill received many messages of support. Even one of his

severest critics in past years, the journalist A. G. Gardiner,[1] declared:
'You *must* be in office in a few weeks. The country would insist upon
it.' On March 16 a Labour supporter, Irene Noel Baker,[2] wrote to
Churchill to urge him to take up the fight for the League 'with *all* the
great intelligence and marvellous compelling force that you can give it'.
Her letter ended: 'For God's sake lead now and put an end to this most
ghastly nightmare in which we are all living.'[3]

On March 18 Professor Morgan, who had supported Churchill during
both the Indian and the Abdication controversies, wrote to him of
how the speech had made 'a profound impression' among the Conservatives who heard it, and he added:

I was discussing it at a dinner-party the other night at which some Conservative MP's were present and one of them said that there was a strong
and growing feeling in the House that our 'Defence Programme' would never
be complete until you were a member of the Cabinet. You may be interested
to know his exact words. They were 'Winston Churchill's presence in the
Cabinet would be worth two battleships to us and would put the fear of God
into the Germans as nothing else could do.' And so say all of us.

On March 17 Oliver Harvey[4] noted in his diary that Churchill was
being spoken of in Whitehall as a possible Air Minister. That same
day, in the House of Commons, Sir Roger Keyes—a former First Sea
Lord—urged Chamberlain to 'delegate to Mr Churchill the task of

---

[1] Alfred George Gardiner, 1865–1946. Author and journalist. Editor of the *Daily News*,
1902–19. President of the Institute of Journalists, 1915–16. Among his essays critical of
Churchill are those published in *Prophets, Priests and Kings* (1908) and *Pillars of Society* (1916).

[2] Irene Noel, only daughter of Frank Noel, a British landowner of Achmetaga, Greece.
She married Philip Baker in 1915, when they both took the surname of Noel-Baker. Her
husband was a Labour MP 1929–31 and 1936–70; their son Francis Noel-Baker was a Labour
MP from 1945–1969. She died in 1956.

[3] On the following day Josiah Wedgwood's daughter Helen, another staunch Labour
supporter and Fabian, wrote to her father: 'For God's sake can't you all shift Chamberlain.
Couldn't Sinclair & Attlee tell Churchill their parties would support him if he will take the
premiership? We haven't a hope of a Labour Govt even if we could force an election which
we can't. But Churchill with the decent Tories and our support could force one, & could get
the country's support. Anything is better than drifting into war with that miserable wobbler
Chamberlain. Churchill may be a reactionary in most ways, but he is sound about foreign
affairs, & his speeches are a joy to read.' On March 26 Josiah Wedgwood replied: 'I entirely
share your views about Winston. So do we all & he knows it.'

[4] Oliver Charles Harvey, 1893–1968. Educated Malvern and Trinity College Cambridge.
On active service in France, Egypt and Palestine (despatches), 1914–18. Entered Foreign
Office, 1919. First Secretary, Paris, 1931–36. Counsellor, and Principal Private Secretary to
successive Secretaries of State for Foreign Affairs, 1936–39, and 1941–43. Minister to Paris
1940. Assistant Under-Secretary of State, 1943–46. Knighted, 1946. Deputy Under-Secretary
of State (Political), 1946–47. Ambassador to France, 1948–54. Created Baron Harvey of
Tasburgh, 1954.

reorganizing the British Navy', and on March 20 Thomas Jones wrote to a friend in the United States:

The last few days have seen a revival of the wish to see Winston in the Government and I should welcome him at the Air Ministry for his driving power would soon be felt throughout the department down to the typists and messengers. But on policy he would have to be kept in chains. He has commended himself to the Labour Party by his support of the League of Nations in his recent speeches and articles. Many would like a reconstruction of the Government on more national lines for this emergency.

For Churchill, the demands of public life were made more difficult by a sudden financial problem. In the second week of March the value of the United States stocks in which he had placed so much trust since 1932 fell so sharply that his share account with Vickers da Costa was in debt to the sum of £18,000. Yet his contract for the *English-Speaking Peoples* would only bring in, before tax, £15,000, and even this sum would not be paid until the book was finished, probably not until December 1939. Not only did it now seem certain that Churchill must sell Chartwell, but also that he would have to spend a far larger portion of his time on literary work in order to try to cover his debt. And yet, as he confided to Brendan Bracken, even his literary earnings, high as they were, could not meet both his share losses and the income tax and super-tax demands. He now feared that he might have to leave public life in order to try to repair his financial plight. On March 18 he set out his dilemma to Bracken, who noted that Churchill, 'apart from the regular literary contracts on which he lives, has a contract for a book on which some progress has been made, deliverable on December 31, 1939 for £15,000. He could accomplish this task within the specified time by laying everything aside; but how is he to do this while events run at this pitch, still less if he should be required to devote his whole energies to public work.' Bracken spoke to Sir Henry Strakosch, who at once agreed to take over Churchill's share account, and to bear full liability. On the following day Churchill wrote to Bracken:

My dear Brendan,

I was profoundly touched and relieved by what you told me last night of the kindness of our friend.

If it were not for public affairs and my evident duty I shd be able to manage all right. But it is unsuitable as well as harrassing to have to watch an account from day to day when one's mind ought to be concentrated upon the great world issues now at stake. I shd indeed be grateful if I cd be liberated during these next few critical years from this particular worry, wh descended upon me so unexpectedly; to the chance of which I shall certainly never expose myself again. I cannot tell you what a relief it would be if I could put it out of my mind; and take the large decisions wh perhaps may be required of me without this distraction and anxiety.

On March 28 Strakosch wrote direct to Churchill: 'My dear Winston, I have today paid to Vickers da Costa & Co £18,162.1.10. being the amount due to them by you. . . . As agreed between us I shall carry this position for three years, you giving me full discretion to sell or vary the holdings at any time, but on the understanding that you incur no further liability.' With these assurances, Churchill no longer needed to sell Chartwell, although on April 2 *The Times* actually announced that it was for sale. A few days later he withdrew the house from the market.

The long-awaited Air Debate had begun on March 15. Of the promise to have 1,500 first-line machines by March 1937 Inskip declared: 'That promise was not accompanied by another promise that they would be modern machines. It was well known to everybody, that they would be to a large extent of obsolescent types.' During the debate Inskip confirmed the Cabinet's decision not to define air parity as equal first-line strength, telling the House: 'I think the Prime Minister is only doing what most men of common sense would do in saying that if you attempt to take first-line strength as the one yard stick in determining parity, you are proceeding on a wholly deceitful basis.' Replying to this new definition a week later, Churchill stated that three and a half years earlier the Government had based their parity promise on a calculation of first-line strength, and he added:

I think it is very unsatisfactory that now, this having been deliberately adopted as the standard by the Government, we should be invited to adopt an entirely new and vague standard. I am quite certain that we should not have been invited to adopt that standard unless it was impossible for the Government to show that they had maintained their pledge upon the standard which they formerly prescribed to the House.

46

Prelude to Munich:
'We Are in an Awful Mess'

O N March 18, in an article in the *Evening Standard*, Churchill
drew his readers' attention to the growing crisis in Czechoslovakia. It was essential, he wrote, for the Czech Government to do
everything possible to ensure that the German-speaking minority was
accorded 'every form of good treatment and equal citizenship, not
incompatible with the safety and integrity of the State'. At the same
time, he welcomed the declaration by the French Government that
France would fulfil its Treaty obligations to Czechoslovakia if she were
to be the victim of an unprovoked attack. 'A further declaration,' he
added, 'of the intentions of the British Government in such an event
must soon be made.'

The Cabinet's Foreign Policy Committee[1] also discussed Czechoslovakia on March 18, when Inskip told his colleagues that he believed
Czechoslovakia to be 'an unstable unit in Central Europe', and that
'he could see no reason why we should take any steps to maintain such
a unit in being'. According to Simon, 'Czechoslovakia was a modern
and very artificial creation with no real roots in the past.' Unlike
Churchill, both Chamberlain and Halifax were worried by the recent
French declaration, and Chamberlain 'wondered whether it would not
be possible to make some arrangement which would prove more
acceptable to Germany'. Halifax stressed the weakness of France as an
ally for Czechoslovakia, telling his colleagues, as the minutes recorded:

No doubt the French authorities would face up to the facts but when he had
put the difficulties to M Corbin the latter had replied to the effect that these

---

[1] Its members were Chamberlain, Simon, Hoare, Malcolm MacDonald, Inskip, Hailsham,
Halifax, Ormsby-Gore and Oliver Stanley. R. A. Butler (Under-Secretary of State for Foreign
Affairs) was also present at the meeting of March 18.

were matters which could profitably be discussed with us. Mr Winston Churchill had a plan under which the French Army was to act on the defensive behind the Maginot Line and there detain large German forces while Czechoslovakia engaged Germany's remaining forces. This seemed to have no relation to the realities of the situation.

Halifax went on to warn that 'the more closely we associated ourselves with France and Russia the more we produced on German minds the impression that we were plotting to encircle Germany'. Halifax added that 'He (Lord Halifax) distinguished in his own mind between Germany's racial efforts, which no one could question, and a lust for conquest on a Napoleonic scale which he himself did not credit.' Halifax then set out for his colleagues his view of what British policy should be:

We should try to persuade France and Czechoslovakia that the best course would be for the latter to make the best terms she could with Germany while there was yet time and that we would use any influence we might have with Germany to induce her to take up a reasonable attitude. If in the result a satisfactory solution of the Sudeten problem was reached we might offer in that event to join with Germany in guaranteeing Czechoslovakia's independence.

As March progressed, the question of whether Czechoslovakia should or should not make concessions to the German-speaking Sudetens, and whether or not she should resist pressure from both Berlin and London to make those concessions, divided British society. The breach cut across political parties and poisoned personal friendships. On March 19 The Times reported a speech by one of Churchill's former India Bill colleagues, and personal friend, Alan Lennox-Boyd, who had told an audience at Biggleswade 'that he could countenance nothing more ridiculous than a guarantee that the frontiers of Czechoslovakia should not be violated when half the people in that country could not be relied upon to be loyal to the Government of the day; and from what he knew of Mr Chamberlain, he did not think he would make a move to give a guarantee of that kind'. Lennox-Boyd went on to say that Germany 'could absorb Czechoslovakia, and Great Britain would remain secure'. In a letter to Churchill on March 19, Boothby described Lennox-Boyd's words as 'an incitement to Germany to get on with the job'.

Chamberlain's dislike of guaranteeing Czechoslovakia was as strong as Lennox-Boyd had suggested. Indeed, on March 20 the Prime Minister wrote in a letter to his sister:

. . . the plan of the 'Grand Alliance', as Winston calls it, had occurred to me long before he mentioned it. . . . I talked about it to Halifax, and we submitted it to the chiefs of the Staff and the FO experts. It is a very attractive idea; indeed, there is almost everything to be said for it until you come to examine its practicability. From that moment its attraction vanishes. You have only to look at the map, to see that nothing that France or we could do could possibly save Czechoslovakia from being overrun by the Germans, if they wanted to do it. The Austrian frontier is practically open; the great Skoda munition works are within easy bombing distance of the German aerodromes, the railways all pass through German territory, Russia is 100 miles away. Therefore we could not help Czechoslovakia—she would simply be a pretext for going to war with Germany. That we could not think of unless we had a reasonable prospect of being able to beat her to her knees in a reasonable time, and of that I see no sign. I have therefore abandoned any idea of giving guarantees to Czechoslovakia, or the French in connection with her obligations to that country.

Two days earlier, on March 18, Lord Halifax had dismissed Churchill's plan for a Grand Alliance with other arguments, writing in a Foreign Office memorandum: 'In order to achieve it, it would be necessary to draw up a formal instrument in Treaty form, and this would be a long and complicated matter. If any undertaking is to be given by us which will help to save the situation in Central Europe, this must be done without undue delay. The long and difficult negotiations which would be necessary to conclude the Grand Alliance would afford both a provocation and an opportunity to Germany to dispose of Czechoslovakia before the grand alliance had been organised.' On March 21 Halifax told the Cabinet Committee on Foreign Policy 'that the great majority of responsible people in the country would be opposed to any new commitments'.

The division of opinion was exacerbated by the attitude of the Press. *The Times* in particular urged the Czechs to make concessions to Germany, and argued that it was Czech obstinacy that was the main obstacle to a peaceful settlement. Yet even the factual reports in *The Times* did not give a true picture of the nature of Nazi rule. On March 18 Churchill was sent a first-hand account of events in Vienna since the German occupation from a young acquaintance, David Hindley-Smith,[1]

[1] David Dury Hindley-Smith, 1916–   . Educated at Uppingham and King's College Cambridge. Studied in Paris and Vienna, 1937–38. Passed the Diplomatic Service examination, 1939. On active service, 1939–45; Liaison Officer to General Leclerc, 1942 and to General de Gaulle's first administration, 1944. Acting Colonel, 1944. Registrar, Dental Board of the UK (later the General Dental Council), since 1947. Executive Chairman, National Association of Youth Clubs, 1970–74. CBE, 1972.

who had been angered by reports in *The Times* that Hitler had received an enthusiastic welcome from an overwhelming majority of Austrians. According to Hindley Smith:

The Viennese are a sentimental intensely patriotic people who love liberty quite as much as we do and whose cultural outlook is very like our own. All my many friends in this city are in the depths of despair. The cultural life of the city must die for it is these people—together with the Embassies and the Jews—who upheld it.

Many hundreds of lorry-loads of NS supporters from Graz and Linz were brought into Vienna, to make it a hell hot enough to hold the Fuhrer—and everyone knows what a noise University students can make.

It avails nothing to speak of the many sickening incidents. A family of six Jews have just shot themselves, a few houses down the street. They are well out of it. Yesterday morning I saw two well-dressed women forced to their knees to scrub out a 'Heil Schuschnigg!' on the pavement. But these things seem to be all part of the Totalitarian's stock in trade.

On March 22 Churchill sent Hindley-Smith's letter to Geoffrey Dawson, who replied on the following day:

No doubt it is true that *The Times*, like every other paper, gave the impression of an enthusiastic street welcome for the new regime. Our Correspondent in Vienna,[1] who is an extreme anti-Nazi and lost no time in leaving the country, talked, for instance, about 'the extraordinary complete emotional surrender of the Austrians' and of 'an apparent change in the Austrian character as the outer world has understood it'. Nobody, he concluded his message, 'can believe Austria could be like that'. There is no doubt, I think, that the impression of jubilation was overwhelming. But we all knew, and said, that this was not the whole of the story. I remember writing myself that same day that the exuberant crowds were composed for the most part of youths and that others had hidden their faces.[2]

The gulf between Churchill and the Government was even greater

[1] Douglas Reed, 1895–1976. A publisher's office boy, 1908; a bank clerk, 1914. Served in the infantry and air force, 1915–18, when he was twice wounded. Joined the staff of *The Times* as a shorthand telephonist, August 1921. Appointed to the Paris Office, 1921; to the Foreign Department, 1922. Assistant Berlin Correspondent, 1928–35. Vienna Correspondent, 1935–38. Central European Correspondent, June–October 1938 (when he resigned). Served as a War Correspondent in Normandy, 1944

[2] The paragraph in *The Times* of March 14 to which Churchill had objected, read: 'Herr Hitler has enjoyed two days of triumphal progress from the Austrian frontier. Our Correspondent leaves no room for doubt about the public jubilation with which he and his army was greeted everywhere. . . .' The paragraph to which Dawson referred, from the same leading article, read: 'No doubt the exuberant crowds were composed for the most part of the youths who would have been excluded under the Austrian constitution from Herr von Schuschnigg's plebiscite and who are at this moment the only visible representatives of the nation. There must be many thousands of thoughtful Germans who are reflecting even now that here are the methods that brought them to grief in the past.'

than he realized. During an important Cabinet discussion on March 22, in the secrecy of the Cabinet room, the Chiefs of Staff sub-committee report was discussed, in which it was stated that 'no pressure that we and our possible allies can bring to bear either by sea, or land, or in the air, can prevent Germany from invading and overrunning Bohemia'. One Minister, unnamed in the minutes, pointed out that 'Today Germany was ill-prepared for a long war. Two years hence she might be much better prepared for that contingency,' but at the end of the discussion it was agreed that pressure should be put on Czecho-slovakia to make concessions to its Sudeten minority. 'It was a disagree-able business,' Halifax told his colleagues, 'which had to be done as pleasantly as possible.'

Despite Chamberlain's promise to the House of Commons on March 14 that the Government would review defence spending, a promise which all MPs assumed must mean an increase, the official minutes of March 22 recorded that 'The Cabinet were reminded that at the present time the Defence Services were working under instructions to cut down estimates, and it was suggested that this was hardly consistent with an announcement that we were accelerating our armaments.' Nevertheless, the Cabinet agreed that an announcement that armaments were being increased should still be made, by Chamberlain himself, when he spoke in the House of Commons on March 24. They also decided to cancel the earlier assumption 'that the course of normal trade should not be impeded' in reconditioning the Services. 'Acceleration of existing plans,' Chamberlain told the Commons on March 24, 'has become essential.' Moreover, he added, 'there must be an increase in some parts of the programme, especially in that of the Royal Air Force and the anti-aircraft defences'.

On the evening of March 24 Churchill spoke in the House of Com-mons, urging MPs to believe that peace in Europe could only be pre-served by means of an 'accumulation of deterrents against the aggressor'. Commenting on Chamberlain's statement earlier in the debate that France and Britain would work together for their mutual defence, he asked whether it was an actual alliance. If so, 'Why not say so?' His speech continued: 'Why not make it effective by a military convention of the most detailed character? Are we, once again, to have all the dis-advantages of an alliance without its advantages, and to have commit-ments without full security?'

An Anglo-French arrangement for mutual defence constituted, Churchill said, 'the great security' for both Britain and France, and he exhorted the Government:

Treat the defensive problems of the two countries as if they were one. Then you will have a real deterrent against unprovoked agression, and if the deterrent fails to deter, you will have a highly organized method of coping with the aggressor.

The present rulers of Germany will hesitate long before they attack the British Empire and the French Republic if those are woven together for defence purposes into one very powerful unit . . .

Churchill then spoke of Czechoslovakia. Unless German pressure were countered, he declared, 'Czechoslovakia will be forced to make continuous surrenders, far beyond the bounds of what any impartial tribunal would consider just or right, until finally her sovereignty, her independence, her integrity, have been destroyed'.

Commenting on Chamberlain's statement that new measures were to be introduced to accelerate the air programme, and to extend the anti-aircraft and air-raid precautions systems, Churchill continued:

It is only a fortnight ago that my right hon Friend told us he was satisfied that we were making the best and the most effective use of our resources. However, it appears that there were other resources not being used which now will be used in a greater effort. I regret very much that these additional resources have not been applied during the last two years, when the air programme was seen to be trailing so far behind. Not only did we start two years too late, but the second two years have been traversed at only half-speed. . . .

Despite Chamberlain's assurances that a greater effort would now be made, Churchill was not entirely convinced that the decision would be properly implemented. 'Ought there not to be created,' he asked, 'however tardily, a Ministry of Supply? Ought there not to be created a far more effective Ministry of Defence?' and he went on to ask:

Is our system of government adapted to the present fierce, swift movement of events? Twenty-two gentlemen of blameless party character sitting round an overcrowded table, each having a voice—is that a system which can reach decisions from week to week and cope with the problems descending upon us and with the men at the head of the dictator States? It broke down hopelessly in the War.

But is this peace in which we are living? Is it not war without cannon firing? Is it not war of a decisive character, where victories are gained and territories conquered, and where ascendancy and dominance are established over large populations with extraordinary rapidity?

Churchill went on to warn of the dangers of allowing any momentary easing of tension to lead to complacency. 'After a boa constrictor has devoured its prey,' he said, 'it often has a considerable digestive spell.'

There had been a pause after each German move—after the revelation that a secret air force had been set up, after the proclamation of conscription, and again after the militarization of the Rhineland. He went on:

Now, after Austria has been struck down, we are all disturbed and alarmed, but in a little while there may be another pause. There may not, we cannot tell. But if there is a pause, then people will be saying, 'See how the alarmists have been confuted; Europe has calmed down, it has all blown over, and the war scare has passed away.' The Prime Minister will perhaps repeat what he said a few weeks ago, that the tension in Europe is greatly relaxed. *The Times* will write a leading article to say how silly people look who on the morrow of the Austrian incorporation raised a clamour for exceptional action in foreign policy and home defence, and how wise the Government were not to let themselves be carried away by this passing incident.

No such attitude was justified, Churchill argued. Day by day the population of Austria was being reduced 'to the rigours of Nazi domination'. Week by week the forces 'of conquest and intimidation' were being consolidated. Presently 'another stroke' would come. 'What I dread,' Churchill told the Commons, 'is that the impulse now given to active effort may pass away, when the dangers are not diminishing, but accumulating and gathering, as country after country is involved in the Nazi system, and as their vast preparations reach their final perfection.'

Churchill's speech ended with a stern warning, and an urgent appeal:

For five years I have talked to the House on these matters—not with very great success. I have watched this famous island descending incontinently, fecklessly, the stairway which leads to a dark gulf. It is a fine broad stairway at the beginning, but after a bit the carpet ends. A little farther on there are only flagstones, and a little farther on still these break beneath your feet. . . .

A few moments later Churchill declared, with foreboding:

. . . if mortal catastrophe should overtake the British Nation and the British Empire, historians a thousand years hence will still be baffled by the mystery of our affairs. They will never understand how it was that a victorious nation, with everything in hand, suffered themselves to be brought low, and to cast away all that they had gained by measureless sacrifice and absolute victory—gone with the wind!

Now the victors are the vanquished, and those who threw down their arms in the field and sued for an armistice are striding on to world mastery. . . .

Churchill's friends were thrilled by his lucid exposition. 'That was a glorious speech of yours this evening,' wrote Sir Roger Keyes. 'I couldn't get near you to say a word.' 'Your speech was *magnificent* from the first word to the last,' Robert Boothby wrote that same evening. 'It makes one very proud to have been associated with you in public life.'

On the day of Churchill's speech, Lord Beaverbrook's *Evening Standard* decided to terminate his contract, and bring his fortnightly articles to an immediate end. For two years they had been his main platform in addressing the British public. It has become evident, R. J. Thompson [1] wrote to Churchill on March 24, 'that your views on foreign affairs and the part which this country should play are entirely opposed to those held by us'.

On the morning of March 25 Churchill flew to Paris, where, for two days, he put his suggestions for an Anglo-French alliance to the leading French politicians, many of whom asked specifically to see him. On the previous day Sir Eric Phipps had written privately to Sir Alexander Cadogan: 'I fervently hope that all these meetings will not unduly excite the French. In any case I shall do my best to calm them down and to convince them that Winston is not the arbiter of our destinies.'

On March 25 Churchill dined with Herriot. On the following day he saw Léger at the Quai d'Orsay, lunched with Reynaud and dined with Blum and Paul-Boncour. [2] On the morning of March 27 Phipps wrote privately to Lord Halifax that Churchill had stressed the 'urgent necessity' for an Anglo-French alliance, immediate Staff talks, 'and the placing at our disposal of all French ports in the Mediterranean'. The French politicians had welcomed Churchill's suggestions, but, Phipps added, they 'naturally realise that he only speaks for himself and a very small section of British public opinion, and I lay great stress on this, and urge liberal sprinklings of salt on what he says'.

On March 27 Churchill lunched with Flandin, who argued in favour of bringing down the Popular Front, and instituting Government by Decree. Then, as Phipps reported to Halifax that same day: 'Mr

---

[1] Reginald John Tanner Thompson, 1896–1956. On active service, Royal Fusiliers and 18th Division, western front, 1914–18. Journalist; worked on the *Daily Express* and the *Evening News*. Editor of the *Evening Standard*, 1938–39. Editor and Managing Director of the Essex Chronicle Series Limited, publishers of the *Essex Chronicle*. His father, mother, brother and two nephews were killed during a raid by a solitary bomber on Chelmsford, 1940.

[2] Joseph Paul-Boncour, 1873–1973. Chef de Cabinet to the Prime Minister, 1899–1902 and 1906–09. Republican Socialist Deputy, 1909. Minister of Labour, 1911. Commanded an infantry battalion, 1914–18 (Croix de Guerre). President of the Foreign Affairs Commission, Chamber of Deputies, 1927–31. Resigned from the Socialist Party, 1931. Minister of War, 1932. Prime Minister, December 1932–January 1933. Foreign Minister, December 1932–February 1934. Minister for League of Nations Affairs, January–June 1936. Foreign Minister for the second time, March–April 1938.

Churchill warned M Flandin that if such procedure were followed it would alienate all Left sympathies in Great Britain for France, and render most difficult that close and loyal collaboration between our two countries now more than ever essential to check further German aggression and to prevent German hegemony.'

'Winston Churchill's stay here,' Phipps wrote to Halifax on March 28, 'has continued in an increasingly kaleidoscopic manner. Almost every facet of French political life has been presented to him at and between meals.' Churchill's theme throughout was that of his Commons speech of March 24: a public, binding Anglo-French alliance, and a joint attempt by France and Britain to persuade the States of Central Europe and the Balkans to unite in resisting German pressure. After dining with Daladier on March 28, Churchill promised that he would discuss the problem on his return with both Chamberlain and Halifax. His views were sought as if he were an official envoy on a special mission, rather than a backbench MP on a private visit. In his letter to Halifax of March 28, Phipps commented:

His French is most strange and at times quite incomprehensible. For instance, to Blum and Boncour the other night he shouted out a literal translation of 'We must make good', by 'Nous devons faire bonne (not even "bon")'. This clearly stumped Boncour, who may even have attributed some improper meaning to it.

You will get a most eloquent first-hand account of this hectic and electric week-end from its brilliant animator.

The Cabinet met in London on the morning of March 30. Halifax read Phipps' letter to his colleagues, who were, he wrote to Phipps later that day, 'greatly amused with the last paragraph of it'. But, Halifax added:

Some of them were disposed to be a little critical of my having encouraged you, as I think I did, to show hospitality to him and generally to keep an eye on his movements. I still think that it was better so, and the Prime Minister was on the whole of the same opinion.

Winston came to see me yesterday and we had some talk. He repeated his desire to see France and Great Britain together forming the nucleus for the rally of smaller Central European and Balkan Powers. I pointed out some of the obvious difficulties in the way of this to him and he did not seem violently interested in that side of the subject.

It would, I think, be useful if, as you get an opportunity of seeing any of those with whom he came in contact, especially perhaps Daladier and Herriot, you were to warn them, as you have no doubt done already, that the right source from which to ascertain British Government policy is the declarations of the British Government, rather than Winston's exuberant interpretations of it. I am always a little bit anxious lest his enthusiasm should lead him, quite unwittingly, to misrepresent HMG's attitude.

Phipps had already acted in the sense of Halifax's advice, for, reporting on March 30 on a talk with Mandel, he wrote of how he took the opportunity 'to rub in, as I have done to all concerned, that Churchill was speaking for himself only during his recent visit to Paris, and that much salt must be taken with what he said'.

Churchill felt his visit to France had been a success, writing to Phipps on April 1:

I had talks both with the PM and your Chief, and I pressed very strongly for Staff conversations and detailed arrangements with the French. I was pleased to find both were responsive.

Halifax told me that he had come round to the view that this would be wise, and even that publicity would be helpful.

Neville also spoke in the same sense, so I hope this at least may be done.

As April progressed, Churchill was increasingly concerned about Czechoslovakia. On April 4 he wrote to Deakin, who was about to visit Prague:

You should call at the Embassy, and ask the best way of getting in touch with the President. Remember he is the head of State. You should encourage him, or anyone he puts you in touch with, to talk to you confidentially for any information about their position, and what they think we can do to help.

Is it true that the fortifications are already complete opposite the new Austrian front? What sort of communications have they from Roumania into Russia? What are their relations with Roumania and Yugoslavia? Is it worth while working out the plan I outlined in the House of Commons for a block of Danubian States planned for economic and ultimately military purposes?

Deakin saw Beneš, and on his return reported to Churchill on the situation in Czechoslovakia. At the same time, Churchill received details of Germany's growing economic strength both from Sir Henry Strakosch and from Robert Boothby, while on April 7 Group Captain MacLean sent Churchill a five-page memorandum comparing British and German air force strengths and warning of the dangers of underestimating Germany's geographical advantage in being able to strike with small forces at vital objectives.

The Cabinet itself now knew about Germany's true air potential. On March 31, the Committee of Imperial Defence discussed a joint memorandum by Desmond Morton and the Air Ministry Intelligence, describing the state of the German aircraft industry. Five Ministers,

Inskip, Swinton, Ormsby-Gore, Hoare and Hore-Belisha were present. During the discussion, Hoare drew the attention of his colleagues 'to the large discrepancy between our own and the German aircraft production, the latter being about 500 air frames and 1,000 aero engines a month, whereas our production figures for last month were only about 118 air frames and about 250 engines'. The situation, Hore-Belisha commented, was 'most alarming . . . it seems that our organisation is not resilient'.

On April 1 Swinton circulated to the Cabinet a further air scheme, L, whereby the total British first-line strength would reach 2,373 by March 1940, with 100 per cent reserves by March 1941.[1] On April 4 Sir John Simon, in a Cabinet paper, urged the adoption of a scheme 'considerably less than that asked for', and he suggested a modified scheme which could be expanded at a later date. At the Cabinet on April 6 Swinton stressed 'that Scheme L was essential to meet the German menace', but Inskip said it would 'wreck the rationing scheme' of the previous February, whereby the defence expenditure of all three Services was not to exceed £1,570 million.

During the Cabinet meeting on April 6 Neville Chamberlain expressed his concern 'that we could not achieve parity without compulsory service and throwing over financial considerations', and he went on to ask whether it might not be possible to produce a 'formidable offensive force' while in fact carrying out a programme 'designed to strengthen our *defensive* strength'. In reply to this, Swinton stated that Scheme L would not produce a 'safe air defence against Germany' and that the Air Staff 'had repeatedly pointed out that they had taken as their basis the minimum *known* German intentions which would be realised this year'. In addition, Swinton pointed out, the Air Staff had 'deliberately put forward a scale of reserves below what they considered a proper insurance' in order to meet 'the financial stringency'. Consequently, Swinton warned, even 'Scheme "L" ' was a minimum dictated not by what the Air Staff considered would give safety from a strategical point of view, but by political considerations of what was possible without control and National Service.'

Swinton pointed out that there was a Budget surplus of £28 million, and he warned his colleagues: 'The proposed accelerated expansion might be an insurance for peace. He himself believed that it was the only insurance. Without it we could not live to use our resources.' But

---

[1] Scheme L was made up of: 1,352 bombers, 608 fighters, 281 General reconnaisance and 132 army cooperation aircraft. It involved the adoption of double shifting throughout the aircraft industry.

Simon reiterated his desire to 'preserve the financial strength of the country' and that it would 'be better to adopt the sound business method of not expanding the business until we were in a position to do so.'

At the end of the Cabinet of April 6 the future of Scheme L was referred to the consideration of four Ministers, Chamberlain, Simon, Inskip and Swinton. Churchill was informed of this decision by Wing-Commander Anderson, who sent him full details both of Scheme J and Scheme L, the latter of which, Anderson wrote in his covering letter, 'has been referred several times to Inskip and the Cabinet sub-committee but is waiting final approval by the Government'. On May 12 Anderson wrote again, enclosing the minutes of an armament conference held on April 8, dealing with 'delays of armament equipment'. Mrs Pearman sent the latter to Churchill with a covering note: 'The Commander wants you particularly to read through this and study it, as it may be very useful to you.'

On April 27, following the discussions of the four Ministers, the Cabinet decided to authorize the Air Ministry to negotiate with individual firms to produce 'as many aeroplanes as they could', even beyond the expenditure planned for the coming two years, provided it did not exceed the previously established upper limit of £1,650 millions allocated to the Defence Services for the next five years. Nor, the minutes added, were the Cabinet 'committed to that rate of expenditure beyond 1940'. At the end of the meeting Chamberlain told his Cabinet:

. . . criticisms must still be expected, especially from Mr Winston Churchill, but he hoped that the Chancellor of the Duchy of Lancaster now felt that he had a good answer, and everything possible was being done to meet the situation and keep the firms extended to their uttermost capacity. It would of course be said that other firms might have been called in to do the work, but that proposal probably emanated from interested quarters who did not really know the business.[1]

---

[1] This decision was taken after discussions with the aircraft industry about how many aircraft it could produce by March 1940. It was agreed to try to produce up to 12,000 aircraft of all types, in order to obtain the 2,373 first-line aeroplanes of Scheme L, with its reduced reserves. Scheme L depended upon adequate supplies of labour. But Chamberlain told Simon, Inskip and Swinton on April 7: 'There could be no question of the compulsory transfer of large blocks of labour until the voluntary method had been tried out.' As a result of these decisions, there were serious labour shortages in 1939, and on 1 August 1939 Kingsley Wood reported to the Committee of Imperial Defence serious delays in Scheme L. 'Most of our permanent work is being delayed,' he said. 'The position in regard to new stations under construction is equally serious and may well result in considerable delay in the formation of new squadrons.'

On April 4, after writing his last article for the *Evening Standard*, Churchill offered his future articles to the owner of the *Daily Telegraph*, Lord Camrose. The provincial circulation in England, he pointed out, was bringing in an extra £25 to £30 an article, while the continental services organized by Dr Revesz added a further £40 to £50. 'As you will see it is a very fine platform,' Churchill wrote, 'though as Nazi power advances, as in Vienna, planks are pulled out of it.' In his letter to Camrose Churchill enclosed a list of 11 British, 9 Colonial and 37 European newspapers in which his articles had been syndicated.[1] Camrose replied to Churchill on April 6 offering to 'try the experiment' for six months. He was afraid, he added, if they were to agree to a longer period 'our policies might well be at serious variance'. Two days later Churchill accepted Camrose's offer, writing to Revesz that same day that there had been a 'rush of papers to secure the articles'. On April 11, once his arrangements with Camrose were agreed, he wrote to R. J. Thompson at the *Evening Standard*:

... With regard to the divergence from Lord Beaverbrook's policy, that of course has been obvious from the beginning, but it clearly appears to me to be less marked than in the case of the Low[2] cartoons. I rather thought that Lord Beaverbrook prided himself upon forming a platform in the Evening Standard for various opinions including of course his own.

With regard to the method of terminating the contract by a month's notice, this was clearly within the formal agreement but the understanding which I had with Mr Cudlipp[3] certainly never led me to expect such abrupt treatment, and I admit I was surprised to receive your communication.

It may interest you to know that I could have placed the articles in three, if not four, different quarters at the same fee. ...

Churchill added: 'The very wide circulation which these articles were commanding throughout Europe also encourages me to feel that you had no reasonable cause for dissatisfaction.' A week later the Syndication

[1] During 1938 Churchill's *Evening Standard* articles were also published in the *Glasgow Evening News*, the *Aberdeen Evening Express*, the *Belfast Telegraph*, the *Adelaide Advertiser*, the *East African Standard*, the *Times of Malta* and the *Madras Mail*. By 1 May 1937 Revesz had placed Churchill's articles in newspapers in Brussels, Rotterdam, Copenhagen, Stockholm, Oslo, Tallinn, Kaunas, Zurich, Lausanne, Prague, Bucharest, Krakow, Buenos Aires, Trondheim, Luzern, Budapest and Belgrade.

[2] David Alexander Cecil Low, 1891–1963. Cartoonist and caricaturist. Born and educated in New Zealand. Joined the *Star*, London 1919; the *Evening Standard*, 1927; the *Daily Herald*, 1950 and the *Manchester Guardian*, 1953. Knighted, 1962.

[3] Percy Cudlipp, 1905–1962. Educated in Cardiff. Dramatic critic and humorous columnist, *Sunday News* (London), 1925–29. Joined the *Evening Standard*, as its film critic, 1929; Assistant Editor, 1931; Editor, 1933–38. Editorial Manager, *Daily Herald*, 1938–40; Editor, 1940–53. Columnist, *News Chronicle*, 1954–56. Editor, *New Scientist*, 1956–62.

Manager, W. H. Robertson,[1] wrote to Churchill: 'I have received expressions of regret from all the papers in England from which we have had to withdraw the series. All the Editors are agreed that the articles were unusually highly appreciated by their readers.'

Churchill was being urged continually to speak in public; friends, acquaintances and strangers all wrote to invite him to address mass meetings, and to set out his thoughts, and suggestions, on the German threat to European peace. In inviting him to speak in Manchester, A. H. Richards, of the Freedom and Peace Movement wrote, on April 2: 'They were emphatic you would receive a tumultuous welcome and be everywhere acclaimed.' Five days later, Sir Malcolm Robertson,[2] who had himself made thirty public speeches in six months, wrote to Churchill of the need for a national speaking campaign 'to enlighten the British public on the grave danger which faces freedom and democracy. . . .' Churchill had already agreed to speak at Manchester on May 9, and in his reply to Robertson on April 11 he wrote: 'I think there is very little doubt we shall have to organize a national campaign, and I am endeavouring to find strength and time for my share in it.' On April 12 he wrote to Lord Derby, who had agreed to take the chair at the Manchester meeting: 'I have felt it my duty to make exertions—so far as I can—to rouse the country in the face of our ever-growing dangers,' and he added:

England must speak with a confident voice. Our party must carry the Trade Unions with them. Non-Conformists, Churchmen and Catholics must work for a common end. The unattached flowing mass (which can nevertheless decide elections) must have a real awakening and a clear goal. The time is very short in which war may be averted. It can only be averted by a great England standing boldly for Peace and Freedom—Freedom first.

[1] William Harris Robertson, 1894–1972. Born in Aberdeen. Left school at the age of 14. Served with the Cameron Highlanders on the western front, 1914–18 (twice wounded). Went to London University after the war. Subsequently editor of the Singapore *Free Press*, then Syndication Manager of the *Daily Express*. Worked with the BBC monitoring service, 1939–45. After the war he edited *Coal*, the magazine of the newly founded National Coal Board. Purchased the *Montrose Review*, 1959; the *Mearns Leader*, 1959 and the *Kincardineshire Observer*, 1965.

[2] Malcolm Arnold Robertson, 1877–1951. Educated at Marlborough. Entered the Foreign Office as a clerk, 1898; 1st Secretary, Washington, 1915–18; the Hague, 1918–19. Deputy British High Commissioner, Rhineland, 1919; High Commissioner, 1920–21. British Agent and Consul-General, Tangier, 1921–25. Knighted, 1924. Minister, Buenos Aires, 1925–27; Ambassador, 1927–29. Privy Councillor, 1927. Retired from the Diplomatic Service, 1930. Conservative MP for Mitcham, 1940–45. Chairman of the British Council, 1941–45.

Even if every effort is made I cannot feel sure that we shall succeed; but I am certain that if we do not make an effort we shall live to see all that we have guarded hitherto, lost.

On April 14, in the first of his new *Daily Telegraph* articles, Churchill commented on the fall of Blum's second Government four days earlier.[1] 'If France broke,' he wrote, 'everything would break, and the Nazi domination of Europe, and potentially of a large part of the world, would seem to be inevitable.' The French Army, he declared, was 'always on the watch', and the new French Government was headed by Edouard Daladier, a 'capable and sincere man' who for nearly two years had been identified 'with the French army and the defence of France'. A stable and firm French Government was essential, he wrote, to the peace of Europe, and he added:

I wonder whether the French people realize how bitter and persistent is the pro-German propaganda in this island? The strongest point, repeatedly made, is that France is on the verge of collapse. She is portrayed as about to go down the same bloody sewer as Spain has done. All the 'Heil Hitler' brigade in London society exploit and gloat over what they are pleased to call 'the Parliamentary impotence of the French democracy'. Thus the amusing game in which French politicians rejoice is turned in deadly fashion to their detriment—and to our common danger.

Fortunately, Churchill wrote, Daladier would receive 'loyal aid' in his task from Léon Blum, who would not fail 'the cause of European freedom'. To Blum himself Churchill wrote that same day:

I have thought much about you in these anxious and trying days, and I feel bound to express to you the gratitude which so many English people cherish towards you for the so great and real advance in the understanding between our two countries which marked your memorable Premierships. It is not for a foreigner, however friendly, to meddle in French politics. But I have never seen the good feeling between Britain and France so strong as during your terms of power.

I am sure that in a private station for a while you will have immense opportunities of carrying forward this great work, so necessary for the rights of the common people in every land, and for the peace and freedom of the world.

As a very old minister now in retirement I thought I might without presumption send these few lines to you. . . .

[1] Léon Blum's second Premiership had lasted only from March 13 to April 10, when Blum was succeeded by Edouard Daladier. At the same time, Georges Bonnet became Foreign Secretary in succession to Joseph Paul-Boncour, while Daladier himself retained the post of War Minister, which he had held since June 1936.

Churchill also wrote to Daladier to congratulate him on coming to power, and to wish him success. His letter continued: 'The time now seems ripe to carry forward those plans for the common safety of our two countries which we talked over together when I had the pleasure to meet you in Paris. You will find the ground well-prepared for you over here; and I do not doubt of success. But strike while the iron is hot.'

On April 16 Neville Chamberlain announced that an Anglo-Italian agreement had just been signed in Rome. In return for the withdrawal of Italian troops from Spain, Britain would recognize Italian sovereignty over Ethiopia. In addition, Italy would reduce the size of her garrison in Libya, and Britain would refrain from further fortifications on the Palestine coast. On April 18 Churchill wrote to Eden: 'It is of course a complete triumph for Mussolini,' and he added:

I think the Anglo-Italian pact is only the first step, and that the second will be an attempt to patch up something even more specious with Germany which will lull the British public, while letting the German armed strength grow, and German designs in the East of Europe develop.

Chamberlain last week told the Executive of the National Union in secret that he 'had not abandoned hopes of similar arrangements with Germany'. They took this rather coldly.

Meanwhile our progress in the Air is increasingly disappointing. . . .

On April 22 Churchill wrote to Philip Guedalla: 'I feel sure that what has happened has done no end of harm in the United States.'

On April 22 Eden wrote to Churchill that he feared the Anglo-Italian agreement would lead to a 'relaxation of national effort'. Churchill was himself much concerned to combat any such mood, and was surprised not to have had any answer from Chamberlain to his air memorandum of March 12. He was also preparing a volume of his past speeches on defence, and on April 27 he asked Hankey if he could include in it both the statements he had made as a member of the two deputations to Baldwin in 1936. 'Looking back now,' he wrote, 'I regret very much that I did not make these two main statements, or the bulk of them, in the House of Commons. They might perhaps then have led to more effective action being taken.'

On April 28, in the second of his *Daily Telegraph* articles, Churchill warned of what he believed were grave set-backs in the pace of aircraft production:

Given an office table, an empty field, and a sufficiency of money and labour, it ought to be possible to produce a steady flow of aircraft from the eighteenth month. It is now the thirty-third month since the Baldwin Government decided to triple the Royal Air Force. Why, then, is there not this copious flow? This remains a mystery to those who had war-time experience. . . .

The Government, though not choosing to equip themselves with emergency powers, have let the Air Ministry enjoy for nearly three years unlimited money and—provided due priorities are given—a superabundant manpower. Yet at the end of the third year of expansion, already tardily begun, we are not overtaking the German monthly outputs. Indeed, if we may credit the allegations which are made more loudly every day, we are at the moment falling back not only relatively but even actually.

These charges must be examined by Parliament at an early date, and it is greatly to be hoped that members will not lack the public spirit necessary to strengthen the hands of the Government in any measures, however drastic, which may be required. . . .

On May 1 Churchill again appealed publicly for greater vigilance in all matters of defence. In the first of a series of political articles for the *News of the World* he argued that it was the scale and scope of Britain's anti-aircraft measures which would be decisive for the country's survival. Nothing must be grudged of money, research or preparations, 'which brings nearer the day when the accursed air-murderer, for such I must judge the bomber of civilian populations, meets a sure doom'.

Churchill's article continued with a plea for bombers to be built in greater quantities, in order to extend the scope of an 'active defence' in wartime:

. . . the greatest safety will be found in having an air force so numerous and excellent that it will beat the enemy's air force in fair fight. It may do this simultaneously in two ways: first, the fighting aeroplanes will rise in the air, meet the bombers, and destroy as many as possible. One may be quite sure that if one in three of the raiding aeroplanes is destroyed at each raid, the raiding will not go on long. Eels are said to get used to skinning; but airmen do not get used to being killed.

Of the even 'more fruitful' policy of bombing the enemy, Churchill wrote:

The attack on the nests from which the hostile vultures come, as well as the attack on the military depots, railway junctions, mobilization centres of the enemy army, if vigorously and successfully maintained, will very soon compel the aggressor State to withdraw their aeroplanes from merely murdering civilians, women and children, the old, the weak and the poor, and come back to the fighting fronts in order to concentrate upon military targets.

Of the bombing of centres of population Churchill declared:

I do not believe in reprisals upon the enemy civilian population. On the contrary, the more they try to kill our women and children, the more we should devote ourselves to killing their fighting men and smashing up the technical apparatus upon which the life of their armies depends. This is far the best way of defending London, and of defending the helpless masses from the bestialities of modern war.

Britain, Churchill wrote, had 'started late in the race', but nevertheless possessed 'great and flexible resources'. Democracy had its own 'moral and intellectual fertility'. Above all, he said, 'we must not despair. The article ended:

I appeal to the readers of the *News of the World*. More than 4,000,000 copies of this article are sold this Sunday, and I am told each may well be read by two or three people, so it may be that ten or twelve millions will read the words I write. If they will only hearken to them and use their influence upon those they meet, upon their political representatives, upon the Government of their country, they will create such an atmosphere of effort and resolve that no Parliament and no Cabinet could fail to do its duty.

These themes and appeals formed the basis of Churchill's public speaking campaign. At Manchester on May 9, at Bristol on May 16, at Chingford on May 23, at Sheffield on May 31 and at Birmingham on June 2 he reiterated, before large and enthusiastic audiences, his concern for a strong Britain and a bold foreign policy.[1] He had been particularly angered in April when Chamberlain negotiated with the Irish Government an end to all British naval rights at Queenstown, Berehaven and Lough Swilly. During the negotiations for the Irish Treaty in 1921, Churchill had himself placed the highest importance on Britain's retention of these naval bases. On May 5, during a debate in the House of Commons, he attacked the decision as 'an improvident

---

[1] In the Far East, Churchill approved the attempt by the Chinese themselves to seek to repel the repeated and violent Japanese attacks, writing in the *Daily Telegraph* on May 26: 'the grand and cardinal event in the Far East is the revival of China. Japan has done for the Chinese people what they could, perhaps, never have done for themselves. It has unified them once more. General Chiang Kai-shek is a national hero, among the most numerous race of mankind. He may well become a world hero, as a patriot and a leader who, amid a thousand difficulties and wants, does not despair of saving China from a base and merciless exploitation. It may thus be that from the opposite side of the earth will come that exemplary discomfiture of a brutal aggression which will cheer the democracies of the Western world and teach them to stand up for themselves while time remains.'

example of appeasement', comparable to the abandonment of Gibraltar or Malta. The House of Commons listened to him with what he later described as 'a patient air of scepticism'. There were frequent, angry interruptions, and his criticisms of Chamberlain were widely resented by his fellow Conservative MPs. Bitterly he told them: 'You are casting away real and important means of security and survival for vain shadows and for ease.'

Among the four million readers of Churchill's article in the *News of the World* was a fellow Conservative MP, Colonel Moore-Brabazon,[1] who wrote to him on May 30: 'I read your article in the News of the World and I must say I was enthralled by it, I really do congratulate you on it. It was absolutely superb, and I am sure many people hundreds of years hence will look back at it and say:—"Here was a man thinking far in advance of his time"—as you often do.' Brabazon also told Churchill that the Directors of Fairey Aviation Company Ltd, whose factory Churchill had visited, were 'staggered at your general knowledge of the subject'.

During the spring of 1938 there was growing German pressure on Czechoslovakia. A series of pronouncements from Berlin championed the rights of the German-speaking minority in Czechoslovakia, about whom Churchill wrote privately to H. C. Vickers on May 7: 'There is no doubt that the Sudeten-Deutsche are the best treated minority in Europe.'

An unexpected opportunity for Churchill to learn of the demands of the Sudeten Germans themselves arose in the first week of May, when Vansittart asked him to meet privately the Sudeten nationalist leader, Conrad Henlein.[2] Churchill gave Henlein lunch at Morpeth Mansions

---

[1] John Theodore Cuthbert Moore-Brabazon, 1884–1964. Educated at Harrow and Trinity College Cambridge. Pioneer motorist and aviator; holder of pilot's Certificate No 1. Won the *Daily Mail* £1,000 for flying a circular mile, 1909. Lieutenant-Colonel in charge of the Royal Flying Corps Photographic Section, 1914–18 (Military Cross, despatches thrice). Conservative MP for Chatham, 1918–29; for Wallasey, 1931–42. Chairman, Air Mails Committee, 1923. Elected to the Other Club, 1936. Minister of Transport, 1940–41. Minister of Aircraft Production, 1941–42. Created Baron, 1942. He published *The Brabazon Story* in 1956.

[2] Conrad Henlein. A schoolteacher by profession. Founded the Sudetendeutsche Heimat-front, 30 September 1933, to replace the banned Nazi Party in Czechoslovakia; renamed the Sudeten German Party (SdP), 1935; Chairman of the Party, 1933–38. Advocated (in a letter to Hitler on 19 November 1937) that not only the Sudetenland, but also the whole of Bohemia should become a part of Germany. Appointed by Hitler to be Reich's Commissioner for the

on May 13. 'His visit is being kept a secret,' Churchill wrote to Archibald Sinclair on May 10, '. . . his wish to come to London to see Van and a few others is a hopeful sign.' Sinclair joined Churchill, Professor Lindemann and Colonel Christie at the lunch. According to the notes taken by Lindemann, Henlein told his hosts that he had never received either orders or even 'recommendations' from Berlin, but that although he himself would accept some form of autonomy for the Sudetens within the Czechoslovak State, many of his followers were 'impatient', and would undoubtedly prefer union with Germany. Pressed to explain the sort of scheme of autonomy which might be 'feasible', Henlein suggested a central Parliament in Prague, with control of foreign policy, defence, finance and communications, and local town and county councils for the Sudetens in which they would exercise 'local autonomy'. In the German-speaking regions, the postal, railway and policy officials 'would of course be German-speaking'. Henlein added: 'The frontier fortresses could be manned by Czech troops, who of course would have unhindered access thereto.'

Churchill at once informed the Czechoslovak Minister, Jan Masaryk,[1] of Henlein's suggestions, with which Masaryk 'professed himself contented'. At the same time, according to Lindemann's notes, it had been made clear to Henlein that if Germany marched against Czechoslovakia, 'France would come in and England would follow'.

Churchill, who sent copies of the Lindemann notes to both Chamberlain and Halifax, subsequently remained faithful to Henlein's proposal of May 13, whereby the territorial integrity of Czechoslovakia would be preserved, and local autonomy granted to the Sudeten Germans within the framework of the Czech State. On May 16, during his plea for collective security at Bristol, Churchill said, as *The Times* reported, that he 'saw no reason why the Sudeten Deutsche should not become trusted and honoured partners in what was, after all, the most progressive and democratic of the new States of Europe'.

The Sudeten Germans themselves appeared to be aware of the nature of Churchill's warning, for, as Colonel Christie wrote to Churchill on May 18:

Sudeten German territories, 1 October 1938. Gauleiter of the Sudetengau, May 1939–May 1945. Captured by the US 7th Army, 9 May 1945; committed suicide on the following day.

[1] Jan Garrigue Masaryk, 1886–1948. Son of Thomas Masaryk. Leader of the Czechoslovak Delegation, Paris Peace Conference, 1919. Czechoslovak Minister to London, 1925–38; resigned after the Munich Conference. Minister of Foreign Affairs, Czechoslovak Government in Exile, 1940–45; in Prague, 1945–48 (Deputy Prime Minister, 1941–45).

Henlein took away with him the firm impression that you incorporated & represented the *real* strength of the British, the intent to tolerate no aggression against the CSR, but at the same time to see fair play given to the SD minority. It seemed to me of utmost importance that Henlein should meet he-men & fighters at this juncture & *not* those wretched defeatists, yes-men whose gutless attitude encourages both ends of the Axis to rev up their demands relentlessly. . . .[1]

The Czech crisis receded momentarily from the public attention after May 16, when Lord Swinton resigned as Secretary of State for Air. Four days earlier, in a stormy debate in the House of Commons, Lord Winterton had defended the Government's air policy on a motion to reduce Lord Swinton's salary. Winterton told the House that the new air scheme would be ready by March 1940, and would consist of 2,370 first-line aircraft in the home forces. During his speech Winterton was continually interrupted by Churchill, Attlee and Sinclair. At one point Churchill asked what had happened to the 1,500 aircraft promised for March 1937: 'We have not completely disposed of that yet,' he insisted. But Winterton had no answer, and although the motion itself was defeated, the debate had shown that there were serious doubts in the House about the actual state of the air programme. Winterton's speech ended, however: 'In passing, I would say to my right Hon Friend the Member for Epping that if the Archangel Gabriel stood at his box and produced an expansion scheme for the present Government, I do not think it would satisfy my right Hon Friend.' To this Churchill replied: 'Considering the many many months my noble friend and I struggled to galvanize the present Government, I think that a little hard. . . .'

Following Swinton's resignation on May 16, many people imagined that in the resultant Cabinet changes Churchill would be given a place. But Chamberlain appointed Sir Kingsley Wood to take Swinton's place, and brought Walter Elliot into the Cabinet as Kingsley Wood's successor at the Ministry of Health. Nor was there to be any Ministry of Supply, although, on May 17, Inskip sought Churchill's views on what such a Ministry should do. In his note on 'W.S.C.'s plan', Inskip pointed out that Churchill saw strategic coordination as different from the work of a Minister 'securing existing programmes & planning British industry'. It was necessary to form a separate department, and to ensure that the chain of responsible authority would 'descend'

---

[1] Ten days later, on May 28, Sir Robert Vansittart wrote to Lord Halifax that Henlein 'is in very bad odour at Berlin today because he wants to negotiate on his London line'.

through the whole of British industry, with design and supply going together. The notes of Churchill's plan continued:

> Progr^{ms} cannot be achieved
> in present atmosphere of
> 'ordinary peace-time
> preparation'
> Don't take *war* powers.
> Declare Emergency Period.
> Legislate Part I Emerg Prep^n
> —II War
> Gliding into war, with
> whole design foreseen

Supply, design and contracts should all be transferred, by instalments, to this new Ministry, Churchill added, and on May 18 Inskip put Churchill's plan to the Cabinet, but without any positive result. Two days later, after Churchill had published his plan in *The Times*, a Cabinet statement was prepared, but not made public, reiterating the Government's view 'of the difficulties of instituting either legislation or any effective control in peace'.

Churchill professed not to be disappointed when no Ministry of Supply was set up, and no other task was found for him. 'I am not at all sure,' he wrote to R. J. Minney[1] on May 20, 'whether I have shown any particular desire to join this Government,' and three days later he wrote to James Watts: 'There is no chance whatever of any action in Parliament being effective. The present majority will remain dumb to the end.' To his friend General Tudor he wrote on May 26: 'We are in an awful mess, and it is the Tory Party, above all others, who have failed in their duty to the country.' To Richard Acland,[2] a Liberal MP since 1935, he wrote that same day: 'The Government have a solid majority, and Chamberlain will certainly not wish to work with me. If of course the foreign situation darkens, something in the nature of a

---

[1] Rubeigh James Minney, 1895–1976. Educated at King's College London. On the Editorial Staff of the *Pioneer*, Allahabad and of the *Englishman*, Calcutta. Represented *The Times* in Calcutta. Worked on the *Daily Express* and *Sunday News*, London. A novelist, he published his first novel in 1921. Editor of *Everybody's Weekly*, 1925–35. Editor of the *Sunday Referee*, 1935–39. Editor, the *Strand Magazine*, 1941–42. In films since 1942. Playwright and biographer. Among his biographies are those of Chaplin (1954), Lord Addison (1958), and Hore-Belisha (1960).

[2] Richard Thomas Dyke Acland, 1906–   . Educated at Rugby and Balliol College Oxford. Unsuccessful Liberal candidate, 1929 and 1931. Liberal MP for Barnstaple, 1935–45. Succeeded his father as 13th Baronet, 1939. Founded the Commonwealth Party during the war. Labour MP for Gravesend, 1947–55. Second Church Estates Commissioner, 1950–51. Lecturer, St Luke's Training College, Exeter, from 1959.

National Government may be forced upon us, but events, and great events alone will rule.'

During his speech at Sheffield on May 31 Churchill declared: 'It is now admitted that there has been a lamentable breakdown and inadequacy in the most vital sphere of all, namely our Air Force and our Air Defences. The Air Minister, Lord Swinton, has been forced to resign, but I will tell you that in my opinion he is one of the least blameworthy among those responsible. He worked night and day. He accomplished a great deal, and his contribution to rearmament was far greater than that of some others who now hold high office of State.'

Throughout June and July Churchill remained vigilant in his efforts to find and to expose all slackness or inefficiency in Britain's defences. He also attended the regular meetings of the Air Defence Research sub-committee. On June 3, at Inskip's invitation, he visited the Austin Shadow Factory near Birmingham, 'a very fine affair', he wrote to Colonel Moore-Brabazon on the following day, 'but what a target, and utterly unprotected. The very first thing they would do would be to send daylight bombers to these places, probably before any declaration of war.' That same day he wrote at length to Hore-Belisha, warning of what he believed to be grave shortages in Britain's anti-aircraft position, and urging him not to commit himself 'to the impossible task of white-washing this horrid scandal'. Of course, Churchill continued, 'you realise that people serving in the existing units are indignant at the failure to supply them with effective arms. They make no secret of the state they are in. The Germans are certainly not making less than three thousand cannon a year, although they have already an enormous accumulation.'

Writing of his visit to the Austin Shadow Factory, Churchill told Hore-Belisha: 'There is no attempt even at camouflage or artificial fog,' while, on the question of Britain's military preparations, he told the Secretary of State for War:

I am assured that the scale of the Expeditionary Force has been steadily reduced in the past few years. Remember, we had fifteen divisions in action before Christmas 1914, and your Army Estimates are far above those of pre-War days.

What I hope above all things to hear from you is that you are preparing the weapons, munitions and equipment for at least twenty divisions. If we should unhappily be drawn into a great war, you will have a million volunteers crowding your recruiting stations in the first few weeks. It will be very bad for all if there are no weapons for them. The new factor of air bombing will infuriate people. . . .

Churchill urged Hore-Belisha to look personally into 'the deficiencies which I alleged existed in the equipment, even of the Guards', and he added:

Of one battalion it is said there are only five Bren guns out of forty, and one anti-tank rifle out of four. The rest are represented, or were a month ago, by coloured rags on sticks. It is incomprehensible to me that such deficiencies can exist now that we are at the end of the third year of re-armament.

'The fact,' Churchill wrote, 'that none of this is yr fault shld give you the greater power to rectify it.' Hore-Belisha replied on June 23. The information which Churchill had obtained, he wrote, 'does not accurately represent facts'. He himself was putting all his energies 'into accelerating production', and he wished to assure Churchill 'that everything that can be done will be done'.

Churchill was not impressed by Hore-Belisha's assurances, particularly as his son-in-law, Duncan Sandys, had told him of grave deficiencies in the anti-aircraft defences of London itself. On June 8 Brigadier-General Edmonds, his former literary assistant, wrote from the Historical Section of the Committee of Imperial Defence: 'Providence looks after us and confounds our enemies, but expects "works" as well as faith. To ensure peace we must be strong.' But many people took it for granted that Britain was already strong, and even the *News of the World*, which had on May 1 published Churchill's major warning, began to assure its readers that all was well. On June 5 Churchill was 'astonished' to read an article on these lines, writing in a 'private & secret' letter to Major Percy Davies:[1]

There is at the present time an almost total absence of defence, apart from the RAF, for our cities and vulnerable points. We have not got a dozen modern anti-aircraft guns in the country. The 3·7 guns which are modern, are now trickling out in small numbers every month, but the total order is itself on a scale hopelessly below our requirements. The Germans have actually between 3,000 and 4,000 modern anti-aircraft guns, all made since 1933. While I would not say the War-time relined 3″ gun is of no value, it is not comparable with modern weapons.[2]

---

[1] David Percy Davies, 1892–1946. Educated at Llandovery College. Joined the editorial staff of the *News of the World*, 1914. Assistant editor of *Tit Bits*, 1914. Major commanding 12 Corps Cyclist Battalion in Italy and France, 1916–18. Captured by the Germans on the western front, April 1918. Called to the Bar 1919. Returned to the editorial staff of the *News of the World*, 1919; deputy editor, 1933; member of the Board, 1935; editor from 1941 until his death. High Sheriff of Glamorgan, 1943–44.

[2] Eleven weeks earlier, on February 16, Sir Samuel Hoare, who, as Home Secretary, had been given the responsibility for Air Raid Precautions, told the Cabinet: 'So far from increasing our output in relation to other countries we were going back. The same considerations applied to anti-aircraft armaments. The key point in AA artillery, for example,

As for the Royal Air Force, Churchill added:

> . . . it is at present less than one-third of the German Air Force, and the rate of production is at present less than one-third. Only about half the Squadrons are equipped with modern machines, and the German fast bombers are so fast that we have not a sufficient margin of speed to catch them, except under very lucky circumstances. In any case we should be heavily outnumbered.

'The Germans know our position very accurately,' Churchill ended, 'and it is our own people who are living in a "Fool's Paradise".'

Four days later, in an article in the *Daily Telegraph* on June 9, Churchill commented on Inskip's statement of May 30 that the Government would introduce compulsory national service in time of war. Such an announcement, Churchill wrote, while welcome in itself, 'ought not to have been thrown out casually to an empty House in an unimportant Debate', but ought to have been made by the Prime Minister himself 'with all formality, in words carefully chosen, and upon a great occasion'. Only by such means could it have exercised 'a beneficial effect upon the European situation'. The prospect of 'an immense British army cast into the scales', Churchill believed, was one of the greatest deterrents to an aggressor, 'and one of the surest bulwarks of peace'. The Government should at once devise 'a scientific, fair, and equal plan' of national service which could be put into operation on the outbreak of war.[1]

Colonel Pakenham-Walsh, who was preparing the maps for Churchill's final *Marlborough* volume, sought to encourage him in his efforts to press for greater army preparedness, writing to him on June 18:

> As a serving soldier one cannot say much, but many like myself, who are perhaps not fully 'in the know', are very disturbed at the situation, and we can only pray that war will not come till we are much more ready. Even when we get equipment we have to learn to use it, and develop suitable tactics. One cannot do everything by imagination.

---

was the 3·7-inch gun. Up to now there was not a single gun with units. He said this not in criticism, but merely as stating a fact. In the next few months we should have a few. The production of the larger gun (4·5-inch) still remained in the dim and distant future. In addition to that, the general defensive position was deteriorating every month.'

[1] In his article Churchill also pressed for measures which would ensure 'social justice' in the event of war, telling his readers that any plan of national service 'would naturally have to be accompanied by legislation "to take the profit out of war". . . .', and he continued: 'The idea of large numbers of men being made liable to be sent abroad on military service is not compatible with others remaining at home to pile up inflated wartime profits, under conditions when free competition is largely suspended.'

During May and June Churchill received important information on French and German military strength from the new French Prime Minister, Edouard Daladier, to whom he wrote on June 6: 'You may be sure I shall use it only with the greatest discretion, in our common interests.' Churchill sent Daladier's figures to Desmond Morton, who commented that in his view the German Air Force was already expanding more rapidly than the French figures indicated. Together with his letter of June 6, Churchill sent Daladier a note based on Morton's comments, asking Daladier to pencil in 'any case where you think I am in error'. The note pointed out that not only were Germany's 36 regular divisions, and 4 armoured divisions, now strengthened by 12 Austrian divisions 'whose formations are well-matured', but that by April 1940 Germany would possess at least 108 'well equipped and armed divisional formations', together with a 'reservoir of trained men' the equivalent of a further 36 divisions. Replying twelve days later, on June 18, Daladier said he was entirely in agreement with Churchill's figures.

Inside Whitehall, Churchill's pressure was still resented, leading to a further acrimonious dispute during the summer with Hankey, Inskip and Tizard. When Churchill had pressed Chamberlain on March 12, and again on June 4, to comment on his list of Air Force deficiencies, Chamberlain had declined to do so, and on June 9 Churchill had been provoked to write to Kingsley Wood about the work of the Air Defence Research sub-committee:

I regret that Professor Lindemann and I accepted Baldwin's invitation to take part in these studies. I am sure that with the support we had from Austen Chamberlain and the Liberal and Labour Parties in the House, we could have enforced more attention to this subject, than by being members of these committees.

The secret information to which we became parties, although going very little further than what we knew ourselves, imposed silence.

'In all my experience of public offices,' Churchill added, 'I have never seen anything like the slow-motion picture which the work of this Committee has presented; and I fear it is typical of a whole group of committees which have been in existence during these vital years.' His letter continued:

One could not have devised a better method of soothing this whole matter down and laying it politely in repose than the elaborate process which has been followed. It proved impossible to get any experiments upon new types of shells carried out except at such lengthy intervals and on so petty a scale as to be futile.

Professor Lindemann, who has a far greater insight in this sphere than anyone I know, was very soon turned out of the Technical Committee for pressing more vigorous action . . .

So far as the ADR Committee is concerned, there seems to be a complete lack of driving power. The final result is that we have nothing that will be of any effective use in the next two years, when much either in war or humiliation may be in store for us all.

Churchill then appealed direct to Kingsley Wood:

Now that you have succeeded Swinton, can we not hope for a renewed effort, for more readiness to carry experiments forward from day to day, and more resolve to take action leading to more tangible results. I earnestly hope so.

When you look into this subject yourself, you will no doubt be given excellent answers to these complaints and quite enough to baffle protests in Parliament, but this will not remove the glaring reproach that we have nothing to shield ourselves with at the present moment. . . .

Churchill's relations with the Admiralty, and in particular with Chatfield and Henderson, were not only amicable but constructive. On June 15 Chatfield personally took Churchill to Portland to show him the new submarine location system, Asdic, which was then a matter of the strictest secrecy. That night Churchill slept on board the flagship, after a long discussion with the Commander-in-Chief of the Home Fleet, Sir Charles Forbes,[1] and on the following morning, accompanied by Chatfield, he went to sea on a destroyer to watch, until late afternoon, an Asdic trial. 'I could see and hear the whole process, he later recalled in his memoirs, 'which was the Sacred Treasure of the Admiralty, and in the culture of which for a whole generation they had faithfully persevered.' After his return to London that night Churchill wrote to Chatfield:

I have reflected constantly on all that you showed me, and I am sure the nation owes the Admiralty, and those who have guided it, an inestimable debt for the faithful effort sustained over so many years which has, as I feel convinced, relieved us of one of our great dangers.

What surprised me was the clarity and force of the indications. I had

---

[1] Charles Morton Forbes, 1880–1960. Entered the Navy, 1894. Served at Jutland (DSO). Director of Naval Ordnance, 1925–28. Third Sea Lord and Controller of the Navy, 1932–34. Vice-Admiral, 1st Battle Squadron, 1934–36. Knighted, 1935. Commander-in-Chief, Home Fleet, 1938–40; Plymouth, 1941–43.

imagined something almost imperceptible, certainly vague and doubtful. I never imagined that I should hear one of those creatures asking to be destroyed, both orally and literally. It is a marvellous system and achievement.

In the second week of June, Churchill had learnt that Hankey was to retire as Secretary to the Cabinet, after more than twenty-two years as the Cabinet's senior civil servant. He and Churchill had worked together over an even longer period, dating back to 1912, when Churchill had been First Lord. On June 15 he wrote to Hankey:

My dear Maurice,

Although we have been in late years divided by differences of view about national safety and the measures to procure it, I cannot allow the momentous announcement of your impending retirement to pass without writing you these few lines of earnest tribute to the magnitude of the services you have rendered in the great days which are gone. At several crises of mortal danger your personal initiative brought about the measures needful to success. The imprint of your long work upon the structure of National Defence, and also upon the workings of the Cabinet system, will form a definite chapter in our history—unless that history is about to be cut short—a fate which even in my most anxious moods I still believe can be averted.

I look back with pleasure upon our own association from the day when Ottley came to me at the Admiralty to tell me about the qualities of a young Captain of Marines who above all men was qualified to guide the CID, and when old Fisher sang your praises in his vibrant tones.[1] I must thank you for many acts of courtesy to me throughout this period—generation-long—when you have so tirelessly discharged your immense function, and formed the chain of continuity which united phases and ministers across the gulfs of party. I wish you all contentment and good fortune in your easier life of rest after unexampled toils.

Hankey replied on June 16:

My dear Winston,

Your letter has touched me more than I can express. What inimitable power you have to touch the hearts of men.

I am a little upset at your suggestion that we have been divided by differences over national defence. That we have been divided, or rather parted, I agree, but that has been due more to my position as a Public Servant than to fundamental differences of opinion, which a frank talk would probably have reconciled.

A few nights ago I dined alone with Lloyd George. He told me he had

---

[1] In 1912, when Churchill was First Lord of the Admiralty, Sir Charles Ottley was the Secretary to the Committee of Imperial Defence (a position he had held since 1907), and Lord Fisher the former First Sea Lord (the position he had held from 1904 to 1910, and was to hold again from October 1914 to May 1915).

avoided me lately, because he was a frequent critic of the Government and had felt it might be embarrassing to me to meet. In the same way, my dear Winston, I have avoided you! For me, in the complete confidence of the Cabinet, their trusted servant, with all their inside knowledge, to discuss the sort of question which you and I can't help discussing, with an intimate friend of many years standing, who is a critic of the Government, was I felt too difficult. I know that you know a lot. But I never know how much you know! . . .

My code you know. I let my chiefs know what I think, but when they have taken their decision, as a public servant, as part of the official machine, I give all the help I can in carrying out their policy.

But all this has never abated my admiration for you nor my affection. And that is why I am so deeply moved by your all too kind references to my past services and to our long and profitable association.

In a few weeks I shall be quit of my official shackles, and then we can meet on the old terms and I hope we shall.

Hankey was not due to retire until July 28. Before he left, he was caught up in one final dispute involving Churchill, of which Churchill himself knew nothing. For some while, Sir Henry Tizard had been 'boiling with indignation', as Hankey explained to Inskip on June 20, as a result of Churchill's criticisms of the work of the Air Defence Research sub-committee in his letter to Kingsley Wood of June 9. Hankey added that while he believed it would be wisest to keep Churchill on the Committee, it was essential that his 'intolerable accusations' be answered, although, as he told Inskip, Churchill's letter was most probably 'prompted by Professor Lindemann, and the latter is in Churchill's entire confidence and very likely sees our secret papers'. Hankey added: 'I cannot prove it. Nevertheless I do not think the moment has come for calling Mr Churchill's bluff openly.' On June 24 Hankey wrote direct to Chamberlain: 'what might interest you in particular is the material available, not only for rebutting Mr Churchill's allegations, but for counter-attacking him'. Hankey added:

Obviously the moment has not yet come to join issue with him because it would not yet be in the public interest to divulge the epoch-making inventions that have been adopted. But the time is not very distant, now that they are coming into use, when they will leak out. Then the Government will be in a position to deliver a withering counter-blast if need be.

In the meantime the obvious tactic is to play for time.

Among themselves the Air Ministry officials were against giving Churchill any chance to expand his questionings. In the draft answer to Churchill's letter of June 9, one draftsman had intended Kingsley

Wood to invite Churchill to send 'any suggestions that you may have for possible new lines of research', but on seeing this draft, Inskip advised striking out this phrase, and pointed out that if it remained 'Churchill might suggest something quite fantastic and the Secretary of State for Air does not want to be obliged to consider anything Churchill throws up'. Sir Henry Tizard was openly personal in his reaction, noting on June 22:

I do most strongly resent Mr Churchill's continual pin pricking, especially as he is in a position which enables him to use large and poisonous pins quite irresponsibly. The effect of these pin pricks is that very many busy people, both inside and outside the Government Service, who are devoting them-selves to the solution of the problems instead of devoting themselves to criticism of people who are trying to solve them, are forced to do a great deal of unnecessary work.

If it were not for this irritating feature of Mr Churchill's attacks his remarks would be highly entertaining. He says that in all his experience he has never seen anything like the slow-motion picture which the work of the ADR Committee has presented. Contrast the development of the last few years with the state of affairs when Mr Churchill was First Lord of the Admiralty before the War. As a result of his total lack of real scientific imagination and foresight we entered the War without any defence what-soever against submarines, and without any method of locating them.

It is well known that the Country only narrowly escaped defeat and 'humiliation' because of this, and that the defeat was only avoided by (a) the convoy system which was opposed by the Admiralty, and (b) the efforts of scientists in developing means for locating submarines. I rather fancy there is evidence to show that Mr Churchill did very little to promote these efforts.[1]

After studying these various comments, Kingsley Wood finally replied to Churchill on June 24. He himself, he wrote, had been 'a good deal impressed' by the research work in progress, and by radar in particular. His letter ended with a caution:

I am a little tempted to take up your statement that you have never in the past known anything so slow as the work of this Committee, but I hope very

---

[1] Churchill had in fact been much concerned about submarine warfare while he was First Lord of the Admiralty. At a meeting of the Committee of Imperial Defence on 11 July 1912 he had challenged the then current view that the submarine would principally be used as a defensive vessel, telling his colleagues: 'If ever there was a vessel in the world whose services to the defensive will be great, and which is a characteristic weapon for the defence, it is the submarine. But the German development of that vessel, from all the information we can obtain, shows that it is intended to turn even this weapon of defence into one of offence, that is to say, they are building not the smaller classes which will be useful for the defence of their somewhat limited coast-line, but the large classes which would be capable of sudden operation at a great distance from their base across the sea.'

much that it will not be necessary for us to go into past history, and that we shall be able to work together to secure the maximum drive behind the experiments on which we are now engaged, and any further experiments which may be necessary to initiate new lines of development.

Churchill replied a month later, on July 26: 'When I think of what might have been done in this period to make us all safe, I find it difficult to express my grief.' He would, he added, be glad to continue to send Kingsley Wood further suggestions 'to help you', for he was sure 'you will not turn and ask me, under penalty, where I got my information from!'

On June 24 George Harrap published the selection of the speeches which Churchill had made on defence and foreign affairs in the ten years since 1928. Entitled *Arms and the Covenant*, the volume had been both suggested and edited by Randolph, and was welcomed by his friends. 'We seem to be more than ever a "Nation of Amateurs",' General Edmonds wrote on publication day, 'especially at the War Office and at the CID.' On the following day Desmond Morton wrote to thank Churchill for the volume, and added:

It is a memory to me of years of struggle and not a little bitterness, as it must in some ways be to you. But you, and in an infinitely less degree I, are not the first to have told the truth to the people and become heartily unpopular for having done so. Modern Governments, whether it be that of an Autocrat or a Party Caucus, which Randolph rightly spurns in his able Preface, hate to be told uncomfortable truths. To that extent both are intensely human. But whether they recognise the truth and mend their ways or reject it, both have the habit of crucifying the prophet of truth or, if this less virile epoch shrinks at such drastic action, they exterminate him with a gas cloud—of propaganda.

However, they have not silenced you yet, thank God, so there is some hope for the Empire still.

'If only our rearmament were more real,' Morton added, 'and our political leaders more truly enthusiastic in regard to it.'[1]

At the end of June, Duncan Sandys' worries about London's lack of

---

[1] *Arms and the Covenant* cost 18/-. Of the 5,000 copies that were printed, only 3,381 were sold at the original price. The book was reissued in June 1940, price 7/6, when a further 1,382 copies were sold. The South African writer Sarah Gertrude Millin, whom Churchill had met during her visit to England that summer, wrote on 15 December 1938, 'The book reads like a toll & knell of doom. All that heartens me is that you yourself, as I saw, have still more heart than any other person I have met in England.'

adequate anti-aircraft defences led to a serious Parliamentary dispute. On June 17 he had sent Hore-Belisha the draft of a question which he wished to ask on London's air defences. As the question was clearly based on secret information, Hore-Belisha, with Churchill's approval, told Sandys to call on the Attorney-General, Sir David Somervell. This Sandys did on June 23, and again on June 24. Somervell told Sandys, as Sandys later declared, that unless he disclosed the name of his informant, he would be liable to prosecution under the Official Secrets Act of 1920. On June 28 Sandys unfolded this story in the House of Commons, and asked for a Select Committee of the House to look into the applicability of the Official Secrets Act to members of the House in the discharge of their Parliamentary duties. That same day Mrs Pearman, who had been forced by illness to leave Chartwell, wrote to Churchill from her home at Edenbridge:

> I am delighted to read in today's paper of the stand Mr Sandys is making (and of course you behind him, as I can guess) over the Official Secrets Act. Every shock the Government has of this kind brings to light the appalling lethargy over defence preparations of which they are guilty. I wish you *every success* in your fight, and only wish I were there to help you.

On June 28 Churchill wrote to Lord Hugh Cecil: 'The fur is likely to fly,' and on the following day Sandys informed the House that, in his capacity as a junior officer in the Territorial Army, he had received orders to appear in uniform before the Military Court of Inquiry. This, he submitted, was a 'gross breach' of the privileges of the House. His submission was at once upheld, and a Committee of Privileges set up. It reported on the following day that a breach of privileges had indeed been committed, and on June 30 the House debated a motion to set up a Select Committee to enquire into Sandys' original complaint. The motion was supported by Attlee and Sinclair, as well as by Churchill, who commented caustically that an Act devised to protect the national defence should not be used to shield Ministers who had neglected national defence. The motion was accepted without dissent. 'I hear Winston is in the brightest spirits over it,' Oliver Harvey noted in his diary on July 2.

Within a few days, however, it emerged that Sandys had not in fact been summoned by the Military Court of Inquiry, but had been ordered to attend the court by Eastern Command. This detail, small in itself, invalidated the decision of the Committee of Privileges. There was at once a demand for a new enquiry, and a lengthy correspondence began on the legal aspects. 'I have the impression,' Sir John Simon wrote to Chamberlain on July 14, 'that Winston & Co are getting thoroughly sick of this business and would not be sorry to see it dropped provided, of course, that they escape the discredit which may come to them.' The matter was finally left in the hands of the Select Committee, whose enquiry was expected to last well into the winter.[1]

Churchill's mood was now one of increasing resignation, as well as pessimism as to the chances of peace. On July 4 he wrote to Anthony Crossley:

It is curious how one's mood changes. In the Spring of 1936, or better still the Autumn of 1935, I should have esteemed it a great privilege to help in the work of rearmament, but now the whole scene has changed. Much has been done, much can never be done. A great deal more is being tried, and I cannot feel that the particular knowledge I possessed in those days is required at the present time. I am, therefore, quite content with my corner seat.

At the end of June Churchill again made public his concern for the future of Czechoslovakia. Writing in the *Daily Telegraph* on June 23 he warned Germany that if attacked, Czechoslovakia would not be left to struggle alone. France, Russia and eventually Britain would be drawn in to help her. The Sudeten Germans, he wrote, must also realize that their future would be far more secure inside a tolerant Czechoslovakia than 'swallowed whole by Berlin and reduced to shapeless pulp by those close-grinding mandibles of the Gestapo'. To the young Lord Birkenhead[2] Churchill had written on the previous day of the Czech Sudeten search for a compromise: 'if the negotiations break down, it will almost certainly be because of malignant outside

[1] In an anonymous paragraph which Churchill himself wrote for the *Evening Standard* Londoner's Diary on September 1 he declared: 'Although the report of the Sandys' case is long delayed and the issues are over-clouded by larger matters, it is well to repeat and inculcate the definite principle upon which Parliament, the Press and the Public will unite, namely, that the Official Secrets Act was intended for spies, crooks, traitors and traffickers in official information, and should never be invoked unless there is a prima facie case on these lines against anyone, be he journalist, Member of Parliament, or merely man-in-the-street.'

[2] Frederick Winston Furneaux Smith, 1907–1975. Only son of the 1st Earl of Birkenhead, to whose earldom he succeeded in 1930. Educated at Eton and Christ Church Oxford. Parliamentary Private Secretary to Lord Halifax (when Foreign Secretary), 1938–39. Joined the 53rd Anti-Tank Regiment, 1938. Captain, 1940; Major, 1942; Political Intelligence Department, Foreign Office, 1942; British Military Mission to the Yugoslav Partisans, 1944–45. Biographer of his father (1935), of Strafford (1938), of Lord Charwell (1961), of Lord Halifax (1965), of Walter Monckton (1969), of Kipling (unpublished) and of Churchill (unfinished). Churchill's godson.

interference'. Unknown to anyone outside his secret circle, Hitler was already contemplating a dramatic outcome. 'I will decide to take action against Czechoslovakia,' he had informed General Keitel[1] on June 18, 'only if I am firmly convinced, as in the case of the demilitarized zone and the entry into Austria, that France will not march, and that therefore England will not intervene.'

On July 6, in a further article in the *Daily Telegraph*, Churchill drew attention to the terrible events which had taken place in Austria since its annexation by Germany. 'It is easy to ruin and persecute the Jews,' he wrote, 'to steal their private property; to drive them out of every profession and employment; to fling a Rothschild into a prison or a sponging-house; to compel Jewish ladies to scrub the pavements; and to maroon clusters of helpless refugees on islands in the Danube;[2] and these sports continue to give satisfaction.' It was part of the policy of German Nazism, Churchill added, 'to treat with exemplary rigour all persons of German race who have not identified themselves with Nazi interests and ambitions'.

Questions of defence remained throughout the summer uppermost in Churchill's mind; on July 9 Wing-Commander Anderson sent him a large map showing the exact location of all RAF aerodromes, landing grounds, bombing ranges, seaplane stations, seaplane moorings and aerodromes under construction. The map also showed the boundaries of the different air commands. Speaking in the House of Commons on July 11, Churchill spoke of his concern about the anti-aircraft programme. On July 12 Colonel Pakenham-Walsh, who was at that very moment at an anti-aircraft training camp, wrote to thank him for his

---

[1] Wilhelm Keitel, 1882–1946. Entered the Saxon Artillery, 1901. Seriously wounded on the western front, September 1914. In 1925 he entered the Government Department designed to replace the General Staff (forbidden by the Versailles Treaty). Head of Army Organization, German General Staff, 1929–32. Chief of the Combined Defence Staff, 1935–38. Married (as his second wife) a daughter of Field-Marshal von Blomberg, 1937. Head of the Armed Forces Office, 1938. One of the twelve Generals created Field-Marshal by Hitler on 19 July 1940. Opposed the conspirators at the time of the anti-Hitler plot, July 1944. One of the signatories who ratified the final German act of surrender in Berlin on 9 May 1945. At his interrogation by the Allies in August 1945 he declared: 'At the bottom of my heart I was a loyal shield-bearer for Adolf Hitler'. Sentenced to death at Nuremberg, 1 October 1946; hanged, October 16.

[2] Following the German annexation of Austria, several hundred Austrian Jews, fleeing southwards across the Danube, had been refused entry into both Czechoslovakia and Hungary, and had been marooned on marshy islands. A report in the *Daily Telegraph* on 2 April 1938 told of 35 such Jews, who were driven back into Austria by the Hungarian authorities, and were at once imprisoned by the Nazis. A further group of refugees were detained at the Yugoslav frontier. All had been deprived of all their property, cash and valuables by the Austrian authorities. Churchill kept this report in his private files.

speech, and adding: 'It is no use the country living in a fool's paradise.'

Churchill and Anderson were right to be worried. At a meeting of the Supply Committee of the Committee of Imperial Defence on June 27, Air Vice-Marshal Welsh[1] pointed out that work on war potential could even now not be embarked upon as the Air Ministry wished, because they 'had been awaiting instructions as to a new hypothesis' from the Cabinet. Welsh added that 'on Lord Weir's advice, the Air Ministry had issued instructions that work should be limited to those programmes, and that work on the war potential should be deferred till a later date'. Later in the discussion the Chairman, Sir Arthur Robinson, himself pointed out 'that we were still a long way short of capacity to meet the present programmes, let alone of the war potential'.

At a Cabinet meeting on July 20, Duff Cooper protested strongly against the Cabinet decision of February 16 to ration the service departments. During the course of an anguished appeal, he pointed out that this rationing continued in spite of a Budget surplus of £20 million and the addition of a further sixpence on the income tax, and went on to warn his Cabinet colleagues that if it was believed by the House that 'all was not going well, and that, owing to financial considerations, the Government were rejecting the advice of their naval experts as to the minimum needed for security, there would be such a storm in the House of Commons that the Government could not hope to survive'.

On July 14 Churchill and Lindemann met the Gauleiter of Danzig, Herr Foerster.[2] As leader of the Nazi Party in the Free City, Foerster had long demanded the city's re-unification with Germany, from which it had been separated by the Treaty of Versailles. 'He did not make a bad impression on me,' Churchill wrote to Halifax two days later,

---

[1] William Lawrie Welsh, 1891–1962. On active service, 1917–18 (Croix de Guerre). Surveyed and pioneered the air route from Jerusalem to Baghdad, 1921. Director of Organization, Air Ministry, 1934–37. Air Member for Supply and Organization on the Air Council, 1937–40. Air Officer Commanding Technical Training Command, 1940–41; Flying Training Command, 1941–42. Commanded RAF operating with Allied Forces in north-west Africa, 1942. Head of the RAF Delegation, Washington, 1943–44.

[2] Albert Foerster. Born in Fürth in 1902. A Catholic. Apprenticed in banking, but dismissed because of his Nazi affiliations. Ortsgruppenführer (Local Group Leader) of the Nazi Party in Fürth, 1925–30. Gauleiter of Danzig, 1930–45. Member of the Reichstag, 1930; Prussian Councillor, 1933. Editor of Der Vorposten. Imprisoned for life by the Polish Government, 1948. Reported killed in Danzig Military Prison, 1953.

'though I am told he is "a tough".' The first topic which Churchill and Foerster discussed was that of the Jews. According to Churchill's memorandum of the conversation:

I remarked that I was glad they had not introduced the Anti-Jewish laws in Dantzig.[1] Herr Foerster said the Jewish problem was not acute in Dantzig, but he was anxious to know whether this type of legislation in Germany would prevent an understanding with England. I replied that it was a hindrance and an irritation, but probably not a complete obstacle to a working agreement, though it might be to comprehension. He appeared to attach great importance to this point. . . .[2]

Foerster had gone on to urge Churchill to visit Hitler, but as Churchill recorded:

I replied that it would be difficult to carry on a useful conversation between an all-powerful Dictator and a private individual, and asked whether August and September would not be unhealthy months to visit Germany. He replied that nobody in Germany was thinking of war; that they had immense social and cultural plans which it would take them years to work out: that the Party Meeting took place in September, and that there was no question of incidents or serious complications. Returning to this point later, his interpreter, Herr Noé[3] said the situation was similar to 1914, when no one in Germany thought of war, but everyone in England feared it. To this I replied that we had unfortunately been right.

Churchill went on to tell Foerster that the Czechoslovak problem ought to be settled 'within the framework' of the Czechoslovak State, and that both England and France were already making 'every effort to persuade the Prague Government to agree'. Foerster then spoke of

---

[1] In 1924 there were 4,678 Jews in Danzig (protected by the League of Nations minority protection rules). But in 1937 Foerster had dismissed almost all the professional Jews from their practices (doctors, lawyers etc). More than 2,000 Jews had fled to Poland by early 1938. On 12 and 14 November 1938 two synagogues were burnt down and others desecrated; many shops and homes were looted. More Jews fled, and by September 1939 only 1,200 remained, mostly elderly people. Of these, only 22 Jews (all partners of mixed marriages) survived the war; the rest were sent by the Nazis to concentration camps, and murdered.

[2] On July 20 Sir Robert Waley Cohen wrote to Churchill: 'We have all been exceedingly anxious about the situation of the persecuted Jewish community in Danzig and I noticed a statement in the Press that you have been seeing the Gauleiter of that unhappy city. I know how much you will have wished to try to say something to him about the cruelties and persecutions which the Nazis are introducing there and I wonder whether you would be willing to tell me something of your talk with the Gauleiter?' Three days later Churchill sent Waley Cohen a copy of his memorandum, noting on his letter: 'I always see these Germans when they ask.'

[3] Ludwig Noé. Born in the Rhineland, 1871. Doctor of Mechanical Engineering. Professor at the Technical College, Danzig, 1919–39. Consul-General in Danzig for the Finnish Government, and a Director of the Danziger Werff. President of the International Shipbuilding and Engineering Company, Danzig.

Russian aerodromes in Czechoslovakia 'from which Berlin could be assailed in half-an-hour'. Churchill replied that in his view 'it would be quite possible as part of the general European settlement for England and France to engage to come to the help of Germany with all their power, if she were the victim of an unprovoked attack by Russia, through Czechoslovakia or otherwise'. Churchill's note of the conversation ended:

Herr F. said he could see no real points of dispute between England and Germany: that if England and Germany would only agree together they could divide the world between them. (This latter remark the interpreter thought it wiser not to translate.)

On July 21, after his return to Danzig, Professor Noé wrote to thank Churchill on his and Foerster's behalf for 'such a thorough conversation'. Five days later Churchill replied sternly:

I am quite sure that any crossing of the Czechoslovakian frontier by German troops would lead to a general war. The French would certainly march and, in my opinion, England would be drawn in. Such a war would be a most terrible catastrophe, as it would last until all the great nations were utterly ruined and exhausted.

The feeling in the United States against Germany is now far stronger than it was even in 1914. In fact, there never has been in time of peace so fierce a feeling against any European country. It seems to me very likely that the United States would not wait so long this time before coming in themselves.[1] Thus what we should see would be a world struggle in which numbers would be once more heavily against Germany.

Therefore, I am especially glad to learn from you and your friend that there is no thought of military violence being used against Czechoslovakia.

Churchill believed that his firm speaking would make an impression on Gauleiter Foerster and Professor Noé. But at the end of July he received evidence that his firmness in speaking earlier to Conrad Henlein had not been so successful. On July 28 Shiela Grant Duff wrote to him:

I am very disturbed by the use which the Germans and Sudeten Germans are making of your words and actions. They claim to have your support against the Czechs and this is used by the more extreme to force the more

---

[1] On August 4 Churchill wrote in the *Daily Telegraph* of how, in the United States, despite strong isolationist feeling, the evils of Nazism had been much publicized, with the result that 'a sombre antagonism to tyranny and aggression in all their various forms is steadily growing'. His article ended: 'It would be foolish of the European democracies, in their military arrangements, to count on any direct aid from the United States. It would be still more foolish for war-making forces in the Dictator Governments of Europe to ignore or treat with contempt this slow but ceaseless marshalling of United States opinion around the standards of freedom and tolerance.'

moderate to raise their claims. You will remember telling me that Herr Henlein had shown himself to be most moderate in his conversation with you. . . . Since his return to Prague, he has in fact raised his original demands. The explanation is partly that Herr Henlein is not a free agent, (and therefore it is of no account that he himself is not an ardent nazi), partly that he is apt to tell a different story in different places, partly that the Henlein party, like any other political party, is out to get the most it can.

You are the one British statesman of whom the Germans are afraid. If you are conciliated, they consider that they can expect much greater support from the British Government whom they think are afraid. . . .

The Czechs recognise you to be the bravest and most outspoken of British statesmen and very strongly opposed to the German advance. The fact that in the Czech–German conflict you stress the acceptability of the *German* claims and the necessity for the *Czechs* to give way still further is interpreted in many Czech and German circles to mean that our armed forces are catastrophically weak and that therefore we will surrender Prague to the Germans rather than fight.

The Czechs, for whom it is a matter of life and death in any case, whether they fight or not, will fight even without us, therefore any intimation which we give to the Germans that we will not fight, only increases the likelihood of a German attack.

'I am told,' Shiela Grant Duff added, 'the only thing to do if one meets a grizzly bear and has no gun, is to wave at him with an umbrella. Yours is the biggest umbrella in the country. . . .'

In the third week of July, when King George VI paid a State visit to Paris, the French Government invited Churchill and his wife as special guests. They attended the principal State functions, including the Elysée banquet on the evening of July 19 when Clementine Churchill sat next to General Pétain,[1] the military review at Versailles on the afternoon of July 21, and the fête at the Quai d'Orsay that same evening. Churchill's daughter Mary later recalled: 'Papa was very down on his political luck. His barometer was very low. But he was highly regarded by the French.'

Throughout the spring and summer of 1938 Churchill spent as much

[1] Henri Philippe Benoni Omer Joseph Pétain, 1856–1951. Commanded an Infantry Regiment, August 1914; an Army Corps, October 1914; the 2nd Army, June 1915. In charge at the siege of Verdun, 1916. Chief of the General Staff, April 1917. Commander-in-Chief, May 1917–November 1918. Vice-President of the Supreme War Council, 1920–30. War Minister, 1934. Ambassador in Madrid, 1939–40. Prime Minister, 16 June 1940; he negotiated the armistice with Germany, 22 June 1940. Chief of State, 1940–44. Condemned to death after the liberation of France, 14 August 1945; the sentence was commuted to life imprisonment.

time as possible at Chartwell, where he worked to complete his final *Marlborough* volume. A formidable team was assembled, with Deakin travelling both in England and in Europe in search of new materials. Working at her own home, Mrs Pearman organized with C. C. Wood the frequent, and at times daily exchange of material to and from the printers. Early in May, Pakenham-Walsh had been put in charge of preparing the maps and plans, while in July Commander Owen had provided notes about the fleet at the time of the accession of George I.

For several months, work on the *Marlborough* volume had gone parallel with work on the *History of the English-Speaking Peoples*. Here too expert advice was sought, and on July 4 Churchill had asked the Keeper of the London Museum, Mortimer Wheeler,[1] to visit Chartwell and lecture on early Britain. 'Your audience,' he explained, 'would be attentive and select, Mr Deakin and me!' To Keith Feiling, Churchill wrote on July 10:

I have definitely plunged into the 'English Speaking Peoples' and am now rollicking with the 'Piltdown Man', Cassivalanus, Julius Caesar, the Scribe Gildas, the Venerable Bede and other hoary figures. How to make anything out of this that is (a) readable, (b) original, (c) valuable and (d) true, is known only to the presiding genius of Britain who has not yet imparted his secrets to Yours most sincerely, Winston S. Churchill.

During August Churchill discussed the technical details of his new book with a director of Cassell & Company, Desmond Flower,[2] and on August 12 he wrote to Flower's father, Newman Flower: 'At last I send you herewith the first tentative and provisional instalment of the new book. It comprises the first and part of the second chapters.' In a letter to Lord Halifax eight days later Churchill wrote of how he was at that moment 'horribly entangled with the Ancient Britons, the Romans, the Angles, Saxons and Jutes all of whom I thought I had escaped from for ever when I left school!'

[1] Robert Eric Mortimer Wheeler, 1890–1976. Franks Student in archaeology, 1913. Major, Royal Field Artillery, 1917, France and Italy (Military Cross, despatches). Lecturer in Archaeology, University of Wales, 1920–24. Keeper and Secretary of the London Museum, 1926–44. Lecturer in Archaeology, University College London, 1934–44. Raised and commanded a Royal Artillery Regiment, North Africa, 1943 (from El Alamein to Tunis). Served with the 10th Corps in Italy (Salerno landing). Director-General of Archaeology in India, 1944–48. Professor of Roman Archaeology, University of London, 1948–55. Knighted, 1952.

[2] Desmond John Newman Flower, 1907– . Only son of Sir Newman Flower. Educated at Lancing and King's College Cambridge. Entered Cassell & Co, 1930; Director 1931; Literary Director, 1938; Acting Director, 1939–40. On active service, 1940–45 (despatches, Military Cross, 1944). As Deputy Chairman of Cassell & Co, 1952–58 and Chairman 1958–71, he supervised the printing, publishing and sale of Churchill's *The Second World War* and *A History of the English-Speaking Peoples*.

The final volume of *Marlborough* was published on September 3. Four days later, Maxine Elliot wrote from the Château de l'Horizon: 'It is incredible to me that one man can possess the genius to write a book like this and at the same time pursue his ordinary life which is a thousand times fuller of grave duties and obligations than that of lesser men.' 'I propose to dive into it this very evening,' Anthony Eden wrote on September 9, 'and seek to forget in its pages the haunting apprehensions of the present age.'

47

The Munich Agreement: 'The Worst of Both Worlds'

DURING the summer of 1938 Churchill's friends urged him to rest. He was sixty-three years old, and the strain of his five-year campaign for rearmament and collective security had begun to take its toll. 'You must not overwork,' Abe Bailey wrote to him on July 29, after they had lunched together. 'You looked as if you wanted a good rest. Why not take a cruise to S Africa?' But during August, as the European situation worsened, Churchill decided to give up all plans for a holiday, including a second visit which he had hoped to make to California at the end of the year.

In Czechoslovakia Dr Beneš had sought throughout the summer some form of compromise with the Sudeten Germans.[1] But they, spurred on by Hitler, had begun to demand, not local autonomy, but complete self-determination. Beneš could not allow the Czech State to be deprived of so large a proportion of its territory, to be denuded of its main strategic protection against German attack from three sides, or to lose so significant a part of its economic wealth. But Hitler was determined to incite the Sudeten Germans to make extreme, unacceptable demands, hoping to create a situation in which Germany would eventually be able to take territorial advantage. On July 23 a British emissary, Lord Runciman, was sent to Prague, where he urged Beneš to meet the Sudeten demands. But Beneš was reluctant to do so, believing that as soon as one demand was met, another more extreme demand would be put forward, and

[1] On April 24 Henlein had put forward eight demands, known as the Carlsbad points, on which he then insisted. Beneš regarded some of the points, such as 'Full self-government for the German areas' and 'Recognition of the principle Within German areas German officials' as possible points for negotiation; but the eighth point, 'Full liberty to profess German nationality and German philosophy,' seemed too open an incitement to Nazi activities throughout Czechoslovakia to be acceptable.

that it was only a matter of time before the deceptive call for self-determination gave way to the open demand for complete union with Germany.

On August 7 the British Military Attaché in Berlin, Colonel Mason-Macfarlane,[1] reported secretly to the Foreign Office that Hitler had already decided to attack Czechoslovakia in September, whatever agreement Beneš might reach with the Sudetens. Six days later the Conservative MP Charles Taylor, who had been travelling in Germany, informed the Foreign Office of massive German troop movements between Nuremberg and the Czech frontier. That same day Churchill wrote to Lloyd George: 'Everything is overshadowed by the impending trial of will-power which is developing in Europe. I think we shall have to choose in the next few weeks between war and shame, and I have very little doubt what the decision will be.'

As the German troop movements grew, with over one and a half million men under arms, Hitler announced that he was holding the usual peace-time manoeuvres. His announcement was widely accepted by the British and French public, for, as Orme Sargent noted in a Foreign Office minute on August 15, the French Press had probably received the same 'hint' as the British 'to write down the German mobilization as much as possible so as not to create a sudden panic'. Churchill, however, in an article in the *Daily Telegraph* on August 18, warned that 'if the optimists were proved wrong', the Governments who shared their views would find themselves 'at an enormous disadvantage in the opening stages of a world war'. His article continued: 'It would be only common prudence for other countries besides Germany to have these same kind of manoeuvres at the same time and to place their precautionary forces in such a position that, should the optimists be wrong, they would not be completely ruined.'

Commenting on the work of the Runciman mission, which was still in Prague, Churchill hoped that a 'practical working compromise' could be secured whereby, within the boundaries of Czechoslovakia, the Sudeten Germans would be given 'a free and equal chance with other races'. But he warned that any attempt to bring about the 'trampling down' of Czechoslovakia 'would change the whole current of human

---

[1] Frank Noel Mason-Macfarlane, 1889–1953. Educated at Rugby and Woolwich. On active service in South Africa, 1900; France, Belgium and Mesopotamia, 1914–18 (Military Cross and two bars); Afghan war, 1919. Military Attaché in Budapest, Vienna and Berne, 1931–34; in Berlin and Copenhagen, 1937–39. Director of Military Intelligence, BEF, 1939–40. Head of British Military Mission to Moscow, 1941–42. Governor and Commander-in-Chief, Gibraltar, 1942–44. Knighted, 1943. Chief Commissioner, Allied Control Commission for Italy, 1944. Lieutenant-General, 1944. Labour MP for North Paddington, 1945–46.

ideas and would eventually draw upon the aggressor a wrath which would in the end involve all the greatest nations of the world'.

Churchill was anxious to know in detail what Hitler intended. From August 18 to August 23 a Major in the German Army von Kleist,[1] was staying in London, incognito, at the Park Lane Hotel. Ian Colvin urged Churchill to see him, for such an occasion, as Colvin wrote to Randolph from Berlin on August 15, 'won't offer itself again'.

Churchill and his son saw von Kleist at Chartwell on August 19. According to the notes taken by Randolph, and sent by Churchill to the Foreign Office on the following day, von Kleist told them:

. . . that he thought that an attack upon Czechoslovakia was imminent and would most likely occur between the Nuremburg Conference and the end of September. There was nobody in Germany who wanted war except H. . . .

The generals, including Reichenau,[2] are for peace and K. believed that if only they could receive a little encouragement they might refuse to march. At least half of them were convinced that an attack upon Czechoslovakia would involve Germany in war with France and Britain.

Churchill told von Kleist that the German generals were correct in their view, and he added:

. . . though many people in England were not prepared to say in cold blood that they would march for Czechoslovakia, there would be few who would wish to stand idly by once the fighting started. He pointed out that the successive Nazi coups had hardened public opinion in Britain.[3]

Our patience in Spain was not so much a sign of weakness as of the conserving of resources for the real struggle which must come if fighting started in Central Europe. He added that public opinion in the United States was immeasurably more advanced than in 1914. He stressed the fact that those who thought as he did were anti-Nazi and anti-war and not anti-German.

Von Kleist told Churchill that he accepted what he said, and that on his return to Germany he would continue 'to emphasise these facts to

[1] Ewald von Kleist-Schmenzin. A gentleman farmer from East Elbia, descendant of the poet Kleist. A member of the German Conservative Party before 1914, and a convinced anti-Nazi since 1933. Author of a pamphlet attacking Hitler's regime. Hanged by the Nazis on 16 April 1945, nine months after the failure of the plot to kill Hitler.

[2] Walter von Reichenau, 1884–1942. Born in Karlsruhe. Chief of Staff, Königsberg, 1932–3. Director, Ministry of War, Berlin, 1933–34; Director of the Wehrmacht, 1934–5. Commanded the Bavarian Corps, 1935. General of Artillery, 1936. A member of the German Olympic Committee, 1936. Commanding Officer of the 6th Army, 1939–41. One of twelve Generals created Field-Marshal on 19 July 1940. Commanding Officer of the Division Süd, Eastern front, from December 1941 until his death at Poltava in January 1942.

[3] But three days earlier, on August 16, Goering told the French Ambassador in Berlin, André François Poncet, that he had received definite assurances from Britain that in the event of war between Germany and Czechoslovakia 'Britain would not lift a finger.'

his friends'. He asked, however, for some British gesture, even from 'private members of Parliament', to help crystallize the 'universal anti-war sentiment in Germany'. He was convinced, he told Churchill, that once the German generals had decided for peace, Hitler would be overthrown 'within forty-eight hours', and a new Government, 'probably of a Monarchist character', would end the fear of war for ever. Churchill told von Kleist that once the world was assured of a peaceful and law abiding government in Germany 'such questions as the colonies and frontier rectifications would be easy of adjustment, and that neither Britain nor France would prove ungenerous once the shadow of aggression and war had passed from Europe'.

As von Kleist wished, Churchill gave him that same day a letter setting out a firm warning of possible future developments. The letter read:

I have welcomed you here as one who is ready to run risks to preserve the peace of Europe and to achieve a lasting friendship between the British, French and German peoples for their mutual advantage.

I am sure that the crossing of the frontier of Czecho-Slovakia by German armies or aviation in force will bring about a renewal of the world war. I am as certain as I was at the end of July 1914 that England will march with France, and certainly the United States is now strongly anti-Nazi. It is difficult for democracies in advance and in cold blood to make precise declarations; but the spectacle of an armed attack by Germany upon a small neighbour and the bloody fighting that will follow will rouse the whole British Empire and compel the gravest decisions.

Do not, I pray you, be misled upon this point. Such a war, once started would be fought out like the last to the bitter end, and one must consider not what might happen in the first few months, but where we should all be at the end of the third or fourth year.

It would be a great mistake to imagine that the slaughter of the civil population following upon air-raids would prevent the British Empire from developing its full war power. Though, of course, we should suffer more at the beginning than we did last time. But the submarine is practically mastered by scientific methods, and we shall have the freedom of the seas and the support of the greater part of the world. The worse the air-slaughter at the beginning, the more inexpiable would be the war. Evidently, all the great Nations engaged in the struggle, once started, would fight on for victory or death.

Churchill had consulted Halifax before sending his letter. In it he also told von Kleist that according to Halifax the British position continued to be that defined by Chamberlain in the House of Commons on March 24. 'The speech must be read as a whole,' Churchill added, 'and I have no authority to select any particular passage out of its context; but I must draw your attention to the final passage. . . .'[1] On August 20 Churchill, while sending Halifax a copy of Randolph's notes of the interview, together with a copy of his letter to von Kleist, added:

He mentioned various Generals in the highest commands to whom he would show it, particularly Beck.[2] I drafted the letter for their benefit. You are committed to nothing except that when I rang you up to ask you about the policy of the Government, you informed me that it was unchanged from that of March 24.

K. was also very emphatic that all the Generals were convinced that they could not possibly fight for more than three months and that defeat was certain, but I did not like what he said about there being no ultimatum, merely an order to troops to advance from all sides at some unexpected moment.

My hope is, however, that the evident distress of the German people at being dragged into a war will create an atmosphere affecting the Generals and the Fuehrer in opposite senses.

On August 23 Halifax replied from the Foreign Office: 'I think, if I may say so, both your language in conversation and your letter are most valuable.' Sending a copy of the interview to Chamberlain on August 24 Churchill added: 'I do not suppose it can do much good, but every little counts.' Sending a further copy to Daladier on August 25 he wrote:

Evidently Hitler will have at least fifteen hundred thousand men under arms for some time to come, and some people tell me that what they are doing now gives them anything from twelve to eighteen days advantage in mobilisation. The newspapers say it is costing them five to six hundred thousand pounds a day, which is a lot for a joke.

---

[1] The passage in Chamberlain's speech to which Halifax and Churchill referred read: 'Where peace and war are concerned, legal obligations are not alone involved, and, if war broke out, it would be unlikely to be confined to those who have assumed such obligations. It would be quite impossible to say where it would end and what Governments might become involved. The inexorable pressure of facts might well prove more powerful than formal pronouncements, and in that event it would be well within the bounds of probability that other countries, besides those which were parties to the original dispute, would almost immediately become involved. This is especially true in the case of two countries like Great Britain and France, with long associations of friendship, with interests closely interwoven, devoted to the same ideals of democratic liberty, and determined to uphold them.'

[2] Ludwig Beck, 1880–1944. An outstandingly brave soldier during the First World War. In 1930, at the Scheringer-Ludin trial in Leipzig, he indicated that he would welcome the advent of National Socialism. Chief of the General Staff, 1933–38, and a leading advocate of rearmament, 1933–35, but from 1936 an opponent of Hitler's expansionist politics. Resigned, 18 August 1938 (his resignation was not made public until 31 October 1938, after the Munich Conference). Subsequently sought to arouse the nations of western Europe into some sense of the danger which confronted them, and became a leader of the clandestine German opposition to Hitler; by 1944 he favoured even the assassination of Hitler, which he had earlier opposed. Committed suicide after the failure of the plot to kill Hitler, July 1944.

I must assure you that I feel grave anxiety, and I do not feel able to believe this immense semi-mobilisation of Germany will be ended before an extreme crisis has been reached over Czechoslovakia or, what is involved in the issue, the Hitler regime.

Negotiations between the Czechs and the Sudeten Germans continued. 'Our latest information from Prague is rather more encouraging,' Chamberlain wrote to Churchill on August 26. But Churchill did not share Chamberlain's optimism. 'The fabricated stories of a Marxist plot in Czechoslovakia,' he told his constituents at Theydon Bois on August 27, 'and the orders to the Sudeten Deutsch to arm and defend themselves, were disquieting signs, similar to those which preceded the seizure of Austria.' Henlein and Beneš, he believed, could easily settle their differences, helped by Lord Runciman. But it was possible, he warned, that 'outside forces, larger and fiercer ambitions, might prevent that settlement'. Were that to happen, and the Germans to invade Czechoslovakia, 'it would be an outrage against civilization and freedom of the whole world. Every country would ask itself, "Whose turn will it be next?" '

On August 30 Halifax reported to the Cabinet that he had discussed the situation with Churchill, who had referred 'to the possibility of a joint note to Berlin from a number of Powers'. But Halifax himself deprecated any such joint policy, warning his colleagues that 'if we were to invite countries to sign a joint note, they would probably ask embarrassing questions as to our attitude in the event of Germany invading Czechoslovakia'. Chamberlain was likewise in a hesitant mood, telling his Cabinet that the policy 'of an immediate declaration or threat might well result in disunity, in this country, and in the Empire'. He did not think that war was a prospect 'which the Defence Ministers would view with great confidence'. Sir Thomas Inskip then explained:

. . . on the question whether we were ready to go to war, in a sense this country would never be ready owing to its vulnerable position. With a country as formidable as Germany so close to us we would be bound to go through a period of suffering and serious injury and loss. It was obvious however, that at the present time we had not reached our maximum preparedness and should not do so for another year or more. . . .

We had based our rearmament programme on what was necessary for our own defence. We had concentrated on Navy and the Air. We could not put an army into the field for many months after the outbreak of war. . . .

At the Cabinet meeting of August 30, three Cabinet Ministers urged a firm policy. Duff Cooper wanted to send the Fleet to Scapa Flow, as a sign of naval preparedness; Oliver Stanley believed that in two years time Germany would be even stronger relative to Britain than she was then; and Lord Winterton argued that Chamberlain's attitude under-estimated the capability of the Czechs themselves to resist an attack. It was decided, however, that no threats should be uttered, and no multi-power cooperation attempted.

Unaware of this decision, Churchill wrote to Halifax on August 31 urging the involvement not only of Russia, but also of the United States, should Henlein turn down any 'fair offer' from Beneš. His proposals were:

First would it not be possible to frame a joint note between Britain, France and Russia stating (a) their desire for peace and friendly relations; (b) their deep anxiety at the military preparations of Germany; (c) their joint interest in a peaceful solution of the Czechoslovak controversy, and (d) that an invasion by Germany of Czechoslovakia would raise capital issues for all three powers.

This note, when drafted, should formally be shown to Roosevelt[1] by the Ambassadors of the three powers, and we should use every effort to induce him to do his utmost upon it. It seems to me not impossible that he would then himself address H. emphasising the gravity of the situation, and saying that it seemed to him that a world war would inevitably follow from an invasion of Czechoslovakia, and that he earnestly counselled a friendly settlement.

This process, Churchill wrote, would give 'the best chance to the peace-ful elements in German official circles to make a stand' while enabling Hitler, when faced with the internal opposition to 'find a way out for himself by parleying with Roosevelt'. Such developments were not certain, he added, 'one only sees them as hopes'.

Churchill also had a proposal to make as far as naval preparations were concerned. There should, he wrote, be 'fleet movements, and the placing of the reserve flotillas and cruiser squadrons into full commis-sion'. His letter continued:

I do not suggest calling out the Royal Fleet Reserve or mobilisation, but there are, I believe, five or six flotillas which could be raised to First Fleet scale, and also there are about two hundred trawlers which would be used for anti-submarine work. The taking of these up and other measures would make a great stir in the naval ports, the effect of which could only be bene-ficial as a deterrent and a timely precaution if the worst happened.

---

[1] Franklin Delano Roosevelt, 1882–1945. United States Assistant Secretary of the Navy, 1913–20. Governor of New York State, 1929–33. President of the United States, 1933–45.

'I venture to hope,' Churchill added, 'that you will not resent these suggestions from one who has lived through such days before. It is clear that speed is vital.'

On September 2 Churchill wrote to Richard Freund:[1] 'I have very strongly the feeling that the veto of France, Britain and Russia would certainly prevent the disaster of war. I hear from many quarters of grave technical hitches in the German mobilization.' That same afternoon the Soviet Ambassador, Ivan Maisky, sent Churchill a message that he wished urgently to see him. Churchill agreed, and Maisky drove down to Chartwell, where he told Churchill that the Soviet Government wished to invoke Article II of the League of Nations Covenant, under which the League Powers were obliged to consult together if war was imminent. According to Maisky, the Soviet Union was anxious to examine with Britain and France various means of defending Czechoslovakia against a German attack. On September 3 Churchill sent Halifax an account of this conversation, but in his reply two days later, Halifax doubted whether action under Article II 'would be helpful'. He preferred, he said, to await the outcome of Henlein's visit to Hitler at Berchtesgaden, telling Churchill: 'Gwatkin[2] telegraphed last night to say that on the whole it was satisfactory.'

The British Government still hoped to deny Hitler any excuse for an attack on Czechoslovakia by persuading Beneš to make substantial concessions. This Beneš did, officially, on September 2, offering 'cantonal self-government' to the Sudetens. Lord Runciman and Ashton-Gwatkin both urged Henlein to accept these terms, but after talking to Hitler at Berchtesgaden, Henlein rejected them, and his followers, taking the cue, began to demand the right to break away altogether from Czechoslovakia. For his part Lord Runciman continued to try to persuade Beneš to make even further concessions. 'I am following the Czechoslovakian problem with keen interest,' Churchill's sixteen-year-

---

[1] Richard Henry Freund, 1900–   . Born in Berlin, of Czech origin and later nationality. Educated at Berlin and Heidelberg Universities. Came to England as a German newspaper correspondent, 1926; dismissed from his job, 1933; naturalized 1935. Published *Zero Hour: Policy of the Powers*, 1936 and *Watch Czechoslovakia*, 1937. Worked as a freelance for the *Yorkshire Post*; joined the *Manchester Guardian*, 1938; Financial Editor, 1939–65. Changed his name to Fry during the Second World War. An authority on Indian Affairs. CBE, 1965.

[2] Frank Trelawny Arthur Ashton-Gwatkin, 1889–1976. Educated at Eton and Balliol College Oxford. Entered the Consular Service, Far East, 1913. Member of the British Delegation at the Washington Disarmament Conference, 1921–22; the Imperial Economic Conference at Ottawa, 1932; the World Monetary and Economic Conference, London, 1933; the Munich Conference, 1938. Counsellor of Embassy, Moscow, 1929. Member of Runciman's mission to Czechoslovakia, 1938. Policy Adviser, Ministry of Economic Warfare, 1939–40. Assistant Under-Secretary, Foreign Office, 1940–47. Novelist, under the *nom de plume* John Paris.

old daughter Mary wrote to him on September 3, 'I think we are making things more difficult by declaring such a feeble policy.'

In an anonymous paragraph which Churchill had written for the *Evening Standard* Londoner's Diary on September 1, he warned of the dangers of 'a marked decline of the will to live, and still more of the will to rule'. That same day the editor of the *Yorkshire Post*, Arthur Mann,[1] wrote to him of how, after an interview with Halifax, 'I did not come away with an impression that the dangers of the European situation were fully appreciated.' Mann added that 'though for patriotic reasons we may not say so now, great numbers, I fancy, are of the opinion that our present menace has been invited by Mr Chamberlain's pursuit of "appeasement" without any true regard for the realities of the European situation'. Three days later, on September 4, Chamberlain wrote to the Chief Whip, David Margesson: 'you won't need to hear from me how anxious the situation has been and still is. But I hope we may avoid any premature summoning of the H of C.'

On September 6 the *Daily Express*, much to Churchill's anger, revealed that the 'latest' of the guests at Chartwell had been the former German Chancellor, Dr Brüning, who 'seemed depressed by a letter he had received from German anti-Nazis, asking Churchill to influence the British Government to "speak plainly to Hitler" '.[2]

The possibility of Britain telling Hitler plainly that the Sudetenland could not be taken from Czechoslovakia was undermined on September 7, when, in its leading article, *The Times* gave its support to what was, in effect, the extreme Henlein position, unacceptable not only to Beneš, but also to that large number of Sudeten Germans for whom union with Germany would mean the loss of all liberty, swift imprisonment, forced labour and death. According to *The Times*:

If the Sudetens now ask for more than the Czech Government are ready to give in their latest set of proposals, it can only be inferred that the Germans

---

[1] Arthur Henry Mann, 1876–1972. Journalist; Editor of the *Evening Standard*, 1918. Editor of the *Yorkshire Post*, 1919–39. Companion of Honour, 1941. Member of the Board of Governors of the BBC, 1941–46.

[2] It was Churchill's sister-in-law Nellie Romilly who had told the *Daily Express* of Brüning's visit to Chartwell. On September 6 Churchill wrote to her in rebuke: 'I was shocked to see the enclosed in the Daily Express, and on making enquiries I have no doubt how this breach of confidence passed. You ought not to have repeated Clemmie's conversation, which was purely private, in any circumstances without permission. In this case Dr B. came under the strict guarantes of secrecy which I gave him personally, and the statement and the visit attributed to him may bring upon him serious consequences. The matter causes me very great anxiety.' Nellie Romilly replied on September 7: 'Dearest Winston, I am so deeply grieved at what I did. Please forgive, is all I can say. It was an absolutely thoughtless act. It has made me very unhappy that I could act in any way badly towards you.'

are going beyond the mere removal of disabilities for those who do not find themselves at ease within the Czechoslovak Republic. In that case it might be worth while for the Czechoslovak Government to consider whether they should exclude altogether the project, which has found favour in some quarters, of making Czechoslovakia a more homogeneous state by the cession of that fringe of alien populations who are contiguous to the nation to which they are united by race.

In this single paragraph *The Times* gave its support to the most extreme of the Nazi demands, the complete cession of the Sudetenland, a demand which, if met, would have condemned Czechoslovakia to disintegration, and placed a majority of the Sudeten Germans under the grim rigours of Nazi rule. That same day, the Foreign Office publicly disassociated itself from the leader, but the damage had been done. Throughout Europe it was believed that *The Times*, in advocating a German annexation of the Sudetenland, spoke for the British Government, and that as a result, Britain clearly would not fight to protect the Czech frontiers against German attack. On September 8 Churchill drafted a 'letter to a correspondent' in which he set out his views. But the letter was never made public. In it he wrote of how he had been 'reassured' by the Foreign Office statement, and he noted, of the suggestion in *The Times*:

Such a proposal, if entertained, would have the effect of handing over to the German Nazis the whole of the mountain defence line which marks the ancient boundaries of Bohemia, and was specially preserved to the Czechoslovak State as a vital safeguard of its national existence.

In taking the unusual course of dissociating themselves so promptly from this suggestion, made by an eminent and friendly newspaper, His Majesty's Government seem to make it clear that they would not countenance proposals which go so far beyond what reason and justice demand.

The Cabinet's newly created 'Situation in Czechoslovakia Committee' met on the afternoon of September 9.[1] Despite the Foreign Office firmness against *The Times* leader, Chamberlain decided to hold back a warning which he had contemplated sending to Hitler, and to seek instead direct negotiations with him; negotiations from which the Czechs were to be excluded. That morning the *Daily Mail* had reported that definite instructions had been sent to the British Ambassador in Berlin, Sir Nevile Henderson, to deliver a stern warning to Hitler.

---

[1] Two Ministers were present, Neville Chamberlain and Sir John Simon. They were accompanied by three senior civil servants, Sir Alexander Cadogan, Sir Robert Vansittart and Sir Horace Wilson.

During the day a specific denial of this was issued from 10 Downing Street.

At a further meeting of the Czechoslovakia Committee on September 10, a telegram was read out from Nevile Henderson, deprecating any further warning to Hitler.[1] While the four Ministers were meeting, Churchill himself had arrived at 10 Downing Street. In his memoirs Samuel Hoare recalled how:

When the talk ended and we left the Cabinet Room, we found Churchill waiting in the hall. He had come to demand an immediate ultimatum to Hitler. He was convinced it was our last chance of stopping a landslide, and according to his information, which was directly contrary to our own, both the French and the Russians were ready for an offensive against Germany.

That night Churchill telephoned Halifax, and, as Oliver Harvey noted in his diary, once more 'urged need for an immediate ultimatum to Germany'. But Churchill's advice was ignored. Harvey added: 'I have a feeling that A. E[den] is right when he says that the present Government will run away if it comes to a show-down. . . . Also I am not reassured by the nature of the Cabinet Committee—especially Simon and Hoare—which is taking all the decisions. None of the younger generation there.' That evening a 'Most Secret' telegram was sent from the Foreign Office to each of the Dominion Prime Ministers, informing them that Lord Halifax had told the French Ambassador, Charles Corbin, that 'although Great Britain might feel obliged to support France in a conflict, if only because our interests were involved in any threat to French security, it did not mean that we should be willing automatically to find ourselves at war with Germany because France might be involved in discharge of obligations which Great Britain did not share and which a large section of opinion in this country had always disliked'.

On September 10 Eleanor Rathbone wrote to Churchill of 'how relieved' she was that he had been to the Foreign Office, and she added: 'There is a great longing for leadership and even those who are far apart from you in general politics realize that you are the one man who has combined full realization of the dangers of our military position with belief in collective international action against aggression. And if we fail again now, will there ever be another chance.'

Churchill saw Halifax again on September 11, and, as Halifax reported to the Cabinet on the following day, proposed 'that we should tell

---

[1] Four Ministers were present at this meeting of September 10, Neville Chamberlain, Lord Halifax, Sir John Simon and Sir Samuel Hoare. Also present were Sir Alexander Cadogan, Sir Robert Vansittart and Sir Horace Wilson.

Germany that if she set foot in Czechoslovakia we should at once be at war with her'. But such a policy did not commend itself, either to the Cabinet, or to Halifax, who had come to the conclusion that same day, as Oliver Harvey wrote in his diary, that no settlement reached between the Czechs and the Sudetens would last, and that therefore the separation of the Sudetenland from Czechoslovakia was 'the only hope of avoiding war'. Thus, within four days of the Foreign Office having rejected *The Times* leader, the Foreign Secretary himself had come to accept its proposal. Halifax now favoured a plebiscite, followed by the transfer to Germany of all Czech territory voting to be a part of Germany. 'In order to enforce such a plebiscite,' Harvey noted, 'the idea would be to summon a Four-Power Conference—Great Britain, France, Germany and Italy.' Under this plan Czechoslovakia was to be excluded from any discussion of its own future.

'This country has been betrayed by its so called leaders,' Boothby wrote to Churchill on September 11, 'whatever the ultimate outcome may be.' Churchill shared Boothby's pessimism. In a letter to Lord Moyne about a possible cruise in the Caribbean at Christmas he wrote:

Alas, a cloud of uncertainty overhangs all plans at the present time, as I cannot pretend to be at all hopeful of the outcome. Owing to the neglect of our defences and the mishandling of the German problem in the last five years, we seem to be very near the bleak choice between War and Shame. My feeling is that we shall choose Shame, and then have War thrown in a little later on even more adverse terms than at present.

Speaking at Nuremberg on September 12, Hitler declared that the 'oppression' of the Sudeten Germans must come to an end, and he described Czechoslovakia as a 'monstrous formation'. The Sudeten Germans, he said, must be granted 'the free right of self-determination', and he continued: 'I am in no way willing that here in the heart of Germany through the dexterity of other statesmen a second Palestine should be permitted to arise. The poor Arabs are defenceless and per-haps deserted. The Germans in Czechoslovakia are neither defenceless nor are they deserted, and folk should take notice of that fact.' The Germans of Austria, Hitler added, 'know best how bitter a thing it is to be separated from the Motherland. They will be the first to recognize the significance of what I have been saying today.'

When the Cabinet met on September 12, Halifax reported, as the minutes recorded, 'that, with the Prime Minister, he had seen Mr Winston Churchill on the previous day. Mr Churchill's proposition was that we should tell Germany that if she set foot in Czechoslovakia we should at once be at war with her. Mr Churchill agreed that this line of action was an advance on the line of action which he had proposed some two or three weeks earlier, but he thought that by taking it we should incur no added risk.' Two days later, on September 14, Josiah Wedgwood wrote to Churchill:

My dear Winston,
    Do our folk really mean business? They seem to have seen everyone but you, & it is inconceivable to me that they should actually be facing up to war if they have not called you in,—inconceivable that we should not be disgraced without you.
    You must have lots of good ideas. I am thinking of Northern Spain, Indian factories, the Baltic, Roumania, enlisting Jewish refugees, Minorca, Turkish co-operation,—& 100 things. Not one of these people had anything to do with the direction of the last war. They are babies, if not cowards. You, or God, will have to help if this country is now to be saved.

When the Cabinet met on September 14 Chamberlain announced that he intended to go to see Hitler in Germany and that he would support the idea of a plebiscite in the Sudetenland, if Hitler insisted on one. No democracy, Chamberlain told his colleagues, could really refuse to accept a plebiscite. 'As regards the rest of Czechoslovakia,' Oliver Harvey noted in his diary, 'he felt it might be necessary to neutralise it under guarantee of Great Britain, Russia, France and Germany.' During the discussion Malcolm MacDonald told his Cabinet colleagues, as the official minutes recorded, that the views of *The Times* of a week before 'represented on this question those of a majority in the country'. Duff Cooper alone dissented, telling the Cabinet that in his opinion 'the choice was not between war and a plebiscite, but war now and war later'.[1]
    Churchill received a continual stream of letters as the crisis intensified. 'Like you I am in close touch with the Czechs and share in their distress,' Sir Bernard Pares[2] wrote on September 14. 'It is unintelligible to me that a paper of the importance of the Times should mess everything up

---

[1] Churchill saw much of Duff Cooper during these weeks; he had visited him at the Admiralty on the evening of September 12, lunched with him after the Cabinet of September 14, and dined with him at Admiralty House on September 26.
[2] Bernard Pares, 1867–1949. Educated at Harrow and Trinity College Cambridge. Historian, he published his first book on Russian history, in 1907. Professor of Russian History, Language and Literature, Liverpool, 1908–17. Attached to the Russian Army, 1914–17. Ambassador in Petrograd, 1917. Knighted, 1919. Director, School of Slavonic and East European Studies, London, 1922–39.

in such a disgraceful way.'[1] On the following day Churchill completed a further article for the *Daily Telegraph*, which was published on the morning of September 15. Inside Czechoslovakia, he wrote, there was 'an absolute determination to fight for life and freedom'. The Czechs, if not 'daunted by all the worry and pressure to which they have been subjected', would fight. For three or four weeks, at enormous cost, they would absorb Germany's time and engage its army, inflicting 'three or four hundred thousand casualties'. The carnage, he believed, would not be 'witnessed impassively by the civilized world', but, 'from the moment that the first shot is fired and the German troops attempt to cross the Czechoslovakian frontier, the whole scene will be transformed, and a roar of fury will arise from the free peoples of the world, which will proclaim nothing less than a crusade against the aggressor'.

No such crusade against the aggressor was, however, being prepared, or even contemplated, by the British Government. Indeed, during September 15 it was announced that Chamberlain would fly that same day to Germany, to see Hitler at Berchtesgaden. 'British press receives news of PM's visit with marked approval,' Oliver Harvey noted in his diary. 'City is much relieved. Reaction in Germany also one of relief. In America it looks as if it were regarded as surrender. Winston says it is the stupidest thing that has ever been done.'

On learning of Chamberlain's journey to Hitler, Randolph Churchill wrote to his father: 'Please in future emulate my deepest distrust of Chamberlain & all his works & all his colleagues. There is no infamy of which they are not capable. When they are with you they are careful to talk in honourable terms; if I have read them more truly it is because their underlings are less discreet with me.' Randolph added: 'Three days ago we were insulted; now we have the submission you have so often predicted. Bless you & please in future steer your own course untainted by contact with these disreputable men.'

Churchill shared his son's distress, and on September 16 sent a telephone message to Dr Revesz, in Paris, for distribution to the European papers. 'The personal intervention of Mr Chamberlain,' he said, 'and his flight to see Herr Hitler, does not at all alter the gravity of the issues at stake. We must hope that it does not foreshadow another complete failure of the Western Democracies to withstand the threats and violence of Nazi Germany.' That same day Sir Eric Phipps reported to Halifax

[1] At six in the evening of September 14 Lord Camrose saw Sir Robert Vansittart at the Foreign Office. According to Camrose's note: 'He regarded the suggestions of a plebiscite as ridiculous, and described the "Times" leading article as having had a deplorable and tremendous effect; he regarded it as "criminal." '

from Paris that he had spoken to Georges Bonnet,[1] who 'actually mentioned Winston Churchill and Spears as being amongst those who had rung him up. Presumably the former breathed fire and thunder in order to binge Bonnet up.'

Chamberlain returned from his visit to Hitler on the evening of September 16. On the following morning he told the Cabinet that he had said to Hitler:

Suppose that all the Sudeten Germans were included in the Reich, was that all that Herr Hitler wanted, or had he some other aims? The point was of importance, because there were a number of people in England who did not believe what Herr Hitler said. They thought that he was trying to deceive us, and they took the view that his real aim was not merely the inclusion of the Sudeten Germans in the Reich, but the dismemberment of Czechoslovakia.

Herr Hitler said that what he was concerned with was the German race. He did not wish to include Czechs in the Reich. . . .

Chamberlain had told Hitler that in principle he had nothing against the separation of the Sudetenland from Czechoslovakia. But such a separation was not even the desire of many Sudeten Germans, for on the evening of September 16 Frank Ashton-Gwatkin had reported to the Foreign Office that the Sudeten leaders had actually wanted to accept the Czech plan for local autonomy, but that since September 12 they had 'received their orders from Berlin'. The Cabinet decided, however, that these important considerations should neither be publicized nor debated. 'As regards Parliament,' Chamberlain told his Cabinet colleagues on the morning of September 17, 'his view was that a discussion would result in wrecking very delicate negotiations', and he added: 'If our rearmament programme had not progressed as far as it had, it would have been impossible for me to have faced Herr Hitler at all.'

Many of those who feared that Czechoslovakia was going to be forced to surrender the Sudetenland as a result of British as well as German pressure turned to Churchill for guidance. On September 17 Vyvyan Adams wrote to him: 'The dismemberment of Czechoslovakia would mean another trench lost to decency. I beg you to use your immense prestige to impress this palpable fact on the Government and the

---

[1] Georges Bonnet, 1889–1973. Born in the Dordogne, for which he was elected a Socialist–Radical Deputy in 1924. Minister for the Budget, 1925; for Pensions, 1926; for Commerce, 1930. President of the Stresa Conference, 1932. Minister of Finance, 1933; of Commerce, 1935. Ambassador to Washington, 1937. Minister of Finance, June–December 1937; of Foreign Affairs, April 1938–September 1939. Honorary knighthood, 1938. Minister of Justice, 1939–40. Member of the National Council, 1941. Member of the Council of State, 1946.

public.' One Conservative junior Minister, Harry Crookshank,[1] told Oliver Harvey on September 17 that he was 'all in favour of the Winston policy of organising all states who will be against aggression and of so confronting the gangsters with a ring of force'. Harvey added: 'I am sure he is right. We shall only defeat the dictators if we show courage and resolution.'

Churchill suspected that all hopes of a firm Government policy were illusory. During September 17 he wrote to A. H. Richards: 'If, as I fear, the Government is going to let Czechoslovakia be cut to pieces, it seems to me that a period of very hard work lies before us all.'

On Sunday September 18 Daladier and Bonnet came to London. Daladier warned Chamberlain that it was not the Sudetenland alone that Hitler wanted, but 'that Germany was aiming at something far greater', and he urged an international guarantee for Czechoslovakia against aggression. This Chamberlain deprecated; Britain, he said, 'had no army which could march to Czechoslovakia, and it was a long way to send an air force'. As for the Sudetenland, he told the French Prime Minister, mediation between Czechs and Sudetens was no longer possible, and there would have to be a plebiscite. After much hesitation Daladier finally agreed that Britain and France should together urge the Czechs to transfer all areas with a German-speaking majority to Germany, while in return Chamberlain agreed to offer a joint Anglo-French guarantee for the remainder of Czechoslovakia, once the cessions had been made. That same day, Shiela Grant Duff wrote to Hubert Ripka,[2] who was in Prague:

I have the impression that things are going very badly. The Labour people who saw Chamberlain yesterday (this is very confidential but quite exact) got a very bad impression. They are not allowed to talk but I have the distinct impression that Chamberlain has a plan, acceptable to Hitler, which he will impose on you, on the French and on public opinion here.

[1] Harry Frederick Comfort Crookshank, 1893–1961. Educated at Eton and Magdalen College Oxford. On active service in France and Salonica 1914–18 (twice wounded). Captain, 1919. Diplomatic Service, 1919–24 (Constantinople and Washington). Conservative MP for Gainsborough, 1924–56. Parliamentary Under-Secretary, Home Office, 1934–35. Secretary for Mines, 1935–39. Financial Secretary to the Treasury, 1939–43. Postmaster-General, 1943–45. Minister of Health, 1951–52. Lord Privy Seal, 1952–55. Created Viscount, 1956.
[2] Hubert Ripka, 1895–1958, Lecturer in International Politics at Prague University, 1930. Combining university work with journalism, he edited a Prague daily newspaper, Lidové Noviny from 1934–39, warning that Hitler always meant to attack Bohemia. Escaped to Paris, March 1939, where he began to organize pro-Czech propaganda. Escaped from France, June 1940. Deputy Secretary of State for Foreign Affairs of the Czechoslovak Government in Exile (in London), 1940–45. Czechoslovak Minister of Foreign Trade, Prague, 1945–48; resigned in February 1948 in protest against the growing power of the Communists. Escaped from Czechoslovakia, 1948. In exile in England from 1948 until his death.

I informed Churchill at once and asked for reassurance. He said he had not been informed, has no idea what is going on but that he too has the impression that there is some 'miserable plan' which Chamberlain and the Government will try and get accepted. He is confident that if Chamberlain tries now to get you to capitulate to the Nazis, that it will let loose a tremendous campaign here and that the country will split. Churchill himself is going to make a very strong declaration on Wednesday. . . . Churchill says everything depends on the willingness of the Czechs to fight at all costs. In that case, Germany will attack you and the situation here will change immediately.

He thinks Germany may attack any time, and the more you establish order in the Sudeten German districts, the more necessary this aggression becomes. In the case of a German attack, it is absolutely certain that we will march.

On September 19 Oliver Harvey noted in his diary: 'every pressure is being applied to Beneš to accept and to accept quickly. Poor Masaryk has taken to his bed with grief. . . .' That evening Churchill saw Halifax at the Foreign Office, where he was told that it was the French who were reluctant to go to war on behalf of the existing Czech frontiers. Sir Alexander Cadogan, who entered Halifax's room while the meeting was still in progress, found Churchill 'tamed somewhat', as he noted in his diary. Yet the information was inaccurate; it was Chamberlain, not Daladier, who had deprecated any international guarantee of the existing frontiers.

To Mortimer Wheeler, Churchill wrote that day of his continuing work on the *History of the English-Speaking Peoples*: 'It has been a comfort to me in these anxious days to put a thousand years between my thoughts and the twentieth century.'

At a meeting of the Cabinet on September 19, Hore-Belisha declared himself sceptical of Czechoslovakia's ability to survive without the Sudeten German areas. But Chamberlain pointed out that Hitler had assured him that Germany had no designs on Czechoslovakia itself, and that he 'would not deliberately deceive a man he respected'. The Minister of Labour, Ernest Brown,[1] told his colleagues: 'There was, no doubt, a section of public opinion which was vocal for war. But in his view the section which thought that this issue should not be allowed to provoke a world war was certainly stronger.'

---

[1] Ernest Brown, 1881–1962. A Baptist lay preacher. On active service in Italy, 1916–18 (Military Cross). Liberal MP for Leith, 1927–31; Liberal National, 1931–45. Parliamentary Secretary, Ministry of Health, 1931–32. Secretary to the Mines Department, 1932–35. Privy Councillor, 1935. Minister of Labour, 1935–40 (and National Service, 1939–40). Secretary for Scotland, 1940–41. Minister of Health, 1941–43. Chancellor of the Duchy of Lancaster, 1943–45. Minister of Aircraft Production, 1945. Companion of Honour, 1945.

On September 20 Churchill left London for Paris, where he spoke to his two friends in Daladier's Cabinet, Paul Reynaud and Georges Mandel, and together with General Spears urged a firm stand to resist the transfer of the Sudetenland to Germany. But Reynaud and Mandel, like Hore-Belisha, Duff Cooper and Oliver Stanley, were in a minority among their colleagues; like their English counterparts, they had no means of influencing policy, and talked gloomily of resignation.[1] Churchill tried to dissuade his friends from resigning, arguing, as he later wrote in a private recollection, that their resignation 'would only leave the French Government weakened by the loss of its two most capable and resolute men'. Churchill added:

This same afternoon I had an impulse to send a telegram myself to Beneš, whom I had known off and on since the days of President Masaryk, urging him to stand firm. I was sure that to throw Czechoslovakia to the wolves was only a putting-off of bad days for worse. This would have been the telegram: 'Fire your cannon, and all will be well.' I pondered anxiously upon the step. In the end I felt I should be grasping responsibilities which I had no right to seek, and no power to bear.

That night, at two o'clock on the morning of September 21, with the approval of both their Cabinets, the British and French Ministers in Prague[2] called on President Beneš to urge him to accept the Anglo-French proposals for the secession of the Sudetenland. Were he to refuse to do so, they said, he would produce a situation 'for which France and Britain could take no responsibility'.

Churchill returned to England on September 21, and at once issued a statement to the Press denouncing Chamberlain's policy:

The partition of Czechoslovakia under pressure from England and France amounts to the complete surrender of the Western Democracies to the Nazi threat of force. Such a collapse will bring peace or security neither to England nor to France. On the contrary, it will place these two nations in an ever weaker and more dangerous situation. The mere neutralisation of Czechoslovakia means the liberation of twenty-five German divisions, which will

[1] On October 2 Sir Maurice Hankey wrote in his diary: 'Winston Churchill's sudden visit to France by aeroplane, accompanied by General Spears, and his visit *only* to the members of the French Government like Mandel, who is opposed to the policy of peace, was most improper—Bonnet, the French Foreign Minister has complained about it, asking what we would say if our prominent French statesmen did the same: he has also protested against being rung up by Churchill and Spears from London for information. . . .' Hankey added that Sir Eric Phipps had also complained to him that Vansittart 'is almost certainly in touch with Churchill, Eden, the Labour leaders and with Léger and the Quai d'Orsay'.

[2] In September 1938 the British Minister in Prague was Basil Newton, the French Minister, Victor de Lacroix.

threaten the Western front; in addition to which it will open up for the triumphant Nazis the road to the Black Sea.

It is not Czechoslovakia alone which is menaced, but also the freedom and the democracy of all nations. The belief that security can be obtained by throwing a small State to the wolves is a fatal delusion. The war potential of Germany will increase in a short time more rapidly than it will be possible for France and Great Britain to complete the measures necessary for their defence.[1]

Churchill knew exactly the state of Britain's air defences at this time. On September 21 Wing-Commander Anderson sent him, at Churchill's request, a diagram of the organization of the Royal Air Force, and its first-line strength on August 31. Of the existing 72 bomber squadrons, Anderson pointed out, 'only 32 have been equipped with new type aircraft', while of the 33 fighter squadrons only 12 had been equipped with the new type aircraft, the Hurricane.

At midday on September 22 Chamberlain flew once more to Germany, to tell Hitler of the Anglo-French plan. That afternoon Churchill went to 10 Downing Street, where he was given details of what Chamberlain was to ask. Then he summoned a meeting at his flat to discuss the crisis. Five peers were present, Cecil, Lloyd, Horne, Wolmer and Lytton,[2] together with three MPs, Sinclair, Bracken and Harold Nicolson. 'While I wait for the lift to ascend,' Nicolson noted in his diary, 'Winston appears from a taxi. We go up together. "This," I say, "is hell." ' To which Winston remarked: 'It is the end of the British Empire.' At the outset of the meeting Churchill reported on his visit to Downing Street, as Nicolson recorded in his diary:

He says that the Cabinet are at last taking a firm stand. Chamberlain is to demand from Hitler (a) early demobilisation; (b) agreement that the transfer of the Sudeten territories should be undertaken gradually by an international commission; (c) that there must be no nonsense about Polish or Hungarian claims; (d) that what remains of the Czechs shall be guaranteed. We say at once: 'But Hitler will never accept such terms.' 'In that case,' says Winston,

[1] Writing from Paris that same day, Emery Revesz told Churchill: 'Your declaration has made a deep impression here. All the newspapers have published it.'

[2] Victor Alexander George Robert Lytton, 1876–1947. Educated at Eton and Trinity College Cambridge. Succeeded his father as 2nd Earl of Lytton, 1891. Civil Lord of the Admiralty, 1916; Additional Parliamentary Secretary, Admiralty, 1917; British Commissioner for Propaganda in France, 1918; Civil Lord of the Admiralty, 1919–20. Under-Secretary of State for India, 1920–22. Governor of Bengal, 1922–27. Acting Viceroy of India, April–August 1925. Head of the League of Nations' Mission to Manchuria, 1932. Chairman of Palestine Potash Ltd; Central London Electricity Ltd; the London Power Company, and the Hampstead Garden Suburb Trust Ltd. His eldest son was killed in a flying accident in 1933 and his younger son was killed in action in 1942.

'Chamberlain will return tonight and we shall have war.' We suggest that in that case it will be inconvenient having our Prime Minister in German territory. 'Even the Germans,' flashes Winston, 'would not be so stupid as to deprive us of our beloved Prime Minister.'

During the meeting Jan Masaryk telephoned to say that the Czechs were withdrawing gradually from the Sudeten regions. Clement Attlee also telephoned, to say that the Opposition were prepared, as Nicolson noted, 'to come in with us if we like'. His account continued:

We continue the conversation. It boils down to this. Either Chamberlain comes back with peace with honour or he breaks it off. In either case we shall support him. But if he comes back with peace with dishonour, we shall go out against him.
'Let us form the focus', says Winston. We say that indeed we will. But it would be better to wait until we hear what has really happened at Godesberg. He agrees that such a delay would indeed be preferable. He stands there behind the fire-screen, waving a whisky-and-soda at us, rather blurry, rather bemused in a way, but dominant and in fact reasonable. I say that there is a worse thing. 'What is worse than worse?' asks Winston. I say this point in the communiqué about a 'general agreement'. What can that mean? They all agree that this is a terrifying prospect. It may mean surrender on fronts far more extended than the Czech front, and in return for such quite valueless concessions as 'a fifty year peace', 'no bombing of open towns'.
We all feel that it is terrifying that a man like Chamberlain should be exposed to such terrors and temptations. . . .

During his second meeting with Hitler, at Godesberg, Chamberlain was subjected to several long harangues, the burden of which was that the Anglo-French plan was 'unacceptable on the ground that its operation would be too slow', and that German troops must be allowed to occupy the areas with a German-speaking majority at once, and without a plebiscite. On the afternoon of September 23, while still at Godesberg, Chamberlain agreed to Hitler's demand that there should be no plebiscite in areas with more than 50 per cent German-speaking people, but a direct transfer to Germany. Chamberlain assured Hitler that he would urge the Czech Government to accept this plan. He made no reference to any possible safeguards for those dissenting Sudeten Germans within the areas to be transferred without even a plebiscite. On September 23 General Tudor wrote to Churchill from Newfoundland:

My dear Winston,
You have been right all along about Hitler and Germany. Also that the Tory Party and its associates have let the country down.

Simon and Runciman wanted to act 'La perfide Albion' in 1914.[1] Halifax is a pious rabbit.

Chamberlain is said to belong to the Astor pro-Hitler group. It is astounding how he can negotiate with Hitler when the latter is already making war on the Czechs, by arming Henlein's party and letting him attack Czech Outposts—surely an act of war. The only possible excuse he may have, is that our rearmament is still in so deplorable a state; that we cannot go to war, except with the odds on our defeat.

Even now he should ask you to replace Inskip. But, unless he has some quite unexpected success in his present parleys, his time as Prime Minister will be short. With you as Prime Minister and Eden as Foreign Secretary of a National Government of 'he-men', instead of rabbits, Hitler would at least realize that bluff is useless.

With Chamberlain's return from Godesberg on September 24, it became clear that he had accepted Hitler's demands and that the German-speaking majority areas of Czechoslovakia were to be transferred to Germany without a plebiscite. In addition, he had urged the Czech Government to accept these terms, and to agree to Hitler's further demand that all fortifications and war materials in the transferred areas should be handed over intact to Germany. That afternoon Chamberlain explained the situation to Simon, Hoare and Halifax, the three other members of the Cabinet's Situation in Czechoslovakia Committee. According to the minutes:

The Prime Minister thought that he had established some degree of personal influence over Herr Hitler. The latter had said to him, 'You are the first man for many years who has got any concessions from me.' Again he had said that if we got this question out of the way without conflict it would be a turning-point in Anglo-German relations. To the Prime Minister that was the big thing of the present issue. He was also satisfied that Herr Hitler would not go back on his word once he had given it to him.

During September 24 Leopold Amery wrote to Lord Halifax: 'Almost everyone I have met has been horrified by the so-called "peace" we have forced upon the Czechs.'[2]

The Cabinet met on September 25. 'PM very pleased with himself,' Oliver Harvey noted in his diary, 'and thinks Hitler's offer not too bad

---

[1] In July 1914 Runciman had been President of the Board of Agriculture and Fisheries, and Simon had been Attorney-General. Six months earlier they had both opposed Churchill's increased Naval Estimates. 'The increase,' they had written to Asquith on 29 January 1914, 'is unexampled at a time of international calm.'

[2] On September 24 Halifax also received a petition, signed by Derrick Gunston, Harold Macmillan, Robert Boothby, Anthony Crossley, General Spears, A. P. Herbert and Sir Sidney Herbert, urging that no further pressure be put on the Czechs to accept the Godesberg terms. A similar protest reached Halifax from Anthony Eden on the morning of September 25.

and should be recommended to the Czechs.' Outside the Cabinet, Harvey wrote, 'Winston, A.E., and Amery are horrified at the possibility of our urging Czechoslovakia to accept.' At the Cabinet meeting of September 25 Chamberlain told his colleagues that he believed he had established an influence over Hitler, and that Hitler trusted him. According to what Hitler had told him, Germany had no further territorial ambitions beyond the Sudetenland. It was essential, he said, to agree to the immediate transfer of the Sudetenland to Germany. But Lord Halifax now expressed his doubts as to whether he was still in agreement with Chamberlain; his own aim, he said, was the destruction of Nazism. Lord Hailsham then expressed doubt as to the wisdom of trusting Hitler's word, while Duff Cooper challenged the value of Hitler's promises, and urged immediate naval mobilization. Both Hore-Belisha and Walter Elliot supported Duff Cooper's plea. But Chamberlain pressed first for a decision on general policy. The Ministers advising acceptance of Hitler's terms were Inskip, Kingsley Wood, Malcolm MacDonald and Lord Stanhope.[1]

That day Churchill lunched with Jan Masaryk, Desmond Morton and Randolph Churchill. That afternoon he issued a statement, which Chamberlain read to the Cabinet on September 26, pressing for the immediate recall of Parliament. But Chamberlain preferred to delay Parliament's recall for a further two days.

During September 26 Churchill received two telegrams from friends. The first was from Lord Rothermere, who declared: 'Have just read your suggestion of a solemn warning to Germany. Think it is admirable. Have been staggered by Germany's further demands after what looked like a settlement.' The second telegram came from Bernard Baruch, who urged: 'In case of war send children and expectant mother to me.' To this Churchill replied: 'Many thanks but Diana is air-raid warden in London. Now is the time for your man[2] to speak.'

Churchill was anxious to encourage Russia, as well as the United States, to take a firm stand. Anthony Crossley, who had hesitated four days earlier to associate himself with Churchill's protests, and who had

---

[1] James Richard Stanhope, 1880–1967. Educated at Eton and Magdalen College Oxford. Grenadier Guards, 1901–08. Succeeded his father as 7th Earl Stanhope, 1905. Served with the Grenadier Guards in France, 1914–18 (despatches twice, Military Cross 1916, DSO 1917). Parliamentary Secretary, War Office, 1918–19. Civil Lord of Admiralty, 1924–29. Privy Councillor, 1929. Under-Secretary of State for War, 1931–34. Parliamentary Under-Secretary of State for Foreign Affairs, 1934–36. First Commissioner of Works, 1936–37. President of the Board of Education, 1937–38. First Lord of the Admiralty, 1938–39. Leader of the House of Lords, 1938–40. Lord President of the Council, 1939–40. His only brother, a Captain in the Grenadier Guards, was killed in action in France on 16 September 1916.

[2] President Roosevelt.

even warned Anthony Eden against any alignment with Churchill, now wrote to a friend:

. . . we received a message from Winston (with whom as you will remember we had declined to co-operate) that his position was a very simple one. He believed that only a joint declaration by England, France & Russia could possibly save peace with honour. Throughout the last two days, we have disapproved the apparent ignoring of Russia by both our own and the French Governments. Even at the dictation of Hitler, the Prime Minister cannot annul geography.

At half past three in the afternoon of September 26 Churchill was received by Chamberlain and Hailfax in the Cabinet room at 10 Downing Street, and pressed them to issue a declaration stressing the solidarity not only between Britain and France, but also of Russia. 'Lord Halifax and I were at one,' Churchill later recounted in his memoirs, 'and I certainly thought the Prime Minister was in full accord.'

Churchill then returned to Morpeth Mansions, where a small, worried group of Peers and MPs had again assembled.[1] Harold Nicolson, who was at Morpeth Mansions awaiting Churchill's return from Downing Street, recorded in his diary not only Churchill's views, but the atmosphere before Churchill arrived:

We began by discussing whether national service should be proclaimed at once. Grigg is very insistent. Lytton wants a Coalition Government immediately, and I agree with him.

At that stage Winston bursts in. He says (as Rob Bernays had also told me) that the Cabinet were in a blue funk last night and that Simon was urging further retreat. But the younger people revolted and the Simon faction began to lose ground. Then came the French, all brave and solid this time, plus Gamelin who restored confidence. In the end the Cabinet were all united in feeling how brave, how strong, how resolute they had always been.

Winston gathers that the memorandum or letter which Horace Wilson is to give to Hitler is not in the least a retreat. It is merely an attempt to save Hitler's face if he wants to climb down. It offers a Conference to decide the means of carrying out the Franco-British plan. It warns him that we do not accept his own post-Godesberg plan and that if he insists, we shall go to war. He had urged the PM to mobilise the Fleet at once and call up all reserves.

[1] According to Churchill's account in *The Gathering Storm* those present included Lord Cecil, Lord Lloyd, Sir Edward Grigg, Sir Robert Horne, Robert Boothby, Brendan Bracken and Richard Law. Leopold Amery, who was also present, recorded in his diary that Lord Lytton and Sir Archibald Sinclair also attended. Another of those at the flat was Harold Nicolson, who, in his diary, gave in addition the names of Harold Macmillan and General Spears. This made a total (with Churchill) of at least fourteen people.

He says he will do so at 9 pm this evening if Hitler's speech at 8 pm tonight is not conciliatory.

The meeting then discussed what should be done. Nicolson recorded the discussion in his diary:

If Chamberlain rats again we shall form a united block against him. We do not think he will rat, and therefore we shall then 'rally behind him' (poor man). We shall press for a Coalition Government and the immediate application of war measures. Above all, the blockade must be put into force at once. Then national service, even if it entails conscription of capital. Then at once we must get in touch with Russia.

Winston says (and we all agree) that the fundamental mistake the PM has made is his refusal to take Russia into his confidence. Ribbentrop always said to Hitler, 'You need never fear England until you find her mentioning Russia as an ally. Then it means that she is really going to war!'

We therefore decide that Winston shall go at once to Halifax and tell him to put out some notice before Hitler's speech. 'We have only got till nine,' says Winston grimly.

Leopold Amery, who was also present, recorded in his diary that Churchill had described Chamberlain as 'an exhausted and broken man'. Amery added that he himself had argued that 'putting Russia in the forefront would not help with wavering Conservatives'. But Churchill spoke strongly in favour of bringing in Russia, even at this late stage. According to Churchill's own account in his memoirs:

The feeling was passionate. It all focused on the point, 'We must get Russia in.' I was impressed and indeed surprised by this intensity of view in Tory circles, showing how completely they had cast away all thoughts of class, party or ideological interests, and to what a pitch their mood had come. I reported to them what had happened at Downing Street and described the character of the communiqué. They were all greatly reassured.

The communiqué, which was issued from the Foreign Office at eight o'clock that evening, was uncompromising. Its main paragraph read: 'If, in spite of the efforts made by the British Prime Minister, a German attack is made upon Czechoslovakia, the immediate result must be that France will be bound to come to her assistance, and Great Britain and Russia will certainly stand by France.'

The final draft of the communiqué had been prepared by Reginald Leeper at the Foreign Office, and approved by Halifax without reference to Chamberlain. Nine years later, on 24 July 1947, Halifax recalled, in a private letter to Churchill, how, 'greatly to my surprise, Neville was much put out when the Communique appeared, and reproached me with not having submitted it to him before publication. I never understood then, and I don't understand now, why he should have been vexed—unless it was that he thought it "provocative"! and not fully consistent with his desire to make a further conciliatory appeal to Hitler.'

The firmness of the Foreign Office communiqué was indeed illusory. On the afternoon of September 27 the Foreign Office telegraphed to both Berlin and Prague, proposing a British initiative to ensure that the Czechs would withdraw from the frontier towns of Eger and Asch on October 1, and from all other majority German-speaking regions on October 10. Any further withdrawals must be completed by October 31, following which negotiations would begin between Britain, France, Germany and Czechoslovakia to guarantee the new frontiers.

During September 27 Jan Masaryk sent Churchill details of what he described as 'the preparation and execution of the "Hitler–Chamberlain auction sale" ', and he added: 'You have my full permission to use them—just please not verbatim so some of my "friends" will not have a pretext to send me away from London. The map will be ready tonight. . . .' During the day Churchill discussed the situation with another dissident Conservative MP, Anthony Crossley, and that night he dined with Duff Cooper at the Admiralty. 'He told me,' Churchill recalled in his memoirs, 'that he was demanding from the Prime Minister the immediate mobilisation of the Fleet. I recalled my own experiences a quarter of a century before. . . .' Just before midnight the warning telegram was sent to all ships, alerting them to the coming mobilization. Writing anonymously in the *Evening Standard* Londoner's Diary on the following day, Churchill declared: 'Mr Duff Cooper is to be congratulated upon having at last obtained authority to issue the necessary mobilisation orders to the Fleet.' The measure was 'most necessary and it is a great pity it was not done some weeks ago'.[1]

On the evening of September 27 Ripka telephoned Shiela Grant Duff from Prague, to say that Britain was putting 'great pressure' on the Czechoslovak Government, warning that 'Bohemia would be militarily crushed' if Hitler's demands were rejected. As Shiela Grant Duff later recalled:

[1] In his anonymous article Churchill linked Duff Cooper's decision of 1938 with his own decision of 1914: 'Mr Duff Cooper's action follows upon the Admiralty tradition of being well in advance of the final moves of diplomacy. In 1914, Mr Churchill, the First Lord of the Admiralty, arranged with the Prime Minister personally to send the Grand Fleet to the North on the Tuesday before the declaration of war. It was therefore able to pass through the Straits of Dover unmolested before the opening of hostilities, and was in its dominant position in the critical days which followed. . . .'

I at once telephoned Churchill. He was very angry with me. He had, only the previous day, himself seen the Prime Minister and Foreign Secretary and they had assured him that all this was at an end. Did I, he asked angrily, really need to draw the attention of the Czechoslovak Government to the statement in the press that morning issued by the Foreign Office that should a German attack be made now on Czechoslovakia 'France will be bound to come to her assistance and Great Britain and Russia will certainly stand by France'? What more, he shouted, did the Czechs want. They were having me on and I better take care and he all but slammed down the receiver.

None of us in England then knew that Chamberlain had gone behind the back of all this brave front and despatched Sir Horace Wilson with yet another appeasing missive. . . .

Chamberlain still believed that the crisis could be resolved without war. On the morning of September 28 he telegraphed to Hitler, asking him if he would agree to one further conference. Early that same afternoon Chamberlain gave the recalled House of Commons an account of all that had happened since August. The only interruptions, Harold Nicolson noted in his diary, were made by messengers bringing in telegrams and messages. 'Mr Winston Churchill,' he wrote, 'who sits at the end of my own row, received so many telegrams that they were clipped together by an elastic band.' Sir Arthur Salter [1] recalled in his memoirs how Churchill 'sat silent in his place below the gangway. With hunched figure and lowering brow he was visibly recalling the past and foreboding the future.'

While Chamberlain was speaking, a message was brought in from the Foreign Office, given to Lord Halifax in the Gallery and then brought down to Chamberlain at the despatch box. It was an invitation from Hitler for a four-power conference at Munich, to which Chamberlain, Daladier and Mussolini were invited. Chamberlain broke off his speech in order to announce the news. Then, amid great excitement and applause, he declared that he would accept the invitation, and fly to Munich. Most MPs rose in their seats and waved their order papers with enthusiasm. Churchill, Eden, Amery and Harold Nicolson remained

---

[1] James Arthur Salter, 1881–1975. Educated at Oxford High School and Brasenose College Oxford. Admiralty Transport Department, 1904; Director of Ship Requisitioning, 1917. General Secretary of the Reparations Commission, 1920–22. Knighted, 1922. Gladstone Professor of Political Theory and Institutions, Oxford, 1933–44. Independent MP for Oxford University, 1937–50. Parliamentary Secretary, Ministry of Shipping, 1939–41. Joint Parliamentary Secretary, Ministry of War Transport, 1941. Privy Councillor, 1941. Head of the British Merchant Shipping Mission to Washington, 1941–43. Chancellor of the Duchy of Lancaster, 1945. Conservative MP for Ormskirk, 1951–53. Minister of State of Economic Affairs, 1951–52. Minister of Materials, 1952–53. Created Baron, 1953.

seated. Those MPs near Churchill called out, as Lennox-Boyd recalled, 'Get up! Get up!' Then, as Chamberlain rose to leave the Chamber—his speech never to be finished, and the House once more adjourned—Churchill rose to shake his hand, and wished him 'God Speed'.

The excitement in the House of Commons at Chamberlain's impending visit to Munich was paralleled by a feeling of anger among many Conservatives at Churchill's earlier statements, protests and private gatherings critical of Chamberlain's policy. On September 29 Anthony Crossley wrote to Churchill:

After yesterday's speech, I went with several Members to a club and drank to our relief. In the course of conversation, one or two of them expressed indignation at what they called the disreputable intrigues which had been going on, and to be perfectly frank, your name was mentioned.

I am glad that I went to your house yesterday morning and the day before, and I only write this to say that if it was ever necessary or if you should ever desire it, I am perfectly ready and willing to stand up in the House and say that it is not true that you were party to intrigues, and that provided the Government took a firm line you were wholly willing to fall in with them as a loyal supporter whether you were asked to take an active part or not. In this matter I shall regard myself as wholly at your disposal. . . .

'Many thanks for your letter,' Churchill replied on the following day. 'I am entirely indifferent to such opinions as you mention. The last word has not been spoken yet.'

After Chamberlain's dramatic announcement in the House of Commons, Churchill prepared a statement for the Press, in which he declared:

I have wished the Prime Minister 'God-speed' in his mission, from the bottom of my heart. The indomitable exertions which he has made to preserve peace make it certain that should he be forced to declare that it is our duty to take up arms in defence of right and justice, his signal will be obeyed by a united nation and accepted by a united Empire. . . .

'The calm, resolute spirit of all classes,' Churchill added, 'particularly the great mass of the people, in the face of danger, shows the strength of the British character in the hour of trial.'

Throughout the evening of September 28 Chamberlain prepared for his flight to Munich by trying to persuade the Czechs in advance to accept Hitler's demands. 'It is essential,' Halifax telegraphed to Basil Newton[1] at 8 pm, 'that Czechoslovak Government should at once

[1] Basil Cochrane Newton, 1889–1965. Educated at Wellington and King's College Cambridge. Entered the Foreign Office, 1912. Acting Counsellor, Peking, 1927–29. Counsellor, Berlin, 1930–35; Minister, 1935–37. Minister to Prague, 1937–39. Knighted, 1939. Ambassador to Baghdad, 1939–41.

indicate their acceptance in principle of our plan and timetable. Please endeavour to obtain this without delay.' Within three hours, at 10.40 pm, Beneš accepted in principle the terms which Chamberlain intended to put to Hitler on the following day.

Chamberlain left London for Munich on the morning of September 29. Churchill lunched that day in a private room at the Savoy Hotel; a luncheon arranged several weeks before by the Freedom and Peace movement. Among those present were representatives of all three political parties, including Lord Lloyd, Lord Cecil, Lord Lytton, Sir Arthur Salter, Sir Walter Layton, Henry Wickham Steed, Sir Archibald Sinclair, Sir Norman Angell and Arthur Henderson. Harold Nicolson, who was also present, recorded in his diary:

Lord Lloyd makes the first speech. He says that Chamberlain is going to run away again and that we must stop him. Then Archie speaks in the same sense. Then I speak, saying that if he does run away I shall vote against him. Then Arthur Salter says that he is all for fighting the Germans, but he would first like to know whether we are likely to win.

Winston says that he has got a telegram which he proposes to send to the PM saying that if he imposes further onerous terms on the Czechs, we shall fight him in the House. He wants to get Eden to sign it.

The Freedom and Peace group reassembled that same evening, again at the Savoy. All afternoon attempts had been made to get further signatures for the telegram to Chamberlain. Both Eden and Attlee were contacted by telephone. But, as Nicolson noted in his diary: 'Anthony Eden refused to sign on the grounds that it would be interpreted as a vendetta against Chamberlain. Attlee had refused to sign without the approval of his Party.' Nicolson's account continued: 'We sat there gloomily realising that nothing could be done. Even Winston seemed to have lost his fighting spirit.' Another of those present, Violet Bonham Carter, later recorded: 'Leaden despair descended upon us as we realised our helplessness; and when we parted there were tears in Winston Churchill's eyes.'

Remaining at the Savoy, Churchill dined that night at the Other Club. Among those present were Lord Moyne, Lloyd George, Lord Horne, Duff Cooper, Lindemann, Garvin, Boothby, Colin Coote, Walter Elliot, Richard Law, Brendan Bracken and Archibald Sinclair. Colin Coote later recalled how, that night:

Churchill was in a towering rage and a deepening gloom. The Focus meeting had been unable to obtain the signatures of Attlee, the Leader of the Labour Party, or of Eden to a telegram adjuring Chamberlain to make no further concession at the expense of the Czechs. Hotly seconded by Archie Sinclair, he turned savagely upon the two ministers present, Duff Cooper and Walter Elliot. One could always tell when he was deeply moved, because a minor defect in his palate gave an echoing timbre to his voice. On this occasion it was not an echo, but a supersonic boom. How, he asked, could honourable men with wide experience and fine records in the Great War condone a policy so cowardly? It was sordid, squalid, sub-human, and suicidal.

'The sequel to the sacrifice of honour', Churchill warned, 'would be the sacrifice of lives, our people's lives'.

There then followed a long and anguished dispute, with Duff Cooper defending as best he could the actions of a Government with which he was so little in sympathy.

Chamberlain reached Munich by air at noon on Thursday September 29. There, for twelve hours, he, Hitler, Daladier and Mussolini worked out the full details of the transfer of the Sudetenland to Germany. Chamberlain began by asking if the Czechs could be present at the discussions, but this Hitler refused. Shortly after midnight, Hitler's demands were ready to be presented to the Czechs. During September 29 Churchill's former Private Secretary P. J. Grigg, wrote to him from India, where he was Finance Member of the Viceroy's Council:

I feel very ashamed at our having forced the Czechs so far and I can't believe that we have done anything but buy a few months of uneasy & expensive peace. However I suppose that Neville had great difficulty with his Simons & his Kingsley Woods and I gather also that Eric Phipps kept on dinning into them that the French weren't going to fight whatever happened.

I do wish that you were in the Government but I daresay that unless & until war actually comes the minnows won't tolerate the presence of a triton.

On the morning of Friday September 30 the Press announced the agreements reached at Munich a few hours earlier. Germany was to begin occupation of the predominantly German-speaking areas of Czechoslovakia on the following day, and there would be a plebiscite in areas where the linguistic majority was uncertain. At the Savoy Hotel several members of the Other Club were still dining when the first newspapers carrying the Munich terms reached the streets. Colin Coote rushed out into the Strand to buy one, and although the full details of the terms were still not known, the appearance of the newspaper caused consternation. Coote later recalled how Duff Cooper seized the paper from him and read the terms out aloud 'with obvious anger and disgust'. Coote's account continued: 'There was a silence as if all had been stricken dumb. Duff rose, and exited without a word.' The members then dispersed to their homes. As Churchill left the hotel, with Richard Law, they passed an open door leading into one of the restaurants, from which echoed the sounds of loud laughter. Churchill stopped in the doorway, watching impassively. 'The restaurant was packed,' Law later recalled, 'and everyone was very gay. I was acutely conscious of the brooding figure beside me. As we turned away, he muttered "those poor people! They little know what they will have to face".'

Throughout the morning the British Government urged the Czechs to accept the 'Munich' terms; at noon Beneš agreed to do so. That afternoon Chamberlain flew back to London. 'Vast crowds in the streets,' Oliver Harvey recorded in his diary, 'hysterical cheers and enthusiasm. PM on balcony at Buckingham Palace. But many feel it to be a great humiliation.' In an unpublished note written ten years later Churchill recalled how, that day, 'My wife and Lord Cecil solemnly discussed marching themselves with a select band to Downing Street and hurling a brick through the windows at N° 10.' During the day Lord Rothermere wrote to Churchill from Scotland:

The agreement signed in the early hours of this morning will lead to much friction, and will end after a period of nine or ten months by the entry of German troops into parts of Czecho-Slovakia outside the territory she has just gained.

A moribund people such as ours is not equipped to deal effectively with a totalitarian State.

Churchill spent Saturday October 1 at Chartwell, where he was visited by a young BBC producer, Guy Burgess,[1] who, after some difficulty, had persuaded the BBC to ask Churchill to give a half-hour talk on the Mediterranean. As a result of the Czech crisis, Churchill asked to cancel the talk; then invited Burgess to visit him and talk it over.

[1] Guy Burgess, 1912–1963. The son of a naval officer (who died when Burgess was 12). Educated at Eton and Dartmouth. Left Dartmouth on account of his poor eyesight, and returned to Eton. History scholar at Trinity College Cambridge, 1930–34; while at Cambridge he joined the Communist Party and the Anti-War Movement. Visited the Soviet Union in 1934, Germany in 1935. Joined the staff of the BBC, 1935; subsequently BBC representative at the House of Commons, responsible for the *Week in Westminster* programme. Joined the British Secret Service, December 1938. Involved in the preparation of Allied propaganda, 1939–40; returned to the BBC, 1941–43. Joined the Foreign Office News Department, 1943; Private Secretary to the Minister of State, 1946; British Embassy, Washington, 1950. Defected to the Soviet Union, 1951; subsequently resident in Moscow, where he died.

Burgess arrived at eleven o'clock. According to Burgess' biographer,[1] Churchill was carrying a trowel when Burgess arrived, as he had been building a wall. The account continued:

Churchill had just received a message from Beneš (he called him 'Herr Beans') asking for his 'advice and assistance'. But, said he, 'what answer shall I give? —for answer I shall and must. What advice can I return, what assistance can I proffer? Here am I'—Churchill added, rising from his seat and thumping his chest—'here am I, an old man, without power and without party. What advice can I give, what assistance can I proffer?'

He paused, and seemed to expect an answer. Guy, who was not then accustomed to consultations at this level, suggested diffidently that Churchill could offer the assistance of his eloquence: he could stump the country with speeches of protest.

Churchill seemed a little pleased. 'My eloquence!' he said. 'Ah, yes, that ... that Herr Beans can rely on in full and indeed'—he seemed to turn aside and wink at himself—'some would say, in overbounding measure. That I can offer him. But what else, Mr Burgess, what else can I offer him in my answer. . . ?'

Guy cannot be described as in general a tongue-tied person, but on this occasion his loquacity deserted him. He could think of nothing else to suggest. After a moment's pause, Churchill went on: 'You are silent, Mr Burgess. You are rightly silent. What else can I offer Herr Beans? Only one thing: my only son, Randolph. And Randolph, who is already'—he growled—'I trust, a gentleman, is training to be an officer.'

They went on to discuss wider aspects of the crisis. Guy found that, as he had expected, Churchill took the view that if Hitler had been resisted by Chamberlain, either the Czechs and therefore France, Britain and Russia would have fought or, quite possibly, there would have been no need to contemplate war at all. . . .

Churchill gave his visitor a copy of *Arms and the Covenant*, which he inscribed: 'To Guy Burgess, from Winston S. Churchill, to confirm his admirable sentiments.' They had talked together for some hours. During that whole time, Burgess recalled, Churchill sat alone in a blue boiler suit, 'with no other callers, no messengers bringing urgent despatches, no important secretaries with papers for him to read or sign; during the hours that this conversation lasted, the telephone did not ring once'. That evening, after his return to London, Burgess wrote to Churchill:

Traditional English policy since the reign of Elizabeth, the policy of Marlborough, of Pitt, of Eyre Crowe, of Vansittart, has been blandly set

---

[1] Tom Driberg (later Baron Bradwell), who visited Burgess in Moscow in 1956, when he took down a verbatim note of Burgess's recollections, which he published later that year in *Guy Burgess, a Portrait with Background*.

aside to suit the vanity, the obstinacy, & the *ignorance* of *one* man, no longer young. We shall be told he has saved the peace, that anything is worth that. This is not true. He has made war inevitable, & lost it. . . .

You spoke of 30 divisions given to Hitler. It is not 30 divisions that have been given to Hitler, but Germany itself—and a Germany that he will in future and for the first time, be able to lead into war with the possibility of success. . . .

Burgess went on to note that he had just heard the news that Duff Cooper had resigned from the Cabinet. 'But you alone,' he added, 'have the force & the authority to galvanise the potential allies into action.' Churchill had also just learned of Duff Cooper's resignation. 'I telephoned the news to Winston,' Lady Diana Cooper later recalled. 'His voice was broken with emotion. I could hear him cry.'

In the Cabinet of October 3, Chamberlain told his colleagues:

Ever since he had been Chancellor of the Exchequer, he had been oppressed with the sense that the burden of armaments might break our backs. This had been one of the factors which had led him to the view that it was necessary to try and resolve the causes which were responsible for the armaments race.

He thought that we were now in a more hopeful position, and that the contacts which had been established with the Dictator Powers opened up the possibility that we might be able to reach some agreement with them which which would stop the armaments race. It was clear, however, that it would be madness to stop rearming until we were convinced that other countries would act in the same way. For the time being, therefore, we should relax no particle of our effort until our deficiencies have been made good. That, however, was not the same thing as to say that as a thank offering for the present détente we should at once embark on a great increase in our armaments programme.

The Munich debate opened in the House of Commons on the afternoon of Monday October 3. The first of the speeches was Duff Cooper's resignation speech. 'The Prime Minister has believed in addressing Herr Hitler through the language of sweet reasonableness,' he said. 'I have believed that he was more open to the language of the mailed fist,' and, a few moments later: 'We have taken away the defences of Czechoslovakia in the same breath as we have guaranteed them, as though you were to deal a man a mortal blow and at the same time insure his life.'

Chamberlain spoke immediately after Duff Cooper. 'the real triumph,' of the Munich agreement he said, 'is that it has shown that representatives of four great Powers can find it possible to agree on a way of carrying out a difficult and delicate operation by discussion instead of by force of arms, and thereby they have averted a catastrophe which would have ended civilisation as we have known it.' Chamberlain also spoke of his hopes for the future, telling the House: 'Ever since I assumed my present office my main purpose has been to work for the pacification of Europe, for the removal of those suspicions and those animosities which have so long poisoned the air. The path which leads to appeasement is long and bristles with obstacles. The question of Czechoslovakia is the latest and perhaps the most dangerous. Now that we have got past it, I feel that it may be possible to make further progress along the road to sanity.'

This road included a 'determination' to fill up 'the deficiencies that yet remain in our armaments and in our defensive precautions' so that Britain would be ready to defend herself, 'and make our ordinary diplomacy effective'. At this suggestion Chamberlain was interrupted, but continued:

. . . yes I am a realist—nevertheless I say with an equal sense of reality that I do see fresh opportunities of approaching this subject of disarmament opening up before us, and I believe that they are at least as hopeful to-day as they have been at any previous time. It is to such tasks—the winning back of confidence, the gradual removal of hostility between nations until they feel that they can safely discard their weapons, one by one, that I would wish to devote what energy and time may be left to me before I hand over my office to younger men.

Speaking for the Labour Party, Clement Attlee declared: 'We have been unable to go in for care-free rejoicing. We have felt that we are in the midst of a tragedy. We have felt humiliation. This has not been a a victory for reason and humanity. It has been a victory for brute force.' For the Liberal Party, Archibald Sinclair stated: 'A policy which imposes injustice on a small and weak nation and tyranny on free men and women can never be the foundation of lasting peace,' and he went on to warn of what 'this surrender means' for the Sudeten-German Jews, and for the Sudeten-German Social Democrats, who, as a result of the Munich agreement, 'must exchange freedom for tyranny, or exile from their homes'. Anthony Eden also spoke against Chamberlain's policy. 'Successive surrenders,' he warned, 'bring only successive humiliation, and they, in their turn, more humiliating demands.'

Among the most outspoken, and courageous, of the Conservatives who spoke on October 3 was Bonar Law's son Richard, who asked: 'Can we really suppose that 3½ million Sudeten Germans were anxious, or have ever been anxious, to put themselves under this Nazi brutality?'

and who declared moments later: 'I believe that we have obtained, by peaceable means, what we have fought four wars to prevent happening, namely, the domination of Europe by a single Power.' On October 4 Josiah Wedgwood and Leopold Amery were among those who spoke against the Government's policy. Peace might have been combined with justice, Amery said, if, during the summer, Chamberlain had 'given real power to a Ministry of Munitions such as my right hon Friend the Member for Epping (Mr Churchill) and others have asked for for years past', had introduced a national register of potential soldiers, had mobilized the Fleet—'a very trifling disturbance of our civil life'—and had avoided repeating the 'guarded and obscure language' of his earlier speech of March 24.

Another speaker on October 4 was the Conservative MP Captain Sir Sidney Herbert, whom Churchill himself had encouraged to speak. 'At the expense of much dishonour,' Herbert told the House, 'we have gained a temporary respite of peace. In the name of all that is decent let us use that for rearmament,' and he went on to urge Chamberlain not to hold a General Election, as it had been rumoured he wished to do, simply in order to seek yet another large majority. It would be better, he argued, to broaden the basis of the Government, and to invite both Labour and the Trade Unions to join it. Above all, Herbert said, the pace of rearmament had been allowed to slacken, and must now be accelerated. Referring to the Sandys case, Herbert told the House of Commons: 'Even a child in my village knows that we have not got Bren guns in the numbers these ought to be for every battalion . . . what is the good of having the men if we are to send them like sheep to the slaughter without armaments. We have talked long enough about "the years which the locusts have eaten". I was led to suppose that the locusts had stopped nibbling about two years ago, but I can still hear their little jowls creaking yet under the Front Bench.'

Churchill did not speak until Wednesday October 5, the third day of the debate, but on October 4, while the debate was in progress, he expressed his thoughts on the crisis in an article in the *Daily Telegraph*, informing his readers that 'unbearable pressure' had been brought by France and Great Britain upon the Czechoslovak Government, 'and beneath that pressure they bent and yielded'. His article continued:

All those statesmen in the minor countries of Europe who have consistently endeavoured to incline their policy towards the Nazi channels; who have pointed out the weakness of the democracies, and the impediments to action provided by their parliamentary systems are now, of course, vindicated. All those who have hitherto laboured with France and Britain, remembering the achievements and results of the Great War, who represented elements opposed to the totalitarian system, are proportionately stultified and discouraged.

Churchill's article ended:

It is a crime to despair. We must learn to draw from misfortune the means of future strength. There must not be lacking in our leadership something of the spirit of that Austrian corporal who when all had fallen into ruins about him, and when Germany seemed to have sunk for ever into chaos, did not hesitate to march forth against the vast array of victorious nations, and has already turned the tables so decisively upon them.

It is the hour, not for despair, but for courage and re-building; and that is the spirit which should rule us in this hour.

48

The Munich Debate and After:
'A Defeat Without a War'

A T ten minutes past five on the afternoon of Wednesday October 5 Churchill rose from his corner seat below the gangway to give the House of Commons his considered opinion of the Munich agreement. He spoke for forty-nine minutes, opening his remarks with a reference to Chamberlain himself:

> If I do not begin this afternoon by paying the usual and indeed almost invariable, tributes to the Prime Minister for his handling of this crisis, it is certainly not from any lack of personal regard. We have always, over a great many years, had very pleasant relations, and I have deeply understood from personal experiences of my own in a similar crisis the stress and strain he has had to bear; but I am sure it is much better to say exactly what we think about public affairs, and this is certainly not the time when it is worth anyone's while to court political popularity.

Churchill then spoke in praise of Duff Cooper's resignation speech. 'We had a shining example of firmness of character,' he said, 'from the First Lord of the Admiralty two days ago. He showed that firmness of character which is utterly unmoved by currents of opinion, however swift and violent they may be.' He also singled out for praise Richard Law's 'compulsive' speech of protest, which had revived, he said, 'the memory of his famous father, so cherished in this House, and made us feel that his gifts did not die with him'.[1] Churchill's speech continued:

---

[1] On October 14 Richard Law wrote to Churchill: '. . . I'd like to congratulate you upon your terrific speech in the House last week (as well as to thank you for your kind & generous reference to myself) & upon your attitude throughout the whole of this affair— I mean from the beginning of "Arms & the Covenant". I hope that one day you will come into your own, although from your own point of view it's not really of very much importance; can't see that office, even the highest, can add much to your fame.'

Having thus fortified myself by the example of others, I will proceed to emulate them. I will, therefore, begin by saying the most unpopular and most unwelcome thing. I will begin by saying what everybody would like to ignore or forget but which must nevertheless be stated, namely, that we have sustained a total and unmitigated defeat, and that France has suffered even more than we have.

Viscountess Astor: Nonsense.

Mr Churchill: When the Noble Lady cries 'Nonsense,' she could not have heard the Chancellor of the Exchequer [Sir John Simon] admit in his illuminating and comprehensive speech just now that Herr Hitler had gained in this particular leap forward in substance all he set out to gain. The utmost my right hon Friend the Prime Minister has been able to secure by all his immense exertions, by all the great efforts and mobilisation which took place in this country, and by all the anguish and strain through which we have passed in this country, the utmost he has been able to gain—[Hon Members: 'Is peace.'] I thought I might be allowed to make that point in its due place, and I propose to deal with it. The utmost he has been able to gain for Czechoslovakia and in the matters which were in dispute has been that the German dictator, instead of snatching his victuals from the table, has been content to have them served to him course by course. . . .

'I am not quite clear,' Churchill continued, 'why there was so much danger of Great Britain or France being involved in a war with Germany at this juncture if, in fact, they were ready all along to sacrifice Czechoslovakia.' Indeed, he went on, 'I will say this, that I believe the Czechs, left to themselves and told they were going to get no help from the Western Powers, would have been able to make better terms than they have got—they could hardly have worse, after all this tremendous perturbation.'

Churchill was convinced that September's 'formidable apparatus of crisis' could have been avoided if, during the summer, the Sudeten German question had been referred for settlement to a League of Nations Commission, 'or some other impartial body', and that the security of Czechoslovakia ought to have been specifically guaranteed by Britain, France and Russia immediately after the German annexation of Austria in March. Such a combination, he believed, might even have stimulated those inside Germany, soldiers and civilians, who did not believe Germany was ready for a world war, or who 'dreaded war', as moderate opinion always did. A few moments later he explained that, in his view:

Between submission and immediate war there was this third alternative, which gave a hope not only of peace but of justice. It is quite true that such a policy in order to succeed demanded that Britain should declare straight out and a long time beforehand that she would, with others, join to defend

Czechoslovakia against an unprovoked aggression. His Majesty's Government refused to give that guarantee when it would have saved the situation, yet in the end they gave it when it was too late, and now, for the future, they renew it when they have not the slightest power to make it good.

'All is over,' Churchill continued. 'Silent, mournful, abandoned, broken, Czechoslovakia recedes into the darkness. She has suffered in every respect by her association with the Western democracies and with the League of Nations, of which she has always been an obedient servant.' He went on to recall that during the summer both Britain and France had favoured Sudeten autonomy within the Czechoslovak State; that Henlein had himself spoken in favour of such a solution; and that the Czechs had finally agreed to it. Then Britain and France had agreed to Hitler's demand for a plebiscite, and finally they had accepted the 'immediate transfer' of large areas to Germany without even the semblance of self-determination. 'It is a fraud and a farce to invoke that name,' he said, and he added:

We in this country, as in other Liberal and democratic countries, have a perfect right to exalt the principle of self-determination, but it comes ill out of the mouths of those in totalitarian States who deny even the smallest element of toleration to every section and creed within their bounds.

As a result of the transfer of the Sudetenland to Germany, Churchill told the House, Czechoslovakia was both politically 'mutilated' and economically in 'complete confusion'. Its fortress defences were in German hands, its railways broken, its industries curtailed. And at any moment Hitler might order Goebbels 'to start again his propaganda of calumny and lies'. Now that the frontier fortresses were lost, what was there, he asked, 'to stop the will of the conqueror?' He continued: 'I venture to think that in future the Czechoslovak State cannot be maintained as an independent entity. You will find that in a period of time which may be measured by years, but may be measured only by months, Czechoslovakia will be engulfed in the Nazi regime.'

The 'abandonment and ruin' of Czechoslovakia was not, Churchill said, to be considered only in the light of the September crisis. There was a far more sombre perspective in which it had to be set:

It is the most grievous consequence which we have yet experienced of what we have done and of what we have left undone in the last five years—five years of futile good intention, five years of eager search for the line of least resistance, five years of uninterrupted retreat of British power, five years of neglect of our air defences. Those are the features which I stand here to declare and which marked an improvident stewardship for which Great Britain and France have dearly to pay.

Churchill then turned to the question of British responsibility:

So far as this country is concerned the responsibility must rest with those who have the undisputed control of our political affairs. They neither prevented Germany from rearming, nor did they rearm ourselves in time. They quarrelled with Italy without saving Ethiopia. They exploited and discredited the vast institution of the League of Nations and they neglected to make alliances and combinations which might have repaired previous errors, and thus they left us in the hour of trial without adequate national defence or effective international security.

Churchill refused to accept the view that the Munich agreement was a triumph for British diplomacy, or that it would open the way, as Chamberlain believed, to a reduction of European tension, and to even closer relations between Britain and Germany. Starkly, he declared:

We are in the presence of a disaster of the first magnitude which has befallen Great Britain and France. Do not let us blind ourselves to that. It must now be accepted that all the countries of Central and Eastern Europe will make the best terms they can with the triumphant Nazi Power.

The system of alliances in Central Europe upon which France has relied for her safety has been swept away, and I can see no means by which it can be reconstituted. The road down the Danube Valley to the Black Sea, the resources of corn and oil, the road which leads as far as Turkey, has been opened. . . .

Churchill went on to say that Hitler need not fire 'a single shot' to extend his power into the Danube basin, telling the House of Commons:

You will see, day after day, week after week, the entire alienation of those regions. Many of those countries, in fear of the rise of the Nazi Power, have already got politicians, Ministers, Governments, who were pro-German, but there was always an enormous popular movement in Poland, Rumania, Bulgaria and Yugoslavia which looked to the Western democracies and loathed the idea of having this arbitrary rule of the totalitarian system thrust upon them, and hoped that a stand would be made. All that has gone by the board. We are talking about countries which are a long way off and of which, as the Prime Minister might say, we know nothing.[1]

Yet the day would come, Churchill warned, when Hitler might choose 'to look westward'. Then France and Britain would bitterly regret the loss of the Czech fortress army, which in the weeks before the Munich

---

[1] In a radio broadcast on September 27 Chamberlain had said: 'How horrible, fantastic, incredible it is that we should be digging trenches and trying on gas-masks here because of a quarrel in a faraway country between people of whom we know nothing. It seems still more impossible that a quarrel which has already been settled in principle should be the subject of war.'

conference was estimated to require 'not fewer than 30 German divisions for its destruction'. A further twelve divisions had already been added to the German Army at the time of the annexation of Austria. But in the current four-year period the Cabinet had agreed to add only four battalions—a single division—to the strength of the British Army. He went on:

Many people, no doubt, honestly believe that they are only giving away the interests of Czechoslovakia, whereas I fear we shall find that we have deeply compromised, and perhaps fatally endangered, the safety and even the independence of Great Britain and France.

This is not merely a question of giving up the German Colonies, as I am sure we shall be asked to do. Nor is it a question only of losing influence in Europe. It goes far deeper than that. You have to consider the character of the Nazi movement and the rule which it implies.

Churchill then exposed what he was convinced was yet another weakness in the policy of appeasement:

The Prime Minister desires to see cordial relations between this country and Germany. There is no difficulty at all in having cordial relations with the German people. Our hearts go out to them. But they have no power.

You must have diplomatic and correct relations, but there can never be friendship between the British democracy and the Nazi Power, that Power which spurns Christian ethics, which cheers its onward course by a barbarous paganism, which vaunts the spirit of aggression and conquest, which derives strength and perverted pleasure from persecution, and uses, as we have seen, with pitiless brutality the threat of murderous force. That Power cannot ever be the trusted friend of the British democracy.

What I find unendurable is the sense of our country falling into the power, into the orbit and influence of Nazi Germany and of our existence becoming dependent upon their good will or pleasure. It is to prevent that that I have tried my best to urge the maintenance of every bulwark of defence—first the timely creation of an Air Force superior to anything within striking distance of our shores; secondly the gathering together of the collective strength of many nations; and thirdly, the making of alliances and military conventions, all within the Covenant, in order to gather together forces at any rate to restrain the onward movement of this Power. It has all been in vain. Every position has been successively undermined and abandoned on specious and plausible excuses.

In order to protect Britain from the 'advance of Nazi power', and to secure 'those forms of life which are so dear to us', Churchill urged a new effort of rearmament 'the like of which has not been seen'.

In the five days since Chamberlain's return from Munich there had been much public rejoicing. Almost every newspaper had been ecstatic in his praise. The enthusiasm of the crowds in Downing Street seemed to have no parallel. Churchill ended his speech by referring to this public jubilation:

I do not grudge our loyal, brave people, who were ready to do their duty no matter what the cost, who never flinched under the strain of last week— I do not grudge them the natural, spontaneous outburst of joy and relief when they learned that the hard ordeal would no longer be required of them at the moment; but they should know the truth.

They should know that there has been gross neglect and deficiency in our defences; they should know that we have sustained a defeat without a war, the consequences of which will travel far with us along our road; they should know that we have passed an awful milestone in our history, when the whole equilibrium of Europe has been deranged, and that the terrible words have for the time being been pronounced against the Western democracies:

'*Thou art weighed in the balance and found wanting.*'

And do not suppose that this is the end. This is only the beginning of the reckoning. This is only the first sip, the first foretaste of a bitter cup which will be proferred to us year by year unless by a supreme recovery of moral health and martial vigour, we arise again and take our stand for freedom as in the olden time.

Churchill was followed in the debate by Page Croft, with whom he had been allied for five years in opposition to the Government's India policy, and who, angered by Churchill's attack on the Government, declared himself 'in complete difference' with all Churchill had said. It was only Chamberlain's 'act of friendship', Page Croft declared, that had 'saved Czechoslovakia from annihilation'.

Churchill was angered that some of his friends and former supporters had voted for the Government's policy. One of those, Alan Lennox-Boyd, later commented that as a result of his support for Munich, Churchill 'regarded me as a renegade', and Patrick Donner likewise recalled, in conversation with the author:

After the debate Churchill came up to me in the corridor and abused me like a Billingsgate fishwife. I was no longer 'Patrick' after ten years, and the intimacy was never recreated. It was the underlying principle for him. You must have principles. He was right in his way. It was very sad for me. I adored him.

It centred around his view of the national interest. There was no bridging the gulf. . . .

Donner went on to explain: 'If somebody took an action which in his judgment was contrary to the national interest he would have absolutely nothing further to do with that person. You could say what you liked, but if you voted against what he regarded as the national interest that was that—he was prosecution counsel and judge combined.'

Press reaction to Churchill's speech was mixed. The *Daily Express* called it 'an alarmist oration by a man whose mind is soaked in the conquests of Marlborough', and believed that his decision not to support the Government 'weakens his influence among the members of the Conservative Party'. According to *The Times*, Churchill 'treated a crowded House to prophesies which made Jeremiah appear an optimist' and went on to refer to Churchill's 'dismal sincerity'. For its part, the *Daily Telegraph* believed that Churchill's warnings 'verified by events, have entitled him to be heard. . . .'

Immediately after his speech, Churchill went to Brendan Bracken's house with a number of Conservative and National Government MPs who shared his opposition to Chamberlain's policy, among them a young Conservative MP who had previously supported Chamberlain's foreign policy, Ronald Cartland.[1] They discussed what tactics they ought to adopt when the House divided at the end of the debate. Some, like Anthony Crossley, wished to abstain, others, like Ronald Cartland, to vote against. In his diary Harold Nicolson, who was present, recorded that although the general view was for abstention, Churchill argued that merely to abstain would mean 'that he half agreed with Government policy'. It was finally decided that each MP must do as he personally thought best. But when the group met again on October 6, shortly before the division, it was decided, as Nicolson recorded, 'that it is better for us all to abstain, than for some to abstain and some to vote against'.

When the vote took place, thirty Conservative MPs abstained. Of these thirty, thirteen, including Churchill, remained seated. Their action in remaining seated 'must enrage the Government', Nicolson—who was among those who did not rise—noted in his diary, 'since it is not our numbers that matter but our reputation'.[2] That same day,

---

[1] John Ronald Hamilton Cartland, 1907–1940. Brother of Barbara Cartland. Their father was killed in action on the western front on 27 May 1918. Educated at Charterhouse. Worked at the Conservative Central Office 1927–35. Conservative MP for King's Norton, 1935–40. Captain, 53rd Anti-Tank Regiment, Royal Artillery, British Expeditionary Force, 1940. Killed in action in France, 30 May 1940. Churchill wrote of him, on 7 November 1941 (in the preface to Barbara Cartland's book *Ronald Cartland*): 'At a time when our political life had become feckless and dull, he spoke fearlessly for Britain. His words and acts were instinct with the sense of our country's traditions and duty. His courage and bearing inspired those who met him or heard him.'

[2] Those who remained sitting were Churchill, Derrick Gunston, Ronald Cartland, Duncan Sandys, Harold Nicolson, Richard Law, Brendan Bracken, Commander Bower, Sir Roger, Keyes, Lord Wolmer, Vyvyan Adams and Captain Alan Graham. The abstainers included

Churchill wrote to his friend General Tudor: 'The Government have thrown everything away, and I am trying now to see what plans can be made to stop the Huns.'

Worried that it was not realized that he too had abstained, Robert Boothby wrote to Churchill on October 7 to assure him that he had in fact done so. 'I have just seen Brendan,' he wrote. 'He did not know that I had abstained from voting. . . .' Churchill replied that same day: 'Of course, you were perfectly free to vote as you chose, and I am very glad to note that you abstained from voting on the Government motion.' And he added:

I do not understand the agitation which seizes you in these moments of what is, after all only petty Parliamentary action. You get so distressed about these matters both at the beginning and at the end, and nearly all our friends thought you had crumpled under the strain. You will certainly live to see many worse things than you have seen at present.

'I feel that the consequences of our defeat . . .' Boothby replied three days later, 'are incalculable; and that we may well have witnessed the first definite step in the downfall of the British Empire. I certainly doubt that we can live to see any worse thing happen than military defeat at the hands of Germany.' He ended on a personal note: 'I do not think I have "crumpled"; but I confess I cannot regard the events of the past few days, which I sincerely believe portend the doom of at any rate my generation, without agitation.'

On October 8 Sir Sidney Herbert wrote to Churchill to congratulate him on his 'magnificent' speech; 'but so is every speech you make', he added, '& I wish to God that the Government had listened to you years ago'. Herbert went on to thank Churchill 'from my heart' for the help he had given him during the Munich debate:

First for your encouragement—secondly for giving me your seat to speak from —(the best that exists in the H of C if one cannot have a Treasury box) & thirdly for all the kind things you were good enough to say to me afterwards.

I remember that you said that I must have been very well fit to make such a speech. Actually I lay in bed from 2 to 4 pm in a mixture of coma & terror—I could write no further notes, nor arrange my speech—& had it not been for you, I think I should have 'run out' on it. So I thank you the

---

Eden, Duff Cooper, Amery, Sir Sidney Herbert, General Spears, Harold Macmillan and Anthony Crossley. Those who supported the Government in the division included several who had earlier supported Churchill on India, including Sir Henry Page Croft, Patrick Donner, Alan Lennox-Boyd, Victor Raikes and Sir Murray Sueter.

more for having both helped & 'gingered' me into a speech which has, I think, proved useful. . . .

Herbert's letter ended: 'Tell me how to help—until we are fully rearmed & able to talk *almost* equally to a Dictator.' Churchill replied from Chartwell on October 9:

You stopped the General Election by your speech; and as you spoke I seemed to hear the voice of that old Conservative Party I once honoured and not of this over-whipped crowd of poor 'whites'.

I hear of the greatest panic in inner circles about the state of their defences now and in the future.

I must send you a copy of my book, which will show how precise, prolonged and detailed have been the warnings I have given.

I am so glad that we are working together again. I should like to talk to you very much, and I wonder whether you could come and spend a night here during the next fortnight or so? You have never seen this small place, which I have constructed largely with my own hands.

Following the division on October 6, Chamberlain moved a motion to adjourn the House until November 1. This was at once opposed by Attlee and Sinclair, as well as by several Conservatives. Harold Macmillan declared: 'We are being treated more and more as a kind of Reichstag to meet only to hear the orations and register the decrees of the government of the day.' It was essential for Parliament to meet before November 1, in what was, Macmillan said, a situation 'more dangerous and more formidable, more terrible than at any time since the beginning of Christian civilisation'. Churchill likewise urged an early recall of Parliament to meet before November 1, suggesting that they meet for two days on October 18. 'It is derogatory to Parliament . . .' he said, 'that it should be thought unfit as it were to be attending to these grave matters, that it should be sent away upon a holiday in one of the most formidable periods through which we have lived.' When Chamberlain said that it was up to the Speaker when Parliament was recalled, Churchill interjected: 'But only on the advice of His Majesty's Government.' Such a remark, Chamberlain retorted, was 'unworthy'. To say that the Government were not aware of the gravity of the crisis was a 'repetition of tittle tattle'.

Churchill protested at Chamberlain calling his remarks unworthy, but Chamberlain was not in a mood to apologize, writing from 10 Downing Street on October 6:

I am sorry if you think my remarks were offensive, but I must say that I think you are singularly sensitive for a man who so constantly attacks others.

I considered your remarks highly offensive to me and to those with whom I have been working.

I had not regarded these remarks, wounding as they were, as requiring a breach of personal relations, but you cannot expect me to allow you to do all the hitting and never hit back.

Churchill's despair at the results of the Munich Agreement was reflected in varying degrees in his correspondence in the days following the Munich debate. To Sir Arthur Longmore,[1] who had asked him to pick a new date for his talk to the Imperial Defence College—a talk postponed because of the crisis—Churchill wrote: 'I am so distressed by the change in the situation that I haven't the heart to address myself to the task to which you invited me at present. Thank you very much all the same for giving me a further opportunity.' In gloomy prophecy he wrote to the Polish Ambassador, Count Edward Raczynski,[2] on October 7, following the Polish seizure of the Czech mining town of Teschen:

We are all in the trough here, but your country has also passed through tragic vicissitudes. I have always thought of Poland as a nation which possessed a strong historical sense. This makes me all the more grieved to contemplate the squalid events which are occurring in Central Europe.

Believe me, all comes out even at the end of the day, and all will come out yet more even when all the days are ended.

To Richard Acland—who had voted against the Government after the Munich debate—Churchill wrote on October 9, of the immediate prospect:

. . . there has been for several years no chance of catching up except by a combination or grand alliance of Powers, great and small, coupled with intense national effort. The disaster of Czechoslovakia has annihilated all possibility of a combination which can restore the situation in Europe.

---

[1] Arthur Murray Longmore, 1885–1970. Entered Navy, 1904. Squadron-Commander, Royal Flying Corps (Naval Wing) 1912; transferred to the Royal Naval Air Service, 1914. Commanded No 1 Royal Naval Air Service Squadron, Dunkirk, December 1914. Served in Flanders, at the Battle of Jutland, and in Italy, 1914–18. Director of Equipment, Air Ministry, 1925–29. Commandant, RAF College Cranwell, 1929–33. Air Officer Commanding Inland Area, 1933–34; Coastal Command, 1934–36. Knighted, 1935. Commandant, Imperial Defence College, 1936–38. Air Officer Commanding in Chief, Training Command, 1939; Middle East, 1940–41. Inspector General of the RAF, 1941. Retired with the rank of Air Chief Marshal, 1942. Vice-Chairman, Imperial War Graves Commission, 1954–57.

[2] Edward Raczynski, 1891–   . Educated at Krakow and Leipzig Universities, and at the London School of Economics. Entered the Polish Ministry of Foreign Affairs, 1919. Polish Minister to the League of Nations and Polish Delegate to the Disarmament Conference, 1932–34; Ambassador to London, 1934–45. Acting Polish Minister for Foreign Affairs (in London), 1941–42; Minister of State for Foreign Affairs in General Sikorski's Cabinet, London, 1942–43. Chairman of the Polish Research Centre, London, 1940–67.

Nevertheless, night and day work by the whole of France and England might put us in a position where the Dictators might find easier prizes elsewhere.

No matter what happened, Churchill added, 'we must do our best'; but he greatly feared 'a demand to cease arming, backed with specious blandishments'. Churchill's nephew Johnny later recalled in conversation with the author: 'The gloom after Munich was absolutely terrific. At Chartwell there were occasions just alone with him when the despondency was overwhelming. The atmosphere became very charged. The faithful came down, but it did not change the situation of this awful thing developing by degrees.'

Churchill's fears of a German hegemony in Europe had been accentuated by the way in which France had been persuaded, partly by the weakness of leaders like Bonnet and Flandin, partly by pressure from Chamberlain, to allow its guarantee to Czechoslovakia to be eclipsed at the very moment when it was most needed by the Czechs. His two friends of the pre-Munich Cabinet, Paul Reynaud and Georges Mandel, had both resigned in protest. On October 10 Churchill wrote to Reynaud:

I feel deeply concerned about the position of France, and about our own course. I cannot see what foreign policy is now open to the French Republic. No minor State will risk its future upon the guarantee of France. I am indulging in no pretensions upon our own account. You have been infected by our weakness, without being fortified by our strength. The politicians have broken the spirit of both countries successively. In the end England was ready to be better than her word. But it was too late.

The magnitude of the disaster leaves me groping in the dark. Not since the loss of the American Colonies has England suffered so deep an injury. France is back to the morrow of 1870.

What are we to do?

I cannot tell what are the forces now governing French action. Flandin is surely only typical of very large interests and moods which are at work beneath the surface of French politics.[1]

The question now presenting itself is: Can we make head against the Nazi domination, or ought we *severally* to make the best terms possible with it—while trying to rearm? Or is a common effort still possible?

For thirty years I have consistently worked with France. I make no defence of my own country; but I do not know on what to rest to-day.

Please show this letter to Monsieur Mandel: but keep it otherwise to yourself.

[1] During the Munich crisis Flandin had urged publicly that France should in no circumstances fight for Czechoslovakia, and he had gone so far as to placard the streets of Paris with a manifesto in this sense. The manifesto had been torn down by the police. Immediately following the Munich Agreement, Flandin had sent a telegram of congratulations to Hitler.

For the first time in his political career—and it was nearly forty years since he had first stood for Parliament—Churchill's optimism deserted him. Despite his appeal in Parliament for a national revival, the events of September 1938 filled him with a deep despondency which pervaded his private correspondence. 'I am now greatly distressed,' he wrote to John Dafoe[1] on October 11, 'and for the time being staggered by the situation. Hitherto the peace-loving Powers have been definitely stronger than the Dictators, but next year we must expect a different balance.

[1] John W. Dafoe, 1866–1944. Born in Canada. Editor of the *Montreal Herald*, 1892–95; the *Winnipeg Free Press*, 1901–44. Represented the Canadian Department of Public Information at the Paris Peace Conference, 1919. Churchill had met him in Winnipeg in August 1929.

49

'I Feel Much Alone'

THE impact of Churchill's Munich speech was considerable. But Violet Bonham Carter wrote to him on October 6, as soon as it was over, 'Will it pierce the shell of those drowsy tortoises? dragging us to our doom?' That same day Emery Revesz wrote from Paris: 'Your speech in the House was grand. It made a very big impression over here on all those who can still be impressed. . . .' Revesz added that in the Chamber everyone had voted for the Munich agreement 'in order to avoid being called a "bellicist"', and he went on: 'There will come a great reaction one day in France, but, of course, too late.' Writing on October 20 Paul Reynaud declared: 'One of your colleagues, a Labour MP, told me of the very great success of your speech and the increasing importance of your position in Britain. I rejoice that this should be so.'[1] On October 22 Churchill received a letter from Germany from an anonymous 'German citizen' who wrote: 'You have no idea of the respect which the German people hold for you, Duff Cooper, Eden, and other English statesmen who defend justice.'

As a result of the Munich debate, relations between Churchill and Chamberlain had worsened considerably. On October 9 Chamberlain revealed his animosity in a letter to his sister, telling her:

I must say that I found the 4 days debate in the House a pretty trying ordeal, especially as I had to fight all the time against the defection of weaker brethren & Winston was carrying on a regular campaign against me with the aid of Masaryk the Czech minister. They, of course, are totally unaware of my knowledge of their proceedings: I had continual information of their doings & sayings which for the nth time demonstrated how completely Winston can deceive himself when he wants to, & how utterly credulous a

---

[1] On November 1 Reynaud was brought back into the Government as Minister of Finance. Churchill telegraphed to him on the following day: 'I am very glad to see you in this great position, and hope it may further the views which we hold in common.'

foreigner can be when he is told the thing he wants to hear. In this case the thing was that 'Chamberlain's fall was imminent'. . . .

I tried occasionally to take an antidote to the poison gas by reading a few of the countless letters & telegrams which continued to pour in expressing in most moving accents the writers' heartfelt relief & gratitude. All the world seemed to be full of my praises except the House of Commons, but of course that was where I happened to be myself, so naturally its voice spoke loudest in my ear. However on Wednesday things began to mend. . . .

The conflict between Churchill and Chamberlain was often referred to by Churchill's correspondents. 'Neville Chamberlain's reputation will not be undermined so long as he is Prime Minister,' Lord Rothermere warned on October 15, 'and any member of his Party who challenges that fact may suffer a complete eclipse. The public is so terrified of being bombed that they will support anyone who keeps them out of the war. . . . I do hope you will soft pedal on the whole position.' That same day Chamberlain wrote to his sister:

Perhaps if I were differently constituted I might just sit & bask in this popularity while it lasted. But I am already a little impatient with it because it seems to assume so much. We have avoided the greatest catastrophe it is true, but we are very little nearer to the time when we can put all thoughts of war our of our minds & settle down to make the world a better place. And unhappily there are a great many people who have no faith that we can ever arrive at such a time & do all they can to make their own gloomy prophecies come true.

On October 16, in a broadcast to the United States, Churchill warned that neither the British nor French publics had yet fully realized the far-reaching consequences 'of the abandonment and ruin of the Czechoslovak republic'. Nevertheless, he added, 'the cause of freedom has in it a recuperative power and virtue, which can draw from misfortune new hope and new strength'. Churchill told his American listeners that only intense, rapid rearmament, and the immediate close cooperation of Britain and the United States, could redress the balance. 'We are left in no doubt where American conviction and sympathies lie,' he said, 'but will you wait until British freedom and independence have succumbed, and then take up the cause, when it is three-quarters ruined, yourselves alone?'

Writing to Churchill on October 17, Sir Sidney Herbert commented: 'One of the things which the Prime Minister appears consistently to ignore is American public opinion, and your broadcast did much to remedy this.' Herbert added: 'I have spent more time than most trying to convince Ministers of the truth of your warnings and of the dangers with which we are faced.' On October 27 Colin Coote wrote to Churchill, appealing to him to attack the Government. According to Coote:

I assume that all decent people must be considering how to excise from the body politic this contaminating canker which calls itself a Government.

Upon this assumption, from the post in the enemy's headquarters which you once enjoined me to keep, I send you my conclusions formed after hearing their plans.

These plans are the mixture of cowardice and cunning with which we have become familiar; but they can be defeated. You will have already observed that Mr Chamberlain has been transformed from the Archangel Gabriel, bringing back peace with honour, to the defendant on a charge of dereliction of duty. . . .

There will be no Ministry of Supply. All that will happen is a Cabinet Committee under Runciman, with instructions to allow manufacturers to profiteer. That is what they call cutting out red tape. There will be no Ministry of National Service. All that will happen is that some Minister will be instructed to play at drawing up a National Register on lines which will not do more than offer jobs to drop-outs. There are three main reasons why Chamberlain does not mean business.

(1) He honestly thinks he can do a deal with Hitler and Mussolini.
(2) He is afraid of the effect of large-scale rearmament on the pound sterling.
(3) He fundamentally wants Nazi ideas to dominate Europe, because of his fantastic dislike of Soviet Russia.[1]

I therefore beg you not to be sidetracked by any of his stupidities into attacking him upon anything except defence. . . .

'It is, of course, possible,' Coote added, 'that the British people themselves are rotted by bad leadership, and that they deserve the Chamberlain policy. But at least they should be given a chance to show whether they are decadent or not; and the defence issue will give them the chance.'

Churchill was determined to maintain the pressure for greater rearmament. 'The exposure of the failure of our defences,' he wrote to

[1] Colin Coote's information and instincts were correct. On October 21 Chamberlain informed Sir Horace Wilson that the demand for a Ministry of Supply was being made 'purely on political grounds', that he had 'already warned' William Hadley, the editor of the *Sunday Times*, against it, and that he would shortly speak to Geoffrey Dawson. The Cabinet decided against a Ministry of Supply on October 26, and confirmed their decision on November 14. Nor was a Ministry of National Service set up until the outbreak of war (when Ernest Brown became Minister of Labour and National Service). As for Chamberlain's belief that he could 'do a deal' with Hitler, on November 10 Chamberlain wrote to his sister: 'Since I last wrote I have seen a very interesting report by young "Bill" Astor who has been visiting Berlin, Sudetenland, Czecho-Slovakia, Austria & France. He, too, has the impression that Hitler definitely liked me & thought he could do business with me. . . .' For Chamberlain's dislike of Soviet Russia, see his letter to his sister of 28 May 1939: 'I had & have deep suspicions of Soviet aims' (quoted on page 1073).

Richard Law on October 18, 'strips Ministers of all credentials to be judges of the national interests,' and he added: 'let us take counsel together as to how we can stem the ebb-tide of British fortunes'. To Ramsay Muir,[1] who had written to him on October 13 to urge him to take the lead 'in a movement of national regeneration', he replied on October 18 about 'the absolutely shameful mismanagement, and indeed betrayal of our interest in the rearmament failure'. It was from Parliament alone, he believed, that the regeneration could come. But if his own constituents were to turn against him, he would fight back in a by-election, the circumstances of which 'would greatly assist the developments you have in mind'.

Churchill's concern about his constituency was not without cause. As was happening with several other Conservative MPs who had abstained on October 6, strong local pressures were building up to force him out of his seat. The Duchess of Atholl at Kinross, Robert Boothby in Aberdeenshire and Richard Law at Kingston-upon-Hull were all in difficulties.[2]

On October 29 Churchill wrote to Page Croft, about his own position in the party:

I see rifts coming in the near future. It seems to me that Hitler will require of Chamberlain to have an Election before he makes his bargain, and to give proofs that he is in a position, at any rate for several years, to 'deliver the goods'. I have no doubt where I stand in that event. It may be possible to fight within the ranks of the Conservative Party, but will there be any rally of the strong forces of the Conservative Party to defend our rights and possessions, and to make the necessary sacrifices and exertions required for our safety, or is it all to go down the drain as it did in the India business, through the influence of the Central Office and the Government Whips? If so, I know my duty. . . .

<hr />

[1] Ramsay Muir, 1872–1941. Historian; he published his first book, on Liverpool Municipal history, in 1906; his *Atlas of Modern History* in 1911. Liberal MP for Rochdale, 1923–24. Chairman of the National Liberal Federation, 1931–33; President, 1933–36. Vice-President, Liberal Party Organization, 1936. His autobiography was published posthumously in 1944.

[2] Both Law and Boothby were finally supported by their constituency associations, but the Duchess of Atholl resigned after her local constituency association had decided by 273 votes to 167 to seek a new candidate at the next election. When she decided to stand as an Independent, Churchill sent her a letter of support in which he declared: 'You are no doubt opposed by many Conservatives as loyal and patriotic as yourself; but the fact remains that outside our island your defeat at this moment would be relished by the enemies of Britain and of Freedom in every part of the world. It would be widely accepted as another sign that Great Britain is sinking under the weight of her cares, and no longer has the spirit and will-power to confront the tyrannies and cruel persecutions which have darkened this age.' The by-election was held on December 21. The Duchess lost by 1,313 votes, to the official Conservative candidate.

If you tell me that our Party is definitely committed to the easy-going life, to the surrender of our possessions and interests for the sake of quietness, to putting off the evil day at all costs, and that they will go along with Chamberlain into what must inevitably be a state of sub-servience, if not indeed actual vassalage to Germany, and that you can do nothing to arrest this fatal tide, then I think the knowledge would simplify my course.

The situation in Churchill's constituency seemed to bear out his pessimism as to the future of the Conservative Party. Even Sir Harry Goschen, one of his staunchest constituency supporters for fourteen years, had been disturbed by his Munich speech, writing privately to Sir James Hawkey on October 20:

I cannot help thinking it was rather a pity that he broke up the harmony of the House by the speech he made. Of course he was not like a small ranting member, and his words were telegraphed all over the Continent and to America, and I think it would have been a great deal better if he had kept quiet and not made a speech at all.

Goschen added that in the outlying areas of the constituency, such as Harlow, the local party members were 'up in arms' about Churchill's criticisms of Chamberlain, and that there had been many complaints to Conservative Central Office. Another of Churchill's former leading supporters in the constituency, Colin Thornton-Kemsley, had been active since the Munich debate in drumming up an anti-Churchill lobby. 'We wanted him to support the Conservative administration, not to discredit them,' Thornton-Kemsley later recalled.

On October 30 Churchill learnt that the next meeting of the Air Defence Research sub-committee had been postponed for two weeks, until November 14, and that Lindemann would not be re-instated. Angrily, he wrote to Sir Kingsley Wood to ask that Lindemann be re-instated, so that he himself could take full advantage of the 'technical knowledge' which Lindemann could provide. Churchill added:

This leads me to draw your attention to what I wrote to you on June 9th, when you first took office as Air Minister. The importance of this subject to our safety has now become paramount. But the Committee, in my opinion, is failing in its task, and is in danger of becoming an actual barrier upon swift progress. . . .

Unless I can feel that the work of this Committee is going to receive a new impulse from your own personal direction, I should consider it my duty to free myself from the silence I have observed for three years upon this branch of our defence and, with due regard to the necessity for secrecy, to endeavour to get something done by Parliamentary action. . . .

On October 25 Kingsley Wood had prepared for the Cabinet a memorandum on air policy, in which he pointed out that the existing British first-line strength was 1,606, with 412 in reserve. The German first-line strength was 3,200 with 2,400 in reserve. Under Britain's existing rate of production, on 1 August 1939 Britain would have 1,890 first-line and 1,502 reserve, as contrasted with the German figure of 4,030 first-line and 3,000 reserve: a comparative strength of 3,392 British to 7,030 German aeroplanes.[1] By April 1940 this ratio would be improved to 5,809 British as against 7,940 German. Kingsley Wood pointed out that the decision taken by the Cabinet six months earlier, in April 1938, 'was dictated mainly by what were then considered to be the limitations on aircraft production and was not related to the possible German air strength by the date when it was due for completion', and he added: 'It is clear that in our previous programmes of expansion we have not taken a sufficiently long range view and have underestimated both the capacity and intentions of Germany.'

Kingsley Wood asked for immediate authority to build half the aeroplanes he believed would be needed by 1942, that is, for the present, 1,850 fighters and 1,750 bombers. It was 'essential', he wrote, 'that at least these orders should be placed at a very early date'.

When the Cabinet met on October 26, Inskip deprecated the setting up of a Ministry of Supply, but argued in favour of an increase in the existing defence programme. As the minutes recorded, 'he pointed out that the present scale of equipment of the Territorial Army would not enable it to train effectively on embodiment, and that it would be necessary to consider some increase in the scale at present authorised'. Chamberlain, while agreeing with Inskip that no Ministry of Supply was needed, rejected his appeal for greater expenditure within the existing Ministerial structure. An extension of the defence programme, Chamberlain stated, 'could not be divorced from the financial issue. We had a small indication the other day that confidence in our financial position had shown some signs of weakness.' Sir John Simon pointed out 'that we should be faced with a deficit in the spring', and that meanwhile 'the revenue was drooping'. But Kingsley Wood argued 'that we must proceed on the basis of a new conception of the position in which safety and security would have first place. We must never again find ourselves

---

[1] But three days later, on October 28, the Director of Plans at the Air Ministry, Group Captain Slessor, told the Cabinet Committee on Defence Programmes and Acceleration: 'The reserves shown on this table might probably last not for more than a week of warfare on a major scale. There was not enough reserve pilots to the reserve aircraft shown on the table. The aircraft were in fact "peace" or "maintenance" reserves. One could not begin to speak of war reserves until one had something in excess of 30% of one's first line strength.'

in the position in which we had been on the 25th September.' Hore-Belisha then said that Britain 'could not continue to tolerate a position in which the equipment of the Territorial Army was sadly deficient and our Regular Army was 20,000 short of establishment'. This led Chamberlain to remark that 'he assumed that the Secretary of State did not propose that Treasury control should be abandoned'.

The Cabinet met again on October 31, when Kingsley Wood once more warned his colleagues in unambiguous terms that at 'the present time' the Royal Air Force was 'seriously deficient as compared with Germany'. Indeed, he added, 'our weakness might be said likely to provoke aggression by others'. But Chamberlain was still reluctant to authorize any great increase in armaments, telling his Cabinet:

> There had been a good deal of talk in the country and in the press about the need for rearmament by this country. In Germany and Italy it was suspected that this rearmament was directed against them, and it was important that we should not encourage these suspicions. . . .
>
> A good deal of false emphasis had been placed on rearmament, as though one result of the Munich Agreement had been that it would be necessary for us to add to our rearmament programmes. Acceleration of existing programmes was one thing, but increases in the scope of our programme which would lead to a new arms race was a different proposition. . . .

Chamberlain's proposition was not to abandon the Munich policies, but to continue with them, 'aimed', as he told his colleagues, 'at securing better relations'.

On November 1 Sir Horace Wilson explained to Kingsley Wood that the Air Ministry's proposed increase in the production capacity 'to a level equal to the estimated German capacity' could not be accepted because Germany would 'take it as a signal that we have decided at once to sabotage the Munich agreement'. That same day Simon argued against a continental Army, telling the Cabinet Committee on Defence Programmes and Acceleration: 'Germany was extremely unlikely to violate the neutrality of Belgium,' and that the Maginot Line 'was probably the strongest system of fortification that had ever been constructed'. But Hore-Belisha pointed out that the 'elimination of Czechoslovakia as a potential ally' meant that Germany could put increased pressure on France. No decision was reached; instead, the issue was left to the Committee of Imperial Defence to discuss.

On November 4 Churchill defended his own criticisms of the Munich agreement at a special meeting of the Central Council of the West Essex Unionist Association, held at Winchester House, in the City of London. Against him, Thornton-Kemsley argued that the policy of seeking to restrain Germany by a 'ring of strongly armed powers' had failed; that there was 'still time' to lay the foundations of peace based on the realization that war would be to no one's advantage, and that Germany's interests 'need at no vital point conflict with our own'. Thornton-Kemsley was convinced, as he told the meeting, that if Germany and Britain, together with France and Italy—the Munich 'partners'—were to 'agree upon a policy of friendship', no other power could start a war in Europe.

Thornton-Kemsley's arguments were nearly successful. But after the forceful intervention of Sir James Hawkey, Churchill's constituents passed a motion regretting that the Government had not heeded Churchill's warnings 'given during the last five years', and expressing the view that had they been heeded, 'the Prime Minister would have found himself in a far better position to negotiate with the heads of dictator States'.

Speaking at Weimar on November 6, Hitler warned the democracies of the dangers of free speech, and especially 'freedom for war-mongering'. Referring to Churchill's frequent appeals to the opponents of Nazism inside Germany to make their voices heard, Hitler declared:

> If Mr Churchill had less to do with traitors and more with Germans, he would see how mad his talk is, for I can assure this man, who seems to live on the moon, that there are no forces in Germany opposed to the régime—only the force of the National-Socialist movement, its leaders and its followers in arms.

That same evening Churchill issued a reply to Hitler's speech, which had gone on to abuse all the other 'gentry' in British politics who had criticized him. Churchill's reply read:

> I am surprised that the head of a great State should set himself to attack British Members of Parliament who hold no official position and who are not even the leaders of parties.
> Such action on his part can only enhance any influence they may have, because their fellow-countrymen have long been able to form their own opinions about them, and really do not need foreign guidance. . . .

When the Cabinet met on November 7, Kingsley Wood again pressed for an increase in air expenditure, particularly for the production of heavy bombers. If Britain's 'real aim', he said, 'was to prevent war, it was necessary that we should also have a sufficient bomber force to ensure that any country wishing to attack us would realize that the game was not worth the candle'. A heavy bomber programme, he added, 'afforded the best means of enabling this country to get on level terms with Germany'. The Cabinet, while agreeing to increase fighter strength by 30 per cent, decided to re-examine Kingsley Wood's appeal for an expanded bomber programme. After Simon had warned that the 'rash outlay' of such a programme might lead to inflation, 'a rise in prices, in wages, in interest rates' and involve 'some real injury to our financial strength', Chamberlain stated: 'In our foreign policy we were doing our best to drive two horses abreast, conciliation and rearmament. It was a very nice art to keep these two steeds in step. It was worth remembering that it was by no means certain that we could beat Germany in an arms race.'

During the Cabinet of November 7, Kingsley Wood suggested that the air position ought to be explained 'in somewhat more detail' to Attlee, Sinclair 'and also to Mr Churchill', but this suggestion met with no support. One Cabinet Minister, Hoare, explained his hostility to Churchill in a letter to Lord Linlithgow that same day. The 'back-biters', Hoare wrote, 'have been at work and have started a violent campaign of recrimination. They have had an easy job as they have been able to fasten upon every conceivable gap and deficiency in our defences. . . . Winston, as you will have seen, has been particularly active, working hand in glove with the Opposition and anyone else who has got a grievance against the Government.'

On November 8 Hitler again attacked Churchill by name, in a speech at Munich marking the fifteenth anniversary of his first, un-successful attempt to seize power. 'In France and Britain,' he said, 'men who want peace are in the Government. But tomorrow those who want war may be in the Government. Mr Churchill may be Prime Minister tomorrow.' Later in his speech he declared: 'Mr Churchill may have an electorate of 15,000 or 20,000. I have one of 40,000,000. Once and for all we request to be spared from being spanked like a pupil by a governess.'

On October 28 the German Government had begun a mass expul-sion of all 20,000 Polish Jews resident in Germany. The expulsions, which took place amid terrible scenes of brutality and hardship, pro-voked the seventeen-year-old son of one of the families expelled to shoot a member of the German Embassy in Paris.[1] The assassination took place on November 7. Two days later the German Press accused Churchill of being linked in the murder plot. The *Angriff* newspaper headlined the murder: 'The work of the instigator-international: A straight line from Churchill to Grynspan.' The article declared that it

---

[1] The young Jew was Herschel Grynspan; the German diplomat vom Rath, Third Secre-tary at the Paris Embassy.

was 'no coincidence' that Grynspan took 'the same line as is pursued by Messrs Churchill, Eden, Duff Cooper and their associates', and it stated: 'While in London the Churchill clique, unmasked by the Führer, was busy with sanctimonious deception, in Paris the murder weapon spat in the hands of a Jewish lout and destroyed the last measurable remnants of credibility in the assertion that agitation for war and murder against the Third Reich has never been carried on or contemplated.'[1]

In fact there had been no plot, only a desperate act by a despairing individual. But it was made the excuse of a violent anti-Jewish pogrom throughout Germany, beginning in the early hours of November 10. Synagogues were set on fire, homes ransacked, hundreds of Jews savagely beaten, and many murdered. Scholars, doctors, lawyers, engineers, bankers, men who had fought in the German army in 1914, men who had once played a leading part in national and civic life were sent to concentration camps, where vile treatment was meted out to them, and more were killed. Then, on November 13, a decree issued by Goering ordered all Jews to cease their trading and business activities by the end of the year, and a massive fine, imposed on the whole Jewish community of Germany for the Paris murder, meant the complete seizure of all Jewish goods and property.

Throughout November Churchill's correspondents kept him informed of the nature of Nazi tyranny inside Germany, and of Nazi intrigue throughout Europe. Ian Colvin from Berlin, Shiela Grant Duff from Prague and Emery Revesz from Paris were among those who sent him full reports of what they had seen and heard. On November 4 Revesz sent Churchill a detailed account of German activity in Scandinavia. 'As you see,' he wrote, 'the terror is spreading all over Europe. This complete change of the situation in the Scandinavian countries is a direct consequence of the Munich agreements. Until that modern peace treaty, the Scandinavian countries were courageously fighting against Nazism, now they are helpless and have to capitulate.'

During November Churchill also received further information on the state of the Royal Air Force, including a copy of Group Captain MacLean's own seven-page report of the September emergency, when he had been Acting Officer Commanding No 3 (Bomber) Group. The report was dated October 11, and read, in part:

The threat of war let loose a flood of schemes from Command Headquarters concerned with the moves to rearward aerodromes, disposal of

---

[1] Hitler's attack on Churchill prompted *The Times* to comment on November 11: 'It is much worse than merely ludicrous. It is wholly intolerable. It demands official notice, and should receive it without delay.'

non-operational aircraft, establishment of refuelling bases, reconnaissance of further advanced landing grounds and so on, none of which were contemplated or catered for in Mobilization Instructions or War Organisation. For each one of these schemes the Group was expected to make all the necessary arrangements, arrangements which were almost entirely administrative. . . .

The frailties and dangers of the Group dependence on Command Headquarters in these respects were clearly shown by the partial collapse of the telephone system at the beginning of the crisis and its failure to recover as the load of traffic increased. To this was added the slowing up of the postal services from Uxbridge to between 48 and 72 hours. . . .

I have refrained from remarking on equipment, since, on the approach of the supreme test, it was necessary to discard two-fifths of our aircraft strength as useless for war (the Heyfords and Hendons) and to depend for our striking power on the Harrow, an aeroplane whose fuel load and 2,000 pounds of bombs, allowed, within the normal permissible limits of its all up weight, of a range of only 700 miles and a safe top speed of 150 mph. The employment of such an aircraft against targets deep in Germany through a fighter defence whose speed is known to be of the order of at least 300 mph, and whose armament consists of both machine guns and cannon guns, provides its own commentary.

MacLean's report ended:

It was very apparent to me throughout the period of tension during the last fortnight in September that if circumstances had forced war upon us when it seemed inevitable, this Group, at all events, would have had to conduct operations with an unsuitably equipped and inadequately trained force, working from ill-prepared and defenceless bases, and depending on a fundamentally defective organisation, and I am left with the awful conviction that our air intervention under these circumstances must inevitably have been not only unavailing—but unavailing at appalling cost, and on this may have depended the very continuance of civilization.

Speaking in the House of Lords on November 2, Duff Cooper's successor as First Lord of the Admiralty, Lord Stanhope, had accused Churchill himself of being 'responsible for the weak state of the defence services because of his economising' policies while Chancellor of the Exchequer. In a statement published in *The Times* three days later, Churchill declared that this line of argument 'shows how hard put to it he and other Government spokesmen must be to defend themselves from the charges of neglect and mismanagement which are made in all quarters, and how eagerly they searched for someone on whom they could shuffle off some of their responsibilities. I have been out of office for nearly ten years. The National Government has been in office with overwhelming majorities in both Houses for the last seven years. The whole process of German rearmament has manifested itself within the last five years. I could not complain, however, of being saddled with the responsibility for the present state of the Navy. It is the only one of our defence services which is in a high state of efficiency and which is far stronger relatively to Europe than in 1914.'

Neither Churchill's knowledge nor his warnings secured him a reliable nucleus of Parliamentary support. To many MPs he was still an outsider. On November 9 Harold Nicolson wrote to his wife of how he had attended a 'hush-hush meeting with Anthony Eden', at which some twelve Conservative MPs, including Duff Cooper, Amery, Spears, Cartland, Crossley, Gunston, Harold Macmillan and Sidney Herbert, agreed to meet together to exchange views, and 'to organize ourselves for a revolt if needed'. This group, he explained, 'is distinct from Churchill's', and he added: 'It was a relief to me to be with people who share my views so completely, and yet who do not give the impression (as Winston does) of being more bitter than determined, and more out for a fight than for reform.'

Churchill sensed this mood of restraint. When A. H. Richards suggested inviting Eden to a Focus luncheon Churchill replied, on November 12: 'I doubt if Mr Eden would come. He is very shy at present.' To R. J. Minney, who had written to Churchill on November 11 urging him to embark on a national speaking campaign to rouse public opinion from its 'state of apathy', Churchill replied pessimistically on November 12:

I am afraid that making speeches in the country no longer has the old effect. In the first place they are not reported or replied to as they used to be before the War.

I did five or six meetings in March and April, in order to warn the country of what was coming this autumn, and everywhere had very large meetings in the best halls and platforms representative of all three parties, but while the labour entailed was enormous, it did not seem to produce the slightest result.

On November 10 Churchill's cousin Lord Londonderry had written to Churchill that in his view an agreement could have been made with Hitler between 1933 and 1935 'when the Germans were weak and defenceless' and that now, with the crisis so acute, it was the duty of both of them to support Chamberlain, as he was 'surrounded by a group of very inferior Ministers who do not know their own minds'. Churchill replied on November 12:

I am quite sure that there never was and there never will be any chance of a satisfactory arrangement between the German Nazi party and the British nation, and I am very sorry that we did not begin to arm on a great scale, especially in the air when the menace of this violent party first appeared.

I do not know what Chamberlain's future policy will entail. I am afraid he is not in earnest about rearmament. I believe he means to surrender the Colonies, and above all things I fear that he may make some Disarmament Convention with Hitler which will stereotype our lamentable inferiority in the Air.

Upon all these matters I shall fight with what strength I have, and I fear that upon all of them you will take a different view.

I doubt very much whether Chamberlain will carry the country with him. He is certainly dividing it on vital matters as it has never been split before. I am ashamed to see the great Conservative Party looking forward to an Election where they will exploit the psychosis of fear; and hope that the old women of both sexes will give a renewal of the present incompetent régime.

On November 14 the Cabinet Committee on Foreign Policy met to discuss the effects of the Munich agreement.[1] Halifax told the Committee that Hitler was reported as saying:

If I were Chamberlain I would not delay for a minute to prepare my country in the most drastic way for a 'total' war and I would thoroughly organise it. If the English have not got universal conscription by the spring of 1939 they may consider their world empire as lost. It is astounding how easy the democracies make it for us to reach our goal.

Halifax then argued in favour of 'increased and hastened' aircraft production, and a National Register of those liable to conscription in war. He told his colleagues: 'This proposal had been rejected and he shared the responsibility for that decision with his colleagues although he thought it to be a wrong decision. There was a tremendous flood of zeal and enthusiasm throughout the country which owing to that decision was evaporating in a sandy desert.'

Later in the discussion, Inskip told his colleagues that Britain's armament programme could be 'greatly accelerated at once' if a three-shift system were begun: this was also the view, he reported, of the Confederation of British Industries. But he added that the effect of 'any such arrangements on cost would of course be devastating', and no decision was reached. At the same time, Chamberlain's decision of October 26 not to set up a Ministry of Supply remained in force.

On November 17, speaking in the House of Commons, Churchill

[1] The members of the Committee were: Chamberlain, Simon, Hoare, Malcolm MacDonald, Runciman, Halifax, Inskip and Oliver Stanley. Sir Alexander Cadogan was also present.

supported a Liberal amendment calling for the immediate establishment of a Ministry of Supply, unaware that in Cabinet on October 26 Chamberlain had decided against such a course. Addressing himself to Chamberlain he declared:

I have used all the arguments of urgency and I have endeavoured to explain many of the processes of detail, three years ago, two years ago, and, finally, only six months ago. I have pleaded this cause in good time; I have pleaded it when it was already late; and perhaps my right hon Friend may remember I have even adjured him not to be deterred from doing right because it was impressed on him by the devil. But neither reason nor persuasion nor coaxing has had the slightest effect against the massive obstinacy of the powers that be, the powers that have led us to where we are now.

It was not, Churchill went on, to the Cabinet that he wished to speak words of warning, but to the Conservative backbenchers, and he continued:

... hon Gentlemen above the gangway—pledged, loyal, faithful supporters on all occasions of His Majesty's Government—must not imagine that they can throw their burden wholly on the Ministers of the Crown. Much power has rested with them. One healthy growl from those benches three years ago —and how different to-day would be the whole lay-out of our armaments production! Alas, that service was not forthcoming. . . .

I put it as bluntly as I possibly can. If only fifty Members of the Conservative Party went into the Lobby to-night to vote for this Amendment, it would not affect the life of the Government, but it would make them act. It would make a forward movement of real energy. We should get our Ministry of Supply, no doubt, but much more than that we should get a feeling of renewed strength and a prestige outside this country which would be of real service and value. . . .

This is no party question. It has nothing to do with party. It is entirely an issue affecting the broad safety of the nation.

Churchill then set out in detail what he believed were the deficiencies in Britain's defences, and urged the need for a secret session in which detailed figures would be examined. His speech ended: 'Is not this the moment when all should hear the deep, repeated strokes of the alarm bell, and when all should resolve that it shall be a call to action, and not the knell of our race and fame?'

Churchill had appealed for fifty Conservatives to vote for the amendment: thirty fewer than had voted repeatedly against their party's India policy less than four years before. But his appeal was a complete failure.

Only two Conservatives followed him into the Lobby, Brendan Bracken and Harold Macmillan.

During the debate on the Ministry of Supply, Duff Cooper, who had resigned in October, felt obliged to defend the Government's record. 'It is quite possible,' he said, 'to be a more loyal supporter of the National Government's policy, even than the Right Hon Member for Epping (Mr Churchill), to believe profoundly that they are a very good government, to support their internal and foreign policy, and yet to think that a Ministry of Supply might possibly help them to carry out that policy.' Speaking for the Government, Inskip told the House that in industrial circles no such Ministry was desired, certainly not in peacetime. Winding up the debate, Chamberlain rejected both the call for a Ministry of Supply, and the call for a secret session. The House seemed perturbed by this, but after the vote had been made one of confidence, the Government's view was upheld by 326 votes to 130, a majority of almost two hundred. In Berlin, this vote was a source of delight for the Nazi Press. 'Great Defeat of Churchill,' read one headline, and another commented: 'Churchill's intrigues collapse. Even Duff Cooper and Eden could not be roped in.'

Churchill had not heard the part of Duff Cooper's speech critical of himself. But after the debate, being much distressed by the Government's refusal to set up a Ministry of Supply, he refused to dine with him. Later, he learnt that some of Duff Cooper's speech had been an attack on him, and privately expressed his resentment. Learning of this, Duff Cooper wrote to him on November 19, seeking to explain why he had not supported him. 'Your great phillipic,' he wrote, 'which I enjoyed immensely and admired still more was an onslaught on the Government's record over a period of three years, during the whole of which, except the last six weeks, I was a member of the Government. You could hardly expect me therefore to say that I entirely agreed with you and to vote accordingly.' Duff Cooper added: 'I hope you will forgive me because your friendship, your comradeship and your advice are very, very precious to me.' Churchill replied on November 22:

Thank you very much for your letter, which I was very glad to get. In the position in which our small band of friends now is, it is a great mistake ever to take points off one another. The only rule is: Help each other when you can, but never harm.—Never help the Bear.

With your facility of speech it ought to be quite easy to make your position clear without showing differences from me. I will always observe this rule. Although there was nothing in what you said to which I could possibly object, yet the fact that you went out of your way to answer me, led several of my friends to wonder whether there was not some purpose behind it: for instance, the desire to isolate me as much as possible from the other Conservatives who disagree with the Government.

I did not credit this myself, and I am entirely reassured by your charming letter. We are so few, enemies so many, the cause so great, that we cannot afford to weaken each other in any way.

'I thought the parts of your speech which I heard,' Churchill added, 'very fine indeed, especially the catalogue of disasters which we have sustained in the last three years. I don't know how you remembered them all without a note.' His letter ended:

I am, of course, sorry about the Debate. Chamberlain has now got away with everything. Munich is dead, the unpreparedness is forgotten, and there is to be no real, earnest, new effort to arm the nation. Even the breathing space, purchased at a hideous cost, is to be wasted. It was my distress at these public matters that made me grumpy when you suggested supper, for I did not then know what you had said in the early part of your speech.

Randolph Churchill later recalled: 'I think my father was rather surprised and disappointed that Duff wasn't a little more *lié* with him—but Duff joined the other group, the more respectable group.'

On November 22, Ian Colvin sent Churchill a secret note of Hitler's character and intentions. Of Hitler himself Colvin wrote: 'The man is furious, vindictive, and more than ever ungovernable. The last excesses in Germany we owe entirely to his temper.' More than eighty Jews, Colvin pointed out, had been killed in the November pogrom. As for Hitler's aims, Colvin sent Churchill a memorandum setting out the text of a secret speech which Hitler had made after Munich to 'three or four of the highest functionaries of the Foreign Ministry', among them Ribbentrop and Weizsäcker.[1] According to the memorandum Hitler had said that internal policy must, for a while, come first:

He wanted to eliminate from German life the Jews, the Churches, and suppress private industry. After that, he would turn to foreign policy again.

In the meantime, Great Britain must be attacked with speeches and in the press. First the Opposition, and then Chamberlain himself. He had learned

[1] Baron Ernst von Weizsäcker, 1882–1951. Served first in the German Imperial Navy, then in the diplomatic service. Political Director at the Foreign Office, Berlin, 1936–38; Head of the Political Department, 1938–43. Ambassador to the Vatican, 1943–44. Sentenced to imprisonment by the Nuremberg military tribunal, 1946; released, 1950.

from the negotiations preceding Munich how to deal with the English—one had to encounter them aggressively (vor dem Bauch treten).

He would deal with England as he had done with France, where he had produced a confusion in political life. Flandin was for Germany, and there were also such men in England. . . .

His (Hitler's) aim was to overthrow Chamberlain. The Opposition would not then be capable of forming a new government, and the same would occur as in France. The political strength of Great Britain would be paralysed. In England too, Fascism would gain the upper hand.

He did not want in the near future to brand as a lie his promise not to make more territorial acquisitions in Europe. Therefore he was first turning to internal policy. But when Mr Chamberlain was no longer prime minister, he would no longer consider himself bound by the Munich Agreement. Memel would at any time fall into the lap of the Reich like a ripe fruit. . . .

On November 30 Churchill celebrated his sixty-fourth birthday. On the following day, at Chartwell, he completed the first 136,000 words of the *History of the English-Speaking Peoples*, the result of four months intensive work, which had been interrupted almost every day by the continuing international crisis, speeches and articles. To Thornton Butterworth he had written, on November 21: 'There will certainly be, if I live, further volumes of the autobiography. . . . But when I see two highly successful books, "My Early Life" and "Thoughts and Adventures", stagnating, I feel somewhat discouraged.'

On December 1, having been inundated with letters from strangers who had evidence of deficiencies in the defence forces, Churchill replied to one such correspondent, R. E. Fearnley-Whittingstall,[1] who had also urged the need for 'new leaders' and a new political party: 'I am sure if there were any reasonable alternative to the present Government, they would be chased out of power by the country. But the difficulties of organizing and forming a new Party have often proved insuperable.'

On December 5 Churchill spoke in the House of Commons on the Sandys report, which exonerated all Ministers from seeking to exercise improper pressure on a member of the House. The report blamed the waywardness of human nature for the 'mass of delays, of cross-purposes, and of misunderstandings' with which the case had been surrounded.

---

[1] Robert Ellison Fearnley-Whittingstall, 1906–   . Educated at Oundle and Corpus Christi Cambridge. Admitted solicitor, 1931. Joined the Territorial Army on the day after Hitler's invasion of Austria, March 1938. 2nd Lieutenant in a Territorial Searchlight Battalion, Royal Engineers, 1938–39. Served in Anti-Aircraft Command, and later in the Judge Advocate General's Office, 1939–45.

During his speech Churchill criticized 'the sudden excess of officialism and authoritarianism' with which Hore-Belisha seemed to have acted. Nor, he said, should the neglect of London's anti-aircraft defences be forgotten. Ministers should allow matters of defence 'to receive higher priority in their mind'. Harold Nicolson, who was present during the debate, noted in his diary how Churchill's speech progressed:

Winston starts brilliantly and we are all expecting a great speech. He accuses Hore-Belisha of being too complacent. The latter gets up and says, 'When and where?' Winston replies, 'I have not come unprepared', and begins to fumble among his notes, where there are some press-cuttings. He takes time. He finds them. But they are not the best cuttings, and the ones he reads out excuse rather than implicate Hore-Belisha. Winston becomes confused. He tries to rally his speech, but the wind has gone out of his sails, which flop wretchedly. 'He is becoming an old man', says Bill Mabane[1] beside me. He certainly is a tiger who, if he misses his spring, is lost.

Churchill's persistence in the Sandys case roused much resentment. But speaking at Chingford, in his constituency, on December 9, he defended his continued concern for every facet of defence, and warned the audience of more than a thousand people of the repeated neglect and shortsightedness of Chamberlain's policies:

The Prime Minister said in the House of Commons the other day that where I failed, for all my brilliant gifts, was in the faculty of judging. I will gladly submit my judgement about foreign affairs and national defence during the last five years, in comparison with his own. . . .

In February the Prime Minister said that tension in Europe had greatly relaxed. A few weeks later Nazi Germany seized Austria. I predicted that he would repeat this statement as soon as the shock of the rape of Austria passed away. He did so in the very same words at the end of July. By the middle of August Germany was mobilising for those bogus manoeuvres which, after bringing us all to the verge of a world war, ended in the complete destruction and absorption of the Republic of Czecho-Slovakia.

At the Lord Mayor's banquet in November at the Guildhall, he told us that Europe was settling down to a more peaceful state. The words were hardly out of his mouth before the Nazi atrocities on the Jewish population resounded throughout the civilised world. When, earlier in the year, the

---

[1] William Mabane, 1895–1969. On active service in France and the Near East, 1914–19. Warden of the University Settlement, Liverpool, 1920–23. Vice-President of the Building Societies Association, and a Director of Kemsley Newspapers Ltd. National Liberal MP for Huddersfield, 1931–45. A staunch supporter of Chamberlain's foreign policy, on 4 October 1938, in the Commons, he praised Chamberlain's 'brilliant initiative' in the Munich crisis. Assistant Postmaster-General, 1939. Parliamentary Secretary, Ministry of Home Security, 1939–42; Ministry of Food, 1942–45. Privy Councillor, 1944. Minister of State, 1945. Knighted, 1954. Chairman of the British Travel Association, 1960–63. Created Baron, 1962.

Prime Minister made a heart-to-heart settlement with Mr de Valera[1] and gave up to him those fortified ports on the South Coast of Ireland, which are vital to our food supply in time of war, he led us to believe that henceforward Mr de Valera and the country now called Eire, were reconciled to us in friendship.

But I warned him, with my defective judgment, that if we got into any great danger Mr de Valera would demand the surrender of Ulster as a price for any friendship or aid. This fell out exactly for Mr de Valera has recently declared that he cannot give us any help or friendship while any British troops remain to guard the Protestants of Northern Ireland. . . .

Churchill then turned his invective on Chamberlain's predecessor:

In 1934 I warned Mr Baldwin that the Germans had a secret Air Force and were rapidly overhauling ours. I gave definite figures and forecasts. Of course, it was all denied with all the weight of official authority. I was depicted a scaremonger. Less than six months after Mr Baldwin had to come down to the House and admit he was wrong and he said, 'We are all to blame' and everybody said, 'How very honest of him to admit his mistake.'

He got more applause for making this mistake, which may prove fatal to the British Empire and to British freedom, than ordinary people would do after they rendered some great service which added to its security and power. Well, Mr Chamberlain was, next to Mr Baldwin, the most powerful Member of that Government. He was Chancellor of the Exchequer. He knew all the facts. His judgment failed just like that of Mr Baldwin and we are suffering from the consequences of it to-day.

Next Churchill referred to Lord Samuel:

Four years ago when I asked that the Air Force should be doubled and redoubled—more than that was being done now—Lord Samuel thought my judgment so defective that he likened me to a Malay running amok. It would have been well for him and his persecuted race if my advice had been taken. They would not be where they are now and we should not be where we are now.

'It is on the background of these proved errors of judgment in the past,' Churchill added, 'that I draw your attention to some of the judgments

---

[1] Eamon De Valera, 1882–1975. Born in New York. A leading figure in the Easter Rebellion, 1916. Sentenced to death; sentence commuted to life penal servitude on account of his American birth. Released under the general amnesty, June 1917. President of the Sinn Fein, 1917–26. Elected to Parliament as a Sinn Fein MP, 1918. Imprisoned with other Sinn Fein leaders, 1918; escaped from Lincoln Jail, February 1919. 'President' of the Irish Republic, 1919–22. Rejected the Irish Treaty and fought with the Irregulars against the Free State Army, 1922–23. President of Fianna Fail, 1926–59. Leader of the Opposition in the Free State Parliament, 1927–32. Minister for External Affairs, 1932–48. Head of the Government of Eire, 1937–48, 1951–54 and 1957–59. President of the Republic of Ireland, 1959–73.

which have been passed upon the future, the results of which have not yet been proved.'

In congratulating Churchill on his Chingford speech, Lord Londonderry's son Robin, himself a Conservative MP, wrote on December 11:

I have listened to practically all your speeches since I have been in the House & your utterances have been strangely prophetic. In this time of emergency & crisis I should have thought that a 'Rather Spineless Cabinet' would have invited the co-operation of a man of energy & proved experience. No doubt when war breaks out you will be asked to compile a National Register, order some guns & quell a Rebellion in Eire. But not before.

I shall have vivid recollections of my talk with Rudolf Hess[1] just over two years ago, about which I told you. He said: 'Why do you not have Winston Churchill in your British Cabinet, then we should know you meant business.' It is so true & Macdonald's pitful cringe to de Valera merely encourages a creature like Göring to ask for more.

'That was a grand speech you made in Essex,' Sir Roger Keyes wrote on December 13, 'and your retort to Chamberlain was simply unanswerable.'

'I feel that for you, it has been a year of great exertion,' A. H. Richards wrote on December 13, 'but not a labour in vain. There are indications that around you are gathering resolute and dynamic forces in your valiant and unsparing efforts for the preservation of our precious heritage, freedom.' Eight days later Richards wrote again, informing Churchill that fifteen different towns had written to ask if Churchill could speak in their main halls. Richards added: 'In moving among people of all classes I find more than ever, that the general feeling is that had we heeded in time, your very wise counsel in the matter of Rearmament and the Covenant—so oft and so resolutely repeated during the past five years, we should not have drifted into such dire peril.'

Churchill was asked so often to speak on public platforms, that every week he was forced to turn down several such appeals. On December 12 he was asked to speak at Oxford by the President of the Oxford Union Society, Edward Heath,[2] who wrote:

---

[1] Rudolf Hess, 1894–1987. Born in Egypt. Joined the National Socialist Party in 1920. Took part in Hitler's unsuccessful Munich putsch of 1923. Imprisoned with Hitler, 1923–24, and became his private secretary. Became Deputy Leader of the Nazi Party in 1933, and Hitler's successor-designate in 1939. Flew to Scotland, May 1941, and held prisoner in Britain until 1945. Tried at Nuremberg in 1946, and sentenced to life imprisonment; thirty years later he was still a prisoner at Spandau, the only Nazi sentenced at Nuremberg still in prison.

[2] Edward Richard George Heath, 1916– . Educated at Chatham House School Ramsgate, and Balliol College Oxford. President of the Oxford University Conservative Association, 1937. Chairman, Federation of University Conservative Associations, 1938. President of the

The present generation of Oxford men has never had the opportunity of hearing you at Oxford, and if you would return to repeat your triumphs of the past—which to us are as mighty legends told us by life-members—I can assure you that the Union Hall could not contain all those who would come to hear you. I cannot promise to find you opponents comparable with those you had in the past but I will willingly invite anyone you may like to suggest to debate opposite you, and the motion for debate would also of course rest with you. The subjects I had in mind were National Service, a National Opposition, or some aspect of Foreign Policy. . . .

Heath continued on a more personal note:

Professor Lindemann will vouch for me as an excellent rebel Tory, which explains why I am so very anxious that you should come, although I realise that it has been many Presidents' ambition that you should. Perhaps however you will think these extraordinary times in which we now live sufficient justification for coming down again to the Union.

Churchill was unable to accept, replying to Heath five days later on 'how much I should like to come and support you in your period of office', but regretting that his work was too heavy to fix a date in advance. Perhaps, he added, 'you will let me keep it open and send you word if I find myself free'.

As 1938 drew to a close Churchill's forebodings intensified. 'Neville leads us from bad to worse,' he wrote to Lord Wolmer on December 12, and on December 21, he wrote bluntly to Hore-Belisha about his claim that the wartime establishment of Bren and anti-aircraft guns in the Guards Battalions was already in being: 'I hope you will not resent it if I say that I still fear you are being misinformed. I wonder you do not ask the Colonels of these battalions to tell you whether they have in fact 50 Bren guns and 22 Anti-tank rifles in their hands at the present time.' His letter continued:

I see a paragraph in 'The Yorkshire Post' states that I am the inspirer of the present attack which is being made on you. There is no truth whatever in this. At no time indeed, except when defending Sandys from the attack you made upon him, which naturally I felt very deeply, have I taken any action personally hostile to yourself.

Oxford Union, 1938–39. On active service, 1939–45 (despatches); Major, 1945; MBE, 1946. Conservative MP for Bexley, 1950–74; for Bexley Sidcup after 1974. Assistant Government Whip, 1951; Deputy Chief Whip, 1953–55; Chief Whip, 1955–59. Privy Councillor, 1955. Minister of Labour, 1959–60. Lord Privy Seal, 1960–63. Secretary of State for Industry, Trade and Regional Development and President of the Board of Trade, 1963–64. Leader of the Opposition, 1965–70. Prime Minister, 1970–74. Leader of the Opposition, 1974–76.

Of Hore-Belisha himself, Churchill wrote a week later, to the editor of the *Yorkshire Post*, Arthur Mann: 'I think he is far less culpable and lethargic than the bulk of them.' To his wife, who was cruising in the West Indies, Churchill wrote on December 22:

Politics tend towards a crisis. Hudson[1] and some of the Under-Secretaries have threatened to resign unless Inskip, Hore-Belisha, Winterton and Runciman are dismissed. This is a new development and very damaging to the Government. The talk now is of a big reconstruction at the end of January, and of Eden being invited back. I do not know what would happen then. It seems to me impossible that it should affect me, either in being asked, or in accepting if I were.

Of European politics Churchill wrote:

Everything goes to show that our interests are declining throughout Europe, and that Hitler will be on the move again in February or March, probably against Poland. Although Poland has lost French and English sympathies by Colonel Beck's[2] cynical, coldhearted behaviour, the great accession to Nazi power which will follow from an eastward advance affects us grievously. It is part of the price we pay for Munich.

On December 24 Churchill wrote to Lord Craigavon, thanking him for a Christmas gift: 'Coming as it does at this time of trouble and mis-understanding in which I feel much alone, tho' constant, it is grateful to me beyond words!' Lord Craigavon's present was an engraved silver cup. Two weeks later Churchill wrote to his wife: 'I think it very beautiful in design. It is quite small and a goblet shape, according to an old Gaelic model, and has been made especially with three supporters, a sword, a brush and a pen. All round are quotations from my father, from me and one from Randolph, about Ulster. I wish some of these dirty Tory hacks, who would like to drive me out of the Party, could see this trophy.'

[1] Robert Spear Hudson, 1886–1957. Educated at Eton and Magdalen College Oxford. Attaché, Diplomatic Service, 1911; First Secretary, 1920–23. Conservative MP for White-haven, 1924–29; for Southport, 1931–52. Parliamentary Secretary, Ministry of Labour, 1931–35. Minister of Labour, 1931–35. Minister of Pensions, 1935–36. Secretary, Department of Overseas Trade, 1937–40. Privy Councillor, 1938. Minister of Shipping, April–May 1940. Minister of Agriculture and Fisheries, 1940–45. Created Viscount, 1952.

[2] Joseph Beck, 1894–1944. An undergraduate at Vienna on the outbreak of war in 1914, when he joined Pilsudski's Legion and took part in the war against Russia. Served first in the Artillery, then on the General Staff. Colonel, 1918. Polish Military Attaché in Paris, 1922–25. Chef de Cabinet to Pilsudski, 1926–29. Minister without Portfolio, 1929–32. Appointed Foreign Minister (at the age of 38) in 1932; remained in office until the German invasion of Poland in 1939. Escaped to Rumania, 1939. Arrested near Bucharest, 1940; died four years later, while still in captivity.

On December 25 Oliver Harvey reflected in his diary on the Ministry for the Coordination of Defence, noting despondently that Chamberlain was not pressing on with rearmament 'fundamentally as the situation demands' and that under Inskip the Committee of Imperial Defence 'goes slower and slower'. Harvey added: 'Inskip must certainly go. A much more vigorous and imaginative personality should be there. Winston is the obvious man, but I believe the PM would rather die than have him.'

50

'The Best Chapter in his Crowded Life'

A T the end of 1938 Churchill was more isolated in Parliament than at any time in the nine years during which he was without office. The groups that gathered around Eden or Amery did not wish to be associated too closely with him. Even at its most marked, Baldwin's hostility towards him had never been as intense as that of Chamberlain after Munich. Yet his wider, public popularity had never been so high, his speeches so in demand, nor his audiences so receptive. The British Press had become attentive to each of his statements, and foreign newspapers reported his pronouncements in detail. His own newspaper articles were widely circulated abroad, and in the three months since Munich he had received several hundred letters of support from ordinary men and women of all classes and every political persuasion.[1]

On December 29 Churchill sent his wife an account of events in England during her absence. Of Chamberlain's policy he wrote:

It may well be that he will have to yield to the force of events, and will adopt my view and policy, while disliking me all the more. I had a talk with Anthony after his return from America. He says nothing will induce him to join the Government unless it is reconstructed in the most drastic manner, and the policy is changed. Even this is not impossible.

Churchill also reported to his wife about his work on the *History of the English-Speaking Peoples*:

I am now doing the Wars of the Roses. They are deeply interesting, and have been much too lightly treated by modern opinion. The causes were

[1] By the end of 1938 Churchill's *Daily Telegraph* articles were being published in five Australian and four New Zealand newspapers, as well as in the Bahamas, Jamaica, Canada, Hong Kong, Singapore, Ceylon, India, the Gold Coast and Kenya. The twenty foreign cities included Cairo, Jerusalem, Athens, Warsaw, Helsinki, São Paulo and Rio de Janeiro.

deep, the arguments equally balanced, and immense efforts were made to avert the disaster which occurred. I have just finished writing about Joan of Arc. I think she is the winner in the whole of French history. The leading women of those days were more remarkable and forceful than the men.

Among the Christmas gifts which Churchill had received was an old French silver snuff box from the Duchess of Buccleuch.[1] He had puzzled over why she had given him such a fine present, writing to his wife, with a reference to the Duchess of Atholl's recent defeat in her by-election:

I think this may be because her friend James Stuart[2] had the cheek to tell me in his exultation about the Duchess's defeat that I ought not to accept the whip any longer. I naturally told him to go to Hell or Epping, and I expect he carried this tale to Molly and was rebuked. Anyhow it was kindly meant.

During the first week of 1939 Churchill continued to work at Chartwell on his book. On January 5 Deakin introduced him to another Oxford graduate, Alan Bullock,[3] who undertook to help with some of the research. Financially, the book promised to provide more than a third of Churchill's income for 1939; it was also to be his principal daily occupation. So much was he influenced by his work on the evolution of British institutions, that in an interview with Kingsley Martin[4] published in the *New Statesman* on January 7 he spoke of Magna Carta, Habeas Corpus and the Petition of Right as the indispensable foundations of freedom and civilization. Without them, he said, the individual would be 'at the mercy of officials and liable to be spied upon and betrayed even in his own home'. Even in wartime, democracy was essential, and such basic features of the democratic system as debate and questions 'far from hindering the conduct of the war, frequently assist it by exposing weak points'. Churchill ended: 'War is horrible but slavery

[1] Vreda Esther Mary Lascelles, 1900– . Known as 'Molly', a descendant of the 1st and 2nd Earls of Harewood. In 1921 she married the 8th Duke of Buccleuch (who died in 1973).

[2] James Gray Stuart, 1897–1971. Third son of the 17th Earl of Moray. Educated at Eton. On active service, 1914–18 (Military Cross and bar). Conservative MP for Moray and Nairn, 1923–59. Entered the Whips Office, 1935; Deputy Chief Whip, 1938–41; Government Chief Whip, 1941–45; Chief Opposition Whip, 1945–48. Privy Councillor, 1939. Secretary of State for Scotland, 1951–57. Created Viscount Stuart of Findhorn, 1959.

[3] Alan Louis Charles Bullock, 1914– . Educated at Bradford Grammar School and Wadham College Oxford. MA, 1936. 1st Class Modern History, 1938. War work, 1939–45. Tutor in Modern History, New College, 1945–52; he published *Hitler: A Study in Tyranny* in 1952. Biographer of Bevin (1960, 1967). Master of St Catherine's College Oxford since 1960. Vice-Chancellor, Oxford University, 1969–73. Knighted, 1972. Created Baron, 1976.

[4] Basil Kingsley Martin, 1897–1969. Educated at Mill Hill School and Magdalene College Cambridge. Assistant Lecturer, London School of Economics, 1923–27. On the editorial staff of the *Manchester Guardian*, 1927–31. Editor of the *New Statesman and Nation*, 1930–60; Editorial Director, 1961–62.

is worse, and you may be sure that the British people would rather go down fighting than live in servitude.'

On the day the *New Statesman* article was published Churchill left England for the South of France, to stay once more with Maxine Elliot at the Château de L'Horizon. On his way south he flew first to Paris, lunching with Paul Reynaud, and talking in the afternoon first to Sir Eric Phipps and Sir Charles Mendl, and then to Léon Blum. That evening he took the night train to Cannes. Writing to his wife from the Château de L'Horizon on January 8 Churchill reported, of his talks in Paris:

They all confirm the fact that the Germans had hardly any soldiers at all on the French frontier during the Crisis. And Blum told me, (secret) that he had it from Daladier himself that both Generals Gamelin and Georges were confident that they could have broken through the weak unfinished German line, almost unguarded as it was, by the fifteenth day at the latest, and that if the Czechs could have held out only for that short fortnight, the German armies would have had to go back to face invasion. On the other side there is their great preponderance in the air, and it depends what you put on that how you judge the matter.

I have no doubt that a firm attitude by England and France would have prevented war, and I believe that history will incline to the view that if the worst had come to the worst, we should have been far better off than we may be at some future date.[1]

During his talk with Blum, Churchill also met Yvon Delbos. 'Both are very anxious,' Churchill told his wife, and he added:

They fear that Mussolini is determined to have his share of the loot, Hitler having had everything so far and he nothing, and they believe that Hitler is bound to him and will support him. I put it that perhaps if Mussolini attacked France we might keep Germany out by saying that we would not come in if she did not. All the Frenchmen seem quite content with this, as they are sure they could smash Italy in an affair à deux. But they doubt very much whether Hitler would stay out, even if they brought the British in against him. It now looks as if he had some sort of deal with Colonel Beck, and that he is more likely in an eastern movement to press towards Hungary and Roumania. Blum seems to think that these two ruffians will be moving again quite soon.

[1] This was true even for air power. According to the Cabinet's own assessment of 25 October 1938, the German first-line air strength would grow from 5,600 (including reserves) in October 1938 to 7,030 (including reserves) in August 1939. The comparative British increase would be from 2,018 to 3,392. Even with Scheme L, on the outbreak of war (as Churchill wrote in his memorandum of 16 October 1939, see page 851) the British figure was not reached. Thus between Munich and the outbreak of war the Germans increased their already substantial lead in first-line aircraft.

Churchill also sent his wife news of the state of opinion at home—for she was still in the West Indies. In London, he told her:

. . . there is a good deal of fear that Hitler may turn towards us and make demands upon us instead of going to the East. The Ambassador told me he heard tales of the pessimism prevailing in so many quarters in London. My feeling is that it is not us that will be singled out at such a time. But what a state to let the world get into!

Meanwhile Chamberlain in endorsing all that Roosevelt said had made a great advance to my point of view. Perhaps you will have noticed that he used the very phrase I have been repeating for the last two years, namely 'freedom and peace', and that he put, as I have always done, 'freedom' first.

Writing of the Air Raid Precautions programme, Churchill told his wife that the ARP volunteers 'are disgruntled and melting away because of the defective organisation'.[1] His letter continued: 'All reports from behind the scenes indicate great disillusion with Hitler and despair about appeasement. . . .[2] Sir John Anderson, although so recently made a Minister, is escaping at St Moritz, and this is a subject of continued comment in the press. . . . Chamberlain does not know the tithe of the things for which he is responsible.'

In his letter to his wife Churchill also reflected on his own political future. 'I do not think it would be much fun to take these burdens and neglects upon my shoulders,' he wrote, 'certainly not without powers such as they have not dreamed of according.'

That same day, January 8, Neville Chamberlain wrote to his sister of his forthcoming visit to Rome, where he hoped 'to establish a relation of confidence in Musso'. Chamberlain added:

I have just had a letter from G. Gwynne[3] in which he warns me that I am embarking on the most perilous adventure of my life & while quite approving of what I have done & being grateful for it, feels it would be much better now

[1] This was also the view of Leslie Hore-Belisha, the Minister responsible for ARP, who wrote to Sir John Simon on January 25, in protest against the Treasury's refusal to increase ARP spending: 'I was extremely sorry to have your letter of the 25th January, because it was the clear opinion of the Cabinet, as it is certainly mine, that our anti-aircraft defences are inadequately conceived.'

[2] Among the many anti-Government letters which Churchill received was one from an organization recently formed in Liverpool, the Progressive Democratic Union, which wrote to him on January 22: 'All over the country there are growing fires of resentment against the short-sighted policy of the Government, and these are ready to be touched into flame.'

[3] Neville Gwyn Gwynne, 1868–1951. Mechanical engineer. Educated at Lancing and Pembroke College Cambridge. Director of Gwynne's Pumps Ltd and of William Foster and Co, Lincoln. A member of the War Pensions Committee, 1917–18. CBE, 1920. President of the London and District Engineering Employers. Chairman of the British Engineers' Association. Chairman of the Engine Section of the Society of British Aircraft Constructors.

to cancel the Rome visit & make a grand alliance against Germany. In other words better abandon my policy & adopt Winston's!

While Churchill was in the South of France the Germans announced that they intended to build sufficient submarines to reach parity with Britain. This decision was in accord with the Anglo-German Naval Agreement of 1935.[1] Writing in the *Daily Telegraph* on January 12, Churchill described the original agreement as 'a heavy blow at all international co-operation in support of public law', which had affected adversely the interests of the Scandinavian and Baltic States. As for Britain herself, he wrote, she had incurred 'an avoidable danger' which, although it could be dealt with, could only be overcome 'with loss and suffering'.

Among those staying at the Château de L'Horizon was Vincent Sheean, who later recalled in his memoirs how Churchill now 'deplored the coming victory of Franco in Spain, pointed out the illusions and misconceptions which had made "well-to-do society" so prejudiced in Franco's favour, and saw with foreboding what this might mean for England. . . .'

Life at Cannes provided Churchill with a brief escape from worry, as he wrote to his wife on January 18:

I have stayed in bed every morning and made great progress with the book. We have averaged fifteen hundred words a day, although nominally on holiday. I shall have a lot for you to read when you come home.

The Windsors dine here and we dine back with them. They have a lovely little palace next door to La D.[2] Everything extremely well done and dignified. Red liveries, and the little man himself dressed up to the nines in the Balmoral tartan with dagger and jabot etc. When you think that you could hardly get him to put on a black coat and short tie when he was Prince of Wales, one sees the change in the point of view. I am to dine with him tomorrow night with only Rothermere. No doubt to talk over his plans for returning home. They do not want him to come, but they have no power to stop him.

Just as at Chartwell I divided my days between building and dictating, so now it is between dictating and gambling. I have been playing very long, but not foolishly, and up to date I have a substantial advantage. It amuses me very much to play, so long as it is with their money. . . .[3]

[1] This Agreement, signed on 18 June 1935, was still in force. At the end of the Munich Conference, Chamberlain and Hitler had signed a document, specially prepared by Chamberlain himself, which described 'the agreement signed last night and the Anglo-German Naval Agreement as symbolic of the desire of our two peoples never to go to war with one another again'.

[2] Lord Rothermere's villa, La Dragonnière, at Cap Martin.

[3] On 1 January 1939 Churchill had made a 'Forecast' of his personal income for the coming year. The total came to £22,420, of which the English Speaking Peoples was to

Commenting on the sudden upsurge of IRA violence in London, Churchill ascribed it to 'the Irish trying to get hold of Ulster', and he added: 'How vain it was for Chamberlain to suppose he could make peace by giving everything away!' Churchill thought, however, that the Government were 'stiffening up on foreign affairs', and he was glad to note that following Chamberlain's visit to Rome 'they certainly gave nothing to the organ grinder or his monkey; not even to pay him to go into the next street'.

Churchill's letter continued with news of the failure of the recent activities of his son and son-in-law, who had decided to form a new party made up only of those who were doing war-preparation work or had fought in the last war. As Churchill reported:

The Duncan-Randolph movement, the Hundred Thousand, has already over-passed its first hundred. Violet made herself very awkward. Just as she upset Eden's Queen's Hall meeting by her violence against the Government, so now she broke up Duncan's little effort by bolting in alarm. I need scarcely say, I did all in my power to dissuade them from it. And no doubt it does me a certain amount of harm. I do not care at all.

At Cannes Churchill was learning a 'very pretty dance'; he was to have lessons after lunch on the following day. 'We take three steps and give a hop,' he wrote. 'I always hop at the wrong time, which I am afraid, provokes small minded people to laugh.' Of his plans for later in the year he told his wife:

In the summer when I am sure the book will be finished, I think I will build a house on the ten acres. It would cost about three thousand pounds to give a lovely dwelling for a man and his wife, two children, one double and one single visiting bedroom, and I expect we could sell it for five or six thousand pounds with the bit of land. It would amuse me all the summer and give me good health.

I should get Lutyens[1] down to give his views as to where it should be put and what it should look like etc. He will do this for nothing, I am sure, as he has always begged to give advice. He has been appointed President of the Royal Academy, so another member of the Other Club is in a distinguished position.

---

provide £7,500, the *Daily Telegraph* articles £4,880, and a series of articles on sport, crime, marriage, health and invention for the *News of the World* £4,200. From Emry Revesz's foreign syndications, including certain sales in the United States, he expected to receive £1,200 and from his articles in *Colliers* a further £2,000. £2,640 came from non-literary sources.

[1] Edwin Lutyens, 1869–1944. Architect; his works included the British Pavilion, Paris, 1900; Government House, Delhi, and the Whitehall Cenotaph. Knighted, 1918. Order of Merit, 1942.

My idea about a house of this kind is that every bedroom must have a bathroom and must be good enough to be a bed-sitting room. Downstairs you have one lovely big room. However, you may be sure nothing will be done until you have passed the plans. I have at least two months work ahead on the present cottage.

Clementine Churchill shared her husband's worries about Europe. 'O Winston,' she wrote on January 19, 'are we drifting into war? without the wit to avoid it or the will to prepare for it?' That same day Franco's forces entered Tarragona, bringing much nearer the fall of the Spanish Republic.[1] That night Churchill dined with the Duke and Duchess of Windsor. Vincent Sheean, who was also present, later recalled:

. . . after the long and stately meal in the white-and-gold dining-room, the Duke of Windsor and Mr Churchill settled down to a prolonged argument with the rest of the party listening in silence. The Duke had read Mr Churchill's recent articles on Spain and his newest one (out that day, I believe) in which he appealed for an alliance with Soviet Russia. We sat by the fireplace, Mr Churchill frowning with intentness at the floor in front of him, mincing no words, reminding HRH of the British constitution on occasion—'When our kings are in conflict with our constitution, we change our kings,' he said—and declaring flatly that the nation stood in the gravest danger of its long history. The kilted Duke in his Stuart tartan sat on the edge of the sofa, eagerly interrupting whenever he could, contesting every point, but receiving—in terms of the utmost politeness so far as the words went—an object lesson in political wisdom and public spirit. The rest of us sat fixed in silence; there was something dramatically final, irrevocable about this dispute.

Churchill remained at Cannes until the third week of January. 'Never have I seen you in such good form . . .' Maxine Elliot wrote to him on January 29, after he had gone, 'and we rocked with laughter continually. Your joie de vivre is a wonderful gift and on a par with your other amazing gifts—in fact you are the most enormously gifted creature in the whole world and it is like the sunshine leaving when you go away.'

On his way back to England Churchill stopped for a short while in Paris. There he saw Alexis Léger, who told him in strictest confidence of intelligence reports of German munitions convoys moving across Czechoslovakia, from the manufacturing centres in the northern part of

---

[1] Barcelona fell to the Nationalist Forces on January 25. On February 28 Neville Chamberlain announced that Britain would recognize General Franco's movement as the Government of Spain. On March 28 Franco entered Madrid, and the civil war ended on April 2.

the Sudetenland, to the Hungarian border areas in the south. Not even the British Embassy in Paris had been informed of this fact. On January 29 Churchill reported the details of what Léger had told him to Desmond Morton, and two days later, when he went to see Halifax at the Foreign Office, he passed them on to him, noting that what Léger feared was that the move heralded a German demonstration against Hungary or Roumania. But Morton believed, as he wrote in a secret note to William Strang[1] on January 30, that the reason was the rearming of the former Austrian army 'to the German scale and with German weapons'.

While Churchill was still in France, it was announced that Sir Thomas Inskip was to leave the Ministry for Coordination of Defence, to become Secretary of State for the Dominions. 'If N.C. does not *beg* you to take on our defences in Inskip's place,' Roger Keyes wrote to Churchill on January 23, 'he will *not* be doing his best for the British Empire in these dangerous times.' But on January 29 it was announced that Lord Chatfield would be appointed. 'I think Chatfield an improvement on Inskip,' Lindemann wrote to Churchill on January 30, 'but it seems a dreadful confession of failure that no member of the House of Commons is considered fit to assume the office.' That same day Churchill wrote to his sister-in-law, Lady Gwendeline Churchill: 'How indescribably bloody everything is!'

Within Churchill's constituency, critical voices had continued, despite the vote of confidence in November, to denounce Churchill's hostile attitude towards the Government's policy. In his own defence, Churchill warned his constituents that unless the 'mood of intolerance in some Party circles at the present time' were firmly resisted, it would 'destroy the quality of the House of Commons'. Much remained to be done before the country was secure. Both towards Air Raid Precautions, and also in the setting up of a compulsory register of those liable for military service in war-time, Churchill feared that there was still insufficient 'clarity of thought or vigour of execution', telling his constituents:

Nearly five months have passed since the trenches in the parks were dug; yet there has not been found the mental and moral grip either to fill them in, or

---

[1] William Strang, 1893–1978. Educated, University College London and the Sorbonne. On active service, 1914–18. Entered Foreign Office, 1919; Counsellor of Embassy, Moscow, 1930; Mission to Moscow, 1939; Assistant Under-Secretary of State, Foreign Office, 1939–43. Knighted, 1943. UK Representative, European Advisory Commission, 1943–45. Political Adviser, British Forces of Occupation, Germany, 1945–47. Permanent Under-Secretary, German Section, Foreign Office, 1947–49; Permanent Under-Secretary of State, Foreign Office, 1949–53. Created Baron, 1954.

make them permanent. They gape, a discreditable advertisement of administrative infirmity, and I am afraid that they are not the only instance which
could be cited in this sphere.

At the time of the Munich agreement, Churchill ended, it had been
hoped by some that Britain had purchased 'even at a great price, a lasting peace', while others felt that at least a 'breathing space' had been
gained. 'Let us make sure,' he declared, 'that this breathing space is not
improvidently cast away.' But on the following day, in rejecting Hore-
Belisha's proposed Army increases, Chamberlain told the Cabinet that
'finances could not be ignored since our financial strength was one of
our strongest weapons in any war which was not over in a short time.
. . . As a former Chancellor of the Exchequer, the financial position
looked to him extremely dangerous.'

The Government's cautious attitude towards defence spending and
the re-organization of industry revealed itself in several ways. On 1
January 1939 an Advisory Panel of Industrialists set up in the previous
month to report on delays and problems in the rearmament programme,
stressed in its report to Chamberlain that as much as possible was being
done by industry 'operating, it must be remembered, on a peace-time
basis'. In suggesting that this particular phrase should be omitted from
the final report, Sir Horace Wilson minuted on January 27: 'There are
previous references to the peace-time basis and I do not see any point in
rubbing it in quite so much. Repetition rather invites the comment that
it might be a good thing to put the country on a war footing and we do
not want to do that just yet. . . .'

On February 6 Chamberlain publicly confirmed an earlier statement
by Bonnet that if either France or Britain were attacked, the whole
resources of the other would be completely at the disposal of the
menaced country. 'I think that even in the great issues we may be
coming closer together,' Churchill had written to Halifax three days
earlier. Also on February 6, at a meeting of the Air Defence Research
sub-committee, Churchill, who sat between the reinstated Professor
Lindemann, and Major-General Ismay, learned of the detailed experimental work being done on anti-aircraft mines and shells.[1] On February

---

[1] Four Cabinet Ministers were present at the meeting of February 6: Kingsley Wood (in
the Chair), Inskip, Hore-Belisha, and W. S. Morrison. Also present were Sir Warren Fisher,
Sir Henry Tizard, Professor A. V. Hill, Sir Frank Smith, Lindemann, and representatives of
the Service Ministries. Ismay had succeeded Hankey as Secretary to the Committee of
Imperial Defence. Among the papers discussed was one by the Air Ministry rejecting as
impracticable Lindemann's proposal for an armed balloon barrage to be placed at 35,000
feet. In its conclusions, the sub-committee agreed with the Air Ministry paper of January 16,
that the strategic value of such a barrage 'would not justify its very high cost'.

7, at Kingsley Wood's invitation, Churchill was shown the Air Ministry's most secret charts of air construction. 'I think we are approaching the show-down,' Churchill wrote to Daisy Fellowes[1] on February 15, 'but there is certainly more confidence and resolution here than before.' On the previous day, however, an indication of the actual pace of rearmament was made clear in a secret Air Ministry estimate that, under the most recent scheme, the first 5 of three hundred Beaufighters ordered from Bristol to replace the older fighters of five fighter squadrons would not be delivered until November or December 1939, the first hundred by late April 1940, and the complete production not until September 1940. The German capacity was known to the Government, and was in stark contrast. On February 26 Lord Zetland wrote to Lord Linlithgow:

We received from Germany an interesting account not long ago of the growth of the German Air Force. The conclusion to be drawn from the information which reached us is that during 1939 the German first line air force will be brought up to 4,000 aircraft, and that she has an aircraft industry employing at the present time over 400,000 hands which is capable of producing on a peace time one shift basis from 800 to 1,000 aircraft of all types per month.

On February 13 A. H. Richards had invited Churchill to address a Jewish Youth Rally for National Service. 'It is perfectly true to say that because of your courageous defence of freedom and denunciation of Nazi-ism you are held in the very highest esteem by all sections of Jewry.' But Churchill declined, explaining on February 14: 'I am refusing practically every engagement at the present time.' To General Spears he explained more fully that same day, in refusing an invitation to dine: 'It is absolutely necessary for me to be in the country every possible night this year in order to complete the history I am writing. . . .'

On February 18 Sir Nevile Henderson sent the Foreign Office an account of a conversation with Goering, who had asked the Ambassador: 'What guarantee had Germany that Mr Chamberlain would remain in office and that he would not be succeeded by "a Mr Churchill or a Mr Eden" Government?' This question, Goering added, 'was

[1] Marguerite Severine Philipinne, daughter of the 4th Duc Decazes and de Glücksbjerg. Known as 'Daisy'. In 1910 she married Prince Jean de Broglie (who died in 1918), hence her nickname 'the Imbroglio'. In 1919 she married the Hon Reginald Ailwyn Fellowes (who died in 1953, and whose mother was Lady Rosamond Spencer Churchill, 2nd daughter of the 7th Duke of Marlborough). In 1929 Daisy Fellowes published *Cats in the Isle of Man*. Her villa in the south of France was Les Zoraïdes; she also lived in Paris and Newbury.

Germany's main preoccupation'. In reply, Henderson urged Goering 'to realize that the policy of a preventative war attributed to some British politicians carried no weight at all with the great mass of British public opinion or had any influence except with a section of the intelligentsia and of London opinion as distinct from the country'. Goering had even better reason than he knew to wish Chamberlain to remain in office, for on February 19 Chamberlain himself wrote to his sister:

I myself, am going about with a lighter heart than I have had for many a long day. All the information I get seems to point in the direction of peace & I repeat once more that I believe we have at last got on top of the dictators. Of course that doesn't mean that I want to bully them as they have tried to bully us; on the contrary I think they have had good cause to ask for consideration of their grievances, & if they had asked nicely after I appeared on the scene they might already have got some satisfaction.

Now it will take some time before the atmosphere is right but things are moving in the direction I want. . . .

I think we ought to be able to establish excellent relations with Franco who seems well disposed to us, & then, if the Italians are not in too bad a temper we might get Franco-Italian conversations going & if they were reasonably amicable we might advance towards disarmament. At any rate that's how I see things working round, & if I were given three or four more years I believe I really might retire with a quiet mind. . . .

On February 21 Chamberlain informed the House of Commons that the Defence Loans were to be doubled, to £800 million. During his speech he went on to say that it was the duty 'of this Government in particular, to watch for every opportunity that may come to try and persuade other Governments of the folly of the course that we are all pursuing which, if persisted in, must bring bankruptcy to every country in Europe'. During his speech, Chamberlain referred to Churchill as 'Bogey No 1 in some parts of Europe'. Replying, Churchill said that it was not his intention to make 'a controversial speech'. Nevertheless, he wished to protest against Chamberlain's remarks earlier in the debate that the League of Nations and collective security had failed. 'I hope he will make it clear,' Churchill said, 'that it was in no spirit of airy satisfaction that he referred to the undoubted downfall of so many hopes and ideals which the Government had encouraged.'

In the course of his speech Churchill said: 'It is evident that the coming financial year will see a very great accretion to our defensive strength. For the first time, the great aircraft production factories will be earning sums upon a scale which has hitherto been attained only in Germany—and it should not be forgotten that most of them were created under the administration of a Minister who is no longer in office, Lord Swinton. I do not in the slightest degree detract from the keenness and energy which the new Minister has imparted, but as so often happens, one sows and another reaps.'

During his speech Churchill again urged the establishment of a Ministry of Supply, whose task would be 'to deliver the goods' needed by the Service Ministries. He also appealed for a far greater production of rifles and ammunition, telling the House:

It seems to me that the production of munitions for an army should long ago have been undertaken upon a scale immensely greater than anything which the War Office have been allowed hitherto to contemplate, and it is another reason for the immediate appointment of a Minister of Supply. It is not a question of allowing plant and factories to come to full fruition, there is a need to provide, quite definitely, for the supply of munitions for very large forces which will be pressing themselves upon us should this hateful evil of war ever come upon us.

Moreover—to continue dealing with unpopular and unpalatable topics— we ought surely to have available in the first few months of war military forces larger than anything of which we have yet heard.

The Government's view, reiterated in the debate, was that a Ministry of Supply would seriously dislocate the smooth working of industry. It was better, W. S. Morrison[1] said on behalf of the Government, 'to trust to cooperation rather than compulsion'; a switch over 'at this moment would mean a check and a delay'. The former Secretary of State for Air, Lord Swinton, who had earlier opposed Churchill's arguments, wrote to him, however, on February 22: 'I think you are right about a Ministry of Supply today . . . the dislocation argument is grossly over-rated. But if it were sound, it is better to have dislocation now than in war.' Swinton also thanked Churchill for his 'generous allusion' to himself during the debate. Two days later Churchill replied:

I am very glad you noticed my remark about yourself. The Press are such lackeys, and do not seem at all to understand that up to the present whatever aeroplanes there are, are due to you. I was shown the other day all the progress charts, which certainly are much better than I had expected. If only you had been in the House of Commons, you should I am sure have fought your way through. Everyone respects the dignity with which you have

---

[1] William Shepherd Morrison, 1893–1961. Known as 'Shakes' Morrison. Served in the Royal Field Artillery, France, 1914–18 (wounded, Military Cross). Captain, 1919. President of the Edinburgh University Union, 1920, Called to the Bar, 1923. Conservative MP for Cirencester and Tewkesbury, 1929–59. King's Counsel, 1934. Privy Councillor, 1936. Minister of Agriculture and Fisheries, 1936–39. Minister of Food, 1939–40. Postmaster-General, 1940–43. Minister of Town and Country Planning, 1943–45. Speaker of the House of Commons, 1951–59. Created Viscount Dunrossil, 1959. Governor-General of Australia, 1960–61.

borne what must have been a most painful, though only I trust a temporary interruption of your political career. I know what I felt about leaving the Admiralty in the War, when I was convinced I was right and master of the event.

On March 2 Hore-Belisha urged the Cabinet to set up a Ministry of Supply. But Neville Chamberlain rejected this request, telling his colleagues that the public believed that they were already 'getting the goods'. Chamberlain went on to say: 'Now that public opinion was becoming satisfied on that point he thought the demand for a Ministry of Supply would die down.'

In Churchill's constituency a second attempt was being made to deprive him altogether of his place in Parliament, and an approach was made to a local landowner, Sir Thomas Fowell Buxton,[1] to stand against Churchill. Buxton refused to do so, but on March 4, at a dinner of the Nazeing Unionist Association, all the local constituency officials denounced Churchill's opposition to Chamberlain, and one speaker said that in other constituencies Churchill's action in opposing the Munich agreement 'would have resulted in his expulsion'. Among the speakers was Colin Thornton-Kemsley, who later recalled: 'I was at this time on the approved list of Conservative candidates and an office bearer in the Essex and Middlesex Provincial Area of the Conservative Party and it was made clear to me that the growing "revolt" in the Epping Division, to use a phrase which was much used in the National press, was welcomed in high places.' During the meeting Thornton-Kemsley told Churchill's constituents that they had been placed in 'an intolerable situation' by his criticisms of Government policy, and he continued: 'I think that unless Mr Churchill is prepared to work with the Conservative Party, National Government, and our great Prime Minister, he ought no longer to shelter under the goodwill and name which attaches to a great Party.'[2]

[1] Thomas Fowell Buxton, 1889–1945. Educated at Eton and Trinity Cambridge. Called to the Bar, 1913. Lieutenant, Essex Yeomanry, 1914–18 (despatches). Succeeded his father as 5th Baronet, 1919. A Justice of the Peace for Essex. High Sheriff of Essex, 1928.

[2] The remarks of two other speakers were reported in the *Hertfordshire Mercury* six days later: 'I entirely disagree,' said Capt. Jones, 'that we require Mr Churchill as Member of Parliament. I have been an opponent of Mr Churchill. He is a menace in Parliament. (A voice: Bogey No 1). I admire his brains and mental capacity, but I decry his judgment—he has no judgment.' Later in the meeting Major Bury said: 'I have never before criticised Mr Churchill in public, but there is an old saying, "the worm turns," and I suppose I am the worm. I have certainly come to the end of my patience and I am inclined to think that Mr Churchill had better look to the organisation of the new council. The new council is very differently constituted to the old council. Branch after branch has come over to support the Prime Minister.'

On March 10 Churchill answered his constituency critics in a speech at Chigwell, defending in detail all his warnings of the previous five years, and all that he had said during the Munich debate. 'I do not withdraw a single word,' he declared. 'I read it again only this afternoon, and was astonished to find how terribly true it had all come.' Now, he said, he would 'cordially support' the Government in their policy of naval and air preparations, while in the sphere of the Government's foreign policy he also found 'much to approve', particularly Chamberlain's recent visit to the Soviet Embassy, 'to show the world that trade and cooperation with Russia was a part of our general policy, so long as Russia continued to show herself an active friend to peace'.

At the end of his speech Churchill referred to his personal position. 'I have been out of office now for ten years,' he said, 'but I am more contented with the work I have done in these last five years as an Independent Conservative than of any other part of my public life. I know it has gained for me a greater measure of goodwill from my fellow-countrymen than I have ever previously enjoyed.' Churchill's spirited defence of his position won him the support of the meeting, and he ended, to applause, 'I am carrying on no factious opposition. I have no axe to grind in the matter. I am simply engaged in trying to get this country strongly armed, properly defended, and to have a foreign policy which will arrive at peace with honour.'

On March 14, in another speech in his constituency, this time at Waltham Abbey, Churchill again defended his right to speak his mind unfettered by party restrictions. 'What is the use of Parliament,' he said, 'if it is not the place where true statements can be brought before the people?' and he went on to ask:

What is the use of sending members to Parliament to say popular things of the moment, and saying things merely to give satisfaction to the Government whips and by cheering loudly every Ministerial platitude? What is the value of our Parliamentary institutions, and how can our Parliamentary doctrines survive if constituencies tried to return only tame, docile, and subservient members who tried to stamp out every form of independent judgment?

'What price politics,' Churchill's daughter Sarah had written to him on March 13, 'since they won't listen to you.'

Churchill's continued warnings of impending danger were in contrast to the views and pronouncements of Cabinet Ministers. On March 10 Sir Samuel Hoare had spoken publicly of the possibility of Europe freeing itself 'from a nightmare that haunts them and from an expenditure on armaments that beggars them' in order to create a new 'Golden Age', based on the friendly collaboration of five European Powers.[1] As well as writing privately to his sister on February 19 of his hopes for disarmament, Chamberlain himself had spoken publicly, on March 10, of the tranquil outlook in international affairs. On the previous day, however, the Slovaks of Czechoslovakia had begun pressing their demand for virtual independence from the Prague Government. In an attempt to preserve the unity of what was left of their State, the Czech Government declared martial law in Slovakia on March 10, and at the same time dismissed the Slovak Prime Minister, Father Tiso.[2] Three days later Tiso fled to Germany, where he was received by Hitler.

Throughout March 14 German troops moved in substantial numbers to the borders of the already truncated Czech State. During his speech that day at Waltham Abbey Churchill declared: 'The Czechoslovakian Republic is being broken up before our eyes. They are being completely absorbed; and not until the Nazi shadow has been finally lifted from Europe—as lifted I am sure it will eventually be—not until then will Czechoslovakia and ancient Bohemia march again into freedom.' A few moments later he declared: 'It is no use going to their aid when they are defenceless, if we would not go to their aid when they were strong. Therefore I agree entirely with those who think we should not intervene at the present time. We cannot. That is the end of it,' but, he added:

. . . to suppose that we are not involved in what is happening is a profound illusion. Although we can do nothing to stop it, we shall be sufferers on a very great scale. We shall have to make all kinds of sacrifices for our own defence that would have been unnecessary if a firm resolve had been taken at an earlier stage. We shall have to make sacrifices not only of money, but of personal service in order to make up for what we have lost.

[1] During the course of his speech Hoare said: 'Five men in Europe, the three dictators and the Prime Ministers of Britain and France, if they worked for a singleness of purpose, and a unity of action to this end, might in an incredibly short space of time transform the whole history of the world. These five men, working together in Europe, and blessed in their effort by the President of the United States, might make themselves the eternal benefactors of the human race. Our own Prime Minister has shown his determination to work heart and soul to such an end. I cannot believe that the other leaders of Europe will not join him in the high endeavour in which he is engaged.'

[2] Josef Tiso. A Slovak priest and active member of the Slovak People's Party. Minister of Health in the Czechoslovak Government, 1927–29. Leader of the Slovak People's Party, August 1938. Prime Minister of the autonomous Slovak Government, October 1938. Proclaimed the independence of Slovakia, 14 March 1939. President of Slovakia from 26 October 1939 until his capture in Austria on 22 May 1945. Tried and condemned to death for collaboration with the Germans, 15 April 1947; hanged three days later.

In the early hours of March 15 the Czechoslovak President, Dr Hacha,[1] was received by Hitler in Berlin. During the meeting, at which Hitler ranted violently about Czech obstinacy, Hacha agreed to place his country under the 'protection' of Germany. Even while their discussion was in progress, German troops had crossed the Czech frontier and were advancing towards the capital. During the day Father Tiso also obtained Hitler's consent for Slovakia to be separated from Bohemia–Moravia, and likewise put under German 'protection'. That night Hitler slept in Prague, at the Hradčany Palace, and on the following day proclaimed a German Protectorate over Bohemia and Moravia. One of the first acts of this new protecting power was to establish a concentration camp, at Milovice, for opponents of the regime.

On the evening of March 15 Churchill dined at Grillions Club. Among those present was the former British Ambassador to Berlin, Sir Horace Rumbold, who wrote to him on the following day:

You asked me last night what I thought of the present situation and I replied that I was profoundly disheartened. This was an understatement. I have had several difficult and depressing situations to deal with in the course of my career and I have, on the whole, been inclined to optimism. But I have never felt so depressed or so nauseated as I feel now and this because it seems to me that our Government have for a year or more, failed to look ahead or to understand the character of the man with whom they are dealing. . . .

I am inclined to think that the northern gangster may go for Memel next and that his fellow brigand in the south will try for Albania.[2] I only hope that it will not enter into the PM's head to pay Hitler another visit. The season ticket he took to Canossa last autumn is more than sufficient and there is no doubt that what the Arabs would call the 'father of appeasement' was outwitted and fooled by the 'father of lies or treachery' ie Hitler at Munich.

The seizure of the Czech aeroplanes and gold etc is such an accession of strength to Hitler that I don't put it past him to challenge us now in a most direct manner.

Churchill replied four days later: 'it seems to me Hitler will not stop short of the Black Sea unless arrested by the threat of a general war, or actual hostilities'.

On March 14 the House of Commons had debated, as previously arranged, the Army estimates. In commenting on Hore-Belisha's

---

[1] Emil Hacha, 1875–1945. An Austro-Hungarian civil servant before 1914. Chief Justice of the Supreme Administrative Court of Czechoslovakia. A devout Catholic, he was elected President of the Czechoslovak National Assembly on 30 November 1938. Appointed 'State President', March 1939, responsible to a Berlin-appointed Reich Protector. In August 1939 he inaugurated the Union of Co-operation with the Germans.

[2] The Germans seized Memel on March 23. The Italians invaded Albania on April 7.

announcement six days earlier that the Government were now equipping the Territorials 'to meet the event of war in a European quarter', Churchill pointed out that the 1936 White Paper had contained a 'shocking sentence' saying that the Territorials could not then be equipped for war. His speech continued:

It seemed such a monstrous thing that we should appeal to the youth of our country to come forward and join the Territorial army . . . and . . . not even give them the ordinary weapons which are necessary and which could put them on equal terms with the contemporary forces they might have to meet. . . .

The Government, no doubt, will protest that they never thought in 1936 that things would turn out so rough. Well, they were wrong.

Churchill ended: 'I quite recognise that the Prime Minister and his colleagues are perfectly safe and will get away with it because there are too many in it . . . they will face only such censure as the course of history may inflict upon them in the pages of history.'

That same day Major F. L. Fraser[1] wrote to Churchill:

In 1916 when you were commanding a battalion of the Royal Scots Fusiliers, I was GSO 3 of the 9th Division; in 1917, when I was wounded, you were kind enough to come & see me in hospital at Eccleston Square. But all this is so long ago now, that I have great hesitation in writing to you.

I am now Chief Intelligence Officer of the ARP Dept and have been with the Dept since 1936.

I should be most grateful if you could spare me a few minutes, as I should like to discuss certain matters with you. . . .

The German occupation of Prague was for many people proof that Hitler's Munich promises were but dust in the eyes of Britain and France.[2] 'I cannot regard the manner or the method . . . as in accord with the Munich agreement,' Chamberlain declared bluntly in the House of Commons on March 15, and the Government at once began considering negotiations with Poland and Roumania, two States clearly in danger should Hitler decide to strike again. Speaking at Birmingham on March 17, Chamberlain pointed out that the German occupation of Prague violated Hitler's often-repeated statement that he did not wish to incorporate any non-Germanic peoples within the borders of his

---

[1] Forbes Leith Fraser, 1885–   . 2nd Lieutenant, Seaforth Highlanders, 1904; Captain, 1914. General Staff Officer, Grade 3, 9th Division, 1917 (wounded). Joined the Air Raid Precautions Department, Home Office, 1936; Chief Intelligence Officer, 1938.

[2] But not for the *Daily Express*, which told its readers on March 14: 'Its Hitler again, but don't worry! Reason No 1: There will be no September crisis, no autumn jitters in the spring. Reason No 2: The Czech trouble, in the British Cabinet's view, cannot in any circumstances involve Britain in military action. Reason No 3: Lord Halifax, Foreign Secretary, at Sunderland last night, warned the public against seeing a crisis in every event.'

Reich. 'Is this the end of an old adventure?' Chamberlain asked, 'or is it the beginning of a new? . . . Is this, in fact, a step in the direction of an attempt to dominate the world by force?' On March 18 A. H. Richards wrote to Churchill: 'At long last it would appear the Prime Minister recognises that you cannot shoo off dictators with an umbrella. His speech struck a new and firm note.' In his letter to Rumbold on March 19 Churchill wrote of how 'Chamberlain in his speech has admitted the altogether wrong opinion which he formed of men and things for which he is responsible.' That same day Margot Asquith wrote to Churchill:

Dearest Winston,

We are *old* friends (I, *very* old!). I think you sd go to 10 Downing St & offer yr services, in whatever the PM wishes to place you. We *must* show Germany that we are united against her wish to dominate Europe.

There was no office of State, and no subordinate position, which Chamberlain had any intention of giving to Churchill. Nor did Churchill feel able to offer his services, as Margot Asquith suggested. 'The Government have now adopted the foreign policy which I and most Liberals have long been pressing,' he replied to her on March 22, 'and consequently I am in very good relations with them, but I am sure it would be a great mistake to make any offer of the kind you suggest.' To Chamberlain he had written on the previous day, after his meeting with Major Fraser, urging an immediate state of 'full preparedness' for Britain's anti-aircraft defences. Churchill went on to explain why he believed this type of action was essential:

Such a step could not be deemed aggressive, yet it would emphasise the seriousness of the action HMG are taking on the Continent. The bringing together of these officers and men would improve their efficiency with every day of their embodiment. The effect at home would be one of confidence rather than alarm.

But it is of Hitler I am thinking mostly. He must be under intense strain at this moment. He knows we are endeavouring to form a coalition to restrain his further aggression. With such a man anything is possible. The temptation to make a surprise attack on London or on the aircraft factories about which I am even more anxious would be removed if it was known that all was ready. There could, in fact, be no surprise, and, therefore, the incentive to the extremes of violence would be removed and more prudent counsels might prevail.

In August 1914 I persuaded Mr Asquith to let me send the Fleet to the North Sea so that it could pass the Straits of Dover and the narrow seas *before* the diplomatic situation had become hopeless. It seems to me that manning the anti-aircraft defences now stands in a very similar position, and I hope you will not mind my putting this before you.

'My dear Winston,' Chamberlain replied that same day from 10 Downing Street, 'Thanks for your note. I have been spending a lot of time on the subject you mention but it is not so simple as it seems.'

Chamberlain's actual view of the future was based on the hope that all was still not lost. 'As always,' he wrote to his sister on March 19, 'I want to gain time for I never accept the view that war is inevitable,' but a week later he wrote again:

> . . . there is always the possibility that Germany will act more cunningly & that instead of invasion we shall be faced with a new 'commercial agreement' which in effect puts Roumania at her mercy. I must confess that even when small states won't face up to this sort of penetration even when backed by us I see nothing for us to do unless we are prepared ourselves to hand Germany an ultimatum. We are not strong enough ourselves & we cannot command sufficient strength elsewhere to present Germany with an overwhelming force. Our ultimatum would therefore mean war & I would never be responsible for presenting it. We should just have to go on re-arming & collecting what help we could from outside in the hope that something would happen to break the spell, either Hitler's death or a realisation that the defence was too strong to make attack feasible.

Later in his letter Chamberlain commented:

> I have to address the 1922 Cttee, on Tuesday evening. It is a very important occasion, as there will be 150 or 200 MPs there including the Anthony & Churchill supporters who will be anxious to exploit any mistakes I make.
> But I agree with you about the undiminished strength of my position in the country. Wherever I go, the crowds at the station, along the routes, in the Guildhall, in the Opera House, give me an astonishing welcome & though no doubt academic circles at Oxford & elsewhere are echoing Attlee's remarks on Friday to the effect that the Govt have now admitted that they were wrong & the opposition right all along, they are only a minority.
> That was not the opinion of De Valera, who spent a couple of hours with me yesterday morning. He is strongly of opinion that I have been right all through & am right now.

Churchill's informants continued to warn him of deficiencies in Britain's defences. On March 21 Lachlan Maclean sent him a memorandum, the aim of which was to show 'how much our requirements in the air differ from what we actually possess, and what we are really doing', particularly in the sphere of bomber ranges and capabilities. Two days later Wing-Commander Anderson offered to send Churchill details of the heavy rate of airmen's applications for discharge, and the unserviceability of many aerodromes 'owing to heavy rains and necessity of laying concrete runways'.

The League of Nations Union were anxious to secure Churchill as a principal speaker at one of their main meetings. On March 23 A. H. Richards had written to him: '*Many* people are asking me why you are not giving a lead.' On March 24 Lord Lytton urged him to speak for the LNU in the north of England. 'I think the tide is definitely running in our direction,' he wrote, 'but the latest utterances of the Government have not been quite definite enough to stop the risk of further aggression.' Churchill replied on March 25. His speaking campaign of April 1938 had not, he wrote, exerted 'the slightest influence upon events', and he added:

I must keep what strength I have for the House of Commons, though there is not much hope of that either. Nothing but the terrible teaching of experience will affect this all-powerful supine Government. The worst of it is that by the time they are convinced, or replaced, our own position will be frightfully weakened.

Following the German occupation of Prague, Churchill received a continual stream of letters of encouragement. These were stimulated by the German annexation of Memel on March 23. Three days later Lord Midleton wrote to Churchill of how 'the fire of youth still burns in you, after 39 years in Parliament', and he added: 'I have always appreciated you even when in controversy, and if we were unhappily at war, should prefer to see you at the Head of our Imperial Defence to anyone.'

On March 27 Churchill received a letter from the Independent Liberal candidate for North Cornwall, T. L. Horabin.[1] In each of his campaign speeches, Horabin wrote, he was advocating Churchill as 'the only possible man for Prime Minister in this hour of danger'. This suggestion had come as a shock at first, and yet it only took 'about two minutes for the idea to sink in, and then there was an outburst of applause'. Replying on March 29, Churchill thanked Horabin 'for the favourable view you take of my usefulness. I greatly appreciate your goodwill and confidence.'[2] The truth of Churchill's warnings had

[1] Thomas Lewis Horabin, 1896–1956. Educated at Cardiff High School. Business consultant. Independent Liberal MP for North Cornwall, 1939–47; Chief Party Whip of the Independent Liberals, 1945. Joined the Labour Party, 1947; Labour MP, 1947–50.

[2] On April 3 T. L. Horabin wrote again, enclosing a copy of a petition which the North Cornwall Liberal Association was to circulate throughout the constituency 'off their own bat calling on Chamberlain to resign, and asking the King to entrust to Churchill 'the formation of a Government of National Defence, comprising all parties in the State'. Churchill alone the petition declared, had 'the moral purpose, courage, experience and capacity to save us

become painfully clear, yet was still unwelcome. On March 30 Harold Nicolson recorded in his diary: 'A meeting of the New Commonwealth which is to be addressed by Winston. It is with difficulty that we whip up a proper audience. They simply do not wish to hear what they fear will be painful things.' Yet two days earlier thirty Conservative MPs had joined Churchill and Eden in tabling a House of Commons resolution calling for an all-Party Government.

On March 27 Churchill had sent Chamberlain, Halifax, Chatfield and Hore-Belisha a memorandum he had written on sea-power, setting out in detail his view of what British naval policy ought to be in the event of war. Complete control of the Mediterranean should be the first goal; then 'domination of the Baltic'. But until German naval power had been broken Singapore would have to hold out with naval aid in the event of war with Japan, although, he wrote, such Japanese attack was unlikely, certainly not until England 'has been decisively beaten, which will not be the case in the first year of the war'.

'With no claim to any special knowledge,' Halifax replied on March 28, 'I find my thought going very much with yours,' while Lord Chatfield replied on April 3: 'I very much agree with nearly all you say and only put in the word "nearly" so as to give myself a loophole of escape in case my mind may work on other lines gradually!' As for the Baltic question, he wrote, that would have to be 'left for a decision until that happy moment that you prophesy arrives when we have settled the Mediterranean question, and the Far East has not developed dangerously'.

Churchill also wrote to Kingsley Wood on March 27. His letter was marked 'For Yourself alone', and contained a strong plea for even greater exertions by the Air Defence Research sub-committee. 'The sole point,' he wrote, 'is to gain a reinforcement of our defences,' and he went on:

You will no doubt be told that everything is going on all right, and that there is no need to disturb the ordinary train of research; and I dare say unless you intervene another year may well be lost. . . .

What we need is an exceptional priority. We go buzzing along with a host of ideas and experiments which may produce results in '41, '42, and '43. Where will you find anything that can operate in June, July and August of 1939? This is the only possible reinforcement. Never will it be more needed than in these months when so much else is lacking. . . .

from these dangers in this hour of peril'. Horabin's own letter ended: 'When they grasp the facts, the determination of the people, men and women alike, to make every sacrifice is wonderful. Given your leadership we can win through.'

Churchill enclosed details of an experiment into explosives which had been held up, in his view, by 'a form of departmentalism very vicious to England'. What was needed in all experimental cases were 'friendly and resolute hands' which condemned such delays. Churchill added: 'Now I do beg you to use your authority. It costs so little; it is such a minute fraction of your sphere of responsibility. But unless you insist that the small primary steps shall be taken at once, day after day, nothing will happen except this vast prolonged grimacing.'

Kingsley Wood followed up Churchill's letter by inviting Lindemann to Farnborough, 'to be au fait with what is going on', as he wrote to Sir Hugh Dowding[1] on March 31, while at the same time he authorized Dowding himself to go to Chartwell in order to discuss with Churchill the details of the new experiments.

On March 28 the first public appeal for a National Government was issued in the form of a Parliamentary motion by more than thirty Conservative MPs, led by Churchill, Eden and Duff Cooper. Harold Macmillan was among those who signed the motion. But Neville Chamberlain was still determined to exclude his critics. On March 31, however, on his own initiative, he drafted and made public a British guarantee to Poland. By this guarantee, Britain promised Poland all the support in her power 'in the event of any action which clearly threatened Polish independence, and which the Polish Government accordingly considered it vital to resist'.

The Polish Guarantee of March 31 reconciled Churchill to the Government's foreign policy; on April 3, during a debate on the European situation, he spoke of the 'almost complete agreement' on foreign policy between the Government and its former critics. 'We can no longer endure,' he said, 'to be pushed from pillar to post.' He was anxious that the new found firmness of the Foreign Office should be properly followed up, and fully understood, telling the Commons:

There was a sinister passage in the Times leading article on Saturday similar to that which foreshadowed the ruin of Czechoslovakia, which sought

---

[1] Hugh Caswall Tremenheere Dowding, 1882–1970. Educated at Winchester. Joined the Royal Artillery, 1900; Royal Flying Corps, 1914. On active service, 1914–19 (despatches). Director of Training, Air Ministry, 1926–29. Commanding the Fighting Area, Air Defence of Great Britain, 1929–30. Air Member for Research and Development, 1930–36. Knighted, 1933. Air Officer Commanding-in-Chief, Fighter Command, 1936–40. Mission to the USA for the Ministry of Aircraft Production, 1940–44. Created Baron, 1943.

to explain that there was no guarantee for the integrity of Poland, but only for its independence. . . .[1]

But the position of the British and French Governments seems to be perfectly clear. We are not concerned at this particular moment with particular rights or places, but to resist by force of arms further acts of violence, of pressure or of intrigue.

Moreover, this is not the time for negotiation. After the crime and treachery committed against Czechoslovakia, our first duty is to re-establish the authority of law and public faith in Europe.

The 'slightest sign of weakness' Churchill warned, would only serve to aggravate the dangers, not only for Britain but for the whole world. Above all, the Soviet Union must be encouraged to come forward as a partner in the gathering together of all threatened States.

Churchill's suspicions about *The Times* leader, were well founded, but even he did not realize that Chamberlain shared the view of *The Times*. On April 3 Chamberlain wrote to his sister: 'I refused to be rushed into making a statement at 11 am on Friday in spite of suggestions that everyone would get the jitters if they weren't told everything at once. This gave a little time to redraft the statement in the light of the latest information & after further reflection. It was of course mostly my own & when it was finished I was well satisfied with it. It was un-provocative in tone, but firm, clear but stressing the important point (perceived alone by the Times) that what we are concerned with is not the boundaries of States, but attacks on their independence. And it is we who will judge whether this independence is threatened or not.'

The Soviet Ambassador, Ivan Maisky, was among those who listened to the debate. In his diary that night Harold Nicolson recorded:

The House rises at 10.50 pm and I am seized upon by Winston and taken down to the lower smoking-room with Maisky and Lloyd George. Winston adopts the direct method of attack. 'Now look here, Mr Ambassador, if we are to make a success of this new policy, we require the help of Russia. Now I don't care for your system and I never have, but the Poles and the Rumanians like it even less. Although they might be prepared at a pinch to let you in, they would certainly want some assurances that you would eventually get out. Can you give us such assurances?'

---

[1] On April 1 *The Times* declared in its leading article: 'The new obligation which this country yesterday assumed does not bind Great Britain to defend every inch of the present frontiers of Poland. They key word in the statement is not integrity but "independence". . . . Mr Chamberlain's statement involves no blind acceptance of the *status quo*. . . . This country has never been an advocate of the encirclement of Germany, and is not now opposed to the extension of Germany's economic activities and influence, nor to the constructive work she may yet do for Europe.'

Lloyd George, I fear, is not really in favour of the new policy and he draws Maisky on to describe the deficiencies of the Polish Army. Apparently many of their guns are pre-Revolution guns of the Russian Army. Maisky contends that the Polish soldiers are excellent fighters and that the officers are well-trained. Winston rather objects to this and attacks Lloyd George. 'You must not do this sort of thing, my dear. You are putting spokes in the wheel of history.'

Churchill's hopes for Soviet involvement in European affairs were not shared by Chamberlain, who was deeply suspicious of Russia's intentions. But before these hopes could be tested, Mussolini began to make fierce accusations against Albania, concentrated the Italian Fleet in the Straits of Otranto and embarked troops at Italy's southern Adriatic ports.

That night Churchill dined with Beaverbrook at Stornoway House. Another of the guests, Arthur Christiansen,[1] recorded in his memoirs how, while Beaverbrook and Brendan Bracken played backgammon, Churchill approached him—they had never met before—and asked:

'Where is the—ah—the British Fleet to-night?' he asked me, rolling the words around his palate and licking them before they are uttered. 'It ish lolling in the Bay of Naples. No doubt, the—ah—the Commander of the British ships at Naples is—ah—being entertained ashore, entertained no doubt on the orders of—ah—Mussholini himself at the Naples Yacht Club.'

Churchill glowered at me and chewed his cigar before continuing: 'And where should the British Fleet be to-night? On the other side of that longheel of a country called Italy. In the Adriatic Sea, not the Mediterranean Sea, to make the rape of Albania impossible. . . .'[2]

On April 7, Good Friday, Mussolini's troops landed on the Albanian coast. Churchill was lunching at Chartwell when the news of this invasion became known. Harold Macmillan, who was at the luncheon, later recalled in his memoirs how:

Maps were brought out; secretaries were marshalled; telephones began to ring. 'Where was the British fleet?' That was the most urgent question. That considerable staff which, even as a private individual, Churchill always maintained to support his tremendous outflow of literary political effort was

---

[1] Arthur Christiansen, 1904–1963. Educated at Wallasey Grammar School. Joined the *Wallasey Chronicle*, 1920. News Editor of the *Sunday Express*, 1926–29; Assistant Editor, 1928–33. Editor of the *Daily Express*, 1933–57; Editorial Director 1957–59. Director, Independent Television News, 1960–62. In 1961 he published his memoirs, *Headlines All My Life*.

[2] On April 8 the First Lord of the Admiralty, Lord Stanhope, told the Cabinet that a number of British warships 'were visiting Italian ports as part of the normal spring cruise and had had a good reception'.

at once brought into play. It turned out that the British fleet was scattered throughout the Mediterranean. Of the five great ships, one was at Gibraltar, one in the Eastern Mediterranean, and the remaining three, in Churchill's words 'lolling about inside or outside widely-separated Italian ports. . . .'[1]

Macmillan's account continued: 'I shall always have a picture of that spring day and the sense of power and energy, the great flow of action, which came from Churchill, although he then held no public office. He alone seemed to be in command, when everyone else was dazed and hesitating.'

On April 9 Churchill wrote to Chamberlain: 'Hours now count,' and he urged that a plan should be put into operation at once to enable Britain 'to recover the initiative in diplomacy'. His suggestion was for an immediate British Naval occupation of the Greek island of Corfu.[2] 'Had this step been already taken,' Churchill wrote, 'it would afford the best chance of maintaining peace,' and he went on to explain:

If it is not taken by us, of course with Greek consent, it seems to me that after the publicity given to the idea in the Press and the obvious needs of the situation, Corfu will be speedily taken by Italy. Its recapture would then be impossible.

On the other hand, if we are there first, an attack even upon a few British ships would confront Mussolini with beginning a war of aggression upon England. This direct issue gives the best chance to all the forces in Italy which are opposed to a major war with England. So far from intensifying the grave risks now open, it diminishes them. But action ought to be taken to-night.

What is now at stake is nothing less than the whole of the Balkan Peninsula. If these States remain exposed to German and Italian pressure while we appear, as they may deem it, incapable of action, they will be forced to make the best terms possible with Berlin and Rome. How forlorn then will our position become! We shall be committed to Poland and thus involved in the East of Europe while at the same time cutting off from ourselves all hope of that large alliance which once effected might spell salvation.

---

[1] On April 13 Churchill told the House of Commons: 'According to published statements in the newspapers of all countries, the Fleet was scattered from one end of the Mediterranean to the other. Of the five great capital ships one was at Gibraltar, another in the Eastern Mediterranean, and the remaining three were lolling about outside various widely separated Italian ports, two of them not attended by their protective flotillas. The destroyer flotillas themselves were dispersed along the European and African shores, and a number of cruisers were crowded in Malta harbour, without the protection which is given by the powerful anti-aircraft batteries of the battleships. I do not understand at all how this situation, which has now been rectified, was allowed to arise.'

[2] Corfu had been a British protectorate from 1815 until 1863, when it was united with Greece. In August 1923 it had been bombarded by Mussolini, who occupied it in 1940. It was restored to Greece in 1945.

'I write the above,' Churchill added, 'without knowledge of the existing position of our Mediterranean Fleet which should of course be concentrated and *at sea*, in a suitable, but not too close supporting position.'

Churchill sent this letter by messenger to 10 Downing Street. Shortly after it had been delivered he telephoned the Prime Minister's Office to say that 'only swift action' by the British Fleet in occupying Corfu could prevent the Greek Government from joining the Rome–Berlin Axis. His message was taken by Cecil Syers,[1] who recorded that Churchill also said that 'his friends in the French Government, with whom he had been in touch, assured him that France would support any vigorous action in this connection taken by us. . . .' A little while later Churchill telephoned a second time to reiterate his points, and to urge the recall of Parliament. Chamberlain was given a written note of both messages and on April 10 took them and Churchill's letter to the Cabinet, but the idea of action such as he proposed met with no support.

In sending his sister an account of Mussolini's attack on Albania, Chamberlain wrote: 'What I had hoped when I went away on Thursday night was that Musso would so present his coup as to make it look like an agreed arrangement & thus raise as little as possible questions of European significance.' Now, he wrote, 'such faith as I ever had in the assurances of dictators is rapidly being whittled away'. Chamberlain's letter continued:

It doesn't make things easier to be badgered for a meeting of Pmt by the two Oppositions & Winston who is the worst of the lot, telephoning almost every hour of the day. I suppose he has prepared a terrific oration which he wants to let off. I know there are a lot of reckless people who would plunge us into a war at once but we must resist them until it becomes really inevitable. I got several abusive telegrams from Communists yesterday & I see Mr Barnes[2] of the Co-ops is calling for my resignation. On the other hand wherever I go the people collect in crowds to give me their good wishes & I don't believe that Hitler & Mussolini have shaken my position.

During the Cabinet of April 10 both Hore-Belisha and Lord de La Warr urged the immediate establishment of a Ministry of Supply.

---

[1] Cecil George Lewis Syers, 1903–81. Educated at St Paul's and Balliol College Oxford. Entered the Dominions Office, 1925; Assistant Private Secretary to the Secretary of State, 1930–34. Assistant Private Secretary to the Prime Minister (Chamberlain), 1937–40. Deputy High Commissioner, South Africa, 1942–46. Assistant Under-Secretary of State, Commonwealth Relations Office, 1946–48; Deputy Under-Secretary of State, 1948–51. Knighted, 1949. High Commissioner, Ceylon, 1951–57.

[2] Alfred Barnes, 1887–1974. Educated at the LCC School of Arts and Crafts. Chairman of the Co-operative Party 1922–45, and Co-operative MP for South East Ham 1922–31 and 1935–55. A Lord Commissioner of the Treasury in the second Labour Government, 1929–30. Privy Councillor, 1945. Minister of War Transport 1945–46; of Transport 1946–51.

But Chamberlain was still reluctant to take such a significant step. On the following day, while Hore-Belisha was at a meeting of the Army Council, a message was brought to him to say that Churchill was on the telephone and was asking if Hore-Belisha could go down to Chartwell 'as he had a bad foot and could not come to London'. Hore-Belisha went on to record:

He said he particularly wanted to have a talk to me. I guessed what he was feeling, being out of it all. I sent a message that I would go down as soon as the meeting was over.

Reached Chartwell about 10 pm. He opened the door himself. He had a felt slipper on his bad foot. We had dinner together. He recalled the difficulties he had had during the war, how he had advocated measures in the Cabinet, which had been turned down by his colleagues, and then had suffered violent opposition because these measures had not been carried out. I arrived back home about 2 am.

Hore-Belisha continued to press, both for a Ministry of Supply, and for a more rapid and thorough equipping of six regular and twenty-six Territorial Divisions to enable them 'to go overseas within 8 months after zero hour'. But on April 13 Lord Chatfield wrote to Sir John Simon telling him that he must not expect the Territorials to be fully equipped that year 'since both from productive capacity, disturbance of industry and finance, a lower aim seems imperative and at the present time the only solution. . . .' Chatfield proposed equipping ten Territorial divisions, but even this limited proposal was too much for Simon, who replied four days later that he feared this was 'more than we can successfully tackle'. Simon added: 'At present four Territorial divisions are to be fully equipped, and this decision was taken only on February 2nd. Does not "doubling the Territorial Army" imply that eight Territorial divisions will be so equipped?'

On April 13 the House of Commons debated the Italian invasion of Albania. Churchill spoke with approval of Chamberlain's decision to give a guarantee to Greece, and to make 'even more effective arrangements' with Turkey. He spoke critically however of the British naval disposition in the Mediterranean when the crisis broke. They did not, he said, conform 'to the ordinary dictates of prudence'. He was also concerned at the apparent lack of information available to Cabinet Ministers on the eve of the invasion, telling the House:

How was it that on the eve of the Bohemian outrage Ministers were indulging in what was called 'sunshine talk', and predicting the dawn of a golden age? How was it that last week's holiday routine was observed at a time when, quite clearly, something of a very exceptional character, the consequences of which could not be measured, was imminent? I do not know. I know very well the patriotism and sincere desire to act in a manner of perfect rectitude which animates Ministers of the Crown, but I wonder whether there is not some hand which intervenes and filters down or witholds intelligence from Ministers.

In 1934, Churchill declared, a similar process of sifting and colouring and reducing had taken place with the figures for German air strength. 'The facts were not allowed to reach high Ministers of the Crown until they had been so modified that they did not present an alarming impression.' There was a tremendous risk, he warned, of Ministers only attaching importance 'to those pieces of information which accord with their earnest and honourable desire that the peace of the world shall remain unbroken', and he went on to urge 'the full inclusion' of Soviet Russia in the emerging defensive bloc, of which Britain, France and Poland, were already a part. He also pressed the Government to try to promote a 'self-protective union' in the Balkans.

In approving Chamberlain's announcement earlier in the debate that Britain had just offered a guarantee to Roumania, Churchill declared: 'One sees a great design which, even now at the eleventh hour, if it could be perfected, would spare the world the worst of agonies,' but he went on to warn that:

The danger is now very near. A great part of Europe is to a very large extent mobilised. Millions of men are being prepared for war. Everywhere the frontier defences are manned. Everywhere it is felt that some new stroke is impending If it should fall, can there by any doubt that we shall be involved? We are no longer where we were two or three months ago. We have committed ourselves in every direction, rightly in my opinion, having regard to all that has happened. . . .

At the end of his speech Churchill asked the House of Commons: 'How can we bear to continue to lead our comfortable, easy life here at home, unwilling even to pronounce the word "compulsion", unwilling even to take the necessary measure by which the armies that we have promised can alone be recruited and equipped?'

'You voiced the opinion of the House,' Colonel Moore-Brabazon wrote to Churchill when his speech was over, 'and it has had a great effect.' Two days later Boothby congratulated Churchill on 'the best speech I have ever heard in the House of Commons. There was nothing more to be said.'

Chamberlain was disappointed and upset by Churchill's speech, explaining in a letter to his sister how, before the debate, he had sent for Churchill 'in the hope of keeping the House as united as possible & had given him much information, after first telling him very flatly that I knew Randolph told journalists and others what his father had reported to him of his talks with me'. Chamberlain's letter continued:

W. took this warning in very good part, expressed his entire approval of what we were doing & declared his intention of making a 'not unhelpful' speech. But there was an acid undertone which brought many cheers from Labour benches & again I felt depressed when he sat down. The first speech in fact which gave me any comfort was A. Eden's with which I thoroughly agreed & I sent him a friendly note & he replied in equally cordial terms.

I heard afterwards that when Winston got my message he thought I was going to offer him the Ministry of Supply & he was therefore smarting under a sense of disappointment, only kept in check by his unwillingness to do anything which might prevent his yet receiving an offer to join the Govt.

When the debate was over, Churchill saw David Margesson, and expressed—as Chamberlain told his sister—a 'strong desire' to enter the Cabinet. Chamberlain's letter went on:

I told D.M. that I would let this suggestion simmer a bit. It caught me at a moment when I was certainly feeling the need of help, but I wanted to do nothing too quickly. The question is whether Winston, who would certainly help on the Treasury bench in the Commons, would help or hinder in Cabinet or in Council. Last Saturday for instance he was at the telephone all day urging that Pmt should be summoned for Sunday & that the Fleet should go & seize Corfu that night! Would he wear me out resisting rash suggestions of this kind?

Churchill remained seriously concerned about the precarious state of Britain's naval alertness. On April 17 he wrote to Halifax about the 'unpreparedness' in Home Waters. 'The Atlantic Fleet,' he commented, 'except for a few anti-aircraft guns, has been practically out of action for some days owing to very large numbers of men having been sent on leave. One would have thought at least the leave could be "staggered" in times like these.' In addition, Churchill pointed out, 'All the mine-sweepers are out of action re-fitting,' and he went on to ask: 'How is it possible to reconcile this with the statement of tension declared to be existing on Tuesday week? It seems to be a grave departure from the procedure of continuous and reasonable vigilance.' Churchill's letter ended: 'I write this to you for your own personal information, and in order that you can check the facts for yourself. Pray, therefore, treat my letter as strictly private, as I do not want to bother the Prime Minister with the matter, but think you ought to know.'

On April 18 Halifax sent Churchill's letter to Lord Chatfield, who replied on the following day: 'There is, of course a good deal in all that he says, though one wishes he would not be quite so restless, because it implies a want of confidence in the Admiralty and ignores certain important considerations altogether.' Chatfield's letter continued with an explanation of why the Home Fleet had not been held together and of Chamberlain's part in that decision:

I asked before the Fleet went on leave whether the Foreign Office and the Admiralty had considered the desirability of this taking place and was informed that a decision had been arrived at by the Prime Minister in conjunction with you and the First Lord approving it, a decision which I have no doubt at the time was a right one, if I may say so.

What Mr Churchill forgets invariably is that the British Fleet is *an old Fleet*, largely due to his own action when he was Chancellor of the Exchequer in opposing its reconstruction, though he is not entirely to blame as you will know. The result is that we are building up our Fleet too late. . . .

Then as regards the Mediterranean Fleet, I think he exaggerates when he talks of them being scattered in 'vulnerable disorder'. It is, of course, a matter of opinion whether paying a friendly visit to our potential enemy and fraternising with them is placing your ship in a state of jeopardy or the contrary, but you will remember that the Admiralty pointed out that the majority of the Fleet was at Malta all the time.

We cannot maintain a continuous reasonable vigilance on our present system and if we have got to do so we must change our principles in my opinion, but you will remember that during the whole of the last twelve months there has been a state of strain and would Mr Churchill say that during the whole of those twelve months the British Navy should have been kept at their war stations?!

For nearly two months there had been frequent articles in the Press putting Churchill's views across to a wide audience. On February 25 *Picture Post* had published a long article by Wickham Steed, illustrated by photographs of Churchill at Chartwell, and stating that 'the greatest moment of his life is still to come'. A second article on March 4 traced his family history in pictures, and a third, a week later, took the form of thirteen questions and answers: 'I think it will be necessary to form a government on a broader base', Churchill said in one of his answers, 'and ensure the cooperation of the working people if we are to carry through a strong foreign policy'. The questions and answers were prepared by the editor of *Picture Post*, Stefan Lorant,[1] who himself went to Chartwell to put them to Churchill. In the following weeks several papers wrote articles or published letters on the theme of Churchill 'The Only Man', while cartoons reflected the call for Churchill's inclusion in the Cabinet. On April 6 the *Evening Advertiser* showed Churchill camping in a tent outside 10 Downing Street, a candidate for the post of Minister of Supply.

On April 14 the Advisory Panel of Industrialists sent a report to Chamberlain. Their principal recommendation was for a Ministry of Supply to be set up as a question of urgency, 'at the first possible opportunity'. The report added: 'We cannot view with equanimity the position that is likely to arise under the present system.' Four days later Chamberlain announced in the House of Commons that he would shortly be making a statement on such a Ministry. This was the step which Churchill had first urged in Parliament three years before, on 23 April 1936, believing it to be even then a question of priority, and which he had reiterated on many occasions. On the day of Chamberlain's announcement Brendan Bracken wrote to Bernard Baruch:

Winston has won his long fight. Our Government are now adopting the policy that he advised three years ago. No public man in our time has shown more foresight, and I believe that his long, lonely struggle to expose the dangers of the dictatorships will prove to be the best chapter in his crowded life.

---

[1] Stefan Lorant, 1901–   . Educated at the Evangelical Gymnasium, and Academy of Economics, Budapest. Left Hungary in 1919, following the establishment of the Horthy Government. Photographer and film maker in Vienna, 1920–25. Editor, *Das Magazin*, Leipzig, 1925; *Bild Courier*, Berlin, 1926; *Muenchner Illustrierte Presse*, 1927–33. Placed in 'protective custody', March 1933; freed six months later following the intercession of the Hungarian Government. Left Germany for London, 1934. Published *I Was Hitler's Prisoner*, 1934. Founded a publishing house, Pocket Publications, in London, 1937. Founder and editor of *Lilliput*, 1937–40. Designed and edited *Picture Post*, 1938–40. Resident in the United States since 1940. Author; pictorial biographer of Abraham Lincoln and Theodore Roosevelt.

51

April–June 1939: 'England Owes You Many Apologies'

D URING the first five months of 1939 Churchill had spent every spare moment at Chartwell working on his *History of the English-Speaking Peoples*. Deakin was put in charge of the organization of the work, and during February two of Churchill's former research assistants, Maurice Ashley and John Wheldon, agreed both to provide material for different topics and to read the proofs. Churchill also engaged the help of the historian G. M. Young,[1] who provided him with copious notes on the early British, Roman, medieval and Tudor periods. John Wheldon also assembled material, and wrote the outlines for the Tudor period. On March 24 Churchill wrote to him:

> I am getting rather hungry for your notes on Henry VIII, which you so kindly promised to give me. Do not let the better be the enemy of the good. Remember 'Sentimental Tommy' who lost his examination because he could not think of the right word in the opening sentence. I know you have a great flair for this reign, and I look forward very much to seeing what you have to say about it.

Another former helper whose expertise was again enlisted was General Edmonds, who had become an authority on the American Civil War, and who sent Churchill detailed notes upon it. As each section was set up in proof, Churchill sent a copy to Sir Edward Marsh for

[1] George Malcolm Young, 1882–1959. Educated at St Paul's School and Balliol College Oxford. British Mission to Petrograd, 1916–17. CB, 1917. Fellow of All Souls College Oxford. Historian, he published his first book, on Gibbon, in 1932; his biography of Stanley Baldwin in 1952. A Trustee of the National Portrait Gallery, 1937–59 and Member of the Standing Commission on Museums and Galleries, 1938–59.

his comments. Working at Oxford, Alan Bullock prepared an outline of 10,000 words on the origins of the Empire in Australia and New Zealand, while Maurice Ashley agreed to return to Churchill's team and to write 10,000 words on the Stuarts and a further 10,000 on Cromwell. 'It is very hard to transport oneself into the past,' Churchill wrote to Ashley on March 24, 'when the future opens its jaws upon us.' On April 12 Churchill wrote to Ashley again:

At this stage, working against time, and with so many distractions, my aim has been to get the narrative through from the beginning to the end, leaving behind many omissions and many general questions. . . .

In the main, the theme is emerging of the growth of freedom and law, of the rights of the individual, of the subordination of the State to the fundamental and moral conceptions of an ever-comprehending community. Of these ideas the English-speaking peoples were the authors, then the trustees, and must now become the armed champions. Thus I condemn tyranny in whatever guise and from whatever quarter it presents itself. All this of course has a current application.

On April 18 Chamberlain formally announced in the House of Commons that a Ministry of Supply was to be established. The person chosen to head it was the Minister of Transport, Leslie Burgin.[1] From Chartwell, Churchill continued to press for yet more measures, including conscription. In this he had an ally in the Cabinet, Hore-Belisha, who pressed Chamberlain to introduce conscription as a matter of urgency. In his memoirs Churchill wrote of how, in urging for conscription, Hore-Belisha 'took his political life in his hands, and several of his interviews with his Chief were of a formidable character. I saw something of him in this ordeal, and he was never sure that each day in office would not be his last.'

By the third week of April, calls in the Press for Churchill's inclusion in the Government had become a daily occurrence. On April 21 the *Daily Telegraph* published a letter from an Oxford don, Frank Pakenham,[2] urging Churchill's return to Cabinet office. That same day

---

[1] Edward Leslie Burgin, 1887–1945. Educated in Lausanne and Paris. Solicitor. Intelligence Officer, 1916–18 (on active service in Italy, despatches). Liberal MP for Luton, 1929–45 (Liberal National since 1931). Charity Commissioner, 1931–32. Parliamentary Secretary, Board of Trade, 1932–37. Privy Councillor, 1937. Minister of Transport, 1937–39. Minister of Supply, 1939–40.

[2] Francis Aungier Pakenham, 1905–   . 2nd son of the 5th Earl of Longford, who was killed in action at Gallipoli in 1915. Educated at Eton and New College Oxford. Worked in the Conservative Party Economic Research Department, 1930–32. Lecturer in Politics, Oxford, 1932. Prospective Labour Party candidate for Oxford City, 1938. Personal Assistant to Sir William Beveridge, 1941–44. Parliamentary Under-Secretary of State, War Office,

Pakenham wrote to Churchill, from Christ Church: 'You have brought it on yourself, if I may say so, by your emergence as the one man of knowledge and purpose whom the public recognise as equal to the military necessities of the moment.' On April 22 the *Evening News* advocated Churchill's return to the Cabinet 'as soon as possible' either as First Lord of the Admiralty, or as Secretary of State for Air, and on April 23 the editor of the *Sunday Pictorial*, Hugh Cudlipp,[1] pressed for Churchill's inclusion in the Government in an article covering the whole front and second pages of the newspaper. 'The jealousy and suspicion of others oblige him to stand idly aside,' the article declared, and went on to suggest that Churchill be made Lord President of the Council in place of Lord Runciman, who had just 'had the impertinence to embark on a four months' holiday'.[2] Two days after the article appeared, Cudlipp telegraphed to Churchill: 'Huge mail has reached me this morning following my Churchill article on Sunday. Letters are overwhelmingly in your favour.' On April 26 Cudlipp wrote again:

. . . following my article last Sunday advocating your entry into the Cabinet, I have received 2,400 letters from readers.

They are overwhelmingly in your favour, and I have never known such an unqualified response. An analysis of the letters shows that they come from all classes. A huge section comes from ex-soldiers and men in the Service today. An interesting point, too, is your appeal to the young.

'No more boot-licking to Hitler' is the general line of comment. 'We want a strong man who is not afraid.' Etc.

So far only 73 out of the growing total of 2,400 letters are against you joining the Cabinet. A number of those are of the cranky type which describe me as a 'dirty Jew in Mr Churchill's pay'—the usual sort of abusive letter of no importance. The more serious objectors blame you for Gallipoli. . . .

1946–47. Chancellor of the Duchy of Lancaster, 1947–48. Minister of Civil Aviation, 1948–51. First Lord of the Admiralty, 1951. Succeeded his brother as Earl of Longford, 1961. Lord Privy Seal, 1964–65. Secretary of State for the Colonies, 1965–66. Lord Privy Seal, 1966–68.

[1] Hugh Cudlipp, 1913–   . Entered provincial journalism, 1927; Features Editor of the London *Sunday Chronicle*, 1932–35; of the *Daily Mirror*, 1935–37. Editor of the *Sunday Pictorial* 1937–40 and 1946–49. On active service, 1940–46. OBE, 1945. Managing Editor, *Sunday Express*, 1950–52. Joint Managing Director, *Daily Mirror* and *Sunday Pictorial*, 1959–63. Chairman, Daily Mirror Newspapers, 1963–68; International Publishing Corporation, 1968–73. Director of Associated Television Ltd, 1956–73. Knighted, 1973; Baron, 1974.

[2] The article was by Raymond Burns, the *Sunday Pictorial's* political correspondent. 'I have always been one of those,' he wrote, 'who shared the majority-Parliamentary view that Mr Churchill, though a distinguished figure, was best out of office except in wartime.' But since 1933, Burns added, 'his vindication has been such that, frankly, it seems fatuous to leave him as a back-bencher any longer'.

'Your name on our street placards,' Cudlipp added, 'aroused tremendous interest, and there is not the slightest doubt of the overwhelming view of the country on this issue.'

On April 24 Churchill had spoken from the balcony of the Mansion House to a large gathering of city workers, on whom he urged the need for compulsory national service. 'Those who now come forward to join the Territorial Army,' he said, 'are discharging the highest duty of citizenship.' That same day Chamberlain announced the Government's intention to introduce a Military Training Bill to Parliament, setting up what Chamberlain described as a 'limited and temporary measure of compulsory service' which would provide 'certain knowledge that on a definite date a definite number of men will be available who can be trained in a definite time'—in all 200,000 youths of twenty and twenty one years of age. At the same time, as a result of Burgin's appointment as Minister of Supply, two Government changes were announced. Euan Wallace[1] was appointed Minister of Transport and Harry Crookshank became Financial Secretary to the Treasury. 'There was much disappointment on both sides of the House,' the *British Weekly* wrote on April 27, 'that the changes in the Cabinet did not include such out-standing figures as Mr Winston Churchill and Mr Anthony Eden.' According to the *News Review* Neville Chamberlain reportedly told friends 'that Winston Churchill's nomination to the Cabinet would be a message of open warfare to Berlin'.

On April 27 Hitler announced that he no longer considered the Anglo-German Naval Agreement to be binding on Germany. That same evening the House of Commons gave its approval to the introduction of the Military Training Bill. According to a report of the debate in the *Daily Telegraph*, Churchill 'was in his most striking and effective form. To hear him, members hurried in, filling the Chamber and side galleries.' The compulsory national service register ought, he said, to have been introduced immediately after Munich. The Military Training Bill did not go far enough. 'A gesture was not sufficient; we

---

[1] David Euan Wallace, 1892–1941. Educated at Harrow and Sandhurst. Joined the 2nd Life Guards, 1911. On active service in France, 1914–18 (wounded, despatches four times, Military Cross). Captain, Reserve of Officers, 1919. Assistant Military Attaché, Washington, 1919–20. Conservative MP for Rugby, 1922–23; for Hornsey, 1924–41. Parliamentary Private Secretary to the First Lord of the Admiralty, 1922–23; to the Colonial Secretary, 1924–28. An Assistant Government Whip, 1928–29. Civil Lord of Admiralty, 1931–35. Secretary, Department of Overseas Trade, 1935–37. Privy Councillor, 1936. Parliamentary Secretary, Board of Trade, 1937–38. Financial Secretary to the Treasury, 1938–39. Minister of Transport, 1939–40.

wanted an army and might want it soon.' During the course of his speech Churchill spoke of how 'everyone is baffled by the now rapid changes of policy upon fundamental issues', changes which give the impression that decisions were being taken 'not after mature planning, but in a hurry, not from design, conviction or forethought, but because of the pressure of events abroad or the pressure of opinion at home'. Churchill went on to say he supported the Government's present policies and the Military Training Bill because the situation was too dangerous to hold an Election to endorse the change of policy, and he went on to warn that if compulsory service were rejected 'the whole resistance of Europe to Nazi domination would collapse. All countries great and small alike, would make the best terms they could with the Nazi Power and we should be left alone with our great possessions to settle up with the dictators ourselves.'

Churchill then asked of the introduction of conscription in peacetime, 'Is this peace?' and went on to answer his own question:

We have had three disastrous campaigns and the battles, the actions of the war have gone not only against us but against the principles of law and freedom, against the interests of the peaceful and progressive democracies. Those battles already make a long catalogue—the Rhineland, Abyssinia, Austria, Munich, Prague and Albania. [Hon Members 'And Spain'] . . . we are all, then, agreed that circumstances are analogous to war actually prevailing.

There was, Churchill told his fellow MPs, 'a common cause in this House' and in Europe, which Parliament must not fail; a common cause which saw Roumania in danger from German pressures, which saw Nazi propaganda active in France, and which a block of nations were now pledging themselves to uphold, and he concluded: 'the impulse, the main impulse, to resist the Nazi principles comes from the mass of the people.'

The *Daily Telegraph* commented: 'Rarely has Mr Churchill been more warmly cheered after a speech, and when he sat down, there was reluctance among members to follow so brilliant an effort.'

Outside the narrow confines of the Cabinet, Churchill's arguments on defence had at last found almost universal approval. On April 28 *The Times* described his speech as 'one of the finest of his Parliamentary performances', and the Press continued its already persistent call for his return to Ministerial office.

Despite the Government's recent decisions Churchill was still dissatisfied with the pace of rearmament. 'Everything moves forward so slowly,' he had written on April 27 to Sir Kingsley Wood, about anti-aircraft research, 'that I fear nothing will be ready should trouble come.' Part of Churchill's unease arose from the evidence which Wing-Commander Anderson continued to send him. On May 2 Anderson sent details of three Bomber Squadrons; No 215 Squadron, he wrote, had, at the end of April 'dropped 28 (250 lb) General Purpose High Explosive bombs, new issue. Eleven of these 28 bombs failed to explode.' Of No 49 Bomber Squadron he wrote:

Delays are experienced in obtaining spare parts, and are also caused by the length of time required for carrying out inspections. For example, when the aircraft has flown 120 hours, a 120-hour inspection is carried out, and the aircraft is unserviceable for one month. The time taken to complete 120 hours flying is approximately eight weeks.

Of No 29 Fighter Squadron, equipped with Blenheim fighters intended to operate from France, Anderson wrote:

The establishment is 21 aircraft, strength is 16, and the number serviceable is 3. This squadron has not a single Browning gun, although it is a fighter Squadron. Mountings and parts are being made by the Southern Railway but the plans and drawings have only just been issued. After completing 120 hours flying, the Blenheim aircraft are unserviceable for six weeks to carry out the inspection, the average time taken to complete 120 hours flying is eight weeks.

In the *Daily Telegraph* on May 4 Churchill published his forecast of the next area in which Hitler planned some 'new outrage or invasion'. It seems 'only too probable', he wrote, 'that the glare of Nazi Germany is to be turned on to Poland'. Hitler's recent denunciation of the German–Polish non-Aggression Pact of 1934 was 'an extremely serious and menacing step', particularly as Hitler did not seem aware 'of the immense change which has been wrought in British public opinion by his treacherous breach of the Munich Agreement, and the complete reversal of policy which this outrage brought about in the British Government, and especially in the Prime Minister'.

In his article Churchill urged the Poles to accept the involvement of Russia in European affairs as a decisive factor 'in preventing war'. While he understood the Polish policy 'of balancing between the German and Russian neighbour', he wished to impress on the Polish Government that 'from the moment when the Nazi malignity is plain, a definite association between Poland and Russia becomes indispensable'. Churchill ended: 'There is no means of maintaining an Eastern front against Nazi aggression without the active aid of Russia.' But it

was the British Government, as much as the Poles, who were resisting
Russia's search for a peace bloc. On the day that Churchill's article
was published in the *Daily Telegraph*, Halifax explained to the newspaper's owner, Lord Camrose, the obstacles, as he saw them, to 'an
alliance with Russia'. Camrose listed Halifax's obstacles in a note which
he made after the meeting:

(1) the effect it would have in Japan; (2) the strong opposition still maintained to such a course by Rumania and Poland; (3) objections in this
country, principally from Roman Catholics; (4) the danger of driving Spain
into the Axis; (5) the probable total and complete alienation of Italy; (6)
the effect on Portugal; and (7) the possibility that such an alliance might
drive Germany into desperate adventures.

The extent of Nazi pressures in Eastern Europe and the Balkans had
continued to affect the syndication of Churchill's articles. On May 6
Emery Revesz informed him that his article on Poland had not been
allowed to appear in Warsaw. In Rumania, Revesz added, there were
twenty-two German language newspapers 'controlled directly by the
Propaganda Ministry in Berlin', and even the most pro-French paper,
Universul, had as a result of German pressure been forced to adopt a
'pro-Nazi' line. In Greece, since the Italian occupation of Albania, and
despite the British guarantee to Greece, 'no article criticizing fascism
or nazism have allowed to be published' and articles by Churchill,
Eden, Attlee, Duff Cooper and Wickham Steed had all been prohibited.
Churchill sent a copy of Revesz's letter to Sir Alexander Cadogan at
the Foreign Office. The growing German control of the press in neutral
countries, was, he wrote in his covering letter, 'a serious matter', and
on May 8 he wrote direct to Revesz: 'I am indeed sorry to hear that
the net is closing round our activities, through fear of Germany.
Luckily, you have already called in the New World to redress the
balance of the Old.'

The campaign for Churchill's inclusion in the Government continued.
On May 6 a front-page headline in *Time and Tide* stated: 'We need
Churchill.' On May 10 the *News Chronicle* published an opinion survey
in which 56% of those questioned said they wanted Churchill in the
Cabinet, 26% were against and 18% did not know.

On May 12 the British Government announced yet another British
commitment, this time to Turkey. Writing in the *Daily Telegraph* on
May 18, Churchill praised this further strengthening of the anti-Nazi
grouping, which would, he hoped, 'have a sobering influence upon the
German Dictator'. But he was suspicious that the new policy was not
as firm as it seemed; for the Government's White Paper on Palestine,

announced on May 19, seemed to him evidence of a weakening and ambiguous attitude, which was likely to prove a blow to the new policy of alliances and agreements, aimed at uniting the anti-dictatorial powers.

In deference to Arab violence in Palestine itself, and following strong Arab pressure from Egypt, Iraq and Saudi Arabia, the Government had set an absolute limit on Jewish immigration into Palestine. Under the terms of the new White Paper, the Jews were to be allowed limited immigration for five more years, after which time no further immigration at all would be permitted 'unless the Arabs of Palestine are prepared to acquiesce in it'. The effect of this policy was two-fold: it cut off the persecuted and desperate Jews of central and eastern Europe from one of the main places of refuge left open to them, and it gave the Arabs power to prevent for all time a Jewish majority in Palestine. In this way the possibility of an eventual Jewish State, an idea which Churchill had supported both in 1920 and in 1937, was totally destroyed.

On the first day of the debate the Secretary of State for the Colonies, Malcolm MacDonald, defended the White Paper.[1] Churchill spoke on May 22, the second day. Before his speech he had invited Dr Weizmann[2] to lunch with him at Morpeth Mansions. Randolph Churchill and Professor Lindemann were also present. In his memoirs Dr Weizmann recalled how Churchill 'produced a packet of small cards and read his speech out to us; then he asked me if I had any changes to suggest. I answered that the architecture was so perfect that there were only one or two small points I might want to alter—but they were so unimportant I would not bother him with them.'

During the debate itself Churchill spoke with force and bitterness against what he believed was both a betrayal of the Balfour declaration, and a shameful act of appeasement. His speech began:

I say quite frankly that I find this a melancholy occasion. Like my right hon Friend the Member for Sparkbrook (Mr Amery), I feel bound to vote

---

[1] Malcolm MacDonald later recalled, in conversation with the author: 'I had prepared a little piece of oratory about the Holy Land with which to end my speech. I said, "Here was the Sea of Galilee, and here Bethlehem—where the Prince of Peace was born . . ." At this point Churchill said in a stage whisper "I never knew that Neville was born in *Bethlehem*." '

[2] Chaim Weizmann, 1874–1952. Born in Russia, educated in Germany. Reader in Biochemistry, University of Manchester, 1906. Naturalized as a British subject, 1910. Director Admiralty Laboratories, 1916–19. President of the World Zionist Organization, and of the Jewish Agency for Palestine, 1921–31 and 1935–46. Chairman, Board of Governors, Hebrew University of Jerusalem, 1932–50. Adviser to the Ministry of Supply, London, 1939–45. First President of the State of Israel from 1949 until his death. His eldest son, Flight-Lieutenant Michael Weizmann, RAF, was killed in action in 1942.

against the proposals of His Majesty's Government. As one intimately and responsibly concerned in the earlier stages of our Palestine policy, I could not stand by and see solemn engagements into which Britain has entered before the world set aside for reasons of administrative convenience or—and it will be a vain hope—for the sake of a quiet life. Like my right hon Friend, I should feel personally embarrassed in the most acute manner if I lent myself, by silence or inaction, to what I must regard as an act of repudiation.

Of the proposed Arab veto on all Jewish immigration after 1944 Churchill declared: 'Now, there is the breach; there is the violation of the pledge; there is the abandonment of the Balfour Declaration; there is the end of the vision, of the hope, of the dream.'

Churchill was particularly concerned about the effect of the Palestine White Paper on world opinion, not only as far as Palestine itself was concerned, but in the wider context of Britain's attempt to rally the democratic and threatened forces of Europe against Nazism and Fascism. His speech continued:

What will our friends say? What will be the opinion of the United States of America? Shall we not lose more—and this is a question to be considered maturely—in the growing support and sympathy of the United States than we shall gain in local administrative convenience, if gain at all indeed we do?

What will our potential enemies think? What will those who have been stirring up these Arab agitators think? Will they not be encouraged by our confession of recoil? Will they not be tempted to say: 'They're on the run again. This is another Munich,' and be the more stimulated in their aggression by these very unpleasant reflections which they make? After all, we were asked by the Secretary of State (Mr Malcolm MacDonald) to approach this question in a spirit of realism and to face the real facts, and I ask seriously of the Government: Shall we not undo by this very act of abjection some of the good which we have gained by our guarantees to Poland and to Rumania, by our admirable Turkish Alliance and by what we hope and expect will be our Russian Alliance.

You must consider these matters. May not this be a contributory factor— and every factor is a contributory factor now—by which our potential enemies may be emboldened to take some irrevocable action and then find out, only after it is all too late, that it is not this Government, with their tired Ministers and flagging purpose, that they have to face, but the might of Britain and all that Britain means?

A few moments later Churchill returned to this sombre theme, telling the House:

Some of us hold that our safety at this juncture resides in being bold and strong. We urge that the reputation for fidelity of execution, strict execution, of public contracts, is a shield and buckler which the British Empire, however it may arm, cannot dispense with and cannot desire to dispense with.

Never was the need for fidelity and firmness more urgent than now. You are not going to found and forge the fabric of a grand alliance to resist aggression, except by showing continued examples of your firmness in carrying out, even under difficulties, and in the teeth of difficulties, the obligations into which you have entered.

I warn the Conservative party—and some of my warnings have not, alas, been ill-founded—that by committing themselves to this lamentable act of default, they will cast our country, and all that it stands for, one more step downward in its fortunes, which step will later on have to be retrieved, as it will be retrieved, by additional hard exertions. That is why I say that upon the large aspect of this matter the policy which you think is a relief and an easement you will find afterwards you will have to retrieve, in suffering and greater exertions than those we are making.

At this point in his speech Churchill had intended to refer to the pressure which the Government was applying in order to secure a majority for its White Paper policy. At the last moment he decided to delete the passage, which, in the notes which he had taken to the Commons, read:

But what is supreme argument upon which Govt rely?
Up till yesterday supporters of Govt
   were summoned to Division
     by a 2-line whip,
   but after speech of S of S.
    and its reception,
       a 3rd line was added to whip.
Not only the *Landwehr* but the *Landsturm*
        were called out.
That was not because case was found to be
        unexpectedly strong.
It was because the case was weak, and
  because it is thought necessary to over ride argument
      by a parade of numbers.

Churchill ended his speech 'upon the land of Palestine', directing his criticisms first against Malcolm MacDonald and then against Chamberlain himself:

It is strange indeed that we should turn away from our task in Palestine at the moment when, as the Secretary of State told us yesterday, the local disorders have been largely mastered. It is stranger still that we should turn away when the great experiment and bright dream, the historic dream, has proved its power to succeed.

Yesterday the Minister responsible descanted eloquently in glowing passages upon the magnificent work which the Jewish colonists have done. They have made the desert bloom. They have started a score of thriving industries, he said. They have founded a great city on the barren shore. They have harnessed the Jordan and spread its electricity throughout the land. So far from being persecuted, the Arabs have crowded into the country and multiplied till their population has increased more than even all world Jewry could lift up the Jewish population.[1]

Now we are asked to decree that all this is to stop and all this is to come to an end. We are now asked to submit—and this is what rankles most with me —to an agitation which is fed with foreign money and ceaselessly inflamed by Nazi and by Fascist propaganda.

It is 20 years ago since my right hon Friend (the Prime Minister) used these stirring words:—

'A great responsibility will rest upon the Zionists, who, before long, will be proceeding, with joy in their hearts, to the ancient seat of their people. Theirs will be the task to build up a new prosperity and a new civilisation in old Palestine, so long neglected and misruled.'

Well, they have answered his call. They have fulfilled his hopes. How can he find it in his heart to strike them this mortal blow?'

'Your magnificent speech may yet destroy this policy,' Dr Weizmann telegraphed that same day. 'Words fail me express thanks.'[2] On May 24 Nathan Laski wrote from Manchester: 'I think it is not exaggerating to say that you will get the blessing of millions of Jews all over the world. . . . I can only hope that the time is not far distant when England will recognize that we have in you a man who can take charge of the affairs of this country and successfully overcome the blunders that others have made.'

On May 27 Robert Boothby wrote to Churchill: 'One of the few things in my life of which I am proud is that in all matters of major policy during the past 5 years I have hitched my waggon to your star,' and he added: 'Long after the names of the miserable creatures who

---

[1] At the beginning of the British Mandate, there were 487,573 Arabs and 83,794 Jews in Palestine (census of 1922). By 1937 the population had increased by a further 350,000 Arabs and 340,000 Jews. Many of the Jews came from eastern Europe and Russia, most of the Arabs from Syria and Transjordan.

[2] Among those Conservatives who voted against the 1939 Palestine White Paper were Churchill, Amery, Bracken, Ronald Cartland, Victor Cazalet, Richard Law, Oliver Locker-Lampson and Harold Macmillan. Others voting against included Lloyd George, Archibald Sinclair and Harold Nicolson. The final vote was 268 to 179 in favour of the Government's policy.

are now supposed to govern us have been lost in a merciful oblivion, the incredible services you have rendered this country since 1933 will be remembered.'

At the end of May the Government considered the question of Russia. Churchill favoured an alliance between the two countries, but Chamberlain was reluctant to consider any formal alliance, even though it was being urged both by France and by Russia. On May 28 Chamberlain wrote to his sister that:

Halifax had written from Geneva to say that he had been unable to shake Maisky on his demand for the 3 party alliance & Daladier had insisted that it was necessary, Poland had raised no objection, the Dominions were divided. It seemed clear that the choice lay between acceptance & the breaking off of negotiations. There could be no doubt that the latter would rejoice the heart of Berlin & discourage Paris & Angora. There was no sign of opposition to the Alliance in the Press & it was obvious that refusal would create immense difficulties in the House even if I could persuade my Cabinet.

On the other hand I had & have deep suspicions of Soviet aims & profound doubts as to her military capacity even if she honestly desired & intended to help. But worse than that was my feeling that the Alliance would definitely be a lining up of opposing blocs & an association which would make any negotiation or discussion with the Totalitarians difficult if not impossible.

The only supporter I could get for my views was Rab Butler & he was not a very influential ally. In these circs I sent for Horace Wilson to see if I could get any light from discussion with him & gradually there emerged an idea which has since been adopted. In substance it gives the Russians what they want, but in form & presentation it avoids the idea of an Alliance & substitutes a declaration of *intentions* in certain circumstances. . . .

Writing in the *Daily Telegraph* on June 8, Churchill pressed for the rapid creation of a Triple Alliance between Britain, France and Russia.[1] Although the three Governments were already negotiating, he doubted whether the British Government were serious. These doubts were fortified when, instead of Halifax going to Moscow to conduct the final negotiations, a Foreign Office official, the Head of the Central Department, William Strang, was sent instead. Churchill saw the British Government's hesitations towards an agreement with Russia as

---

[1] Churchill had sent a copy of his article in advance to Sir Alexander Cadogan, at the Foreign Office. On June 6 Cadogan replied: 'Very many thanks for letting me see the copy of your proposed article to be published in the press next Thursday. This article seems to me to be admirable and I have no comments to make.'

symptomatic of a less firm attitude towards Nazi Germany itself. On June 11 Halifax spoke in the House of Lords about Anglo-German relations. At one point in his speech he referred to 'the really dangerous element in the present situation, which is that the German people as a whole should drift to the conclusion that Great Britain had abandoned all desire to reach an understanding with Germany and that any further attempt at such a thing must be written off'. That same day Churchill wrote to Halifax of how he had been 'a little disturbed' by this speech:

I am sure you realise that to talk about giving back colonies, or *lebensraum*, or any concession, while nine million Czechs are still in bondage, would cause great division among us.

Very bad reports are coming from Bohemia and Moravia about the oppression and terrorism of the Nazi Regime upon these conquered people, and similar conditions are developing in Slovakia. At any moment bloody episodes may occur, and it is even said that many executions by the Gestapo have already taken place. Therefore, it seems to me quite impossible even to enter into discussions with Hitler at the present time. . . .

As the summer progressed, Churchill became increasingly worried about the sense of defeatism and despair which he began to feel around him. At dinner on June 14, when he found himself sitting next to the American columnist Walter Lippmann[1] he was shocked to learn from Lippmann that the United States Ambassador, Joseph Kennedy,[2] was telling his friends that when war came Britain, facing defeat, would negotiate with Hitler. Harold Nicolson who was present at the dinner recalled that the moment Churchill heard the word 'defeat' he turned to Lippmann and declared:

No, the Ambassador should not have spoken so, Mr Lippmann; he should not have said that dreadful word. Yet supposing (as I do not for one moment suppose) that Mr Kennedy were correct in his tragic utterance, then I for one would willingly lay down my life in combat, rather than, in fear of defeat, surrender to the menaces of these most sinister men. It will then be for you, for the Americans, to preserve and to maintain the great heritage of the English-speaking peoples. . . .

[1] Walter Lippmann, 1889–1974. Educated at Harvard. Associate Editor, *New Republic*, 1914–17. Assistant to the Secretary of War, 1917; Captain, Military Intelligence, USA, 1918. Editor, *New York World*, 1919–31. Special writer to the *New York Herald Tribune* syndicate, 1931–62. Pullitzer Prize for International Reporting, 1962.

[2] Joseph Patrick Kennedy, 1888–1969. Born in Boston. Graduated from Harvard, 1912. Assistant General Manager, Fore River Plant, Bethlehem Shipbuilding Corporation, 1917–19. Investment banker. Chairman of the Securities Exchange Commission, 1934–35 and of the US Maritime Commission, 1937. Ambassador to London, 1937–41. Of his four sons, Joseph was killed in action in 1944; John (President of the United States) was assassinated in 1963; and Robert (a Senator) was assassinated in 1968.

Walter Lippmann also kept a note of what Churchill had said to him. The note, though cryptic, gives a picture of Churchill's reaction to Kennedy's belief that Germany would be victorious. The note read:

German army can't pierce French carapace; Spain negligeable; British territorials can hold Spanish army and blockade of Spain would ruin her. Would rather Turks than Italians as allies. Italy a prey, Turkey a falcon. Would cut losses in Far East; no disperson of the fleet; settle with Japan after the war. Central Europe mobilised as a unit in 1914. Then Germany had ten divisions from Czecho-Slovakia; now they need six divisions to hold it. Hungary, Jugoslavia, Rumania, dangerous and unreliable. Poland, a new force, and behind it, the Russian pad. No use to say to Germany they are not being encircled. Better to overwhelm them with righteous indignation. Only argument that counts is force. No use shaping policy in accordance with Goebbels' propaganda. Take your own line and make them follow. In event of German mobilisation, mobilise fleet; at first provocative action, cut German railway communications with Europe and defy them to do anything about it. As for negotiated peace, there never can be peace in Europe while eight million Czechs are in bondage.

In his newspaper articles, Churchill continued to argue against defeatism in any form. On June 18, in the *News of the World,* he insisted that even the 'atrocity' of bombing attacks on civilians could be countered and overcome, by adequate shelters and defences, skilful and prompt evacuation, and bold aerial attacks on the incoming and departing bombers. His article ended: 'Of these grievous events, the people of the United States may soon perhaps be the spectators. But it sometimes happens that the audience become infuriated by a revolting exhibition. In that case we might see the spectators leaving their comfortable seats and hastening to the work of rescue and of retribution.' Reading this article a few days later, Sir John Anderson was prompted to write to Churchill, on June 29: 'I entirely agree with your view as to the danger of allowing the public to slip into a defeatist attitude. . . .'

During June, Sir Kingsley Wood had offered to show Churchill the progress of radar at the air stations in which it had been installed. On June 20, guided by Sir Henry Tizard and Robert Watson Watt, he visited Biggin Hill, Martlesham and Bawdsey. What he saw, he wrote to Kingsley Wood on the following day was 'profoundly interesting, and also encouraging'. The one point on which he felt concern was the protection of the radar stations themselves, and once more he advocated the use of a 'smoke cloud' protective screen. Many of the radar stations,

Churchill wrote, were on or near the coast, and he went on to explain that:

> . . . from a barge or buoy in the sea, or from a container a mile to the right or to the left along the coast, and another inland, it might be possible according to the wind by pressing an electric button on the alarm, which they will be the first to receive, to make a white sea mist which will envelope the towers and the buildings during the quarter of an hour of danger. This would be inexpensive, and above all, soon provided.
>
> Even when the B guns come, they could with their special appliances fire through the mist, which would prevent the actual towers or buildings being precisely located in daylight or moonlight.

Churchill was also worried about the tracking of enemy aircraft once they had crossed the coast, when radar ceased to operate, 'and we become dependent upon the Observer Corps'. His letter continued:

> This would seem a transition from the middle of the 20th Century to the Early Stone Age. Although I hear that good results are obtained from the Observer Corps, we must regard following the raider inland by some application of RDF as most urgently needed. It will be some time before the RDF stations can look back inland, and then only upon a crowded and confused air theatre. Here is where the 'lambs'[1] come in.
>
> The marvellous progress of the process of investing the 'lambs' with smelling-power (as I saw at Martlesham) should give us exactly what we need. The 'lambs' directed by RDF would meet the raiders out at sea, and keep continually with hostile squadron formations, explaining their whereabouts as they go.

Churchill ended his letter by congratulating Kingsley Wood on the progress that had been made. 'We are on the threshold of immense securities for our island,' he noted. 'Unfortunately we want to go further than the threshold and time is short.'

On June 22 Sir Stafford Cripps went to see Churchill at Morpeth Mansions. In his diary Cripps recorded Churchill's feelings:

> He inveighed strongly against the PM; said he, Eden and others had been ready to join the Cabinet since Hitler went into Prague but would not be admitted as it would stop all possibility of appeasement. . . .
>
> He was opposed to the idea of Broadcasts (to Germany) as he was afraid the

---

[1] The fast, unarmed single-seater aircraft, equipped with wireless, whose aim was to follow invading air forces after these had been located by radar, and to radio back to ground-bases the location and direction of the invading forces. It was Churchill himself who had first suggested this idea, on 23 July 1935.

German Government would look upon it as appeasement and that it would not have any value otherwise. He agreed on the need of an all-in Government but despaired of any way of getting rid of or convincing Chamberlain.

I got the impression that he could do nothing at all in the matter though he agreed.

Writing in the *Daily Telegraph* that same day, Churchill noted the growing German efforts to put pressure on Poland. The strident German claims for Danzig were an attempt 'to cut Poland from the sea', while the massing of German troops on the Slovak frontier could be for no other purpose than encircling Poland's 'southern flank'. Two days later Churchill wrote to G. M. Young: 'I am afraid I continue to take a sombre view of our affairs.' Speaking at the City Carlton Club on June 27, to what the *Yorkshire Post* described as 'the largest audience ever gathered there on such an occasion', again he appealed for 'a full and solid alliance' with Russia. In the course of his speech he declared:

I wish I could convince Herr Hitler of the fact that the British nation and, surely also, the British Empire, have reached the limit of their patience. We have receded and acquiesced time after time in breaches of solemn promises and treaties. Herr Hitler would make a profound mistake if he persuaded himself that all these retreats were merely the results of cowardice and degeneracy. . . .

One junior Minister who wished to see Churchill in the Government was the head of the Overseas Trade Department, Robert Hudson, who wrote to Churchill on June 30:

Although since December I have scrupulously abstained from encouraging civil servants' confidences, in the last ten days I have had increasing evidence of a sort of administrative malaise arising from the lack of decision on the part of their elders and betters.

In my own experience I am appalled at the lackadaisical method in which we are dealing with the question of supplying the Poles, the Turks, and the Rumanians with munitions and raw materials of which they sorely stand in need, and the lack of any agreed plan between the French and ourselves how best to utilise what supplies we can afford.

It seems to me that if Halifax's speech fails as I am afraid it may, there is no alternative under present leadership but a steady drift into war.

I understand from a fairly good source that the Prime Minister in conversation a day or two ago, indicated that he felt his policy had failed, and that he was contemplating handing it over to someone else, according to my informant that someone else being Kingsley Wood.

Surely the time has come when we ought to form in this country a War Government. It seems to me that this is the only step left which might still at the eleventh hour convince Hitler and his entourage that we mean business.

Another member of the Government, Malcolm MacDonald, later recalled in conversation with the author:

The Government was divided over whether Churchill should come in. On balance the younger members were for him, the older members sceptical. Some of us were trying to press Neville to have a government of national unity. We had begun to think this is war, we must get Churchill in, not as PM but as a very important war minister, or a war-to-be minister, but Neville was reluctant.

Churchill was a genius towering above us.

In the last week of June Churchill sent out fifty-four personal copies of a volume of his *Evening Standard* and *Daily Telegraph* articles, entitled *Step by Step*, which was published on June 27. 'It must be a melancholy satisfaction to see how right you were. . . .' Clement Attlee wrote on July 1: 'Let's hope its not too late.' Desmond Morton wrote on July 2:

Many years on, historians will read this and your speeches in Arms and the Covenant. They will wonder but I doubt if they will decide what devil of pride, unbelief, unselfishness or sheer madness possessed the English people that they did not ride as one man, depose the blind guides, who have certainly 'swallowed camels' even if they have not 'strained at gnats', and call on you to lead them to security, justice and peace.

There is a Polish proverb about the Poles themselves: 'Mądry Polak po szkodzie,' or 'Wise is the Pole after the event.' The English electorate is growing more Polish daily.

'What a happier world we should be living in today if you had stood at the helm during the last few years,' Sir Henry Strakosch wrote on July 2, and Sir Reginald Barnes, Churchill's subaltern friend of more than forty-four years, wrote to him on July 4:

My dear old Winston,
How nice of you to send me your latest book. I have read some of the letters, but not all, but to do so, is only to underline the fact, that I instinctively knew all the time, that you have been *right* about the Nazis.

It is a great triumph for you, dear old pal.

Now, our rather slow movers in command, having gone rather more than the whole hog, & burnt their last remaining boat, seem to be realizing at last, that you might be of some help to them, in the fight that still seems to be ahead. If we stick to this line, & continue to make our position all round stronger, I can't believe that a nation of good soldiers like the Germans, will embark on a war which they can't see a victorious end to. I pray I shall see you in the Cabinet soon.

'The reading of it is somewhat painful,' Anthony Eden wrote on July 5, 'but no doubt salutary,' and on July 7 Lord Wolmer wrote: 'The book is a record of perspicacity and courage on your part. England owes you many apologies.'

52

July 1939:
'Bring Back Churchill'

FROM the first day of July, the Press demand for Churchill's return
to Ministerial office grew in intensity. Many papers assumed he
would be brought into the Cabinet almost at once. On July 1 the *Star*
told its readers: 'Mr Chamberlain will shortly strengthen his Cabinet. It
is expected that he will invite Mr Churchill to enter the Government.'
The paper reported that the Chief Whip, Captain Margesson, had
already begun to take 'soundings' among the Conservative rank and
file. 'In nearly every case,' it added, 'the Chief Whip was told that the
appointment of Mr Churchill to one of the key posts in the Cabinet
would create fresh confidence.' That same day, in an editorial, the
Daily Telegraph described Churchill as 'the most experienced of our
political leaders out of office'. On July 2 the *Sunday Graphic* reported
speculation that Churchill would soon replace Lord Stanhope as First
Lord of the Admiralty, and the *Observer* declared: 'That one who has
so firm a grasp of the realities of European politics should not be
included in the Government must be as bewildering to foreigners as it
is regrettable to most of his own countrymen.'

On July 3 the *Yorkshire Post* reported a speech by the Liberal leader,
Sir Archibald Sinclair, two days earlier, calling on Chamberlain to
bring both Churchill and Eden into the Cabinet's 'inner counsels'.
That same day the *Manchester Guardian* advised Chamberlain to swallow
his prejudices and make use of Churchill's ability 'in any capacity'.
The paper added: 'We need Ministers of vision and power as well as
administrators.' The *Daily Telegraph* devoted the whole of its main
leading article on July 3 to demanding that Churchill be brought into
the Government. Appraising his vision, energy, 'gift of exposition and
popular appeal', the article continued: 'He might not be welcome as a

colleague to all the members of the present Cabinet, some of whom have felt the sting of his criticism and the lash of his oratory; but private feelings cannot be allowed to weigh against national interests.'

The *Daily Telegraph* sought to convince Chamberlain himself of the urgent need for Churchill's participation in the affairs of state. Above all, it wrote, 'no step would more profoundly impress the Axis Powers with the conviction that this country means business'.

'I hope the Daily Telegraph push will result in your being brought in to the Government,' Leopold Amery wrote to Churchill on July 3, and he added: 'I would sooner see you as the driving power in a small War Cabinet, with a general supervision on all three services, than attached to a single department.' But Chamberlain was determined not to bring Churchill into the Cabinet in any capacity. He had himself read the *Daily Telegraph* leader, and later that day spoke to Lord Camrose about it. Immediately after their conversation Camrose recorded what Chamberlain had told him:

. . . while he appreciated Churchill's ability, his own experience in Cabinet work with him had not been such as to make him feel that his (Churchill's) inclusion in the Cabinet would make his own task any easier. He admitted that Baldwin had not attempted to control his Cabinet, and that therefore Winston had had a much freer rein than he should have done. In any case, however, the result was that Winston's ideas and memoranda tended to monopolise the time of the whole Ministry. If you did not agree with him he was liable to lose his temper in argument and a number of his colleagues had found that the easier way was not to oppose him. Personally he had had two discussions with him which had ended in rather violent disagreement; but in each case he found that in a week's time Churchill had forgotten the matter and had some fresh idea which he regarded as being more important. His own personal relations with him were quite cordial and they had never had any lasting differences.

His own responsibility at the present time was so onerous that he did not feel that he would gain sufficiently from Winston's ideas and advice to counterbalance the irritation and disturbance which would necessarily be caused.

In our article we had suggested other names that came readily to the mind. One was, of course, Anthony (Eden). Well, Winston was Public Enemy No 1 in Berlin, and Eden was the same in Italy. Their inclusion in the Cabinet might strike both ways.

We agreed that the question of Eden ('while he has a following in the country') was not of the same consequence as that of Winston. He did not strongly demur to my emphasis of the psychological effect Winston's inclusion would have on the country, but he was the only person who could properly judge the question from every angle. Simon's judgment, and Hoare's, might have been wrong at times, but Winston's was notorious. As a recent instance, on the Saturday after the Italians marched into Albania the latter warned them persistently ('he was on the doorstep all day') to at once seize Corfu as the essential and immediate counterstroke. He emphasised the privacy of this statement.[1]

During their talk, Chamberlain told Camrose that he 'had not yet given up hopes of peace'. If Hitler were asking for Danzig 'in the normal way', he said, 'it might be possible to arrange things'. Even Colonel Beck, he added, would be willing to make concessions over Danzig. On the previous day Chamberlain had elaborated on these hopes in a letter to his sister, to whom he wrote:

> It is very difficult to see the way out of Danzig but I don't believe it is impossible to find, provided we are given a little time and also provided that Hitler doesn't really want war. I can't help thinking that he is not such a fool as some hysterical people make out and that he would not be sorry to compromise if he could do so without what he would feel to be humiliation. I've got one or two ideas which I am exploring though once again it is difficult to proceed when there are so many to cry 'nous sommes trahis' at any suggestion for a peaceful solution.

Chamberlain's determination to keep Churchill out of the Government was matched by an equal determination elsewhere to see him included. 'I earnestly hope we will not have long to wait,' Lord Craigavon wrote to Churchill on July 4, 'till the Country has your services at its full disposal.' That same day there were appeals for Churchill's return in the *Manchester Guardian*, the *Yorkshire Post*, the *News Chronicle*, the *Daily Mirror*, the *Evening News*, the *Star* and again in the *Daily Telegraph*. Even the Communist *Daily Worker* supported Churchill's inclusion as 'the outstanding opponent of the "Munich policy" '. But the *Evening Standard* predicted that despite this 'terrific barrage from the newspaper artillery', Chamberlain would 'stand fast on this occasion'.

On July 5 Sir Stafford Cripps, for ten years one of the most outspoken Labour critics of Churchill's ideas on defence, wrote to him of 'the insane resistance of Chamberlain to your entry into the Cabinet', and he added:

> Could you not make a public statement—to your Constituents or otherwise—stating your preparedness to give your services to the country and

---

[1] It was also a misleading statement, as Churchill had not gone to 10 Downing Street that day (April 9). He had telephoned twice, and had sent a letter by messenger (see page 1055).

emphasizing the need for some spectacular act to confirm the avowed change in Foreign Policy. I feel that it would make a tremendous impact just now on the country and would intensify enormously the demand that is growing everywhere for your inclusion in the Government.

Somehow or another Chamberlain must be forced to yield to this demand, and such a clear statement by you would I believe make it much more difficult for him to hold out.

Please think this over and decide to act upon it!

Churchill replied three days later:

Many thanks for your most kind letter which I have carefully weighed.

I am quite sure that any such demarche on my part would be unwise, and would weaken me in any discussion I might have to have with the gentleman in question.

Many thanks for writing.

Also on July 5, Lord Wolmer wrote to his father, the Earl of Selborne:[1]

My friends in the H of C all think it would help very much if you would write a letter to The Times urging Neville to bring into his Govt men like Anthony Eden & Winston just to prove to Hitler that England is united. . . . They do not think Neville will pay any attention to private representations but will take notice of a public demand. Vide yesterday's & today's DT.

Churchill was careful not to encourage in any way the campaign for his inclusion in the Cabinet. But he did continue to send his thoughts privately to Ministers. On July 5 Wing-Commander Anderson gave him a further detailed note on Bomber deficiencies, this time in Bomber Squadrons No 102 and No 78. The peace-time establishment of each squadron was meant to be 16 aircraft, but No 102 had only nine and No 78 had five. 'The shortage of aircraft in these squadrons,' Anderson wrote, 'is due to unserviceability, difficulty in obtaining spare parts, and the necessity of sending aircraft to manufacturers for installation of later type engines.' Anderson also wrote of the poor state of the aircraft used for target-towing. As had become his custom, Churchill sent these complaints direct to Kingsley Wood, exactly in the form that Anderson had passed them to him. Commenting on Anderson's

---

[1] William Waldegrave Palmer, 1859–1942. Educated at Winchester and University College Oxford. Liberal MP, 1885–6; Unionist MP, 1886–95. 2nd Earl of Selborne 1895. First Lord of the Admiralty, 1900–5. High Commissioner for South Africa 1905–10. President of the Board of Agriculture and Fisheries in Asquith's Coalition Government, from May 1915 to June 1916, after which he received no further Cabinet appointment. Served in the Ministry of Economic Warfare, 1940. His second son, Robert, was killed in action in Mesopotamia in 1916.

memorandum, Kingsley Wood's Private Secretary, Folliott Sandford,[1] noted on July 27: 'I think there can be little doubt that the author was the Camp Commandant at Catfoss who has been a frequent purveyor of information in the past to Mr Churchill.' The actual points in the memorandum were not, however, seriously disputed, nor was any disciplinary action taken against Anderson, whose links with Churchill were now clearly known, and recorded.

The pro-Churchill Press campaign continued on July 5, with the *Daily Mail* adding its voice to the chorus. So too did the *Evening Standard* cartoon. 'I see that Low portrays us together "on the Step" tonight,' Eden wrote to Churchill that same evening.[2] On July 7 the *Spectator* argued that the return of Churchill and Eden would be 'a decisive contribution to our cause', and might convince Hitler to pause before he sought to seize Danzig by force. 'Oh Winston dear,' wrote Maxine Elliot on July 6, 'was there ever such a triumph for a public man! Press and public alike hotly demanding its one man who has told them the frightening truth all these years and now they run to him to try and pull their burning chestnuts out of the fire.' But that same day Colin Coote wrote to Robert Boothby from *The Times*:

You will have observed the agitation in favour of Mr Winston Churchill. I will offer you a small bet that the other Mr C. won't listen to it for a moment; for his motto is still peace at any price except loss of office, and he is rightly sure that the inclusion of Winston means his own proximate exclusion. So you will come to a Carlton Club meeting in the end, if the British Empire is to survive.

There was even one member of Hitler's Government who argued in favour of Churchill's inclusion in the Cabinet, for on July 6 Colonel Beaumont-Nesbitt had reported to the Foreign Office on a conversation which he and General Marshall-Cornwall[3] had had with Count

---

[1] Folliott Herbert Sandford, 1906–86. Educated at Winchester and New College Oxford. Entered the Air Ministry, 1930; Private Secretary to successive Secretaries of State (Swinton, Kingsley Wood, Samuel Hoare, and Archibald Sinclair), 1937–40. Attached to RAF Ferry Command, Montreal, 1941–42. Secretary, Office of Minister Resident in West Africa, 1942–44. Assistant Under-Secretary of State, Air Ministry, 1944–47; Deputy Under-Secretary of State, 1947–58. Knighted, 1959. Registrar of Oxford University, 1958–72.

[2] The Low cartoon showed Churchill and Eden on the steps of 10 Downing Street, with a man called 'Public Opinion' knocking at the door, holding in his hand a newspaper with the headline: 'The Need for a Stronger Government'. Neville Chamberlain appeared peeping out behind a downstairs window.

[3] James Handyside Marshall-Cornwall, 1887–1985. Entered Royal Artillery, 1907. Served as an Intelligence Officer in France and Flanders, 1914–18; Military Cross, despatches five times. Attended the Paris Peace Conference, 1919. Intelligence Officer Constantinople, 1920–22. Served with the Shanghai Defence Force, 1927. Military Attaché, Berlin, April 1928–April 1932. Took the surname Marshall-Cornwall, 1929. Director-General, Air and

Schwerin von Krosigk[1] on the previous day, when the Count had advised:

Take Winston Churchill into the Cabinet. Churchill is the only Englishman Hitler is afraid of. He does not take the PM and Lord Halifax seriously, but he placed Churchill in the same category as Roosevelt. The mere fact of giving him a leading ministerial post would convince Hitler that we really meant to stand up to him.

But in reply to this suggestion both Marshall-Cornwall and Beaumont-Nesbitt had, according to Beaumont-Nesbitt's report, 'pointed out to Schwerin . . . that Winston's entry into the Cabinet might make for discord rather than unity'. Schwerin was not convinced by this reply, and went on to stress that 'Churchill's admission to the Cabinet would be the most effective measure. Otherwise trouble would start again very soon.' A further account of Schwerin's advice was sent direct to Lord Halifax on July 8 by Lieutenant-Colonel C. Gray,[2] who wrote: 'I asked him what he thought the effect would be if Winston were included in the Cabinet. He said—there would be a tremendous outcry in Germany: but that Hitler thinks that Churchill is the only dangerous Englishman, and it might perhaps do good, because it might perhaps *make* him realise that Great Britain really intends to fight if there is any further aggression.'

On July 8 the *New Statesman* reported rumours that in the Cabinet itself both Sir Samuel Hoare and Sir Kingsley Wood supported Churchill's return but that Sir John Simon was 'vehemently against', and that Chamberlain feared 'it would very quickly be Mr Churchill's Cabinet and that whatever last-minute hopes there are of appeasement over Danzig would be frustrated by his inclusion'. That same day the *Daily Telegraph* published a letter from Lord Selborne. 'I have never been a follower of Mr Churchill,' he wrote, 'but I agree with those who think that the inclusion of Mr Churchill or of Mr Eden in the Government at

---

Coast Defence, 1938–39. Knighted, 1940. General Officer Commanding the British Troops, Egypt, 1941; Western Command, 1941–42. Editor-in-Chief, captured German archives, 1948–51. President, Royal Geographical Society, 1954–58. Military historian.

[1] Johann Ludwig (Lutz), Count Schwerin von Krosigk, 1887-   . Born in Anhalt. Studied law at Oxford. Entered the Reich Ministry of Finance, 1924. Financial Secretary of the Reich (Reichsfinanzminister) under Papen, Schleicher and Hitler, June 1932–May 1945. Foreign Secretary during the Dönitz Government, May 1945. Imprisoned by an American military court, 1947; released, 1951.

[2] Clive Osric Vere Gray, 1882–1945. 2nd Lieutenant, 1901; on active service on the north-west frontier of India, 1908 (dangerously wounded); in the European War (despatches eight times, DSO). Lieutenant-Colonel, 1918. One of His Majesty's Body Guard, Corps of Gentlemen at Arms from 1932 until his death.

this particular moment would be a gesture which even Dr Goebbels could not fail to understand.'

'Pro-Churchill campaign dying down,' Oliver Harvey wrote in his diary that Sunday, 'no sign whatever of a move in No 10.' Reflecting on this 'campaign', Chamberlain saw it as a plot, but one that had failed. On July 8 he wrote to his sister:

This has been a comparatively quiet week only enlivened by the drive to put Winston into the government. It has been a regular conspiracy in which Mr Maisky has been involved as he keeps in very close touch with Randolph and no doubt Randolph was responsible for the positive statements in the Mail that it was all settled as well as the less definite paragraphs in the Express. I don't mind them, but I am vexed that Camrose who used to be such a firm supporter should now have committed himself. As soon as I saw the leader in the Telegraph I sent for him and explained just why I was not prepared to invite Winston. I did not convince him, but perhaps the interview was useful as at any rate I was assured that there was no bitterness in his mind. But since his illness Camrose is a changed man. . . .

Anyway they have as usual over-played their hand and annoyed both my friends and Anthony's who don't see why their hero should be given such a second place. It is significant that Bruce[1] came to see me and expressed his consternation at the idea. It is evident that Australia and South Africa are rather alarmed at the bellicose tone in the country and they think as I do that if Winston got into the Government it would not be long before we were at war.

Churchill remained at Chartwell working on his history. 'It has been a comfort in this anxious year to retire into past centuries,' he wrote to Newman Flower during Sunday July 9, 'but I have had to work very hard, and many a night have sat up until two or three in the morning.' Four days later he wrote to Desmond Flower that he had already completed 490,000 words, and needed only 20,000 more to complete the narrative.

A further meeting of the Air Defence Research sub-committee was held in London on July 11, when Churchill, who was present, learned that there were now twenty radar stations in operation between Scapa Flow and Portsmouth 'with temporary equipment' with a range from 50 to 12 miles at 10,000 feet. According to the minutes: 'The Air

---

[1] Stanley Melbourne Bruce, 1883–1967. Born and educated in Melbourne, Australia. Called to the Bar (London) 1907. On active service with the Worcestershire Regiment, 1915 (severely wounded at Suvla Bay). Military Cross, 1915. Captain, Royal Fusiliers, France, 1916 (wounded). Prime Minister and Minister of External Affairs, Australia, 1923–29. Resident Minister in London, 1932–33; High Commissioner, 1933–45. Represented Australia at the Imperial Conferences of 1923, 1926 and 1937, and at the League of Nations Assembly, 1933–38. Created Viscount, 1947.

Ministry were urged to accelerate the planned date of December for replacement of temporary by (longer ranging) permanent equipment.'

While Churchill returned to Chartwell and to his book, the Press campaign continued. Leading articles, letters to the editor and a spate of cartoons all demanded the same result. On July 11 Sir Samuel Hoare wrote to William Astor,[1] deprecating 'the drive to get Winston into the Government'. His letter went on:

> Your father and mother have been, for some reason, very excited over this attempt—both of them being very anxious to get Winston in on the ground that his presence in the Government would act as a deterrent to Germany.
>
> I have adopted with them and other people a completely detached attitude, holding as I do the view that these personal matters are solely in the discretion of the Prime Minister. As a matter of fact, I was convinced that the attempt would fail. Anything that Winston attempts is overdone, and in this case it was so overdone that it has stirred up a great reaction against him.
>
> I believe that if there was a ballot of Conservative Back Bench members on the subject, four out of five would be against him. This is to some extent the result of the papers of the Left and the important papers of the Right shouting with one voice for his inclusion.
>
> All this has made Neville's position stronger rather than weaker. . . .

Echoing Hoare's complaints, on July 13 *The Times* described the pro-Churchill campaign as 'mischievous and futile'. Nevertheless, it added, 'Mr Churchill may well be needed in a Government again.' But two days later Chamberlain wrote to his sister:

> There are more ways of killing a cat than strangling it, and if I refuse to take Winston into the Cabinet to please those who say it would frighten Hitler, it doesn't follow that the idea of frightening Hitler or rather of convincing him that it would not pay him to use force need be abandoned.
>
> In fact I have little doubt that Hitler knows quite well that we mean business. The only question to which he is not sure of the answer is whether we mean to attack him as soon as we are strong enough . . .

'Danzig at present is the danger spot,' Chamberlain continued, and he went on: 'I doubt if any solution short of war is practicable at present but if Dictators would have a modicum of patience I can imagine that a way could be found of meeting German claims while safe guarding Poland's independence and Economic Security. I am thinking of

---

[1] William Waldorf Astor, 1907–1966. Son of the 2nd Viscount Astor and Nancy Astor. Educated at Eton and New College, Oxford. Conservative MP for East Fulham, 1935–45, and for Wycombe, 1951–2. Parliamentary Private Secretary to Sir Samuel Hoare, 1936–39. Lieutenant-Commander, RNVR, 1939. Succeeded his father as 3rd Viscount, 1952.

making a further proposal to Musso that he should move for a twelve months truce to let the temperature cool down.'

Writing in the *Daily Mirror* on July 13, Churchill criticized the 'unaccountable delay' in concluding 'a solid, binding, all-in alliance between Britain, France and Russia'. Such a delay, he wrote, 'aggravates the danger of a wrong decision by Herr Hitler. It is lamentable indeed that this broad mainsail of peace and strength, which might carry the ship of human fortunes past the reef, should still be flapping half-hoisted in the wind.' But on July 2 Neville Chamberlain had written to his sister from 10 Downing Street: 'I am so sceptical of the value of Russian help that I should not feel that our position was greatly worsened if we had to do without them.'

On July 14 Churchill flew to Paris, as a guest of the French Government, to watch the annual military review. During the ceremony he asked General Gamelin whether he could visit the Maginot Line once more, at some time in August, and Gamelin gave the scheme his approval. After the ceremony was over Consuelo Balsan commented to Churchill on the size of the tanks in the parade; they were so large that they had shaken the Champs Elysées in their progress. In her memoirs she recorded Churchill's response. The French Government, he said, had to show its people 'that their economics had been transferred from the idleness of the stocking to the safety of the tank'.

On his return to Chartwell, Churchill learnt that T. L. Horabin had been elected for North Cornwall, largely on a 'bring back Churchill' platform. It was, wrote A. H. Richards to Churchill on July 15, 'a signal victory'.[1] That weekend Churchill worked with Deakin to finish Book Two of the *History of the English-Speaking Peoples*, the revised and polished narrative of which had now reached the reign of Edward III.

On July 17 Lord Rothermere wrote to Churchill that he could see 'a great responsibility' being on him 'at an early date', and offering him a further £600 if he would again give up drinking cognac for a year. 'Everyone,' Rothermere explained, 'including especially myself, will wish you to be in the finest fettle when the day arrives.' Rothermere's letter continued:

Carefully handled I don't think there will be war over Danzig. Hitler left upon me the indelible impression that overtly he will never take the initiative

---

[1] The election was held on July 13 and the result was declared on the following day. Horabin (Liberal) secured 17,072 votes, his Conservative opponent, E. R. Whitehouse, 15,608 votes. Three days later Chamberlain wrote to his sister: 'I get pretty sick of the perpetual personal attacks on me at home. I heard that in Cornwall the feeling in my favour was unmistakeable yet it hasn't shown itself in the by-election and sometimes I wonder what *would* happen in a General Election.'

in resorting to bloodshed. I suppose when I had my long talk with him he mentioned this matter at least a dozen times.

All the same we must go on arming night and day using up if necessary whatever available resources we can lay our hands on.

I think Hitler has been badly handled. Instead of the language of reproach and rebuke constantly applied to him, I should have tried out the language of butter because these Dictators live in such an atmosphere of adulation and awe-struck reverence that the language of guns may not go nearly so far as the language of butter.

I have never yet seen an authoritative statement made in England complimenting Hitler on his tremendous record of achievement in Germany.

'On the few occasions on which I have written to Hitler,' Rothermere added, 'I have always interlarded my letter with plenty of compliments and butter. Strange as it may seem he is a shy and solitary man. How few people know this.'

Churchill replied to Rothermere on July 19:

You may well be right about Dantzig; but does it really matter very much what the thing is called? Evidently a great 'crunch' is coming, and all preparations in Germany are moving forward ceaselessly to some date in August. Whether H. will call it off or not is a psychological problem which you can probably judge as well as any living man. I fear he despises Chamberlain, and is convinced that the reason he does not broaden his Government is because he means to give in once Parliament has risen. But I do not know whether, in the present state of public opinion, this will in fact come to pass.

I am remaining entirely quiescent at the present time. Like you, I have given my warnings, and I am consoled for being condemned to inaction by being free from responsibility.

I am very glad to have my 'History of the English-speaking Peoples' to work at. It is now nearly finished. . . .

Work on his history kept Churchill busy at Chartwell for the rest of July. 'I am staggering along to the end of this job,' he wrote to Edward Marsh on July 20, 'and am glad to have found the strength to have accomplished it.'[1] More than half of the chapters were now in proof, most of the others well advanced. There remained much careful checking of facts, the amalgamation of the comments of critics, and the fitting in of a few special studies still being drafted by Deakin and Bullock. On July 20 Churchill wrote to General Spears: 'I am so rarely

[1] On completion of his history at the end of 1939, but not before, Churchill would receive £7,500. This constituted nearly half of his income for 1939, and made completion of the book a financial necessity. Of a total for his literary earnings in 1939 of £15,781, the other main sources were the *News of the World*, £4,200; *Colliers*, £700 (for two articles); the *Daily Mirror*, £600 and foreign syndications, £450, somewhat less than his January forecast.

in London now, and so busy on my "History" that I find it difficult to make appointments, but why do you not come down and lunch with me one day?' Churchill also decided to make further plans of his own for a second visit to the Maginot Line. On July 21 he wrote to General Gamelin: 'You received very kindly the suggestion I made of visiting another sector of the Maginot Line. Upon reflection, I think I should like to see the Rhine front, as I know nothing of that country, whereas I have seen a lot of Flanders.'

Churchill remained at Chartwell while the Press campaign for his inclusion in the Government entered its third week. On Sunday July 23 he was a guest at Taplow Court.[1] A fellow guest, Compton Mackenzie,[2] recalled in his memoirs:

I was sharply aware of the overriding question at the back of Churchill's mind. Was war coming? I recall saying I hoped if war did come that the British Government would behave more sensibly over Ireland than in the last war. He flushed and said almost truculently:

'We cannot let down those who have remained faithful to the Union Jack,' and then perhaps feeling he was talking too much like a Conservative candidate in the Khaki election of 1900 the blue eyes twinkled and he said,

'I've invented a wonderful new tank.'

We asked what kind of a tank it was.

'It can dig itself in and turn itself into a machine-gun post if required.'

On July 22 Harold Laski wrote in *Time and Tide* that despite Churchill's 'defects', including 'sudden lapses from balance in judgement', and a 'naturally rhetorical mind', in the past five years 'the whole democratic world has recognized the eminence of the part he has played'. Not only in Britain, Laski wrote, but in France and the United States, as well as Germany and Italy, Churchill's return to the Cabinet would be taken as 'the outstanding proof available of this Government's determination to resist aggression'. This view, Laski added, was shared 'by most Liberals and by the great bulk of the Labour Party. Yet it makes no impression on Mr Chamberlain.'

Churchill's admission to the Government, Garvin wrote in the *Observer* on July 22, 'would be accepted as the conclusive proof of

---

[1] Near Maidenhead, the home of Lord and Lady Desborough.

[2] Compton Mackenzie, 1883–1972. Educated at St Paul's and Magdalen College Oxford. 2nd Lieutenant, 1st Herts Regiment, 1900–01. Poet and novelist, he published the first of more than a hundred volumes in 1907; one of his best known novels, *Sinister Street*, in 1913–14. Lieutenant, Royal Marines, 1915; on active service with the Royal Naval Division at the Dardanelles (invalided, September 1915). Military Control Officer, Athens, 1916. Director of the Aegean Intelligence Service, 1917. OBE, 1919. Captain, Home Guard, 1940–44. Knighted, 1952. In 1929 he published *Gallipoli Memories*; in 1946 a biography of Beneš; in 1963 the first volume of his memoirs *Octave One* (*Octave Ten* in 1971).

national efficiency and resolution'. Even now, Garvin added, German official propaganda 'persistently suggests that Herr Hitler will secure peace with triumph because Mr Chamberlain will put pressure on the Poles to give way'. In a letter to his sister on July 23, Chamberlain reported on the reason why pressure was being put on Poland, telling her that:

I heard last week that Hitler had told Herr Förster the Danzig Nazi Leader that he was going to damp down the agitation. True the German claim that Danzig should be incorporated in the Reich was to be maintained but that could wait until next year or even longer. Meanwhile the city would be demilitarized and the press muzzled but particular stress was laid on the necessity for secrecy at present and for restraint on the Polish side.

Accordingly we sent all sorts of warnings to the Poles accompanied by exhortations to let nothing leak out. . . .

Unfortunately, Chamberlain added, the Germans themselves had 'let the cat out of the bag', with the result that it gave occasion, as he put it, 'to all my enemies to say "There I told you so. He means to sell the Poles", and makes it impossible for me to enter into conversations with Germans on any subject'.

In his letter, Chamberlain also told his sister of his wider hopes:

One thing is I think clear namely that Hitler has concluded that we mean business and that the time is not ripe for the major war. Therein he is fulfilling my expectations. Unlike some of my critics I go further and say the longer the war is put off the less likely it is to come at all as we go on perfecting our defences and building up the defences of our allies. That is what Winston and Co never seem to realise. You don't need offensive forces sufficient to win a smashing victory. What you want are defensive forces sufficiently strong to make it impossible for the other side to win except at such a cost to make it not worth while. That is what we are doing and though at present the German feeling is it is not worth while *yet* they will presently come to realise that it never *will* be worth while, then we can talk.

Commenting on the pro-Churchill campaign, Chamberlain noted: 'As for the Churchill episode it has in Joe Kennedy's picturesque phrase "Fallen out of bed" and although I see Garvin in an insufferably dull and boring article tries to keep it alive it has lost all life and even Camrose has now dropped it in the Telegraph.' But the campaign continued. On July 23 Edward Hulton,[1] writing in *Picture Post*, urged

---

[1] Edward George Warris Hulton, 1906– . Educated at Harrow and Brasenose College Oxford. Unsuccessful Conservative candidate, 1929 and 1931. Practised as a barrister on the South-Eastern Circuit. Chairman and Managing Director of Hulton Publications Ltd, including *Picture Post*. Knighted, 1957.

Churchill's appointment as First Lord of the Admiralty, in view of his achievements there in 1914, and asked, in answer to Churchill's critics: 'can it be seriously implied that Mr Churchill desires war?' Hulton went on to say that, on the contrary, Churchill's 'implacable firmness would be the greatest guarantee of peace. His inclusion might indeed irritate Herr Hitler. But if we are to leave men out because they are efficient and resolute, we may as well give up the ghost here and now.'

As the pro-Churchill campaign continued, those who opposed it declared it to be a deliberate, organized attempt to overthrow Chamberlain. This was hinted at several times by *The Times*, the *Daily Express* and the *Sunday Express*. In answer to these insinuations, Churchill drafted a statement for publication in the Press. Although he finally decided not to send it, the statement set out his position with clarity, as well as giving his reasons for wishing to be included in the Government:

I have taken no part in the movement in favour of broadening His Majesty's Government, in which my name has been mentioned. But in view of the assertions now so loudly made that I am concerned in an agitation to drive Mr Chamberlain from office, I think it right to state that this has not been, and is not, my wish, nor I am sure, the wish of any of those Conservatives with whom I am in political contact.

From the moment when the Prime Minister entered upon a policy of forming a strong block of peace-minded States in harmony with the Covenant of the League of Nations, in order to resist further acts of aggression, no major difference in principle has existed between me and the Government.

These are not times when considerations of tactics and personal interest should be a bar to plain speaking; and I therefore feel it is my duty to place on record that I am willing to serve under Mr Chamberlain on the basis of the policy declared by him and by Lord Halifax, and give him any loyal help in my power.

The only condition which I should feel bound to make would be that the process of broadening the Government should include those Conservative ex-Ministers who have consistently advocated courses similar to that on which the Government is now embarked, and who have testified to their convictions on important occasions. Such a step would, to the best of my belief, have a unifying effect throughout this country, and be welcomed in all countries friendly to Great Britain. It might have a restraining effect on dangerous intentions elsewhere. It would prevent the growth of a schism at home, which might otherwise be serious. It would prepare the way and render more smooth that further broadening of the Government, which is upon all sides admitted to be necessary, should unhappily the Prime Minister's efforts to prevent war not be attended by success.

I feel sure that my fellow-countrymen will not think less of me for speaking with the simplicity and frankness which the gravity of the hour requires from all.

On July 24 General Ironside visited Churchill at Chartwell. 'I dined alone with him,' Ironside recorded in his diary, 'and then we sat talking till 5 am this morning.' According to Ironside's record of their discussion:

He remarked that he would have to pull in his horns considerably if he ever took office, because he would have to cease making money by writing. Last September, had there been a war, he would have been given the Admiralty and perhaps the War Office. Now he might even be Prime Minister.

He had made friends with Belisha because he says that it was Belisha who got conscription through, 'taking his life in his hands'. He nearly got the sack and acted with great courage. . . .

Neville Chamberlain is not a war Prime Minister. He is a pacifist at heart. He has a firm belief that God has chosen him as an instrument to prevent this threatened war. He can never get this out of his mind. He is not against Winston, but he believes that chances may still arrive for averting war, and he thinks that Winston might be so strong in a Cabinet that he would be prevented from acting.

Churchill told Ironside 'that it was now too late for any appeasement. The deed was signed, and Hitler is going to make war.' This thought led Churchill to an exposition of what might happen once war were declared. Ironside's account continued:

He walked about in front of the map and demonstrated his ideas, repeating, 'You are destined to play a great part, you will be the Commander-in-Chief. You must be clear on what is going to happen:

(i) The crippling or annihilation of Poland.
(ii) The employment of Italy to create diversions. Mussolini had sold his country for his job.
(iii) The capture of Egypt, chiefly by Italian forces.
(iv) A pressing on to the Black Sea *via* Roumania.
(v) An alliance with Russia, when the latter sees how the land lies.'[1]

Ironside told Churchill that in his view 'we were in for a bad time', as the War Office had no considered plans; no plan to deal with the war in general', and that it would need 'guts' to withstand the first German and Italian attacks. In reply, Churchill told Ironside about his plan for sending British battleships into the Baltic, in order to 'paralyse the Germans and immobilize many German divisions', and to

---

[1] The Russo-German Alliance was signed a month later, on August 23.

deal with the German submarine menace. 'All his schemes,' Ironside added, 'came back to the use of the Navy. It ran through my head that here was a grand strategist imagining things, and the Navy itself making no plans whatever.'

On July 25, while Churchill was explaining to Ironside the sort of initiatives Britain ought to take on the outbreak of war, Lord Kemsley[1] was in Berlin talking to leading Nazis. Both Dr Rosenberg[2] and von Weizsäcker spoke with anxiety of the strength of the opposition in England, 'particularly Mr Winston Churchill', as Kemsley noted. On July 27 Kemsley visited Hitler at Bayreuth, where, according to Kemsley's own note of the conversation:

Herr Hitler talked about the strength of the opposition to the Prime Minister, and referred particularly to Mr Winston Churchill and his powers of expression. Lord Kemsley replied that in his opinion far more notice was taken abroad of the Opposition than in England, and whilst giving every credit to Mr Winston Churchill for his ability as a writer and as a speaker, he reminded Herr Hitler that Mr Churchill had been unfortunate in his campaigns on at least four occasions in the past, starting with the Abdication of King Edward VIII.

Despite Kemsley's minimizing of Churchill's influence, for the general public in Britain his prestige was growing from day to day, and Churchill received a stream of letters from strangers with words of encouragement and support. Yet he remained at Chartwell, decided not to issue his statement, made no public speeches, and awaited with foreboding the march of events. On July 27 General Ironside noted in his diary:

I keep thinking of Winston Churchill down at Westerham, full of patriotism and ideas for saving the Empire. A man who knows that you must act to win. You cannot remain supine and allow yourself to be hit indefinitely. Winston must be chafing at the inaction. I keep thinking of him walking up and down the room.

---

[1] James Gomer Berry, 1883–1968. Newspaper proprietor, and brother of Lord Camrose. Created Baronet, 1928. Created Baron Kemsley, 1936. Chairman, Kemsley Newspapers Ltd 1937–59; Editor-in-Chief, *Sunday Times*, 1937–59. A Trustee of Reuters, 1941 (Chairman, 1951–59). Created Viscount, 1945. One of his six sons was killed in action in Italy in 1944.
[2] Alfred Rosenberg, 1893–1946. Editor of the Nazi Party Newspaper, *Völkischer Beobachter*, 1921–38. Elected a Member of the Reichstag, 1930. The leading Nazi authority on Russian and Baltic questions; Director of the National Socialist Party Foreign Bureau. Supervisor of Youth Education, 1940–41. Minister for the Occupied Eastern Territory, 1941–45. Tried at Nuremberg by the Allied War Crimes Tribunal, and hanged, 16 October 1946.

53

The Coming of War

FOR the first two weeks of August Churchill continued to work at Chartwell on his *History of the English-Speaking Peoples*. Deakin, who had joined the Territorials and been at camp, spent much of those two weeks with Churchill working on the proofs. On August 1 General Spears lunched at Chartwell to discuss the visit Churchill planned to make to the Maginot Line in mid-August. Spears later recalled how:

Winston thought war imminent, but he was certain the German General Staff would try to dissuade Hitler from becoming involved in a war on two fronts. What was the real attitude of Russia? Although an Anglo-French Military Mission was discussing plans in Moscow, he felt grave doubts concerning Stalin's policy. He thought, as I did, that we had deeply, perhaps irretrievably, offended the Russians at the time of Munich, and that they would not hesitate to turn the tables on us, as they considered we then had on them, if they considered it to their advantage to do so.

'What worried Winston most,' Spears noted, 'apart from fearing the Government would run out over Poland as it had over Czechoslovakia, was our weakness in the air. He came back to this again and again.' The two men also spoke of the 'immense advantage' Germany had gained by the seizure of Czechoslovakia. As Spears wrote: 'Neither of us doubted that in the year that had since elapsed Germany had armed infinitely faster than had either the French or ourselves.' Spears added: 'I knew Czechoslovakia well. There was no doubt that the already vast German arms industry, driven at furious pace, had gained an enormous accession of strength by the possession of the Skoda and Witkowitz works.'

In discussing the Government's policy, Churchill told Spears that Chamberlain's decision to adjourn Parliament from August 4 to October 3 was a grave error of judgement, which could only encourage the Germans to believe that Britain would not take decisive action when the crisis came, and would also convince the Russians that Britain was not in earnest about an alliance. Churchill had decided to speak against this two-month adjournment, and read Spears a draft of the speech which he intended to deliver on August 2, asking for Parliament to be recalled on August 22 or 25. Both Attlee and Sinclair, for the Labour and Liberal Parties, urged a similar course. In preparation for the debate, Churchill and Eden alerted several of their friends. 'Try to come on Wednesday,' Churchill had written to Lord Wolmer on July 29, 'because the scattering of Parliament is a serious snub.' But Wolmer replied two days later, in pessimistic vein:

I am afraid I do not quite agree with you and Anthony about this. The assumption is I take it that Neville, having got rid of the House, proposes to do another Munich. Even if this were true I cannot believe that he would be deterred from making an agreement which he considered right, by anything that was said or done in the House of Commons. The House is so obedient to him that he can rely on securing a big majority for any policy he may like to propose.

The real tribunal before which he has to justify himself is the bar of public opinion, and that is in session whether the House of Commons is or not. Therefore, the demand that the house shall continue to sit seems to me unreal and pin-pricky.

'Abroad,' Churchill said during the debate itself, 'the House of Commons is counted, and especially in dictator countries, as a most formidable expression of the British national will and an instrument of that will in resistance to aggression.' His speech continued:

This is an odd moment for the House to declare that it will go on a two months' holiday. It is only an accident that our summer holidays coincide with the danger months in Europe, when the harvests have been gathered, and when the powers of evil are at their strongest.

The situation in Europe is graver than it was at this time last year. The German Government have already 2,000,000 men under arms actually incorporated in their Army. When the new class joins before the end of August more than 500,000 will be added to this number automatically. All along the Polish frontier from Danzig to Cracow there are heavy massings of troops, and every preparation is being made for a speedy advance. There are five German divisions in a high state of mobility around Breslau alone. . . .

I have been told—I may be wrong, but I have not always been wrong—that many of the public buildings and of the schools in large parts of Czechoslovakia, Bohemia certainly, have been cleared and prepared for the accommodation of wounded. But that is not the only place. There is a definite movement of supplies and troops through Austria towards the east.

The details he had given, Churchill went on, constituted 'terribly formidable signs'. Even the Government recognized this. The Fleet was largely mobilized, the anti-aircraft gunners were at their stations and there were similar 'great preparations' among Britain's allies. 'Is this, then,' he asked, 'the moment that we should separate and declare that we separate until the 3rd October? Who can doubt that there is going to be a supreme trial of will power, if not indeed a supreme trial of arms.' He added:

At this moment in its long history, it would be disastrous, it would be pathetic, it would be shameful for the House of Commons to write itself off as an effective and potent factor in the situation, or reduce whatever strength it can offer to the firm front which the nation will make against aggression. . . .

It is a very hard thing, and I hope it will not be said, for the Government to say to the House, 'Begone! Run off and play. Take your masks with you. Do not worry about public affairs. Leave them to the gifted and experienced Ministers' who, after all, so far as our defences are concerned, landed us where we were landed in September last year, and who, after all—I make all allowances for the many difficulties—have brought us in foreign policy at this moment to the point where we have guaranteed Poland and Rumania, after having lost Czechoslovakia, and not having gained Russia.

Churchill had been disturbed by the continuing severity of Chamberlain's attitude towards him and his criticisms. Towards the end of his speech he declared:

I noticed a sort of spirit on these benches to try and run this matter through on ordinary party loyalty, but we are not going to get through these troubles on the basis of party loyalty and calling everyone who differs unpatriotic. If that sort of atmosphere were created I am sure that it would be absolutely swept away by the country.[1]

'To the astonishment of the House,' as Harold Nicolson recorded in

---

[1] For nearly a year, Chamberlain had been irritated by the general attitude of the House of Commons towards his foreign policy. During the Munich crisis he had hoped to avoid 'premature summoning' of the House (see page 969); he had feared that the recall of Parliament in September 1938 'would result in wrecking very delicate negotiations' (page 975); and he had commented after Munich in a letter to his sister, that 'all the world seemed to be full of my praises except the House of Commons' (see page 1009). On June 13 Sir Eric Phipps had informed Chamberlain that Daladier wished to prorogue the Chamber for two years, and hoped therefore that Chamberlain would not announce a British General Election until after August. On the following day Chamberlain wrote to Phipps: 'Your account of Daladier's intentions concerning prorogation of Parliament makes my mouth water!'

his diary, Chamberlain rejected the appeal for the recall of Parliament in the last week of August, and told MPs that he would regard the vote on the adjournment as a vote of confidence in himself. As a result of this display of Party strength, Parliament was adjourned for two months. 'Mr Chamberlain,' the *Manchester Guardian* wrote on August 3, 'forgetting all his pretentions as leader of a united country, fell back on stale party gibes, cracked the disciplinary whip, and warned his supporters to obey. It is a regrettable episode.' Among those Conservatives who had argued during the debate in favour of an early recall were Leopold Amery, Harold Macmillan and Ronald Cartland. Cartland later told his sister Barbara [1] how:

After Neville's speech our little group shuffled disconsolately into the lobby. Winston came out. 'Well,' I said to him, 'We can do no mor*x*.'

'Do no more, my boy?' he echoed. 'There is a lot more we can do. This is the time to fight—to speak—to attack!'

A few moments before the debate itself, Chamberlain saw Churchill in the lobby, where they had spoken together, as Chamberlain wrote to his sister three days later. But, Chamberlain's account continued:

. . . he is so sensitive to criticism that he couldn't stand even my joking remark about a tu quo que when he said he couldn't trust my judgement. That annoyed him so much that he actually went out of his way to associate himself with Sinclair's fatuous and imbecile proposition that if Parliament had met earlier last September we could have mobilised the fleet, made an agreement with Russia, and saved the independence of Czechoslovakia. I did turn upon him savagely then and barked out that I totally and utterly disagreed with him. He was in a state of red fury after that and burst out at David Margesson whom he met subsequently in the lobby. But yesterday he appeared to have recovered his temper and repeatedly cheered my remarks about Japan. [2]

That is Winston all over. His are summer storms violent but of short duration and often followed by sunshine. But they make him uncommonly difficult to deal with.

---

[1] Barbara Hamilton Cartland, 1904–   . Authoress and playwright, she published her first novel at the age of 21. Carried the first aeroplane-towed glider mail in her own glider, from Manston to Reading, 1931. Junior Commander, ATS, 1941–45. In 1942 she published a biography of her brother, and in 1943 she edited his speeches, *Common Problem*.

[2] During his speech on August 4 Chamberlain stated: 'We have been compelled by force of circumstance to undertake some very heavy liabilities and commitments in Europe. The effect of these commitments is that if certain things were to happen, this country would have to go to war. It would not be possible to undertake the same commitments in the far East. I do not want to do that . . . there are limits to what it would be prudent to undertake. . . .'

On August 8, in a fifteen-minute broadcast to the United States, Churchill put into practice his advice to Ronald Cartland of six days before, telling his American listeners:

Holiday time, ladies and gentlemen! Holiday time, my friends across the Atlantic! Holiday time, when the summer calls the toilers of all countries for an all too brief spell from the offices and mills and stiff routine of daily life and bread-winning, and sends them to seek if not rest at least change in new surroundings, to return refreshed and keep the myriad wheels of civilised society on the move.

Let me look back—let me see. How did we spend our summer holidays twenty-five years ago? Why, those were the very days when the German advance guards were breaking into Belgium and trampling down its people on their march towards Paris! Those were the days when Prussian militarism was—to quote its own phrase—'hacking its way through the small, weak, neighbour country' whose neutrality and independence they had sworn not merely to respect but to defend.

There was, Churchill said, 'a hush all over Europe, nay, over all the world'. Only in China was it broken by the continuing dull thud of Japanese bombs. The Chinese, he said, were fighting 'our battle—the battle of democracy'. They were defending 'the soil, the good earth, that has been theirs since the dawn of time', and defending it 'against cruel aggression'. He went on:

Give them a cheer across the ocean—no one knows whose turn it may be next. If this habit of military dictatorships breaking into other people's lands with bomb and shell and bullet, stealing the property and killing the proprietors, spreads too widely, we may none of us be able to think of summer holidays for quite a while.

As to the hush that he had said was 'hanging over Europe', what kind of a hush was it, he asked, and answered his own question:

Alas! it is the hush of suspense, and in many lands it is the hush of fear. Listen! No, listen carefully; I think I hear something—yes, there it was quite clear. Don't you hear it? It is the tramp of armies crunching the gravel of the parade-grounds, splashing through rain-soaked fields, the tramp of two million German soldiers and more than a million Italians—'going on manoeuvres'—yes, only on manoeuvres!

Of course it's only manoeuvres—just like last year. After all, the Dictators must train their soldiers. They could scarcely do less in common prudence, when the Danes, the Dutch, the Swiss, the Albanians—and of course the Jews—may leap out upon them at any moment and rob them of their living-space, and make them sign another paper to say who began it.

Besides these German and Italian armies may have another work of liberation to perform. It was only last year they liberated Austria from the horrors of self-government. It was only in March they freed the Czechoslovak Republic from the misery of independent existence. It is only two years ago that Signor Mussolini gave the ancient kingdom of Abyssinia its Magna Charta. It is only two months ago that little Albania got its writ of Habeas Corpus. . . .

No wonder the armies are tramping on when there is so much liberation to be done, and no wonder there is a hush among all the neighbours of Germany and Italy while they are wondering which one is going to be 'liberated' next.

On August 10 Churchill again visited the RAF station at Biggin Hill, where, as the guest of Sir Kingsley Wood, he watched fighter exercises. Three days later he sent Kingsley Wood a note by Lindemann on a new type of weapon of which there had been some talk both in Britain and Germany. In his covering note Churchill told Kingsley Wood: 'There are a lot of rumours going about this atomic explosive, and Ribbentrop has made remarks to people on the subject. I expect Lindemann's view is right, ie that there is no immediate danger, although undoubtedly the human race is crawling nearer to the point when it will be able to destroy itself completely.'

At Chartwell, Churchill and Deakin continued their work on the *English-Speaking Peoples*, and on August 13 Churchill wrote to enlist G. M. Young's help once more, on the last section of the book, which covered the reign of Queen Victoria. Perhaps, Churchill wrote, 'we may have a talk about this period towards the end of September (if we ever get there)'. To General Ironside he wrote that same day: 'Of course I think this fortnight may enable us to see more clearly through the mist. Personally I take the graver view; but as we have lost the initiative, one is baffled by the many uncertainties.'

On the morning of August 14 Churchill flew from London to Paris, arriving in time for lunch with General Georges. General Spears, who was present, later recorded:

Georges was convinced war was almost upon us, and that the Germans, unless given all they wanted, were prepared to launch it. It went without saying that if Poland gave way, they would present other demands which would be insisted upon the more arrogantly because their might and confidence would have grown.

As we ate wood strawberries soaked in white wine, it emerged that there was no more doubt in General Georges' mind than in ours that it was the Germans rather than we who had benefited by the time gained at Munich, always supposing they had really intended fighting then, which he doubted.

He thought Hitler had been bluffing. He pointed out, as proof of the good use the Germans had made of the time granted them, that a year ago they had no defences facing France. Now they had the Western Wall, a formidable obstacle built according to modern ideas, in great depth, whereas the Maginot Line was linear. And another thing: a year ago the French artillery was incomparably superior to the German, but now? And Georges lamented, as a major disaster, the gain by Hitler of Skoda, one of the greatest armament firms in the world.

And the air? All agreed that the Germans had forged ahead and that the results were very serious; all we could do now was to build and build, and place the largest possible orders in the United States.

General Spears' account continued:

One question in particular, I remember, preoccupied Churchill. It was the shoulder of the Maginot Line, the point where it came to an end about Montmédy and was thence prolonged by field works opposite the Ardennes, and on to the sea. I have no note of what Georges answered. What I do remember, for I recalled it a few months later with great vividness, was Churchill's pursed mouth, his look centred on the fruit on the table as if he were crystal-gazing.

His face had ceased smiling, and the shake of his head was ominous when he observed that he hoped these field works were strong, that it would be very unwise to think the Ardennes were impassable to strong forces, as he understood Marshal Pétain had held in his time. 'Remember,' he said, 'that we are faced with a new weapon, armour in great strength, on which the Germans are no doubt concentrating, and that forests will be particularly tempting to such forces since they will offer concealment from the air.'

Churchill's visit to the Maginot Line began on August 15. In a gesture of confidence by the French military authorities he was shown sections no other foreign politician had been allowed to see, including underground railways in the sector facing the Siegfried Line, anti-tank obstacles, strong points on the Rhine and guns sited to shell German troops advancing into France from Switzerland.

Churchill lunched that day with General Gamelin, the Chief of the French General Staff, and Commander-in-Chief designate. After lunch he was driven east of Strasbourg to the bridge over the Rhine which linked France with Germany. There, the German sentries on the far side were within shouting distance of their French counterparts. On August 16, after a night at Colmar, Churchill drove to the French fortified position at Neufbrisach. 'Mr Churchill was amazed,' *The Times* reported 'to observe that the Germans had put up on the other side of the river, right opposite Neufbrisach, an enormous hoarding on which was painted the words "Ein Volk, ein Reich, ein Führer".

In reply to this the French have put up an equally large hoarding which proclaims "Liberté, Egalité, Fraternité".'

From Neufbrisach Churchill continued his tour of the French defences as far south as the Swiss border. That evening, in a hotel at Belfort, he discussed with General Georges his impressions of the day. Spears later recalled:

The trip tore to shreds any illusion that it was not Germany's intention to wage war and to wage it soon. There was no mistaking the grim, relentless and barely concealed preparations she was making, in spite of the fact that silence and secretiveness characterised the right bank of the Rhine. Every commander had tales to tell and they all led to the same conclusion.

Winston Churchill was pleased with the aspect of the men, who greatly liked being inspected by him. He knew how to look every man in the eyes as he passed him, thus convincing him he had been recognised by someone already known, even in France, to be a very important person.

The nightly discussions had borne on the efficacy of the tank obstacles, the danger from parachutists, and attacks in a fog or under cover of artificial fog, which Churchill strongly emphasised. . . .

Our backwardness in tank construction was deplored, and the consensus of opinion certainly favoured the heaviest type that bridges could carry, unless indeed means could be found of lightening a tank for river-crossings or devising machines capable of crossing river-beds.

As I listened I remembered how in 1915 I had heard this same Winston developing his theory of 'land cruisers' to a French General and his staff on the Vimy Ridge, and how heartily they had laughed, after he had gone, at this absurd idea. 'Your politicians are even funnier than ours,' they had exclaimed.

On August 17 Churchill and Spears returned to Paris, where they stayed at the Ritz. 'My most vivid recollection of the trip,' Spears later recalled, 'was Winston's incredible vitality.' On the following day Churchill left Paris for Dreux, where he stayed with Consuelo Balsan at her château, St Georges Motel. That same day *The Times* published an appeal to Chamberlain signed by 375 members of the staffs of every British university, 'strongly urging' Churchill's inclusion in the Government. Among the signatories were seventy professors and six heads of colleges. On August 19 Captain A. H. Henderson-Livesey[1] wrote to Churchill from the City:

---

[1] Alfred Herbert Henderson-Livesey, 1882–   . Joined the Essex Yeomanry as a private, 1914. 2nd Lieutenant, 1915; Lieutenant, 1917. Captain, Army Educational Corps, 1920. Pharmacologist; in the second world war his firm specialized in the treatment of pilots' burns.

At this grave hour I write on behalf of some of my friends here informally assembled to say that we pray that God will give you health and strength to discharge the great task which awaits you.

We feel that the continued exclusion of yourself from the ranks of the Government is a monstrous scandal which cannot long continue.

We note that you have been spending your vacation inspecting the defences of France while the First Minister of the Crown has been absorbed in the mysteries of rod and line in remote Highland streams. . . .

In the Strand, and at other prominent points in London, an enormous poster had been displayed since July. 'What Price Churchill?' it asked. No one knew who was responsible for it.[1] Churchill remained at Consuelo Balsan's château, reading the books he had brought with him on the Victorian era, and painting. Paul Maze, who was also at the château, recorded the painting sessions in his diary on August 20:

I worked alongside him. He suddenly turned to me and said: 'This is the last picture we shall paint in peace for a very long time.' What amazed me was his concentration over his painting. No one but he could have understood more what the possibility of war meant, and how ill prepared we were. As he worked, he would now and then make statements as to the relative strength of the German Army or the French Army. 'They are strong, I tell you, they are strong,' he would say. Then his jaw would clench his large cigar, and I felt the determination of his will. 'Ah,' he would say, 'with it all, we shall have him.'

On the following day Churchill again painted at the Moulin, before returning to Paris. Paul Maze recorded that final day of relaxation in his diary:

We talked about his visit to the Maginot Line with Georges—very impressed with what he saw. Dined at the Chateau. Winston was fuming but with reason as the assemblée didn't see any danger ahead.

As Charteris[2] was walking up the stairs to go to his bedroom he shouted to me, 'don't listen to him. He is a warmonger.'

He was depressed as he left. I had written a letter to him 'only to read when he was over the Channel': 'Don't worry Winston you *know* that you will be Prime Minister and lead us to victory. . . .'

---

[1] The 'What Price Churchill' posters were paid for by an advertising agent, J. M. Beable, Managing Director of AA sites. On 17 August 1939 he told the *Advertisers' Weekly:* 'I was more anxious to get people thinking of the reinstatement of Churchill than necessarily to advocate that policy.'

[2] Evan Charteris, 1864–1940. 6th son of the 10th Earl of Wemyss. Educated at Eton. Staff Captain, Royal Flying Corps, 1916; General Staff Officer, Grade 3, Tank Corps, 1916–18. King's Counsel, 1919. Knighted, 1932. A Trustee of the National Gallery, 1932–39. Chairman of the Tate Gallery, 1934–40. His nephew Hugo was killed in action in 1916.

On August 23 Churchill returned to London. The news that greeted
him was of an impending agreement between Germany and the Soviet
Union. On the following day the *Daily Mirror* published his article 'At
the Eleventh Hour!' In view of the Soviet–German 'intrigue', he
wrote, it was becoming 'increasingly difficult to see how war can be
averted . . . events are moving forward from every quarter and along
all roads to catastrophe. The German military preparations have
already reached a point where action on the greatest scale is possible
at any moment.'

That evening Archibald Sinclair telephoned Churchill to find out
his reaction to the Nazi–Soviet agreement. 'The latter has just returned
from Paris,' Harold Nicolson recorded in his diary, 'and is in high
fettle. The French are not at all perturbed by the Russo-German Pact
and are preparing to support Poland nevertheless. They are half-
mobilizing. Winston has just rung up Paul Reynaud, who asserts that
all is going well: by which he means war, I suppose.' That same day
Kingsley Wood wrote to Churchill: 'I hope that you found your visit
to France interesting and encouraging.'

During August 24, with the worsening crisis, Chamberlain recalled
Parliament. As MPs gathered, a group of six men and women walked
up and down the pavement past which Chamberlain was to reach the
Commons, carrying sandwich boards with the word CHURCHILL in
a blue circle. Among the protesters was the novelist Phyllis Bottome,[1]
who had helped organize the demonstration. Her husband, Captain
Forbes Dennis,[2] told a *Star* reporter on the following day: 'We just
represent the point of view of the exasperated—the very exasperated—
man in the street, who is eighty per cent of the population. We know
how the eyes of people here and in other countries have been turned
towards Churchill in the past weeks and months. We do not necessarily

---

[1] Phyllis Bottome, 1884–1963. Author and Novelist, she published her first book in 1905,
her fortieth in 1961. Did relief work for Belgian refugees, 1914–15. Lecturer, Ministry of
Information, 1940–43. In 1917 she married Captain Ernan Forbes Dennis, grandson of
General Sir John Forbes, GCB, of Inverernan, a hero of the Afghan war of 1842.

[2] Ernan Forbes Dennis, 1884–1972. Helped organize the London Festival of Empire, 1911.
Interpreter, 33rd Light Cavalry Regiment, 1914–15; on active service in France with the
5th Indian Cavalry Division, 1915–18 (badly gassed and wounded). Captain, 1918. Commanded British Intelligence HQ, Marseilles, 1919. Vice Consul, Vienna, and Passport
Control Officer, for Austria, Hungary and Yugoslavia, 1920–23. Ran a language school for
British and American boys (including Ian Fleming), Kitzbühel, 1925–29. Active in London
on behalf of refugees from Nazi persecution, 1935–39. A friend of Adler, he became a practising
psychiatrist. Uncle of the novelist Nigel Dennis. His brother Lieutenant Colonel M. F. B.
Dennis (Nigel Dennis' father) was killed in action on 19 May 1918.

demand that Churchill should be Prime Minister, but that his services should be utilised at this eleventh hour.'

During the meeting on August 24, Parliament passed an Emergency Powers Bill. That same day the Fleet was ordered to its war stations. That night Churchill dined at the Savoy with Eden, Sinclair, Sandys and Duff Cooper. 'We were all very gloomy,' Duff Cooper recorded in his diary.

On August 25, recognizing the immediate dangers of a German attack on Poland now that Russia had decided to stand aside, the British Government signed a formal Treaty of Alliance with Poland. Thus the unilateral guarantee of March 31 was turned into a binding and bilateral pact. Previously Halifax had used the guarantee to try to put pressure on the Poles to make concessions, now, by the Treaty she was much more strictly bound to come to Poland's aid.

On August 29, after speaking to Churchill on the telephone, Sir Edward Marsh noted in his diary: 'He said Hitler was evidently rattled, but he didn't see how he could climb down, which would cost him his life.' That same day the British Government sent a note to Hitler, urging him not to seek to conquer Danzig by force. Churchill was worried lest the message was not strong enough, and, as Duff Cooper recorded in his diary, 'rang up the Polish Ambassador . . . who said that he was now completely satisfied with the support he was receiving from our Government'.

Still worried about the problems of air defence, on August 30 Churchill dictated a 'Secret' memorandum for Kingsley Wood, in which he pointed out some of the deficiencies at Croydon airport, at which he arrived on his return from France a week before. His points were terse and practical:

Scheme of Camouflage for Airport Buildings and concrete aprons not yet given to airport authorities: nor have they any instructions to proceed with Camouflage work although it is a very lengthy and extensive job.

Obstruction from the airport authorities to the digging of trenches outside the aerodrome boundary for the protection of pilots and crews standing by their aircraft dispersed around the aerodrome.

The scheme of underground shelters (being carried out by contractors) is proceeding far too slowly—no special extra shifts of workmen are employed— and they are very inadequate at present.

Churchill also wrote to Chamberlain on August 30. But having signed the letter, he then decided not to send it. Nevertheless, he kept a copy among his private papers. The letter read:

My dear Prime Minister,

I think you are quite right to let things drag on, if they will; more especially because one feels a certain hesitation on the other side as the *act* approaches. But would it not be helpful to call up the reserves and mobilize the TA? If events turn out badly, it would prove a timely precaution. If they continue undefined, it would be an invaluable testing of machinery which is probably very rusty. Anyhow the effect would surely add to the force of your exertions to preserve peace; and the people involved would gladly respond.

I do not see myself how Hitler can escape from the pen in which he has put himself. But a victory without bloodshed would be the best; and this would help, not hinder it.

On Thursday August 31 Churchill was at Chartwell, working on his book. To Sir Newman Flower, who had asked him to write a preface for a biography of Austen Chamberlain he replied that day: 'I am, as you know, concentrating every minute of my spare life and strength upon completing our contract. These distractions are trying. . . . You will understand, more than anyone else, how difficult it is for me to spend a night upon another form of work.' Nevertheless, Churchill added, he now had 530,000 words in print 'and there is only the cutting and proof reading, together with a few, special points, now to be done'. That same day Churchill wrote to G. M. Young: 'I have completed the Commonwealth story (Lambeth and Monk), but have still not cleared away the Queen Elizabeth block. I am now working on the Chatham period, which is very inspiriting.' He added: 'It is a relief in times like these to be able to escape into other centuries. Happily there are good hopes that Chamberlain will stand firm.'

As was his custom, Churchill worked that night until the early hours of Friday morning, September 1. Towards dawn, while he was asleep, the German armies invaded Poland. At 8.30 that morning the Polish Ambassador, Count Raczynski, telephoned Chartwell to give him the news. At ten o'clock Churchill himself telephoned to General Ironside at the War Office. 'They've started,' he told him. 'Warsaw and Cracow are being bombed now.'

Telegrams were at once sent out from the War Office, ordering full mobilization for two o'clock that afternoon. The House of Commons was summoned for six o'clock. Churchill drove up to London from Chartwell, and at Chamberlain's request, called at 10 Downing Street that afternoon. According to Churchill's post-war account:

He told me that he saw no hope of averting a war with Germany and that he proposed to form a small War Cabinet of Ministers without Departments to conduct it. He mentioned that the Labour Party were not, he understood, willing to share in a national coalition. He still had hopes that the Liberals would join him. He invited me to become a member of the War Cabinet. I agreed to his proposal without comment, and on this basis we had a long talk on men and measures.

Chamberlain and Churchill were agreed that the best war-making instrument would be a small War Cabinet of six members, from which the three Service Ministers would be excluded. Churchill, therefore, would enter the War Cabinet as Minister without Portfolio.

At six o'clock that evening Churchill was in his place below the gangway when Chamberlain entered the House of Commons. During their meeting that morning Chamberlain had told Churchill: 'the die is cast'. To the House of Commons, he explained that documents were being prepared for a White Paper that would 'make it perfectly clear that our object has been to bring about discussions of the Polish–German dispute between the two countries themselves on terms of equality, the settlement to be one which safeguarded the independence of Poland'—a settlement to be secured 'by international guarantees'. The Germans had not responded. Chamberlain then read out the British note to Germany, which had been delivered that day in Berlin. The note read:

Unless the German Government are prepared to give His Majesty's Government satisfactory assurances that the German Government have suspended all aggressive action against Poland and are prepared promptly to withdraw their forces from Polish territory His Majesty's Government in the United Kingdom will without hesitation fulfill their obligation to Poland.

That evening Churchill returned to Morpeth Mansions, writing to Chamberlain shortly after midnight, in the early hours of September 2:

Aren't we a very old team? I make out that the six you mentioned to me yesterday aggregate 386 years or an average of over sixty-four! Only one year short of the Old Age Pension! If however you added Sinclair (49) and Eden (42) the average comes down to 57½.

If the *Daily Herald* is right that Labour will not come in, we shall certainly have to face a constant stream of criticism, as well as the many disappointments and surprises of which war largely consists. Therefore it seems to me all the more important to have the Liberal Opposition firmly incorporated in our ranks. Eden's influence with the section of Conservatives who are associated with him, as well as with moderate Liberal elements, also seems to me to be a very necessary reinforcement.

The Poles have now been under heavy attack for thirty hours, and I am much concerned to hear that there is talk in Paris of a further note. I trust you will be able to announce our Joint Declaration of War at *latest* when Parliament meets this afternoon.

The *Bremen* will soon be out of the interception zone unless the Admiralty take special measures and the signal is given to-day. This is only a minor point, but it may well be vexatious.[1]

Churchill's letter ended: 'I remain here at your disposal.'

Throughout September 2 Churchill waited for a summons to 10 Downing Street. On the following day Lord Hankey,[2] who had also been invited to join the Government, wrote to his wife: 'As far as I can make out, my main job is to keep an eye on Winston!' and he continued:

I spent 1½ hours with him yesterday morning. He was brimful of ideas, some good, others not so good, but rather heartening and big. I only wish he didn't give one the impression that he does himself too well!

I went into the House of Commons smoking room yesterday. The amount of alcohol being consumed was incredible! Winston too was in a corner holding forth to a ring of admiring satellite MPs!

He has let it get into the Press that he will be in the War Cabinet—to the great annoyance of many.

Mrs Hill later recalled how throughout September 2, Churchill 'was pacing up and down like a lion in a cage. He was expecting a call, but the call never came.'

When the Cabinet met at 4.30 on the afternoon of September 2, Count Raczynski, who was present, urged the immediate implementation of the Anglo-Polish Treaty, while Hore-Belisha told his Cabinet colleagues, as he recorded in his diary: 'I was strongly opposed to further delay, which I thought might result in breaking the unity of the country. Public opinion was against yielding an inch.' According to Hore-Belisha, as a result of the discussion 'Unanimous decision was taken that the ultimatum should end at midnight.' But when Chamberlain went to the House of Commons three hours later, at 7.30, he spoke not of an immi-

---

[1] The German liner *Bremen* escaped British interception and, after finding shelter in the Soviet port of Murmansk, returned to Germany, being spared on her return journey by the British submarine *Salmon* which (as Churchill wrote in *The Gathering Storm*) 'observed rightly and punctiliously the conventions of International Law'.

[2] Sir Maurice Hankey had been created Baron on 3 February 1939. He became Minister Without Portfolio on 3 September 1939, when he was also made a Privy Councillor.

nent ultimatum with only 4½ hours to run, but of the possibility of further negotiations. Although the Germans had not yet replied to the Anglo-French warning, he said, this might be because they were considering a new Italian proposal for a conference to discuss a possible German-Polish settlement.

'If the German Government should agree to withdraw their forces,' Chamberlain announced, 'then His Majesty's Government would be willing to regard the position as being the same as it was before the German forces crossed the Polish frontier.' Were German troops to withdraw, Chamberlain added, 'the way would be open to discussions' between Germany and Poland, a discussion with which the British Government would be 'willing to be associated'. Leopold Amery recalled in his memoirs:

The House was aghast. For two whole days the wretched Poles had been bombed and massacred, and we were still considering within what time-limit Hitler should be invited to tell us whether he felt like relinquishing his prey! And then these sheer irrelevancies about the terms of a hypothetical agreement between Germany and Poland. . . .

Was all this havering the prelude to another Munich? A year before the House had risen to its feet to give Chamberlain an ovation when he announced a last-moment hope of peace. This time any similar announcement would have been met by a universal howl of execration.

'There was no doubt,' Churchill later recorded, 'that the temper of the House was for war. I deemed it even more resolute and united than in the similar scene on August 3, 1914, in which I had also taken part.'

Even Chamberlain's Cabinet colleagues, as Hore-Belisha wrote in his diary, 'were completely aghast' that negotiations might still be contemplated, or that the German invasion of Poland might not automatically lead to the honouring of the terms of the Anglo-Polish Treaty. Immediately after Chamberlain's speech five Ministers, Simon, Hore-Belisha, Sir John Anderson, Walter Elliot and Lord de la Warr went to Simon's room in the House of Commons, where they agreed that the Cabinet's earlier decision ought to be implemented at once; they then proceeded to Chamberlain's room where they 'put the case very forcibly', as Hore-Belisha noted, against any further delay.

Duff Cooper had gone from the House of Commons to the Savoy Grill. There, as he wrote in his diary, he met two members of the Government. One, Harold Balfour, when asked if he were still a member of the Government, made a gesture of 'shame and despair'; the other, Euan Wallace, left Duff Cooper a message that Chamberlain's announcement in the Commons had 'taken the whole Cabinet by surprise'.

Duff Cooper went at once from the Savoy to see Churchill at Morpeth Mansions. Eden, Boothby, Brendan Bracken and Duncan Sandys had already gathered there. 'We were all in a state of bewildered rage' Duff Cooper noted. Churchill himself recalled in his memoirs how 'a number of gentlemen of importance in all Parties' had arrived at Morpeth Mansions, to express 'their deep anxiety lest we should fail in our obligations to Poland'. In his diary Duff Cooper recorded how Churchill:

considered that he had been very ill-treated, as he had agreed the night before to join the War Cabinet but throughout the day he had not heard a word from the Prime Minister. He had wished to speak that night in the House but feeling himself already almost a member of the Government had refrained from doing so. . . .

Bob was convinced that Chamberlain had lost the Conservative Party forever and that it was in Winston's power to go to the House of Commons tomorrow and break him and take his place. He felt very strongly that in no circumstances now should Winston consent to serve under him. Was it better to split the country at such a moment or bolster up Chamberlain? That seemed at one time the decision that Winston had to take.

The six men argued long into the night, their discussion punctuated by the thunder-claps of a fierce storm. Shortly after midnight Churchill wrote again to Chamberlain:

I have not heard anything from you since our talks on Friday, when I understood that I was to serve as your colleague, and when you told me that this would be announced speedily. I really do not know what has happened during the course of this agitated day; though it seems to me that entirely different ideas have ruled from those which you expressed to me when you said 'the die was cast'.

I quite realise that in contact with this tremendous European situation changes of method may become necessary, but I feel entitled to ask you to let me know how we stand, both publicly and privately, before the debate opens at noon.

It seems to me that if the Labour Party, and as I gather the Liberal Party, are estranged, it will be difficult to form an effective War Government, on the limited basis you mentioned. I consider that a further effort should be made to bring in the Liberals, and in addition that the composition and scope of the War Cabinet you discussed with me requires review.

There was a feeling to-night in the House that injury had been done to the spirit of national unity by the apparent weakening of our resolve. I do not underrate the difficulties you have with the French; but I trust that we shall now take our decisions independently, and thus give our French friends any lead that may be necessary. In order to do this we shall need the strongest and most integral combination that can be formed. I therefore ask that there should be no announcement of the composition of the War Cabinet until we have had a further talk.

As I wrote to you yesterday morning, I hold myself entirely at your disposal, with every desire to aid you in your task.

The British ultimatum to Germany was sent from London to Berlin at nine in the morning of Sunday September 3. It gave the Germans three hours to halt their advance into Poland, or to face war with Britain. Hitler made no reply. Meanwhile, German troops continued their advance and German aeroplanes their bombing. Churchill, convinced that Hitler would not halt his troops, prepared a short speech for Parliament. At eleven fifteen that morning Neville Chamberlain broadcast to the nation that Britain was at war with Germany.

No sooner had Chamberlain finished speaking than the air raid sirens sounded. Churchill, who was at Morpeth Mansions, went first on to the roof 'to see', as he later recalled, 'what was going on', and was impressed to see thirty or forty barrage balloons 'in the clear, cool September light'. Then, 'armed with a bottle of brandy and other appropriate medical comforts', he and his wife went into the basement shelter down the street. 'Everyone was cheerful and jocular,' he wrote, 'as is the English manner when about to encounter the unknown.' As soon as the All-Clear sounded, Churchill went to the House of Commons. No sooner was he in his seat than he received a note from Chamberlain, asking him to come and see him when the debate was over. 'As I sat in my place, listening to the speeches,' Churchill recalled, 'a very strong sense of calm came over me, after the intense passions and excitements of the last few days. I felt a serenity of mind and was conscious of a kind of uplifted detachment from human and personal affairs.'

There was no formal debate that morning. Chamberlain gave a short account of the events leading up to Britain's ultimatum, and declared, to the cheers of the House, 'I hope I may live to see the day when Hitlerism has been destroyed.' Speaking for the Labour Party, Arthur Greenwood[1] told the House to further cheers, that the 'intolerable

---

[1] Arthur Greenwood, 1880–1954. Lecturer in economics, Leeds University, and Chairman of the Yorkshire District Workers' Educational Association. Assistant Secretary, Ministry of Reconstruction, 1917–19. Labour MP for Nelson and Colne, 1922–31; for Wakefield, 1932–

agony of suspense' was over, and paid tribute to the Poles, now fighting desperately for survival. Churchill spoke next, to an attentive, apprehensive House: 'In this solemn hour it is a consolation to recall and to dwell upon our repeated efforts for peace. All have been ill-starred, but all have been faithful and sincere. This is of the highest moral value. . . .' Outside, Churchill added, 'the storms of war may blow and the lands may be lashed with the fury of its gales, but in our own hearts this Sunday morning there is peace. Our hands may be active, but our consciences are at rest.' His speech continued:

We must not underrate the gravity of the task which lies before us or the severity of the ordeal, to which we shall not be found unequal. We must expect many disappointments, and many unpleasant surprises, but we may be sure that the task which we have freely accepted is one not beyond the compass and the strength of the British Empire and the French Republic. . . .

This is not a question of fighting for Danzig or fighting for Poland. We are fighting to save the whole world from the pestilence of Nazi tyranny and in defence of all that is most sacred to man. This is no war of domination or imperial aggrandisement or material gain; no war to shut any country out of its sunlight and means of progress. It is a war, viewed in its inherent quality, to establish, on impregnable rocks, the rights of the individual, and it is a war to establish and revive the stature of man. . . .

After the speeches were over Boothby wrote to Churchill: 'Your immediate task seems to have been made much easier by the PM today. His was not the speech of a man who intended to lead us *through* the struggle.' In his diary Leopold Amery described Chamberlain's speech as 'good, but not the speech of a war leader', and he added: 'I think I see Winston emerging as PM out of it all by the end of the year.'

Immediately after a final speech by Lloyd George, Churchill went to see Chamberlain in his room in the House of Commons. There, Chamberlain told him that the Liberals would not join the Government, but that if the three Service Ministers were to join the War Cabinet, as they were most anxious to do, the average age would be less than sixty. Sir Kingsley Wood would remain at the Air Ministry, and Hore-Belisha at the War Office, but Chamberlain was willing to let Churchill go to the Admiralty in place of Lord Stanhope. He would then have both a Ministry, and a place in the War Cabinet. Churchill later recorded:

---

54. Parliamentary Secretary, Ministry of Health, 1924. Minister of Health, 1929–31. Privy Councillor, 1929; Deputy Leader of the Labour Party, 1935. Member of the War Cabinet, 1940–42. Lord Privy Seal, 1945–47. Chairman of the Labour Party, 1952.

I was very glad of this because, though I had not raised the point, I naturally preferred a definite task to that exalted brooding over the work done by others which may well be the lot of a Minister, however influential, who has no Department. It is easier to give directions than advice, and more agreeable to have the right to act, even in a limited sphere, than the privilege to talk at large. Had the Prime Minister in the first instance given me the choice between the War Cabinet and the Admiralty, I should of course have chosen the Admiralty. Now I was to have both.

During the early afternoon Churchill sent a message to the Admiralty, to say that he would arrive later that day to take up his office. On receiving this message the Board of Admiralty signalled to the Fleet: 'Winston is Back.' Early that evening Churchill himself went to Admiralty House, and returned to the First Lord's Room for the first time since his departure more than twenty-four years before, at the height of the Dardanelles crisis of May 1915. Mrs Hill, who accompanied him, later recalled how 'he rushed up to the First Lord's Room, and went up to a cupboard in the panelling. I held my breath. He flung the door open with a dramatic gesture—there, behind the panelling was a large map showing the disposition of all German ships on the day he had left the Admiralty in 1915.' On the following day Churchill wrote to his predecessor at the Admiralty, Lord Stanhope:

Fortune of war which chased me a quarter of a century ago from the Admiralty, has now reversed its action. I am sure you know that I have done nothing to disturb you. Indeed I had already accepted a seat in the War Cabinet 'without portfolio', when a change of plan brought me into this office. The few hours I spent there last night show me the excellent condition in which you have left it; and I have no doubt that this impression will be deepened as my knowledge grows. I should like very much however to learn from you the points you had especially in mind, in order that nothing may be overlooked in changing guard. Perhaps you will let me know when I may call upon you.

I hope we are to be colleagues, as well as neighbours,[1] and that I may count on your assistance.

Among the hundreds of letters which Churchill received on his return to the Admiralty were many from those of his friends who had never wavered in their belief that his unique skills ought to be used by the nation, and who had long looked forward to his return to office. 'My dear old Winston,' his Sandhurst subaltern friend Sir Reginald

---

[1] Lord Stanhope had become Lord President of the Council on September 3 (he received no office after May 1940). He lived at Chevening, near Sevenoaks, Kent, seven miles from Chartwell.

Barnes wrote on September 3, 'I am *so* glad that you are in your right place, & will knock that l--r Hitler out. Personally I am miserable, as they say I am too old.' That same day Paul Maze, who had first met Churchill on the western front in 1916, wrote to him from the Moulin de Montreuil: 'I feel happy to know that the responsibility of the Navy is in your hands at this juncture. I am writing this only a few yards from the spot where your easel stood ten days ago. Now we are at war and we can meet the future with confidence.'

'Thank whatever God there be,' Josiah Wedgwood wrote on September 4. 'Now we shall win.' Margaret, Countess of Birkenhead wrote that same day from Charlton:

My dear Winston,
    A cry of 'Thank God' went up from the whole family when we read the good news, & I am sure the same cry has gone up from the whole nation. I cannot tell you how thankful I am to feel that your great gifts & wonderful brain are being used in the War Cabinet, as there is no one else in the country to compare with you at a time like this. If only Fred was here to be working with you!

'May I thank you once more,' Eduard Beneš wrote from his home in exile at Putney on September 4, 'for all the great services you have rendered to my unfortunate country during the last year. . . . I hope that even in this great struggle my people and myself personally we shall have occasion to collaborate with you effectively. . . .' and G. D. Birla wrote from Calcutta on September 6, of how, in India, 'even those who do not appreciate your politics would acclaim your appointment with whole-hearted approval . . . the sympathies of most of us who belong to the Gandhi school of thought are whole-heartedly with Great Britain'. 'It may be,' Churchill replied to Birla on September 21, 'that larger unities and deeper understandings will grow out of the storm of this severe war. I shall always be on the lookout for this.'

'You would have been gratified I know if you could have heard the gasp of relief from the French when you went back to the Admiralty,' Maxine Elliot wrote from the Château de L'Horizon on September 20. 'All sorts and conditions of people have even shaken hands over it, but I personally resent the government that waited so long to take advantage of your overwhelming superiority of brain and experience!'

Despite his own preoccupations, Churchill followed the actions of his friends. Learning that James Scrymgeour-Wedderburn, whom he had known since his youthful visit to Chartwell in 1928, had resigned as Parliamentary Under-Secretary of State for Scotland in order to join his regiment, Churchill telegraphed on September 12: 'Let me congratulate you on your fine and spirited conduct in resigning your Office of State for active Service.'

Colin Thornton-Kemsley, who six months earlier had tried to remove Churchill from Parliament, and had himself become an MP in March, wrote on September 12 from his Army camp:

> You won't welcome a letter from me & it will not be a long one, but war puts things into proportion, and I should not be happy to go off to my job until I had said something which has been on my mind of late.
>
> For fourteen years I worked as hard as most in your support, and from September until the time of my By-Election in March (since when I have scrupulously refrained from taking any part at all in the affairs of your Division) I have opposed you as hard as I knew how for reasons, and in ways, which you know all about.
>
> I want to say only this. You warned us repeatedly about the German danger & you were right: a grasshopper under a fern is not proud now that he made the field ring with his importunate chink.
>
> Please don't think of replying—you are in all conscience busy enough in an office which we are all glad that you hold in this time of Britain's danger.

Churchill had received so many letters in the week after reaching the Admiralty that he could not read them all, and most of them were not even put before him. But Mrs Hill put this one on his desk with the message '*Please* read this,' and he did so. He also showed it to his wife and read it over the telephone to Sir James Hawkey. Then, on September 13, he replied, accepting Thornton-Kemsley's apology, and adding:

> I certainly think that Englishmen ought to start fair with one another from the outset in so grievous a struggle and so far as I am concerned the past is dead.

List of Sources

List of Sources

I have divided this list of sources into three parts: a page-by-page list of original documents; a person-by-person list of previously unpublished individual recollections; and an alphabetical list of printed sources. Unless otherwise indicated, all Churchill's letters to his wife are from the Baroness Spencer-Churchill papers. The other archives used in this volume are as follows:

PART ONE

ORIGINAL DOCUMENTS

PREFACE: **p. xx**, Churchill to Sir Alexander Hardinge (2 June 1940), Churchill papers, 20/4; **p. xxi**, Churchill to Desmond Morton (15 October 1947), Premier papers, 7/1; Desmond Morton to Churchill (in reply) Churchill papers, 4/141.

CHAPTER 1. 'GETTING MUCH BETTER IN MYSELF': **p. 3**, Churchill to Spears, Spears papers; **p. 5**, Churchill to Bernau, Churchill papers 28/144; Jack Churchill to Churchill, Churchill papers 1/170; Stevenson to Churchill, Churchill papers, 2/126; **p. 6**, Churchill to the Duke of Marlborough, Blenheim Palace archive; **p. 7**, Prince of Wales to Churchill, and Margot Asquith to Churchill, Churchill papers, 8/46; **p. 12**, Garvin to Churchill, Churchill papers, 8/45; **p. 13**, Churchill to Spears, Spears papers; Churchill private note, Churchill papers, 2/128; **p. 14**, Amery diary, Amery papers; Baldwin to Churchill, and Lawrence to Churchill, Churchill papers, 8/47; **p. 15**, Amery to Churchill, Churchill papers, 8/47; **p. 16**, Rothermere to Churchill, Churchill papers, 2/126; **p. 21**, Tyrrell to Churchill, and Lady Wilson to Churchill, Churchill papers, 2/126; **p. 22**, Douglas to Churchill, A. Chamberlain to Churchill, and Greene to Churchill, Churchill papers, 2/127; **p. 23**, Kellaway to Churchill, Churchill papers, 2/127; **p. 24**, Churchill to Violet Bonham Carter and reply, Churchill papers, 2/132; **p. 25**, MacDonald to Churchill, Churchill papers, 2/132; **p. 26**, Churchill to the Bristol Labour Association, Churchill papers, 2/132.

CHAPTER 2. 'TOWARDS THE CONSERVATIVES': **p. 30**, A. Chamberlain to Birkenhead, A. Chamberlain papers; **p. 31**, A. Chamberlain to Churchill, Churchill papers, 6/2; **p. 32**, A. Chamberlain to his wife, A. Chamberlain papers; Sassoon to Churchill, Churchill papers, 6/2; Churchill to Baldwin, Baldwin papers; **p. 33**, Gwynne to Baldwin, Baldwin papers; **p. 34**, A. Chamberlain to his wife, A. Chamberlain papers; **p. 35**, Churchill to Balfour, Balfour papers; **p. 36**, Derby to Rawlinson, Derby papers; **p. 37**, Conway, Lady Birkenhead and Duff Cooper to Churchill, Churchill papers, 6/2; **p. 38**, Spears to Churchill, Churchill papers, 6/2; Erskine to Baldwin, Baldwin papers; Londonderry to Churchill, Churchill papers, 2/132; **p. 39**, Birkenhead to Derby, Derby papers; Churchill to Balfour, Churchill papers, 2/132; Churchill to Baldwin, Baldwin papers; **p. 40**, Marlborough to Churchill, and Salvidge to Churchill, Churchill papers, 2/132; **p. 42**, Jackson to Churchill, and Hoare to Churchill, Churchill papers, 2/133; **p. 43**, Churchill to Baldwin, May 10, Baldwin papers; Baldwin to Churchill, Churchill papers, 2/133; Churchill to Baldwin,

May 30, Baldwin papers; **p. 44**, Baldwin to Churchill, Churchill papers, 2/133; Locker Lampson to Baldwin, Baldwin papers; Hoare to Churchill and reply, Churchill papers, 2/133; **p. 45**, Baldwin to A. Chamberlain, A. Chamberlain papers; Goschen to Churchill and reply, Churchill papers, 7/1; **p. 46**, Churchill to Jackson, Churchill papers, 2/134; **p. 47**, Churchill to Horne, and Jackson to Churchill, Churchill papers, 2/134; **p. 49**, Lady Hozier to a friend, Lady Hozier papers; **p. 50**, Churchill to Lindemann, April 3, April 21 and May 10, Cherwell papers; **p. 52**, Churchill to Cecil and reply, Chelwood papers.

CHAPTER 3. 'THE JOLLIEST BIT OF NEWS FOR MONTHS': **p. 53**, Jackson and Londonderry to Churchill, Churchill papers, 2/135; **p. 55**, Baring to Churchill, Churchill papers, 2/135; Harmsworth and Hamilton to Churchill, Churchill papers, 7/1; **p. 56**, Lawrence to Churchill, Churchill papers, 7/1; Tyrrell to Baldwin, Baldwin papers; Churchill note, Churchill papers, 4/96; **p. 57**, Wimborne to Churchill, and Churchill to Burgoyne, Churchill papers, 2/136; **p. 58**, A. Chamberlain to Baldwin, Baldwin papers; Churchill private note, Churchill papers, 4/96; **p. 59**, Churchill private note, Churchill papers, 4/96; **p. 60**, Churchill private note, Churchill papers, 4/96; A. Chamberlain to Baldwin, and N. Chamberlain to Baldwin, Baldwin papers; **p. 61**; Horne, Consuelo Balsan, and Lambert to Churchill, Churchill papers, 2/138; **p. 62**, A. Chamberlain's sister, A. Chamberlain papers; Churchill to Sheepshanks, Churchill papers, 1/172; Churchill to Rosebery, Rosebery papers; McKenna to Beaverbrook, Beaverbrook papers.

CHAPTER 4. GREAT ISSUES IN THE SOCIAL SPHERE: **p. 65**, Churchill to Baldwin, Baldwin papers; **p. 66**, Churchill to Barstow, Churchill papers, 18/2; Churchill to Fisher, Churchill papers, 18/3; Churchill to Hopkins, Treasury papers, 171/239; **p. 67**; Churchill to Hopkins, Churchill papers, 18/3; **p. 68**, Cabinet minutes (November 26), Cabinet papers, 23/49; **p. 69**, Churchill to Baldwin, Treasury papers, 171/247; N. Chamberlain diary, N. Chamberlain papers; **p. 70**, Churchill to Barstow, Churchill papers, 18/3; Churchill to Bridgeman, Churchill papers, 18/2; Churchill to A. Chamberlain, A. Chamberlain papers; **p. 71**, Churchill memoranda, (December 2 and 4), Churchill papers, 22/21; Churchill to Hankey, Churchill papers, 18/3; **p. 72**, Churchill to Barstow, Churchill papers, 18/3, Churchill to Hoare, Churchill papers, 18/2; Hoare to Churchill, Treasury papers, 172/1440; **p. 73**, Churchill to Hopkins, Churchill papers, 18/3; Churchill to Salisbury, Salisbury papers; **p. 74**, Churchill to Hopkins, Treasury papers, 171/239; Churchill to Barstow, Churchill papers, 18/3; Churchill to Baldwin, Churchill papers, 18/2; **p. 77**, Churchill to Bridgeman, and A. Chamberlain, Churchill papers, 18/2; Churchill to N. Chamberlain, Treasury papers, 172/1452; Churchill Cabinet note (December 29), Churchill papers, 22/22; **p. 78**, N. Chamberlain to Churchill, Treasury papers, 171/247; Baldwin to Churchill, Treasury papers, 171/247; Clementine Churchill to Lindemann, Cherwell papers; Committee of Imperial Defence minutes, Cabinet papers, 27/273; **p. 79**, Churchill to Niemeyer, Churchill papers, 18/3; **p. 80**, Churchill to A. Chamberlain, A. Chamberlain papers; Cabinet minutes (January 5), Cabinet papers, 23/49; Paris Conference, Treasury papers, 188/6; **p. 82**, Grey to Churchill, Churchill papers, 1/178; Cabinet minutes (January 15), Cabinet papers, 23/49; Phipps to Churchill, Churchill papers, 2/141; Barstow to Churchill, Churchill papers, 18/6; Churchill to Bridgeman, Churchill papers, 18/10; **p. 83**, Churchill to Cecil, Churchill papers, 18/10; Churchill to Bridgeman, Churchill papers, 18/4, Churchill to Baldwin, Baldwin papers; **p. 84**, Bridgeman to Churchill, Churchill papers, 18/4; Churchill memorandum, Churchill papers, 22/28; **p. 85**, Birkenhead to Reading, Reading papers; **p. 86**, Barstow to Fisher, Baldwin papers; Churchill to Beatty (February 3), Churchill papers, 18/4; Churchill to Beatty (February 4), Churchill papers, 22/68; **p. 87**, Churchill to Bridgeman, Churchill papers, 18/4; Churchill to Baldwin, Churchill papers, 18/10; **p. 88**, Churchill Cabinet memorandum (February 7), Churchill papers, 22/30; Bridgeman to Churchill, Churchill papers, 18/4; Cecil to Churchill and reply, Churchill papers, 22/68; Cabinet minutes (February 11), Cabinet papers, 23/49; **p. 89**, Cabinet minutes, (February 12), Cabinet papers, 23/49; Churchill to Bridgeman and reply, Churchill papers, 22/30; **p. 90**, Cabinet minutes (February 18), Cabinet papers, 23/49; Churchill to Baldwin and N. Chamberlain to Churchill, Treasury papers, 171/247; Watson minute, Treasury papers, 171/247; **p. 91**, Barstow to Churchill, Treasury papers, 171/247.

CHAPTER 5. RETURN TO THE GOLD STANDARD: **p. 93**, Churchill to Baldwin, A. Chamberlain papers; Churchill to Niemeyer, Treasury papers, 171/245; **p. 94**, Bradbury to Niemeyer, Treasury papers, 171/245; Churchill memorandum, Treasury papers, 171/245; **p. 95**, Niemeyer and Norman to Churchill, Treasury papers, 171/245; **p. 96**, Churchill to Niemeyer, Treasury papers, 171/245; Churchill to A. Chamberlain, Churchill papers, 18/10; **p. 97**, Niemeyer to Churchill and reply, Churchill papers, 18/12; **p. 99**, Churchill to Beaverbrook, Beaverbrook papers; Churchill to Grigg (19 May 1930), Grigg papers; **p. 100**, Churchill to the King, Churchill papers, 18/7.

CHAPTER 6. 'KEEPING HIS NOSE TO THE GRINDSTONE': **p. 101**, Naval Programme Committee minutes, Churchill papers, 22/65; Churchill to Birkenhead, Churchill papers, 18/10; **p. 102**, Naval Programme Committee minutes, Churchill papers, 22/65; **p. 103**, Bridgeman memorandum, Churchill papers, 22/66; Cabinet Committee minutes (March 5), Cabinet papers, 27/273; Churchill to Birkenhead, Churchill papers, 18/10; **p. 104**, Naval Programme Committee minutes, Churchill papers, 22/65; Cabinet minutes (March 18), Churchill papers, 22/69; Keyes to Churchill, Keyes papers; **p. 105**, Churchill to Keyes, Keyes papers; Churchill notes (March 31), Churchill papers, 22/68; **p. 108**, Employers' Deputation and Weir to Churchill, Treasury papers, 171/247; Churchill to N. Chamberlain, Treasury papers, 171/247; **p. 109**, Churchill to Watson, Churchill papers, 18/19; Churchill to N. Chamberlain, Churchill papers, 18/9; Steel-Maitland to Churchill and reply, Churchill papers, 18/9; **p. 110**, Niemeyer to Churchill and reply Churchill papers, 18/7; Watson to Churchill, Treasury papers, 171/247; Baldwin to the King, Baldwin papers; Churchill to Baldwin, Churchill papers, 18/8; **p. 111**, Cabinet minutes (April 22), Cabinet papers, 23/50; Churchill to the King, and Stamfordham's reply, Churchill papers, 18/7.

CHAPTER 7. 'THE APPEASEMENT OF CLASS BITTERNESS': **p. 112**, Guest and Seely to Churchill, Churchill papers, 2/141; **p. 115**, Mildmay to Churchill, Churchill papers, 2/141; **p. 116**, Wimborne to Churchill, Churchill papers, 2/141; Baldwin to the King, Baldwin papers; **p. 118**, Baldwin to the King, Baldwin papers; **p. 119**, N. Chamberlain diary, N. Chamberlain papers; **p. 120**, Beaverbrook to Bracken, Beaverbrook papers; Baldwin to the King, Baldwin papers.

CHAPTER 8. 'ALARM BELLS RINGING': **p. 121**, Committee of Imperial Defence minutes (4 December 1924), Churchill papers, 22/31; **p. 122**, Churchill to A. Chamberlain, A. Chamberlain papers; Committee of Imperial Defence minutes (13 February 1925), Churchill papers, 22/31; **p. 123**, Churchill to Balfour, Balfour papers; **p. 124**, Churchill to A. Chamberlain, A. Chamberlain papers; **p. 125**, Baldwin and Crowe to A. Chamberlain, A. Chamberlain papers; Bridgeman note, Baldwin papers; **p. 126**, Silk Deputation, Treasury papers, 172/1517; Churchill to Hamilton, Treasury papers, 172/1474; **p. 127**, Churchill to Hopkins, Treasury papers, 172/1474; Hamilton to Churchill, Treasury papers, 172/1474; Scott note, Scott papers; **p. 128**, Naval Programme Committee minutes (May 11), Churchill papers, 22/65; **p. 129**, Churchill to A. Chamberlain (July 17), A. Chamberlain papers; A. Chamberlain to Churchill, Churchill papers, 22/69; Churchill to A. Chamberlain (July 20), A. Chamberlain papers; Ministerial Conference minutes (July 22), Churchill papers, 22/69; **p. 130**, Rothermere to Churchill, Churchill papers, 2/142; **p. 131**, Cabinet Committee (July 30), Cabinet papers, 23/50; Hankey diary, Hankey papers; **p. 132**, N. Chamberlain to Baldwin, N. Chamberlain papers; **p. 133**, Churchill to his brother (end 1924), Churchill papers, 1/172; Baldwin to Churchill, Churchill papers, 18/9; **p. 134**, Churchill to the French Ambassador, Treasury papers,

188/7; Churchill to A. Chamberlain, A. Chamberlain papers; **p. 135**; Churchill to A. Chamberlain, A. Chamberlain papers, Churchill to Caillaux (October 15, and 29 and reply November 7), Churchill papers, 2/142; **p. 136**, Churchill to Loucheur, Loucheur papers; **p. 137**, Churchill to Baldwin, Baldwin papers; **p. 138**, Craig to Churchill, Churchill papers, 2/142; Churchill memorandum, Churchill papers, 18/7; **p. 139**, Standing Committee minutes, Churchill papers, 22/50; Churchill departmental memorandum, Churchill papers, 18/7; **p. 140**, Joynson-Hicks and Barstow to Churchill, and Churchill minutes, Treasury papers, 171/250; **p. 141**, Cabinet Committee (December 10 and 18), Churchill papers, 22/50; Churchill to Betting Deputation, Treasury papers, 172/1494; Churchill to Niemeyer and Hamilton, Churchill papers, 18/7; House of Lords Reform Committee minutes, Churchill papers, 22/58; **p. 142**, Churchill to Hamilton, Barstow and Hopkins, Churchill papers, 18/30; Churchill Volpi negotiations, Treasury papers, 172/1505; **p. 143**, Churchill to Bridgeman, and Steel-Maitland, Churchill papers, 18/29; **p. 144**, Beaverbrook to Mackenzie King, Beaverbrook papers; **p. 145**, Hoare to Beaverbrook, Beaverbrook papers.

CHAPTER 9. THE GENERAL STRIKE AND THE BRITISH GAZETTE: **p. 147**, Coal Committee Report on Report of the Royal Commission on the Coal Industry, Cabinet papers, 27/316; Harold Macmillan to Churchill, Churchill papers, 2/147; **p. 150**, Birkenhead memorandum, Churchill papers, 22/94; Amery diary, Amery papers; **p. 151**, Hoare diary, Templewood papers; Churchill newspaper programme, Churchill papers, 22/142; **p. 152**, meeting with editors, transcript, Churchill papers, 22/142; **p. 157**, Churchill unsigned articles, Churchill papers, 22/142; **p. 158**, Churchill to Lindemann, Treasury papers, 172/1558; Fraser memorandum, and Churchill to Fraser, Churchill papers, 22/143; **p. 159**, Sassoon to Hoare, Templewood papers; **p. 160**, Davidson to Baldwin, Baldwin papers; **p. 161**, Churchill to Worthington-Evans, Churchill papers, 22/141; **p. 162**, Churchill notes, Churchill papers, 22/141; Davidson to Irwin, Halifax papers; **p. 163**, Cabinet Committee report (May 8), Churchill papers, 22/94; **p. 164**, Dawson to Baldwin, Baldwin papers; Churchill to Dawson, *The Times* archive.

CHAPTER 10. 'TONIGHT SURRENDER: TOMORROW MAGNANIMITY': **p. 167**, Fraser to Churchill, Churchill telegram to newspaper proprietors, and Cadbury to Churchill, Churchill papers, 22/143; **p. 169**, Beaverbrook to Churchill and reply, Beaverbrook papers; **p. 170**, Amery diary, Amery papers; Cabinet minutes, (May 11), Cabinet papers, 23/52; Churchill to Beaverbrook, Beaverbrook papers; **p. 171**, Churchill to Baldwin, draft, Cherwell papers; meeting with editors, transcript, Churchill papers, 22/142; Churchill to Gwynne, Churchill papers, 22/142; **p. 172**, Gwynne to Churchill, Churchill papers, 22/142; Goschen to Churchill and reply, Treasury papers, 172/1558; Crawford, Lane-Fox, Dawson and Davidson to Irwin, Halifax papers; **p. 173**, Churchill to Hogg, Churchill papers, 18/29; Hogg to Churchill, Churchill papers, 2/147; **p. 174**, Baldwin to the King, Baldwin papers; Churchill to Gwynne, Churchill papers, 2/152.

CHAPTER 11. THE SEARCH FOR A SETTLEMENT: **p. 175**, Cabinet Coal Committee minutes, Churchill papers, 22/116; **p. 176**, Cabinet Committee on Trade Union Legislation, Committee minutes (June 3), Cabinet papers, 27/326; Cabinet minutes (June 9), Cabinet papers, 23/53; Churchill to Baldwin, Baldwin papers; **p. 177**, Coal Committee minutes (June 14), Churchill papers, 22/116; **p. 178**, Churchill to Baldwin, and Baldwin to the King, Baldwin papers; **p. 180**, Churchill to Balfour, Balfour papers; N. Chamberlain diary, N. Chamberlain papers; N. Chamberlain to Irwin, Halifax papers; **p. 181**, Lane-Fox to Irwin, Halifax papers; Joynson-Hicks to Baldwin, Baldwin papers; **p. 182**, Coal Committee minutes, Churchill papers, 22/116; **p. 183**, meeting with miners' leaders, stenographic notes, Churchill papers, 22/100; **p. 185**, Coal Committee minutes, Churchill papers, 22/116; **p. 186**, Jones to Baldwin, Baldwin papers; Joynson-Hicks to the King, Baldwin papers; **p. 187**, Churchill-MacDonald discussions, Baldwin papers; Churchill telegram to Baldwin, Churchill papers, 22/112; **p. 188**, Lane-Fox to Irwin, Halifax papers; Churchill telegram to Baldwin, Churchill papers, 22/112; **p. 189**, Lane-Fox to Irwin, Halifax papers; Churchill-MacDonald negotiations, Baldwin papers; Baldwin to Churchill, Baldwin papers; Jones to Baldwin, Baldwin papers; Coal Committee minutes, Churchill papers, 22/116; **p. 190**, Churchill to Baldwin, and Gower to Davidson, Baldwin papers; **p. 191**, Jones to Hankey, Hankey papers; Churchill to Baldwin, Churchill papers, 22/112; Steel-Maitland to Baldwin, Baldwin papers; **p. 192**, Jones to Baldwin, Baldwin papers; Baldwin to Churchill, Churchill papers, 22/112; Coal Committee minutes, Churchill papers, 22/117; **p. 193**, meeting with mine owners, stenographic notes, Churchill papers, 22/101; **p. 196**, Beaverbrook to Derby, Beaverbrook papers; **p. 197**, Londonderry to Churchill, Churchill papers, 22/112; Cabinet Committee (September 7), Churchill papers, 22/117; **p. 198**, Churchill to Baldwin, and Jones to Baldwin, Baldwin papers; **p. 199**, Churchill to Williams, Churchill papers, 22/113; Steel-Maitland to Baldwin, Baldwin papers; **p. 200**, Lane-Fox to Churchill, Churchill papers, 22/113; Jones to Baldwin, Baldwin papers; **p. 201**, Churchill to Stamfordham, Churchill papers, 22/113; Churchill to Baldwin, Churchill papers, 22/112; **p. 202**, Londonderry to Churchill, Churchill papers, 22/112; **p. 203**, Birkenhead to Churchill and reply, Churchill papers, 18/28; Churchill to Londonderry, Churchill papers, 22/112; **p. 204**, Coal Committee minutes, Churchill papers, 22/117; **p. 205**, Churchill to Gwynne, Churchill papers, 2/147; **p. 207**, Birkenhead to Irwin, Halifax papers; **p. 208**, Amery diary, Amery papers; **p. 211**, Baldwin to the King, Baldwin papers; **p. 212**, Baldwin to the King, Baldwin papers; Coal Committee minutes, Churchill papers, 22/117; **p. 213**, Lane-Fox to Irwin, Halifax papers; **p. 214**, Birkenhead to Irwin, Halifax papers; Coal Committee minutes, Churchill papers, 22/117; Boothby to Churchill, Churchill papers, 18/28; **p. 215**, Churchill to Boothby, Churchill papers, 18/29; **p. 216**, Churchill Cabinet memorandum, Churchill papers, 22/103; **p. 217**, Londonderry to Churchill and reply, Churchill papers, 18/28; Guest to Churchill, Churchill papers, 2/147; **p. 218**, Coal Committee minutes (November 5), Churchill papers 22/125 (November 10) Churchill papers, 22/117; **p. 219**, Lane-Fox to Irwin, Halifax papers; **p. 220**, Churchill to Hawkey, Churchill papers, 2/147; **p. 221**, Baldwin to the King, Baldwin papers.

CHAPTER 12. 'THE SMILING CHANCELLOR': **p. 222**, Churchill to Keyes, Keyes papers; Churchill to his son, Randolph Churchill papers; Sheepshanks to Churchill, Churchill papers, 1/188; **p. 223**, Churchill to Beaverbrook, Beaverbrook papers; **p. 224**, Churchill to Baldwin, Baldwin papers; **p. 225**, Graham to A. Chamberlain, and Churchill press statement, A. Chamberlain papers; **p. 227**, Baldwin to Churchill and reply, Churchill papers, 22/151; Grigg to Churchill, Churchill papers, 18/41; Churchill to Worthington-Evans, Churchill papers, 18/43; **p. 229**, Blumenfeld, N. Chamberlain, Boothby and Scribner to Churchill, Churchill papers, 8/208; **p. 230**, Le Maitre to Churchill, Churchill papers, 8/208; Churchill to Worthington-Evans, Churchill papers, 18/45; Niemeyer to Churchill, Churchill papers, 18/40; Churchill to Worthington-Evans, Churchill papers, 18/41; **p. 231**, Churchill to Niemeyer, and Churchill memorandum, Churchill papers, 18/45; Cabinet Committee minutes (February 10), Cabinet papers, 27/338; Deputation of March 9, Treasury papers, 171/264; Churchill note (February 18), Churchill papers, 2/155; **p. 232**, Churchill note (April 2), Churchill papers, 22/169; Cabinet Committee minutes (April 5), Churchill papers, 22/168; Cabinet minutes (April 6), Cabinet papers, 23/54; Churchill to the King, Churchill papers, 18/40; **p. 233**, Stamfordham to Churchill, Churchill papers, 18/40; Amery to Baldwin, and Baldwin to the King, Baldwin papers; **p. 234**, Goschen and McNeill to Churchill, Churchill papers, 2/151; Baldwin to the King, Baldwin papers; **p. 235**, Baldwin to the King, Baldwin papers; Churchill to Geddes, Churchill papers, 18/43; **p. 236**, Lane-Fox and Winterton to Irwin, Halifax papers.

CHAPTER 13. 'A PLAN FOR PROSPERITY': **p. 237**, Churchill to Niemeyer, Churchill papers, 18/45; Churchill to Niemeyer, Churchill papers, 18/71; **p. 238**, Churchill to

Hurst, Churchill papers, 18/64; **p. 239**, Churchill to Baldwin, Churchill papers, 18/43; **p. 241**, Churchill to N. Chamberlain, Churchill papers, 18/43; **p. 242**, Hurst to Churchill, Churchill to Hopkins, and N. Chamberlain to Churchill and reply, Churchill papers, 18/64; Hurst to Churchill, Churchill papers, 18/64; **p. 243**, Churchill note, Churchill papers, 22/151; Churchill to Beaverbrook, Beaverbrook papers; Irwin to N. Chamberlain, Halifax papers; Lloyd to Irwin, Halifax papers; **p. 244**, Churchill to Stamfordham, Churchill papers, 1/194; Churchill to Beaverbrook, Beaverbrook papers; **p. 245**, N. Chamberlain to Irwin, Halifax papers; **p. 246**, Baldwin to Irwin, and Wedgwood to Irwin, Halifax papers; Churchill to Hopkins and Hurst, and Hurst to Churchill, Churchill papers, 18/64; Churchill to N. Chamberlain, Churchill papers, 18/63; **p. 247**, Churchill to Baldwin, Baldwin papers; **p. 248**, Cabinet Committee minutes (October 26), and Churchill to Bridgeman, Churchill papers, 22/175; **p. 249**, Bridgeman to Churchill, Churchill papers, 22/175; Churchill to N. Chamberlain, Churchill papers, 18/64; **p. 250**, Churchill to Bridgeman, Churchill papers, 22/175; Churchill memorandum, Churchill papers, 22/173; Naval Programme Committee minutes, Cabinet papers, 27/355; **p. 252**, Churchill to Hopkins and Hurst, Churchill papers, 18/42; Treasury Conference minutes, Treasury papers, 175/12; **p. 253**, Churchill to Duckham and Hopkins, Churchill papers, 18/65; **p. 254**, Churchill memorandum, Grigg, Hopkins and Hurst to Churchill, Churchill papers, 18/65; **p. 255**, Churchill to Fisher and Hopkins, Churchill papers, 18/65; **p. 256**, Churchill revised memorandum, Churchill papers, 18/65; **p. 257**, Churchill to Baldwin, Baldwin papers; Churchill to N. Chamberlain, Churchill papers, 18/65; **p. 258**, Churchill to Cunliffe-Lister, Churchill papers, 18/44; N. Chamberlain to Churchill, Churchill papers, 18/65; Fisher to Churchill, Treasury papers, 175/13; Churchill to Fisher, and Duckham memorandum, Churchill papers, 18/65; **p. 259**, Churchill to Grigg, N. Chamberlain memorandum, and Macmillan memorandum, Churchill papers, 18/65; **p. 260**; N. Chamberlain to Irwin, Halifax papers; N. Chamberlain to Cunliffe-Lister, Swinton papers; **p. 261**; Weir to Churchill, and Churchill to Fergusson, Churchill papers, 18/65; Macmillan to Churchill, Churchill papers, 18/85; **p. 262**, Churchill to Hopkins, and Baldwin, Churchill papers, 18/85; **p. 263**, Churchill to Baldwin, Baldwin papers; Weir to Churchill and Churchill to Macmillan, Churchill papers, 18/85; **p. 264**, Baldwin to Churchill, Churchill papers, 18/85.

CHAPTER 14. 'EVERYONE BUT YOU IS FRIGHTENED': **p. 266**, Cabinet minutes (January 20), Churchill papers, 18/85 and Cabinet papers, 23/57; **p. 267**, Churchill to Balfour, Balfour papers; Cabinet Policy Committee minutes, Churchill papers, 18/86 and Cabinet papers, 27/364; **p. 268**, Churchill to his son, Randolph Churchill papers; **p. 269**, Cabinet minutes (February 15), Cabinet papers, 23/57; Churchill to Baldwin, Baldwin papers; Baldwin to Churchill, Churchill papers, 22/190; Churchill to his son, Randolph Churchill papers; **p. 270**, Cabinet minutes (February 17), Churchill papers, 18/77; Amery diary, Amery papers; Cabinet Committee minutes (February 27 and March 5), Churchill papers, 18/86; **p. 271**, Churchill to Grigg, Grigg papers; Grigg to Churchill, Churchill papers, 18/72; Churchill memorandum, Churchill papers, 18/87; **p. 272**, Cabinet Policy Committee minutes, Cabinet papers, 27/364; Churchill to N. Chamberlain, Churchill papers, 18/87; **p. 273**, N. Chamberlain to Churchill, and Macmillan to Churchill, Churchill papers, 18/87; Cabinet Committee minutes, Cabinet papers, 27/364; **p. 274**, Churchill to Anderson, and N. Chamberlain, Churchill papers, 18/88; Cabinet Committee minutes (March 26), Cabinet papers, 27/364; Cabinet Committee minutes (March 28), and Cabinet Committee report (March 29), Churchill papers, 18/89; **p. 275**, N. Chamberlain diary, N. Chamberlain papers; Baldwin to Churchill, Churchill papers, 18/72; Hoare to Irwin, Halifax papers; Cabinet minutes, (April 2), Cabinet papers, 23/57; **p. 276**, Amery diary, Amery papers; Cabinet minutes (April 3), Cabinet papers, 23/57; Churchill to Chamberlain and reply, Churchill papers, 18/89; **p. 277**, N. Chamberlain diary, N. Chamberlain papers; Cabinet minutes (April 4), Cabinet papers, 23/57; **p. 278**, Churchill to Cunliffe-Lister, and N. Chamberlain, Churchill papers, 18/73; Churchill to Baldwin,

Baldwin papers; **p. 279**, Cunliffe-Lister to Churchill, Churchill papers, 18/73; N. Chamberlain to Baldwin, Baldwin papers; Churchill to Baldwin, Baldwin papers, Baldwin to Churchill, Churchill papers, 18/89; **p. 280**, N. Chamberlain to Churchill, and Churchill to Grigg, Churchill papers, 18/75; Cabinet minutes (April 19), Cabinet papers, 23/57; **p. 281**, Cabinet minutes (April 20), Cabinet papers, 23/57; Amery diary, Amery papers; Churchill to the King, Churchill papers, 18/71; Baldwin to the King, Baldwin papers; **p. 283**, Baldwin to the King, Baldwin papers; Derby, Tyrrell and Balfour to Churchill, Churchill papers, 18/76; **p. 284**, Churchill to Balfour, Balfour papers; Guest to Churchill, Churchill papers, 18/76; Boothby to Churchill, Churchill papers, 2/158.

CHAPTER 15. 'VY INDEPENDENT OF THEM ALL': **p. 285**, Churchill to Hopkins, Churchill papers, 18/75; Churchill to Baldwin, Baldwin papers; **p. 286**, Baldwin to Churchill, Churchill papers, 18/90; **p. 287**, Churchill to Beaverbrook, Beaverbrook papers; Churchill to Baldwin, Baldwin papers; Churchill to N. Chamberlain, Churchill papers, 18/90; **p. 288**, Churchill to Baldwin and Baldwin to the King, Baldwin papers; Churchill to Bridgeman, Churchill papers, 18/73; Churchill to Grigg, Churchill papers, 18/75; **p. 289**, Churchill to Hopkins, Churchill papers, 22/218; Churchill memorandum, Churchill papers, 22/198; **p. 290**, Committee of Imperial Defence minutes, Churchill papers, 22/202; **p. 292**, Cabinet minutes (July 4), Cabinet papers, 23/58; Amery diary, Amery papers; Lane-Fox to Irwin, Halifax papers; **p. 293**, Churchill to Baldwin, and Derby to Churchill, Churchill papers, 2/158; **p. 294**, Randolph Churchill to his father, Churchill papers, 1/199; Amery diary, Amery papers; Beaverbrook to Mackenzie King, Beaverbrook papers; **p. 295**, N. Chamberlain to Irwin, Halifax papers; Page Croft to Baldwin (September 17), Baldwin papers.

CHAPTER 16. THE LAST YEAR OF THE BALDWIN GOVERNMENT: **p. 299**, Churchill to O'Malley, Churchill papers, 8/217; Baldwin to Churchill, Churchill papers, 1/200; Wilson to Churchill, (September 14), Churchill papers, 1/201; **p. 300**, Baldwin to Churchill, Churchill papers, 1/200; Churchill to Baldwin, Baldwin papers; Churchill to Alderman Lane (September 23), Churchill papers, 1/201; **p. 301**, Scrymgeour-Wedderburn diary, Dundee papers; **p. 304**, Churchill to Fergusson and Fisher, Churchill papers, 18/75; Cabinet minutes (October 17), Cabinet papers, 23/59; **p. 305**, Churchill memorandum of his Paris discussions, Churchill papers, 22/206; **p. 306**, Baldwin to Churchill, Churchill papers, 2/159; Amery diary, Amery papers; Beaverbrook to Amery, Beaverbrook papers; **p. 307**, Churchill to Rothermere, Churchill papers, 18/72; **p. 308**, Churchill Cabinet memorandum, Churchill papers, 22/208; Churchill to Lints Smith (December 27), Churchill papers, 8/219; **p. 309**, Churchill to Morton, Churchill papers, 8/217; Baldwin to Churchill, Churchill papers, 1/200; **p. 310**, Baldwin to Churchill, Churchill papers, 1/205; Churchill to Baldwin, Baldwin papers; Randolph Churchill to his father, Churchill papers, 1/205; Birley and Sheepshanks to Churchill, Churchill papers, 1/200; **p. 311**, Cabinet minutes (February 7), Cabinet papers, 23/60 and Churchill papers 22/326; **p. 314**, Beaverbrook to Borden, Beaverbrook papers; Amery diary, Amery papers; Amery to Baldwin, Baldwin papers; **p. 315**, Amery diary, Amery papers; **p. 316**, N. Chamberlain diary, N. Chamberlain papers; **p. 317**, Hoare, Snowden, Rosebery and Balfour to Churchill, Churchill papers, 8/224; **p. 318**, Morton, Vansittart and Lawrence to Churchill, Churchill papers, 8/224; **p. 319**, Churchill to Katherine Asquith, Churchill papers, 8/224; Churchill to Scribner and reply, Churchill papers, 8/225; Churchill to Marlborough, Churchill papers, 8/244; **p. 320**, Beaverbrook to Borden, Beaverbrook papers; Macmillan (March 27 and April 8), to Churchill, Churchill papers, 18/101; **p. 321**, Irwin to Churchill, Churchill papers, 8/224; Irwin to Baldwin, Baldwin papers; **p. 323**, Churchill to Baldwin, Baldwin papers; Grigg to Churchill, and Baldwin to Grigg, Churchill papers, 18/97; **p. 324**, Churchill to the King, Churchill papers, 18/97; **p. 325**, N. Chamberlain diary, N. Chamberlain papers; Baldwin to Churchill, Churchill papers, 18/101; **p. 326**, Amery to Baldwin, Baldwin papers; Churchill note, Churchill papers, 4/96; **p. 327**, Runciman to

Churchill, Churchill papers, 1/205; **p. 328**, Amery diary, Amery papers; **p. 329**, Lawrence to Marsh, Marsh papers.

CHAPTER 17. 'TRAVELS IN THE NEW WORLD': **p. 333**, Churchill to Ashley, Churchill papers, 8/223; **p. 334**, Churchill to Camrose, Churchill papers, 8/225; Churchill to Baruch, and Hearst, Churchill papers, 1/206; **p. 335**, Churchill to Baldwin, Baldwin papers; **p. 336**, Churchill to Beaverbrook, Churchill papers, 2/164; Amery diary, Amery papers; Inchcape to Churchill, Churchill papers, 1/211; **p. 337**, Churchill note, Churchill papers, 4/113; Churchill to Camrose, Churchill papers, 8/225; **p. 338**, Churchill to Beaverbrook, Beaverbrook papers; Amery diary, Amery papers; **p. 349**, Campbell to Churchill, Churchill papers, 1/207; **p. 350**, Churchill's unpublished 'American Impressions', Churchill papers, 8/592.

CHAPTER 18. A GROWING ISOLATION: **p. 352**; Hoare to Irwin, Halifax papers; **p. 353**, Salisbury to Baldwin, Baldwin papers; Irwin to Dulverton, Halifax papers; **p. 354**, Irwin to Lane-Fox, Halifax papers; Irwin to Hoare, Templewood papers; Davidson and Dawson to Irwin, Halifax papers; **p. 355**, Hoare, Lane-Fox, Davidson and Winterton to Irwin, Halifax papers; **p. 357**, Irwin to Churchill, Churchill papers, 2/164; **p. 358**, Churchill to Reith, Churchill papers, 2/169; **p. 359**, Rothermere to Beaverbrook, Beaverbrook papers; **p. 360**, Beaverbrook to Rothermere, Beaverbrook papers; Randolph Churchill to his father, Churchill papers, 1/214; **p. 362**, Fisher to Irwin, Halifax papers; **p. 363**, Churchill to Baldwin, Baldwin papers, Baldwin to Churchill, Churchill papers, 2/159; **p. 364**, Lawrence to Churchill, Churchill papers, 8/269; Churchill to Baldwin, Baldwin papers; **p. 365**, Grigg, Ramsay MacDonald and Trevelyan to Churchill, Churchill papers, 8/269; Churchill to Beaverbrook, Beaverbrook papers.

CHAPTER 19. 'A REAL PARTING OF THE WAYS': **p. 367**, Lane-Fox, MacDonald, Dawson and Hoare to Irwin, Halifax papers; **p. 368**, Irwin to Curtis and to Dawson, Halifax papers; **p. 369**, Lane-Fox to Irwin, Halifax papers; Churchill to Baldwin, Baldwin papers; Jacob to Churchill, Churchill papers, 2/174; **p. 370**, Burnham to Churchill, Churchill to Jacob, and Hunter to Churchill, Churchill papers, 2/174; **p. 371**, Churchill to Baldwin, Churchill papers, 2/169; **p. 372**, Baldwin to Churchill, Churchill papers, 2/169; Bismarck memorandum, German Diplomatic archives, A2386–K567889–92; **p. 373**, Baldwin and N. Chamberlain to Churchill, Churchill papers, 2/169; Davidson to Baldwin, Baldwin papers; Weir to Churchill, and Knutsford to Churchill, Churchill papers, 8/269; Amery diary, Amery papers; Clementine Churchill to her son, Randolph Churchill papers; **p. 375**, N. Chamberlain to Donner, Donner papers; **p. 377**, Irwin to Dawson, and Hailey to Irwin, Halifax papers; **p. 378**, Dawson, Schuster and Hailey to Irwin, Halifax papers; **p. 379**, Churchill to his son, Randolph Churchill papers; Churchill to Marlborough, Churchill papers, 8/289; **p. 380**, Irwin to Baldwin, Baldwin papers; **p. 382**, Lane-Fox to Irwin, Halifax papers; **p. 383**, Churchill to Baldwin, Baldwin papers; Baldwin to Churchill, Churchill papers, 2/177; **p. 384**, Cadogan to Baldwin, Baldwin papers.

CHAPTER 20. 'THE CONSERVATIVE PARTY IS WITH ME': **p. 385**, Hunter and Rothermere to Churchill, Churchill papers, 2/180; **p. 386**, Churchill to Rothermere, Churchill papers, 2/180; **p. 387**, Churchill to Whitley, Churchill papers, 2/183; Rothermere to Churchill, Churchill papers, 2/180; Churchill to his son, Randolph Churchill papers; **p. 388**, Amery diary, Amery papers; **p. 389**, Churchill to Rothermere, Churchill papers, 2/180; Bracken to Randolph Churchill, Randolph Churchill papers; **p. 391**, Churchill to Lindemann, Churchill papers, 8/292; Topping to N. Chamberlain, Baldwin papers; Churchill to his son, Randolph Churchill papers; **p. 392**, Brooke to Baldwin, Baldwin papers; Lane-Fox to Irwin, Halifax papers; **p. 394**, Dawson, Spender-Clay and Davidson to Irwin, Halifax papers; **p. 396**, Bridgeman to Baldwin, Baldwin papers; **p. 400**, Beaverbrook to Garvin, Beaverbrook papers; Churchill to Hunter, Churchill papers, 2/180;

Churchill to Butterworth, Churchill papers, 8/294; **p. 401**, Amery diary, Amery papers; Churchill to Irwin, and Irwin to Davidson, Halifax papers; Churchill to Boothby, Boothby papers; **p. 403**, Ameer Ali to Churchill, Churchill papers, 2/180.

CHAPTER 21. CHURCHILL'S FINAL ISOLATION: **p. 406**, Bismarck memorandum, German Diplomatic archives, A2386–K567887–889; **p. 407**, Bernstorff minute, German Diplomatic archives, A2386–K567878; Churchill to his son, Randolph Churchill papers; **p. 411**, Churchill to Marsh, Marsh papers; Horne to N. Chamberlain, Baldwin papers; **p. 412**, Hordern to Churchill, Churchill papers, 8/287; Churchill to Bracken, Churchill papers, 8/290; Hoare to N. Chamberlain, Templewood papers; **p. 413**, Churchill to Reading (13 May 1933), Churchill papers, 2/201; **p. 414**, Hankey diary, Hankey papers; **p. 415**, Butterworth to Churchill, Churchill papers, 8/294; **p. 416**, Hordern to Churchill, Churchill papers, 8/287; Butterworth to Churchill, Churchill papers, 8/294; **p. 417**, Churchill to Hordern, Churchill papers, 8/287; Dewar to Churchill, Churchill papers, 8/291; **p. 419**, Hoare to Willingdon, Willingdon papers.

CHAPTER 22. A SERIOUS ACCIDENT: **p. 420**, Churchill to Baruch, Baruch papers; Bracken to Churchill, Churchill papers, 8/290; Churchill to his son, Randolph Churchill papers; **p. 421**, Clementine Churchill to her son, and Randolph Churchill to his father, Randolph Churchill papers; Lindemann to Churchill, Cherwell papers; **p. 422**, Churchill to Harrap, Churchill papers, 8/289; Churchill to his son, Randolph Churchill papers; Churchill to Harmsworth, Churchill papers, 8/289; Churchill to his son (November 3), Churchill papers, 1/226; **p. 423**, Churchill to his son, and Clementine Churchill to her son, Randolph Churchill papers; Lady Leslie to Churchill, Churchill papers, 1/284; **p. 424**, Churchill to his son, Randolph Churchill papers; **p. 425**, Churchill to Hawkey, Hawkey papers; Churchill to Boothby, Boothby papers; **p. 426**, Churchill to Harmsworth, Churchill papers, 8/309; **p. 427**, Scribner to Churchill, Churchill papers, 8/314; Churchill to Butterworth, Churchill papers, 8/312.

CHAPTER 23. 'NOT EXHIBITING THIS YEAR': **p. 428**, Churchill to Salisbury, Salisbury papers; Churchill to Marsh, Marsh papers; Royal Academy speech notes, Churchill papers, 9/102; **p. 430**, Baldwin to Churchill, Churchill papers, 1/231; **p. 431**, Churchill to Baldwin, Baldwin papers; Churchill broadcast to the USA, transcript, Churchill papers, 9/102; Churchill to his son, Randolph Churchill papers; **p. 432**, Churchill to Boothby, Boothby papers; **p. 433**, Hoare to Willingdon, Willingdon papers; Hoare to MacDonald, Templewood papers; **p. 434**, Churchill to Simon, Foreign Office papers, 800/287; Marsh to Clementine Churchill, Spencer-Churchill papers; **p. 435**, Stanley to Churchill and reply, and Churchill to Crawford, Churchill papers, 1/232; Churchill to Vickers, Churchill papers, 1/235; **p. 436**, Churchill to Alber, Alber papers; **p. 437**, Churchill to Feiling, Churchill papers, 8/307; Churchill to Marlborough, Churchill papers, 8/315; **p. 438**, Jack Churchill to Churchill, Churchill papers, 1/236; **p. 439**, Churchill to Marsh, Marsh papers; Butterworth to Churchill, Churchill papers, 8/312; Churchill to Marlborough, Pakenham-Walsh and Harrap, Churchill papers, 8/315; **p. 440**, Amery diary, Amery papers; Hoare to MacDonald, Templewood papers; **p. 441**, Hoare to Anderson, Templewood papers; Hoare to Willingdon, Willingdon papers; Mrs Pearman to Miss Pearn, Churchill papers, 8/313; Churchill to Flower, Churchill papers, 8/307.

CHAPTER 24. 'TELL THE TRUTH TO THE BRITISH PEOPLE': **p. 447**, Simon to Rumbold Rumbold papers; **p. 450**, Amery to Churchill and reply, Churchill papers, 2/184; **p. 453**, Noyes to Churchill, Churchill papers, 8/307; Guest to Churchill, Churchill papers, 2/184; **p. 454**, Baldwin to Hoare, Templewood papers; **p. 455**, Cabinet minutes (February 15), Cabinet papers, 23/75; **p. 456**, Donner to Churchill, Churchill papers, 2/192; Churchill to Cecil, Quickswood papers; **p. 458**, Cabinet minutes (March 15), Cabinet papers, 23/75; **p. 462**, Custance to Churchill, Churchill papers, 2/192; Morton to Churchill, Churchill papers, 9/103.

CHAPTER 25. A PARTY DIVIDED: **p. 464**, Sydenham to Churchill and reply, Churchill papers, 2/192; Hoare to Baldwin, Baldwin papers; Hoare to Willingdon, Templewood papers; **p. 465**, Salisbury to Churchill and reply, Churchill papers, 2/192; **p. 466**, Hoare to Willingdon, Templewood papers; Duchess of Atholl to Baldwin, Baldwin papers; **p. 467**, Carson, and Knox, to Churchill, Churchill papers, 2/192; Amery diary, Amery papers; Hoare to Willingdon, Templewood papers; **p. 468**, Willingdon to Hoare and reply, Templewood papers; **p. 469**, Churchill to Margesson, Churchill papers, 2/192; **p. 470**, Cabinet minute (March 10), Cabinet papers, 23/75; **p. 471**, Hoare to Willingdon, Templewood papers; **p. 472**, Willingdon to Hoare and reply, Templewood papers; **p. 473**, Gretton to Churchill, Churchill papers, 2/192; Hoare to Willingdon, Templewood papers; **p. 474**, Churchill to Banks, and Carson, Churchill papers, 2/192; Churchill to Gretton, Churchill papers, 2/193; Churchill to Page Croft, Croft papers; Hoare to Churchill, Churchill papers, 2/192; **p. 475**, Churchill to Salisbury, and Hoare and Gwynne to Churchill, Churchill papers, 2/193; **p. 476**, Churchill to Hoare and reply, Churchill papers, 2/193; Hoare to Willingdon, Templewood papers; **p. 477**, Burnham to Churchill and Churchill to Diggle, Churchill papers, 2/193; Hoare to Willingdon, Templewood papers; **p. 479**, Linlithgow to Churchill and reply, and Churchill to Rothermere, Churchill papers, 2/193; **p. 480**, Linlithgow to Churchill and reply, Churchill papers, 2/193; **p. 481**, Hoare to Willingdon, Templewood papers; Churchill to Salisbury, Salisbury papers; Willingdon to Hoare, Templewood papers; **p. 482**, Hoare to Willingdon, Templewood papers; Linlithgow to Churchill, Churchill papers, 2/193.

CHAPTER 26. 'THERE IS NO TIME TO LOSE': **p. 485**, Churchill to Linlithgow, Churchill papers, 2/193; Rumbold to Simon, Rumbold papers; **p. 487**, Cabinet minutes (May 5 and 10), Cabinet papers, 23/76; Herring memorandum, Foreign Office papers, 371/16733; **p. 488**, Cabinet minutes (July 26), Cabinet papers, 23/76; **p. 489**, Duff Cooper to Churchill, Churchill papers, 2/201; Cabinet minutes (September 5 and 20), Cabinet papers, 23/77; **p. 490**, Cabinet minutes (October 9), Cabinet papers, 23/77; **p. 491**, Cabinet minutes (October 18), Cabinet papers, 23/77; Londonderry memorandum, Cabinet papers, 24/243; **p. 492**, Cabinet minutes (October 23), Cabinet papers, 23/77; **p. 493**, Hamilton to Churchill, Churchill papers, 8/326; **p. 495**, Cabinet minutes (November 15 and 29), Cabinet papers, 23/77.

CHAPTER 27. AUTHORSHIP, INDIA AND REARMAMENT: **p. 496**, Baldwin, N. Chamberlain, Grigg and Riddell to Churchill, Churchill papers, 8/326; **p. 497**, Hoare to Anderson, Templewood papers; Churchill to Ashley, Churchill papers, 8/324; Duchess of Atholl to Churchill, Churchill papers, 2/194; **p. 498**, Ameer Ali to Churchill, Churchill papers, 2/194; Hoare to Willingdon, Templewood papers; **p. 499**, Baldwin to Churchill, Churchill papers, 8/325; Churchill to Baldwin, Baldwin papers; Churchill to Edmonds, Churchill papers, 8/483; **p. 500**, Churchill to Owen, Churchill papers, 8/483; Churchill to Ashley, Churchill papers, 8/484; **p. 501**, Namier to Churchill and Churchill to Wheldon, Churchill papers, 8/484; **p. 505**, Hutchison, diary, Hutchison papers; **p. 506**, Vansittart to Hankey and reply, Cabinet papers, 21/434; **p. 509**, Cabinet minutes (March 14 and 19), Cabinet papers, 23/78; **p. 510**, Creedy to Hankey, Cabinet papers, 21/384; Beaverbrook to Borden, Beaverbrook papers.

CHAPTER 28. THE COMMITTEE OF PRIVILEGES: **p. 512**, McWhirter, and Crawford, to Churchill, Churchill papers, 2/213; **p. 513**, Savoy Hotel meeting notes, Churchill papers, 2/213; **p. 514**, Churchill to Lloyd George, Churchill papers, 2/213; **p. 515**, Hoare to Willingdon (five letters) and Willingdon to Hoare (two letters), Templewood papers; **p. 516**, Robinson to Churchill and Churchill to Salisbury, Churchill papers, 2/213; Streat to Derby, Derby papers; **p. 517**, Salisbury to Churchill, Churchill papers, 2/213; Hoare to Bond, Derby papers; Robinson to Churchill, Churchill papers, 2/213; **p. 518**, Robinson to Churchill and Churchill to the Speaker, Churchill papers, 2/213; **p. 519**, Churchill to

Hoare and Derby, and Derby to Churchill, Churchill papers, 2/213; India Mission telegram, Derby papers; Downie to Churchill (11 June 1934), Churchill papers, 2/214; **p. 523**, Robinson to Churchill, Churchill papers, 2/213; **p. 524**, Hoare to Willingdon, Templewood papers; **p. 525**, Committee of Privileges transcript, Churchill papers, 2/213; **p. 528**, Cyril Asquith to Churchill, Churchill papers, 2/213; **p. 529**, Committee of Privileges to Churchill, Churchill papers, 2/213; India Office discussion, Derby papers; **p. 530**, Derby to Kershaw and reply, and Derby to Streat, Derby papers; **p. 531**, Derby to Streat, Derby papers, Hoare to Willingdon, Templewood papers, Churchill to Mac-Donald, Premier papers, 1/162; MacDonald to Churchill, Churchill papers, 2/214; Brabourne to Hoare, Templewood papers; **p. 532**, Churchill to MacDonald, Premier papers, 1/162 and MacDonald to Churchill, and Robinson to Churchill, Churchill papers, 2/214; Hoare to Derby, Derby papers; Churchill memorandum, Randolph Churchill papers; **p. 533**, Derby to Streat, Derby papers; **p. 534**, Cyril Asquith to Churchill, Churchill papers, 2/214; **p. 535**, Hoare to Stanley (May 11 and 17), Templewood papers; **p. 536**, Hoare to Stanley (May 22 and June 1), Templewood papers; O'Connor to Churchill, Churchill papers, 2/214; **p. 538**, Hoare to Stanley, Templewood papers; Cannell, Lygon and Halsbury to Churchill, Churchill papers, 2/214; **p. 542**, Select Committee of Witnesses, evidence, Churchill papers, 2/242; **p. 546**, Wolmer and Rankin to Churchill, Churchill papers, 2/205; Cyril Asquith to Churchill, Churchill papers, 2/214; **p. 547**, Churchill to Asquith and Sinclair to Churchill, Churchill papers, 2/214; Hoare to Stanley, Templewood papers; **p. 548**, Lady Lambton to Churchill, Churchill papers, 2/205; Wolmer to Churchill, Selborne papers; Lloyd to Churchill, Churchill papers, 2/215.

CHAPTER 29. 'SOUNDING A WARNING': **p. 549**, Sinclair to Churchill, Churchill papers, 1/255; **p. 550**, Lady Lambton to Churchill, Churchill papers, 2/205; Machin to Churchill, Churchill papers, 2/204; **p. 551**, Cabinet minutes (April 13), Cabinet papers, 23/78; Cabinet Committee minutes (May 3, June 25 and July 2), Cabinet papers, 27/507; Cabinet sub-committee minutes, Cabinet papers, 21/389; **p. 552**, Cabinet committee minutes (July 6 and 10), Cabinet papers, 27/514; **p. 553**, Hankey note, Cabinet papers, 21/389; Londonderry to Baldwin, Baldwin papers; Cabinet minutes (July 31), Cabinet papers, 23/79; **p. 554**, Fellowes to Churchill, Churchill papers, 2/228; **p. 556**, Secret Air Ministry memorandum of May 1938, Air Ministry papers, 8/238; **p. 557**, O'Connor to Churchill, Churchill papers, 2/221; Rothermere to Churchill and reply, Churchill papers, 2/228; **p. 558**, Rothermere and Morton to Churchill, Churchill papers, 2/228; **p. 559**, Hankey to Baldwin, Baldwin papers; **p. 560**, Riddell to Churchill, Churchill papers, 8/491; Wedgwood to Churchill, Churchill papers, 2/208; Baldwin to Churchill, Churchill papers, 1/255; Siepmann to Churchill, Churchill papers, 8/495; **p. 561**, Churchill to Korda, Churchill papers, 8/495; Churchill to Feiling, Churchill papers, 8/486; **p. 562**, Churchill to Korda, Churchill papers, 8/495; **p. 563**, Churchill to Korda, Churchill papers, 8/495; Corfield to Churchill, Churchill papers, 8/481; **p. 564**, Churchill to Geddes, Churchill papers, 2/209; Edmonds, Baldwin, Morton, McGowan and Darling to Churchill, Churchill papers, 8/487; **p. 565**, Churchill draft note, Churchill papers, 4/113; Barnes to Churchill, Churchill papers, 8/481; **p. 566**, Sargent to Churchill, Churchill papers, 2/229; **p. 567**, Filson Young to Churchill, Churchill papers, 2/210; Captain Balfour to Churchill, Churchill papers, 2/211; **p. 568**, Harmsworth to Churchill, Churchill papers, 2/221; Londonderry to MacDonald, Premier papers, 1/155; Cabinet minutes (November 21), Cabinet papers, 23/80; **p. 569**, Cabinet Committee minutes, Cabinet papers, 27/572; Morton to Churchill, Churchill papers, 2/228; **p. 570**, Lindemann and Morton to Churchill, Churchill papers, 2/228; **p. 571**, Churchill to Lloyd George, Churchill papers, 2/228; Cabinet Committee minutes, and Air Ministry memorandum, Cabinet papers, 27/572; Wigram memorandum, Foreign Office papers, 371/17696; **p. 572**, Cabinet minutes (November 26), Cabinet papers, 23/80; Simon to Phipps, Air Ministry papers, 2/1355; **p. 577**, Morton to Churchill, Churchill papers, 2/228; **p. 578**, Morton and Lindemann to Churchill, Churchill papers, 2/228; **p. 579**, Coote to Churchill, Churchill papers, 2/228;

Hoare to Willingdon, Templewood papers; **p. 580**, Nellie Romilly to Randolph Churchill, Randolph Churchill papers; Pakenham-Walsh and Fitzroy to Churchill, Churchill papers, 1/256; O'Connor to Churchill, Churchill papers, 1/255.

CHAPTER 30. 'A VERY STERN FIGHT BEFORE US': **p. 581**, Donner to Churchill, Churchill papers, 2/226; Baldwin to Derby, Derby papers; **p. 582**, Derby to Baldwin, Baldwin papers; Hoare to Stanley, Templewood papers; Churchill to his son, Randolph Churchill papers; Churchill to Watts, Churchill papers, 2/215; **p. 583**, Page Croft to Churchill, and Churchill to Watts, Churchill papers, 2/215; Hoare to Stanley, Templewood papers; Churchill to Chorlton, Churchill papers, 2/215; **p. 584**, Churchill to Cyril Asquith, Churchill papers, 2/207; Churchill to Spencer-Churchill, Churchill papers, 2/225; Churchill to Ray, Churchill papers, 2/227; Hoare to Willingdon, Templewood papers; **p. 585**, Willingdon to Reading, Reading papers; Page Croft to Churchill, Churchill papers, 2/225; Diggle to Churchill, Churchill papers, 2/215; Churchill to Colvin, Churchill papers, 8/486; Brabourne to Baldwin, Baldwin papers; **p. 586**, Churchill to Wolmer, and Page Croft and Melchett to Churchill, Churchill papers, 2/225; **p. 587**, Hoare to Brabourne, Templewood papers; **p. 588**, Donner to Churchill, Churchill papers, 2/227; Hoare to Willingdon, Templewood papers; O'Connor, Emery and Morton to Churchill, Churchill papers, 2/221; **p. 589**, N. Chamberlain to Hoare, Templewood papers; **p. 591**, Churchill to Rothermere, Churchill papers, 2/246; Hoare to Willingdon, Templewood papers; **p. 592**, Churchill press statement, Churchill papers, 2/246; Churchill to his wife, Churchill papers, 1/273; Churchill to Pickhardt, Churchill papers, 2/234; **p. 593**, Churchill to his wife, Churchill papers, 1/273; **p. 594**, Churchill to Carson and to Duff Cooper and reply, Churchill papers, 2/246; **p. 597**, Hoare to Willingdon, Templewood papers; Churchill to Westminster, Churchill papers, 2/246; Churchill to his wife, Churchill papers, 4/141; **p. 599**, Churchill to his son, Churchill papers, 2/246; **p. 600**, Churchill to his wife, Churchill papers, 1/273; **p. 601**, Hoare to Willingdon, Templewood papers.

CHAPTER 31. THE FINAL CHALLENGE: **p. 604**, Hoare to Willingdon, Templewood papers; **p. 605**, Hoare to Willingdon, Templewood papers, **p. 608**, Hoare to Willingdon, Templewood papers; **p. 611**, Willingdon to Hoare, Templewood papers; Churchill to his wife, Churchill papers, 1/273; **p. 613**, Donner to Churchill, Churchill papers, 2/235; **p. 614**, Hoare to Willingdon, Templewood papers; Page Croft to Churchill, Churchill papers, 2/240; **p. 615**, Addison to Churchill, Churchill papers, 2/236; **p. 616**, Churchill to Morgan, and to Butler, Churchill papers, 2/236; **p. 617**, Churchill to Linlithgow, Churchill papers, 2/236; **p. 618**, Birla to Gandhi, Birla papers; **p. 619**, Birla to Churchill, Churchill papers, 2/240.

CHAPTER 32. 'WE CAN NEVER CATCH UP': **p. 623**, Cabinet minutes (December 11), Cabinet papers, 27/572; Churchill to Londonderry, Churchill papers, 2/211; Churchill to Trevelyan, Churchill papers, 2/234; Lindemann to Londonderry, Premier papers, 1/253; **p. 624**, Lindemann to Churchill and reply and Lindemann to Churchill (January 22), Churchill papers, 2/243; **p. 625**, Wigram and Vansittart minutes, Foreign Office papers, 371/18828; **p. 626**, Fisher to Baldwin, Baldwin papers; **p. 630**, Phipps to the Foreign Office, Foreign Office papers, 371/18828; **p. 631**, Creswell memorandum and Wigram minute, Foreign Office papers, 371/18828; **p. 632**, Creswell note, Foreign Office papers, 371/18828; Captain Don's report, and Creswell and Wigram minutes, and Bullock to the Foreign Office, Foreign Office papers, 371/18833; **p. 633**, Vansittart minute, Foreign Office papers, 371/18833; **p. 634**, Wigram minute, Foreign Office papers, 371/18832; Simon to MacDonald, Baldwin papers; **p. 635**, Air strength correspondence (of 1947 and 1948), Churchill papers, 4/143; **p. 636**, Londonderry memorandum, Weir papers; Wigram to Churchill, Churchill papers, 2/235; Creswell minute, and Vansittart to Simon, Foreign Office papers, 371/18836; **p. 637**, Churchill memorandum, Cabinet papers, 21/419; **p. 639**, Creswell minute, Foreign Office papers, 371/18837; Page Croft to Churchill, Churchill papers, 2/243; Churchill to Tyrrell, Churchill papers, 2/235; Churchill to MacDonald, Churchill papers, 2/243; Churchill to Baldwin, Baldwin papers; **p. 640**, Londonderry to Churchill, and Churchill to Rothermere, Churchill papers, 2/243; Ministerial Committee minutes, Foreign Office papers, 371/18839; Morton to Churchill (May 13), Churchill papers, 2/243; **p. 642**, Stanhope note (September 20), Foreign Office papers, 371/18850; **p. 643**, Ava Wigram to Churchill, Churchill papers, 2/235; **p. 644**, Air strength correspondence (of 1947 and 1948), Churchill papers, 4/143; **p. 645**, Wigram to Churchill, Churchill papers, 2/235; Hankey to MacDonald, Cabinet papers, 21/406; **p. 646**, Churchill to Camrose, Churchill papers, 2/235; Churchill to Pakenham-Walsh, Churchill papers, 8/503.

CHAPTER 33. 'EVERY DAY COUNTS': **p. 647**, Defence Requirements Committee report (May 8), Weir papers; Defence Requirements Committee minutes (May 10), Foreign Office papers, 371/18840; **p. 648**, Hitler to Rothermere, and Churchill to Rothermere, Churchill papers, 2/235; **p. 649**, Rothermere to Churchill, Churchill papers, 2/243; Camrose to Churchill, Churchill papers, 2/235; Gwynne to Churchill and reply, Churchill papers, 2/243; Wigram and Creswell minutes, Foreign Office papers, 371/18839; **p. 650**, Cabinet conclusions (May 21), Weir papers; Ava Wigram and Tyrrell to Churchill, Churchill papers, 2/235; **p. 651**, Wigram to Churchill (and enclosures), Churchill papers, 2/243; **p. 653**, Morton to Churchill, Churchill papers, 2/243; Churchill to his son, Churchill papers, 1/271; Churchill to Horne, Churchill papers, 2/243; Churchill to Eidenow, Churchill papers, 8/502; **p. 654**, Churchill to Ava Wigram, Churchill papers, 1/271; Churchill to Baldwin, Baldwin papers; Baldwin to Churchill, Churchill papers, 2/236; **p. 655**, Churchill to Baldwin, Baldwin papers; Wigram to Churchill, Churchill papers, 2/236; **p. 656**, Morton to Churchill, and Churchill to Flandin, Churchill papers, 2/236; Committee of Imperial Defence memorandum (ADR 21), Churchill papers, 4/81–3; Churchill to Cunliffe-Lister, Swinton papers; **p. 657**, Cunliffe-Lister to Churchill, Churchill papers, 25/4; **p. 658**, Air Defence Research sub-committee minutes (July 25 and September 16), Cabinet papers, 16/132; **p. 659**, Weir to Cunliffe-Lister, Weir papers; **p. 660**, Churchill draft letter, Churchill papers, 25/4; **p. 661**, Morton to Churchill, Churchill papers, 2/244; Industrial Intelligence memorandum (28 January 1938), Foreign Office papers, 371/21666; Committee of Imperial Defence minutes, (31 March 1938), Cabinet papers, 24/276; **p. 662**, Hoare, Eden, Churchill conversation, record, Templewood papers; **p. 663**, Churchill to Hoare, Churchill papers, 4/84–5; **p. 664**, Hoare to Churchill, Churchill papers, 2/236; Churchill to Hoare, Churchill papers, 2/244; Garvin to Churchill, Churchill papers, 2/237; **p. 667**, Thornton Kemsley diary, Thornton Kemsley papers; Churchill to Chatfield, Churchill papers, 2/244; **p. 668**, Churchill to Keyes, Churchill papers, 2/244; Baldwin to Churchill, Churchill papers, 2/237; **p. 669**, A. Chamberlain, McGowan, Sitwell and Bateman to Churchill, Churchill papers, 2/237; **p. 670**, Churchill to Vansittart, Churchill papers, 4/84–5, Vansittart to Churchill and Churchill to A. Chamberlain, Churchill papers, 2/237; **p. 671**, Churchill unpublished note, Churchill papers, 4/84–5; Winterton and Morton to Churchill, Churchill papers, 2/244; **p. 672**, Churchill to Winterton, Churchill papers, 2/244; Morton to Churchill (October 1), Churchill papers, 2/247; Admiralty minute (28 September 1939), and Churchill minute (8 October 1939), Churchill papers, 19/3; **p. 673**, Churchill memorandum (September 30), Foreign Office papers, 371/18852; **p. 674**, Churchill to Cunliffe-Lister, Churchill papers, 25/4; **p. 675**, Churchill to Feiling, Churchill papers, 8/506; **p. 676**, Baldwin to Churchill, Churchill papers, 2/237; Churchill to Baldwin, Baldwin papers; Consuelo Balsan and Sinclair to Churchill, Churchill papers, 2/237.

CHAPTER 34. NO PLACE FOR CHURCHILL: **p. 677**, Marjorie Maxse to Churchill, Churchill papers, 2/245; Morton to Churchill, Churchill papers, 2/237; **p. 678**, Morton to Churchill (October 26 and 16), 2/237; **p. 679**, Phipps telegram, Foreign Office papers, 371/18878; Muirhead Gould to Churchill, Churchill papers, 2/237; Wigram minutes (October 29 and 30), and Phipps telegram, Foreign Office papers, 371/18880; Morton to Churchill (June 26), Churchill papers, 8/518; **p. 681**, Phipps telegram, Foreign Office papers, 371/18880; **p. 682**, Phipps telegram and Wigram minute, Foreign Office papers, 371/18880; Randolph Churchill to his father, Randolph Churchill papers; Churchill to Bailey, Churchill papers, 2/237; Richard Law, and the Conservative Central Office, to Churchill, Churchill papers, 2/245; **p. 683**, Law and Lennox-Boyd to Churchill, Churchill papers, 2/245; Strakosch to Churchill and reply, and Morton to Churchill (November 4 and 7), Churchill papers, 2/244; **p. 684**, Phipps to Hoare, Foreign Office papers, 371/18851; **p. 685**, Vansittart minute, Foreign Office papers, 371/18851; Churchill note, Churchill papers, 4/141; Cabinet minutes (December 4), Cabinet papers, 23/82; **p. 686**, Nancy Astor to Baldwin, Baldwin papers; Keyes to Churchill, Churchill papers, 2/245; Churchill note, Churchill papers, 4/141; Bridges and Greene to Churchill, Churchill papers, 1/272; George Spencer-Churchill to Churchill, Churchill papers, 2/238; **p. 687**, Churchill to Flandin, and Guest and Tudor to Churchill, Churchill papers, 2/238; Feiling to Churchill, Churchill papers, 8/506; **p. 688**, Feiling to Churchill and reply, Churchill papers, 8/506; Air Defence Research sub-committee minutes (December 9), Cabinet papers, 16/132; Churchill note, Foreign Office papers, 371/18852; Churchill private letters of 15 February 1939, Churchill papers, 1/343 and 29 April 1939, Churchill papers, 2/235; **p. 689**, Lawford and Wigram minutes, Foreign Office papers, 371/18852.

CHAPTER 35. HOPING FOR A CABINET POST: **p. 691**, Randolph Churchill to his father Churchill papers, 2/238; **p. 692**, Randolph Churchill to his father (December 16 and 17), Churchill papers, 2/238; **p. 693**, Morton to Churchill, Churchill papers, 2/238; **p. 694**, Churchill to his son, Randolph Churchill papers; Churchill to Hoare, Templewood papers; **p. 696**, Grigg to Churchill, Churchill papers, 2/261; **p. 698**, Churchill to Rothermere, Churchill papers, 2/287; **p. 699**, Bracken to Churchill, Churchill papers, 2/287; **p. 700**, Barnes to Churchill, Churchill papers, 1/284; Carr to Churchill, Churchill papers 8/533; **p. 701**, Churchill to Barnes, Churchill papers, 1/284; Hankey to Churchill, Cabinet papers, 21/419; Churchill to Hankey (not sent, draft), Churchill papers, 27/5; **p. 702**, Churchill to Hankey, Cabinet papers, 21/419; Randolph Churchill to his father, Churchill papers, 2/287; Beaverbrook to Hoare, Beaverbrook papers; **p. 703**, Churchill to Astor and reply, Churchill papers, 2/287; Boothby to Churchill, Churchill papers, 2/251; **p. 704**, Morton to Churchill, Churchill papers, 2/281; Duchess of Atholl to Churchill, Churchill papers, 2/275; Defence Policy and Requirements Committee report, Cabinet papers, 23/83; **p. 705**, Swinton memorandum, Cabinet papers, 24/259; Cabinet minutes (February 25), Cabinet papers, 23/83; Ormsby-Gore to Baldwin, Premier papers, 1/196; **p. 706**, Hankey to Fisher, and Fisher to N. Chamberlain, Cabinet papers, 21/424; A. Chamberlain to his sister, A. Chamberlain papers; A. Chamberlain to Sandys, Churchill papers, 2/251; Jones to Lady Grigg, Grigg papers; **p. 707**, Hoare to N. Chamberlain, Templewood papers; Keyes to Churchill, Churchill papers, 2/251; **p. 708**, Crossley poem, Churchill papers; **p. 708**, Chiozza Money to Churchill, Churchill papers, 2/252; **p. 710**, Swinton minute, Cabinet papers, 21/422A; **p. 712**, Melchett to Churchill, Churchill papers, 2/266; Cabinet minutes (March 11), Cabinet papers, 23/83; **p. 713**, Foreign Office Affairs Committee minutes, Premier papers, 1/194; **p. 714**, Chiozza Money and Taylor to Churchill, Churchill papers, 2/252; Crossley poem, Churchill papers, 2/330; Cabinet minutes (February 24), Cabinet papers, 23/83; **p. 715**, N. Chamberlain diary, N. Chamberlain papers; Goodenough and Morton to Churchill, Churchill papers, 2/252; **p. 176**, Lloyd to his son, Lloyd papers.

CHAPTER 36. TURNING TO CHURCHILL: **p. 717**, Maze to Churchill, Churchill papers 2/252; Cabinet minutes (March 17), Cabinet papers, 23/83; Wigram portfolio, note and letter, Churchill papers, 2/273; **p. 718**, Eden to Churchill, Churchill papers, 2/253; Warburton to Churchill, Churchill papers, 25/7; **p. 719**, Churchill to Morton, Churchill papers, 2/274; Morton to Churchill, Churchill papers, 25/7; **p. 720**, Jones to Lady Grigg,

Grigg papers; **p. 721**, Morrison-Bell to Churchill, Churchill papers, 2/253; Churchill to Cecil, Churchill papers, 2/282; **p. 722**, Cecil to Churchill, Churchill papers, 2/282; Churchill to Eleanor Rathbone, Churchill papers, 2/274; **p. 723**, Hankey to Inskip, Cabinet papers, 21/435; **p. 724**, Leeper to Churchill, Churchill papers, 2/253; Leeper memorandum and Vansittart minute, Foreign Office papers, 395/538; **p. 725**, Leeper memorandum and Vansittart minute, Foreign Office papers, 395/541; **p. 727**, Margot Asquith to Churchill, Churchill papers, 2/253; Morton to Churchill, Churchill papers, 2/266; **p. 728**, Churchill to Strakosch, Churchill papers, 2/277; Weir to Churchill, Churchill papers, 2/253; **p. 729**, Cabinet minutes, (April 29), Foreign Office papers, 371/19904; Churchill to Feiling, Churchill papers, 8/532; Churchill to Weir (envelope note), Weir papers; **p. 731**, Londonderry to Churchill, Churchill papers, 2/266; **p. 732**, Churchill to Londonderry, Churchill papers, 2/266; **p. 733**, Thorneycroft and Boucher to Churchill, Churchill papers, 2/272; **p. 734**, Henderson, Portal and Chatfield to Churchill, Churchill papers, 2/272; Churchill unpublished draft, Churchill papers, 4/143; **p. 735**, Williams to Churchill, Churchill papers, 2/280; **p. 736**, Churchill to Weir, Weir papers, Weir to Churchill, Churchill papers, 2/234; **p. 737**, Morton to Churchill, Churchill papers, 2/266; Long to Churchill, Churchill papers, 2/254; Churchill to A. Chamberlain and reply, Churchill papers, 2/272; **p. 738**, Wigram portfolio, Churchill papers, 2/273; Vansittart to Churchill, Churchill papers, 1/284; Churchill to Flandin and reply, Churchill papers, 2/274; **p. 739**, Anti-Nazi Council minutes, and Violet Bonham Carter to Churchill, Churchill papers, 2/282; **p. 740**, Churchill to Violet Bonham Carter, Churchill papers, 2/282; **p. 741**, Hankey to Inskip, Cabinet papers, 21/573; **p. 742**, Ralegh Club speech, transcript, Churchill papers, 9/120; Morton to Churchill, Churchill papers, 2/266; Mrs Pearman to Churchill and Anderson portfolio, Churchill papers, 2/271; **p. 743**, Churchill to Inskip, Cabinet papers, 64/5; **p. 744**, Inskip to Churchill, Churchill papers, 2/269; Churchill to Clark, and Elles to Churchill, Churchill papers, 2/280; Churchill to Weir, and Inskip, Churchill papers, 2/269; **p. 745**, Churchill to Swinton, Cabinet papers, 21/426; Hankey to Churchill, Churchill papers, 25/7; Swinton to Hankey, Cabinet papers, 64/5; Churchill to Bailey, Churchill papers, 2/255; Morton to Churchill, Churchill papers, 2/266; **p. 746**, Inskip to Churchill and reply, Churchill papers, 2/269; **p. 747**, Inskip Departmental note (June 7), Cabinet papers, 64/31; Cabinet Committee minutes (June 11), Cabinet papers, 16/136; **p. 748**, Churchill to Davies and Hawkey, Churchill papers, 2/284; Tudor to Churchill, Churchill papers, 2/266; **p. 749**, Wigram to Churchill and portfolio, Churchill papers, 2/273; Duchess of Atholl to Churchill, Churchill papers, 2/275.

CHAPTER 37. 'A REMORSELESS PRESSURE': **p. 750**, Tizard to Swinton (June 10 and 12), Cabinet papers, 21/426; **p. 751**, Tizard to Lindemann, Cherwell papers; Watson-Watt to Churchill, Churchill papers, 25/10; Churchill to Swinton, Cabinet papers, 21/426; **p. 752**; Swinton to Churchill, Churchill papers, 25/7; Lindemann to Tizard, Cherwell papers; Tizard to Swinton, Cabinet papers, 64/5; Churchill memorandum (June 12) (Committee of Imperial Defence paper 1241B enclosure 1), Foreign Office papers, 371/19933; **p. 754**, Air Staff notes (June 26) (Committee of Imperial Defence paper 1241B enclosure 2), Foreign Office papers, 371/19933; **p. 755**, Wigram minute, Foreign Office papers, 371/19933; **p. 756**, Christie's memorandum, Christie papers; Morton to Churchill, Churchill papers, 25/7; **p. 756**, Swinton to Hankey, and Inskip minute, Cabinet papers, 21/426; **p. 758**, Hankey to Baldwin, Cabinet papers, 21/573; Inskip to Churchill and reply, Churchill papers, 2/269; **p. 759**, Inskip to Churchill and reply, Churchill papers, 2/269; Guest to Churchill, Churchill papers, 2/255; **p. 760**, Bailey to Churchill, Churchill papers, 2/255; Waley minute, Foreign Office papers, 371/19946; **p. 761**, Wigram minute, Foreign Office papers, 371/19946; Churchill to Purbrick, Churchill papers, 2/256; Churchill to A. Chamberlain, A. Chamberlain papers; Cabinet minutes (July 6), Cabinet papers, 23/85; **p. 762**, Bateman to Churchill, Churchill papers, 2/256; Henderson to Churchill, Churchill papers, 2/266; **p. 763**, Churchill to Hankey and reply, Churchill papers, 2/267; Churchill to Tudor, Churchill papers, 2/266; Churchill New Commonwealth speech, transcript,

Churchill papers, 9/120; **p. 765**, Locker-Lampson to Churchill, Churchill papers, 2/256; Churchill to Rothermere, Churchill papers, 2/266; Morton memorandum, Churchill papers, 2/268; **p. 767**, Cabinet Committee minutes (July 23), Cabinet papers, 16/136; Cabinet minutes (July 29), Cabinet papers, 23/85.

CHAPTER 38. THE DEFENCE DEPUTATION: **p. 768**, Churchill to A. Chamberlain, Churchill papers, 2/270; **p. 769**, Anti-Nazi Council discussion, transcript, Churchill papers, 2/283; Hankey to Baldwin, Premier papers, 1/193; **p. 770**, Hankey to Swinton, Cabinet papers, 21/437; Parliamentary Deputation, transcript, Premier papers, 1/193; **p. 773**, Admiralty Oil storage information, Churchill papers, 19/3; **p. 777**, Hankey to Swinton, Hoare, and Duff Cooper, Premier papers, 1/193; **p. 778**, Morton to Ismay, Cabinet papers, 21/437; Departmental observations, Premier papers, 1/193; **p. 780**, Hankey to Sargent, Cabinet papers, 21/441; Cabinet Committee minutes, Air Ministry papers, 2/1873.

CHAPTER 39. TOWARDS FRANCE OR GERMANY?: **p. 781**, Churchill to Corbin, Churchill papers, 2/257; **p. 782**, Churchill to Eden and reply, Churchill papers, 2/257; **p. 783**, Churchill to Eden, Churchill papers, 2/257; Churchill to Deakin, Churchill papers, 8/530; Churchill to Hunt, Churchill papers, 1/285; Mrs Pearman (October 31) to Eden's private secretary, Churchill papers, 2/267; **p. 785**, Ava Wigram to Churchill, Churchill papers, 2/258; Churchill to Blum, Churchill papers, 2/267; **p. 787**, Churchill to Beaumont-Nesbitt, Churchill papers, 2/267; Churchill to Dawson, and Barrington-Ward to Churchill, Churchill papers, 2/258; **p. 786**, Churchill Paris Speech, transcript, Churchill papers, 9/121; Fisher to Lindsay, Churchill papers, 2/258; **p. 789**, Churchill to Bailey, Churchill papers, 2/259; Anti-Nazi Council lunch, transcript, Churchill papers, 2/283; Morton to Churchill, Churchill papers, 2/259; **p. 790**, Adams to Churchill, Churchill papers, 2/259; **p. 791**, Phipps telegram, Foreign Office papers, 371/19914; Peake, N. Chamberlain, Hankey and Baldwin to Churchill, Churchill papers, 8/531; **p. 792**, Cabinet minutes (November 7), Cabinet papers, 23/86; Hankey to Phipps, Cabinet papers, 21/570; **p. 793**, Eden to Churchill, Churchill papers, 2/260.

CHAPTER 40. 'THE ILLUSION OF SECURITY': **p. 794**, Herbert to Churchill, Churchill papers, 2/267; Rowley to Anderson, Churchill papers, 2/271; **p. 795**, Anderson portfolio, Churchill papers, 2/271; Churchill to Baldwin, Churchill papers, 2/267; **p. 798**, Donner to Churchill, Churchill papers, 2/260; Londonderry to Churchill, Churchill papers, 2/267; **p. 799**, Boyd Carpenter to Churchill and reply, Churchill papers, 2/267; Churchill to Richards and reply, and Churchill to A. Chamberlain, Churchill papers, 2/283; **p. 800**, Churchill to Fleetwood Wilson, Churchill papers, 2/260; Churchill to his son, Churchill papers, 2/283; Churchill to Wolmer, Churchill papers, 2/260; Anderson notes (November 18), Churchill papers, 2/271; **p. 802**, Anderson notes (November 19), Churchill papers 2/271; **p. 803**, Anderson to Mrs Pearman (November 20), Churchill papers, 2/271; Myers to Churchill, Churchill papers, 2/267; Parliamentary Deputation, Premier papers, 1/193; **p. 806**, Churchill memorandum (December 20) (Committee of Imperial Defence paper, 1295B) Foreign Office papers, 371/20733; **p. 807**, Guest to Churchill, Churchill papers, 2/260.

CHAPTER 41. THE ABDICATION: **p. 809**, Churchill to Edward VIII, Churchill papers, 1/284; **p. 810**, Churchill narrative of the abdication of Edward VIII, Churchill papers, 2/264; **p. 812**, Salisbury to Churchill, Churchill papers, 2/264; N. Chamberlain diary, N. Chamberlain papers; **p. 817**, Churchill to Baldwin (December 5) and Churchill to the King, Churchill papers, 2/264; **p. 818**, Salisbury to Churchill, and Churchill press statement, final draft, Churchill papers, 2/264; **p. 819**, Spender to Churchill, Churchill papers, 2/264; **p. 820**, Churchill to Morton, Churchill papers, 2/264; **p. 821**, Churchill to the King, Churchill papers, 2/264; Churchill to Boothby, Boothby papers; **p. 822**, Amery diary, Amery papers; Boothby to Churchill, Churchill papers, 2/264; **p. 823**, Churchill to

Diggle, Churchill papers; 2/264; **p. 824**, Jones to Lady Grigg, Grigg papers; Boothby to Churchill, Churchill papers, 2/264; **p. 825**, Churchill to Spender, Salisbury and Diggle, Churchill papers, 2/264; **p. 827**, Amery diary, Amery papers; **p. 828**, Guedalla and Dawson to Churchill, Churchill papers, 2/264; **p. 829**, Churchill to Wedgwood and Boothby, and Edward VIII to Churchill (telegram), and reply, Churchill papers, 2/264; **p. 830**, Churchill to Dawson and Westminster, Churchill papers, 2/264; **p. 831**, Churchill to Colvin and Lloyd George, Churchill papers, 2/264.

CHAPTER 42. 'EVERYTHING IS VERY BLACK': **p. 832**, Keyes to Churchill, Churchill papers, 2/261; Russell to Inskip, Cabinet papers, 64/5; 1922 Committee minutes, Cabinet papers, 64/5; **p. 833**, Churchill to Baruch, Churchill papers, 1/298; Churchill to Grigg, Churchill papers, 2/294; **p. 834**, Churchill to Ava Wigram, Countess Waverley papers; Ava Wigram to Churchill, Churchill papers, 1/300; Churchill to Lady Islington, Islington papers; **p. 835**, Davies to Churchill and reply, Churchill papers, 2/312; Cabinet minutes (30 March 1936), Cabinet papers, 27/603; **p. 836**, Churchill to Inskip, Churchill papers, 2/306; Rothermere to Churchill, Churchill papers, 2/294; **p. 837**, Gibbs, d'Eyncourt and Beveridge to Churchill, Churchill papers, 2/302; **p. 838**, Anderson to Churchill (with MacLean memorandum) Churchill papers, 2/303; **p. 839**, Anderson memorandum, Churchill papers, 2/303; Inskip note, Cabinet papers, 64/15; Torr minute, Foreign Office papers, 371/20654; **p. 840**, Hankey to Baldwin and Inskip, and Hankey diary, Hankey papers; Lindemann notes, Churchill papers, 25/12; Swinton memorandum, Cabinet papers, 24/267; **p. 841**, Cabinet minutes (January 27), Cabinet papers, 23/87; **p. 842**, Cabinet minutes (February 3), Cabinet papers, 23/87; **p. 843**, Swinton memorandum, Cabinet papers, 24/268; Cabinet minutes (February 24), Cabinet papers, 23/87; Air Staff memorandum (8 October 1937), Cabinet papers, 27/648; Swinton memorandum (27 October 1937), Swinton papers; **p. 844**, Churchill to Flower, Churchill papers, 8/550; **p. 845**, Churchill to Rothermere (February 21 and March 1), Churchill papers, 2/294; Churchill to Reeves Shaw, Churchill papers, 8/554; **p. 847**, Peel Commission minutes of evidence (12 March 1937), Churchill papers, 2/317; **p. 850**, Angell to Churchill, Churchill papers, 2/311; Dawson to Lothian, Lothian papers; **p. 851**, Churchill to Lady Chamberlain, A. Chamberlain papers; Lady Chamberlain to Churchill, Churchill papers, 1/299; Churchill memorandum (16 October 1939), Churchill papers, 4/143; **p. 852**, Mountbatten to Churchill, Churchill papers, 2/305; Inskip to Churchill (April 8), Churchill papers, 2/303; Churchill to Duke of Windsor, Churchill papers, 2/300; Anderson memorandum (March 16), Churchill papers, 2/303; **p. 855**, Eden to Churchill, Churchill papers, 2/296; Churchill to Rothermere, Churchill papers, 2/295; Churchill to Duke of Windsor, Churchill papers, 2/300; **p. 856**, Churchill to Marsh, Churchill papers, 4/2; Churchill to Duke of Windsor, Churchill papers, 2/302; Churchill to Bailey and Pakenham-Walsh, Churchill papers, 1/299; **p. 857**, Lady Snowden to Churchill, Churchill papers, 1/299; **p. 858**, Churchill to Duff Cooper, Churchill papers, 1/299; Churchill to Bernays and reply, Churchill papers, 2/296; Churchill Caxton Hall speech, transcript, Churchill papers, 9/126; **p. 859**, Melchett to Churchill, Churchill papers, 2/302; Churchill to Nathan Laski, Churchill papers, 2/296; Churchill to Harold Laski, Laski papers; **p. 860**, Ramsay to Churchill, Churchill papers, 2/310; Anderson to Churchill, (enclosing MacLean letter and memorandum), Churchill papers, 2/303; **p. 861**, Sandeman Allen to Churchill, and Deverell to Churchill and reply, Churchill papers, 2/302; **p. 862**, Morton to Churchill, and Churchill to Cot, Churchill papers, 3/307; **p. 863**, Shiela Grant Duff to Churchill, Churchill papers, 2/307; Churchill to Salisbury, and MacLean memorandum (June 22), Churchill papers, 2/303; Hamilton to Churchill, Churchill papers, 2/297; **p. 864**, MacLean to Anderson, and Salisbury to Churchill, Churchill papers, 2/303; Supply Committee minutes, Cabinet papers, 60/4; Churchill to Flower, Churchill papers, 8/550; **p. 865**, Churchill to Harrap, Churchill papers, 8/595; Norton to Mrs Pearman and reply, Churchill papers, 8/548; Churchill to Swinton, Churchill papers, 2/298; **p. 867**, Anderson and MacLean to Churchill, Churchill papers, 2/304; **p. 868**, Churchill to Eden (September 3),

Churchill papers, 2/302; Defence inventions and suggestions, Churchill papers, 2/278, 2/279 (1936), 2/310 (1937), 2/342 (1938) and 2/375 (1939); **p. 869**, Churchill to Eden (September 14), Churchill papers, 2/314; Eden to Churchill (September 14) and reply (September 20), and Eden to Churchill (September 25), Churchill papers, 2/302; **p. 870**, Churchill to Linlithgow, Churchill papers, 2/301; Churchill to Eden (October 3), Churchill papers, 2/311; **p. 871**, Churchill to Diston, Churchill papers, 8/546; Fedden letter, Churchill papers, 2/328; Churchill to Diston (10 October 1937), 8/546; **p. 872**, Nicholls and Vansittart minutes, Foreign Office papers, 371/21666; Trevelyan to Churchill, Churchill papers, 8/495; Chamberlain to Churchill, 8/549; **p. 873**, Churchill to Beaverbrook, Breaverbrook papers; Londonderry to Churchill, Churchill papers, 8/549; Churchill to Londonderry, Churchill papers, 2/299; Morton to Churchill (October 6), Churchill papers, 2/311.

CHAPTER 43. 'INFORMATION IN THE PUBLIC INTEREST': **p. 874**, Mrs Pearman to Churchill and Anderson notes, Churchill papers, 2/304; **p. 875**, Hankey to Churchill, Churchill papers, 8/549; MacLean to Anderson, Churchill papers, 2/304; **p. 876**, Hankey to Inskip, Cabinet papers, 21/626; Kirkpatrick report, Cabinet papers, 64/18; **p. 877**, Churchill to Hankey, Hankey papers; **p. 878**, Hankey to Churchill, Churchill papers, 2/304; **p. 881**, Churchill to Hankey, Hankey papers; Air Staff memorandum, and Air Ministry memorandum, Cabinet papers, 27/648; **p. 882**, Swinton memorandum, Swinton papers, Swinton to Inskip, and Air Staff memorandum, Cabinet papers, 64/9; **p. 883**, MacLean memorandum (November 16), Churchill papers, 2/304; Mrs Pearman to Churchill and Anderson to Churchill, Churchill papers, 2/304; **p. 884**, Churchill to Swinton and reply, and Churchill to Swinton, Churchill papers, 2/299.

CHAPTER 44. 'THE VISION OF DEATH': **p. 885**, Churchill to Carr, Churchill papers, 8/551; Churchill to Derby, Churchill papers, 2/311; **p. 886**, Churchill to Linlithgow, Churchill papers, 2/301; **p. 887**, Eden to Churchill, Churchill papers, 2/302; Ironside diary, Ironside papers; Churchill to Bailey, Churchill papers, 2/330; **p. 888**, Cabinet minutes (December 8), Cabinet papers, 23/90; Cabinet minutes (November 24), Cabinet papers, 21/700; Churchill to Chenery, Churchill papers, 8/604; **p. 890**, Ava Wigram to Churchill, Churchill papers, 1/300; Morton to Churchill, Churchill papers, 2/299; Creswell to Churchill, Churchill papers, 2/307; **p. 891**, Inskip Defence Survey, Cabinet papers, 24/273; Hotblack Report, and Rumbold and Mallet minutes, Cabinet papers, 21/575; Cabinet meeting (27 October 1937), Cabinet papers, 23/90; **p. 892**, Cabinet minutes (December 22), Cabinet papers, 23/90; **p. 893**, Morton to Churchill, Churchill papers, 2/302; **p. 894**, Churchill to Phipps, Churchill papers, 2/299; Mrs Pearman to Richards, Churchill papers, 2/343; Phipps to Hankey, Phipps papers; **p. 895**, Simon to Chamberlain, Premier papers, 1/250; Zetland to Linlithgow, Zetland papers; Air Ministry report (January 21), Swinton papers; **p. 896**, Chamberlain to his sister, Templewood papers; Cabinet Committee minutes, Cabinet papers, 27/623; Horace Wilson to Grigg, Grigg papers; Colvin to Churchill, Churchill papers, 2/341; **p. 897**, Shiela Grant Duff to Churchill, Churchill papers, 2/328; Anderson to Mrs Pearman, Churchill papers, 2/338; Mrs Pearman to Lindemann, Cherwell papers; Churchill to his son, Randolph Churchill papers; Churchill to Maxine Elliot, Churchill papers, 1/323; **p. 898**, Randolph Churchill to his father, and reply, Churchill papers, 1/325; Hore Belisha to Clementine Churchill, Spencer-Churchill papers; **p. 899**, Randolph Churchill to his father and Churchill to his son, Churchill papers, 1/325; Randolph Churchill to his father, Churchill papers, 1/325; **p. 900**, Ludlow-Hewitt report, Churchill papers, 2/339; Munster to Churchill, Churchill papers, 2/336; **p. 901**, Inskip Report, Cabinet papers, 24/274; **p. 902**, Cabinet minutes (February 16), Cabinet papers, 23/92; **p. 904**, telegrams to Churchill, Churchill papers, 2/346; Churchill to Eden, Churchill papers, 2/328; Hankey to Phipps, Phipps papers; **p. 905**, Mrs Chamberlain to her sister-in-law, Templewood papers; **p. 907**, Churchill to Feiling, Churchill papers, 8/595.

CHAPTER 45. 'SURRENDERING THE FUTURE': **p. 908**, Unity Mitford to Churchill, Churchill papers, 2/328; Churchill to Franckenstein, and reply, Churchill papers, 2/328; **p. 911**, Churchill to Unity Mitford, Churchill papers, 2/328; Horace Wilson note, Premier papers, 1/238; **p. 912**, Swinton memorandum, Swinton papers; Cabinet minutes (March 12), Cabinet papers, 23/91; **p. 913**, Cabinet minutes (March 14), Cabinet papers, 23/92; **p. 914**, Anderson to Churchill, Churchill papers, 2/339; Ludlow-Hewitt report, Churchill papers, 2/339; Anderson to Churchill, Churchill papers, 2/336; Morton to Churchill, Churchill papers, 2/336; Churchill memorandum, Churchill papers, 2/336; **p. 917**, Cabinet minutes (March 16), Cabinet papers, 23/93; **p. 918**, Gardiner, Noel Baker and Morgan to Churchill, Churchill papers, 2/328; Helen Pease to her father, and his reply, Wedgwood papers; **p. 919**, Bracken note, Churchill papers, 1/328; Churchill to Bracken, Churchill papers, 1/328; **p. 920**, Strakosch to Churchill, Churchill papers, 1/328.

CHAPTER 46. 'WE ARE IN AN AWFUL MESS': **p. 921**, Cabinet Committee (March 18), Cabinet papers, 27/623; **p. 922**, Boothby to Churchill, Churchill papers, 2/328; Chamberlain to his sister, Templewood papers; **p. 923**, Halifax memorandum, Cabinet papers, 27/623; Hindley-Smith to Churchill, Churchill papers, 2/328; **p. 924**, Dawson to Churchill, Churchill papers, 2/328; **p. 925**, Cabinet minutes (March 23), Cabinet papers, 23/93; **p. 927**, Keyes to Churchill, Churchill papers, 2/328; **p. 928**, Boothby to Churchill, Churchill papers, 2/328; Thompson to Churchill, Churchill papers, 8/600; Phipps to Cadogan, Phipps papers; Phipps to Halifax (morning letter), Phipps papers; Phipps to Halifax (later letter), Foreign Office papers, 800/311; **p. 929**, Phipps to Halifax and his reply, Foreign Office papers, 800/311; **p. 930**, Phipps to Halifax, Foreign Office papers, 800/311; Churchill to Phipps, Churchill papers, 2/329; Churchill to Deakin, Churchill papers, 8/595; Committee of Imperial Defence minutes, Cabinet papers, 24/276; **p. 931**, Simon memorandum, Cabinet papers, 24/276; Cabinet minutes (April 6), Cabinet papers, 23/93; **p. 932**, Anderson notes (post April 6), Churchill papers, 9/129; Anderson notes (May 12), Churchill papers, 9/129; Mrs Pearman to Churchill, Churchill papers, 9/129; Cabinet minutes (April 27), Cabinet papers, 23/93; Chamberlain to Simon, Inskip and Swinton, Air Ministry papers, 8/237; Kingsley Wood report, Air Ministry papers, 8/275; **p. 933**, Churchill to Camrose, Camrose papers; Camrose to Churchill, Churchill papers, 8/601; Churchill to Revesz, Churchill papers, 8/607; Churchill to Thompson, Churchill papers, 8/600; **p. 934**, Robertson to Churchill, Churchill papers, 8/600; Richards to Churchill, Churchill papers, 2/343; Robertson to Churchill and his reply, Churchill papers, 2/343; Churchill to Derby, Churchill papers, 2/343; **p. 935**, Churchill to Blum, copy, Walter Lippmann papers; **p. 936**, Churchill to Daladier, Eden and Guedalla, Churchill papers, 2/329; Eden to Churchill, Churchill papers, 2/329; Churchill to Hankey, Churchill papers, 8/598; **p. 939**, Moore-Brabazon to Churchill, Churchill papers, 2/336; Churchill to Vickers, Churchill papers, 2/347; **p. 940**, Churchill to Sinclair, Churchill papers, 2/329; Lindemann notes, Churchill papers, 2/340; Christie to Churchill, Churchill papers, 2/329; **p. 941**, Inskip note on Churchill's plan, Cabinet papers, 64/31; Vansittart to Halifax, Foreign Office papers, 800/309; **p. 942**, Churchill to Minney, Churchill papers, 8/594; Churchill to Watts, Tudor and Acland, Churchill papers, 2/329; **p. 943**, Churchill to Moore-Brabazon, Churchill papers, 2/336; Churchill to Hore-Belisha, Churchill papers, 2/336; **p. 944**, Edmonds to Churchill, Churchill papers, 2/330; Churchill to Davies, Churchill papers, 8/602; Cabinet minutes (February 16), Cabinet papers, 23/92; **p. 945**, Pakenham-Walsh to Churchill, Churchill papers, 8/595; **p. 946**, Churchill to Daladier, Churchill papers, 2/341; Churchill to Kingsley Wood, Churchill papers, 25/17; **p. 947**, Churchill to Chatfield, Churchill papers, 4/82; **p. 948**, Churchill to Hankey and reply, Churchill papers, 2/330; **p. 949**, Hankey to Inskip, Cabinet papers, 64/5; Hankey to Chamberlain, Cabinet papers, 21/634; Air Ministry draft, Cabinet papers, 64/5; **p. 950**, Tizard memorandum, Cabinet papers, 64/5; Kingsley Wood to Churchill, Churchill papers, 25/14; **p. 951**, Churchill to Kingsley Wood, Churchill papers, 25/14; Edmonds, Morton and Sarah Millin to Churchill, Churchill papers, 8/599; **p. 952**, Mrs Pearman to

Churchill, Churchill papers, 1/323; Churchill to Cecil, Quickswood papers; Simon to Chamberlain, Premier papers, 1/283; **p. 953**, Churchill to Crossley, Churchill papers, 2/330; Churchill to Birkenhead, Churchill papers, 2/330; Churchill Londoner's Diary notes, Churchill papers, 8/610; **p. 954**, Anderson to Churchill, Churchill papers, 9/129; Pakenham-Walsh to Churchill, Churchill papers, 2/330; **p. 955**, Committee of Imperial Defence minutes (June 27), Cabinet papers, 60/4; Cabinet minutes (July 20), Cabinet papers, 23/94; Churchill to Halifax, Foreign Office papers, 800/314; **p. 956**, Waley Cohen to Churchill, Churchill papers, 2/330; Noé to Churchill and reply, Churchill papers, 2/340; Shiela Grant Duff to Churchill, Churchill papers, 2/330; **p. 959**, Churchill's letters to Wheeler and Feiling, Churchill papers, 8/597; **p. 960**, Churchill to Flower, Churchill papers, 8/595; Churchill to Halifax, Foreign Office papers, 800/309; Maxine Elliot to Churchill, Churchill papers, 8/596; Eden to Churchill, Churchill papers, 8/596.

CHAPTER 47. 'THE WORST OF BOTH WORLDS': **p. 961**, Bailey to Churchill, Churchill papers, 1/323; **p. 962**, Churchill to Lloyd George, Lloyd George papers; Sargent minute, Foreign Office papers, 371/21668; **p. 963**, Colvin to Randolph Churchill, Randolph Churchill papers; Churchill–Kleist discussion notes, Churchill papers, 2/340; **p. 964**, Churchill to Kleist, Churchill papers, 2/331; **p. 965**, Churchill to Halifax, Foreign Office papers, 800/309; Halifax to Churchill, Churchill papers, 2/331; Churchill to Chamberlain, and Daladier, Churchill papers, 2/331; **p. 966**, Chamberlain to Churchill, Churchill papers, 2/331; Cabinet minutes (August 30), Cabinet papers, 23/94; **p. 967**, Churchill to Halifax, Churchill papers, 2/331; **p. 968**, Churchill to Freund, Churchill papers, 2/341; Churchill to Halifax, Foreign Office papers, 800/322; Halifax to Churchill, Churchill papers, 2/331; Mary Churchill to her father, Churchill papers, 1/325; **p. 969**, Churchill Londoner's Diary notes, Churchill papers, 8/610; Mann to Churchill, Churchill papers, 2/331; Chamberlain to Margesson, Margesson papers; Churchill to Romilly and reply, Churchill papers, 2/331; **p. 970**, Churchill draft letter, Churchill papers, 2/331; **p. 971**, Foreign Office telegram to the Dominions, Foreign Office papers, 371/21771; Eleanor Rathbone to Churchill, Churchill papers, 2/331; Cabinet minutes (September 12), Cabinet papers, 23/95; **p. 972**, Boothby to Churchill, Churchill papers, 2/331; Churchill to Moyne, Churchill papers, 2/331; Cabinet minutes (September 12), Cabinet papers, 23/95; **p. 973**, Wedgwood to Churchill, Churchill papers, 2/331, Cabinet minutes (September 14), Cabinet papers, 23/95; Pares to Churchill, Churchill papers, 2/331; **p. 974**, Randolph Churchill to his father, Churchill papers, 1/325; Churchill to Revesz, Churchill papers, 8/612; Phipps to Halifax, Foreign Office papers, 800/311; Camrose note, Camrose papers; **p. 975**, Cabinet minute (September 17), Cabinet papers, 23/95; Adams to Churchill, Churchill papers, 2/331; **p. 976**, Churchill to Richards, Churchill papers, 2/343; Shiela Grant Duff to Ripka, Grant Duff papers; **p. 977**, Churchill to Wheeler, Churchill papers, 8/597; Cabinet minutes (September 19), Cabinet papers, 23/95; **p. 978**, Churchill notes, Churchill papers, 4/92; Churchill's statement, Churchill papers, 9/132; Hankey diary, Hankey papers; **p. 979**, Anderson to Churchill, Churchill papers, 9/129; Revesz to Churchill, Churchill papers, 8/607; **p. 980**, Tudor to Churchill, Churchill papers, 2/331; **p. 981**, Cabinet Committee minutes (September 24), Cabinet papers, 27/646; Amery to Halifax, Foreign Office papers, 800/309; **p. 982**, Rothermere to Churchill, Churchill papers, 1/324; Baruch to Churchill and reply, Churchill papers, 1/324; **p. 983**, Crossley to a friend, Crossley papers; **p. 984**, Amery diary, Amery papers; Halifax to Churchill, Churchill papers, 4/143; **p. 985**, Masaryk to Churchill, Churchill papers, 2/331; Churchill Londoner's Diary, Churchill papers, 8/610; **p. 987**, Crossley to Churchill and reply, Churchill papers, 2/331; **p. 989**, Grigg to Churchill, Churchill papers, 8/596; **p. 990**, Churchill note, Churchill papers, 4/92; Rothermere to Churchill, Churchill papers, 9/130; **p. 991**, Burgess to Churchill, Churchill papers, 2/350; **p. 992**, Cabinet minutes (October 3), Cabinet papers, 23/95.

CHAPTER 48. 'A DEFEAT WITHOUT A WAR': **p. 996**, Law to Churchill, Churchill papers, 2/323; **p. 1002**, Churchill to Tudor, Churchill papers, 2/332; **p. 1003**, Boothby to Churchill and replies, Churchill papers, 2/332; Herbert to Churchill and reply, Churchill papers, 2/332; **p. 1004**, Chamberlain to Churchill, Churchill papers, 2/332; **p. 1005**, Churchill to Longmore, Churchill papers, 2/336; Churchill to Raczynski, and Acland, Churchill papers, 2/332; **p. 1006**, Churchill to Reynaud, Churchill papers, 2/332; **p. 1007**, Churchill to Dafoe, Churchill papers, 2/332.

CHAPTER 49. 'I FEEL MUCH ALONE': **p. 1008**, Bonham Carter to Churchill, Churchill papers, 2/332; Revesz to Churchill, Churchill papers, 8/607; Reynaud to Churchill, Churchill papers, 2/332; anonymous letter to Churchill, Churchill papers, 2/332; Chamberlain to his sister, Templewood papers; Churchill to Reynaud, Churchill papers, 2/332; **p. 1009**, Rothermere to Churchill, Churchill papers, 2/332; Chamberlain to his sister, Templewood papers; Churchill broadcast to the USA, Churchill papers, 9/132; Herbert to Churchill, Churchill papers, 2/332; **p. 1010**, Coote to Churchill, Churchill papers, 2/332; Chamberlain to Horace Wilson, Premier papers, 1/296; Chamberlain to his sister, Templewood papers; **p. 1011**, Churchill to Law, Churchill papers, 2/332; Ramsay Muir to Churchill and reply, Churchill papers, 2/332; Churchill to Page Croft, Churchill papers, 2/332; Churchill to the Duchess of Atholl, Churchill papers, 2/333; **p. 1012**, Goschen to Hawkey, Hawkey papers; Churchill to Kingsley Wood, Churchill papers, 25/14; **p. 1013**, Kingsley Wood memorandum, Cabinet papers, 27/648; Cabinet minutes (October 26) Cabinet papers, 23/96; Cabinet Committee minutes (October 28), Cabinet papers, 27/648; **p. 1014**, Cabinet minutes (October 31) Cabinet papers, 23/96; Horace Wilson to Kingsley Wood, Premier papers, 1/236; Cabinet Committee minutes (November 1), Cabinet papers, 27/648; **p. 1015**, Churchill reply to Hitler, Churchill papers, 9/133; Cabinet minutes (November 7), Cabinet papers, 23/96; **p. 1026**, Churchill attack on Hitler, Churchill papers, 2/355; **p. 1017**, Revesz to Churchill, Churchill papers, 8/607; MacLean report, Churchill papers, 2/339; **p. 1019**, Churchill to Richards, Churchill papers, 2/343; Churchill to Minney, Churchill papers, 2/333; Londonderry to Churchill and reply, Churchill papers, 2/333; **p. 1020**, Cabinet Committee (November 14), Cabinet papers, 27/624; **p. 1022**, Duff Cooper to Churchill and reply, Churchill papers, 2/333; **p. 1023**, Colvin to Churchill and memorandum, Churchill papers, 2/340; **p. 1024**, Churchill to Butterworth, Churchill papers, 8/595; Churchill to Fearnley-Whittingstall, Churchill papers, 2/334; **p. 1027**, Castlereagh, Keyes, Richards and Heath to Churchill, Churchill papers, 2/334; **p. 1028**, Churchill to Heath, Churchill papers, 2/334; Churchill to Wolmer, Churchill papers, 8/597; Churchill to Hore-Belisha, Churchill papers, 2/336; **p. 1029**, Churchill to Mann, Churchill papers, 2/336; Churchill to his wife, Churchill papers, 1/325; Churchill to Craigavon, Churchill papers, 1/324; Churchill to his wife, Churchill papers, 1/325.

CHAPTER 50. 'THE BEST CHAPTER IN HIS CROWDED LIFE': **p. 1031**, Churchill to his wife, Churchill papers, 1/325; **p. 1033**, Churchill to his wife (January 8), Churchill papers, 1/344; **p. 1034**, Chamberlain to his sister, Templewood papers; Hore-Belisha to Simon, Cabinet papers, 21/624; Progressive Democratic Union to Churchill, Churchill papers, 2/357; **p. 1035**, Churchill to his wife, Churchill papers, 1/344; Churchill income forecast, Churchill papers, 1/347; **p. 1037**, Clementine Churchill to her husband, Churchill papers, 1/332; Maxine Elliot to Churchill, Churchill papers, 1/343; **p. 1038**, Morton to Strang, Foreign Office papers, 371/22963; Keyes to Churchill, Churchill papers, 8/624; Lindemann to Churchill, Churchill papers, 25/17; Churchill to Lady Gwendeline Churchill, Churchill papers, 1/343; **p. 1039**, Cabinet minutes (January 25), Cabinet papers, 23/97; Advisory Panel of Industrialists and Horace Wilson minute, Premier papers, 1/358; Air Ministry paper (January 16), Churchill papers, 25/18; **p. 1040**, Churchill to Daisy Fellowes, Churchill papers, 1/343; Air Ministry estimate, Churchill papers, 2/3291; Zetland to Linlithgow, Linlithgow papers; Richards to Churchill and reply, Churchill papers, 2/376; Churchill to Spears, Churchill papers, 8/624; Henderson to Foreign Office, Foreign Office papers, 371/22965; **p. 1041**, Chamberlain to his sister, Templewood papers; **p. 1043**,

Cabinet minutes (March 2), Cabinet papers, 23/97; **p. 1044**, Sarah Churchill to her father, Churchill papers, 1/344; **p. 1046**, Rumbold to Churchill and reply, Churchill papers, 2/358; **p. 1047**, Fraser to Churchill, Churchill papers, 2/358; **p. 1048**, Richards to Churchill, Churchill papers, 2/376; Margot Asquith to Churchill and his reply, Churchill papers, 2/358; Churchill to Chamberlain and Chamberlain's reply, Churchill papers, 2/358; **p. 1049**, Chamberlain to his sister, Templewood papers; MacLean to Churchill, Churchill papers, 2/371; Anderson to Churchill, Churchill papers, 2/372; **p. 1050**, Richards to Churchill, Churchill papers, 2/376; Lytton to Churchill and reply, Churchill papers, 2/378; Midleton to Churchill, Churchill papers, 2/358; Horabin to Churchill and reply, Churchill papers, 2/358; **p. 1051**, Churchill to Chamberlain, Halifax, Chatfield and replies, Churchill papers, 2/371; Churchill to Kingsley Wood, Churchill papers, 25/17; **p. 1052**, Kingsley Wood to Dowding, Air Ministry papers, 19/26; **p. 1053**, Chamberlain to his sister, Templewood papers; **p. 1054**, Cabinet minutes (April 8), Cabinet papers, 23/98; **p. 1055**, Churchill to Chamberlain, Churchill papers, 2/358; **p. 1056**, Syers note, Premier papers, 1/323; Chamberlain to his sister, Templewood papers; **p. 1057**, Chatfield to Simon, Cabinet papers, 21/653; **p. 1058**, Moore-Brabazon to Churchill, Churchill papers, 2/358; Chamberlain to his sister, Templewood papers; **p. 1059**, Churchill to Halifax, Foreign Office papers, 800/323; **p. 1060**, Chatfield to Halifax, Foreign Office papers, 800/323; Advisory Panel of Industrialists, Premier papers, 1/358; **p. 1061**, Bracken to Baruch, Baruch papers.

CHAPTER 51. 'ENGLAND OWES YOU MANY APOLOGIES': **p. 1062**, Churchill to Wheldon, Churchill papers, 8/626; **p. 1063**, Churchill to Ashley, Churchill papers, 8/626; Pakenham-Walsh to Churchill, Churchill papers, 2/358; **p. 1064**, Cudlipp to Churchill, Churchill papers, 8/624; **p. 1066**, Churchill to Kingsley Wood, Churchill papers, 25/17; **p. 1067**, Anderson to Churchill, Churchill papers, 2/372; **p. 1068**, Camrose note, Camrose papers; Revesz to Churchill, Churchill papers, 8/638; **p. 1071**, Churchill speech notes, Churchill papers, 2/379; **p. 1072**, Weizmann to Churchill, Weizmann papers; Laski to Churchill, Churchill papers, 2/379; Boothby to Churchill, Churchill papers, 2/373; **p. 1073**, Chamberlain to his sister, Templewood papers; Cadogan to Churchill, Churchill papers, 8/646; **p. 1075**, Lippmann notes, Lippmann papers; Anderson to Churchill, Churchill papers, 8/624; Churchill to Kingsley Wood, Churchill papers, 25/17; **p. 1076**, Cripps diary, Churchill papers, 4/19; **p. 1077**, Churchill to Young, Churchill papers, 8/626; Hudson to Churchill, Churchill papers, 2/365; **p. 1078**, Attlee, Morton, Strakosch and Barnes to Churchill, Churchill papers, 8/628; **p. 1079**, Eden and Wolmer to Churchill, Churchill papers, 8/628.

CHAPTER 52. 'BRING BACK CHURCHILL': **p. 1081**, Amery to Churchill, Churchill papers, 2/371; Camrose notes, Camrose papers; **p. 1082**, Chamberlain to his sister, Templewood papers; Craigavon to Churchill, Churchill papers, 8/628; Cripps to Churchill and reply, Churchill papers, 2/364; **p. 1083**, Wolmer to Selborne, Selborne papers; Anderson to Churchill, Churchill papers, 2/372; **p. 1084**, Sandford note, Air Ministry papers, 19/26; Maxine Elliot to Churchill, Churchill papers, 8/628; Coote to Boothby, Churchill papers, 2/363; Beaumont Nesbitt note, Foreign Office papers, 371/22974; **p. 1085**, Colonel Gray note, Foreign Office papers, 371/22974; **p. 1086**, Chamberlain to his sister, Templewood papers; Churchill to Flower, Churchill papers, 8/629; Air Defence Research minutes, Churchill papers, 25/18; **p. 1087**, Hoare to Astor, Templewood papers; Chamberlain to his sister, Templewood papers; **p. 1088**, Chamberlain to his sister, Templewood papers; Richards to Churchill, Churchill papers, 2/376; Rothermere to Churchill and reply, Churchill papers, 2/360; **p. 1089**, Churchill to Marsh, Churchill papers, 8/626; Churchill to Spears, Churchill papers, 2/367; **p. 1090**, Churchill to Gamelin, Churchill papers, 2/365; **p. 1091**, Chamberlain to his sister, Templewood papers; **p. 1092**, Churchill draft statement, Churchill papers, 2/360; **p. 1093**, Ironside diary, Ironside papers; **p. 1094**, Kemsley note, Foreign Office papers, 800/316; Ironside diary, Ironside papers.

CHAPTER 53. THE COMING OF WAR: **p. 1096**, Churchill to Wolmer and reply, Selborne papers; Chamberlain to his sister, Templewood papers; **p. 1098**, Chamberlain to Phipps, Phipps papers; **p. 1099**, Churchill broadcast to USA, Churchill papers, 9/137; **p. 1100**, Churchill to Kingsley Wood, Air Ministry papers, 19/26; Churchill to Young, Churchill papers, 8/626; Churchill to Ironside, Churchill papers, 2/365; **p. 1102**, Henderson-Livesey to Churchill, Churchill papers, 2/361; **p. 1103**, Maze diary, Maze papers; **p. 1104**, Kingsley Wood to Churchill, Air Ministry papers, 19/26; **p. 1105**, Duff Cooper diary, Lord Norwich papers; Churchill to Kingsley Wood, Churchill papers, 25/17; Churchill to Chamberlain, Churchill papers, 2/364; **p. 1106**, Churchill to Flower, Churchill papers, 8/624; Churchill to Young, Churchill papers, 8/625; Ironside diary, Ironside papers; **p. 1107**, Churchill to Chamberlain, Churchill papers, 4/96; **p. 1108**, Hankey to his wife, Hankey papers; **p. 1109**, Amery diary, Amery papers; Duff Cooper diary, Lord Norwich papers; **p. 1110**, Churchill to Chamberlain, Churchill papers, 4/96; **p. 1112**, Boothby to Churchill, Churchill papers, 2/363; Amery diary, Amery papers; **p. 1113**, Churchill to Stanhope, Churchill papers, 2/367; Barnes to Churchill, Churchill papers, 2/363; **p. 1114**, Maze to Churchill, Churchill papers, 2/368; Margaret, Countess of Birkenhead, Churchill papers, 2/363; Beneš to Churchill, Churchill papers, 2/381; Birla to Churchill and reply, Churchill papers, 2/363; Maxine Elliot to Churchill, Churchill papers, 2/367; **p. 1115**, Churchill to Scrymgeour Wedderburn, Churchill papers, 2/367; Thornton Kemsley to Churchill and reply, Churchill papers, 2/368.

PART TWO

AUTHOR'S RECORDS OF INDIVIDUAL RECOLLECTIONS

Recollections of Group Captain Torr Anderson, quoted on pp. 828, 838; of Maurice Ashley, p. 439; of Sarah, Lady Audley, pp. 392, 442–3, 707 n. 2; of Lord Boyd of Merton, pp. 302, 987, 1001; of the late Randolph Churchill, p. 1023; of Lord Coleraine, pp. 468, 990; of Lady Diana Cooper, p. 992; of Sir Colin Coote, p. 579 n. 1; of Sir F. W. Deakin, pp. 729–30, 784; of Sir Patrick Donner, pp. 595, 602–3, 1001–2; of Sir Keith Feiling, pp. 437, 731; of Shiela Grant Duff, pp. 985–6; of Grace Hamblin, pp. 362 n. 4, 857; of Sir John Hathorn Hall, p. 563; of the Hon. Sylvia Henley, p. 707; of Kathleen Hill, pp. 865–6, 1108, 1113; of James Lees-Milne, p. 265; of Malcolm MacDonald, pp. 1069 n. 1, 1078; of Air Commodore Lachlan MacLean, pp. 838–9; of Adolf Schlepegrell, p. 505; of the Hon. Lady Soames, p. 958; of Baroness Spencer-Churchill, p. 11; of John Spencer-Churchill, pp. 442, 1006; and of John Wheldon, pp. 500–1, 507 n. 2.

PART THREE

PRINTED SOURCES

The Earl of Avon, *The Eden Memoirs, Facing the Dictators*: quoted on pp. 897 and 903.

Consuelo Vanderbilt Balsan, *The Glitter and the Gold*: quoted on p. 1088.

Lord Beaverbrook, *The Abdication of King Edward VIII*: quoted on pp. 820 and 822.

David Ben Gurion, *Diaries*: quoted on p. 848.

Brian Bond (ed.), *Chief of Staff* vol 1: the diaries of Lieutenant-General Sir Henry Pownall, 1933–9: quoted on p. 553 n. 1.

Fenner Brockway, *Inside The Left*: quoted on p. 34.

Rear-Admiral W. S. Chalmers, *The Life and Letters of David, Earl Beatty*: quoted on pp. 78 84, 86 and 87 (Beatty's letters to his wife).

Barbara Cartland, *The Isthmus Years*: quoted on p. 1098.

Arthur Christiansen, *Headlines All My Life*: quoted on p. 1054.

Randolph S. Churchill, *Twenty-One Years*: diary quoted on pp. 226 n. 1, 339, 343, 345, and 348.

Winston S. Churchill, *Thoughts and Adventures*: quoted on pp. 33 and 37.

Winston S. Churchill, *The Second World War*, volume 1, *The Gathering Storm*: quoted on pp. 46 n. 1, 634, 693–4, 713, 896 n. 3, 903, 910–11, 947–8, 983, 984, 985, 1063, 1107, 1109, 1111, 1112–13.

Walter Citrine, *Men and Work, An Autobiography*: quoted on pp. 161, 171, and 813.

Colin R. Coote, *Editorial*: quoted on pp. 988–99 and 990.

Mark de Wolfe-Howe (ed.), *Holmes-Laski Letters*: quoted on p. 219.

David Dilks (ed.), *The Diaries of Sir Alexander Cadogan*: quoted on p. 977.

Tom Driberg, *Guy Burgess*, quoted on p. 991.

Keith Feiling, *The Life of Neville Chamberlain*: diary extracts quoted on pp. 59, 69 and 275.

P. J. Grigg, *Prejudice and Judgment*: quoted on pp. 99, 157, 158 and 264.

Ernst Hanfstaengel, *Hitler—The Missing Years*: quoted on pp. 447–8.

John Harvey (ed.), *The Diplomatic Diaries of Oliver Harvey*: quoted on pp. 918, 952, 971, 972, 973, 974, 976, 977, 981–2, 990, 1030 and 1086.

Christopher Hassall, *Edward Marsh*: Marsh's diary quoted on p. 1105.

The Memoirs of General The Lord Ismay: quoted on pp. 163–4.

Robert Rhodes James, *Victor Cazalet*: Cazalet's diary quoted on p. 243.

Robert Rhodes James, *Chips. The Diaries of Sir Henry Channon*: quoted on pp. 855 and 859.

Robert Rhodes James, *John Colin Campbell Davidson*: Davidson's diary and notes quoted on pp. 150, 196, 197, 199, 316, 360, 375, 387, 467–8, 687, and 822.

Thomas Jones, *A Diary with Letters 1931–1950*: quoted on pp. 531, 539, 686, 741, 762, 824, 860 and 919.

Frederick Leith-Ross, *Money Speaks*: quoted on pp. 96 and 279.

The Memoirs of Captain Liddell Hart: quoted on p. 705, n. 1.

Compton Mackenzie, *My Life and Times, Octave Eight 1939–1946*: quoted on p. 1090.

Harold Macmillan, *Winds of Change 1914–1939*: quoted on pp. 1054–5.

Keith Middlemas (ed.), *Thomas Jones, Whitehall Diary*: quoted on pp. 35, 57–8, 59, 69, 131, 132, 143, 149, 150, 155, 163, 166–7, 175–6, 178, 181–2, 182–3, 185, 186, 186–7, 188, 189, 190–2, 193, 198, 205–7, 207–8, 208–9, 212, 213, 268, 303, 314, 321, 327, 328, 395, and 398.

R. J. Minney, *The Private Papers of Hore-Belisha*: quoted on pp. 1057, 1108 and 1109.

Harold Nicolson, *Diaries and Letters 1930–1939*: quoted on pp. 359–60, 363, 410, 686, 764, 797, 814, 824, 826–7, 903, 906, 907, 917, 979–80, 983, 986, 988, 1002, 1019, 1025, 1051, 1053–4, 1074, 1098, 1104.

Owen O'Malley, *The Phantom Caravan*: quoted on pp. 298–9.

F. W. Pethick-Lawrence, *Fate Has Been Kind*: quoted on p. 20.

J. C. W. Reith, *Into The Wind*: quoted on pp. 167–8 and 358.

Lord Riddell, *Diary of the Peace Conference and After*: quoted on page 8.

Cecil Roberts, *The Bright Twenties*: quoted on pp. 19 and 20.

Cecil Roberts, *Sunshine and Shadow*: quoted on p. 860.

Arthur Salter, *Slave the Lamp*: quoted on p. 986.

Vincent Sheean, *Between the Thunder and the Sun*: quoted on pp. 665, 666, 1035 and 1037.

Major-General Sir Edward Spears, *Assignment to Catastrophe*, volume 1, *Prelude to Dunkirk*: quoted on pp. 1095, 1100–1, and 1102.

Eugen Spier, *Focus*: with an introduction by Lady Violet Bonham Carter: text quoted on p. 862, introduction on p. 988.

A. J. P. Taylor (ed.), *Lloyd George—A Diary*: Frances Stevenson's diary, quoted on pp. 524, 532, 535, 546 and 576.

Viscount Templewood, *Nine Troubled Years*: quoted on p. 971.

Colin Thornton-Kemsley, *Through Winds and Tides*: quoted on pp. 1012 and 1043.

Lord Vansittart, *The Mist Procession*: quoted on pp. 625, 630 and 640 n. 1.

Chaim Weizmann, *Trial and Error*: quoted on p. 1069.

The Duke of Windsor, *A King's Story*: quoted on pp. 814, 816–7 and 829.

Earl Winterton, *Orders of the Day*: quoted on p. 822.

Kenneth Young (ed.), *The Diaries of Sir Robert Bruce Lockhart*: quoted on pp. 359, 726 and 789.

Index

Index

Compiled by the Author